CONTEMPORARY

MANAGEMENT

David D. Van Fleet   Arizona State University West

Tim O. Peterson   University of Tulsa

in collaboration with

Ricky W. Griffin, Texas A & M University

Houghton Mifflin Company   Boston   Toronto
Geneva, Illinois   Palo Alto   Princeton, New Jersey

CONTEMPORARY

MANAGEMENT

THIRD EDITION

Sponsoring Editor: *Diane L. McOscar*
Development Editor: *Susan Kahn*
Senior Project Editor: *Linda Hamilton*
Production/Design Coordinators: *Patricia Mahtani, Jill Haber*
Senior Manufacturing Coordinator: *Priscilla Bailey*
Marketing Manager: *Robert D. Wolcott*

Chapters 3 and 5 are adapted from chapters in *Management,* Fourth Edition, by Ricky W. Griffin, copyright © 1993 by Houghton Mifflin Co. Chapter 4 is adapted from a chapter in *The Management of Organizations* by Jay Barney and Ricky W. Griffin, copyright © 1992 by Houghton Mifflin Co.

Cover image by Dieter Leistner/Architekturphoto. Cover design by Harold Burch, Harold Burch Design, New York City.

Chapter 21 Self-Assessment, Experimental Exercise from MANAGEMENT, Second Edition, by Richard L. Daft, copyright © 1991 by The Dryden Press, reprinted by permission of the publisher.

Chapter 22 Self-Assessment, Self feedback Exercise from ORGANIZATIONAL BEHAVIOR: THEORY AND PRACTICE by Steven Altman, Enzo Valenzi and Richard M. Hodgetts, copyright © 1985 by Harcourt Brace & Company, reprinted by permission of the publisher.

Notes: Chapter 1: 1. Russell Mitchell, "The Gap," *Business Week,* March 9, 1992, pp. 58–64 and "Crowding into The Gap," *Business Week,* September 23, 1991, p. 36; "A Bit of a Rut at The Gap," *Business Week,* November 30, 1992, p. 100; "Outlook 1990," *Stores,* December 1, 1989, p. 19. (Notes continued on page 561.)

Printed in the U.S.A.

Library of Congress Catalog Card Number: 93–78700

Student Book ISBN: 0-395-67342-9

Examination Copy ISBN: 0-395-69216-4

123456789-VH-96 95 94 93

For Ella, Marijke, and Dirk

Joys to Balance the Trials of Life

DDVF

For Ron Johnson, Brian Hawkins,

Larry Penley, and David Van Fleet

My Mentors

TOP

About the Authors

David Van Fleet and Tim Peterson constitute a team with a unique blend of experience and expertise. Together, with their diverse consulting and teaching backgrounds, they have revised this text to help make management interesting and practical—to make the subject come alive for tomorrow's managers.

Dr. David D. Van Fleet   ARIZONA STATE UNIVERSITY   WEST

David Van Fleet received his Ph.D. in Economics and Management from the University of Tennessee, Knoxville. He is a Fellow of the Academy of Management and has over 30 years of full-time teaching experience. His executive education experience includes over 145 programs on topics such as leadership, motivation, time management, and performance appraisal.

He is a past Editor of the *Journal of Management* and has over 150 publications and presentations including journal articles in the United States, Australia, Germany, Great Britain, Norway, and Russia. His consulting clients are from both profit and nonprofit organizations including Shell Oil; the Arizona Division of the American Cancer Society; the Kuwait Oil Company; the State of Kuwait; the Texas cities of Corpus Christi, Denison, and Seguin; the Coastal Zone Management Study Group of Texas A & M University; and the Ohio Department of Health.

He is currently President-Elect of the Southern Management Association.

Dr. Tim O. Peterson   UNIVERSITY OF TULSA

Tim Peterson received his Ph.D. in Business Administration from Texas A & M University. In 1993, he was named Teacher of the Year by the Mortar Board Society at the University of Tulsa. His current areas of research are total quality management, knowledge-based systems, managerial communication, performance feedback, leadership, and creativity.

Prior to joining the faculty at the University of Tulsa, he served in the U.S. Air Force, where he acted as a management consultant, taught at the Air Force Academy, and was involved in the How-To-Study program.

While with the University of Tulsa, he has conducted professional seminars on managerial skills, creativity, leadership, team building, strategic planning, and computer-based learning. He has consulted with corporations such as U.S. Sprint, AMOCO, Dowell Schlumberger, and Defense Logistics Agency. His other work includes his roles as editor of *Human Resource Management: Readings and Cases* and ad hoc reviewer for the *Journal of Management* and the *Academy of Management Journal.*

Brief Contents

Contents

Chapter 6

The Ethical and Social Environment   122

Chapter 9

Planning Tools and Techniques

Chapter 10

Managerial Problem Solving and Decision Making   216

Chapter 19

Managerial Communication   428

PART SIX   **Chapter 20**

Controlling   **Organizational Control**   450

Chapter 21

Total Quality Management 471

Appendix 1: Managerial Careers

Appendix 2: Control Techniques and Methods

Preface

Today's students preparing to enter the workforce must prepare to face a tremendous host of challenges. They may choose to join a large corporation or start their own, enter the public or private sector, or work with a not-for-profit agency. Regardless, they must be ready to competitively address the challenges and opportunities presented by the global marketplace, the diverse workforce, and the increasing importance of quality and productivity.

Instructors face the great task of helping students prepare for the challenge. Management students today need to learn not only the "what" of management, but also the "how." *Contemporary Management,* Third Edition and its complete teaching/learning package has been revised with the dual goal of providing both a strong foundation in the principles of management, using a traditional functional approach, and a basis for students to develop the skills needed to become successful practicing managers.

The management of organizations is routinely discussed on television and radio as well as in newspapers and magazines. It is taught in virtually all universities and colleges and in many high schools. It is also taught for credit as part of degree programs and non-credit in continuing education programs. It is taught in formal classroom situations and in the day-to-day life of all organizations. Books are used in much of that teaching. *Contemporary Management* continues to be among those books because of its adherence to the standards set in the very first edition.

High Standards for a Solid Foundation

The first and second editions of *Contemporary Management* stressed four standards. Those were that the book be *readable, interesting, up-to-date,* and *accurate.* The first two standards assure that the book is highly accessible to students, while the latter two assure that it is of high quality. The third edition continues those standards.

Reader-Friendly Text

To assure readability, *Contemporary Management* is not filled with unnecessary jargon, detailed summaries of research findings, nor irrelevant names and dates. The material flows smoothly and logically from one point to another throughout the book. The use of straightforward language that involves the reader, a logical sequencing of material, and the use of numerous examples all contribute to making the material clear and understandable to the reader. Beyond writing style, clarity is achieved through the use of exhibits, tables, photographs, marginal notes, and a strong heading structure.

Holds Student Interest

Contemporary Management draws readers in by making the material realistic. Text material is tied to examples from organizations from all over the world and all aspects of life. There is something here to reach every student. Text examples, opening vignettes, boxed inserts, cases, and illustrations are all used to make applications of the material relevant and understandable to readers.

Up-To-Date, Quality Research

Students should learn that to be on the cutting edge means to have the most up-to-date material. This text, their first reference point in a long series of lifelong learning about management, is extremely current in its content. All of the cases in the third edition are new, and research-based text material has been updated to reflect current thought. This assures that timely material is included in the book to further enhance its utility to readers.

Accuracy Ensures Well-Informed Readers

Although the text is not burdened with strings of references, it is firmly grounded in both recent and historical research. And as mentioned above, the text has been revised to include the most up-to-date material. Every effort has been made, then, by the authors and with the help of reviewer input, to assure that recent, major developments in the field of management are included in this edition. Careful use of current research assures that the material is correct, while use of relevant practical examples assures that it is believable.

Improvements in the Third Edition to Prepare Tomorrow's Managers

Every effort has been made to ensure that those who used and liked the earlier editions will continue to find the same benefits in this edition. But in response to an emerging need among students, cognitive content has been greatly complemented by the addition of skills content. That is, we have recognized that skills development is an important part of educating students so that they will be able to face the challenges of management. In addition, we have made adjustments to the book's organization in order to highlight important emerging and continuing trends.

New Skills Material Prepares Students to Act as Managers

To assure that you will get the maximum benefit from *Contemporary Management,* we have added a whole range of new material to this edition. That material deals with the skills of effective management.

Today it is more important than ever for business schools and programs to teach both the "what" *and* the "how" of management. Managers have to know more than just the language and issues of management, they must also be able to apply specific skills to those management issues facing their organizations. We have taken on the challenge of integrating both the issues of management and the skills of management.

In *Contemporary Management,* you will find that Chapter 2 is dedicated to managerial roles and skills. The chapter builds on Chapter 1 by developing an integrative framework using the schools of management thought presented in Chapter 1. Next, the roles managers perform are integrated into the framework. This is followed by an explanation of the skills and knowledge needed by each manager to perform these roles. This chapter sets the tone for the skill building which will take place in the rest of the textbook.

Each chapter has both a self-assessment and skill builder. These items have been placed at the end of the chapter to make the readability of the main text continue to flow smoothly. These self assessments and skill builders were not chosen just to add exercises to the textbook. Each was chosen because it would help students develop a skill or knowledge necessary to be an effective manager. In addition, a self-assessment and a skill builder appear at the end of every part in the book.

Each self-assessment was chosen based on two criteria. First, based on each chapter's content, we identified knowledge that would be useful for a student to learn through a self-awareness activity. Based on this information, we selected multiple self-assessments that could be used in that specific chapter. Second, we selected the specific self-assessment based on which seemed most popular in other exercise and skill books. Now you have proven self-assessments integrated into your textbook.

Each skill builder went through similar scrutiny. Before being selected, each skill builder had to aid in the development of a conceptual, human, or technical skill needed by managers. In addition, the skill builder had to fit into one of the managerial roles presented in Chapter 2. So, each skill builder is specifically tailored to the issue presented in the chapter and also is consistent with the integrated framework presented in Chapter 2.

Improved Organization Highlights Key Trends

Contemporary Management continues to be organized around the management functions of planning and decision making, organizing, leading, and controlling. However, in response to requests from users of earlier editions and reviewers for this edition, chapters have been moved as well as rewritten and a new part has been added to recognize the special nature and importance of competition, global economics, ethics, and other aspects of the environment of management.

- Part One introduces you to management, including its historical development, and the skills and behaviors critical to managerial effectiveness.
- The four chapters in the new Part Two deal with the environment of management—the general environment, competition, the impact of a global economy, and social and ethical aspects of management—to help students understand the context of business, as mandated by AACSB guidelines. Moving the global chapter to the front of the book places the emphasis on this topic that it deserves and lays the foundation for the integration of global coverage throughout the text. The chapter on the competitive environment is new to this edition and addresses issues such as downsizing, entrepreneurship, productivity, quality, technology, innovation, and diversity.
- Part Three focuses on planning and decision making. Furthering the skills theme, the discussion of planning tools and techniques has been expanded to a full chapter.
- Part Four, which deals with organizing, now includes the chapter on change and innovation.
- Part Five deals with the human side of management. A strong emphasis is placed on organizational behavior topics for students who might not proceed with this area of study or for students who might want more of a preview of this topic. A new chapter on interpersonal processes complements the chapters on leadership, motivation, groups and teams, and communication.
- The final section, Part Six, describes control, quality management, operations management. In response to user and reviewer feedback, the chapter on information systems has been moved to this part.
- There are also appendices dealing with managerial careers and control techniques and methods.

Special Features to Help Students Succeed

Themes for the 90s

Throughout the text, in separate chapters, boxed inserts, cases, and integrated text discussions and examples, several themes are evident. These are the themes of great importance to managers today:

- Skills associated with effective managers—Covered in Chapter 2, end-of-chapter and end-of-part self-assessments and skill builders.
- Ethics and social responsibility—Covered in Chapter 6 and boxed inserts such as "Waste Management" and "Privacy at Work."
- Quality management—Covered in Chapter 21 and boxed inserts such as "General Motors and Suppliers Try to Catch Up" and "Chaparral Teams Up for Quality."
- The environment of management—Covered in Part 2 and boxed inserts such as "Nike, Reebok, and L.A. Gear Run a Tough Race" and "NAFTA: Promise or Peril."

- Small business and entrepreneurship—Integrated throughout the text and in boxed inserts such as "Small Airlines Can Succeed" and "Small Companies Have Big Motivational Impact."
- The global character of the field of management—Covered in Chapter 5, boxed inserts such as "Recruiting in Japan" and "Blockbuster Grows Around the World," and in end-of-chapter cases.

Skills Connect Concepts with Practice

The self-assessments and skills builders are integrated into the main text starting with the first chapter. Students are informed at the appropriate point in each chapter that a self-assessment or skill builder is available. All of the *self-assessments,* which are referred to in the text and which begin with a link to the chapter's content, can be completed without instructor assistance. It is just-in-time learning for students. The interpretation of the self-assessments are at the back of the book, so students can complete the self-assessment and then interpret the tool themselves.

On the other hand, while the *skill builders* are also introduced in each chapter, the information necessary to complete the skill builder is located in the Instructor's Resource Manual. Quite often skill builders require processing for maximum learning to occur. By putting some of the information in the Instructor's Resource Manual, we have ensured that instructors will be able to facilitate these exercises for maximum student benefit. Like the self-assessments, the skill builders are referenced in each chapter and begin with a statement linking the activity to chapter content. It also identifies the model, role, and skill that is being developed as part of the integrative framework in Chapter 2.

Pedagogical Aids Facilitate Learning

Contemporary Management is designed to make learning as interesting and effective as possible.

- Each chapter begins with a *Chapter Outline* and a set of *Learning Objectives* to serve as a road map through the chapter and to point out its "landmarks."
- There are two kinds of questions at the end of each chapter designed to assist students in learning and reviewing the chapter material. *Discussion Questions* are intended to cause students to review and consider the meaning and importance of material. *Analysis Questions* ask students to integrate the material as well as go beyond the basic material to understand applications.
- There is a *Chapter Summary,* which covers the major points of the chapter.
- A list of important terms is presented in *The Manager's Vocabulary* at the end of each chapter. These terms are introduced in boldface type and defined in the chapter and included in the *Glossary* at the end of the text.
- There are also *marginal notes* to highlight key concepts, *photographs* with informative captions, and colorful *exhibits* to reinforce the learning process and make it more interesting.

Applications to Stimulate Student Interest

To spark and sustain student interest, applications from real world organizations are distributed throughout *Contemporary Management.* Considerable time and effort have gone into taking these examples from a wide variety of levels of management, types of organizations, countries of operations, and the like to assure that students are exposed to the full, rich diversity of management. In addition to the numerous examples within the body of the text, the following are included:

- An *Opening Vignette* to draw the student into each chapter with an actual incident with which the student may already be familiar.
- Two end-of-chapter cases, one focusing on a domestic organization, the other focusing on an international organization. All of these cases are new with this edition.

- Four types of boxed inserts, two of which appear in every chapter. *A Matter of Ethics, The Environment of Management, The Quality Challenge,* and *The Entrepreneurial Spirit* extend points made in the text. All of these are new with this edition.
- Self assessment and skill builder activities tied to chapter and part topics. These activities were carefully selected to provide students with increased self-awareness and to aid in their managerial skill development.

The Teaching/ Learning Package

A complete instructional package is available to supplement this text. As with the earlier editions, this package has been revised and coordinated by Dr. Fraya Wagner and the text authors so that they form a truly integrated whole. Dr. Wagner is particularly qualified for this work. She received her Ph.D. in management from Memphis State University and has taught graduate and undergraduate courses in human resource management, general and supervisory management, social responsibility, and organizational behavior at Eastern Michigan State University for over ten years. In addition to being an active member in the Academy of Management, the Society for Human Resource Management, and the American Association of University Professors, she has worked in industry and served as a consultant in the private and public sectors in the areas of compensation, leadership, and supervisory management. Like the text authors, she brings to her work on *Contemporary Management* a great deal of both teaching and industry experience.

Videotapes

A complete selection of videos to complement the text feature real-world examples from leading organizations. In general, the tapes are under twenty-minutes in length to allow for classroom discussion.

Instructor's Resource Manual

The *Instructor's Resource Manual* is designed to be the basic source of information to support the text material. For each chapter the following items are identified: chapter summary, learning objectives, extended chapter outline including box summaries and new extra examples, the manager's vocabulary, answers to review and analysis questions, skills material, concluding case summaries and answers, additional activities, audio-visual guide, and material for the Study Guide skill exercises. This resource also contains suggested class schedules.

Test Bank and Computerized Test Bank

The *Test Bank* contains 2500 items including true/false, multiple-choice, completion, matching, and essay questions. In addition, the multiple-choice items are now identified as either application (process or procedural knowledge) or factual (declarative knowledge) questions. A computerized version of the Test Bank is available. It includes all of the materials from the Test Bank in easily usable form for IBM PC or compatible computers.

Color Transparencies

There are 106 color transparencies available, fifty percent from the text and fifty percent from outside the text.

Study Guide and Computerized Study Guide

A *Study Guide* is available to assist students in learning the definitions and concepts presented in *Contemporary Management.* It has chapter summaries, chapter outlines, and restates the chapter learning objectives to keep the student focused. In addition, it has practice test questions and exercises designed to help students prepare for examinations. The *Study Guide* also includes additional skill exercises linked to chapter content. The computerized Study Guide includes all the review elements in the printed Study Guide so that students can complete the work in a computer lab and print out notes and reports of their progress. This program is available for the IBM PC or compatible computers.

Manager: A Simulation

Manager, written by Jerald R. Smith of Florida Atlantic University, is a business game that provides students, acting as management teams, with simulated real-world experience in managerial decision making. An instructor's disk is provided to explain how to play the game, provide suggestions for grading, and analyze and evaluate student decisions.

Acknowledgments

E very work such as this is a team effort. Ricky Griffin continued as a collaborator in this edition. He shared his ideas, experience, and resources to help assure that this work would be an excellent text for both students and faculty alike. We owe him a great deal for, without his collaboration, this would not be the high quality it is.

We wish to acknowledge our students who have been some of our best teachers over the years. They certainly helped make this work the success that it is.

Colleagues over the years have greatly influenced our thinking and, hence, this work. We owe a considerable debt of gratitude to those with whom we have studied, worked, collaborated, argued, and hopefully always learned.

Houghton Mifflin's outstanding team of professionals was also critical to the success of this venture. Patrick Boles, who has moved to another position, was the original sponsoring editor for earlier editions of this work and helped assure its quality every step of the way before turning it over to the capable hands of Diane McOscar. Susan Kahn guided the total project and was invaluable in shaping the final product. Nancy Doherty Schmitt and Linda Hamilton, in particular, merit recognition for the way in which they made the necessary adjustments so that this work could be as up-to-date, readable, and high quality as possible. Bob Wolcott, Marketing Manager, and the dedicated Houghton Mifflin sales staff also deserve thanks for their input and continued hard work.

In addition to that team, numerous reviewers contributed to the final form of the work. Those reviewers are indispensable in shaping the final work you see here. However, any and all errors of omission, interpretation, and emphasis remain the responsibility of the authors. Each of these reviewers deserves special thanks for their suggestions and assistance in developing this text.

Dave Aiken
Hocking Technical College

James Baird
Community College of Finger Lakes

Roger K. Baker
Illinois Central College

Becky Tyler Bechtel
Cincinnati Technical College

John D. Bigelow
Boise State University

Michael Cicero
Highline Community College

M. Lou Cisneros
Austin Community College

Ronald Courchene
Community College of Allegheny County

R. J. Dick
Missouri Western State College

Winola F. Emory
Northern Virginia Community College

Benjamin Findley, Jr.
University of Sarasota

Elaine Fry
Nicholls State University

Matthew Gross
Moraine Valley Community College

Lisa Gundry, Ph.D.
DePaul University

Anthony Jurkus
Louisiana Technical University

Sylvia Keyes
Bridgewater State College

Kenneth Lacho
University of New Orleans-Lakefront

David Lang
*City University of New York—
Kingsborough Community College*

Martin Lecker
Rockland Community College

Rick A. Lester
University of North Alabama

Paul D. Maxwell
Bridgewater State College

Dr. Fredric L. Mayerson
Kingsborough Community College

Coenraad L. Mohr, Ph.D.
Illinois State University

Lee H. Neumann
Bucks County Community College

Joseph O'Grady
Champlain College

James W. Peelle
Carl Sandburg College

Donald Pettit
Suffolk County Community College

Gary Poorman
Normandale Community College

Kathy Pullins
Columbus State Community College

Deborah A. Reed
Community College of Beaver County

Mary Reed
Delta Junior College

Susanne Schmalz
University of Southwestern Louisiana

Gene Schneider
Austin Community College

Michael Shaner
St. Louis University

Thomas J. Shaughnessy
Illinois Central College

Suzanne D. Taylor
University of Tulsa

Dr. Deborah L. Wells
Creighton University

Ron Weston
Contra Costa College

Douglas Wozniak
Ferris State College

Penny Wright
San Diego State University

John Zeiger
Bryant College

All of the ancillaries for *Contemporary Management* were prepared by Dr. Fraya Wagner at Eastern Michigan University. Fraya worked closely with everyone involved in this edition to ensure that each supplement is of the highest quality. She is delightful to work with, and the ancillaries are exceptional teaching and learning aids.

Writing a textbook is hard work. It requires tremendous sacrifices from everyone concerned and from their families. Our families had to put up with the pressure of deadlines and a lot of work. Without their help and understanding this work would never have been completed. They serve to demonstrate that love can grow even during turbulent times.

Management Today

Learning Objectives

After studying this chapter you should be able to

· Define management and describe its complexity and pervasiveness.

· Define successful management in terms of efficiency and effectiveness.

· Identify the major functions of management.

· Discuss the importance of history and theory to the field of management.

· Discuss the origins of management and trace its development.

· Describe and assess the classical, behavioral, and quantitative schools of management theory.

· Identify major components of contemporary management theory.

From the late 1980s and into the 1990s, the United States was in an economic recession. Many retailing businesses had to cut back on operations because consumer spending was down. A major exception was The Gap, Inc. Its rate of growth slowed during that time, but it continued to be a huge success while its competitors struggled.

Donald Fisher began The Gap in 1969 in San Francisco to sell jeans and records. Seven years later there were more than two hundred stores throughout the United States. In 1983, The Gap bought Banana Republic, another casual clothing retail chain. That same year, Fisher brought in a new president and reorganized all of The Gap's operations. Then, in 1986 a new chain was started, Baby Gap, which also quickly grew to more than two hundred stores.

In the five-year period 1988 to 1992, average annual growth in earnings at The Gap was approximately 43 percent. This phenomenal growth was expected to slow during the 1990s, but the top managers were developing ways to sustain growth as The Gap became the number 2 clothes brand in the United States in 1991 (Levi Strauss was number 1).

Progress has not always been smooth, however. Although sales in the Banana Republic stores grew from more than $40 million in 1985 to about $190 million by 1987, Banana Republic later lost about $10 million dollars in only two years. Changes were made quickly in both management and merchandise, and by 1992 its 150 stores were again profitable.

The Gap has plenty of markets in which to move should it so desire. As of early 1992, it had thirty-five stores in both Canada and Britain but had not expanded into any other countries. And there were still areas within the United States in which The Gap did not operate or did so with only a small presence.

The president of The Gap, Mickey Drexler, got an undergraduate business degree from the State University of New York at Buffalo and a Masters of Business Administration degree from Boston University. He gained experience in retailing at a department-store chain in Brooklyn, Bloomingdale's, Inc., R.H. Macy & Co., Inc., and AnnTaylor, where he was president before joining The Gap in 1983.[1] ■

The history of The Gap illustrates the world of management and managers extremely well. The company was being run by one manager, its founder; when he needed help, he hired another top manager to assist him. Together they developed a vision of what the company should be doing and tried to accomplish goals based on that vision. The current president is well educated and has extensive experience in the industry. Such a background is common in management.

Nancy Bajer owns and operates Plants Plus, an artificial plant decorator business in Scottsdale, Arizona. John Van Fleet owns and is involved with the operation of VMF, Inc., of Scranton, Pennsylvania. George Steinbrenner, principal owner of the New York Yankees professional baseball team, is known for his frequent managerial changes and his acquisitions of high-priced players in the annual attempt to win the World Series. The chief executive officer (CEO) of General Motors must make decisions every day that affect thousands of people and involve millions of dollars.

Each of these people is a manager. Each leads and directs the activities within his or her organization, and each is accountable for the performance of that organization. Moreover, each of these organizations and the people who manage them illustrate the complexity noted in The Gap.

This book is about the world of management and managers. Together we will explore the dynamic nature of the management process in all its forms. As you read and study the book, you will come to better appreciate the nature of organizations and the manager's job. And you will develop insights into how you can function effectively as a successful manager.

This preparatory chapter provides you with an overview of management, including its history. First it describes the manager's job—defining management, noting the importance of both efficiency and effectiveness, and identifying managerial functions. Then the history of management is outlined—noting the importance of history and theory, origins of management theory, major schools of management, and contemporary developments in the field. The chapter concludes with an overview of the entire book.

The Manager's Job

Definition of Management

Management *is a set of activities directed at the efficient and effective utilization of resources in the pursuit of one or more goals.*

Management can be defined as a set of activities directed at the efficient and effective utilization of resources in the pursuit of one or more goals. Three distinct elements of this definition, illustrated in Exhibit 1.1, warrant special discussion.

First, the manager's job involves activity.[2] Managers do not sit around all day and think. Instead, they talk, listen, read, write, meet, observe, and participate. Their days are filled with action. As we will see, most managerial activities can be classified into one of four categories: planning, organizing, leading, and controlling.

Second, management involves the efficient and effective use of resources. These may be human resources (assembly-line workers, managers, and dealers for Ford Motor Co.), physical resources (buildings, office furniture, and raw materials for Dow Chemical), financial resources (retained earnings, product sales, and bank loans for Safeway Stores, Inc.), and informational resources (sales projections and market research for the Procter & Gamble Co.).

Third, our definition of management notes the importance of organizational goals. Goals are targets organizations aim for. They can be developed for many different areas and levels of an organization. The setting of appropriate goals is a very important part of the manager's job.

The Complexity of Management As you might have gathered from the preceding points, management is an extremely complex process. Part of this complexity stems from the different activities managers engage in.[3] Another part is due to the fact that managers must change activities frequently. In the United States about half of a manager's activities take less than nine minutes to perform. That is, the typical manager stops doing one thing and starts something else every nine minutes. This pattern contrasts sharply with the duration of activities of managers in other countries, however.[4]

Whatever the reasons for these patterns, there are clear differences in the complexity of the manager's job across national boundaries. Nevertheless, the complexity of the managerial job continually serves as a source of new excitement, and its diversity is a reward for those seeking new challenges. The manager's job requires enormous energy and has many rewards. One of those rewards, pay (and particularly that for top executives), has recently come under fire, as indicated on the next page in *A Matter of Ethics: CEO Pay.*

Exhibit 1.1
The Manager's Job

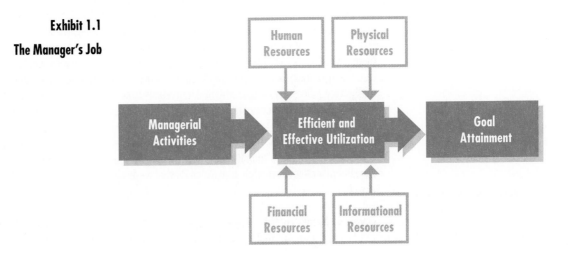

A Matter of Ethics

CEO Pay

In 1992, Texas Instruments posted a loss of more than $400 million. At that time its chief executive officer (CEO) received total compensation of just over $2 million. The situation of CEO's receiving compensation in the millions of dollars while their companies are losing money or have negative return on equity has been repeated numerous times in corporations across the United States. (A few other well-known companies where this happened in 1991 include CPOS Inc., United Technologies, and Digital Equipment.) CEOs in the United States earn nearly twice as much as their counterparts worldwide. When coupled with poor corporate performance, this situation raises questions about the magnitude and value of their pay.

Most corporations have compensation committees that analyze and make recommendations about executive pay. If those committees were doing their jobs, it would seem that the situation described in the opening paragraph would not occur frequently, and yet it does. One problem, at least in some cases, is that members of such compensation committees have potential conflicts of interest: they are not independent enough to make free and unimpeded judgments.

Often companies or individuals hired by the firm in question sit on the compensation committees. Lawyers, investment bankers, and consultants whose companies earn large sums from the corporations frequently are not only members of the board of directors but also sit as members of the compensation committee. For instance, the compensation committee at Merck & Co., Inc. had a member who was chairman of a company that performed the corporation's banking services. A law firm that had earned more than $24 million from Philip Morris sat on that corporation's committee. At Coca-Cola, a member's firm had drawn more than $20 million in investment banking fees from Coca-Cola subsidiaries..

These sorts of potentially conflicting arrangements certainly raise questions about CEO pay and how ethical the processes are by which such pay is determined. Note that these arrangements represent *potential* conflict. There is no hard evidence that in any of these situations any conflict of interest actually was present, but the existence of the practice is so troubling that some have even suggested that it be made illegal. The result of this is that the U.S. Congress, the Financial Accounting Standards Board, and the Securities and Exchange Commission are considering restrictions on executive pay.[5] ∎

The Pervasiveness of Management   Another characteristic of managerial work is its pervasiveness—its influence in contemporary society and its applicability in many different situations.[6] Imagine, for example, how many organizations influence your daily life. You waken in the morning to a G.E. alarm clock, shower with Procter & Gamble toiletries, eat General Foods products for breakfast, get into your Ford automobile, fill it with Texaco gas, and go off to your place of business. And that is all before noon. All of those businesses are run by managers. But management is not limited to businesses. It is also practiced in universities, government agencies, health care organizations, social organizations, and families. Indeed, management can be found in virtually every collection of people who find it necessary to coordinate their activities. Thus, it is well worth developing a better understanding of how these organizations function and of the people who lead them.

This book is generally focused on management as it is applied to business firms, although it gives some attention to management in government, universities, and health care situations. You should remember, though, that much of what we discuss is applicable to other organizations as well.

Levels of management are vertical differences among managers from the lower part of the organizational structure to the top.

Levels of Management   There are many kinds of managers. If we take a hypothetical organization and draw horizontal lines through it, as in Exhibit 1.2, we have a common way of classify-

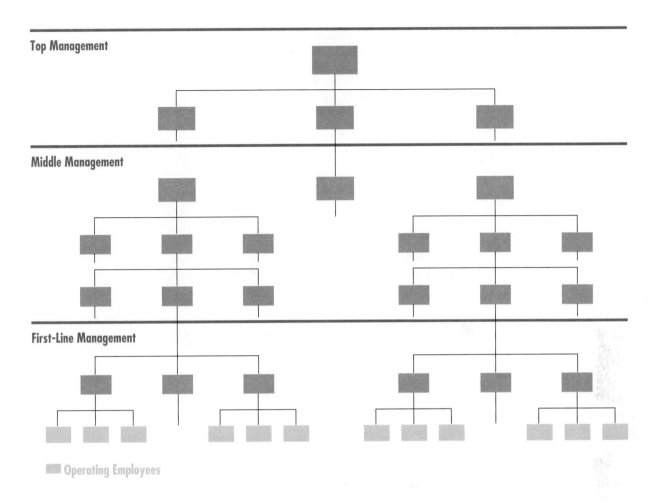

Top Management

Middle Management

First-Line Management

 **Operating Employees**

Exhibit 1.2   Levels of Management

ing managers: top, middle, and first-line. The dividing lines are arbitrary, but **top management** refers to those at the upper levels of the organization and usually includes the chief executive officer and vice presidents of the organization. Julie Nguyen Brown, the head of Plastech Engineered Products Inc., is a top manager. So is John Sculley, president of Apple Computer, Inc. Top managers set overall organizational goals, determine strategy and operating policies, and represent the organization to the external environment. The job of CEO is demanding, and turnover is common.[7]

Middle managers make up the largest group in most companies. Their ranks extend from top management all the way down to those immediately above first-line management. They include such titles and positions as plant manager, division manager, and operations manager. Although the middle manager's job is changing and some experts warn that the future of such positions is questionable, these managers generally implement the strategies and policies set by top managers and coordinate the work of lower-level managers.[8]

First-line managers are those who supervise operating employees. They are called supervisors, department managers, office managers, and foremen. These are usually the individu-

Highly effective executives maintain close contact with their environment, customers, organizations, and employees. Bernard Marcus, Chairman of Home Depot, visits stores to assure that Home Depot's special selling culture is maintained. (Ann States/SABA)

als' first management positions. In contrast to middle and top managers, first-line managers spend much of their time directly overseeing the work of operating employees. As is the case with middle managers, the job of the first-line manager is changing dramatically.[9]

Areas of management are the primary activities in which the manager is engaged.

Areas of Management   Another useful way of differentiating among kinds of managers is by area. The most common areas of management are marketing, operations, finance, and human resources. **Marketing managers** are those who are responsible for pricing, promoting, and distributing the products and services of the firm. In the Kmart Corp., the top marketing manager is a vice president. **Operations managers** are those responsible for actually creating the goods and services of the organization. The vice president of manufacturing for Procter & Gamble (top), the regional transportation manager for Safeway (middle), and the quality control manager for the Texas Instruments plant in Lubbock, Texas (first-line), are all operations managers. **Finance managers** are responsible for managing the financial assets of the organization. They oversee the firm's accounting systems, manage investments, control disbursements, and are responsible for maintaining and providing relevant information to the CEO about the firm's financial health. Another important area of management is human resources management, HRM. **Human resource managers** are responsible for determining future human resource needs, recruiting and hiring the right kind of people to fill those needs, designing effective compensation and performance appraisal systems, and ensuring that various legal guidelines and regulations are followed. Other kinds of managers include public relations, research and development, international, and administrative or general managers. **Administrative managers** are generalists, overseeing a variety of activities in several different areas.

Efficiency and Effectiveness

At several points in the discussion so far, the notion of successful management has been raised. Exactly what is successful management? As indicated in the definition, successful management is the achievement of both efficiency and effectiveness in reaching goals.

Efficiency *means operating in such a way that resources are not wasted.*

Efficiency

Efficiency means operating in such a way that resources are not wasted. Allowing surplus funds to sit idly in a bank account drawing little interest, having employees do nothing while waiting for new work, generating large amounts of waste by-products from a poorly designed production system, and acquiring but not using valuable information are all examples of inefficiency. Note that inefficiency can relate to any category of resources. One key to successful management is to avoid this kind of situation. An efficient manager invests surplus funds promptly and wisely, devises employee work schedules so that people always have something to do, designs production systems so that little is wasted, and uses all the relevant information available.

Effectiveness *means doing the right things in the right way at the right times.*

Effectiveness

Successful managers are also effective. **Effectiveness** means doing the right things in the right way at the right times. It is also important to recognize that what might appear to be effective in the short term could prove to be ineffective in the long term. A manager who enters a new market just before it starts expanding, gets out of a market before it collapses, and maintains an appropriate competitive posture is more effective than one who enters a market as it starts to decline, gets out of a market just before it starts growing, and does not maintain an appropriate competitive posture. Wal-Mart managers, for instance, started carrying under-the-cabinet kitchen appliances well before most other merchants, dropped home computers just before the market slumped, and always stay in touch with competitors' pricing policies.[10] Consistent actions such as these are a hallmark of effectiveness. Effectiveness combined with efficiency is the hallmark of successful management.

Managerial Functions

With an understanding of the levels and areas of management as a foundation, we can now take a closer look at its basic functions. Management functions are the sets of activities inherent in most managerial jobs. Many of these activities can be grouped into one of four general functions: planning and decision making, organizing, leading, and controlling. The relationships among these functions are shown in Exhibit 1.3.

Planning *and* ***decision making*** *involve determining the organization's goals and deciding how best to achieve them.*

Planning and Decision Making

As noted in Exhibit 1.3, **planning** and **decision making** involve determining the organization's goals and deciding how best to achieve them. The purpose of planning is to provide managers with a blueprint of what they should be doing in the future. That is, just as a carpenter looks at a blueprint to determine which rooms to put in a new house, how they are to be configured, and so forth, a manager looks at plans to determine what course has been charted for the organization. For example, suppose top managers at Eastman Kodak Company decide that the firm should attempt to increase its market share of 35mm film by 10 percent

Exhibit 1.3   Basic Management Functions

| Planning and Decision Making: Determining the organization's goals and how best to achieve them | → | Organizing: Grouping activities and resources so as to facilitate goal attainment | → | Leading: Guiding and directing employees toward goal attainment | → | Controlling: Monitoring and adjusting organizational activities toward goal attainment |

by the year 2000 and that ten new photographic products should be developed and put on the market within that same time frame. These targets serve as blueprints for other managers to follow. Marketing managers must launch new advertising campaigns, production managers must figure out how to cut costs (so that prices may be reduced), and finance managers must determine the effects of increased promotional expenditures and product revenues on cash flows. Similarly, market research managers must begin to determine what new products will be successful, and R&D managers must start searching for ways to create them.

In general, the planning process consists of three steps. First, goals and objectives are established. This is usually done by top management. Next, strategic plans are developed. Strategic plans serve as the broad, general guidelines that chart the organization's future. Strategic planning is also performed by top management. Finally, tactical plans are developed, often by middle managers. Decision making pervades each of these activities.[11] It is also important that plans be consistent and integrated across both organizational levels and management areas. It is important for managers to juggle and improve on decision making and planning, but not to the exclusion of other primary responsibilities. The self-assessment provided at the end of the chapter allows you to examine which management functions you excel at and which functions may need additional development.

Organizing is the process of grouping activities and resources in a logical and appropriate fashion.

Organizing   The second basic managerial function is organizing. **Organizing** is the process of grouping activities and resources in a logical and appropriate fashion. In its broadest sense, organizing is creating the organizational shape of a firm. Quaker Oats, for example, has a domestic foods division, an international foods division, and a division for Fisher-Price toys. Decisions that brought about the creation of this specific set of divisions, as opposed to a different set, were a part of the organizing process at Quaker Oats. The determination of how much power each division head is to have, how many subordinates each will have, and the kinds of committees that will be needed are also a part of the organizing process.[12] In like manner, when a supervisor groups the activities to be performed by her team members, she is organizing.

Leading is the set of managerial activities associated with guiding and directing employees toward goal attainment.

Leading   The third basic function inherent in the manager's job is **leading,** the set of processes associated with guiding and directing employees toward goal attainment. When Michael Eisner became president of Disney, he sold its real estate unit to clearly show his intended direction for the company, he convinced old and new employees to work together rather than to battle one another, he improved communication and motivation, and he linked rewards to performance. Each of these activities was part of the leading function and all but the first could have been done by managers at any organizational level. Eisner served as an effective role model and as a prime motivator for people at Disney. Key parts of leading are motivating employees, managing group processes, and dealing with conflict and change. Note that each of these activities relates to behavioral concepts and processes.[13]

Controlling is the process of monitoring and adjusting organizational activities toward goal attainment.

Controlling   The final basic managerial function is controlling. **Controlling** is the process of monitoring and adjusting organizational activities toward goal attainment. Consider Kodak's attempt to increase its market share by 10 percent by the year 2000. Now assume that this goal was set in the year 1990, and that managers at Kodak believe that market share growth will be evenly distributed across the ten-year period; that is, there should be an increase of about 1 percent each year. In 1991 an increase of 1.2 percent would indicate that growth is on target. No increase in 1992, however, would signify a problem; increased advertising may be required. An increase of 3 percent during 1996 may suggest that advertising can be reduced somewhat. This method of monitoring progress and making appropriate adjustments is controlling.[14] When a supervisor monitors the performance of members of his or her group and assists them in achieving their objectives, that supervisor is also engaged in controlling.

The sets of activities inherent in most managerial jobs, then, can be grouped into the four general functions of planning and decision making, organizing, leading, and controlling. All managers enact each of these, although the exact mixture will vary over time and with the manager's position in the organization.

The Evolution of Management

To understand how The Gap or any organization arrived at its current approach to management, it is useful to know its origins. For instance, a Polaroid plant in upstate New York began to suffer from problems of low morale and declining productivity a few years ago. Company officials tried to solve those problems but were unable to do so because they were at a loss to account for the causes. Then the corporate historian went to work and soon explained what was going on: over a fifteen-year period, management had gradually increased its control over the work, which in turn had resulted in negative reactions from workers. No single manager had seen the problem because each had taken a narrow view of the situation.[15]

What can we learn from this example? Among other things, we can learn to better appreciate the value of history. That is the topic to which we next turn.

The Importance of History and Theory

An understanding of history helps managers to understand current developments better and to avoid repeating mistakes.

There are several reasons why it is useful for managers to be familiar with history and theory. An understanding of history serves two primary purposes. First, it helps managers to better understand current developments. This is what happened at Polaroid. History also helps managers avoid repeating mistakes. If a certain course of action did not work well several years ago, it might not be any more successful today. Of course, if circumstances have changed, previous actions very well might work now.

In similar fashion, an understanding of management theory and an appreciation of the value of theory in general are helpful. Theory helps the manager organize information. Systems theory, for example, allows the manager to categorize a large, complex network of variables into a single framework. This framework in turn helps the manager develop a better understanding of how the variables are related to one another. (Systems theory is covered later in this chapter.) Theory also helps the manager approach problems in a systematic fashion. Using a framework like the one just mentioned, the manager can classify certain variables as causes and others as effects. The manager might then be able to predict certain effects based on certain causes. For example, if advertising is a cause and sales increases are effects, the manager can develop a theory (or model) of how various advertising increases or decreases will affect sales.

A knowledge of both history and theory helps the manager understand and appreciate current conditions and developments. This understanding also facilitates his or her ability to predict various future conditions. For example, a plant manager in the Chrysler Corp. who remembers bad decisions made by the company in the past and who understands why those decisions were made can avoid repeating them today. Similarly, if she understands the interrelationships among critical conditions affecting the plant, that manager can better predict the future effects of changes in those conditions. Thus, history and theory are both valuable parts of the manager's tool kit.[16]

Origins of Management Theory

As a scientific discipline, management is only a few decades old. Examples and illustrations of management in use, however, go back thousands of years. In this section we first consider several of these ancient examples and then trace the conditions that led to the emergence of contemporary management.

Ancient Management   If we look at the accomplishments of many ancient civilizations, we can clearly see that they must have used management concepts and techniques. For example, consider the complexities inherent in building the Egyptian pyramids or managing the vast Roman Empire. It is doubtful that such things could have been done without using effective management. One of the earliest recorded uses of management is the Egyptians' construction of the pyramids, but the Babylonians, the Greeks, the Chinese, the Romans, and the Venetians also practiced management. Management concepts were also discussed by Socrates, Plato, and Alfarabi, who developed one of the earliest codes of government operations.[17]

In spite of the widespread practice of management, however, there was little interest in management as a scientific field of study until about a hundred years ago. There are several reasons for this. For one thing, there were few large businesses until the late nineteenth century. Governments and military organizations were not interested in increasing profits and therefore paid little attention to efficiency or effectiveness. For another thing, the first field of commerce to be studied was economics, and economists were initially more concerned with macroeconomic issues than they were with micromanagement concerns. This pattern began to change during the nineteenth century, however.

Precursors of Modern Management   During the Industrial Revolution, the factory system began to emerge. Factories brought together for the first time large numbers of workers performing a wide variety of different jobs. Managers in charge of these factories had to cope with new problems that related to coordinating and supervising this kind of arrangement. They also had to contend with emerging societal concerns about child labor, working hours and conditions, and minimum wage levels.

One of the first people to confront these issues was the British industrialist Robert Owen, who improved working conditions in his plants, set a higher minimum working age for children, provided meals for his employees, and shortened working hours. Charles Babbage, another Englishman, recognized the importance of efficiency and the human element in the workplace. Andrew Ure was among the first to teach management concepts in a university, and many of his students went on to hold management positions in Great Britain. Charles Dupin studied these British advances and applied them in his native France. In America, Daniel McCallum saw the need for systematic management in the railroad industry and implemented many innovative practices.[18]

Thus, throughout the nineteenth century there was a growing awareness of the need for more systematic approaches to management. As a result of these early efforts, schools of management thought soon began to emerge. Today there are three major schools. These three management theories are known as the classical school, the behavioral school, and the quantitative school.

The Classical School

The **classical school** of management emerged around the turn of this century. It is actually composed of two distinct subareas: scientific management and administrative management. Historically, scientific management focused on the work of individuals, whereas administrative management was concerned with how organizations should be put together.

*Scientific management, one important subarea of the **classical school** of management, attempted to design jobs to increase individual output.*

Scientific Management   The goal of **scientific management** in the early days was to determine how jobs should be designed so as to maximize the output of an employee. The pioneers of scientific management were Frederick W. Taylor and Frank and Lillian Gilbreth.

Taylor was an industrial engineer interested in labor efficiency. At his first job, for Midvale Steel Company in Philadelphia, Taylor observed a phenomenon he subsequently labeled "soldiering": laborers working at a reduced pace. When he talked to other managers about the problem, he discovered that they were unaware of its existence. This was because they actually knew very little about the jobs their employees were performing.

Taylor decided that something needed to be done. First he studied each job and determined the most efficient way to perform it. He then installed a piece-rate pay system, which means that a worker is paid according to what he or she has actually produced at the end of the day.

Encouraged by his results at Midvale, Taylor left the company and became an independent consultant. Much of his most significant work was done at Simonds Rolling Machine Company and at Bethlehem Steel Corp. At Simonds he studied and redesigned jobs, introduced rest breaks, and adapted the piece-rate pay system. The results were improved output and morale. At Bethlehem he applied his ideas to the tasks of loading and unloading railcars, with equally impressive results.

Over the years Taylor gradually solidified his thinking about work and developed what came to be called scientific management.[19] The practice of scientific management rests on four distinct steps, which are summarized in Exhibit 1.4. First the manager should develop a science for each element of the job; that is, he should study the job and determine how it should be done. This replaced the "rule-of-thumb" methods that managers had been using. Second, the manager should scientifically select and then train, teach, and develop workers. This replaced the previous system in which each worker trained himself or herself. Third, the manager should cooperate with workers to ensure that they are using the scientific steps already developed; that is, he should monitor their work to be sure they adhere to the one best way. Fourth, the manager assumes all planning and organizing responsibilities while the workers perform their tasks.

Taylor's ideas and methods created quite a stir. There were protests from organized labor and a congressional investigation. In recent years evidence has been uncovered that suggests that some of Taylor's experiments were not carefully performed and that someone else did part of his writing for him. However, his ideas have had a profound influence on contemporary business in areas ranging from assembly-line technology to compensation systems.[20]

Frank and Lillian Gilbreth were also notable pioneers in the scientific management movement. Their work was popularized first in a book and later in a movie entitled *Cheaper by the Dozen,* a reference to their application of scientific management practices to their family of twelve children.

Frank's work contributed to the craft of bricklaying and to medicine. He observed that even though bricklaying was one of the oldest construction technologies known, there were no generally accepted work guidelines on how to lay bricks efficiently. He applied the principles of scientific management by first studying and then standardizing the steps involved. His methods reduced the total number of steps undertaken by the bricklayer from eighteen to five and more than doubled output. He also made major contributions to the medical field by helping the handicapped and by

Exhibit 1.4 Scientific Management

| First: Develop a science for each element of the job. | Second: Scientifically select and then train, teach, and develop the worker. | Third: Cooperate with workers to ensure that the scientific steps are used. | Fourth: Assume all the planning and organizing, leaving the workers to do their jobs. |

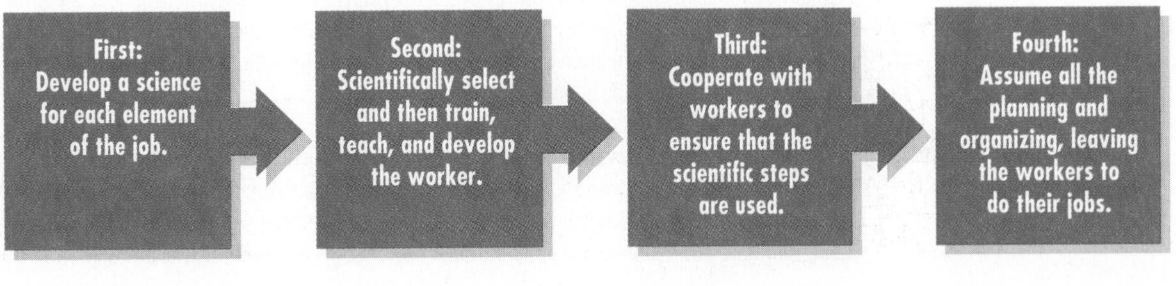

streamlining operating room procedures, thus greatly reducing the time the average patient spent on the operating table.[21]

Lillian also made a variety of important contributions. She was primarily interested in ensuring that the welfare of the worker was not forgotten. She assisted Frank in the areas of time and motion studies and industrial efficiency and was an early contributor to personnel management.

In addition to Taylor and the Gilbreths, several other people made important contributions to scientific management. Henry Gantt, an associate of Taylor's, developed the Gantt Chart, which is a device for scheduling work over a span of time. It is still used today. He also worked in the area of pay systems. Harrington Emerson applied scientific management to the railroad industry and was an eloquent spokesperson before government audiences. Morris Cooke did some writing for Taylor and applied scientific management to the public sector.[22]

Administrative management, the second important subarea of the classical school, dealt with the structure of organizations.

Administrative Management   The second important subarea of classical management theory is called **administrative management.** Whereas scientific management focused on the work of individual employees, administrative management was concerned with how organizations should be structured. The primary contributors to this area were Henri Fayol and Max Weber.

Henri Fayol was the Taylor of administrative management; that is, he was perhaps its greatest contributor and most visible proponent. Drawing on more than fifty years of industrial experience, Fayol developed fourteen general guidelines, or principles, of management, including "authority": managers have the right to give orders so that they can get things done; "remuneration": compensation for work done should be fair to both the employee and employer; and "*esprit de corps*": promoting team spirit will give the organization a sense of unity.[23] Fayol believed that these principles were universally valid and that if they were applied and followed, they would always enhance managerial effectiveness.

Bureaucracy is an organizational form based on rational rules with an emphasis on technical competence.

Max Weber was a German sociologist who was the first to describe the concept of **bureaucracy.**[24] The bureaucratic form of organization is one based on a comprehensive set of rational rules and guidelines with an emphasis on technical competence as the basis for determining who would get what jobs. Weber's guidelines were similar in concept to Fayol's fourteen principles and were designed for managers to use in structuring their organizations. Weber assumed that the resulting structure would be the most appropriate one, regardless of the situation.

Other noteworthy contributors to administrative management included Chester Barnard, who added to our understanding of authority and power distributions in organizations; Mary Parker Follett, who worked in the areas of goal setting and conflict resolution; and Lyndall Urwick, who tried to integrate some of the central ideas of scientific management with those of administrative management.

Assessment of the Classical School   The classical school of management has a number of strengths and weaknesses. On the plus side, managers today are still using many of the insights and developments of these pioneers. The early theorists also helped bring the study of management to the forefront as a valid scientific concern. On the negative side, many of their ideas now seem quite simplistic and relevant only in isolated settings. For example, many people are motivated by a variety of factors beyond economic incentive. Moreover, the classical school tended to underestimate the role of the individual. This flaw was primarily responsible for the growth of the second school of thought, the behavioral school.[25]

The Behavioral School

Although many early theorists ignored, or at least neglected, the human element in the workplace, there were a few scattered voices in the wilderness. Mary Parker Follett, for example, recognized the potential importance of the individual. So did Hugo Munsterberg. Munsterberg, a German psychologist, published a pioneering book in 1913 that subsequently became the cornerstone of in-

*The **behavioral school** focused on the potential importance of the individual in the workplace.*

*The **Hawthorne studies** were a series of research studies that provided the catalyst for the behavioral school.*

dustrial psychology.[26] The real catalyst for the emergence of the **behavioral school,** however, was a series of research studies conducted at the Hawthorne plant of Western Electric between 1927 and 1932.[27] This research has come to be known as the **Hawthorne studies.**[28]

The Hawthorne studies actually consisted of several experiments which had little impact on performance. Three are particularly noteworthy, however.[29] In one, researchers manipulated the lighting for a group of workers and compared their performance with that of a group whose lighting had not been changed. Quite surprisingly, performance changed in both groups. In another experiment, the researchers established a piecework pay system for a group of nine men. If they had been motivated solely by money, they should have produced as much as possible in order to get as much pay as possible. However, the researchers found an unexpected pattern of results. They discovered that the group established a standard level of acceptable output for its members. People who fell below this standard were called chiselers and were pressured to do more, those above were labeled rate-busters and were pressured to bring their output into line with that of the rest of the group. In the third study, a group of female workers was paid to participate in a series of experiments while assembling relays. While their output increased, it was unclear how much was due to the paid participation and how much was due to social factors.

As a result of these studies, researchers concluded that a variety of social factors previously unknown to managers were important. For example, the researchers attributed the results in the lighting study to the fact that the workers were receiving special attention for the first time. They concluded from the findings of the piecework experiment that social pressure was a powerful force to be reckoned with. The relay experiments were widely misinterpreted for years but clearly showed not only the impact of social forces but also the impact of money.[30]

*The **human relations** model recognizes that people have their own unique needs and motives that they bring to the workplace with them.*

Human Relations   The Hawthorne studies gave birth to an new way of thinking about workers. This view focuses on the importance of the individual in the workplace. Whereas previous views ignored the role of the individual, the **human relations** model recognizes that people have their

One of the experiments at the Hawthorne Plant of the Western Electric Company involved mica splitting. While most of the experiments resulted in little or no improvement in performance, these studies precipitated a change toward the human element in the workplace. (Courtesy of AT&T Archives)

own unique needs and motives that they bring into the workplace with them. While at work, an individual is exposed to the task, a supervisor, and so forth, but she or he also experiences a social context. This context includes the possible satisfaction of social needs, membership in the work group, and the possible satisfaction of special needs such as the need to be with others and to be liked and accepted by them. These factors then combine to influence such responses as satisfaction and performance.

Two writers are particularly identified with the human relations movement. Abraham Maslow proposed an approach to the understanding of human needs.[31] The other primary proponent of human relations is Douglas McGregor, who described two quite different opinions of workers that managers might hold. These opinions, called **Theory X** and **Theory Y,** are summarized in Table 1.1. According to McGregor, Theory X typified pessimistic managerial thinking. The more optimistic Theory Y was the view he felt was more appropriate.[32]

Contemporary Behavioral Science   Although the views espoused by early human relations theorists had some validity, they were also somewhat naive and simplistic. For example, these theorists believed that if managers made workers happier, the employees would work harder. Contemporary behavioral science, known as the **human resources** approach, takes a more complex view. It acknowledges and attempts to explain a variety of individual and social processes as both determinants and consequences of human behavior. For example, performance is caused by many things, including motivation and ability. As a consequence of performing at a high level, people may achieve a variety of rewards. These rewards may in turn affect future motivation and, consequently, future performance. Thus, instead of presenting simple, universal principles, contemporary behavioral science presents complex, contingency views, which are discussed in later chapters. Today, an understanding of human behavior is seen as an important tool that managers can use to do a better job of drawing on the important human resources that all organizations have.

Table 1.1
Theory X and Theory Y

Theory X Assumptions	Theory Y Assumptions
1. People do not like work and try to avoid it.	1. People do not naturally dislike work; work is a natural part of their lives.
2. People do not like work, so managers have to control, direct, coerce, and threaten employees to get them to work toward organizational goals.	2. People are internally motivated to reach objectives to which they are committed.
3. People prefer to be directed, to avoid responsibility, to want security; they have little ambition.	3. People are committed to goals to the degree that they perceive personal rewards when they reach their objectives.
	4. People will both seek and accept responsibility under favorable conditions.
	5. People have the capacity to be innovative in solving organizational problems.
	6. People are bright, but under most organizational conditions their potentials are underutilized.

Source: Used by permission of McGraw-Hill, Inc. from *The Human Side of Enterprise* by Douglas McGregor, copyright © 1960.

Assessment of the Behavioral School   The behavioral school yielded some significant but simplistic insights into the role of the individual in the workplace. Behavioral scientists today continue to work toward a better understanding of human behavior in organizational settings. Like the classical school, the behavioral view is an important but incomplete theory of management. Another important piece of the puzzle is the quantitative school of management thought.[33]

The Quantitative School

The third school of management thought is the **quantitative school.** As the term implies, this approach focuses on quantitative, or measurement, techniques and concepts of interest to managers. It has its roots in World War II, when the military sought new and better ways to deal with troop movement, arms production, and similar problems. There are three branches of the quantitative school: management science, operations management, and management information systems.

*Management science, one branch of the **quantitative school,** develops advanced mathematical and statistical tools and techniques for managers.*

Management Science   **Management science** is concerned with the development of sophisticated mathematical and statistical tools and techniques that the manager can use, primarily to enhance efficiency.[34] For example, a manager might use a management science model to help her decide how large a new plant needs to be. The model would contain a number of equations related to such things as projected production volume at the plant, construction cost per square foot, utility costs for plants of different dimensions, and so forth, and the solutions would give the manager useful guidelines as to how big to make the plant. Companies such as Delta Air Lines and American Airlines use management science models to plan flight schedules, to set rate structures, and to schedule maintenance.

Advancements in the management science area have been greatly helped by breakthroughs in computers and other forms of electronic information processing. Such innovations as the personal computer enhance managers' access to the tools and techniques of management science. On the other hand, in the country most associated with high technology, Japan, some managers still adhere to traditional approaches to problem solving and encourage employees to use an abacus rather than a computer to make rapid calculations.

Operations management focuses on the application of mathematical and statistical tools to managing an organization's processes and systems.

Operations Management   **Operations management** is somewhat like management science but is focused more on application.[35] It concerns the various processes and systems an organization uses to transform resources into finished goods and services. Decisions about where a plant should be located, how it should be arranged, how much inventory it should carry, and how its finished goods should be distributed are all elements of operations management, which is used by General Motors, Black & Decker, and IBM in managing their assembly plants. Since many aspects of operations management are related to control, an entire chapter (Chapter 22) is devoted to it later in the book.

*A **management information system (MIS)** is a system created specifically to store and provide information to managers.*

Management Information Systems   **Management information systems,** or **MISs,** make up the third branch of the quantitative school. An MIS is a system created specifically to store and provide information to managers. For instance, an MIS for a large manufacturer like Westinghouse might contain information about everything from the finished goods inventory of a plant in Seattle to the number of operating employees at a service center in St. Louis. The data are kept as current as possible, so a marketing manager in New York can tap into the system and check the inventory levels in Seattle while a human resource manager in Houston is verifying the number of employees in St. Louis. Of course, most systems of this type make extensive use of computer technology. We will learn more about MIS in Chapter 23, "Information Systems."

Assessment of the Quantitative School   The primary value of the quantitative school lies in the portfolio of tools it provides for management. These tools can greatly enhance a manager's decision making, planning, and control. At the same time, we should remember that tools cannot replace human intuition and insight. A manager needs to choose the right tools for the job, apply them properly, and then understand what the results mean.

Contemporary Management Theory

I n recent years, several new perspectives on management have emerged. These have not yet attained the stature of schools of thought, but they still provide useful techniques and approaches that managers should understand. In this section we will explore systems theory, the contingency approach, and TQM and high involvement management.

Systems Theory

Systems theory is an approach to understanding how the different elements of an organization function and operate.

Systems theory is an approach to understanding how organizations function and operate.[36] It is illustrated in Exhibit 1.5. A system is an interrelated set of elements that function as a whole. Note that it has four basic parts. First, the system receives from the environment the four kinds of inputs, or resources, that were included in the definition of management. For an organization like Texaco, human resources include managers and oil field personnel, physical resources include oil and pipelines, financial resources are derived from product sales and stockholder investment, and informational resources include OPEC proclamations and demand forecasts.

Second, these various resources are transformed through a variety of processes into outputs. These processes represent the organization's technology. The third part of the model, outputs, includes products or services, behaviors, and profits or losses. For Texaco, products are gasoline and oil, behaviors are the impact of its employees on the environment, and profits or losses are reflected in the level of funds put back into or taken from the environment. Finally, feedback from the environment provides the system with additional information about how well its actions are being accepted.

Interaction with the environment is one of the major contributions systems theory makes to the manager. This notion comes from the concept of open systems. An *open system* is one that actively interacts with its environment, whereas a *closed system* does not. Because all organizations are open systems, managers need to remember that they must always monitor and be sensitive to their environments. Organizations with managers who forget this are almost invariably left behind. For example, for years American Motors assumed it could just go on producing Ramblers and not worry about what other car manufacturers were doing. As a result of this attitude, the company eventually fell so far behind its competitors that it could never hope to catch up again. The company was subsequently bought by Chrysler and ceased to exist as an independent entity. A

Exhibit 1.5   The Systems Model

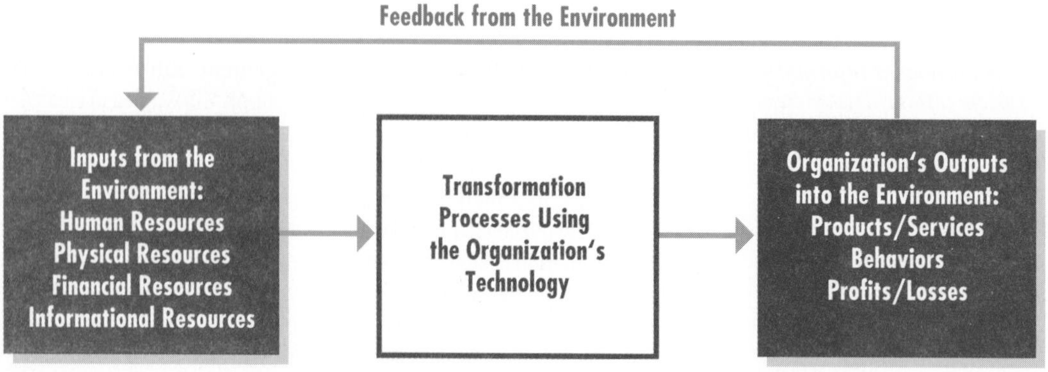

Feedback from the Environment

Inputs from the Environment: Human Resources Physical Resources Financial Resources Informational Resources	→	Transformation Processes Using the Organization's Technology	→	Organization's Outputs into the Environment: Products/Services Behaviors Profits/Losses

The Environment of Management

Globalism

Globalism refers to the growing impact of international issues and events on management and organizations. One element of globalism is the extent to which many organizations are becoming so widely international in terms of their ownership, operations, and markets that they can no longer be thought of as having particular national identities. Another element is the extent to which even smaller organizations deal with suppliers and/or customers on an international level. Yet another element is the extent to which no single country or even small group of countries can be said to dominate world economic conditions or affairs.

As late as 1960, about three-fourths of the world's one hundred largest businesses were American. By 1990 only about one-third were. Japanese companies like Hitachi, Matsushita Electrical, and Toyota; European companies like Royal Dutch/Shell, Daimler-Benz, Fiat, IRI, Unilever, and Volkswagen; companies from Korea (Samsung), Australia (Elders IXL),

and Mexico (PEMEX) had now joined the list of the world's largest businesses. And companies in many countries were investing heavily in other companies in other countries. The top investors in the United States were companies in Great Britain, the Netherlands, and Japan. U.S. companies with substantial foreign investments included Exxon, Mobil, and IBM, each of which had half or more of its assets in foreign investments, as well as Citicorp, Dow Chemical, Ford, General Motors, and many others.

Not only is the environment of management becoming global, the rate of globalization is increasing as developments in transportation and telecommunications take place. Equally important are developments in political alliances. New collaborative markets are developing, old barriers are dropping, and innovative ventures across national boundaries are springing up. Managers must develop new competitive skills to be able to function effectively in the global environment. These changes are so profound that Chapter 5 is devoted entirely to their discussion, and one case at the end of each chapter features an international or global organization.[37] ■

---

major change in environments impacting all organizations is *globalism,* which is discussed above in *The Environment of Management.*

Subsystem interdependencies are the different ways in which a change in one part of an organization affects other parts.

Another useful contribution of systems theory is the notion of **subsystem interdependencies.** A subsystem is a system within a system, and managers need to be aware that a change in a subsystem within a parent system is highly likely to affect other subsystems. A good example of subsystem interdependencies occurred in 1986, when General Motors Corporation automobile dealerships were beset by falling sales and bloated inventories. To help alleviate the problem, GM decided to finance cars for consumers at a previously unheard-of 2.9 percent interest rate. However, GM's financing division, General Motors Acceptance Corp., or GMAC, could not handle this level of financing. Such interest rates would have hurt its profit margins and consequently lowered its bond ratings. General Motors itself had to underwrite the low interest rates, even though this would ordinarily have been the responsibility of GMAC. Thus, the needs of one subsystem, GM's dealerships, necessitated a certain course of action, but the environmental circumstances surrounding another subsystem, GMAC, kept it from responding appropriately.[38]

When two or more people or units working together produce more than they could working alone, **synergy** *has occurred.*

Entropy is failure caused by a closed-system approach to management.

Equifinality suggests that the same goal may be achieved through different means.

Three other concepts of systems theory are also useful. **Synergy** suggests that two people or units can achieve more working together than working individually. When a retail chain like Kmart purchases Walden Book Co., it is partially because managers recognize that the two businesses complement one another. **Entropy** is what happens when organizations take a closed-system perspective: they falter and die. Studebaker and W. T. Grant Co. made this mistake. The key is to stay in tune with the environment and work hard at keeping the organization stimulated and vital. Finally, **equifinality** is the idea that two or more paths may lead to the same place. Dow

Chemical and Union Carbide can pursue different strategies, for example, and yet be equally effective in the chemical industry.

Contingency Approach

*The **contingency approach** argues that appropriate managerial actions depend on certain major elements of situations.*

A second important contemporary perspective on management is the **contingency approach,** which argues that appropriate managerial actions in a situation depend on, or are contingent on, certain major elements of that situation.[39] Early approaches to management problems sought universal answers. As illustrated in the top portion of Exhibit 1.6, the premise was that a given problem or situation could be solved or acted upon in "one best way." In the bottom portion is the

Exhibit 1.6

Universal and Case Versus Contingency Approaches

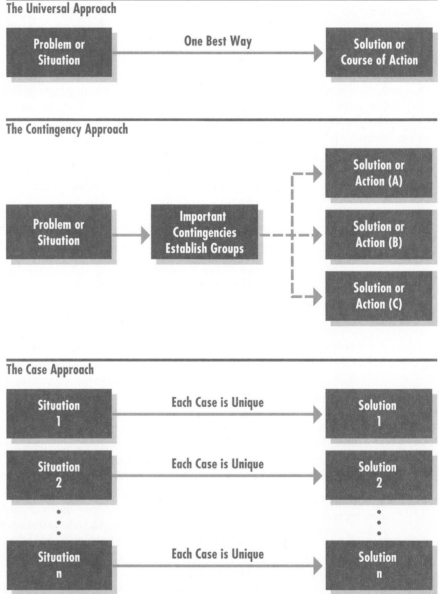

extreme contrast, the case approach, which argues that each situation is completely unique so that common solutions do not exist. A synthesis of these two extremes, the contingency approach, dominates management theory today.

The contingency approach recognizes that there are few, if any, "one best ways" in management, because the complexities of human behavior and social systems like organizations make situations different. Not every situation, however, is unique. As shown in Exhibit 1.6, the contingency approach acknowledges these differences and suggests that when a manager is confronted with a problem or situation, he or she must examine important contingencies to determine which of several potential solutions or actions may be appropriate. What will work best in one situation might not be best in another, but groups of similar situations can be identified by contingencies such that within those groups similar solutions hold while across groups they do not. The contingency approach, then, does not suggest that every single problem is unique. Theories are still useful guides to thinking, and, although situations may vary, different problems can often be handled quite similarly.

Almost every aspect of management has embraced the contingency philosophy. For example, there are contingency theories of goal setting, planning, organization design, job design, leadership, motivation, and control. We will look at these theories in later chapters. Before moving on, however, we will examine a couple of real situations in which companies did not take a contingency orientation and paid a high price.

One such organization was People Express Airlines. In its early days it was small and used few controls, had minimal organizational structure, and involved its employees in many aspects of management. As it grew, however, many of those practices were not changed with the changing situational contingencies, and the company went into decline, eventually being bought by Texas Air in 1986.[40] Similarly, Sears seemed to have trouble adapting to changing contingencies in the retailing market. That, coupled with problems with its automotive unit, led it into financial troubles, which by 1993 saw it dropping its catalog sales, making top management changes, and restructuring to try to turn itself around.[41]

Other Emerging Perspectives: TQM and High Involvement

In addition to systems and contingency theory, other emerging perspectives are worth noting. These ideas are very new and have not yet withstood the test of time. Thus, they may continue to evolve into more fully framed theories of management, or they may go the way of fads and be replaced by new ideas.

*TQM, or **Total Quality Management**, refers to the entire quality movement in business organizations.*

TQM

TQM or **total quality management** is used here to refer to the entire quality movement that has become ubiquitous in business organizations.[42] It began with the emergence of statistical quality control in the United States during the 1920s and 1930s. However, the real impetus was its adoption by Japan following World War II.[43] This topic has become so important in contemporary management that Chapter 21 is devoted exclusively to it.

***High involvement management** includes all forms of participative management as well as self-control and self-management to achieve commitment from all organizational participants.*

High Involvement Management

High involvement management is used to include not just all forms of participative management but also a fundamentally different approach to management than has been traditional.[44] The traditional, control-oriented approach to management, which is based on the assumption that hierarchical organizations represent the best way to assure performance, will not easily be displaced.[45] Nevertheless, many elements of high involvement management are already being tried in organizations around the world.

High involvement management relies much more on self-control and self-management at the lowest levels of organizations.[46] Quality circles, employee survey feedback, job enrichment, work teams, quality-of-life programs, gainsharing, and what are called new design plants are

General Electric strives to get innovative ideas from its personnel. The diverse workforce regularly contributes to making the firm more efficient, such as meeting to plan strategies for parts of the company. GE Medical Systems personnel from the U.S., Japan, and India are shown here working on global strategies. (Photo by Brownie Harris/Courtesy of GE.)

among the most common techniques being tried.[47] Each of these will be discussed at a later point in the book.

It is still too early to assess the full impact of either TQM or high involvement management. Each offers the manager many useful concepts, but each should be followed with discretion. Managers should consider ideas such as these within their own situational context and use them only as they are appropriate. The skill builder at the end of the chapter allows you to apply many of the management schools of thought in solving a problem for the president of a student association.

Plan for the Book

Exhibit 1.7 presents the blueprint we will follow as we explore specific aspects of management today. As you can see, the framework for the book follows the management functions described earlier in this chapter. Part One, Management: An Introduction, provides a foundation for further study. This chapter introduces you to the manager's job and deals with past and contemporary management theory. Chapter 2 discusses managerial roles and skills. Part Two covers the important environment of management. In that part, Chapter 3 covers organizational environments; Chapter 4, the competitive environment; Chapter 5, the global environment; and Chapter 6 discusses managerial ethics and the social responsibility of managers.

"Planning and Decision Making," which make up the first management function, are discussed in Part Three. The four chapters in this part deal with planning, strategy, and decision making. Part Four, "Organizing," treats the second basic management function. Its four chapters focus on organizing concepts, organization and job design, organizational change and innovation, and staffing and human resources.

Part Five, "Leading," has five chapters that deal with interpersonal processes, leadership, motivation, groups and teams, and interpersonal communication. The final management function, "Controlling," is the subject of Part Six. The chapters in this part discuss controlling concepts, quality, operations management, and information systems. The book ends with an appendix on managerial careers and one on control techniques and methods.

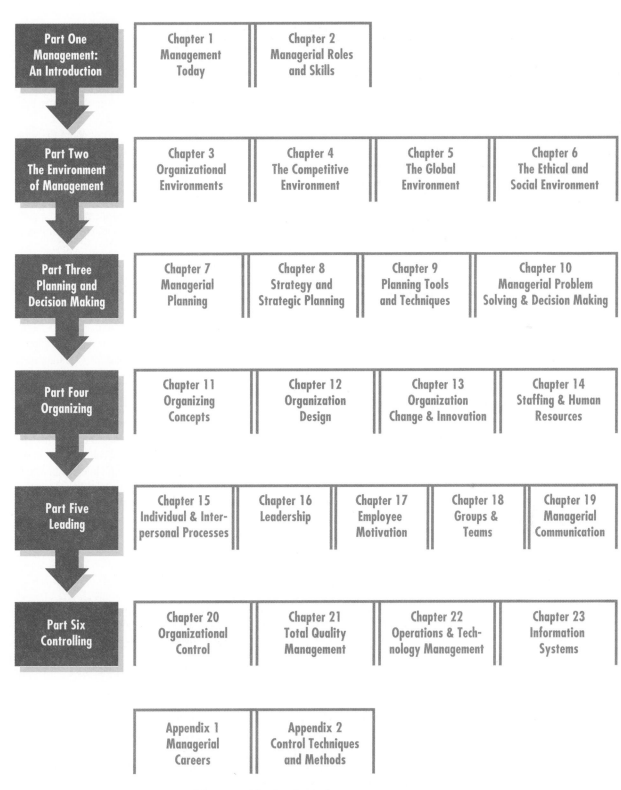

Exhibit 1.7   Plan for the Book

Chapter Summary

Management can be defined as a set of activities directed at the efficient and effective utilization of resources in the pursuit of one or more goals. Management is complex because of the large number of different activities managers must engage in and because they must change activities frequently. Management is also pervasive, occurring in all organizations.

Managers exist at all organizational levels. Although the actual number of levels varies among organizations, most companies have three general levels: top, middle, and first-line. Additionally, there are different kinds of managers such as marketing managers, operations managers, finance managers, human resource managers, and administrative managers.

All managers perform four general functions, to varying degrees: planning and decision making, organizing, leading, and controlling. Successful management involves achieving both efficiency and effectiveness. Efficiency means operating in such a way that resources are not wasted. Effectiveness means doing the right things in the right way at the right times. Most managers are not able to achieve equal amounts of efficiency and effectiveness, and some organizations might require more of one than the other, but a combination is always the hallmark of success.

Knowledge of history will help you better understand current developments and avoid repeating mistakes. An understanding of theory helps you organize and further comprehend information that is available to you as a manager. It also enables you to be more systematic in your approach to problems so that you can reach better solutions.

The classical school of management emerged around the turn of this century and consists of two major subareas: scientific management and administrative management. Scientific management focused on the work of individuals and sought to determine how jobs could be designed to maximize employee output. Administrative management focused on how organizations should be structured for best performance.

The behavioral school actually began at about the same time as the classical school, but it did not have a significant impact on the field until later. This movement did much to advance the view that more humanistic approaches to the treatment of workers were needed. Contemporary behavioral science takes a more complex view of the worker, acknowledging and attempting to explain a variety of individual and social processes as both determinants and consequences of human behavior.

The quantitative school of management theory emerged during World War II, when the military sought new and better ways to deal with the managerial problems of modern warfare. Management science is concerned with the development of mathematical and statistical tools and techniques for managers. Operations management is similar but tends to focus on the application of techniques to operational aspects of management. Management information systems (MIS) are created to store and provide information for managers.

The major components of contemporary management theory include systems theory, the contingency approach, and the emerging perspectives of Total Quality Management and high involvement management. Among the useful contributions of systems theory are the study of an organization's interaction with its environment, subsystem interdependencies, and the concepts of synergy, entropy, and equifinality. The contingency approach suggests that there is no "one best way" to manage; however, it does not hold that every case is unique.

The Manager's Vocabulary

management	leading	management science
top management	controlling	operations management
middle managers	classical school	management information systems (MIS)
first-line managers	scientific management	systems theory
marketing managers	administrative management	subsystem interdependencies
operations managers	bureaucracy	synergy
finance managers	behavioral school	entropy
human resource managers	Hawthorne studies	equifinality
administrative managers	human relations	contingency approach
efficiency	Theory X	TQM
effectiveness	Theory Y	high-involvement management
planning and decision making	human resources	
organizing	quantitative school	

Review Questions

1. What is management? Identify different kinds of managers, both by levels and by areas.
2. What are efficiency and effectiveness?
3. What are the major functions of management? Briefly describe each.
4. Briefly explain why history and theory are important to the field of management.
5. What are the important contributions and weaknesses of the three schools of management?

Analysis Questions

1. Think of someone you know who is a manager. Describe that person's management position in terms of the type of organization, level in the organization, and the area of management in which he or she practices.
2. Given the importance of history and theory, how can many managers operate successfully without a good understanding of either? Would they do better with such an understanding? Why?
3. Which school of management theory do you feel most closely matches your present ideas about how management should function? Why?
4. Why were management theories of the past relatively simple? Was it because the theorists did not know much or because the managerial world the theorists were describing was relatively simple? Defend your view.
5. Illustrate the concepts of synergy, entropy, and equifinality in a system other than a business one. (You may need to go to the library and look up some articles on systems to answer this question fully.)

Self-Assessment

How Do I Rate as a Manager?

Introduction The following self-assessment should help you understand your current views about the practice of management and your approach to management. This assessment outlines five important dimensions of management: management style, planning, information/communication, time management, and delegation. You should respond to this in one of three ways:
1. Respond about your own managerial practices if you are currently a manager;
2. Respond about effective (or ineffective) managers you have observed in your work experience; or
3. Respond in terms of how you think an ideal manager should behave.

Think of a situation in which you worked with a group or team completing a project, either in a work setting, class group, church group, or club and review and assess your style in each of the following categories.

Instructions For each question listed, rate yourself as follows:

10–9	Definite strength
8–7	Moderately effective
6–5	Average performance
4–3	Rarely effective
2–1	Definite weakness

I. Management Style

_____ 1. Am I sensitive to the influence my actions have on others?
_____ 2. Do I understand their reactions to my actions?
_____ 3. Do I find an appropriate balance between encouragement and pressure?
_____ 4. Do I allow others to express ideas and opinions?
_____ 5. Am I effective at motivating others?
_____ 6. Am I able to resolve conflicts in a constructive way?
_____ 7. Have I developed a spirit of teamwork?
_____ 8. Do I have a clear understanding of my role in the organization?
_____ 9. Am I tactful in expressing discipline?
_____10. Do I have a personal plan for self-improvement?

SECTION TOTAL _____

II. Planning

_____ 1. Are the operations of my organization balanced so that the pace of change is neither too routine nor too disruptive?

_____ 2. Do I sufficiently analyze the impact of particular changes on the future of my organization?

_____ 3. Am I sufficiently well informed to pass judgment on the proposals that others make?

_____ 4. Do I schedule my meetings appropriately?

_____ 5. Are my meetings planned in advance?

_____ 6. Do I have a clear vision of direction for my organization?

_____ 7. Are these plans in written form to guide me as well as others?

_____ 8. Do I make these plans explicit in order to better guide the decisions of others in the organization?

_____ 9. Are these plans flexible enough to be changed, if necessary, to meet the changing needs of the organization?

_____ 10. Does the day-to-day work in my organization run smoothly?

SECTION TOTAL _____

III. Information/Communication

_____ 1. Do I have good sources of information and methods for obtaining information?

_____ 2. Is my information organized so that it is easy to locate and use?

_____ 3. Do I have other people do some of my scanning for me?

_____ 4. Do I make good use of my contacts to get information?

_____ 5. Do I balance the collection of information with action?

_____ 6. Do people have the information they need when they need it?

_____ 7. Do I put information in writing so that others are not at an informational disadvantage?

_____ 8. Do I use interoffice communication media appropriately?

_____ 9. Do I make the most of meetings for which I am responsible?

_____ 10. Do I spend enough time visiting other areas in the office to observe firsthand the results accomplished?

SECTION TOTAL _____

IV. Time Management

_____ 1. Do I have a time-scheduling system?

_____ 2. Do I avoid reacting to the pressures of the moment?

_____ 3. Do I avoid concentrating on one particular function or one type of problem just because I find it uninteresting?

_____ 4. Do I schedule particular kinds of work at special times of the day or week to take advantage of my own energy/effectiveness levels?

_____ 5. Am I in control of the amount of fragmentation and interruption of my work?

_____ 6. Do I balance current, tangible activities with time for reflection and planning?

_____ 7. Do key problems/priorities receive the attention they deserve?

_____ 8. Do I make use of time-saving devices such as electronic mail, dictating machines, and PCs?

_____ 9. Do I have my priorities clearly in mind most of the time?

_____ 10. Do I have the necessary information available to me at the right times to meet my deadlines?

SECTION TOTAL _____

V. Delegation

_____ 1. Do my group members understand our objectives and know what is to be done when, and by whom?

_____ 2. Do I know which of my responsibilities I must meet myself and which I can delegate?

_____ 3. Do I encourage initiative in the people I supervise?

_____ 4. Do I leave the final decision to my group often enough?

_____ 5. Do I avoid doing others' work?

_____ 6. Do I show genuine interest in other people's work?

_____ 7. Am I confident that others can handle the work I give them?

_____ 8. Do I give group members the guidance, training, and authority they need to make decisions independently?

_____ 9. Do I regularly assess the quality of my work and that of my organization?

_____ 10. Do I use delegation to help others gain new skills and grow in the organization?

SECTION TOTAL _____

For interpretation, turn to the back of the book.

Source: From *What Managers Need to Know,* copyright © Roger Fritz and Associates, Inc., 500 Technology Drive, Naperville, Illinois 60563.

Skill Builder

Management Theory Applied: Which Managerial Model Do You Use?

Purpose All managers must develop three sets of skills: conceptual, technical, and human. We will talk more about these skills in Chapter 2. For now, we will define and develop conceptual skills. Conceptual skills allow the manager to develop relationships between factors that other people may not see. Managers who have well-developed conceptual skills are able to apply different management theories to the same situation.

    This skill builder focuses on the development of conceptual skills. It will help you develop the ability to see different management theories applied to a specific situation.

Introduction This exercise has been developed to assist you in honing your skills to meet the complexity of management. It allows you to examine all of the different managerial schools of thought and the more contemporary theories by applying them to a specific problem.

The Dilemma To be able to have entertainment that students find interesting, such as top name comedians and bands, the student association must raise additional funds to match those provided by the university. The association has determined that it must have one major fund raiser. The previous year's fund raiser was a disaster. Consequently, only mediocre entertainment could be provided and students did not attend in any great numbers. Because of the mediocre entertainment the association ran a $1000 deficit.

    The members of the association are determined that this year's fund raiser be a success. They have elected to sponsor a sidewalk sale. They have divided up the responsibilities, and are getting close to the date when things must be done.

    The president of the student association, Leigh, has been informed by the university administration that her goals of high-level entertainment may be too ambitious based on last year's fund raiser. Leigh is trying to figure out ways to make this year's fund raiser successful.

Part I (Individual) The following five statements are activities that Leigh thinks must be done to make the sidewalk sale a success. Using the management schools of thought, match the activities with appropriate school of thought.

_____1. Leigh should assign tasks to individuals according to their skills.

_____2. Leigh should do a market analysis to determine whether the sidewalk sale would be profitable.

_____3. Leigh should use pride as a motivator for the members.

_____4. Leigh should adjust her efforts and be flexible based on the information she receives through a series of informal interviews.

_____5. Leigh should review the comments provided from the feedback she was given about last year's project.

a. Classical (administrative and scientific)
b. Behavioral (organizational behavior & human relations)
c. Quantitative (operations management and management science)
d. Open Systems Model
e. Contingency Model

Part II (Group) For each school of thought and contemporary theory write a statement of what Leigh needs to do, similar to the statements in Part I.

a. Classical (administrative and scientific)
b. Behavioral (organizational behavior & human relations)
c. Quantitative (operations management and management science)
d. Open Systems Model
e. Contingency Model

CONCLUDING CASES

1.1   Goodyear's Bumpy Ride

Frank and Charles Seiberling began making rubber for bicycle tires in 1898 but quickly moved to making tires for all kinds of vehicles, including airplanes in 1909 when there were only one hundred planes in the entire United States. By 1916 the company was the largest tire maker in the United States and soon was leading the world. Poor financial management of this expansion, however, led to major problems. The Seiberling brothers were bought out after World War I, although a friend, Paul Litchfield, headed production (and the company) for over thirty years. Goodyear is still the leading U.S. tire maker, but France's Michelin surpassed it worldwide in 1990, and Japan's Bridgestone is developing a strong presence in the industry as well.

As competition increased, Goodyear's dominance began to shrink. To deal with that competition during the 1980s, Goodyear began substantial restructuring. It got rid of Goodyear Farms in Litchfield Park, Arizona. It began making off-brand tires under the Kelly-Springfield Tire Co., Lee Tire & Rubber Co., and Atlas names. And thousands of employees were dropped from the payroll. Those measures were not enough, however.

Goodyear had incurred a large debt to stave off a takeover attempt in 1986. American car sales were down. Further, it had an oil pipeline that, although completed, was still consuming cash and operating at less than capacity. Net income per share dropped every year from 1987 through 1991. Then the retired CEO of Rubbermaid Inc., Stanley Gault, was hired to try to turn Goodyear around.

Gault is described as a blizzard of activity who manages without having to give direct orders. He believes in organizations built on trust, prefers people to call him by his first name, and regularly visits tire stores on Saturdays. He installed closed-circuit television so that workers can keep abreast of the company's fi-

nancial position and plays video tapes of his quarterly question and answer meetings at corporate headquarters. To hold down costs, he removed light bulbs from most of the lamps in his office, replaced company limousines with sedans, and sold three of the five corporate jets. He introduced new products, issued new stock, and opened new channels of distribution such as using the Sears network of stores.

All of these attempts seemed to work. Sales and profits were up in 1992, and Goodyear's prospects for the future looked bright. And Gault was named CEO of the year by a leading trade publication.[48]

Discussion Questions

1. In what way does an understanding of where Goodyear came from (its history) aid you in comprehending its current activities?
2. Describe management as practiced by Gault. How does that description compare to the description in the text?
3. Can you identify all of the functions of management in this brief case? Explain.
4. Can you identify all of the schools of management theory in this case? Explain.

1.2   International Training on the Rise

Ever since the megatrend from a national to a world economy was documented by John Naisbitt, training in international business has been steadily increasing. Such training helps when the German manager of an American company in Europe is moved to head up a Spanish plant. International training has proven useful not just for the globalization of business but also for dealing with diversity in organizations. In 1990, for instance, a Digital Equipment Corporation plant in Boston had 350 employees from 44 countries who spoke 19 languages. The plant printed announcements in English, Chinese, French, Spanish, Portuguese, Vietnamese, and Haitian Creole. Today, with many foreign corporations taking direct investment in U.S. companies, many U.S. employees find that their superior is from another country. Training can help to ease problems in all such situations.

Leading experts in the education field suggest that an ability to communicate effectively both orally and in writing as well as mastery of at least one foreign language and culture are fundamental. Businesses are training people in these fundamentals, and business school training is increasing outside of the United States. L'Institut Européen d'Administration des Affaires (INSEAD) in

Fontainebleau, France, the International Management Institute in Geneva, Switzerland, and the International Management Development Institute in Lausanne, Switzerland, all have far more applicants than they are able to accept. This is also true in business programs at Bocconi University in Italy and Spain's three top-rated business programs.

Indeed, most overseas managers do not fail because they lack the usual job skills. They fail because of an inability to adapt to an unfamiliar culture. Because doing business requires specialized language knowledge—of labor laws, tax codes, legal constraints, and accounting concepts—one key component to such adaptation is the ability to communicate in the language of that culture. But understanding culture goes beyond understanding language. Some cultures, for instance, put great emphasis on punctuality, while others are far more casual about time. In some cultures it is considered bad taste to get right to business before exchanging social pleasantries. In the United States managers generally "make" decisions, while in many other cultures managers "take" decisions, that is, obtain decisions from others in a more highly participative manner.

Companies that recognize the importance of international

and cross-cultural training are reaping the benefits of such under-standing. Of eight hundred employees so trained and then sent to Saudi Arabia, Shell Oil found that only three returned to the United States early, a considerable improvement over their past experience. At S.C. Johnson Wax, the use of training has reduced the failure rate for overseas managers to less than 2 percent, again a significant improvement.[49]

Discussion Questions

1. In what way does this case suggest that the environment of management is changing? Is management becoming even more complex? If so, how; if not, why?
2. How should companies respond to this change?
3. In terms of both efficiency and effectiveness, what might the costs and benefits be of international training?

CHAPTER

2

Managerial Roles and Skills

Learning Objectives

After studying this chapter you should be able to

· Describe the challenges facing managers of today and tomorrow.

· Discuss the integrative framework for the different managerial schools of thought.

· Identify the essential managerial roles.

· Identify the essential managerial skills and knowledge.

· Summarize how managers develop managerial skills and knowledge.

Twenty-one years ago, the first Hard Rock Cafe opened in London. Today there are eighteen Hard Rock Cafes across Europe and eleven in the United States. One of the Hard Rock's central strategies has been to cater to the rock music business and its fans. All of the cafes have a rock theme with rock and roll memorabilia. In addition, each cafe plays rock and roll music nonstop. Over the last twenty years, Robert Earl, president of the European division, has served many rock stars and their fans. The cafe has also provided free backstage catering at rock concerts, all in an effort to get the rock stars and other celebrities to frequent the cafe. Hard Rock Cafes have done more than survive with this strategy, they have thrived. Most of this success has occurred without spending large sums of money on traditional methods of advertising.

But nothing stays the same for very long in business. Competition, changing demographics, and social pressures have caused managers at the Hard Rock Cafe chain to seek new ventures and change their methods of operation. For example, as economic competition heated up in the restaurant business, Hard Rock Cafes diversified their product line not by introducing new food items but by introducing souvenir T-shirts. Over 11 million of these shirts have been sold from the London cafe alone. In addition, Peter Morton, president of the U.S. division, is planning to open the Hard Rock Hotel & Casino in Las Vegas in 1993. The marketing research indicates that the Hard Rock patrons "really enjoy gambling with friends in a more social environment." For that reason, the hotel will have not only a large pool but also a sandy "beach" for socializing. The casino will also have a larger proportion of slot machines than other casinos to cater to the more casual crowd that usually frequents the Hard Rock Cafes.

As society's values change, so must business. In 1987 Morton created a Save the Planet Department in response to environmental concerns of air and water pollution and the solid waste crisis. The restaurants now recycle intensively, attempt to serve food free of chemicals and pesticides, and donate excess food to hunger projects. In addition, the department acts as a training department for employees and serves as a clearinghouse on environmental information for other companies. As Morton views it, "The Hard Rock Cafe chain is in the entertainment business," but they must always stay alert for new ventures and changes in society's wants and desires.[1] ■

Peter Morton and Robert Earl are managers who run the international organization called Hard Rock Cafe. Although they have been very successful in the past, they are not resting on their laurels. They are planning for the future by opening new cafes in Berlin, Italy, and Las Vegas. They have made important decisions about environmental issues and the make-up of their clientele. All of these actions required the use of specific managerial knowledge and skills such as strategic planning, decision making, and environmental scanning. You will learn more about these specific managerial topics in later chapters. For now, recognize that Morton and Earl are examples of real managers in action just like Mo Hatton, manager of Ken's Pizza in Tulsa, Oklahoma. He too has to apply managerial skill and knowledge to operate his pizzeria.

Developing managerial knowledge and skills is what this book is all about. This chapter begins with a brief discussion of the challenges facing managers today and tomorrow. Next, we present an integrative framework that synthesizes the different managerial schools of thought presented in Chapter 1. Using the integrative framework, we will explore the different roles managers play. Then we present the essential managerial skills and knowledge every manager needs to activate the managerial roles. Finally, we discuss how managers develop managerial skills and acquire managerial knowledge. After completing this chapter, you will have started to develop important conceptual skills for the field of management.

The Challenges of Today's and Tomorrow's Managers

Today's manager faces many challenges and will continue to do so in the future. One of the more pressing challenges is how to compete successfully not just against local or national competition but against global competition. You will learn more about these challenges in Chapter 5. The challenge of global competition has managers rethinking how organizations should be structured and how work should be done. Self-managing work teams, total quality management, and just-in-time inventory are all examples of managers trying to find better ways to compete.

As international competition heats up, organizations will need to turn to their most valuable resource for new ways to compete. That resource is people. But this means *all* people, not just a select class or group of people. One of our greatest resources is the diversity of our culture, but in the past we have often wasted this resource. As Jim Preston, president and CEO of Avon Products, Inc., said, "Talent is color blind. Talent is gender blind. Talent has nothing to do with dialects, whether they're Hispanic or Irish or Polish or Chinese."[2] He went on to say that if the United States is to regain its competitive advantage, managers will have to harness the human power of all the diverse groups that make up the work force. It will be the challenge of management to do so, including harnessing the abilities of the disabled as required by the Americans with Disabilities Act.

Another challenge that managers face is the production of quality goods and services. The concept of total quality management has become a hallmark of progressive companies. Total quality management (TQM) has to do with making an organization-wide commitment to continuous improvement and to completely meeting the customers' needs. In Chapter 21, the topic of TQM is discussed more fully. For example, as part of Xerox Corporation's quality movement, the company has been able to reduce the component defect rate by more than 80 percent and improve customer service too.[3] But a commitment to total quality does not just happen. Every manager in the organization must accept the challenge for this to happen.

At the same time that managers are trying to satisfy customer needs, they are also trying to increase productivity within the organization. Productivity is a measure of output (product or service) as it relates to inputs (people, materials, money, and information). While the United States is still the productivity leader in the world, it is slipping. For example, in 1992, the United States increased its productivity by only .5 percent while Japan increased its by 3.0 percent and West Germany increased its by 1.6 percent.[4] The decline could spell trouble for the American standard of living. Managers will be challenged to find new methods to increase productivity. As Jack Welch, CEO of General Electric put it, "For a company and for a nation, productivity is a matter of survival."[5]

These are only a few of the many challenges facing managers today and tomorrow. In *A Matter of Ethics,* Anita Roddick, founder and owner of Body Shop International, balances the challenges of making a profit and being socially responsible. To be able to effectively deal with these challenges, a manager must know which managerial roles to play and which managerial skills to apply.

An Integrative Framework

Models are representations of a more complex reality.

In Chapter 1 we presented a historical perspective of management. Three different schools of thought were presented: the classical school, the behavioral school, and the quantitative school. In addition, contemporary theories such as systems theory, the contingency approach, TQM, and high involvement were introduced. While these schools of thought may appear unrelated, each represents one part of the whole story of management.

Many of these may be thought of as specific **managerial models.** Models are representations of a more complex reality. A toy train is a physical model that represents a real train. Social models like the managerial schools of thought represent a set of assumptions and a way of viewing the world. The contingency approach to management argues that there is no one best way to

A Matter of Ethics

Body Shop Balances Responsibility and Profitability

Body Shop International founder and managing director, Anita Roddick, combines her personal values and her professional mission. Although altruism is often viewed as polarized thinking with profit orientations, Roddick has made herself one of the richest women in Britain by selling natural skin and hair care products with social consciousness. Her formula is working. Sales in 1991 reached $391 million, and earnings were $21 million. She monitors the progress of more than seven hundred stores in thirty-nine countries, including a mail-order business that sells nonanimal-tested products developed with naturally based ingredients.

Roddick's approach is based on a belief that businesses can improve the world, a belief that fits with the company's carefully crafted image. Instead of appealing to vanity, like the conventional cosmetics business, "run by men who create needs that don't exist," Body Shop appeals to individuals concerned with environmental and social issues. The Body Shop has a commitment to these concerns that goes beyond lip service to popular issues. For example, Body Shop contributes $5,000 each month to keeping up three orphanages in Romania.

Every success breeds competition, and, as would be expected, competition using her strategy is coming from such lofty contenders as The Limited and Estee Lauder Inc. Roddick claims little concern, believing that her politics will set her apart from the imitators. As the competition rides on her approach toward "naturalness," she refuses to counter with advertising. In fact, she states that she does not believe in advertising; the company has no advertising or marketing department. The cynical have deemed this approach a clever ploy to attract attention and thus receive free publicity.

Roddick is a liaison and figurehead manager and in fact finds finances "bloody boring." She intends to keep her organizational culture intact in part by her hiring practices. Applicants are asked questions that range from whom they admire to what they read. One prospective employee lost a retail director position when Roddick learned that he liked to hunt. Roddick believes that a leader should be committed to a forceful vision in order to focus the energies of the entire organization. Roddick is an effective manager who wins commitment and sets an example for the organization by being ethical and inspiring.[6] ■

---

manage across all situations. Therefore, each management model explains only one part of the whole management process. But each model does contribute its own unique insight to the process. Together the different models provide a manager with a useful framework.

For example, the challenge of coordinating an organization's activities increases as the organization increases in size. A large organization may therefore have more policy manuals and scheduled meetings than a small firm. Some organizations face complex and turbulent environments while others face definable and stable environments. An organization that faces a turbulent environment must use open systems thinking to remain adaptive to these external forces. On the other hand, an organization with a more stable environment will most likely use administrative management school thinking to routinize the work. The important point here is that the application of different managerial schools of thought (managerial models) are contingent on key factors experienced by the organization.

An **integrative framework** has been developed to help managers better understand this relationship.[7] The framework is built around two continua (Exhibit 2.1). The horizontal continuum runs from an internal focus to an external focus. The manager moves along this continuum trying to satisfy both the internal needs or forces of the organization and the external needs or forces of the environment. The **internal focus** helps to maintain the organization. It might in-

*The **integrative framework** provides a process model for the four managerial models.*

***Internal focus** helps to maintain the organization.*

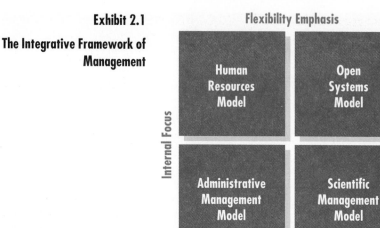

Source: Adapted from Robert E. Quinn, Sue R. Faerman, Michael P. Thompson, and Michael R. McGrath, *Becoming a Master Manager: A Competency Framework* (New York: John Wiley, 1990), p. 13.

External focus helps to make the organization competitive.

clude activities such as employee participation in decision making and the management of information. At the other end of the spectrum, an **external focus** helps to make the organization competitive. This focus might include such things as organization growth and productivity.

The vertical continuum extends from an efficiency emphasis to a flexibility emphasis. The manager moves along this continuum trying to make the organization as efficient as possible yet simultaneously flexible enough to adapt to environmental forces. The **efficiency emphasis** helps the manager to use resources the best way possible. The **flexibility emphasis** helps the manager to adapt to change. While the efficiency dimension seeks stability and direction, the flexibility dimension seeks employee participation and innovation. The two axes demonstrate the dynamic tension placed on a manager. As you can see in Exhibit 2.1, each of the management models fits into one of the quadrants.

Efficiency emphasis helps to use resources wisely.

Flexibility emphasis helps to adapt to change.

Scientific Management Model

The **scientific management model** focuses on making the best product in the most efficient way. In some ways, it was a forerunner to the current quality movement. The central idea was to identify the best way to do a task and then to make sure that the task was done that way.[8] One reason for making a product as efficiently as possible is to keep its cost low. By doing so, the product is more attractive to customers. Therefore, the scientific management model focuses on satisfying the customer (an external focus) by producing the product the best way possible at the lowest cost.

Administrative Management Model

The **administrative management model** focuses on the internal operation of the organization. It attempts to make administrative procedures more efficient by finding better ways to coordinate and monitor the work of the organization. By doing this, the organization becomes more stable and predictable. Just as the scientific management model pleases customers, the administrative management model satisfies managers. One reason for making the work of the organization as predictable as possible is so that managers can more easily evaluate the productivity of the organization. In addition, when the work is predictable, it is clear when management must take action to correct deficiencies.

Human Resources Model

The **human resources model** emphasizes flexibility in adapting to internal organizational changes by focusing on the people inside the organization. It attempts to build both team orientation and employee involvement among members of the organization. By doing so, the organization hopes that employees will become committed to the organization and willing to adapt to organizational changes. In that way the organization becomes more cohesive and adaptable. Just as the administrative management model pleases managers, the human resources model satisfies organizational members. One reason for this emphasis on people is that while people are an organization's most valuable resource, they are also its most expensive resource. In addition, organizations that have shown that they value their employees' involvement are also widely respected and are considered good places to work.[9]

Open Systems Model

The **open systems model** emphasizes flexibility in adapting to external changes. It attempts to focus on adapting to the feedback from external forces in a creative and innovative manner. In addition, it requires the application of the entrepreneurial role. *The Entrepreneurial Spirit: Paliafito Gets a Grip on New Market* box shows how one group of entrepreneurially spirited friends turned a creative idea into a hot toy. Chapter 4 explores the topic of entrepreneurship in more detail. By seeking new ideas and developing new ways of producing old products, organizations try to remain competitive in the global economy. If, on the other hand, an organization does not adapt, it runs the risk of failing. Just as the human resources model pleases organizational members, the open systems model satisfies organizational owners such as stockholders. One reason for emphasis on adapting to environmental forces such as economic, competitive, and sociocultural elements is the survival of the organization. In addition, while worldwide boundaries of business are disappearing rapidly,[10] organizations that do adapt to environmental changes will continue to be able to offer employment and improved standards of living.

An Analysis of the Integrative Framework

The integrative framework provides the manager with a way of making sense out of the different managerial models. If you examine Exhibit 2.1 again, you can see that it includes both complementary and opposing schools of thought.

Microsoft employees spend long hours frequently interacting as teams in an open system organization. They dress casually and decorate their work spaces to make a comfortable environment. Note here the numerous mermorabilia on the bookcase and wall. (Peter Sibbald 1992.)

The Entrepreneurial Spirit

Paliafito Gets a Grip on a New Market

"The Super Grip Ball craze is a dream come true," says Gregory Waylock, executive vice president for Paliafito, the company that produces Super Grip Ball. Even the klutziest kid can field like a big leaguer. How? Put stick-to-itself Velcro on a sphere that is roughly the size of a tennis ball. Apply the same stuff to two mitt-size disks that have straps across the back for a handhold, and presto! The Velcro-covered ball and mitts have been stocked, and have subsequently sold out, in traditional toy stores like Toys "Я" Us, as well as in upscale executive toy stores like Sharper Image.

One of the advantages of the games played with Super Grip Ball is that they can be played in the house, and they surpass the specified age range that most toys must accommodate. Entrepreneurs know they have been successful when competition appears, and several other companies now produce similar versions of the Super Grip Ball. Another variation of this fad involves a cap with Velcro. Individuals "catch" the ball on their hat for scores that are outlined on the cap. Marketers of the Super Grip Ball also are planning new versions. One of these involves a seven-foot mitt for team play.

How do entrepreneurs find ideas like this? In Mark Pali-afito's case it was coaching a young baseball league. Paliafito had a set of Velcro grips and a ball made in South Korea. He tried it out and found that kids love it. Paliafito immediately started thinking about other potential uses. He contacted six of his friends who played basketball and football together in high school. They ventured together to market and distribute the Super Grip Ball.

In January 1991, Paliafito bought the U.S. marketing rights by promising wide exposure of the product. In fact, Paliafito promised to spend at least $1 million on advertising. In the spirit of a true entrepreneur his promotions involved more ingenuity and effort than money. For example, Paliafito gave away thousands of the games to college students on beaches in Texas and Florida during the traditional spring break. The results were sales of 650,000 Super Grip Balls and orders for nearly 1 million more.

One problem successful entrepreneurs have is keeping ahead of demand. "We have accounts calling us every day, but our warehouse is empty," laments Waylock, one of the co-founders. Cash-flow constraints, a classic problem for new ventures, particularly small companies, has also limited Paliafito.

Fads usually change, decline, and die very quickly. In an attempt to expand its audience, Paliafito offers Super Grip Ball paddles with corporate logos on them. Regardless of the future whims of the consumer, at present Paliafito is enjoying its success. Says Waylock: "We're having a ball."[11] ∎

For example, the administrative management and the scientific management models both emphasize efficiency and stability. The human resources and open systems models share a common emphasis on flexibility and adaptation. The human resources and administrative management models focus on internal processes in the organization. The open systems and scientific management models both focus on external forces and their effect on the organization.

In addition, each model has its opposing point of view. The human resources model, with its emphasis on team orientation and employee involvement, is in direct contrast to the scientific management model, which emphasizes worker efficiency and task simplification. Likewise, the models of administrative management and open systems are diametrically opposed. The administrative management model emphasizes developing stable and efficient organizations, while the open systems model argues for an adaptive and fluid organization.

These differences among the managerial models reflect the challenges managers face every day. Remember, no one model is always right or always wrong. Effective managers use all of the different managerial models daily to perform their jobs. The self-assessment tool at the end of this chapter will help you determine which managerial model is most appropriate for a given situation. For now, we will conclude that managers must use all managerial models to be both effective and efficient.

Is it enough just to know which managerial model applies to be an effective manager? The answer to this question is an emphatic no. But knowing the appropriate managerial school is an excellent place to start, because it provides a conceptual framework for focusing the manager's attention. Once a manager has determined the appropriate managerial model for the specific challenge at hand, the manager must next be able to act. Managers activate the different managerial models through **managerial roles.** A manager's role in an organization is similar to an actor's role in a play. It consists of certain actions that the manager is expected to perform and ways in which he or she is expected to behave.

Managerial roles are actions a manager is expected to perform and ways in which he or she is expected to behave.

Managerial Roles: Essential Activities

Managers work long hours at an intense pace.[12] They are frequently interrupted. Most of their work is disjointed and fragmented. Most of their encounters are brief and seldom with the same person or group. While managers use many different communication methods, they prefer face-to-face communication with subordinates, peers, superiors, and others inside and outside the organization. In addition, managers play definite roles to get their work done.

Managerial roles fall into three general categories. Roles begin with the formal authority bestowed on managers by their organization. This authority is accompanied by a certain amount of status. This status causes all managers to be involved in interpersonal relationships with subordinates, peers, and superiors, who in turn provide managers with information they need to make decisions.[13] Table 2.1 presents the ten roles grouped according to those primarily concerned with interpersonal relationships, those concerned with information exchange, and those concerned with decision making.

Interpersonal Roles

There are three **interpersonal roles** in the manager's job. The first is that of **figurehead.** When serving as a figurehead, the manager simply puts in an appearance as a representative of the organization. Although there is little serious communication and no important decision making in the figurehead role, it should not be overlooked. At the interpersonal level, the figurehead role symbolizes what the organization is all about and its attitude toward others. When a manager takes a visitor to dinner, attends a ribbon-cutting ceremony, or serves as a company representative at a wedding or funeral, he or she is playing the figurehead role.

The second interpersonal role is that of **leader.** As a leader, the manager hires employees, motivates them to work hard, and deals with behavioral processes. The manager is responsible for coordinating the efforts of subordinates. When a manager inspires employees by creating a vision of the future, emphasizes the importance of high quality performance, and clarifies the roles of each subordinate, the manager is enacting the leadership role.

The third interpersonal role is that of **liaison,** which involves dealing with people outside the organization on a regular basis. Managers must be able to work well with outside agencies that can help them achieve their organizational goals. In a sense, the liaison role is about developing a network of mutual obligation with others. For example, a vice president of human resources might serve as a trustee on your university's board of trustees. By doing this, the manager develops a network of contacts outside of her organization. Some of these contacts may prove to be useful to her organization. In addition, when the university asks for information on what industry is seeking in new undergraduates, the manager successfully fills the liaison role when she provides insightful information about necessary skills of undergraduates.

Categories/roles	Description	Identifiable activities
Interpersonal		
Figurehead	Symbolic head; obliged to perform a number of routine duties of a legal or social nature	Ceremony, status requests, solicitations
Leader	Responsible for the motivation and activation of subordinates; responsible for staffing, training, and associated duties	Virtually all managerial activities involving subordinates
Liaison	Maintains self-developed network of outside and informers who provide favors and information	Acknowledgements of mail; external board work; other activities involving outsiders
Informational		
Monitor	Seeks and receives wide variety of special information (much of it current) to develop thorough understanding of organization and environment; emerges as nerve center of internal and external information of the organization	Handling all mail and contacts categorized as concerned primarily with receiving information (e.g., periodical news, observational tours)
Disseminator	Transmits information received from outsiders or from other subordinates to members of the organization; some information factual, some involving interpretation and integration of diverse value positions of organizational influencers	Forwarding mail into organization for informational purposes, verbal contacts involving information flow to subordinates (e.g., review sessions, instant communication flows)
Spokesperson	Transmits information to outsiders on organization's plans, policies, actions, results, etc.; serves as expert on organization's industry	Board meetings; handling mail and contacts involving transmission of information to outsiders
Decisional		
Entrepreneur	Searches organization and its environment for opportunities and initiates "improvement projects" to bring about change; supervises design of certain projects as well	Strategy and review sessions involving initiation or design of improvement projects
Disturbance handler	Responsible for corrective action when organization faces important, unexpected disturbances	Strategy and review sessions involving disturbances and crises
Resource allocator	Responsible for the allocation of organizational resources of all kinds—in effect, the making or approval of all significant organizational decisions	Scheduling; requests for authorization; any activity involving budgeting and the programming of subordinates' work
Negotiator	Responsible for representing the organization at major negotiations	Negotiation

Source: Table "Mintzberg's Managerial Roles" from *The Nature of Managerial Work* by Henry Mintzberg. Copyright © 1973 by Henry Mintzberg. Reprinted by permission of HarperCollins, Publishers, Inc.

Table 2.1   Original Managerial Roles

Informational Roles

There are also three basic **informational roles** in the manager's job. The first is the role of **monitor,** in which the manager actively watches the environment for information that might be relevant to the organization. A manager who reads *The Wall Street Journal,* asks employees about work-related problems they are having, and closely scrutinizes television commercials for competitors is acting as a monitor.

The opposite of the monitor role is that of **disseminator.** In this role the manager relays information gleaned through monitoring to the appropriate people in the organization. For instance, an article in *Fortune* may be of little direct use to one manager but of considerable value to a colleague. To fill the role of disseminator successfully, the first manager clips the article and passes it on.

The third informational role is that of **spokesperson.** The spokesperson role is similar to the figurehead role, but the manager in the spokesperson role presents information of meaningful content and/or answers questions on the firm's behalf. For example, during the Union Carbide disaster in India in 1985, when a plant's poison gas leak killed thousands of people, managers regularly appeared at news conferences to make statements about new events and to answer reporters' questions. The Exxon *Valdez* oil spill in 1989 showed how crucial the spokesperson role can be. In this case, the slowness with which Exxon's CEO responded to the disaster damaged the public's trust in the company. In contrast, Johnson & Johnson's response in 1982 and 1986 to the Tylenol incidents demonstrated how critical the spokesperson role is in a crisis and in maintaining the public's trust.

Decisional Roles

The final category of managerial roles is **decisional** in nature; that is, these are the roles that managers play when they make decisions. First, there is the role of **entrepreneur,** in which the manager looks for opportunities that the organization can pursue and takes the lead in doing so. If a manager at Dow Chemical notices that a particular waste by-product can easily be transformed into a new, potentially marketable product and then submits a proposal offering to take charge of the initiative, the manager is being an entrepreneur.

The role of **disturbance handler** is also important. This role involves the manager in resolving conflicts between, for example, two groups of employees, between a sales representative and an important customer, or between another manager and a union representative. If a manager at the Ford glass plant resolves a grievance, he or she is being a disturbance handler.

The **resource allocator** role focuses on determining how resources will be divided among different areas within the organization. If there is $275,000 to divide among three departments, each of which has requested $100,000, the manager has to decide how to distribute the funds. While this task may involve using some quantitative procedure to analyze the best use of the funds, it also requires interpersonal skill in explaining the decision to each department. In this situation, the manager is combining the resource allocator role with the leader role. The example here talks about financial resources, but the manager also allocates material, people, and information as part of the resource allocator role.

Finally, there is the role of **negotiator.** In this role, the manager attempts to work out agreements and contracts that operate in the best interests of the organization. Such agreements might be labor contracts, purchasing contracts, or sales contracts. The negotiator's role occurs both inside and outside of the organization. For example, a company president may negotiate a contract with a consulting firm, or a procurement officer may negotiate for janitorial services for the organization. Both managers are performing the negotiator role. Inside the organization, a manager may facilitate the settlement of an equal opportunity grievance or negotiate a labor contract. Each of these activities also represents the negotiator role.

Cross-cultural decision making is an increasingly important challenge to contemporary managers. Hayward P. Gipson, Jr., Vice President and General Manager for Corning's Vitro International group wrestles with a decision about selling square-shaped dishes and round-shaped dishes in different countries. (Photolink/John Reis.)

An Analysis of Managerial Roles

Since the original managerial roles were identified, there have been many follow-up studies attempting to validate the roles.[14] The results generally support the earlier findings. However, managers at different levels within the organization place different emphasis on some of the roles.[15] For example, top managers say they place great importance on the roles of liaison, spokesperson, and resource allocator. On the other hand, middle managers and first-line managers list the leader role as one of their most important roles.

How do these ten managerial roles fit into the integrative framework? The figurehead, liaison, spokesperson, and entrepreneur roles all fit nicely into the open systems model. Each of these roles has something to do with an effort to improve the effectiveness and competitiveness of the organization. The roles of leader, disseminator, and disturbance handler fit into the human resources model. These roles deal primarily with people inside the organization. Negotiator is a role that fits into both the open systems and human resources models because it deals with negotiating both inside and outside of the organization. Finally, monitor and resource allocator are roles necessary in the administrative management model. These two roles focus on the internal functioning of the organization.

As you can see, these roles do not satisfy all four of the managerial models in the integrative framework. One reason is that the integrative framework point of view was not used in developing these roles. Other management scholars have identified additional managerial roles that are believed to be critical for a successful and effective manager.[16]

Recently, two essential managerial roles have been identified for each of the four models in the integrative framework.[17] Table 2.2 presents the eight roles grouped by managerial model. Studies using this newer set of managerial roles have confirmed that the eight roles do indeed appear in the four indicated quadrants of the integrative framework.[18] If you compare the two lists of roles, you can see that some of the roles such as the monitor role are the same. In other cases, some of the earlier roles such as spokesperson and entrepreneur are combined into a single role such as

Roles	Description	Identifiable activities
Scientific Management		
Producer	Task oriented; usually involves motivating others to increase production and to accomplish stated goals	High interest, energy, and personal drive
Director	Goal setter; a take-charge and decisive individual; usually involves planning and initiating goals, defining roles, and giving instructions	Develops goals, defines tasks to be accomplished, and provides direction to accomplish the tasks
Administrative Management		
Coordinator	Reliable; expected to maintain the structure and flow of the organization	Schedules, organizes, and coordinates staff efforts
Monitor	Desire for details; knows what is going on in the unit and checks on progress	Reviews, analyzes, and responds to work processes
Human Resources		
Facilitator	Process oriented; fosters teamwork and manages interpersonal conflict	Develops a cohesive and group problem-solving atmosphere
Mentor	Caring oriented; helpful, considerate, approachable, open, and fair	Develops people through personal involvement
Open Systems		
Innovator	Creative; envisions new ways, packages them invitingly, and convinces others of the need	Facilitates adaptation and change
Broker	Powerful; represents, negotiates, and acquires resources for the organization	Politically astute, persuasive, and influential

Source: Robert E. Quinn, Sue R. Faerman, Michael P. Thompson, and Michael R. McGrath, *Becoming a Master Manager: A Competency Framework* (New York: John Wiley, 1990).

Table 2.2   Managerial Roles of the Integrative Framework

innovator. As you can see the two lists of managerial roles, while created from different viewpoints do complement each other. However, since the newer set of managerial roles was created specifically with the integrative framework in mind, we will focus on these roles in this book. This does not mean that the older set of managerial roles is unimportant or wrong. You can find each of these roles in the integrative framework, but they do not provide complete coverage of all the quadrants in the integrative framework. The skill builder at the end of this chapter starts to develop the mentor role. To be a mentor to an employee means to help develop that employee by providing career information and performance feedback. Good mentors understand how they achieved the position they currently hold. They understand their strengths and weaknesses. In other words, they are self aware. The Johari window skill builder helps you develop the skill of self-awareness.

In summary, managers activate the different managerial models through enacting different managerial roles. Each role is important and must be properly executed. Whether a manager performs a role successfully is determined by the extent to which he or she possesses the necessary management skills and knowledge.

Managerial Skills and Knowledge: Essential Competencies

Managerial skills reflect the ability to perform the various behaviors managers need to execute their roles effectively. Effective managers tend to possess a certain mix of skills that sets them apart from others. Skills, then, are behavioral in nature, such as the ability to present a strategic plan to the board of directors or conduct a performance feedback session with an employee. **Managerial knowledge,** on the other hand, is the special information and mental activity a manager uses to decide how to behave. Again, effective managers have a mix of different types of knowledge that they combine in unique ways to be effective. Knowledge, then, is cognitive in nature, such as formulating a new way to solve the company's parking problem or calculating the estimated return on investment for a new venture.

From these examples, it should be clear that skills and knowledge work together. The process comprises three components: 1) the existence of knowledge, 2) a method for accessing this knowledge, and 3) the ability to enact a set of behaviors using the retrieved knowledge to perform the given task. The third component is what people observe and label as a skill. Actually, the first two components are indispensable prerequisites to the actual execution of the observable actions, and these components are knowledge.

Managerial Skills

The core managerial skills have been identified as technical, human, and conceptual and can be developed in managers by providing them with managerial knowledge.[19] It was believed that if managers were to perform effectively in their managerial roles, they needed specific managerial skills and knowledge. Exhibit 2.2 illustrates the relative importance of these skills by level of management.

Technical skills are the skills a manager needs to perform specialized tasks within the organization.

Technical skills are the skills a manager needs to perform specialized tasks within the organization. In the Mayo Clinic, technical skills are those possessed by physicians, nurses, and lab technicians. At Dean Witter Reynolds, they are the skills associated with understanding investment opportunities, tax regulations, and so forth. The electrical and mechanical engineering skills possessed by the professional engineers at Hewlett-Packard are the relevant technical skills for that organization. At Wal-Mart, a manager who decides on an advertising campaign, the promotional items, and pricing for a new product is using technical skills.

As shown in Exhibit 2.2, technical skills are very important for first-line managers. Because they spend much of their time working with operating employees, they must have a good understanding of the work those employees are doing. Technical skills are slightly less important for middle managers, since a greater proportion of their time is devoted to other managerial activity, and even less important (although not unimportant) for top managers.

Exhibit 2.2

The Importance of Managerial Skills by Level

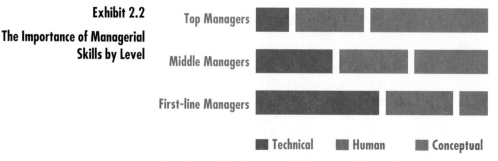

Source: Based on information presented in Robert L. Katz, "Skills of an Effective Administrator," *Harvard Business Review,* January–February 1955, pp. 33–42.

Even in international planning, technical skills are important. Arco Chemical's regional Technical Center in Singapore provides product application services and technical support for its Asia-Pacific customers. The Technical Center also plays a role in Arco research efforts by adapting research to regional needs. (Reprinted with permission of Arco Chemical.)

__Human skills__ are the skills a manager needs to work well with other people.

Human skills are the skills a manager needs to work well with other people. They include the ability to understand someone else's position, to present one's own position in a reasonable way, to communicate effectively, and to deal effectively with conflict. Managers with well-developed human skills can create a climate of trust and security in which organizational members feel free to express themselves without fear of punishment or humiliation.[20]

Because all managers must interact with others, human skills are equally important at all managerial levels. In fact, some say they are the most critical and the least developed skills in managers.[21] In general, the better any manager's human skills are, the more effective the manager is likely to be. While some managers have been successful in spite of limited human skills, it is rare. If it happens, it is only because another managerial skill is critically needed by the organization at the time. More often it is managers such as Jack Welch, CEO of GE, and David Glass, CEO of Wal-Mart, who demonstrate that human skills are very important in running successful organizations.

__Conceptual skills__ relate to a manager's ability to think in the abstract.

Conceptual skills relate to a manager's ability to think in the abstract. Managers need to be able to see relationships between forces that others may not see, to understand how a variety of factors are interrelated, and to take a global perspective of the organization and its environment. A manager who recognizes an opportunity that no one else has seen and then successfully exploits that opportunity has drawn on conceptual skills.

Conceptual skills also include the ability to define and understand situations. If a plant manager at Alcoa notices that turnover at the plant is increasing, the manager needs to address the situation in some way. The first step is to define the problem: unacceptable turnover. Next, the manager must determine what is causing the problem and identify one or more ways to reduce it. For example, closer inspection may show that only one department is affected, which suggests a problem specific to that department. Appropriate action might include discussions with the department manager, the entire work group, or both.

As shown in Exhibit 2.2, conceptual skills are most important for top managers, because their job is to identify and exploit new opportunities. These skills are moderately important for middle managers and of less importance to first-line managers.

Technical, human, and conceptual skills are all necessary for effective management. As we have seen, top managers need a large measure of conceptual skills and a lesser amount of technical skills, whereas first-line managers need the reverse combination. Middle managers need equal measures of technical and conceptual skills. Finally, all managers need an equal portion of human skills.

Managerial Knowledge

In order to enact a skill, a manager must possess managerial knowledge. Cognitive psychologists have identified three types of knowledge that a person has to have to perform any task.[22] The three types of knowledge are declarative, procedural, and process. For example, for a manager to make an investment requires knowledge of investment terms (declarative), of tax procedures (procedural), and of the stock market process (process).

Declarative knowledge deals with facts and definitions.

Declarative knowledge deals with facts and definitions. It is sometimes called the "what" of a topic. For example, the boldface words in this text are definitions and therefore a kind of declarative knowledge. The words in the margins are also a kind of declarative knowledge. Without this type of knowledge, we could not think or communicate. This form of knowledge assists a manager in describing a situation. It also allows two managers to interact intelligently about a specific problem within the organization.

Procedural knowledge outlines a set of steps to be taken to accomplish a task.

Procedural knowledge outlines a set of steps to be taken to accomplish a task. It has often been called the "how to" of a task. A manager who sits down to prepare a budget is following a set of steps to accomplish this task. Procedural knowledge activates technical skills. For example, when a manager at British Petroleum prepares a scheduling chart, procedural knowledge is being used to carry out this technical skill.

Process knowledge provides a manager with a mental map for a specific topic.

Process knowledge provides a manager with a mental map for a specific topic. It is often referred to as knowledge about "how something works." Just like a road map helps you get around town by providing you with a model, a mental map helps the manager understand the relationships between different factors by providing a mental picture of the situation. The integrative framework is a good example of process knowledge. It provides a mental map that helps you understand the relationship among the different managerial models. Throughout this book, the exhibits provide excellent mental maps to assist you in developing process knowledge. Process knowledge activates the conceptual skills. A product manager at Sony who conceptualizes a new use or a new market for a product line is using process knowledge.

An Analysis of Managerial Skills and Knowledge

Since the original work on managerial skills, many studies have been conducted that confirm the three broad skill areas identified in this early research.[23] The more recent research done on knowledge types also seems to be consistent with the original conceptualization of skills. Declarative knowledge is a foundation. A great deal of what is covered in this book is declarative knowledge. The managerial vocabulary list at the end of each chapter is an example. By learning the definitions and meanings of these words, you will be able to better understand the lectures in class. You will also be able to ask better questions and formulate more intelligent answers during class discussion.

Process knowledge and procedural knowledge build on declarative knowledge. Process knowledge helps us explain how something works. For example, being able to explain how the brake system in a car works would indicate that you had process knowledge about a car's brake system, just as being able to explain how an oil company converts oil into gasoline would indicate process knowledge of the refining method. But to be able to explain how anything works, we also rely on our declarative knowledge about the topic.

Procedural knowledge specifies how to do a task. When you do multiplication or long division, you are using procedural knowledge. A manager redesigning a job is using procedural knowledge. In fact, anytime a person executes a set of steps to complete a task, he is using procedural knowledge. Procedural knowledge builds on both declarative knowledge and process knowledge. For example, imagine that you were asked to prepare a PERT chart for an upcoming project in your organization. Not only would you have to know the steps in the PERT chart procedure (procedural knowledge), but you would also have to be able to formulate a work flow diagram of the project (process knowledge). In addition, you would have to know the definition (declarative knowledge) of a node, an activity, and the critical path. You would also have to know the facts (declarative knowledge) such as the constants in calculating the expected time of completion for each activity in the chart. As you can see, procedural knowledge is dependent on both process knowledge and declarative knowledge. When actually preparing the PERT chart, you would be demonstrating both a conceptual skill (diagraming the work flow) and a technical skill (preparing the PERT chart).

Knowledge is critical to performing any skill, but generally it goes unseen. Knowledge is stored either internally in our minds or externally in books or computer systems. When the knowledge is stored externally, the manager must know where and how to access the knowledge. By reading this book, you are not only storing some of the knowledge internally, you are learning where to access knowledge that is stored externally in this book. On the other hand, skills are what we actually see people do. In this chapter, we have identified three broad skills. Each relies on different types of knowledge.

Conceptual skills rely heavily upon process knowledge. A manager formulating a new strategic plan for J C Penney's may use a SWOT analysis to determine the strengths and weaknesses of Penney's, but this skill is based on process knowledge of the relationship between the organization's structure and current environmental forces which impact on the organization. We will talk more about the impact of environmental forces in Part Two of the book and we will also assist you in developing the conceptual skill of SWOT analysis.

While conceptual skills depend heavily on process knowledge, technical skills rely most heavily on procedural knowledge. Technical skills generally have some procedure to follow to complete the task. For example, the planning and decision-making tools in Chapter 10 and the control methods in Appendix 2, all have defined procedures. When you have mastered these procedures and can perform the specified tasks, you will have mastered a set of managerial technical skills.

Finally, human skills depend equally on all of the knowledge types. This could be because the human element in an organization is the most complex and difficult to manage. For example, when a manager prepares to do a performance appraisal of an employee, the manager must conceptualize how the performance appraisal system relates to organizational entry, development, performance, and exit. In this case, the manager is using both process and declarative knowledge. When the manager prepares the performance appraisal form, he is using both procedural and declarative knowledge. Finally when the manager sits down with the employee to discuss past performance and to discuss future performance, the manager is using all three types of knowledge.

In summary, whenever a manager exhibits a managerial skill, it is done to satisfy some managerial role. Skills build on knowledge and roles build on skills to form the managerial storehouse. Exhibit 2.3 shows how managerial skills, knowledge, and roles fit together.

At the end of every chapter, we provide you with a managerial skill builder. This skill builder is to help you develop the skills you will need to become an effective manager. In addition, the skill builder will allow you to apply the managerial knowledge you learned while reading the chapter. Each skill builder will specify both the managerial role and managerial skill being developed. We have also provided a self-assessment tool at the end of each chapter. The self-assessments are designed to provide you with further insight into your professional development as a manager. Not all management development goes on in a formal classroom setting. You can en-

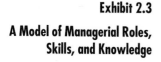

Exhibit 2.3

A Model of Managerial Roles, Skills, and Knowledge

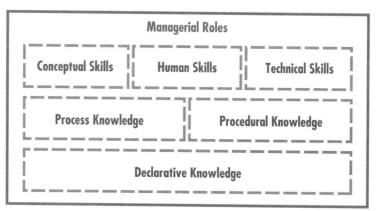

hance your ability to be a successful and effective manager by completing the self-assessment and then developing strategies for increasing your knowledge and developing your skills on specific topics of management.

Developing Managerial Skills and Acquiring Managerial Knowledge

s it just luck when managers combine effectiveness with efficiency? It is true that managers are sometimes just plain lucky, but more often than not they become successful because they are prepared.[24] This preparation usually consists of a combination of education and experience that gives an individual the technical, human, and conceptual skills and the declarative, procedural, and process knowledge necessary to contribute to an organization's efficiency and effectiveness.

Education

An education leading to a college degree is the first step in most people's managerial careers. In fact, a college degree is almost a requirement for promotion to upper levels of management in most organizations today. In 1990, over 90 percent of the CEOs of *Business Week*'s top one thousand corporations held a college degree.[25] Education does not stop with an undergraduate degree, however. Many managers return to school and get a graduate degree, usually a Master of Business Administration, or M.B.A. Often, many of these managers return to school because their undergraduate degree was in some other area such as chemistry or engineering. But just as many managers who majored in business return each year to update their managerial knowledge and skills.

In addition, managers attend advanced training and professional development programs sponsored by universities, private consulting firms, or other own companies.[26] These activities are apt to continue throughout a manager's career. This phenomenon is referred to as lifelong learning. It is a philosophy that learning, gaining new knowledge, and developing new skills is a lifelong process, not something that ends with a degree. The major accrediting organization for business schools (American Assembly of Collegiate Schools of Business, AACSB) has recognized the importance of this lifelong learning philosophy and has incorporated it into the new standards governing business schools' curriculums.[27]

The primary advantage of education and professional development as sources of managerial knowledge and skills is that learning can be well organized and planned. The process focuses the learner's attention on a specific body of knowledge. This reduces the time it takes to learn the material. One drawback to this method of learning is that the knowledge must be made more general in nature to satisfy a wide variety of learners.

Experience

An education alone, of course, does not promise a person an executive position. Making an "A" in your management class will not guarantee you a management position. Most people must still work their way up in an organization, sometimes making mistakes and suffering setbacks along the way.

Experience adds to your managerial knowledge. It provides you with specific declarative knowledge about your industry. It provides process knowledge in the form of specific work flows for your company. It provides specific procedural knowledge for tasks such as budgeting, hiring, and goal setting.

Experience comes in a variety of forms. Some people often work while in college. Others may even hold full-time jobs before they enter college. Quite often, these people return to school as non-traditional students seeking a degree in business. In these cases, the individuals have experience, but not the more structured and well-organized learning that an education provides. Others enter college directly from high school. After finishing college they might accept an initial job assignment with a company that offers them an entry-level position plus a management training program. Later, they may accept transfers to different departments to broaden their experience within the company.

Company changes are also common, and many people leave the first firm they work for and take a new job with another. Indeed, companies such as Procter & Gamble, General Foods, General Mills, and IBM have such good training programs that other organizations actively recruit people who have worked there for a few years.[28] Over the course of a lifelong career, a person is likely to work in a number of different jobs, usually for more than one company. Throughout this process, the individual develops managerial knowledge and skills through a combination of education and experience. Both are necessary to producing a successful and effective manager.

Chapter Summary

Managers are facing many new challenges in the business world today. One of those challenges is global competition. Another challenge managers will face is how to manage the diverse work force. Besides these two challenges, managers will also have to increase productivity while at the same time increasing quality. To meet these challenges, managers must develop knowledge and skills so that they can perform their roles efficiently and effectively.

The integrative framework organizes the different managerial schools of thought into a coherent whole. The framework revolves around two continuums. The horizontal continuum is anchored at one end by an external focus and at the other end by an internal focus. The vertical continuum emphasizes efficiency and flexibility. Each of the different managerial models fits into the contingency framework. Managers should be aware of the different situations in which each model will be most effective.

Managers activate the different managerial models through enacting different managerial roles. A role is a set of behaviors expected in a given situation. Earlier work identified ten different managerial roles in three different categories. The three general categories are interpersonal roles, informational roles, and decisional roles. Interpersonal roles are those of figurehead, leader, and liaison. Monitor, disseminator, and spokesperson are the informational roles. The four decisional roles are the roles of entre-

preneur, disturbance handler, resource allocator, and negotiator. More recent findings identified eight managerial roles, two for each managerial model. The managerial models are those of scientific management, administrative management, human resources, and open systems. The two essential roles for the scientific management model are those of producer and director; for the administrative management model, coordinator and monitor; for the human resources model, facilitator and mentor; and for the open systems model, innovator and broker. Other management scholars have identified their own lists of managerial roles. The key point is that managers perform roles to accomplish their managerial duties.

Whether a manager performs a role successfully is determined by the extent to which he or she possesses the necessary management skills and knowledge. Managerial skills consist of technical, human, and conceptual skills. These three skills provide the manager with the essential skills to enact the managerial roles. Managerial knowledge consists of declarative, procedural, and process knowledge. Each of these knowledge types assists the manager in performing some specific skill. It takes both knowledge and skill to enact a managerial role.

Managers obtain skill and knowledge by combining education and experience. Education may consist of schooling such as college or professional development conducted by the company.

Experience may be gained by job rotation, lateral movement within the company, or by moving from one company to another.

Both education and experience allow managers to acquire the skills and knowledge they need to be successful and effective.

The Manager's Vocabulary

managerial model	managerial roles	entrepreneur
integrative framework	interpersonal roles	disturbance handler
internal focus	figurehead	resource allocator
external focus	leader	negotiator
efficiency emphasis	liaison	technical skills
flexibility emphasis	informational roles	human skills
scientific management model	monitor	conceptual skills
administrative management model	disseminator	declarative knowledge
human resources model	spokesperson	procedural knowledge
open systems model	decisional roles	process knowledge

Review Questions

1. What are some of the challenges facing managers today and tomorrow?
2. Sketch the integrative framework of management and describe the managerial models of thought that are opposing forces.
3. Compare and contrast the original roles with those in the integrative framework.
4. List and describe the three essential managerial skills and the three essential managerial knowledge types. Give examples of each.
5. What are the roles of education and experience in acquiring managerial skills and knowledge?

Analysis Questions

1. Identify ten advantages to work force diversity.
2. It has been argued that there is no one best way to manage. Do you agree or disagree with this assertion? Why?
3. Which roles do you think managers spend most of their time playing? Is an effective manager more likely to use one or two roles exclusively, or does an effective manager go back and forth between all of the roles? Why?
4. For each of the integrative framework roles, provide an example of a managerial skill or managerial knowledge an effective manager might need.
5. You hear two classmates arguing over which is more important for a manager: education or experience. How would you help them see that it is not an either/or question? Which managerial role are you enacting during this discussion?

Self-Assessment

Which Management Model Applies?

Introduction Before a manager can apply specific managerial roles or skills the manager must know which managerial model applies for a given situation. The integrative framework presented in this chapter identifies four possible managerial models. This self-assessment assists you in defining which model is most applicable for a specific situation.

Instructions Think about a situation that you are facing with a job, campus organization, or club. Rate the following items on a scale from 1—Almost Never True, to 5—Almost Always True.

_____ 1. Effort is expended to find people to help with group tasks.

_____ 2. Our group is flexible.

_____ 3. Rules and policies are important in the organization.

_____ 4. My organization is productive.

_____ 5. Help is usually forthcoming for new people in our group.

_____ 6. Demands on our organization are predictable.

_____ 7. The work flow in our organization is understandable and coordinated.

_____ 8. Planning is emphasized in our organization.

_____ 9. Most people in my organization know how they are performing.

_____ 10. Outside sources criticize our organization.

_____ 11. Crisis management creeps into the work flow.

_____ 12. Most people in my organization plan their own tasks.

_____ 13. Overall, most people are committed to their jobs.

_____ 14. Outside sources support our organization.

_____ 15. Computerization is significant to our group.

_____ 16. Intensity is evident in the work effort.

_____ 17. Teamwork matters in this organization.

_____ 18. Our organization would be considered "information rich."

_____ 19. My work is fairly predictable from day to day.

_____ 20. Organizational objectives are clear.

For interpretation, turn to the back of the book.

Discussion Questions

1. Now that you have plotted your perspective of your organization, discuss why you believe that the indicators are correct or incorrect.
2. Which area could you have the greatest effect on for change within your organization?
3. Was there a great deal of difference between your highest score and your lowest score? Can you explain this difference for your organization?

Source: Adapted from Robert E. Quinn, *Beyond Rational Management: Mastering the Paradoxes and Competing Demands of High Performance* (San Francisco: Jossey-Bass, 1988).

Skill Builder

Johari Window

Purpose This exercise has two purposes: to encourage you to analyze yourself more accurately, and to start you working on small group cohesiveness. This exercise encourages you to share data about yourself and then to assimilate and process feedback. Small groups are typically more trusting and work better together, and you will be able to see this after this exercise has been completed. The Johari Window is a particularly good model for understanding the perceptual process in interpersonal relationships.

This skill builder focuses on the *human resources model*. It will help you develop your *mentor role*. One of the skills of a mentor is self-awareness.

Introduction Each individual has four sets of personality characteristics. One set, which includes such characteristics as working hard, the individual is well aware of and so are others. A second set is unknown to the individual but obvious to others. For example, in a working situation a peer might observe that your jumping in to get the group moving off dead center is appropriate. At other times, you jump in when the group is not really finished, and you seem to interrupt. A third set is known to the individual but not others. These are situations that you have elected not to share, perhaps because of a lack of trust. Finally, there is a fourth set, which is not known to the individual or to others, such as why you are uncomfortable at office parties.

Instructions Look at the Johari window on page 48. In quadrant #1 list three things that you know about yourself and that you think others know. List three things in quadrant #3 that others do not know about you. Finally, in quadrant #2, list three things that you did not know about yourself last semester that you learned from others.

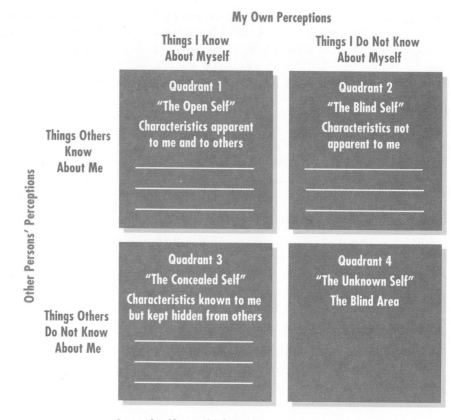

Sources: Adapted from Joseph Luft, *Group Processes: An Introduction to Group Dynamics* (Palo Alto, Ca.: Mayfield Publishing Co., 1970), pp. 10–11, and William C. Morris and Marshall Sashkin, *Organizational Behavior in Action* (St. Paul, Minn.: West Publishing Co., 1976), p. 56.

CONCLUDING CASES

2.1   Marriott Adapts to Meet Challenges

Marriott has a tough job for its new chief financial officer, but the organization has found an able manager in Stephen F. Bollenbach. Marriott has a specific task for Bollenbach: trim a $3.2 billion debt from the organization. Most people are assuming Bollenbach is the right person for the task.

Bollenbach was the financial officer of the Trump Organization until the offer from Marriott came in March 1992. His style has been that of both a tough-nosed negotiator and a soothing dealer with people. Both skills were exhibited throughout his tenure with Trump, when he endeared himself to Trump by persuading bankers to reduce Trump's personal liability for bank loans from more than $800 million to about $165 million.

Bollenbach has been successful in the financial arena throughout his career, utilizing both his finance degree and his M.B.A. What distinguishes his expertise is the level of creativity he brings to the financial side of business. Marriott is eager for his expertise. The company's current debt service is a worrisome $245 million, which is more than one-third of Marriott's $700-million annual cash flow.

J. W. Marriott, Jr. said he wants consumers to associate the Marriott chain with quality and consistency. To achieve his vision, he is betting that the company will grow through conversions, franchises, and management contracts. This growth pattern is consistent with expectations for Bollenbach: to put the hotel chain in a position to access additional sources of capital that were previously unattainable. Marriott believes that the recession cannot end until banks and bank regulators stop believing that all real estate is bad. He also states that until the economy improves, the competitive edge will be provided by better price value. The assignments for Bollenbach have been coupled with myriad changes to the organization.

One of the new approaches to efficiency is the reservation system that was initiated in the summer of 1992. Marriott introduced fourteen-day and twenty-one-day nonrefundable, advance-purchase pricing structure, similar to the airline industry's pricing structure differentials. Critics are quick to allege that the new system will provide less flexibility for guests and will allow rooms to be sold at too low a price.

Marriott is also attempting to adjust space and activities to current social norms. For example, as consumers have cut back on alcohol consumption, Marriott has had low utilization of lounges. The chain has begun to consider changing from the lobby appearance of the lounges to a theme concept. One successful venture has been the expansion of the Champion's Sports Bars.

Marriott has ventured into some uncharted territory in the areas of social responsibility and consumer voice requests. Although many hotels have responded with token improvements in waste and environmental issues, Marriott has taken bold steps to assess consumer conscientiousness. The Miami Marriott Dadeland converted 19 of its 303 rooms to "green" rooms, that is, rooms that feature advanced equipment designed to purify the air and drinking water. The response was so great that the number of green rooms was increased to 28.

Equally important to the clients of the future will be the reflection of cultural diversity in the workplace at Marriott. In an attempt to persuade minorities to select Marriott as a management career path, the company has created the INROADS program, which gives minority college students the financial means to experience four years of hotel management training. Marriott is attempting to stay ahead of the demands and concerns of society by adapting and leading with its mission and vision.[29]

Discussion Questions

1. What skills will Bollenbach need to enhance if he is to be successful at Marriott?
2. Some people believe that social responsibility programs like green rooms are not compatible with cost reduction. What is your opinion?
3. What cultural norms or issues might Marriott consider that would result in a competitive advantage for its organization?

2.2   Maytag Expands Its Market

In the fickle world of consumers, Maytag holds a secure position, recognizable by the long-running ads in which a repairman laments that Maytag's trouble-free products make him a lonely guy. Maytag's reputation is one of assumed quality. *Consumer Reports* has rated Maytag Corp. the leader in dependability for the last twenty-six years, far outdistancing competitors. But every company has its share of challenges, as Maytag learned when rumors hinted at possible takeovers. To assertively counter these rumors, Maytag chairman Daniel J. Krumm proposed a $1-billion acquisition of Chicago Pacific Corp., the maker of vacuum cleaners and other appliances. Maytag had to borrow heavily to acquire Chicago Pacific, yet Krumm asserts the company had no choice if it was to remain competitive. Some analysts believe that the price was too great.

The Maytag organization scrambled to maintain its reputation for quality in 1989, when *Consumer Reports* rated Maytag's washers no more durable than other brands. Maytag reacted with a revamping of its washers' transmission for the first time in thirty-five years. The average life expectancy for the new transmission is now at least twenty years. The new transmission uses few parts, reducing manufacturing expenses even further.

In order to expand its base, Maytag has cut the work force by one-eighth. Since 1990 the savings, estimated at $75 million a year, was put into capital spending. CEO Leonard A. Hadley states that capital expenditures are an important part of productivity. The new capital spawned an overseas opportunity with the purchase of Hoover Company. This purchase showed an interesting change of heart for Krumm, who had previously declined the notion of chasing business abroad.

In fact, Maytag expanded abroad reluctantly. Traditionally, 98 percent of the appliances sold in the United States have been made in the United States. However, Maytag started to feel the letdown in the U.S. appliance market. The company's 1988 earnings dropped an estimated 9 percent to $139 million. Maytag had to diversify from its high-margin niche to survive in a business that was consolidating around four or five major players. Suddenly, Krumm had reason to turn internationalist.

One of the difficulties of the new market is the fierce loyalty of Europeans to domestic brands. With the purchase of Hoover, Maytag has options for advancement in Australia, although this market is not large in comparison to others. The company to beat in Europe is Electrolux, with more than 20 percent of the market and a strong presence in every country from Finland to Portugal.

Another concern of the industry is the effect of the working culture on current appliance usage. The initial pass at designing electronic controls for laundry appliances was discounted as overequipping a machine that was often placed in a basement. Many felt that consumers would not pay the price of the electronics. Maytag proved that consumers' lifestyles force change in washing patterns. Consumers wash more frequently, and, consequently, appliances are more visible. This change also explains the surge of stacked laundry models since 1991. Although past consumers seemed reluctant to use membrane-input devices to key in their selections, the current single-touch approach allows users to let the machine's fuzzy-logic controller determine load size and fabric mix.

Maytag has built sizable breathing room for change and

new ventures. Yet it may be years, if ever, before Krumm's overseas approaches pay off. History has yet to determine if, in Europe, the Maytag salesman and not the repairman gets lonely.[30]

Discussion Questions

1. Discuss the concept of investing in capital while cutting back on human resources. What can Maytag do to ensure high morale for surviving organizational members?
2. What roles will be essential for managers at Maytag as they move toward a more global market?
3. If you were going to work for Maytag as a sales manager, what managerial school of thought do you think would apply most often? Why?

Part One   Management: An Introduction

Self-Assessment

A Twenty-First–Century Manager

Introduction This assessment captures the focus of Part One: It offers a self-described profile of your management foundations (MF). The items on the list are recommended by the American Assembly of Collegiate Schools of Business (AACSB) as skills and personal characteristics that should be nurtured in college and university students of business administration.

Instructions Rate yourself on the following personal characteristics. Use this scale:

S = Strong, I am very confident about this one
G = Good, but I still have room to grow
W = Weak, I really need work on this one
? = Unsure, I just don't know

_____ 1. *Resistance to stress:* The ability to get work done even under stressful conditions.

_____ 2. *Tolerance for uncertainty:* The ability to get work done even under ambiguous and uncertain conditions.

_____ 3. *Social objectivity:* The ability to act free of racial, ethnic, gender, and other prejudices or biases.

_____ 4. *Inner work standards:* The ability to personally set and work to high performance standards.

_____ 5. *Stamina:* The ability to sustain long work hours.

_____ 6. *Adaptability:* The ability to be flexible and adapt to changes.

_____ 7. *Self-confidence:* The ability to be consistently decisive and display one's personal presence.

_____ 8. *Self-objectivity:* The ability to evaluate personal strengths and weaknesses and understand one's motives and skills relative to a job.

_____ 9. *Introspection:* The ability to learn from experience, awareness, and self-study.

_____ 10. *Entrepreneurism:* The ability to address problems and take advantage of opportunities for constructive change.

For interpretation, turn to the back of the book.

Source: See Outcome Measurement Project, Phase I and Phase II Reports (St. Louis: American Assembly of Collegiate Schools of Business, 1986 & 1987). Reprinted with permission.

Skill Builder

Planners and Operators

Purpose This skill builder draws on several of the concepts introduced in the first part of the text. Recall that managers have to be effective and efficient in their roles regarding planning and leading in an organization. This skill builder focuses on the *human resources* and *administrative management models*. It will help you develop the *coordinator* and *facilitator roles*. One of the skills of the coordinator is planning; one of the skills of the facilitator is communications.

Introduction This experience combines elements of plan-ning, communication, group dynamics, and managerial interrelationships into one exercise. Clusters of about ten people will be formed and divided into three subgroups. Four persons will serve as "planners," four as "operators," and the remaining participants as observers.

Instructions Your instructor will give you directions for completing this exercise.

Source: Permission granted by Richard Schmuck, Center for OD in Education. University of Oregon, Eugene, OR 97403.

CHAPTER

3

Organizational Environments

Learning Objectives

After studying this chapter you should be able to

· Discuss the nature of the organizational environment.

· Identify and describe the components of the general environment.

· Identify and describe the components of the task environment.

· Discuss the internal environment of organizations.

· Identify and describe how the environment affects organizations and how organizations respond to their environment.

Fashion merchandising is one of the world's most competitive businesses. Clothing tastes and styles change almost overnight, and firms that compete in the industry are always on the alert for ways to get an edge. Until recently, one of the most successful fashion merchandising businesses was The Limited.

The Limited operates several different retail chains. Limited stores have offered trend-setting clothes for career women. Lerner has focused more on economy-priced clothing for customers on a tight budget. Express sells more contemporary clothing for younger consumers. Victoria's Secret sells lingerie in both retail outlets and through a lucrative mail-order business. Other specialty divisions of The Limited include Structure, Henri Bendel, Lane Bryant, and Abercrombie and Fitch.

During the early 1980s The Limited was hailed as one of the world's most innovative and successful fashion retailers. Buyers saw hot new trends in designer lines and had them copied in Hong Kong and Taiwan. Limited stores used a state-of-the-art-information system to monitor sales, transmit reorders of popular items to factories in Pacific Asia, and have its inventory replenished within days. By 1990 The Limited's revenues surpassed $5.5 billion, while profits exceeded $421 million.

In the early 1990s, however, The Limited's star began to dim. Other retailers, copying the firm's inventory control system, gained ground on its ability to keep high fashion goods in stock. And the lines separating the clothes carried by different Limited stores began to blur. For example, customers began to find some of the same items in Limited, Express, and Lerner stores in the same malls—but with different prices.

Sales at Limited stores and Lerner stalled in 1992. Managers, however, moved quickly to develop a new strategy for getting them going again. Both The Limited and Lerner began an ambitious effort to upgrade the overall quality of their product lines. These moves are intended to move each chain farther from Express but still keep them distinct from one another. Only time will tell, of course, whether The Limited will regain its momentum or whether it will stall out completely.[1] ∎

Like every organization in the world today, The Limited is profoundly affected by its environment. Suppliers, customers, and competitors, for example, must all be closely monitored, and care must be taken to stay abreast of changing tastes and trends in every phase of the firm's operation. Indeed, managers who fail to keep pace with changes in their environment are doomed to fall behind their competitors and may cause irreparable damage to their organization's revenues and profit margins.

This chapter is the first of four devoted to the environmental context of management. We begin by introducing the nature of organizational environments. Next we discuss the general environment of organizations. The task environment is then described. After an analysis of the internal organization, we conclude with an examination of organization-environment relationships.

The Nature of Organizational Environments

To underscore the importance of organizational environments, consider the situation of a swimmer crossing a wide river. The swimmer must first assess the current, obstacles, and distance before setting out. If these elements are properly evaluated, the swimmer will arrive at the expected point on the far bank of the river. But if they are not properly understood, the swimmer might end up too far up- or downstream. The organization is like a swimmer, and the environment is like the river. The organization's managers must understand the basic elements of its environment in order to properly maneuver among them.[2]

Managers need to pay close attention to the external environment, including those aspects that impact on their employees' health. As part of this effort, Bell Atlantic contracts with U.S. Healthcare to provide free mammogram testing to its personnel. (Lynn Johnson/Black Star.)

*The **external environment** consists of everything outside an organization that might affect it.*

The **external environment** consists of everything outside an organization that might affect it. Of course, the boundary that separates the organization from its external environment is not always clear and precise. In one sense, for example, stockholders are part of the organization, but in another sense they are part of its environment. As shown in Exhibit 3.1, the external environment is composed of two layers: the general environment and the task environment. An organization's **internal environment,** also shown in Exhibit 3.1, is best reflected by its culture. Of course, not all aspects of the environment are equally important for all organizations. A small, nonunion firm may not need to concern itself too much with unions, for example. A private university with a large endowment like Harvard may be less concerned about general economic conditions than might a state university like the University of Oregon that is dependent on state funding from tax revenues. Still, organizations need to fully understand which environmental forces are important and how the importance of others might increase.[3]

*An organization's **internal environment** is best reflected by its culture.*

The General Environment of Organizations

As noted above, an organization's external environment consists of two layers. The **general environment** of an organization consists of the broad dimensions and forces in its surroundings that provide opportunities and impose constraints on the organization. These elements are not necessarily associated with other specific organizations. The general environment of most organizations is composed of economic, technological, sociocultural, political-legal, and international dimensions. Each of these dimensions of the general environment has the potential to influence the organization in significant ways. The general environment of The Limited is shown in Exhibit 3.2.

Exhibit 3.1

Organizations and Their Environments

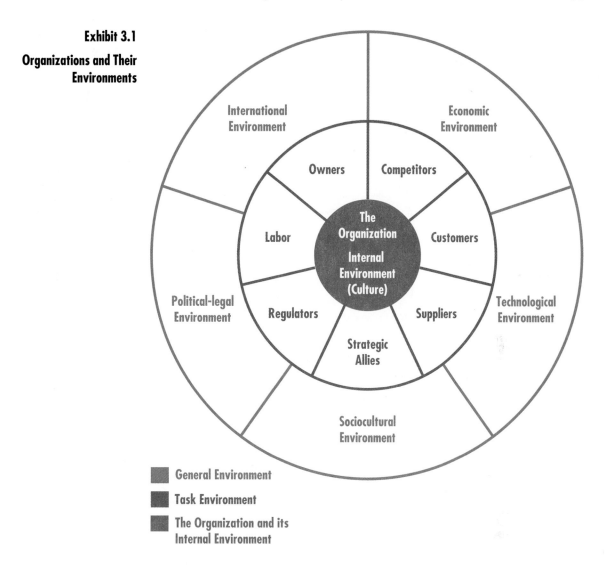

- General Environment
- Task Environment
- The Organization and its Internal Environment

The Economic Environment

*The **economic environment** is the overall health of the economic system in which the organization operates.*

An organization's **economic environment** is the overall health of the economic system in which the organization operates.[4] Particularly important economic factors are inflation, interest rates, unemployment, and demand. During times of inflation, for example, a company pays more for resources and must raise its prices to cover the higher costs. When interest rates are high, consumers are less willing to borrow money, and the company itself must pay more when it borrows. When unemployment is high, the company is able to be very selective about whom it hires, but consumer buying may decline. The economic recession in the United States during the early 1990s no doubt contributed to declining sales at The Limited.

The economic environment is also of importance to nonbusiness organizations. For example, poor economic conditions affect funding for state universities. Charitable organizations like the Salvation Army are asked to provide greater assistance during bad times, while their incoming contributions simultaneously dwindle. Hospitals are affected by the availability of government grants and the number of cases they must treat for free.

Exhibit 3.2
**The Limited's General
Environment**

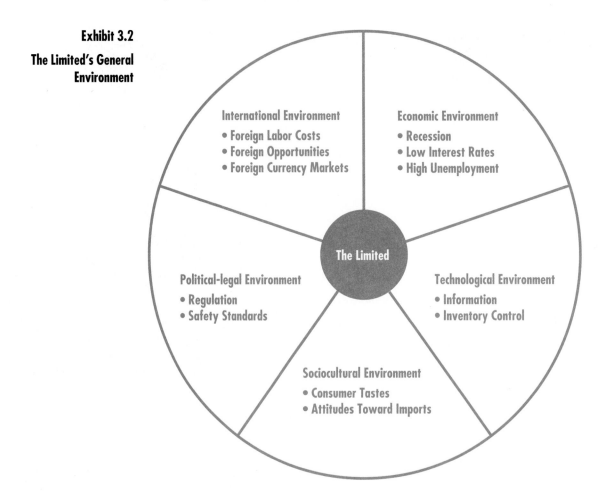

International Environment
- Foreign Labor Costs
- Foreign Opportunities
- Foreign Currency Markets

Economic Environment
- Recession
- Low Interest Rates
- High Unemployment

The Limited

Political-legal Environment
- Regulation
- Safety Standards

Technological Environment
- Information
- Inventory Control

Sociocultural Environment
- Consumer Tastes
- Attitudes Toward Imports

The Technological Environment

*The **technological environment** refers to the methods available for converting resources into products or services.*

The **technological environment** of an organization refers to the methods available for converting resources into products or services. Although technology is applied within the organization, the forms and availability of that technology come from the general environment. Computer-assisted manufacturing and design techniques, for example, allow McDonnell Douglas to simulate the three miles of hydraulic tubing that run through a DC-10. The results include decreased warehouse needs, higher-quality tube fittings, fewer employees, and significant time savings.[5] New innovations in robotics and other manufacturing techniques also have implications for managers. The availability of high-speed information processing systems, for instance, provided The Limited with a competitive advantage for several years.

The Sociocultural Environment

*The **sociocultural environment** of an organization includes the customs, mores, values, and demographic characteristics of the society in which the organization functions.*

The **sociocultural environment** of an organization includes the customs, mores, values, and demographic characteristics of the society in which the organization functions. Sociocultural processes are important because they determine the products, services, and standards of conduct that the society is likely to value. In some countries, for example, consumers are willing to pay premium prices for designer clothes. But the same clothes have virtually no market in other countries. Consumer tastes also change over time. Drinking hard liquor and smoking cigarettes are far less acceptable than they were just a few years ago. And sociocultural factors influence how workers in a society feel about their jobs and organizations.

Communication that deals with the external community can be handled in many ways. At the Travis County Court House in Austin, Texas, foreclosed properties are auctioned off each month. Susan Mills of Trustees of Texas, shown here, represents banks that hold defaulted loans. (Charles O'Rear/Westlight.)

Appropriate standards of business conduct also vary across cultures. In the United States accepting bribes and bestowing political favors in return are considered unethical and are illegal as well. In other countries, however, payments to local politicians may be expected in return for a favorable response to common business transactions such as applications for zoning and operating permits. The ethics of political influence and attitudes in the work force are only some of the many ways in which culture can affect an organization. The sociocultural environment partially shapes consumer tastes and standards, which in turn affect fashion merchants like The Limited.

The Political-Legal Environment

*The **political-legal environment** includes government regulation of business and the relationship between business and government.*

An organization's **political-legal environment** includes government regulation of business and the relationship between business and government. It is important for three basic reasons. First, the legal system partially defines what an organization can and cannot do. Although the United States is basically a free market economy, there is still significant regulation of business activity.[6] The Limited, for example, is subject to strict rules about labeling the content of its garments.

Second, pro- or antibusiness sentiment in government influences business activity. For example, during periods of probusiness sentiment, firms find it easier to compete and have fewer concerns about antitrust issues. On the other hand, during less favorable periods firms may find their competitive strategies more restricted and have fewer opportunities for mergers and acquisitions because of antitrust concerns. Finally, political stability has ramifications for planning. No company wants to set up shop in another country unless trade relationships with that country are relatively well-defined and stable. Hence, U.S. firms are more likely to do business with England, Mexico, and Canada than with Iran and El Salvador. Similar issues are also relevant to assessments of local and state governments. A change in the mayor's or the governor's position can af-

The Environment of Management

Blockbuster Grows Around the World

A new industry spawned in just the last few years has already been dramatically changed by the presence of a single firm. Video rental stores started out in the 1970s as locally owned mom-and-pop stores and flourished throughout the United States. But their prosperity lasted just a few years as big national chains emerged, came into town, and gobbled up the local markets. Chief among these national chains is Blockbuster Entertainment Corp.

Blockbuster's incredible growth started in 1987 when investor Wayne Huiszenga acquired the firm. He began a major growth campaign that as recently as 1991 resulted in a new Blockbuster Video store opening every seventeen hours. The firm's ability to buy in bulk and provide national advertising has resulted in Blockbuster earning more revenues than its next largest one hundred competitors combined. There were more than three thousand Blockbuster stores open in 1992.

But Huiszenga realizes that there is only room for so many video stores. Moreover, the growth in video rentals is slowing, and the firm faces increased competition from pay-per-view movies available from cable operators.

Blockbuster has now turned to foreign markets for much of its future growth. The firm's goal is that by 1995 25 percent of its revenues will come from abroad. Presently there are only fifteen Blockbuster stores in Japan, for example, but the firm plans to expand to at least one thousand stores there in the next ten years. And Blockbuster recently bought Britain's largest home-video company, Citivision PLC, for $81 million and 3.9 million shares of stock. The firm is also expanding in Mexico, Chile, Venezuela, Austria, and Spain and is exploring joint venture opportunities in France, Germany, and Italy.[7] ∎

fect many organizations, especially small firms that do business in only one location and are susceptible to deed and zoning restrictions, property and school taxes, and the like.

The International Environment

*The **international environment** of an organization refers to forces that extend beyond national boundaries.*

A final component of the general environment for many organizations is the **international environment,** forces that extend beyond national boundaries. As we discuss in Chapter 5, multinational firms such as The Boeing Co., IBM, Monsanto Company, and Exxon Corporation clearly affect and are affected by international conditions and markets. Boeing, for example, earns more than half of its revenues from outside the United States. Even firms that do business in only one country may face foreign competition at home, and they may use materials or production equipment imported from abroad. The Limited acquires most of its products from Pacific Asia. *The Environment of Management: Blockbuster Grows Around the World* describes how Blockbuster Video is attempting to expand into more international markets.

The international dimension also has implications for not-for-profit organizations. For example, the Peace Corps sends representatives to underdeveloped countries. Medical breakthroughs achieved in one country spread rapidly to others, and cultural exchanges of all kinds take place between countries. As a result of advances in transportation and communication technology in the past century, almost no part of the world is cut off from the rest. Virtually every organization is affected by the international dimension.[8]

The Task Environment of Organizations

Because the impact of the general environment is often ambiguous and gradual in its effects, most organizations focus more on their task environment. Although it is also quite complex, the task environment provides useful information more readily than does the general environment. The **task environment** consists of other specific organizations or groups that are

*The **task environment** consists of other specific organizations or groups that are likely to influence an organization.*

likely to influence an organization. The task environment may include competitors, customers, suppliers, labor, regulators, owners, and strategic allies. The manager can identify environmental factors of specific interest to the organization rather than having to deal with the more abstract dimensions of the general environment. It may be easier for you to understand this concept if you think about an organization with which you are familiar. The skill builder for this chapter allows you to determine the environmental forces that affect your university. Exhibit 3.3 depicts the task environment of The Limited. In The Limited's case, competitors include The Gap, Liz Claiborne Inc., Levi Strauss, and Nordstrom. Customers are individual fashion consumers. Suppliers are the textile mills in Pacific Asia that manufacture the fabric and the sewing concerns that make the garments the firm orders. The Limited currently has no strategic allies but is considering a joint venture with a European clothing firm. Key regulators of The Limited are the Federal Trade Commission and the Equal Employment Opportunity Commission. Important labor unions include the Garment Workers of America. Owners include both Leslie Werner, the firm's founder, and one of the authors of this book, who recently bought one hundred shares of stock in The Limited.

Competitors

*uparse **Competitors** are other organizations that compete with an organization for resources.*

An organization's **competitors** are other organizations that compete with it for resources. The most obvious resources that competitors vie for are customer dollars. Reebok, Adidas, and Nike are competitors, as are A & P, Safeway, and Kroger. Competition also occurs between substitute products. Thus, Chrysler competes with Yamaha (motorcycles) and Schwinn (bicycles) for your transportation dollars, and Walt Disney, Club Med, and Carnival Cruise Lines compete for your vacation dollars. Nor is competition limited to business firms. Universities compete with trade schools, the military, other universities, and the job market to attract good students. Art galleries compete with each other to attract the best exhibits.

Organizations may also compete for different kinds of resources besides consumer dollars. Two totally unrelated organizations may compete to acquire a loan from a bank that has only lim-

Exhibit 3.3

The Limited's Task Environment

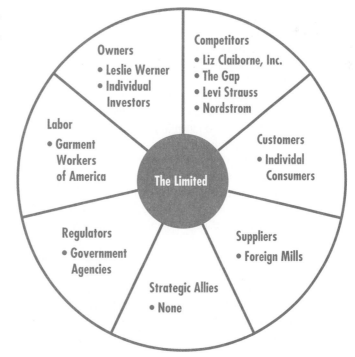

ited funds to lend. In a large city, the police and fire departments may compete for the same tax dollars. Firms compete for quality labor, technological breakthroughs and patents, and scarce raw materials. Information about competitors is often quite easily obtained. Kmart can monitor J.C. Penney's prices by reading its newspaper advertisements or by sending someone to a store to inspect price tags. Other kinds of information may be more difficult to obtain. Research activities, new product developments, and future advertising campaigns, for example, are often closely guarded secrets.[9]

Customers

Customers *are whoever pays money to acquire an organization's product or service.*

A second dimension of the task environment consists of customers. The **customer** is whoever pays money to acquire an organization's product or service. In many cases, however, the chain of customer transactions is deceivingly complex. As consumers, for example, we do not buy a bottle of Coke from The Coca-Cola Company. We buy it from Safeway, which bought it from an independent bottler, which bought the syrup and the right to use the name from Coca-Cola. Customers need not be individuals. Schools, hospitals, government agencies, wholesalers, retailers, and manufacturers are just a few of the many kinds of organizations that may be major customers of other organizations. Common sources of information about customers include market research, surveys, consumer panels, and reports from sales representatives.

Dealing with customers has become increasingly complex in recent years. Many firms have found it necessary to focus their advertising on specific consumer groups or regions. General Foods Corporation, for example, has found it necessary to promote its Maxwell House coffee differently in different regions of the country, even though doing so costs two or three times what a single national advertising campaign would cost.[10] Pressures from consumer groups about packaging and related issues also complicate the lives of managers.

Suppliers

Suppliers *are organizations that provide resources for other organizations.*

Suppliers are organizations that provide resources for other organizations. Disney World buys soft-drink syrup from Coca-Cola, monorails from Daewoo, food from Sara Lee and Smucker, and paper products from The Mead Corporation. Suppliers for manufacturers like Corning Glass include the suppliers of raw materials as well as firms that sell machinery and other equipment. Another kind of supplier provides the capital needed to operate the organization. Banks and federal lending agencies are both suppliers of capital for businesses. Other suppliers provide human resources for the organization. Examples include public and private employment agencies like Kelly Services and college placement offices. *The Quality Challenge: General Motors and Suppliers Try to Catch Up* explains how General Motors is pressuring its suppliers to help the firm enhance its overall product quality.

Still other suppliers furnish the organization with the information it needs to carry out its mission. Many companies subscribe to periodicals such as The Wall Street Journal, Fortune, and *Business Week* to help their managers keep abreast of news. Market research firms are used by some companies. And some firms specialize in developing economic forecasts and in keeping managers informed about pending legislation. Most organizations try to avoid depending exclusively on particular suppliers. A firm that buys all of a certain resource from one supplier may be crippled if the supplier goes out of business or is faced with a strike. Most organizations try to develop and maintain relationships with a variety of suppliers.[11]

Labor

Labor *refers to people who work for the organization, especially when they are organized into unions.*

Organizations must also concern themselves with **labor.** Labor refers to people who work for the organization, especially when they are organized into unions. The National Labor Relations Act of 1935 requires organizations to recognize and bargain with a union if that union has been legally established by the organization's employees. Presently, around 23 percent of the American labor force is represented by unions. Some large firms such as Ford, Exxon, and General Motors have to deal with a great many unions. Even when an organization's labor force is not unionized, its man-

The Quality Challenge

General Motors and Suppliers Try to Catch Up

Like most firms today, General Motors is taking steps to upgrade the quality of its products. Unfortunately for the auto giant, it got a late start and is only now just beginning to catch up with its domestic rivals. In the 1980s, Chrysler, for example, began to ask suppliers how they could work together to both upgrade product quality and lower costs. And Ford set very specific quality standards in the mid-1980s and announced that beginning in 1992 only suppliers who met those standards could bid on new business.

General Motors, on the other hand, was focusing its efforts on changing its organization design and dealt with quality improvement only as a secondary consideration. But in the last few years GM has put quality improvement at the forefront. One key dimension of its quality improvement efforts involves its suppliers. The firm is working to get suppliers to upgrade their own quality while also lowering their costs.

Some observers believe that GM is dealing with its suppliers in the wrong way. Toyota has two long-term suppliers for every part it buys who compete vigorously, but no other firms can bid for business. In an effort to follow this model, GM tore up existing contracts and put all parts out for new bids. In one case, the firm sought new bids on the same part twice in three weeks. Toyota takes blueprints from one supplier and shares them with the other. Those two suppliers then continue to share Toyota's business. But GM took blueprints from one supplier, shared them with many other firms, and asked who could make the same part for a lower price.

GM's suppliers agree that the firm needs to upgrade its quality and realize that it's in their own best interests to help. But they also want to protect their own self-interests and avoid being abused by the auto giant. Only time will tell if these tenuous collaborations will be smoothed out.[12] ∎

agers do not ignore unions. For example, Kmart, J.P. Stevens & Co., Inc., Honda Motor Company of America, and Delta Air Lines all actively seek to avoid unionization. And even though people think primarily of blue-collar workers as union members, many government employees, teachers, and other white-collar workers are also represented by unions.

Regulators

Regulators are units in the task environment that have the potential to control, regulate, or influence an organization's policies and practices.

Regulatory agencies are created by the government to protect the public from certain business practices or to protect organizations from one another.

Regulators are units in the task environment that have the potential to control, regulate, or influence an organization's policies and practices. There are two important kinds of regulators. The first, **regulatory agencies,** are created by the government to protect the public from certain business practices or to protect organizations from one another. Powerful federal regulatory agencies include the Environmental Protection Agency (EPA), the Occupational Safety and Health Administration (OSHA), the Securities and Exchange Commission (SEC), the Food and Drug Administration (FDA), and the Equal Employment Opportunity Commission (EEOC).

Many of these agencies play important roles in protecting the rights of individuals. The FDA, for example, helps ensure that the food we eat is free from contaminants. The costs a firm incurs in complying with government regulations may be substantial, but these costs are usually passed on to the customer. Even so, many organizations complain that there is too much regulation at the present time. One study found that forty-eight major companies spent $2.6 billion in one year —over and above normal environmental protection, employee safety, and similar costs—because of stringent government regulations. On the basis of these findings, the extra costs of government regulations for all businesses have been estimated at more than $100 billion per year.[13] Obviously, the impact of regulatory agencies on organizations is considerable.

Although federal regulators get a lot of publicity, the effect of state and local agencies is also significant. California has more stringent automobile emission requirements than those established by the EPA. And not-for-profit organizations must also deal with regulatory agencies. Most states, for example, have coordinating boards that regulate the operation of colleges and universities.

Interest groups are organized by their members to attempt to influence organizations.

The other basic form of regulator is the **interest group.** An interest group is organized by its members to attempt to influence organizations. Prominent interest groups include the National Organization for Women (NOW), Mothers Against Drunk Drivers (MADD), the National Rifle Association (NRA), the League of Women Voters, the Sierra Club, Ralph Nader's Center for the Study of Responsive Law, Consumers Union, and industry self-regulation groups like the Council of Better Business Bureaus. Interest groups lack the official power of government agencies. They can, however, exert considerable influence by using the media to call attention to their positions. MADD, for example, puts considerable pressure on alcoholic-beverage producers (to put warning labels on their products), automobile companies (to make it more difficult for intoxicated people to start their cars), local governments (to stiffen drinking ordinances), and bars and restaurants (to limit sales of alcohol to people drinking too much).

Owners

Owners are those people, organizations, and institutions that legally control an organization, most commonly through owning stock in a corporation.

Owners—those people, organizations, and institutions that legally control an organization—are also becoming a major concern of managers in many businesses.[14] Until recently, stockholders of major corporations were generally happy to sit on the sidelines and let top management run their organizations. Of late, however, more and more of them are taking active roles in influencing the management of companies they hold stock in. This is especially true of owners who hold large blocks of stock. For example, in 1991 Time Warner announced that it was going to issue new stock to reduce its debt. Current stockholders were to be given first option on buying the stock, but its price was not going to be known at the time options had to be exercised. Several large stockholders complained and some threatened lawsuits. Time Warner eventually backed down and canceled its plans.[15]

Another group exerting more influence is the managers of large corporate pension funds. These enormous funds control 50 percent of the shares traded on the New York Stock Exchange and 65 percent of Standard & Poor's 500 stocks. AT&T's pension fund, for example, exceeds $35 billion. Since pension funds are growing at twice the rate of the U.S. GNP, it follows that their managers will have even more power in the future.[16] And given the increased power wielded by owners (and their willingness to use that power), some fear that managers are sacrificing long-term corporate effectiveness for the sake of short-term results. For example, managers at the Carnation Company were afraid to increase advertising costs too much for fear of attracting the attention of institutional investors. As a result, sales declined. After Nestlé Enterprises took over and loosened the purse strings, sales took off again.[17] Thus, while organizations should never ignore their owners, they are having to be considerably more concerned about them now than in the past.

Strategic Allies

Strategic allies are two or more companies that work together in joint ventures.

A final dimension of the task environment is **strategic allies,** two or more companies that work together in joint ventures. Ford has a number of strategic allies, including Volkswagen (to make cars in South America) and Nissan (to make vans in the United States). Ford and Mazda also jointly make the Probe automobile. Alliances such as these have been around for a long time, but they became popular in the 1980s and are now increasing at a rate of about 22 percent per year.[18] IBM used to shun strategic alliances but now has forty active partnerships around the globe.[19]

Strategic alliances help companies get from other companies the expertise they may lack. They also help spread risk. Managers must be careful, however, not to give away sensitive competitive information. For example, when Sperry entered into a strategic alliance with Hitachi, a Japanese computer maker, it found that it had to divulge valuable trade secrets in order to make the partnership work. Strategic alliances need not always involve business. Texas A&M University

Strategic alliances and partnerships are more common as businesses strive to compete. Some of these alliances are designed to contribute to the firms' total quality management efforts. One such alliance is that between Parker Hannifin Corporation and Harley-Davidson. Parker products—pumps, valves, fluid connectors, and seals are used not only throughout Harley-Davidson plants but also in the brake systems of their motorcycles. (Reprinted with permission by Harley-Davidson.)

and the University of Texas, for example, often work together to secure government grants. And some churches sponsor joint missionary projects.

The Internal Environment: Corporate Culture

The Importance of Culture

*The **culture** of an organization is the set of values that helps its members understand what the organization stands for, how it does things, and what it considers important.*

The **culture** of an organization is the set of values that helps its members understand what the organization stands for, how it does things, and what it considers important. Culture is an amorphous concept that defies objective measurement or observation. Nevertheless, because it is the foundation of the organization's internal environment, it plays a major role in shaping managerial behavior.[20]

Several years ago, executives at Levi Strauss felt that the company had outgrown its sixty-eight-year-old building. Even though everyone enjoyed its casual and relaxed atmosphere, more space was needed. So Levi Strauss moved into a modern office building in downtown San Francisco, where its new headquarters spread over twelve floors in a skyscraper. It quickly became apparent that the change was affecting the corporate culture, and that people did not like it. Executives felt isolated, and other managers missed the informal chance meetings in the halls. Within just a few years, Levi Strauss moved out of the skyscraper and back into a building that fosters informality. For example, there is an adjacent park area where employees gather for lunchtime conversation. Clearly, Levi Strauss has a culture that is important to everyone who works there.[21]

Culture determines the "feel" of the organization. The stereotypic image of the IBM executive is someone wearing a white shirt and dark suit. In contrast, Texas Instruments likes to talk about its "shirt-sleeve" culture, in which ties are avoided and few managers ever wear jackets. Of course, the same culture is not necessarily found throughout an entire organization. For example, the sales and marketing department may have a culture quite different from that of the operations and manufacturing department. Regardless of its nature, however, culture is a powerful force in organizations, one that can shape the firm's overall effectiveness and long-term success. Companies that can develop and maintain a strong adaptive culture, such as Hewlett-Packard and Procter & Gamble, tend to be more effective than companies that have trouble developing and maintaining such a culture.[22]

Origins of Culture

Where does a culture come from? Typically, it develops and blossoms over a long period of time. Its starting point is often upper management, or even the organization's founder. For example, James Cash Penney believed in treating employees and customers with respect and dignity. Employees at J.C. Penney are still called associates rather than employees (to reflect partnership), and customer satisfaction is of paramount importance.

As an organization grows, its culture is modified, shaped, and refined by symbols, stories, heroes, slogans, and ceremonies. For example, a key value at Hewlett-Packard is the avoidance of bank debt. A popular story still told at the company involves a new project that was being considered for several years. All objective criteria indicated that HP should incur bank debt to finance it, yet Bill Hewlett and David Packard rejected it out of hand simply because "HP avoids bank debt." This story, involving two corporate heroes and based on a slogan, dictates Hewlett-Packard's corporate culture today.[23]

Corporate success and shared experiences also shape culture. For example, Hallmark Cards has a strong culture derived from its years of success in the greeting card industry. Employees speak of the Hallmark family and care deeply about the company; many of them have worked at the company for years. At Atari Corp., in contrast, the culture is quite weak, the management team changes frequently, and few people sense any direction or purpose in the company. The differences in culture at Hallmark and Atari are in part attributable to past successes and shared experiences.

Managing Organizational Culture

How can managers deal with culture, given its clear importance but intangible nature? The key is for the manager to understand the current culture and then decide if it should be maintained or changed. By understanding the organization's current culture, managers can take appropriate actions. At Hewlett-Packard, the values represented by "the HP way" still exist. Moreover, they guide and direct most significant activities undertaken by the firm. Culture can also be maintained by rewarding and promoting people whose behaviors are consistent with the existing culture and by articulating the culture through slogans, ceremonies, and so forth.

To change culture, managers must have a clear idea of what it is they want to create. Many organizations today are attempting to create a strong culture like that found in consistently effective firms like Eastman Kodak, Walt Disney, Procter & Gamble, and Levi Strauss. Another way to shape culture is by bringing outsiders into important managerial positions. The choice of a new CEO from outside the organization is often a clear signal that things will be changing. Adopting new slogans, telling new stories, staging new ceremonies, and breaking with tradition can also alter culture. Culture can also be changed by methods discussed in Chapter 13.

Organization-Environment Relationships

The preceding discussion identifies and describes the various dimensions of organizational environments. Because organizations are open systems, they interact with these various dimensions in many different ways. We now turn our attention to these interactions. We first discuss how environments affect organizations and then note a number of ways in which organizations respond to their environments.

How Environments Affect Organizations

Three basic frameworks can be used to describe how environments affect organizations. The first is environmental change and complexity. The other two are competitive forces and environmental turbulence.

Environmental Change and Complexity   James D. Thompson was one of the first people to recognize the importance of organizational environments.[24] Thompson suggests that an organization's environment can be described along two dimensions: its degree of change and its degree of homogeneity. The degree of change is the extent to which the environment is relatively stable or

Uncertainty *is created by the*
degree of change and the degree of
homogeneity that characterize an
organization's environments. Uncer-
tainty adds unpredictability and
complexity to the environment.

relatively dynamic. The degree of homogeneity is the extent to which the environment is relatively simple (few elements, little segmentation) or relatively complex (many elements, much segmentation). These two dimensions interact to determine the level of **uncertainty** faced by the organization. Uncertainty, in turn, is a driving force that influences many organizational decisions by adding unpredictability and complexity to the environment. Exhibit 3.4 illustrates a simple view of the four levels of uncertainty defined by different levels of homogeneity and change.

The least environmental uncertainty is faced by organizations with stable and simple environments. Although no environment is totally without uncertainty, many franchised food operations (such as Subway and Taco Bell) and many container manufacturers (like Ball and Federal Paper Board) have relatively low levels of uncertainty to contend with. Subway, for example, focuses on a certain segment of the consumer market, produces a limited product line, has a constant source of suppliers, and faces relatively consistent competition.

Organizations with dynamic but simple environments generally face a moderate degree of uncertainty. Examples of organizations functioning in such environments include clothing manufacturers (targeting a certain kind of clothing buyer but sensitive to fashion-induced changes) and CD producers (catering to certain kinds of record buyers but alert to changing tastes in music). Levi Strauss faces few competitors (Wrangler and Lee), has few suppliers and few regulators, and uses limited distribution channels. However, this relatively simple task environment also changes quite rapidly as competitors adjust prices and styles, consumer tastes change, and new fabrics become available.

The third combination of factors is one of stability and complexity. Again, a moderate amount of uncertainty results. General Motors faces these basic conditions. Overall, the organization must deal with myriad suppliers, regulators, consumer groups, and competitors. Change, however, occurs quite slowly in the automobile industry. Despite many stylistic changes, cars of today still have four wheels, a steering wheel, an internal-combustion engine, and so forth.

Exhibit 3.4
Environmental Uncertainty

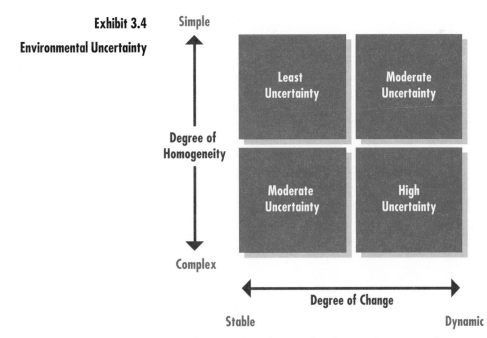

Source: Adapted by permission of McGraw-Hill, Inc. from *Organizations in Action* by J.D. Thompson, copyright © 1967.

Finally, very dynamic and complex environmental conditions yield a high degree of uncertainty. The environment has a large number of elements, and the nature of those elements is constantly changing. Intel, IBM, and other firms in the electronics field face these conditions because of the rapid rate of technological innovation and change in consumer markets that characterize their industry, their suppliers, and their competitors.

Five Competitive Forces   Although Thompson's general classifications are useful and provide some basic insights into organization-environment interactions, in many ways they lack the precision and specificity needed by managers who must deal with their environments on a day-to-day basis. Michael E. Porter, a Harvard professor and expert in strategic management, proposed a more refined way to assess environments. In particular, he suggests that organizations view their environments in terms of **five competitive forces.**[25]

Competitive forces that may affect an organization are the threat of new entrants, jockeying among contestants, the threat of substitute products, the power of buyers, and the power of suppliers.

The *threat of new entrants* is the extent to which new competitors can easily enter a market or market segment. It takes a relatively small amount of capital to open a dry-cleaning service or a pizza parlor, but it takes a tremendous investment in plant, equipment, and distribution systems to enter the automobile business. Thus, the threat of new entrants is fairly high for a local hamburger joint but fairly low for General Motors and Toyota.

Jockeying among contestants is the nature of the competitive relationship between dominant firms in an industry. In the soft-drink industry, Coke and Pepsi often engage in intense price wars, comparative advertising, and new-product introductions. And U.S. auto companies continually try to outmaneuver each other with warranty improvements and rebates. Local car-washing establishments, in contrast, seldom engage in such practices.

The *threat of substitute products* is the extent to which alternative products or services may supplant or diminish the need for existing products or services. The electronic calculator eliminated the need for slide rules. The advent of microcomputers, in turn, has reduced the demand for calculators as well as for typewriters and large mainframe computers. And Nutra-Sweet is a viable substitute product threatening the sugar industry.

The *power of buyers* is the extent to which buyers of the products or services in an industry have the ability to influence the suppliers. For example, there are relatively few potential buyers for a Boeing 747. Only companies such as American Airlines, United Air Lines, and KLM can purchase them; hence, these companies have considerable influence over the prices they are willing to pay, the delivery date for the order, and so forth. On the other hand, Japanese car makers charged premium prices for their cars in the United States during the energy crisis of the late 1970s because if the first customer wouldn't pay the price, there were two more consumers waiting in line who would.

The *power of suppliers* is the extent to which suppliers have the ability to influence organizations. The local electric company is the only source of electricity in your community. Hence, subject to local or state regulation (or both), it can charge what it wants for its product, provide service at its convenience, and so forth. Likewise, even though Boeing has few potential customers, those same customers have few suppliers that can sell them a three-hundred-passenger jet. So Boeing, too, has power. On the other hand, a small vegetable wholesaler has little power in selling to restaurants because if they don't like the produce, they can easily find an alternative supplier.

Environmental Turbulence   Although always subject to unexpected changes and upheavals, the five competitive forces can be studied and assessed systematically, and a plan can be developed for dealing with them. At the same time, though, organizations also face the possibility of environmental change or turbulence, occasionally with no warning at all.[26] The most common form of organizational turbulence is a crisis of some sort. Table 3.1 lists a number of crises that different organizations have had to confront in recent years.

Table 3.1
Recent Organizational Crises

Date	Organization	Crisis
1979	Metropolitan Edison	Near meltdown at Three Mile Island nuclear power plant
1982	Johnson & Johnson	Cyanide poisoning of Tylenol capsules resulting in 8 deaths
1984	Union Carbide	Poison gas leak at plant in Bhopal, India, kills 3,000 and injures another 300,000
1985	Jalisco	Bacteria in cheese kills 84
1986	NASA	Space shuttle *Challenger* explodes, killing 7 crew members
1989	Exxon	Tanker *Valdez* runs aground off coast of Alaska, spilling millions of gallons of oil.
1993	Jack-in-the-Box	Tainted meat sold in Washington state restaurants kills 2 and poisons over 400 others.
1993	Pepsi	Unsubstantiated claims about sewing needles in cans of Pespi-Cola make national headlines.

Source: Based on Ian Mitroff, Paul Shrivastava, and Firdaus E. Udwadia, "Effective Crisis Management," *The Academy of Management Executive,* August 1987, pp. 283–292.

The effects of crises like those can be devastating to an organization, especially if managers are unprepared to deal with them. At NASA, for example, the shuttle disaster essentially paralyzed the U.S. space program for almost three years. The cost to Johnson & Johnson of the Tylenol poisonings has been estimated at $750 million in product recalls and changes in packaging and product design.[27] Exxon's legal problems arising from the Alaskan oil spill will not be settled for years.

Such crises affect organizations in different ways, and many organizations are developing crisis plans and teams. When a Delta Air Lines plane crashed in 1988 at the Dallas–Fort Worth airport, for example, fire-fighting equipment was at the scene in minutes. Only a few flights were delayed, and none had to be canceled. In 1987 a grocery store in Boston received a threat that someone had poisoned cans of its Campbell's tomato juice. Within six hours, a crisis team from Campbell Soup Co. removed two truckloads of juice from all eighty-four stores in the grocery chain. Still, fewer than half of the major companies in the United States have a plan for dealing with major crises.[28]

How Organizations React to Their Environment

Given the myriad issues, problems, and opportunities in an organization's environments, how should the organization respond? Obviously, each organization must assess its own unique situation and then react according to the wisdom of its senior management.[29] Exhibit 3.5 illustrates the six basic ways in which organizations react to their environment. One reaction, social responsibility, is discussed in Chapter 6.

Information Management   One way organizations respond to the environment is through information management. This is especially important in forming an initial understanding of the environment and in monitoring the environment for signs of change. Organizations use several techniques for managing information. One is defining boundary spanners. A **boundary spanner** is someone like a sales representative or a purchasing agent who spends much of his or her time in contact with others outside the organization. Such people are in a good position to learn

*A **boundary spanner** is someone who spends much of her or his time in contact with others outside the organization.*

Environmental scanning *is the process of actively monitoring the environment through observation, reading, and so forth.*

Information systems *gather and organize relevant information for managers and assist in summarizing that information in the form most pertinent to each manager's needs.*

what other organizations are doing. All effective managers engage in **environmental scanning,** the process of actively monitoring the environment through observation, reading, and so forth. Merrill Lynch, Federal Express, Ford Motor Company, and many other firms have also established elaborate **information systems** within the organization to gather, organize, and summarize relevant information for managers and to assist in summarizing that information in the form most pertinent to each manager's needs. (Information systems are covered more fully in Chapter 23.)

Strategic Response   Another way organizations respond to their environment is through a strategic response. The response may involve doing nothing (for example, if they feel they are doing very well with their current approach), altering their strategy a bit, or adopting an entirely new strategy. If the market that a company currently serves is growing rapidly, the firm might decide to invest even more heavily in products and services for that market. Likewise, if a market is shrinking or does not provide reasonable possibilities for growth, the company may decide to cut back. For example, when Tenneco's managers recently decided that oil and gas prices were likely to remain depressed for some time to come, they decided to sell the company's oil and gas business and invest the proceeds in its healthier businesses like Tenneco Automotive.[30]

Mergers, Takeovers, Acquisitions, and Alliances   A merger occurs when two or more firms combine to form a new firm. For example, Time and Warner recently merged to create Time-Warner. A takeover occurs when one firm buys another, sometimes against its will (a hostile takeover). Usually, the firm that is taken over ceases to exist and becomes part of the other company. For example, when AT&T took over NCR, it folded that company into its existing operations. After an acquisition, the acquired firm often continues to operate as a subsidiary of the acquiring company. As already discussed, in strategic alliance the firm undertakes a new venture with another firm. Companies engage in these kinds of strategies for a variety of reasons. For example, they can ease entry into new markets or expand a firm's presence in a current market.

Organization Design   Another organizational response to environmental conditions is through its structural design. For example, a firm that operates in an environment with relatively low levels of uncertainty might choose to use a design with many basic rules, regulations, and standard operating procedures. Alternatively, a firm that faces a great deal of uncertainty might choose a design with relatively few standard operating procedures, instead allowing managers considerable discretion over how they do things. The former type is characterized by formal and rigid rules and relationships. The latter is considerably more flexible and permits the organization to respond more quickly to environmental change.[31] We learn much more about these and related issues in Chapter 12.

Direct Influence of the Environment   Organizations are not necessarily helpless in the face of their environments.[32] Indeed, many organizations are able to directly influence their environment in many different ways. For example, firms may influence their suppliers by signing long-term contracts with fixed prices as a hedge against inflation. Or they may become their own supplier. Sears, for example, owns some of the firms that produce the goods it sells. Du Pont bought Conoco Inc. a few years ago partially to ensure a reliable source of petroleum for its chemical operations.

Almost any major activity a firm engages in affects its competitors. If JVC lowers the prices of its CD players, Sony may be forced to follow suit. If Prudential lowers its life insurance rates, New York Life is likely to do the same. Organizations may also influence their customers. Examples include creating new uses for a product, finding entirely new customers, and taking customers away from competitors. Developing new kinds of software expands the customer base of computer firms. Organizations also influence their customers by convincing them that they need something new.

Exhibit 3.5

How Organizations Respond to Environments

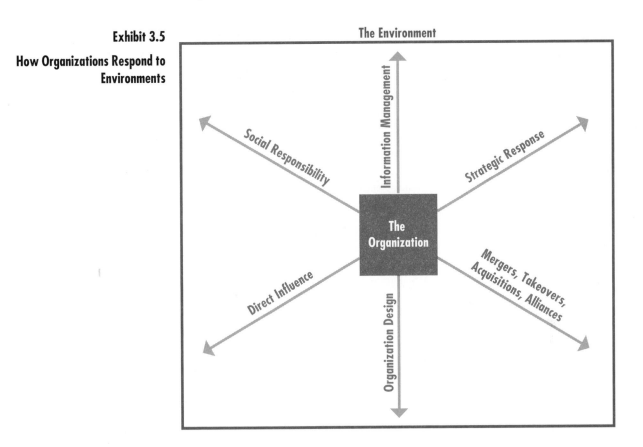

Automobile manufacturers use this strategy in their advertising to convince people that they need a new car every two or three years. Developing creative and innovative approaches ensures the survival of organizations. The self-assessment at the end of the chapter tests your creative approaches to situations.

Organizations influence their regulators through lobbying and bargaining. Lobbying involves sending a company or industry representative to Washington in an effort to influence relevant agencies, groups, and committees. For example, the U.S. Chamber of Commerce lobby, the nation's largest business lobby, has an annual budget of more than $100 million. The automobile companies have been successful on several occasions in bargaining with the EPA to extend deadlines for compliance with pollution control and mileage standards.[33] Mobil Corporation tries to influence public opinion and government action through an ongoing series of ads about the virtues of free enterprise.

Most bargaining sessions between management and unions are also attempts at mutual influence. Management tries to get the union to accept its contract proposals, and unions try to get management to sweeten its offer. When unions are not represented in an organization, management usually attempts to keep them out. When Honda opened its first plant in the United States, it helped establish a plant union to head off efforts by the United Auto Workers to set up a branch of its own union in the plant. Corporations influence their owners with information contained in annual reports, by meeting with large investors, and by pure persuasion. And strategic alliance agreements are almost always negotiated through contracts. Each party tries to get the best deal it can from the other as the final agreement is hammered out.

Chapter Summary

Environmental factors play a major role in determining an organization's success or failure. All organizations have both external and internal environments.

The external environment consists of general and task environment layers. The general environment of an organization is composed of the broad elements of its surroundings that might affect the activities of the organization. The general environment includes the economic, technological, sociocultural, political-legal, and international environments. The effects of these dimensions on the organization are broad and gradual.

The task environment consists of specific dimensions of the organization's surroundings that are very likely to influence the organization. It consists of seven elements: competitors, customers, suppliers, labor, regulators, owners, and strategic allies.

Since these dimensions are associated with specific organizations in the environment, their effects are likely to be direct.

The internal environment of an organization is its culture. Managers must understand not only its importance but also how it is determined and how it can be managed.

Organizations and their environments affect each other in several ways. Environmental influence on the organization can occur through uncertainty, competitive forces, or turbulence. Organizations, in turn, use information management, strategic response, mergers, takeovers, acquisitions, alliances, organization design, direct influence, and social responsibility to influence their task environments, and they occasionally try to influence broader elements of their general environment as well.

The Manager's Vocabulary

external environment	task environment	owners
internal environment	competitors	strategic allies
general environment	customers	culture
economic environment	suppliers	uncertainty
technological environment	labor	five competitive forces
sociocultural environment	regulators	boundary spanner
political-legal environment	regulatory agencies	environmental scanning
international environment	interest groups	information systems

Review Questions

1. What is an organization's general environment? Identify and discuss each major dimension of the general environment.
2. What is an organization's task environment? What are the major dimensions of that environment?
3. What is an organization's internal environment? How is it formed?
4. Describe the basic ways in which the environment can affect an organization.
5. Describe the basic ways in which an organization can respond to its environment.

Analysis Questions

1. Identify five different types of companies that are likely to be especially concerned about each one of the five dimensions of the general environment.
2. Identify examples of organizations in each dimension of the task environment of your college or university.
3. How are the general and task environments interrelated?
4. Think of an organization with which you have some familiarity. Describe its culture and suggest how that culture was created.
5. What are some recent examples of how the environment has affected specific organizations?

Self-Assessment

How Creative Are You?

Introduction The following exercise is designed to help you understand your creativity, a characteristic that is very valuable in assessing and responding to your organizational environment. If managers do not hone their creativity, they are likely to be passive reactors to the environment, rather than shapers of the future.

Instructions After each statement, indicate the degree to which you agree or disagree with it: A–strongly agree, B–agree, C–in between or don't know, D–disagree, E–strongly disagree. Mark your answers as accurately and frankly as possible. Try not to guess how a creative person might respond to each statement.

_____ 1. I always work with a great deal of certainty that I'm following the correct procedures for solving a particular problem.

_____ 2. It would be a waste of time for me to ask questions if I had no hope of obtaining answers.

_____ 3. I feel that a logical, step-by-step method is best for solving problems.

_____ 4. I occasionally voice opinions in groups that seem to turn some people off.

_____ 5. I spend a great deal of time thinking about what others think of me.

_____ 6. I feel that I may have a special contribution to make to the world.

_____ 7. It is more important for me to do what I believe to be right than to try to win the approval of others.

_____ 8. People who seem uncertain about things lose my respect.

_____ 9. I am able to stick with difficult problems over extended periods of time.

_____ 10. On occasion I get overly enthusiastic about things.

_____ 11. I often get my best ideas when doing nothing in particular.

_____ 12. I rely on intuitive hunches and the feeling of "rightness" or "wrongness" when moving toward the solution of a problem.

_____ 13. When problem solving, I work faster when analyzing the problem and slower when synthesizing the information I've gathered.

_____ 14. I like hobbies that involve collecting things.

_____ 15. Daydreaming has provided the impetus for many of my more important projects.

_____ 16. If I had to choose, I would rather be a physician than an explorer.

_____ 17. I can get along more easily with people if they belong to about the same social and business class as I.

_____ 18. I have a high degree of aesthetic sensitivity.

_____ 19. Intuitive hunches are unreliable guides in problem solving.

_____ 20. I am much more interested in coming up with new ideas than I am in trying to sell them to others.

_____ 21. I tend to avoid situations in which I might feel inferior.

_____ 22. When I evaluate information, its source is more important to me than its content.

_____ 23. I like people who follow the rule "Business before pleasure."

_____ 24. Self-respect is much more important than the respect of others.

_____ 25. I feel that people who strive for perfection are unwise.

_____ 26. I like work in which I must influence others.

_____ 27. It is important for me to have a place for everything and everything in its place.

_____ 28. People who are willing to entertain "crackpot" ideas are impractical.

_____ 29. I enjoy fooling around with new ideas, even if there is no practical payoff.

_____ 30. When a certain approach to a problem doesn't work, I can quickly reorient my thinking.

_____ 31. I don't like to ask questions that show ignorance.

_____ 32. I am able to change my interests to pursue a job or career more easily than I can change a job to pursue my interests.

_____ 33. Inability to solve a problem is frequently due to asking the wrong questions.

_____ 34. I can frequently anticipate the solution to my problems.

_____ 35. It is a waste of time to analyze one's failures.

(con't. on page 72)

_____ 36. Only fuzzy thinkers resort to metaphors and analogies.

_____ 37. At times I have so enjoyed the ingenuity of a crook that I hoped he or she would go scot-free.

_____ 38. I frequently begin work on a problem that I can only dimly sense and not yet express.

_____ 39. I frequently forget things such as names of people, streets, highways, and small towns.

_____ 40. I feel that hard work is the basic factor in success.

_____ 41. To be regarded as a good team member is important to me.

_____ 42. I know how to keep my inner impulses in check.

_____ 43. I am a thoroughly dependable and responsible person.

_____ 44. I resent things being uncertain and unpredictable.

_____ 45. I prefer to work with others in a team effort rather than alone.

_____ 46. The trouble with many people is that they take things too seriously.

_____ 47. I am frequently haunted by my problems and cannot let go of them.

_____ 48. I can easily give up immediate gain or comfort to reach the goals I have set.

_____ 49. If I were a college professor, I would rather teach factual courses than those involving theory.

_____ 50. I'm attracted to the mystery of life.

For interpretation, turn to the back of the book.

Source: From E. Raudsepp, *How Creative Are You?* Copyright © 1981. Reprinted by permission of Dominick Abel Literary Agency.

Skill Builder

Mapping Environmental Forces

Purpose This skill builder focuses on the *open systems model*. This model argues that an organization must be able to adapt to its environment. In order to maximize an organization's strengths, the managers must be able to assess the organization's culture, its external environment, and the task environment. This skill builder will help you develop the *innovator role*. One of the skills of the innovator is the ability to analyze the environmental facts that affect the organization.

Instructions Part I: In small groups, complete the University General Environment Worksheet and develop responses to the discussion questions. Select a group spokesperson to present the group's findings.

Discussion Questions

1. Which of the general elements have had the greatest impact on your education?
2. Which of the general elements have had the greatest impact on university administration? The faculty?
3. In what ways do the university's general elements differ from those of a giant organization like IBM?

University General Environment Worksheet

Identify the various elements in each general environment category that affect the university.

Economic Elements

_____

_____

Technological Elements

_____

_____

_____

Sociocultural Elements

_____

_____

_____

Political-Legal Elements

_____

_____

_____

International Elements

_____

_____

_____

Instructions Part II: Working in small groups, complete the University Task Environment Worksheet and develop responses to the discussion questions. Select a group spokesperson to present the group findings.

Discussion Questions

1. Which of the task environment factors has had the greatest impact on your education?

2. Which of the task environment factors has had the greatest impact on the university administration? The faculty?
3. In which ways does the university's task environment differ from that of a large organization like General Motors?

University Task Environment Worksheet

Identify the various elements in each task environment category that affect the university.

Competitors

_____

_____

_____

Regulators

_____

_____

_____

Customers

_____

_____

_____

Owners

_____

_____

Suppliers

_____

_____

_____

Strategic Allies

_____

_____

Source: Adapted from *Management: Function and Strategy,* 2nd ed. by Thomas S. Bateman and Carl P. Zeithaml. Reprinted by permission of the publisher, Richard D. Irwin, Inc. © Richard D. Irwin, Inc., 1987, 1990, and 1993.

Unions

_____

_____

_____

_____

CONCLUDING CASES

3.1   Safeway Keeps Adapting

Safeway Stores, Inc. was once the world's largest grocery store chain. The company was formed by a merger of two regional chains in 1926. Several other acquisitions and an aggressive expansion program resulted in 3,527 Safeway stores — the most ever — in 1931. During this time the firm also expanded internationally, opening stores in Canada, the U.K., and Australia. For the next several decades the firm was content to maintain its market share and concentrate on the profitability of its existing operations.

In 1986, however, events occurred that would forever change the venerable grocer. To avoid a hostile takeover by the Dart Group, Safeway management took the firm private. To accomplish this move, the company affiliated with KKR, a firm specializing in leveraged buyouts, and borrowed heavily. A leveraged buyout involves borrowing money to buy a firm while using assets of that firm as collateral. In order to make its new ownership structure work, Safeway managers also recognized that they had to change the firm's strategy.

In order to survive, management decided to narrow the firm's market and cut costs. Accordingly, it sold more than one thousand of its stores to other chains. These stores were primarily in Texas, Oklahoma, and other Southern states and were selected in part because of their high labor costs. Safeway also sold its international operations. The firm chose to retain its stores in the West and concentrate on being a regional grocer.

Safeway did indeed emerge from these changes as a strong regional chain with a significant share of the market in California and other Western states. The firm also gained some very favorable publicity in the aftermath of the San Francisco earthquake in 1989. At one store, for example, the manager kept the doors open and gave away bottled water, flashlights, batteries, and other essentials until they were all gone. About 140 of the firm's 300 northern California stores were damaged, with 30 suffering major damage. Yet, most stores were open by 6 A.M. the morning after the quake, and all were open in less than three days.

But problems still exist for the firm. For one thing, its labor costs are still high. The firm has repeatedly tried to negotiate with the United Food and Commercial Workers union for lower wages and fewer work rules but has often been stymied. Safeway suffered another setback during the early 1990s. Though the U.S. economy was in recession just about everywhere, California was especially hard hit. Because the firm acquires over one-third of its revenues from California alone, bad economic times for the region spelled bad economic times for Safeway as well. Compounding its difficulties, Safeway must still service the huge debt it took on as part of its leveraged buyout in 1986.[34]

Discussion Questions

1. Identify as many examples as you can in this case of how its environment has affected Safeway.
2. How is Safeway similar to and different from other grocery chains?
3. What steps has Safeway taken to affect its environment?

3.2   Sony Takes Control

When most people think of Sony, they think of the Walkman and other popular consumer electronics products like televisions, CD players, and stereos. Indeed, the name Sony is derived from the Latin *sonus*, for "sound." Founded by three Japanese engineers in 1946, the firm remains a market leader in electronics around the world today, generating an incredible eight hundred product extensions and two hundred totally new products every year!

A few years ago, however, managers at Sony started to grow concerned because the firm was so dependent on consumer electronics. They feared that increased competition or major industry shifts could leave the firm weakened. Accordingly, they developed a plan calling for diversification away from consumer electronics.

Part of this effort involved entering the semiconductor market and building computers and workstations.

The firm's boldest moves, however, were into the entertainment industry. Sony executives recognized that most of their consumer electronics products depended on inputs from other sources, including prerecorded music for CD players and videotaped movies for VCRs. Thus, if Sony could enter the market that created those products, it could accomplish two different goals: it could earn profits on the initial sales of those entertainment products, and it could partially control the input side of its electronics business.

Sony started its move into entertainment in 1988 by buying CBS Records for $2 billion. But it made its biggest splash when it bought Columbia Pictures from Coca-Cola in 1989 for $4.9 billion. These moves accomplished exactly what Sony wanted. They immediately gave the firm a vast library of prerecorded material and also provided Sony with a major presence in the entertainment industry.

The first few years were not without their pitfalls, however. During this period, for example, there was a major backlash in the United States against Japanese investors. At about the same time Sony bought Columbia, another Japanese firm, Matsushita, was buying MCA, parent of Universal Studios, prompting concerns about the Japanese presence in Hollywood. And at first, Columbia looked like anything but a star. Many pictures, like *Hook* and *Hudson Hawk*, were running over budget, bombing at the box office, or both.

By 1992, however, Sony seemed to be getting the hang of things. The firm succeeded in implementing tighter cost controls without undermining the creative forces that contribute to popular movies. And its roster of stars now includes such luminaries as Steven Spielberg, Tom Cruise, and Arnold Schwarzenegger. Columbia continues to score with some of the biggest movie hits in the industry—*A League of Their Own, In the Line of Fire,* and *A Few Good Men* among them. Thus, Sony may be well on its way to a happy ending.[35]

Discussion Questions

1. Note areas in which Sony's general and task environments have affected it.
2. How has Sony attempted to influence its own environment?
3. Identify several recent Columbia movies and determine their profitability.

CHAPTER 4

The Competitive Environment

Chapter Outline

Learning Objectives

After studying this chapter you should be able to

· Characterize the changing environment of management.

· Identify and describe the basic economic challenges of managers today.

· Identify and describe the basic competitive challenges faced by managers today.

· Identify and describe the basic workplace challenges faced by managers today.

· Summarize the legal and social challenges faced by managers today.

PepsiCo, Inc. is one of the world's most successful food products companies. Most people know the firm through its line of soft drinks—Pepsi-Cola, Diet Pepsi, Slice, Mountain Dew, and others. But PepsiCo is far more than just soft drinks. For example, it also owns one of the world's largest snack food businesses, Frito-Lay, maker of such popular snack food items as Doritos, Fritos, Lay's, Chee-Tos, Ruffles, and Tostitos. Moreover, PepsiCo also owns the world's largest chain of restaurants, comprised of more than eighteen thousand Pizza Hut, Taco Bell, and KFC food outlets.

Over the years, PepsiCo has been enormously successful. For example, it has eight different brands that generate more than $1 billion a year each in revenues. And the firm is well positioned abroad, with strong operations in Europe and South America. PepsiCo also has a presence in Asian markets and projects strong future growth there. PepsiCo's strengths come from its thorough understanding of consumer markets, aggressive sales strategy, deep pool of managerial talent, and tight cost controls.

Of course, even PepsiCo stumbles occasionally. For example, in the 1980s its Frito-Lay division in Dallas hired too many managers and grew into a bloated and lethargic bureaucracy. When Roger Enrico took over Frito-Lay in 1991, however, he eliminated eighteen hundred managerial jobs. He also invested in new technology, began discounting prices to retailers, and quickly restored the division's growth and profitability. Moreover, these changes were implemented with a minimum of dissatisfaction among members of the work force. PepsiCo's aggressive recruiting, promotion, and compensation practices have allowed the firm to have some of the most harmonious labor relations in the industry.

Over in the restaurant business, Pizza Hut has passed Domino's Pizza for the leadership in the home delivery business. And the new KFC name for Kentucky Fried Chicken was an attempt to get away from the "fried" label in today's health-conscious times. New manufacturing methods are also being used in all of PepsiCo's businesses in an effort to keep costs low and improve profit margins. The soft drink business, for example, recently installed new processing equipment in all its bottling plants that operate much more efficiently than did the old equipment.[1] ▪

Managers at PepsiCo have been very successful in confronting the basic competitive environment that is faced by all managers. Among other hurdles, they have had to deal with changing economic conditions, numerous competitive challenges, and a number of fundamental workplace challenges. Their ability to deal with these challenges has been a primary ingredient in the firm's effectiveness.

These issues and challenges are the focus of this chapter. Many of them are detailed extensions of some of the basic ideas introduced in Chapter 3. First we will characterize the changing environment faced by managers. Subsequent sections will introduce and explore particular economic, competitive, workplace, and legal and social challenges (and opportunities) that organizations and their managers must address.

The Changing Environment of Management

Though small businesses have existed for centuries, most big companies have been around for less than two centuries. In the grand scope of human history, then, professional managers and large business organizations are relative newcomers. But consider the vast changes that they have had to confront in their brief lifetimes. Electric motors, automobiles, airplanes, and telephones have each been around for less than 150 years.[2] Early industrialists like Vanderbilt and Carnegie could not take a transcontinental flight from New York to San Francisco.

Messages were sent by telegraph. Workers did not have sophisticated equipment to use in performing their jobs. And they worked long hours, often with little pay.

Now consider other tools and equipment that modern managers have come to rely on. Personal computers, xerographic machines, electronic calculators, overnight delivery services, facsimile machines, video cassette recorders, compact disc players, industrial robots, and many other things that have become commonplace in organizations today have been around for only a brief period of time.

To bring the impact of these changes into sharper focus, consider the changes faced by managers in a single organization such as Ford Motor Co. When Henry Ford first started his company in 1903, he did not have to contend with governmental regulation or organized labor because there were few regulations and no auto workers unions. He had a handful of domestic competitors, but demand for his automobiles was so great that quality was not a major issue. Indeed, most early Ford automobiles were not of particularly high quality. The firm made a single make of car—the Model T—from 1908 until 1927. Ford himself also owned the company so he did not have to concern himself with hostile stockholders. And because his firm was such a large purchaser of raw materials, he could virtually dictate what prices he would pay, when materials would be delivered by his suppliers, and so forth.

Over the years since 1903, the situation faced by Ford has changed dramatically and in every way imaginable. Ford now has operations around the world and must contend with myriad international competitors. The United Auto Workers is a major union that bargains aggressively for wages, benefits, and worker rights, and various governmental agencies regulate and control many of Ford's activities in areas ranging from pollution to hiring practices. Quality has become of paramount importance. Suppliers often have several large customers, thus limiting Ford's importance to them. Consumer tastes and demands continue to change, necessitating new models and new features on a regular basis. Today Ford makes twenty-three different models, each of which has to be redesigned every few years. The price of gasoline can also dramatically affect demand for different models. When gas prices go up, so too does demand for small, fuel-efficient cars like the Escort. When the price of gas goes down or stabilizes, demand jumps for larger cars like the LTD or Lincoln series. In short, then, the environment that Ford managers must cope with is vastly more complex and more prone to change today than it was just a few decades ago.

In a sense, the various forces and changes that affect managers today can be viewed as challenges. Competing for resources is seldom easy. If it were, all organizations would be successful and none would ever fail. Thus, confronting major economic, competitive, workplace, and legal and social changes are indeed challenges. Managers who do not deal with them effectively will suffer and perhaps fall by the wayside.[3] At the same time, we should also remember that a natural complement to challenge is opportunity. Just as failing to meet a challenge can have negative consequences, overcoming it or meeting it successfully can lead to increased profitability, effectiveness, and reputation.

Economic Challenges of Managers

Economic challenges of managers consist of various forces and dynamics associated with the economic system within which their organization competes.

Economic challenges of managers consist of various forces and dynamics associated with the economic system within which their organization competes. Thus, they reflect the economic environment of organizations, as described in Chapter 3. Far more complex than the simple supply and demand curves that students learn to interpret, the real economic world of managers is fraught with perils and opportunities, challenges and payoffs. General economic factors such as inflation rates, levels of unemployment, interest rates, budget deficits or surpluses, and the international balance of trade are all major dimensions of an economic system that affect managers. Four somewhat more specific areas that have become particularly significant are downsizing and cutbacks, entrepreneurship, the emerging service sector, and corporate ownership.

As organizations downsize to cut costs and become more competitive, sometimes divisions must be eliminated. Sears closed some of its stores as a result of its efforts to compete with other major merchandising firms. This one shown here was in Oakland, California. (Mark Richards/DOT Pictures.)

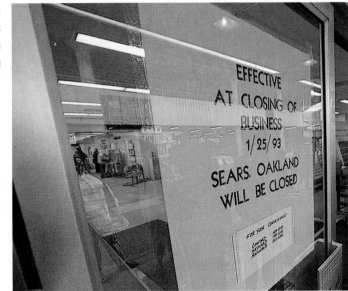

The Trend Toward Downsizing

Downsizing is a planned reduction in organizational size.

Cutbacks are reductions in the scope of an organization's operations.

Over the past several years many firms have been forced to go through a period of downsizing and/or cutbacks. **Downsizing** is a planned reduction in organizational size (for example, the number of employees, the number of businesses, the number of markets served, and so forth). **Cutbacks** are reductions in the scope of an organization's operations (such as operating budgets, travel expenses, R&D expenditures, and expansion plans). For years managers of U.S. firms in particular saw so much demand for their products and services that they had few concerns about costs. Likewise, quality was of only token importance (thus, a Ford had to be only as good as a Chevrolet), and prices could be raised as necessary with consideration for only a handful of competitors. This atmosphere changed dramatically, however, when global competition became more widespread and productivity and quality took on greater importance as competitive advantages. Many organizations began to experience loss of market share and declining income.

Many firms found themselves with excessive payroll costs (too many employees), excess capacity (too many offices and plants), and technology that was far too inefficient and outdated to rise to the competitive challenge. In response, they closed plants, refurbished others, and slashed payrolls. In the process they also eliminated hundreds of thousands of jobs. For example, American Airlines recently laid off one thousand managers. On a much more dramatic level, IBM has cut 25 percent of its payroll since 1985, including more than forty thousand employees in 1992 alone.[4] And we have already noted the cutbacks at Frito-Lay. Though downsizing has helped many businesses regain a competitive position, it has also undermined worker confidence in the traditional job security they have long expected from large organizations.

Entrepreneurship and New Careers

Entrepreneurship is the process of starting a new business.

People decide to engage in **entrepreneurship** and go into business for themselves for a variety of reasons. Many want the freedom of setting their own goals and objectives. Others want the challenge of creating something new—their own product or firm, for example. Still others have attractive opportunities in a family-owned business that may seem safer and/or be more lucrative than working for a big corporation. In addition, many former employees of large businesses that have cut back on their payrolls (as discussed above) decide to start their own business or go to work in someone else's small business. *The Entrepreneurial Spirit: Little Switzerland in the Caribbean* describes the successes enjoyed by one such firm.

The Entrepreneurial Spirit

Little Switzerland in the Caribbean

Little Switzerland sounds like a quaint European principality. But in reality it is a small but prosperous retail chain scattered across several exotic Caribbean islands. Based on the island of St. Thomas, there are nineteen Little Switzerland outlets that specialize in selling watches and jewelry to tourists. Every day, for example, two or three cruise ships with thousands of tourists dock at St. Thomas. And those tourists head into town looking for bargains and souvenirs.

Because of local government regulations, Little Switzerland is able to import watches and jewelry from other countries and pay little or no import tariff. Its tax rate in the Virgin Islands is also very low. Combined with a state-of-the-art in-

ventory system, these conditions allow Little Switzerland to sell its merchandise for lower prices than retailers in the United States. Customers can buy a Rolex watch or a piece of Baccarat crystal at a Little Switzerland store for 20 percent less than they would pay in New York City.

The firm's CEO, Walter Fischer, is from Switzerland. He admits that this has allowed him to build closer ties with Swiss manufacturers and to get better deals for his firm. They frequently grant him exclusive dealerships, thereby eliminating potential competition from other retailers.

Fischer thinks that Little Switzerland has ample opportunity for additional growth in the Caribbean. Tourism is up in the region, and European travelers are especially attracted to the Virgin Islands and other destinations served by Little Switzerland. Fischer plans to expand gradually and add at least two more stores in the next couple of years.[5] ∎

Small businesses play a vital role in the U.S. economy and in the economies of most industrialized nations around the world. For example, more than half of all new private sector jobs created in the United States in the 1980s were in businesses with fewer than one hundred employees (a common benchmark for defining small business).[6] And in many Eastern European countries just opening their markets to a free enterprise–based system, small businesses are also expected to play a major role in economic growth and development.

Unfortunately, many new businesses fail within a relatively short period of time. Though there are sometimes significant consequences of failing (including financial setback, social censure, damage to reputation, and so forth), it is also the case that many successful entrepreneurs fail one or more times before they finally succeed. Henry Ford, for example, went bankrupt twice before finally succeeding with the Ford Motor Co. One way to aid in determining whether you would be comfortable starting and running your own business is to compare your attributes with those of others who have been successful as entrepreneurs. The self-assessment at the end of the chapter aids you in discovering your potential as an entrepreneur.

Many other small businesses survive from the very beginning, however. They establish a comfortable niche for themselves—serving a well-defined market—and allow the owner-entrepreneur to remain in business and set her or his own course. These businesses may remain small or grow slowly over a period of years. Finally, a few businesses take off and become large businesses within just a few years. For example, Compaq Computer Corporation has grown from a three-person operation in 1982 to a multimillion dollar enterprise with more than twelve thousand employees.

The Service Sector   For many decades U.S. industry was based primarily on manufacturing. The manufacturing sector is composed of firms such as automobile companies, steel mills, oil refineries, and computer companies, which all make tangible products that are sold for profit. In recent decades, however, the service sector has taken on increased importance.

*In contrast to manufacturing, **services** provide some sort of utility for consumers.*

Services provide some sort of utility for consumers, as opposed to providing a tangible product. Examples of service firms range from small architectural or accounting partnerships to neighborhood beauty shops, aerobics studios, and pizza parlors to giant service firms like AT&T (with 1991 revenues of $63 billion), Wal-Mart Stores (whose 1991 revenues were $44 billion), and GTE (with 1991 revenues of $29 billion).[7]

In 1947 the service sector accounted for less than half of America's gross national product. By 1975, however, its proportion had grown to 65 percent, and by 1985 it had climbed to more than 70 percent. By 1990 it was approaching 75 percent. As shown in Exhibit 4.1, by the year 1995, approximately 90 million workers will be employed in service-producing industries, while only 30 million workers will be employed in goods-producing industries.

Ownership Challenges

*Basic **corporate ownership** issues include the power of mutual funds and institutional investors and hostile takeovers.*

A final economic challenge we will discuss relates to **corporate ownership.** Corporations sell stock to investors who then own a share of the business. Until the last few decades, each corporation had so many owners—individual investors—that no single one of them could exert much influence over the firm. Two major changes, however, have led to significant shifts in how managers respond to owners.

The first change in ownership patterns involved the emergence of the mutual fund market and the growth of institutional investing. Mutual funds are collections of stocks handled by professional fund managers. Individual investors who put their money in a mutual fund gain the expertise of a financial professional who decides which stocks to buy and sell. That is, the fund itself buys and sells stocks, passing along dividends and resale gains to the investors. Since mutual funds may have the resources to buy and sell hundreds of millions of dollars in stock, they have much more power than do the individual investors themselves. At the same time, managers who handle investments for institutions (such as universities) and retirement funds can also control large blocks of stock. Since these managers themselves, however, are responsible for showing a return to their investors, there has been some concern that managers may feel pressured to focus too much on short-term returns and not enough on long-term strength.[8]

Exhibit 4.1

Impact of the Service Sector

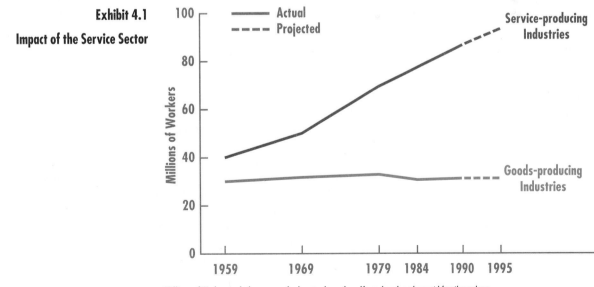

Millions of Workers includes wage and salary workers, the self-employed, and unpaid family workers.

Source: From Ricky W. Griffin/Ronald J. Ebert, *Business,* 3e, © 1993, p. 323. Reprinted by permission of Prentice-Hall, Englewood Cliffs, New Jersey.

A **takeover** *occurs when one corporation or group of investors buys or trades for enough stock in a company to gain control over it. Such a takeover is considered hostile when the target company does not wish to be taken over.*

Another ownership challenge has been the growth in hostile takeovers. A **hostile takeover** occurs when one corporation or group of investors buys or trades for enough stock in a company to gain control over it. Such a takeover is considered hostile when the target company does not wish to be taken over. The acquiring firm may want the target firm as a way of entering a new market, buttressing existing positions, or for other reasons. After it is acquired, the target firm may be left alone to continue doing what it was already doing, integrated into the acquiring firm, or have its assets sold individually for profit.

Competitive Challenges of Managers

Competitive challenges *of managers involve efforts to gain an advantage in acquiring scarce resources.*

Competitive challenges of managers involve efforts to gain an advantage in acquiring scarce resources. In the soft-drink market, for example, Coca-Cola and Pepsi-Cola are close competitors. IBM, Dell, and Compaq compete in the computer industry. Likewise, Stanford and Harvard compete for the best students, and neighboring states may compete for tourist dollars or industrial development opportunities.

Virtually all organizations compete with other organizations in some way, be it for consumer dollars, good students, or budget appropriations. *The Environment of Management: Nike, Reebok, and L.A. Gear Run a Tough Race* describes the highly competitive environment in the market for footwear. There are several different aspects to effective competition. Many of the broader and more general aspects are covered later in Chapter 8. Our concern here is with three specific sets of challenges that affect managers—productivity and quality, technology and automation, and innovation and intrapreneurship.

Productivity and Quality

Productivity *is a measure of efficiency—how much is created relative to the resources used to create it.*

Quality *is a measure of value.*

During the last decade managers have increasingly come to recognize the importance of productivity and quality as ingredients in successful competition. **Productivity** is a measure of efficiency—how much is created relative to the resources used to create it. **Quality,** on the other hand, is a measure of value. For example, consider two inexpensive watches with the same selling price. One runs flawlessly for five years, while the other must be discarded after only three. The longevity of the first watch is evidence of its higher quality. Or consider the experience of returning a sweater to a store. If you are treated cordially and receive a prompt refund with no questions asked, you might assess the quality of the service you received as high. On the other hand, if you are treated rudely, asked a number of probing questions about why you are returning the sweater, and then told that you will get a refund check in the mail in several weeks, you would likely feel the quality of service you received was poor. Thus, productivity and quality are relevant for both manufacturing and services.

At one time managers believed that quality and productivity were inversely related—that spending more to achieve higher quality resulted in higher total costs and, therefore, lower productivity. Now, however, managers recognize that just the opposite is true. Higher quality means fewer defects, more efficient use of resources, and fewer quality inspections, thereby actually boosting productivity.[9] Of course, quality is a relative concept. Among automobiles, for example, most knowledgeable consumers would expect a Lincoln Mark VIII to be of higher quality than a Ford Escort. But there are also major price differences between the two cars. Each may actually be of high quality relative to its price. When assessing quality, then, we must understand that it can have both absolute (as compared to some objective standard) and comparative (as compared to substitute products or services) dimensions.

Managers have come to see an important competitive role for both productivity and quality. An organization that falls behind its competitors in either area will be hard pressed to catch up. Indeed, more and more organizations are attempting to compete on the basis of both productivity and quality. We will return to quality and productivity in Chapter 21.

The Environment of Management

Nike, Reebok, and L.A. Gear Run a Tough Race

Though athletic fields are often the site of intense competition, that competition pales beside that for the right to equip those athletes with shoes and other apparel. Indeed, firms like Reebok, Nike, and L.A. Gear live and die on the whims of consumers who pay big bucks for shoes bearing the name of famous athletes.

Nike is perhaps the most successful firm in the industry. Nike was started in 1962 as Blue Ribbon Sports by a former runner from the University of Oregon and his coach. Blue Ribbon shoes soon attracted the attention of serious athletes because they were technologically superior to existing shoes and because the firm was interested in knowing what those athlete-consumers wanted in their shoes.

After changing its name to Nike in 1978, the firm's success was assured when Jimmy Connors won Wimbledon wearing Nikes and when the Boston Celtics and the Los Angeles Lakers adopted Nike as their official shoe. With spokespersons like Michael Jordan and Bo Jackson and slogans like "Just do it," Nike is on top of its game. A recent survey found that the Nike name was as well known around the world as IBM and Coke.

Reebok, meanwhile, has both streaked and sputtered. For several years Reebok was one of the fastest-growing firms in the United States. The firm started as a trendy maker of fashionable aerobic shoes and took several years before it became accepted by serious athletes. Its latest innovation, a street shoe called the Blacktop, has stopped a declining marketshare pattern and given new momentum to the firm.

L.A. Gear has yet to effect such a turnaround, however. Like Reebok, L.A. Gear started out focusing on fashion. But unlike Reebok, the firm has not been able to shift away from this narrow segment of the market. Indeed, L.A. Gear has few professional sportspersons promoting its shoes and recently sunk $20 million into an ill-fated endorsement by Michael Jackson. The jury is still out on the fate of the firm.[10] ■

Technology and Automation

Technology consists of processes and steps used to transform various inputs such as raw materials and component parts into something else.

Automation is the use of machinery, especially computers and robots, to replace human labor as part of the technological transformation process.

Technology consists of processes and steps used to transform various inputs such as raw materials and component parts into something else—a stereo, a book, or a shirt, for example. **Automation** is the use of machinery, especially computers and robots, to replace human labor as part of the technological transformation process. Technology has become a major competitive battlefield around the world. Indeed, many managers are finding that focusing on technology allows them both to introduce new products and improve existing products more effectively than in the past. Much of this advantage flows from automation. Managers of both manufacturing and service firms are recognizing that robotics and other approaches to automation can help them boost productivity and quality while lowering costs. At the same time, however, automation sometimes eliminates jobs and makes other jobs less challenging than before.

For example, when Steven Jobs launched his new computer firm Next, he decided early on that manufacturing and technology would be the core of his business. He created an almost fully automated plant that operates with only six hourly workers. Whenever company engineers design a new circuit board on their office computers, they can transmit the specifications to the plant by modem and pick up the completed board in twenty minutes. Moreover, the boards are made with such precision that there are fewer than twenty defects per one million units produced.[11]

Innovation and Intrapreneurship

Innovation is the process of creating and developing new products or services and/or identifying new uses for existing products and/or services. Without innovation, firms would become stagnant as competitors continued to introduce new products into the marketplace. 3M, based in Minnesota, has a goal of generating 25 percent of its profits from products less than five years old. Re-

Innovation is the process of creating and developing new products or services and/or identifying new uses for existing products and/or services.

cent successes for 3M include Post-It Notes and removable Scotch magic tape. Post-It Notes were a new product, while the removable tape was an extension of an existing product.

U.S. firms have typically been among the world leaders in innovation. Frequently, after U.S. scientists have achieved new product breakthroughs, businesses in other countries have figured out better ways of making the products. This has been the case for a number of products, ranging from televisions to cameras to hard disks. In recent years, however, many U.S. businesses have renewed their commitment not only to developing new products but also to applying their innovative methods to manufacturing and marketing them.[12] For example, Kodak, IBM, and Merck & Company have all made significant commitments in the last few years to increase spending on R&D, automate plants, and strive for greater innovation.

Intrapreneurship is the process of starting new ventures within a larger organization.

Many managers are finding that **intrapreneurship** is an effective approach to stimulating innovation. An intrapreneur is like an entrepreneur, but he or she works within the framework of an existing larger organization. Instead of going out and starting a new business, the intrapreneur starts new ventures within a larger organization. That is, he or she develops new ideas and then champions them through the various organizational channels that lead to their introduction into the marketplace. At 3M it was an intrapreneur who developed the Post-It Note and then fought for it over the objections of his boss, who did not think it was a good idea. Now, many managers are actively encouraging and rewarding intrapreneurship. For example, some firms give engineers and scientists a fixed amount of time each week that they can use to pursue pet projects.

Global Competition

Global challenges of managers are those that come from international competition.

Global challenges of managers are those that come from international competition. Many managers today really have no choice but to adopt a global perspective on doing business. Even if a company wants to compete only within a single economic system, it is very likely that competitors that draw on global financial resources, design and technology breakthroughs, and production efficiencies will have a marked advantage. Thus, the globalization movement is such that many organizations must choose either to participate in that movement or else gradually lose their ability to compete effectively.

Organizations that are competing in a global environment face myriad challenges and opportunities. At the simplest level, managers must determine which market to enter and how to enter it. One way would be to hire a foreign broker to sell the firm's goods in the chosen market. Another would be to license a company already in the market both to make and sell the firm's products. Some managers might decide to build a new plant in the foreign market and make their own products there. Others might enter into a joint venture with another firm to help get a foothold. We discuss the global environment more fully in Chapter 5.

Workplace Challenges of Managers

Workplace challenges involve the relationships among organizations, their managers, and their operating employees. Three important sets of workplace issues today are work force diversity, employee expectations and rights, and workplace democracy.

Work Force Diversity

Work force diversity exists in a group or organization when its members differ from one another along one or more important dimensions.

Work force diversity has become a very important issue in many organizations. **Work force diversity** exists in a group or organization when its members differ from one another along one or more important dimensions.[13] As more women and minorities have entered the labor force, for example, the available pool of talent from which organizations hire employees has changed in both size and composition.[14] A related factor that has contributed to diversity has been the increased awareness of managers that they can improve the overall quality of their work force by hiring and promoting the most talented people available.[15] Another reason for diversity has been legislation and legal actions that have forced organizations to hire more broadly.

Dimensions of Work Force Diversity   There are many different dimensions of diversity that can be used to characterize an organization. Some of these are illustrated in Exhibit 4.2. Another key dimension of diversity is the age distribution of workers. The average age of the U.S. work force is gradually increasing and will continue to do so for the next several years. How does this trend affect organizations? Older workers tend to have more experience, may be more stable, and can, therefore, make greater contributions to productivity. On the other hand, despite improvements in health and medical care, older workers are nevertheless likely to require higher levels of insurance coverage and medical benefits. The declining labor pool of younger workers will continue to pose problems for firms as they find fewer potential new entrants into the labor force.[16]

Exhibit 4.2

Trends in Work Force Diversity

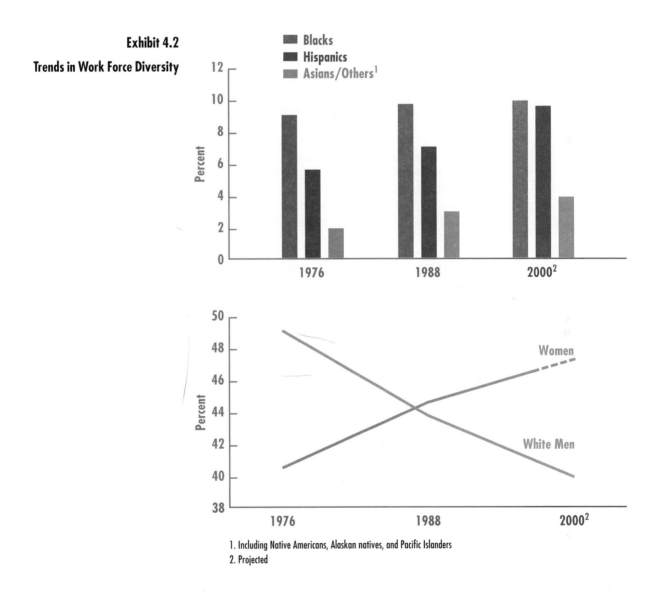

1. Including Native Americans, Alaskan natives, and Pacific Islanders
2. Projected

Most organizations have already experienced changes in the relative proportions of male and female employees. In the United States, for example, it is projected that the percentage of male employees will shrink from 55 percent in 1988 to 53 percent by the year 2000. Simultaneously, the percentage of female employees will increase from 45 percent in 1988 to 47 percent by the year 2000.[17] There are still relatively few female top managers, but this pattern is gradually changing as well.

Ethnicity refers to the ethnic composition of a group or organization.

Another major dimension of cultural diversity in organizations is ethnicity. **Ethnicity** refers to the ethnic composition of a group or organization. Within the United States, most organizations reflect varying degrees of ethnicity comprised of whites, blacks, Hispanics, and Asians. By the year 2000 the percentage of whites in the U.S. work force is expected to drop to 74 percent. At the same time the percentage of Hispanics is expected to climb to 10 percent. The percentages of blacks, Asians, and others are expected to climb only about 1 percent each.[18]

In addition to age, gender, and ethnicity, managers are confronting other dimensions of diversity as well. Some of the more important ones include country of national origin, handicapped and physically challenged employees, single parents, dual-career couples, gays and lesbians, people with special dietary preferences (for example, vegetarians), and people with different political ideologies.[19] The skill builder at the end of this chapter allows you to experience diversity first hand.

The Impact of Diversity   There is no question that organizations are becoming ever more diverse. But what is the impact of this diversity on organizations? As we will see, diversity provides both opportunities and challenges for managers. For example, many managers are finding that diversity can be a source of competitive advantage in the marketplace. There are six arguments that have been proposed for how diversity contributes to competitiveness.[20] These arguments are summarized in Table 4.1.

The *cost argument* suggests that managers who learn to cope with diversity will generally have higher levels of productivity and lower levels of turnover and absenteeism. Ortho Pharmaceuticals estimates that it has saved $500,000 by lowering turnover among women and ethnic minorities.[21] The *resource acquisition argument* for diversity suggests that organizations that manage diversity effectively will become known among women and minorities as good places to work. These organizations will thus be better able to attract qualified employees from among these groups. The *marketing argument* suggests that managers with diverse work forces will be better able to understand different market segments than will less diverse organizations. For example, a cosmetics firm like Avon that sells its products to women and blacks can better understand how to create and effectively market such products if women and black managers are available to provide input into product development, design, packaging, advertising, and so forth.[22]

The *creativity argument* for diversity suggests that organizations with diverse work forces will generally be more creative and innovative than will less diverse firms. Related to the creativity argument is the *problem-solving argument*. In a more diverse organization, there is more information that can be brought to bear on a problem and therefore a higher probability that better solutions will be identified. Finally, the *systems flexibility argument* for diversity suggests that organizations must become more flexible as a way of managing a diverse work force. As a direct consequence, the overall organization will also become more flexible.

Unfortunately, diversity in an organization can also become a major source of conflict. One potential avenue for conflict is when people think that someone has been hired, promoted, or fired to promote diversity. For example, suppose a male executive loses a promotion to a female executive. If he believes that she was promoted simply because the firm wanted to have more female managers rather than because she was the better candidate for the job, he will likely feel resentful toward both her and the organization itself.

Another source of conflict stemming from diversity is through misunderstood or inappro-

Table 4.1

Diversity and Competitiveness

Argument	Rationale
Cost	Effective management of diversity leads to higher levels of productivity and lower levels of turnover and absenteeism
Resource acquisition	Effective management of diversity leads to women and minorities wanting to work for the organization
Marketing	Effective management of diversity helps managers understand different market segments
Creativity	Effective management of diversity fosters creativity in organizations
Problem solving	Effective management of diversity leads to more effective problem solving because of more information being brought to bear on problems
Systems flexibility	Effective management of diversity helps organizations become more flexible

Source: Based on data in Taylor H. Cox and Stacy Blake, "Managing Cultural Diversity: Implications for Organizational Competitiveness," *The Academy of Management Executive,* August 1991, pp. 45–56.

priate interactions between people. For example, suppose a male manager tells a sexually explicit joke to a new female manager. He may intentionally be trying to embarrass her, he may be clumsily trying to show her that he treats everyone the same, or he may think he is making her feel like part of the team. Regardless of his intent, however, if she finds the joke offensive she will feel anger and hostility. These feelings may be directed only at the offending individual or, more generally, toward the entire firm if she believes that its culture facilitates such behavior. And of course, sexual harassment itself is both unethical and illegal.

Conflict can also arise as a result of cultural phenomena. For example, suppose a U.S. manager publicly praises the work of a Japanese employee. The manager's action stems from the cultural belief in the United States that recognition is important and rewarding. But because the Japanese culture places a higher premium on group loyalty and identity, the employee will likely feel ashamed and embarrassed. Thus, a well-intentioned action may backfire and result in unhappiness.

Conflict may also arise as a result of fear, distrust, or individual prejudice. Members of the dominant group in an organization may worry that newcomers from other groups pose a personal threat to their own position in the organization. For example, when U.S. firms have been taken over by Japanese firms, U.S. managers have sometimes been resentful or hostile to Japanese managers assigned to work with them. People may also be unwilling to accept people who are different from themselves. Personal bias and prejudices are still very real among some people today and can lead to potentially harmful conflict.[23]

Managing Diversity in Organizations Because of the tremendous potential that diversity holds for competitive advantage, as well as the possible consequences of diversity-related conflict, much attention has been focused in recent years on how individuals and organizations can better manage diversity.[24] Some of these are summarized in Table 4.2. The four basic things individuals can do is to strive for understanding, empathy, tolerance, and communication.[25]

The first of these individual strategies is understanding the nature and meaning of diversity. Some managers have taken the concepts of equal employment opportunity to an unnecessary extreme. They know that, by law, they cannot discriminate against people on the basis of sex, race, and so forth. In following this mandate they attempt to treat everyone the same. But this belief can cause problems when it is translated into workplace behaviors among people after they have been hired. The fact is that people are not the same. While people need to be treated fairly and equitably, managers must understand that differences do, in fact, exist among people. Thus, any effort to treat everyone the same, without regard to fundamental human differences, will only lead to problems.

Related to understanding is empathy. People in an organization should try to understand the perspective of others. For example, suppose a group that has traditionally been comprised of white males is joined by a female member. Hopefully, the males will be interested in making her feel comfortable and welcome. They may be able to do this most effectively by empathizing with how she may feel. For example, she may feel disappointed or elated about her new assignment, she may be confident or nervous about her position in the group, and she may be experienced or inexperienced in working with male colleagues. By learning more about her situation the existing group members can further facilitate their ability to work together.

A third related individual approach to dealing with diversity is tolerance. Even though managers may learn to understand diversity, and even though they may try to empathize with others, they may still not accept or enjoy some aspect of their interactions with others. For example, one firm recently reported considerable conflict among its U.S. and Israeli employees. The Israeli employees seemed to want to argue about every issue that arose. The U.S. managers preferred a more harmonious way of conducting business and became uncomfortable with the conflict. Finally, after considerable discussion it was learned that many Israeli employees simply enjoy arguing and

Diverse, cross-functional teams present tremendous opportunities and challenges to contemporary managers. At Hallmark Cards, artists, designers, printers, and finance personnel used to work a city block apart from each other. After Hallmark reorganized the work, the staff now works together. Such changes are expected to reduce by one-half the time it takes to get a new product to market. (James Schnepf.)

Table 4.2
Managing Diversity

Individual strategies	Organizational strategies
Understand the nature of diversity	Policies and procedures
Empathy	Diversity training
Tolerance	Language training
Communication	Corporate culture

see it merely as part of getting work done. The firm's U.S. employees still do not enjoy the arguing, but they are more willing to tolerate it as a fundamental cultural difference between themselves and their colleagues from Israel.[26]

A final individual approach to dealing with diversity is communication. Problems about diversity issues often get magnified because people are afraid or otherwise unwilling to openly discuss issues that relate to diversity. For example, suppose a younger employee has a habit of making jokes about the age of an older colleague. Perhaps the younger colleague means no harm and is just engaging in what she sees as good-natured kidding. But the older employee may find the jokes offensive. If there is no communication between the two, the jokes will continue and the resentment will grow. Eventually, what started as a minor problem may erupt into a much bigger one. For communication to work, it must be a two-way street. If a person wonders whether a certain behavior on her or his part is offensive to someone else, the curious individual should probably just ask. Similarly, if someone is offended by the behavior of another person, he or she should explain to the offending individual how the behavior is perceived and request that it be stopped. As long as such exchanges are handled in a friendly, low-key, and nonthreatening fashion they will generally have a positive outcome.

Though individuals can play an important role in managing diversity, the organization itself must play a fundamental role. Through its various policies and practices people in the organization come to understand what behaviors are and are not appropriate. The organization's culture is the ultimate context within which diversity must be addressed. The starting point in managing diversity is the policies that an organization adopts that directly or indirectly affect how people are treated. Obviously, for instance, the extent to which an organization embraces the premise of equal employment opportunity will to a large extent determine the potential diversity within an organization. But there are differences in the organization that follows the law to the letter and still practices passive discrimination and the organization that actively seeks a diverse and varied work force.

Another aspect of organizational policies that affects diversity is how the organization addresses and responds to problems that arise from diversity. Consider the example of a manager charged with sexual harassment. If the organization's policies put an excessive burden of proof on the individual being harassed and invoke only minor sanctions against the guilty party it is sending a clear signal as to the importance of such matters. But the organization that has a balanced set of policies for addressing questions like sexual harassment sends its employees a different message about the importance of diversity and individual rights and privileges.

Organizations can also help manage diversity through a variety of ongoing practices and procedures. Benefit packages, for example, can be structured to better accommodate individual situations. An employee who is part of a dual-career couple and who has no children may require relatively little insurance (perhaps because her spouse's employer provides more complete coverage) and would like to be able to schedule vacations to coincide with those of her spouse. Another employee, who happens to be a single parent, may need a wide variety of insurance coverage and prefer to schedule his vacation time to coincide with school holidays. Flexible working hours are another useful organizational practice to accommodate diversity. Differences in family arrangements, religious holidays, cultural events, and so forth may dictate that employees have some degree of flexibility regarding when they work. For example, a single parent may need to leave the office every day at 4:30 in order to pick up the children from their day care center. An organization that truly values diversity will make every reasonable attempt to accommodate such a need.

Organizations can also facilitate diversity by making sure that there is diversity in its key committees and executive teams. Even if diversity exists within the broader organizational context, an organization that does not reflect diversity in groups like committees and teams implies that diversity is not a fully ingrained element of its culture. In contrast, if all major groups and related work assignments reflect diversity, the message is a quite different one.

Many organizations are finding that diversity training is an effective means for managing diversity and minimizing its associated conflict. **Diversity training** is training that is specifically designed to better enable members of an organization to function in a diverse workplace. This training can take a variety of forms. For example, many organizations find it useful to help people learn more about their similarities to and differences from others. Men and women can be taught to work together more effectively and can gain insights into how their own behaviors affect and are interpreted by others. In one organization a diversity training program helped male managers gain insights into how various remarks they made to one another could be interpreted by others as being sexist. In the same organization female managers learned how to point out their discomfort with those remarks without appearing overly hostile.[27]

Similarly, white and black managers may need training in order to better understand each other. Managers at the Mobil Corporation noticed that four black colleagues never seemed to eat lunch together. After a diversity training program they came to realize that the black managers felt that if they ate together, their white colleagues would be overly curious about what they might be talking about. Thus, they avoided close associations with one another because they feared calling attention to themselves.[28]

Some organizations even go so far as to provide language training for their employees as a vehicle for managing diversity. Motorola, for example, provides English language training for its foreign employees on assignment in the United States. At Pace Foods in San Antonio, with a total payroll of 350 employees, staff meetings and employee handbooks are translated into Spanish for the benefit of the company's 100 Hispanic employees.[29]

The ultimate test of an organization's commitment to managing diversity is its culture. Regardless of what managers say or put in writing, unless there is a basic and fundamental belief that diversity is valued, it cannot ever become truly an integral part of an organization. An organization that really wants to promote diversity must shape its culture so that it clearly underscores top management commitment to and support of diversity in all of its forms throughout every part of the organization. With top management support, however, and reinforced with a clear and consistent set of organizational policies and practices, diversity can become a basic and fundamental part of an organization.

Diversity training is training that is specifically designed to better enable members of an organization to function in a diverse workplace.

Employee Expectations and Rights

For many years managers generally believed that workers were motivated only by opportunities for economic gain. Later, with more emphasis on human relations, it was thought that personal satisfaction was the driving force in motivation. Eventually, managers came to see that employee motivation is actually a very complex process. Each individual has his or her own unique set of needs and perceptions of how best to fulfill them. These individual needs continue to change. For example, more fathers want to participate in the raising of their children, and more women are seeking professional careers. Thus, managers today are finding it necessary to be more flexible in how they treat their employees.[30] They are allowing workers to have more say in how they do their jobs, providing more information about what the organization has planned, and allowing workers more freedom in selecting job assignments.

Managers seeking to motivate a diverse work force and enhance employee performance must work harder than ever to understand their employees. At the same time, however, new concerns are being raised about worker rights and privacy.[31] For example, some managers argue that organizations should seek to help employees with drug or alcohol problems. They believe that helping with these problems is the socially responsible thing to do and that organizations have an obligation to fulfill this function. On the other hand, some managers argue that organizations should essentially "mind their own business" as long as their employees are meeting performance expectations. They reason that what a person does outside the workplace is his or her own business and that the organization should not attempt to intervene.

Workplace Democracy

Many managers are also having to contend with issues of workplace democracy, the practice of giving workers a greater voice in how the organization is managed. Some managers have come to believe that letting workers have a say in what the organization does will enhance employee commitment to the organization while also improving its effectiveness. The workers, in turn, get to have a voice in determining what happens to their employing organization.

As we will see in Chapter 17, many managers have started increasing the participation that workers have in deciding how they do their jobs. Together with this participation, however, is an expectation on the part of employees that they will have a greater say in a wide variety of organizational issues—including, but not limited to, working hours, organizational practices, hiring decisions, and compensation decisions. Sometimes this voice gets legitimized in very specific ways. The United Auto Workers union was granted a seat on Chrysler's board of directors in return for wage concessions made during the automaker's financial crisis in the early 1980s.

In some parts of the world, workplace democracy has been part of organizational life for a long time. In Germany, for example, organizations are required by law to have a specified number of employees and managers on their governing boards. In the United States, however, workplace democracy is a relatively new concept that managers are just beginning to address. For example, in traditional General Motors plants workers are gradually getting a bigger voice in what goes on. However, in the firm's new Saturn division, workers have started out with a significant role in deciding how work will be done. A number of different worker councils, for example, review a wide variety of activities and projects and make recommendations to management about whether or not they should be adopted.

Legal and Social Challenges of Managers

Legal challenges *of managers are those that reflect the judicial context in which an organization operates.*

Social challenges *are those that are related to prevailing social customs and mores.*

Legal challenges of managers are those that reflect the judicial context in which an organization operates. **Social challenges** relate more to prevailing social customs and mores. Recent concerns about legal and social challenges were in part stimulated by several widely publicized ethical scandals during the 1980s and early 1990s. For example, Ivan Boesky, David Levine, and Michael Milken were all involved in Wall Street scandals.[32] Major ethical scandals plagued Japan, Great Britain, and Germany as well.

Virtually all managers face ethical dilemmas as an inherent part of their jobs. Thus, both organizations and the managers who work for them must strive to better understand the ethical context in which decisions are made. Consider the case of a manager deciding what to do about a minor pollution problem. His plant operates within governmental guidelines for his industry. Even though the manager knows his firm is generating a small amount of "acceptable" pollution, one choice he has is to do nothing. Another alternative is to invest in modest equipment that might further lower but not eliminate the pollution. Finally, he could spend heavily on state-of-the-art equipment that would eliminate all of his firm's pollution. None of these three choices is technically the best or the worst one. Different people can make very compelling arguments for each of these three choices.

Managers must make a variety of decisions every day about how they treat their employees, how they interact with suppliers, customers, lenders, regulators, and competitors, and so forth. Virtually all of these decisions have an ethical component. We return to issues of ethics and social responsibility in Chapter 6.

Governmental Regulation

In theory, free market economies are characterized by relatively little governmental regulation. That is, businesses and their managers are free to compete however they see fit. Even though the United States has a free market economy, there is still an abundance of governmental regulation that both proscribes and prescribes business activity. There are a variety of reasons why governmental regulation has been considered necessary during the history of U.S. business. For one, large and powerful firms have sometimes been known to try to drive their weaker competitors out of business by using unfair business practices. For another, governmental regulation is sometimes necessary to support various laws such as the Occupational Safety and Health Act, the Environmental Protection Act, and so forth. There is also a feeling among some people that the government should strive to maintain a reasonable level of competition for the public good. Finally, many people believe that unscrupulous businesspeople would resort to unethical and illegal behavior on a regular basis if they were not regulated.

On the other hand, critics of regulation argue that, if we are indeed a free market, businesses should be free to do whatever they want. The logic behind this belief is that if a business does something people object to, they will "punish" that business by not buying its products or services. In the United States there has been a trend to reduce or lower regulation of business. For example, in recent years many regulations regarding the airline, the financial, and the trucking industries have been softened. How has reduced regulation worked? In the airline industry many weaker carriers have been absorbed by larger ones, but fares are considerably lower than they were during the days of extreme regulation. In the financial industry, however, managers in many savings and loan firms took advantage of decreased regulation and prompted one of the biggest financial crises in history. We discuss regulation more fully in Chapter 6.

The Natural Environment

Though concerns about pollution and the environment have been raised for decades, they are increasingly coming to center stage.[33] Greater consumer awareness, growing alarm about problems ranging from global warming to the scarcity of landfills for trash, and media attention have all served to sensitize everyone about these issues. There are an increasing variety of controversial environmental issues that organizations of all types must address, from air pollution to toxic waste disposal to water pollution. For example, some environmentalists protest the plastic containers that many firms use to package their products.

Still another issue that has emerged is the increasingly widespread organizational practice of promoting products as being environmentally sound. Sometimes these claims are legitimate, while on other occasions they are overstated. For example, Procter & Gamble recently had to drop claims that its disposable diapers were biodegradable. A growing global concern is the extent to which businesses are defying conventional wisdom or generally accepted practices concerning the environment. For example, many environmentalists are concerned about unregulated fishing practices in Japan that result in Japanese fishing fleets hunting whales or destroying dolphins while catching tuna. The Canadian government has for years tried to get the United States to curb the pollution that results in forest-destroying acid rain. Others worry about how Brazil is destroying its rain forests for the sake of industry and expansion. And many countries in Eastern Europe are among the most polluted on earth. For example, 70 percent of the rivers in Czechoslovakia are

The social challenges of managers seem to expand every day. Anita Roddick, founder of the Body Shop, views that as an opportunity and has developed a highly successful organization that is socially and environmentally responsible. Her products are made from natural ingredients and are packaged in recyclable materials. She is shown here with members of the Wodaabe tribe in Nigeria, a group about whom she sponsored a documentary film. (Carol Beckwith/Courtesy of the Body Shop.)

heavily polluted, one-third of Bulgaria's forests are damaged by unrestricted air pollution, and East Germany has major toxic waste problems.[34] Again, we return to these issues in Chapter 6.

Chapter Summary

Because managers today operate in an ever-changing world, they must confront a variety of issues. This confrontation carries with it both challenges and opportunities. The basic sets of challenges include economic, competitive, workplace, and legal and social issues.

Economic challenges of managers include various forces and dynamics associated with the economic system within which their organization functions. Some of the more important economic considerations are downsizing and cutbacks, the role of entrepreneurship and new careers, the emerging role of service organizations, and corporate ownership.

Competitive challenges are associated with the efforts of managers to gain an advantage for their organization in acquiring scarce resources. Four specific sets of competitive challenges

that organizations have to address today are productivity and quality, technology and automation, innovation and intrapreneurship, and global competition.

Workplace challenges are those associated with the relationships among organizations, their managers, and their operating employees. Work force diversity is perhaps the most significant of these challenges today. Employee expectations and rights and workplace democracy are also important.

Legal challenges of organizations are those reflecting the judicial context of the organization. Social challenges involve prevailing social customs and mores. Key legal and social issues today include the ethical standards of managers, governmental regulation, and the relationship between business and the natural environment.

The Manager's Vocabulary

Economic challenges	Corporate ownership	Technology
Downsizing	Hostile takeover	Automation
Cutbacks	Competitive challenges	Innovation
Entrepreneurship	Productivity	Intrapreneurship
Services	Quality	Global challenges

Workplace challenges   Ethnicity   Legal challenges
Work force diversity   Diversity training   Social challenges

Review Questions

1. Identify and briefly describe the four basic sets of managerial challenges discussed in this chapter.
2. Why have many businesses been forced to go through downsizing?
3. How are productivity and quality different and how are they related? Can you change one without changing the other?
4. Why is innovation important to managers?
5. What are some of the arguments for and against governmental regulation of business? Can there really be a "free market?" Why or why not?

Analysis Questions

1. How is entrepreneurship affected by downsizing and cutbacks? Is there anything resembling a logical cycle between the two?
2. Suppose you are a plant manager considering the purchase of an automated assembly line. What issues would you consider before proceeding?
3. It is fairly easy to identify U.S. firms such as Ford that have stiff international competition. Identify some U.S. firms that have no direct foreign competitors, at least in North America.
4. What are some recent controversies that have arisen regarding the natural environment and business? (Give specific examples and cite the basic issues involved in each.)
5. Suppose you had a subordinate with a drug problem. The subordinate was capable of working adequately, but was having personal problems resulting from drug use. Should you try to help, or should you stay out of it? What if your boss had the drug problem?

Self-Assessment

Are You an Entrepreneur?

Introduction The increase in entrepreneurial activity discussed in the chapter may indicate that some of you are interested in becoming entrepreneurs. This self-assessment helps to evaluate your entrepreneurial tendencies.

Instructions This quiz is designed to give you an idea of whether you have the entrepreneurial spirit. Circle your answer to each of the following twenty-six questions.

1. How were your parents employed?
   a. Both worked and were self-employed for most of their working lives.
   b. Both worked and were self-employed for some part of their working lives.
   c. One parent was self-employed for most of his or her working life.
   d. One parent was self-employed at some point in his or her working life.
   e. Neither parent was ever self-employed.
2. Have you ever been fired from a job?
   a. Yes, more than once.
   b. Yes, once.
   c. No.

3. Are you an immigrant, or were your parents or grandparents immigrants?
   a. I was born outside of the United States.
   b. One or both of my parents were born outside of the United States.
   c. At least one of my grandparents was born outside of the United States.
   d. Does not apply.
4. Your work career has been:
   a. Primarily in small business (under 100 employees).
   b. Primarily in medium-sized business (100 to 500 employees).
   c. Primarily in big business (over 500 employees).
5. Did you operate any businesses before you were 20?
   a. Many.
   b. A few.
   c. None.

6. What is your present age?
    a. Under 31.
    b. 31–40.
    c. 41–50.
    d. 51 or over.
7. You are the _____ child in the family.
    a. Oldest.
    b. Middle.
    c. Youngest.
    d. Other.
8. You are:
    a. Married.
    b. Divorced.
    c. Single.
9. Your highest level of formal education is:
    a. Some high school.
    b. High school diploma.
    c. Bachelor's degree.
    d. Master's degree.
    e. Doctor's degree.
10. What is your primary motivation in starting a business?
    a. To make money.
    b. I don't like working for someone else.
    c. To be famous.
    d. As an outlet for excess energy.
11. Your relationship to the parent who provided most of the family's income was:
    a. Strained.
    b. Comfortable.
    c. Competitive.
    d. Nonexistent.
12. If you could choose between working hard and working smart, you would:
    a. Work hard.
    b. Work smart.
    c. Both.
13. On whom do you rely for critical management advice?
    a. Internal management teams.
    b. External management professionals.
    c. External financial professionals.
    d. No one except myself.
14. If you were at the racetrack, which of these would you bet on?
    a. The daily double—a chance to make a killing.
    b. A 10-to-1 shot.
    c. A 3-to-1 shot.
    d. The 2-to-1 favorite.

15. The only ingredient that is both necessary and sufficient for starting a business is:
    a. Money.
    b. Customers.
    c. An idea or product.
    d. Motivation and hard work.
16. If you were an advanced tennis player and had a chance to play a top pro like Boris Becker, you would:
    a. Turn it down because he could easily beat you.
    b. Accept the challenge but not bet any money on it.
    c. Bet a week's pay that you would win.
    d. Get odds, bet a fortune, and try for an upset.
17. You tend to "fall in love" too quickly with:
    a. New product ideas.
    b. New employees.
    c. New manufacturing ideas.
    d. New financial plans.
    e. All of the above.
18. Which of the following personality types is best suited to be your right-hand person?
    a. Bright and energetic.
    b. Bright and lazy.
    c. Dumb and energetic.
19. You accomplish tasks better because:
    a. You are always on time.
    b. You are superorganized.
    c. You keep good records.
20. You hate to discuss:
    a. Problems involving employees.
    b. Signing expense accounts.
    c. New management practices.
    d. The future of the business.
21. Given a choice, you would prefer:
    a. Rolling dice with a 1-in-3 chance of winning.
    b. Working on a problem with a 1-in-3 chance of solving it in the allocated time.
22. If you could choose between the following competitive professions, it would be:
    a. Professional golf.
    b. Sales.
    c. Personnel counseling.
    d. Teaching.
23. If you had to choose between working with a partner who is a close friend and working with a stranger who is an expert in your field, you would choose:
    a. The close friend.
    b. The expert.

(con't. on page 96)

24. You enjoy being with people:
    a. When you have something meaningful to do.
    b. When you can do something new and different.
    c. Even when you have nothing planned.
25. In business situations that demand action, clarifying who is in charge will help produce results.
    a. Agree.
    b. Agree, with reservations.
    c. Disagree.

26. In playing a competitive game, you are concerned with:
    a. How well you play.
    b. Winning or losing.
    c. Both of the above.
    d. Neither of the above.

For interpretation, turn to the back of the book.

Source: From "The Entrepreneur in You," by Joseph R. Mancuso. Reprinted from *Across the Board,* July–August 1984; The Conference Board, 845 Third Avenue, New York, NY 10022, and The Center for Entrepreneurial Management Inc., 180 Varick Street, 17th Floor, New York, NY 10014.

Skill Builder

Becoming a Minority: Being Exposed to Cultural Diversity

Purpose Managers must get the best out of all people. They cannot allow the color of a person's skin, a person's age, or a person's gender to cause them to behave in a way that would reduce an employee's performance. One way of understanding how others experience life is to try and experience it yourself. This skill builder will allow you to do just that.

This skill builder focuses on the *human resources model.* It will help you develop your *facilitator* role. One of the skills of a facilitator is the ability to accept other people's differences.

Introduction Because we are moving into more of a diverse work environment, it is important to understand and appreciate people's backgrounds that are different from our own. The following assignment exposes you to a new situation, requires you to carefully observe your surroundings, and asks you to describe what you felt and what others might feel to have you among them.

Instructions Your task is to go by yourself (you may not take anyone with you) to a place where you have not been before and to observe what you see. After this experience, write a two-page paper that reports on the following:
1. Date and address of where the experience took place.
2. Length of time you were there.
3. Brief description of the setting.
4. Your reaction to the situation in terms of your behavior and feelings.
5. Your perception of other individuals' reactions toward you.
6. What this experience teaches you about being different from others in your environment.
7. How such an experience might influence your development if you were to live or work in such a setting all your life.

8. Concluding comments about the experience.

Whenever possible, relate your experience to the literature covered in the course. To give some ideas about possible places to visit, below are examples of previous students' choices:
a. Protestants visited a Catholic service and vice versa.
b. Caucasians visited Black churches and student organizations.
c. A student went to a Japanese birthday party.
d. A student visited a Croatian wedding.
e. Students went to the School for the Deaf or the School for the Blind.
f. White-collar workers went to a blue-collar cafeteria.
g. A student visited a body-building club.
h. A younger student visited a nursing home.
i. A female student went to a car auction with predominantly male customers.
j. A student sat in the Faculty Lounge.

Source: Renate R. Mai-Dalton, "Becoming a Minority: Being Exposed to Cultural Diversity," *Organization Behavior Teaching Review,* vol. 9 (3), 1984–85, pp. 76–82.

CONCLUDING CASES

4.1   ConAgra, Inc. Faces New Challenges

Few people have ever heard of ConAgra, but many people use its products on a regular basis. When Charles Harper took over a nearly bankrupt Midwest grain company in 1974, he had visions of greatness for the firm. He cut costs to the bone, sold some of the firm's flour mills, and then used the surplus cash to begin buying other firms in the food-processing industry. Today ConAgra is the largest independent firm in its industry. Some of its better-known brand names include Banquet frozen foods, Armour luncheon meat, Hunt's tomato sauce, Peter Pan peanut butter, Orville Redenbacher popcorn, and Healthy Choice frozen entrees.

A big key to ConAgra's success has been innovation. The firm is constantly looking for new products and for new ways of making current products. One of its most recent innovations has been a ground-meat blend that has only 4 percent fat. And its Healthy Choice line was hailed by *Advertising Age* as the most successful new food brand introduced in twenty years. Managers at ConAgra think of themselves as entrepreneurs and run their business as though it was a small operation.

But like managers in all businesses, managers at ConAgra face challenges. ConAgra stole market share from industry giants like Stouffer (a division of Nestlé) and Kraft (a division of Philip Morris), but those firms have started fighting back. Each, for example, has introduced a line of frozen entrees aimed directly at Healthy Choice's market. Though ConAgra has held its market share, price cutting has substantially trimmed its profit margins.

Investors also wonder about the firm's long-term prospects. Harper will be retiring soon, and some observers question the ability of his hand-picked successor, Philip Fietcher, to continue ConAgra's aggressive strategy of innovation and growth. For example, one large investor, the Teacher Retirement System of Texas, recently cut its holdings of ConAgra stock by 10 percent because its manager sees little growth in the firm's stock price. Fietcher, meanwhile, argues that he fully understands Harper's approach to running the business and plans to keep things on track.

One area where Fietcher sees considerable opportunities for growth is in foreign markets. But critics also worry that the firm is moving too slowly in this area. Some of ConAgra's competitors, like Sara Lee Corp. and H. J. Heinz Company, get more than 40 percent of their revenues from abroad while ConAgra gets only about 5 percent of its revenues from foreign markets. ConAgra managers point out that they first had to rebuild the firm's financial strength and then establish strong domestic operations. Only now, they contend, is the firm well positioned for international expansion. But they also plan to move slowly and cautiously into foreign markets.[35]

Discussion Questions

1. Which managerial challenges are most relevant to ConAgra today?
2. Are different challenges likely to become more important to the firm in the future?
3. What are the advantages and disadvantages of moving slowly into international markets?

4.2   Europe Opens New Markets for Automakers

The European market is shaping up as the next big battlefield for the world's automakers. As the final trade barriers come down on the European continent, the European Community (EC) is emerging as the largest unified marketplace on the globe. And automakers from every corner of the globe are scrambling for a piece of the action.

For years the European market has been dominated by six major firms, plus several niche companies. The big six firms are Volkswagen, Fiat, General Motors, Ford, Peugeot, and Renault. Strong niche players are Mercedes, BMW, Porsche, Rover, Volvo, and Saab. Though competition among these firms was often fierce, everyone knew the rules. Strict import quotas limited the number of cars any given firm could ship to other countries, for example, and local regulation forced most firms to operate relatively autonomous units within each country where they conducted business.

But with the opening of the EC in 1993 comes the elimination of quotas and tariffs. Thus, rather than dealing with a dozen or so medium-size markets, firms will find themselves dealing with one huge one. And most of the companies in Europe are already jockeying for position. Fiat, for example, has closed most of its manufacturing facilities in its home country of Italy and relocated most of its manufacturing in Poland to capitalize on lower labor costs and higher worker productivity. Volkswagen has started making many of its parts in China and Mexico for the same reason. Ford, meanwhile, has cut its European employment from 150,000 down to 100,000. To cut costs both it and GM are building several new manufacturing facilities in Europe.

Besides the enormous opportunities available in Europe, there is also a looming threat: Japanese automakers. At the present time Japanese firms have only a small presence in Europe, in part because of strict import quotas and in part because they have been so focused on the U.S. market for the past ten years. But now they are beginning to implement the same strategy in Europe that worked so well in North America—heavy advertising, competitive pricing, local production, and a strong dealership.

For example, Japanese firms have already captured a significant market share in those European countries—including Finland, Norway, and Switzerland—that do not produce their own cars. They are also setting up dealerships across the continent. And it seems as though they are building plants everywhere. Nissan, Toyota, and Honda are building plants in Great Britain, and Mitsubishi is building one in the Netherlands.

But some observers believe that the Japanese will have a harder time than they expect. For one thing, many governments seem to welcome Ford and GM because they have been doing business in Europe for years but resent the Japanese for coming in so late. And Europeans still tend to be somewhat nationalistic. Thus, they are less likely to buy a Japanese product if they see that it will hurt domestic firms.[36]

Discussion Questions

1. What are the major economic challenges facing automakers in Europe today?
2. What are the major competitive challenges facing automakers in Europe today?
3. Are there any major issues associated with work force diversity that firms entering the European market may encounter?

CHAPTER

5

The Global Environment

Learning Objectives

After studying this chapter you should be able to

- Describe the global environment, including its forms and levels, growth, managing internationalization, and managing in an international market.

- Discuss the elements of the international economy and how they impact international management.

- Identify and discuss the basic challenges inherent in international management.

- Describe the basic issues involved in managing in an international economy, including the influence of organization size and the management functions.

Toys "Я" Us Inc. was founded in 1958 by Charles Lazarus. Using personal savings and a bank loan, he opened a 25,000-square-foot toy discount store in Washington, D.C. Growth in the new venture was initially slow. Gradually, however, as Lazarus refined his operating formula growth and profits began to escalate. That formula involves stringent site selection procedures, providing a wide array of toys for discount prices, high volume, and relentless cost cutting.

In the mid-1980s Lazarus decided to take the Toys "Я" Us concept to foreign markets. By 1990 there were almost one hundred stores outside U.S. borders, concentrated mainly in Canada, the United Kingdom, Germany, and France. Just like at home in the United States, each of these markets proved to be a virtual gold mine for the firm. Because of its successes abroad, Lazarus then decided to take the Toys "Я" Us concept to one of the world's most attractive but troublesome marketplaces—Japan.

A big hurdle faced by the company was Japan's so-called "big store" review process. Designed to protect small local retailers, it requires that all businesses planning to open a large retail outlet in Japan undergo an exhaustive review process that can take as long as three years. Toys "Я" Us and McDonald's decided to team up and try to shorten this review process. McDonald's already had considerable success in cracking the Japanese bureaucracy. In return for its efforts, Toys "Я" Us agreed to sell McDonald's a 20-percent stake in its Japanese operation. Through extensive lobbying efforts they were indeed able to shorten the review cycle to eighteen months and also eliminate several other administrative hurdles.

Finally, amid considerable hoopla, the first Toys "Я" Us in Japan opened its doors in 1991. The opening of its second store, in early 1992, was attended by President George Bush. All told, at least one hundred stores are planned for Japan by the end of this decade. Not surprisingly, Japan has proved to be just as profitable for the firm as the other markets where it does business. Now Lazarus is busy surveying his globe looking for other opportunities.[1] ∎

The path chosen by Toys "Я" Us is an increasingly common one. Firms from every industrialized country in the world are entering new markets, taking on new challenges, and forming alliances with other firms. And all for the same reason: to compete more effectively in the international business environment. To be successful today, managers have to understand the global context within which they function. This holds true regardless of whether the manager runs a *Fortune* 500 firm or a small independent manufacturing concern.

This chapter explores the global environment of management. We start by describing the influence of the global environment. We then discuss international economy in terms of different economies and economic systems. Basic challenges of international management are introduced and discussed next. We then focus on managing in the international economy. To survive in the next century, all managers will have to be prepared for a global environment. The skill builder at the end of the chapter assesses your preparation for globalization.

The Influence of the Global Environment

You probably woke up this morning to the sound of an alarm clock made in Japan. The clothes you put on were probably made in Korea, Mexico, or Taiwan. The coffee you drank was probably made from beans grown in South America. To get to school, you may have driven a Japanese car. Even if you drove a Ford or a Chevrolet, some of its parts were manufactured abroad. Perhaps you did not drive a car to school but rather rode a bus (manufactured by Volvo, a Swedish company) or a motorcycle (manufactured by Honda or Yamaha, both Japanese firms).

Our daily lives are strongly influenced by businesses from around the world. But we are not unique in this respect. People living in other countries have much the same experience. They drive Fords in Germany, use IBM computers in Japan, eat McDonald's hamburgers in France, and snack on Mars candy bars in England. They drink Pepsi and wear Levi Strauss jeans in China. The Japanese buy Kodak film and use American Express credit cards. People around the world fly on United or American Airlines in planes made by Boeing. Their buildings are constructed with Caterpillar equipment and they buy Mobil oil.

In truth, we have all become part of a global village and have a global environment in which no organization is insulated from the effects of foreign markets and competition. More and more firms are viewing themselves as international or multinational businesses.[2] What do these terms mean, and why has this pattern developed? These and related questions are addressed first.

International Business Defined

*A **domestic business** acquires essentially all of its resources and sells all of its products or services within a single country.*

*An **international business** is primarily based in a single country but acquires some meaningful share of its resources or revenues from other countries.*

*A **multinational business** has a worldwide marketplace where it buys raw materials, borrows money, manufactures its products, and subsequently sells its products.*

*A **global business** transcends national boundaries and is not committed to a single home country.*

There are many different forms and levels of international business. Though the lines that distinguish one from another are perhaps arbitrary, we will identify four forms of international business. These are illustrated in Exhibit 5.1.[3] A **domestic business** acquires essentially all of its resources and sells all of its products or services within a single country. Many (but not all) small businesses are essentially domestic. However, there are few, if any, large domestic businesses left in the world today.

Most large firms today are either international or multinational operations. An **international business** is primarily based in a single country but acquires some meaningful share of its resources or revenues from other countries. The Limited fits this description. Most of its stores are in the United States, but many of the clothes it sells are manufactured abroad. A **multinational business** has a worldwide marketplace where it buys raw materials, borrows money, manufactures its products, and subsequently sells its products. General Motors is an excellent example of a multinational company. It has design and production facilities around the world. For example, its Geo Storm was designed and engineered in Europe, manufactured in Mexico, and is sold in the United States. GM makes and sells cars in Europe that are never seen in the United States. GM cars are designed and produced for and sold in individual markets, wherever they are and without regard for national boundaries.[4] Multinational businesses are often called **MNEs,** for multinational enterprises.

The final form of international business is the global business. A **global business** transcends national boundaries and is not committed to a single home country. Though no business has truly achieved this level of international involvement, Nestlé comes close. Nestlé is based in Vevey, Switzerland, but has a German CEO. The firm gets over 98 percent of its revenues and has over 95 percent of its assets outside Switzerland. The firm has ten general managers, only five of whom are Swiss. What makes Nestlé a Swiss firm is that its headquarters are in Switzerland and Swiss investors still own over half the firm's stock.[5]

The Growth of International Business

To understand why these different levels of international business have emerged, we must briefly look back to the past. After World War II, the United States was by far the dominant economic force in the world. Many countries in Europe and Asia had been devastated. There were few passable

Exhibit 5.1
Levels of International Business

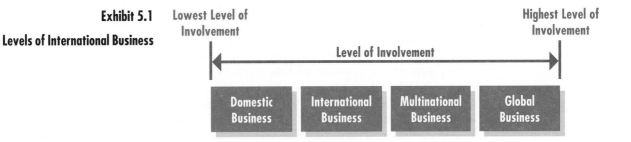

roads, few standing bridges, and even fewer factories dedicated to the manufacture of peacetime products. Places less affected by the war—Canada, South and Central America, and Africa—did not have the economic muscle to threaten the economic pre-eminence of the United States. Thus, when anyone in the world wanted to buy automobiles, electronic equipment, or machine tools, there was only one place to shop—the United States. Breakthroughs in communication and transportation only served to make it easier for businesses to buy and sell around the world.

Companies in war-torn countries had no choice but to rebuild from scratch. They were in the unfortunate but eventually advantageous position of having to rethink every facet of their operations, from technology to production to finance to marketing. Although it took many years for them to recover, they eventually did so and were poised for growth. During the same era, U.S. companies grew complacent. Increased population spurred by the baby boom and increased affluence resulting from the postwar economic boom greatly raised the average individual's standard of living and expectations. The U.S. public continually wanted new and better products and services. U.S. companies profited greatly from this pattern but were perhaps guilty of taking it for granted.

U.S. firms are no longer isolated from global competition or the global market.[6] A few simple numbers help tell the full story. First of all, the volume of international trade increased more than 2,000 percent from 1960 to 1990. Foreign investment in the United States was more than $37 billion in 1990 alone, while U.S. firms invested more than $33 billion in foreign markets. In 1960, seventy of the world's one hundred largest firms were American. This figure dropped to sixty-four in 1970, to forty-five in 1985, and to thirty in 1991.[7] Clearly, U.S. dominance of the global economy is a thing of the past.

U.S. firms are also finding that international operations are an increasingly important element of their sales and profits. For example, in 1990 Exxon realized 74.9 percent of its revenues and 83.5 percent of its profits abroad. For Citicorp, these percentages were 54.9 percent and 56 percent, respectively.[8] From any perspective it is clear that we live in a truly global economy. The days when U.S. firms could safely ignore the rest of the world and concentrate only on their U.S. market are gone forever. Now these firms must be concerned with the competitive situations they face in lands far from home and with how companies from distant lands are competing in the U.S.

Managing the Process of Internationalization

Managers should recognize that the international environment dictates two related but distinct sets of challenges. Each challenge carries with it its own unique set of skill demands. One set of challenges must be confronted when an organization chooses to change its level of international involvement. For example, a firm that wants to move from being an international to a multinational business has to manage that transition. The other set of challenges occur when the organization has achieved its desired level of international involvement and must then function effectively within that environment. This section highlights the first set of challenges, and the next section introduces the second set of challenges. When an organization makes the decision to increase its level of international activity, there are several alternative strategies that can be adopted. The most basic ones are shown in Exhibit 5.2.[9]

Importing and Exporting

Exporting means making the product in the firm's domestic marketplace and selling it in another country.

Importing occurs when a good, service, or capital is brought into the home country from abroad.

Importing or exporting (or both) is usually the first type of international business in which a firm gets involved. **Exporting** means making the product in the firm's domestic marketplace and selling it in another country. Both merchandise and services can be exported. **Importing** occurs when a good, service, or capital is brought into the home country from abroad. For example, automobiles (Toyota, Volkswagen, Mercedes-Benz, Audi), stereo equipment (Sony, Bang and Olufsen, Sanyo), and wine (Riunite, Dom Perignon, Swartzkatz) are imported into the United States. And firms in the United States routinely export grain to Russia, gas turbines to Saudi Arabia, locomotives to Indonesia, jeans to Great Britain, and diapers to Italy.

An import/export operation has many advantages. For example, it is the easiest way of entering a market with a small outlay of capital. Because the products are usually sold "as is," there

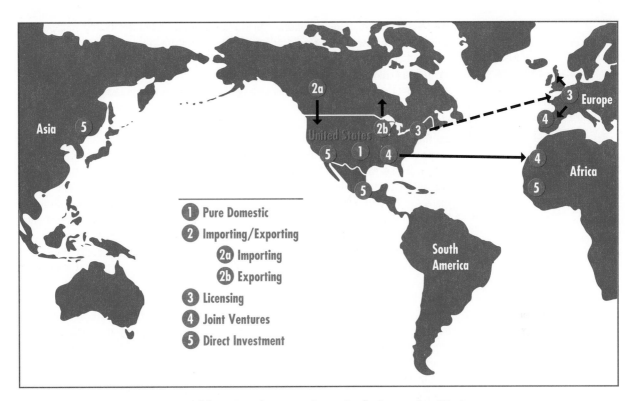

① **Pure Domestic**
② **Importing/Exporting**
  ②ⓐ **Importing**
  ②ⓑ **Exporting**
③ **Licensing**
④ **Joint Ventures**
⑤ **Direct Investment**

Exhibit 5.2   Alternative Strategies for International Business

is no need to adapt the product to the local conditions, and very little risk is involved. However, there are also disadvantages. For example, imports and exports are subject to taxes, tariffs, and higher transportation expenses. Furthermore, because the products are not adapted to local conditions, they may miss the needs of a large segment of the market. Finally, some products may be restricted and thus can be neither imported nor exported.

*Under a **licensing agreement**, a firm allows another company to use its brand name, trademark, technology, patent, copyrights, or other assets.*

Licensing   There are times when a company may prefer to arrange for a foreign company to manufacture or market its products under a **licensing agreement.** Factors that may lead to this decision include excessive transportation costs, government regulations, and home production costs. Under a licensing agreement, a firm allows another company to use its brand name, trademark, technology, patent, copyrights, or other assets. In return, the licensee pays a royalty, usually based on sales. For example, General Instrument Corp. recently signed a licensing agreement with Hyundai Electronics Industries Company in South Korea. Under the agreement, Hyundai will manufacture some of General Instrument's integrated circuit products. General Instrument initiated the arrangement because it felt the demand for its products would exceed the capacity of its plant in Chandler, Arizona. Under licensing agreements actual goods do not pass from one country to another. Thus, a dotted line is used to show this relationship in Exhibit 5.2.

Two advantages of licensing are increased profitability and extended profitability. This strategy is frequently used for entry into less developed countries where second-generation technology is still acceptable and, in fact, may be state of the art. A primary disadvantage of licensing is inflexibility. A firm can tie up its product or expertise for a long period of time. And if the licensee does not develop the market effectively, the licensing firm can lose profits. A second disadvantage is that licensees can take the knowledge and skill that they have been given access to for a foreign market and exploit them in the licensing firm's home market. When this happens, what used to be a business partner becomes a business competitor.

Joint Ventures/Strategic Alliances   An increasingly common form of international business is the **joint venture** or **strategic alliance.** When two firms enter into a joint venture, they share in the control and ownership of a new enterprise.[10] Chrysler and Austrian Motors recently established a joint venture called Eurostar to manufacture and sell mini-vans in Europe. A strategic alliance, on the other hand, is a cooperative agreement that does not necessarily involve ownership. Kodak, Fuji, Canon, and Minolta have recently agreed to work together to develop new types of film. After these new types of film have been developed, Kodak and Fuji will manufacture them, and Canon and Minolta will produce cameras to use them.

Joint ventures and strategic alliances have both advantages and disadvantages. They allow quick entry into a market by taking advantage of the existing strengths of participants. For example, Japanese automobile manufacturers used this strategy to their advantage to enter the U.S. market by using the already established distribution systems of U.S. automobile manufacturers. They are also an effective way of gaining access to technology or raw materials. And they allow firms to share the risk and cost of new venture. The major disadvantage of these approaches lies with the collaborative nature of the operation. Although it reduces the risk for each participant, it also limits the control and the return that each firm can enjoy.

Direct Investment   Another level of commitment to internationalization is direct investment. **Direct investment** occurs when a firm headquartered in one country builds or purchases operating facilities or subsidiaries in a foreign country. The foreign operations then become either a natural part of the organization or else a wholly owned subsidiary of the firm. Kodak recently made a direct investment when it built a new research lab in Japan. Each new Toys "Я" Us store the firm builds is also a direct investment.

Like the other approaches for increasing a firm's level of internationalization, direct investment carries with it a number of benefits and liabilities. Managerial control is more complete, and profits do not have to be shared as they do in joint ventures and strategic alliances. Purchasing an existing organization provides additional benefits because the human resources, plant, and organizational infrastructure are already in place. Acquisition is also a way to purchase brand-name identification of a product. This could be particularly important if the cost of introducing a new brand is high. For example, when Nestlé bought the U.S. firm Carnation a few years ago, it retained the firm's brand names for all of its products sold in the United States. Notwithstanding these advantages, Nestlé is now operating a part of itself entirely within the borders of a foreign country. The additional complexity in decision making, the economic and political risks, and so forth may outweigh the advantages that can be obtained by international expansion.

One special form of direct investment is called **outsourcing.** Outsourcing, sometimes referred to as global sourcing, involves transferring production to locations where labor is cheap. Japanese businesses have moved much of their production to Thailand, because labor costs are much lower there. Many U.S. firms are using maquiladoras for the same purpose. **Maquiladoras** are light-assembly plants built in northern Mexico close to the U.S. border. The plants are given special tax breaks by the Mexican government, and the area is populated with workers willing to work for very low wages. There are now more than one thousand plants in the region employing 300,000 workers, and more are planned. The plants are owned by major corporations, primarily from the United States, Japan, South Korea, and several European industrial countries. This concentrated form of direct investment benefits Mexico, the investing companies, and workers who might otherwise be without jobs. Some critics argue, however, that the low wages paid by the maquiladoras amount to little more than slave labor.[11]

We should also note that these approaches to internationalization are not mutually exclusive. Indeed, most large firms use all of them simultaneously. MNEs and global businesses have a global orientation and worldwide approach to foreign markets and production. They search for

Joint ventures are not limited to business firms; non-profit organizations and governments can also form joint ventures. The Canadian and Chinese governments collaborated five years on joint dinosaur expeditions. The more than eighty tons of specimens collected in the two countries are changing our picture of how dinosaurs lived. Workers in the photo are assembling some of the dinosaurs that will go on a world tour. (Louis Psihoyos/MATRIX.)

opportunities all over the world and select the best strategy to serve each market. In some settings they may use direct investment, in others licensing, in others joint ventures and strategic alliances. In still others they might limit their involvement to exporting and importing.

Managing in International Markets

Even when a firm is not actively seeking to increase its level of internationalization, its managers are still responsible for seeing that it functions effectively within whatever level of international involvement the organization has achieved. In one sense the job of a manager in an international business may not be much different from the job of a manager in a domestic business. Each may be responsible for acquiring resources and materials, making products, providing services, developing human resources, advertising, and monitoring cash flow.

In another sense, however, the complexity of these activities is much greater for many managers in international firms. Thus, a wider array and greater sophistication of management skills are necessary for effectively managing in the international economy. Rather than buying raw materials from sources in California, Texas, and Missouri, an international purchasing manager may buy materials from sources in Peru, India, and Spain. Rather than training managers for new plants in Michigan, Florida, and Oregon, the international human resources executive may be training new plant managers for facilities in China, Mexico, and Scotland. And instead of developing a single marketing campaign for the United States, an advertising director may be working on promotional efforts in France, Brazil, and Japan. Exhibit 5.3 illustrates the complexities associated with a single firm operating in international markets.

The key question that must be addressed by any manager trying to be effective in an international market is whether to focus on globalization or regionalism.[12] A global thrust requires

Exhibit 5.3

The Complexities of Competing in International Markets

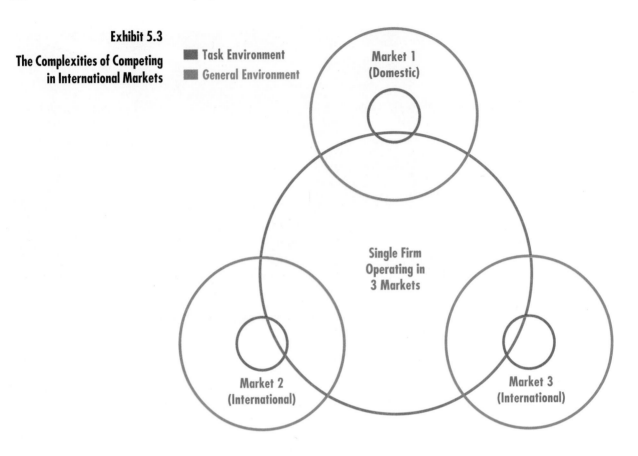

■ Task Environment
■ General Environment

Market 1
(Domestic)

Single Firm
Operating in
3 Markets

Market 2
(International)

Market 3
(International)

that activities be managed from an overall global perspective and as part of an integrated system. Regionalism, on the other hand, involves managing within each region with less regard to the overall organization. In reality, most larger MNEs manage some activities globally (for example, finance and manufacturing) and others locally (such as human resources management and advertising). We will explore these approaches more fully later in this chapter.

The International Economy

One thing that can be helpful to managers seeking to operate in a global environment is to better understand the structure of the international economy. Though each country, and indeed each region within the country, is unique, there are still some basic similarities and differences among countries that can be noted. We will describe three different elements of the international economy: mature market economies and systems, developing economies, and other economies.

Mature Market Economies and Systems

*A **market economy** is based on the private ownership of business and allows market factors such as supply and demand to determine business strategy.*

A **market economy** is based on the private ownership of business and allows market factors such as supply and demand to determine business strategy. Mature market economies include the United States, Japan, the United Kingdom, France, Germany, and Sweden. These nations have several things in common. For example, they tend to employ market forces in the allocation of resources. They also tend to be characterized by private ownership of property, although there is some variance along this dimension. France, for example, has a relatively high level of government ownership.

U.S. managers have relatively few problems operating in market economies. Many of the business "rules of the game" that apply in the United States, for example, also apply in Germany

When planned economies started to falter in the late 1980s, worldwide economies grew dominant. Although some former planned economies—now market economies—are struggling, others seem to be entering prosperity. In this picture, shoppers in Bombay, India, are enthusiastically crowding to stores to take advantage of the new goods available in its emerging market economy. (Raghu Rai/Magnum.)

or England. And consumers there often tend to buy the same kinds of products that U.S. consumers do. For these reasons it is not unusual for U.S. firms seeking to expand geographically to begin operations in some other market economy. Recall, for example, that the first countries that Toys "Я" Us entered were market economies. Although the task of managing an international business in an industrial market country is somewhat less complicated than operating in some other type of economy, it still poses some challenges. Perhaps the foremost challenge is that the markets in these economies are typically quite mature. This means in part that many industries are already dominated by large and successful companies. Thus, competing in these economies poses a major challenge.[13]

Market systems are clusters of countries that engage in high levels of trade with each other.

The map in Exhibit 5.4 highlights two relatively mature market systems. **Market systems** are clusters of countries that engage in high levels of trade with each other. One mature market system is Europe. Until recently, Europe was two distinct economic areas. The eastern region consisted of communist countries such as Poland, Czechoslovakia, and Rumania. These countries relied on government ownership of business and greatly restricted trade. In contrast, Western European countries with traditional market economies have been working together to promote international trade for decades. In particular, the **European Community** (or **EC** as it is often called) has long been a formidable market system. The formal members of the EC are Denmark, the United Kingdom, Portugal, the Netherlands, Belgium, Spain, Ireland, Luxembourg, France, Germany, Italy, and Greece. For years these countries have been following a basic plan that called for the elimination of most trade barriers by 1992. The European situation has recently grown more complex, however. Communism has collapsed in most eastern countries, and they are trying to develop market economies. They also want greater participation in trade with the Western European countries. In some ways the emergence of the east has slowed and complicated business activities in the west. In the long run, however, the new markets in the east are likely to make Europe an even more important part of the world economy.

*The **European Community (EC)** is a mature market system that consists of Denmark, the United Kingdom, Portugal, the Netherlands, Belgium, Spain, Ireland, Luxembourg, France, Germany, Italy, and Greece.*

*The **Pacific Rim** consists of Japan, China, Thailand, Malaysia, Singapore, Indonesia, South Korea, Taiwan, Hong Kong, the Philippines, and Australia.*

A second mature market system is the so-called **Pacific Rim.** The Pacific Rim includes Japan, China, Thailand, Malaysia, Singapore, Indonesia, South Korea, Taiwan, Hong Kong, the Philippines, and Australia. Though Japan has been a powerhouse for years, Taiwan, Hong Kong,

Europe

Pacific Rim

Exhibit 5.4   Mature Market Systems

Singapore, and South Korea have only recently become major economic forces. Trade among these nations is on the rise, and talk has started about an Asian economic community much like the EC.[14]

A third mature market system is North America. The United States, Canada, and Mexico are major trading partners with one another. More than 70 percent of Mexico's exports go to the United States, and more than 65 percent of what Mexico imports comes from the United States. Over the last several years these countries have negotiated a variety of agreements to make trade even easier. *The Environment of Management: NAFTA—Promise or Peril?* details how the **North American Free Trade Agreement** may represent another step toward the development of a unified North American market.

The Environment of Management

NAFTA—Promise or Peril?

For years the world has been talking about the European Community and 1992—the year that the continent's major economic powers would drop their trade barriers and create a unified market. But as 1992 drew to a close, another economic community with the potential to be just as important was also edging closer to reality.

For years politicians in the United States, Canada, and Mexico have been exploring the formation of a unified North American market. The idea behind a North American market is that by allowing easier movement of goods and services across the borders of the three countries each would benefit. A preliminary agreement on a unified market was tentatively reached late in 1992. The framework behind the agreement is the North American Free Trade Agreement, or NAFTA.

But NAFTA faces a long, hard climb before it is approved.

Mexico appears to be the country with the most to gain from the agreement. Because their labor costs are so high, many more U.S. and Canadian firms would be expected to move manufacturing facilities into Mexico, resulting in higher employment and standards of living for its citizens.

In the United States and Canada, however, the picture is less clear. Some businesses would clearly profit because they would be able to compete in a larger market with fewer constraints. But others would be hurt by increased competition from firms in the other two countries.

For example, one recent report has suggested that U.S. manufacturers of auto parts, furniture, and household glass, as well as producers of sugar, peanuts, citrus fruits, seafood, and vegetables, would all suffer from the agreement. All told, U.S. firms are expected to gain a total of 95,000 jobs in some sectors but lose as many as 170,000 in others. Not surprisingly, then, many unanswered questions have to be resolved before the U.S. and Canadian legislatures buy into NAFTA.[15] ∎

Developing Economies

*A **developing economy** is one that is relatively underdeveloped and immature, characterized by weak industry, weak currency, and relatively poor consumers.*

In contrast to the highly developed and mature market economies described above, other countries have what is termed a **developing economy.** These economies are relatively underdeveloped and immature. They are generally characterized by weak industry, weak currency, and relatively poor consumers. However, the government in each of these countries is actively working to strengthen its economy by opening its doors to foreign investment and by promoting international trade. Some of these countries have only recently adopted market economies, while others still use a command (i.e., government-controlled) economy. Even though it is technically part of the Pacific Rim, the People's Republic of China is largely underdeveloped. Many of the countries in South America and Africa are only now developing in an economic sense. And the various states and republics that previously comprised the U.S.S.R. are also viewed as developing economies.

The primary challenges presented by countries with developing economies to those interested in conducting international business there are the lack of wealth on the part of potential consumers and the underdeveloped infrastructure. Developing economies have enormous economic potential, but much of it remains untapped. Thus, international firms entering these markets often have to invest heavily in distribution systems, in training consumers how to use their products, and in providing facilities for their workers to live in.

Other Economies

There are also economic systems around the world that defy classification as either mature markets or developing economies. One major area that falls outside these categories is the oil-exporting region generally called the Middle East. The oil-exporting countries present mixed models of resource allocation, property ownership, and the development of infrastructure. Because these countries all have access to significant amounts of crude oil, they are major players in the international economy.

These countries include Iran, Iraq, Kuwait, Saudi Arabia, Libya, Syria, and the United Arab Emirates. High oil prices in the 1970s and 1980s created enormous wealth in these countries. Many of them invested heavily in their infrastructures. Whole new cities were built, airports were constructed, and the population was educated. As oil prices have fallen, many of the oil-producing countries have been forced to cut back on these activities. Nevertheless, they are still quite wealthy. The per capita incomes of the United Arab Emirates and Qatar, for example, are among the highest in the world. Although there is great wealth in the oil-producing nations, they also provide major challenges to managers. Political instability (as evidenced by the Persian Gulf War in 1991) and tremendous cultural differences, for example, combine to make doing business in the Middle East both very risky and very difficult.

Other countries pose risks to business of a different sort. Politically and ethnically motivated violence, for example, still characterizes some countries. Foremost among these are Peru, El Salvador, India, Turkey, Colombia, and Northern Ireland.[16] Cuba presents special challenges because it is so insulated from the outside world. Because of the fall of communism, some experts believe that Cuba will eventually join the ranks of the market economies. If so, its strategic geographic location will quickly make it an important business center.

Challenges of International Management

We noted earlier that managing in an international environment poses additional challenges and creates additional opportunities for the manager. Three challenges in particular warrant additional exploration at this point: economic challenges, political-legal challenges, and sociocultural challenges.[17]

Economic Challenges of International Management

Every country is unique and creates a unique set of challenges for managers trying to do business there. However, three characteristics in particular can help managers anticipate the kinds of economic challenges they are likely to face in working abroad.[18]

Economic System   The first characteristic is the economic system used in the country. As we described earlier, most countries today are moving toward market economies. In a mature market economy, the key element for managers is freedom of choice. Consumers are free to make decisions about which products to purchase, and firms are free to decide which products and services to provide. As long as both the consumer and the firm are free to decide to be in the market, then supply and demand determine which firms and which products will be available.

A related characteristic of market economies that is relevant to managers has to do with the nature of property ownership. There are two pure types — complete private ownership and complete public ownership. In systems with private ownership, individuals and companies — not the government — own and operate the companies that conduct business. In systems with public ownership, the government directly owns the companies that manufacture and sell products. Few countries have pure systems of private ownership or pure systems of public ownership. Most tend toward one extreme or the other, but usually a mix of public and private ownership exists.

Natural Resources   Another important dimension for understanding the nature of the economic environment in different countries is the availability of natural resources. There is a very broad range of resource availability in different countries. Some countries, like Japan, have relatively few natural resources. Japan is thus forced to import virtually all of the oil, iron ore, and other natural resources it needs to manufacture products for its domestic and overseas markets. The United States, in contrast, has enormous natural resources and is a major producer of oil, natural gas, coal, iron ore, copper, uranium, and other metals vital to the development of a modern economy. One natural resource that is particularly important in the modern global economy is oil.

Global opportunities exist in expanding and changing economies. Senie Kerschner International Housing Ltd. of Westport, Connecticut, recognized the possibility of using modular construction to take housing units manufactured in the United States and erect them in Russia. Construction, shown here, began outside of Moscow in 1991 and the first tenants moved in during 1992. (Chuck Nacke/Picture Group.)

As noted earlier a small set of countries in the Middle East, including Saudi Arabia, Iraq, Iran, and Kuwait, controls a very large percentage of the world's total known reserves of crude oil. Access to this single natural resource has given these oil-producing countries enormous clout in the international economy.

Infrastructure   A final important attribute of the economic environment of relevance to international management is infrastructure. A country's infrastructure comprises its schools, hospitals, power plants, railroads, highways, ports, communication systems, airfields, commercial distribution systems, and so forth. The United States has a highly developed infrastructure. For example, we have a modern educational system, roads and bridges are well developed, and most people have access to medical care. Overall, we have a relatively complete infrastructure sufficient to support most forms of economic development and activity.

Many countries, on the other hand, lack a well-developed infrastructure. In some countries there is not enough electrical-generating capacity to meet demand. Such countries often schedule periods of time during which power is turned off. These planned power failures reduce power demands but can be an enormous inconvenience to business. In the extreme, when a country's infrastructure is greatly underdeveloped, firms interested in beginning business may have to build an entire township, including housing, schools, hospitals, and perhaps even recreation facilities, to attract a sufficient overseas work force.

Political-Legal Challenges of International Management

A second set of challenges facing international managers is the political-legal environment in which they will do business. Four important aspects of the political-legal environment of international management are government stability, incentives for international trade, controls on international trade, and the influence of economic communities on international trade.

Government Stability   Stability can be viewed in two ways — as the ability of a given government to stay in power in spite of opposing factions in the country and as the permanence of government policies toward business. A country that is stable in both respects is preferable, since then managers have a higher probability of successfully predicting how government will affect their business. Civil war in countries such as Lebanon has made it impossible for international managers to predict what government policies are likely to be and whether the government will be able to guarantee the safety of international workers. Consequently, international firms have been reluctant to invest in Lebanon.

In many countries—the United States, Great Britain, and Japan, for example—changes in government occur with very little disruption. In other countries—such as India, Argentina, and Greece—changes are likely to be more disruptive. Even if a country's government remains stable, there are risks that the policies adopted by that government might change. In some countries foreign businesses may be nationalized (taken over by the government) with little or no warning. For example, the government of Peru recently nationalized Perulac, a domestic milk producer owned by Nestlé, because of a local milk shortage.

Incentives for International Trade   Another facet of the political environment is incentives to attract foreign business. For example, municipal governments in Texas have offered such foreign companies as Fujitsu huge tax breaks and other incentives to build facilities there.[19] In like fashion, the French government sold land to Disney at a price far below its market value and agreed to build a connecting freeway in exchange for the company agreeing to build a theme park outside Paris. Incentives can take a variety of forms, including reduced interest rates on loans, construction subsidies, and tax breaks. Less-developed countries tend to offer different packages of incentives. In addition to lucrative tax breaks, for example, they can also attract investors with duty-free entry of raw materials and equipment, market protection through limitations on other importers, and the right to take profits out of the country.

Controls on International Trade   A third element of the political environment that managers need to consider is the extent to which there are controls on international trade. In some instances the government of a country may decide that foreign competition is hurting domestic trade. To protect domestic business such governments may enact barriers to international trade. These barriers include tariffs, quotas, export restraint agreements, and "buy national" laws. In our opening case we noted some of the barriers in Japan. Indeed, the Japanese market is one of the world's most difficult to enter.

*A **tarrif** is a tax collected on goods shipped across national boundaries.*

A **tariff** is a tax collected on goods shipped across national boundaries. Tariffs can be collected by the exporting country, countries through which goods pass, and the importing country. Import tariffs, which are the most common, can be levied to protect domestic companies by increasing the cost of foreign goods. For example, Japan charges U.S. tobacco producers a tariff on cigarettes imported into Japan as a way to keep their prices higher than domestic cigarette prices. Tariffs can also be levied, usually by less-developed countries, to raise money for the government.

*A **quota** is a limit on the number or value of goods that can be traded.*

Quotas are the most common form of trade restriction. A quota is a limit on the number or value of goods that can be traded. The quota amount is typically designed to ensure that domestic competitors will be able to maintain a certain market share. For example, Honda is allowed to export 425,000 autos each year to the United States. This quota is one reason Honda opened manufacturing facilities here. The quota applies only to cars imported into the United States, and the company can produce as many other cars within our borders as it wants. **Export restraint agreements** are designed to convince other governments to voluntarily limit the volume or value of goods exported to a particular country. They are, in effect, export quotas. For example, Japanese steel producers voluntarily limit the amount of steel they send to the United States each year.

***Export restraint agreements** are designed to convince other governments to voluntarily limit the volume or value of goods exported to a particular country.*

"Buy national" legislation gives preference to domestic producers through content or price restrictions. Several countries have this type of legislation. For instance, Brazil requires that

Brazilian companies purchase only Brazilian-made computers. The United States requires that the Department of Defense purchase only military uniforms manufactured in the United States, even though the price of foreign uniforms might be half as much. And Mexico requires that 50 percent of the parts of cars sold in Mexico be manufactured in Mexico.

Economic Communities   Just as government policies can either increase or decrease the political risk facing international managers, trade relations among countries can either help or hinder international business. If these relations are dictated by quotas, tariffs, and so forth, they can hurt international trade. However, there is currently a strong movement around the world to reduce many of these barriers. This movement takes its most obvious form in international economic communities.

*An international **economic community** is a set of countries that agrees to significantly reduce or eliminate trade barriers among its member nations.*

   An international **economic community** is a set of countries that agrees to significantly reduce or eliminate trade barriers among its member nations. The first, and in many ways still the most important, of these economic communities is the European Community (EC), discussed earlier. Other important economic communities include the Latin American Integration Association (Bolivia, Brazil, Colombia, Chile, Argentina, and other South American countries) and the Caribbean Common Market (the Bahamas, Belize, Jamaica, Antigua, Barbados, and twelve other countries). *The Entrepreneurial Spirit: Rules for Doing Business in the EC* describes how rules and regulations in the European Community may limit small firms wanting to enter that market.

Sociocultural Challenges of International Management

The final set of challenges for the international manager is the cultural environment and how it affects business. A country's culture includes all the values, symbols, beliefs, and language that guide behavior.

Values, Symbols, and Beliefs   Cultural values and beliefs are often unspoken, even taken for granted by those who live in a particular country. Cultural factors do not necessarily cause problems for managers when the cultures of two countries are similar. Difficulties can arise, however, when there is little overlap between the home culture of a manager and the culture of the country in which business is to be conducted. For example, most U.S. managers find the culture and traditions of England familiar. People in both countries speak the same language, they share strong historical roots, and there is a history of strong commerce between the two countries. However, when U.S. managers begin operations in Japan or the People's Republic of China, most of those commonalities disappear.[20]

   Even when the cultures of two countries are similar, there is still substantial room for misunderstanding and embarrassment. For example, when someone from the United Kingdom tells you that he is going to knock you up, take a lift, and put the telly in the boot, he has told you that he will (1) wake you up in the morning, (2) take an elevator, and (3) put a television set in the trunk of your car.

   Things become even more complicated when the cultures are truly different. In Japanese, for example, the word *hai* (pronounced "hi") means "yes." In conversation, however, this word is used much like people in the United States use *uh-huh.* That is, it moves a conversation along or shows the person you are talking to that you are paying attention. So when does *hai* mean "yes," and when does it mean "uh-huh"? This turns out to be a relatively difficult question to answer. If a U.S. manager asks a Japanese manager if she agrees to some trade arrangement, the Japanese manager is likely to say *hai,* which may mean "yes, I agree," or "yes, I understand," or "yes, I am listening." Many U.S. managers become frustrated in negotiations with the Japanese, because they feel that the Japanese continue to raise issues that have already been agreed upon, based on the fact that the Japanese managers said *yes.* What many of these managers fail to recognize is that *yes* does not always mean "yes" in Japan.

The Entrepreneurial Spirit

Rules for Doing Business in the EC

The creation of a single, unified European market has been a long, painstaking process. It began with the signing of the Treaty of Rome in 1957. The goal was to reduce or eliminate virtually all trade barriers among member nations by 1992. This would enable businesses to function more efficiently across a large, single, integrated market and would contribute to the overall prosperity of all members.

As the target date approached, more attention was focused on specific details necessary to achieve this integration. Each member nation had its own standards for safety, health, environment protection, and quality. For all firms to be on a level playing field, it was necessary to make these standards uniform for all nations wishing to do business in the EC.

Initially the EC concentrated on 1,500 basic standards to be made consistent across all its member nations. These standards govern everything from the fat content of ice cream to the width of airline seats. Eventually there may be as many as 10,000 standards, many of them new. So far, highly detailed standards have been created for about 190 products. For example, the set of standards for a washing machine's electrical system is more than one hundred pages long.

Small businesses figure to be hit the hardest by this burgeoning set of rules and regulations. One U.S. firm had to buy $5 million worth of new equipment to meet EC-mandated testing equipment and add ten inspectors to its staff, even though its own internal standards were already higher than those set by the EC. A small firm that makes scenic props for model railroads (a hobby usually pursued by adults) has already hit a major snag. The EC has defined the products as toys, and they cannot be sold in the European market because of their lead content. Many more problems and roadblocks are likely to emerge in the future. Some U.S. officials are concerned that the jungle of rules may eventually force many small exporters to stop doing business with the EC altogether.[21] ∎

Cultural differences between countries can have a direct impact on business practice. For example, the religion of Islam teaches that people should not make a living by exploiting the misfortune of others and that making interest payments is immoral. In practice this means that in Saudi Arabia there are no businesses that provide auto-wrecking services to tow a car to the garage should it break down (because that would be capitalizing on misfortune). It also means that, in the Sudan, banks cannot pay or charge interest. Given the cultural and religious constraints, those two businesses—auto towing and banking—do not seem to hold great promise for international managers in those particular countries.

Some cultural differences between countries can be even more subtle and yet have a major impact on business activities. For example, in the United States there is a very clear agreement among most managers about the value of time. Most U.S. managers schedule their activities very tightly and then adhere to their schedules. Other cultures do not put such a premium on time. In the Middle East, for example, managers do not like to set appointments, and they rarely keep appointments set too far into the future. U.S. managers interacting with managers from the Middle East might misinterpret the late arrival of a potential business partner as a negotiation ploy or an insult, when it is rather a simple reflection of different views of time and its value. As a condition to entry into Japan, Toys "Я" Us had to agree to close its doors thirty days a year, a practice followed by Japanese retailers. To test your cultural awareness, refer to the self-assessment at the end of the chapter. Regardless of how sensitive we think we are to other cultures, this quiz will probably indicate that more insight is needed.

Language Language itself can be a significant factor in the sociocultural environment. Beyond the obvious and clear barriers posed by people who speak different languages, subtle differences in meaning can also pose difficulties. For example, Esso realized it was in trouble when it learned that its name meant "stalled car" in Japanese. Ford began to understand why its profits were lower than expected in Spain when it realized that some Spaniards read its name as *Fabrica Ordinaria Reparaciones Diariamente,* meaning "ordinarily, make repairs daily." The color green is used extensively in Moslem countries, but it signifies death in some other countries. Toys "Я" Us realized that the backwards "R" in its name could confuse customers in non-English-speaking countries. Its managers therefore decided to miniaturize the existing logo with the reversed "R" and to list the store's name in the local language in larger letters.

Managing in the International Economy

As already noted, managing in the international economy is both a significant challenge and an opportunity for businesses today. The nature of these challenges depends on a variety of factors, including the size of the organization. In addition, international management also has implications for the basic functions of planning, organizing, leading, and controlling.

The Influence of Organization Size

Though organizations of any size may compete in international markets, there are some basic differences in the challenges and opportunities faced by MNEs, medium-size organizations, and smaller organizations. Each also requires the application of appropriate management skills in order to succeed.

Multinational Organizations The large MNEs have long since made the choice to compete in global marketplaces. In general these firms take a global perspective on everything they do. They transfer capital, technology, human resources, inventory, and information from one market to another. They actively seek new expansion opportunities wherever feasible. MNEs tend to allow local managers a great deal of discretion in addressing local and regional issues. At the same time, each operation is ultimately accountable to a central authority. Managers at this central authority (called headquarters, a central office, or some other term) are responsible for setting the overall strategic direction for the firm, making major policy decisions, and so forth. MNEs need senior managers who understand the global economy and who are comfortable dealing with executives and government officials from a variety of cultures.

Medium-Size Organizations Many medium-size businesses are still primarily domestic organizations. But they may also buy and sell products made abroad and compete with businesses from other countries in their own domestic market. Increasingly, however, medium-size organizations are expanding into foreign markets as well. For example, Molex Inc. is a medium-size firm based in Chicago. Its recent annual sales have been in the range of $300 million to $400 million. Molex manufactures electronic connectors. The firm operates several plants in Japan and derives more than half its sales from the Pacific Rim.[22] In contrast to MNEs, medium-size organizations doing business abroad are much more selective about the markets they enter. They also depend more on a few international specialists to help them manage their foreign operations.

Smaller Organizations More and more smaller organizations are also finding they can benefit from the global economy. Some, for example, serve as local suppliers for MNEs. A dairy farmer who sells milk to Carnation, for example, is actually transacting business with Nestlé. Local parts suppliers also have been successfully selling products to the Toyota and Honda plants in the United

States. Beyond serving as local suppliers, some small businesses also buy and sell products and services abroad. For example, the Collin Street Bakery, based in Corsicana, Texas, ships fruitcakes around the world. In 1990 the firm shipped 145,000 pounds of fruitcake to Japan.[23] Most small businesses rely on simple importing and/or exporting operations for their international sales. Thus only a few specialized management positions are needed. Collin Street Bakery, for example, has one local manager who handles international activities. Mail-order activities within each country are subcontracted to local firms in each market.

The Management Functions in a Global Economy

The management functions that constitute the organizing framework for this book—planning, organizing, leading, and controlling—are just as relevant to international managers as to domestic managers. International managers need to have a clear view of where they want their firm to be in the future; they have to organize to implement their plans; they have to motivate those who work for them; and they have to develop appropriate control mechanisms.

Planning in a Global Economy   To plan effectively in a global economy, managers must have a broad-based understanding of both environmental issues and competitive issues. They need to understand local market conditions and technological factors that will affect their operations. At the corporate level, executives need a great deal of information in order to function effectively. Which markets are growing? Which markets are shrinking? What are our domestic and foreign competitors doing in each market? Managers must also make a variety of strategic decisions about their organization. For example, if a firm wishes to enter the market in France, should it buy a local firm there, build a plant, or seek a strategic alliance? Critical issues include understanding environmental circumstances, the role of goals and planning in a global organization, and how decision making affects the global organization. We will note special implications for global managers as we discuss planning in Chapters 7 through 10.

Organizing in a Global Economy   Managers in international businesses must also attend to a variety of organizing issues. For example, Texas Instruments has operations scattered around the globe. The firm has made the decision to give local managers a great deal of responsibility for how they run their business. In contrast, many Japanese firms give managers of their foreign operations relatively little responsibility. As a result, those managers must frequently travel back to Japan to present problems or get decisions approved. Managers in an international business must address the basic issues of organization structure and design, managing change, and dealing with human resources. We will address the special issues of organizing in Chapters 11 through 14.

Leading in a Global Economy   We noted earlier some of the cultural factors that affect international organizations. Individual managers must be prepared to deal with these and other factors as they interact with people from different cultural backgrounds. Supervising a group of five managers, each of whom is from a different state in the United States, is likely to be much simpler than supervising a group of five managers, each of whom is from a different culture. Managers must understand how cultural factors affect individuals, how motivational processes vary across cultures, the role of leadership in different cultures, how communication varies across cultures, and the nature of interpersonal and group processes in different cultures. In Chapters 15 through 19 we will note special implications for international managers that relate to leading and interacting with others.

Controlling in a Global Economy   Finally, managers in international organizations must also be concerned with control. Distances, time differences, and cultural factors also all play a role in control. For example, in some cultures close supervision is seen as being appropriate, and in other cultures it is not. Likewise, executives in the United States and Japan may find it difficult to communicate vital information to one another because of time differences. Basic control issues for the international manager revolve around operations management, productivity, quality, technology, and information systems. These issues are integrated throughout our discussion of control in Chapters 20 through 23.

Chapter Summary

International business has grown to be one of the most important features of the world's economy. Learning the skills necessary to operate in an international economy is a significant challenge facing many managers today. Businesses can be primarily domestic, international, multinational, or global in scope. Managers need to understand both the process of internationalization as well as how to manage within a given level of international activity.

To compete in the international economy, managers must understand its structure. Mature market economies and systems dominate the global economy today. North America, Europe, and the Pacific Rim are especially important. Developing economies in Eastern Europe, South America, and Africa may play bigger roles in the future. The oil-exporting economies in the Middle East are also important.

Many of the challenges of international management are unique issues associated with the international environmental context. Economic, political-legal, and sociocultural challenges of international management are especially critical.

Basic issues of competing in the international economy vary according to whether the organization is a MNE, a medium-size organization, or a smaller organization. In addition, the basic managerial functions of planning, organizing, leading, and controlling must all be addressed in international organizations.

The Manager's Vocabulary

domestic business
international business
multinational business
MNE (multinational enterprise)
global business
exporting
importing
licensing agreement
joint venture

strategic alliance
direct investment
outsourcing
maquiladoras
market economy
market system
European Community
  (EC)
Pacific Rim

North American Free Trade Agreement
  (NAFTA)
developing economy
tariff
quota
export restraint agreement
"Buy national" legislation
economic community

Review Questions

1. What are the four basic levels of international business activity? Give examples for each.
2. Why has international business grown so much in recent years?
3. Summarize the basic structure of the international economy. What are some of the major changes occurring today within the international economy?
4. Identify and briefly describe some of the basic challenges of international management.
5. What are some of the competitive differences for MNEs, medium-size organizations, and smaller organizations?

Analysis Questions

1. Identify industries that are most and least global.
2. In what ways are the processes of managing an increase in internationalization versus managing in a steady state of international involvement likely to be the same and different?

3. In which situations might an organization want to decrease its level of international activity? Comment on some of the basic issues that might be involved.
4. Some experts argue that free trade eventually helps everyone. Others, however, believe that domestic governments have an obligation to protect local businesses from foreign competition. What do you believe and why?
5. Identify several businesses and/or products that affect you on a regular basis that are owned by foreign companies.

Self-Assessment

The Culture Quiz

Introduction The environment of business is becoming more global, which, in turn, suggests that it will be more diverse. The following assessment is designed to help you understand your readiness to respond to managing in a global environment.

1. In Japan, loudly slurping your soup is considered to be
   a. rude and obnoxious.
   b. a sign that you like the soup.
   c. okay at home but not in public.
   d. something only foreigners do.
2. In Korea, business leaders tend to
   a. encourage strong commitment to teamwork and cooperation.
   b. encourage competition among subordinates.
   c. discourage subordinates from reporting directly, preferring information to come through well-defined channels.
   d. encourage close relationships with their subordinates.
3. In Japan, virtually every kind of drink is sold in public vending machines except for
   a. beer.
   b. diet drinks with saccharin.
   c. already sweetened coffee.
   d. soft drinks from U.S. companies.
4. In Latin America, managers
   a. are most likely to hire members of their own families.
   b. consider hiring members of their own families to be inappropriate.
   c. stress the importance of hiring members of minority groups.
   d. usually hire more people than are actually needed to do a job.
5. In Ethiopia, when a woman opens the front door of her home, it means
   a. she is ready to receive guests for a meal.
   b. only family members may enter.
   c. religious spirits may move freely in and out of the home.
   d. she has agreed to have sex with any man who enters.
6. In Latin America, business people
   a. consider it impolite to make eye contact while talking to one another.
   b. always wait until the other person is finished speaking before starting to speak.
   c. touch each other more than North Americans do under similar circumstances.
   d. avoiding touching one another as it is considered an invasion of privacy.
7. The principal religion in Malaysia is
   a. Buddhism.
   b. Judaism.
   c. Christianity.
   d. Islam.
8. In Thailand
   a. it is common to see men walking along holding hands.
   b. it is common to see a man and a woman holding hands in public.
   c. it is rude for men and women to walk together.
   d. men and women traditionally kiss each other on meeting in the street.
9. Pointing your toes at someone in Thailand is
   a. a symbol of respect, much like the Japanese bow.
   b. considered rude even if it is done by accident.
   c. an invitation to dance.
   d. the standard public greeting.
10. American managers tend to base the performance appraisals of their subordinates on performance, whereas in Iran, managers are more likely to base their performance appraisals on
    a. religion.
    b. seniority.
    c. friendship.
    d. ability.

11. In China, the status of every business negotiation is
    a. reported daily in the press.
    b. private, and details are not discussed publicly.
    c. subjected to scrutiny by a public tribunal on a regular basis.
    d. directed by the elders of every commune.

12. When rewarding an Hispanic worker for a job well done, it is best not to
    a. praise him or her publicly.
    b. say "thank you."
    c. offer a raise.
    d. offer a promotion.

13. In some South American countries, it is considered normal and acceptable to show up for an appointment
    a. ten to fifteen minutes early.
    b. ten to fifteen minutes late.
    c. fifteen minutes to an hour late.
    d. one to two hours late.

14. In France, when friends talk to one another,
    a. they generally stand about three feet apart.
    b. it is typical to shout.
    c. they stand closer to one another than Americans do.
    d. it is always with a third party present.

15. When giving flowers as gifts in Western Europe, be careful not to give
    a. tulips and jonquils.
    b. daisies and lilacs.
    c. chrysanthemums and calla lilies.
    d. lilacs and apple blossoms.

16. The appropriate gift-giving protocol for a male executive doing business in Saudi Arabia is to
    a. give a man a gift from you to his wife.
    b. present gifts to the wife or wives in person.
    c. give gifts only to the eldest wife.
    d. not give a gift to the wife at all.

17. If you want to give a necktie or a scarf to a Latin American, it is best to avoid the color
    a. red.
    b. purple.
    c. green.
    d. black.

18. The doors in German offices and homes are generally kept
    a. wide open to symbolize an acceptance and welcome of friends and strangers.
    b. slightly ajar to suggest that people should knock before entering.
    c. half-opened, suggesting that some people are welcome and others are not.
    d. tightly shut to preserve privacy and personal space.

19. In West Germany, leaders who display charisma are
    a. not among the most desired.
    b. the ones most respected and sought after.
    c. invited frequently to serve on boards of cultural organizations.
    d. pushed to get involved in political activities.

20. American managers running businesses in Mexico have found that by increasing the salaries of Mexican workers, they
    a. increased the number of hours the workers were willing to work.
    b. enticed more workers to work night shifts.
    c. decreased the number of hours workers would agree to work.
    d. decreased production rates.

For interpretation, turn to the back of the book.

Source: From *OB in Action: Cases and Exercises* by Janet W. Wohlberg and Scott Weighart. Copyright © 1992 by Houghton Mifflin Company. Used with permission.

Skill Builder

Are You Prepared for Globalization?

Purpose The environment of business is becoming more global. All managers must be prepared for globalization. To assist you in honing your skills in responding to globalization, the following brief activity has been provided. The results of this activity should give you information to determine in what aspects of globalization you are deficient. Follow your instructor's directions to learn as much as you can from this activity.

This skill builder focuses on the *open systems model.* It will help you develop the *innovator role* of the open systems model. One of the skills of the innovator is the ability to live with change.

Introduction A global environment requires that U.S. managers learn to deal effectively with people in other cultures. To believe that all leaders and businesspeople negotiate and practice business like those in the United States is not realistic. How well prepared are you to live with globalization?

Instructions Think carefully, and answer the following questions honestly.

Are you guilty of:	Definitely No				Definitely Yes
1. Impatience? Do you think "Time is money" or "Let's get straight to the point"?	1	2	3	4	5
2. Having a short attention span, bad listening habits, or being uncomfortable with silence?	1	2	3	4	5
3. Being somewhat argumentative, sometimes to the point of belligerence?	1	2	3	4	5
4. Ignorance about the world beyond your borders?	1	2	3	4	5
5. Weakness in foreign languages?	1	2	3	4	5
6. Placing emphasis on short-term success?	1	2	3	4	5
7. Believing that advance preparations are less important than negotiations themselves?	1	2	3	4	5
8. Being legalistic? Of believing "A deal is a deal," regardless of changing circumstances?	1	2	3	4	5
9. Having little interest in seminars on the subject of globalization, failing to browse through libraries or magazines on international topics, not interacting with foreign students or employees?	1	2	3	4	5

TOTAL SCORE _____

Source: Cynthia Barmun and Netasha Wolninsky, "Why Americans Fail at Overseas Negotiations." Reprinted by permission of the publisher from *Management Review*, October 1989 © 1989. American Management Association, New York. All rights reserved.

CONCLUDING CASES

5.1   Disney Moves into Europe

Though some people think of Disney as strictly an American social institution, the fact is that the popular entertainment company has been engaged in international business for years. For example, its movies are as popular abroad as they are at home. Moreover, the firm earns more than $40 million a year simply from licensing fees from firms that manufacture and sell Disney-related merchandise in other countries.

After the successful openings of its Disneyland theme park (in California) in 1955 and the Disney World resort (in Florida) in 1966, managers at the firm began to think of foreign locations for future development. Its first foray abroad was Tokyo Disneyland, which opened in 1984. To minimize its risks in the Japanese market, Disney found local investors in Japan to put up the cash for the park and to assume its ownership. In return, Disney planned and coordinated the construction of the park. Disney also has a contract whereby it manages the park and earns royalty income.

Tokyo Disneyland was even more successful than the firm's existing parks, welcoming its one-hundred-millionth visitor after only eight years (it took Disneyland twice as long to reach that milestone). Managers therefore quickly began to consider other sites for expansion. This time, however, Disney committed to ownership participation and a bigger investment in the new enterprise.

The firm spent months exploring possible sites in Europe. It narrowed its decision to two possibilities, one in Spain and one in France. After careful deliberation managers chose the French site, just outside of Paris. Though the site in Spain would have provided better weather, the French site was more centrally located. Indeed, more than 350 million people live within a two-hour plane ride of

Paris. In addition, the French government provided several incentives to attract the firm. For example, it condemned the land Disney wanted and then sold it to the firm for a bargain price. It also agreed to extend the Parisian rail system to the park's main entrance. A final part of the agreement was that Disney could retain up to 49 percent ownership in Euro Disneyland, with the rest made available for trade on European stock exchanges.

Unfortunately, Euro Disneyland was quickly overtaken by controversy and problems. Some French observers lambasted the project as a symbol of the Americanization of Europe. Farmers were upset about the prices the French government forced them to accept for their land. And the firm itself encountered resistance to its stringent grooming codes and training procedures.

Nevertheless, Euro Disneyland opened its gates on schedule in April 1992. To date, the results are mixed. Visitors seem pleased with the park, and most indicate that they will return. But overall attendance has been running behind Disney's projections, and those who are coming are spending less money than Disney had forecast. Disney managers remain optimistic, however, and believe that as Europeans become more familiar with the Disney park, its attendance and profitability will skyrocket.[24]

Discussion Questions

1. Is Disney an international business or a multinational business? Explain.
2. Would a Disney theme park succeed in a developing economy? Why or why not?
3. Identify some of the economic, political-legal, and sociocultural challenges Disney confronted in Europe.

5.2   Northern Telecom Soars at Home and Abroad

Few people associate Northern Telecom Limited with such communications giants as AT&T, Siemens, NEC, or Philips. But the Canadian firm is indeed well on its way to joining those illustrious firms among the world's largest and most profitable businesses in the international marketplace for telecommunications equipment.

Until 1962 Northern Telecom was a subsidiary of AT&T. That year, however, AT&T divested itself of what it saw as a marginal unit with little growth potential. The firm's new management believed that AT&T had made a mistake, however, and began investing heavily in research and development and manufacturing. Both its revenues and its profits soon began to grow, and by the early 1980s Northern Telecom was entering foreign markets. When U.S. courts ordered the breakup of AT&T in 1984, Northern Telecom saw a golden opportunity and aggressively entered the U.S. market.

For the remainder of the decade, the firm enjoyed spectacular growth. The basis of its success has been digital central-office switching systems, the heart of any telephone system. Northern Telecom has also performed well in markets for cellular telephone equipment and related technology.

Northern Telecom received an additional boost in 1989 when Paul Stern was appointed CEO. Stern was born in Czechoslovakia, raised in Mexico City, educated in England, and now has U.S. citizenship. Stern brought to the company an enormous ambition for growth. More specifically, Stern made it clear from the beginning that he wanted Northern Telecom to become one of the world's largest communication businesses by the end of the present decade.

Stern used Northern Telecom's existing strengths — world-class research and development and low-cost manufacturing capabilities — as a foundation. He then worked to make the firm more flexible and adaptable. He wants to be able to tailor every product and service offered by the firm to best fit local market conditions. In addition, he has instilled throughout the firm a strong sense of urgency and competitiveness.

So far, Stern's efforts appear to be paying dividends. For one thing, he has succeeded in making Northern Telecom a truly international firm. Although still based in Canada, the firm today acquires half its revenues from the United States, 24 percent from its home country, 18 percent from Europe, and 8 percent from other areas. Moreover, Northern Telecom is the largest foreign supplier in Japan.

More recently, Northern Telecom has been aggressively pursuing joint venture and strategic alliance opportunities. For example, it has a joint venture with the French firm Matra to build digital mobile telephone equipment. It has other joint ventures in Spain, the United States, and Japan. And its global market share, revenues, and profits continue to climb. Only a few years ago critics would have scoffed at the notion that Northern Telecom could become a world player. Now the only question is whether the firm will be among the leaders or claim the undisputed title of leader.[25]

Discussion Questions

1. Characterize the internationalization process at Northern Telecom.
2. Should Northern Telecom be paying more attention to developing economies? Why or why not?
3. What are the major challenges ahead for Northern Telecom?

CHAPTER

6

The Ethical and Social Environment

Chapter Outline

Learning Objectives

After studying this chapter you should be able to

- Define ethics and discuss how they are formed.

- Describe the relationship between ethics and management, particularly the ethical context of management.

- Understand the management of ethics, including the necessity for top-management support and codes of conduct.

- Define social responsibility, discuss arguments both for and against it, and identify the general areas of social responsibility.

- Discuss approaches to social responsibility.

- Discuss the role of government in business's social responsibility.

- Describe how organizations manage social responsibility.

One of the biggest challenges faced by both business and the government today is the delicate balance between economic growth and environmental protection. For the last several years environmentalists have fought to protect tracts of old timber in the Northwest where the endangered spotted owl nests. While logging companies have argued that saving the owl has cost jobs and dollars, the issue is the tradeoff between protecting the environment versus allowing business to do whatever it wants to fuel revenues and profits.

Environmental protection does indeed carry with it several costs. U.S. companies spent over $100 billion in 1990 in meeting environmental protection rules. Moreover, protection of the environment is projected to leave the U.S. economy 2.6 percent smaller by the year 2000 than it would otherwise be. Environmental protection also causes economic upheaval. In the Northwest alone, for example, over eleven thousand logging jobs have been lost. And finally, environmental protection affects such industries as the coal, oil, and automobile industries.

On the other hand, in addition to its obvious intrinsic benefits, protecting the environment also has several economic benefits. First, it has spawned the $120-billion environmental services industry. Second, more than a million new jobs associated with environmental protection have been created in the U. S. alone. Third, clean water and healthy ecosystems save jobs in tourism. And finally, curtailing pollution has often cut waste and increased productivity. Regardless of which side you take, then, it's clearly not an open-and-shut case.[1] ▪

The debate about the environment and the role of business in protecting it clearly demonstrates the increasingly important relationship between business and its social environment. If a large company is not socially responsible, it may receive well-deserved criticism. But even companies that put forth their best efforts can quickly become embroiled in an issue like the projected demise of the spotted owl that captures the public's attention. Some organizations know how to function within their social environment; others think they know how to function, only to occasionally stumble; still others have little clear understanding of what it means to function within the social environment.

We introduced the nature of the social environment of business in Chapter 3. This chapter deals more substantively with that environment. We first examine individual ethics and then discuss managerial ethics and how organizations can manage their members' ethical behavior. We then look at the nature of corporate social responsibility and approaches to it. Next we analyze relationships between the government and business in a social context. Finally, we explore how organizations go about managing social responsibility.

The Nature of Ethics

One critical component necessary to the understanding of the social environment of business is the understanding of the nature of ethics. Ethics are an individual-level phenomenon. By this we mean that the concept of ethics does not apply to an entire organization. It makes no sense, for example, to talk about an organization's ethics. But each individual manager within an organization has his or her own personal set of ethics. And the ethical standards and behaviors of those managers can impact the organization in profound ways.

What Are Ethics?

What are ethics? Ask any four experts and you will probably get four different answers, and you may even get more. For our purposes, let us define **ethics** as those standards or morals a person

Ethics *are those standards or morals*
a person sets for himself or herself
regarding what is good and bad or
right and wrong.

sets for himself or herself regarding what is good and bad or right and wrong.[2] Thus, while some behavior is clearly ethical or unethical, much of the behavior in an organization tends to be relatively ethical or relatively unethical.

It is important to note the distinction between something that is ethical and something that is legal. The law defines various kinds of acts as acceptable or unacceptable. In contrast, ethics often go beyond the law and are based more on prevailing societal norms and expectations. Thus an action can be both legal and ethical, legal but unethical, or both illegal and unethical. There are differences of opinion as to whether an action can be ethical but illegal.

For example, suppose you are a manager for a large manufacturing company. Today you found a $100 bill on the floor and turned it in to the company lost-and-found department. This action is both legal and ethical. You also suspect that another manager may be stealing company property for her own use, but you decide to ignore it. Although your action here is not illegal, it is probably unethical. The other manager's actions, though, are both unethical and illegal. Suppose you take $20 from petty cash to help a janitor who has no money to feed his family. Some would argue that this action, though illegal, is ethical. Clearly, then, the determination of ethical behavior is complex, and it is clouded by individual values, opinions, and logic.

The Formation of Ethics

One's ethics are determined by one's
family, past experiences, values and
morals, and situational factors.

Where do ethics come from? How are they formed? Exhibit 6.1 illustrates the most common factors that determine individual ethics.

Family Influences   Family influences play a key role in determining an individual's beliefs as to what is and is not right. For example, a person who grows up in a family with high ethical standards and whose members adhere consistently to those standards is likely to develop higher ethical standards than is someone who grows up in a family environment characterized by low or inconsistently practiced ethical standards.

Peer Influences   Peer influences are also quite important in determining a person's ethics. Childhood friends, classmates, and others in a person's social network can shape his ethics. Peer pressure, for instance, can help determine how much a person will engage in such questionable activities as shoplifting, experimenting with drugs, and so forth.

Past Experiences   As a person grows, her past experiences can also play a role in determining the evolution of her ethical standards. If she behaves unethically in a given situation and suffers negative consequences (feelings of guilt, for example, or getting caught), her behavior will probably be more ethical next time. Conversely, if her unethical behavior does not lead to feelings of guilt but instead leads to rewards, she may choose to behave the same way when she is next confronted with a similar situation.

Values and Morals   At a more general level, basic values and morals influence ethics. A person who is profoundly religious, for example, will almost certainly have strong feelings about what is right and wrong. Such beliefs will probably carry over to help shape this individual's personal ethics as well. The Self-Assessment at the end of the chapter will help you determine your own personal values. These values help form your individual ethics.

Situational Factors   Finally, situational factors are important. These are events that occur in a perhaps random way and that have the potential to determine behavior that may or may not be consistent with a person's ethics. For example, consider an employee who is very honest and hard working. His wife loses her job, and the family begins to have trouble making ends meet. One day, when things look especially bad, he is offered an opportunity to make some extra money by sell-

Exhibit 6.1
The Formation of an Individual's Ethics

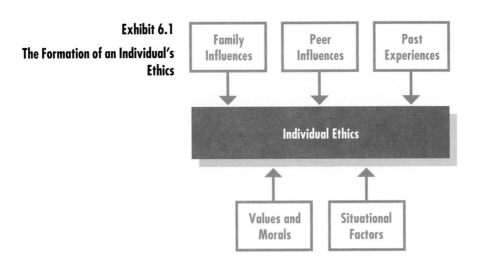

ing a company secret to a competitor. His financial situation and his despair at seeing his family suffer might cause him to accept the unethical offer. This factor is situational because if his wife had not lost her job or if he had not been offered the opportunity to sell company secrets, he might well have remained a dedicated, honest, and loyal employee throughout his career.

Managerial Ethics

Managerial ethics refers to the ethics of a person performing a managerial role.

Ethics and Management

Managers of organizations are not robots. They are not programmed to always do the same thing regardless of the circumstances. Indeed, one of the most important factors in the behavior of managers is their ethics, because of the multitude of situations that confront managers and the ethical context of their jobs.[3] **Managerial ethics,** then, refers to the ethics of a person performing in a managerial role.

Managers face ethical dilemmas almost every day. Ethical dilemmas occur when a manager is faced with two or more conflicting ethical issues. Table 6.1 highlights several of the more common situations that require ethical decisions.

Relationship of the Firm to the Employee   The relationship of the firm to the employee involves the ways in which the organization chooses to treat its employees in different situations in which ethics can come into play. In the area of hiring and firing, for instance, managers must make ethical decisions regarding who is the most qualified, how to treat minorities, and so forth.

Wages and working conditions must also be considered. Managers must establish a pay level that will satisfy employees but that is not excessive. A major ethical issue today involves the compensation of top managers. For example, the CEO of H. J. Heinz recently received over $75 million in annual compensation. Critics argue that this is excessive.[4] The employer also needs to provide a work environment that is relatively safe and free from hazards. A reasonable degree of job security is also something most people consider to be an ethical concern.

There are also ethical issues regarding privacy and the private lives of employees.[5] Employees who have drinking or drug problems may be of concern to the organization, even if they are keeping their problems separate from the workplace. An area of related interest is garnishment of wages, which happens when a creditor forces the organization to pay a portion of an employee's wages toward that employee's debts.

Table 6.1

The Ethical Dilemmas of Management

Situations involving the . . .	May lead to ethical dilemmas regarding . . .
Relationship of the firm to the employee	Hiring and firing Wages and working conditions Privacy
Relationship of the employee to the firm	Conflicts of interest Secrecy and espionage Honesty and expense accounts
Relationship of the firm to the environment	Customers Competitors Stockholders Suppliers and dealers Unions Community

Source: Adapted from Thomas M. Garrett and Richard J. Klonoski, *Business Ethics,* 2nd ed., © 1986, pp. viii–x. Reprinted by permission of Prentice Hall, Englewood Cliffs, New Jersey.

Relationship of the Employee to the Firm   Other issues relate to the relationship of the employee to the firm. The focus here is how the individual behaves in relation to the organization. Conflicts of interest are one major consideration. A **conflict of interest** exists when an employee is put into a situation in which his or her decisions may be compromised because of competing loyalties. Suppose a purchasing manager accepts a free vacation from a major equipment supplier. The next time the company needs to buy a new piece of equipment, the manager may feel obligated to give the contract to that supplier. Wal-Mart feels so strongly about this situation that it will not allow a merchandise buyer to accept meals or gifts from sales representatives.[6] Moonlighting is also an issue: When an employee has another job in addition to the primary one, fatigue may hinder performance in both jobs.

*In a **conflict of interest,** an employee is put into a situation in which his or her decisions may be compromised because of competing loyalties.*

Secrecy and espionage are also valid considerations. For example, an employee of a computer firm might have plenty of opportunities to sell information about new products to other companies. Finally, basic issues such as stealing and dishonest handling of expense accounts are relevant. When an employee takes home a pad of paper from the office or makes a long-distance call on the company telephone to an old friend or family member, he is technically stealing. Likewise, a manager who has lunch with a friend and writes it off on her expense account is stealing.

Relationship of the Firm to the Environment   There are also broad ethical considerations in how the organization interacts with various elements of its environment. A critical component of this relationship is the customer. Managers must contend with a number of issues involving customers, answering such questions as the following: What should we say when we advertise? What should our warranty be? How should we price our products? How concerned should we be with product safety?[7]

Relations with competitors are also important. Price cutting and unfair competition can drive smaller firms out of business. A group of small, independent druggists in Arkansas is suing

Individual concepts of ethics vary greatly. Today many organizations strive to be caring and ethical places to work. Levi Strauss & Company was one of many companies that participated in making a quilt calling attention to AIDS. Levi's "square" commemorates their employees who died of AIDS-related illnesses. (Richard Morgenstein.)

Wal-Mart. The druggists claim that the discounter is selling many products below cost in order to drive them out of business.[8] Price fixing—developing an agreement with competitors to sell competing products or services for the same price—is also both unethical and illegal.

Relations with stockholders are obviously crucial. Managers have the responsibility of working in stockholders' best interests and of reporting appropriate information to them on a timely basis. Similarly, questions about appropriate levels of executive compensation and benefits (as noted earlier) affect stockholders. Large companies with considerable power over their suppliers and dealers are often in situations in which ethical dilemmas arise. For example, if Chrysler does not keep its dealers properly informed about upcoming model changes, price adjustments, and so forth, the dealers can become resentful. On the other hand, too much information might leak into the hands of competitors.

Relations with unions also involve ethical issues. If a firm divulges too much information about its profitability, the union might increase its wage demands. Too little disclosure, however, is not conducive to ethical bargaining. A last factor is the community and surrounding environment. In recent years there has been a trend for communities that are hungry for industry to offer concessions on taxes and utilities, free land, and other incentives. When a company plays competing communities against one another, it may be violating ethical norms. Where building business networks is critical, managers may be tempted to grant favors or provide inside information to establish those connections.[9] Additional issues of particular interest might be pollution and other environmental impacts, participation in United Way activities, and so forth.

The Ethical Context of Management

It is obvious from this discussion so far that many management activities occur within an ethical context. (The Skill Builder at the end of the chapter focuses on the performance appraisal process and the ethical dimensions of this process.) The key dimensions of this context are illustrated in Exhibit 6.2.[10] First, the manager's personal ethics, as explored earlier in this chapter, are a major

Exhibit 6.2

The Ethical Context of Management

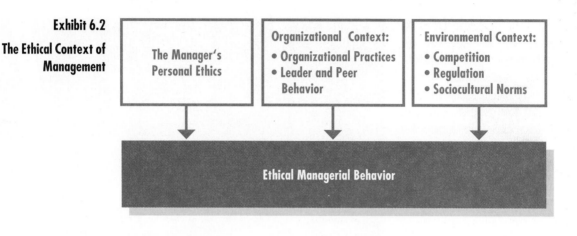

| The Manager's Personal Ethics | Organizational Context:
• Organizational Practices
• Leader and Peer Behavior | Environmental Context:
• Competition
• Regulation
• Sociocultural Norms |

Ethical Managerial Behavior

determinant of his or her ethical behavior. Values, predilections about right and wrong, and sense of justice and fairness all come into play. Susceptibility to situational factors is also relevant.

Second, the specific organizational context is important to the ethical managerial context. Of special interest are organizational practices and the behavior of leaders and peers. Organizational practices are ways in which the organization deals with the ethical situations it encounters. Some organizations reward people who report improprieties and punish those guilty of committing them. Other firms tend to punish those who make misdeeds public and do little or nothing to the guilty parties.[11] For instance, a few years ago a manager at Citibank reported to his superiors that one division of the bank was engaging in illegal activities to increase its profits. He was fired.[12] The behavior of leaders and peers can also be a big influence on the individual manager's ethical behavior. If those surrounding a manager routinely engage in unethical behavior, the manager is likely either to start such practices too or to leave the organization. *A Matter of Ethics: Waste Management* summarizes how the organizational context at Waste Management may have inadvertently led to problems.

The environmental context is the third vital factor. Competition, as we have seen, is a major force to consider. When competition is keen, there is strong pressure to resort to whatever means are available to get an advantage. Regulation by the government also determines the ethical context. Too much regulation can handcuff the manager so much that he or she feels forced to bend the rules or the law to compete. By the same token, too little regulation can provide too many opportunities to engage in questionable ethical practices. The norms of the sociocultural environment make up the last major part of the ethical context of management. In some countries bribes, price gouging, and industrial espionage are normal business practices. In other countries managers are expected to follow accepted ethical behavior.

Managing Ethics

Because managers have become increasingly aware of the importance of ethics, they have also taken a greater interest in how they and their organizations should attempt to manage this area. In fact, a retired executive recently gave $30 million to the Harvard Business School to fund the teaching of ethics. And the Graduate School of Business at Bentley College has made ethics an integral part of its curriculum for years.[13] Today the two most common approaches to the management of ethics are through top-management support and formal codes of conduct.

A Matter of Ethics

Waste Management

Waste Management Inc. has been both helped and hurt by growth in the waste treatment industry. The firm got its start in 1956 by taking over garbage collection operations from cities. Today the firm is the world's largest waste collection, disposal, and recycling enterprise.

But Waste Management has also come under the microscope for some of its practices. For several years the firm held up its Chicago incinerator as a model for waste disposal. It gave tours of the facility and widely publicized its impeccable safety record. But in 1992 allegations surfaced that have cast a cloud over Waste Management and its Chicago incinerator. The firm conceded that since 1988 it has turned off the pollution-monitoring system at least four times, then admitted that a key supervisor at the facility had put phony labels on one hundred barrels of toxic waste to evade safety requirements.

In March 1992 the firm announced that it was suspending operation of the facility and laid off most of its workers. But it will likely be several years before the myriad legal implications of Waste Management's actions will be untangled. For example, state officials in Illinois have launched a criminal investigation into activities at the facility.

What led to these problems? Some observers believe that Waste Management itself created a culture that facilitated the problems in Chicago. In particular, critics argue that managers at Waste Management are under intense pressure to perform and that the firm's highly decentralized practices give them far too much leeway in how they do their jobs. At the same time, defenders of Waste Management point out the many other facilities in the firm where no problems have been detected. Thus, as with many issues dealing with ethics and social responsibility, there seem to be two sides to the story.[14] ∎

Top-Management Support

For organizations to develop and maintain a culture in which ethical managerial behavior can thrive, top management must support such behavior. There are several things that executives can do to demonstrate such support.

First, they can adhere to ethical standards themselves. This is probably the most important thing that can be done to promote ethical behavior throughout the organization. If middle and lower-level managers see top managers behaving unethically, they are likely to follow suit.

Another important action is to provide and encourage training in ethics. After the aforementioned ethical scandal at Citibank, managers there created an ethics game to help develop better insights into what is and is not acceptable behavior. Boeing has a program to sensitize employees to ethical conflicts, the Sun Company, Inc. supplements a compliance questionnaire with talks by its corporate counsel, and at Hercules Inc. managers must sign forms saying that they have abided by policy.[15] In addition, General Dynamics, McDonnell Douglas, Chemical Bank, and American Can Company have initiated ethics training for their employees.[16]

Codes of Conduct

*Company **codes of conduct** state the importance of following ethical business practices.*

Another important step in the management of ethics is establishing **codes of conduct,** which usually state the importance of following ethical business practices in all areas of the organization's activities. These codes are symbolic but meaningful statements of the company's concern.

Professional groups such as the American Psychological Association and the American Management Association have long had such codes for their members. More and more often, however, individual companies are developing their own codes of ethical conduct. One recent survey found that 75 percent of the United States's twelve hundred largest companies had formal ethics codes such as Johnson & Johnson's, shown in Exhibit 6.3.[17]

Exhibit 6.3

Johnson & Johnson's Code of Ethical Conduct

Our Credo

We believe our first responsibility is to the doctors, nurses and patients,
to mothers and fathers and all others who use our products and services.
In meeting their needs everything we do must be of high quality.
We must constantly strive to reduce our costs
in order to maintain reasonable prices.
Customers' orders must be serviced promptly and accurately.
Our suppliers and distributors must have an opportunity
to make a fair profit.

We are responsible to our employees,
the men and women who work with us throughout the world.
Everyone must be considered as an individual.
We must respect their dignity and recognize their merit.
They must have a sense of security in their jobs.
Compensation must be fair and adequate,
and working conditions clean, orderly and safe.
We must be mindful of ways to help our employees fulfill
their family responsibilities.
Employees must feel free to make suggestions and complaints.
There must be equal opportunity for employment, development
and advancement for those qualified.
We must provide competent management,
and their actions must be just and ethical.

We are responsible to the communities in which we live and work
and to the world community as well.
We must be good citizens — support good works and charities
and bear our fair share of taxes.
We must encourage civic improvements and better health and education.
We must maintain in good order
the property we are privileged to use,
protecting the environment and natural resources.

Our final responsibility is to our stockholders.
Business must make a sound profit.
We must experiment with new ideas.
Research must be carried on, innovative programs developed
and mistakes paid for.
New equipment must be purchased, new facilities provided
and new products launched.
Reserves must be created to provide for adverse times.
When we operate according to these principles,
the stockholders should realize a fair return.

Johnson & Johnson

Source: Used with permission of Johnson & Johnson.

The Nature of Social Responsibility

Whereas ethical behavior is a phenomenon primarily at the individual level, social responsibility applies more to the organizational level. **Social responsibility** refers to the obligations of the organization to protect and/or enhance the society in which it functions.[18] As we will see, however, people hold different opinions as to its real nature.

Historical Evolution

Social responsibility refers to the obligations of an organization to protect and/or enhance society.

Over the years both society and organizations have taken many different views of social responsibility.[19] In general, the historical development of these views has progressed through three distinct periods in the United States.[20]

The first period occurred between 1860 and 1890. During this era the so-called captains of industry — Andrew Carnegie, John D. Rockefeller, J. P. Morgan, Cornelius Vanderbilt, and others — were creating the giant steel, oil, banking, and railroad corporations that came to dominate U.S. industry. In contrast to earlier organizations, these mammoth entities held enormous power in our emerging industrial society. Abuses of this power — labor lockouts, kickbacks, discriminatory pricing, and predatory business practices — caused both a public outcry and governmental action, and several laws were passed to regulate the way in which business was carried out. These early laws indicated for the first time the interdependence of business, government, and the general public.[21]

The second period spanned the few years following the stock market crash of 1929. Mergers and general business growth had continued, and by the 1920s big business had truly come to dominate the U.S. economy. Because of this, most Americans blamed large corporations for the Great Depression, and President Roosevelt and other supporters of the New Deal succeeded in passing more legislation targeted at those corporations. In particular, laws from this era specifically delineated the social responsibilities of businesses and reinforced the importance of fairness and ethical practices at all levels.

The third period took place during the 1960s and early 1970s, an era characterized by a great deal of social unrest and public awareness. Young people lashed out at the government, big business, and other dimensions of what they called the Establishment. There were campus sit-ins, business boycotts and bombings, and protest marches about dozens of social causes. Government began to take a greater role in business, getting involved in everything from regulations for packaging over-the-counter drugs to consumer warnings on cigarettes, and business tried to respond by espousing a greater commitment to benefiting society. The effects of this period of crisis are still being felt today.

Arguments About Social Responsibility

As we might infer from this brief history, the debate about the proper role of business organizations in society is far from over. In fact, today there are several factors that argue against social responsibility and several others that argue for a high level of social responsibility. The most prominent of these are summarized in Table 6.2.[22]

Proponents argue that a business's social responsibility derives from its power and resources and its position as a citizen in partnership with government and the public.

Arguments for Social Responsibility   Several compelling arguments can be made in favor of social responsibility. These views tend to be broader and have a longer time perspective. One argument here is that corporations are citizens, in the same way that individuals are. As such, they have the same responsibilities as individual citizens to improve society as a whole.

Proponents of social responsibility also argue that the great power enjoyed by business carries with it great responsibility. In particular, business has the power to produce products, set prices, influence consumer preferences, pay employees, and so forth. Further, since business cre-

Table 6.2

Arguments for and Against Social Responsibility

For	Against
1. Like individuals, corporations are citizens.	1. Social responsibility will decrease profits, thus contradicting the real reason for corporations' existence.
2. Since business creates some problems, it should help solve them.	2. Social responsibility gives corporations too much power.
3. Organizations have ample resources to help society.	3. Corporations are not accountable for the results of their actions.
4. Business, government, and the general public are partners in our society.	4. Corporations may lack the expertise to be socially responsible.
5. Arguments against social responsibility can be logically refuted.	5. Corporations may have conflicts of interest in how they spend their money.

Socially responsible companies are proactive. FINA continually strives to improve its performance on environmental, health, and safety issues. Here FINA employees return young alligators to their original nesting sites in Louisiana. (Courtesy of FINA, Inc.)

ates some problems (water and air pollution, for example), it can be argued that business should help solve them. Social responsibility can be seen as an important way to limit or constrain the power of business.

It can also be argued that the vast resources available to companies can be used most effectively by being returned to society, at least in part. By and large, the business sector is in at least as good a position as the government to return wealth to its users in some way. The idea of partnership is also important. If indeed business, government, and the public are partners in our society, each must attempt to protect, maintain, and nourish that society.

Last, simple arguments of logic can be used to defend social responsibility. In particular, logic can be used to refute each of the arguments against social responsibility. For example, it can be argued that existing laws sufficiently constrain corporate power so that socially responsible corporate behavior provides business with no additional power. With all such arguments out of the way, social responsibility seems quite desirable.

Arguments Against Social Responsibility   One major argument against social responsibility is that by definition it decreases corporate profits. When Exxon gives thousands of dollars to support the arts, for instance, the money is actually being taken out of the pockets of stockholders. Economists like Milton Friedman believe that such practices run counter to the basic premises underlying U.S. capitalism.[23] This argument is an economic view that tends to be narrow, focuses on the short term, and assumes competitive markets with little impact on one another.

Another argument against social responsibility is that it may give big business even more power, destroying the checks and balances among government, business, and the general public. Increased activities of a socially responsible nature might tip the scales in favor of business. Accountability is also an issue. Since a business can use its money in any way it wants, the company is not accountable for the results of its activities.

Some people also argue that business organizations have no expertise in the area of social responsibility. Therefore it would be better to leave such activities in the hands of people more skilled in social programs, such as teachers, social workers, and art administrators, for instance.

Finally, some critics of social responsibility argue that such activities lead to conflicts of interest. Suppose that a large chemical manufacturing firm was contemplating a donation of $100,000 to charity. If one of its managers learned that a member of Congress who favored a certain charity was working on legislation affecting the chemical industry, this knowledge, theoretically, could influence the company's decision about where to spend the money.

Areas of Social Responsibility

Basic areas of social responsibility include organizational constituents, the natural environment, and general social welfare.

These various arguments aside, in the United States a relatively strong norm dictating social responsibility has evolved. That is, U.S. organizations are generally expected to behave in socially responsible ways. Those organizations may exercise social responsibility toward their constituents and the natural environment and in promoting general social welfare. Social entities closer to the organization will have a clearer and more immediate stake in what the organization does, while those further removed will have a more ambiguous and longer-term stake in the organization and its practices.

Organizational Constituents   In Chapter 3 we characterized the task environment as those specific elements of the environment that directly affect a particular organization. Another view of that same network is in terms of **organizational constituents,** those people and organizations that are directly affected by the practices of an organization and that have a stake in its performance. Major constituents are depicted in Exhibit 6.4.

Organizational constituents are those people and organizations that are directly affected by the practices of an organization and that have a stake in its performance.

The interests of people who own and invest in an organization will be affected by virtually anything the firm does. If the firm's managers are caught committing criminal acts or violating acceptable ethical standards, the resulting bad press and public outcry will likely hurt the organization's profits and stock prices. Organizations also have a responsibility to their creditors. If poor social performance hurts an organization's ability to repay its debts, those creditors and their employees will also suffer.

A firm that engages in socially irresponsible practices toward some of its constituents is asking for trouble. For example, managers at Allegheny International once spent a half million dollars to buy a lavish Pittsburgh home in which to entertain clients. The firm maintained a fleet of five corporate jets so that its managers could travel anywhere, anytime. While entertaining and travel are normal parts of doing business in the eyes of many, Allegheny went too far. The company also made large loans to employees at a 2 percent interest rate. Nepotism in hiring was rampant. A close analysis of Allegheny's performance during this period suggested that it spent too much on executive perquisites, that conflicts of interest clouded executive judgment, that improper accounting methods were employed, that managers withheld information from shareholders, and that the board of directors inadequately monitored top management. Consequently, other constituents such as investors (who received lower dividends), the government (which received fewer tax dollars), the court system (which was eventually forced to deal with Allegheny's improprieties), and employees (who might have been paid higher wages under other circumstances) all were affected.[24]

On the other hand, consider the case of Ben and Jerry's Homemade, Inc. The ice cream company gives 7.5 percent of its pretax earnings to social causes, treats its employees and suppliers with dignity and respect, has had no major ethical scandals, is respected by its competitors, maintains good relations with government regulatory agencies, and contributes to college and university scholarship programs. This record suggests that managers at Ben and Jerry's are doing an excellent job of maintaining good relations with the firm's constituents.[25]

Not all organizations can do as well as Ben and Jerry's in attending to constituents, but most make an effort to take a socially responsible stance toward three main groups: customers, employees, and investors. Lands' End, a mail-order firm, is a good example of a company that has profited from good customer relations. Its telephone operators are trained to be completely informed

Exhibit 6.4

Organizational Constituents

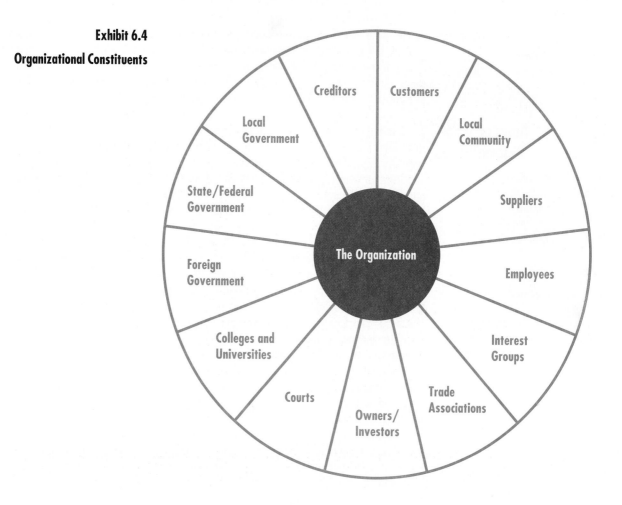

about company policies and products, to avoid pushing customers into buying unwanted merchandise, to listen to complaints, and to treat customers with respect. As a result, the company's sales have been increasing 20 percent each year.[26] Organizations that are socially responsible in their dealings with employees treat workers fairly, make them a part of the team, and respect their dignity and basic human needs. Companies such as 3M and Golden West Financial Corp. go to great lengths to find, hire, train, and promote qualified minorities.[27]

To maintain a socially responsible stance toward investors, managers should follow proper accounting procedures, provide appropriate information to shareholders about the financial performance of the firm, and manage the organization so as to protect shareholder rights and investments. Insider trading, illegal stock manipulation, and the withholding of financial data are examples of recent wrongdoings attributed to many different businesses. The former chairman of Ashland Oil, for example, was accused of selling important Ashland documents to Iran in order to manipulate the supply and price of oil for personal gain.[28]

The Natural Environment   A second critical area of social responsibility relates to the natural environment. Not long ago many organizations indiscriminately dumped sewage, waste products from production, and trash into streams and rivers, into the air, and on vacant land. Now, however, many different laws regulate the disposal of waste materials. In many instances companies themselves have seen the error of their ways and have become more socially responsible in their release

An interesting blend of public and private, profit-making and not-for-profit organizational cooperation resulted in posters such as this for the National Parks. Hi-Tec Sports sponsored the posters, the Sierra Club made space for advertisements for the posters, and the National Parks got contributions from the sale of the posters. (Reprinted with permission of the National Parks and Conservation Association and Hi-Tec Sports.)

of pollutants. Consequently, most forms of air and water pollution have decreased, although there is still widespread ocean dumping of sewage sludge, and much remains to be done. Companies need to develop economically feasible ways to avoid contributing to acid rain, to depletion of the ozone layer, and to global warming. Alternative methods are required for handling sewage, hazardous wastes, and ordinary garbage.[29] Procter & Gamble, for example, is an industry leader in using recycled materials for containers, and Hyatt has a new company to help recycle waste products from its hotels.

Companies also need to develop safety policies that cut down on accidents with potentially disastrous environmental results. When one of Ashland Oil's storage tanks ruptured, spilling over 500,000 gallons of diesel fuel into Pennsylvania's Monongahela River, the company moved quickly to clean up the spill but was still indicted for violating U.S. environmental laws.[30] After the Exxon oil tanker *Valdez* spilled millions of gallons of oil off the coast of Alaska, it adopted new and more stringent procedures to keep another disaster from happening.

General Social Welfare   Some people feel that in addition to treating constituents and the environment responsibly, business organizations also should promote the general welfare of society. Examples include making contributions to charities, philanthropic organizations, and not-for-profit foundations and associations; supporting museums, symphonies, and public radio and television; and taking a role in improving public health and education.[31] Some people also believe that organizations should act so as to correct, or at least not contribute to, the political inequities that exist in the world. A well-publicized expression of this viewpoint in the late 1980s was the argument that U.S. businesses should end their operations in South Africa to protest that nation's policies of apartheid.[32] Companies like Kodak and IBM responded to these concerns by selling their operations in South Africa. As we shall see, this area of social responsibility is a source of much controversy for the managers of modern organizations.

Approaches to Social Responsibility

Given the persuasive arguments both for and against social responsibility and the varied interpretations of socially responsible behavior toward organizational constituents and the natural environment and in promoting general social welfare, it comes as no surprise that businesses take dramatically different views of how they should behave. In general, there are four basic approaches that characterize business postures.[33] These are summarized in Exhibit 6.5.

Social Obstruction

Social obstruction involves doing as little as possible to solve social or environmental problems.

The few organizations that take what might be called a **social obstruction** approach to social responsibility usually do as little as possible to solve social or environmental problems. When they cross the ethical or legal line that separates acceptable from unacceptable practices, their typical response is to deny or cover up their actions. A few years ago managers at Beech-Nut learned that the firm was mixing chemical additives in apple juice but advertising it as being pure juice with no additives. Rather than losing money on the existing supply of juice, they decided to do nothing and continue selling it under false pretenses until the existing inventory was gone. Ashland Oil also has an unfortunate history of alleged social wrongdoing followed by less-than-model responses. For example, Ashland was found guilty of rigging bids with other contractors in order to charge higher prices for highway work in Tennessee and North Carolina.[34] It was also charged with wrongfully firing two employees because they refused to cover up illegal payments the company made.

Social Obligation

Social obligation refers to meeting economic and legal responsibilities but not going beyond them.

The **social obligation** view is most consistent with the argument that any business activity that is not directly aimed at profits is inadvisable. The company that takes this approach is willing to meet its social obligations as mandated by societal norms and government regulation, but it is not willing to do more. Thus it meets its economic and legal responsibilities but does not go beyond them. Tobacco companies such as Philip Morris have reduced their advertising in the United States and have put consumer warnings on every package of cigarettes they sell. However, they did not choose to take these measures; they were forced to by government regulation. In other parts of the world where such regulation is not in force, tobacco companies are still heavily promoting their products. Hence, although they are doing nothing illegal, they are following the letter of the law and not its spirit.[35]

Exhibit 6.5

Approaches to Social Responsibility

Lowest   Highest

Degree of Social Responsibility

| Social Obstruction | Social Obligation | Social Response | Social Contribution |

Social Reaction

Social reaction *goes beyond social obligation by also responding to appropriate societal requests.*

The firm using a **social reaction** approach is one that meets its social obligations and is also willing to react to appropriate societal requests and demands. That is, the company will make limited and specific positive contributions to social welfare. For example, many large corporations such as Exxon and IBM routinely match employee contributions to worthwhile charitable causes with contributions of their own. These actions fall under the heading of social reaction. So do the actions of the company that agrees to help local charities and civic organizations by providing free meeting space or that donates funds to support Little League baseball teams. The key point to note is reaction: the normal pattern is for the civic group to knock on the company's door and ask for help, which the firm then agrees to give.

Social Involvement

Social involvement *goes beyond obligations and requests and actively seeks ways to benefit society.*

The firm using the **social involvement** approach to social responsibility fulfills its obligations and responds to requests, just as the social reaction and social obligation types of companies do. In addition, however, it actively seeks other ways in which to help. One example of the social involvement view is provided by McDonald's, which has established Ronald McDonald houses to help the families of sick children. This action is clearly above and beyond the call of corporate duty. Another example is the recent trend toward corporate support of the arts. Some corporations, such as Sears and General Electric, have taken an active role in supporting artists and cultural performers. Such actions may well lead to higher profits, but this is by no means guaranteed, and the corporate motive appears to be primarily altruistic. Another example is that of Lands' End, as described earlier. The mail-order house goes far beyond conventional levels of customer responsiveness.[36]

The Government and Social Responsibility

 nother area of significance is the link between the government and social responsibility. Generally, the government is actively working to regulate and control business, while business is attempting to influence the government, as summarized in Table 6.3.

Government Regulation of Business

Since the period of the late 1800s, already discussed, the government of the United States has taken an active role in the regulation of business. Much government regulation has been concerned with enhancing the social responsiveness and awareness of business and with protecting the best interests of society from abuse by big business.

Government regulation has generally focused on four basic areas. First, the government has attempted to ensure fair labor practices by passing legislation regarding hiring wages, union rela-

Table 6.3

How Business and the Government Interact

Government regulation of business	Business influence on government
1. Ensures fair labor practices 2. Protects the environment 3. Protects consumers 4. Guarantees safety and health	1. Gains favorable legislation and lessened scrutiny through personal contacts 2. Enhances the company image to government officials and the general public 3. Influences legislation by using lobbyists 4. Aids political candidates through donations

Government regulation is concerned with enhancing business's social responsiveness and awareness and with protecting the best interests of society.

tions, and so forth. Second, it has worked for environmental protection from pollution by business as well as by other organizations. Third, consumer protection has theoretically been achieved by numerous laws dealing with truth in advertising, pricing, and warranties. Fourth, a set of regulations has been developed to guarantee the safety and health of both employees and consumers.

In general, the enforcement of these regulations has been assigned to several different and sometimes conflicting governmental agencies. Businesses today must contend with the Occupational Safety and Health Administration (OSHA), the Environmental Protection Agency, the Fair Labor Standards Board, the Equal Employment Opportunity Commission, the Federal Trade Commission, and the Food and Drug Administration.[37]

Critics argue that this level of regulation is excessive and does more harm than good. For example, Goodyear Tire & Rubber once had to generate 345,000 pages of computer reports to comply with one new OSHA regulation. Moreover, the company reported that it spent over $35 million each year to comply with federal regulations and that it took thirty-four employee-years just to fill out the necessary forms.[38] OSHA seems to be responding to criticisms, however, and advocates of government regulation argue that we would all be subjected to business abuses without it.[39]

Business Influence on Government

Just as the government regulates business, so does business attempt to influence the government. Such efforts, of course, must be relatively subtle and are often quite indirect. In general, there are four common approaches businesses use to influence government.

First, company managers try to develop personal contacts with influential government leaders, because such contacts can lead to favorable legislation and lessened scrutiny from the government. Second, many companies, especially large ones, employ public relations firms to enhance their image with government officials and the general public.

*A **lobbyist** is a person who works in a seat of government specifically to influence legislators.*

Third, many businesses employ lobbyists. A **lobbyist** is someone based in a seat of government—either Washington or a state capital—for the express purpose of influencing the legislative body. A lobbyist for the oil industry, for example, might work to persuade key congressional leaders to vote for an upcoming bill that would result in increases in oil prices. Finally, some organizations make direct contributions to political candidates. Such contributions are heavily restricted and can be made only under certain circumstances. In recent years organizations have started creating **political action committees,** or **PACs,** that solicit money from a variety of

*P**olitical action committees (PACs)** solicit funds from organizations and then make contributions to political candidates in order to gain their favor.*

organizations and then make contributions to several candidates for office in order to gain their favor. For example, between 1987 and 1988 Federal Express's political action committee Fepac contributed more than $200,000 to Democratic campaigns. In 1988, as the congressional session came to a close, Democratic sponsors pushed a controversial bill through both the House and the Senate that allowed certain tax benefits for Federal Express employees.[40]

These days there is no apparent widespread opposition to business influence on government, but there have been times when things have gone too far. Some financial contributions have been so large that they almost constituted a direct bribe, and some have been made on the condition that the candidate take a certain position on a specific issue. Clearly, such practices are unethical and violate all premises of social responsibility. In all likelihood business and government will continue to work hard to influence one another legally and publicly, but occasional abuses will probably still occur.

Managing Social Responsibility

The demands for social responsibility placed on contemporary organizations by an increasingly sophisticated and educated public are probably stronger than ever. As we have seen, there are pitfalls for managers who fail to adhere to high ethical standards and for companies that try to circumvent their legal obligations. Organizations therefore need to fashion an approach to social responsibility the way they develop any other business strategy. That is, they should view social responsibility as a major challenge that requires careful planning, decision making, consideration, and evaluation. They may accomplish the effective management of social responsibility through both official and unofficial approaches to managing social responsibility.[41]

Official Approaches to Social Responsibility

Some dimensions of managing social responsibility are formal and planned activities on the part of the organization. Formal organizational dimensions that can help manage social responsibility are legal compliance, ethical compliance, and philanthropic giving.[42]

Legal Compliance   **Legal compliance** is the extent to which the organization complies with local, state, federal, and international laws. The task of managing legal compliance is generally assigned to the appropriate functional managers. For example, the organization's top human resource executive is generally responsible for ensuring compliance with regulations concerning recruiting, selection, pay, and so forth. Likewise, the top finance executive generally oversees compliance with securities and banking regulations. The organization's legal department is also likely to contribute to this effort, by providing general supervision and answering queries from managers about the appropriate interpretation of laws and regulations.

Ethical Compliance   **Ethical compliance** is the extent to which the members of the organization follow basic ethical (and legal) standards of behavior. We have already noted that organizations have started doing more in this area by providing training in ethics and developing guidelines and codes of conduct, for example. These activities serve as vehicles for enhancing ethical compliance. Many organizations also establish formal ethics committees, which may be asked to review proposals for new projects, help evaluate new hiring strategies, or assess a new environmental protection plan. They might also serve as a peer review panel to evaluate alleged ethical misconduct by an employee.

Philanthropic Giving   Finally, **philanthropic giving** is the awarding of funds or other gifts to charities or other social programs. Dayton-Hudson Corporation routinely gives 5 percent of its taxable income to charity and social programs. Indeed, most organizations give a specified amount of their pretax income to social causes. Common causes include charities, colleges and universities, and arts programs like museums and symphonies. Unfortunately, during the recent period of cutbacks and retrenchment, many corporations have had to decrease their charitable gifts. Firms that do engage in philanthropic giving usually have a committee of top executives who review requests for grants and decide how much and to whom money will be allocated. *The Environment of Management: Giving Internationally* summarizes patterns of giving by international firms.

Unofficial Approaches to Social Responsibility

In addition to these official dimensions for managing social responsibility, there are also unofficial dimensions. Two of the more effective ways to clarify the organization's approach are to provide appropriate leadership and culture and to allow for whistle blowing.

Organization Leadership and Culture   Leadership practices and organization culture can go a long way toward defining the social responsibility stance an organization and its members will adopt. For example, Johnson & Johnson executives for years provided a consistent message to employees that customers, employees, communities where the company did business, and shareholders were all important, but only in that order. Thus, when packages of poisoned Tylenol showed up on store shelves in 1982, Johnson & Johnson employees did not need to wait for orders

The Environment of Management

Giving Internationally

Most people understand that businesses in the United States have a history of philanthropic giving. But what few people realize is that corporate giving has become an international operation as U.S. firms increase their contributions abroad and foreign firms increase contributions within the United States.

For example, Alcoa recently donated $112,000 to a small town in Brazil to build a waste sewage treatment plant. Alcoa reaped some benefits since it had employees stationed there, but several thousand local residents also benefited. Du Pont recently donated 1.4 million water-jug filters to eight African nations to help remove parasites from local drinking water.

And IBM has given equipment to Costa Rican researchers working to save that country's rain forests. All told, U.S. firms distribute about 6 percent of their total philanthropic giving in other countries.

Many firms in other countries, especially Japan, have mirrored this practice by giving more in the U. S. For example, in 1991 Japanese firms donated approximately $500 million to U.S. charities, sixteen times as much as they had contributed as recently as 1986. Hitachi, for example, has tripled the amount it gives to support minority causes in the U. S.

Why has this trend emerged? Firms believe that they can do good while also doing good for themselves. The Japanese, for example, are desperate to improve their image in this country. And large, well-publicized contributions go a long way in helping meet this goal.[43] ∎

---

from headquarters to know what to do: they immediately pulled all the packages from the shelves before any other customers could buy them.[44] By contrast, the irresponsible behavior by top managers of Beech-Nut, as described earlier, sent a far different message to that firm's employees.

Whistle blowing is the disclosure by an employee of illegal or unethical conduct on the part of others within the organization.

Whistle Blowing   **Whistle blowing** is the disclosure by an employee of illegal or unethical conduct on the part of others within the organization. How an organization responds to this practice often indicates its stance toward social responsibility. Whistle blowers may have to proceed through a number of channels to be heard and may even get fired for their efforts. Many organizations, however, welcome their contributions. Individuals who observe questionable behavior typically report the incident to their boss first. If nothing is done, the whistle blower may then inform higher-level managers or an ethics committee if one exists. Eventually, the person may have to go to a regulatory agency or even the media in order to be heard.[45] For example, the apple juice scandal at Beech-Nut, noted earlier, started with a whistle blower. A manager in the firm's R&D department began to suspect that its apple juice was not "100% pure." His boss, however, was unsympathetic, and when the manager went to the president of the company, he too turned a deaf ear. Eventually, the manager took his message to the media.

Evaluating Social Responsibility   Any organization that is serious about social responsibility must ensure that its efforts are producing the desired benefits. Producing the desired benefits requires applying the concept of control to social responsibility. Many organizations now require employees to read their guidelines or code of ethics and then sign a statement agreeing to abide by it. An organization should also evaluate how it responds to instances of questionable legal or ethical conduct. Does it follow up immediately? Does it punish those involved? Or does it use delay and cover-up tactics? Answers to these questions can help an organization form a picture of its approach to social responsibility.

*A **corporate social audit** is a formal and thorough analysis of the effectiveness of a firm's social performance.*

Additionally, some organizations occasionally conduct corporate social audits. A **corporate social audit** is a formal and thorough analysis of the effectiveness of the firm's social performance. It requires that the organization clearly define all its social goals, analyze the resources devoted to each goal, determine how well the various goals are being achieved, and make recommendations about which areas need additional attention. Unfortunately, such audits are not conducted very often because they are expensive and time consuming. Indeed, most organizations probably could do much more to evaluate the extent of their social responsibility than they do.[46]

Chapter Summary

E thics are the standards or morals a person sets for himself or herself about what is good and bad or right and wrong behavior. Ethics are formed by a variety of factors: family influences, peer influences, past experiences, values and morals, and situational factors.

Managers face ethical dilemmas or conflicts every day. These dilemmas occur in the relationship of the firm to the employee, the relationship of the employee to the firm, and the relationship of the firm to the environment. The key dimensions of the ethical context of management are personal ethics, the organizational context, and the environmental context.

Managers must understand ethics and know how their organizations should attempt to manage them. For organizations to develop and maintain cultures that lead to ethical managerial behavior, it is essential for top management to support such behavior. In addition, the organization can develop a code of conduct that serves as a guide to managers and a reminder of the importance of ethical behavior to the organization.

Social responsibility is the obligation of the organization to protect and/or enhance the society in which it functions. There are several arguments both for and against social responsibility. The basic areas of social responsibility include organizational constituents, the natural environment, and general social welfare.

There are four general approaches to social responsibility. These different approaches are social obstruction, social obligation, social reaction, and social involvement.

Government regulates and controls business. Critics feel that the burden of regulation is too great; proponents of regulation feel it is the lesser of two evils. Business also tries to influence government in various ways. These attempts to influence government do not appear to be generating widespread negative reaction in the general public, so they are likely to continue in the future, even though abuses occasionally are made public.

Because of its obvious importance, organizations proactively attempt to manage social responsibility. There are both official and unofficial approaches that organizations can use to address social responsibility. In addition, most businesses make an effort to evaluate the effectiveness of their social responsibility programs and activities.

The Manager's Vocabulary

ethics
managerial ethics
conflict of interest
codes of conduct
social responsibility
organizational constituents

social obstruction
social obligation
social reaction
social involvement
lobbyist
political action committees (PACs)

legal compliance
ethical compliance
philanthropic giving
whistle blowing
corporate social audit

Review Questions

1. What are the three general types of situations in which ethics are important to managers? What are the key dimensions of the manager's ethical context?

2. How can ethics be managed by organizations?

3. What is meant by social responsibility? What are the arguments for and against it?

4. What four general approaches to social responsibility do organizations take?

5. What is the government's role with regard to business's social responsibility? Why has it assumed that role? How does business influence government?

Analysis Questions

1. Make a list of five ways in which you feel it is ethical for students to behave. Then list five that you feel are unethical. What are the strongest influences on your feelings about what is ethical and unethical student behavior?

2. Identify an action that is both legal and ethical, legal but unethical, illegal but ethical, both illegal and unethical.

3. How useful are codes of conduct or codes of ethics to business firms? Explain your response.

4. The proponents of social responsibility claim that the arguments against responsibility are flawed. Study those arguments and explain how each might be flawed. Give details to support your claim.

5. Which area of social responsibility do you feel is most in need of action? Which is least in need of action? Why?

Self-Assessment

Personal Values—What Is Important to You?

Introduction As Exhibit 6.1 shows, personal values help determine an individual's ethics. This self-assessment will help identify the personal values which have shaped your ethics.

Instructions Each of the following questions has six possible responses. Rank these responses by assigning a 6 to the one you prefer the most, a 5 to the next, and so on, to 1, the least preferred of the alternatives. Sometimes you may have trouble making choices, but there should be no ties; you should make a choice.

1. Which of the following branches of study do you consider to be most important for the human race?

    _____ A. philosophy

    _____ B. political science

    _____ C. psychology

    _____ D. theology

    _____ E. business

    _____ F. art

2. Which of the following qualities is most descriptive of you?

    _____ A. religious

    _____ B. unselfish

    _____ C. artistic

    _____ D. persuasive

    _____ E. practical

    _____ F. intelligent

3. Of the following famous people, who is most interesting to you?

    _____ A. Albert Einstein—discoverer of the theory of relativity

    _____ B. Henry Ford—automobile entrepreneur

    _____ C. Napoleon Bonaparte—political leader and military strategist

    _____ D. Martin Luther—leader of the Protestant Reformation

    _____ E. Michelangelo—sculptor and painter

    _____ F. Albert Schweitzer—missionary and humanitarian

4. What kind of person do you prefer to be? One who:

    _____ A. is industrious and economically self-sufficient

    _____ B. has leadership qualities and organizing ability

    _____ C. has spiritual or religious values

    _____ D. is philosophical and interested in knowledge

    _____ E. is compassionate and understanding toward others

    _____ F. has artistic sensitivity and skill

5. Which of the following is most interesting to you?

_____ A. artistic experiences

_____ B. thinking about life

_____ C. accumulation of wealth

_____ D. religious faith

_____ E. leading others

_____ F. helping others

6. In which of the following would you prefer to participate?

_____ A. business venture

_____ B. artistic performance

_____ C. religious activity

_____ D. project to help the poor

_____ E. scientific study

_____ F. political campaign

7. Which publication would you prefer to read?

_____ A. *History of the Arts*

_____ B. *Psychology Today*

_____ C. *Power Politics*

_____ D. *Scientific American*

_____ E. *Religions Today*

_____ F. *Wall Street Journal*

8. In choosing a spouse, who would you prefer? One who:

_____ A. likes to help people

_____ B. is a leader in his or her field

_____ C. is practical and enterprising

_____ D. is artistically gifted

_____ E. has a deep spiritual belief

_____ F. is interested in philosophy and learning

9. Which activity do you consider to be more important for children?

_____ A. scouting

_____ B. junior achievement

_____ C. religious training

_____ D. creative art

_____ E. student government

_____ F. science club

10. What should government leaders be concerned with?

_____ A. promoting creative and aesthetic interests

_____ B. establishing a position of power and respect in the world

_____ C. developing commerce and industry

_____ D. supporting education and learning

_____ E. providing a supportive climate for spiritual growth and development

_____ F. promoting the social welfare of citizens

11. Which of the following courses would you prefer to teach?

_____ A. anthropology

_____ B. religions of the world

_____ C. philosophy

_____ D. political science

_____ E. poetry

_____ F. business administration

12. What would you do if you had sufficient time and money?

_____ A. go on a retreat for spiritual renewal

_____ B. increase your money-making ability

_____ C. develop leadership skills

_____ D. help those who are disadvantaged

_____ E. study the fine arts such as theater, music, and painting

_____ F. write an original essay, article, or book

13. Which courses would you promote if you were able to influence educational policies?

_____ A. political and governmental studies

_____ B. philosophy and science

_____ C. economics and occupational skills

_____ D. social problems and issues

_____ E. spiritual and religious studies

_____ F. music and art

14. Which of the following news items would be most interesting to you?

_____ A. "Business Conditions Favorable"

_____ B. "Relief Arrives for Poor"

_____ C. "Religious Leaders Meet"

_____ D. "President Addresses the Nation"

_____ E. "What's New in the Arts"

_____ F. "Scientific Breakthrough Revealed"

(con't. on page 144)

15. Which subject would you prefer to discuss?

_____ A. music, film, and theater

_____ B. the meaning of human existence

_____ C. spiritual experiences

_____ D. wars in history

_____ E. business opportunities

_____ F. social conditions

16. What do you think the purpose should be for space exploration and manned space flight?

_____ A. to unify people around the world

_____ B. to gain knowledge of our universe

_____ C. to reveal the beauty of our world

_____ D. to discover answers to spiritual questions

_____ E. to control world affairs

_____ F. to develop trade and business opportunities

17. Which profession would you enter if all salaries were equal and you felt you had equal aptitude to succeed in any one of the six?

_____ A. counseling

_____ B. fine arts

_____ C. science

_____ D. politics

_____ E. business

_____ F. ministry

18. Whose life and works are most interesting to you?

_____ A. Madame Curie—discoverer of radium

_____ B. Gloria Vanderbilt—business woman

_____ C. Elizabeth I—British monarch

_____ D. Mother Teresa—religious leader

_____ E. Martha Graham—ballerina and choreographer

_____ F. Harriet Beecher Stowe—author of _Uncle Tom's Cabin_

19. Which television program would you prefer to watch?

_____ A. "Art Appreciation"

_____ B. "Spiritual Values"

_____ C. "Investment Opportunities"

_____ D. "Marriage and the Family"

_____ E. "Political Power and Social Persuasion"

_____ F. "The Origins of Intelligence"

20. Which of the following positions would you like to have?

_____ A. political leader

_____ B. artist

_____ C. teacher

_____ D. theologian

_____ E. writer

_____ F. business entrepreneur

For interpretation, turn to the back of the book.

Source: George Manning and Kent Curtis, _Ethics at Work: Fire in a Dark World_ (Cincinnati: South-Western, 1988), pp. 99–111.

Skill Builder

Ethics of Employee Appraisal

Purpose Many management activities occur within an ethical context. The appraisal of employees' performance is one of those activities that can raise ethical issues. This skill builder focuses on the _human resources model_. It will help you develop the _mentor role_ of the human resources model. One of the skills of the mentor is the ability to develop subordinates.

Introduction Much attention has been given in recent years to ethics in business, yet one area often overlooked is ethical issues when hiring or appraising employees. Marian Kellogg developed a list of principles to keep in mind when recruiting or appraising.

How to Keep Your Appraisals Ethical: A Manager's Checklist
1. Don't appraise without knowing why the appraisal is required.
2. Appraise on the basis of **representative** information.
3. Appraise on the basis of **sufficient** information.
4. Appraise on the basis of **relevant** information.
5. Be honest in your assessment of all the facts you obtain.
6. Don't write one thing and say another.
7. In offering an appraisal, make it plain that this is only your personal opinion of the facts as you see them.
8. Pass appraisal information along only to those who have good reason to know it.
9. Don't imply the existence of an appraisal that hasn't been made.
10. Don't accept another's appraisal without knowing the basis on which it was made.

Instructions Read each incident individually and decide which of the ten rules is violated, marking the appropriate number on the right. In some cases, more than one rule is violated. In your group go over each case and come to a consensus on which rules are violated.

Incidents

1. Steve Wilson has applied for a transfer to Department O., headed by Marianne Kilbourn. As part of her fact finding, Marianne reads through the written evaluation, which is glowing, and then asks Steve's boss, Bill Hammond, for information on Steve's performance. Bill starts complaining about Steve because his last project was not up to par, but does not mention Steve's wife has been seriously ill for two months. Marianne then decides not to accept Steve's transfer.
   Rule violation # _____
2. Maury Nanner is a sales manager who is having lunch with several executives. One of them, Harvey Gant, asks him what he thinks of his subordinate George Williams, and Nanner gives a lengthy evaluation.
   Rule violation # _____

3. Phillip Randall is working on six-month evaluations of his subordinates. He decides to rate Elisa Donner less-than-average on initiative because he thinks she spends too much time, energy, and money making herself look attractive. He thinks it distracts the male employees.
   Rule violation # _____
4. Paul Trendant has received an application from an outstanding candidate, Jim Fischer. However, Paul decides not to hire Jim because he heard from someone that Jim only moved to town because his wife got a good job here. Trendant thinks Jim will quit whenever his wife gets transferred.
   Rule violation # _____
5. Susan Forman is on the fast track and tries to make herself look good to her boss, Peter Everly. This morning she has a meeting with Pete to discuss which person to promote. Just before the meeting, Pete's golf buddy, Harold, a coworker of Susan, tells Susan that Alice, Jerry, and Joe are favored by Pete. Susan had felt Darlene was the strongest candidate, but she goes into the meeting with Pete and suggests Alice, Jerry, and Joe as top candidates.
   Rule violation # _____
6. Sandy is a new supervisor for seven people. After several months Sandy is certain that Linda is marginally competent and frequently cannot produce any useful work. Looking over past appraisals Sandy sees all of Linda's evaluations were positive, and she is told that Linda "has problems" and not to be "too hard on her." Realizing this is not healthy, Sandy begins documenting Linda's inadequate performance. Several supervisors hint that she should "lighten up because we don't want Linda to feel hurt."
   Rule violation # _____

Source: Marian S. Kellogg, *"What to Do About Performance Appraisal,"* AMACON, a division of the American Management Association, New York, 1975; Marian S. Kellogg, *Personnel,* July–August 1965, American Management Association, New York; Dorothy Marcic, *Organizational Behavior: Experiences and Cases,* 3rd ed. (West Publishing Company, 1992).

CONCLUDING CASES

6.1 Phar-Mor

It seems that every few years a serious financial scandal comes to light in a major corporation. One of the latest concerns Phar-Mor, Inc., a rapidly growing chain of drugstores. Phar-Mor was founded in 1982 by David Shapira and Michael Monus. Their strategy was to position Phar-Mor as a high-volume discounter.

Shapira's family owns Giant Eagle Inc., a large supermarket

chain in Pittsburgh. In 1981 Giant Eagle bought a grocery distribution firm called Tamarkin Co., Inc. Monus was a vice president at Tamarkin at the time and met Shapira following the acquisition. The two of them then developed the plan for Phar-Mor. Giant Eagle provided the financing, and the first Phar-Mor store opened soon thereafter. The company enjoyed immediate success, growing to 68 stores by 1987 and 169 stores by 1989.

Shapira served as CEO, and Monus assumed the position of chief financial officer. While Shapira continued to concentrate on Phar-Mor, Monus branched out into the world of professional sports. In 1987, for instance, he launched the World Professional Basketball League. In 1990 he began sponsoring two Ladies Professional Golf Association tournaments. In that same year he signed on as an investor in the Colorado Rockies, a new major league professional baseball team. Also in 1990 Phar-Mor opened its two-hundredth store and its sales topped $2 billion.

In 1992, however, things began to come apart for Phar-Mor in general and for Monus in particular. For some time Shapira had suspected that Monus was not managing the company's funds appropriately. Quietly investigating behind the scenes, he determined that Monus had been siphoning off Phar-Mor funds to support his sports activities. Shapira has alleged that Monus and two confederates misappropriated more than $10 million from Phar-Mor. Even more damaging, however, Shapira has also alleged that Monus overstated the firm's inventories and profit levels, to the tune of $350 million.

In retrospect, it seems unlikely that Phar-Mor earned any real profits. It fueled its growth by taking on new debt, by not paying suppliers, and by selling new stock on the strength of misleading financial reports. Shortly after Shapira made his charges public, he fired Monus and called in the FBI to conduct a more thorough investigation. Monus, in turn, folded the World Basketball League, sold his stake in the Rockies, and dropped out of sight. At the same time, other participants began pointing fingers. The firm's auditors, Coopers & Lybrand, claimed that the board of directors were negligent and gave Monus too much authority with too little accountability. The board, meanwhile, argued that Coopers & Lybrand should have detected what Monus was doing and has replaced them with the firm of Deloitte Touche.

And what of Phar-Mor? Shapira concedes that the firm has been severely damaged. He has laid off nearly seven hundred employees, suspended a three-hundred-store expansion plan, and stopped construction of a new distribution center in Florida. But he also believes that he can turn things around and that the firm can eventually regain its magic touch.[47]

Discussion Questions

1. Identify the major ethical and social responsibility issues in this case.
2. Was the involvement by Monus in professional sports a conflict of interest?
3. Research how well Phar-Mor has done in overcoming this scandal.

6.2   United Distillers p.l.c.

A continuing source of controversy among international firms is the extent to which it is ethical and proper for a business to promote products in some markets when it is legally prohibited from promoting them in others. The controversy becomes more heated when those products pose known health concerns and their misuse can create hazardous situations. During the 1980s a frequent focal point for this kind of controversy was cigarettes. For the 1990s it seems that alcohol is becoming just as controversial.

Over the last several years, consumers in the United States have dramatically altered their consumption patterns of alcoholic beverages. The trend has been toward relatively light alcoholic beverages like beer and wine and away from beverages with higher alcoholic content such as whiskey and bourbon.

For example, in 1975 more than 30 million cases of bourbon were sold in the United States. In recent years consumption has fallen to under 17 million cases per year. And because whiskey and bourbon distillers cannot advertise their products on television in this country, there are few opportunities for them to turn things around.

Not so abroad, however. Because advertising is much less regulated in most other countries than it is in the United States, makers of alcoholic beverages have found many opportunities for foreign market expansion. The biggest success story to date has been in Japan and the rest of Pacific Asia. Led by United Distillers p.l.c., bourbon exporters have been able to triple bourbon and whiskey sales in that region since 1990. In Australia, United pushes Rebel Yell and Jim Beam products aggressively. In Japan,

United and other distributors advertise their various products through every available media.

Now that sales in Pacific Asia have begun to level off a bit, United and the other firms are turning their attention to Europe. For years whiskey and bourbon had a decidedly low-brow image in Europe. But now distributors are linking those beverages to an image of American pop culture and are again finding a receptive and growing market. Sales of top brands such as Jack Daniels are growing at a rate of 25 percent a year in England. And product managers throughout the industry say this is only the beginning.[48]

Discussion Questions

1. Do you think it is ethical for firms to promote products abroad using methods that they cannot use at home?
2. Are there other products besides cigarettes and alcohol that might fit this pattern?
3. Some people might argue that if a firm does not pursue every market opportunity as aggressively as possible, it is not working in the best interests of its stockholders. What do you think?

Part Two   The Environment of Management

Self-Assessment

International Business IQ Test

Introduction In this part of the book, you have been introduced to many different environmental forces managers must deal with as they manage their organizations. One of the most challenging is the international competition most businesses face today. This self-assessment examines your knowledge of the international business environment. Whether your instructor assigns this self-assessment or not, you may want to do it to give yourself a competitive advantage in the job market.

Instructions How informed are you about the everyday vocabulary of international business? Test yourself by answering the following questions.

1. Where in the world is:
   a. Suriname?
   b. The Seychelles?
   c. Belize?
   d. Dar es Salaam?
   e. Lagos?
   f. Vientiane?
   g. Kiev?
   h. Myanmar?
   i. Kazakstan?

2. What do the following acronyms stand for?
   a. EC
   b. UNDP
   c. ILO
   d. EFTA
   e. OAS
   f. GATT
   g. IMF

3. Define the following terms:
   a. balance of payments
   b. devaluation
   c. trade barrier
   d. floating exchange rate

4. Match the following with the correct country from this list: Jordan, Ireland, Peru, Zaire, China, Hong Kong, Honduras, Somalia, South Africa, Saudi Arabia, Chile.
   a. Ruled for many years by Mobutu Sese Seko
   b. Home of the "ANC"
   c. Home of the "Shining Path"
   d. Location of the infamous "Tianenmen" incident
   e. Where Mecca is located

For interpretation, turn to the back of the book.

Source: John R. Schermerhorn, Jr., *Management for Productivity*, 4th ed., copyright © 1993 by John Wiley & Sons, Inc. Reprinted by permission of John Wiley & Sons, Inc.

Skill Builder

Bargaining, United Nations Style: Exploring the Impact of Cultural Values

Purpose In Part Two of the textbook, we examined different environmental factors impacting business today. As the world becomes more of a global village, business people will have to learn to negotiate and do business with many different types of people. They will have to be sensitive to other people's values and culture. This skill builder starts to help you develop those skills. This skill builder focuses on the *human resources and open systems models.* It will help you develop both the *broker role* and the *mentor role.* One of the skills of the broker is the ability to negotiate with others, while one skill required of the mentor role is understanding others.

Introduction This skill builder allows you an opportunity to experience being a person from a different culture. It allows you to experience the effects of cultural differences on interactions and negotiations between different cultures.

Instructions Your instructor will provide additional materials for this exercise.

Source: J. William Pfeiffer, (ed.), *The 1992 Annual: Developing Human Resources,* San Diego, CA: Pfeiffer and Company. 1992.

Learning Objectives

After studying this chapter you should be able to

- Discuss the nature of planning, including its purpose and where the responsibilities for planning lie within the organization.

- Define goals, note their purpose, and identify the steps in the goal-setting process.

- Identify and define three major kinds of plans.

- Describe three major time frames for planning and how these time frames are integrated within organizations.

- Define contingency planning and describe contingency events.

- Discuss how to manage the planning process by avoiding the roadblocks to effective planning.

When a unique product is suddenly swamped by a lot of low-priced imitators, the manufacturer can adopt one of two plans. The company can defend its product and hope to survive through attrition, or it can adopt a plan of introducing new products to stay ahead. Intel follows the latter plan.

Intel is phasing in a "sleep" mode to make computers using its technology more energy efficient. Computers using this technology will automatically go into the sleep mode when not in use. In the sleep mode the computer will use thirty watts or less of power, compared to several hundred in the awake mode. The computer will not, however, be shut off. The touch of a key will instantly shift it from the sleep mode back to the awake mode.

Intel has also switched names. Instead of giving its most recent chip another in the series of "86" names (the 486 followed the 386 and was due to be followed in turn by the 586), the chip is called Pentium, a name that can more easily be protected through trademark rights. Well over three thousand suggestions were gathered from all over the world before the name was selected. The name suggests the fifth generation of chip (*pent* is Greek for "five") and a fundamental element (suggested by the *-ium* ending). It is hoped the name will have market appeal as well as more protectability.

Another part of Intel's plan involves speed. Previously, Intel had waited until one generation of chip was unveiled in the marketplace before beginning on the next generation. For that reason, design on the Pentium chip (previously known as the 586) did not begin until the 486 was introduced. The design on the 486 began with the introduction of the 386, which, in turn, began with the introduction of the 286. Not so now. Design on the next generation overlaps that of its predecessor so that instead of three-year lapses between introductions of each new generation, now only one year is planned. This pace makes it very hard for imitators to keep up.

Intel is also carefully developing products other than microprocessors. It makes video chips, flash memory, personal and super computers, and personal computer enhancement products such as networking boards. These products help Intel withstand cyclic swings in its microprocessor business. More importantly, they help Intel keep in touch with customers and stay on the cutting edge of product technology.

Intel's CEO, Andrew Grove, who fled the Soviet invasion of Hungary in 1956, is planning his product line farther into the future than ever before. To accomplish those plans, Intel is spending huge amounts on research and development as well as on plant and equipment. The continued success of Intel depends on the quality of its managerial planning.[1] ∎

When most people think of large, fast-growing businesses, they think of retailers like Wal-Mart (145 new stores in 1988), McDonald's (600 new stores in 1988), Benetton (more than 200 stores in 1989), and Woolworth (more than 1,100 new stores in 1988). Yet one of the larger, fastest-growing organizations in the United States is ConAgra.

As you read in Chapter 4, ConAgra is the largest independent food processor in the United States.[2] Like Intel's success, ConAgra's lies in innovation and effective planning. Managers at ConAgra looked carefully at their environment and purchased Beatrice to have access to its grocery-store distribution network and brands including Hunt's tomato products, Peter Pan peanut butter, Armour meats, and Banquet frozen foods.[3] In doing so, ConAgra developed a path to success.[4]

This chapter focuses on planning as a basic management function. First it looks at the nature of goals, which are the basis of planning. It then identifies major kinds of plans and discusses time frames for planning. After investigating contingency planning, it concludes by discussing ways in which the planning process can be more effectively managed.

Planning in Organizations

Why Managers Plan

*A **plan** is a blueprint or framework an organization uses to describe how it expects to achieve its goals.*

***Planning** is the process of developing plans.*

What is planning? To better understand it, we must first define and clarify its purpose and then identify who in the organization is responsible for planning.

A **plan** is a blueprint or framework used to describe how an organization expects to achieve its goals. **Planning,** then, is simply the process of developing plans. In essence, planning is determining which path among several to follow.[5] Planning activities also serve to project an image of managerial competence to the organization's constituencies.[6] The steps and procedures of the formal planning process become a symbol of the effectiveness of management.[7]

For example, when Harry Hoffman became CEO of Waldenbooks in 1979, he developed several plans for achieving his goal of making the bookseller the leader in its industry. His plans called for rapidly increasing the number of stores in the chain, increasing promotional activities to boost the sales of each store, and expanding the product line. Each of these activities was part of a systematic effort to dramatically increase the company's sales. In terms of planning, Hoffman could have chosen to maintain the status quo, branch out into other markets, maintain a pattern of slow growth, or any of several other alternatives. His choice of rapid growth, then, was the creation of his particular blueprint for action.[8]

In other words, any goal might be approached in several ways. Planning is the process of determining which is the best way to approach a particular goal. Waldenbooks chose the path that seemed best for it. The same holds true for Intel and ConAgra. Of course, it is also possible to choose a wrong path. This fact makes planning all the more important.

Responsibilities for Planning

Given the obvious importance of planning, it is essential to identify planning responsibilities: that is, who does an organization's planning? The answer is quite simple: all managers are involved in the planning process.

By careful planning, companies such as Campbell have expanded to worldwide markets. Recent expansion into Eastern Europe has U.S. brands popping up everywhere and ads becoming highly visible. The Campbell's soup here is being advertised at a tram stop in Warsaw, Poland. (Wojtek Laski/Sipa Press.)

All managers need to be involved in the planning process.

Exhibit 7.1 identifies several important planning centers within an organization. Planning starts with top management, which, working with the board of directors, establishes the broad goals and strategies of the firm. The usual approach is for the top management team to develop these goals and strategies and then submit them to the board for approval.

Many large organizations, such as Tenneco, General Motors, General Electric, Boeing, and Ford, also make use of a planning staff.[9] As noted in the exhibit, a planning staff is a group of professional planners at the top level of the organization. The staff assists line managers, providing expertise and various resources necessary to develop appropriate kinds of plans. The planners also coordinate and integrate the planning activities of other levels of the organization. Even some smaller organizations utilize more formal approaches to planning.[10]

Middle managers play several roles in the planning process.[11] They work together to assist with strategic planning, and they undertake tactical planning (these types of planning are discussed below).[12] They also work individually to develop and implement planning activities within their respective divisions or units.[13]

First-line managers must also be actively involved in planning. Like middle managers, they work together to make plans that affect more than one department or unit and work individually to plan for their own units. Their efforts mostly involve assisting with tactical planning and developing operational plans.[14] A well-integrated planning system that links all levels of the organization and takes into account the other managerial functions (organizing, leading, and controlling) can be a major ingredient in organizational success.

Exhibit 7.1

Planning Centers in an Organization

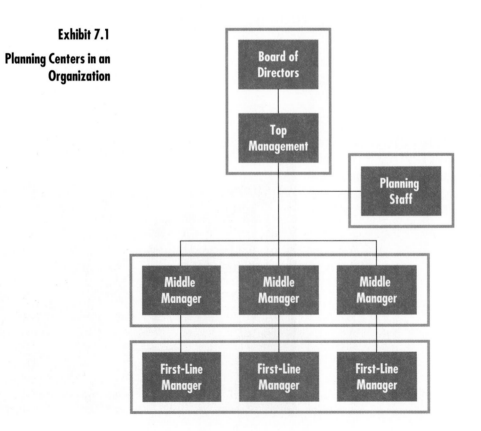

The Nature of Organizational Goals

What are goals? Why are they important in planning? How are they established? Before discussing planning, these basic questions must first be answered.

Definition and Purpose of Goals

*A **goal** provides direction for an organization and represents a desired state or condition that the organization wants to achieve.*

A **goal** can be defined as a desired state or condition that the organization wants to achieve, a target the organization wants to hit. When General Electric says that it wants to be number one in all of its markets, or when Kellogg states that it wants to control 50 percent of the cereal market, each company is specifying a market share goal it wants to achieve and then maintain.

Like targets, goals are supposed to provide a clear purpose, or direction, for the organization. When Stanley Gault became CEO of Rubbermaid, he decided to make the company much more innovative. He set a goal of increasing sales 15 percent annually. He also pledged increased employee participation and promised greater rewards for innovation. Rubbermaid's employees enthusiastically accepted these ideas and met the sales goal every year. And the company is now recognized as one of the most innovative in the world.[15] At Rubbermaid, then, goals are clearly serving their intended purpose: they are providing guidance and direction. It was this success at Rubbermaid that led to Gault's being brought out of retirement to head Goodyear.[16]

Types of Goals

Organizational goals vary in terms of levels, areas, and time frame and specificity.

Goals come in a variety of types and are called by many different names, including missions, purposes, objectives, ends, and aims. While there is no universally agreed-on set of definitions, goals can be readily differentiated by organizational level, area, and time frame and specificity.

Goals by Level   One useful perspective for describing goals is their level in the organization. For example, we noted in Chapter 1 the various levels of management that characterize most organizations. It follows logically, then, that each level is likely to have its own goals. At the top are the purpose and mission of the organization, as determined by the board of directors. An organization's **purpose** is its reason for existence. For instance, the purpose of Corning Glass, Reebok, and Compaq Computers is to make a profit, whereas the purpose of the Mayo Clinic is to provide health care. An organization's **mission** is the way it attempts to fulfill its purpose.[17] Honda Motor Company attempts to fulfill its purpose — making a profit — by manufacturing and selling automobiles, motorcycles, and lawn mowers. Kmart's mission is to sell large quantities of merchandise at a small markup.

*An organization's **purpose** is the reason it exists.*

*An organization's **mission** is the way in which it attempts to fulfill its purpose.*

Top-management goals are those that define the organization's strategy, or the broad plans that set the overall direction (see Chapter 8). Several years ago the former CEO of Citicorp, Walter Wriston, set three broad goals for the bank that determined the strategy that Citicorp would follow: earnings' growth of 15 percent per year, a 20-percent return on stockholders' equity, and becoming the world's first truly international banking system. Wriston's successor, John Reed, continued to work toward the same set of goals.[18]

Middle managers also set goals. These goals follow logically from the strategic goals set by top managers. A plant manager for Dow Chemical, for example, might have goals for reducing costs and increasing output for the next year by a certain amount. Likewise, the head of one of Citicorp's large banks will have goals designed to contribute to the three general goals noted above.

Of course, first-line managers also have goals. These might relate to specific projects or activities pertinent to the manager's job. For instance, a first-line supervisor in a Dow Chemical plant might have the goal of reducing costs in his or her unit by 5 percent. And a Citicorp banker sent to open a small branch in a new overseas location will have goals consistent with the corporation's goal of internationalization.

As you might have figured out, every job has goals. These goals affect how the jobholder feels about the job. The self-assessment in this chapter examines job goals. It provides an understanding of the effect goals have on a job.

Goals by Area   It is possible as well to differentiate goals by areas of management, also discussed in Chapter 1. That is, goals can be established for each organizational area. Managers in the marketing area might develop goals for sales, sales growth, market share, and so forth. Operations managers establish goals for costs, quality, and inventory levels. Financial goals relate to return on investment and liquidity. Human resource goals relate to turnover, absenteeism, and employee development. Research and development goals might include innovations, new breakthroughs, and so forth. These same goals could, of course, result in product or geographic areas. Finally, in a slightly different vein, managers might set social goals such as contributions to the community through the United Way and so forth.

As shown in Exhibit 7.2, goals can also be established for each area across different levels. For example, within the marketing area of Lever Brothers there are goals for top managers (for example, to increase total sales by 10 percent), middle managers (increase sales of three different products by 8 percent, 10 percent, and 13 percent, respectively), and first-line managers (increase sales of one product within a certain territory by 6 percent).

Goals by Time Frame and Specificity   The last dimension along which we can classify goals is time frame and specificity. Most organizations establish long-range, intermediate, and short-

Exhibit 7.2   Kinds of Goals

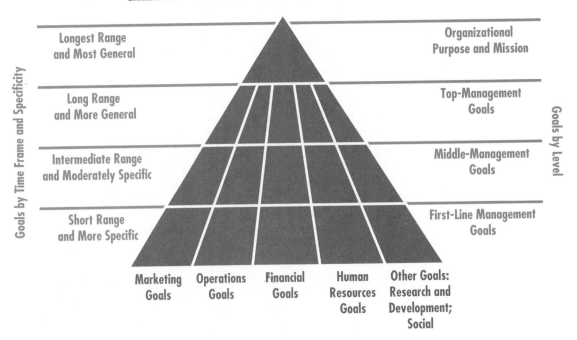

range goals. At Kodak long-range goals might extend ten years ahead; intermediate goals, for the next five years; and short-term goals, for the next year.

Specificity refers to the extent to which the goal is precise or general. A precise goal for Sears might be to increase sales in a certain store by 14 percent next year. Note that the goal specifies the unit, the target amount, and a time frame. As noted above, Citicorp has a goal of providing worldwide banking services. This is a very general goal in that it specifies no time frame and establishes only a broadly stated target.

As we can see in Exhibit 7.2, goals tend to take more time and be more general at the top of the organization, and they are usually shorter range and more specific at the lower levels of the organization.

Steps in Setting Goals

Goal setting is a six-part process resulting in a set of consistent and logical goals that permeate the entire organization.

Goal setting is a six-part process, as shown in Exhibit 7.3. The end result of this process should be a set of consistent and logical goals that permeate the entire organization.

The managers in the organization first scan the environment for opportunities and threats (step 1) and then assess organizational strengths and weaknesses (step 2). For a company such as Disney, opportunities might include new overseas markets for its theme parks and new ideas for movie projects, and threats could include other entertainment companies and movie producers. Disney's organizational strengths might involve marketing savvy in the theme park industry, a solid reputation, and surplus capital. Its weaknesses could be the firm's dependence on its theme parks for operating funds and an image that does not appeal to teen-agers and young adults.

The next step in goal setting is to establish general organizational goals that match strengths and weaknesses with opportunities and threats (step 3). Disney's managers might decide to open three new theme parks in other countries by the year 2020 and make fifteen new movies per year for the next ten years. This leads to steps 4 and 5, setting unit and subunit goals. The theme park unit might decide that one new park every ten years is the best target, and its subunits would then set specific goals for new rides and attractions, attendance levels at existing parks, and so forth. The last step (step 6) is for managers to monitor progress toward goal attainment at all levels of the organization. This progress subsequently affects all of the other steps as the cycle repeats itself. For example, a string of bad movies might cause Disney to halt film production until managers can straighten out the problems.[19]

Throughout the goal-setting process, managers can follow several guidelines to ensure effective organizational goal setting. First, managers should understand the purpose of goal setting so that they will set appropriate, realistic goals. Second, managers should state goals as specifically and briefly as possible so that they will be easily understood. A well-stated goal should include a time frame as well as both desired quantitative and qualitative results. Third, goals across areas and levels should be consistent so that managers are working together to achieve optimization (discussed below). Fourth, managers should communicate goals to others in the organization. Again, this helps to ensure that everyone in the organization is working together. And fifth, managers at all levels should take care to reward effective goal setting. By rewarding appropriate behavior, an organization reinforces what is important and helps to ensure that effective behavior will continue. (The Skill Builder at the end of this chapter will help you learn how to set appropriate goals.)

Managing Multiple Goals

One fact that should be apparent is that an organization does not have merely a single goal. Regardless of its size or diversity, any organization must pursue a variety of goals in order to survive. Suppose a plant manager in an organization sets a goal of reducing costs by 10 percent. One way to do this might be to buy cheaper materials and put more pressure on workers. Now suppose a

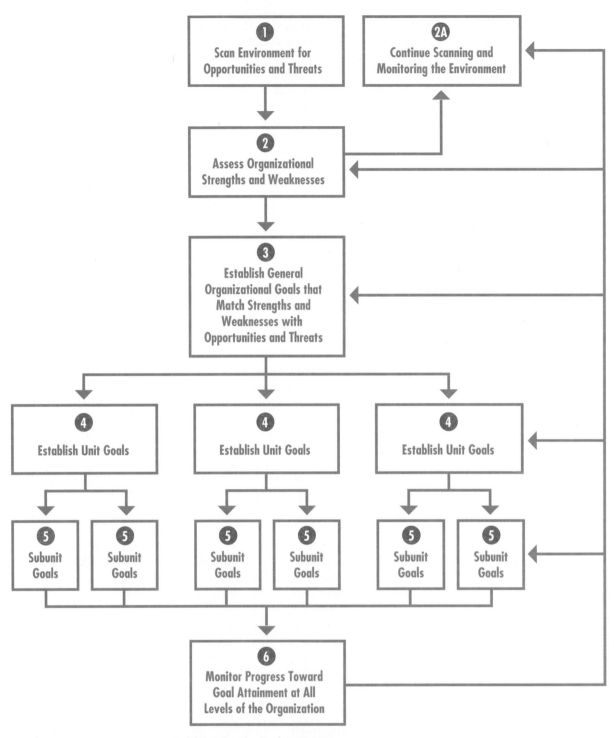

Exhibit 7.3   The Goal-Setting Process

marketing manager in that organization has decided to increase sales by 5 percent by promoting product quality, and a human resource manager in the same organization has decided to cut turnover by 20 percent. In all likelihood, the actions of the first manager will hurt the chance of the other two managers achieving their goals.

Goal optimization is the process of achieving an effective balance among the different goals of an organization.

This is where goal optimization becomes important. **Goal optimization** is the process of balancing and trading off among different goals for the sake of organizational effectiveness. Achieving the balance called for in goal optimization is a difficult task. The manager usually starts with a set of conflicting, disparate, and diverse goals. Using talent, insight, and experience, and with the appropriate level of flexibility and autonomy, the manager then arranges them into a unified, consistent, and congruent set of organizational goals. It takes skill, both conceptual and technical skill, to do this well.

The optimization process allows the organization to pursue a unified vision and helps managers maintain consistency in their actions. In the example mentioned earlier, a middle manager might help the marketing, plant, and human resource managers arrive at a new set of goals so that each can make progress in his or her area without getting in the way of the others. For the kinds of optimizing necessary at Intel, for instance, the chief executive officer and his vice presidents were no doubt involved in the decisions that had to be made.

Kinds of Planning

Given the fact that organizations naturally have a large number of goals, they also have a number of plans at any one time. Given the variety of areas for which these plans can be developed, it is not surprising that planning falls into different categories. This section identifies and discusses the three major kinds of planning activities that go on in organizations. As shown in Exhibit 7.4, these can be described in terms of different levels of scope and different time frames.

Strategic Planning

Strategic planning involves formulating the broad goals and plans of the organization.

Strategic planning formulates the broad goals and plans developed by top managers to guide the general directions of the organization.[20] As illustrated in Exhibit 7.4, strategic plans are very broad in scope and have an extended time frame. Strategic planning follows from the major goals of the organization and indicates what businesses the firm is in or intends to be in and what kind

Exhibit 7.4

Kinds of Planning Activities

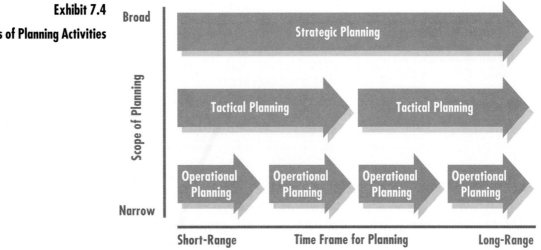

Walgreens developed its integrated network plan for customers from a base of retail stores distributed over a wide geographic area and computer-assisted mail service capability. The mail service facility is able to take advantage of expanding air service into and out of Orlando, Florida, because it is located across the street from Orlando's Wet 'N Wild water park. (Walgreen Company 1992 Annual Report.)

of company its top managers want it to be. The key components of a strategy, then, outline how resources will be deployed and how the organization will position itself within its environment.

PepsiCo provides an excellent example of a firm with a well-conceived and well-executed strategic plan. Specifically, managers at PepsiCo have decided that the company will compete in three general areas of the food industry: soft drinks, fast food restaurants, and packaged snack foods. Its soft drink business, led by Pepsi-Cola and Slice, is so well established that many people equate it with PepsiCo. The fast food business is also thriving, however, led by Pizza Hut, Taco Bell, and KFC. And finally, the snack food business, called Frito-Lay, has such successful products as Fritos Corn Chips, Lays Potato Chips, and Doritos.[21]

Tactical Planning

Tactical planning has a moderate scope and an intermediate time frame.

Whereas strategic planning has a broad scope and an extended time frame, tactical planning has a moderate scope and an intermediate time frame. **Tactical planning** tends to focus on people and action. That is, it is concerned with how to implement the strategic plans that have already been developed. It also deals with specific resources and time constraints. Tactical planning is more closely associated with middle management than with top management.

When PepsiCo first bought KFC, for example, managers developed several tactical plans to implement an aggressive growth strategy. First, managers noted that most of KFC's business was done at night, whereas McDonald's does most of its business at lunch. So tactical plans were developed to increase KFC's lunchtime business while retaining current levels of evening business. Second, PepsiCo managers planned to expand KFC's menu to include such things as roasted chicken and salad bars. Finally, PepsiCo also planned to offer home delivery in some markets.

Operational Planning

The third kind of planning is **operational planning,** which can take a variety of forms. In general, operational planning has the narrowest focus and the shortest time frame. Such plans are

Operational planning has a relatively narrow scope and a short time frame. Two basic kinds of operational plans are standing plans and single-use plans.

Standing plans are designed to handle recurring and relatively routine situations. Three forms are policies, standard operating procedures, and rules and regulations.

usually supervised by middle managers but executed by first-line managers. As illustrated in Table 7.1, there are two basic kinds of operational plans, standing plans and single-use plans.

Standing Plans

Plans that are developed to handle recurring and relatively routine situations are called **standing plans.** Basic kinds of standing plans include policies (the most general), standard operating procedures, and rules and regulations (the most specific).

Policies are general guidelines that govern relatively important actions within the organization. For example, PepsiCo might establish a policy that no individual owning a stake in a McDonald's franchise will be allowed to acquire a franchise for a Pizza Hut restaurant. Similarly, the company could also establish policies concerning the control of advertising campaigns, restaurant appearance, and sources of cooking supplies.

Standard operating procedures, or **SOPs,** are more specific guidelines for handling a series of recurring activities. The manager of a Taco Bell restaurant, for example, might have a set of SOPs for inventory management. Following the SOPs, the manager could set desired levels of ingredients for each menu item, determine appropriate reorder schedules and amounts, and line up local suppliers. Following a set of SOPs, then, is fairly mechanical.

Finally, **rules and regulations** are statements of how specific activities are to be performed. A rule for a KFC restaurant, for example, might dictate company policy regarding employee tardiness. Such a rule might state that if an employee is late to work three times in a two-month period, she or he is to be warned and told that the next incident may result in termination. The use of operational plans is indicated in *The Quality Challenge: IHOP Sizzles.*

Single-use plans are developed to handle events that only happen once. Two forms are programs and projects.

Single-Use Plans

The second major category of operational plans is **single-use plans,** plans set up to handle events that happen only once. The two types of single-use plans are programs and projects.

A **program** is a single-use plan for a large set of activities. The integration of KFC into the PepsiCo system is a good example of a program. This integration was a major operation involving thousands of people and hundreds of operating systems. In all likelihood, several task forces were created to handle the transition, and millions of dollars were spent to make KFC an integral part of the PepsiCo organization.

A **project** is similar to a program but usually has a narrower focus. A menu addition at KFC, for example, can be considered a project. Market research determines that a particular new product will sell well, a recipe is developed and tested, relevant information is relayed to restaurant managers, the product is advertised and becomes a part of the regular menu, and managers move on to new things.

Table 7.1

Operational Planning in Organizations

Kinds of operational planning	
Standing plans	**Single-use plans**
Policies	Programs
Standard operating procedures	Projects
Rules and regulations	

The Quality Challenge

IHOP Sizzles

Assuring that the food you eat and the service you receive in a restaurant is of high quality is no easy task. The industry has high turnover among its personnel, and many establishments obtain supplies from a variety of sources. However, despite the recession and lots of competition, the International House of Pancakes, IHOP, has been flourishing and providing consistently high quality.

A major way in which IHOP, with its central headquarters in Glendale, California, maintains quality is through careful planning and control of its franchising system. For instance, when a new facility opens, IHOP operates it for at least six months before contracting with a franchisee to assume operations. IHOP is thus able to establish the operating plans, standing operating procedures, rules, and regulations of the facility.

Those operating plans initially involve having an IHOP employee at the facility to train the franchisee. This training serves to focus the attention of everyone involved on the importance of maintaining high quality. IHOP generally owns or holds leases on its facilities so that, if a franchisee is unable to maintain the quality expected, he or she can be replaced.

IHOP's plans also help to assure quality by avoiding fads that could detract from maintaining taste and service on its main menu items. However, customer satisfaction is an important component of quality, so local favorites can be added to menus. Atlanta serves grits while Albuquerque serves *huevos rancheros* to keep customers happy and coming back.

This careful planning not only has assured high-quality food and service, but it has also assured good economic performance. During 1992 sales at existing stores rose an average of 7 percent, and overall sales were up approximately 12 percent. This performance was excellent, especially when one considers the poor state of the economy during 1992.[22] ■

Time Frames for Planning

Regardless of what kind of plan a manager is developing, it is important for him or her to recognize the role of the time factor. As noted earlier in this chapter, goals are often long range, intermediate, or short range in scope. Similarly, plans also focus on long-range, intermediate, and short-range time frames.

Long-Range Planning

Long-range planning spans several years to several decades.

Long-range planning covers a period that can be as short as several years to as long as several decades. Virtually all large companies have long-range plans. Suppose, for example, that Boeing is planning to introduce a new generation of airplanes in ten years. This is a long-range plan. Given this plan, Boeing's managers can begin to develop other pertinent long-range plans. They may need to find a site for a new factory in six years so that the plant can be operational in eight years. They must arrange financing for the purchase of plant materials, construction costs, and raw materials for the new planes. Because they will need to be ready to take over operations at the plant in eight years, after four years the managers might want to identify who will be in charge and subsequently train those people.

Long-range plans are primarily associated with activities such as major expansions of products or facilities, development of top managers, large issues of new stocks and bonds, and the installation of new manufacturing systems. Top managers are responsible for long-range planning in most organizations. For example, Michael D. Eisner, CEO of Disney, recently said, "I think in terms of decades. The nineties are EuroDisneyland. I've already figured out what we can do for 1997, and I've got a thing set for 2005."[23]

Long-range planning is particularly important when the product takes years of preparation for the market. Pine trees are just such a product. Helped through the first stages of growth by being protected in a nursery like this state forest nursery in Davis, California, young pine trees are then planted to grow to maturity. (Mark E. Gibson.)

Intermediate Planning

Intermediate planning focuses on a time horizon of from one to five years.

Intermediate planning generally involves a time perspective of between one and five years. Because of the uncertainties associated with long-range plans, intermediate plans are the primary concern of most organizations. Accordingly, they are usually developed by top managers working in conjunction with middle managers.

Intermediate plans are often seen as building blocks in the pursuit of long-range plans. If Dell Computer has a long-range plan to have ten major computer systems available for sale in ten years, its managers might begin by developing an intermediate plan to get four new systems under way within the next three years. At the end of three years, they would assess the situation and devise a new intermediate plan for the next time period to assure achievement of the long-range plan.

Short-Range Planning

Short-range planning covers a period of less than one year.

Finally, **short-range planning** covers time periods of one year or less. These plans focus on day-to-day activities and provide a concrete base for evaluating progress toward the achievement of intermediate and long-range plans. To use the Dell example, a short-range plan might be to get two new projects under way within the next year. The managers can thus focus on a specific set of activities (getting two new products under development) that need to be accomplished within the time frame (one year). One danger to short-range planning is that it becomes separated from longer-term planning and leads to a dysfunctional overemphasis on short-term results.[24]

Integrating Time Frames

We have seen that intermediate plans should build toward the pursuit of long-range plans, but all three time frames ideally should be integrated. A company might develop a long-range plan spanning ten years, an intermediate plan for five years, and a short-range plan for one year. Conceptually, at least, the short-range plan should be identical to the first year of the intermediate plan, which in turn should correspond to the first five years of the long-range plan.

At the end of one year, the short-range plan may or may not have been fulfilled, of course, so managers must develop a new short-range plan and modify the intermediate and long-range plans as appropriate. Suppose, for example, that Dr Pepper has developed a short-range plan to increase total sales by 5 percent and a long-range plan to increase sales by 25 percent. At the end of the first year, however, sales have increased by only 2 percent. Dr Pepper's managers might then revise their plans, i.e., drop the long-range plan down to 22 percent. This process of monitoring and adjusting plans relates to another important part of the process, contingency planning.

Contingency Planning

Contingency planning is the part of the planning process in which managers identify alternative courses of action that the organization might follow if various conditions arise.[25] Again, this is something that most companies do.

The Nature of Contingency Planning

Contingency planning is identifying alternative courses of action that might be followed if various conditions arise.

The general nature of contingency planning follows the process shown in Exhibit 7.5. As illustrated, managers develop an initial plan (A) that specifies possible contingency events that might dictate modification of the original plan. The organization then monitors ongoing activities so that it will know if and when the events occur. Depending on the nature of the contingencies, the organization might continue its original plan (A), change to a contingency plan (B), or change to another contingency plan (C).[26]

Contingency Events

Obviously, the identification of contingency events is a critical part of contingency planning. If the events are not properly identified, or if their relevant indicators are poorly understood, the entire process of contingency planning can fall apart.[27]

In general, critical contingency events relate either to the extent to which the ongoing plan is being accomplished or to environmental events that might change things in the future. For example, Burger King is in the midst of a major expansion program in the United States and Europe. Its managers might break down their intermediate plan into a series of five short-range plans,

Exhibit 7.5

Contingency Planning

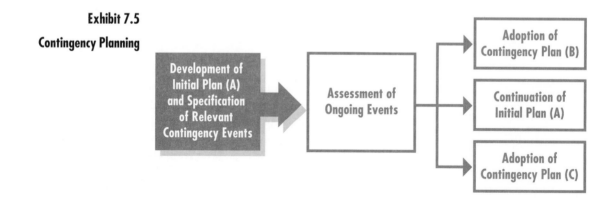

The Environment of Management

Gatorade Great!

Gatorade, the superstar of the sports-drink world, is one of the top performing brands of Chicago-based Quaker Oats. Along with Quaker Oats, Aunt Jemima, the "Roni" products (Rice-a-Roni and Noodle-Roni), and Ken-L-Ration and Gaines pet foods, Gatorade has helped to make Quaker Oats a dominant firm in packaged foods.

Gatorade was developed in 1965 by the University of Florida to help its football team, the Gators, avoid dehydration. Its market potential was quickly seen, and Stokely-Van Camp bought it in 1967. When Quaker acquired Gatorade from Stokely-Van Camp Inc. in 1983, Quaker developed an intense marketing plan for the product. That plan effectively expanded the Gatorade market nationally and carved out a strong market niche—sports drinks—by aggressively promoting it at amateur and professional sporting events. The National Football League, the National Basketball Association, and major league baseball all adopted Gatorade as an "official" drink endorsed by those organizations. The advertising budget was increased dramatically, especially to appeal to physical activity enthusiasts who engage in some form of exercise at least once a week. The impact of the plan was clear. Sales of Gatorade more than doubled in just the first three years after the acquisition. Clearly the marketing plan worked.

This very success, however, altered the competitive environment. Numerous smaller companies tried to get in on the market. Brands such as 10K, UltraFuel, PowerBurst, Recharge, and Exceed were introduced, although none seemed to make much of an impact. The double-digit growth of Gatorade sales, however, caught the attention of the soft-drink industry, and Coke and Pepsi entered the market in the mid-1980s. Coke's initial foray, Max, failed, but it introduced another product, PowerAde, in 1990 with more success. Pepsi approached the market cautiously through regional test marketing of Mountain Dew Sport and seemed to make some headway, too.

This intense competition caused Quaker to respond. That response included an increased promotional effort and new product development. The market impact of this increased competition could be to increase the size of the total market so that, even if Gatorade were to lose some market share, it could continue to be a huge financial success for Quaker.[28] ■

each of which calls for one hundred new U.S. restaurants and fifty new European restaurants at the end of each calendar year. One contingency event would then be the extent to which the short-range plans are being realized. If there are ninety-six new U.S. restaurants and fifty-one new European restaurants at the end of the first year, the managers may conclude that things are going well. In contrast, sixty new U.S. and fifteen new European restaurants would indicate a problem. The managers' contingency plans might call for a revision of the original plan or increased efforts to catch up in the second year as well as efforts to determine why the plan was not met.

The other kind of contingency event, as noted above, relates to the environment. Burger King's managers might have based their European expansion plans on the assumption that McDonald's and Wendy's would continue to expand at current rates. If McDonald's unexpectedly begins to double its rate of European expansion, Burger King might be forced to change its own plans. Changes in the competitive environment are clearly being felt in the sports-drink market, as discussed in *The Environment of Management: Gatorade Great!*

Clearly, contingency planning is an important part of any organization's overall planning process. Contingency planning should never be neglected but should instead be an integral part of ongoing planning activities. In addition, there are other things managers should do to facilitate effective planning. The next section addresses some of these.

Managing the Planning Process

Roadblocks to Effective Planning

As we have seen several times already, planning is a vital part of all managerial jobs and requires considerable skill. Two additional dimensions of planning, understanding the roadblocks to effective planning and knowing how these roadblocks can be avoided, are critical if planning is to be carried out properly.

What can go wrong when managers set out to develop plans? In truth, any number of factors or roadblocks can disrupt effective planning.[29] Let us look at Table 7.2 and consider five of the most common ones.

The Environment   In Chapters 3 through 6 we looked at the importance of the environment in goal setting and planning. Most organizations operate in environments that are both complex and dynamic. That is, managers must contend with a great many environmental forces and dimensions (complexity) and with the fact that these forces and dimensions change rapidly (dynamism). In combination, these factors make it harder to develop effective plans. For example, General Electric recently plunged into factory automation. Demand dropped, other automation systems turned out to be more advanced than GE's, and soaring costs drove prices up. Each of these factors resulted from environmental complexity and dynamism. Consequently, GE's original plans for sales and income from automation were not realized.[30]

Resistance to Change   Another factor that can impede effective planning is resistance to change. By its very nature, planning involves change. Fear of the unknown, preference for the status quo, and economic insecurity can combine to cause managers to resist change and, as a result, to avoid planning that might begin that change. General Electric has the goal that all of the company's businesses should be number one or two in their respective industries. A GE manager who had little hope that his or her business would be able to meet this standard might recognize that planning could undermine the managerial role in the company and might therefore avoid planning activities.

Situational Constraints   Similarly, various situational constraints can hinder effective planning. Suppose that Westinghouse would like to undertake a full-scale expansion program, but its human resource managers learn that the company does not have enough managerial talent to support expansion at the desired rate. As a consequence, the rate of expansion has to be scaled back to fit the availability of managers. Other constraints that can affect planning include labor unions

Table 7.2
Roadblocks to Effective Planning

Roadblocks
1. The environment might be so complex and/or changing that managers fail to plan effectively.
2. Managers might resist change for a variety of reasons and avoid planning that might lead to change.
3. Effective planning might be constrained by labor contracts, government regulations, or scarce resources.
4. Managers might not plan effectively because the plans are developed from poor or inappropriate goals.
5. Lack of time and/or money can limit managers' ability to plan effectively.

and contracts, government regulations, a scarcity of raw materials, and a shortage of operating funds.

Poor Goal Setting   Poor goal setting is a significant roadblock to effective planning. Since goal setting is the first step in the planning process, any of the things that might impede proper goal setting by definition also hinder effective planning. The ability to develop specific, measurable, achievable, realistic, and temporal goals is an important technical skill all managers must possess. The Skill Builder in this chapter helps develop this skill through a series of short exercises.

Time and Expense   Finally, effective planning can be limited by the time and expense involved. Like most things worth doing, planning takes a considerable amount of time. Because of the pressures that affect them, most managers occasionally find it difficult to undertake planning activities. Similarly, acquiring the necessary information to develop effective plans can cost money. Managers at Polaroid who want to know about future trends in amateur photography, for instance, might need to conduct extensive market research or buy the information from private market research firms. Faced with such expenses, they may be tempted to take short cuts or evade the issue altogether.

Avoiding the Roadblocks

Fortunately for managers, there are some useful guidelines that can help them avoid these roadblocks. Six of the most basic ones are summarized in Table 7.3.

Start at the Top   For planning to be effective, it must start at the top. Top managers must set the goals and strategies that lower-level managers will follow. Andrew Grove, CEO of Intel, leads each of his company's planning groups. This leadership conveys a strong and clear message to everyone that planning is important.

Recognize the Limits   Managers must also recognize that no planning system is perfect. Because of its very nature, planning has limits and cannot be done with absolute precision. Coca-Cola spent years planning to introduce a new formula (New Coke) in 1985 to replace its flagship product (Classic Coke). Even though the company did everything "by the book," the change was disastrous and Classic Coke was reintroduced within a short time.

Communicate   Communication, especially vertical communication within the organizational hierarchy, can also facilitate effective planning. If top managers know what middle and first-line

Table 7.3

Avoiding the Roadblocks to Effective Planning

Improving planning effectiveness
1. Planning should start at and be led by the top level of an organization.
2. Managers should recognize the limits and uncertainties of planning.
3. Managers should communicate what they are doing to other levels in the organization.
4. Managers should actively participate in planning.
5. Managers should make sure that long-range, intermediate, and short-range plans are well integrated.
6. Managers should develop contingency plans.

managers are doing, they can continue their own planning activities better. At Intel, great efforts are made to ensure that every manager who might potentially be affected by a decision or plan is made aware of it.

Participate   In similar fashion, participation aids effective planning. Managers who are fully involved in planning are more likely to know what is going on, to understand their own place in the organization, and, consequently, to be motivated to contribute. One of the keys to Ford's recent success has been increased participation by managers in all aspects of planning.

Integrate   We have already noted that long-range, intermediate, and short-range plans must be properly integrated. The better these plans are integrated, the more effective the organization's overall planning system will be. Toyota has always done a good job of integrating the various time frames across which it plans. Short-term model changes, for example, almost always mesh nicely with longer-term new model introductions.

Develop Contingency Plans   The final technique for enhancing planning is to develop contingency plans. As we have discussed, contingency plans are alternative actions that a company might follow if conditions change. If competitors such as Honda and Nissan change their approach to marketing, for example, Toyota will no doubt have several different contingency plans from which to choose.

Recent years have seen a revolution in information technology, based largely on developments in personal computing. That revolution has added a powerful tool to every manager's kit for use in planning. It has also increased the need for having technical skills in the computer area. Tomorrow's managers will be even better equipped to handle the complex and dynamic nature of the planning process although the demand for needed skills will also be greater for those managers. Tools and techniques of use in planning are covered in more detail in Chapter 9.

Chapter Summary

A plan is a blueprint or framework used to describe how an organization expects to achieve its goals. Planning is the process of developing plans or of determining how best to approach a particular goal. Because it is so important, every manager must be involved in the planning process.

A goal is a desired state or condition that an organization wants to achieve. Goals may be differentiated by level of management, area, and time frame and specificity. The steps in the goal-setting process are (1) to scan the environment for opportunities and threats, (2) to assess organizational strengths and weaknesses, (3) to establish general organizational goals, (4) to establish unit and (5) subunit goals, and (6) to monitor progress toward goal attainment and provide feedback as the cycle repeats. Goal optimization is the process of balancing and trading off among different goals for the sake of organizational effectiveness.

The three major kinds of plans are strategic, tactical, and operational. Strategic plans are the broad, long-term plans developed by top managers to guide the general directions of the organization. Tactical plans are designed to implement strategic plans and hence have a moderate scope and intermediate time frame. Operational plans have the narrowest focus and the shortest time frame and are executed by first-line managers.

The three major time frames for planning are long-range, intermediate, and short-range planning. Long-range planning covers a period that can be as short as several years or as long as several decades. Intermediate planning generally takes a time perspective of about one to five years. Short-range planning covers time periods of one year or less and focuses on day-to-day activities, thus providing a basis for evaluating progress toward the achievement of intermediate and long-range plans. Each of these time frames should be integrated with the others to ensure smooth functioning of the organization.

Contingency planning is the part of the planning process that identifies alternative courses of action that an organization might follow if various different conditions arise. Critical contingency events relate either to the extent to which the ongoing plan is being accomplished or to environmental events that might change things in the future.

Roadblocks to an effective planning include the environment, resistance to change, situational constraints, poor goal setting, and the time and expense of planning. Guidelines for avoiding these roadblocks include starting at the top, recognizing the limits to planning, communicating, participating, integrating, and developing contingency plans.

The Manager's Vocabulary

plan	strategic planning	program
planning	tactical planning	project
goal	operational planning	long-range planning
purpose	standing plans	intermediate planning
mission	policies	short-range planning
specificity	standard operating procedures (SOPs)	contingency planning
goal setting	rules and regulations	
goal optimization	single-use plans	

Review Questions

1. What are the six steps in the organizational goal-setting process?
2. Identify and describe the three basic kinds of planning done by most organizations.
3. How should organizations integrate plans that span different periods of time?
4. What are contingency plans? How are they developed?
5. Identify several roadblocks to effective planning. Suggest ways around these roadblocks.

Analysis Questions

1. Do you think an organization could function effectively without planning? Why or why not?
2. What kinds of goals would a not-for-profit organization such as your college or university have? What might be the similarities and differences between those goals and the goals of a business operating for a profit? Why?
3. If all managers are supposed to plan, why should planning start at the top? Could it start at the bottom? How?
4. Describe a contingency plan you once developed. How closely did the steps you followed coincide with those outlined in this chapter?
5. Why might different kinds of organizations have different concepts of what long-range planning means?

Self-Assessment

Job Goals Questionnaire

Introduction This chapter spent considerable time talking about different types of goals. In addition, the chapter explains how goals are developed. This self-assessment examines how goals affect a jobholder's attitude about the job.

Instructions The following statements refer to a job you currently hold or have held. Read each statement and then select a response from the scale below that best describes your view.

Scale: Almost Never   1   2   3   4   5   Almost Always

_____ 1. I understand exactly what I am supposed to do on my job.

_____ 2. I have specific, clear goals to aim for on my job.

_____ 3. The goals I have on this job are challenging.

_____ 4. I understand how my performance is measured on this job.

_____ 5. I have deadlines for accomplishing my goals on this job.

_____ 6. If I have more than one goal to accomplish, I know which ones are most important and which are least important.

_____ 7. My goals require my full effort.

_____ 8. My superior tells me the reasons for giving me the goals I have.

_____ 9. My superior is supportive with respect to encouraging me to reach my goals.

_____ 10. My superior lets me participate in the setting of my goal.

_____ 11. My superior lets me have some say in deciding how I will go about implementing my goals.

_____ 12. If I reach my goals, I know that my superior will be pleased.

_____ 13. I get credit and recognition when I attain my goals.

_____ 14. Trying for goals makes my job more fun than it would be without goals.

_____ 15. I feel proud when I get feedback indicating that I have reached my goals.

_____ 16. The other people I work with encourage me to attain my goals.

_____ 17. I sometimes compete with my co-workers to see who can do the best job in reaching their goals.

_____ 18. If I reach my goals, my job security will be improved.

_____ 19. If I reach my goals, my chances for a pay raise are increased.

_____ 20. If I reach my goals, my chances for a promotion are increased.

For interpretation, turn to the back of the book.

Skill Builder

You and Goal Setting

Purpose The first step in planning is setting goals. This is a critical skill required of all managers. This skill builder focuses on the _scientific management model._ It will help you develop the _director role_ of the scientific management model. One of the skills of the director is the ability to set goals.

Introduction The purpose of this exercise is to provide an opportunity to determine whether you understand how to write goal statements, set goals that are challenging but realistic, and select appropriate measures of results. The exercise has three parts: (1) writing goal statements, (2) setting goal levels, and (3) selecting indicators.

Instructions

Part I   Goal Statements
Read each goal statement, determine what is wrong with it, and write a better one.

Goal 1—Complete the required training of new employees as soon as possible.

_____

_____

Goal 2—Reduce the error rate in the department to an acceptable level by the end of the year.

_____

_____

Goal 3—Eliminate all customer complaints by summer.

_____

_____

Goal 4—Reduce unit cost on the new product to $80 by implementing new work procedures immediately.

_____

_____

Part II   Goal Difficulty

For each goal, consider the background information and determine whether the goal is easy (E), challenging (C), or unrealistic (U). Put the appropriate letter code on the line provided next to the goal to indicate your evaluation of goal difficulty. Note that deadlines are worded in a way to indicate how much time is available to implement the goal.

_____ 1. Goal: Reduce average daily error rate to 5 percent by the end of next quarter.

The error rate for the department was 7 percent during the last quarter and 8% the quarter before last. The error rate last quarter for three similar departments was 5 percent, 4 percent, and 6 percent, respectively.

Notes: _____

_____

_____ 2. Goal: Attain a production level of 75 units/day for the next two quarters.

The production output for a manufacturing plant was 70 units/day for the quarter just ended. Production for the three previous quarters was 80, 75, and 85 units/day. The company is in a stable industry without major changes in products or technology.

Notes: _____

_____

_____ 3. Goal: Increase the number of safety inspections by 25 percent next year.

The budget does not allow for any increase in inspection personnel for next year. The inspectors in the department are currently making approximately 10 percent more safety inspections than last year or the year before.

Notes: _____

_____

_____ 4. Goal: Attain a productivity index score of 75 for the next year.

For the year just ended, a composite productivity index for the data-processing department was 60 on a scale of zero to 100. The new computer system to be installed next month is expected to increase productivity by approximately 25 percent.

Notes: _____

_____ 5. Goal: Reduce absenteeism in the department to 5 percent by the next quarter.

The rate of absenteeism for the department last year was 10 percent. The average rate of absenteeism was 6 percent and 5 percent for two other operating departments in the company with similar employees and type of work.

Notes: _____

_____

_____ 6. Goal: Reduce unit cost to $85 by the end of the coming year.

Unit cost for output in a production department was $100 for the year just ended. In the previous three years it was $95, $90, and $92. Unit cost for another production department in the company that makes the same product and has comparable employees was $80 last year.

Notes: _____

_____

Part III   Selecting Relevant Indicators

For each results area, determine which three indicators are likely to provide the most relevant and accurate measure of a manager's performance. Place a check on the line next to your three choices. Briefly explain why each of the three rejected choices is not as relevant or accurate.

1. Maintain efficient operation of a service center (such as equipment repair, consulting services, or information gathering services).

_____ a. Monthly operating cost of the service program.

_____ b. Number of clients per month given service.

_____ c. Average cost per client of service provided.

_____ d. Operating costs as a percentage of budgeted costs.

_____ e. Average employee-hours/client required to provide service.

_____ f. Monthly cost of salaries for service personnel.

_____

_____

_____

(con't. on page 170)

2. Design and conduct effective training programs (personnel department or training center).

_____ a. Number of training hours conducted per month.

_____ b. Number of employees trained to required levels of proficiency.

_____ c. Average cost per trainee of training provided.

_____ d. Ratings by trainees at end of training on how much they learned.

_____ e. Ratings by trainees at end of training on how much they enjoyed it.

_____ f. Improvement in knowledge determined by comparing scores on a test given before and after training.

_____

_____

_____

3. Maintain effective interpersonal relations with subordinates.

_____ a. Turnover among subordinates.

_____ b. Ratings of a manager's interpersonal skills made by subordinates.

_____ c. Number of subordinate grievances and complaints about the manager.

_____ d. Subordinate productivity.

_____ e. Ratings by subordinates of satisfaction with the manager.

_____ f. Monthly quality index for subordinate performance.

_____

_____

_____

4. Process applicant requests for social services and notify applicants promptly (government agency or welfare office, or volunteer social service organization).

_____ a. Average response time from receipt of application to response.

_____ b. Number of applicant complaints about delays.

_____ c. Average number of visits to center required before decision is made.

_____ d. Number of applicants processed each month.

_____ e. Average employee-hours required to process an application.

_____ f. Percentage of applicants processed within a specified number of days.

_____

_____

_____

Source: Gary A. Yukl, _Leadership in Organizations_ © 1981, p. 27. Reprinted by permission of Prentice Hall, Inc., Englewood Cliffs, New Jersey.

CONCLUDING CASES

7.1 VISA

In 1958 Bank of America began to issue credit cards called the BankAmericard. Other banks began to issue the card too. In 1966 Banc One Corp. began to issue that card, followed by Citicorp in the 1970s. In 1977 the name was changed to the VISA card, and Merrill Lynch joined the banks by issuing VISA cards too. By the 1990s, VISA was the number one credit card in the United States, with approximately 120 million cardholders, far in front of MasterCard, which was second with approximately 90 million cardholders. So strong had VISA become that, in 1992, its CEO, H. Robert Heller, wondered if it might be in danger of becoming a monopoly.

Many people do not realize that VISA is actually a franchis-ing organization so that many different banks (and now nonbanks as well) offer VISA cards. Citibank, Chase Manhattan, and Bank of America are among the largest bank issuers of VISA cards. The VISA organization must have plans with which to deal with the numerous institutions that issue its cards and with its fierce competitors. The unique way in which the credit field has come to operate presents both advantages and disadvantages to VISA.

In 1991, for instance, Sears acquired a failed Utah savings firm, MountainWest Savings & Loan, which issued VISA cards. Because Sears is the parent company of the third-largest card, Discover Credit Corp., VISA refused to issue any more VISA cards through MountainWest. Sears got a federal judge to rule that VISA had to issue new cards, but the United States Justice Department began to study the situation because of the unique nature of the relationships involved. Many banks began to worry that Sears would move to convert all of its Discover cards into VISA cards and, hence, drastically alter the nature of the competitive environment in the credit field. Clearly such a move would be something that VISA would need to plan for as well.

Meanwhile AT&T got into the act and began issuing cards through its Universal group. It quickly became a major force in the credit card industry, but it also spurred the interest of other organizations. Soon General Motors, Ford, Prudential, and John Hancock, among others, began issuing credit cards. The banks claim that because these organizations do not have to meet the federal capital requirements that the banks do, it represents unfair competition for them to be able to issue cards. While that is being argued, more nonbanks enter the field. As a result, the credit card industry has become one of the more competitive and volatile businesses around.

This increased competition has forced VISA to develop new strategic plans for expansion. Those strategic plans are currently being acted on and include such things as the introduction of new products like debit and cobranded cards.[31]

Discussion Questions

1. What might VISA's goals be? Why?
2. What different kinds of planning can you identify at VISA? Give specific examples.
3. What time frames for planning has VISA used? What time frame should it be using to cope with the increasing competition? Why?
4. Should VISA engage in contingency planning? Why or why not?

7.2   Subaru of America, Inc.

Subarus are made by Fuji Heavy Industries of Japan. They have long enjoyed a reputation as sturdy, rugged automobiles and have been the official cars of the U.S. Olympic ski teams since 1976. Consistent with its tough reputation, about half of the Subarus sold in the United States are four-wheel-drive vehicles. The bulk of U.S. sales have been in New England and California and have been handled since 1968 through Subaru of America, Inc., headquartered in Cherry Hill, New Jersey.

Despite its favorable reputation and some success, however, Subaru sales began falling throughout the 1980s. Subaru began making plans to rectify that situation. In 1989 Subaru-Isuzu Automotive was formed and opened a production plant in Lafayette, Indiana. Subaru sedans and Isuzu trucks are produced on the same assembly line, providing both organizations with economies otherwise not attainable, given their relatively low sales volumes in the United States.

The rising value of the yen made it difficult to continue to compete as effectively in the United States. Further, other four-wheel-drive vehicles began to become more popular, including the Jeep Cherokee and the Ford Explorer. Nissan Motor Company quietly took control of Fuji Heavy Industries in 1990. That action was largely nonfinancial and was done with the approval of Fuji's bank, the Industrial Bank of Japan Ltd., but nevertheless was aimed at providing some much-needed marketing and financial assistance to Subaru.

Subaru developed plans to try to take its solid reputation at the low end of the car market and move it upward. It revitalized its line of compacts and introduced its Legacy sedans and wagons in the mid-priced market. Those efforts met with some success even though those moves put Subaru in an even more competitive confrontation with Honda and Toyota. Then, in 1991, it introduced a more expensive sports car, the SVX, to try to get into the high-margin sporty market. Though the SVX received high praise from many automotive analysts and car experts, an advertising campaign led to strong objections from highway safety promoters. They felt that the advertising was suggesting illegal and dangerous driving.

Much of Subaru's planning has seemed to be reactive, adjusting to competition and changing consumer preferences, rather than proactive, innovating to lead the market and anticipate consumer wants. Nevertheless, Subaru continues to be a force in the automotive world.[32]

Discussion Questions

1. What might Subaru's goals be? What do you think they should be? Why?
2. What different kinds of planning can you identify at Subaru? Does any kind seem missing? Give specific examples.
3. What strengths and weaknesses seem to exist for Subaru? How could better managerial planning help the company? Why?
4. What should Subaru do now?

CHAPTER

8

Strategy and Strategic Planning

Learning Objectives

After studying this chapter you should be able to

· Describe the nature of strategic planning, including the components and levels of strategy and strategy formulation and implementation.

· Explain the environmental forces important to strategic planning and how managers position their organizations within those forces.

· Identify major approaches to corporate strategy.

· Identify major approaches to business strategy.

· Identify the major functional strategies developed by most organizations.

· Describe the process of strategy implementation.

Tyco Industries Inc., the Mt. Laurel, New Jersey, toy company, was losing money in 1973 when it hired Richard E. Grey to take charge. Through cost cutting and inventory control, he was able to turn it around in eighteen months. Tyco's parent company, Sara Lee, sold it in 1981, and a ten-year battle for control ensued. During most of that time, Tyco was not a particularly notable toymaker; it ranked only twenty-second in its industry in 1986. About that time, however, Grey began to assert his control over the firm.

Grey developed a sound strategy for Tyco with which to cope with the increasingly global toy market. His strategy called for Tyco to broaden its line, make careful acquisitions, and expand overseas. Tyco bought New-Master Ideal Group, Inc., in 1989 and Playtime Products, Inc. in 1990. In 1992 Tyco bought New York–based Illco Toy Co. U.S.A. to move into the preschool market since Illco held licenses for several Sesame Street characters. That same year it also bought Universal Matchbox Group Ltd. Though the Matchbox purchase was costly, it provided Tyco with a much-needed international distribution network. That network enabled Tyco to expand into fast-growing overseas markets.

In 1992 it had the hottest toy on the market with its Incredible Crash Dummies. It launched Catechic, a Trivial Pursuit board game with questions based on religion, in an effort to develop a market niche. As a result, by the end of 1992, Tyco reached $600 million in sales and had become the third-largest U.S. toymaker behind Mattel and Hasbro.[1] ■

By most objective indicators, Tyco's strategy has enabled it to be a very effective organization. And even though the complexity of its environment has changed, Tyco executives are convinced that they can still manage the firm successfully. Because of changing environmental conditions, it is difficult to always make exactly the right decisions and do exactly the right things. But managers must still make a concerted effort to understand their environment and take appropriate action. The activities involved in doing these things are a part of strategy and strategic planning.

This chapter is about the various elements of strategy and strategic planning. First it describes the nature of strategic planning. It then focuses on environmental analysis and discusses corporate, business, and functional strategies. The chapter concludes with a description of strategy implementation.

The Nature of Strategic Planning

In Chapter 7 we learned that strategic plans are the broad plans developed by top management to guide the general direction of the organization. To expand on that definition and to describe the nature of strategic planning better, we need to identify the components of strategic planning, draw a distinction between strategy formulation and strategy implementation, and note the levels of strategy.

The Components of Strategy

Strategy has four basic components: scope, resource deployment, competitive advantage, and synergy.

In general, strategy can be thought of as having four basic components: scope, resource deployment, competitive advantage, and synergy.[2]

The **scope** of strategy specifies the position the firm wants to have in relation to its environment. More specifically, it details the markets or industries in which the firm wants to compete.[3] For example, the scope of Ford's strategy specifies that the company wants to produce and sell automobiles around the world, whereas Timex's specifies that it wants to produce and market low-priced watches.

Resource deployment indicates how the organization intends to allocate resources.[4] General Electric wants each of its businesses to be either number one or number two in its industry. This suggests that GE might sell a business that is number five and losing ground, allocate enough resources to a business firmly entrenched as number one for it to stay there, and provide new resources to a business that is number three and gaining ground on number two.

Competitive advantage is the specification of what advantage or advantages the firm holds relative to its competitors. Levi's competitive advantages include its well-known name and dominance of the jeans market. Likewise, Kodak used its strengths in name recognition and distribution channels to introduce a new line of batteries.

Synergy is the extent to which various businesses within the firm can expect to draw from one another. Disney, for example, realizes considerable synergy from its theme parks, movies, and merchandising businesses. Families familiar with Disney characters from movies and books are motivated to visit the theme parks. After an enjoyable experience, they are subsequently motivated to buy merchandise and see future movies.

Strategy Formulation and Implementation

Another important element of strategic planning is the distinction between **strategy formulation** and **strategy implementation**.[5] Actually, the words themselves convey the meaning of the two terms. Formulation is the set of processes involved in creating or developing strategic plans. Implementation is the set of processes involved in executing them, or putting them into effect.[6] Most of our attention in this chapter is directed to formulation issues, although the end of the chapter touches on implementation.

The Levels of Strategy

The three general levels of strategy are ***corporate, business,*** *and* ***functional.***

A final important perspective to understanding the nature of strategic planning is the levels of strategy. As indicated in Exhibit 8.1, there are three such levels: corporate, business, and functional.

Strategic planning has clearly been valuable to Chrysler. Robert Eaton, Lee Iacocca, and Robert Lutz comprised the top executive team involved in the strategies that turned the organization around. Its newly designed cars (a model is shown here at Chrysler's technical center) helped it to be profitable in 1992 when other U.S. automakers were not. (James Schnepf.)

As Woolworth's principal line of business fell into hard times, it changed its corporate strategy. Instead of pursuing mass merchandising, Woolworth moved to develop niche chains in specialty areas. These could be started and stopped relatively quickly to keep abreast of consumer tastes. Foot Locker is among the more successful of those chains. (Doug Knutson.)

The **corporate strategy** charts the course for the entire organization and attempts to answer the question What businesses should we be in? Kmart has developed a corporate strategy that calls for continued growth and emphasis on volume retailing.

A **business strategy** is charted for each individual business within a company. Managers at Kmart have set strategies for its discount store division, its bookstore division, and its home improvement store division. Although there may be some similarities in business strategies across divisions, there are also clear differences.

Similarly, **functional strategies** are developed to correspond to each of the basic functional areas within the organization. As indicated in Exhibit 8.1, common functional strategies include marketing, financial, and production strategies, as well as human resources, organiza-

Exhibit 8.1

Levels of Strategy

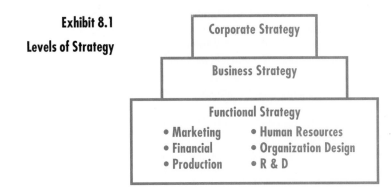

Having a functional strategy that supports research and development has proven to be a key to success for many organizations. Tyco is no exception. It spends considerable time and resources to assure that potential users will enjoy their products. The Crash Dummies went on numerous test rides before reaching the marketplace. (Jodi Buren.)

tion design, and R&D. Kmart has a marketing strategy of low-cost, volume retailing, a financial strategy that calls for low debt, and a human resource strategy that emphasizes hiring college graduates as management trainees.

Clearly, each level of strategy is important. If any level is neglected, the entire organization can and will suffer. We shall therefore consider each one in more detail, but first we will look at another important dimension of strategic planning, environmental analysis.

Environmental SWOT Analysis

The starting point in strategic planning is developing a thorough understanding of the organization's environment. Many of the key issues involved here are discussed in Chapters 3 through 6. However, from a strategic management perspective, managers need to think in terms of how to balance the organization's position in terms of its strengths and weaknesses [**SW**ot] against basic environmental forces that present opportunities and threats [sw**OT**] to the firm. At the end of this chapter, the Skill Builder provides you with an opportunity to work with the SWOT analysis technique. It provides you with a conceptual skill for modeling your organization and the environmental forces.

Organizational Position — Strengths and Weaknesses

Strengths   **Organizational strengths** are those aspects of the organization that let the organization compete effectively.[7] Different strengths call for different strategies.[8] For instance, Intel has tremendous strengths as an innovative computer chip manufacturer, but those strengths might not support a strategic move into the health care industry. It is important for an organization to know which of its strengths are common to similar organizations and which are distinctive. The distinctive strengths are more important to shaping distinct strategies for the organization.

In evaluating strengths, one approach is to use the VRIO framework.[9] The **VRIO framework** consists of asking for each strength identified if it is valuable, rare, difficult to imitate, and exploitable. The organization would then use the information to help in establishing its strategic plan.

Weaknesses **Organizational weaknesses** are those aspects of the organization that prevent or deter it from competing effectively. Weaknesses can either be overcome through investing in whatever resources are necessary, or they can be allowed to exist with corresponding changes in the mission and strategy of the organization. ConAgra's acquisition of Beatrice was an investment of resources to overcome a weakness in its grocery-store distribution system.[10] The March of Dimes, on the other hand, changed its mission from finding a cure for polio, which happened in the 1950s, to supporting research on birth defects because the weakness, a nonexistent target, could not be overcome.[11]

Environmental Forces— Opportunities and Threats

The five critical environmental forces are the threat of new entrants, the power of suppliers, jockeying among contestants, the threat of substitute products, and the power of buyers.

As can be seen in *The Entrepreneurial Spirit: Small Airlines Can Succeeed,* opportunities and threats can be highly significant to organizations. The five competitive *environmental forces* discussed in Chapter 3 must be considered in strategic planning.[12] As indicated in Chapter 3, these forces generally relate to the competitor dimension of the firm's task environment. They are illustrated in Exhibit 8.2 and are useful in identifying opportunities and threats facing the firm.

Opportunities **Organizational opportunities** refer to those aspects of the organization's environment that, if properly acted upon, would enable the organization to achieve higher than planned levels of performance. When the cost of entry into a market is high or if innovation or copying is hard, an organization already in that market has the opportunity to solidify and even expand its market share and establish brand loyalty. If the organization has numerous buyers and suppliers such that none of them have any significant power, that organization has an opportunity to influence product design and/or characteristics to lower costs, facilitate delivery, or in other ways establish itself as dominant in the market. Finally, if other companies are not actively engaged in attempting to increase market share or establish brand/product identity and loyalty, the organization has an opportunity to jump ahead of its competition.

Threats **Organizational threats** refer to those aspects of the organization's environment that, if not countered in some way, would impede the organization's progress to achieve its plans. If entry and innovation are easy, the possibilities of new entrants and/or substitute products are clear threats. If there are few buyers or suppliers such that one or more of them could exercise

Exhibit 8.2
Environmental Forces Affecting Strategic Planning

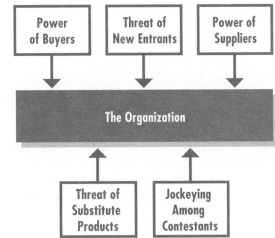

The Entrepreneurial Spirit

Small Airlines Can Succeed

The airline industry is extremely price competitive since all carriers (except Southwest Airlines Co.) can simply be called up on the computer of any other carrier or travel agent. To cope with this price competition, American Airlines rearranged its fares to attract more passengers with lower fares. Robert Crandall, CEO of American Airlines, believes that in such a market, there is room for only three to six major carriers. There were seven as of mid-1992.

However, even though this is a highly competitive industry, with proper planning smaller carriers can do quite well under certain conditions. Smaller airlines, for instance, can plan to add comparatively small cargo volumes to their passenger flights and make the difference between a profit and a loss on a flight. In Canada, where there are several smaller

carriers, airline workers made wage concessions and put money into their companies in an effort to make their carriers more competitive and save jobs. Canadian airlines were also planning possible mergers or joint ventures with American carriers as a way to survive.

Even so, it is difficult for smaller carriers, and numerous Canadian government officials have urged a merger policy to protect small carriers and allow new ones to enter the market. Without such a policy, fares are likely to increase, and passenger choice will shrink as competition is extinguished. A changed government policy could enable small airlines to win more routes in large, profitable international markets.

Despite these efforts, however, smaller airlines cannot afford to be complacent or not pay attention to their customers. City Express was among those small carriers that seemed to ignore its competition and alienate its customers. The result was that it did not survive in this market.[13] ■

power over the organization, that would represent a threat. Finally, if other competitors are strongly jockeying for market position and brand identity, the organization is constantly threatened with a loss of its position unless it continually responds to such moves.

The Organization-Environment Interface

After managers have developed a clear understanding of relevant environmental forces, they must come to grips with how they want to interact with those forces. Indeed, the purpose of strategy is to determine what position in the environment the firm wishes to take. As shown graphically in Exhibit 8.3, the key to developing effective strategy is to understand environmental opportunities and threats and organizational strengths and weaknesses.

For example, in 1989 Ford found itself with several billion dollars in surplus funds (an organizational strength). Managers at Ford believed, however, that the company lacked a strong enough presence in the luxury car market (an organizational weakness). Meanwhile, Toyota and Nissan were introducing new luxury car divisions (both environmental threats). Managers at Ford learned that Jaguar Ltd. was for sale (an environmental opportunity) but that General Motors was already negotiating a purchase (still another threat). Ford jumped in and paid a premium price to acquire Jaguar first. The result was a successful organization-environment interface achieved by matching environmental opportunities and threats with organizational strengths and weaknesses.

Corporate Strategy

As defined earlier, corporate strategy involves the determination of which businesses the firm expects to compete in. The two most common approaches to corporate strategy are the development of a generic, or grand, strategy and the use of a portfolio approach.

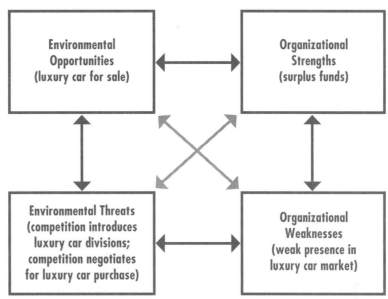

Exhibit 8.3

The Organization-Environment Interface

Generic Strategies

*Three alternative **generic strategies** are **growth**, **retrenchment**, and **stability**.*

A **generic strategy,** which is also called a grand strategy, is an overall framework for action developed at the corporate level. It is generally used when the corporation competes in a single market or in a few highly related markets. There are three basic generic strategies that organizations adopt: growth, retrenchment, or stability.

A **growth strategy** is adopted when the corporation wants to generate high levels of growth in one or more areas of operations.[14] For example, Wal-Mart is pursuing a growth strategy by opening more than one hundred new stores each year and moving rapidly into markets all across the United States.

A **retrenchment strategy** is employed when managers want to shrink operations, cut back in some areas, or eliminate unprofitable operations altogether. Firestone pursued a retrenchment strategy when it recently cut its work force from 107,000 to 55,000, closed eight plants, and sold several unrelated businesses.

Finally, a **stability strategy** is used when the organization wants to maintain its status quo. Such an approach is often adopted immediately after a period of sharp growth or retrenchment. For example, following its recent shift in pricing strategy, Sears is attempting to maintain stability.

Portfolio Approaches

*The **portfolio approach** involves identifying **strategic business units (SBUs)** and then classifying them in some meaningful framework.*

When the firm competes in several different markets simultaneously, it often uses one of several different portfolio approaches. A **portfolio approach** to corporate strategy views the corporation as a collection of different businesses. The foundation of portfolio approaches is the concept of the strategic business unit.

Strategic Business Units   A **strategic business unit,** or **SBU,** is an autonomous division or business operating within the context of another corporation. The SBU concept was born in the early 1970s at General Electric. Managers at G.E. felt that they needed some sort of framework to help them manage the diverse businesses under the corporate umbrella. Close scrutiny suggested that G.E. was actually engaged in forty-three distinct businesses. Each of these businesses was clearly defined as an SBU for purposes of corporate strategy. In short order, several other large firms, including Union Carbide and General Foods, began to realize that they too comprised a set of SBUs.

In general, an SBU has the following characteristics:

1. It is a single division or set of closely related divisions within the corporation.
2. It has its own set of competitors.
3. It has its own distinct mission.
4. It has its own strategy that sets it apart from other SBUs within the organization.

For example, the strategic business units of the candy company, Mars, include their candy business, pet food business, packaged food business, and electronics business.

The Portfolio Matrix   Of course, the notion of SBUs by itself is of only marginal value to managers. It is only when managers can logically group the SBUs into meaningful categories that this approach becomes truly significant. The best known of several different portfolio approaches is the **portfolio matrix** method. The portfolio matrix method classifies SBUs along two dimensions: market growth rate and relative market share. Market growth rate is the extent to which demand for a product is growing rapidly, at a modest pace, or not at all. Relative market share is the proportion of that market controlled by the product.

*In the **portfolio matrix**, SBUs are classified as **stars, cash cows, question marks**, or **dogs**.*

If we classify market growth rate as high or low and relative market share as high or low, we get the two-by-two matrix shown in Exhibit 8.4. Note that this creates four different categories of products. Classifying SBUs into the appropriate cells helps managers figure out how to manage them better.

Stars are businesses whose products have a high share of a fast-growing market. When IBM personal computers were first introduced, they were clearly stars. The market was expanding dramatically, and the IBM PC controlled a large portion of it. Of course, since market growth rates

Exhibit 8.4
The Portfolio Matrix

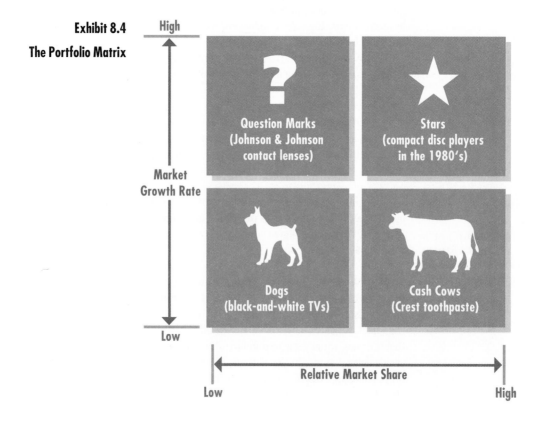

The Environment of Management

L.A. Gear Off Stride

L.A. Gear had an astounding beginning. By using ads featuring top stars and athletes, flamboyant styles, and some aggressive financial techniques, L.A. Gear rose to number three in the industry. From its beginning in 1984, sales went from $11 million in 1985 to more than $900 million in 1990. L.A. Gear planned to overtake Nike and Reebok to become number one in the industry by 1994. However, by the early 1990s it was in trouble; 1991 losses were estimated at from about $4 million to more than $60 million. As the economy worsened, poor planning became evident.

In reaching buying decisions for athletic shoes, particularly performance shoes, customers began to pay more attention to utility and performance rather than glitz and the endorsements of stars. L.A. Gear's reputation, which was based on its star-studded ads, seemed to hurt rather than help. Poor quality control was also damaging. Its sales began to fall off almost as dramatically as they had grown earlier.

When this occurred, its inventory policy, which had been based on ever-growing sales, led to massive stockpiles. These could be sold only by deep discounting, which further upset some distributors and cost it contracts. It sued Michael Jackson in 1992, saying that he signed a contract and cashed their check but then refused to wear their shoes and deliberately messed up their marketing schedules.

In 1992 L.A. Gear got a new president and hired marketers from Reebok, a major competitor, in an effort to turn things around. It changed management and marketing strategies. Asia became the focus market since it seemed not to be suffering the sluggish growth of U.S. and European markets.[15] ∎

must eventually stabilize, stars tend to be fairly short-lived.[16] Other recent stars have included Chrysler's mini-vans, compact disc players, and Diet Coke. Obviously, managers like stars. Stars need little investment to be sustained and generate large amounts of revenue.

Cash cows are products that control a large share of a low-growth market. If market growth stabilizes and the product can still control a large portion of it, it has become a cash cow. Since the market is stable, there is little need to promote products aggressively, so they generate large amounts of cash with relatively little support. Current cash cows include Crest toothpaste, Right Guard deodorant, and Coca-Cola Classic.

Question marks are products with a small share of a growing market. When confronted with a question mark, a manager must decide whether to invest more resources in the hope of transforming it into a star, simply maintain the status quo, or drop the product or business from the portfolio. For example, Bausch & Lomb controls the lion's share of the market in the contact lens industry. Divisions of Revlon and Johnson & Johnson have been trying to gain a larger share of the market for the past few years but have made little headway. For them, the contact lens business is a question mark, whereas it is a star for Bausch & Lomb.

Dogs are products or businesses with a small share of a stable market. Trying to salvage dogs is very difficult because growth has to come at the expense of competing products. Given their unappealing nature, dogs tend not to stay around long. An example might be a small division of an electronics division that still produces black-and-white televisions. Similarly, because of the growing popularity of compact discs and disc players, businesses that produce vinyl records and turntables might turn into dogs in the future.

The key to using the portfolio matrix is to manage the portfolio effectively. For instance, cash cows can be used to generate the resources needed to support stars and maintain question marks. Dogs are usually sold or dropped, although occasionally they are turned into viable products again.

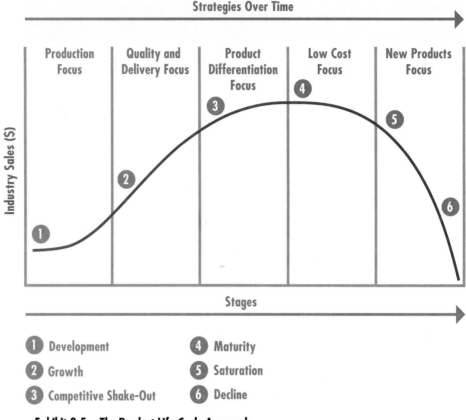

Exhibit 8.5   The Product Life Cycle Approach

On balance, the portfolio matrix is the dominant view of corporate strategy today. Managers are comfortable with it, and research generally supports its validity.[17] Nonetheless, it should be seen for what it is—a guiding framework to be used with caution and judgment.

Product Life Cycle Approaches

The **product life cycle** refers to how sales volume for a product changes during the existence of the product. Analyzing the life cycles of different products can also be useful in shaping corporate strategy. As shown in Exhibit 8.5, generally the product life cycle goes from development, growth, competitive shake-out, maturity, saturation, to decline.[18] In the development stage, demand for the product may be high, and the organizational response is primarily on production. In the growth stage, more firms enter the market, and the organizational response usually turns to quality, service, and delivery. Then competition intensifies, and some firms are driven from the market. As the market matures, demand slows down, and the number of competitors drops off. The organizational response is usually to focus on low costs and product differentiation. As the market becomes saturated and begins to decline, organizations continue to lower costs and also to explore new products or services. Consider what happened at L.A. Gear, as described in *The Environment of Management: L.A. Gear Off Stride.*

Most products, ranging from dolls to computer chips, have life cycles measured in a few years, although the actual time period involved may vary from extremely short to extremely long.[19] Fads like hula hoops and pet rocks may go through the cycle in a matter of months (although they may recur periodically), while a product like Levi's 501 jeans has a life measured in decades.

In assessing an organization's response during the life cycle, it is important to keep in mind the competitive position and the market share of the organization. Having a small market share, for instance, in the development stage might not be so bad if the organization had a strong competitive position based on its other strengths. However, a small market share coupled with a weak competitive position is not encouraging and would probably suggest that the organization drop that product from its line.

Each of these approaches (generic, portfolio, and product life cycle) should be used in strategic planning. One is not "better" or an alternative to another. They are complementary ways of visualizing an organization's position and possibilities. The important thing is to carefully and accurately analyze the organization's SWOT situation to determine the strategy most likely to be effective.

Business Strategy

As we saw earlier, business strategy is the strategy managers develop for a single business. A business strategy is developed for each SBU within a portfolio matrix and for single-product firms that are not broken down into SBUs. The following sections explore a useful conceptual framework for understanding business strategy and identify and discuss the major kinds of business strategies that firms adopt.

The Adaptation Process

*According to the **adaptation model**, managers must solve **entrepreneurial**, **engineering**, and **administrative problems**.*

One popular approach to business strategy is the **adaptation model,** which suggests that managers should focus on solving three basic managerial problems by adopting one of three forms of strategy.[20] The model is illustrated in Exhibit 8.6.

Problems of Management   The first of the three managerial hurdles is the **entrepreneurial problem.** This problem involves determining which business opportunities to undertake, which to ignore, and so forth. Decisions regarding the introduction of a new product or the purchase of another business relate to the entrepreneurial problem. One of the underlying factors that affects this managerial hurdle is the willingness of the manager or the organization to take a risk. Deciding to introduce a new product requires a higher level of risk that to just repackage a current product. All entrepreneurial activities involve risk. The Self-Assessment in this chapter examines your willingness to take risks.

The **engineering problem** involves the production and distribution of goods and services. For example, Canon might elect to manufacture its own facsimile machines, to have them

Exhibit 8.6

The Adaptation Model

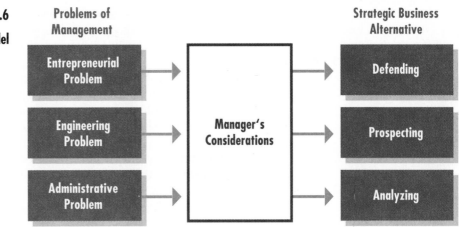

manufactured by someone else, or to combine the two methods in some way. Similarly, the plant that produces the facsimile machines might use traditional assembly lines staffed by employees, total automation, or some combination of the two. Finally, the company might do its own distribution or subcontract distribution to a wholesaler. Each of these decisions relates to the engineering problem.

The **administrative problem** involves structuring the organization. Top managers at Canon might choose to give operating managers considerable power and autonomy to make important decisions or to retain most of that power at the top. They might also choose to have a large number of different divisions or to maintain only a handful of divisions. These are aspects of the administrative problem.

*Three common strategic business alternatives are **defending**, **prospecting**, and **analyzing**.*

Strategic Business Alternatives   According to the model, firms can use a variety of strategies to address these problems. In general, managers usually choose one of three basic alternatives, as shown in Exhibit 8.6: defending, prospecting, and analyzing.

Defending is the most conservative approach to business strategy. Defenders attempt to carve out a clearly defined market niche for themselves and then work hard to protect that niche from competitors. They tend to ignore trends and remain within their chosen domain. They concentrate on efficiency and attempt to create and maintain a loyal group of customers. Mobil, Levi Strauss, many regional universities, and most local community hospitals use the defending mode of strategy.

Prospecting is the exact opposite of defending. Prospectors attempt to discover and explore new market opportunities. They prefer to avoid dependence on a narrow product or product group. Indeed, they attempt to shift frequently from one market to another. 3M is a good example of a prospector. One of its goals is to have 25 percent of its sales coming from products that did not exist five years ago.[21] Other well-known prospectors include Westinghouse, Bendix, and Litton Industries.

Analyzing is a midrange approach that falls between defending and prospecting. Analyzers attempt to move into new market areas, but at a deliberate and carefully planned pace. The analyzer keeps a core set of products that provide predictable revenues but at the same time systematically looks for new opportunities. Examples of analyzers are Procter & Gamble, Unilever, and Nestlé.

Overall, the adaptation model is a useful framework for helping managers understand business strategy. It has been supported by research and is well known among practicing managers.[22]

Competitive Strategies

*Three competitive strategies are **differentiation**, **overall cost leadership**, and **targeting**.*

In addition to the adaptation model, there are three competitive strategies that are pursued by some businesses: differentiation, overall cost leadership, and targeting. **Differentiation** is the process of setting the firm's products apart from those of other companies. Such differentiation might be in terms of quality (Volvo, IBM, Rolex), style (Ralph Lauren, Calvin Klein), or service (Maytag, Federal Express, American Express).

Overall cost leadership involves trying to keep costs as low as possible so that the firm is able to charge low prices and thus increase sales volume and/or market share. Examples of companies that use the cost leadership strategy are discount retailers like Kmart and Wal-Mart, manufacturers like Bic Corp. and Black & Decker, and companies that provide services like Southwest Airlines and Motel 6.

Finally, **targeting** occurs when a firm attempts to identify and focus on a clearly defined and often highly specialized market. Some companies produce cosmetics just for African Americans, for instance, or food for regional markets (chili in the Southwest, clam chowder in the Northeast). Others attempt to focus on special categories of consumers (the young, the upper class, and so forth).

Functional Strategies

 e saw earlier that the lowest level of strategy in the organization includes functional strategies. The six basic types of functional strategy are listed in Table 8.1, along with their major areas of concern.

*Functional strategies are often developed for **marketing, finance, production, research and development, human resources,** and **organization design**.*

Marketing Strategy   The **marketing strategy** is the functional strategy that relates to the promotion, pricing, and distribution of products and services by the organization. For example, Reebok has determined that it will sell only to fashionable retailers and will avoid discount chains. The firm also limits the amount of apparel it produces, even though it could sell more.[23] These decisions are a part of the firm's marketing strategy. Similarly, decisions about how many variations of each product to market (six versus nine sizes of Crest toothpaste dispensers), desired market position (Sears versus Kmart for the number one position in retailing), pricing policies (high prices with an emphasis on quality versus lower prices with an emphasis on quantity), and distribution

Table 8.1

Basic Functional Strategies

Functional area	Major concerns
Marketing	Product mix
	Market position
	Distribution channels
	Sales promotions
	Pricing issues
	Public policy
Finance	Debt policies
	Dividend policies
	Assets management
	Capitalization structure
Production	Productivity improvement
	Production planning
	Quality
	Production
	Plant location
	Government regulation
Research and development	Product development
	Technological forecasting
	Patents and licenses
Human resource	Human resource policies
	Labor relations
	Executive development
	Governmental regulation
Organization design	Degree of decentralization
	Methods of coordination
	Bases of departmentalization

Source: Adapted from *Management*, 4th ed., by Ricky W. Griffin. Copyright © 1993 by Houghton Mifflin Company. Adapted by permission.

channels (Timex's early decision to sell only through drugstores) are all part of the development of the marketing strategy. In any event, an emphasis on quality has become important in strategic planning.[24]

Financial Strategy   The **financial strategy** of a firm is also important. Companies need to decide whether to pay out most of their profits to stockholders as dividends, retain most of the earnings for growth, or take some position between these extremes. They must also make decisions about the proper mix of common stock, preferred stock, and bonds, and establish policies regarding how surplus funds will be invested and how much debt the organization can and is willing to support. For example, Disney's financial strategy calls for low debt. It managed to spend almost $1 billion from operating funds on Epcot Center without incurring any debt.[25] At the other extreme, Texas Air, the parent company of Continental and Eastern, is hundreds of millions of dollars in debt.

Production Strategy   In many ways, **production strategy** follows from marketing strategy. For example, if a company emphasizes quality, production costs may be of secondary importance. On the other hand, if price is to be emphasized, low-cost production techniques may become critical. Several areas of concern are usually addressed in this strategy. The location of plant sites is a production issue. So too are production planning and productivity improvement efforts. Production managers must also deal with governmental agencies such as the Environmental Protection Agency. In recent years the production strategy has become even more complex because more and more companies subcontract the manufacture and assembly of their products to other firms. For example, Kodak's new line of 35mm cameras is made by various Japanese manufacturers.

Research and Development Strategy   The **research and development strategy** relates to the invention and development of new products and services as well as the exploration of new and better ways to produce and distribute existing ones.[26] Some firms, such as IBM, Rubbermaid, and Texas Instruments, spend large sums of money on R&D, whereas others spend less. Long-term gains from R&D investment can be impressive, as in the case of Bridgestone Tire Company, where a strong R&D program has increased worker productivity by 10 percent each year for over a decade.[27]

Human Resource Strategy   Most organizations also develop a **human resource strategy.** This might deal with issues such as whether the firm plans to pay premium wages to get better-qualified workers, whether it will welcome unions, how it will attempt to develop executives more effectively, and how it will comply with federal regulations such as the equal employment opportunity guidelines.

Organization Design Strategy   Finally, companies often develop an **organization design strategy,** which is concerned with how the various positions and divisions within the organization will be arranged. For example, some organizations allow field managers to make fairly important decisions without consulting the home office, whereas others require home office personnel to approve virtually all field decisions. The determination of which policy to follow is a part of the organization design strategy. (Organization design is discussed more fully in Chapter 12.)

Integration as well as development of the six major functional strategies is crucial. Specifically, managers must make sure that all functional strategies follow logically from a unified corporate and business strategy and that they fit logically together. For example, if the marketing strategy calls for a sales increase of 50 percent, the production strategy might be to build a new plant to come on line in five years. This strategy in turn means that the human resource strategy will include a provision for developing the necessary managerial talent to run the plant and that a financial strategy must be developed to pay for the plant. The organization design strategy needs to specify how the new plant will fit into the existing organizational structure.

Strategy Implementation and Control

Strategy implementation is achieved through tactical planning, contingency planning, and integration with organization design.

The final part of strategic planning, and one we will only briefly review, is the implementation and control of strategic plans by managers of the organization.[28] Exhibit 8.7 summarizes the process of strategy implementation.[29] First, it must follow logically from strategy formulation: that is, managers must think strategically by first formulating and then systematically implementing strategies.[30] Implementation itself consists of three elements. Tactical planning, as detailed in Chapter 7, is the real way in which strategy is implemented. Contingency planning, also described in Chapter 7, is also important for the proper implementation of strategic plans. Finally, strategy and organization design must be properly integrated. A mismatch can result in numerous problems for organizations and can serve as a major barrier to the effective accomplishment of strategic plans.

In reality, of course, strategy implementation is far more comprehensive and complex than this simple overview implies. Process improvement and other such techniques have been shown to be tools that can be useful in strategy implementation.[31] In addition, modeling and scenario generation have become widely used tools.[32] As a result, each strategy and its corresponding organizational context are unique, making each effort to implement a strategy unique as well. Much of the material in other chapters of this book is in some way an attempt to show how all or part of a strategic plan developed by top management is implemented.

Strategic control refers to the process whereby management assures that the strategic planning process itself is effective.[33] Such control involves evaluating the organization's progress with its strategy, its flexibility in meeting changing environmental conditions, and the resources actually consumed by the strategic planning process. This latter evaluation involves the strategic budget as opposed to the operations budget, which is separate in many companies such as Texas Instruments and 3M.[34] Strategic control necessitates having indicators of the performance of the strategic planning process as well as mechanisms for corrective action should it not be accomplishing its objectives.

Exhibit 8.7   Strategy Implementation

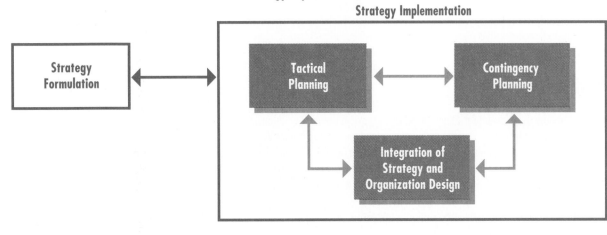

Chapter Summary

S trategic planning is the broad planning of top management to guide the general direction of an organization. There are four basic components of strategy: scope, resource deployment, competitive advantage, and synergy. Strategy formulation is the set of processes involved in creating or developing strategic plans, and strategy implementation is the set of processes involved in executing those plans. Finally, there are three levels of strategy: corporate strategy, business strategy, and various functional strategies.

Environmental analysis is the specific study of the company's environment and how it affects the company. Managers must understand the environmental forces and use them as a framework to match environmental threats and opportunities with organizational strengths and weaknesses.

Corporate strategy means determining what businesses the firm expects to compete in. Three generic, or grand, strategies are growth, retrenchment, and stability. Some organizations also use a portfolio approach involving strategic business units, or SBUs. The portfolio matrix is a system for analyzing SBUs in terms of relative market share and the growth rate of the market.

A business strategy is the strategy developed for a single business within an organization. The adaptation model is the most popular view of business strategy and suggests that managers should focus on solving three basic managerial problems—entrepreneurial, engineering, and administrative—by adopting one of three strategies: defending, prospecting, or analyzing. Competitive alternatives include differentiation, overall cost leadership, and targeting.

Functional strategies constitute the lowest level of strategy in an organization. There are six basic types: marketing, financial, production, research and development, human resource, and organization design.

Strategy implementation involves three elements: tactical planning, contingency planning, and integration of the strategy with the organization's design.

The Manager's Vocabulary

strategic plans
scope
resource deployment
competitive advantage
synergy
strategy formulation
strategy implementation
corporate strategy
business strategy
functional strategies
organizational strengths
VRIO framework
organizational weaknesses
organizational opportunities
organizational threats

generic strategy
growth strategy
retrenchment strategy
stability strategy
portfolio approach
strategic business unit (SBU)
portfolio matrix
stars
cash cows
question marks
dogs
product life cycle
adaptation model
entrepreneurial problem
engineering problem

administrative problem
defending
prospecting
analyzing
differentiation
overall cost leadership
targeting
marketing strategy
financial strategy
production strategy
research and development strategy
human resource strategy
organization design strategy
strategic control

Review Questions

1. What are the three levels of strategy? Do all firms have all three levels? Why or why not?
2. What are the five competitive environmental forces that organizations must consider when developing strategies? How do organizations go about positioning themselves relative to those forces?
3. Identify three generic strategies that organizations might choose to pursue.

4. What are the three problems of management and the three strategic business alternatives described in the adaptation model?
5. What are the six basic functional strategies most organizations develop?

Analysis Questions

1. Apply the concepts of corporate, business, and functional strategies to your university or college.
2. Which of the five environmental forces are more likely to exist together than others? Identify other examples of organizations likely to be affected by each of the five forces.
3. What are the risks involved in selling dogs quickly? Why would anyone want to buy a dog?
4. Identify examples beyond those noted in the chapter to illustrate defenders, prospectors, and analyzers.
5. What are the critical issues in implementing a new strategy within an organization?

Self-Assessment

Are You a Risk Taker?

Introduction Taking risks is part of business. Whether it is opening a new branch office or hiring a new college graduate, the decision maker (manager) is taking a risk. Not everyone is comfortable taking risks. This Self-Assessment examines your level of comfort with risk taking.

Instructions As a decision maker, do you tend to steer clear of risky situations, or do you find them tantalizing and invigorating? For example, if you had saved $20,000 would you keep it in the bank or invest it in a friend's new business venture? This quiz, designed by psychologist Frank Farley, measures how likely you are to take risks with finances and your career. Answer true or false for each question.

1. I'd rather start my own business than work for someone else.
   TRUE   FALSE
2. I would never take a job that requires lots of traveling.
   TRUE   FALSE
3. If I were to gamble, I would be a high roller.
   TRUE   FALSE
4. I like to improve on ideas.
   TRUE   FALSE
5. I would never give up my job before I was certain I had another one.
   TRUE   FALSE
6. I'd never invest in highly speculative stocks.
   TRUE   FALSE
7. I'd be willing to take risks just to broaden my horizons.
   TRUE   FALSE
8. Thinking about investing in stocks doesn't excite me.
   TRUE   FALSE

9. I'd consider working strictly on a commission basis.
   TRUE   FALSE
10. Knowing that any new business can fail, I'd always avoid investing in one, even if the potential payoff was high.
    TRUE   FALSE
11. I would like to experience as much of life as possible.
    TRUE   FALSE
12. I don't feel that I have a strong need for excitement.
    TRUE   FALSE
13. I have a lot of energy.
    TRUE   FALSE
14. I can easily generate lots of money-making ideas.
    TRUE   FALSE
15. I'd never bet more money than I had at the time.
    TRUE   FALSE
16. I enjoy proposing new ideas or concepts when the reactions of others—my boss, for example—are unknown or uncertain.
    TRUE   FALSE
17. I have never written checks without having enough money in the bank to cover them.
    TRUE   FALSE
18. A less secure job with a large income is more to my liking than a more secure job with an average income.
    TRUE   FALSE
19. I'm not very independent-minded.
    TRUE   FALSE

For interpretation, turn to the back of the book.

Source: Frank Farley, 1025 West Johnson Street, University of Wisconsin, Madison, WI 53706. Copyright 1986 by Frank Farley.

Skill Builder

The SWOT Analysis

Purpose SWOT analysis provides the manager with a cognitive model of the organization and its environmental forces. By developing this ability, the manager builds both process knowledge and a conceptual skill. This skill builder focuses on the *administrative management model*. It will help you develop the *coordinator role* of the administrative management model. One of the skills of the coordinator is the ability to plan.

Introduction This exercise helps you understand the complex interrelationships between environmental opportunities and threats and organizational strengths and weaknesses.

Instructions Step 1: Study the exhibit below, Strategy Formulation at Marriott, and the text materials concerning the matching of organizations with environments.
Step 2: The instructor will divide the class into small groups. Each group will conduct a SWOT (strengths, weaknesses, opportunties, threats) Analysis for Marriott and prepare group responses to the discussion questions. Marriott has been successful in its hotel and food services businesses but less than successful in its cruise ship, travel agency, and theme park businesses.

Strategy formulation is facilitated by a SWOT Analysis. First the organization should study its internal operations in order to identify its strengths and weaknesses. Next the organization should scan the environment in order to identify existing and future opportunities and threats. Then the organization should identify the relationships that exist among the strengths, weaknesses, opportunities, and threats. Finally, major business strategies usually result from matching an organization's strengths with appropriate opportunities or from matching threats with weaknesses. To facilitate the environmental analysis in search of opportunities and threats, it is helpful to break the environment down into its major components—international, economic, political-legal, sociocultural, and technological.

Step 3: One representative from each group may be asked to report on the group's SWOT Analysis and to report the group's responses to the discussion questions.

Discussion Questions

1. What was the most difficult part of the SWOT Analysis?
2. Why do most firms not develop major strategies for matches between threats and strengths?
3. Under what conditions might a firm develop a major strategy around a match between an opportunity and a weakness?

Source: From *Exercises in Management*, 4th ed., by Gene E. Burton. Copyright © 1993 by Houghton Mifflin Co. Used with permission.

Strategy Formulation at Marriott

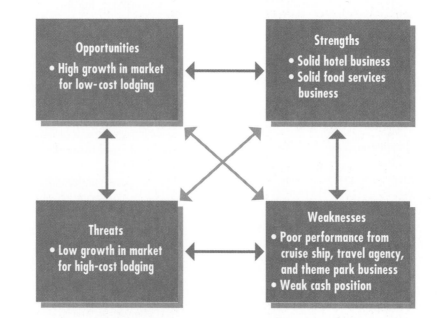

From *Management*, 4th ed., by Ricky Griffin. Copyright © 1993 by Houghton Mifflin Company. Used by permission.

Marriott SWOT Analysis Sheet

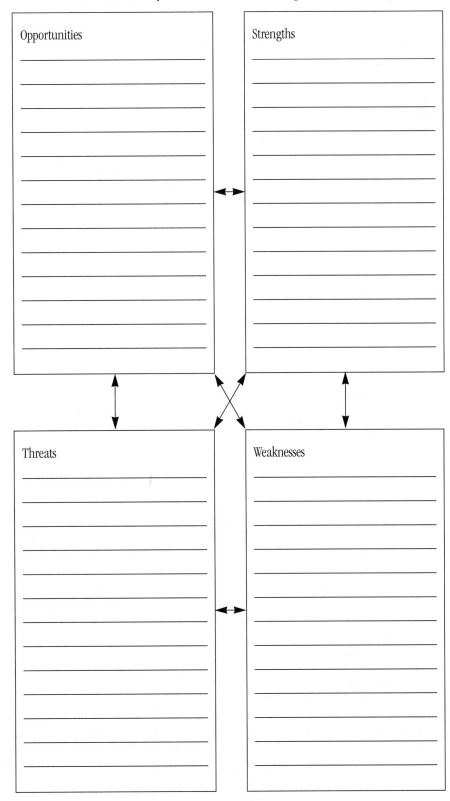

Environmental Analysis

Opportunities

Organizational Analysis

Strengths

Threats

Weaknesses

Relationships Between Opportunities and Strengths

1. _____
2. _____
3. _____

**Relationships Between Opportunities
and Weaknesses**

1. _____
2. _____
3. _____

Relationships Between Threats and Strengths

1. _____
2. _____
3. _____

Relationships Between Threats and Weaknesses

1. _____
2. _____
3. _____

**Major Strategies Matching Opportunities
with Strengths**

1. _____
2. _____
3. _____
4. _____

Major Strategies Matching Threats with Weaknesses

1. _____
2. _____
3. _____
4. _____

CONCLUDING CASES

8.1   Du Pont Adjusts Its Strategy

From the very early 1800s when it was founded as a gunpowder company until around the turn of the next century, Du Pont was strictly a family business. Early this century, however, it began to emerge as the epitome of the professionally managed corporation with a strong divisional structure based on products. The family clearly maintained a strong interest in it, including serving as the top executives until the early 1970s. At about that same time, Du Pont began to expand its operations into paints, dyes, artificial fibers, and plastics, and from there into all forms of chemistry. Today Du Pont is the largest chemical company in the United States (followed closely by Dow).

Du Pont has six principal business segments—industrial products, fibers, polymers, petroleum, coal, and diversified businesses. However, its purchase of Conoco in 1981 seemed to signal a change. During the 1980s Du Pont's performance slipped from excellent to only average, and it seemed to suffer more from cyclical impacts than it had in the past. Four different CEOs battled with varying degrees of success to overcome these problems and to keep the firm on a steady growth course. In addition, Du Pont became

known as the number one corporate polluter in the United States because of problems with both emissions from its plants and its disposal of hydrochloric acid. College students in the United States organized "Red Wednesday" on October 28, 1982, to protest Du Pont's pollution. Nevertheless, by the end of the 1980s, total sales had nearly tripled while the total number of employees stayed almost the same. Clearly Du Pont had a remarkable record.

Then came the 1990s. Battelle Memorial Institute filed suit, charging that Du Pont had deliberately misappropriated Battelle's trade secrets during a joint research project. A major fungicide, Benlate, proved a disappointment because it ended up damaging some crops. By the end of 1992, Du Pont's net income had fallen for two years, and return on equity had dropped. Du Pont began making strategic and tactical plans to rectify these situations.

Top management was reorganized, managerial and supervisory positions were eliminated, early retirements were pushed, and whole levels of management disappeared. Decision making was decentralized further than before, cutting the red tape with which customers had had to deal. Pharmaceuticals were spun off into a joint venture with Merck & Company, yearly operating costs were slashed, and efforts were made to reduce Du Pont's problems with pollution.

Research and development expenditures were kept high, and joint projects were developed to keep innovation occurring. To ensure fewer market failures, closer contact with customers is being stressed, both in large ventures such as automotive products and small ones like the Bob Evans Design operation, which makes swim fins. Weak businesses, particularly those that lack strong market shares or potential, such as its acrylics products business, were cut. Offshore businesses were developed, and the company's global role is expanding.[35]

Discussion Questions

1. What would Du Pont's strengths and weaknesses seem to be? Why?
2. What would Du Pont's opportunities and threats seem to be? Why?
3. Can you see any applications for the portfolio approach at Du Pont? Be specific.
4. Which competitive strategies has Du Pont employed? Which ones might it consider using? Why?

8.2 New is a Key at Kellogg

Kellogg was founded early this century as a result of a mistake. Two brothers were experimenting with ways to make health foods more appetizing and nutritious for medical patients when they accidentally discovered how to make wheat flakes. One of the brothers developed the idea commercially and quickly discovered how to also make corn and rice flakes. Kellogg began selling the cereal to the public in 1906 and, through innovative marketing techniques, changed the way in which people thought about breakfast. Competition quickly grew, however, as companies like General Mills and General Foods entered the market.

Kellogg is a believer in new ideas. New products have continually been developed and introduced. Marketing innovations, beginning with the world's largest sign in 1912, are constantly being tested. Since nutrition was a major concern in the development of its first product, Kellogg was a pioneer in nutrient labeling of its products. It introduced new packaging approaches too. To expand its markets, Kellogg began to grow internationally early in its life (Canada in 1914, Australia in 1924, and England in 1938).

During the 1950s and 1960s, Kellogg's market share grew very close to 50 percent. In the 1970s, however, trouble began. The company seemed to have lost touch with its customers and, as overall demand for breakfast cereals started to decline, Quaker Oats and Nabisco began to take market share away from Kellogg. Further, health-conscious consumers began to turn away from many of its heavily sweetened brands that had previously been so popular. Kellogg's market share began to drop, falling to around 37 percent by 1990.

Kellogg responded with new plans. It increased advertising to shore up the overall market and convince adults to return to eating cereal. It developed numerous healthy cereals, especially those based on oat bran. Managers began to focus on quality control to assure uniformly nutritious products. And Kellogg moved to strengthen its foreign markets, which existed in 130 different countries. These efforts quickly paid off as Kellogg's market share began to climb again. Nevertheless, as the 1990s began, it was in the foreign markets, particularly Europe, that the competitive battle became most fierce.

Kellogg dominated the European market prior to the 1990s. Then in 1989 General Mills formed CPW (Cereal Partners Worldwide), a partnership with Nestlé, to bring the General Mills family of cereals into the European market. However, every time CPW introduced a cereal, Kellogg responded by also introducing one that was packaged very similarly and tasted almost identical. This strategy effectively reduced the impact of the competition and enabled Kellogg to take advantage of the expanding market. Kellogg had six plants in Europe and in 1991 had six of the top ten cereal brands. Clearly, even if it lost some market share, it would be a winner in an expanding market. When advertising sharply increases in product markets, the overall size of the market frequently expands. That is Kellogg's hope for the European cereal market.[36]

Discussion Questions

1. Identify the strengths and weaknesses of Kellogg in the United States and then in Europe.
2. Identify its opportunities and threats in those two markets as well.
3. Can you see any applications for the adaptation process at Kellogg? Be specific.
4. Which competitive strategies has Kellogg employed? Which ones might it consider using? Why?

CHAPTER

9

Planning Tools and Techniques

Learning Objectives

After studying this chapter you should be able to

· Describe the different organizational planning techniques used today by business.

· Discuss when to utilize appropriate project planning tools.

· Identify personal planning techniques that a manager must develop.

As we become more of a global village, planning will be essential for countries as well as for organizations. As president of Mexico, Carlos Salinas has put planning into action. Salinas, forty-four, joins the sophistication of a Harvard-educated economist with the understanding of the culture of Mexico to address the challenge of the North American Free Trade Agreement (NAFTA). This dynamic president intends to bring down the trade barriers between Mexico, the United States, and Canada to create the largest trading bloc in the world.

Salinas is a believer that the three countries must unite to compete with the European Community, stating that this is the trend of the world. This increased competition will help all three countries. To counter the criticism that the United States will lose jobs to Mexico, Salinas offers the logic that, "if wages alone were the main element to decide the logistics of industrial activity, Haiti would be the capital of the world. The United States is losing jobs not to countries with lower wages but to ones with higher wages, like Japan and Germany."

For Mexico, Salinas believes that reform is an ongoing permanent approach. The young president is stabilizing the country and intends to plan for its future. Not only is Salinas planning Mexico's future, unknowingly, he is also a role model for Hispanics living outside Mexico. One Hispanic student at a U.S. university declared that Carlos Salinas is "one of the great leaders for today." As Salinas prepares his country for the future, he is also helping Hispanics plan for their future.[1] ∎

The agreement between the United States and Mexico (NAFTA) will have tremendous planning consequences for companies as well as for the countries involved. The planning approaches are critical to the success of any project, regardless of how large, such as the NAFTA agreement, or how small. This chapter addresses techniques and tools specifically designed to increase planning efficiency and effectiveness. Planning tools are described for the macrolevel (strategic planning management), the mesolevel (monitoring within and between projects), and the microlevel (planning tools for the individual manager).

Organizational Planning Techniques

Organizational members have the responsibility to plan for future events. To do a credible job in this function, managers must make assumptions about the future, using their experience and, increasingly, appropriate planning tools. Planning tools assist us with planning the future, rather than having to merely react to it. Increasingly, a manager's task is not only to forecast the future but to create it and mold it to the organization's needs. "The objective of planning should be to design a desirable future and to invent ways to bring it about."[2] How we design the future has everything to do with planning, with less emphasis on reacting than in the past.

Environmental Scanning

Environmental scanning is a proactive approach to monitoring trends and anticipating changes that might affect an organization at the strategic and tactical levels of planning.

There is an emerging group of organizational members who are referred to as "information rich" members. These individuals control the majority of the useful information about the environment and competitors and can discern quickly what information is valuable and what information is not. The majority of information about the future of an organization resides external to the organization. In order to access this information, the process of **environmental scanning** is the tool and skill utilized. Environmental scanning is a proactive approach to monitoring trends and anticipating changes that might affect an organization at the strategic and tactical levels of

Environmental scanning, especially in terms of customer wants and needs, can prove valuable to organizations. For instance, Delchamps of Mobile, Alabama, has taken numerous steps to better serve its customers. Shown here is the closed-circuit TV system it installed in stores. Customers can keep up-to-date on special features so that shopping will be easier and less time-consuming. (Reprinted with permission of Delchamps, Inc.)

planning. The vast amounts of information available remain passive and useless until they are connected with active intelligence.[3]

For example, knowing the smoking policy for another company is relatively useless information that might be shared among coworkers who play racquetball together. It might become very useful information if the company decides to adopt a smoking policy and is therefore looking for examples from other companies that have been implemented.

Scanning the environment does not always involve information provided by an information system. Information can be valuable without coming through a computerized method. For example, Philips Petroleum Company established an advantageous relationship with the highly technical retirement community in Bartlesville, Oklahoma. Many of the community members were avid ham radio operators who listened to news from all over the world late into the night. Philips's marketing department arranged for a security guard to pick up their "listenings" early each morning and then transcribed and placed the newsworthy items on the desks of department members before eight in the morning.[4]

Organizations can gather intelligence in a variety of ways, but it is a unified approach to sharing the information that makes it valuable. *The Entrepreneurial Spirit: Maybelline Reaches Out for a New Market* provides an example of how environmental scanning can lead to a competitive advantage.

A more expansive approach to environmental scanning is the attempt to review relevant information for the company. This can be a major task, given that the number of articles written each day is estimated at more than twenty thousand. On-line retrieval systems facilitate access to this vast amount of information by allowing individuals to sort through the massive quantities of data and

The Entrepreneurial Spirit

Maybelline Reaches Out for a New Market

The cosmetics industry has finally recognized the needs of a previously underserved population—African American, Asian, Hispanic, and Native American women—that has not been able to wear mainstream make-up lines because the colors and formulations were developed specifically for white skin. How did Maybelline recognize this need first? The company did research (scanning) on demographic characteristics and identified a niche that was not being filled.

Maybelline was first to offer a new cosmetics line, Shades of You, that management expected would bring in $15 million in 1991. Although most cosmetics companies plan products for people of color, the diversification and decline in traditional markets have made this venture a reality for Maybelline. The African American population is the largest ethnic group in the United States, and it is growing at twice the rate of the white population. Further, blacks spend an average of three times more than white consumers do for cosmetics. Unlike the aging white population, the median age of the African American population is expected to remain in the eighteen to thirty-five range. Another underrepresented group—the 9.6 million Hispanic women in the United States—spends $1.4 billion on cosmetics and fragrances annually. Research indicates that Hispanics spend more than the average consumer on products they perceive to be of high quality. Also, Hispanics reportedly are more brand loyal than whites.

Another dynamic market is evolving as a traditional market declines. With the number of U.S. teen-age girls decreasing, cosmetics manufacturers must address the needs of women thirty-five and older who will be the growth market for their products. More value-conscious and with less time to shop, these women represent a variety of needs that has not been served in the past. It is also believed that this group of consumers is more demanding, requiring more precise marketing and incentives than previous groups. The wise company is viewing this new market as an entrepreneurial opportunity.[5] ■

random facts. But, more information is not necessarily better information, and it certainly is not a managerial asset until it has been scanned for relevance and quality. Consequently, better information is not a luxury but a critical tool to help deal with environmental uncertainties.[6]

During the decade of the 1980s, companies gained access to external databases through communications networks. Previously, these huge databases were inaccessible to individual organizations because of their cost and storage problems. Access to these databases is often provided through connect time costs. Using public access telecommunications systems, the databases charge the user a fee based on the amount of time that is spent connected. This is similar to the way charges are computed for long-distance phone service.

On-line searching is the expression used for computerized literature searches using public databases. These services allow people to search for information for a fee. All of these databases allow searching through the use of key words from the articles. Databases have become easier to use because they allow the stringing together of key words. For example, a person might ask a database for all of the citations on Fortune 500 companies *and* strategic planning in the future *or* forecasting.

On-line searching is the expression used for computerized literature searches using public databases.

A major difficulty involved with environmental scanning is the wide range of available choices. Systematic searching with consistent databases, rather than a scattered approach to information, reveals the greatest advantage. It is essential to understand this because one database (from over a total of one hundred databases offered by one service to access) might include all of the United Press International coverage since 1976.

The CD-ROM, a laser-generated disc with a thousand times the storage capacity of the floppy disk, is now used by many of the major distributors to store more databases for easier and more frequent searching. But if an organization must pay for individual searches, environmental scanning can become an expensive and time-consuming venture. Consequently, there are guidelines for appropriate searching. Table 9.1 illustrates when on-line retrieval searching is most appropriate.

The currently available external databases may be divided into four categories of assistance for organizations.[7] All of the sources listed in Table 9.2 may be useful for organizational assistance.

Three of the most popular on-line services are Dow Jones News/Retrieval, CompuServe, and The Source. Dow Jones began providing information to the financial community in the early 1970s with brokerage services, news, shopping, education, and entertainment information as well as financial data. CompuServe and The Source provide microcomputer owners with access to other computer systems, college courses, shopping, news, weather, sports, travel planning, games, financial data, and information on home, health, and family matters. One of largest database services is Dialog, from Lockheed. Dialog provides abstracts of more than four hundred periodicals and includes Standard and Poor's corporate reports, the government printing office index, and full indices to several daily newspapers. Dialog services include summaries of competitors' Securities and Exchange Commission (SEC) filings, patent information, income and balance sheet data, and in-depth profiles on key executives in competitors' firms.

NEXIS, from Mead Data Central, is the sister service to the LEXIS legal data database. NEXIS provides access to the full text of the *Washington Post,* Associated Press and United Press International dispatches, *Dun's Review,* the *Congressional Quarterly,* the *Economist, Newsweek,* and *U.S. News and World Report.* It even includes the *Encyclopaedia Britannica.* The LEXIS database could be used to secure information about the court cases that a competitor has been engaged in, as well as the "win" record of law firms the company may be considering for employment. Access to and appropriate utilization of these sources aids in keeping individuals and organizations headed toward the "information rich" philosophy. In fact, it is fair to say that the information revolution is transforming the nature of competition.[8]

Table 9.1

Guidelines for On-line Data Searching

Appropriate reason	Example
Searches that require the coordination of two or more distinct topics that could not be accomplished manually	S&L loans and takeovers
Searches on topics so new or specialized that they may not appear as subject headings in printed indexes	rightsizing; Americans with Disabilities Act
Searches on topics that may be stated in so many synonymous ways that manual searching would be extremely time consuming	quality teams, super teams, self-managed teams
Searches that are relatively narrow in scope and are likely to result in fairly small retrievals	natural gas liquids and environmental compliance

Full-text services	Access to	Applications to
I. Informational data bases		
LEXIS	legal info.	company research
NewsNet	corporate researchers	industry trends
VU/Text	analysts	competitor intelligence
DataTimes	managers	consumer trends
Info Globe	new products	technological development
II. Financial & statistical databases		
Dow Jones News/Retrieval	brokers	day-to-day operations of stocks, bonds, and commodities
Data Resources International (DRI)	bankers	bank operations
Chase Econometrics	accountants	financial disclosures
National Automated Accounting Research Systems (NAARS)	accountants	standard industrial codes (SIC), *Fortune* rankings
III. Consumer-based information services		
CompuServe	individuals	airline tickets, e-mail, conferencing
The Source	individuals	investing
IV. Multifaceted services		
Dialog	social scientist	research
ORBIT	natural scientist	research
BRS/SEARCH	college students	Business Periodicals Index (BPI)

Dow Jones News/Retrieval is a registered trademark of Dow Jones & Co., Inc. CompuServe is a registered trademark of CompuServe Inc. The Source is a service mark of Source Telecomputing Corp. Dialog is a registered trademark of DIALOG Information Services. ORBIT is a registered trademark of the ORBIT Search Service. BRS/SEARCH is a registered trademark of BRS Information Technologies.

Table 9.2   Available Databases for Corporations

Competitor Intelligence

Competitor intelligence is the active approach of scanning information available publicly about competitors.

One of the fastest-growing specific areas of environmental scanning is competitor intelligence. Competitor intelligence is a form of environmental scanning that uses external sources to assure that a company has adequate information for competition. **Competitor intelligence** is an attempt to scan the information available publicly about competitors. Intelligence-gathering techniques are vital in maintaining a competitive advantage. An organization keeps a competitive advantage by moving from identifying to satisfying market needs faster than its competitors or the industry leader.[9] Like environmental scanning, competitive intelligence does not have to involve a computer.

For example, personnel can have a major impact on the information brought into an organization from external sources. Some organizations may select an applicant for a position in part because the job seeker has worked for a competitor recently. To ward off such potential raids on their talented professionals, many companies are examining their hiring policies relating to nondisclosure after leaving the company. A source of competitor intelligence for marketing is the sales force. A firm's advertising department may scan the environment for competitors' ads, including recordings of radio and TV advertisements. The purchasing department staff could work with vendors who also sell to the competition. A company's real estate department often gets information on competitors' expansion plans, since many of the plans are filed with the local courthouse.

It is important to separate the concept of competitor intelligence from industrial espionage. For example, industrial espionage, selling information about the product plans of your company, is illegal. On the other hand, the information retrieved from public databases such as ProQuest is considered competitor intelligence.

Human resource management professionals know which people in the organization have worked for competitors. In fact, companies have become so effective with these databases that they are aware that their competitors are checking on them frequently. It is not unusual for a company to practice a form of counterintelligence by providing confusing or contradictory information in the public databases. For example, a pharmaceutical company could file a patent for compounds that its competitor assumes is a breakthrough in a drug they are both working on. This patent sends a false signal to the competitor about the pharmaceutical company's actual status on the drug.

International business competition continually heats up. The more successful your product, the more likely will competitors emerge to challenge it. NuTek USA Corp. spent four years developing software for a computer that would "act like a Macintosh" but sell for much lower prices. Companies in the United States, Europe, and the Far East were quick to sign up to sell the machines. (William Mercer McLeod.)

Conceptual Modeling

Conceptual modeling is the formation of patterns and models in an efficient way for problem solving, especially in handling and even looking for information.

Another tool for strategic planning is **conceptual modeling.** Conceptual modeling helps members think of their organization as a whole with many interrelated parts by forming patterns and creating models. Conceptual modeling focuses on process: how we seek data, turn it into information, and use it to help reach conclusions.[10]

The most common way in which people reflect what is going on in their heads is through lists and hierarchies. Everyone jots down a list in a hurry to guide thinking. In order to give the list shape and significance, people may then sequence the list, relating and numbering items, shifting them around into an order that better reflects how they want to attack the problem. Turning a list into a map instantly improves the thinking tool. The special feature of maps is that questions are built into them. Maps provide structure and links that help people think up ways to handle a task.

Rules and questions are exactly what expert systems attempt to capture from humans. Expert systems are computer-based programs that provide advice to the user just like a human expert does. The approach simulates the rules of thumb based on experience and education that we use in making decisions. This conceptual technique may aid us in recognizing whether something essential in the planning is not known or is not right and then to work out the thinking that is needed. The questions that drive thinking reflect mental patterns. These patterns are in fact models, but most people are unaware of them. For example, by your third year of college, how you select a course has become a simple procedure. You consider many things almost at once: the time of the course, work schedule, assignments that are listed for the course, family obligations, and so on. You have become information rich in your environment. Though once it might have been an agonizing problem for you to decide which courses to select, now it is routine. If the model that we use remains unconscious, we will not have access to the patterns that drive similar questions. We will be trapped in routines of thinking over which we have limited control. On the other hand, if we are alert to our pattern-making capacity, we can better use this effective skill. Once we are aware, we can manipulate the models in our mind and create and recreate them. We can use them to understand, predict, plan, map, and observe our own thinking.

The mentor map becomes the essential link required for a task like making a decision or developing a plan. A good conceptual map is actually a blueprint for the future, generic enough in its design to be useful for many people. Wise managers are more likely to make a plan for thinking ahead to avoid the dangers of being forced to react inadequately, starting fires that they later have to put out. Managers who are too busy are often those who have failed to think things through in advance. They wind up spending an exorbitant amount of time because they had not given enough forethought to something that later became a problem.

Quantitative Tools and Techniques

Forecasting is the systematic development of predictions about the future.

In this section we briefly look at a variety of quantitative tools and techniques that can assist managers in their planning activities: forecasting, linear programming, and break-even analysis.

Forecasting   **Forecasting** is the systematic development of predictions about the future. One of the most critical kinds of forecasting that managers must do is revenue forecasting. All organizations depend on revenues to remain in operation. For businesses, revenues come from the sales of products and services. For banks, revenues come from interest paid by borrowers. The government derives its revenues from taxes, and schools and universities get much of their revenues from the government and student tuition.

It follows logically that managers need to know what their future revenues will be so they can plan effectively. For example, if Alcoa wants to open a new plant, its managers need to know that they will have enough funds available to pay for it. Similarly, the University of Tulsa needs to know what its budget will be next year so it can hire instructors, schedule classes, pay the staff, and so forth.

Thus, one of the first pieces of information most managers seek when developing plans is a projection of future revenues. This is developed through revenue forecasting, which involves statistical projections based on past earnings.

Managers can use numerous quantitative techniques to assist them in developing forecasts. One technique is time-series forecasting, which involves plotting the subject of the forecast (sales, demand, or whatever) against time for a period of several years. A "best-fit" line is then determined and extended into the future. An example is given in Exhibit 9.1, which plots the number of units sold for the years 1988 though 1994. As the line moves beyond 1994, it can forecast a demand of 2,750 in 1995 and 3,000 in 1996.

Delphi forecasting is the system-atic refinement of forecasting that takes advantage of expert opinion to make various predictions.

Another common technique utilized for planning is **Delphi forecasting.** Delphi fore-casting is the systematic refinement that takes advantage of expert opinion. Under the Delphi method, a panel of experts is asked to make various predictions. Each individual then shares his or her response with the rest of the panel, and the process is repeated. After a few repetitions, the experts fine-tune their opinions and a consensus—the forecast—usually emerges.[11]

Linear Programming   A very useful method for determining the optimal combination of resources and activities is called **linear programming,** or **LP.** Consider a small manufacturer who produces sofas, chairs, and ottomans. Each product is made of a wood frame, fabric covering, and wooden legs. Further, each goes through the same production and inspection system. Employees can work on only one product line at a time. Since it is costly to change frequently from one line to another, and since each product has a different profit margin, the question is how to schedule the work: how many sofas, chairs, and ottomans should be produced during a given period in order to optimize the efficient use of resources and simultaneously satisfy demand?

Linear programming (LP) is a method for determining the optimal combination of resources and activities.

LP quantifies the required raw materials and human resources, profit margins, and demand for each product into an equation. The entire set of equations is then solved, and the resulting solution suggests the best number of units of product to produce.

Exhibit 9.1

Time-series Forecasting

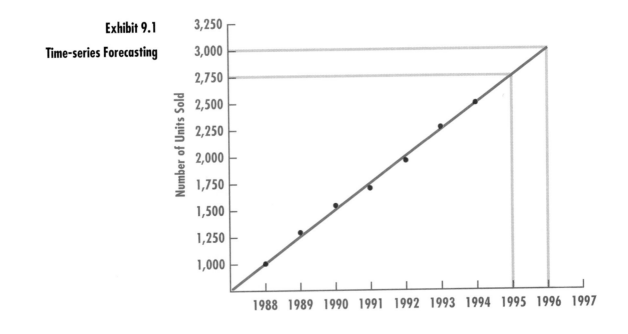

Break-even analysis helps the manager determine the point at which revenues and costs will be equal.

Break-Even Analysis Another useful planning technique is **break-even analysis.** Break-even analysis helps the manager determine the point at which revenues and costs will be equal. For example, suppose that a manager is trying to decide whether or not to produce a new product. There are two kinds of costs associated with the product, fixed and variable. Fixed costs are costs that are incurred regardless of the level of output: rent or mortgage payments on the plant, taxes, guaranteed wages and salaries, and so forth. Variable costs are costs that result from producing the product: raw materials, direct labor, and shipping. Total costs, then, are the fixed costs plus variable costs. Because fixed costs always exist, the total cost line never begins at zero but at the minimum level of fixed costs if nothing is produced. Total costs rise from there in direct proportion to the volume of output.

To determine the break-even point, the manager plots total costs and total revenues on the same graph, as shown in Exhibit 9.2. Total revenues are simply the projected selling price times the volume of output. The point at which the lines cross is the break-even point. If the company produces and sells less than this, it will have a loss because total costs exceed total revenues for the product at the given selling price.

If the company produces and sells more, it will make a profit. If the break-even point is too high, the manager might decide to raise the selling price in order to reach it sooner.

Using the Tools and Techniques In using various tools and techniques for planning, the manager needs to remember two things: the relative strengths and weaknesses of these aids and the increasingly important role of the computer. To use an analogy, most carpenters know how to use a handsaw, a table saw, a saber saw, and a ripsaw, and good carpenters know when to use each one. When the carpenter selects the right saw, he or she is using a conceptual skill. When the carpenter actually uses the saw, he or she is demonstrating a technical skill. In a similar fashion, managers should recognize that the various techniques described here are tools that provide tech-

Exhibit 9.2
Break-Even Analysis

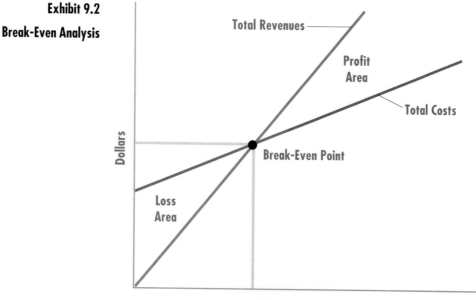

nical skill. Some are useful in some situations, whereas others are useful in other situations. When the manager has developed the skill to select the best planning tool for the situation, the manager has developed a conceptual skill for planning.

When choosing a technique, a manager needs to consider several points. On the positive side, these tools offer powerful ways to address certain kinds of problems. They help simplify and organize information, they make planning easier, and they are applicable in a wide variety of situations. On the negative side, they may not reflect reality accurately, some factors may not be quantifiable, the tools may be costly to use, and the manager may use a technique too rigidly without giving enough credibility to either intuition or insight.

As virtually everyone knows, the last several years have seen a revolution in information technology. The foundation of this revolution has been the computer, in particular the personal computer. This machine greatly enhances the manager's ability to use quantitative techniques in a meaningful fashion. Today's managers have certainly added another powerful tool to their kit. Tomorrow's managers will be even better equipped to handle the complex and dynamic nature of the planning process.

Project Planning Techniques

Project planning tools are designed to assist in the development of an acceptable solution to a problem within a reasonable time frame and at minimum cost.

In order to best utilize the previous tools, it is important to schedule and plan who will be responsible for employing them and when. **Project planning tools** are designed to assist in the development of an acceptable solution to a problem within a reasonable time frame and at minimum cost. There are several reasons why projects require special techniques for their management. Projects are different than traditional tasks in that projects typically have a specific beginning and ending point. A project is normally a one-time effort and tends to be complex in nature. Tools are needed to break down the complexity into segments for analysis to make the project more approachable and plannable.

Without techniques for scheduling and keeping track of milestones and key individuals, missed deadlines become what has been referred to as the mythical man-month.[12] As a project gets behind, the typical leader solution is to try to solve the problem by assigning more people to the project team in an effort to "catch up." But the problem does not work that logically. There is no linear relationship between time and number of personnel. The addition of personnel creates more communications and political interfaces. The result is that the project gets even further behind schedule. This is one reason that project leaders need project planning tools such as PERT and Gantt charts. These tools help project leaders plan and control the project. In the next section of this chapter, we will introduce these tools to you. By mastering the ability to use these tools you develop both conceptual and technical skills.

Project Planning and Scheduling

Because of the complexity of tasks and the number of individuals involved, it becomes essential for managers to be competent in scheduling. Scheduling in any environment becomes part of a typical day. For example, in your personal life, you have tailored your study habits around your work, course schedules, meals, and family obligations. The more complicated your individual schedule becomes, the more likely you are to use a device such as a scheduling calendar to help you plan.

Project Planning Tools

Two of the most popular tools used by project managers are **PERT charts** and **Gantt charts.** PERT charts are helpful for project planning. Gantt charts are best for project scheduling and progress reporting. As the project becomes more complicated, it is also helpful to use computer software such as Harvard's Project Manager, ABT's Project Management Workbench, SuperProject Plus, or Microsoft's Project.

PERT charting identifies the various activities necessary in a project, developing a network that specifies the interrelationships among those activities, determining how much time each activity will take, and refining and controlling the implementation of the project using the network.

*A **Gantt chart** is a bar chart with each bar representing a project task.*

As projects become large and have multiple tasks, it is necessary to have a method for monitoring the project performance and for reaching decisions about changes in project tasks. A well-known and often-used graphic tool for displaying time relationships and monitoring progress toward a project's completion is the Gantt chart.

Although the Gantt chart was developed in 1917, it is still a useful tool for time scheduling projects that involve a graphic approach. The popularity of Gantt charts is based on their simplicity: they are easy to prepare, read, and use.

The Gantt chart is a bar chart with each bar representing a project task. Gantt charts depict the overlap of scheduled tasks. When a task has been completed, a shaded bar corresponds to that task. Exhibit 9.3 shows a Gantt chart created by students for a class project.

PERT stands for Program Evaluation and Review Technique. It was developed in the late 1950s to assist the Navy in scheduling, coordinating, and controlling the Polaris submarine project. Thanks to PERT, the Navy saved two years in the development of the submarine. PERT is usually recommended for larger projects where the tasks are very dependent on each other for completion. PERT and Gantt can be used in a complementary manner to plan, schedule, evaluate, and control systems development projects.

PERT involves identifying the various activities necessary in a project, developing a network that specifies the interrelationships among those activities, determining how much time each activity will take, and refining and controlling the implementation of the project using the network. For the planning process, PERT charts assist by determining the approximate time required to complete a given project, in deriving actual project dates, and in allocating the necessary resources to accomplish the task. PERT charts allow projects to be organized in terms of events and tasks.

*An **event** represents a point in time, such as the start or completion of a task or tasks.*

Before drawing a PERT chart, **events** must be determined. Events represent points in time when the project begins, when a set of tasks are completed, or when the project is completed. A variety of symbols has been used to depict events on PERT charts. The PERT diagram in Exhibit 9.4 uses circles to represent the events. The numbers in the circles represent events that are specific, definable accomplishments. For example, Event 1 in the exhibit might be "Start home construction."

The arrows identified by letters are activities or tasks necessary to complete the various events. The number in parentheses beside each activity letter is an estimate of how much time will be needed to complete the activity. An estimate of the time needed for each task or activity must be calculated. The Skill Builder at the end of this chapter will help you develop this skill. For now, we will assume that the time estimates have been calculated as shown in Exhibit 9.4.

The direction of the arrow indicates the order in which events must be completed. Note that some activities can be worked on simultaneously, whereas others must be completed in sequence. For example, contractors cannot do anything toward building a house until the foundation has been poured. After the framing is complete, however, one crew can be putting on the roof while an electrical crew is wiring the walls and a plumbing crew is working on the pipes. In the PERT diagram in Exhibit 9.4, Activities a, b, and c can all be undertaken at the same time, but Event 6 will not be completed nor Activity h started until Activities g and e are accomplished. Similarly, at the other end of the network, all other events must be completed before Activity i can be started, so that Event 8 can be attained.

*The **critical path** is the longest path of connecting tasks in a PERT chart.*

A specific advantage of PERT charts over Gantt charts is the determination of the **critical path,** the longest path through the entire project. The critical path is calculated by summing up the time estimates for each possible path through the network and then selecting the path with the longest time estimate. It is called the critical path because if any task on the path gets behind schedule, the entire project is in jeopardy of being delayed.

In the example given, the critical path is 1-2-5-6-7-8. This combination of tasks should take twenty units of time to complete. A different path, and not critical to the overall project, is the path

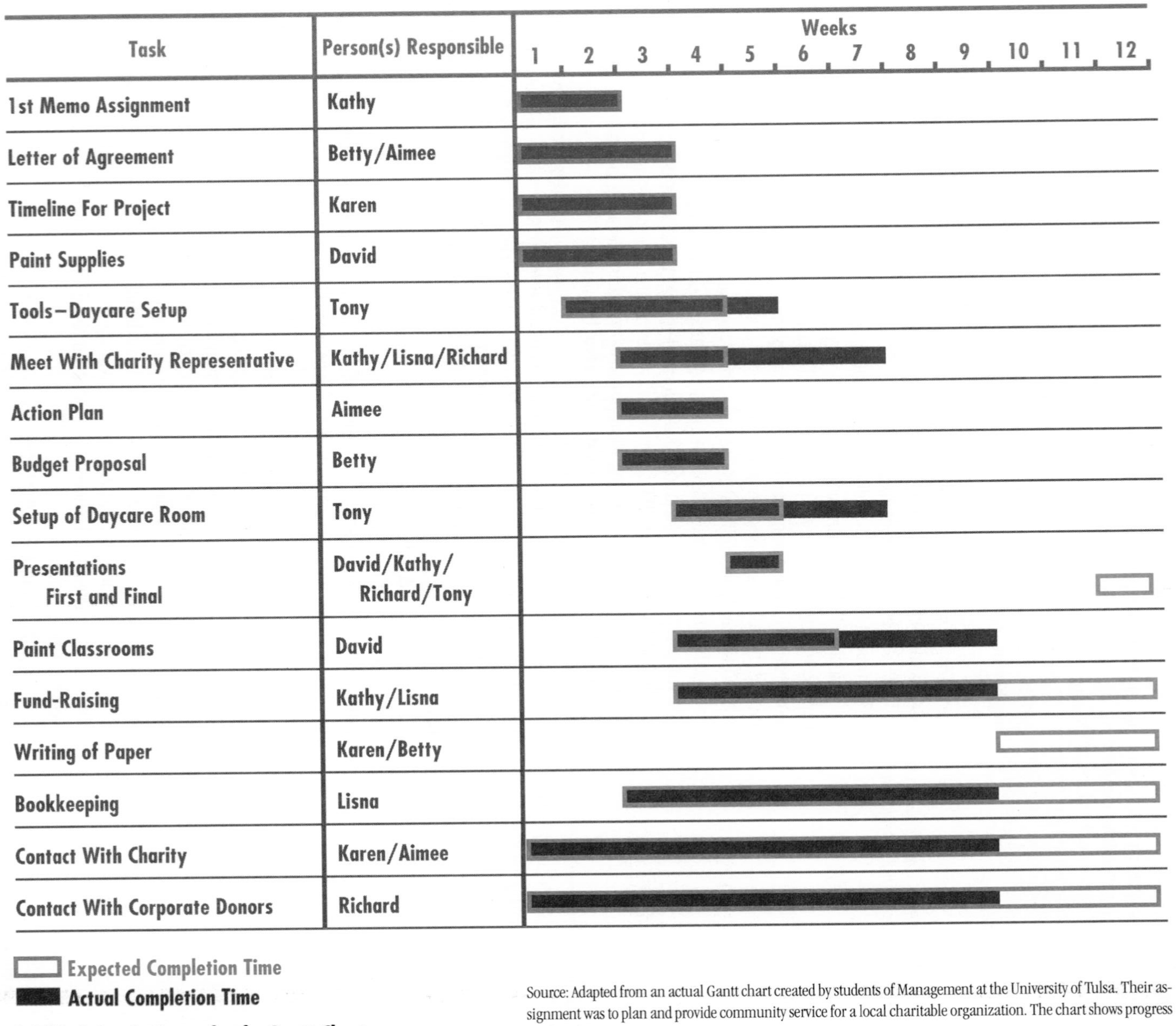

Task	Person(s) Responsible	1	2	3	4	5	6	7	8	9	10	11	12
							Weeks						
1st Memo Assignment	Kathy												
Letter of Agreement	Betty/Aimee												
Timeline For Project	Karen												
Paint Supplies	David												
Tools—Daycare Setup	Tony												
Meet With Charity Representative	Kathy/Lisna/Richard												
Action Plan	Aimee												
Budget Proposal	Betty												
Setup of Daycare Room	Tony												
Presentations First and Final	David/Kathy/ Richard/Tony												
Paint Classrooms	David												
Fund-Raising	Kathy/Lisna												
Writing of Paper	Karen/Betty												
Bookkeeping	Lisna												
Contact With Charity	Karen/Aimee												
Contact With Corporate Donors	Richard												

☐ Expected Completion Time
■ **Actual Completion Time**

Exhibit 9.3   An Example of a Gantt Chart

Source: Adapted from an actual Gantt chart created by students of Management at the University of Tulsa. Their assignment was to plan and provide community service for a local charitable organization. The chart shows progress as of Week 9.

Exhibit 9.4

A PERT Chart

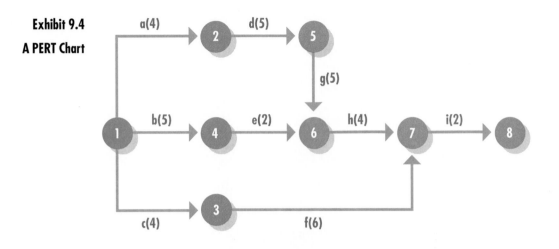

1-4-6-7-8. This path takes thirteen units of time. A final option of 1-3-7-8 takes twelve units of time to complete all tasks on the network. An understanding of the critical path helps managers in two ways. First, the manager recognizes that a delay in any activity along the critical path delays the entire project. If Activity c takes five units of time instead of four, no real harm has been done. On the other hand, if Activity d takes six units of time instead of five, the entire project has been delayed by one unit of time. Of course, the manager may be able to regain the lost time by working overtime, hiring extra help, or providing additional machinery.

Understanding the critical path allows managers to reallocate resources to shorten the overall project. For example, after seeing the PERT diagram in Exhibit 9.4, the manager might decide to move some workers from Activity e to Activity d. As a result, Activity e now takes three units of time to complete, but Activity d is finished in four units. The overall time of completion — that is, the critical path — has therefore been reduced by one unit of time.

Personal Planning Techniques

M any of our current expressions deal with time as a scarce resource. For example, we talk about saving time, using time wisely, being short of time, and a time crisis. Managers get the same amount of time as everyone else. Because it is definitely a finite resource, managers must plan to use what time they have as effectively and efficiently as possible.

Time Management

Time management is the act of setting priorities for how our time will be used in achieving our needs and desires.

Time is a scarce resource that requires planning and monitoring. **Time management** is the act of setting priorities for how our time will be used in achieving our needs and desires. The Self-Assessment activity at the end of the chapter provides you with a profile of your use of time. Table 9.3 provides a brief overview of indicators that might signify that you are not managing information correctly and consequently are being time inefficient.

Recently, links have been established between job-related stress and job satisfaction or dissatisfaction.[13] Stress can be measured through time-related characteristics such as boredom (too much time with little of value to fill it) or procrastination (misuse of time resulting in crisis and anxiety).

There are beginning to be clear separations between what is a healthy work attitude and the attitude of a work addict. Workaholics are addicted to activity. **Peak performers,** individuals who excel at their performance, are committed to results. Job obsession and job addiction are not the same.[14]

Peak performers are individuals who excel at their performance.

Time management is a necessary managerial skill and technology helps managers and others to organize their time more efficiently than ever. In this picture a New York broker, Walter Kaczor, watches the U.S. Open tennis matches, monitors the stock market on a portable quote receiver, keeps in touch with his office on a cellular phone—all at the same time. (Charles O'Rear/Westlight.)

Table 9.3

Are You Information Anxious?

For example, are you:

1. Chronically talking about not keeping up with what's going on around you?

2. Feeling guilty about that ever-higher stack of periodicals waiting to be read?

3. Nodding your head knowingly when someone mentions a book, an artist, or a news story that you have actually never heard of before?

4. Finding that you are unable to explain something that you thought you understood?

5. Blaming yourself for not being able to follow the instructions for putting a bike together?

6. Buying high-tech electronics because you feel that through osmosis you'll become more technologically knowledgeable?

7. Calling a book "prophetic" even though you couldn't even understand the review of it, which is all you read?

8. Looking down at your watch to sign in the exact time in an office building logbook even though you know that no one really cares?

9. Giving time and attention to news that has no cultural, economic, or scientific impact on your life?

10. Feeling depressed because you don't know what all of the buttons are for on your VCR?

11. Thinking that the person next to you understands everything you don't?

12. Too afraid or too embarrassed to say "I don't know"?

Source: From *Information Anxiety by* Richard Saul Wurman. Copyright © 1989 by Richard Saul Wurman. Used by permission of Doubleday, a division of Bantam Doubleday Dell Publishing Group, Inc.

The Quality Challenge

Dell Computer

The Dell Computer Corporation announced that as of August 18, 1992, its net income rose 76.6 percent in the second quarter. This growth took place in the personal computer business that has been deemed in a slump, and in an area that has been traditionally known as the "mail-order business." The twenty-six-year-old chairman prefers that the public become aware of Dell's research, manufacturing, service and marketing expertise, however. In fact, Michael S. Dell does not want his $546-million personal computer company to be referred to as a mail-order business. Dell, the pioneer behind the company, began his business at the age of nineteen from a University of Texas dorm room. Dell maintains that his advantage is service that is unexpected from mail-order approaches. Salespeople train for six months before they are allowed the headsets to receive phone calls. Dell claims that 91 percent of customer problems are solved over the phone by his staff of 150 technicians. The service mentality overrides the size of an organization. Large or small, mail-order or on-site, service is a primary concern of all organizations.

To counter difficulties during the PC slump, Dell has reduced salaries for himself (5 percent) and his chief executive staff. He maintains that Dell's success is due to cost cutting and efficiency. In fact, Dell Computer has cut corners by buying used furniture, insisting that executives travel coach class and stay at budget inns, and eliminating perks.[15] ■

Too much stress has a multiplying effect, so that your judgment may be slowed down to the point that it will take you longer to reach the right decision, and it may prevent you from making a decision at all. Stress can cause you to exaggerate the importance of one class of problems at the expense of another to the point of obsession, in which case you can neither settle the problems nor lay them aside long enough to consider the other ones, which may be equally important. For example, it may be difficult for a manager to give a negative performance appraisal to a cooperative employee. Consequently, the manager delays and worries about the appraisal to the point of missing a deadline for a proposal.

There are many difficulties with managing time, yet the most common ones can be identified and analyzed. The following guidelines may help you master your time. First, do not let being busy pass for being productive, and do not confuse visibility with productivity. Everyone knows someone who is always in motion. For them, the crisis and the urgent situation may crowd out the important tasks. For example, a manager on the *Apollo 11* project that put the first people on the moon impressed on his subordinates (many of them extremely bright young scientists hired to make creative contributions to the space program) that his three main values were arriving early, staying late, and looking busy. He was interested in seeing people at their desks, in case he was visited by senior managers. He worried about having people out of sight doing experiments or research in libraries. The staff knew he checked the coat rack when he came in to see who had arrived early each morning. One enterprising individual hired a janitor who started work at six A.M. to hang up his coat so that he could go to the library and work.[16]

Secondly, have confidence in your ability to proceed. Several personal symptoms force individuals into a cycle that is destined to delay decision making and induce procrastination. Underestimating oneself paralyzes an individual from action for fear of not being able to handle the correct outcome. Henry Kissinger said that in the final analysis, the decision is yours, and after the decision is made there is a kind of calm that settles around you.[17] Michael Dell, owner of Dell Computer Corporation, is an excellent example of a person who has confidence in his ability to proceed. Not only does he run a personal computer company valued at $546 million, but the company is also one of the quality leaders. You can read about this amazing young man in *The Quality Challenge: Dell Computer.*

If you constantly distrust your own judgment, you may be so cautious that much time elapses before you are able to act. Many managers, distrusting their experience or intuition, may request increasing amounts of information to shed new light on an issue. The assumption is that more information is better, and that more information will increase decision-making expertise. It does not indicate, however, that a manager knows how to use this additional information.

An additional time waster is the person who is not willing to trust subordinates with decisions. This individual is unable to delegate important tasks to others for fear that they will not be able to accomplish them correctly. Consequently, this person gathers the task back from the employee, very often after much time has already been spent on a project.

In today's approach toward participative management, many individuals are concerned that if a decision is made too quickly, or singularly, they may be perceived as misusing their authority, rather than being decisive.[18]

Finally, do not get sidetracked from making decisions. It has often been stated that the less we understand something, the more we require to explain it.[19] This tendency may be an avoidance of proceeding to closure and consequently is a time waster. If the next step is to venture into unpopular or difficult tasks, it is not unusual to stall at the stage where we are most comfortable. For example, term papers are often difficult to pull together. Therefore, you may be stuck at the stage of gathering information about your topic, as opposed to beginning the writing of the paper.

There are several approaches to help you improve your time management skills. First, do not let adversity defeat you. Individuals who manage time effectively become skilled jugglers, "able to change focus back and forth among a network of enterprises."[20] Barriers to your time, including unexpected crises, are not insurmountable for achieving sound time management accomplishments. Bertrand Russell was a mathematician and a political activist. When the British government imprisoned him toward the end of World War I for his antiwar writings, he used the time in jail to write articles and the *Introduction to Mathematical Philosophy.*

Secondly, use technology to assist you. One of the techniques to assist in time management is the environmental scanning approach to the wealth of information available. To keep your stress in check, remember that you do not need to know everything. It is more advantageous to know where to find information.[21] Additionally, many good ideas have been left just sitting on the shelf. Simply begin, and do not procrastinate. This approach may amount to doing the hardest thing first. Often we cannot find time for the really difficult tasks. We unconsciously let more task-oriented activities crowd out long-term accomplishment goals.

One of the more difficult problems is being selfish with your time to accomplish your goals. That is, manage your own time rather than letting others manage your time. Set your patterns and get to know your tendencies. If you are most productive in the late afternoon for interpersonal communications, let people know that is when you will return their phone calls. Do not let the phone dictate your time management. All time wasters can be rationalized or blamed on someone else. Once identified, time wasters can be replaced with more productive activities. The key is to know exactly what you want to do with the time you free up when you eliminate a time waster. Otherwise the time will quickly be dominated by another low-payoff activity.[22]

Just as it is necessary to monitor the time you spend with others, it is necessary to determine high-payoff activities from low-payoff activities. High-payoff activities are often long-range goals and consequently do not seem urgent. They are also not day-to-day tasks and may seem fuzzy, or ill defined. Therefore, low-payoff activities crowd into each day. Consciously evaluate yourself and these low-payoff activities. Do you continue to do low-payoff activities because you have always done them or feel like you have to do these low-payoff activities to be valued?

Finally, self-correct when you determine a time waste problem. Another common illusion in managing time is to think you are being effective (doing the right job right) when actually you are being efficient (doing the job right, but not doing the right job). A good example of this problem is studying very hard for an examination, although one of the chapters you have been studying is not on the exam.

The concept of path correction is an integral skill for peak performers. Rather than spinning in one place, a perceptive manager develops the skill to know when to alter the course. A critical path in a personal planning horizon is the most efficient or appropriate route to take toward a goal. Along the way, there is room for mistakes and corrections.[23]

The tools for projects and overall organizational planning benefit large groups. What PERT and Gantt charts do for accomplishing a large project, action planning does for individual perspective on time scheduling.

One common illusion in managing time is that you think you know where your time goes. Make a personal time study not only to determine where the time goes but also to determine how you feel about the way it is used. Managers have recognized and given credit to project planning techniques and scheduling. If the purpose of scheduling is to ensure that the right things are done at the right time with the right items and/or people to create them, it only makes good sense that we need the advantage of scheduling techniques for our hectic personal planning.

Action Planning

Action plans specify decisions that call for actions for specific project completion.

An **action plan** is used to explain detailed implementation plans to organizational members.[24] Action plans specify decisions that call for actions; for example, to market new products, build new factories, or sell old machines. Some of the proposed actions may be taken within single units, but others can cut across unit boundaries.

If a company's performance goal states that there should be an increase in sales by 10 percent a year, an action plan might state to do it by introducing blue widgets. Although the action plan may have different formats, it should answer who, what, when, where, and how, and consider the obstacles and aids for success of the goal.

An action plan should provide better estimates of the time needed to carry out a strategy, thereby resulting in more realistic deadlines for completing projects. Action plans may help avoid delays caused by failure to carry out a critical action step or to start the action step early enough.

Action planning differs from strategic (or tactical or operational) planning in that it compels an individual to add specific steps to the ideas presented in the original plan. For example, if your goal is to achieve an overall grade point average of 3.6 upon graduation, an action plan would provide specific steps to ensure that your goal would be met. Some of these action steps might include limiting course enrollment to fifteen hours during the spring semester while working; taking only two courses in your major during any one semester; studying at least two hours an evening during the week; and not procrastinating on assignments.

Chapter Summary

All managers must spend some time planning for the future if their organization is going to survive. Environmental scanning is an attempt to monitor the external factors that affect an organization so that the manager can determine which objectives to pursue. Competitor intelligence is a specific form of environmental scanning that tracks competitors and what they are doing. Conceptual models allow managers to develop mental maps of related topics. These conceptual models assist managers in scanning the environment and in making decisions. In addition, managers have specific planning tools for specific organizational situations. Forecasting is the systematic development of predictions about the future. Linear programming and break-even analysis are other tools that managers can use in planning. These two planning tools focus on resource planning (linear programming) or costs (break-even analysis).

In addition to planning for organizational achievement, managers must also plan for specific projects. There are many techniques for planning projects, such as PERT and Gantt charts.

These techniques provide managers with technical skills to plan projects to achieve organizational objectives.

Personal planning tools aid managers in planning their time and actions. Time management focuses on a scarce resource called time. Action planning focuses on what actions should be accomplished and the necessary steps to accomplish the activity. Each of these personal planning tools assists the manager in achieving the overall organizational goals.

The Manager's Vocabulary

environmental scanning
on-line searching
competitor intelligence
conceptual modeling
forecasting
Delphi forecasting

linear programming (LP)
break-even analysis
project planning tools
program evaluation and review
    technique (PERT)
Gantt chart

event
critical path
time management
peak performers
action planning

Review Questions

1. Why is environmental scanning a planning tool?
2. What is the reason for break-even analysis?
3. If you are sure of your resources, why would you want to spend the time on a PERT chart for a project?

4. What are some barriers to effective time management?
5. What is the difference between an action plan and strategic planning?

Analysis Questions

1. Review the assignments you have for the entire semester: (a) develop a Gantt chart for the semester projects, (b) develop an action plan for the semester, and (c) develop a time management schedule for the semester.
2. Comment on this statement: "Time management is just common sense. Either you have the ability to be organized or you don't."
3. Describe a situation where competitor intelligence borders on industrial espionage.

4. If you were going to graduate school immediately after graduation, which environmental sources would be helpful to you in making your selection of a program?
5. Try to map your thought process for determining your major. Which steps did you take for granted and almost leave out of your notes?

Self-Assessment

Time Management Profile

Introduction Time is a finite resource. Each of us only gets twenty-four hours a day to achieve our goals, needs, and desires.

This self-assessment activity explores how effectively you use your time.

Instructions Complete the following questionnaire by indicating Y (yes) or N (no) for each item. Force yourself to respond yes or no. Be frank and allow your responses to create an accurate picture of how you tend to respond to these kinds of situations.

_____ 1. When confronted with several items of similar urgency and importance, I tend to do the easiest one first.

_____ 2. I do the most important things during that part of the day when I know I perform best.

_____ 3. Most of the time I don't do things someone else can do; I delegate this type of work to others.

_____ 4. Even though meetings without a clear and useful purpose upset me, I put up with them.

_____ 5. I skim documents before reading them and don't complete any that offer a low return on my time investment.

_____ 6. I don't worry much if I don't accomplish at least one significant task each day.

_____ 7. I save the most trivial tasks for that time of day when my creative energy is at its lowest.

_____ 8. My work space is neat and organized.

_____ 9. My door is always "open"; I never work in complete privacy.

_____ 10. I schedule my time completely from start to finish every workday.

_____ 11. I don't like "to do" lists, preferring to respond to daily events as they occur.

_____ 12. I "block" a certain amount of time each day or week that is dedicated to high-priority activities.

For interpretation, turn to the back of the book.

Source: John R. Schermerhorn, Jr., *Management for Productivity*, 4th ed., Copyright © 1993 by John Wiley & Sons, Inc. Reprinted by permission of John Wiley & Sons, Inc.

Skill Builder

Robbery Planning with PERT

Purpose In this chapter you were introduced to many different planning tools and techniques. To be able to plan requires the development of both your conceptual and technical skills. This skill builder focuses on developing those skills as part of the *administrative management model*. It will help you develop the *coordinator role* of the administrative management model. Two of the skills of the coordinator are the abilities to plan and control.

Introduction This skill builder is designed to illustrate the use of the Program Evaluation and Review Technique (PERT) and Critical Path Method (CPM) in planning. In order to experience the scheduling and timing of simultaneous and sequential activities, you will create a basic PERT chart.

Instructions

Background: You are members of a notorious bank-robbing gang. The secret of your success is that your robberies are always well planned. For your next caper you have selected a rural branch of the Second National Bank. From your surveillance you have discovered that it will take the police seven minutes and thirty seconds to reach the bank once the alarm has sounded.

To complete the robbery two members of your gang (one gun person and a safe cracker) will be dropped off behind the bank and will be responsible for picking the lock on the rear door. The rest of the gang will be driven to the front of the bank to wait. Once the alarm has sounded, the entire gang will enter the bank. The gun people will point their weapons at the guards and the customers, the counter leaper will leap over the counter and empty the teller drawers, and the safe cracker will crack or blow the safe and empty it. Once these things have been accomplished, the gang will leave.

Your task is to determine whether the robbery can be accomplished in the allotted time and, if so, what the critical path is.

Your task: To create a PERT chart for the bank robbery scenario.

Robbery Informational Worksheet

Participants

2 gun people	1 counter leaper
1 safe cracker	1 driver

Activities

1. Drop off one gun person and the safe cracker in the alley behind the bank.
2. Drop off the other gang members in front of the bank.
3. Everyone enters the bank at the same time.

4. The gun people take up their positions and point their weapons at everyone in the bank.
5. The counter leaper leaps over the counter and empties the teller drawers.
6. The safe cracker cracks open the safe and empties it.
7. All members of the gang leave the bank at the same time.
8. The driver meets the rest of the gang in front of the bank when the robbery is completed.

Timing
1. Two minutes to pick the lock on the rear door.
2. The alarm goes off when the back door is picked; the police arrive after seven minutes and thirty seconds.
3. Forty-five seconds to drive from the alley to the front of the bank.
4. Thirty seconds for the gun people to enter the bank and take up their positions.
5. Sixty seconds for the safe cracker to reach the safe from the back door.

6. Thirty seconds for the counter leaper to leap over the counter and start to empty the drawers.
7. Three minutes to empty the teller drawers.
8. Two minutes to open the safe.
9. Two minutes to empty the safe.
10. Forty-five seconds to exit from the bank and reach the car at the front curb.

Decisions to Be Made
1. Can the robbery be accomplished in the seven minutes and thirty seconds before the police arrive?
2. How quickly can it be accomplished?
3. What is the critical path?
4. Are there any rearrangements of resources or objectives that would reduce the time it takes to conduct the robbery?

Source: Adapted from L.D. Goodstein and J.W. Pfeiffer (eds.), *The 1983 Annual for Facilitators, Trainers, and Consultants,* San Diego, CA: Pfeiffer & Company, 1983. Used with permission.

Concluding Cases

9.1 Microsoft and Bill Gates

Bill Gates is known as the founder of Microsoft. At the young age of thirty-seven, this CEO need not be worried about the future with his 30 percent of Microsoft's stock reaching $7.3 billion dollars. Yet Bill Gates continues to shake up the industry by pushing and changing. This future-oriented dynamo has plans for the future, and he intends to provide the users of his software with all of the information that they could want.

Many personal computer-oriented companies viewed 1992 as the year of the slump. Microsoft, however, hired 2,500 people in 1992 and plans to add that many again in 1993. Currently Microsoft controls more than 30 percent of the market, yet Gates is not content with the past. Perhaps the memory of the challenge of 1984's introduction of Microsoft's Windows keeps him striving. Regardless of the reasons, the effect of his relentless pursuit of his own long-term strategy on the rest of the industry is evident.

Gates's plan for Microsoft, revealed as the Microsoft Vision to the 7,200 staff members at the annual employee meeting, is another trend setter. The planning vision is for PC users to tap into information from anywhere and everywhere. He sees his company as meeting the challenge of the information age. His long-range vision will take at least a decade to realize, and he confidently refers to it as "Information at Your Fingertips." He believes that any piece of information the public wants should be available. Because of the relentless pace, plans and objectives are usually met, although

Microsoft has sometimes failed at meeting Gates' self-imposed delivery dates. There is a tenacious belief that eventually the product will succeed even if the product is late to market.

It has not always been a straight spiral up toward success for Gates or Microsoft. As would be expected with an entrepreneur so successful and young, Gates has had his share of adversity. In the past his outspoken confidence has placed him in direct competition with the giants of the industry, like IBM. On the other hand, when he decided to link plans for the future with IBM, some accused him of selling out Microsoft and the entrepreneurial spirit. But recently Microsoft's value ($26.76 billion) surpassed IBM's value ($26.48 billion), with no stop in sight. Clearly, the entrepreneurial spirit is still alive and well at Microsoft.[25]

Discussion Questions

1. Discuss how Bill Gates's idea of "Information at Your Fingertips" is consistent with environmental scanning and competitor intelligence gathering.
2. Discuss different databases that you think would be useful for business and your major.
3. Discuss how Microsoft might use a PERT chart to plan the software development for "Information at Your Fingertips." What are some of the events and activities that will need to be completed?

9.2   Bristol-Myers

Bristol-Myers had a difficult year in 1992, to say the least. Richard L. Gelb, chief executive officer of Bristol-Myers Squibb Co., had to announce an unheard-of goof in sales projections for the second quarter in a row. The company reported second-quarter earnings would grow in the single digits, instead of climbing 13 percent. In reaction to this news, several lawsuits were filed against the Bristol-Myers Squibb Co., charging the company's executives with misleading the public about the strength of its earnings. The company has countered the charges by saying that it made no specific earnings projections. Subsequently, the week after the announcement the drug giant's stock slid 11 percent. Stockholders have become accustomed to expecting 15 percent earnings increases since Bristol-Myers merged with Squibb in 1989. But since this initial profitable merger, the company has been struggling with a range of problems that engulf the entire organization.

Although Bristol-Myers has primarily a domestic orientation, the company has recently been moving into Japan, which is the world's number two drug market, but has little presence in the country. Bristol-Myers has also opened its first pharmaceutical plant in Russia, which will produce Capoten and Corgard, two of its cardiovascular drugs. The plant will be operated by Akrihin Chemical Co.

Even with these attempts, many state that the moves are not bold enough to recoup Bristol-Myers's downward spiral. Of course Bristol's problems are not unique to this company. Many typical woes evolved during 1992; some have been dealt with successfully, others continue to haunt the company. Sometimes what seemed like a sure bet leaves everyone baffled with the results. For example, Bristol's successful campaign for Nuprin, the high-visibility "Nupe-It" ads featuring tennis pro Jimmy Connors, failed to deliver increased sales. Actually, for the first quarter of 1992, Nuprin's share of the $1 billion pain-reliever market dropped by half a point. The commercial that aired during the U.S. Open tennis matches featured an exchange between tennis stars Jimmy Connors and Michael Chang in which Connors declared that he would make a comeback with the help of Nuprin pain reliever.

Regardless of how aggressively the company tried to head off difficulties, it was in court more than it anticipated. In April 1992 the company pleaded guilty to federal charges of illegally polluting waters in a Syracuse, N.Y., lake. The firm agreed to pay $3.5 million in fines and build a pretreatment plant to handle industrial wastes generated at its plant in East Syracuse.

The company continues to pursue advances in its research niches. It planned a $23-million expansion of its antitumor research facilities at its Candiac Quebec research center. Bristol has reason to feel confident that these will be fruitful expansions. In August of 1992, Bristol-Myers applied to the FDA for approval to market taxol, an anticancer drug. Most likely the firm will seek the approval to treat ovarian cancer since taxol has been shown effective against ovarian tumors.

The promise of marketing taxol also has its difficulties because it has been a controversial drug. Because taxol is extracted from the bark of the rare Pacific yew tree, it has caused a battle between conservationists and medical researchers. Fortunately for the company, a unit of Inverni Della Beffa Group of Italy has agreed to provide a precursor chemical for taxol that can be extracted from common yew trees. In a development that will help avert the extinction of the Pacific yew tree, Bristol-Myers Squibb and Rhone-Poulenc Rorer have come up with methods of creating a promising cancer drug without cutting down yews for taxol. Bristol-Myers has already sunk $100 million into developing the product, but other companies are close behind.

Bristol-Myers has also submitted an application to the FDA to expand the use of its AIDS drug Videx (DDI), even though an advisory panel declined to recommend any label change in April 1992 attesting to additional abilities the drug may hold. A new study on the drug, which was approved as a backup drug to Wellcome PLC's AZT in 1991, shows that it may be as good as AZT for some patients and better for those with AIDS-related complex. Burroughs Wellcome's AZT and Bristol-Myers Squibb's DDI are the only two compounds that have been approved by the FDA for AIDS treatment. Just three and one-half months after the company submitted its new drug application, the FDA voted for its approval.

Bristol-Myers is actively planning for the future. Whatever setbacks have been dealt them, the company is fighting back.[26]

Discussion Questions

1. Discuss some of the possible reasons that Bristol-Myers may have misforecast its earnings.
2. Given that forecasting depends on historical data both from the organization and the environment, explain why environmental scanning will be important as Bristol-Myers moves into Japan and Russia.
3. If you were a consultant hired by Bristol-Myers, which computer databases would you recommend the company scan to help solve some of its current problems?

CHAPTER

10

Managerial Problem Solving and Decision Making

Learning Objectives

After studying this chapter you should be able to

- Define problem solving and decision making and explain how they are related.

- Describe the problem-solving and decision-making process.

- Identify the conditions within which managers must make decisions and solve problems.

- Describe the rational and behavioral models of decision making.

- Describe decision-making techniques, including payoff matrices and decision trees.

The idea of a television network that televises news twenty-four hours a day seems obvious today. However, in 1980 when Ted Turner started the Cable News Network, or CNN, most experts said that it would never work and predicted that it would be off the air in a few months. Although CNN has had its rocky moments, it is now firmly entrenched as a regular on the cable television list of choices. Ted Turner and the three hundred people he hired to make CNN a reality dreamed that through the capacity of modern telecommunications systems news from all over the world could be available to viewers at all hours of the day anywhere in the world. The staff now numbers more than 1,700, and its signal is received by more that 75 million homes worldwide.

The network has revolutionized the news business, especially the televised news business. No longer does the news tell only what happened as recently as earlier today or yesterday. CNN tells what is happening right now, whether it is happening in a courtroom, in the capital of a country halfway around the world, or in a political campaign. How different this type of news-as-it-happens is becomes readily apparent in coverage of events such as the Persian Gulf War in 1991 when CNN had continuous broadcasts from Iraq. The broadcasts were so up to the minute that when U.S. military advisers heard that a SCUD missile had been launched, they often turned on CNN to find out where the missile would land.

Providing immediate, current, and complete coverage of historic events is not always easy, however. Making decisions about what to put on network television every minute of the day can become harrowing when headline-making news is happening around the world. Of course, truly newsworthy items do not usually come along at the same time, but when they do, there are plenty of headaches for everyone in the newsroom.

CNN executives had to make some difficult choices during the trial of William Kennedy Smith in 1991. As the network continued to provide complete gavel-to-gavel coverage of the trial, other world events began to transpire. Should CNN interrupt the trial coverage? If so, which events would warrant breaking in? As the most important witness was about to take the stand, CNN learned that the last American hostage, Terry Anderson, was about to make his first appearance in Damascus. In Atlanta, CNN producer Bob Furnad leaned toward the TV monitors and yelled directions to the staff. Then Furnad made the decision. The network televised Anderson's statement, went to commercial, and returned to the trial, missing only seven minutes of testimony. Normal decisions about daily CNN broadcasts are made in orderly staff meetings each morning. However, in unusual situations, decisions are made each minute in a "seat of the pants" fashion.[1] ∎

The executives at CNN make many different types of decisions as they deliver the news twenty-four hours a day. Routine decisions are made in the morning planning meetings. On the other hand, problems can arise when fast-breaking stories occur and regular programming must be interrupted. At CNN, producer Bob Furnad is responsible for making the minute-by-minute programming decisions. But decision making is a critical part of every manager's job and almost all organizational activities and requires a lot of skill to do successfully. Decision making is covered here because it is perhaps most closely linked to planning. However, the organizing, leading, and control functions also involve problem solving and decision making.

This chapter first explores the nature of problem solving and decision making with a focus on the individual. Group decision making will be covered in Chapter 18. Chapter 10 then outlines the problem-solving and decision-making process in detail, discusses various types and conditions of managerial problems, and identifies major approaches to making decisions. It concludes with a brief discussion of some useful problem-solving and decision-making techniques.

The Nature of Problem Solving and Decision Making

A s noted earlier, problem solving and decision making are pervasive parts of all managerial activities. Virtually every action managers take involves making one or more decisions. For example, a simple decision to raise prices must be made within the context of its probable effects on consumer and competitive behavior. A manager must also consider how much to raise prices, when to initiate the new prices, and a variety of other issues. Decision making is most closely linked to planning, since all planning involves making decisions.[2]

Managers As Problem Solvers

Problem solving occurs when a manager is faced with an unfamiliar situation for which there are no established procedures that specify how to handle the problem.

Problem solving occurs when a manager is faced with an unfamiliar situation for which there are no established procedures that specify how to handle the problem. Managers may receive information from their boss, their subordinates, their customers, or some other source that indicates that something is not going as planned. Usually the manager is aware of only some symptoms of the problem and must do some research, data gathering, or fact finding to uncover the true cause of the problem. It takes a lot of skill to separate symptoms from causes and properly diagnose the situation. Quite often this skill is affected by the way managers prefer to gather and evaluate information which they receive from the organization or the environment. This preference for how information is gathered and evaluated is called a problem-solving style. The Self-Assessment in this chapter helps identify your problem-solving style. Rather than considering problem solving as a negative situation and one that managers should fear, some optimists have suggested that problems are really opportunities for making something new and creative happen. Whether problems are crises or opportunities, managers are often faced with situations with which they have little or no experience, no decision rules, and little or no guidance as to what to do.

Suppose that a plant manager for a small electronics firm realizes that turnover in the plant has increased substantially over the past year. Having never encountered this problem before, the manager does some investigation and discovers that employees are leaving to take higher-paying jobs in other companies because wage rates in the plant have not kept up with the prevailing wage

Otis Jones and Sydney Wayman, owners of the nation's lone African-American-owned coffee roasting facility, use their problem-solving skills to upgrade their personnel. They strive to maintain a commitment to quality and lower costs and to increase sales. (Mark M. Lawrence.)

The Entrepreneurial Spirit

Gateway 2000

Every decision is driven by the corporate philosophy: the lowest price for a viable product. That philosophy has driven Gateway 2000 from nineteenth largest in the PC market in 1990 to sixth largest in 1991, when the firm sold 235,000 personal computers—all IBM clones—for an annual revenue of $635 million. Very simply, Gateway 2000 manufactures no parts, buying the best personal computer parts from other suppliers and assembling exactly what each customer orders in their only plant in North Sioux City, South Dakota. All orders are taken over the telephone, and the finished PC is shipped in black and white (as in Holstein cow) boxes directly to the customer. The company stands behind its computers with quick service provided by an outside supplier but has experienced very few quality problems. Assembly costs are low, and there is no corporate or personal income tax in South Dakota. Prices are lowered every two months, and there is no

intention to begin any manufacturing of any parts, as its predecessors in the low-cost market have done.

Starting with ten thousand dollars (his grandmother's CD) as collateral, a good idea, and a partner named Mike Hammond, company founder and president Ted Waitt has stuck by his original philosophy to provide a viable computer directly to the customer at the lowest price. The company has nearly tripled its growth and added over one thousand employees in 1991. Waitt knows the problems of adding employees, bureaucratic levels of management, and increasing decision-making complexity. He vows, however, not to stray from his original philosophy. He has hired one specialist to redesign the assembly process and another from Coopers & Lybrand to run daily operations and teach the company how to be big. He says that everyone was able to meet in the halls and make decisions. But with the increases in size, the decision makers now have to have meetings, and no one knows what the others are doing. Clearly, problem solving and decision making will have to change if the company is to continue to succeed.[3] ■

---

rate in the area. The manager therefore must address the wage issue. The problem involves a basic question: which alternative will best solve the problem—raise wages, keep them where they are and live with higher turnover, or offer incentives other than higher wages? The skills required are in differentiating between symptoms and root causes of the problem, developing alternatives, and choosing the best alternative for solving the problem. Managers increasingly find themselves in large organizations with complex situations and difficult problems to solve. *The Entrepreneurial Spirit: Gateway 2000* addresses this issue.

Managers As Decision Makers

Decision making is the process of choosing one alternative from among a set of alternatives.

Decision making is the process of choosing one alternative from among a set of alternatives. When managers make decisions, therefore, they identify a number of potentially feasible alternatives and choose what they believe to be the single best alternative for their situation. For example, before Harry Cunningham made the decision to open the first Kmart stores, he had several options: to open only one or two on a trial basis, to stay in variety retailing with the Kresge stores, to move into another branch of retailing (such as food or specialty retailing), or to open several Kmart stores. Cunningham chose the fourth alternative, and the rest, as they say, is history. Decision making and problem solving are slightly different processes, but they are also interrelated.[4]

The Problem-Solving and Decision-Making Process

Many times every day managers are faced with decisions that will enable them to take advantage of new opportunities and solve problems. At each opportunity managers need to be prepared to make the best decision possible. Many managers seem to make decisions quite easily, while others seem to agonize over each and every one. Either way, managers must utilize their best skills to make the appropriate decision. The steps in the problem-solving and decision-making process, which are summarized in Exhibit 10.1, include recognizing and diagnosing

Exhibit 10.1

The Problem-Solving and Decision-Making Process

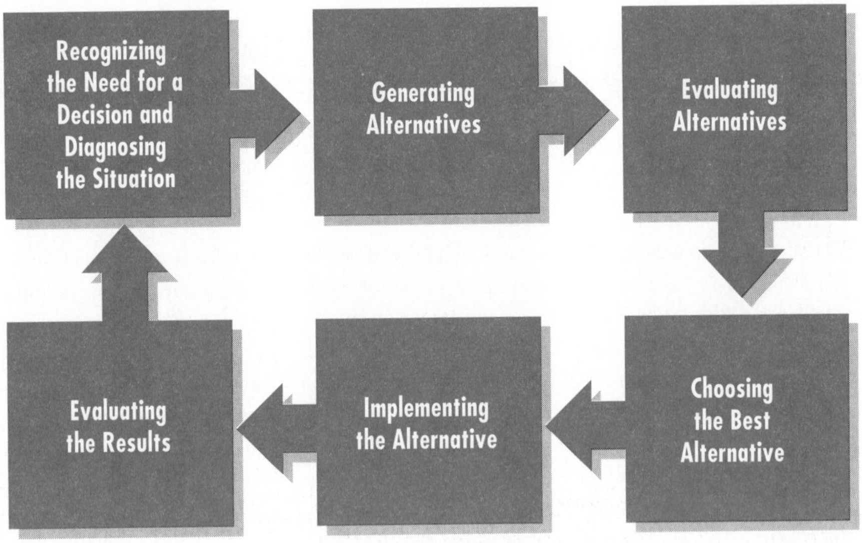

```
Recognizing          Generating          Evaluating
the Need for a   →   Alternatives   →    Alternatives
Decision and
Diagnosing
the Situation

Evaluating       ←   Implementing    ←   Choosing
the Results          the Alternative     the Best
                                         Alternative
```

the situation, generating alternatives, evaluating alternatives, selecting the best alternative, implementing the chosen alternative, and evaluating the results. Following these steps is the key skill that a manager needs to make the best decisions and solve problems effectively.[5]

Recognizing and Diagnosing the Situation

The first step for the manager is to recognize the need for a decision and to define its parameters. In the earlier chapter on strategic planning (Chapter 8), the SWOT analysis was shown to precede many decisions about the strategy of the firm. In fact, the SWOT analysis serves as the guide for all managerial decision making. Sometimes the catalyst for a decision is the recognition that a problem exists. For example, if company turnover increases by 10 percent, profits unexpectedly drop by 15 percent, or a customer files a lawsuit against the company, a problem clearly exists, and the manager needs to respond by making appropriate decisions.

Positive developments can also prompt the need to make a decision. For example, the manager of an organization with surplus profits needs to decide how those profits should be used. Likewise, a manager who makes offers to five outstanding engineers and then has all of them accept must decide about their initial job assignments.

A new business opportunity can also act as a catalyst. For example, managers at Kodak reacted to such an opportunity when the firm entered the battery market. Increased demand and cost-cutting technological breakthroughs combined to provide a perfect opportunity. Kodak had high name visibility and resources to back the venture, and it was looking for new markets to enter.

In recognizing and diagnosing the situation, it is often useful to refer back to the strategy and goals of the organization.

Recognizing and diagnosing a situation is a stage at which individual factors may come into play. An individual's predispositions and motives might influence how he or she sees the decision situation. For example, if a manager has a negative attitude about labor unions, he or she might define a situation prompted by a union-organizing campaign strictly in terms of how to avoid unionization. In any case, recognizing and diagnosing the situation are key skills in solving problems and making decisions.

Generating Alternatives

The second step of the process is to generate alternatives. Since one of the characteristics of a decision-making situation is that the manager must choose from several alternatives, the identification of those alternatives is a very important part of the process. After all, if the "best" alternative is never considered, the "right" decision can never be made.

alternative is most appropriate. The essence of this process is to try to predict the short- and long-run outcomes of each alternative in terms of the short- and long-run goals of the organization.

Selecting the Best Alternative

After evaluating the alternatives, the manager must choose one of them. The initial evaluation phase will probably eliminate some of the alternatives, and the few that remain will have many positive and negative points. The manager must decide which alternative best solves the problem or takes advantage of the opportunity.

The manager should also consider the way in which the decision was originally defined. This may provide clues as to which alternative is truly best. For example, assume that the original goal was to reduce turnover as much as possible, regardless of the costs. If that is still the goal, the manager might choose an alternative that promises to reduce turnover substantially but that carries a high cost rather than an alternative that would reduce turnover by a moderate level and cost only a moderate amount. If the original goal was to reduce turnover by a reasonable amount, or if that goal is more desirable now, the second alternative might be better.

Finally, the manager may be able to choose more than one of the alternatives simultaneously by developing contingency plans. Contingency plans, described in Chapter 7, are alternative courses of action to pursue if certain conditions occur in the future. A manager might select one preferred alternative but note that if something unusual occurs in the future, then another alternative will be put into action. Contingency planning can also be part of effective problem solving and decision making. Suppose the manager is hiring an assistant and has two strong candidates for the position. One strategy is to offer the position to one candidate and keep the other candidate on hold. If the first offer is refused, the manager still has a very acceptable alternative. Knowing when to put contingency plans into effect is a key managerial skill.

Choosing alternatives is frequently an extremely difficult process. Consider the problem faced by IBM in deciding whether to leave South Africa, where the corporation had a long history and 1,500 employees. Only after months of internal agonizing as to the best course of action did IBM's managers decide that the deteriorating political situation warranted a change in the company's policy. A related issue that occasionally arises pertains to the ethics of the various alternatives available.

Implementing the Alternative

After choosing the preferred alternative, the manager must still put it into effect. In some instances, this is fairly easy: the manager calls the chosen job applicant and offers her the job, or he buys the plot of land chosen for a new plant. In other situations, however, implementation can be quite complicated. Members of the organization might resist changes brought about by the decision to hire someone for a new position. Similarly, even though it might be easy to buy the land for a new plant, it might be nearly impossible to convince townspeople that the plant should be built.

The key to effective implementation is proper planning, including both contingency planning, as discussed in Chapter 7, and strategic planning, as discussed in Chapter 8. Changes take time, they are subject to unexpected pitfalls, and they do not always work as expected. Managers need to exercise patience and understanding during this phase.

Evaluating the Results

The final step of the problem-solving and decision-making process is to evaluate the results or consequences of the implementation of the chosen alternative. One big mistake managers occasionally make is to implement an alternative and then assume that the problem has been corrected. Things seldom go this smoothly. It is necessary to follow up and evaluate the results of the alternative in light of the original situation. One general way to handle this stage is shown in Table 10.1. First, restate the desired consequences of the decision and estimate how long it will take to realize those consequences (step 1). For example, suppose the catalyst for the decision was an unusually high absenteeism level. The manager might conclude that the desired consequence of the chosen alternative is to reduce absenteeism by 10 percent within one year. The chosen alternative is to pay a bonus to workers with a low absenteeism rate. This alternative is implemented as part of normal or-

Table 10.1

Steps in Evaluating a Decision

Basic steps in evaluating a decision
Step 1   State the desired consequences of the decision and estimate how long it will take to realize those consequences.
Step 2   Implement the alternative chosen as part of the decision-making process.
Step 3   Assess the actual consequences of the decision in light of the desired consequences.

ganizational procedures (step 2). After a year, the manager measures absenteeism again (step 3). If it has declined to the appropriate level, the problem has been solved. If not, more time, a different solution that might have been set up in contingency plans, or both might be needed to solve it.

One of the reasons why so many managers neglect the last step is that they fear what might happen if their idea has been unsuccessful. In some organizations this kind of "failure" is considered a major black mark against the manager responsible for making the decision.

Managerial Problems: Types and Conditions

 anagers must make many different types of decisions under many different conditions. The skilled manager must be able to understand these differences and react accordingly.

Routine Decisions and Nonroutine Problems

Programmed decisions are situations that occur frequently when the decision maker can utilize a decision rule or company procedure to make the decision.

Nonprogrammed decisions are decisions that have significant or expensive consequences or that have not occurred in the past and for which there is no established decision rule or procedure.

One of the important ways in which decision situations differ is in the degree of routineness of the situation. In some situations managers are faced with factors that are familiar and have occurred in the past. In such situations managers may be able to fall back on company policy, previously established procedures, or other decision rule to use in making the decision. These types of decisions are **programmed** and are quite common in organizations.

On the other hand, some situations are unique, have never occurred before, or have such large consequences that managers cannot apply corporate procedures or some decision rule and must go through extensive information gathering and alternative search and evaluation before making the decision. These are called **nonprogrammed decisions.**

Managers need to develop the skills to be able to differentiate between these two types of situations in order to be effective problem solvers and decision makers in organizations. If the problem is really nonprogrammed, yet the manager thinks it is programmed, there is the danger that an inappropriate decision rule or procedure may be used to solve the problem. Very poor outcomes could result. On the other hand, if the situation is really a programmed one, and the manager thinks that it is a nonprogrammed one, then many hours and much expense could be wasted to generate a solution that was already available. Either type of error results in less than the best utilization of organizational resources. Therefore, it is essential that managers learn the skills necessary to properly differentiate between programmed and nonprogrammed situations.

Certainty, Risk, and Uncertainty

*There are three possible decision-making conditions managers may face: **certainty, risk,** and **uncertainty.***

Just as important as understanding the type of situation, managers also need to understand the conditions within which decisions are made. All decisions are made under one of three conditions: certainty, risk, or uncertainty.[9] These situations are illustrated in Exhibit 10.3.

Certainty   Decision making under a condition of **certainty** occurs when the manager knows exactly what the alternatives are and that each alternative is guaranteed. That is, the manager knows that if Alternative 1 is chosen, it will result in certain outcomes. In reality, of course, man-

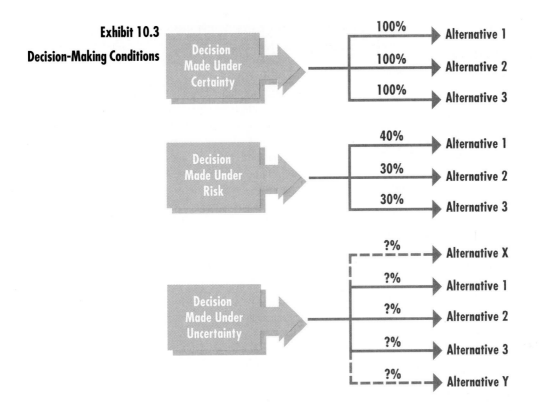

Exhibit 10.3
Decision-Making Conditions

agers encounter few situations of this nature. One example that approximates this condition occurs when American Airlines decides to buy a new jumbo jet. The company has exactly three alternative suppliers—Boeing, McDonnell Douglas, or Airbus—and knows the probable reliability, cost, delivery time, and so forth for each.

Risk Under a condition of **risk,** the manager has a basic understanding of the available options and can estimate with some confidence the probabilities associated with each alternative. That is, some element of risk is associated with each outcome. For example, suppose Dow Chemical is considering two possible sites for a new plant. Except for taxes, the two sites are equal. Site 1 has a relatively high tax rate, but the rate is not likely to be increased for several years. Site 2 has a low tax rate that will be increased next year. Managers at Dow might make several conclusions: that there is a 40-percent chance that the new tax rate at Site 2 will be higher than that at Site 1, that there is a 30-percent chance that it will be slightly lower, and that there is a 30-percent chance that the tax rate will be increased only a little beyond its current level. Dow's managers must consequently deal with a large element of risk in making their decision. Decision making under conditions of risk occurs frequently. The key to making effective decisions in these circumstances is correctly estimating the probabilities.[10] Managers at NUCOR are encouraged to take risks to improve quality and productivity and may be rewarded handsomely for it. See *The Quality Challenge: NUCOR* box.

Uncertainty The most common decision-making condition that managers must confront is **uncertainty.** In this case, not only are the probabilities hard to assess, but the list of available alternatives is as well. That is, the manager might not even be able to identify all the feasible alternatives that should be considered. This is the situation managers face in today's changing scene in Eastern Europe and Russia. Developments in those areas toward a free market economy appear to hold considerable promise for businesses and managers who are able and willing to supply the

The Quality Challenge

NUCOR

"Good managers can make bad decisions," says Ken Iverson, CEO of NUCOR Corp., the little steel "mini-mill" that is threatening the large integrated steel manufacturers. In fact, Iverson believes that good managers make about 60 percent good decisions and 40 percent bad decisions and asks that managers let him know when those 40 percent occur. Managers readily do that without being afraid of retribution. When a decision does not go well, Iverson still congratulates the manager for trying something new in an effort to make something better. He does this in the never-ending attempt to generate new ideas and make improvements. Still, Iverson does not think of himself as a revolutionary.

NUCOR is a technological leader in the steel industry, the seventh largest in the industry, with almost $1 billion in revenue. It is far different from the six companies ahead of it because it has concentrated on the mini-mill concept rather than being a fully integrated mill. Its technological leadership comes mostly from empowering its employees, which has re-sulted in its ability to make a ton of sheet steel in forty-five man-minutes compared to three man-hours for the integrated steel producers and to make it for sixty-five dollars less.

NUCOR constantly communicates with its employees and sets standards of quality and output for groups of twenty-five to thirty people who are responsible for a specific work task. Employees are paid weekly bonuses that run about 120 to 150 percent of base pay for exceeding the weekly standards. Therefore there is substantial incentive for individual employees and groups to make suggestions for improvements in quality and productivity efficiency.

NUCOR's orientation toward quality management rests on four principles. The first is few management levels—specifically, four layers in its current structure. Second, NUCOR has an absolute minimum of staff people, with only twenty-two people in its corporate office. Third, decision-making responsibility is pushed down to the lowest level of employee. The fourth principle is the generous bonus incentive system. The total effect of these four principles has been increased technological innovation, quality, and productivity for NUCOR.[11] ■

---

right goods and services at the right price. Still, considerable uncertainty persists regarding a possible reversion to a command economy, competition from other countries, the spending power of consumers in those countries, and many other unknown factors. Therefore managers contemplating a decision to enter one or more of those markets face considerable uncertainty.

Creativity, Problem Solving, and Decision Making

Creativity is a way of thinking that generates new ideas or concepts.

Regardless of their types or conditions, problem solving and decision making often require that managers develop new ideas and approaches. A key ingredient in developing these new ideas and approaches is the creativity of the manager. **Creativity** is a way of thinking that results in the generation of new ideas or concepts.[12] This chapter's Skill Builder provides you with one method for developing new ideas when you are faced with an unfamiliar situation.

Creativity is useful at every step of the decision-making process. For example, creativity can help managers see problems or opportunities looming in the future before specific symptoms are evident. Similarly, creativity can help in the generation, evaluation, and selection of alternatives. Creative people, for instance, are more likely to think of novel alternatives. And creativity can also help managers figure out new ways of implementing and evaluating alternatives.

How does the creative process work? Some see it as a spontaneous event, while others think of it as a much more complex process. One writer suggests that "sudden insights [are] not sudden at all, but [are] preceded by early premonitions and hints, which [are] then developed through an orderly and logical process."[13] As shown in Exhibit 10.4, most experts see creativity as a five-step process: preparation, frustration, incubation, illumination, and verification.

Exhibit 10.4

Steps in the Creativity Process

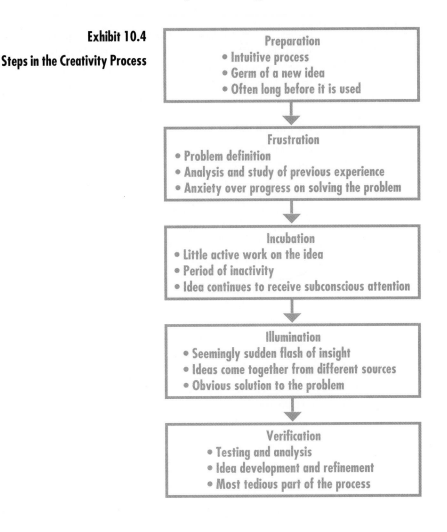

Preparation
- Intuitive process
- Germ of a new idea
- Often long before it is used

Frustration
- Problem definition
- Analysis and study of previous experience
- Anxiety over progress on solving the problem

Incubation
- Little active work on the idea
- Period of inactivity
- Idea continues to receive subconscious attention

Illumination
- Seemingly sudden flash of insight
- Ideas come together from different sources
- Obvious solution to the problem

Verification
- Testing and analysis
- Idea development and refinement
- Most tedious part of the process

The first step, preparation, relies heavily on intuition and often carries with it the germ of a new idea long before it has been used. A medical student, for example, might develop an interest in a particular illness or ailment while still in school. She may think of her interest as only a curiosity and do little formal work on it.

During the second stage, frustration, people more actively define the problems they are interested in, begin to manipulate ideas, and analyze and study previous experiences. The medical student may be drawn to a field of specialization that is especially pertinent to the illness she is interested in, without specific plans to pursue its cure. At the same time, however, her subconscious may occasionally think about the illness and link it with her current studies. Quite often this stage is frustrating because the individual does not feel much success with solving the problem.

Incubation, the third stage of the creative process, is a period of inactivity and carries with it little active work on the idea. It still receives subconscious attention, however. During her residency, the medical student may have little time or energy to work on her interests, but at the same time her thought process continues to work on it and develops new and complex insights.

Stage four is illumination. The original interests, preparation, and incubation all combine to yield what seems like a sudden flash of insight. Ideas come together from different sources and an obvious solution to the problem emerges. While treating a patient one day, or while reading a new research report in a medical journal, the former medical student—now physician—sees the potential for treating an old illness with a new drug developed for a totally different situation.

Finally, in stage five, the veracity of the idea must be confirmed. Testing and analysis are necessary to make sure that the idea will work, and additional development and refinement may be necessary. The physician will need to conduct exhaustive tests before using the new drug to treat an illness for which it has not been tested.

The time frame across which the creative process unfolds varies widely. The example we used with the medical student/physician extended across a several year period. But the entire process can also occur in a matter of days, hours, or minutes. Thinking of an idea for a term paper and determining its appropriateness, for example, might take only a few minutes.

Because of its significant role in organizational effectiveness, managers are keenly interested in creativity.[14] Firms often provide management training programs for their executives that are intended to help them become more creative. For decades Japanese managers have deemphasized creativity, preferring instead to identify ideas created in other countries and then figuring out how to exploit them. More recently, however, firms throughout Japan have started to place more value on creativity. Companies like Shiseido, Fuji, Omron, and Shimizu, for example, have recently initiated new executive training programs that emphasize creativity.[15]

Approaches to Decision Making

Managers approach decision making and problem solving in many different ways. Most managers, of course, like to think that they are completely rational in their decision making. However, the complexities and variations of problems and decision situations make the utilization of consistently rational decision processes virtually impossible.[16] There is a general consensus that most managerial decision making follows one of two models: the rational model or the behavioral model.[17]

The Rational Model

*The **rational model** of decision making assumes that managers are objective, have perfect information, and consider all alternatives and consequences.*

The **rational model** of decision making assumes that decision makers are objective, have complete information, and consider all alternatives and consequences when making decisions. The rational approach is the one that many managers claim to follow. The basic premises of the rational model are summarized in Table 10.2.[18]

First, this model assumes that managers have perfect information; that is, they have all the information that is relevant to the situation, and the information is completely accurate. Second, the model assumes that the decision maker has an exhaustive list of alternatives from which to choose. If there are eight potential alternatives, the rational model assumes that the manager has complete knowledge and understanding of all of them.

Next, as the model's name implies, it holds that managers are always rational. It assumes that managers are capable of systematically and logically assessing each alternative and its associated probabilities and making the decision that is best for the situation. Finally, the rational model assumes that managers always work in the best interests of the organization. Even if their decision makes them suffer, managers will still be motivated to make the decision that other managers in the same organization would make in that situation. Thus, even if the clearest course of action will result in budget cuts for a manager's own department, the manager is expected to choose that alternative anyway.

Clearly, the rational model is not always realistic in its depiction of managerial behavior. A variety of forces, including imperfect information, emotions, fatigue, personal motives, individual preferences, and organizational politics and reward systems often intervene in most decision situations. The behavioral model represents an attempt to incorporate these individual processes into managerial decision making.

Table 10.2

Rational and Behavioral Models of Decision Making

Rational model	Behavioral model
1. The decision maker has perfect information (relevant and accurate).	1. The decision maker has imperfect information (incomplete and possibly inaccurate).
2. The decision maker has an exhaustive list of alternatives from which to choose.	2. The decision maker does not have a complete set of alternatives or does not completely understand those he or she does have.
3. The decision maker is rational.	3. The decision maker has bounded rationality and is constrained by values, experiences, habits, etc.
4. The decision maker always has the best interests of the organization at heart.	4. The decision maker will select the first minimally acceptable alternative (satisficing).

The Behavioral Model

*The **behavioral model** of decision making recognizes that managers do not always have complete information and are limited in their ability to make rational decisions.*

The **behavioral model** of decision making recognizes that managers have incomplete information about the situation, alternatives, and their evaluation, thus limiting their potential for making the best possible decision. The behavioral approach was first explained by Herbert Simon, who was subsequently awarded a Nobel prize for his contributions.[19] The basic premises of the behavioral model are also summarized in Table 10.2.

First, this view assumes that managers have imperfect information. That is, the information might be incomplete and/or parts of it might be inaccurate. Second, the behavioral model assumes that managers also have an incomplete list of alternatives. There may be alternatives that managers simply do not know about, they may not completely understand some of the alternatives, and the probabilities associated with various alternatives may be difficult to predict.

***Bounded rationality** suggests that rationality is constrained by values and experiences and by unconscious reflexes, skills, and habits.*

Managers are also assumed to be characterized by **bounded rationality**. This means that managers may attempt to be rational, but this rationality is constrained by their own values and experiences and by unconscious reflexes, skills, and habits. For example, if a manager has a history of making decisions in a certain fashion, he or she will probably continue to follow that same pattern, even when an objective observer might see the need for a new approach. Finally, the behavioral model assumes that decision makers engage in what is called satisficing. **Satisficing** is selecting the first minimally acceptable alternative even though a more thorough search could uncover better ones. For example, suppose a college student wants a job in marketing, preferably in marketing research, with a minimum salary of $25,000 and within one hundred miles of his hometown. When he is offered a job in marketing (although it is in sales) for $25,500 at a company eighty miles from home, he may be inclined to take it. A more comprehensive search, however, could have revealed a job in marketing research for $30,000 only twenty-five miles from home.

***Satisficing** occurs when a manager selects the first minimally acceptable alternative without conducting a thorough search.*

Other Behavioral Processes

Beyond the concepts of bounded rationality and satisficing, there are also other important behavioral processes that affect how decisions are made. One such process is called **escalation of commitment**.[20] This is the tendency of people to continue with a course of action when evidence indicates that the course of action or project is doomed to failure. The idea behind escalation of commitment is that people sometimes make a decision and then become so committed to it that

Escalation of commitment is the tendency of people to continue to pursue an ineffective course of action even when current information indicates that the project will fail.

they fail to see that it was incorrect. For example, suppose an investor buys stock in a company for fifty dollars a share. As the price starts to drop, the investor may doggedly hold on to the stock — not wanting to take a loss — when others see that it is a lost cause. Instead of selling the stock for forty dollars and taking a 20-percent loss, the investor may continue to hold on to it or even buy more at the lower price until the total investment is lost. Managers at ABC may have been guilty of this error with their 1988 production of the costly mini-series "War and Remembrance," which was the sequel to the highly successful mini-series "Winds of War." The sequel was expected to also be a big hit. Halfway through the project everyone involved knew that it could not possibly make money, because of extremely high production costs. Managers at ABC, however, continued production and probably lost about $20 million.[21]

Decision framing is the tendency of people to let the way that a decision is stated, either as a potential gain or loss, affect their choice of risky or cautious alternatives.

Another behavioral process that affects managers when they make decisions is **decision framing.** This is the way the decision situation is perceived by the decision maker, either in terms of a potential gain or a potential loss.[22] When a decision is framed in terms of a loss, decision makers tend to choose more risky alternatives. On the other hand, when the decision is framed in terms of a gain, decision makers tend to choose less risky alternatives. Disastrous consequences have occurred when decision makers have framed their decisions as the choice between two losses and have subsequently chosen the more risky alternative. Examples include the decision by Coca-Cola to change the formula for its Coke product and introduce the new Coke, the decision by President Jimmy Carter to attempt to rescue the American hostages held in Iran, and the Iran-Contra affair in which arms were sent to Iran in exchange for hostages during the Reagan administration. In each situation evidence exists that suggests that the decision was framed as a choice between losses, which could have led to the selection of a risky alternative. Suggestions on how to avoid the problems associated with decision framing include (1) training decision makers to be aware of the effects of framing a problem in certain ways, (2) trying to approach problems from multiple frames of reference, and (3) avoiding reacting with a first impulse.[23]

Other behavioral forces that affect decision making include power, political behavior, and coalitions. Power, discussed more fully in Chapter 16, is the ability to affect the behavior of others. Political behaviors are activities carried out for the specific purpose of acquiring, developing, and using power to obtain a preferred course of action.

Finally, coalitions are informal alliances of people or groups formed to achieve a common goal.[24] For example, suppose a ten-person board of directors is deciding on a new CEO for a corporation. If the board is split into factions of three, three, and four members, no single faction can get its way. However, by forming a coalition, any two factions that can compromise on a candidate will control a majority vote. The coalition can then force the group to make a decision in the way that it wants.

Tools for Improving Problem Solving and Decision Making

The Payoff Matrix

*A **payoff matrix** determines the expected values for two or more alternatives, each of which is associated with a probability estimate.*

As with planning, there are several useful techniques that managers can utilize to enhance their decision-making skills. Two of the more popular techniques are the payoff matrix and decision trees.

The **payoff matrix** involves the calculation of expected values for two or more alternatives, each of which is associated with a probability estimate.[25] A payoff matrix is useful when the probability of occurrence of each outcome can be estimated. **Probability** is the likelihood, expressed as a percentage, that an event will or will not occur. If something is certain to happen, its probability is 1.00. If it is certain not to happen, its probability is 0. If there is a fifty-fifty chance, its probability is .50.

The **expected value** of an alternative is the sum of all its possible outcomes multiplied by their respective probabilities. Thus, if there is a 50-percent chance that an investment will earn

Probability *is the likelihood that an event will or will not occur.*

The ***expected value*** *of an alternative is the sum of all its possible outcomes multiplied by their respective probabilities.*

$100,000, a 25-percent chance that it will earn $10,000, and a 25-percent chance that it will lose $50,000, the expected value (EV) of the investment is

$$EV = .50(\$100,000) + .25(\$10,000) + .25(-\$50,000)$$
$$= \$50,000 + \$2,500 - \$12,500$$
$$= \$40,000.$$

The following example of an extended version of an investment decision illustrates how this concept relates to the payoff matrix. Suppose that we are considering buying either a computer business or a sailboat business. We have determined that the success of each business is dependent on inflation. If inflation increases, we will make $5 million from the computer business or $3 million from the sailboat business. If inflation decreases, however, we will lose $4 million in the computer business but lose only $2 million in the sailboat business. We have also estimated that there is a 70-percent chance that inflation will increase and a 30-percent chance that it will decrease.

The resultant payoff matrix is shown in Exhibit 10.5. The expected values are calculated as described above. For the computer business, the expected value is

$$EV = .70(\$5 \text{ million}) + .30(\$-4 \text{ million})$$
$$= \$3.5 \text{ million} - \$1.2 \text{ million}$$
$$= \$2.3 \text{ million}.$$

For the sailboat business, the expected value is

$$EV = .70(\$3 \text{ million}) + .30(\$-2 \text{ million})$$
$$= \$2.1 \text{ million} - \$.6 \text{ million}$$
$$= \$1.5 \text{ million}.$$

Thus, investing in the computer business is likely to result in a higher profit than investing in the sailboat business.

Payoff matrices have a number of applications in organizational settings, and the popularity of personal computers promises to make them even more pervasive. Of course, the manager always needs to remember that the estimates of expected value are only as good as the quality of the estimates for potential payoffs and their associated probabilities.

Exhibit 10.5

The Payoff Matrix

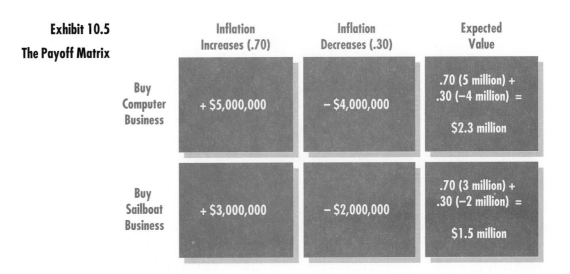

	Inflation Increases (.70)	Inflation Decreases (.30)	Expected Value
Buy Computer Business	+ $5,000,000	− $4,000,000	.70 (5 million) + .30 (−4 million) = $2.3 million
Buy Sailboat Business	+ $3,000,000	− $2,000,000	.70 (3 million) + .30 (−2 million) = $1.5 million

Decision Trees

Decision trees are extensions of payoff matrices that diagram alternatives and the first-, second-, and third-level outcomes.

A **decision tree** is an extension of a payoff matrix that diagrams alternatives and includes second- and third-level outcomes that can result from the first outcome.[26] Consider a medium-size manufacturing company that is thinking about building a new plant. It needs the plant because demand for the company's products is projected to increase. There is some chance that the increase will be large, or high, and some chance that it will be small, or low, so the manager is trying to decide whether to build a large or a small plant. This decision scenario is illustrated in decision tree format in Exhibit 10.6.

First, the manager must decide on the size of the new plant. Regardless of the size of the plant that is chosen, demand will either be high or low. If there is high demand and a small plant is built, another decision will be necessary. Probable alternatives include building another small plant, selling the new small plant and building a bigger one, and leaving the demand unsatisfied. Of course, if the manager builds a small plant and demand is low, no further action is needed.

If the manager builds a large plant and demand is high, again no action is needed. On the other hand, if a large plant is built and demand is low, there are again new alternatives to consider: should the plant produce at partial capacity, with the rest of the plant sitting idle; should the plant produce at capacity and create an excess inventory in hopes of future increases in demand, or should the manager again wait for more information?

To use the decision tree, the manager needs to estimate probabilities for each alternative on all branches of the tree. Then, working backward from the right to the left, the manager is able to estimate the expected values of building a large and a small plant.

Exhibit 10.6   The Decision Tree

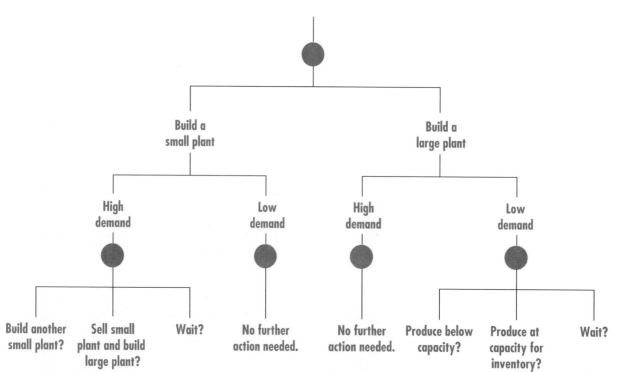

As with payoff matrices, the key managerial skill needed to effectively use a decision tree is to be able to forecast potential outcomes and to estimate the probabilities of each potential outcome accurately. Again, computers make decision trees much easier for managers to use.

Other Techniques

*Other decision-making techniques include **inventory, queuing,** and **distribution** models.*

Other fairly common quantitative techniques for decision making are inventory models, queuing models, and distribution models.

An **inventory model** is a decision-making technique that helps the manager plan the optimal level of inventory to carry. For example, ordering large quantities of raw materials decreases the chances that the organization will run out but increases storage costs. Ordering smaller quantities reduces the storage costs but increases the chances of running out. An inventory model can help estimate how much material should be ordered, how often, when, and at what cost.

A **queuing model** is a decision-making technique that helps plan waiting lines—in a Safeway grocery store, for instance. Having one check-out operator will reduce costs but increase waiting lines and therefore customer dissatisfaction. Having twenty check-out operators on duty at all times will keep customers happy but will dramatically increase personnel costs. Queuing models help determine the best number of operators to have on duty at various times of the day.

Finally, a **distribution model** helps managers plan routes for distributing products. Suppose a company needs to drop off shipments of products at twenty different points around the city. Left to their own devices, drivers might not proceed from one stop to another in the best sequence. A distribution model helps develop that sequence so as to minimize travel time and fuel expenses and maximizes employee productivity.

Chapter Summary

P roblem solving occurs when a manager is faced with an unfamiliar situation for which there are no established procedures that specify how to handle the problem. Decision making is the process of choosing one alternative from among a set of alternatives.

The problem-solving and decision-making process involves six steps. Recognizing and diagnosing the situation, the first step, involves recognizing the need for a decision and defining its parameters. The second step calls for generating alternatives from which to choose. Next the manager must evaluate, or judge, the alternatives. The fourth step is selecting the best alternative from those available. Implementing the alternative, or putting it into effect, is the fifth step, and involves careful planning. The final step is evaluating the results of the process.

Programmed decisions occur in situations that are routine in nature, have occurred in the past, and for which there exists a decision rule or company procedure for handling the problem. Nonprogrammed decisions are nonroutine decision situations that do not occur frequently, for which there is no decision rule or company procedure, or for decisions that have very significant

consequences. In addition, decisions are made under three conditions: certainty, risk, and uncertainty. Creativity is a way of thinking that generates new ideas or concepts and is a five-step process: insight, preparation, incubation, illumination, and verification.

There are two general approaches to decision making, the rational model and the behavioral model. The rational model assumes perfect information, an exhaustive list of alternatives, managers who are capable of systematically and logically assessing those alternatives, and managers who will always work in the best interests of the organization. The behavioral model is a modification of this approach and assumes imperfect information, an incomplete list of alternatives, bounded rationality, and satisficing behavior. Escalation of commitment, decision framing, power, political behaviors, and coalitions also influence how decisions are made.

Numerous techniques have been developed to aid managers in making decisions. Two general techniques are the payoff matrix and decision trees. Other techniques include inventory, queuing, and distribution models.

The Manager's Vocabulary

problem solving
decision making
brainstorming
programmed decisions
nonprogrammed decisions
certainty
risk
uncertainty

creativity
rational model
behavioral model
bounded rationality
satisficing
escalation of commitment
decision framing
payoff matrix

probability
expected value
decision tree
inventory model
queuing model
distribution model

Review Questions

1. List and describe the steps in the decision-making process.
2. What is the difference between programmed and nonprogrammed decision situations?
3. Describe the three basic conditions under which managers make decisions.

4. What is the role of creativity in decision making?
5. Compare and contrast the rational and behavioral models of decision making.
6. Describe the differences and similarities between payoff matrices and decision trees.

Analysis Questions

1. Identify a decision-making circumstance that has elements of both certainty and uncertainty.
2. Which model of decision making do you think is most common? Is a manager most likely to follow one of the models almost exclusively, or will the same manager go back and forth between models? Why?
3. Identifying all the potential alternatives to a decision situation may be too costly, if not impossible. Yet satisficing is a problem if too few alternatives are explored. How might a manager guard against these extremes?

4. Can creativity be practiced apart from decision making, or are the two always linked? Why?
5. Identify a recent situation in which you framed a decision in terms of a choice between losses. Did you eventually choose the riskier of the two alternatives? How could you have framed the decision differently so that your perspective of the choices might have been different?

Self-Assessment

Problem-Solving Style Questionnaire

Introduction One of the critical skills needed by all managers is the ability to solve problems. One of the underlying characteristics of problem solving is how the managers prefer to gather and evaluate information. This self-assessment will aid you in determining your preferred problem-solving style.

Instructions Indicate the response that usually describes your concerns and behaviors. There are no right or wrong answers to the questions. For each question, indicate which of the two alternative statements is more characteristic of you. Some statements may seem to be equally characteristic or uncharacteristic of you. While we anticipated this, try to choose the statement that is relatively more characteristic of what you do or feel in your everyday life. You will be working with pairs of statements and will have 5 points to distribute among the statements. Points may be divided between each A and B statement in any of the following combination pairs.

- If A is completely characteristic of you and B is completely uncharacteristic, write a 5 on your answer sheet under A and 0 under B, thus:

$$\frac{A}{5} \bigg| \frac{B}{0}$$

- If A is considerably more characteristic of you and B is somewhat characteristic, write a 4 on your answer sheet under A and a 1 under B, thus:

$$\frac{A}{4} \bigg| \frac{B}{1}$$

- If A is only slightly more characteristic of you than B, write a 3 on your answer sheet under A and a 2 under B, thus:

$$\frac{A}{3} \bigg| \frac{B}{2}$$

- Each of the above three combinations may be used in reverse order. For example, should you feel that B is slightly more characteristic of you than A, write a 2 on your answer sheet under A and a 3 under B, thus: (And so on, for A = 1, B = 4; or A = 0, B = 5)

$$\frac{A}{2} \bigg| \frac{B}{3}$$

Be sure that the numbers you assign to each pair sum to 5 points. Relate each question in the index to your own behavior. Remember, there is no right or wrong answer. Attempts to give a "correct" response merely distort the meaning of your answers and render the inventory's results valueless.

Questions   Score

1. Are you more
   (a) pragmatic   A | B
   (b) idealistic

2. Are you more impressed by
   (a) standards   A | B
   (b) sentiments

3. Are you more interested in that which
   (a) convinces you by facts   A | B
   (b) emotionally moves you

4. It is worse to
   (a) be practical   A | B
   (b) have a boring routine

5. Are you more attracted to
   (a) a person with common sense   A | B
   (b) a creative person

6. In judging others, are you more swayed by
   (a) the rules   A | B
   (b) the situation

7. Are you more interested in
   (a) what has happened   A | B
   (b) what can happen

8. Do you more often have
   (a) presence of mind   A | B
   (b) warm emotions

9. Are you more frequently
   (a) a realistic sort of person   A | B
   (b) an imaginative sort of person

10. Are you more
    (a) faithful   A | B
    (b) logical

11. Are you more
    (a) action oriented   A | B
    (b) creation oriented

12. Which guides you more
    (a) your brain   A | B
    (b) your heart

13. Do you take pride in your
    (a) realistic outlook   A | B
    (b) imaginative ability

14. Which is more of a personal compliment
    (a) you are consistent in reasoning   A | B
    (b) you are considerate of others

15. Are you more drawn to
    (a) basics   A | B
    (b) implications

16. It is better to be
    (a) fair   A | B
    (b) sentimental

17. Would you rather spend time with
    (a) realistic people   A | B
    (b) idealistic people

18. Would you describe yourself as
    (a) hard   A | B
    (b) soft

19. Would your friends say that you are
    (a) someone who is filled by new ideas A | B
    (b) someone who is a realist

20. It is better to be called a person who shows
    (a) feelings   A | B
    (b) reasonable consistency

(con't. on page 236)

Answer Form

Please enter the numbers for your response to each question in the appropriate columns.

Questions	Column I A	Column II B	Questions	Column III A	Column IV B
1	——	——	2	——	——
3	——	——	4	——	——
5	——	——	6	——	——
7	——	——	8	——	——
9	——	——	10	——	——
11	——	——	12	——	——
13	——	——	14	——	——
15	——	——	16	——	——
17	——	——	18	——	——
19	——	——	20	——	——
TOTAL SCORE	——	——		——	——
	S	N		T	F

For interpretation, turn to the back of the book.

Source: Reprinted by permission from pages 144–146 of *Organizational Behavior*, 6th ed., by Hellriegel, Slocum, and Woodman. Copyright © 1992 by West Publishing Company. All rights reserved.

Skill Builder

Metaphorically Speaking

Purpose The ability to come up with new, novel, and useful ideas to old problems is critical in the highly competitive business environment that managers face today. To be able to generate new ideas, means developing your creative skills. This skill builder focuses on the *open systems model*. It will help you develop the *innovator role* of the open systems model. One of the skills of the director is taking initiative, while one of the skills of the innovator is the ability to solve problems creatively.

Introduction Creating metaphors can help to develop new insights into a particular problem. The metaphor can provide a greater understanding of the problem and possibly identify a new solution to the problem. Metaphors can also be used to explain a complex idea in simple language. This activity uses the power of the metaphor to help you understand a specific problem. By developing this skill you will improve your ability to think creatively.

Instructions

Your instructor will provide additional materials for this exercise.

Source: From Geof Cox, Chuck Dufault and Walt Hopkins, *50 Activities on Creativity and Problem Solving*. Reprinted by permission of Gower Publishing Company Limited.

CONCLUDING CASES

10.1   Cargill's Three Big Decisions

Family-owned businesses usually stay pretty small and struggle through hard times with every economic downturn. If they grow very large, they often have difficulty dealing with the differences caused by sheer size. If they clear this hurdle and become very successful, the second generation often has problems with internal bickering between heirs who want control or who want to get their share of the fortune and get out of the business. Cargill somehow has survived these transitions and has become a commodities giant with 1991 revenues of $49.1 billion. Starting in 1865 the first Cargill bought grain from farmers and sold it to larger markets in cities. Currently it is nearly three times the size of the next largest privately held company and is the second-largest diversified services company, the nation's largest grain merchandiser, the second-largest beef packer, and the eighth-largest steel producer.

A marriage in the second generation to the MacMillan family has led to members of the families owning and running the business ever since. The heirs now number about seventy-five and own 100 percent of the company stock. Management has always been characterized as very conservative. Decisions are made by a council of elder family members who meet for coffee every day at ten A.M. at company headquarters in a suburb of Minneapolis. The guiding principle for decisions is to do what is right for the family and the business.

Currently Cargill is facing three major decisions that will change the company and determine its future. First, its leadership, from the chairman down through the vice presidential level, is nearing retirement age, and no family member is ready for these top jobs. A family crisis looms as members debate if, when, and how to turn the company over to nonfamily leadership. Quite naturally, feelings run high throughout the clan. Second, many members of the family are not pleased with the low rate of return their shares are providing. The company usually returns about 3 percent of income to shareholders, and in 1991 its earnings were only about 1 percent of sales revenue. The estimates of what shares of the company might bring on the market have been about $10 billion, and a group of heirs would strongly like to get their share.

Third, in many of Cargill's commodity businesses the problems are many: thin margins, increasing worldwide competition, and changing buying patterns worldwide. The natural remedy is to move "up the food chain" into retail markets, which have much higher margins and the potential for huge profits. In the few efforts to do so to date, Cargill's inexperience in mass-market retailing has shown and products have been withdrawn.

These three issues will severely test the more conservative decision making of the past. These three decisions will have to be made soon since the retirements will hit within the next three to five years, the younger relatives are eager to get their hands on some of the money, and the mass-marketing opportunities for food products changes rapidly.[27]

Discussion Questions

1. How would you classify these three decisions in terms of risk, certainty, and uncertainty? Why?
2. Which type of decision-making process would you use to make these decisions?
3. Which decision-making techniques do you think would be appropriate for these three decisions?

10.2 Royal Dutch/Shell: Masters at Decision Making in Uncertainty

Royal Dutch/Shell is the most common name for the oil company giant that was formed in 1907 by the merger of two firms: the Dutch firm Royal Dutch Petroleum and the British firm Shell Transport & Trading. It now has nine service divisions and more than nine hundred operating companies in one hundred different countries with more than 120,000 employees. Once the weakest of the top seven major oil companies in 1970, Shell surpassed Exxon as the world's largest oil company in 1990. It is second only to General Motors of the world's largest industrial corporations, with sales revenues of $107 billion in 1990. Shell and the rest of the industry are facing extremely difficult times as development costs for new crude oil reserves are skyrocketing, refining costs are increasing, environmental concerns are causing new problems, and prices are weakening all over the world. The environment within which the major oil companies operate is one of the most dynamic in the world, with the price of raw crude oil moving between four dollars and forty dollars per barrel as only one example. Shell's top management, specifically Sir Peter Holmes, current chairman of the management committee, claims that the best is still ahead of them and that Shell is ready to take on the new challenges.

How has Shell developed into such a major power and continued to increase in every aspect of the business when all of the others are shrinking? How has it continued to succeed and grow in the face of political, economic, and technological chaos taking place all over the world? The answer may lie in its approach to planning, problem solving, and decision making. First, in planning Shell attempts to take the risk out of making decisions by constantly forecasting future events under every scenario imaginable. The planning team attempts to foresee every possible future catastrophic event and plan the proper organizational response. The team even practices different organizational responses, much like practice fire drills. Therefore, when actual events do transpire, Shell has a system in place ready to be activated.

Second, the decision-making process is unique in major corporations anywhere. There are six managing directors, representing the major divisions, all of whom have extensive experience in managing at least one major operating division. These six directors must agree on every major decision. If anyone disagrees, the issue is discussed until true consensus is reached; otherwise the proposal is not agreed to or acted upon. This group even moves back and forth between the corporate offices in the Netherlands and London to keep in touch with activities in both offices. Consensus problem solving and decision making and a revolutionary planning process are keeping Shell on top.[28]

Discussion Questions

1. Which types of decision-making conditions does Shell face?
2. Does Shell use the rational or the behavioral model of decision making? Why?
3. Which kinds of decision-making techniques do you think Shell probably uses?

Part Three   Planning and Decision Making

Self-Assessment

Decision Making in the Daily Life of Managers

Introduction The abilities to solve problems, plan, and make decisions go hand in hand. A manager's life is filled with decision points. Many of these decisions must be made under a condition of uncertainty. This self-assessment examines your ability to make decisions under uncertainty.

Instructions For each incident below, indicate your degree of approval for each of the interpretations by assigning any number of points from 0 to 100 to any of the interpretations. Total points assigned must equal 100. Assign a number to each interpretation, even if that number is 0.

1. You are the manager of a small group of workers. Unfortunately, your philosophy and the company's philosophy conflict and your influence with upper management is limited. Your group is dissatisfied with company policy.

   Would you ask employees:

   a. _____ To fall in line in almost all cases.

   b. _____ To make up their own minds.

   c. _____ To follow the majority decision of all members.

   d. _____ To follow your position on issues.

   e. _____ To communicate their concern to management.

   f. _____ Not to fall in line in almost all cases.

2. A group of employees under you develops an improved tool capable of increasing productivity by 50 percent. Actual productivity increases 10 percent and quality improves as well. The group withholds information about the tool from the methods engineer.

   Would you:

   a. _____ Tell the methods engineer in almost all cases.

b. _____ Attempt to convince the employees to divulge the information.

c. _____ Be satisfied with the 10 percent increase.

d. _____ Speak to each worker individually to assess the situation.

e. _____ Ask the workers to increase their output.

f. _____ Not tell the methods engineer in almost all cases.

3. You are a manager in the production department of your firm. The firm has stringent regulations against the consumption of alcohol on business premises. One hot afternoon you find an "old timer" drinking a bottle of beer.

   Would you:

   a. _____ Report the person in almost all cases.

   b. _____ Reprimand the person and give a warning.

   c. _____ Ask for an explanation of this behavior.

   d. _____ Lay off the person as allowed in the union contract.

   e. _____ Overlook the incident after making certain that the person sees you.

   f. _____ Not report the person in almost all cases.

4. You find out that a shipper has been "working a deal" with the majority of your best salespeople whereby they all gain financially at the expense of the organization. The amounts are not large but the practice is widespread. You are the sales manager.

   Would you:

   a. _____ Fire all the guilty parties in almost all cases.

   b. _____ Fire the shipper and keep the salespeople.

c. _____ Call a meeting to tell them you know what they are doing but not fire anyone.

d. _____ Overlook the situation, assuming it to be a "bonus."

e. _____ Try to catch them in the act.

f. _____ Not fire all guilty parties in almost all cases.

5. Due to rapid expansion of your organization, your "open door" policy is taking up a disproportionate amount of time.

Would you:

a. _____ "Close the door" in almost all cases.

b. _____ Try to have your secretary screen employees before they reach you.

c. _____ Institute a formal communication system such as a company newsletter.

d. _____ Work after hours so as to maintain your close relationship with employees.

e. _____ Set up an appointment book.

f. _____ Not close the door in almost all cases.

6. A new production process will increase profits by an estimated 10 percent. It will also significantly pollute a large river running through a nearby town. Government regulations do not affect your firm.

Would you:

a. _____ Introduce the process in almost all cases.

b. _____ Introduce the process only if profits are lower than usual.

c. _____ Introduce the process only if your competitor does.

d. _____ Not introduce the process unless pressured by upper management.

e. _____ Not introduce the process if residents of the town complain.

f. _____ Not introduce the process in almost all cases.

7. A friend is having difficulty at work with subordinates. Informally you have heard it said that your friend is too autocratic and disorganized. The friend has asked you for your opinion of why problems exist.

Would you:

a. _____ Tell your friend what you have heard in almost all cases.

b. _____ Tell your friend that he/she is too autocratic but not discuss organizational ability.

c. _____ Tell your friend that he/she is disorganized but not discuss his/her autocratic behavior.

d. _____ Tell your friend that what he/she does at work is his/her own business.

e. _____ Ask your friend what he/she thinks the problem is.

f. _____ Not tell your friend what you have heard in almost all cases.

8. As manager of a radio station, you are faced with a dilemma. Your program manager works a twelve-hour day, but the popularity of the station is declining and it is losing money. The program manager has worked for your organization for five years.

Would you:

a. _____ Fire the program manager in almost all cases.

b. _____ Replace the person and give him/her another job.

c. _____ Take over some of the program manager's duties yourself.

d. _____ Ask the person to look for another job but continue to employee him/her.

e. _____ Try to determine the person's weaknesses so that you can help.

f. _____ Not fire the program manager in almost all cases.

9. Your best salesperson has difficulty relating to peers. The position of sales manager is open and this salesperson has told you that he/she plans to leave if not promoted.

Would you:

a. _____ Give the person the job in almost all cases.

b. _____ Tell the person that he/she needs more management training.

c. _____ Tell the person that you hate to lose a great salesperson to gain a questionable sales manager.

d. _____ Ask the person what qualities he/she has to do a good job.

e. _____ Tell the person to prove he/she can get along with others first.

f. _____ Not give the person the job in almost all cases.

(con't. on page 240)

10. A bright young scientist has joined your research team in the past few months. The scientist has come to you with a letter from a competing firm offering a job with a 25 percent salary increase.

Would you:

a. _____ Offer an equal salary in almost all cases.

b. _____ Ask why he/she is showing you the letter.

c. _____ Try to sell the advantages of your firm.

d. _____ Tell the scientist that he/she can make as much at your firm after a time.

e. _____ Tell the person that loyalty should count for something.

f. _____ Not offer to increase salary in almost all cases.

For interpretation, turn to the back of the book.

Source: Reprinted from J. William Pfeiffer and Leonard D. Goodstein (Eds.), *The 1982 Annual for Facilitators, Trainers, and Consultants*. San Diego, CA: Pfeiffer & Company, 1982. Used with permission.

Skill Builder

Establishing Policies, Procedures, and Rules

Purpose Planning requires managers to use their conceptual, human, and technical skills. Throughout this part of the textbook, we have provided you with knowledge about how a manager might carry out the planning task. In this skill builder, you get the chance to apply your hand to the planning process. This skill builder focuses on the *administrative management model*. It will help you develop the *coordinator role* of the administrative management model. One of the skills of the coordinator is the ability to plan. In this exercise, you expand on your technical skills in planning, whereas the exercise in Chapter 8 developed your conceptual skills in planning.

Introduction Policies are standing plans that are general statements defining the organization's general approach to an issue and are designed to serve as guides for individual attitudes and behaviors. Procedures, on the other hand, are standing plans that outline the sequential steps necessary to accomplish a particular task. Rules and regulations are standing plans that specify exactly how tasks are to be done.

Instructions Each group will complete the Policies, Procedures, and Rules Worksheet for the corporation assigned by your instructor. The group will also develop group responses to the discussion questions. One representative from each group will report on the group's activities and on the group's responses to the discussion questions.

Discussion Questions

1. If large organizations have large books of procedures and rules, why do they still write policies?
2. If a corporation is unionized, what role does the union play in developing these categories of standing plans?
3. For the average employee, which of these standing-plan categories is most familiar? Is that good or bad?

POLICIES, PROCEDURES, AND RULES WORKSHEET

Corporation Assigned: _____

For each corporate issue listed, write: (1) a policy to guide employee thinking and behavior, (2) a short outline of a procedure related to the policy, and (3) a rule for enforcing the policy.

Corporate Issues	Policies, Procedures, and Rules	
Equal Employment Opportunity	Policy	_____
	Procedure	_____

Equal Employment
Opportunity (con't.)

                    Rule _____

_____

Employee Layoffs   Policy _____

                  Procedure _____

_____

_____

                  Rule _____

_____

Employee Safety   Policy _____

                  Procedure _____

_____

_____

                  Rule _____

_____

Product Quality   Policy _____

                  Procedure _____

_____

_____

                  Rule _____

_____

Product Safety   Policy _____

                  Procedure _____

_____

_____

                  Rule _____

_____

Corporate Tax   Policy _____

                  Procedure _____

_____

_____

                  Rule _____

Environmental
    Pollution   Policy   _____

                             Procedure   _____

                                         _____

                                         _____

                             Rule   _____

                                         _____

Advertising   Policy   _____

                             Procedure   _____

                                         _____

                                         _____

                             Rule   _____

                                         _____

Public Image   Policy   _____

                             Procedure   _____

                                         _____

                                         _____

                             Rule   _____

                                         _____

Social Responsibility   Policy   _____

                             Procedure   _____

                                         _____

                                         _____

                             Rule   _____

                                         _____

Organizing Concepts

Learning Objectives

After studying this chapter you should be able to

· Discuss the nature of organizing, describe the organizing process, and identify key components and concepts involved in organizing.

· Discuss job design in organizations, including job specialization and alternatives to it.

· Indicate how jobs are grouped, giving particular attention to grouping by function, product, and location.

· Define and discuss authority and responsibility and the related concepts of delegation and decentralization.

· Discuss the concept of group effectiveness, its impact on the shape of organizations, and how a manager might determine what will make a group effective.

· Define line and staff positions and indicate their role in organizational analysis.

The Bechtel Group, Inc., one of the largest construction and engineering companies in the world, is a privately owned, family-controlled company. It has had only two presidents who were not family members. It began in the late 1800s, doing contract construction for the government building railroads across the United States. It quickly moved to get contracts for irrigation canals, highways, pipelines, and any other form of construction. It led the 1931 consortium to build Hoover Dam and then moved to other dam and bridge construction.

Bechtel thrived on huge projects, including the construction of nuclear power plants, although it came under criticism for its role in constructing those power plants as well as an Iraqi petrochemical facility. However, it had former officers in top government posts to stave off any strong regulatory responses to its work. Nevertheless, the worldwide construction slump in the 1980s caused Bechtel to restructure, laying off nearly half of its more than forty thousand professional employees and changing the way in which it did business.

In 1991 Bechtel had projects, in seventy-seven countries, nine major U.S. offices, and thirteen international field offices. The international offices were in Europe, the Middle East, Canada, South America, and Southeast Asia. The diversity of those projects was considerable. They included an airport in Hong Kong, management of the tunnel between Britain and France, a giant technology center near Moscow, the Barcelona Olympics, a major highway project in Boston, a theme park in Spain, San Francisco's Museum of Modern Art, and an international airport in Tokyo.

Each of these projects is organized as a unit, although it is coordinated by a field office and headquarters. Bechtel also now can assist clients with financing and operating projects. It has expanded into all phases of the construction process rather than limiting itself to building only. Bechtel has also developed a specialization in managing and cleaning up the mistakes of others, as it did with the English Channel tunnel project and with numerous nuclear power plant decommissioning projects (many of which it had built in the first place).[1] ■

*The **organizing** process involves shaping the organization as it grows, shrinks, or changes.*

Bechtel is a complex organization that handles not just building but all aspects of the construction business, including financing and operating projects. The pattern of organization that might have worked well in its early years had to give way to one better suited to its expanded strategy. It had to change its organization to fit a newer, more complex environment. In Chapter 1 we noted that **organizing** was the second basic managerial function, following planning and decision making. Organizing was defined as the process of grouping activities and resources in a logical and appropriate fashion. At Bechtel the former organization might have been eminently logical, but it became obsolete over time and was no longer appropriate. This chapter is the first of four devoted to the organizing function and to helping you understand when different organizations are and are not logical and appropriate.

Our discussion here will revolve around defining and describing five basic concepts of organizing: designing jobs, grouping jobs, dealing with authority and responsibility, establishing group effectiveness, and managing line and staff positions. The next chapter focuses on how these components are put together to form organization designs. Chapter 13 addresses approaches to organizational change and innovation, and we explore staffing the organization in Chapter 14.

The Nature of Organizing

We have already defined organizing. However, to develop a more comprehensive understanding of this critical function, we need to elaborate on this definition by addressing the nature of organizing and identifying its key components.

The Environment of Management

EDS Adapts

The largest single customer of EDS, Electronic Data Systems, was General Motors. That situation proved fateful for both organizations when GM bought EDS in 1984. The idea was to make GM a powerful force in computerized data processing systems as well as to improve GM's internal operations and controls.

The founder, owner, and CEO of EDS, Ross Perot, quickly became a thorn in GM's side. Perot argued that GM had too many things that separated people and caused warring camps. He felt that the top executives at GM were too far from their customers, employees, dealers, and even shareholders because of their unwieldy organizational structure. GM paid Perot $742 million to leave. He did, but the problems remained.

In 1992 GM began to make the kind of organizational structural changes that Perot had advocated.

Meanwhile, the environment in which EDS operated underwent substantial change. Instead of being an independent computer data processing company, it was now part of the GM organization. But it was still a computer data processing company that was expected to compete in that industry.

EDS immediately set about working with GM divisions to develop methods and procedures to improve performance. EDS grew even stronger under GM's mantle and became what is generally regarded as the first truly global computer services firm. It became a major firm as other companies turned to outsiders to do their computer data processing rather than do it themselves. Finally, EDS began to form unique organizational arrangements in deals with Texas Air and Sun Microsystems to expand markets and better serve customers.[2] ∎

The Organizing Process

Giant, complex organizations such as AT&T, Du Pont, Exxon, and General Motors were not created in a day. Nor were your neighborhood dry-cleaning establishment and favorite pizza parlor. Instead, most organizations start out in one form and then evolve into other forms as they grow, shrink, or otherwise change.[3] EDS Corp. is an organization that has had to change, as indicated in *The Environment of Management: EDS Adapts*.

Consider the case of a programmer who develops a new applications software package for personal computers. She starts out writing code and preparing copies of the materials on her home computer in the morning. She then tries to sell them in the afternoon. On Saturday she updates her records, and on Sunday she works on new developments.

Suppose, however, that her new circuit is a real breakthrough, and she has trouble performing all of these activities. Eventually she looks for help. She hires a part-time salesperson and a part-time bookkeeper, which allows her more time for production and invention. Sales continue to expand; soon she moves out of her home and into a small workshop. The salesperson and the bookkeeper became full-time employees, and she must also hire a production assistant.

In a few years the programmer may be in charge of two sales managers, each of whom oversees eight sales representatives. She may also have larger facilities and several dozen production workers, in addition to a production manager, a full-time accountant, and a personnel manager. At this point the programmer's scope of operations has expanded from a one-person effort to a full-fledged organization.

Each of the steps the programmer takes along the way, such as creating new jobs, grouping those jobs under new management positions, and delegating authority to those managers, is a part of the organizing process. Moreover, she can never truly be finished organizing. New circumstances, opportunities, and threats will always cause her to modify and adjust her organization to more efficiently and effectively meet competition.[4]

Key Organizing Components and Concepts

The above example touches on three of the basic concepts of organizing: creating or designing jobs, grouping jobs, and delegating authority. The five components that make a complete picture of organizing concepts are described below.[5]

Designing jobs is one basic component. As we will see, this process involves determining the best level of job specialization to use and grouping jobs into meaningful categories. This grouping, called departmentalization, is necessary in order to facilitate supervision and coordination.

Authority and responsibility must also be properly defined. Between a manager and those reporting to him, these definitions are accomplished through delegation. Across the entire organization, the process of defining these two is called decentralization.

Organizing for group effectiveness is the fourth critical component. Managers may coordinate the efforts of a few or many others in the organization. Characteristics of the manager, those reporting to him or her, and the situation determine what leads to group effectiveness.

Finally, attention needs to be directed to the management of line and staff positions. Line positions are usually conceived of as those in the direct chain of command who hold the responsibility for accomplishing organizational goals. Staff positions, in contrast, are generally thought to be advisory positions primarily used to facilitate the work of line managers.[6]

Designing Jobs

*The basis of **job design** is **job specialization**, defining the tasks that set one job apart from others.*

Job design is the process of determining what procedures and operations are to be performed by the employee in each position. For example, a new employee at a Honeywell assembly plant or even a local travel agency does not simply sit down and start working. Instead, the manager shows the new employee how to do the job. Moreover, this manager is not making the job up as he or she goes along. Other operating managers and managers from the human resource department at some time carefully decided how the job should be performed, basing their decisions on what was the best design for the job.

The basis for all job-design activities is job specialization. Let us investigate the nature of job specialization and then identify several alternative approaches to designing jobs.

Job Specialization

We first considered the topic of **job specialization** back in Chapter 1, during our discussion of scientific management. As you recall, Frederick W. Taylor, the chief proponent of scientific management, advocated extremely high levels of specialization and standardization as ways to increase the efficiency of organizations.[7]

The nature of job specialization at an abstract level is illustrated in Exhibit 11.1. Let us use the Goodyear Tire & Rubber Company as an example. Essentially, Goodyear has one "job": making and selling tires. In order to execute this job, however, it must break this job down into smaller jobs. One job is buying the raw materials, another is transforming these materials into tires; still another is distributing the tires to dealers. And, of course, there are dozens more. Further, several

Exhibit 11.1

Job Specialization

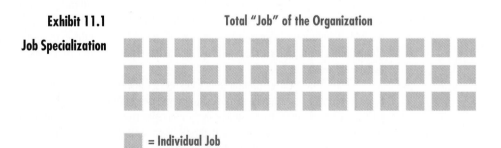

Total "Job" of the Organization

☐ = Individual Job

people are needed to perform most of these jobs. Specialization can involve managerial and professional jobs as well as those of nonmanagerial personnel.[8]

We can note from the exhibit that the smaller jobs that are created through specialization add up to the total. That is, if it were possible to add up the contributions of each of the individual jobs, the total would equal the original overall job of the organization, including managerial coordination.

Specialization has a number of advantages and disadvantages. On the plus side, it allows each employee to become an expert. If the job is simple and straightforward, people trained to do it should become very proficient. Specialization also allows managers to exercise greater control over workers, since they can easily observe and monitor employees doing simple jobs. Specialization is also presumed to facilitate the development of equipment and tools that can increase the efficiency of the job holder.[9]

On the other hand, it is possible to overspecialize. If the job is simplified too far, employees may spend so much time passing the work from person to person that efficiency is actually decreased. Even more significant is the problem of boredom and job dissatisfaction. If jobs are too simple and specialized, workers quickly get bored performing them. They become dissatisfied, and their performance may drop, or they might consider looking for more exciting work elsewhere.[10] To counter these problems, managers have begun to search for alternatives that will still maintain the positive benefits that specialization can provide.

Alternatives to Specialization

The three most common alternatives to job specialization are shown in Exhibit 11.2, which uses a single square to represent job specialization. Specialized jobs can be thought of as narrowly defined and standardized. The three alternatives are job rotation, job enlargement, and job enrichment.

*Overspecialization can lead to boredom and dissatisfaction. Managers often use such alternatives as **job rotation, job enlargement,** and **job enrichment.***

Job Rotation   **Job rotation** involves systematically moving employees from one job to another. As noted in the exhibit, the jobs themselves are still narrowly defined and standardized. For instance, suppose an employee works in a Sunbeam toaster-assembly plant. The assembly operation involves four sets of jobs. During the first week of the month, the employee plugs preassembled heating units into a base. The next week the employee connects four wires that make the heating unit operational. The third week is spent installing the chrome cover over the toaster unit, and the next week is devoted to testing each toaster and packing it in its box. In the fifth week the employee rotates back to the first job again.

Ford, Prudential Insurance, and Bethlehem Steel have all experimented with job rotation, and many companies use this system in one form or another. Unfortunately, job rotation by itself

Exhibit 11.2   Alternatives to Job Specialization

| Job Specialization:
Narrowly Defined
and Standardized Job | Job Rotation:
Employee Rotates Across
Several Narrowly Defined
and Standardized Jobs | Job Enlargement:
Job is Changed
to Include More
Activities | Job Enrichment:
Job is Changed to Include
More Activities *and* More
Discretion in How to Do Them |

Cross training is used by many organizations to break down the tedium of some jobs. At Ciba-Geigy Canada Ltd.'s agricultural chemical plant, workers set schedules, handle costs, develop job descriptions, and are involved in many aspects of the business. Formerly, Martha Nichol's job consisted only of working on this liquid herbicide filling line; now she and five colleagues are cross trained to move between jobs, including maintaining equipment. (Edward Gajdel/Courtesy of Ciba-Geigy, Canada, LTD.)

is not very successful at decreasing the boredom associated with highly specialized jobs. Each of the jobs our toaster assembler performs is still fairly monotonous. In general, job rotation is used as a way to train employees in a variety of skills and/or as a part of a more comprehensive job design strategy.[11]

Job Enlargement   In contrast to job rotation, **job enlargement** actually changes the nature of the job itself. As shown in Exhibit 11.2, this system involves adding more activities to the job. Job enlargement might be used in the toaster factory to decrease the total number of jobs from four to two. One set of workers might now plug in the heating element and attach the wires, and the other set could then attach the covers and pack the toasters into boxes.

IBM, Maytag, AT&T, and Chrysler have all tried job enlargement. In general, the results have been somewhat more positive than those of job rotation, and workers report slightly less boredom with enlarged jobs. Still, adding more and more simple activities to a job that is already simple does not really change the nature of the work that much.[12]

Job Enrichment   The final alternative to job specialization to be considered here is job enrichment. Exhibit 11.2 points out the critical difference between job enlargement and job enrichment: under **job enrichment,** workers are given more activities to perform and more discretion as to how to perform them.[13]

Job enrichment *gives the worker* *more discretion in deciding how to* *perform various activities.*

Suppose, for example, that workers at the Sunbeam toaster plant are told that they have to insert the heating element first, and then attach the wires in a specified order, using standard equipment. After enrichment they are given various options: they can attach the wires before inserting the element, use a different kind of tool to attach the wires, and so on. Similarly, the inspection operation might dictate that defective toasters should be turned over to a supervisor, who then decides what to do. Enrichment can give the inspector more discretion: he or she might repair small problems personally, take the defective toaster back to the worker who caused the defect, or still give it to a supervisor. When enrichment is combined with cross-training, training people in multiple skills so that they can do more than one job, it is frequently called re-engineering.[14]

AT&T, Texas Instruments, General Foods, Texaco, and John Hancock have all used job enrichment. Whereas this approach is far from being universally successful, it does frequently decrease employee boredom and dissatisfaction. Many organizations are continuing to experiment with new and innovative ways to design employee jobs.[15] The Skill Builder in this chapter provides you with a tool to examine ways to enrich a job through the use of the job-characteristics model.

Grouping Jobs

*Departmentalization frequently groups jobs according to one of three bases: **function, product,** and **location.***

After jobs have been designed, the next part of the organizing process is the grouping of those jobs into logical sets. This step is important because properly grouped jobs make it easier to coordinate and integrate activities and, hence, achieve the goals of the organization. The process of grouping jobs is called **departmentalization,** or departmentation.

The key word here is, of course, *logical.* Managers do not just randomly pull together whatever jobs are at hand and call them a department. Instead, they must use a plan or a set of guidelines. These guidelines are the basis for departmentalization. The most common groupings are by function, by product, and by location. First let us discuss each of these bases for departmentalization, and then we can briefly note others that are occasionally used.

Departmentalization by Function

*Many small companies use **functional departmentalization,** which leads to easy coordination of activities, expert staffs, and clear definitions of responsibilities.*

When organizations departmentalize by function, they group together employees who are involved in the same or very similar functions or broad activities.[16] An illustration of how a company that uses **functional departmentalization** is organized appears in Table 11.1. Note that this organization has a marketing department, a finance department, and a production department. Thus, marketing researchers, product managers, advertising managers, sales managers, and sales representatives are all included in the marketing department; and operations managers, distribution managers, plant managers, and quality control managers are all in the production department.

The key advantages of this approach are that, since each department is staffed by experts in that particular function or activity, the managers in charge of each function can easily coordinate and control the activities within the department, and areas of responsibility are clearly defined. On the other hand, functional departmentalization also has certain disadvantages. Decision making tends to be slow. Employees might concentrate so much on their functional specialties that they lose sight of the total organization, and communication between departments is difficult.[17]

Smaller organizations tend to use the functional approach to departmentalization. As they grow they often change bases. Frequently they go on to adopt departmentalization by product.

Departmentalization by Product

Product or process departmentalization is common among large organizations and enables them to keep activities together, speed up decision making, and monitor the performance of product groups.

When organizations use **product or process departmentalization,** they group together all the activities associated with individual products or closely related product groups or processes. A simple example of this approach is also shown in Table 11.1. Product Group A might be a line of packaged foods, such as cereals, instant breakfast mixes, and so forth. All of the financial, marketing, and production activities associated with this line of products are grouped together in this department. Product Group B could consist of several different small retail chains. As in Group A, all the marketing, financial, and operations functions for these chains are grouped together in Group B.

There are several advantages of product/process departmentalization. For one thing, all of the activities associated with unique products or processes are kept together. Marketing cereal might be quite different in nature from marketing a retail chain. For another, decision making is faster, because managers responsible for individual products are closer to those products. Finally, it is easier to monitor the performance of individual product groups under this arrangement.

As you might expect, of course, product/process departmentalization also has several disadvantages. First, administrative costs are higher, because each department has its own marketing research team, its own financial analysis team, and so forth. Second, conflict or resentment occasionally arises between departments as each thinks the other is getting more than its fair share of attention or resources.[18]

Table 11.1

Departmentalization by Function, Product, and Location

Structure	Departments	Positions
Functional organization	Marketing	Marketing researchers, product managers, sales managers, etc.
	Finance	Budget analysts, accountants, financial planners, etc.
	Production	Operations managers, plant managers, quality control specialists, etc.
Product organization	Product Group A	Financial, marketing, and production managers for packaged foods
	Product Group B	Financial, marketing, and production managers for small retail chains
	Product Group C	Financial, marketing, and production managers for a third product
Locational organization	North American Operations	Production, distribution, financial, marketing, and human resource managers for the U.S.A., Canada, and Mexico
	European Operations	Production, distribution, financial, marketing, and human resource managers for Europe
	Southeast Asian Operations	Production, distribution, financial, marketing, and human resource managers for Southeast Asia

Departmentalization by Location

Locational departmentalization is especially appropriate for multinational organizations because it keeps expert managers close to their operations.

The third major form of departmentalization is **locational.** In this situation, jobs that are in the same or nearby locations are grouped together in a single department. Table 11.1 presents a simplified view of a company that uses this approach. All of the activities of the organization that pertain to North America—production facilities, distribution systems, financial considerations, marketing activities, and human resource management activities—are grouped together in one department. Likewise, similar activities that relate to European operations are grouped together, as are those that relate to Southeast Asian operations.

This approach to departmentalization gives managers the basic advantage of being close to the location of their decision-making responsibilities. Managers in North America might not be fully in tune with cultural and social norms in Europe, understand the nature of European marketing, or appreciate the financial difficulties involved in foreign exchange rates. By putting a manager with the requisite insights and authority directly on the scene, however, the company might achieve more effective operations.

On the other hand, this approach results in a duplication of staff, just as product departmentalization does. For instance, the company would need a marketing manager in North America, one in Europe, and one in Southeast Asia. Nonetheless, this approach is becoming more widely used, especially by firms that decide to go multinational.[19]

Other Considerations in Departmentalization

Some companies use other bases of departmentalization, and it is very common to mix bases of departmentalization within the same organization.

One approach occasionally used by organizations is to departmentalize by customer. Using

Departmentalization by location is used by Ray-Ban, a product division of Bausch & Lomb. Ray-Ban is divided by region for all its sites, such as Asia, Europe, and the United States. This enables the products to be redesigned for each region to provide better service to customers and to increase sales. (Seiji Ibuki.)

this approach, the company groups together activities associated with individual customers or customer groups. A Midwestern bank, for example, might have departments for consumer loans, business loans, and agricultural loans.

Time also serves as a base for departmentalization. For instance, a plant might operate on three shifts, and the company might view each shift as a department.

Departmentalization by sequence occurs when a sequence of numbers or other identifying characteristics defines the separation of activities. When going through registration, students frequently get into different lines on the basis of their last names, their student numbers, or their class standing.

Our discussion of departmentalization has considered each base in its pure form, but in reality most organizations use multiple bases and/or combine bases. One way to mix approaches is by level. For example, a firm might use product departmentalization at the top but departmentalize each product group by function. Each marketing department could then be broken down by location or customer.

Similarly, bases of departmentalization might be mixed at the same level to suit individual circumstances. A firm doing business in Europe on a moderately small scale might decide to establish a marketing group in Paris but keep all production in the United States, at least until sales grow. Thus the marketing activities are broken down by location, but the production activities are not.

Authority and Responsibility

Another important part of the organizing process is the determination of how authority and responsibility will be managed.[20] At the level of an individual manager and his or her group, this is the delegation process. At the total organizational level, it is related to decentralization.

Delegation

Delegation is the process through which the manager assigns a portion of his or her task to those reporting to him or her.[21] In discussing delegation, let us first identify the steps in the process

Exhibit 11.3
The Delegation Process

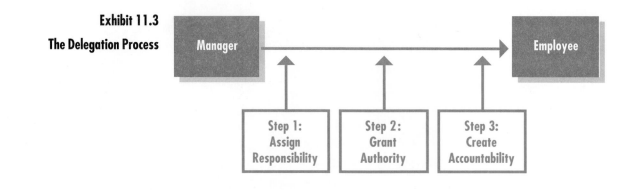

Manager ⟶ Employee

| Step 1: Assign Responsibility | Step 2: Grant Authority | Step 3: Create Accountability |

Delegation—*assigning tasks to group members*—*involves giving the emploee the **responsibility** for a job, the **authority** to perform it, and **accountability** for seeing that it gets done.*

and then address barriers to effective delegation. Some people have more of an inclination to delegate work than others. The Self-Assessment at the end of the chapter measures your willingness to delegate work to others.

Steps in Delegation   Delegation essentially involves three steps, as shown in Exhibit 11.3.

First, the manager assigns **responsibility.** That is, the manager defines the employees' duty to perform a task. For example, when a manager tells someone reporting to him to prepare a sales projection, order additional raw materials, or hire a new assistant, he is assigning responsibility.

Second, the manager must also grant the **authority** necessary to carry out the task. Preparing a sales projection may call for the acquisition of sensitive sales reports, ordering raw materials may require negotiations on price and delivery dates, and hiring a new assistant may mean submitting a hiring notice to the human resource department. If these activities are not a formal part of the group member's job, the manager must give her the authority to do them anyway.

Finally, the manager needs to create **accountability.** This suggests that the group member incurs an obligation to carry out the job. If the sales report is never prepared, if the raw mate-

President Clinton delegated the development of a national health care plan to Hillary Rodham Clinton. She was assigned the responsibility, granted the authority, and held accountable for the results. Rodham Clinton developed a task force to hold hearings, study the situation, and develop recommendations for health care reform. (Cynthia Johnson/Gamma Liason.)

A Matter of Ethics

Nu Skin

Nu Skin was formed in the early 1980s and quickly became a major player in the personal care product industry. Headquartered in Provo, Utah, Nu Skin has offices in Atlanta, Toronto, Hong Kong, Taiwan, and other cities around the world. However, 1992 saw drastic changes in the conduct of Nu Skin's business as a result of the culmination of legal actions brought against it.

State attorneys general in six states—Connecticut, Florida, Illinois, Michigan, Ohio, and Pennsylvania—reached an agreement with Nu Skin to stave off massive law suits against the firm. Nu Skin had achieved its massive growth through a pyramid sales effort that relied on people selling its products to their friends and neighbors. In addition to commissions on their own sales, Nu Skin distributors were paid extra commissions on the sales of their recruits. While not in and of itself illegal, this arrangement can quickly become illegal if the distributors begin to put more emphasis on recruiting new salespeople than they do on selling the products themselves. Clearly a lot of people felt that Nu Skin had crossed that line.

Nu Skin agreed to several conditions. It agreed to fire distributors who use the appeal of huge earnings to recruit new distributors. It agreed to let disgruntled distributors sell back 90 percent of unopened stock. And it agreed to ensure that 80 percent of sales are from at least five customers who are not also distributors.[22] ■

---

rials are not ordered, or if the assistant is never hired, the group member is accountable to her boss for failing to perform the task. Indeed, if the manager is not careful, it is possible for some personnel to lose sight of their major task because they become focused on the wrong objectives, as indicated in *A Matter of Ethics: Nu Skin*.

Of course, these steps are not carried out in rigid, one-two-three fashion. Indeed, in most cases they are implied by past work behavior. When the manager assigns a project to a group member, for instance, the group member probably knows without asking that he has the authority necessary to do the job and that he is accountable for seeing to it that it does, indeed, get done.

Barriers to Delegation   Unfortunately, the ideal delegation process never materializes. Several factors can contribute to this failure. For one thing, the manager might be too disorganized to delegate systematically. For another, she may be afraid that the group member will do such a good job that she will look bad in comparison. Alternatively, she may be afraid that the group member is incapable of doing the job properly. Finally, the group member may be unwilling or unable to accept the job.[23]

Decentralization

*Decentralized organizations delegate power and control to lower levels, whereas **centralized** organizations keep power and control at the top level.*

A closely related issue is **decentralization,** the result of maximum delegation throughout the organization. General Electric, Sears, and Xerox are extremely decentralized; McDonald's, Kmart, and Boeing, however, are just the opposite. IBM has recently moved from being centralized to becoming much more decentralized in an effort to speed decision making and respond more quickly to its customers.[24] Even Japanese companies, which have traditionally been centralized, have begun to become more decentralized.[25]

Under conditions of decentralization, power and control are systematically delegated to lower levels in the organization. Under conditions of **centralization,** however, power and control are systematically kept at the top of the organization.

Some organizations choose to practice decentralization in order to keep managers who are close to problems responsible for making decisions about them. That is, managers who come into contact with customers, suppliers, and competitors on a daily basis may be in a better position to make decisions than managers who are isolated back at headquarters.

In general, decentralization is usually pursued when the environment is complex and uncertain, when lower-level managers are talented and want more say in decision making, and when the decisions are relatively minor. In contrast, centralization is often practiced when the environment is more stable, when the home office wants to maintain control, when lower-level managers are either not talented enough to have or do not want a stronger voice in decision making, and when decisions are more significant.[26]

Part of the reason behind decentralization is to speed up decision making, while another part is to assure that the individual companies can respond quickly to customer wants and needs. These are precisely the kinds of reasons why General Motors reorganized in the early 1990s.

Group Effectiveness and the Shape of Organizations

Another important concept in organizing is group effectiveness. Group effectiveness is thought to be partly a function of the **span of management,** which is the number of people who report directly to a given manager. Companies must consider the relation of this number to group effectiveness and to overall organizational effectiveness. Let us look at the notions of the span, its effect on the "height" of the organization, and other factors that influence group effectiveness even more strongly than does the span.

Group Size and Span of Management

*A manager who has a large number of people reporting to him or her has a wide **span of management**, whereas a manager with only a few people reporting to him or her has a narrow span.*

If a manager has a large group, she is said to have a wide span of management. Similarly, having a relatively small group defines a narrow span of management.

What difference does it make? At the request of an early management pioneer, a French mathematician attempted to illustrate the impact of wide and narrow spans.[27] He noted that groups contain three basic kinds of relationships: direct (the manager's one-on-one relationship with each group member), cross (relationships among group members), and group (relationships between clusters of group members). A mathematical formula for these relationships showed that as the number in a group increases linearly, the number of total relationships increases exponentially. That is, the number of interactions or relationships increases rapidly as more people are added to the group. This means that if a manager has two people reporting to him or her, there are six relationships; for three people, the number of relationships increases to eighteen; and five people in the group means one hundred relationships. Adding one person to an existing group of five is quite different from adding one to an existing group of seventeen.

Although this work is not based on business organizations, it does carry an important message: groups involve a complex network of interrelationships, and the complexity of that network increases greatly as the group grows larger.

Other early writers sought to identify the ideal span for all managers, but they quickly realized that an ideal number did not exist. Indeed, the appropriate span varies considerably from one setting to another and may be much larger than these early writers speculated.[28] This fact suggests that the effects of the span of management on organizations is not as important as other factors that influence group effectiveness.

Organizational Levels: Tall vs. Flat Organization

*Large groups or a wide span of management means that there are relatively few managerial levels; therefore, the organization is **flat**. A narrow span leads to **tall** organizations.*

One key effect of span of management on organizational structure concerns the "height" of the organization. A wide span of management results in an organization that has relatively few levels of management, or a **flat organization.** On the other hand, a narrow span of management adds more layers of management and therefore leads to a **tall organization.** These relationships are illustrated in Exhibit 11.4.

In general, flat organizations tend to be characterized by greater communication between upper- and lower-level management, an increased capacity to respond to the environment, and lower total managerial costs than tall organizations. In recent years many corporations, including Sears, Roebuck and Co., CBS, Avon, General Motors, and IBM, have taken steps to eliminate

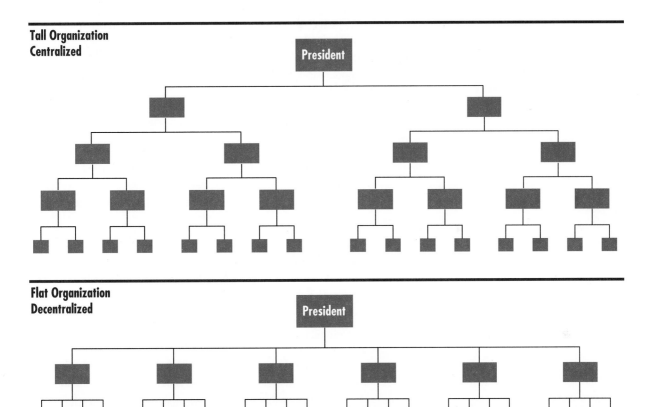

Tall Organization Centralized

Flat Organization Decentralized

Exhibit 11.4   Tall Versus Flat Organizations

layers of management in an effort to create a more streamlined and efficient organization.[29] Reducing the number of levels in an organization is known as downsizing.[30] Improved organizational communication enables substantially larger spans and correspondingly flatter organizations, thus making both the groups and the overall organization more effective.[31]

Factors Influencing Group Effectiveness

Since a group's effectiveness and the impact of the span of management depend on the circumstances of the situation, what exactly are those circumstances? Several of the more important ones are noted in Exhibit 11.5.

The competence of both the manager and the group is one significant factor. If both are competent, a larger group or wide span is possible, but if either is less competent, a smaller group or narrower span may be dictated.

Physical dispersion is another important variable. In general, if the manager and the group are scattered throughout a building or territory, the group must be smaller. If, on the other hand, everyone works in close proximity, a larger group can be used.

Preferences are also an important factor in some situations. If everyone wants a bigger group, then that is what should be used. A smaller group may be desirable, though, if that is preferred.

Task similarity is significant, too. The manager will probably want a narrower span if each group member is doing a different job, whereas a wider span can be adopted when everyone is performing similar tasks.

Exhibit 11.5

Factors Influencing Group Effectiveness and the Span of Management

A Group With a Wide Span of Management May Be More Effective When:

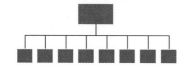

1. Managers and group are highly competent.
2. Managers and group work in close proximity.
3. People prefer low supervision.
4. Group members perform similar tasks.
5. A manager's sole task is supervising the group.
6. Little interaction between managers and the group is necessary.
7. Work is highly standardized.
8. New problems seldom arise.

A Group With a Narrow Span of Management May Be More Effective When:

1. Managers and/or group are not highly competent.
2. Managers and group are widely dispersed.
3. Managers want close control over their group.
4. Each group member performs a different task.
5. Managers have nonsupervisory tasks to perform.
6. Managers and the group must interact with each other on a regular basis.
7. Work is not highly standardized.
8. New problems arise frequently.

The degree to which the manager has nonsupervisory work to do is also an important consideration. If all the manager has to do is supervise the group, he or she can use a wider span. On the other hand, if the manager has a lot of other tasks to perform, a narrower span may be indicated.

A related factor is the required interaction between the manager and the members of the group. Since interaction takes time, it follows that the more interacting a manager needs to do, the smaller the group will need to be. Similarly, less required interaction will allow for a larger group.

Standardization is another important variable. Highly standardized work, like task similarity, can accommodate a larger group or wider span than lack of standardization can.

Finally, the frequency of new problems should be considered. If new problems arise often, a narrow span may be necessary, whereas few new problems will allow for a wider span.

In summary, the company must consider several factors when organizing a group and establishing its size.[32] Each of these factors, along with others which might be relevant, must be properly assessed and considered by the manager in order to achieve effective group performance.[33] Today, the trend is toward larger groups and correspondingly flatter organizations.

Line and Staff Positions

The last element of the organizing process is the idea of line and staff positions. **Line positions** are traditionally defined as those in the direct chain of command with specific responsibility for accomplishing the goals of the organization. **Staff positions** are positions outside the direct chain of command that are primarily advisory or supportive in nature. These differences are shown in Exhibit 11.6.

Exhibit 11.6
Line and Staff Positions

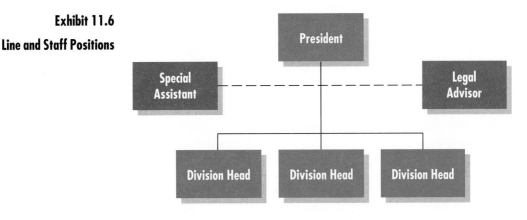

The traditional distinction between **line positions** *and* **staff positions** *is fading as managers become better educated and more experienced.*

The roles of president and division head are line positions. Each has goals that derive from and contribute to those of the overall organization. The positions of special assistant and legal adviser are staff positions. These people perform specialized functions that are primarily intended to help line managers. For example, the legal adviser is not expected to contribute to corporate profits. Instead, the adviser answers questions from and provides advice to the president about legal issues that confront the firm. Historically, staff managers tended to be better educated, younger, and more ambitious than their line counterparts. They were frequently hired directly out of school, whereas line managers usually worked their way up the corporate ladder. Moreover, there tended to be considerable conflict between line and staff managers, especially when staff managers were given the responsibility of finding shortcomings in the efforts of line managers.[34]

In recent years, however, this state of affairs has begun to change. The results of one survey show that top managers have started redirecting the efforts of their staff managers in more cooperative and constructive directions.[35] Staff positions are also beginning to lose part of their glamor. Recent corporate cutbacks and downsizing have often reduced the number of staff positions, and line managers have been given greater decision-making power and discretion. These jobs have therefore become more attractive to people graduating from college as well as to those managers already in staff positions.[36]

In the future, the distinction between line and staff managers is likely to become vaguer. Effective managers are starting to see that everyone within the company is really on the same team and that the best approach is to promote participation and cooperation among all members of the organization rather than labeling different groups.

Chapter Summary

Organizing is the process of grouping activities and resources in a logical and appropriate fashion. The basis for job design is job specialization. Specialization allows employees to become experts at their jobs, it allows managers to control workers more easily, and it makes it simpler to design equipment and tools that can increase efficiency. Overspecialization can lead to increased movement of work, which decreases efficiency. Much more important, it can cause boredom and dissatisfaction, which can lead to negative consequences that outweigh the advantages of specialization.

Three common alternatives to specialization are job rotation, job enlargement, and job enrichment. Job rotation involves systematically moving employees from one job to another. Although useful in training, job rotation has not been very effective in reducing dysfunctional aspects of overspecialization. Job enlargement changes the nature of the job by adding activities; some short-term alleviation in boredom may result, but the impact is limited. Job enrichment has had more success. In job enrichment, employees are given more activities to perform and more discretion over how to perform them.

The process of grouping jobs into logical sets to make coordination and integration easier is known as departmentalization. Common bases are by function, product, and location. Functional departmentalization refers to grouping together those jobs that call for similar work. Product departmentalization refers to grouping together all activities associated with one product (project, process, program, and so forth). Departmentalization by location involves recognizing the advantages of physical or geographical proximity as a basis for grouping jobs.

Authority is the power to get things done; responsibility refers to who is supposed to get them done. Delegation involves both as a manager assigns a portion of his or her task to group members. The manager assigns responsibility to do a task, grants the authority necessary to accomplish the task, and creates accountability for the group member to carry out the job.

Decentralization is the result of delegation. In decentralization, power and control are systematically delegated to lower levels of the organization. Decentralization enables organizations to respond more rapidly to their environments by keeping in close touch with customers, suppliers, and competitors.

Span of management refers to the number of people who directly report to a given manager. Large groups or wide spans result in fewer levels of management, or flat organizations, whereas smaller groups or narrow spans result in more levels, or tall organizations. Flat organizations tend to have better communication, an increased capacity to respond to the environment, and lower total managerial costs.

Eight factors influence group effectiveness. They are the competence of the manager and workers, physical dispersion, individual preferences, the degree of task similarity, the amount of nonsupervisory work done by the manager, the extent of necessary interaction among group members, the degree of standardization of the work, and the frequency with which new problems occur.

Traditionally, line positions carry specific responsibility for accomplishing the goals of the organization. Staff positions are primarily advisory or supportive in nature. As line managers have become better educated, they have taken on certain staff functions; as staff managers have become more experienced, they have acquired certain line functions. The distinctions are becoming less clear. Effective managers realize that everyone in the organization is part of the same team and that all are important to effectiveness.

The Manager's Vocabulary

organizing	functional departmentalization	decentralization
job design	product or process departmentalization	centralization
job specialization	locational departmentalization	span of management
job rotation	delegation	flat organization
job enlargement	responsibility	tall organization
job enrichment	authority	line positions
departmentalization	accountability	staff positions

Review Questions

1. What is job specialization? What are its benefits and limitations?
2. What is meant by departmentalization? What are the common bases for departmentalization?
3. Identify and describe the major parts of the delegation process. What are centralization and decentralization?
4. What are the major differences between tall and flat organizations? Why are these differences important?
5. What are the major factors influencing group effectiveness?

Analysis Questions

1. Specialization has dominated organizations for centuries. Do you think it is likely to continue, or will companies move toward less specialization in the future? Why or why not?
2. How can organizations deal with the boredom and dissatisfaction created by specialization? Suggest some ways other than those mentioned in the chapter.

3. Comment on this statement: "You can delegate authority, but you can't get rid of your obligation."
4. Do companies that are heavily centralized have managerial processes similar to or different from those of companies that are heavily decentralized? Why?

5. Which kind of position is more important to an organization, line or staff? Why? Could an organization function with only one of these kinds of positions? Why or why not?

Self-Assessment

Inclinations Toward Delegation

Introduction Most organizational goals are too large or too complex for one individual to accomplish. This is where the manager comes in. It is the manager's task to delegate the work to different people in manageable units, so the whole goal is accomplished. But the manager must be willing to delegate. This self-assessment will help you determine your willingness to delegate work to others.

Instructions This instrument is designed to help you understand the assumptions you make about people and human nature. Ten pairs of statements follow. Assign a weight from 0 to 10 to each statement to show the relative strength of your belief to the statement. The points assigned for each pair must always total 10. Be as honest with yourself as you can and resist the tendency to respond as you would like to think things are. This instrument is not a test; there are no right or wrong answers. It is designed to stimulate personal reflection and discussion.

1. _____ a. It's only human nature for people to do as little work as they can get away with.

_____ b. When people avoid work, it's usually because their work has been deprived of meaning.

2. _____ c. If employees have access to any information they want, they tend to have better attitudes and behave more responsibly.

_____ d. If employees have access to more information than they need to do their immediate tasks, they will usually misuse it.

3. _____ e. One problem in asking for the ideas of employees is that their perspective is too limited for their suggestions to be of much practical value.

_____ f. Asking employees for their ideas broadens their perspective and results in the development of useful suggestions.

4. _____ g. If people don't use much imagination and ingenuity on the job, it's probably because relatively few people have much of either.

_____ h. Most people are imaginative and creative but may not show it because of limitations imposed by supervision and the job.

5. _____ i. People tend to raise their standards if they are accountable for their own behavior and for correcting their own mistakes.

_____ j. People tend to lower their standards if they are not punished for their misbehavior and mistakes.

6. _____ k. It's better to give people both good and bad news because most employees want the whole story, no matter how painful.

_____ l. It's better to withhold unfavorable news about business because most employees really want to hear only the good news.

7. _____ m. Because a supervisor is entitled to more respect than those below her in the organization, it weakens her prestige to admit that a subordinate was right and she was wrong.

_____ n. Because people at all levels are entitled to equal respect, a supervisor's prestige is increased when he supports this principle by admitting that a subordinate was right and he was wrong.

8. _____ o. If you give people enough money, they are less likely to be concerned with such intangibles as responsibility and recognition.

_____ p. If you give people interesting and challenging work, they are less likely to complain about such things as pay and supplemental benefits.

(con't. on page 260)

9. _____   q.   If people are allowed to set their own goals and standards of performance, they tend to set them higher than the boss would.

_____   r.   If people are allowed to set their own goals and standards of performance, they tend to set them lower than the boss would.

10. _____   s.   The more knowledge and freedom a person has regarding her job, the more controls are needed to keep her in line.

_____   t.   The more knowledge and freedom a person has regarding her job, the fewer controls are needed to ensure satisfactory job performance.

For interpretation, turn to the back of the book.

Source: David A. Whetten and Kim S. Cameron, *Developing Management Skills* (Glenview, Ill.: Scott, Foresman and Company, 1984), pp. 351–352.

Skill Builder

Enriching Jobs Through Job Design

Purpose This exercise illustrates how particular characteristics of work relate to the motivation and satisfaction of those who perform the work. Understanding the job characteristics model will provide you with valuable conceptual skill on how jobs should be organized. Learning to calculate the internal motivation potential score and growth need strength score for a specific job provides you with an important technical skill. Finally, learning how to apply this model and the calculations to a specific job, so the individual's motivation to perform rises will develop your human skills. This skill builder focuses on the *administrative management model*. It will help you develop the *coordinator role* of the administrative management model. One of the skills of the coordinator is to organize the work.

Introduction This skill builder is designed to develop your skills on how to enrich jobs by improving on the job characteristics in the job. All jobs can be thought of having several characteristics. These job characteristics are not present at the same level in all jobs. These characteristics are key factors in determining the motivational potential of the job. The five job characteristics are: skill variety, task identity, task significance, autonomy, and feedback.

Instructions There are three different approaches to this exercise. Your instructor will give you directions on how to proceed.

Source: From *Management: Experiences and Demonstrations* by Henry L. Tosi and Jerald W. Young. Rerpinted by permission of the publisher, Richard D. Irwin, Inc. © Henry L. Tosi, 1982.

JOB TITLE _____

(Title of the job to be analyzed)

JOB DESCRIPTION Briefly describe the major responsibilities of the job.

_____

_____

This part of the questionnaire asks you to describe your (the) job, as *objectively* as you can. *Please do not use the questionnaire to show how much you like or dislike your job.* Questions about that will come later. Make your descriptions as accurate and as objective as you possibly can.

1. How much variety is there in your job? That is, to what extent does the job require you to do *many different things* at work, using a *variety of your skills and talents?*

1 - - - - - - - - - - 2 - - - - - - - - - - 3 - - - - - - - - - - 4 - - - - - - - - - - 5 - - - - - - - - - - 6 - - - - - - - - - - 7

Very little; the job requires me to do the same routine things over and over again.

Moderate variety.

Very much; the job requires me to do many things using a number of skills and talents.

2. To what extent does your job involve doing a *"whole" and identifiable piece of work?* That is, Is the job a complete piece of work that has an obvious beginning and end? Or is it only a small *part* of the overall piece of work, which is finished by other people or by automatic machines?

1 - - - - - - - - - - 2 - - - - - - - - - - 3 - - - - - - - - - - 4 - - - - - - - - - - 5 - - - - - - - - - - 6 - - - - - - - - - - 7

My job is only a tiny part of the overall piece of work; the results of my activities cannot be seen in the final product or service.

My job is a moderately sized chunk of the overall piece of work; my own contribution can be seen in the final outcome.

My job involves doing the whole piece of work from start to finish; the results of my activities are easily seen in the final product or service.

3. In general, how much impact on others does your job have? That is, are the results of your work likely to significantly affect the lives or well-being of other people?

1 - - - - - - - - - - 2 - - - - - - - - - - 3 - - - - - - - - - - 4 - - - - - - - - - - 5 - - - - - - - - - - 6 - - - - - - - - - - 7

Not very significant; the outcomes of my work are *not* likely to have important effects on other people.

Moderately significant.

Highly significant; the outcomes of the work can affect other people in very important ways.

4. How much autonomy is there in your job? That is, to what extent does your job permit you to decide *on your own* how to go about doing the work?

1 - - - - - - - - - - 2 - - - - - - - - - - 3 - - - - - - - - - - 4 - - - - - - - - - - 5 - - - - - - - - - - 6 - - - - - - - - - - 7

Very little; the job gives me almost no personal say about how and when the work is done.

Moderate autonomy; many things are standardized and not under my control but I can make some decisions about the work.

Very much; the job gives me almost complete responsibility for deciding how and when the work is done.

5. To what extent does *doing the job itself* provide you with information about your work performance? That is, does the actual *work itself* provide clues about how well you are doing—aside from any "feedback" co-workers or supervisor may provide?

1 - - - - - - - - - - 2 - - - - - - - - - - 3 - - - - - - - - - - 4 - - - - - - - - - - 5 - - - - - - - - - - 6 - - - - - - - - - - 7

Very little; the job itself is set up so I could work forever without finding out how well I am doing.

Moderately; sometimes doing the job provides "feedback" to me; sometimes it does not.

Very much; the job is set up so that I get almost constant "feedback" as I work about how well I am doing.

(con't. on page 262)

Listed below are a number of statements which could be used to describe a job. You are to indicate whether each statement is an *accurate* or an *inaccurate* description of *your* job. Once again, please try to be as objective as you can in deciding how accurately each statement describes your job—regardless of whether you *like* or *dislike* your job.

Write a number in the blank beside each statement, based on the following scale:

How accurate is the statement in describing your job?

1	2	3	4	5	6	7
Very inaccurate	**Mostly inaccurate**	**Slightly inaccurate**	**Uncertain**	**Slightly accurate**	**Mostly accurate**	**Very accurate**

_____ 6. The job requires me to use a number of complex or high-level skills.

_____ 7. The job is arranged so that I have the chance to do an entire piece of work from beginning to end.

_____ 8. Just doing the work required by the job provides many chances for me to figure out how well I am doing.

_____ 9. This job is not at all simple or repetitive.

_____ 10. This job is one where many other people can be affected by how well the work gets done.

_____ 11. The job allows me a chance to use my personal initiative or judgment in carrying out the work.

_____ 12. The job provides me the chance to completely finish the piece of work I begin.

_____ 13. The job itself provides many clues about whether or not I am performing well.

_____ 14. The job gives me considerable opportunity for independence and freedom in how I do the work.

_____ 15. The job itself is quite significant or important in the broader scheme of things.

Listed below are a number of characteristics which could be present on any job. People differ about how much they would like to have each one present in their own jobs. We are interested in learning *how much you personally would like* to have each one present in your job.

Using the scale below, please indicate the *degree* to which you *would like* to have each characteristic present in your job.

1 ----------- 2 ----------- 3 ----------- 4 ----------- 5 ----------- 6 ----------- 7

Would like having this only a moderate amount (or less)   Would like having this very much   Would like having this *extremely* much

_____ 16. Stimulating and challenging work.

_____ 17. Chances to exercise independent thought and action in my job.

_____ 18. Opportunities to learn new things from my work.

_____ 19. Opportunities to be creative and imaginative in my work.

_____ 20. Opportunities for personal growth and development in my job.

_____ 21. A sense of worthwhile accomplishment in my work.

Computation Work Sheet for Internal Motivation Potential Score

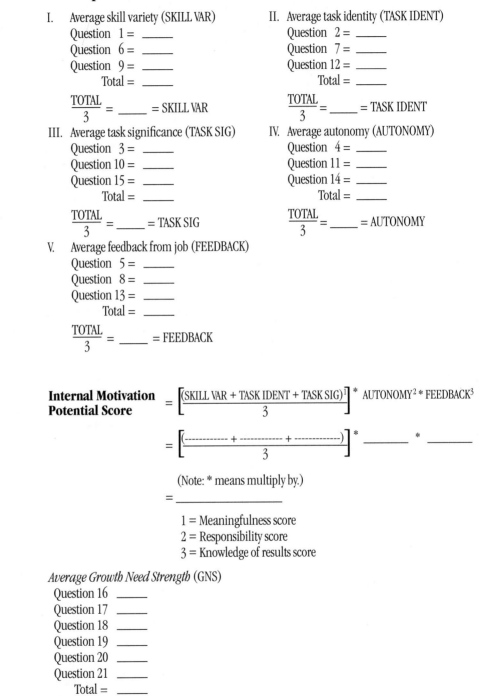

I. Average skill variety (SKILL VAR)

Question 1 = _____

Question 6 = _____

Question 9 = _____

Total = _____

$$\frac{TOTAL}{3} = \_\_\_\_\_ = SKILL\ VAR$$

II. Average task identity (TASK IDENT)

Question 2 = _____

Question 7 = _____

Question 12 = _____

Total = _____

$$\frac{TOTAL}{3} = \_\_\_\_\_ = TASK\ IDENT$$

III. Average task significance (TASK SIG)

Question 3 = _____

Question 10 = _____

Question 15 = _____

Total = _____

$$\frac{TOTAL}{3} = \_\_\_\_\_ = TASK\ SIG$$

IV. Average autonomy (AUTONOMY)

Question 4 = _____

Question 11 = _____

Question 14 = _____

Total = _____

$$\frac{TOTAL}{3} = \_\_\_\_\_ = AUTONOMY$$

V. Average feedback from job (FEEDBACK)

Question 5 = _____

Question 8 = _____

Question 13 = _____

Total = _____

$$\frac{TOTAL}{3} = \_\_\_\_\_ = FEEDBACK$$

Internal Motivation Potential Score $= \left[\frac{(SKILL\ VAR + TASK\ IDENT + TASK\ SIG)^1}{3}\right] * AUTONOMY^2 * FEEDBACK^3$

$= \left[\frac{(\text{-----------} + \text{-----------} + \text{-------------})}{3}\right] * _____ * _____$

(Note: * means multiply by.)

$= _____$

1 = Meaningfulness score

2 = Responsibility score

3 = Knowledge of results score

Average Growth Need Strength (GNS)

Question 16 _____

Question 17 _____

Question 18 _____

Question 19 _____

Question 20 _____

Question 21 _____

Total = _____

Total ÷ 6 = _____   GNS =

(con't. on page 264)

Job Characteristics Worksheet

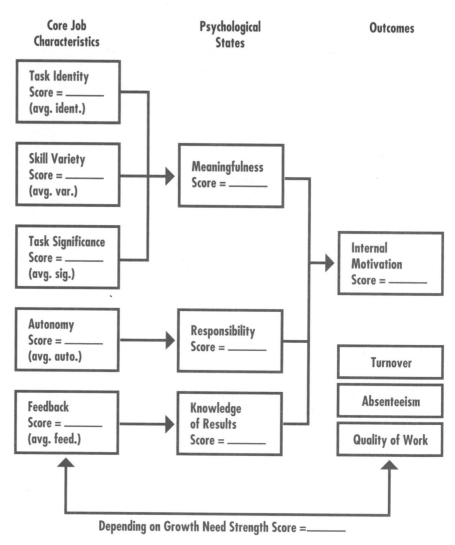

11.1   Johnson & Johnson

The three Johnson brothers began making antiseptic surgical dressings in 1896. The next year Edward Mead Johnson left to form his own firm, Mead Johnson, now a subsidiary of Bristol-Myers Squibb. Johnson & Johnson went on to develop their now-famous Band-Aid and to become number one in several products—adhesive bandages, sanitary napkins, painkillers, and baby-care products. The company, headquartered in New Brunswick, New Jersey, employs more than eighty thousand people worldwide to make not only these products but dental-care items, contraceptives, and personal-care products, too.

Johnson & Johnson is not only big and dominant in many markets, it is also well thought of. *Fortune* named it the most admired company in community and environmental responsibility in 1990. More than half of its business is in health products other than drugs, and half comes from outside the United States. It has European subsidiaries like Cilag and Janssen Pharmaceutica, Inc., and Janssen-Kyowa in Japan.

In 1989 Johnson & Johnson bought L'Oreal's sanitary-protection business and the Piz Buin sun-protection products firm. That same year it formed a joint venture with Merck to sell Mylanta and other nonprescription products from ICI Americas, the U.S. branch of the British drug firm. In 1992 Johnson & Johnson was organized into 166 separately chartered companies, each with its own president. Each of these prepares its own budgets and marketing plans, and many of them do their own research and development work. While they all technically report to the top executive group at headquarters, quarterly contact is all that some have.

This form of organization actually began in the 1930s when Robert Wood Johnson decentralized operations. He created smaller, self-governing units to make them more responsive to their markets and more easily managed. Permitting autonomy while assuring integration is not easy and has been likened to running an orchestra where musicians must be permitted individual creativity while still assuring quality music. Costly mistakes can occur because tighter home-office controls are not present, but, at the same time, innovation prospers.

Johnson & Johnson tries to get its companies to share back-office functions such as payroll processing and other forms of accounting, computer services, purchasing, and distribution. To maintain low costs Johnson & Johnson reviews its companies and sometimes moves to merge several of them to achieve greater efficiency. However, innovation is always the primary basis for organizational decisions.

When a product developed in one of Johnson & Johnson's companies seems to have promise, it is spun off into a separate unit. In this unit everyone can concentrate on nothing but getting it to market as a high-quality, affordable product. It may then grow into a separate division and later, after becoming solidly established, become part of another company again.

This form of organizational structure assures that the management associated with any given product or product line will remain close to the customers. In addition, it also keeps people working within the unit closer to one another simply because such units are somewhat smaller and have much more narrowly focused goals. To make this form of organization work well, company managers must be held accountable for results. Successes can lead to sizable rewards, including raises and stock options, and failures can lead to ouster from the organization. The corporate benefits from such an organizational structure are clear. From 1980 through 1992 profits increased about 19 percent per year at Johnson & Johnson.[37]

Discussion Questions

1. What best describes the organization of Johnson & Johnson?
2. How does the Johnson & Johnson organization work?
3. Is the Johnson & Johnson organization effective? Why or why not?

11.2 Glaxo

Glaxo Holdings p.l.c., the British pharmaceutical firm, is one of the ten leading drug companies worldwide. Tracing its origins to a New Zealand import-export business begun in 1873, Glaxo started producing powdered milk as a baby food in the early 1900s. By the 1920s it had entered pharmaceuticals, grew rapidly, and diversified into related areas such as veterinary and medical instrumentation and drug distribution.

Glaxo survived a takeover bid by Beecham Inc., in the 1970s, which led it to consider innovative organizational arrangements as well as product innovation. One such organizational arrangement was formed in the 1980s when Glaxo combined with Hoffmann-La Roche to have its large sales force market Glaxo's new ulcer medication, Zantac. By the late 1980s Zantac's market share was expanding rapidly and had grown to more than half by the early 1990s. This sort of unique organizational arrangement is becoming more common as firms worldwide strive to compete more effectively and efficiently.

Other Glaxo organizational moves included investment in a new development facility in the late 1980s; development of a new and controversial distribution system for its products in 1991; entering into an agreement with the Baker Institute, an Australian research center, to share developments, also in 1991; and organizing a pharmacy division in 1992.[38]

Discussion Questions

1. What forms of organization seem to be in use by Glaxo?
2. What are the advantages and disadvantages of the organization design of Glaxo?
3. What suggestions might you make to the top management of Glaxo about their organization design? Why?

CHAPTER 12

Organization Design

Chapter Outline

The Nature of Organization Design

The Meaning of Organization Design
The Role of Organization Charts

Early Approaches to Organization Design

The Bureaucratic Design
System 4 Design

Contingency Factors Affecting Organization Design

Size and Life Cycle
Technology
Environment

Contemporary Organization Design Alternatives

The Functional Design (U-Form)
The Conglomerate Design (H-Form)
The Divisional Design (M-Form)
The Matrix Design
Other Designs

Corporate Culture

Determinants of Culture
Components of Culture
Consequences of Culture

Learning Objectives

After studying this chapter you should be able to

· Discuss the meaning of organization design and the role of organization charts.

· Describe early approaches to organization design, including the bureaucratic design and System 4 design.

· Name and discuss several major contingencies that affect organization design.

· Name and discuss several major contemporary organization design alternatives.

· Define and discuss corporate culture, including its determinants, components, and consequences.

Chrysler, the third-largest U.S. automobile maker, produced a new model, the Viper, with Japanese-style teams, careful budgets, and deadlines. The Viper is a 10-cylinder, $50,000 sports car. Its production involved an entirely new manufacturing platform. Even more importantly it presented a new image for the Chrysler corporation. The new image was designed to lure customers into showrooms where, if they did not buy a Viper, they might buy another Chrysler product.

On the other hand, even if customers do not come to see the Viper in showrooms, Chrysler has already achieved huge benefits from the project. The Viper was first introduced at automobile shows early in 1989. That same year feasibility studies and research and development projects were begun. Early in 1991 it had fallen behind schedule and was not meeting the weight goals set for it. However, it was brought back on target during that year and deliveries were begun in 1992. Normally it took Chrysler five years to put a new car into production, so this effort was record breaking.

The lessons learned in achieving this effort are being applied to other aspects of Chrysler's operations. In that way Chrysler hopes to hold down costs and shorten production cycles for all of its products. Instead of using a huge hierarchical organization, the Viper was developed by a team of eighty-five people working in a large room with managers ready to make decisions on the spot.[1] ▪

One of the keys to understanding a company is to understand its organization. Chrysler has numerous divisions, most of which make cars. Its central headquarters is in Michigan, but it has facilities in several other locations as well. It has a financial unit; three rental car units, Collar, Snappy, and Thrifty; a joint venture with Mitsubishi (Diamond-Star); and it bought American Motors in 1987. It is a large, complex organization, and understanding it involves not only the concepts introduced in Chapter 11 but others as well.

Chapter 11 identified and discussed a number of basic organizing concepts. This chapter considers how these concepts are integrated into one overall organization design. First it discusses the nature of organization design and summarizes some early approaches to it. Then it describes three important contingency factors that can affect organization design and several contemporary approaches to this design. To conclude, it considers the nature of organizational culture. Each of these subjects will help us better understand companies like Chrysler.

The Nature of Organization Design
The Meaning of Organization Design

Organization design refers to the overall arrangement of positions and the interrelationships among positions within an organization.

What do we mean by organization design? We must answer this question before we discuss the idea of the organization chart.

We can define **organization design** as the overall configuration of positions and interrelationships among positions within an organization. More specifically, let us think of the design of an organization as being like a puzzle: it consists of a number of pieces that can be put together in certain ways.

All organizations have certain things in common: they use one or more bases of departmentalization, they have different kinds of positions, and so forth. At the same time, however, no two organizations are exactly the same. Some use functional departmentalization, and others use product departmentalization; some have wide spans of management, and others have narrow spans of management; some are decentralized, and others are centralized. Describing exactly how the pieces of a specific organization are to be put together results in its organization design.

One way to simplify a retailer's organizational design is to establish a link to a single supplier. Designs Inc. of Chestnut Hill, Massachusetts, has done just that with Levi Strauss. Designs deals only with Levi's and is tied into Levi's automated inventory system, LeviLink. Linking enables Designs to reduce its buying staff and eliminate warehouses and distribution centers since supplies are shipped directly to the store. (Steve Woit.)

The Role of Organization Charts

Organization charts—pictures or maps of organizations—may be useful to small companies for clarifying relationships.

To some people, organization design is best represented by an **organization chart.** Throughout this book organization charts are used to present examples and to illustrate important points. Now let us examine the chart itself, using the simplified chart for a small manufacturing company, shown in Exhibit 12.1. Note that this chart is a vertical chart composed of a series of boxes, each of which is connected to others with one or more lines. Each box represents a management position within the firm, and each line represents the nature of the relationship between that position and other positions.

Several things about the company can be gleaned from the organization chart in the exhibit. For one thing, we can see that the firm is departmentalized by function. Each function is headed by a vice president; the four vice presidents report to a president. We can also see that the marketing vice president has three sales managers under his control and the operations vice president has three plant managers under her control. Finally, we can see that the president has a staff assistant.

The organization chart can be thought of as a picture or map of the organization. Such charts are especially useful to outsiders and newcomers to an organization. They help outsiders know whom to contact in the organization to get certain things done. They help newcomers better understand their place in the overall scheme of things, and they clarify reporting relationships between positions.

However, as an organization grows in size, it becomes more difficult to use organization charts because of the large number of positions and the complex relationships that can exist among those positions. For example, in large, complex firms such as AT&T, Du Pont, and Union Carbide, some managers report to more than one higher-level manager. Further, in the contemporary world, organizations change so frequently that a chart drawn at any one point is not accurate shortly thereafter. In such cases, organization charts may not be used at all. If they are, they usually show only the major positions in the organization.

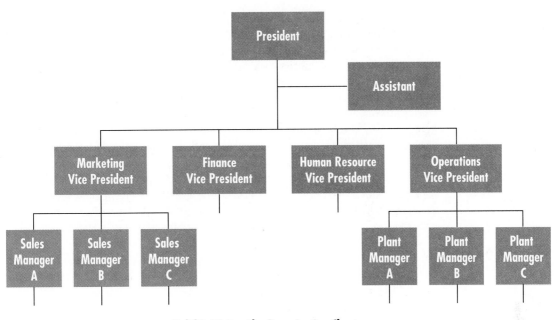

Exhibit 12.1   The Organization Chart

Early Approaches to Organization Design

I n Chapter 1 you were introduced to administrative management, the area of classical management theory concerned with organizational structure. The chapter briefly noted the contributions of the German sociologist Max Weber. Weber was one of the first to describe how organizations should be designed to promote effectiveness.

The Bureaucratic Design

*According to Weber, the formal system of authority of a **bureaucracy** should lead to rational and efficient organizational activities.*

Weber coined the term **bureaucracy** to describe what he saw as the ideal kind of organization design.[2] His goal was to identify and prescribe a set of guidelines that, if followed, would result in efficient and effective organizations. The foundation of his bureaucratic guidelines was the creation of a formal and legitimate system of authority. This system, he argued, would serve to guide rational and efficient organizational activities.

The guidelines Weber developed to create this system are summarized in Table 12.1. First, managers should strive for a strict division of labor. Each position should be clearly defined and filled by an expert in that particular area to take advantage of the specialization of labor. Second, there should be a consistent set of rules that all employees must follow in performing their jobs.

Table 12.1

The Ideal Bureaucracy

Weber's organizational guidelines
1. The division of labor should be clearly defined.
2. One consistent set of rules should apply to all employees.
3. A clear chain of command and communication should exist.
4. Business should be conducted in an impersonal manner.
5. Advancement should be based solely on expertise and performance.
6. Careful records should be kept for organizational learning.

These rules are supposed to be impersonal and rigidly enforced so that family connections and political favoritism are minimized. Third, to minimize confusion there should be a clear chain of command: everyone should report to one, and only one, direct supervisor. Moreover, communication should always follow this chain and never by-pass individuals. Fourth, business should be conducted in an impersonal manner. In particular, managers should maintain an appropriate social distance from the members of their group and not play favorites. Fifth, advancement within the organization should be based on technical expertise and performance rather than on seniority or favoritism. Finally, careful records should be kept so that organizational learning can take place.[3] Weber expected this form of organization to enhance employee loyalty to the organization.

Over the years, however, the term *bureaucracy* has come to connote red tape and slow, hassle-ridden decision making. Many universities, hospitals, and governmental agencies have a bureaucratic flavor to them. In fact, the bureaucratic approach to organization design may be appropriate when the environment of the organization is stable and simple. However, since few organizations today have such environments, this approach should be used only with great care.[4]

System 4 Design

*The flexibility of **System 4** often leads to increased effectiveness, but it is not appropriate for every organization.*

As the human relations school of thought emerged, new perspectives on organization design naturally also emerged.[5] One of the more popular views has come to be known as the **System 4** approach.[6] This view holds that the bureaucratic model has numerous drawbacks and deficiencies and advocates an entirely different way of designing organizations. Its basic premises are summarized in Table 12.2.

The proponents of System 4 design argue that organization design can be described as a

Table 12.2   System 1 and System 4 Organization Designs

System 1 organization	System 4 organization
1. **Leadership process** includes no perceived confidence and trust. Subordinates do not feel free to discuss job problems with their superiors, who in turn do not solicit their ideas.	1. **Leadership process** includes perceived confidence and trust between superiors and subordinates. Subordinates discuss job problems with their superiors, who solicit ideas.
2. **Motivational process** taps only physical, security, and economic motives through the use of fear and sanctions. Unfavorable attitudes prevail among employees.	2. **Motivational process** taps a full range of motives through participatory methods. Attitudes are favorable toward the organization and its goals.
3. **Communication process** is such that information flows downward and tends to be distorted, inaccurate, and viewed with suspicion by subordinates.	3. **Communication process** is such that information flows freely—upward, downward, and laterally. The information is accurate and undistorted.
4. **Interaction process** is closed and restricted; subordinates have little effect on goals, methods, and activities.	4. **Interaction process** is open and extensive; superiors and subordinates affect goals, methods, and activities.
5. **Decision process** occurs only at the top of the organization; it is relatively centralized.	5. **Decision process** occurs at all levels through group processes; it is relatively decentralized.
6. **Goal-setting process** is located at the top of the organization; discourages group participation.	6. **Goal-setting process** encourages group participation in setting high, realistic objectives.
7. **Control process** is centralized and emphasizes fixing of blame for mistakes.	7. **Control process** is dispersed and emphasizes self-control and problem solving.
8. **Performance goals** are low and passively sought by managers, who make no commitment to developing the human resources.	8. **Performance goals** are high and actively sought by superiors, who make a commitment to developing, through training, human resources.

Source: Adapted from Rensis Likert, *The Human Organization* (New York: McGraw-Hill, 1967), pp. 197–211. © 1967. Reprinted by permission.

The Quality Challenge

ITW

ITW, Illinois Tool Works Inc., is a Chicago-based conglomerate organization. It operates in more than thirty countries and has worldwide revenues of more than $2 billion. It is frequently named by *Fortune* magazine as one of the most admired corporations in the United States. Its organizational design enables it to focus on quality, keep close to its customers, and be highly innovative. ITW holds 2,400 active U.S. patents, including the plastic loops that hold six-packs of canned drinks together, for instance.

ITW is a complex organization with many products to control. ITW works with General Motors on fasteners. With Dow Chemical it produced the Zip-Pak resealable food packages. New Zealanders use its Kiwi-Lok to secure their kiwi plants. It developed a quick-change couple for machine tools to assist Caterpillar and Toyota. The Buildex division, which makes construction products, worked with Owens-Corning Fiberglas to develop small retainer plates for fastening insulation to roofs.

In one of its plants, located in Elgin, Illinois, ITW makes nuts, bolts, screws, and other metal products in a hot, noisy manufacturing facility. Functional departmentalization was replaced by cellular groupings of equipment arranged around high-volume products. These cellular groupings were actually located in small, focused factories with a high degree of participation by the workers involved to encourage entrepreneurism and high quality.

In a similar way, ITW restructured one of its packaging subsidiaries, Signode, to get better quality. Signode had been highly centralized, with all of its operations managed by a giant computer. ITW got rid of the computer, decentralized decision making and operations, flattened the organization, and began creating focused factories. Millions of dollars of overhead were cut, and productivity and quality improved.[7] ∎

---

continuum. At one end of the continuum is a hierarchical design, largely bureaucratic in nature, called System 1 in the table. At the other end is System 4, a design that has more openness, flexibility, communication, and participation. In between are other organization designs that show characteristics relatively similar to System 1, called System 2, or relatively similar to System 4, called System 3.

The premise is that most organizations start out as hierarchical bureaucracies like System 1 organizations. Theoretically, through a series of prescribed steps managers can transform the organization first to a System 2, then to a System 3, and ultimately to a System 4 design.

Those who designed this approach helped demonstrate that the bureaucratic model is not the only way in which organizations can be designed, and one early study at General Motors found that a System 4 design was indeed more effective.[8] On the other hand, the System 4 model, like the bureaucratic model before it, was presented as a universal guideline that all managers should follow. As we see in the next section, research has shown that there are no universal guidelines. Instead, the appropriate form of organization design for any given company is contingent on a variety of critical factors.

Contingency Factors Affecting Organization Design

Size and Life Cycle

In Chapter 1 we saw that the contingency approach to management suggests that no single method of management will always be successful. So, too, no single organizational design is best. Three major situational elements that have been found to affect the appropriate design for an organization are size and life cycle, technology, and the environment.[9]

The size of an organization can be assessed in any number of ways—by number of employees, assets, sales, and so forth. In most cases, however, these characteristics are closely related. Regardless of what criteria are used, Du Pont, General Motors, Exxon, and Tenneco are large companies, and a neighborhood dry cleaner, a locally owned pizza parlor, and a small-town automobile garage are small organizations.

Size, life cycle, technology, and the environment are contingency elements that affect the appropriate design for an organization.

The effects of size on organization design are summarized in Exhibit 12.2. In particular, research has found that large and small organizations differ from one another in three important ways.[10] First, smaller organizations tend to be less specialized than large organizations. It is not uncommon for every employee in a small company to have to be able to do a number of different jobs, but as the company grows each employee tends to stick to one well-defined job.

Second, smaller organizations tend to be somewhat less standardized than large ones. This means that they have fewer rules for how things should be done and more flexibility in how employees can confront problems. Again, as the organization grows, it has a tendency to create more rules and to eliminate some of the individual flexibility in problem solving. It should be noted, however, that some small business owners seem to feel that having lots of rules is a good way to manage, while most large organizations are moving to reduce the number of rules and regulations they have.

Finally, organizations tend to be more centralized when they are small. This relates to the fact that the original owner or founder is probably still in charge and is accustomed to having the final say in decision making. In larger organizations decision making tends to become more and more decentralized. Indeed, as indicated in *The Quality Challenge: ITW,* larger companies find that decentralization can aid in achieving high quality. Managers of growing organizations should recognize that alterations in the design of the company may be necessary as it becomes larger and larger.

Life cycle is also important because it tends to be related to size. Most organizations are created small, grow and mature over a period of years, become stable as mature organizations, and then undergo change. That final stage may be one of decline or regrowth, depending on the or-

Exhibit 12.2

The Effect of Size on Organization Design

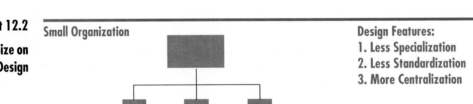

Small Organization

Design Features:
1. Less Specialization
2. Less Standardization
3. More Centralization

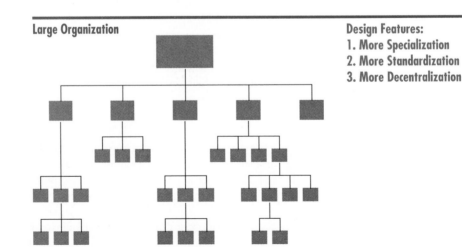

Large Organization

Design Features:
1. More Specialization
2. More Standardization
3. More Decentralization

ganization's response to its environment. Clearly, the organization design needed by an organization in each stage of its life cycle is different from that needed in other stages.

Technology

Technology is the set of conversion processes used by an organization to transform inputs into outputs. Obviously, the job of transforming crude oil into refined petroleum at Shell is quite different from the job of repairing a fuel pump in the garage at a local Chrysler dealership. It follows, then, that the Shell refinery and the Chrysler dealership will have quite different management needs, one manifestation of which is the kind of organization design that is appropriate.

The most common approach to describing technology is to classify it as unit or small-batch, large-batch or mass-production, or continuous-process technology.[11]

*System 4 design works best in **unit** or **small-batch technology** and **continuous-process technology**. A System 1 design may be more appropriate for companies using **large-batch** or **mass-production technology**.*

Unit or **small-batch technology** is used when the product is made in small quantities, usually in response to customer orders. For example, Boeing does not keep an inventory of 747s on hand. Instead, it makes them to customer specifications after they have been ordered. Tailor shops and printing shops use a similar approach to production.

Large-batch or **mass-production technology** occurs when the product is manufactured in assembly-line fashion by combining component parts into a finished product. Products are made for inventory instead of according to customer specifications. Examples include a Nissan assembly plant for manufacturing cars and a Maytag plant that makes washing machines.

Finally, **continuous-process technology** means that the composition of the raw materials is changed through a series of mechanical or chemical processes. A Pennzoil refinery, a Miller brewery, and a Union Carbide chemical plant all use continuous-process technology.

Many people think of the automotive industry when they visualize large-batch technology. There are, however, numerous industries both in the United States and overseas that employ large-batch technology. Shown here is a Baxter plant in Malaysia, which makes rubber gloves in a mass-production operation. (R. Ian LloydProductions Pte LTD.)

In general, the appropriate form of organization design used by a company depends at least in part on its dominant technology. Organizations that rely on unit or small-batch technology are often more effective if they use a System 4 design, which allows them the flexibility to react quickly to customer needs and expectations. Large-batch or mass-production organizations, on the other hand, may be more effective if they use a System 1 type of design. Such organizations are more amenable to rules, regulations, and other formal practices. Continuous-process firms, like unit or small-batch companies, may be most effective if they adopt a System 4 organization design. They need its flexibility to oversee their complete technology as well as to enhance the introduction of automated production processes into the system.[12]

Within the System 4 framework, some new organizational arrangements have emerged. Most involve the use of employee groups working as teams rather than as isolated individuals. **Quality circles** are groups of employees who focus on how to improve the quality of products. **Semi-autonomous work groups** are groups of workers who operate with no direct supervision to perform some specific task, such as assembling an automobile or producing a circuit board for an electronic product. These will be discussed in more detail in Chapter 18.

Environment

A third factor that has been found to directly affect the appropriate design of an organization is the environment. Part Two discussed the environment extensively. Now we need to relate it more directly to organization design.

Several different perspectives on the impact of the environment have been developed, and a synthesized view that captures the essential points of each is shown in Exhibit 12.3.[13] (The Self-Assessment at the end of the chapter assesses your feelings about how an organization with which you are familiar is organized.) The basic idea is that **environmental uncertainty** can be captured by two dimensions, **environmental change** and **environmental complexity.** The exhibit places these two dimensions in a graph.

Environmental uncertainty is affected by complexity and change. High complexity and frequent change create a high level of uncertainty.

When the environment changes frequently, is dynamic, and is difficult to predict, it has a high rate of change. In contrast, if the environment seldom changes, is fairly static, and is relatively easy to predict, it has a low rate of change. Similarly, if the environment contains many dif-

Exhibit 12.3

The Environment and Organization Design

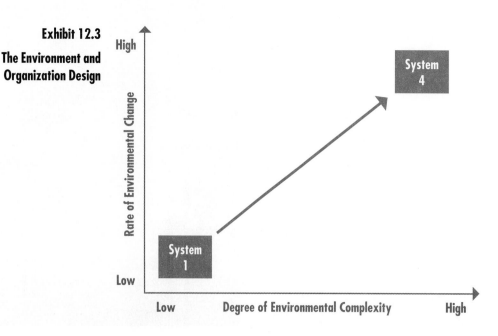

ferent elements, it can be considered to have a high level of complexity. When the number of elements is low, however, the complexity of the environment is also low.

When change and complexity are both high, uncertainty is also high. In this instance, a System 4 or organic type of organization design will probably be most effective. However, when both change and complexity are low, so too is uncertainty. For this condition, a System 1 or bureaucratic or mechanistic design might work best.

For example, let us consider Intel Corporation and a small liberal arts college. Intel competes in a complex and rapidly changing environment, the electronics industry. Faced with uncertainty, it uses a System 4 design, which allows it to respond quickly and relatively easily to shifts, threats, and opportunities in the environment. In contrast, the college functions in a relatively stable and simple environment, higher education. Confronted with little uncertainty, it uses a System 1 design, akin to a bureaucracy.

It is up to the manager to analyze the three factors of size, technology, and environment effectively and then properly match the design of the organization to them. Now let us explore some of the more common design alternatives that many companies currently adopt.

Contemporary Organization Design Alternatives

As we have repeatedly seen, there is no one best method for organization design. Managers must therefore carefully consider their circumstances and choose the one that is most appropriate for those circumstances. Among the options that are being chosen with increasing regularity are the functional design, the conglomerate design, the divisional design, and the matrix design.[14]

The Functional Design (U-Form)

Traditionally, the most common design is the **functional design,** based on functional departmentalization as discussed in Chapter 11. It is also known as the U-Form, because it uses a unitary or uniform approach to design.[15] This form of organization makes maximum use of functional specialization and therefore achieves the benefits of that specialization. However, it also requires considerable integration and coordination.

The functional design (see Exhibit 12.1) is popular because it lends itself to centralized coordination. With this design an individual CEO can integrate and coordinate the entire organization, at least up to some fairly large size. That is the reason this design is so common among smaller firms. However, as the organization grows in either size or complexity, it becomes increasingly difficult for a single person or even a single group of persons to perform such coordination.

The Conglomerate Design (H-Form)

The **conglomerate design** is typically found in an organization that has grown through the development of new and perhaps relatively unrelated product lines. It is also called the H-Form because such conglomerates may be holding companies for groups of diverse products. This design uses the product form of departmentalization and takes advantage of specialization based on knowledge of specific products or services, their production and marketing.

In the conglomerate design the units are separate businesses usually headed by general managers. These general managers are responsible for the profits and losses of their units and operate independently of one another. These units report to a central, corporate group. That group evaluates their performance, allocates resources, and guides the decision making of the general managers. *The Environment of Management: Synergy at Newell* indicates how one company uses this approach.

Duplication of costs and efforts, lack of communication and coordination, and the difficulties associated with trying to integrate highly diverse companies are among the limitations to this form of organization. Most companies using this design find that they achieve only average financial performance and are therefore moving away from the H-Form.[16]

The Environment of Management

Synergy at Newell

Newell Co., headquartered in Freeport, Illinois, was founded in 1921 and grew slowly until the 1970s. Newell's operating environment is complex. It makes a wide variety of products—from baking dishes, pots, pans, and other housewares to bathroom scales, paintbrushes, blowtorches, window shades, and mini-blinds. Newell began to use mass-market retailers such as Kmart, Wal-Mart, and Home Depot to expand its sales during the 1970s, a move which has proved to be extremely effective. It saw sales rocket from about $19 million on sales of $343 million in 1985 to more than $100 million on sales of more than a billion in 1991.

A major factor in this success was a strategy of acquiring faltering companies that had established products in lines similar to those already handled by Newell. By carefully integrating such acquisitions, synergy could be obtained in not only warehousing, distribution, and customer service but in manufacturing as well. The 1987 acquisition of Anchor Hocking is a case in point. Anchor Hocking makes glasses, cookware, and related products and was nearly twice Newell's size when it was acquired. It had to be completely reorganized to integrate it into the Newell organization, but afterward it was one of the more successful such acquisitions.

After acquisitions have had time to become integrated and coordinated, they are evaluated by Newell's corporate headquarters. Those that are not profitable or that no longer fit into the similar business frame-work are sold to keep Newell financially fit and focused in its environment.[17] ■

The Divisional Design (M-Form)

*Under the **divisional design**, an organization establishes fairly autonomous product departments that operate as strategic business units.*

A third popular approach to organization design is the **divisional design,** called the M-Form for its multidivisional characteristics. This form, popular with multinational organizations, combines a product approach to departmentalization with strategic business unit strategy, as discussed in Chapter 8. An example of this kind of design is shown in Exhibit 12.4.

Each division of the organization is responsible for all aspects of the management of a given product or product family. A company such as General Foods, for example, establishes a division for each of its major types of food products. Each division then takes care of its own suppliers and handles its own advertising campaigns. The head of the division is usually given the title of vice president, although titles such as **division head** and **division manager** are also common.

Each division is also thought of as a strategic business unit, or SBU. That is, each has its own market and competitors. Moreover, a division might be a star, a cash cow, a question mark, or a dog, so it might be sold, used to generate cash for other divisions, given extra cash, or put on a "wait and see" basis.

Note that positions in the different divisions in the exhibit are linked by dashed lines. These indicate that cooperation between divisions is encouraged, although usually not required. For instance, two divisions of General Motors might link up to negotiate a better contract with a supplier, or two divisions of General Foods might use the same advertising agency. Each division, however, is free to undertake and terminate such collaborative arrangements as it chooses.

Finally, we should note that even though the divisions are given considerable autonomy, certain functions are probably retained at a centralized level. At General Motors, for instance, all labor negotiations for all divisions are handled at the corporate level.[18] Although the divisional design generally is the most effective approach to organizational design,[19] it is not perfect, however, which is one reason other designs are also used.

The Matrix Design

Another important contemporary form of organization design also used by international firms is the **matrix design,** which is created by superimposing a product-based form of departmental-

Exhibit 12.4

The Divisional Design

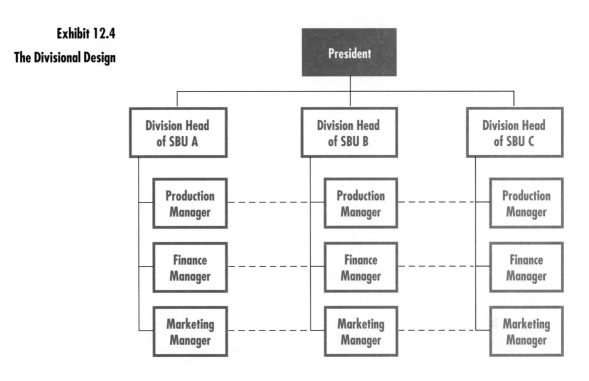

*An organization can retain the efficiency of functional departments and gain the advantages of product departmentalization through the use of the **matrix design.***

ization on an existing functional or locational departmentalization.[20] An example is shown in Exhibit 12.5.

Note that in the exhibit four functional departments are arrayed across the top of the organization, and each is headed by a vice president. Down the side of the organization are listed three project managers. Each of these managers is similar to the head of a product-based department (as shown by the dashed lines). In the matrix design, each project manager heads a project that cuts across functional areas (shown by the shaded areas). Thus the employees within the matrix design are part of two (or more) departments and report to two (or more) bosses at the same time.

The rationale for a matrix is really quite simple: the functional departments allow the firm to develop and retain unified and competent functional specialists, and the product design directs special and focused attention to individual products or product groups. The matrix design allows the firm to use the advantages of both forms simultaneously.

For example, suppose a firm using the matrix design wants to create and produce a new product. Specialists from each of the functional departments are brought together and formed into a team under the direction of the project manager. The new product gets the specialized attention it needs from each functional area, but each specialist can work on many projects at the same time and still have a functional "home."

In recent years many companies, including Monsanto, NCR, the Chase Manhattan Bank, and Prudential Insurance, have adopted the matrix form of organization design. There are generally clear indications of when a matrix should be used, although the design has disadvantages as well as advantages.

When to Use a Matrix   In general a matrix design is most likely to be effective in one of three situations.[21] First, it may be useful when the firm has a diverse set of products and a complex environment. Although the diverse set of products suggests product departmentalization, the

Exhibit 12.5

The Matrix Design

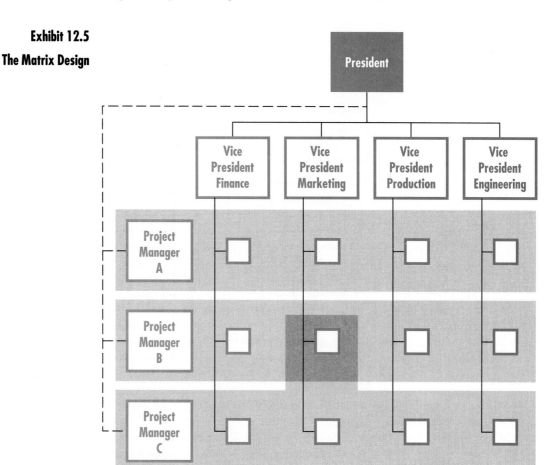

strength provided by the functional approach might be necessary to retain the requisite number of specialists.

The matrix might also be called for when there is a great deal of information to be processed. In highly uncertain environments accentuated by broad product lines, for example, the organization is confronted with a mountain of information. The matrix allows managers to categorize this information systematically and direct it to a group of key individuals.

Finally, the matrix organization design might be appropriate when there is pressure for shared resources. A company may need eight product groups yet have the resources to hire only four marketing specialists. The matrix provides a convenient way for the eight groups to share the talents of the four specialists.

Advantages of the Matrix   Clearly the matrix design has certain advantages.[22] For one thing, it is very flexible. Teams can be created, changed, and dissolved without major disruption. For another, it often improves motivation. Since the team has so much responsibility, its members are likely to be committed to its success and will feel a great sense of accomplishment.

Another significant advantage of the matrix is that it promotes the development of human resources. Managers get a wide range of experiences and can thus take increasingly important roles in the firm. The matrix can also enhance cooperation. Since there is so much interdependence among team members, it is important that they work well together. A final advantage is that managerial planning is facilitated. Because so much of the day-to-day operation of the organization is delegated to the teams, top managers have considerably more time to concentrate on planning.

Disadvantages of the Matrix   There are also major disadvantages to the matrix approach to organization design. Paramount among these is the potential conflict created by having a number of bosses. If a marketing specialist is part of three project groups and still has work to do within his functional role, he may not be able to satisfy all of his bosses when he is pressured for time. Another disadvantage is that coordination is difficult in a matrix. When two or more groups need the same information, each could end up paying a market research firm to get the information without realizing that the other group or groups could use it too. A final drawback is the fact that group work tends to take longer than individual work. Each manager in a matrix is likely to spend considerable amounts of time meeting and talking with other managers and putting one set of activities aside and picking up others. Thus the manager may have less individual time to devote to task accomplishment.[23]

Other Designs

Organizations that are becoming truly multinational in character have evolved the **global design.** This design refers to modifications of the functional, conglomerate, and divisional designs rather than to another single specific design. A global design might be relatively decentralized, as is Nestlé, or relatively centralized, as is Matsushita.[24] The key to a successful global design is the development of a design that will provide the necessary coordination and integration for worldwide business while also enabling the flexibility and autonomy necessary to compete in regional and local markets.[25]

*An **organic design**, in contrast to a **mechanistic design**, is based on open communication systems, a low level of specialization and standardization, and cooperation.*

The **organic design** was developed in the early 1960s by two British researchers and is similar in some ways to the System 4 design.[26] Its designers' goal was to help managers better align their organizations with their environments. They found that some firms could effectively use what they called a **mechanistic design,** a design similar to System 1 that was found to work best in stable conditions. For example, the Singer Sewing Machine Company operates in an environment that is fairly stable, has few domestic competitors, and so forth, so Singer might be best designed along mechanistic lines. In contrast, firms such as Hewlett-Packard and Levi Strauss use an organic design, which is presumed to be most effective when the environment is fluid and when constant adjustments are necessary to respond to shifts and changes. The organic organization is based on open communication systems, a low level of specialization and standardization, and cooperation. These characteristics are summarized in Table 12.3.

The view that seems to be emerging in organization design is that there is no one best way to organize and that companies should use whatever design seems most appropriate for them to accomplish their objectives. As a result, numerous **hybrid designs** have appeared in ongoing organizations. *Hybrid* means that different parts of the same organization are designed along different lines. One part may be divisional, another may use a matrix, and still others may be more or less bureaucratic in design. Some of those designs that merit noting include new venture units, alternate ownership patterns, and front-end-back-end and network organizations.

***New venture units** are small, semi-autonomous, voluntary work units that develop new products or ventures for companies.*

New venture units, or "skunkworks," as they are informally called, are small, semi-autonomous, voluntary work units. They are protected from many normal day-to-day corporate activities and pressures so that they can concentrate on the generation of new ideas or the development of new products or ventures. Companies that have used this design include Boeing, Genentech, Hewlett-Packard, IBM, Monsanto, NCR, Westinghouse, and 3M.[27]

Alternate ownership patterns have also emerged as a variety of designs are increasingly being used in an attempt to bring new ideas or new monies into the organization. For instance, **Employee Stock Ownership Plans (ESOPs)** transfer stock ownership to employees in an

Mechanistic	Organic
1. Tasks are fractionated and specialized; low emphasis on clarifying tasks relation between tasks and organizational objectives.	1. Tasks are more interdependent; emphasis on relevance of and organizational objectives.
2. Tasks tend to remain rigidly defined unless altered formally by top management.	2. Tasks are adjusted and redefined through interaction of organizational members.
3. Specific role definition (rights, obligations, and technical methods prescribed for each member).	3. Generalized role definition (members accept general responsibility for task accomplishment beyond individual role definition.)
4. Hierarchic structure of control, authority and communication. Sanctions derive from employment contract between employee and organization.	4. Network structure of control, authority, and communication. Sanctions derive more from community of interest than from contractual relationship.
5. Information relevant to situation and operations of the organization is formally assumed to rest with CEO.	5. Leader not assumed to be omniscient; knowledge centers identified where located throughout organization.
6. Communication is primarily vertical between superior and subordinate.	6. Communication is vertical and horizontal, depending on where information resides.
7. Communications primarily take the form of instructions from superiors and of information and requests for decisions from inferiors.	7. Communications primarily take form of information and advice.
8. Insistence on loyalty to organization and obedience to superiors.	8. Commitment to organization's tasks and goals valued over loyalty or obedience.
9. Importance and prestige attached to identification with organization and its active members.	9. Importance and prestige attached to affiliations and expertise in external environment.

Source: Adapted from Tom Burns and G. M. Stalker, *The Management of Innovation* (London: Tavistock Publications, 1961), pp. 119–122. Used with permission.

Table 12.3   Mechanistic and Organic Designs

effort to increase their commitment, involvement, and motivation. This also means, however, that executives cannot set corporate policy and strategy without involving the employees. **Research and Development Limited Partnerships (RDLPs)** are consortia, usually among high technology firms, that are designed to do basic research. The resources come from participating firms' contributions, and those firms then share in the results of the research. **Joint ventures,** whereby two firms jointly form a third one to produce a new product, are also becoming more common. The joint venture between GM and Toyota to produce the Saturn automobile is an example. Finally, many firms are buying into other companies to establish **equity positions** through the purchase of significant portions of stock. This financial interdependency tends to lead to endeavors that benefit both firms.[28]

Many newer organizational designs are early forms of what has been called the **high involvement organization.**[29] These designs are based on a process orientation, open communications, a low level of functional specialization and standardization, and cooperation. These designs have also been labeled as horizontal organizations, as opposed to the traditional, vertical organization.[30] Exhibit 12.6 illustrates the nature of such an organization in which parallel processes consisting of self-managed teams coordinated by process owners, who may be team representatives, are focused by an executive team on customers' needs. Versions of such high involvement organizations are the front-end-back-end and network organization as well as the new plant design.

Exhibit 12.6

The Horizontal Process Organization

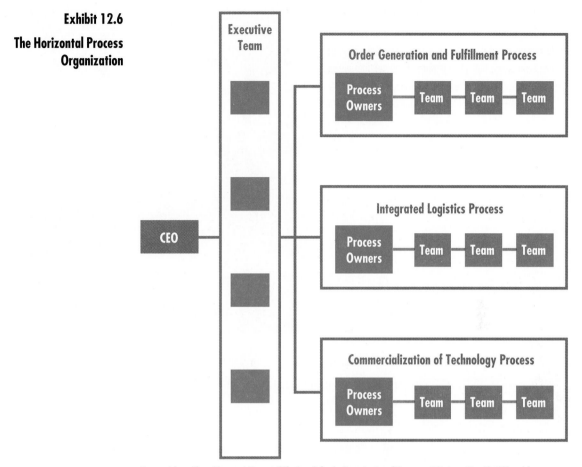

Source: Adapted from Thomas A. Stewart, "The Search for the Organization of Tomorrow," *Fortune,* May 18, 1992, p. 94.

Front-end-back-end organizations are those in which product and customer departmentalization are simultaneously employed. The "back end" produces the goods and services that are marketed by the "front end." This form of organization seems to be increasingly used by organizations that are selling complex sets of products or services to numerous groups of customers.[31]

Still another emerging organizational design is the **network organization.** Also known as a value-added partnership or a hollow corporation, network organizations usually engage in **outsourcing,** which is the contracting to other firms of many of their usual functions. Such organizations are the center of a network of companies that perform the activities of the business. Apple Computer, Reebok, Nike, and Benetton are examples of firms moving toward this form of organization.[32]

Finally, Procter & Gamble, Mead, TRW, Sherwin-Williams, Cummins Engine, General Foods, and other companies have used a high involvement approach in some of their newest plants. That approach, therefore, has come to be called the **new plant approach.** It has six characteristics.[33] The selection process is long and realistic about the kind of management to be used to increase the fit between those employed and the organization design. The physical layout is designed to suggest an egalitarian and team approach. Jobs are enriched and are performed by autonomous teams. All employees are salaried (there are no time clocks), and pay is based on skills and performance. There are wide spans, few levels, and high decentralization. Lastly, exten-

A General Electric factory in Bayamón, Puerto Rico instituted self-managed teams and a compensation system that rewards learning and performance. The workers, who make arresters (surge protectors that guard power stations and transmission lines from lightning strikes) are enthusiastic and productive. Profits rose 20 percent in the first year of the new system.
(Brian Smith.)

sive training is used to support the personal growth of all employees and to enable everyone to maintain and increase their skills.

Corporate Culture

*The shared experiences, stories, beliefs, norms, and actions of an organization are called its **corporate culture.***

A final element of organizations we should consider here is a concept that was introduced in Chapter 3, the internal environment, or **corporate culture.** Corporate culture is the shared experiences, stories, beliefs, norms, and actions that characterize an organization and influence its design.[34] Although the concept has been around for centuries, it has only recently become widely regarded as an important issue for managers. The catalyst for this interest was a popular book by Terrence Deal and Allen Kennedy, *Corporate Cultures: The Rites and Rituals of Corporate Life*, published in 1982.[35] Since that time, much attention has been focused on the concept.[36] The Skill Builder in this chapter helps you develop a better awareness of an organization's culture. The basic nature of corporate culture is illustrated in Exhibit 12.7.[37]

Determinants of Culture

As noted in the exhibit, three basic factors determine the culture of an organization. One key determinant is the values held by top management. If top executives are antagonistic toward the government, if they want to stamp out all competition, or if they just want to earn fat profits, they set a certain tone for the firm. On the other hand, if they want to cooperate with the government, if they want to coexist peacefully with competitors, or if they want to treat customers honestly and fairly, a different atmosphere is prevalent.

The history of the organization also helps determine its culture. A company founded by a strong personality, one who leaves a mark on the firm, will follow the original model. For example, Steve Jobs left an indelible imprint on Apple Computer, and Sam Walton did the same for Wal-Mart. Similarly, Les Wexner has imbued Limited, Inc. with a self-confidence that is overwhelming. Those in the organization seem to believe that Limited can do no wrong. Even relatively old companies such as Ford still carry vestiges of their founders.

Finally, top management's vision for the firm also helps shape its culture. If the CEO decides

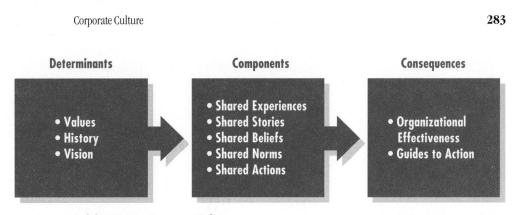

Exhibit 12.7   Corporate Culture

that the company needs to undertake significant new ventures and aim for rapid growth and expansion, this vision will permeate the entire organization. On the other hand, if the CEO is content to maintain the status quo and takes a defensive posture, this, too, will shape the culture. At Hewlett-Packard, a story about the founders declining a project because it involved bank financing has made the slogan "HP avoids bank debt" part of its culture.[38]

Components of Culture

How is an organization's design translated into culture? In general, it shapes five basic components or dimensions that we can use to characterize corporate culture.

Shared experiences are the common events that people participate in that become a part of their thinking. For instance, if a group of employees work closely together for an extended period, putting in twelve-hour days and seven-day weeks to create a new product on schedule, this experience becomes a part of the culture. Even after the group breaks up, its members will always have this experience in common.

Shared stories also become a part of the culture. "Do you remember . . . ," "That was the time . . . ," and "This company has always . . ." are common beginnings to stories that have entered an organization's mythology.

Shared beliefs are those things that all members of the organization accept as fact about the company. Employees at IBM, for example, believe that the company will win any battle it chooses to undertake. Likewise, associates (employees) at Wal-Mart believe that they can sell more this month than they sold last month.

Similarly, shared norms are generally accepted ways of doing business. A norm at Delta Air Lines is that all employees are expected to help get the job done, so if there is a back-up in passenger luggage at an airport, managers are expected to jump in and help clear the logjam.

Finally, shared actions are day-to-day behaviors that most people perform. At Texas Instruments the "shirt-sleeve" culture suggests that men do not wear ties to work. In contrast, at IBM the more formal culture dictates that all the men wear ties. Other common actions involve work hours, social interactions, and so forth.

Consequences of Culture

Two factors influencing a company's effectiveness are the creation and transmission of a strong corporate culture and the consistency of that culture with the organization's strategy.

Although relevant research is scant, one consequence of culture is that it impacts organizational effectiveness.[39] In particular, three aspects of culture can affect a company's success.

One, it seems to be important for top management to create and transmit a clear, strong but not arrogant culture.[40] There may not be a single best culture, but it does seem that everyone in the company needs to understand what the culture is. Common reasons cited for the past success of firms such as IBM and Digital Equipment and the current success of Disney and Southwest Airlines are that everyone in the organization understands the culture. Two, the culture must fit the strategy. Effectiveness tends to be enhanced if the corporate culture is consistent with the organization's strategy. When the culture and strategy do not seem to be in tune, effectiveness often suffers[41]. Three, it seems important that top management keep the culture adaptable to respond to changes in the organization's environment.[42] The organization comes to value the importance of satisfying its numerous constituencies and balancing their various needs.

The second consequence of culture, which is actually a corollary of the first, is that it provides a guide to actions for newcomers. A new employee at Texas Instruments can look around the plant, see everyone working in shirt sleeves, and know immediately how he or she should dress the next day. Newcomers also quickly learn whether high performance is expected or not.

Chapter Summary

Organization design refers to the overall configuration of positions and interrelationships among positions within an organization. The ideal bureaucracy was to have a strict division of labor, consistent rules, a clear chain of command, impersonal decision making, advancement based on expertise and performance, and well-kept records. Such organizations possess some desirable features but are most appropriate only in relatively simple and stable environments. Another early design was the System 4 view, which uses eight characteristics to describe organizations along a continuum. The characteristics include leadership, motivation, communication, interaction, decisionmaking, goalsetting, control processes, and the performance goals sought by managers.

Three major contingencies affect organization design: size, technology, and the environment. Technology refers to the set of conversion processes used by an organization to transform inputs into outputs. Environmental uncertainty seems to be accounted for by two components, rate of change and degree of complexity. When these are high, uncertainty is high, and when they are low, uncertainty is low.

There is no one best organization design. Contemporary organizations seem to recognize this by having changeable, flexible designs. Major contemporary approaches to organization design are the functional, conglomerate, divisional, and matrix designs.

New designs are emerging to deal with differing environments. New venture units, ESOPs, RDLPs, joint ventures, and equity positions are among those based on ownership. Early forms of high involvement organizations are also beginning to appear. Those include front-end-back-end and network organizations and new plant designs. Designs based on a process orientation, open communications, a low level of functional specialization and standardization, and cooperation seem to be increasingly used.

The major determinants of corporate culture are values held by the top management of the organization, the history of the firm, and the top managers' vision of the firm. These translate into culture through shared experiences, memories or stories, beliefs, norms (generally accepted ways of doing business), and actions. There is a link between corporate culture and organizational effectiveness. Effective organizations have strong, clear cultures that are consistent with their strategies. Further, the corporate culture provides a guide to action for newcomers and for new situations.

The Manager's Vocabulary

organization design
organization chart
bureaucracy
System 4
technology
unit technology
small-batch technology
large-batch technology
mass-production technology
continuous-process technology
quality circles
semi-autonomous work groups
environmental uncertainty

environmental change
environmental complexity
functional design
conglomerate design
divisional design
division head
division manager
matrix design
global design
organic design
mechanistic design
hybrid design
new venture units

employee stock ownership plans (ESOPs)
research and development limited partnerships (RDLPs)
joint ventures
equity positions
high involvement organization
front-end-back-end organization
network organization
outsourcing
new plant approach
corporate culture

Review Questions

1. What is meant by organization design?
2. Describe two major early approaches to organization design.
3. What are three major contingency factors that affect organization design? How do they do so?

4. Briefly describe the major contemporary organization design alternatives.
5. What is corporate culture, and why is it important?

Analysis Questions

1. Comment on these sentences: "The only real value of an organization chart is in doing the analysis necessary to draw it. Once it is drawn, the only value it has is covering cracks in plaster walls."
2. Can bureaucratic organizations avoid red tape and other problems usually associated with them? If so, how? If not, why not?
3. Rensis Likert, who developed the System 1–4 approach, said that when he asked managers to describe the best organization with which they had ever been associated, they invariably described a System 4 design. When asked to describe the worst,

they described System 1. Yet when he asked, "What would you do if you took over a company in trouble?" they all described actions that characterize System 1 more than System 4. What reasons can you give for this? How could you prevent it?
4. Would you rather work in an organic or a mechanistic organization? Why? Which form of organization would be more likely to appeal to someone who believes "there is a place for everything and everything should be in its place"? Why?
5. What factors could influence corporate culture besides the ones mentioned in the book?

Self-Assessment

How Is Your Organization Managed?

Introduction This self-assessment helps you define how an organization you are familiar with is organized. With this information, you can refer to Exhibit 12.3 to see if this organizational design is consistent with the environmental forces your organization is facing.

Instructions In this questionnaire, we want you to focus either on an organization you are currently working for or on one that you have worked for in the past. This organization could be a club, sorority, fraternity, or the university you are attending. Please circle the letter on the scale indicating the degree to which you agree or disagree with each statement. There is no "right answer." Respond according to how you see your organization being managed.

Strongly Agree (SA)	Agree (A)	Don't Know (DK)	Disagree (D)	Strongly Disagree (SD)

1. If people feel they have the right approach to carrying out their job, they can usually go ahead without checking with their superior.

    SA   A   DK   D   SD

2. People in this organization don't always have to wait for orders from their superiors on important matters.

    SA   A   DK   D   SD

3. People in this organization share ideas with their superior.

    SA   A   DK   D   SD

4. Different individuals play important roles in making decisions.

    SA   A   DK   D   SD

5. People in this organization are likely to express their feelings openly on important matters.

    SA   A   DK   D   SD

6. People in this organization are encouraged to speak their minds on important matters, even if it means disagreeing with their superior.

    SA   A   DK   D   SD

7. Talking to other people about the problems someone might have in making decisions is an important part of the process of decision making.

    SA   A   DK   D   SD

8. Developing employees' talents and abilities are major concerns of this organization.

    SA   A   DK   D   SD

(con't. on page 286)

9. People are encouraged to make suggestions before decisions are made.

   SA   A   DK   D   SD

10. In this organization, most people can have their point of view heard.

    SA   A   DK   D   SD

11. Superiors often seek advice from their subordinates before decisions are made.

    SA   A   DK   D   SD

12. Subordinates play an active role in running this organization.

    SA   A   DK   D   SD

13. For many decisions, the rules and regulations are developed as we go along.

    SA   A   DK   D   SD

14. It is not always necessary to go through channels in dealing with important matters.

    SA   A   DK   D   SD

15. The same rules and regulations are not consistently followed by employees.

    SA   A   DK   D   SD

16. There are few rules and regulations for handling any kind of problem that may arise in making most decisions.

    SA   A   DK   D   SD

17. People from different departments are often put together in task forces to solve important problems.

    SA   A   DK   D   SD

18. For special problems, we usually set up a temporary task force until we meet our objectives.

    SA   A   DK   D   SD

19. Jobs in this organization are not clearly defined.

    SA   A   DK   D   SD

20. In this organization, adapting to changes in the environment is important.

    SA   A   DK   D   SD

Questions	Strongly Agree	Agree	Don't Know	Disagree	Strongly Disagree
1.	5	4	3	2	1
2.	5	4	3	2	1
3.	5	4	3	2	1
4.	5	4	3	2	1
5.	5	4	3	2	1
6.	5	4	3	2	1
7.	5	4	3	2	1
8.	5	4	3	2	1
9.	5	4	3	2	1
10.	5	4	3	2	1
11.	5	4	3	2	1
12.	5	4	3	2	1
13.	5	4	3	2	1
14.	5	4	3	2	1
15.	5	4	3	2	1
16.	5	4	3	2	1
17.	5	4	3	2	1
18.	5	4	3	2	1
19.	5	4	3	2	1
20.	5	4	3	2	1
Total Score:	_____	_____	_____	_____	_____

Source: From *Type of Management System* by Robert T. Keller. Copyright © 1988. Used by permission of the author.

For interpretation, turn to the back of the book.

Skill Builder

Caught Between Corporate Cultures

Purpose The values, history, and vision of the corporate leaders all help determine the organization's culture. The culture then affects what is considered acceptable behavior within the organization. This skill builder focuses on the *open systems model*. It will help you develop the *broker role* of the administrative management model. One of the skills of the broker is the ability to live with change and change is often caused by the organizational culture.

Introduction Every organization has a culture. It guides and directs the actions and the behaviors of the organizational members. The organization's culture is so ubiquitous that often members of the organization don't even think about it. Yet it is always there, and if a member of the organization doesn't eventually conform to the culture, the organization usually removes the individual from the organization.

Quite often new members of the organization learn about the organization's culture through the socialization process. On some occasions this socialization process is very formal such as a new employees' orientation. On other occasions, the process is very informal such as when a veteran employee tells a new employee about an unwritten rule over lunch. But no matter what, everyone must learn about and live within the organization's culture.

Instructions Below is an incident about organizational culture. Read over the incident and prepare your thoughts based on the discussion questions provided.

The Consolidated Life Case

It all started so positively. Three days after graduating with his degree in business administration, Mike Wilson started his first day at a prestigious insurance company—Consolidated Life. He worked in the Policy Issue Department. The work of the department was mostly clerical and did not require a high degree of technical knowledge. Given the repetitive and mundane nature of the work, the successful worker had to be consistent and willing to grind out paperwork.

Rick Belkner was the division's vice president, "the man in charge" at the time. Rick was an actuary by training, a technical professional whose leadership style was laissez-faire. He was described in the division as "the mirror of whomever was the strongest personality around him." It was also common knowledge that Rick made $60,000 a year while he spent his time doing crossword puzzles.

Mike was hired as a management trainee and promised a supervisory assignment within a year. However, because of a management reorganization, it was only six weeks before he was placed in charge of an eight-person unit.

The reorganization was intended to streamline workflow, upgrade and combine the clerical jobs, and make greater use of the computer system. It was a drastic departure from the old way of doing things and created a great deal of animosity and anxiety among the clerical staff.

Management realized that a flexible supervisory style was necessary to pull off the reorganization without immense turnover, so they gave their supervisors a free hand to run their units as they saw fit. Mike used this latitude to implement group meetings and training classes in his unit. In addition he assured all members raises if they worked hard to attain them. By working long hours, participating in the mundane tasks with his unit, and being flexible in his management style, he was able to increase productivity, reduce errors, and reduce lost time. Things improved so dramatically that he was noticed by upper management and earned a reputation as a "superstar" despite being viewed as free spirited and unorthodox. The feeling was that his loose, people-oriented management style could be tolerated because his results were excellent.

A Chance for Advancement After a year, Mike received an offer from a different Consolidated Life division located across town. Mike was asked to manage an office in the marketing area. The pay was excellent and it offered an opportunity to turn around an office in disarray. The reorganization in his present division at Consolidated was almost complete and most of his mentors and friends in management had moved on to other jobs. Mike decided to accept the offer.

In his exit interview he was assured that if he ever wanted to return, a position would be made for him. It was clear that he was held in high regard by management and staff alike. A huge party was thrown to send him off.

The new job was satisfying for a short time but it became apparent to Mike that it did not have the long-term potential he was promised. After bringing on a new staff, computerizing the office, and auditing the books, he began looking for a position that would both challenge him and give him the autonomy he needed to be successful.

Eventually word got back to his former vice president, Rick

Belkner, at Consolidated Life that Mike was looking for another job. Rick offered Mike a position with the same pay he was now receiving and control over a 14-person unit in his old division. After considering other options, Mike decided to return to his old division feeling that he would be able to progress steadily over the next several years.

Enter Jack Greely: Return Mike Wilson Upon his return to Consolidated Life, Mike became aware of several changes that had taken place in the six months since his departure. The most important change was the hiring of a new divisional senior vice president, Jack Greely. Jack had been given total authority to run the division. Rick Belkner now reported to Jack.

Jack's reputation was that he was tough but fair. It was necessary for people in Jack's division to do things his way and "get the work out."

Mike also found himself reporting to one of his former peers, Kathy Miller, who had been promoted to manager during the reorganization. Mike had always "hit it off" with Kathy and foresaw no problem in working with her.

After a week Mike realized the extent of the changes that had occurred. Gone was the loose, casual atmosphere that had marked his first tour in the division. Now, a stricter, task-oriented management doctrine was practiced. Morale of the supervisory staff had decreased to an alarming level. Jack Greely was the major topic of conversation in and around the division. People joked that MBO now meant "management by oppression."

Mike was greeted back with comments like "Welcome to prison" and "Why would you come back here? You must be desperate!" It seemed like everyone was looking for new jobs or transfers. Their lack of desire was reflected in the poor quality of work being done.

Mike's Idea: Supervisors' Forum Mike felt that a change in the management style of his boss was necessary in order to improve a frustrating situation. Realizing that it would be difficult to affect his style directly, Mike requested permission from Rick Belkner to form a Supervisors' Forum for all the managers on Mike's level in the division. Mike explained that the purpose would be to enhance the existing management-training program. The Forum would include weekly meetings, guest speakers, and discussions of topics relevant to the division and the industry. Mike thought the forum would show Greely that he was serious about both his job and improving morale in the division. Rick gave the okay for an initial meeting.

The meeting took place and ten supervisors who were Mike's peers in the company eagerly took the opportunity to "Blue Sky" it. There was a euphoric attitude about the group as they drafted their statement of intent. Their memo to Rick Belkner appears below.

The group felt the memo accurately and diplomatically stated their dissatisfaction with the current situation. However, they pondered what the results of their actions would be and what else they could have done.

To: Rick Belkner
From: New Issue Services Supervisors
Subject: Supervisors' Forum

On Thursday, June 11, the Supervisors' Forum held its first meeting. The objective of the meeting was to identify common areas of concern among us and to determine topics that we might be interested in pursuing.

The first area addressed was the void that we perceive exists in the management-training program. As a result of conditions beyond anyone's control, many of us over the past year have held supervisory duties without the benefit of formal training or proper experience. Therefore, what we propose is that we utilize the Supervisors' Forum as a vehicle with which to enhance the existing management-training program. The areas that we hope to affect with this supplemental training are: a) morale/job satisfaction; b) quality of work and service; c) productivity; and d) management expertise as it relates to the life insurance industry. With these objectives in mind, we have outlined below a list of possible activities that we would like to pursue.

1. Further utilization of the existing "in-house" training programs provided for manager trainees and supervisors, i.e., Introduction to Supervision, E.E.O., and Coaching and Counseling.

2. A series of speakers from various sections in the company. This would help expose us to the technical aspects of their departments and their managerial style.

3. Invitations to outside speakers to address the Forum on management topics such as managerial development, organizational structure and behavior, business policy, and the insurance industry. Suggested speakers could be area college professors, consultants, and state insurance officials.

4. Outside training and visits to the field. This could include attendance at seminars concerning management theory and development relative to the insurance industry. Attached is a representative sample of a program we would like to have considered in the future.

In conclusion, we hope that this memo clearly illustrates what we are attempting to accomplish with this program. It is our hope that the above outline will be able to give the Forum credibility and establish it as an effective tool for all levels of management within New Issue. By supplementing our on-the-job training with a series of speakers and classes, we aim to develop prospective management personnel with a broad perspective of both the life insurance industry and management's role in it. Also, we would like to extend an invitation to the underwriters to attend any programs at which the topic of the speaker might be of interest to them.

cc: J. Greely
Managers

Source: Joseph Weiss, Mark Wahlstrom, and Edward Marshall, *Journal of Management Case Studies,* Fall 1986, pp. 238.

Discussion Questions

1. Compare and contrast the organizational culture of the Policy Issue Department before and after Jack Greely.
2. Which set of organizational culture characteristics was Mike Wilson working under when he suggested the Supervisors' Forum and wrote the memo?
3. How do you think Rick Belkner and Jack Greely will respond to this initiative?

CONCLUDING CASES

12.1   A Picture of Kodak

Global competition impacts even huge, highly successful, and market-dominant firms. One such firm, Eastman Kodak, the Rochester, New York–based photography company, underwent at least four restructurings beginning in the 1980s in its efforts to respond to increased global competition. More than twenty thousand people left the company through early retirements, resignations, or dismissals. Despite these efforts, however, Kodak's profits declined from more than $1 billion in 1980 to just a little more than $300 million in 1985. Profits began to recover after that though, reaching more than $500 million by 1989.

Kodak is organized around its major market sectors at the corporate level. The imaging sector includes such products as cameras, films and papers, batteries, and audiovisual equipment. The information sector makes copiers, computer disks, electronic publishing equipment, and related products. The health sector consists of Sterling Drugs and Lehn & Fink, which make Bayer aspirin, Campho-Phenique, d-Con, Lysol, and many other products. The chemical sector is Eastman Chemical with its Tennessee and Texas locations, which make polyester, plastics, adhesives, and resins.

For several years now, however, within these sectors, Kodak has been moving toward high involvement organization approaches. For instance, in its Kodak Apparatus Division in Elmgrove, New York, Kodak has turned to the use of teams to achieve its goals. That teamwork takes the form of employee involvement and self-direction linked with a continuous improvement philosophy and has been achieving outstanding results.

Process or horizontal organization is also being used. The 1,500 employees who make black and white film began to work in "the flow" in 1989. Through the use of flow charts, the process of producing black and white film was re-engineered from departments into customer streams or business units. One such stream makes the hundreds of types of film used by the Health Sciences Division. Before the restructuring, the black and white film activities were poor performers. The division averaged 15 percent over budgeted costs, was late more than 30 percent of the time, had poor morale, and took up to forty-two days to fill an order. After restructuring, it was under budget, late only 5 percent of the time, had much improved morale, and had cut response time in half.

Productivity, profitability, and morale at Kodak have all improved with the use of high involvement, process organization. The picture at Kodak is better than ever.[43]

Discussion Questions

1. Which of the approaches to organization design discussed in the chapter seem best to describe that used at Kodak?
2. Which contingency factors are influential in shaping Kodak's organization design? How?
3. What changes seem to be taking place in Kodak's corporate culture?
4. What recommendations would you make to Kodak's board of directors regarding its organization design? Why?

12.2   ABB Produces More Than Power

Asea Brown Boveri Ltd., ABB, is a truly multinational company. It began when ASEA, a Swedish engineering group, joined a Swiss competitor, BBC Brown Boveri, to form a new company. The new company, ABB, quickly added 70 other companies throughout the world and now operates through 1,300 companies worldwide although it has only just over 200,000 employees.

It is impossible to buy stock directly in ABB since ASEA and BBC Brown Boveri continue as separate companies, each of which owns 50 percent of ABB. They kept certain assets, such as ASEA's portion of Electrolux, and continue to be listed separately on several world stock exchanges. ABB is now one of the largest global electrical equipment companies—larger than Westinghouse and second only to General Electric.

The firm's top managers meet frequently in different countries but use English to conduct their business. They do so despite the fact that ABB's home office is in Zurich, Switzerland, and the Wallenberg family in Sweden is a major owner of ASEA.

Some of ABB's acquisitions needed a lot of work. America's Combustion Engineering, purchased in 1989, for example, was reorganized, had its staff cut, and some divisions were sold. After all of that it became more profitable and has been kept by ABB. Other acquisitions were quickly dropped when they were not able to be made into profitable additions.

ABB strives to enhance its strategic position and its effectiveness through its acquisitions and joint ventures. For instance, ABB formed a joint venture in the United States with Gould in 1979 to produce electrical equipment. In 1988 it formed two such ventures with Westinghouse to produce electrical generation and transmission equipment. In 1989 ABB bought the electrical transmission and distribution equipment division of Westinghouse, which had been the original business of George Westinghouse. It bought the robotics production of Cincinnati Milacron in 1990 to enhance its automation business. That same year it joined with Germany's Thyssen to form a transportation venture, ABB Henschel.

ABB also strives to keep a very small headquarters staff and decentralize operations. ASEA had about 2,000 personnel when it was merged but has only about 150 now. Most of the rest moved to subsidiaries or were absorbed in other acquisitions.

ABB uses a loose version of a matrix organization with all employees reporting to both a country manager and a business sector manager. These managers are not usually equal in power, however, and the country manager may well be the more powerful one. This approach makes it easier for ideas about local or regional markets as well as for technology to be recognized and used by ABB.[44]

Discussion Questions

1. Describe ABB's organization design. Which of the approaches discussed in the chapter seem to fit ABB?
2. Which contingency factors seem to be important in shaping ABB's organization design? Why?
3. How would you describe ABB's corporate culture?
4. What recommendations would you make to ABB's board of directors regarding its organization design? Why?

CHAPTER

13

Organization Change and Innovation

Chapter Outline

Learning Objectives

After studying this chapter you should be able to

· Discuss the nature of change, including the reasons and need for change, planned organizational change, and the steps in change.

· Explain why people resist change and how to overcome that resistance.

· Identify strategic, structural, technological, and people-focused approaches to change.

· Define and discuss the nature and techniques of organization development.

· Explain why and how organizations may need to undergo revitalization.

· Discuss the importance of innovation in organizations and describe how it can be facilitated.

Weyerhaeuser Corporation is the third-largest forest products company in the United States. The firm owns 5.5 million acres of timberland in the United States and has cutting rights to another 13 million acres in Canada. Weyerhaeuser is a major exporter of newsprint to the Pacific Rim and has one subsidiary that builds homes and commercial buildings and another in the financial services industry.

Unfortunately, Weyerhaeuser has not performed very well for the last several years. Beginning more than a decade ago managers at the firm have undertaken one major change after another in an effort to boost both sales and profits. In 1982, for example, Weyerhaeuser reduced its salaried work force by 25 percent. In 1983 it bought GNA Corporation, its current financial services unit, and other unrelated businesses in an effort to diversify. And in 1984 Weyerhaeuser opened a branch operation in China to capitalize on growth opportunities in that country. To management's consternation, however, none of these changes produced meaningful results.

In 1988 the board of directors finally brought in a new president, John Creighton, and gave him the charge to turn things around. Creighton began by developing a new strategy calling for renewed emphasis on the firm's forest products businesses. He also announced a major reorganization of Weyerhaeuser's organization design. At that time the firm was organized by geographic region. Creighton changed the firm's structure to a product-based design.

Creighton also sold several marginal businesses and initiated a sweeping modernization program that closed several older facilities and upgraded many others. Finally, he installed a new incentive system to reward individual mills for their own profitability. While it's too early to assess the effects of the most recent changes, observers hope that the firm may have finally figured out how to do it right.[1] ■

Weyerhaeuser presents a vivid portrait of the complexities and issues involved in the management of organization change in today's business environment. All organizations must change if they are to maintain an effective alignment with their environment. Indeed, an organization's ability to effectively manage change is often a critical ingredient in its very survival. At the same time, however, if change is not properly managed, it may do as much harm as good.

This chapter explores organization change and three of its most important related areas. We first discuss the nature of change. We then describe ways that change can be more effectively managed, highlighting why people resist change and ways to overcome that resistance. Four general areas of organization change are then identified. The final three sections focus on organization development, organization revitalization, and innovation in organizations. Each of these areas represents special forms of change that are often managed as distinct activities.

The Nature of Organization Change

Organization change is a fundamental change in some aspect of the organization.

IBM has announced that it will eliminate almost fifty thousand jobs. Bank of America is in the midst of a major expansion program across the United States. Goodyear has altered virtually every facet of its organization design in the last three years. Tenneco is trying to motivate its employees to work harder in an effort to boost profitability. And Weyerhaeuser has installed new production equipment in many of its mills.[2] What do these examples have in common?

They all represent a fundamental change in some aspect of the organization—a form of **organization change.** IBM is shrinking while Bank of America is growing. Goodyear is changing its organization design. Tenneco is changing people's behavior. And Weyerhaeuser is changing the technology it uses to make paper products. Why were these changes felt to be necessary? To answer this question, we must explore some of the reasons for organization change and look at the steps that managers usually follow in making such changes.

Reasons for Change

Reasons for change are associated with forces in the organization's task and/or general environments.

An organization might find it necessary to change for a variety of different reasons. As shown in Exhibit 13.1, the most common reasons for change stem from one or more forces in the organization's general and/or task environments, as discussed previously in Chapter 4.[3]

Consider, for example, how shifts in an organization's general environment might cause it to have to respond. Technological forces might provide new equipment or make existing technology obsolete. For example, newly automated work processes might have to be implemented to reduce labor costs and improve quality and productivity. Political-legal forces might introduce new legislation or regulations that affect the organization. For example, a new law that increases safety standards for the firm's products might alter the parts the firm buys to use in assembling the product.

Economic forces could impact an organization in several different ways. For example, inflation or changes in unemployment might affect how the organization hires new employees. Similarly, shifts in interest rates might change a firm's ability or willingness to borrow money. International forces are also becoming increasingly important. For example, new markets and/or competition might emerge in other countries. Finally, sociocultural forces are also important in many different circumstances. For example, general shifts in consumer values and preferences about alcohol are changing how alcohol-producing companies like Miller and Coors do business.

In similar fashion, the task environment can also bring about organization change. Suppliers can raise or lower prices, alter quality standards, or change delivery schedules. Customers might turn to alternative products or demand higher quality or lower prices. Competitors might raise or lower prices, introduce new products or services, or adjust their advertising techniques. Unions might demand higher wages or better working conditions or a greater voice in making decisions. Regulators might impose new restrictions on how the organization does business or mod-

Exhibit 13.1 Reasons for Change

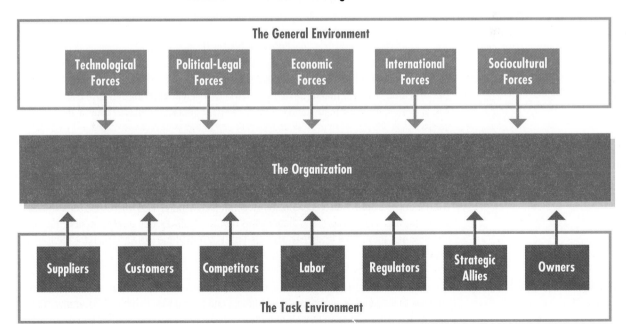

Economic conditions are a major factor in organizational change. While Boeing has been highly successful in exporting its products worldwide, an economic slump during the 1990s brought many changes. At its Seattle base, the number of inventoried planes, costs, and employees were reduced. (Ed Kashi.)

ify the ways the organization can do certain things. Owners might exert pressure for higher profitability. And strategic allies might want to negotiate new joint venture agreements or modify or cancel existing ones.

Planned Organization Change

One of the ways in which organizations can deal with these forces in the general and task environments is to try to anticipate them ahead of time. In most cases the company that senses the need for a change before the change is actually needed and then plans for that change in a careful and systematic fashion will be more effective than the company that waits to be forced to respond.[4]

Planned organization change is the anticipation of possible changes in the environment and how the organization should most likely respond to those changes.

The former approach is called **planned organization change.** In general, planned organizational change involves the anticipation of possible changes in the environment to which the organization will have to respond and some consideration of how that response will occur ahead of time. Of course managers cannot always accurately predict the future. Even an imperfect vision of what the future holds for a business, however, is almost certain to be better than no vision at all.

Reactive change is an unplanned response to environmental changes as they occur.

In contrast, **reactive change** is more likely to occur when the organization pays little attention to anticipating environmental shifts and must consequently react to the environment as dictated by what happens. For example, some critics argue that IBM has struggled in recent years primarily because its managers did not anticipate the need for change. When worldwide computer sales slumped just as new competitors were emerging, IBM found itself with excess capacity and a heavy payroll. The changes it is undergoing now to regain its lost competitiveness are more painful than they might have been had the firm taken the time earlier to plan for them in an orderly fashion.

Steps in Planned Change

When an organization is successful in its efforts to anticipate the need for change, it will be able to manage that change in a comparatively rational and logical way. Exhibit 13.2 summarizes the steps that can be followed in this circumstance.[5]

Exhibit 13.2

Planned Organization Change

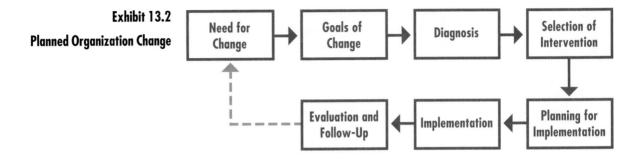

Logically, the process must first start with the recognition of a need for change. This recognition might come in the form of an anticipated event. For example, a manager may read about a new technological breakthrough that will soon be available and that she believes will be applicable to her organization. Or an employee might casually mention that workers in the organization would greatly appreciate an on-site child-care facility.

After deciding that a change is needed, the manager must set goals for the change. That is, she must consider why the change is being considered and what should be gained from it. For instance, she might decide that adopting the new technology should cut costs or that the on-site day-care facility should lower employee absenteeism. Obviously, if the change will not benefit the organization in some way, it might be advisable to delay making it until it has more potential.

The third step is diagnosis. This means that the manager should look carefully at the organizational system to identify all of the possible effects of the change. The new technology she is considering might call for training of employees, a new performance appraisal system, and higher pay. The child-care facility might require the services of a full-time nurse and other additional employees.

Next, the manager chooses the actual intervention to use. For example, several forms of the technology might be available, and it might be possible to buy or lease it. The child-care facility could be operated by the organization itself or managed by an outside company. Each of these options, as well as others, needs to be considered.

The dynamics associated with the intervention must also be carefully planned. The manager must ask herself when the technology will be introduced, whether it will be introduced in stages or all at once, and whether it will be installed in all plants or just in one, as a pilot. When will the training be done, who will do it, and who will be eligible for the training? When will the child-care center be opened, what are its potential hours of operation, how much will employees pay, and what are the insurance implications?

When these and myriad other questions have been answered, implementation can take place. Of course, some period of time will probably be necessary to get things fully operational, and some problems will probably have to be worked out. The manager should anticipate and expect these problems so as not to abandon the change before it has had ample time to demonstrate its usefulness. The adoption of new technology, for example, might need to be phased in gradually.

Finally, after the change has been fully installed and is operating smoothly, the manager should evaluate it carefully to ensure that it has met its original goals. After the new technology has been installed, productivity should go up and costs should go down. Absenteeism should also go down once the child-care facility is in place. Assuming that the goals have been reasonably met, the process is essentially complete, and the manager can wait for the next opportunity for change. If the goals are not being met (for example, if the child-care facility is not being used or absenteeism has not dropped), additional fine-tuning may be in order.

Managing Organization Change

Resistance to Change

People resist change because of uncertainty, self-interests, perceptions, and loss.

O bviously, many of these points relate to the management of organizational change, but there are also other aspects of the process. Two that are especially critical are recognizing that people often resist change and subsequently understanding ways to overcome this resistance.[6]

People in organizations resist change for a variety of reasons. As summarized in Table 13.1, the four most common reasons for resisting change are uncertainty, self-interests, perceptions, and loss.

First, for a variety of reasons, change breeds uncertainty. For instance, some people may fear for their place in the organization. They may worry that they cannot meet new job demands or that their job will be eliminated. Or they may dread the ambiguity that frequently accompanies change. As a result of this uncertainty, they may also feel anxious and nervous. They resist the change in order to cope better with these feelings. Many U.S. government workers resisted efforts to automate their work because of their uncertainty about the new technology they were having to learn about.[7]

People also resist change because it threatens their own self-interests. A plant manager might resist a change to automate his plant because he fears it threatens his control of the plant's human resources. Likewise, another manager may resist a new automated information network because it will give others access to information that she alone previously controlled. Or an impending change in a firm's organization design may eliminate several higher-level management positions, thereby increasing loyalty among managers wanting to be promoted to management positions.

Different perceptions also cause resistance to change. For example, a manager with a marketing background might conduct the diagnostic phase of the change process and conclude that a change in promotion and advertising is needed. However, a manager with an operations background might see the problem in terms of quality and productivity. Thus the manager sees the situation in a different light and will likely conclude that a different intervention is needed. Consequently, the second manager might resist the change as first proposed by the marketing manager because of perceiving the situation differently.

Finally, an individual might resist change because of feelings of loss. Many changes involve alterations in work assignments and work schedules and thus informal groups and close working relationships among peers are broken up. Loss of power, status, security, or familiarity with existing procedures can also be a problem. For example, when J. C. Penney moved its corporate headquarters from New York to Dallas a few years ago, many people resisted the change because, among other things, they did not want to leave their friends and existing working relationships.

Overcoming Resistance to Change

Resistance to change can sometimes be overcome through participation, communication, facilitation, and force-field analysis.

Fortunately, managers can at least partially overcome resistance to change in several ways. Four especially useful ones are also noted in Table 13.1. One key approach is to encourage participation by those people who will be involved in the change. When people participate, they feel less threatened, recognize that they have a say in what happens, and are less concerned about feelings of loss. Logically, then, they will come to lower their resistance to the change.

Open communication also helps overcome resistance. Complete and accurate information helps remove the uncertainty that so often accompanies change, as we have noted. Managers should provide information that is relevant to the change as often as they can. This can be achieved by disseminating information as it becomes available and by being open and receptive to questions and inquiries from employees about the impending change.

Facilitation can also reduce resistance. Facilitation simply means that managers need to recognize that resistance may be present and must therefore actively work to manage it. For example, introducing change gradually helps minimize its impact. Being sensitive to people's concerns and helping them to resolve those concerns rationally can also be effective.

Table 13.1
Resistance to Change

Common reasons for resistance	Ways to overcome resistance
1. Uncertainty	1. Participation
2. Self-interests	2. Communication
3. Differing Perceptions	3. Facilitation
4. Feelings of Loss	4. Force-Field Analysis

Force-field analysis is one management approach to overcoming resistance to change.

Another management approach to overcoming resistance to change is to use **force-field analysis.** The first step in using force-field analysis is to systematically look at the pluses and minuses associated with the change from the standpoint of the employees. Next, the manager should make efforts to increase the pluses and decrease the minuses in order to tip the scales toward acceptance. For example, if a major barrier to an impending change is that a certain work group will be broken up, the manager might try to figure out a way to keep the group intact. If that can be arranged, one minus has been eliminated. Likewise, if one thing working in favor of the change is greater autonomy over how the job is done, providing even more autonomy and making sure employees see how this will benefit them will further increase acceptance of the change.

Areas of Organization Change

So far we have talked a lot about organizational change but have not really focused on exactly what the organization might actually be changing. In this section we identify the four major areas of organizational change. As shown in Table 13.2, these are strategy, structure, technology, and people.[8]

Strategic Change

Strategic change occurs when the organization modifies or adopts a new strategy.

Whenever an organization modifies its strategy or adopts a new strategy, it has engaged in **strategic change.** At the corporate level, for example, a firm might move from a growth to a retrenchment strategy (as IBM is currently doing). Or it might move from a retrenchment strategy to one of stability. From a portfolio perspective, a corporation might eliminate one or more strategic business units and/or acquire new ones (as when Weyerhaeuser sold some of its unrelated businesses).

Table 13.2
Areas of Organization Change

Strategic change	Structural change	Technological change	People-focused change
Corporate Strategy	Components of Structure	Equipment	Skills
Business Strategy	Organization Design	Work Processes	Performance
Functional Strategy	Reward System	Work Sequence	Attitudes
	Performance Appraisal System	Automation	Perceptions
	Control System	Information-Processing System	Behaviors
			Expectations

The Environment of Management

Sara Lee

Most people think of Sara Lee as a small, regional food producer. And while it's true that Sara Lee does make a mean brownie, it also makes far more than just pastries. What else comes under the Sara Lee umbrella? Think of Hanes men's underwear, L'eggs nylons, Bali bras, and Coach leather goods, just to name a few products.

How did Sara Lee achieve this array of consumer success stories? Other food processors like Quaker Oats and General Mills had tried unsuccessfully to diversify. Learning from their mistakes, Sara Lee CEO John Bryan developed a new strategy for diversification that has paid big dividends for the firm, at least so far.

Bryan starts by identifying target markets dominated by private-label goods — underwear and sweat clothes, for exam-

ple. He then buys firms in the industry to acquire both capacity and market share. The economies of scale that result from this approach allow the firm to keep costs and prices low. Bryan then reinforces brand identity through extensive marketing and sells his products through as many distribution channels as is feasible.

In nylons, for example, Sara Lee has acquired and developed four distinct product names. L'eggs and Just My Size are dominant in the low-end market, while Hanes and Donna Karan compete successfully in upscale department stores. But all four product lines are made in the same factories. By maintaining distinct images, the firm can tailor promotions for each at the same time.

So far, Bryan's formula has worked. But he is facing his biggest challenge now as he leads Sara Lee into Europe. His preliminary acquisitions and consolidations seem to be working there just as well as they have in the United States.[9] ■

At the business level, an organization might shift among the defending, prospecting, and analyzing approaches. Likewise, it might move from a differentiation strategy to one of cost leadership, or from cost leadership to targeting. Finally, the organization might also change one or more of its functional strategies. These changes might occur in any or all of the areas of marketing, finance, production, research and development, human resources, or organization design. *The Environment of Management: Sara Lee* describes how Sara Lee has changed not only its strategy but other parts of the organization as well.

Structural Change

Structural change focuses on part of the formal organization itself.

Structural change is any change directed at a part of the formal organizational system.[10] In general, such changes relate to structural components, overall organization design, or other aspects of the organization.

In Chapter 11 we identified several basic components of organization structure. One or more of these components will need to be changed from time to time. That is, the organization might change its degree of decentralization, its span of management, or its bases of departmentalization (as Weyerhaeuser has done). Other structural components can also change. The organization may adopt new methods of coordination, change the degree of job specialization, or modify working hours for employees.

On a larger scale, the company might need to change its overall design. It has been estimated that most companies need changes of this magnitude every five years or so.[11] In Chapter 12 we looked at several forms of organization design. Whenever a firm changes its design, it is embarking on a major organizational change. In the late 1970s, for instance, Texas Instruments changed from a functionally organized firm to a matrix organization. In the early 1980s it made modifications in its matrix design.[12] And more recently the firm decided to alter its design once again in order to more effectively compete in the international arena.[13]

There are also other areas in which structural changes may be made. Common changes in this category include changes in the organization's reward system, its performance appraisal system, its degree of participation, and/or its control system.[14]

Technological Change

Technological change involves equipment, work processes or sequences, and so forth.

A third major type of change is that related to technology. **Technological change** has been increasingly widespread in the last few years.[15] Like strategic and structural change, it comes in many forms. One obvious area is new equipment. As new and more efficient machines are introduced into the market, manufacturers occasionally need to upgrade in order to keep pace.

Changes may also affect work processes or sequences. For instance, a decision to produce plastic flashlight casings instead of metal ones necessitates major changes in the work processes. Similarly, the sequence of work can change as management considers new ways of arranging the workplace. This area will become increasingly important as flexible manufacturing systems come to replace traditional assembly lines.

Automation is a major form of technological change. Such changes as those made by Nissan, which recently installed more than two hundred computer-controlled robots in its Tennessee plant, greatly increase productivity but also represent a major capital investment.

Finally, significant changes can also be made in the organization's information-processing system. For example, a mainstay of many offices, the typewriter, has been widely replaced with word processors, and most managers now use personal computers. Each individual piece of equipment can be tied with the others in an integrated network to provide access to large blocks of data. Such data-processing capabilities represent major changes.

Technological change can affect any and all organizations, even in areas that have not changed for long periods of time. Dole Food Co., Inc., for instance, invested millions of dollars to design and manufacture its own harvesting and packing systems such as the Precision Pack Harvester used for lettuce harvesting. Such applications of technology reduce the labor required, lower costs, and improve quality. (Photo by Ken Whitmore/Courtesy of Dole Foods Co., Inc.)

People-Focused Change

People-focused change can address skills and performance or attitudes, perceptions, behaviors, and expectations.

Finally, change can be focused on people within the organization. **People-focused change** can actually affect two distinct areas: (1) skills and performance and (2) attitudes, perceptions, behaviors, and expectations.

In general, managers can take three approaches to upgrade skills and performance. First, current employees can be replaced. This is clearly a difficult route to choose and usually should be taken only when no other options are available. Alternatively, managers can gradually upgrade selection standards. With this approach, existing employees are not dismissed, but when someone leaves for a better job, retires, or is fired, his or her replacement is selected according to higher standards. A third option is to train existing employees to upgrade their performance-related skills. Change focused more on attitudes, perceptions, behaviors, and expectations is often undertaken from the perspective of organization development. We discuss this area in more detail in our next section. Many of the underlying causes of optimistic development are also discussed in depth in chapters 14–19.

Organization Development

The Nature of Organization Development

Organization development is a planned, organizationwide effort intended to improve the health of the organization by systematically applying behavioral science techniques.

A s we noted above, organization development focuses on changing attitudes, perceptions, behaviors, and/or expectations.

Organization development can be defined as a planned, organizationwide effort to enhance organizational health and effectiveness through the systematic application of behavioral science techniques.[16] Rather than being a single, isolated change, organization development actually represents a complete philosophy of management. It assumes that people want to grow and develop, that they are capable of making useful contributions, and that one of the missions of the organization is to help facilitate personal growth as a way of enhancing employees' contributions.

Many large organizations practice organization development on a regular basis.[17] For example, American Airlines, Federated Department Stores, ITT, Polaroid, Procter & Gamble, and B. F. Goodrich each have major organization development programs under way at all times. Goodrich, in fact, has trained sixty people in organization development processes and techniques. They serve as internal consultants, helping other managers use organization development.

Organization Development Techniques

*Common organization development techniques include the **Leadership Grid**, team building, survey feedback, third-party peace making, and process consultation.*

A number of change techniques fall under the organization development umbrella. One of the best known is the **Leadership Grid,** which is used to assess current leadership styles in an organization and then to train leaders to practice an ideal style of behavior.[18] The basic Grid framework is shown in Exhibit 13.3. The axes of the Grid represent concern for people and concern for production. Each leader is scored from 1 to 9 along each dimension. The five main leadership styles (1,1; 1,9; 9,1; 5,5; and 9,9) are shown in the exhibit.

The Grid assumes that the 9,9 combination is the ideal style of behavior for leaders. Managers in the organizations go through a six-phase training program to move them in the general direction of the 9,9 coordinates. Although some people are critical of the Grid's effectiveness, others claim it has been quite beneficial.

In addition to the Grid, other organization development techniques are used by many organizations.[19] **Team building,** for example, is used to enhance the motivation and satisfaction of people in groups. It is a series of activities and exercises designed to foster mutual understanding, acceptance, and group cohesion. **Survey feedback,** surveying subordinates about their perceptions of their leader and then providing feedback to the entire group, is used to increase communication between leaders and their subordinates.

A separate set of organization development activities focuses on improving coordination and communication among different groups. **Third-party peace making** is an organization

Exhibit 13.3
The Leadership Grid

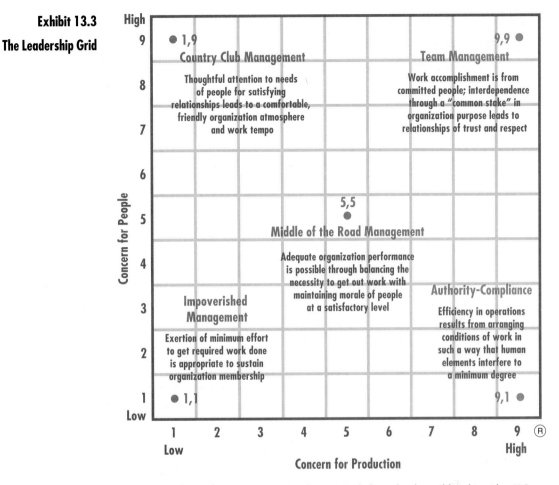

Source: The Leadership Grid ® Figure from *Leadership Dilemmas—Grid Solutions,* by Robert R. Blake and Anne Adams McCanse. Houston: Gulf Publishing Company, p. 29. Copyright © 1991, by Scientific Methods, Inc. Reproduced by permission of the owners.

development effort concentrated on resolving conflict, especially conflict that is quite strong and that has existed for a long time. **Process consultation** involves having an organization development expert observe the communication, decision-making, and leadership processes in the organization and then suggest ways to improve them. Other activities are directed at specific areas such as life and career planning and individual goal setting.

Organization Revitalization

Reasons for Revitalization

A second related area of organization change that organizations occasionally must use is revitalization. **Organization revitalization** is a planned effort to bring new energy, vitality, and strength to an organization.

Why is revitalization necessary? For the most part, organizations do an imperfect job of maintaining an effective alignment with their environments. Given that environments change rapidly, the best most organizations can do is to approximate the best strategy, design, and so forth that fits their unique situation. Even such well-managed organizations as Disney and American Airlines

Exhibit 13.4

Stages in Organization Revitalization

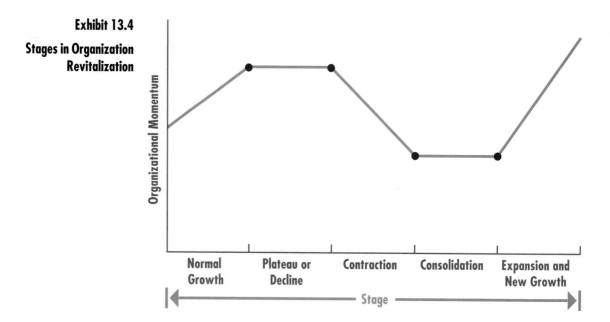

must occasionally step back and work to improve their alignment with their environments. Sometimes, however, an organization falls so far out of alignment with its environment that simple adjustments and shifts are not enough. When this happens, the organization must undergo a major change in order to get back in proper alignment with its environment.

Stages in Revitalization

Exhibit 13.4 shows the general cycle that revitalization can follow. First of all, an organization has what might be called normal momentum. It is growing and effectively reaching its goals regularly. At some point, however, the organization falls so far out of alignment with its environment that its growth reaches a plateau or goes into a decline. For example, U.S. automakers were not aligned with their environment when they were turning out gas-guzzling, low-quality products. Economy-minded consumers were concerned about quality.

If this happens and the firm cannot turn things around, it may have to enter a planned period of contraction. During this stage the organization cuts back on its operations, eliminates unnecessary facilities, and so forth. Next comes consolidation. During this phase the organization learns to live with a leaner and tighter budget. Eventually, if things go well, the organization will be able to start expanding and growing once again.

During these various stages the company may undertake a number of initiatives to facilitate its revitalization. For example, it may bring in a new management team. It may also seek an infusion of new capital through extended bank loans or new investment. Some firms even go so far as to change their names altogether. After extensive programs of revitalization, International Harvester became Navistar International Corp., for example, and United States Steel became USX.

Innovation in Organizations

Finally, many organizations today are recognizing the critical importance of yet another aspect of change, innovation. **Innovation** is the managed effort of an organization to develop new products or services and/or new uses for existing products or services. *The Entrepreneurial Spirit: Charles and Patricia Lester* summarizes how two Welsh entrepreneurs have succeeded in the fashion world through innovation.

The Entrepreneurial Spirit

Charles and Patricia Lester

For years Patricia Lester wanted to hit the big time. Lester was a fashion designer but of the small-time variety. Working out of her home in Wales, she made tie-dyed and batik garments and sold them at craft fairs and markets.

Her first love was silk fabric. But because silk wrinkles so easily, fashion dresses made from the fabric tend to be impractical. For example, a typical silk dress folded and packed in a suitcase comes out too wrinkled to wear. Patricia's husband, Charles, worked in a research laboratory and was assigned to a project to develop a synthetic silk alternative. He applied some of the things he learned at work to Patricia's problem, and soon the two of them arrived at a solution.

Specifically, the Lesters developed a technology for creasing silk in a way that allows it to keep its shape when folded. The result was a new line of clothing, made from silk and silk-like fabrics, that is much more durable and wearable.

The Lesters have begun to successfully market their clothing to a number of high-fashion outlets. For example, in the United States their clothing is sold by Lord & Taylor, Henri Bendel, and Barney's of New York. Annual revenues are approaching one million dollars. Patricia Lester may not have hit the big time yet, but she and her husband seem well on their way.[20] ∎

The Innovation Process

Innovation is the managed effort by organization to develop new products or services and/or new uses for existing products or services.

The *organizational innovation process* consists of developing, applying, launching, and managing the maturity and decline of a creative idea.

Organizations that emphasize innovation usually start with a culture that values innovation and then use that culture to attract creative employees and managers. You may be one of those innovative people a company is looking for today. The Self-Assessment in this chapter will help you determine how innovative you are. To harness this creativity, however, the organization must keep itself focused on managing the innovation process itself. The process of developing, applying, launching, and managing the maturity and decline of a creative idea is called the **organizational innovation process.**[21] This process is depicted in Exhibit 13.5.

Innovation Development   Once an idea for innovation is identified and approved, product prototypes are usually built. Most original ideas are not ready to be instantly transformed into new products or services. Innovation development is the stage in which an organization evaluates, modifies, and improves on a potential innovation before turning that idea into a product or service to sell. Rather than just read about this important skill, we have included a Skill Builder in this chapter that allows you to experience innovation development first hand. As you develop this skill, you will improve your value to your organization. Innovation development can transform a product or service with only modest potential into a product or service with significant potential. Parker Brothers, for example (manufacturers of the board games Monopoly, Risk, and Life), was developing plans for an indoor volleyball game. During innovation development managers decided not to market the game itself but instead to sell separately the appealing little foam ball that designers had created for the game. That product, the Nerf ball, has generated millions of dollars in revenues for Parker Brothers.[22]

Innovation Application   Even after development, the idea has yet to be applied to real products or services. Innovation application is the stage in which an organization takes a developed idea and uses it in the design, manufacturing, or delivery of new products, services, or processes. At this point the innovation emerges from the laboratory and is transformed into tangible goods or services. One example of innovation application is the use of radar-based focusing systems in Po-

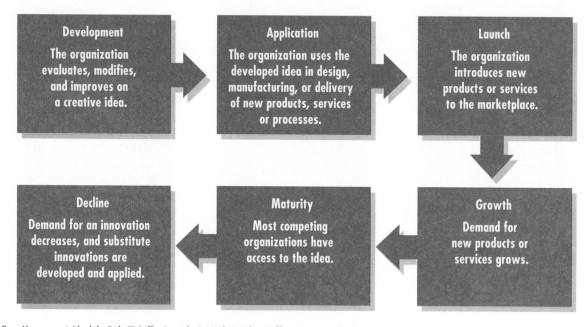

Exhibit 13.5   The Innovation Process

laroid's instant cameras. The idea of using radio waves to discover the location, speed, and direction of moving objects was first applied extensively by Allied forces during World War II. As radar technology developed over the following years, the electrical components became smaller and more streamlined. Researchers at Polaroid hit on radar as a creative idea and applied this well-developed technology in a new way.[23]

Application Launch   Application launch is the stage in which an organization introduces new products or services to the marketplace. The key question is not "does the innovation work?" but "will customers want to purchase the innovative product and service?" History is full of creative ideas that did not generate enough interest among customers to be successful. Some notable innovation failures include the Sony's seat warmer, the Edsel automobile (with its notoriously homely front end), and Polaroid's SX-70 instant camera (which cost $3 billion to develop but never sold more than 100,000 units in a year). Despite individual creativity, development, and application, it is still possible for new products and services to fail at the application launch phase of innovation.[24]

Application Growth   Once an innovation has been successfully launched, it then enters the stage of application growth, where demand for an innovation increases. This is a period of high economic performance for an organization, because there is often more demand for the product or service than supply. Organizations that fail to anticipate this stage may unintentionally limit their growth, as Gillette did by not anticipating demand for its Sensor razor blades. At the same time, overestimating demand for a new product or service can be just as detrimental to performance. This situation occurred for many retailers of Western wear when the popularity of the John

Innovation is a must for any organization and innovative technology in management is no exception. Sharp Electronics introduced the Wizard OZ-9600 Electronic Organizer as part computer and part secretary for managers. It has pen-touch technology so that the manager can use a pen-shaped stylus to make notes or drawings, and to control the clock, calendar, schedule, and other features built in. (John Parnell.)

Travolta movie *Urban Cowboy* suddenly—but very briefly—increased demand for cowboy boots, shirts, and other clothes. Many stores lost money anticipating higher demand than what actually existed and purchasing a great deal of Western wear inventory that took years to sell.

Innovation Maturity   After a period of growing demand, an innovative product or service often enters a period of maturity. Innovation maturity is the stage in which most organizations in an industry have access to an innovation and are applying it in approximately the same way. The technological application of an innovation during this stage can be very sophisticated. However, because most firms have access to the innovation (either because they have developed the innovation on their own or have copied the innovation of others), it does not provide a competitive advantage to any one of them. The time that elapses between innovation development and innovation maturity varies significantly, depending on the particular product or service. Whenever an innovation involves the use of complex skills (such as a complicated manufacturing process or highly sophisticated teamwork), it will take longer to move from the growth phase to the maturity phase. In addition, if the skills needed to implement these innovations are rare and difficult to imitate, then strategic imitation may be delayed and the organization may enjoy a period of sustained competitive advantage.

One innovation that has taken a very long time to move from growth to maturity (and may not have matured even yet) is the user-friendliness of Apple's Macintosh computer. When the Macintosh was first introduced, it immediately provided a level of user-friendliness that was unique in the personal computer industry. Over the years, efforts to make other types of PCs as user-friendly as the Macintosh have not succeeded. Only recently has Microsoft's Windows software begun to address user-friendliness as effectively. During all this time, customers who wanted to purchase user-friendly PCs were limited to the Macintosh. On the other hand, when the implementation of an innovation does not depend either on rare or difficult-to-imitate skills, then the time between the growth and maturity phases can be very brief. In the market for computer memory devices, for example, technological innovation by one firm can be very quickly duplicated by other firms, because the skills needed to design and manufacture these electronic devices are widespread. Computer memory devices thus move very rapidly from growth to maturity.

Innovation Decline   Every successful innovation bears its own seeds of decline. Since an organization does not gain a competitive advantage from an innovation at maturity, it must encourage its creative scientists, engineers, and managers to begin looking for new innovations. It is this continued search for competitive advantage that usually leads new products and services to move from the creative process through innovative maturity and finally to innovative decline. Innovation decline is the stage during which demand for an innovation decreases and substitute innovations are developed and applied.

Types of Innovation

Each creative idea an organization develops poses a different challenge for the innovation process. Innovations can be radical or incremental and technical or managerial.

Radical innovations are new products or technologies.

Incremental innovations modify existing products or technologies.

Radical Versus Incremental Innovations   **Radical innovations** are new products or technologies developed by an organization that completely replace the existing products or technologies in an industry. **Incremental innovations** are new products or processes that modify existing products or technologies. Many radical innovations have been introduced by organizations over the last several years. For example, compact disk technology has virtually replaced long-playing vinyl records in the recording industry, and high definition television seems likely to replace regular television technology (both black and white and color) in the near future. Whereas radical innovations like these tend to be very visible and public, incremental innovations actually are more numerous. One example is GM's aerodynamic mini-van, the Lumina. Manufacture of this sleek product pioneered the use of plastic autobody panels and employed a new process for forming the front windshield. However, while the van's exterior is the result of innovation, the engine, drive train, and other mechanical parts remain quite standard. Thus, it's an evolutionary change—one logical step following another.

Technical innovations involve the physical appearance or performance of a product.

Managerial innovations involve the management process itself.

Technical Versus Managerial Innovations   **Technical innovations** are changes in the physical appearance or performance of a product or service, or the physical processes by which a product or service is manufactured. Many of the most important innovations over the last fifty years have been technical. For example, the serial replacement of the vacuum tube with the transistor, the transistor with the integrated circuit, and the integrated circuit with the microchip has greatly enhanced the power, ease of use, and speed of operation of a wide variety of electronic products. **Managerial innovations** are changes in the management process by which products and services are conceived, built, and delivered to customers. Managerial innovations do not necessarily affect the physical appearance or performance of products or services directly, but they can. Many Japanese firms have used managerial innovations to improve the quality of their products or services. One of the most important of these innovations developed in the last thirty years is called the quality circle. It helped Oki Electronics become one of the premier electronics companies in the world. Organizations that have been able to incorporate quality circles and total quality management (in which small groups of concerned workers discuss how to improve product quality) have found that quality improves dramatically and the costs of operations decrease.[25]

Barriers to Innovation

To remain competitive in today's economy, it is necessary to be innovative. And yet many organizations that should be innovative are not successful at bringing out new products or services or do so only after innovations created by others are very mature. There are at least three reasons why organizations may fail to innovate.

Lack of Resources   Implementing innovative change can be expensive, in terms of dollars, time, and energy. If a firm does not have sufficient money to fund a program of innovation or does not currently employ the kinds of creative individuals it needs to be innovative, it may find itself lagging behind in innovation. Even highly innovative organizations cannot become involved in every new product or service its employees think up. For example, other commitments in the electronic instruments and computer industry kept Hewlett-Packard from investing in two young inventors who came to the firm with an idea for a personal computer. Those inventors, Steve Jobs and Steve Wozniak, eventually became frustrated and formed their own company called Apple Computer.

Failure to Recognize Opportunities Since organizations cannot pursue all innovations, they need to develop the capability to carefully evaluate innovations and to select the ones that hold the greatest potential. In order to obtain a competitive advantage, an organization usually must make investment decisions before the innovation process reaches the mature stage. If organizations are not skilled at recognizing and evaluating opportunities, they may be overly cautious and fail to invest in innovations that turn out later to be successful for other firms.

Resistance to Change As already noted, there is a tendency in many organizations to resist change. Innovation means giving up old products and old ways of doing things in favor of new products and new ways of doing things. These kinds of changes can be personally difficult for managers and other members of an organization.

Facilitating Innovation

A wide variety of ideas for promoting innovation in organizations has been developed over the years. Three specific ways for promoting innovation are described below.

The Reward System An organization's reward system is the means it uses to encourage and discourage certain behaviors by employees. Key components of the reward system include salaries, bonuses, perquisites, and so forth. Using the reward system to promote innovation is a fairly mechanical but nevertheless effective management technique. The idea is to provide financial and nonfinancial rewards to people and groups that develop innovative ideas. Once the members of an organization understand that they will be rewarded for their innovations, they are more likely to work creatively. With this end in mind, Monsanto Company gives a fifty-thousand-dollar award each year to the scientist or group of scientists that develops the biggest commercial breakthrough.

While it is important for organizations to reward innovative ideas, it is just as important to avoid punishing people when their innovative ideas are not successful. At 3M, nearly 60 percent of the innovations suggested each year do not succeed in the marketplace. If innovative failure is due to incompetence, systematic errors, or managerial sloppiness, then an organization should respond with appropriate sanctions (such as withholding raises or reducing promotion opportunities). However, people who act in good faith to develop an innovation that simply does not work out should not be punished for failure. If they are, they will probably not be as motivated to innovate in the future. To avoid punishing failure inappropriately, managers must thoroughly understand both the skills and capabilities of a creative individual and the goal the individual was attempting to accomplish that did not come to fruition. By developing this understanding, managers will be able to distinguish among activities that simply did not work out and other activities that reflect managerial incompetence, stupidity, or poor judgment.

Intrapreneurs are similar to entrepreneurs, except that they work in the context of a larger organization.

Intrapreneurship Intrapreneurship also helps organizations encourage innovation. **Intrapreneurs** are similar to entrepreneurs, except that they develop a new business in the context of a larger organization. There are three intrapreneurial roles in large organizations.[26] To successfully use intrapreneurship to encourage creativity and innovation, the organization must find one or more individuals to perform these roles. The *inventor* is the person who actually conceives of and develops the new idea, product, or service by means of the creative process. However, because the inventor may lack the expertise or motivation to oversee the transformation of the product or service from an idea into a marketable entity, a second role comes into play. A *product champion* is usually a middle manager who learns about the project and becomes committed to it. He or she helps overcome organizational resistance and convinces others to take the innovation seriously. The product champion may have only limited understanding of the technological aspects of the innovation. However, product champions are skilled at knowing how the organization works, whose support is needed to push the project forward, and where to go to secure the resources necessary for successful development. A *sponsor* is a top-level manager who approves of and supports a project. This person may fight for the budget needed to develop an idea, overcome arguments against a project, and use organizational politics to ensure the project's survival. With a sponsor in place, the inventor's idea has a much better chance of being successfully developed.

Several firms have embraced intrapreneurship as a way to encourage creativity and innovation. Colgate-Palmolive has created a separate unit, Colgate Venture Company, staffed with intrapreneurs who develop new products. General Foods developed Culinova Group as a unit to which employees can take their ideas for possible development. S. C. Johnson & Son, established a $250,000 fund to support new product ideas, and Texas Instruments refuses to approve a new innovative project unless it has an acknowledged inventor, champion, and sponsor.

Organizational Culture   As we discussed in Chapter 3, an organization's culture is the set of values, beliefs, and symbols that help guide behavior. A strong, appropriately focused organizational culture can be used to support creative and innovative activity. A well-managed culture can communicate a sense that innovation is valued and will be rewarded and that occasional failure in the pursuit of new ideas is not only acceptable but even expected. Firms such as 3M, Corning, Monsanto, Procter & Gamble, Texas Instruments, Johnson & Johnson, and Merck are all known to have strong, innovation-oriented cultures. These cultures value individual creativity, risk taking, and inventiveness.[27]

Chapter Summary

Organizational change is a meaningful alteration in some part of the organization. Forces in the general and task environments can prompt the need for change. To the extent possible, organizations should plan for change. Planned change can be pursued through a series of rational and logical steps.

People resist change for a variety of reasons, including uncertainty, self-interests, different perceptions, and feelings of loss. There are four common methods for overcoming this resistance: participation, open communication, facilitation, and force-field analysis.

Organizational change generally takes place in one or more of four areas—strategy, structure, technology, and people. Strategic change can occur at the corporate, business, or functional levels. Structural change involves changes in the formal organizational system. Technological change might involve new and differ-

ent machines or work processes. People-focused change involves changes in the skills, performance, attitudes, perceptions, behaviors, and expectations of the people in the organization.

Organization development is a planned, organizationwide effort to enhance organizational health and effectiveness through the systematic application of behavioral science techniques.

Organization revitalization is a planned effort to infuse new energy, vitality, and strength into an organization. The general stages in revitalization include growth, plateau or decline, contraction, consolidation, and renewed expansion and new growth.

Innovation is a managed effort to develop new products or services or new uses for existing products or services. The innovation process includes development, launch, growth, maturity, and decline. Forms of innovation include radical or incremental and technical or managerial. While several barriers to innovation can be identified, managers can also actively facilitate innovation.

The Manager's Vocabulary

organization change	organization development	organizational innovation process
planned organization change	Managerial Grid	radical innovation
reactive change	team building	incremental innovation
force-field analysis	survey feedback	technical innovation
strategic change	third-party peace making	managerial innovation
structural change	process consultation	intrapreneur
technological change	organization revitalization	
people-focused change	innovation	

Review Questions

1. Distinguish between planned and reactive change.
2. What are the basic steps to be followed in planned change? Identify the basic reasons people resist change and the most common methods for overcoming that resistance.
3. Provide at least two examples of each area of organization change.
4. What is organization development? What are some of its more common techniques?
5. What is innovation? Describe the innovation process.

Analysis Questions

1. Heraclitus once said, "There is nothing permanent except change." Is change, in fact, inevitable? Why or why not?
2. The text notes that people tend to resist change. Are there some people who like change? Is it possible for people to initiate too much change?
3. Think of a change you recently experienced. How was it managed? How did you feel about it?
4. Can you identify an organization that has never had to go through a period of revitalization?
5. Can creativity—as part of the innovation process—really be managed? Can an organization concentrate too much attention on managing innovation?

Self-Assessment

How Innovative Are You?

Introduction Innovative people are in great demand today. Organizations have realized that to survive and grow, they must come up with new and useful ideas. In fact, a great deal of the total quality management movement is about innovation and change. Are you one of those innovative people? Take the self-assessment and see.

Instructions To find out how innovative you are, react to the following eighteen statements. Remember that there is no right or wrong answer. Rather, we are interested in exploring your attitudes. Answer using the following scale.

Strongly Agree (SA)	Agree (A)	Undecided (?)	Disagree (D)	Strongly Disagree (SD)

1. I try new ideas and new approaches to problems.
   SA   A   ?   D   SD
2. I take things or situations apart to find a new use for existing methods or existing equipment.
   SA   A   ?   D   SD
3. I can be counted on by my friends to find a new use for existing methods or existing equipment.
   SA   A   ?   D   SD

(con't. on page 310)

4. Among my friends, I'm usually the first person to try out a new idea or method.

   SA   A   ?   D   SD

5. I demonstrate originality.

   SA   A   ?   D   SD

6. I like to work on a problem that has caused others great difficulty.

   SA   A   ?   D   SD

7. I plan on developing contacts with experts in my field located in different companies or departments.

   SA   A   ?   D   SD

8. I plan on budgeting time and money for the pursuit of novel ideas.

   SA   A   ?   D   SD

9. I make comments at meetings on new ways of doing things.

   SA   A   ?   D   SD

10. If my friends were asked, they would say I'm a wit.

    SA   A   ?   D   SD

11. I seldom stick to the rules or follow protocol.

    SA   A   ?   D   SD

12. I discourage formal meetings to discuss ideas.

    SA   A   ?   D   SD

13. I usually support a friend's suggestion on new ways to do things.

    SA   A   ?   D   SD

14. I probably will not turn down ambiguous job assignments.

    SA   A   ?   D   SD

15. People who depart from the accepted organizational routine should not be punished.

    SA   A   ?   D   SD

16. I hope to be known for the quantity of my work rather than the quality of my work when starting a new project.

    SA   A   ?   D   SD

17. I must be able to find enough variety of experience on my job or I will leave it.

    SA   A   ?   D   SD

18. I am going to leave a job that doesn't challenge me.

    SA   A   ?   D   SD

For interpretation, turn to the back of the book.

Source: J. E. Ettlie and R. D. O'Keefe, "Innovative Attitudes, Values, and Intentions in Organizations," *Journal of Management Studies,* 1982, 19: p. 176.

Skill Builder

Innovation in Action: Egg Drop

Purpose Managers are continuously improving on the work flow, the product, and the packaging of products. This is what Total Quality Management is all about. To do this means both thinking creatively and acting innovatively. This skill builder focuses on the *open systems model*. It will help you develop the *innovator role*. One of the skills of the innovator is thinking creatively and acting innovatively.

Introduction This activity is a practical and entertaining demonstration of creativity and innovation in action. "Egg Drop"

provides practice in identifying, defining, or refining a problem or opportunity, developing options and alternatives, choosing the best option or alternative, actually launching the alternative into reality, and verifying the results within a specified time period. Your instructor will provide you with further instructions.

Source: Reproduced with permission from *50 Activities on Creativity and Problem Solving,* by Geof Cox, Chuck DuFault and Walt Hopkins, Gower, Aldershot, 1992.

CONCLUDING CASES

13.1   Xerox

Xerox Corporation has its roots in the Haloid Company, founded in 1906. For the first several decades of its existence, Haloid worked to develop and refine xerography, the process of transferring electro-static images onto plain paper. In 1959 the firm introduced the first simplified office copier, the Xerox 914. Sales and profits skyrocketed immediately, and the Xerox 914 became an office staple around the world. Sales soared from $37 million in 1960 to $268 million in 1965. The firm changed its name to Haloid Xerox in 1958 and simply to Xerox in 1961.

For years thereafter Xerox maintained two distinct patterns that proved to be both blessing and curse. On the positive side, Xerox copiers dominated the market and continued to generate huge revenues and profits. On the negative side, Xerox gradually grew complacent in the copier market and did a poor job of developing innovations in other key markets. For example, Xerox scientists were among the first to dabble in personal computers, and its research labs actually pioneered laser printers. But failure to promote innovation caused the firm to miss the boat in both industries.

In the 1980s its neglect of its copier business also began to create problems. Indeed, by the time Xerox recognized the threat from Canon and Ricoh, those two firms had drastically cut into its market share. And Canon did leapfrog Xerox in the color copier market. Observers blamed the fall of Xerox on its bureaucratic organization design and its lethargic approach to new product development.

In 1990 the board of directors at Xerox named Paul Allaire as its CEO and gave him a mandate to get the firm back on track. At the time Allaire was a twenty-six-year Xerox veteran and was widely regarded for his forward-looking and aggressive approach to management.

As a starting point Allaire arranged for him and his executive team to undergo an extensive organization development program to make sure they were in synch on what they were going to do and how they were going to do it. This activity involved a battery of personality tests followed by several days at a Connecticut monastery to process the results and address their differences.

After the executives had established a common frame of reference and agreed on their plan of attack, Allaire began changing the organization. In particular, he and the other executives decided to create the culture and atmosphere of several smaller companies under the umbrella of the Xerox corporation. They felt that this change would promote innovation while also enhancing peoples' commitment to and involvement with the organization and its goals.

To accomplish these objectives the entire organization design of the firm was changed. Previously the firm had been organized as a tall hierarchy based on functional departmentalization. Allaire changed it to more of a matrix, defining relatively autonomous units. Today Xerox has nine product divisions, ranging from personal document copiers to a software unit to an advanced office document unit, and three geographic sales divisions. Each of these twelve units reports directly to Allaire and the executive group. While some managers balked at the changes, and a few chose to leave the firm, most of the key people at Xerox feel that the firm is now poised to regain its standing in the industry.[28]

Discussion Questions

1. What kinds of change can you identify at Xerox?
2. Do you think the changes will help Xerox compete more effectively?
3. Would you call Xerox's changes revitalization or simply a typical change program?

13.2   Philips

Philips Electronics N.V. is the world's second-largest electronics firm, ranking behind only Matsushita, the Japanese giant. Philips is responsible for developing the videocassette recorder, laser disk technology, and, in conjunction with Sony, compact disk technology. For years the firm has had a reputation for being a leader in electronics innovation.

Its reputation aside, the firm has struggled for years. For one thing, its profit margins have been too small. For another, it has failed to take full advantage of technology developed in its research laboratories. On several different occasions Philips scientists have made significant breakthroughs only to have the firm license the new technology to competing firms without fully exploiting the innovations itself.

In 1990 Jan Timmer was appointed CEO of Philips. He surveyed the organization and decided that major changes were necessary. His vision for the firm was to make it more like Sony, emphasizing innovation but then taking full advantage of that in-novation in the marketplace. To fulfill this vision Timmer realized that many changes were needed.

First of all Timmer decided that the firm was too large and overly bureaucratic. To address this he began by eliminating 45,000 jobs at Philips. At the same time he eliminated three levels from the corporate hierarchy and streamlined operations to make decision making both faster and easier. He also sold several peripheral businesses in areas such as appliances and computers.

Next, Timmer took steps to link research and development more directly with marketing. His thinking was that if marketing knew what new technology was coming, it could do a better job of penetrating the market with that technology. Conversely, marketing could perhaps provide additional insights for research and development as to what new technology might be most exciting in the market. The first major product to result from this collaboration has been an interactive compact disk system called The Imagination Machine. The machine will play new Nintendo games as well as music and video disks. In addition, it will display digital photographic images and serve as an archival source for various statistics and records.

But, so far at least, Timmer has been disappointed with the results of these changes. In particular, he believes that even though Philips is no longer a bureaucracy, its employees still think and act like they did during the earlier era. For example, even though managers have more decision-making latitude, many are reluctant to take advantage of their new autonomy. And even when various administrative procedures and channels do not need to be followed, many people still adhere to them as though they still existed.

Timmer has realized that though he changed the objective nature and character of Philips, its culture remains entrenched in its previous configuration. Accordingly, he is now undertaking a major new program aimed at changing the firm's culture to better fit its new approach to doing business.[29]

Discussion Questions

1. What changes can you identify at Philips?
2. Why does so much change seem to be reactive, rather than planned?
3. How would you go about trying to change the entire culture of an organization?

CHAPTER 14

Staffing and Human Resources

Learning Objectives

After studying this chapter you should be able to

- Discuss the nature of staffing, including the staffing process and legal constraints.

- Describe human resource planning and indicate how to use job analysis and forecasts to match supply and demand.

- Discuss the selection of human resources, including recruiting, selection, and orientation.

- Describe the assessment of training and development needs, various training and development techniques, and the importance of evaluating those techniques.

- Define performance appraisal and discuss both objective and judgmental methods, management by objectives, and feedback.

- Discuss compensation decisions regarding wages and salaries, as well as various kinds of benefits.

- Discuss labor relations, including how unions are formed and the nature of collective bargaining.

"**A**von calling" was once a familiar part of popular culture in the United States. Avon Products, Inc. started out as a door-to-door operation selling inexpensive cosmetics to housewives. Each so-called "Avon lady" sold perfume and make-up to her neighbors, friends, and relatives. For decades the firm was highly successful with this strategy. The Avon ladies were able to work part-time and set their own hours, and their customers appreciated the ease and convenience of the personal sales calls.

Over the past several years, however, Avon has had to dramatically change its approach to doing business. A major force in this shift has been the changing role of women in U.S. business. And this force has affected Avon from two different perspectives. For one thing, many women who were previously content working part-time as Avon ladies and earning small commissions decided they wanted more fulfilling and rewarding professional careers. For another, Avon's traditional customer base of housewives also dwindled as more and more of those individuals also entered the work force.

Avon has responded to this shift in several ways. From a strategic vantage point, the firm has shifted more to retail outlets for selling its products. For example, Avon owns Giorgio and several other labels that are sold only through upscale retailers. And it has also expanded the array of products it sells through its direct marketing network to include toys, fashions, videos, and gift items.

Avon has also changed the way it manages its work force. For one thing, it has made direct sales jobs more flexible. For example, most direct marketers are now full-time employees, receive professional sales training, and earn significantly higher income. Employees holding these jobs also have more frequent contact with management and have more opportunities for promotion into managerial positions.

Like many firms, Avon has had an Affirmative Action program that facilitated the identification and employment of qualified minorities. But few of them were advancing into higher levels of management, and many left for better jobs elsewhere. To cope with this problem, Avon created networks of minority workers. Members of each network meet regularly to discuss common experiences and to help one another better understand the organization. So far the program seems to be working. For example, Avon reports that its retention rate has improved, and more minorities are being promoted.[1] ■

Like many organizations, Avon has had to change the way it does business in order to remain competitive. One major aspect of this change involved a new business strategy. Another involved an entirely new approach to managing human resources. The firm had to fundamentally alter its approach to hiring, developing, and rewarding its employees. That is, it had to develop a new philosophy about staffing.

*The process of obtaining and managing the human resources of an organization is termed **staffing.***

Staffing is the process of procuring and managing the human resources an organization needs to accomplish its goals. Staffing, however, is more than just hiring new employees. When Avon hires new direct marketers it is engaged in staffing. But if General Motors gives one hundred managers early retirement, it is also engaging in the staffing process. And when UPS sends 450 employees to a training seminar, it is engaging in staffing. Xerox is involved in staffing when its employees get a new health insurance option. And if Alcoa Aluminum has to close a plant because of safety hazards, it is also exercising part of the staffing process.

This chapter explores the staffing process in detail. First, we provide more background information about the nature of staffing. We then examine human resource planning. Next we look at the selection process and training and development. Performance appraisal and compensation are covered next. Finally, labor relations are explored in the last section.

The Nature of Staffing

Having already defined staffing, now let us develop a more complete framework for understanding staffing and for organizing our discussion. Then we can discuss the legal environment of the staffing process.[2]

The Staffing Process

Exhibit 14.1 presents the basic staffing process in detail. First, as indicated at the top of the framework, the staffing process must take place within a series of legal constraints that restrict what a firm can do. Within this legal environment the first actual step in staffing is human resource planning. This involves developing a complete understanding of the various tasks within the organization, forecasting how many people are needed and will be available to perform those tasks, and taking steps to match supply with demand.

Several steps follow the initial planning. If Texas Instruments needs more employees, it must recruit qualified applicants to consider employment with the firm and then choose the ones best suited for the jobs that need to be performed. After joining the company the new employees then need to be trained and developed. In addition, while they are working, their performance must be evaluated so that managers can provide appropriate rewards or remediation. Of course, they must be compensated from the time they begin work and must also have the opportunity to participate in relevant benefit programs. Their base level compensation may be adjusted as a result of the performance appraisal process. Finally, as the exhibit indicates, labor unions may also affect these various activities.

*Human resources, traditionally called **personnel**, recruits qualified applicants, trains and develops new employees, and evaluates performance.*

Who performs these functions? In small firms, one person, often called the personnel manager, handles them. As an organization grows, a department of personnel or human resources is created. (**Personnel** is the traditional name, but the term **human resources** is increasingly used instead.) Line managers also assist in performing many of the human resource functions in most organizations. In the past line managers and human resource managers did not always work well together, but this is changing. Increasingly, line managers and the human resource department jointly try to act in the best interests of the organization.

Exhibit 14.1   The Staffing Process

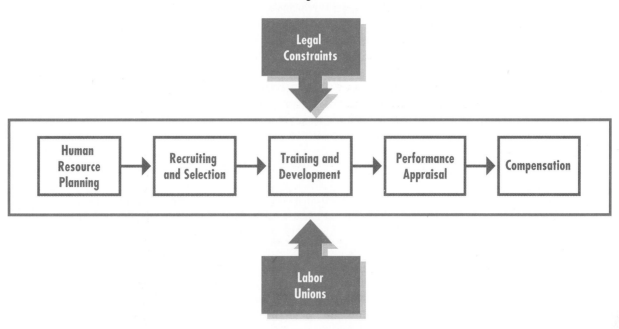

Table 14.1
Legal Constraints That Affect Staffing

Staffing considerations	Legislation
Employee Selection	Title VII of the 1964 Civil Rights Act Age Discrimination Act Executive Orders
Compensation and Benefits	Fair Labor Standards Act Equal Pay Act
Labor Relations	National Labor Relations Act Labor-Management Relations Act
Working Conditions	Occupational Safety and Health Act Americans with Disabilities Act

The Legal Environment

One factor that has contributed to the increased importance of human resource managers in organizations is the number and complexity of legal constraints any organization faces. These constraints affect selection, compensation and benefits, labor relations, and working conditions. The most significant of these are listed in Table 14.1.

Among constraints on the selection of employees is *Title VII of the 1964 Civil Rights Act,* which prohibits discrimination on the basis of sex, race, color, religion, or national origin in all areas of employment, including hiring, layoff, compensation, access to promotion, and training. The *Age Discrimination Act* prohibits discrimination against people between the ages of forty and seventy. In addition, various executive orders prohibit discrimination in organizations that do business with the government, provide extra protection for Vietnam era veterans, and so forth.[3]

Wages and salaries are affected by the *Fair Labor Standards Act,* which sets minimum wages that have to be paid to employees. Over the years the minimum wage has been raised several times and as of 1991 was $4.25 per hour. Another important law in this area is the *Equal Pay Act,* which prohibits wage discrimination on the basis of sex.

Labor relations are strongly influenced by legal constraints as well. For example, the *National Labor Relations Act* governs the collective bargaining process between companies and organized labor unions. Another important law, the *Labor-Management Relations Act* provides additional guidelines for dealing with labor unions.

Working conditions are also affected by legal constraints. For example, the *Occupational Safety and Health Act* requires organizations to provide safe, nonhazardous working conditions for employees. Another recently passed law, the *Americans with Disabilities Act,* prohibits discrimination on the basis of physical handicaps and requires that all employers make their workplace accessible to the disabled.[4]

Because of these and other laws, the staffing process is perhaps more affected by the legal environment than any other area of management. It is little wonder, then, that human resource managers have come to be vital members of organizations.

Human Resource Planning

s we have seen, the first actual phase of the staffing process is human resource planning. This phase consists of three steps: job analysis, forecasting human resource supply and demand, and matching supply and demand. These steps are illustrated in Exhibit 14.2.

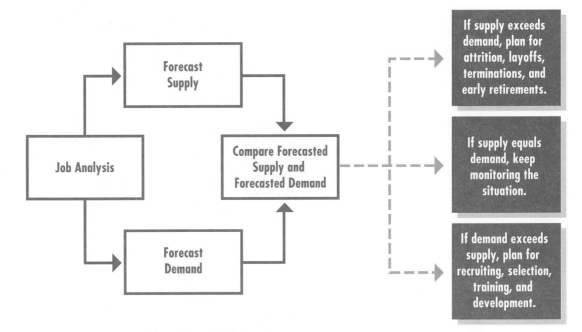

Exhibit 14.2   Human Resource Planning

Job Analysis

*Job analysis refers to the systematic investigation of the nature of the job, which results in a **job description** and an identification of the skills and credentials needed to perform the job, known as a **job specification.***

Job analysis is the systematic collection and recording of information about jobs in the organization.[5] It actually consists of two different activities. One of these is the development of a **job description.** A job description summarizes the duties encompassed by the job, the working conditions where the job is performed, and the tools, materials, and equipment used on the job. The other part of job analysis is the development of the **job specification.** A job specification lists the skills, abilities, and other credentials necessary to perform the job. Taken together, the job description and the job specification provide the human resource manager with the information he or she needs to forecast the supply and demand of labor within the organization. (Job analysis information is also used for a variety of other purposes as well, including compensation and performance appraisal.)

Forecasting Supply and Demand

Forecasting the supply and demand for various kinds of employees involves using any number of sophisticated statistical procedures.[6] Such actual techniques are beyond the scope of our discussion, so we will focus on the forecasting process at a general and descriptive level.

Forecasting demand involves determining the numbers and kinds of employees that the organization will need at some point in the future. If General Mills plans to open three new food processing plants in five years, its human resource managers must begin planning now to staff those plants. Likewise, if the company intends to close a plant, there will be less demand for employees. Demand, then, is based partly on the projected overall growth of the organization and partly on where in the organization that growth is expected to occur.

Forecasting supply involves determining what human resources will be available, both inside and outside the organization. Many upper-level management positions, for example, will be filled by employees currently working for the firm, whereas technical employees like engineers and programmers are usually brought in from the outside. The identification of highly skilled specialists may need to be done months or even years in advance, whereas the identification of lower-level and unskilled workers can be done according to a much more immediate timetable.

Finding employees with good managerial skills is easier to do in the San Francisco area thanks to M2. M2's founders, Marion McGovern and Paula Reynolds, built the organization to provide managerial skills to organizations especially when female managers take time off for childbearing. Their success enabled them to build an extensive network of experienced managers and to assist organizations in many ways. (Anne Hamersky.)

Matching Supply and Demand

After the appropriate forecasts have been prepared, the results must be compared and actions must be planned. As shown earlier in Exhibit 14.2, managers can select from among three alternatives. If the supply of labor is projected to exceed the demand for labor, management must plan for normal attrition, layoffs, terminations, and early retirement.

But if the demand for labor exceeds its projected supply, management must plan to recruit, select, train, and develop new employees. Finally, if supply and demand are roughly the same, no immediate action is necessary, although the situation should be monitored in case either supply or demand changes.

The human resource planning process can be especially difficult in international business. For example, international firms must engage in human resource planning within each country where they do business. Given the high costs of moving employees between countries, different patterns of supply and demand within each country, and tremendous variations in both cultural and legal contexts, planning within each country must be undertaken with great care and with the assistance of local experts who understand the regional labor situation.[7]

Selecting Human Resources

If an organization needs to hire more permanent employees, either because of growth or just to replace current employees who leave, it must begin the selection phase of human resource management. This phase consists of three distinct steps: recruiting, the actual selection, and orientation. (The use of temporary workers is commonly used today when the need for additional employees is short-term.)

Recruiting

Recruiting is the process of attracting a pool of qualified applicants who are interested in working for the organization. Suppose, for example, that Du Pont wants to add an extra shift of one hundred employees at one of its chemical plants. The company would like to recruit more than

The Environment of Management

Recruiting in Japan

For years Western companies hiring in Japan had to take second best. Japanese graduates uniformly favored working for Japanese firms, and Western recruiters knew little about the subtle intricacies of recruiting in Japan. When recent forecasts predicted an increased labor shortage in Japan, U.S. companies began to realize that they needed to develop aggressive recruiting approaches.

Many firms started by learning more about the recruiting process in Japan. Like most business negotiations, recruiting in Japan is a slow process based on trust and interpersonal relations. Thus U.S. firms began to foster relations with both professors and parents. These same companies also began to promote themselves more aggressively to students.

U.S. firms in Japan have long paid higher starting salaries than their Japanese counterparts (averaging 10 percent). But many prospective employees were not aware that the U.S. companies also practiced shorter workweeks, offered more flexibility, and paid on the basis of merit. As U.S. firms began to promote these features, the number of applicants grew.

U.S. firms also began to recruit women more aggressively. Japanese firms have a long-standing history of sex discrimination. Career-oriented females in Japan are therefore very attracted to U.S. firms that offer them equal job and promotion opportunities. Of course, fearing the loss of employees, Japanese firms have begun to fight back. Still, Western firms are steadily achieving a bigger and bigger presence in the Japanese job market.[8] ∎

Internal recruiting is finding current employees who would like to change jobs, whereas external recruiting is finding qualified applicants outside the company.

one hundred qualified applicants to select from. Fewer than one hundred applicants does not give the company ample choice, but several thousand applicants would pose a big logistical problem. Therefore, the key is to attract enough recruits, but not too many.[9]

One type of recruiting is internal recruiting. This approach involves identifying existing employees who want to be transferred and/or promoted. How a manager goes about making these staffing decisions has a direct impact on the employees. The Skill Builder at the end of this chapter helps you develop the skill necessary to make these staffing decisions effectively. Often called **job posting**, this method may increase worker motivation because employees see that they have opportunities to advance within the organization. On the other hand, it may also lead to numerous job changes as each internal recruit vacates his or her position.[10] External recruiting is advertising for and soliciting applicants from outside the organization, often through want ads. This approach brings in new talent and perspective, but may also upset existing workers who would like to have been considered for the opening.

Many organizations frequently use external placement firms and private employment agencies. This strategy is especially common when the organization is recruiting for managerial and/or professional positions. As technology develops, computerized databases will also increasingly be used to assist human resource professionals in the recruitment task.[11] *The Environment of Management: Recruiting in Japan* provides insights into recruiting in Japan.

Each of these sources, internal and external, has distinct advantages. Table 14.2 summarizes these from the standpoint of internal recruiting. However, the advantages of internal recruiting tend to be the disadvantages for external recruiting and vice versa. For instance, an advantage for internal recruiting is that work histories are readily obtained whereas a disadvantage for external recruiting is that work histories are not so easily obtained. Most organizations use a combination of both internal and external to try to obtain the advantages of both.

Selection   Once applicants have been recruited, the organization must attempt to hire the ones that best fit its needs and opportunities. It makes this choice through the selection process. The **selection**

Table 14.2

Advantages and Disadvantages of Internal Recruiting

Advantages

From the organization's standpoint
current employees' work history easily obtained and evaluated
no time delays for visits, interviews, etc.
current employees already socialized

From the current employees' standpoint
it may serve to motivate if contingent on performance
they already know the organization so the process may be easier

Disadvantages

From the organization's standpoint
limits the pool, which may lead to inferior decisions
limits ability to bring in "new blood" that could speed up innovation and lead to rapid change

From the current employees' standpoint
resultant competitive pressures could make working together cooperatively more difficult
inability to get desired positions could lead to decrements in work performance

process is a systematic attempt to determine how well the skills, abilities, and aspirations of a job applicant match the needs, requirements, and opportunities within the organization. Managers can use a variety of techniques to assess an individual's current and potential skills, abilities, and aspirations during the selection process. However, each technique must be job related and have no discriminatory effects.

Although the discussion here focuses on the selection of full-time personnel, it is also applicable to the selection of temporary or free-lance workers. "Outsourcing," the use of workers who are not full-time personnel of the organization, is becoming common in organizations as a cost reduction technique.

Application blanks, tests, interviews, and assessment centers help managers decide which applicants to select for employment.

Application Blanks　　The typical first step in selection is to have prospective employees complete application blanks. An **application blank** is a standardized form that requests information from job applicants about their background, education, experience, and so forth. An example of an application blank is presented in Exhibit 14.3.

An application blank generally serves as a screen or filter to eliminate some applicants and retain others for further consideration. For example, if a particular job requires a college degree, application blank data can easily separate those who meet this requirement from those who do not. Some firms use more sophisticated application blanks that allow managers to weight some items mathematically and then combine various scores to provide an overall predictor of performance.[12]

Application for Employment

Houghton Mifflin Company

PLEASE PRINT OR TYPE

DATE _____

POSITION FOR WHICH
YOU ARE APPLYING _____

SALARY
EXPECTATION _____

PERSONAL INFORMATION

NAME

PRESENT
ADDRESS

PERMANENT
ADDRESS

SOCIAL
SECURITY NO.

HOME PHONE
NUMBER

WORK PHONE
NUMBER

HOW WERE YOU REFERRED TO US?

SPECIAL SKILLS, ABILITIES, KNOWLEDGE, FOREIGN LANGUAGES, ETC.
(In addition to paid experience, you may also list skills gained as a volunteer.)

PROFESSIONAL REFERENCES (PLEASE INCLUDE TITLE, BUSINESS, AND TELEPHONE NUMBER)

IF HIRED, YOU WILL BE REQUIRED TO PROVIDE PROOF OF AUTHORIZATION TO WORK IN THE UNITED STATES PRIOR TO
BEGINNING EMPLOYMENT (The Immigration Reform and Control Act of 1986)

To the best of my knowledge all of the information in this application and attached resume is true and is given voluntarily.

SIGNATURE _____

FA-268R

NAME

EXPERIENCE

LIST MOST CURRENT POSITION FIRST

COMPANY, ADDRESS, SUPERVISOR	DATES OF SERVICE	TITLE AND DUTIES	REASON FOR LEAVING

EDUCATION

	NAME AND ADDRESS OF SCHOOL ATTENDED	DATES ATTENDED FROM	TO	MAJOR MINOR	DEGREE · DATE
HIGH SCHOOL					
COLLEGE OR UNIVERSITY					
POST GRADUATE					

Exhibit 14.3   A Job Application Blank

321

Tests   **Tests** are also frequently used to select employees. Common types used in the selection process include ability, skill, aptitude, and knowledge tests.[13] A typing test would be given to applicants for a typist's job, and swimming tests to a potential lifeguard. Physical ability tests such as these are relatively easy to administer and interpret.

On the other hand, organizations that use aptitude tests or personality assessments in selection must be much more careful in their administration and interpretation. These characteristics are much harder to measure accurately and the tests are also more prone to have bias and/or to discriminate in ways that are unrelated to job performance. Physical examinations are also used by some firms as part of their test program.

Interviews   The most common selection technique is the interview. In its simplest format an **interview** is a conversation between the job applicant and a representative of the organization. Besides evaluating the applicant, the interviewer can use this occasion to promote the company. Many organizations use multiple interviews. Interviews may be relatively structured (with a set of prescribed questions to be asked and answered) or unstructured (open-ended, with no prescribed questions).

Unfortunately, despite their widespread use, interviews are rather poor predictors of job success.[14] Judgments of interviewers tend to have low or zero correlation with the later job performance of employees. One reason for this may be that many people are relatively unskilled in asking probing questions and interpreting responses. Another is that job applicants may not be completely truthful during the interview in order to avoid making a bad impression.

Assessment Centers   Finally, **assessment centers** are specially designed techniques used to select managerial employees. During an assessment center prospective managers spend an extended period of time (perhaps two or three days) undergoing a battery of tests, interviews, and simulated work experiences. These simulated work experiences attempt to imitate various parts of the managerial job, such as decision making, time management, giving feedback to subordinates, and so forth. Each potential manager performs these tasks under the observation of skilled human resource managers. Assessment centers are an excellent way to predict an individual's managerial potential. On the other hand, they take a lot of time for both applicants and human resource managers and are expensive to operate.

Regardless of which selection techniques an organization uses, it must be able to demonstrate that it is not discriminating on the basis of irrelevant factors. For example, suppose an organization uses a selection test with a maximum potential score of 100. During the development of the test a manager asks thirty current employees to answer the test questions. It turns out that the ten highest performers all score between 90 and 100, the next ten performers all score between 70 and 80, and the ten lowest performers all score below 60. The manager now has evidence that the test is a valid predictor of performance. On the other hand, if the test proves to be unrelated to subsequent performance, its use is discriminatory and could result in problems for the organization.

Such discriminatory practices were the catalyst for much of the legislation that so tightly controls the human resource area today.[15] Most organizations now work hard not to discriminate in their employment practices.

Orientation   After a new employee accepts an offer to join the organization, such as Bethlehem Steel or Turner Construction, he or she must go through an **orientation** procedure. Such orientation procedures vary widely from company to company. Orientation for operating employees might simply be telling them when to come to work, when they get paid, and whom to see if they have a problem. Orientation for managerial and professional employees tends to be more involved. It may take several weeks or months of work with other employees for the newcomer to become totally acquainted with all phases of the organization.

Training and Development

After new employees have been recruited, selected, and oriented, the next logical step is to train and develop them. **Training** typically involves specific job skills and applies more to operating employees. **Development** usually refers to training for managers. Development is more general in nature and focuses on a wider array of skills, including conceptual, problem-solving, and interpersonal skills.[16]

Assessing Training and Development Needs

Before a manager can properly plan training and development activities, she or he must ascertain the training and development needs of both the employees and the organization. For example, if labor market conditions are such that a university has to hire librarians who are not totally qualified for the job (that is, if skilled librarians are scarce), training needs will be great. On the other hand, if qualified employees are readily available, an organization's training needs are considerably less.

Employee training and skill development are increasingly important to organizations as they strive to create learning environments to improve productivity. Customers benefit from such training in a variety of ways. Cincinnati Gas & Electric, for instance, has trained some of its customer service representatives in the use of sign language to serve the special needs of some of its customers. (Photo by Ron Rack for The Cincinnati Gas & Electric Company.)

Training generally means teaching job skills, whereas *development* involves more general abilities.

Regardless of how much formal training is necessary, employees will need at least some basic work to learn exactly how the organization requires them to perform their tasks. And management development is a long-term, ongoing process that never really stops.

In recent years organizations have intensified their training and development efforts in a number of specific areas. For one thing, with the growth of international business many companies now provide extensive language and/or cross-cultural training for their employees. For another, increased sensitivity regarding work force diversity within organizations has also prompted training in the area of multiculturalism.[17]

Popular Training and Development Techniques

Several common techniques used for training and development are noted in Table 14.3. The key, of course, is to match the technique with the goals of the training and development effort. For example, if the goal is for employees to learn about new company procedures, assigned reading

Table 14.3　Common Training and Development Techniques

Method	Comments
Assigned Readings	Readings may or may not be specially prepared for training purposes.
Behavior Modeling Training	Use of a videotaped model displaying the correct behavior, then trainee role playing and discussion of the correct behavior. Used extensively for supervisor training in human relations.
Business Simulation	Both paper simulations (such as in-basket exercises) and computer-based business "games" are used to teach management skills.
Case Discussion	Real or fictitious cases or incidents are discussed in small groups.
Conference	Small-group discussion of selected topics, usually with the trainer as leader.
Lecture	Oral presentation of material by the trainer, with limited or no audience participation.
On the Job	Ranges from no instruction, to casual coaching by more experienced employees, to carefully structured explanation, demonstration, and supervised practice by a qualified trainer.
Programmed Instruction	Self-paced method using text or computer followed by questions and answers. Expensive to develop.
Role Playing	Trainees act out roles with other trainees, such as "boss giving performance appraisal" and "subordinate reacting to appraisal" to gain experience in human relations; also used in international training.
Sensitivity Training	Also called T-group and laboratory training, this is an intensive experience in a small group, wherein individuals give each other feedback and try out new behaviors. It is said to promote trust, open communication, and understanding of group dynamics.
Vestibule Training	Supervised practice on manual tasks in a separate work area where the emphasis is on safety, learning, and feedback rather than productivity.
Interactive Video	Newly emerging technique using computers and video technology.

might be an effective approach. If Motorola has a goal to teach people how to relate better to others or how to make decisions more effectively, it might use role playing or case discussion groups. Training supervisors in conducting performance reviews might involve behavior modeling.[18] If the idea is to teach a physical skill such as operating a new kind of machine, vestibule or on-the-job training could be the most appropriate option. Whichever technique is used, however, it is important to get the trainees to accept the training.[19]

Evaluating the Effectiveness of Training

The final component of a well-managed training and development program is evaluation. Considering how much time, effort, and money companies invest in training and development, they should make sure that the goals of the program are met.[20]

If an employee training program is designed to increase the proficiency of word-processing operators, for instance, the operators' performance should be measured both before and after the training program. If the program is effective, their performance should improve. Lack of improvement might suggest that the training should be revised.

Evaluation is more difficult in the case of management development, but it is not impossible. Managers who participate in many development activities and get high marks in those activities should subsequently have a good record of promotions, performance, and so forth. If this is indeed the case, then the organization has evidence that its development efforts are paying off. But again, if involvement and performance in management development activities are unrelated to future job performance, the organization should reassess its approach to developing managers.

Performance Appraisal

Performance appraisal is important for verifying the validity of selection methods, providing rewards fairly, and helping employees improve.

After employees have been trained and have adjusted to their jobs, managers usually begin to evaluate their performance. There are several purposes behind this evaluation, or **performance appraisal.** First, the organization needs evidence to justify, or validate, the selection techniques it used to hire the person in the first place. Second, since performance is frequently a basis for rewards, it is important to evaluate performance so that those rewards can be provided fairly. In addition, the individual needs to know how well he or she is performing in order to improve.[21] And finally, performance appraisal helps determine what additional training the employee may need. Managers can use several different kinds of techniques for performance appraisal. The Self-Assessment in this chapter examines your ideas about performance appraisal. Before you continue reading about performance appraisal, you might want to complete the Self-Assessment to determine your current thinking about this topic.

Objective Measures

Objective measures of performance appraisal are quantifiable indicators of how well the employee is doing. For instance, it may be possible to count how many units of a product an employee assembles, adjust this number for quality, and arrive at an objective index of performance. Similarly, the number of sales dollars generated by a sales representative reflects performance objectively.

Unfortunately, objective measures are often unavailable or, worse still, misleading. Assembly-line workers have little control over how many units they produce, and a sales representative with a lot of major customers in his or her territory should have more sales than a rep with only a few large customers. For these reasons, managers may need to adjust objective indicators of performance in order to have a valid representation of actual performance.

Judgmental Methods

Another common approach to performance appraisal used by many organizations is **judgmental methods.** These methods involve having someone, usually the employee's immediate supervisor, subjectively evaluate that person's performance via a ranking or a rating procedure.

*A **ranking** system measures employees against one another, whereas a **rating** system compares each employee with a standard of performance.*

Ranking, as the term implies, means that the supervisor ranks subordinates in a continuum from high to low performance. Such a procedure forces the manager to differentiate among high, moderate, and low performers. At the same time, however, it also makes feedback more difficult to deliver as each rank must be dependent, and the last person on the list may still be a solid performer.

Rating is comparing each employee with one or more absolute standards and then placing the employee somewhere in relation to that standard. These scales rate the individual's level of conscientiousness and degree of initiative on the job. The manager considers the questions, judges how well the person stacks up, and then circles the appropriate numbers along the scales. Managers usually sum or average the various ratings to arrive at an overall index of performance.

Because they are flexible and relatively easy to use and to interpret, rating scales such as these are probably the most common kinds of performance appraisal devices currently in use. Unfortunately, however, they also suffer from a number of problems. For one thing, managers are sometimes inclined to give everyone the same relative rating (all high, all average, or all low). This rating makes it impossible to differentiate among them. For another thing, many people tend to be influenced by an employee's most recent behavior rather than by his or her overall level of performance over longer periods of time.

To help overcome these shortcomings some organizations develop guidelines to improve the process used in rating systems.[22] Some organizations also develop more sophisticated and intricate rating scales to make them more accurate. Two examples of these are Behaviorally Anchored Rating Scales (BARS) and Behavior Observation Scales (BOS). While each is complicated and takes considerable time and effort to develop, they are also a vast improvement over traditional rating scales.[23] Two example rating scales are shown in Exhibit 14.4.

Management by Objectives

Management by objectives, a popular vehicle for managing the goal-setting process, also serves as a useful method for evaluating the performance of those managers who set the goals to begin with. For example, suppose a sales manager for Colgate-Palmolive sets a goal of increasing sales next year by 15 percent. At the end of the year, this goal provides an effective framework for performance appraisal. If sales have indeed increased by 15 percent or more, a positive performance appraisal may be in order. But if sales have increased by only 4 percent, and if the manager is directly responsible for the disappointing results, a more negative evaluation may be forthcoming.

Feedback

The final part of performance appraisal, and often the most difficult, is providing **feedback** to the employee by telling him or her the results of the appraisal.[24] Because it is often so difficult, software has even been written to assist managers with the feedback task.[25]

Exhibit 14.4

Performance Rating Scales

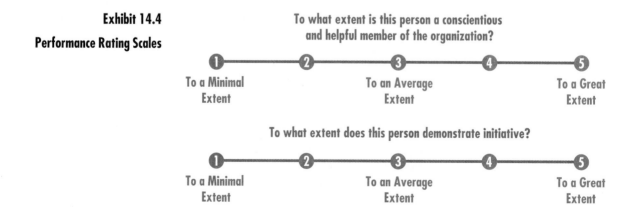

To what extent is this person a conscientious and helpful member of the organization?

① ② ③ ④ ⑤

To a Minimal   To an Average   To a Great
Extent   Extent   Extent

To what extent does this person demonstrate initiative?

① ② ③ ④ ⑤

To a Minimal   To an Average   To a Great
Extent   Extent   Extent

A Matter of Ethics

Food Lion

Food Lion Inc., based in North Carolina, is one of the strongest grocery chains in the United States. After struggling for a few years after its formation in 1957, the firm has grown steadily over the last several years. In contrast to other chains like Kroger and Safeway, Food Lion builds only medium-size stores and carries few nongrocery items.

The firm is rapidly expanding nationally, moving into contiguous states and opening stores in major metropolitan areas. The firm's annual sales and profit growth have been nothing short of spectacular. In 1980, the firm operated 106 stores; now there are almost 1,000 Food Lion stores. And a single share of Food Lion bought in 1957 for $10 would today have been split into 12,000 shares and be worth more than $200,000.

But some critics argue that Food Lion's growth is tainted.

To achieve its high level of profitability managers at Food Lion put tremendous emphasis on efficiency. Labor costs at Food Lion are only 7 percent of sales, half the industry average. Some employees have charged that Food Lion keeps its costs low by forcing employees to work for free.

That is, each worker is given a set number of tasks that must be performed within a forty-hour week. If the workers do not get the work done, some say, they feel pressured to keep working on their own time. Moreover, a few former employees have charged that they were fired either for seeking overtime pay or for refusing to work extra hours.

Food Lion denies the charges and points to a written policy that prohibits employees from working "off the clock." Still, a few former employees and the United Food & Commercial Workers Union have filed several complaints with the Labor Department. Food Lion has lost some of these cases, but it has won others.[26] ■

Feedback is a difficult part of performance appraisal, but it is essential if employees are to understand why subsequent actions are taken.

In most instances feedback is given in a private meeting between the superior and the subordinate. The superior typically begins by summarizing the results of the appraisal, then answers any questions, suggests ways to improve, and explains the immediate consequences of the appraisal. A poor evaluation might result in no salary increase, a cutback in authority, or even a warning that the employee will be fired if things are not turned around. In contrast, a good evaluation can lead to a raise, a bonus, a promotion, or increased responsibilities.

The employee being evaluated is usually given an opportunity to respond to the results of the evaluation. For example, the employee may argue that the manager was unfair or that the evaluation itself did not tell the complete story. The manager may or may not choose to adjust the evaluation, but the employee can usually document her or his perceptions and add them to the official evaluation before it becomes official.

Compensation and Benefits

The management of compensation and benefits is another important part of the human resource process. Employees must be paid **compensation**—wages and salaries—and they usually expect to receive various kinds of benefits. The organization also often uses financial incentives to increase motivation and reward past performance of productive workers.[27] As described in *A Matter of Ethics: Food Lion* the management of compensation and benefits can be a controversial process.

Wages and Salaries

The central part of compensation management involves determining wages and salaries for employees. This determination, in turn, consists of three parts: wage level decisions, wage structure decisions, and individual wage decisions.

Wage Level Decisions

Management's **wage level** decision is the decision about whether the organization wants to pay higher wages, the same wages, or lower wages than the prevailing rate in the industry or geographic area. If Microsoft Corporation decides that it wants to attract the best possible computer scientists, it would set a policy of paying recent college graduates starting salaries that are several percentage points higher than those of other companies hiring computer scientists. Similarly, a small manufacturer might decide to pay the same rates as other local companies and not to attract people on the basis of a high starting wage but to keep wages from being a factor that could force current employees to seek other jobs.[28]

Wage Structure Decisions

Another important decision pertains to the **wage structure** within the organization. The essential issue here is how much people performing one job should be paid relative to people performing another job. That is, is Job A worth a higher salary than Job B, is Job B worth a higher salary than Job A, or are Jobs A and B worth exactly the same salary? The wage structure is usually determined through job evaluation. **Job evaluation,** closely related to job analysis, is the process of determining the relative value of jobs within the organization.[29]

Probably the most widespread approach to job evaluation is the **point system.** The point system starts with a committee of workers and managers determining what factors are most appropriately used to differentiate and characterize jobs within the organization. As shown in Table 14.4, these factors might include such things as education, responsibility, skill, and physical demand.

After the factors have been identified, each is assigned points based on its perceived importance to the organization. For example, points awarded for education required to perform the job might range from 20 to 100. Table 14.5 shows how these points might then be allocated for three jobs: secretary, office manager, and janitor. In the table the job of office manager warrants 80 points for education needed, 70 for responsibility, 60 for skill, and only 20 for physical demand. Its total, then, is 230 points. This job should therefore be worth more than the secretarial job, which totals 200 points. It in turn is worth more than the janitorial job, with 145 points.

Individual Wage Decisions

Finally, the manager must address individual wage decisions. These decisions involve deciding how much each person within a job classification is to be paid. Most organizations set wage ranges for jobs within certain point ranges. For instance, a company might decide to pay people $8 to $10 an hour for jobs worth 350 to 375 points. Initial wages are

Table 14.4

Sample Point System for Wage Determination

Compensable factors	Points associated with degrees of the factors				
	Very little	Low	Moderate	High	Very high*
Education	20	40	60	80	100
Responsibility	20	40	70	110	160
Skill	20	40	60	80	100
Physical Demand	10	20	30	45	60

* The job evaluation committee that constructed the system believed that responsibility should be the most heavily weighted factor and physical demand the least. That is why the maximum points for these factors are different.

Table 14.5

An Application of the Point System

Compensable factors	Job		
	Secretary II	**Office manager**	**Janitor**
Education	Moderate = 60	High = 80	Very low = 20
Responsibility	Low = 40	Moderate = 70	Low = 40
Skill	High = 80	Moderate = 60	Low = 40
Physical Demand	Low = 20	Low = 20	High = 45
Total points	200	230	145

The job analysis committee carefully reviews the content of each job and decides what degree of each factor best describes the job.

then set according to the employee's experience. A person who is just starting his or her career might be paid $8, whereas a more experienced person might receive $8.75.

Later, wages are adjusted according to seniority and/or performance. The new employee might get a fifteen-cents-an-hour raise after six months and another thirty-cent raise for very good performance, bringing the total to $8.45 an hour. The other employee, meanwhile, might be given the same fifteen-cent raise after six months but no additional increase for performance.

Benefits

Payments to employees other than wages or salaries are known as **benefits.**

Another important part of compensation is the benefit package to be provided. **Benefits** are payments other than wages or salaries. Benefits add substantial costs to the total compensation received by employees, averaging slightly over 40 percent above the cost of wages and salaries.[30] The most common benefits include health, dental, disability, and life insurance coverage for the employee (and sometimes the employee's family). Costs for these benefits may be borne entirely by the organization or shared with the employee. Employees also usually receive some pay for time when they do not work, such as vacations, sick days, and holidays. Retirement programs are also common benefits. Not as prevalent but still provided by some organizations are benefits such as counseling programs, physical fitness programs, credit unions, and tuition reimbursement for educational expenses related to the job. On-site day-care facilities are also becoming more common, especially in larger firms.

An organization's benefit package is clearly significant for several reasons. In addition to representing a major cost to the organization, it is an important factor in attracting and retaining employees. Some organizations have experimented with what is called a "cafeteria benefits package." Under such an arrangement each benefit is priced and employees can choose those they want within a total price. This arrangement recognizes the diverse work force and individuals' varying needs. For example, a married worker with several children can concentrate on insurance programs, a single employee can choose more vacation time, and an older worker can put more into retirement. Such cafeteria programs are expensive to administer but are an attractive feature to many employees.[31]

Labor Relations

The final aspect of human resource management to be discussed here is labor relations. The term **labor relations** generally refers to dealing with employees when they are organized in a labor union.[32] In this section we first describe how unions are formed and then address collective bargaining.

How Unions Are Formed

The process of forming a union is carefully defined by the government, which created the National Labor Relations Board (NLRB) to oversee union creation.

Given the turbulent history of union-management relations, it should come as no surprise that government regulation closely defines the processes involved in forming a union.[33] The National Labor Relations Board (NLRB) was created to oversee these processes.

The actual steps in forming a union are summarized in Exhibit 14.5. First, someone must generate interest among employees. For example, either disgruntled employees or representatives of large national unions might initiate this action within a particular organization. Next, em-

Exhibit 14.5

How Unions Are Created

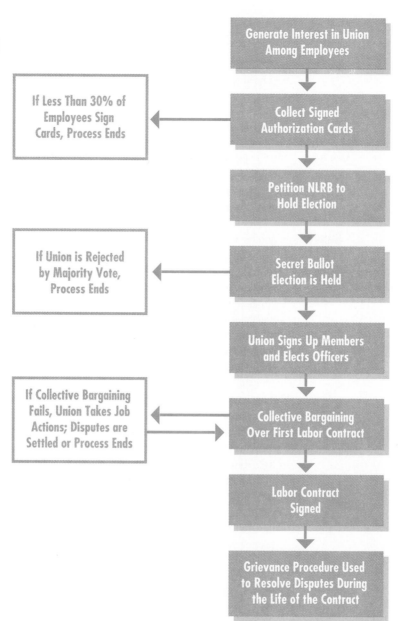

ployees must collect signatures on what are called authorization cards. These cards simply indicate that the individuals who sign them believe that an election should be held to determine whether employees are interested in unionization. If fewer than 30 percent of the eligible employees sign the cards, the process ends. But if 30 percent or more sign authorization cards, however, the NLRB conducts a certification election.

A simple majority of those who vote—as opposed to all eligible employees in the organization—determines the outcome of the election. If the majority votes against the certification of a union, the process ends. But if a majority votes in favor of unionization, the union is officially certified by the NLRB and becomes the official bargaining representative for all eligible employees.

Immediately following certification, the union recruits members and elects officers. Members pay dues (to cover administrative costs) and expect to gain improved employment conditions as a result. After the membership is signed up, the union sets out to negotiate a labor contract with management. Either management and the union agree on a contract, or the union takes various job actions. These actions might include strikes, work slowdowns, or similar activities. The contract also specifies a grievance procedure that will be used to settle disputes during the term of the contract.[34]

Obviously, management prefers employees not to belong to unions. In general, the best way to avoid unionization is to treat employees fairly and to give them a voice in how the workplace is governed. Establishing clear guidelines for performance appraisals, reward allocations, and promotions, avoiding favoritism, and creating a mechanism for handling disputes are frequently cited ways to help make employees feel that they do not need unions.[35] But unions can help management and employees resolve their differences through the formal collective bargaining process, which is our next topic.

Collective Bargaining

*Management and union officials reach agreement on wages, layoff policies, and the like through **collective bargaining**, which results in a mutually binding contract.*

Collective bargaining is a discussion process between union and management that focuses on agreeing to a written contract that will cover all relevant aspects of the relationship between the organization and members of the union.[36] In particular, it defines wages, work hours, promotion and layoff policies, benefits, and decision rules for allocating overtime, vacation time, and rest breaks. The union also frequently pushes for a security clause, which is designed to protect the union by requiring that all new employees join the union and that all current employees remain members. In turn, management pushes for a stipulation that it has total control over any and all areas not specifically covered in the contract.

In most cases, strikes are prohibited during the term of the contract. Any strikes that do occur are called *wildcat strikes* and do not have the official endorsement of the union. Of course, the union can call strikes after the existing contract has expired and when the union and management representatives cannot agree on a new one.

Discipline   Labor contracts frequently devote considerable attention to discipline. Everyone seems to agree that management can discipline employees for just cause, but disputes frequently arise over the meaning of "just cause." In general, management and union representatives make an effort to define work rules very clearly and to define penalties for violating those rules. For example, the first time an employee is late he or she might receive a reminder about work hours; the second time a note might go in the employee's file; a third offense could lead to a short suspension without pay. If everyone knows the rules and the penalties for breaking them, there will be few legitimate complaints.[37]

Grievance Procedure   Of course, no contract is perfect, and differences of opinion are inevitable. Thus the contract also specifies procedures that everyone will follow to resolve disputes.

An employee who feels mistreated often files a written **grievance** with the union and discusses it with his or her supervisor. If the problem cannot be resolved, union officials and higher-level managers become involved. Ultimately, it may be necessary to make use of an arbitrator. An **arbitrator** is a labor law specialist jointly paid by the union and the organization. The arbitrator listens to both sides of the argument, studies the contract, and makes a decision as to how the dispute is to be settled. Both the union and management agree to abide by his or her ruling.

Chapter Summary

Staffing is the process of procuring and managing the human resources an organization needs to accomplish its goals. Staffing is vitally important to all organizations and is usually the shared responsibility of human resource specialists and line managers.

Human resource planning is the first phase of the staffing process. It involves job analysis, forecasting human resource supply and demand, and matching supply with demand. Job analysis is the systematic collecting and recording of information about jobs in the organization, resulting in descriptions of jobs and specifications that explain what kind of person is needed for them. With this information forecasts of the demand for and supply of human resources are made. If supply exceeds demand, the manager must make plans to reduce employment through attrition, layoffs, terminations, and early retirements. If demand exceeds supply, the manager must engage in the next process, selection.

The selection phase of human resource management consists of recruiting, selecting, and orienting employees. Recruiting is the process of attracting a pool of qualified applicants interested in working for the organization. Selection is choosing which applicants to hire, using techniques such as application blanks, tests, interviews, and assessment centers. Orientation is the procedure whereby new employees are brought into and informed about the company, its purpose, and their job.

Training is usually job specific, whereas development is more general. Before engaging in such activities, the organization should determine how much and what kinds of training are needed. Training and development involve a wide range of techniques, including role playing, reading, and on-the-job training. All training and development activities should be evaluated in terms of effectiveness and efficiency.

Performance appraisal—the evaluation of each employee's performance—is used to justify the selection techniques used, to provide a basis for reward distribution, and to give feedback to the employee. Where employees exert considerable control over their work, the best measures are objective, quantifiable indicators such as units assembled or dollars sold. In other cases judgmental methods such as ranking or rating tend to be used. One approach that has some value when individuals have a fair amount of control over their jobs is management by objectives, whereby performance is appraised by how well the objectives have been accomplished.

The determination of employee compensation or wages and salaries, is central to management. It involves three types of decisions: wage level, wage structure, and individual wage decisions. Wage level decisions are external; wage structure decisions are internal. Job evaluation is the process used to determine the relative value of jobs within an organization. Benefits are yet another part of compensation management. Health care, dental care, disability, and/or life insurance, vacations, sick leave, and holidays are all part of benefits that must be managed.

Labor relations refers to dealing with employees when they are organized into a labor union. The best way to avoid unions is by making them unnecessary. This means treating employees fairly, having them participate in setting clear guidelines for performance appraisal, reward allocation, and personnel decisions, and creating a mechanism for handling disputes. Negotiating a contract—collective bargaining—may be a complex process, since all relevant aspects of the relationship between the organization and members of the union are covered in such contracts.

The Manager's Vocabulary

staffing
personnel
human resources
job analysis
job description

job specification
recruiting
job posting
selection
application blanks

tests
interview
assessment centers
orientation
training

development
performance appraisal
objective measures of performance
   appraisal
judgmental methods of performance
   appraisal
ranking

rating
management by objectives
feedback
compensation
wage level
wage structure
job evaluation

point system
benefits
labor relations
collective bargaining
grievance
arbitrator

Review Questions

1. What are the major components of human resource planning? How are they related?
2. What is selection? What are some of the techniques used in it?
3. What are some popular training and development techniques? Where might each be appropriate?

4. What are some methods used in performance appraisal? What are the advantages and disadvantages of each?
5. Describe the general process through which unions are formed.

Analysis Questions

1. What are the advantages and disadvantages of internal and external recruiting? Which do you feel is best in the long term? Why?
2. How can you determine whether or not a particular technique is valid for selection? What are the costs and benefits of using invalid techniques?
3. An objective measure of performance for a research chemist

might be the number of patents obtained. Why might this be a poor method for evaluating the chemist's performance? What might be a better approach?
4. Do you think wages or salaries are more important than benefits? Why or why not?
5. Respond to this statement: "Unions would not exist if it weren't for poor management."

Self-Assessment

What Are Your Ideas About Performance Appraisal?

Introduction Performance appraisals are completed in all walks of life. In fact, grades are your performance appraisal and your transcript is a summary of your performance over many different subjects. This self-assessment examines your ideas about performance appraisal.

Instructions The following seventeen statements ask your opinion about performance appraisals in general. For these statements, indicate the extent to which you agree or disagree with each by indicating the number that most closely corresponds to your opinion.

   1 = Strongly Disagree
   2 = Disagree
   3 = Slightly disagree
   4 = Neither agree nor disagree

5 = Slightly agree
6 = Agree
7 = Strongly agree

_____ 1. Performance appraisals can be objectively and unemotionally carried out by managers.

_____ 2. Many people really understand what the objectives of performance appraisal are.

_____ 3. Most people have a real understanding of how performance appraisal results are to be used in organizations.

_____ 4. In organizations, salary decisions should be based on performance appraisal results.

_____ 5. In organizations, promotion decisions should be based on performance appraisal results.

_____   6. Supervisors and subordinates pretty much agree on what constitutes good or poor performance.

_____   7. Performance appraisal practices should provide accurate feedback to the subordinate.

_____   8. Most managers would not participate in performance appraisals unless their organization required them to.

_____   9. Most subordinates would not participate in performance appraisals unless their organizations required them to.

_____   10. Performance appraisals are fairly and honestly done in most organizations.

_____   11. Performance appraisals motivate individuals to improve their performance.

_____   12. Performance appraisals typically lead to productive changes in the subordinate's behavior.

_____   13. Performance appraisals should lead to better supervisor and subordinate understanding of what the subordinate's role should be.

_____   14. Salary decisions should be based on performance appraisal results.

_____   15. Promotion decisions should be based on performance appraisal results.

_____   16. A subordinate's self-appraisal should be an important part of the performance appraisal process.

_____   17. Performance appraisals should be based on goals previously agreed to by the supervisor and subordinate.

For interpretation, turn to the back of the book.

Source: Edward E. Lawyer, III, Steve Kerr, Chuck Maxey, Monty Mohrman, Bruce Prince, Janet Schriesheim, Center for Effectiveness Organizations, Graduate School of Business Administration, University of Southern California, Los Angeles, California, 90007. Reprinted by permission of the author.

Skill Builder

Whom Do You Promote?

Purpose In this chapter we discuss the importance of staffing to the organization. One method of staffing the organization is through promotion. To staff through promotion requires special skill on the part of the manager. This skill builder focuses on both the human resources and scientific management models. It will help you develop the director role of the scientific management model and the mentor role of the human resources model. One of the skills of the director is taking initiative, while one of the skills of the mentor is developing subordinates.

Introduction Consider, first by yourself, and then within a group, which of the following individuals should be promoted. Keep in mind what criteria you are using for making these decisions.

Instructions

Your company recently developed a plan to identify and train top hourly employees for promotion to first-line supervisor. As part of this program, your boss has requested a ranking of the six hourly workers who report to you with respect to their promotion potential. Given their biographical data, rank them in the order in which you would select them for promotion to first-line supervisor; that is, the person ranked number one would be first in line for promotion.

Biographical Data:

1. *Sam Nelson:* White male, age forty-five, married, with four children. Sam has been with the company for five years, and his performance evaluations have been average to above average. He is well liked by the other employees in the department. He devotes his spare time to farming and plans to farm after retirement.

2. *Ruth Hornsby:* White female, age thirty-two, married, with no children; husband has a management-level job with the power company. Ruth has been with the company for two years and has received above-average performance evaluations. She is very quiet and keeps to herself at work. She says she is working to save for a down payment on a new house.

3. *Joe Washington:* Black male, age twenty-six, single. Joe has been with the company for three years and has received high performance evaluations. He is always willing to take on new assignments and to work overtime. He is attending college in the evenings and someday wants to start his own business. He is well liked by the other employees in the department.

4. *Ronald Smith:* White male, age thirty-five, recently divorced, with one child, age four. Ronald has received excellent performance evaluations during his two years with the company. He seems to like his present job but has removed himself from the line of progression. He seems to have personality conflicts with some of the employees.

5. *Betty Norris:* Black female, age forty-four, married, with one grown child. Betty has been with the company for ten years and is well liked by fellow employees. Her performance evaluations have been average to below-average, and her advancement has been limited by a lack of formal education. She has participated in a number of technical training programs conducted by the company.

6. *Roy Davis:* White male, age thirty-six, married with two teenage children. Roy has been with the company for ten years and received excellent performance evaluations until last year. His most recent evaluation was average. He is friendly and well liked by his fellow employees. One of his children has had a serious illness for over a year, resulting in a number of large medical expenses. Roy is working a second job on weekends to help with these expenses. He has expressed a serious interest in promotion to first-line supervisor.

Source: Reproduced from *Supervisory Management: The Art of Working With and Through People,* 2nd ed., by Donald C. Mosley, Leon C. Megginson, and Paul H. Pietri, Jr. with the permission of South-Western Publishing Co. Copyright 1989 by South-Western Publishing Co. All rights reserved. (Cincinnati: South-Western Publishing, 1989).

CONCLUDING CASES

14.1   Caterpillar

Caterpillar has a well-entrenched reputation for making high-quality earth-moving equipment. It sells its products under a variety of brand names, including Cat, Caterpillar, Barber-Greene, and Solar. The firm is one of the largest exporters in the United States, with total 1991 exports of almost $4 billion.

While Caterpillar encounters few rough spots in the marketplace, its dealings with its labor union have been a different story altogether. The most recent problem involved a bitter five-month strike that lasted from late 1991 until the early summer of 1992.

Many of Caterpillar's workers are represented by the United Auto Workers, or UAW. The UAW is generally considered to be among the world's most powerful labor unions. The UAW likes to engage in what is widely called pattern bargaining. Under pattern bargaining, the union contract negotiated with one company becomes the pattern the union uses to establish subsequent contracts with other companies in the same industry whose workers it represents.

Since 1958 the UAW has been using pattern bargaining in its dealings with Caterpillar, John Deere, and J. I. Case. The union also uses pattern bargaining in its dealings with large U.S. automakers. Thus the UAW has long been motivated to protect its pattern bargaining platform and has been loath to deviate from it too much.

Caterpillar, on the other hand, has for several years been interested in breaking the UAW's pattern approach. The firm argues that since it ships so much of its output abroad and competes in international markets, it should not be grouped with Deere and Case, both of which sell primarily in the U.S. domestic market.

Caterpillar first tried to break the UAW pattern in 1982 when the firm weathered a 205-day strike before finally accepting a slightly modified pattern agreement. While Caterpillar may have

scored a symbolic victory, the UAW still got most of the major pattern provisions it was seeking.

In 1991 Caterpillar again rejected the UAW pattern offer. The UAW promptly sent 2,400 workers out on strike. Caterpillar fought back by locking out another 5,650 workers and settling in for a protracted battle. About half of the firm's unionized workers stayed on the job. Managers moved in to operate the plants that were struck and locked out. The UAW countered by refusing to bargain until Caterpillar agreed to entertain a pattern agreement.

The strike lasted about five months. From the beginning, Caterpillar held the upper hand. For one thing, the United States was in recession and jobs were scarce. For another, in preparation for a possible strike the firm had built up huge inventories and did not experience any lost sales.

In June 1992 the firm announced that it would hire replacement workers and began accepting employment applications from prospective nonunion employees. One week later the UAW called off the strike and and sent its members back to work. The union refused to sign a contract but did agree to the last set of employment terms that Caterpillar had offered before the strike. Most observers agreed that in round two, Caterpillar scored both a symbolic and a substantive victory.[38]

Discussion Questions

1. What effects did the environment have on labor relations at Caterpillar?
2. What are the pros and cons of pattern bargaining?
3. Research current conditions at Caterpillar and the UAW.

14.2   Lufthansa

Deutsche Lufthansa AG, more popularly known simply as Lufthansa, is the government-owned airline of Germany. Lufthansa has an excellent on-time record. It is the world's twelfth-largest airline and the world's second-largest air cargo carrier (after Federal Express).

Because the German government owns Lufthansa, the airline has never had to worry too much about profitability. Moreover, because European airline activity has been so heavily regulated there were relatively few competitive measures the airline could take. Thus for years Lufthansa carried out its mission as efficiently as it could, functioning in a relatively protected and insulated environment.

In recent years, however, things have changed. For one thing, the German government, strapped for cash by the financial pressures of its reunification program, has mandated better financial performance by Lufthansa. Indeed, there is even talk that the airline may be privatized. For another, the opening of the European market in 1992 following deregulation has increased competition among all European airlines.

To fight back, Lufthansa recently brought in a new CEO, Juergen Weber. Weber quickly realized that the airline had to cut its costs if it wanted to remain competitive. Indeed, analysis revealed that Lufthansa had the lowest profit margins of any major European carrier.

Weber decided to start with labor. His first step was to announce plans to cut seven thousand jobs. Workers affected by the cuts are represented by two unions, the German Corporate Employees union (DAG) and the Public Workers' Union (OTV). The two unions, however, had quite different responses to Weber's plan.

The OTV, representing flight attendants and ground-services staff, took a hard line. It demanded that Lufthansa first trim management and administrative payrolls. Moreover, the union threatened strikes and/or work slowdowns if its demands were not met.

The DAG, which represents pilots, engineers, and technicians, took a more conciliatory stance. Like the OTV, the DAG also urged that Lufthansa cut administrative costs. But the DAG also volunteered to take an 8-percent wage cut and to increase work hours from 37.5 hours per week to 40 hours per week.

One thing the unions did agree on, however, was concern about a new airline Lufthansa is planning to start. Lufthansa wants to keep its current organization for international flights but also intends to create an entirely new airline called Lufthansa Express for all domestic flights. Lufthansa Express will pay wages 30 percent below those it currently pays. It will also provide fewer benefits for its workers.[39]

Discussion Questions

1. How has Lufthansa's environment affected its human resource practices?
2. How should Lufthansa approach its two unions?
3. What potential advantages and disadvantages can you identify from a staffing perspective for Lufthansa Express?

Part Four   Organizing

Self-Assessment

Inventory of Effective Organization Design

Introduction Throughout this part of the book we have examined why and how managers organize to effectively and efficiently achieve the organization's goals. This self-assessment aids in determining whether you feel the organizational design of a organization you are currently involved with is effective.

Instructions Listed below are a number of statements describing an effective organization design. Please indicate the extent to which you agree or disagree with each statement as a description of an organization you currently or have worked for. If you don't currently work, this could be an organization such as a club or society to which you belong. Write the appropriate number next to the statement.

1	**2**	**3**	**4**	**5**	**6**	**7**
Strong Disagree	**Disagree**	**Somewhat Disagree**	**Uncertain**	**Somewhat Agree**	**Agree**	**Strongly Agree**

_____ 1. Employees who try to change things are usually recognized and supported.

_____ 2. The organization makes it easy to get the skills needed to progress.

_____ 3. Employees almost always know how their work turns out, whether it is good or bad.

_____ 4. Employees have flexibility over the pace of their work.

_____ 5. Managers facilitate discussion at meetings to encourage participation by subordinates.

_____ 6. Few policies, rules, and regulations restrict innovation in this organization.

_____ 7. Boundaries between departments and/or divisions rarely interfere with solving joint problems.

_____ 8. There are few hierarchical levels in this organization.

_____ 9. Everyone knows how their work will affect the work of the next person or the quality of the final product or service.

_____ 10. The organization is well informed about technological developments relevant to its processes, goods, or services.

_____ 11. The organization is constantly trying to determine what the customer wants or how to meet customer needs.

_____ 12. The organization can adapt to most changes because its policies, structure, and employees are flexible.

_____ 13. Different parts of the organization work together; when conflict arises, it often leads to constructive outcomes.

_____ 14. Everyone can state the values of the organization and how they are used to make decisions.

_____ 15. A great deal of information is shared openly.

For interpretation, turn to the back of the book.

Source: Adapted from W. A. Pasmore, _Designing Effective Organizations: The Sociotechnical Systems Perspective_ (New York: John Wiley & Sons, 1988), 157–186.

Skill Builder

The Quick Brown Fox

Purpose Throughout this part of the textbook the emphasis has been on how to organize to achieve organizational goals. This skill builder allows you to experience first hand the process of organizing. By experiencing different types of organizational designs, you will develop an ability to know when one type of design will be effective and/or efficient or when an alternate design might be more effective and/or efficient. This skill builder focuses on the administrative management model. It will help you develop the coordinator role of the administrative management model. One skill of the coordinator is the ability to organize organizational resources for effective and efficient accomplishment of organizational goals.

Introduction You are a company that manufactures sentences for students to use in typing classes in U.S. high schools. Each sentence must contain all twenty-six letters of the alphabet. The initial sentence is, "The quick brown fox jumps over the lazy dog." Product quality depends on criteria such as legibility, completeness, neatness, and correct spelling. Appointed Quality Assurance (QA) and Quality Control (QC) inspectors, as well as customers, will evaluate inputs and outputs for acceptability.

Production Standards: Production Standards will be created by groups at each stage of the production process. Obvious standards include legibility, completeness, neatness, and correct spelling. Other standards might include consistency (e.g., handwriting or printing style, color of ink), writing tool standards (e.g., absence of pencil), and minimal use of correction fluid.

Measuring Performance: Quality Control and Quality Assurance inspectors appointed for each group will have the responsibility for assessing the quality of inputs, as well as finished goods. The QC inspector will inspect finished goods inventory based on the criteria determined by the work group. Unacceptable outputs will be corrected, returned to the line for further processing, or scrapped.

Your instructor will provide you with further instructions on this skill builder.

Source: Michael M. Beyerlein and Susan Tull Beyerlein, "The Quick Brown Fox," _Journal of Management Education,_ Vol. 15 (2), May 1991, p. 268–270.

CHAPTER

15 Individual and Interpersonal Processes

Learning Objectives

After studying this chapter you should be able to

- Describe the relationship between individuals and the organization.

- Identify and discuss basic individual differences and how they can affect work performance.

- Identify and discuss performance-based differences at work.

- Describe the role of stress in organizations.

- Discuss basic interpersonal processes at work.

J ob satisfaction and morale are becoming increasingly important concerns for managers in many different businesses. Survey after survey seems to suggest that managers and workers in the United States are becoming less enthusiastic about their work and less loyal and committed to their organizations.

While a number of solutions to this trend are being explored, one especially interesting strategy has been to focus on humor in the organization. By concentrating on making the workplace fun, some organizations are finding that they can make people want to come to work.

Ben and Jerry's ice cream, for example, has an appointed committee called the joy gang. Its charge is to keep the workplace light and enjoyable. One recent gag: they held Slinky races to inaugurate a new staircase built at corporate headquarters. At a recent meeting of senior executives at Apple Computer, managers were asked to hold their applause and to indicate their approval of speakers by tooting on kazoos instead. And employees at Domino's Pizza headquarters are invited to bring their pets to work every Friday.

Some companies have even taken steps to institutionalize humor. Levi Strauss recently modified its corporate mission statement to include this statement: "Above all, we want satisfaction from accomplishments and friendships, balanced personal and professional lives, and to have fun in our endeavors." It seems that some firms take their fun seriously![1] ∎

H umor plays an important role in most organizations. So, too, do other fundamental individual and interpersonal processes. People's attitudes, for instance, shape how they feel about the organization. Conflict may determine how healthy or dysfunctional various interactions between people will prove to be. And motivation to perform will clearly help determine the effectiveness of the organization.

This chapter introduces and discusses several basic individual and interpersonal processes in organizations. We first discuss the basic relationship between individuals and organizations. Then we examine such psychological individual differences as personality, attitudes, and perception. Performance-based differences are then discussed. Stress is examined next. Finally, we introduce and discuss several basic interpersonal processes. Other critical individual and interpersonal processes—leadership, employee motivation, group dynamics, and managerial communication—are covered in the next four chapters in this part.

Individuals and Organizations

O rganizations are comprised of a collection of individual people—managers, clerical workers, administrators, custodial workers, scientists, and dozens of others. Each of these individuals brings a unique set of contributions to the organization. And each expects to receive certain things from the organization. We begin by examining psychological contracts and the person-job fit.

Psychological Contracts

*A **psychological contract** is the set of expectations held by an individual about what he or she will contribute to the organization and what it will provide in return.*

A **psychological contract** is the set of expectations held by an individual about what he or she will contribute to the organization and what it will provide in return.[2] The nature of a psychological contract is illustrated in Exhibit 15.1. The individual makes a variety of contributions to the organization—effort, skills, ability, time, loyalty, and so forth. These contributions satisfy various needs and requirements of the organization.

In return for these contributions, the organization provides inducements to the individual. Some inducements, like pay, are tangible. Others, like status, are intangible. Just as the contributions from the individual must satisfy needs of the organization, the inducements offered by the

Exhibit 15.1   The Psychological Contract

organization must serve the needs of the individual. That is, if a person accepts employment with an organization because he thinks he will earn an attractive salary and have an opportunity to advance, he will subsequently expect that those rewards will actually be forthcoming.

If both the individual and organization perceive that the psychological contract is fair and equitable, they will be satisfied with the relationship and continue it. But if either party sees an imbalance or inequity in the contract, it may initiate a change. For example, the individual may request a pay raise or promotion, decrease her efforts, or look for a better job elsewhere. The organization can also initiate change by requesting that the individual improve skills through training, transfer the person to another job, or terminate the person's employment altogether.

A basic challenge faced by a firm, then, is to manage psychological contracts. An organization must ensure that it is getting value from its employees. At the same time, it must also be sure that it is providing employees with appropriate inducements. If a firm is underpaying its employees for their contributions, for example, they may perform poorly or leave for better jobs elsewhere. On the other hand, if they are being overpaid relative to their contributions, the firm is incurring unnecessary costs.

The Person-Job Fit

*The **person-job fit** is the extent to which the contributions made by the individual match the inducements offered by the organization.*

One specific aspect of managing psychological contracts is managing the **person-job fit,** the extent to which the contributions made by the individual match the inducements offered by the organization. In theory, each employee has a specific set of needs that he or she wants fulfilled and a set of job-related behaviors and abilities to contribute. If the organization can take perfect advantage of those behaviors and abilities and exactly fulfill the employee's needs, it will have achieved a perfect person-job fit.[3] (Needs and motivation are discussed in Chapter 17.)

Of course, such a precise level of person-job fit is seldom achieved. For example, because organizational selection procedures are imperfect, firms can only estimate employee skill levels when making hiring decisions. Similarly, both people and organizations change. An individual who finds a new job exciting may find the same job monotonous after a few years of performing it. And when the organization adopts new technology it changes the skills it needs from its employees. Finally, because each individual is unique, assessing individual differences simply cannot be done with complete precision.

The Nature of Individual Differences

Individual differences are personal attributes that vary from one person to another. Are specific differences that characterize a given individual good or bad? Do they contribute to or detract from performance? The answer, of course, is that it depends on the circumstances. One person may be dissatisfied, withdrawn, and negative in one job setting but satisfied, outgoing, and positive in another. Working conditions, coworkers, and leadership are also all important ingredients.

Thus, whenever a manager attempts to assess or account for individual differences among

The person must fit the job. As simple as this idea sounds, many times it is not carefully applied. What specifications would you employ, for instance, to assure a good person-job fit for a job such as this one—repairing pipes in highly elevated locations? (William Taufic/Courtesy of Tyco Labs.)

Individual differences are personal attributes that vary from one person to another. Three important individual differences are personality, attitudes, and perception.

employees, he or she must also be sure to consider the situation in which behavior occurs. Individuals who are satisfied or productive in one context may prove to be dissatisfied or unproductive in another. Attempting to consider both individual differences and contributions in relation to inducements and contexts, then, is a major challenge for managers as they attempt to establish effective psychological contracts with their employees and achieve optimal fits between people and jobs.

Personality and Work

Personality is the relatively stable set of psychological and behavioral attributes that distinguish one person from another.

Personality is the relatively stable set of psychological and behavioral attributes that distinguish one person from another.[4] Understanding basic personality attributes is important because they affect people's behavior in organizational situations and their perceptions of and attitudes toward the organization.[5]

Personality Formation An individual's basic personality is formed before he or she ever becomes a member of an organization. But a person's personality can still change as a result of organizational experiences. For example, suppose a manager is subjected to prolonged periods of stress or conflict at work. As a result, the manager may become more withdrawn, anxious, and irritable. While removal of the stressful circumstances may eventually temper these characteristics, the individual's personality may also reflect permanent changes.

From a more positive perspective, continued success and accomplishment at work may cause an individual to become more self-confident and outgoing. But managers should recognize that they can do little to change the basic personalities of their subordinates. Instead, they should

Leslie Harris typifies successful small business operators and entrepreneurs. They seem to have a tenacious personality devoted to making their ideas come to fruition. When Hollywood was cool to Harris's script—a story of a young girl whose plans to get out of the projects are wrecked when she becomes pregnant—she quit her advertising career, lined up backers, and made the film, *Just Another Girl on the IRT.* (Robin Holland.)

work to understand the basic nature of their subordinates' personalities and how attributes of those personalities affect the subordinates' work behavior.

Personality Attributes in Organizations   Several important personality attributes that are particularly relevant to organizations are listed and defined in Table 15.1.

Locus of control is the degree to which a person believes that behavior has a direct impact on its consequences.[6] Some people believe that if they work hard they will succeed. They also believe that people who fail do so because they lack ability or motivation. Because these people believe that each person is in control of his or her life, they have an *internal locus of control.* Other people think that what happens to them is a result of fate, luck, or the behavior of other people. An employee who fails to get a promotion may attribute that failure to a politically motivated boss or to bad luck, rather than to his or her own lack of skills or poor performance. Because these people think that forces beyond their control dictate what happens to them, they have an *external locus of control.*

Locus of control has several implications for managers. Internal locus of control individuals may have a strong desire to participate in the governance of the firm and have a voice in how they do their jobs. Thus they may prefer a decentralized organization and a leader who gives them freedom and autonomy. And they may be most comfortable under a reward system that recognizes individual performance. External locus of control people, on the other hand, may prefer a centralized organization where decisions are made by others. They may also gravitate to structured jobs where standard procedures are defined for them. And they may prefer a leader who makes most of the decisions and a reward system that puts a premium on seniority.

Another important personality characteristic is **authoritarianism**—the extent to which a person believes that power and status differences are appropriate within organizations.[7] A person who is highly authoritarian may accept orders from someone with more authority purely because

Locus of control is the degree to which a person believes that behavior has a direct impact on its consequences.

Authoritarianism is the extent to which a person believes that power and status differences are appropriate within organizations.

A Matter of Ethics

Privacy at Work

Where does an individual's right to privacy begin and end at work? Workplace privacy is shaping up as a major issue in the 1990s. And the authoritarian personality most likely plays a role in how people see this issue.

The issue itself starts with two changes in the workplace. First, new technology has made it easier than ever before to monitor the actions of individuals. Firms like American Express and Disney monitor telephone calls between customers and customer service representatives in order to improve service quality and efficiency. And firms like AT&T and Electronic Data Systems can monitor keyboard activity to better measure individual productivity.

The other change has been a move toward fewer private offices and more open office areas. This shift both allows better use of space and makes people more accessible to one another. But each of these changes—electronic monitoring and open office space—also makes it harder for individuals to maintain privacy at work. Conversations can be easily overheard, for example, and in many instances electronic mail is not as secure as people might think.

Authoritarianism most likely plays a role in how people respond to a loss of workplace privacy. People who are highly authoritarian, for instance, may well feel that everything they do at work is the business of the organization and that privacy is not necessarily a workplace right. But people who are not authoritarian are much more likely to resent any invasion of their privacy by the organization. Thus managers need to be sure to account for individual differences when trying to understand the whole privacy issue in today's organization.[8] ■

the other person is "the boss." But while a person who is not highly authoritarian may still carry out appropriate directives from the boss, he or she is also more likely to question things or express disagreement with the boss. A manager who is highly authoritarian may be autocratic and demanding, and subordinates who are highly authoritarian will be more likely to accept this behavior from their leader. But a manager who is less authoritarian may allow subordinates a bigger role in making decisions, and less authoritarian subordinates will prefer this behavior.[9] A potentially related aspect of authoritarianism is the individual's right to privacy, as explored more fully in *A Matter of Ethics: Privacy at Work.*

Dogmatism is the rigidity of a person's beliefs and his or her openness to other viewpoints.

Dogmatism, another important attribute, is the rigidity of a person's beliefs and his or her openness to other viewpoints.[10] The popular terms for dogmatism are *close-minded* and *open-minded.* For example, suppose a manager has such strong beliefs about how procedures should be carried out that she is unwilling to even listen to a new idea for doing it more efficiently. This

Table 15.1

Key Personality Attributes

Locus of control is the degree to which a person believes that behavior has a direct impact on its consequences.

Authoritarianism is the extent to which a person believes that power and status differences are appropriate within organizations.

Dogmatism is the rigidity of a person's beliefs and his or her openness to other viewpoints.

Self-esteem is the extent to which an individual believes that her or she is a worthwhile and deserving person.

Risk propensity is the degree to which an individual is willing to take chances and make risky decisions.

person is close-minded, or highly dogmatic. Another manager might be very receptive to listening to and trying new ideas. He is more open-minded, or less dogmatic.

Self-esteem is the extent to which an individual believes that he or she is a worthwhile and deserving person.[11] A person with high self-esteem is more likely to seek higher status jobs, be more confident in his or her ability to achieve high levels of performance, and derive greater intrinsic satisfaction from his or her accomplishments. In contrast, a person with less self-esteem may be more content to remain in a lower-level job, be less confident of her or his ability, and focus more on extrinsic rewards.[12]

Risk propensity is the degree to which an individual is willing to take chances and make risky decisions. A manager with a high risk propensity might be expected to experiment with new ideas and gamble on new products. This manager might also lead the organization in new and different directions and be a catalyst for innovation. But the same individual might also jeopardize the continued well-being of the organization if the risky decisions prove to be bad ones. A manager with low risk propensity might lead the organization to a stagnant and overly conservative situation, or help the organization successfully weather turbulent and unpredictable times by maintaining stability and calm. Thus, the potential consequences to a firm of risk propensity are heavily dependent on that firm's environment.

Attitudes and Work

Another aspect of individuals in organizations is their attitudes. **Attitudes** are sets of beliefs and feelings that individuals have about specific ideas, situations, or other people. Attitudes are important because they are the mechanism through which most people express their feelings. An employee's statement that he feels underpaid by the organization reflects his feelings about his pay. Similarly, when a manager says that she likes the firm's new advertising campaign, she is expressing her feelings about the organization's marketing efforts.

Attitudes have three components.[13] The *affective component* reflects feelings and emotions an individual has toward something. The *cognitive component* is derived from knowledge an individual has about something. It is important to note that cognition is subject to individual perceptions (something we discuss more fully later). Thus one person might "know" that a certain political candidate is better than another, while someone else may "know" just the opposite. Finally, the *intentional component* reflects how an individual expects to behave toward or in the situation.

To illustrate these three components, consider the case of a manager who places an order for some supplies for his firm with a new office supply company. Many of the items he orders are out of stock, others are overpriced, and still others arrive damaged. When he calls someone at the supply firm for help, he is treated rudely and gets disconnected before his claim is resolved. When asked how he feels about the new supplier, he might respond, "I don't like that company (affective component). They are the worst office supply firm I've ever dealt with (cognitive component). I'll never do business with them again (intentional component)."

People try to maintain consistency among the three components of their attitudes. However, circumstances sometimes arise that lead to conflicts called **cognitive dissonance**.[14] For example, an individual who has vowed never to work for a big, impersonal corporation intends instead to open her own business. Unfortunately, a series of financial setbacks causes her to have to take a job with a large company. Thus, cognitive dissonance occurs; the affective and cognitive components of the individual's attitude conflict with intended behavior. In order to reduce dissonance, which is usually uncomfortable, the individual might tell herself the situation is only temporary. Or she might revise her cognitions and decide that working for a large company is more pleasant than she had expected.

Attitude Change   Attitudes are not as stable as personality attributes. For example, attitudes may change as a result of new information. A manager may have a negative attitude about a new

---

Margin glossary definitions:

Self-esteem *is the extent to which an individual believes that he or she is a worthwhile and deserving person.*

Risk propensity *is the degree to which an individual is willing to take chances and make risky decisions.*

Attitudes *are sets of beliefs and feelings that individuals have about specific ideas, situations, or other people.*

Cognitive dissonance *occurs when there is a conflict among the three components of an attitude.*

colleague because of the person's lack of job-related experience. After working with the new person, however, the manager may realize that the colleague is actually very talented. The manager may subsequently develop a more positive attitude. Attitudes can also change as a result of changes in the object of the attitude. For example, if employees feel underpaid and have a negative attitude about their pay, a big salary increase may result in more positive attitudes about their pay.

Attitude change can also occur when the object of the attitude becomes less important or relevant to the person. For example, suppose an employee has a negative attitude about the firm's health insurance. When the employee's spouse gets a new job with an organization that has outstanding health insurance benefits, the person's attitude toward his or her own insurance may become more moderate simply because it is no longer a worry. Finally, as noted earlier, individuals may change their attitudes as a way of reducing cognitive dissonance.[15]

Work-Related Attitudes

People form attitudes about many different things. For example, employees may have attitudes about their salary, promotion possibilities, their boss, employee benefits, the food in the company cafeteria, and the color of the company softball team uniforms. But some attitudes are especially critical.

Job satisfaction or *dissatisfaction* is an attitude that reflects the extent to which a person is gratified by or fulfilled in his or her work. Extensive research conducted on job satisfaction suggests that factors such as individual needs and aspirations determine this attitude, along with factors such as relationships with coworkers and supervisors and working conditions, work policies, and compensation.[16] A satisfied employee tends to be absent less often, to make positive contributions, and to stay with the firm. But a dissatisfied employee may be absent more often, may experience stress that disrupts coworkers, and may be continually looking for another job. Contrary to what many managers believe, however, high levels of job satisfaction do not necessarily lead to higher levels of performance. *The Environment of Management: Trends in Morale* discusses recent trends in job satisfaction.

Organizational commitment, another important attitude, reflects an individual's identification with and attachment to the firm. A person with high commitment is likely to see herself as a true member of the organization (for example, referring to the organization in personal terms like "we make high quality products"), to overlook minor sources of dissatisfaction, and to see herself remaining a member of the firm. In contrast, a person with less commitment is more likely to see himself as an outsider (using less personal terms like "they don't pay their employees very well"), to express more dissatisfaction about things, and to not see himself as a long-term member of the organization.

Perception and Work

As noted earlier, an important element of an attitude is the individual's perception of the object about which the attitude is formed. **Perception** is the set of processes by which an individual recognizes and interprets information about the environment. As Exhibit 15.2 illustrates, perception can be deceiving. Since perception plays a role in workplace behaviors, managers need to have a general understanding of basic perceptual processes. At the end of this chapter, the Skill Builder helps you build a better understanding of basic perceptual processes. Two basic perceptual processes that are particularly relevant to managers are selective perception and stereotyping.

Selective perception is the process of screening out information that we are uncomfortable with or that contradicts our beliefs. Suppose a manager is exceptionally fond of a worker. The manager has a positive attitude about the worker and thinks she is a top performer. One day the manager sees that the worker seems to be loafing. Selective perception may cause the manager to ignore what he observed. Similarly, suppose a manager has a negative image of a worker and thinks he is a poor performer. When she sees him working hard, she, too, may ignore it. Selective perception allows us to disregard minor bits of information. On the other hand, if selective perception causes us to ignore important information, it can become a problem.

Job satisfaction or dissatisfaction is an attitude that reflects the extent to which a person is gratified by or fulfilled in his or her work.

Organizational commitment reflects an individual's identification with and attachment to the firm.

Perception is the set of processes by which an individual recognizes and interprets information about the environment.

Selective perception is the process of screening out information that we are uncomfortable with or that contradicts our beliefs.

The Environment of Management

Trends in Morale

The landscape of American business has changed significantly over the past decade or so. One major shift has involved middle managers, those managers between the ranks of supervisors and top management. For decades middle managers dominated organizations, had secure futures, and could pursue a variety of advancement opportunities.

But as U.S. firms went through prolonged periods of cutbacks and downsizing, these conditions changed. Many middle management positions have been eliminated, and those that remain are no longer secure. Moreover, even those middle managers who kept their jobs recognize that they have far fewer doors open above them than they once thought.

Not surprisingly, then, job satisfaction and other attitudes held by middle managers have begun to change, usually negatively. One survey has assessed job-related attitudes for a sample of 750,000 middle managers in the United States for the periods 1985–1987 and 1988–1990. Virtually every attitude reflected a decline between periods.

For example, in the 1985–1987 period, 54 percent of the middle managers expressed a positive attitude about the ability of top management. This figure dropped to 38 percent in the 1988–1990 period. Similar drops were reported in positive attitudes toward the company as a place to work (65 percent versus 55 percent), their company treating them with respect (51 percent versus 43 percent), and top management listening to their complaints and problems (42 percent versus 35 percent).

A bit of a surprise, though, was the change in positive attitude toward pay. It actually increased from 47 percent in 1985–1987 to 52 percent in 1988–1990. Perhaps people are just so happy to have jobs now that any pay is better than none.[17] ∎

Stereotyping is the process of categorizing people on the basis of a single attribute.

Stereotyping is the process of categorizing people on the basis of a single attribute. Common attributes from which people often stereotype are race and sex. Of course, stereotypes along these lines are inaccurate and can be harmful. For example, suppose a manager holds the stereotype that women can only perform certain tasks and that men are best suited for other tasks. To the extent that this affects the manager's hiring practices, he or she is (1) costing the organization valuable talent, (2) violating the law, and (3) behaving unethically. But certain forms of stereotyping can be useful and efficient. Suppose, for example, that a manager believes that communication skills are important for a job and that speech majors tend to have exceptionally good communication skills. As a result, whenever he interviews candidates for jobs he pays close attention to speech majors. To the extent that communication skills do predict performance and that majoring in speech does indeed provide those skills, this form of stereotyping can be beneficial.

Performance-Based Differences and Work

Performance Behaviors

Performance behaviors are the set of work-related behaviors that a firm expects people to display.

Performance behaviors, derived from the psychological contract, are the set of work-related behaviors that a firm expects people to display. Performance behaviors can be narrowly defined and easily measured for some jobs. An assembly line worker who sits by a moving conveyor and attaches parts to a product as it passes by has relatively few performance behaviors. He or she is expected to remain at the work station and correctly attach the parts. Performance can often be assessed quantitatively by counting the percentage of parts correctly attached.

For many other jobs, performance behaviors are more diverse and difficult to assess. For example, consider the case of a research scientist at Merck. The scientist works in a lab trying to find new breakthroughs that have commercial potential. The scientist must apply knowledge with experience. Intuition and creativity are also important elements. The desired breakthrough may take months or even years to accomplish. As we discussed in Chapter 14, organizations rely on a

Exhibit 15.2

Perception Can Be Deceiving. Is "A" a young woman or an old woman? Can the object in "B" exist? Is the hat in "C" taller or wider? Is "D" a goblet or two faces?

A   **B**

C   **D**

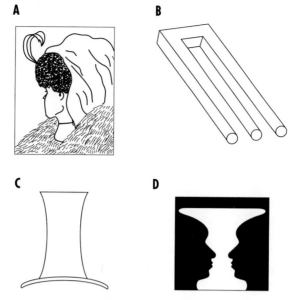

number of different methods for evaluating performance. The key, of course, is to match the evaluation mechanism with the job being performed.

Withdrawal Behaviors

Absenteeism occurs when an individual does not come to work.

Another work-related behavior is that which results in withdrawal from being a committed and contributing member of the organization. **Absenteeism** occurs when an individual does not come to work. The cause may be legitimate (illness or jury duty, for example) or feigned (reported as legitimate but actually just an excuse to stay home). When an employee is absent, his or her work does not get done, or a substitute must be hired to do it. In either case, the quantity or quality of actual output may suffer.[18] Obviously, some absenteeism is expected. The concern of managers is to minimize feigned absenteeism and reduce legitimate absences as much as possible. High absenteeism may be a symptom of other problems, such as dissatisfaction and low morale.

Turnover occurs when people quit their jobs.

    Turnover occurs when people quit their jobs. A firm always incurs costs in replacing individuals who have quit, but if turnover involves especially productive people it is even more costly. Turnover results from aspects of the job, the firm, the individual, the labor market, family influences, and other factors. Of course, some turnover is inevitable and may even be desirable. For example, if the organization is trying to cut costs by reducing its work force, having people choose to leave is preferable to having to terminate them. And if the people who choose to leave are low performers or express high levels of job dissatisfaction, the organization may also benefit from turnover.

Organizational Citizenship

Organizational citizenship is the behavior of individuals that makes a positive overall contribution to the organization.

Organizational citizenship is the behavior of individuals that makes a positive overall contribution to the organization.[19] Consider, for example, an employee who does work that is acceptable in terms of both quantity and quality. However, she refuses to work overtime, will not help newcomers learn the ropes, and is generally unwilling to make any contribution to the organization beyond the strict performance of her job. While this person may be seen as a good performer, she is not likely to be seen as a good organizational citizen. Another employee may exhibit the same level of performance. In addition, however, he always works late when the boss asks, takes time to help newcomers learn their way around, and is helpful and committed to the organization's success. While his level of performance may be seen as equal to that of the first worker, he is also likely to be seen as a better organizational citizen.

The determinant of organizational citizenship behaviors is a complex mosaic of individual, social, and organizational variables. For example, the personality and attitudes of the individual have to be consistent with citizenship behaviors. Similarly, the situation in which the individual works needs to facilitate and promote such behaviors. And the organization itself, especially its culture, must be capable of promoting, recognizing, and rewarding these types of behaviors if they are to be maintained.[20]

Stress at Work

Stress is an individual's response to a strong stimulus.

A stimulus that causes stress is called a stressor.

Stress generally follows a cycle referred to as the General Adaptation Syndrome, or GAS.

Another important individual process in organizations is stress. **Stress** is an individual's response to a strong stimulus.[21] This stimulus is called a **stressor.** Stress generally follows a cycle referred to as the **General Adaptation Syndrome,** or GAS,[22] shown in Exhibit 15.3. According to this view, when an individual first encounters a stressor, the GAS is initiated and the first stage, alarm, is activated. He or she may feel panic, may wonder how to cope, and may feel helpless. For example, suppose a manager is told to prepare a detailed evaluation of a plan by the firm to buy one of its competitors. His first reaction may be, "How will I ever get this done by tomorrow?"

If the stressor is too intense, the individual may feel unable to cope and never really try to respond to its demands. In most cases, however, after a short period of alarm, the individual gathers some strength and starts to resist the negative effects of the stressor. For example, the manager with the evaluation to write may calm down, call home to say he's working late, roll up his sleeves, order out for coffee, and get to work. Thus, at Stage 2 of the GAS, the person is resisting the effects of the stressor.

In many cases, the resistance phase may end the GAS. If the manager is able to complete the evaluation earlier than expected, he may drop it in his briefcase, smile to himself, and head home tired but satisfied. On the other hand, prolonged exposure to a stressor without resolution may bring on Stage 3 of the GAS, exhaustion. At this stage, the individual literally gives up and can no longer resist the stressor. The manager, for example, might fall asleep at his desk at three A.M. and never finish the evaluation.

We should note that stress is not all bad.[23] In the absence of stress, we may experience lethargy and stagnation. An optimal level of stress, on the other hand, can result in motivation and

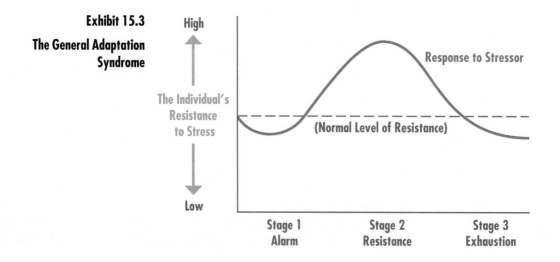

Exhibit 15.3

The General Adaptation Syndrome

High

The Individual's Resistance to Stress

Low

Response to Stressor

(Normal Level of Resistance)

Stage 1
Alarm

Stage 2
Resistance

Stage 3
Exhaustion

Table 15.2 **Common Causes of Stress**	*Organizational Stressors* (stressors derived primarily from the organizational context in which the person works)
	Task demands associated with the task itself
	Physical demands associated with the job setting
	Role demands associated with position in group or organization
	Interpersonal demands associated with working relationships
	Life Change (stressors derived from the rate of change in a person's life)

excitement. Too much stress, however, can have negative consequences. It is also important to understand that stress can be caused by "good" as well as "bad" things. Excessive pressure, unreasonable demands on our time, and bad news can all cause stress. But receiving a bonus and then having to decide what to do with the money can be stressful. So, too, can receiving a promotion, gaining recognition, and similar "good" things.

Type A individuals are extremely competitive, very devoted to work, and have a strong sense of time urgency.

Type B individuals are less competitive, less devoted to work, and have a weaker sense of time urgency.

One important line of thinking about stress focuses on **Type A** and **Type B** personalities.[24] Type A individuals are extremely competitive, very devoted to work, and have a strong sense of time urgency. They are likely to be aggressive, impatient, and very work-oriented. They have a lot of drive and want to accomplish as much as possible as quickly as possible. Type B individuals are less competitive, less devoted to work, and have a weaker sense of time urgency. Such individuals are less likely to experience conflict with other people and more likely to have a balanced, relaxed approach to life. They are able to work at a constant pace without time urgency. Type B people are not necessarily more or less successful than are Type A people. But they are less likely to experience stress. The Self-Assessment in this chapter measures your Type A or Type B personality. Whether or not your instructor assigns this activity, it might be useful for you to complete the Self-Assessment to understand yourself better.

Causes of Stress

Stress is obviously not a simple phenomenon. As listed in Table 15.2, several different things can cause stress.[25]

Organizational Stressors Organizational stressors fall into one of four categories—task, physical, role, and interpersonal demands.[26] *Task demands* are associated with the task itself. Some occupations are inherently more stressful than others. Having to make fast decisions, decisions with less than complete information, or decisions that have relatively serious consequences are some of the things that can make some jobs stressful. The jobs of surgeon, airline pilot, and stockbroker are relatively more stressful than the jobs of general practitioner, airplane baggage loader, and office receptionist. Though a general practitioner makes important decisions, he is also likely to have time to make a considered diagnosis and fully explore a number of different treatments. But during surgery the surgeon must make decisions quickly, while realizing that the wrong one may endanger her patient's life.

Physical demands are stressors associated with the job setting. Working outdoors in extremely hot or cold temperatures or even working in an improperly heated or cooled office can lead to stress. A poorly designed office, which makes it difficult for people to have privacy or promotes too little social interaction, can result in stress, as can poor lighting and inadequate work surfaces. Even more severe stressors are actual threats to health. Examples include jobs like coal miner, toxic waste handler, and police officer.[27]

Role demands can also cause stress. (Roles are discussed more fully in Chapter 18). A role is a set of expected behaviors associated with a position in a group or organization. Stress can result either from role ambiguity or role conflict that people can experience in groups.[28] For exam-

Table 15.3

Life Change and Stress

Rank	Life event	Mean value
1	Death of spouse	100
2	Divorce	73
3	Marital separation	65
4	Jail term	63
5	Death of close family member	63
6	Personal injury or illness	53
7	Marriage	50
8	Fired at work	47
9	Marital reconciliation	45
10	Retirement	45
11	Change in health of family member	44
12	Pregnancy	40
13	Sex difficulties	39
14	Gain of new family member	39
15	Business readjustment	39
16	Change in financial state	38
17	Death of close friend	37
18	Change to different line of work	36
19	Change in number of arguments with spouse	35
20	Mortgage over $10,000	31
21	Foreclosure of mortgage or loan	30
22	Change in responsibilities at work	29
23	Son or daughter leaving home	29
24	Trouble with in-laws	29
25	Outstanding personal achievement	28

ple, an employee who is feeling pressure from her boss to work longer hours while also being asked by her family for more time at home will almost certainly experience stress. Similarly, a new employee experiencing role ambiguity because of the organization's poor orientation and training practices will also suffer from stress.

Interpersonal demands are stressors associated with relationships that confront people in organizations. For example, group pressures regarding restriction of output (producing less than people are capable of producing) and norm conformity (meets the expectations of others) can lead to stress. Leadership style may also cause stress. An employee who feels a strong need to participate in decision making may feel stress if his or her boss refuses to allow participation. And individuals with conflicting personalities may experience stress if required to work too closely together. A person with an internal locus of control might be frustrated when working with someone who prefers to wait and just let things happen.

The causes of stress may also lie in events that are less connected to people's daily work lives. Some of these may have nothing to do with a person's work at all, while others may be work-related only in a general way. One early perspective was called life change, that is, any meaningful change in a person's personal or work situation.[29] According to this view, major changes in a per-

Rank	Life event	Mean value
26	Spouse beginning or stopping work	26
27	Beginning or ending school	26
28	Change in living conditions	25
29	Revision of personal habits	24
30	Trouble with boss	23
31	Change in work hours or conditions	20
32	Change in residence	20
33	Change in schools	20
34	Change in recreation	19
35	Change in church activities	19
36	Change in social activities	18
37	Mortgage or loan less than $10,000	17
38	Change in sleeping habits	16
39	Change in number of family get-togethers	15
40	Change in eating habits	15
41	Vacation	13
42	Christmas	12
43	Minor violations of the law	11

The amount of life stress that a person has experienced in a given period of time, say one year, is measured by the total number of life change units (LCUs). These units result from the addition of the values (shown in the right-hand column) associated with events that the person has experienced during the target time period.

Source: Reprinted from the *Journal of Psychosomatic Research*, Vol. 11, Thomas H. Holmes and Richard H. Rahe, "The Social Adjustment Rating Scale," pp. 213–218, 1967, with kind permission from Pergamon Press, Ltd., Oxford, U.K.

son's life can lead to stress. For example, when people finish college they have more responsibilities, usually have more money, often get married, and so forth. And each of these events represents a significant life change.

Table 15.3 summarizes the relative effects of different types of life change. Some of these changes (such as marriage and outstanding personal achievement) are positive while others (such as the death of a spouse and serving a jail term) are negative. Early research suggested that higher total point values were likely to lead to health problems. It was suggested that a total of 150 life change units within a one-year period was associated with a 50 percent chance of major illness the following year.[30] While this view provides some instructive viewpoints on stress, current thinking has advanced beyond these relatively simplistic ideas.

Consequences of Stress

As noted earlier, the results of stress may be positive or negative. The negative consequences may be behavioral, psychological, or medical.[31] Behaviorally, for example, stress may lead to detrimental or harmful actions, such as smoking, alcoholism, overeating, and drug abuse. Other stress-induced behaviors are accident proneness, violence toward self or others, and appetite disorders.

High-performance, high-involvement organizations may also be high stress organizations. Such organizations may provide testing to monitor the stress of members, such as that shown here, as well as programs to reduce that stress. These programs may include counseling as well as physical exercise at organizational facilities. (Jeffrey Lowe/ONYX.)

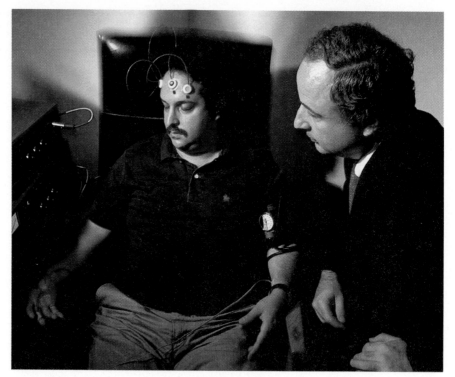

Psychological consequences of stress interfere with an individual's mental health and well-being. These outcomes include sleep disturbances, depression, family problems, and sexual dysfunction. Managers are especially prone to sleep disturbances when they experience stress at work.[32] Medical consequences of stress affect an individual's physiological well-being. Heart disease and stroke have been linked to stress, as have headaches, backaches, ulcers and related disorders, and skin conditions such as acne and hives.[33]

Individual stress also has direct consequences for businesses. For an operating employee, stress may translate into poor quality work and lower productivity. For a manager, it may mean faulty decision making and disruptions in working relationships. Withdrawal behaviors can also result from stress. People who are having difficulties with stress in their jobs are more likely to call in sick or to leave the organization. More subtle forms of withdrawal may also occur. A manager may start missing deadlines, for example, or start taking longer lunch breaks. Employees may also withdraw by developing feelings of indifference.[34] The irritation displayed by people under great stress can make them difficult to get along with. Job satisfaction, morale, and commitment can all suffer as a result of excessive levels of stress. So, too, can motivation to perform.

Burnout is a feeling of exhaustion that may develop when someone experiences too much stress for an extended period of time.

Another consequence of stress is **burnout,** a feeling of exhaustion that may develop when someone experiences too much stress for an extended period of time.[35] Burnout results in constant fatigue, frustration, and helplessness. Increased rigidity follows, as do a loss of self-confidence and psychological withdrawal. The individual dreads going to work, often puts in longer hours but gets less accomplished than before, and exhibits mental and physical exhaustion. Because of the damaging effects of burnout, some firms are taking steps to help avoid it. For example, British Airways provides all of its employees with training designed to help them recognize the symptoms of burnout and develop strategies for avoiding it.[36]

Managing Stress

Given the potential consequences of stress, it follows that both people and organizations should be concerned about how to limit its more damaging effects. Numerous ideas and approaches have been developed to help manage stress. Some are strategies for individuals, while others are strategies for organizations.[37]

Exercise One way people manage stress is through exercise. People who exercise regularly feel less tension and stress and are more self-confident and more optimistic. Their better physical condition also makes them less susceptible to many common illnesses. People who do not exercise regularly, on the other hand, tend to feel more stress and are more likely to be depressed.[38] They are also more likely to have heart attacks. And because of their physical condition they are more likely to contract illnesses.

Relaxation Another method people use to manage stress is relaxation. Relaxation allows individuals to adapt to, and therefore better deal with, their stress. Relaxation comes in many forms, such as taking regular vacations. A recent study found that people's attitudes toward a variety of workplace characteristics improved significantly following a vacation.[39] People can also learn to relax while on their jobs. For example, some experts recommend that people take regular rest breaks during their normal workday.

Time Management People can also use time management to control stress. The idea behind time management is that many daily pressures can be reduced or eliminated if individuals do a better job of managing time. One approach to time management is to make a list every morning of the things to be done that day. The items on the list are then grouped into three categories: critical activities that must be performed, important activities that should be performed, and optional or trivial things that can be delegated or postponed. The individual performs the items on the list in their order of importance.

Support Groups Finally, people can manage stress through support groups. A support group can be as simple as a group of family members or friends to enjoy leisure time with. Going out after work with a couple of coworkers to a basketball game or a movie, for example, can help relieve stress built up during the day. Family and friends can help people cope with stress on an ongoing basis and during times of crisis. For example, an employee who has just learned that she did not get the promotion she has been working toward for months may find it helpful to have a good friend to lean on, to talk to, or to yell at.[40] People also may make use of more elaborate and formal support groups. Community centers or churches, for example, may sponsor support groups for people who have recently gone through a divorce, the death of a loved one, or some other tragedy.

Organizational Stress Programs Organizations are also beginning to realize that they shouldbe involved in helping employees cope with stress. One argument for this is that since the business is at least partially responsible for stress, it should also help relieve it. Another is that stress-related insurance claims by employees can cost the organization considerable sums of money. Still another is that workers experiencing lower levels of detrimental stress will be able to function more effectively. AT&T has initiated a series of seminars and workshops to help its employees cope with the stress they face in their jobs. The firm was prompted to develop these seminars for all three of the reasons noted above.[41]

A wellness stress program is a special part of the organization specifically created to help deal with stress. Organizations have adopted stress management programs, health promotion programs, and other kinds of programs for this purpose. The AT&T seminar program noted earlier is similar to this idea, but true wellness programs are ongoing activities that have a number of different components. They commonly include exercise-related activities as well as classroom instruction programs dealing with smoking cessation, weight reduction, and general stress management.

Some companies are developing their own programs or using existing programs of this type.[42] Johns-Manville, for example, has a gym at its corporate headquarters. Other firms negotiate discounted health club membership rates with local establishments. For the instructional part of the program, the organization can either sponsor its own training or perhaps jointly sponsor seminars with a local YMCA, civic organization, or church. Organization-based fitness programs facilitate employee exercise, a very positive consideration, but such programs are also quite costly. Still, more and more companies are developing fitness programs for employees.[43]

Interpersonal Processes at Work
The Nature of Working Relationships

Thus far we have focused primarily on characteristics of individuals in organizations. But work in organizations is done by people working together. Therefore we also need to examine some fundamental interpersonal processes at work.

The nature of working relationships in an organization is as varied as the individual members themselves. Personality and attitudes, as well as numerous other factors, affect working relationships in many different ways. At one extreme these relationships can be personal and positive. This occurs when the parties know each other, share mutual respect and friendship, and enjoy interacting with one another. Two managers who have known each other for years and are close personal friends will likely interact at work in a relaxed and effective fashion. At the other extreme, relationships at work can have quite a negative cast. This is most likely the case when the parties dislike one another, do not have mutual respect, and do not enjoy interacting with one another. Suppose, for example, one manager has fought openly for years to block the advancement of another manager. If the second manager eventually gets promoted, their relationship will most likely be strained and difficult.

Effective working relationships promote collaboration and cooperation, people working together toward the best interests of the organization. Good working relationships throughout a firm can be a tremendous source of synergy.

Most working relationships fall between these extremes, as members of the organization interact in a professional way focused on goal accomplishment. A professional relationship is more or less formal and structured and highly task directed. Two managers may respect each other's work and recognize the professional competence that each brings to the job. The fact that they may have few common interests and little to talk about other than their jobs will probably not be a factor in the quality of their work.

Poor interpersonal relations at work can result in excessive competition and conflict.

Working relationships, whether positive and professional or negative, exist among individuals, among groups, and among individuals and groups. They can also change over time. Two managers with a negative relationship, for example, might eventually resolve their disputes and develop a more positive and professional relationship. Similarly, people may also expand mutual professional respect into real friendship.

Collaboration and Cooperation

From a pure performance standpoint, effective working relationships promote collaboration and cooperation, people working together toward the best interests of the organization. Good working relationships throughout a firm can be a tremendous source of synergy. People who support one another and who work well together can accomplish much more than people who do not. They focus more fully on meeting their goals and accomplishing their tasks, for example, and they are more inclined to help each other. And even when people are working individually, the presence of good relations minimizes emotional distractions.

Positive working relationships can also serve as a solid basis for social support in a firm.

When people offer reassurance and encouragement to one another, they are providing social support. Suppose an employee receives a poor performance review or is denied a promotion. Others in the firm can commiserate because they share a common frame of reference—the organization's culture, an understanding of the causes and consequences of the event, and so forth.[44]

Competition and Conflict

On the other side of the coin, poor interpersonal relations at work can result in excessive competition and conflict. Like stress, competition and conflict may be either good or bad.[45] When there is absolutely no competition or conflict, performance often tends to be very low. This stems primarily from the fact that people are often motivated by competition and spurred to action because they think their way of doing something is better than someone else's. Thus, as conflict increases, so too may performance. At some point, however, conflict reaches its highest effective point. Additional conflict then begins to hurt performance.

Causes of Conflict

Several things can cause conflict. One very common reason for conflict is the interdependencies that exist among people or groups within the organization.[46] For example, consider the case of an assembly line in a Volvo automobile plant. Work is performed in large blocks by teams of workers and then is passed from one team to another. If one team does not do its job properly, or gets too far ahead or behind in its work, it causes problems for the next group.

Competition among people or groups can also cause conflict, especially when the stakes are high. For example, if a company establishes a sales contest among sales groups and plans to award a two-week vacation in Hawaii to the winning group, conflict is likely: the stakes are high, and when one group wins, all the others lose. Differences in goals and activities can also lead to conflict. For example, if marketing wants to increase product lines to boost sales while production wants to reduce product lines to cut costs, conflict may result. Finally, personalities might also come into play. Two people may be unable to work together, or simply not be able to get along.

Consequences of Conflict

Just as there are several causes of conflict, there are also several consequences. One major consequence is hostility. Withdrawal is also a distinct possibility. The withdrawal may be confined to such things as refusing to socialize with others, or it might extend to actually leaving the organization. On a more positive note, conflict may also increase motivation. People who have a mild disagreement may each become more motivated to prove that the other is wrong. Finally, performance can also be increased via conflict. For example, consider the case of two plant managers within the same company who disagree over the best way to improve productivity. Each may be allowed to pursue his or her own ideas, and each may develop new techniques that do actually improve productivity. Thus the overall performance of the company increases, and each manager can feel like a "winner."

Controlling Conflict

Given the importance of competition and conflict to managers, it follows that they need to know how to control them. One approach is to increase resources. For example, if two departments are competing for access to a new computer network, it may be wise to expand the network so that each department can have full access. Rules and standard operating procedures can be established to better manage interdependencies. Setting overall goals can also help prevent conflict. We earlier used an example of potential conflict between the marketing department's goal to increase sales and the production department's goal to cut costs. The manager may get the two departments to agree that an overall goal of optimizing sales increases and cost cuts is best. Finally, interpersonal relations may also be manageable. For example, if a manager knows that one employee is a chain smoker and another is an aggressive nonsmoker, the manager might make sure that their offices are as far apart as possible and try to minimize their interactions.

Resolving Conflict   Of course, regardless of the manager's best intentions, conflict is still likely to occur. Fortunately, there are several things that can be done to resolve conflict. One technique is avoidance. As the term implies, avoidance involves ignoring the problem and hoping it will go away. If the conflict is minimal, avoidance may work. However, it should not be used simply because the manager does not want to deal with the problem. Smoothing is similar to avoidance. Here, though, the manager acknowledges the existence of the conflict but also downplays its importance. Like avoidance, smoothing may be effective if used wisely, but sometimes the conflict is simply too great to go away on its own.

Compromise involves reaching a point of agreement between what each of the conflicting parties initially wanted. Of course, like other strategies, compromise must be used with care. It is possible that both parties will end up feeling like they lost. Finally, the conflict might be resolved through confrontation. Confrontation is the direct approach of addressing the conflict and working together to resolve it. For example, Control Data Corporation recently established a peer review committee to deal with grievances. Two randomly chosen peers of the aggrieved employee and one "disinterested" executive hear the complaints and help determine the best course of action.

Chapter Summary

The basic relationship between individuals and organizations is defined by a psychological contract, the expectations of an individual about what he or she will contribute to the organization and what it will provide in return. One key aspect of managing psychological contracts is enhancing the person-job fit.

Individual differences are personal attributes that vary from one person to another. Key personality attributes include locus of control, authoritarianism, dogmatism, self-esteem, and risk propensity. Important job-related attitudes include job satisfaction or dissatisfaction and organizational commitment. Important perceptual processes are selective perception and stereotyping.

Actual performance is an important performance behavior. So, too, are withdrawal behaviors like absenteeism and turnover. Organizational citizenship is also important.

Individual stress usually follows the General Adaptation Syndrome. Type A and B individuals react to stress quite differently. Stress is caused by such organizational stressors as task, physical, role, and interpersonal demands. Life change also causes stress. Consequences of stress include behavioral, psychological, and medical outcomes, lower performance, and burnout. Individuals and organizations can each help manage stress.

Working relationships vary significantly. Collaboration and cooperation are most effective. Competition has some benefits but can also lead to difficulties. Conflict is an important outcome that has to be carefully managed.

The Manager's Vocabulary

psychological contract	attitudes	absenteeism
person-job fit	cognitive dissonance	turnover
individual differences	job satisfaction	organizational citizenship
personality	job dissatisfaction	stress
locus of control	organizational commitment	stressor
authoritarianism	perception	General Adaptation Syndrome (GAS)
dogmatism	selective perception	Type A
self-esteem	stereotyping	Type B
risk propensity	performance behaviors	burnout

Review Questions

1. What is a psychological contract?
2. Identify and define several basic personality attributes relevant to organizations.
3. What are the three components of an attitude? What does an individual experience if there is a conflict or inconsistency among these components?

4. Identify several factors that cause stress. Identify several consequences of stress.
5. Name several things that can cause conflict.

Analysis Questions

1. What can an individual do if he or she wants to change the psychological contract he or she has with an organization?
2. Characterize yourself on each of the personality traits discussed in the chapter.
3. Select an important attitude that reflects how you feel about something. Try to recall how this attitude was formed, and break it down into its three components.

4. What causes stress for you? How do you deal with it?
5. Suppose a manager thought there was too little conflict in the organization. Would it be ethical to stimulate conflict? What are the inherent dangers in doing this?

Self-Assessment

Behavior Activity Profile: A Type A Measure

Introduction In this chapter, we discuss many different dimensions of an individual's personality, attitudes, and behaviors. One of the topics is the cause of stress. This Self-Assessment allows you to understand better the traits that might cause stress for you.

Instructions Each of us displays certain kinds of behaviors and thought patterns of personal characteristics. For each of the twenty-one sets of descriptions below, circle the number that you feel best describes where you are between each pair. The best answer for each set of descriptions is the response that most nearly describes the way you feel, behave, or think. Respond in terms of your regular or typical behavior, thoughts, or characteristics.

DESCRIPTIONS

1. I'm always on time for appointments.

   7 6 5 4 3 2 1   I'm never quite on time.

2. When someone is talking to me, chances are I'll anticipate what he or she is going to say by nodding, interrupting, or finishing sentences.

   7 6 5 4 3 2 1   I listen quietly without showing any impatience.

3. I frequently try to do several things at once.

   7 6 5 4 3 2 1   I tend to take things one at a time.

4. When it comes to waiting in line (at banks, theaters, etc.), I really get impatient and frustrated.

   7 6 5 4 3 2 1   It simply doesn't bother me.

5. I always feel rushed.

   7 6 5 4 3 2 1   I never feel rushed.

6. When it comes to my temper, I find it hard to control at times.
7 6 5 4 3 2 1
I just don't seem to have one.

7. I tend to do most things like eating, walking, and talking rapidly.
7 6 5 4 3 2 1
Slowly.

TOTAL SCORE 1–7 _____ = S

8. Quite honestly, the things I enjoy most are job-related activities.
7 6 5 4 3 2 1
Leisure-time activities.

9. At the end of a typical workday, I usually feel like I needed to get more done than I did.
7 6 5 4 3 2 1
I accomplished everything I needed to.

10. Someone who knows me very well would say that I would rather work than play.
7 6 5 4 3 2 1
I would rather play than work.

11. When it comes to getting ahead at work, nothing is more important.
7 6 5 4 3 2 1
Many things are more important.

12. My primary source of satisfaction comes from my job.
7 6 5 4 3 2 1
I regularly find satisfaction in nonjob pursuits, such as hobbies, friends, and family.

13. Most of my friends and social acquaintances are people I know from work.
7 6 5 4 3 2 1
Not connected with my work.

14. I'd rather stay at work than take a vacation.
7 6 5 4 3 2 1
Nothing at work is important enough to interfere with my vacation.

TOTAL SCORE 8–14 _____ = J

15. People who know me well would describe me as hard driving and competitive.
7 6 5 4 3 2 1
Relaxed and easygoing.

16. In general, my behavior is governed by a desire for recognition and achievement.
7 6 5 4 3 2 1
What I want to do—not by trying to satisfy others.

17. In trying to complete a project or solve a problem, I tend to wear myself out before I'll give up on it.
7 6 5 4 3 2 1
I tend to take a break or quit if I'm feeling fatigued.

18. When I play a game (tennis, cards, etc.), my enjoyment comes from winning.
7 6 5 4 3 2 1
The social interaction.

19. I like to associate with people who are dedicated to getting ahead.
7 6 5 4 3 2 1
Easygoing and take life as it comes.

20. I'm not happy unless I'm always doing something.
7 6 5 4 3 2 1
Frequently, "doing nothing" can be quite enjoyable.

21. What I enjoy doing most are competitive activities.
7 6 5 4 3 2 1
Noncompetitive pursuits.

TOTAL SCORE 15–21 _____ = H

For interpretation, turn to the back of the book.

Source: From *Organizational Behavior and Management*, 3rd ed. by John M. Ivancevich and Michael T. Matteson, pp. 274–276. Reprinted by permission of the publisher, Richard D. Irwin, Inc. © Richard D. Irwin, Inc., 1990 and 1993.

Skill Builder

Assumptions that Color Perceptions

Purpose Perceptions rule the world. In fact, everything we know or think we know is filtered through our perceptions. Our perceptions are rooted in past experiences and socialization by significant others in our life. This skill builder focuses on the human resources model. It will help you develop the mentor role of the human resources model. One of the skills of the mentor is self-awareness.

Introduction This skill builder is designed to help you become aware of how much our assumptions influence our perceptions and evaluations of others. It also illustrates how we compare our perceptions with others to find similarities and differences.

Instructions

1. Read the descriptions of the four individuals provided in the Personal Descriptions below.
2. Decide which occupation is most likely for each person and place the name by the corresponding occupation in the Occupations list that follows. Each person is in a different occupation and no two people hold the same one.

Personal Descriptions

R. B. Red is a trim, attractive woman in her early 30s. She holds an undergraduate degree from an eastern woman's college and is active in several professional organizations. She is an officer (on the national level) of Toastmistress International.

Her hobbies include classical music, opera, and jazz. She is an avid traveler, who is planning a sojourn to China next year.

W. C. White is a quiet, meticulous person. W. C. is tall and thin with blond hair and wire-framed glasses. Family, friends, and church are very important and W. C. devotes any free time to community activities.

W. C. is a wizard with figures but can rarely be persuaded to demonstrate this ability to do mental calculations.

G. A. Green grew up on a small farm in rural Indiana. He is an avid hunter and fisherman. In fact, he and his wife joke about their "deer-hunting honeymoon" in Colorado.

One of his primary goals is to "get back to the land" and he hopes to be able to buy a small farm before he is fifty. He drives a pickup truck and owns several dogs.

B. E. Brown is the child of wealthy professionals who reside on Long Island. Mr. Brown, B. E.'s father, is a "self-made" financial analyst who made it a point to stress the importance of financial security as B. E. grew up.

B. E. values the ability to structure one's use of time and can often be found on the golf course on Wednesday afternoons. B. E. dresses in a conservative upper-class manner and professes to be "allergic to polyester."

Occupations

Choose the occupation that seems most appropriate for each person described. Place the name in the spaces next to the corresponding occupations.

_____   Banker

_____   Labor negotiator

_____   Production manager

_____   Travel agent

_____   Accountant

_____   Teacher

_____   Computer operations manager

_____   Clerk

_____   Army general

_____   Salesperson

_____   Physician

_____   Truck driver

_____   Financial analyst

Source: Jerri L. Frantzve, *Behaving in Organizations,* Boston: Allyn & Bacon, 1983, pp. 63–65.

CONCLUDING CASES

15.1 Attitudes at General Motors

Attitudes play a major role in all organizations. And at few places are they more critical today than at General Motors. GM is going through the painful process of closing plants and terminating thousands of workers. The attitudes of those workers, combined with those of managers involved in making critical decisions, are key to the potential success of GM's efforts.

Two plants in particular provide a marked contrast in workers' attitudes at GM. Workers at each plant know that they are working at a plant that may be closed and that they are fighting for job survival. One plant is the GM facility in Orion Township, in Michigan. Orion is one of GM's newest plants, built in the late 1980s. Most workers at Orion were transferred to the plant when older plants were shut down.

Orion workers take a very adversarial posture toward GM. Most are long-time members of the United Auto Workers, or UAW. Moreover, because they are primarily from Michigan and grew up in the auto industry, they are accustomed to the relatively high wages and benefits paid to UAW members.

The UAW leadership at Orion wants as little as possible to do with employee involvement. Some of the union leaders believe that product quality is something that should not concern them. They feel that their workers should follow orders but do nothing more, and that it's management's job to worry about quality and improvement.

There is also considerable hostility among the workers themselves at Orion. Fights are common, for example, and police investigations are routine. Company data suggests that Orion ranks twenty-second among GM's twenty-eight plants in terms of productivity, and a recent spot check found unacceptable defects in eighty-eight of one hundred cars.

The GM factory in Oklahoma City provides a sharp contrast to Orion. Most workers at this plant are in their first UAW-represented job. The wages and benefits they receive, while comparable to those in other auto plants, are somewhat higher than those of other Oklahoma workers in the manufacturing sector.

When the Oklahoma City workers realized that their jobs were endangered, they rallied behind management to help improve productivity and quality at the plant. For example, they have willingly adopted several popular Japanese management techniques, such as just-in-time and employee involvement. These and other changes have helped make the Oklahoma City plant one of the most productive facilities owned by GM.

Many of the workers there eagerly volunteer for the plant's various training programs. Between fifty and one hundred employees per day receive training in everything from equipment operation to computer manufacturing to preparation for high-school equivalency tests. In contrast to most GM facilities, the training at Oklahoma City is provided by union members rather than by management.[47]

Discussion Questions

1. Speculate about how attitudes were formed at these two GM plants.
2. What other individual and interpersonal processes are illustrated in this case?
3. If GM chooses to close one of these plants, which do you think it will be?

15.2 Perceptions and Attitudes Between Japan and the United States

Japan and the United States are a marked study in contrasts. The two countries dominate the world's economy. Consumers freely buy the same products and services. U.S. consumers, for example, drive Honda and Toyota automobiles and listen to Sony stereos. Just as eagerly, consumers in Japan wear U.S. clothing and eat U.S. fast food.

Given these similarities in buying and consuming behavior, it seems a bit strange that each should see the other country so very differently. But cultural differences are so great and centuries of misunderstanding are so strong that differences in perceptions and attitudes between the two countries are indeed quite profound.

Take people from the United States, for example. One recent survey found that only 13 percent of Americans believe they know a lot about Japan. Forty-two percent indicated they knew some things, and 45 percent indicated that they did not know very much about Japan. When a sample of Japanese was asked the same question, 5 percent said they knew a lot, 42 percent said they knew some things, and over half (51 percent) said that they did not know very much.

In terms of specific characteristics, Americans and Japanese do hold a few similar perceptions about the other. For example, people in each country admire the degree of scientific and technical accomplishment and respect for family life about the same. And each group sees the other as being relatively friendly and nonviolent.

But again the differences far outweigh the similarities. For example, the Japanese have much higher admiration for Americans for their form of government (63 percent), role in world leadership (84 percent), freedom of expression (89 percent), variety of lifestyles (86 percent), leisure time (88 percent), and treatment of women (68 percent) than Americans do for the Japanese (23, 31, 27, 25, 15, and 20 percent, respectively). Similarly, Americans admire the Japanese for their industriousness (88 percent) and educational institutions (71 percent) much more than the Japanese admire Americans for the same characteristics (27 and 48 percent, respectively).

Moreover, Japanese people see Americans as being moderately competitive, somewhat lazy, not very hard working, not very crafty, and somewhat poorly educated. Along these dimensions, Americans see Japanese as being extremely competitive, not lazy at all, extremely hard working, very crafty, and quite well educated.

Finally, Americans and Japanese see their competitive strengths and weaknesses quite differently as well. For example, two-thirds of Americans believe that Japan unfairly keeps U.S. products out of its country, while only one-third of the Japanese feel this same way. Almost half of the Japanese, in contrast, feel that U.S. firms do so poorly in Japan primarily because their products are not as good as those made by Japanese firms. Only 22 percent of Americans hold this same opinion.[48]

Discussion Questions

1. What are the implications of the survey data reported in this case for a U.S. manager doing business in Japan?
2. What are the implications of the survey data reported in this case for a Japanese manager doing business in the United States?
3. Which survey results came as a surprise to you? Which data do you agree with? Which do you disbelieve?

CHAPTER

16

Leadership

Learning Objectives

After studying this chapter you should be able to

· Define leadership, indicate the difference between leadership and management, and identify the challenges of leadership.

· Name and describe several types of power, including their uses, limits, and outcomes.

· Briefly discuss the trait approach to the study of leadership.

· Discuss leadership behaviors and compare and contrast the Michigan and Ohio State studies with contemporary views.

· Describe several situational approaches to leadership, including the LPC model, the path-goal model, the participation model, and an integrative framework for these models.

· Discuss such contemporary perspectives on leadership as charismatic, transformational, and symbolic leadership; and substitutes and neutralizers of leadership.

T. J. Rogers, CEO of Cyprus Semiconductor Corporation, is a bit of a maverick even in an industry noted for unique managers. Rogers originally gained national attention with his "killer software," software that monitors inventories or delivery dates and shuts down vital systems when items sit too long in inventory or deliveries are not on time. Because people who succeed get credit for it, the software has worked wonders at Cyprus. Parts that used to sit for up to two hundred days in inventory now never exceed ten days, and on-time delivery went from only 65 percent to more than 90 percent in one year.

Five feet eight inches tall, Rogers nevertheless played both high school and college football. In 1975 with a Ph.D. in electrical engineering, he failed at a project at Advanced Microsystems Inc. and was fired. He next went to Advanced Micro Devices and in 1983 got the financial backing to form Cyprus. These experiences led him to expect a great deal of himself (he routinely puts in thirteen-hour workdays, for instance) as well as of everyone else who works for his company.

He uses stress interviews for employees to assure that they can handle the pressure of high performance in a company where mottoes such as "Be realistic—demand the impossible" abound. Rogers can be abrasive and blunt in criticizing managers, but turnover averages only about 12 percent a year. Rogers feels that the small size of Cyprus is an advantage and says that his philosophy of management is to "Think small, think efficient, think flexible."

Rogers is a private person. He tries to keep his weekends free for cooking, visiting restaurants, or taking in a movie. Arnold Schwarzenegger movies are among his favorites. When he takes a vacation, he pushes to do as much as he can during that time, relentlessly pursuing experiences on vacation as he pursues success in his business.

Though Cyprus lost about $10 million in its first year of operation (1984), it has made money every year from 1986 on, and earnings were approaching $60 million in 1992. A soft market in the early 1990s decreased its earnings as it did for virtually all of the firms in the industry, but with careful cost controls, Rogers expected to recover quickly when the market improved.[1] ∎

T. J. Rogers reflects a valuable but relatively uncommon mix of two key ingredients that are often needed to run a major corporation—managerial ability and leadership ability. Whereas managerial ability relies heavily on relatively objective talents and skills, leadership ability is more intangible. Most observers agree that it is difficult to understand, much less practice, effective leadership.

This chapter first explains the nature of leadership and then defines power and its relationship to leadership. After looking briefly at early trait models of leadership, it examines in more detail behavioral approaches. Much of its attention, however, is focused on situational approaches. The chapter concludes by discussing other contemporary perspectives on leadership.

The Nature of Leadership

Leadership is an influence process that is directed at shaping the behavior of others.

We can define **leadership** as an influence process directed at shaping the behavior of others.[2] Various tactics can be used when attempting to influence others.[3] When Don Shula exhorts the members of the Miami Dolphins to play harder, he is leading with one set of influence tactics. When Jack Welch, CEO of General Electric, encourages his managers to work harder, he is leading with another. And when a friend convinces you to try a new restaurant you have been avoiding, he is also leading.

The study of leadership covers more than a century, and the books, articles, and papers on it number in the thousands.[4] While this chapter is not intended to be a comprehensive review of that literature, the material in this chapter does reflect major consensus views supported by extensive research.[5] Thus popularized views of leadership for which supporting research does not exist

Leaders face many challenges. When Patricia Flynn became Dean of the Graduate School of Business at Bentley College, one of her major challenges was to develop programs through which students would learn to routinely examine decisions with an ethical angle. Her vision was for students to become actively involved with the community and to work with non-profit organizations as ways of developing this ability. (Joanne Rathe/The Boston Globe.)

are not included. This does not imply that to follow their prescriptions would be in error; it does imply that sufficient research to support their claims does not now exist.

Leadership occurs in a variety of settings and in a variety of ways. Before discussing the various forms of leadership, however, let us first make a clearer distinction between leadership and management and then explore some of the challenges of leadership.

Leadership Versus Management

Leadership and management are in some ways similar but in more ways different.[6] People can be leaders without being managers, managers without being leaders, or both managers and leaders at the same time. Nevertheless, there do appear to be some differences between the two roles, as indicated in Table 16.1.

In creating an action agenda, managers are more likely to emphasize planning and budgeting, while leaders tend to focus more on direction. In focusing on the human element necessary to achieve that agenda, managers tend to think in terms of organizing and staffing, while leaders seem more concerned with communication and cooperation. In carrying out that agenda, managers tend to focus on problem solving and control, while leaders emphasize motivation.

The bases of power used by managers and leaders also tend to differ. Managers can direct the efforts of others because of their formal organizational power and control of resources. If a department head tells a member of the department to do three things and the person does exactly what was dictated but nothing else, the department head is probably being a manager but not a leader. When Bill Marriott instructs a hotel manager to increase the size of the hotel's catering staff, he is acting as a manager. A leader, on the other hand, does not have to rely on the formal position to influence someone but may rely more on expertise or personality. If a secretary organizes a group effort to help a coworker who has personal problems, this person is acting as a leader but not as a manager.

From the standpoint of organizational effectiveness, people who are both leaders and managers are a valuable resource.[7] Such individuals are able to carry out their managerial responsibilities effectively while also commanding the loyalty and respect of those they lead. But they are

Table 16.1

Differences Between Management and Leadership

	Management	Leadership
Creating an Action Agenda	Focuses on planning and budgeting	Concentrates on establishing direction
Achieving That Agenda	Thinks in terms of organizing and staffing	Concerned with communication and cooperation
Carrying Out That Agenda	Focuses on problem solving and control	Emphasizes motivation
Bases of Power	Formal organizational position and control of resources	Expertise and personality

Source: Adapted with the permission of The Free Press, A Division of MacMillan, Inc. from *A Force for Change: How Leadership Differs from Management* by John P. Kotter. Copyright © 1990 by John P. Kotter, Inc.

also quite scarce and usually quite successful at doing almost anything they set out to do. To help you understand leadership better, the Skill Builder in this chapter asks you to prepare a set of interview questions and then interview someone you think is a leader and someone you think is a manager. This will help you develop a conceptual framework for leadership.

The Challenges of Leadership

In order to fulfill others' expectations of them, leaders must confront numerous challenges. In large measure, the success of any leader depends on his or her ability to address these challenges in a way that people will accept. Although any number of challenges are inherent in a given situation, three are relatively constant: multiple constituencies, unpopular decisions, and diversity.

*One leadership challenge is having to satisfy **multiple constituencies,** different groups that may want different things from the organization.*

Multiple Constituencies   Satisfying **multiple constituencies** means that the leader must attempt to deal with several different people and groups at the same time in a way that is relatively acceptable to every party. This concern is compounded by the fact that the different constituencies often desire conflicting things from the organization. Employees may demand higher wages, while stockholders desire bigger dividends. Consider the case of Lee Iacocca. While at Chrysler, Iacocca has had dealings with the government, union officials, suppliers, creditors, competitors, and employees. One of his major challenges has been to see that each is in basic agreement with what he feels needs to be done to rebuild the company's health. T. J. Rogers must also deal with unions, customers, suppliers, competitors, and stockholders.

Another leadership challenge is having to make decisions that are unpopular with others.

Unpopular Decisions   Hand in hand with the notion of multiple constituencies is the simple fact that leaders occasionally have to make decisions that are unpopular, at least among some of their constituents. When Iacocca closed plants, employees at those plants clearly were unhappy. Bill Marriott encountered considerable resistance when he announced the decision to sell some of the company's restaurant operations. The mark of a good leader is the ability to recognize when such decisions must be made and having the perseverance to see them through.[8]

Diversity holds tremendous promise for management.

Diversity   Managers and leaders are both becoming more diverse as a group and are having to deal with groups that are composed of more diverse members than in the past. Organizations can gain a great deal by taking advantage of the skills such diverse groups possess, but if organizations are not careful, they could also alienate members of these diverse groups and suffer rather than gain from the increasingly diverse labor force worldwide.

Clearly, organizational members from different nations bring rich and valuable perspectives to bear on problems. They may also bring communication problems and misunderstandings. Developing organizational members versed in international experience and capable of communicating in more than one language is vital to all organizations attempting to do business internationally, but it can also be useful to any organization.

Demographic issues—race, gender, age, ethnic origins, region of the country—are also becoming significant to leadership and organizations. There is some evidence that effective leaders display the same behaviors regardless of sex.[9] On the other hand, there is also some evidence that suggests that the behaviors are different.[10] Race has likewise been a subject with mixed results.[11] Age issues have received less attention, but there is some research to suggest that managers who lead groups composed of people who are older than they are face considerable difficulties.[12] Despite the difficulties inherent in highly diverse organizations, the potential benefits certainly seem to outweigh the costs.

In addition to these three critical challenges, leaders have others. They must set good examples for their followers, they must continually monitor situations so that new actions can be taken as needed, and they must develop the potential of employees in the organization. Leaders need to use their power wisely and without infringing on the rights and privileges of others. Finally, leaders must be ethical in all of their dealings. *A Matter of Ethics: What's True at America West* indicates the complexity of some of these issues to managers. In the next section we turn our attention to a more detailed consideration of power in organizational settings.

Power and Leadership

The foundation of leadership is power. Leaders have power over their followers and wield this power to exert their influence. The various kinds of power can be used in several different ways.

Types of Power

Legitimate, reward, and coercive power derive from a person's formal position in an organization; expert and referent power involve personal abilities and traits.

Most people agree that there are five basic types of power: legitimate, reward, coercive, expert, and referent power.[13]

Legitimate power is power created and conveyed by the organization. It is the same as authority. The person formally in charge of a group can generally tell group members how they should be doing their jobs, how they should allocate their time at work, and so forth. Legitimate power alone does not make someone a leader. All managers have legitimate power, but only some of them are leaders. As we have seen, orders and requests from someone with legitimate power may be carried out by others but only to the minimum extent needed to satisfy the person in charge.[14]

A second type of power is **reward power**—the power to grant and withhold various kinds of rewards. Typical rewards in organizations include pay increases, promotions, praise, recognition, and interesting job assignments. The greater the number of rewards a manager controls and the more important they are to others, the more reward power the manager has.

Coercive power is the power to force compliance through psychological, emotional, or physical threat. In some settings, such as the military and prisons, coercion may take the form of physical force. In most settings today, though, coercion is practiced more subtly, through verbal reprimands, disciplinary layoffs, fines, demotions, the loss of privileges, and excessive public criticism. As with reward power, the more punitive elements a manager can bring to bear and the more important they are to those reporting to that manager, the more coercive power he or she has. However, the use of coercion also tends to increase hostility and resentment.

A Matter of Ethics

What's True at America West

In 1981 Edward R. Beauvais founded America West Airlines, one of the last upstarts begun during the deregulation of the airline industry. After an ambitious start the company lost $45 million in 1987 and looked doomed. But in 1988 it reported a profit of just over $9 million. Further, Beauvais stunned critics, who felt that the airline had gotten into trouble by expanding too fast, by announcing expansion to Hawaii, Australia, and other points in the Pacific Basin as well as new routes to New York and Washington, D.C.

By 1991, America West was again in serious trouble. As losses mounted, it filed for protection under Chapter 11 of the bankruptcy laws in June 1991. Laid-off employees who had been loaned money to buy stock as a condition of employment were asked to repay the loans. Meanwhile the value of the stock plummeted though the dollar amount of the loans stayed constant. Needless to say, the employees felt abused and angry.

By mid-1992, Beauvais was out. His CEO, Michael J. Conway, who had been instrumental in cutting costs by reshuffling routes and reducing the number of employees, took over. Conway was quoted as saying that Beauvais had to leave because he was associated with the expansionist practices that had gotten the company in trouble. The move was also meant to show investors that America West was serious about turning things around. Beauvais, on the other hand, told a radio talk show host that the company continued to be in bad trouble. He said that more layoffs were imminent, flights would be cut, and the Hawaii route would soon be terminated. Conway responded that Beauvais had misstated the situation and given misinformation. Customers, investors, and employees wondered whom to believe and what the future would bring.[15] ■

Expert power is power based on knowledge and expertise. A manager who knows the best way to deal with a difficult customer or a secretary who knows the ins and outs of the organization's bureaucracy has expert power. The more important the knowledge is and the fewer people who are aware of it, the more expert power the person has.

The fifth type of power is **referent power.** It is referent power that generally sets leaders apart from nonleaders. This type of power is based on personal identification, imitation, and charisma. If a child dresses and talks like his favorite rock singer, the rock singer has referent power over the child. If an ambitious middle manager starts to emulate a successful top manager (dressing like her, going to the same restaurants for lunch, playing the same sports, and so on), the top manager has referent power. This aspect of leadership is covered again later, when we look at charisma.

Most leaders use several different bases of power at the same time. For example, no matter how effective an individual is as a leader, he or she will sometimes find it necessary to rely on legitimate power. Indeed, many managers who lack leadership characteristics are still somewhat effective by using legitimate and reward power together. Likewise, leaders are often successful by combining expert and referent power.

Uses, Limits, and Outcomes of Power

Uses of Power   There are numerous ways in which power may be used.[16] For one, the manager can make a legitimate request—that is, simply ask someone to do something that falls within the normal scope of the job. The manager may also try to gain instrumental compliance—that is, use reward power by letting the person know that if he or she does what is needed, a reward will be forthcoming.

Coercion is the use of coercive power to get one's way. In the business context, it involves

Position power, which is derived from titles and locations within organizations, can be useful to a leader. However, expertise is even more useful. Carl Ware began as an urban specialist with Coca-Cola before rising from manager of corporate external affairs in 1986 to President of Coca-Cola's Africa Group in 1991. (Ann States/SABA.)

threatening a group member. For example, a manager might tell a group member that he will be fired if he does not perform a specific action. A more reasonable approach might be rational persuasion, convincing the group member that compliance is in everyone's best interest. Suppose a manager is trying to initiate a wage reduction. Clearly, most employees will not be enthusiastic, but if the manager can convince everyone that the cuts are necessary and that they will be temporary, people may be more receptive.

Personal identification and inspirational appeals are also used. These approaches derive from referent power. The idea is that the leader strives to set a good example and attempts to inspire others to follow it. For example, Sam Walton, founder of Wal-Mart, was one of the richest men in America. Yet he lived very unpretentiously and treated all Wal-Mart employees as his equal.

Finally, managers occasionally distort information to get their way. Of course, this misuse of expert power can be dangerous and frequently backfires. Consequently, it should seldom, if ever, be used.

Limits and Outcomes of Power   Regardless of the manager's skill, power always has its limits. As a general rule, people can only be influenced up to a point. Moreover, their willingness to follow someone may be quite short-lived. Few leaders can maintain long-term support for their ideas and programs when mistakes are made and faulty decisions are implemented.

*When managers attempt to use power, they may encounter **commitment, compliance,** or **resistance.***

When group members are confronted with an attempt by the person in charge to influence them, they usually have one of three basic responses: commitment, compliance, and resistance. **Commitment** is the outcome when the manager is also a leader. People are committed to the person and therefore respond favorably to her attempt to influence them. **Compliance** occurs when the person in charge is strictly a manager but has little leadership quality; employees go along with the request but do not have any stake in the result. Finally, **resistance** occurs when the manager's power base is weak or inconsistent with the situation. In this case employees actively resist the attempt to influence them.

Table 16.2 summarizes the outcomes of different kinds of power uses. In particular, it shows

Source of leader influence	Type of outcome		
	Commitment	*Compliance*	*Resistance*
Legitimate Power	*Possible*—If request is polite and very appropriate	*Likely*—If request or order is seen as legitimate	*Possible*—If arrogant demands are made or request does not appear proper
Reward Power	*Possible*—If used in a subtle, very personal way	*Likely*—If used in a mechanical, impersonal way	*Possible*—If used in a manipulative, arrogant way
Coercive Power	*Very unlikely*	*Possible*—If used in a helpful, nonpunitive way	*Likely*—If used in a hostile or manipulative way
Expert Power	*Likely*—If request is persuasive and subordinates share leader's task goals	*Possible*—If request is persuasive but subordinates are apathetic abooout task goals	*Possible*—If leader is arrogant and insulting or subordinates oppose task goals
Referent Power	*Likely*—If request is believed to be important to leader	*Possible*—If request is perceived to be unimportant to leader	*Possible*—If request is for something that will bring harm to leader

Source: Table adapted by Gary A. Yukl from information in John R. P. French, Jr., and Bertram Raven, "The Bases of Social Power," in *Studies in Social Power*, Dorwin P. Cartwright, ed. (Ann Arbor: Institute for Social Research, the University of Michigan, 1959), pp. 150–167. © 1955. Data used by permission of the Institute for Social Research.

Table 16.2   Outcomes of the Uses of Power

when commitment, compliance, and resistance are likely or possible in different power bases and situations.

In sum, then, various kinds, uses, and outcomes of power are relevant in organizational settings. We are now ready to look more closely at leadership itself. Through the years writers have focused on three distinct approaches to studying and describing leadership, called the trait, behavioral, and situational approaches.[17]

Leadership Traits

Leadership traits *were thought to be stable and enduring characteristics that set leaders apart from nonleaders.*

One early systematic approach to the study of leadership was the trait approach, whose adherents assumed that great leaders such as Napoleon, Lincoln, and Gandhi possessed a set of stable and enduring **leadership traits** or characteristics that set them apart from followers. Their goal was to identify these traits so that they could be used as a basis for selecting managers.

A great deal of attention was focused on the search for traits, and researchers studied common traits such as intelligence, height, self-confidence, attractiveness, and vocabulary.[18] But, unfortunately, traits proved to be ineffective predictors of leadership. For one thing, the list of characteristics soon grew to such lengths that it became unmanageable. For another, the list of exceptions was almost as long as the list of leaders who possessed each trait. For instance, it has been suggested that leaders are taller than nonleaders, but many historical leaders (such as Napoleon and Hitler) and contemporary leaders (like H. Ross Perot) are of slight build.

Scholars soon realized that the search for leadership traits was interesting but of little scientific merit. Consequently, they started focusing attention on other areas instead. However, despite the failure of researchers to identify a replicable set of traits, many people cling to the trait notion.[19] Scholars, on the other hand, next turned to the study of leadership through what we now call the behavioral approach.

Leadership Behaviors

Whereas the trait approach attempted to identify characteristics that differentiated leaders from nonleaders, the behavioral approach sought to define behaviors that set effective leaders apart from ineffective leaders. Although numerous **leadership behaviors** have been found, those identified by two major sets of studies have received special attention.[20]

The Michigan Studies

*The **leadership behavior** approach attempted to differentiate leaders from nonleaders on the basis of their behaviors.*

The Michigan studies identified two forms of leadership behavior: job centered and employee centered.

Researchers at the University of Michigan identified two critical leadership behaviors, called job-centered behavior and employee-centered behavior.[21] A leader who practices job-centered behavior engages in close supervision so that the performance of those reporting to him can be monitored and controlled. His interests are primarily in getting the job done, and he takes an active role in explaining this task.

In contrast, employee-centered behavior focuses on reaching high levels of performance by building a sense of team spirit through the human element of the workplace. An employee-centered leader is concerned with developing a desire to achieve high levels of performance among her group members through paying attention to the members of the group. She is willing to let employees have a voice in how they do their jobs, and she tries to develop job satisfaction and group cohesion.

The Michigan researchers felt that job-centered and employee-centered behaviors represent a single dimension, with one of the two basic behaviors at each end. That is, they believed that if leaders become more job centered, they simultaneously become less employee centered, and vice versa. They also felt that leaders who were employee centered would generally be more effective managers than leaders who were primarily job centered. That is, their employees would perform at a higher level and also be more satisfied.

The Ohio State Studies

The Ohio State studies suggested that leaders could choose initiating structure and/or consideration behaviors.

Researchers at Ohio State University identified many of the same concepts as those developed in Michigan but also extended and refined them.[22] They agreed that there were two critical leadership behaviors, which they called initiating structure behavior and consideration behavior. Initiating structure behavior, similar but not identical to job-centered behavior, focuses on getting the job done. Consideration behavior involves employee satisfaction and friendliness. It is like only part of employee-centered behavior since it does not have the high performance focus found in employee-centeredness.

The basic difference between the Ohio State and Michigan findings is shown in Exhibit 16.1. As we have noted, the Michigan researchers argued that leaders could be job centered or employee centered, but not both. The Ohio State researchers, however, found that the two forms of leader behavior they identified were independent. Therefore, as the exhibit shows, a leader can use initiating structure behavior and consideration at the same time.

Much of the early research of Ohio State was conducted with managers from International Harvester (now known as Navistar). In general, the researchers found that high initiating structure behavior resulted in higher performance but also led to lower levels of job satisfaction. High levels of consideration behavior caused higher levels of job satisfaction but lower levels of performance. However, they also found that there were numerous other types of leader behavior that could be important, depending on the situation. Clearly, the dynamics of leader behavior are complex and anything but straightforward.

Exhibit 16.1
Leadership Behaviors

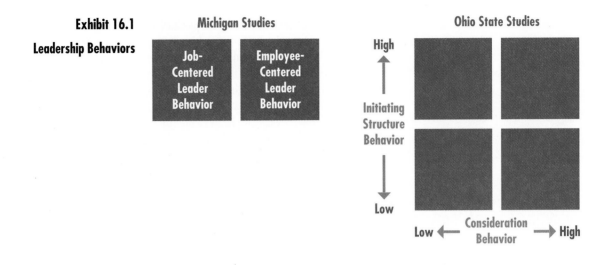

Michigan Studies

| Job-Centered Leader Behavior | Employee-Centered Leader Behavior |

Ohio State Studies

High ↑ Initiating Structure Behavior ↓ Low

Low ← Consideration Behavior → High

A Contemporary View

As behavioral research continued, numerous categories of leader behavior were identified. As each researcher used his or her own labels, a bewildering array of lists of leader behaviors emerged. However, one approach to integrating them seems both defensible in terms of research and understandable and useful to practicing managers.[23] That approach is shown in Exhibit 16.2.

This approach suggests that the previously identified two categories of leader behavior can readily be seen to consist of four major categories: Building Relationships, Giving-Seeking Infor-

Exhibit 16.2
Leader Behaviors

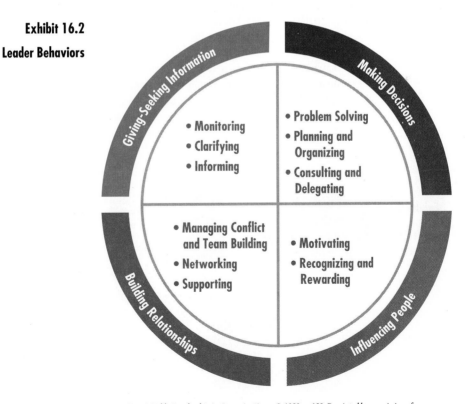

Giving-Seeking Information

- Monitoring
- Clarifying
- Informing

Making Decisions

- Problem Solving
- Planning and Organizing
- Consulting and Delegating

Building Relationships

- Managing Conflict and Team Building
- Networking
- Supporting

Influencing People

- Motivating
- Recognizing and Rewarding

Source: Gary A. Yukl, *Leadership in Organizations,* © 1989, p. 129. Reprinted by permission of Prentice-Hall, Englewood Cliffs, New Jersey.

mation, Making Decisions, and Influencing People. Each of those categories, in turn, can be refined still further (and, indeed, even further refinements are obviously possible). The resulting eleven categories are readily understandable and learnable. However, as had been found in the Ohio State studies, research has shown that effective leaders use different combinations of these behaviors in different situations. Thus, there is no one best set of leader behaviors.

Further, numerous skills have been found to be associated with effective leadership.[24] While considerably more research is needed to clearly identify those skills, some are rather obvious. Leaders need interpersonal skills, particularly those associated with communication, persuasiveness, and tact. Leaders need conceptual skills, particularly those associated with problem solving. And leaders need technical and administrative skills. However, the particular technical skill needed will vary with the situation. Indeed, it is clear from this research that no one type of skill or leadership fits all situations. **Leadership style** refers to combinations of skills and behaviors. This means that there is no one best style but rather that style must fit circumstance.

Leadership style refers to combinations of skills and behaviors.

Indeed, the notion that one style of leadership will always be appropriate has been unacceptable for many years. Researchers have shifted their efforts to the development of contingency models of leadership, which attempt to define those circumstances in which one style of leadership is best and those in which an alternative style will be more appropriate. The next section introduces several interesting contingency models of leadership.

Situational Approaches

Contingency, or situational, approaches to leadership attempt to specify circumstances under which different kinds of leadership behavior are appropriate.

Earlier in the book we investigated the nature of **contingency,** or **situational, approaches** to management. Leadership was one of the very first areas in which situational theories were developed. Exhibit 16.3 illustrates the differences between behavioral approaches and situational approaches. The behavioral approach is represented by the two boxes linked with the solid arrow. The basic premise is that appropriate leadership behaviors lead to desired group member responses. For instance, the Michigan researchers assumed that employee-centered behavior would always lead to employee performance and satisfaction.

Situational approaches, in contrast, introduce the third box into the exhibit. They suggest that situational, or contingency, factors must be considered. Whereas one kind of behavior will work in one setting, a different setting may well dictate a different form of behavior. The goal of situational approaches is to define the situational variables that managers need to consider in assessing how different forms of leadership will be received.

Exhibit 16.3

Situational Approaches to Leadership

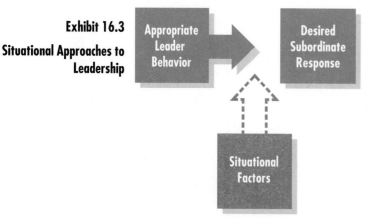

Although a few early researchers noted the potential importance of situational factors, these factors did not receive widespread attention until the 1960s. Since then, however, virtually all approaches to leadership have adopted a situational view. The three most widely known situational theories—the LPC model, the path-goal model, and the participation model—are described next.[25]

The LPC Model

*The **LPC model** suggested that appropriate leadership behavior is a function of the favorableness of the situation.*

The first of these contingency models of leadership, called the **LPC** (for least preferred coworker) **model**, was developed by Fred E. Fiedler.[26] Fiedler suggested that appropriate forms of leadership style varied as a function of the favorableness of the situation.

Leadership Styles The LPC model includes two basic forms of leadership style, task oriented and relationship oriented. The task-oriented style is similar to the earlier job-centered and initiating structure behaviors, and the relationship-oriented style is like employee-centered and consideration behaviors. The name of the model is derived from a questionnaire developed to measure task-oriented and relationship-oriented style. People who complete the questionnaire do so in reference to the employee with whom they least prefer to work, their least preferred coworker.

One interesting aspect of the LPC model is that leadership style is assumed to be a stable personality trait of the leader. That is, some leaders use one style and others use a different style, and these styles are basically constant. Any given leader is unable to change his or her behavior.

*In the LPC model, the favorableness of the situation is determined by **leader-member relations, task structure,** and **position power.***

Favorableness of the Situation As we noted, the LPC model sees appropriate leadership behavior as a function of the favorableness of the situation. Favorableness is defined by three elements—leader-member relations, task structure, and position power.

Leader-member relations defines the nature of the relationship between the leader and the members of the group. If the relationship is characterized by confidence, trust, liking, and respect, it is defined as good and is favorable for the leader. In contrast, if the relationship lacks confidence, trust, and respect, and if the leader and the followers do not like each other, the relationship is bad and unfavorable for the leader.

Task structure is the degree to which the group's task is well defined and understood by everyone. If the task is highly structured, the situation is probably more favorable.

Finally, **position power** is the power vested in the leader's position. Strong power is favorable for the leader, and weak power is unfavorable. Thus the best possible situation is good leader-member relations, a structured task, and strong position power. The worst situation is poor relations, an unstructured task, and weak power.

Styles and Situations Exhibit 16.4 illustrates how leadership styles combine with the situation to determine group effectiveness. Note that the situation can be defined in eight unique ways. The left side of the chart represents the best situation. As the situation progresses to the right, however, it gets gradually worse.

The line above the situations predicts which style of leadership will be most effective in each situation. A task-oriented leader (using controlling, active, structuring leadership) will be most effective in the best and the worst situations, whereas a relationship-oriented leader (permissive, passive, considerate) will have better chances in situations of intermediate favorableness.

For example, suppose John has just been appointed the chairman of a task force to develop a new grievance procedure. The task force contains several of John's peers, so his position power is weak. The company has no grievance procedure at present, and John has been given no guidelines to follow, so the task is unstructured. Finally, John has had some interpersonal problems—poor

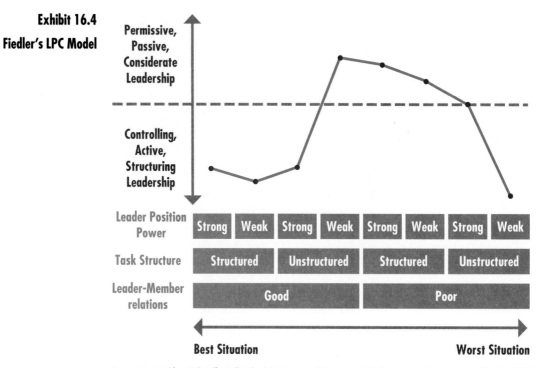

Exhibit 16.4
Fiedler's LPC Model

Source: Reprinted from "The Effects of Leadership Training and Experience: A Contingency Model Interpretation," by Fred. E. Fiedler published in *Administrative Science Quarterly,* Vol. 17, No. 4, December 1972, p. 455, Figure 1, by permission of *Administrative Science Quarterly.*

relations—with a few of the other committee members in the past. If John is by nature a task-oriented leader, the contingency model predicts he will have greater success with the group than if he is a relationship-oriented leader.

On balance, the LPC model has received mixed research support. For example, people have questioned its assumptions about the flexibility of leadership style and how it defines situations. There are also major questions about the questionnaire that is used to measure leadership behavior. At the same time, it was a major approach that attracted our attention to the situation as an important part of leadership.[27]

The Path-Goal Model

*The **path-goal model** of leadership suggests that leaders should attempt to determine their group members' goals and then clarify the paths to achieving them.*

The **path-goal model** also provides interesting insights into the situational nature of leadership. This model essentially suggests that the purpose of leadership in organizational settings is to clarify for organization members the paths to desired goals. That is, leaders should determine what employees want from their jobs and then show them how to acquire those things through their work.[28] The basic framework of the path-goal model is shown in Exhibit 16.5.

Leadership Styles   Like the other models discussed so far, the path-goal model includes one task-oriented style and one employee-oriented style, called directive and supportive leadership. It also includes an additional one, however, called participative leadership. Participative leadership is the extent to which the leader allows group members to participate in decisions that affect them.

Exhibit 16.5

The Path-Goal Model

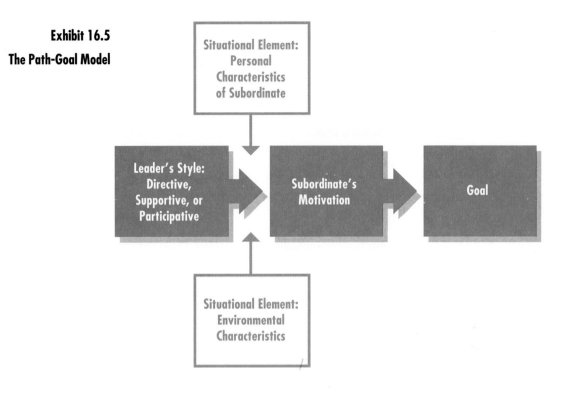

Situational Elements   As shown in the exhibit, there are two sets of situational factors that intervene between the leader's behavior and the group member's motivation: the group member's personal characteristics and environmental characteristics.

The personal characteristics of group members include such things as perceptions of their own ability, desire to participate in organizational activities, and willingness to accept direction and control. Environmental characteristics include the extent to which the task is highly structured, the nature of the work group, and the authority system within the organization.

Styles and Situations   The LPC model is very precise. In contrast, the path-goal model is very general and suggests that the leader needs to use a lot of common sense. The path-goal model also assumes that a leader's style is flexible and that he or she can change this style as needed.

In using the model, then, a manager should assess the relevant dimensions of the situation and choose an appropriate combination of behaviors that will complement that situation. For instance, suppose that a group member lacks confidence in her abilities and is assigned to a new task that is highly unstructured. It may be appropriate in this situation for the group leader to be highly directive in order to clarify the member's task demands and reduce her anxiety about being able to get the job done. Similarly, if group members want to participate, the leader needs to consider allowing them to do so, whereas if they have no desire to participate, the leader may not even have to think about it.

The path-goal model is still in the early stages of development, and several variations exist. It has received generally favorable support from research, however, and will probably continue to be developed and used in the future.[29]

The Participation Model

*The **participation model** helps managers determine how much participation employees should be allowed in making various kinds of decisions.*

The final situational model to be discussed here is the **participation model,** which involves a much more narrow aspect of leadership than do the preceding models. In particular, it addresses the specific question of how much group members should be allowed to participate in decision making.[30] As with the other models, the participation model includes alternative styles and situational factors to consider.

Leadership Styles   The model includes five different degrees of participation:

AI: The manager makes the decision alone, with no input from group members (the A stands for autocratic).

AII: The manager asks group members for information that he or she needs to make the decision but still makes the decision alone. Group members may or may not be informed of the decision.

CI: The manager shares the situation with selected group members and asks for information and advice. The manager still makes the decision but keeps the group actively informed (the C stands for consultative).

CII: The manager meets with the whole group at one time to discuss the situation. Information is freely shared, although the manager still makes the decision.

GII: The manager and the group meet and freely share information, and the entire group makes the decision (the G stands for group).

Situational Elements   The participation model suggests that a manager needs to ask several questions before choosing a degree of participation. Moreover, different questions are used for different circumstances. In some cases, the manager will have a group-related problem to address, whereas in other cases the problem will relate more to an individual. In addition, in some cases the goal will be to make a decision as quickly as possible, whereas in other situations the manager will be striving to help an individual or group improve its decision-making skills.

Styles and Situations   Styles and situations are combined in a very structured and precise fashion in the participation model, as illustrated in the decision tree presented in Exhibit 16.6. This particular tree is suggested for a group problem when time is important. The questions involved in the situation are listed above the diagram. The manager asks each in order and answers high or low, yes or no. Depending on the manager's answer to any given question, he or she follows the appropriate path on the tree to the next question. Ultimately, each path ends with a suggested decision-making style. This style is the one that optimizes group members' acceptance of the decision, the quality of the decision (from the organization's standpoint), and the demands on the manager's time.

In general, the participation model has been supported by research and accepted by managers.[31] Of course, it should not be followed too rigidly. Managers should recognize that it provides a set of guidelines rather than a set of rules that should always be followed.

An Integrative Framework

An integrative framework suggests that different elements of the various approaches to leadership can be combined to produce effective leadership in different situations.

Recently, a framework to integrate these diverse results has been devised.[32] As shown in Exhibit 16.7, the framework includes all of the major factors discussed so far—power, traits, behavior, and situations.

This framework essentially suggests that leadership is a complex phenomenon rather than a simple one. It also suggests that all the approaches to leadership have merit and that they should be seen as complementary rather than contradictory. All other things being equal, traits do make a difference in leadership. Given the careful selection process in many organizations, however, managers will have such similar traits that power or behavior will essentially make the difference in terms of performance.

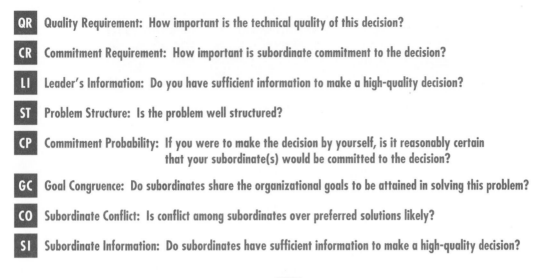

QR Quality Requirement: How important is the technical quality of this decision?

CR Commitment Requirement: How important is subordinate commitment to the decision?

LI Leader's Information: Do you have sufficient information to make a high-quality decision?

ST Problem Structure: Is the problem well structured?

CP Commitment Probability: If you were to make the decision by yourself, is it reasonably certain
        that your subordinate(s) would be committed to the decision?

GC Goal Congruence: Do subordinates share the organizational goals to be attained in solving this problem?

CO Subordinate Conflict: Is conflict among subordinates over preferred solutions likely?

SI Subordinate Information: Do subordinates have sufficient information to make a high-quality decision?

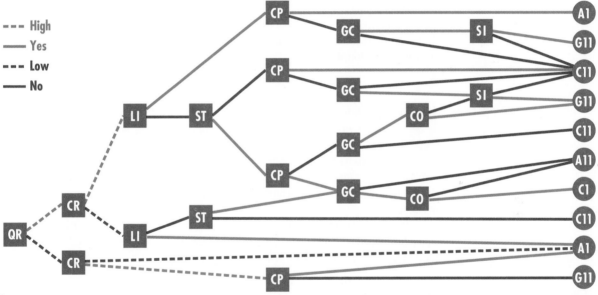

Source: Reprinted from *The New Leadership: Managing Participation in Organizations* by Victor H. Vroom and Arthur G. Jago, 1988, Englewood Cliffs, N.J.: Prentice-Hall. Copyright 1987 by V. H. Vroom and A. G. Jago. Used with permission of the authors.

Exhibit 16.6   Time-Driven Group Problem Decision Tree for the Participation Model

The situation is shown as surrounding the other components of the framework in order to convey the idea that its impact is general rather than particular. That is, it affects everything, not just one or a few aspects. The situation can influence which behavior is appropriate for leaders, as in the situational models, and it can influence which forms of power are available to the leader. Also, of course, it can directly influence results beyond the leader's impact. For example, a shortage of materials may hinder performance in ways the leader cannot control. Understanding the situation, then, is the key to being an effective managerial leader.[33]

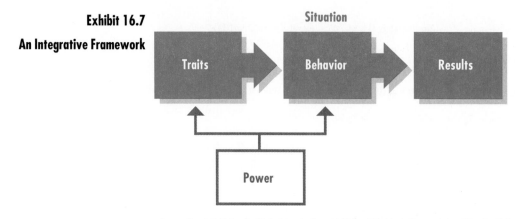

Exhibit 16.7

An Integrative Framework

Source: Gary A. Yukl, *Leadership in Organizations*, © 1981, p. 270. Adapted by permission of Prentice-Hall, Inc., Englewood Cliffs, New Jersey.

Contingency theories suffer from their reality. Reality is complex, and so are these theories. They do not translate into simple, behavioral guides for practicing managers. Nevertheless, they are useful and important to practitioners because they call attention to the role of the situation and the many variables, all of which must be considered in managing an effective organization in the contemporary world of business.

Other Contemporary Perspectives

Given the obvious importance of leadership, we should not be surprised that researchers are always devoting a lot of attention to identifying new and even more insightful perspectives. Cross national differences, such as those between Japan and the United States, are being investigated in an effort to determine what, if any, important differences in leadership styles exist across different cultures.[34] Japanese leaders, for instance, have been found to demonstrate very strong performance—or task-oriented behavior coupled with maintenance—or people-oriented behavior.[35]

At present, five contemporary perspectives particularly noteworthy are charismatic leadership, transformational/entrepreneurial leadership, and symbolic leadership, and the notion of substitutes and neutralizers of leadership. These are discussed next.

Charismatic Leadership

Charismatic leadership relies on attributes of the leader that inspire loyalty and enthusiasm.

Charisma is an intangible attribute in the leader's personality that inspires loyalty and enthusiasm. Certain leaders, such as Ronald Reagan, Mike Ditka, Jesse Jackson, and Mary Kay Ashe, seem to have charisma. Others, such as Dan Quayle, Jimmy Carter, IBM's John Akers, and former Dallas Cowboys coach Tom Landry, tend to have less charisma although they still seem to accomplish a great deal. Recently, researchers have tried to link charisma with leadership. In general, it has been suggested that when a leader has charisma, followers trust his or her beliefs, adopt those beliefs themselves, feel affection for the leader, obey the leader unquestioningly, and develop an emotional involvement with the mission of the organization. The Self-Assessment in this chapter measures your charismatic leadership potential.

One view suggests that charismatic leaders articulate a vision, radiate self-confidence, communicate high expectations, and express confidence in group members.[36] Another view suggests that followers tend to attribute charisma to leaders based on the success of those leaders.[37] Although the study of charismatic leadership is still in its infancy, it will probably become more popular in the future.

The Environment of Management

Southwest Flies High

Southwest Airlines was founded in 1967 by Herb Kelleher, a lawyer, and Rollin King, a Texas businessman. Originally called Air Southwest (the name was changed in 1971), it served the three major Texas cities: Dallas, Houston, and San Antonio. Kelleher took over the presidency in 1978. As competition has increased, he has used his zany style of leadership to continue the company's profitability. Indeed, it has earned a profit every year since 1972.

Southwest seems to love short-haul flights that are shunned by other airlines. Kelleher has kept the company different in other ways, too. Southwest does not have any hubs, it does not subscribe to major computer reservations systems, it does not use a feeder airline system, there are no reserved seats, and there are no meals served in flight. All of this saves money. Southwest then passes some of that saving along to its customers by keeping its fares extremely low.

Kelleher has also engaged in unique marketing efforts. Playing on its original location at Love Field in Houston, in the 1970s flight attendants served love potions (drinks) and love bites (peanuts). Fun Fares (discounted fares) were introduced in 1986, and a frequent flyer program based on number of flights instead of miles began in 1987. In 1988 Southwest Airlines became the official airlines for Sea World of Texas. Fittingly, Kelleher had a plane painted like Shamu, the park's killer whale. Kelleher also has appeared in many of Southwest's television commercials. And flight attendants continue to project a "fun" theme by dressing in costumes on Halloween.

Kelleher's leadership style seems to work. While many other airlines were experiencing financial difficulties during the late 1980s and early 1990s, Southwest continued to make a profit. Further, it expanded. It opened service in Phoenix to compete directly with America West, moved into California, the Midwest, and Las Vegas. It achieved over a billion dollars in sales in 1989 and by 1993 was the seventh-largest carrier in terms of number of passengers carried. And it has won awards for Best On-Time Record, Best Baggage Handling, and Fewest Customer Complaints in a single month.[38] ∎

Transformational/ Entrepreneurial Leadership

Transformational/entrepreneurial leadership attempts to foster innovation and vision.

Transformational leadership, sometimes called entrepreneurial leadership, is also a fairly new concept. The focus here is on how some managers are always able to be at the forefront of innovation and vision in shaping their organizations for the future.[39] The key elements of transformational leadership seem to be developing a full grasp of the organization's environment, understanding the organization's place in that environment, attending to proper strategic management, developing human resources, and anticipating rather than reacting to the need for change and development.

Transformational leadership seems to overlap charismatic leadership. Indeed, it has been suggested that charisma is a necessary component of transformational leadership, although there does not appear to be research to support that claim.[40] Like charismatic leadership, transformational leadership will no doubt receive greater attention in the future, although the term "cultural leadership" may come to be used in recognition that these leaders change organizational cultures.[41] *The Environment of Management: Southwest Flies High* indicates an example of this form of leadership at Southwest Airlines.

Symbolic Leadership

Symbolic leadership involves creating and maintaining a strong organizational culture.

A third contemporary concept is **symbolic leadership,** leadership associated with establishing and maintaining a strong organizational culture, as discussed in Chapters 12 and 13. In fact, leadership is usually seen as the primary determinant of culture. For example, in a company like Levi Strauss, top management takes a very casual approach to leadership, emphasizing informality, open communication networks, and individualism. This is translated into a unique culture

Transformational leadership is not unique to young people in high technology organizations. Patricia McGee was in her sixties when, as President of the Yavapai tribe in Prescott, Arizona, her vision transformed the economic well-being of the tribe. She secured a grant to build a resort hotel, persuaded the town to issue bonds to finance the project, and obtained a developer's assistance in finalizing both the hotel and a shopping mall. (Peter Sibbald.)

that members of the organization recognize and adopt. In contrast, top management at IBM set a different tone; it emphasized formality and conformity, and managed communication flows. The wrong symbols can lead people into unethical behavior. Once again, the notion of symbolic leadership is a new one. Hence, managers are just becoming aware of the importance of symbolism in their work.

Substitutes and Neutralizers

The notion of **substitutes** and **neutralizers** for leadership arose to account for situations in which leadership does not seem to be necessary.[42] Many situations exist where people go about doing their jobs without any specific direction from either managers or leaders. They know their jobs so well or the situation is so specific that they act without the presence of a leader. Thus group member expertise can substitute for leadership, as can the nature of the task itself (emergency conditions, for instance).

Indeed, in situations where group members have considerable expertise, efforts by an individual to influence them may be rendered ineffectual, that is, be neutralized. The efforts of the individual may also be inappropriate in, say, attempting to offer rewards that group members do not need or want. Here, too, the effort is neutralized by aspects of the situation or characteristics of the group.

Finally, characteristics of the organization can also substitute for or neutralize leadership. Formal and inflexible policies and procedures can be developed such that leadership is not needed. A rigid reward system may neutralize a leader's attempts at using reward power to influence group members. Group solidarity may also resist influence attempts.[43]

Leadership is a complex phenomenon. There is no one style, no one basis of power, no one set of behaviors, no one use of skills that fit every situation and so can be universally recommended for managers. Rather, contemporary managers must understand different styles, bases of power, and combinations of behaviors and skills and shape them to fit the situations in which they are trying to effectively manage.

Chapter Summary

L eadership is an influence process directed at shaping the behavior of others. People can be managers but not leaders, leaders but not managers, or both. The most valuable people are those who combine the two qualities, but they are scarce. Leadership depends on the use of one of the five types of power: legitimate, reward, coercive, expert, and referent. Leaders may use each of these forms to influence people to pursue certain goals. When people are confronted with someone's attempt to influence them, their response can be commitment, compliance, or resistance.

Leadership traits are those characteristics of leaders that set them apart from followers. Unfortunately, no one has ever established that any single set of traits can reliably distinguish leaders from nonleaders in a wide variety of situations.

The behavioral approach attempted to differentiate successful or effective leaders from unsuccessful or ineffective ones on the basis of their behaviors. The Michigan studies identified two major leadership behaviors termed job-centered and employee-centered behaviors. They regarded these behaviors as mutually exclusive and felt that employee-centeredness was more effective. The Ohio State researchers also tended to emphasize two major forms of behavior, which they called initiating structure and consideration behaviors. Unlike the Michigan group, the Ohio State researchers felt that these two forms of behavior could and should be combined for most effective leadership.

Situational approaches to leadership attempt to define circumstances in which one form of leadership is more appropriate than another. The LPC model assumes that the behavior of managers is not changeable and is either task oriented or relationship oriented. The path-goal model suggests that the purpose of leadership is to clarify for followers the paths to desired goals. The participation model focuses on a narrow but important aspect of leadership: determining how much group members should be allowed to participate in decision making. A framework to integrate these diverse models has recently been developed. It suggests that leadership is a complex phenomenon rather than a simple one and that all approaches to leadership have merit and should be seen as complementary rather than contradictory. Three new and insightful perspectives on leadership focus on charismatic, transformational, and symbolic leadership.

The Manager's Vocabulary

leadership
multiple constituencies
legitimate power
reward power
coercive power
expert power
referent power
commitment
compliance

resistance
leadership traits
leadership behaviors
leadership style
contingency (situational) approaches
LPC model
leader-member relations
task structure
position power

path-goal model
participation model
charisma
transformational/entrepreneurial
　leadership
symbolic leadership
substitutes
neutralizers

Review Questions

1. Explain how someone could be a manager but not a leader, a leader but not a manager, or both a leader and a manager.
2. List and define the five types of power.
3. What are the major forms of leadership behavior identified in the Michigan and Ohio State studies?

4. Summarize the LPC, path-goal, and participation models.
5. Describe three contemporary perspectives on leadership.

Analysis Questions

1. Many people have heard the saying "Power corrupts, but absolute power corrupts absolutely." What does this mean? What implications does it have for organizations and for managers?
2. What leadership traits do you think are most important?
3. What forms of leadership behavior can you identify beyond those discussed in the chapter?
4. Compare and contrast the three situational approaches to leadership.
5. Who do you think are today's charismatic leaders?

Self-Assessment

Are You a Charismatic Leader?

Introduction Charismatic leaders articulate a vision, show concern for group members, communicate high expectation, and create high-performing organizations. This Self-Assessment measures your charismatic potential.

Instructions The following statements refer to the possible ways in which you might behave toward others when you are in a leadership role. Please read each statement carefully and decide to what extent it applies to you. Then put a check on the appropriate number.

To a Very Great Extent	1
To a Considerable Extent	2
To a Moderate Extent	3
To a Slight Extent	4
To Little or No Extent	5

You . . .

1. pay close attention to what others say when they are talking.   1 2 3 4 5
2. communicate clearly.   1 2 3 4 5
3. are trustworthy.   1 2 3 4 5
4. care about other people.   1 2 3 4 5
5. do not put excessive energy into avoiding failure.   1 2 3 4 5
6. make the work of others more meaningful.   1 2 3 4 5
7. seem to focus on the key issues in a situation.   1 2 3 4 5
8. get across your meaning effectively, often in unusual ways.   1 2 3 4 5
9. can be relied on to follow through on commitments.   1 2 3 4 5
10. have a great deal of self-respect.   1 2 3 4 5
11. enjoy taking carefully calculated risks.   1 2 3 4 5
12. help others feel more competent in what they do.   1 2 3 4 5
13. have a clear set of priorities.   1 2 3 4 5
14. are in touch with how others feel.   1 2 3 4 5
15. rarely change once you have taken a clear position.   1 2 3 4 5
16. focus on strengths, of yourself and of others.   1 2 3 4 5
17. seem most alive when deeply involved in some project.   1 2 3 4 5
18. show others that they are all part of the same group.   1 2 3 4 5
19. get others to focus on the issues you see as important.   1 2 3 4 5
20. communicate feelings as well as ideas.   1 2 3 4 5
21. let others know where you stand.   1 2 3 4 5
22. seem to know just how you "fit" into a group.   1 2 3 4 5
23. learn from mistakes, do not treat errors as disasters, but as learning.   1 2 3 4 5
24. are fun to be around.   1 2 3 4 5

For interpretation, turn to the back of the book.

Source: Marshall Sashkin and William C. Morris, *Experiencing Management,* © 1987 by Addison-Wesley Publishing Company, Inc. Reprinted with permission of the publisher.

Skill Builder

The Leadership/Management Interview Experiment

Purpose Leadership and management are in some ways the same, but more often they are different. This skill builder allows you to develop a conceptual framework for leadership and management. This skill builder focuses on the *scientific management model and open systems model.* It will help you develop the *director role* of the scientific model. One of the skills of the director is taking initiative. In addition, it will help you develop the *broker role* of the open systems model. One of the skills of the broker is the ability to present ideas orally.

Introduction Since most management behaviors and leadership behaviors are a product of individual work experience, each leader/manager tends to have a unique leadership/management style. An analysis of leadership/management styles and a comparison of such styles with different organizational experiences are often rewarding experiences in learning.

Instructions

Fact-Finding and Execution of the Experiment

1. Develop a list of questions relating to issues studied in this chapter that you want to ask a practicing manager and leader during a face-to-face interview. You may want to draw those questions from the Leadership Versus Management (page 364) discussion or from Table 16.1. Prior to the actual interview, submit your list of questions to your instructor for approval.
2. Arrange to interview a practicing manager and a practicing leader. For purposes of this assignment, a manager or leader is a person whose job priority involves supervising the work of other people. The leader/manager may work in a business, or in a public or private agency.

3. Interview at least one manager and one leader using the interview you have developed. Take good notes on their comments and on your own observations. Do not take more than one hour of each leader/manager's time.

Oral Report:

Prepare an oral report using the questions here and your interview information. Complete the following report after the interview. (Attach a copy of your interview questions.)

The Leadership/Management Interview Experiment Report:

1. How did you locate the leader/managers you interviewed? Describe your initial contacts.
2. Describe the level and responsibilities of your leader/managers. Do not supply names—their responses should be anonymous.
3. Describe the interview settings. How long did the interview last?
4. In what ways were the leader/managers similar or in agreement about issues?
5. What were some of the major differences between the leader/managers and the ways in which they approached their jobs?
6. In what ways would the managers agree or disagree with ideas presented in this course?
7. Describe and evaluate your own interviewing style and skills.
8. How did your managers feel about having been interviewed? How do you know that?
9. Overall, what were the most important things you learned from this experience?

Source: Adapted from Stephen C. Iman, "The Management Interview Experiment," in *Introducing Organizational Behavior: Exercises and Experiments,* 2nd ed., by Peter P. Dawson and Stephen C. Iman (Lexington, Mass.: Ginn and Company, 1981), pp. 135–138.

CONCLUDING CASES

16.1   Leadership at Merck

Merck & Co., Inc., is the world's largest maker of prescription drugs, with about 5 percent of the market. While it shares common roots with E. Merck of Germany, the two companies have been completely independent of one another since the early part of this century. Merck & Co. became the world leader by having consistent sales and earnings growth brought about by innovative products. Indeed, in 1990 Merck had eighteen products that each earned more than $100 million. To develop those products, Merck invests heavily in research and development, usually spending the most in the industry. Its emphasis on research can be traced to the formation of its first laboratory in 1933, where its scientists did pioneering work on vitamin B-12 and developed cortisone. During the 1940s and 1950s, five Merck scientists received the Nobel prize.

Dr. P. Roy Vagelos, the biochemist who has been Merck's CEO since 1985, has stated that the more original thinkers Merck has, the better he likes it. He feels that having people thinking along different lines but with similar objectives is the key to innovation and success. But Merck stands for more than innovative products. It is also one of the best-managed companies in the world. For more than ten years *Fortune* magazine has determined the "most admired corporations" in the United States. Only one company has been in that group every time—Merck. Not only has it been in the group, it has dominated the ratings and been number one six times. Merck says the reason is that it attracts, develops, and keeps good people in its organization. Indeed, the promotions and merit evaluations of senior executives are impacted by the number of people recruited and trained by those executives. Further, women seem able to advance successfully at Merck. One of the highest-ranking women in a *Fortune* 500 company was Merck's chief financial officer in 1990.

In a communication to employees, Vagelos stressed the need to carefully monitor the environment and plan to respond to changes in it. He said that the trick is for Merck to anticipate environmental change and to move to take advantage of it before anybody else does. In that way, Merck would continue to be successful. "The best—really, the only—guarantee of true employment stability is a successful business."

Careful monitoring of the environment at Merck includes not just research linked to product developments but also market opportunities. Merck bought half of Banyu, the Japanese drug company, to open up the Japanese market as well as to gain access to the thinking of Japanese scientists. Alliances with other drug companies have been formed to open access to other new markets as well. Merck and Du Pont formed a joint venture to expand the global markets for each other's products. Merck and Johnson & Johnson formed a joint venture to market products resulting from a merger of Merck with the nonprescription part of ICI Americas (the major product involved was Mylanta).[44] Clearly, Merck's leaders are staying in touch with these situations.

Discussion Questions

1. How would you describe Vagelos's leadership?
2. Which approach to leadership seems most nearly to "fit" Vagelos? Why?
3. Can you identify aspects of all parts of the integrative framework in the leadership situation at Merck? If so, what are they? If not, what parts are missing?

16.2   British Air Leaders

John King was chairman of a large engineering firm, Babcock International, in 1981, when he was chosen to become chairman of troubled British Airways (BA) and move it from a government organization to a private business. He slashed employment, sold surplus aircraft as well as some real estate holdings, switched insurance agencies, transformed the board of directors, changed advertising agencies, and hired a new chief executive. The new chief executive was chosen specifically because he understood service organizations and management but had had no previous experience in the airline industry and so would be open to new ways of operating. That person was Colin Marshall.

Colin Marshall left home as a teen-ager to go to sea with the Orient Steam Navigation Company. He spent seven years sailing from Britain to Australia before going to Chicago as a management trainee with Hertz. He left Hertz for Avis, where he worked first in the European division and then in its New York headquarters. Later he moved to its parent company, Norton Simon Inc., as an executive. Marshall learned a great deal about tough competitive battles by having worked for both Hertz and Avis. In 1981 he moved to apply his experience in retailing as deputy chief executive of Sears PLC (the parent company of the Selfridges retail empire and not related to Sears, Roebuck). In 1983 he moved from there to the chief executive position at BA.

King and Marshall worked well together. The merger of British Airways and British Caledonia, which took place in 1988, a year after the privatization of BA, was so difficult and protracted that many employees were depressed by the time it ended. To ease the tension and enable the new organization to quickly become effective, King and Marshall had a consulting firm throw a party for all employees. The party for forty thousand people was held in an unused hanger and was highly effective in reducing tensions and bringing everyone together.

As Marshall assumed control of BA, he applied his experience with Hertz and Avis to make BA highly competitive and profitable. He emphasized customer service as the way to win competitive battles and won high praise for improvements in service in all areas of BA. In 1990 BA and Aeroflot formed Air Russia to establish routes from Moscow to Europe, the United States, and the Far East. In 1991, thanks to an excellent information system and continued tight cost controls under Marshall's leadership, BA was the world's most profitable carrier. Then, in 1992, BA agreed to buy 44 percent of USAir in a move to become the world's first truly global airline.

The USAir deal was fought by other large U.S. carriers so that its final form was yet to be determined as of 1993. Regardless of the final form of the cooperative arrangement between USAir and BA, each party stood to gain. The arrangement provided a way to feed passengers from USAir to BA and vice versa. Further, USAir benefited from the customer service emphasis of BA while BA benefited from the attention to reduced costs of operations so characteristic of U.S.-based airline companies. The kind of arrangement under consideration also suggested the possibility for opening British and European routes to other U.S. carriers. Such increases in international competition would benefit the industry in the long term.[45]

Discussion Questions

1. Which approach to leadership seems most nearly to fit Marshall? Why?
2. How would you describe King's leadership? Marshall's leadership?
3. Do any of the contemporary perspectives on leadership seem to be applicable to the situation at British Air? If so, which one(s)?

CHAPTER

17

Employee Motivation

Chapter Outline

Learning Objectives

After studying this chapter you should be able to

· Discuss the nature of human motivation and explain the basic motivational process.

· Identify important human needs and discuss two theories that attempt to outline the way in which those needs motivate people.

· Describe employee motivation from the perspectives of expectancy, satisfaction, equity, goal setting, and participation.

· Discuss reinforcement processes, including kinds of reinforcement and schedules of reinforcement.

· Identify several kinds of rewards, indicate how reward systems can be effective in motivation, and describe several new reward systems.

ncreasingly, members of organizations are looking for evidence that their organizations are loyal to them before they are willing to demonstrate any significant loyalty to their organizations. Many people feel that Apple Computer is among the leaders in demonstrating loyalty to its personnel.

Apple had long been known as a benevolent organization where employees could work on projects that interested them without being overly concerned about meeting schedule, costs, or marketability. Like many other firms, Apple set up fitness programs to assist employees in maintaining their health and for reducing stress. But unlike most other firms, Apple was among the first to establish communication networks, educate its personnel, and push for reforms in benefit provisions to prevent homosexuality from hindering employee careers and to assure that there was no discrimination based on sexual preferences. In addition, it established a manager for multicultural programs to assure that cultural diversity would be an effective reality in the workplace at Apple.

While such moves may bolster loyalty, it remains to be seen if their effect on employees will translate into performance. Does loyalty lead to higher performance among organizational members? Can improved loyalty increase productivity sufficiently to offset the negative impacts of frequently changing strategies, reorganizations, layoffs, and increased competition?[1] ■

pple has prospered because it provides an open organizational environment for its members. Apple seems to have learned what many contemporary managers are just beginning to learn: the success of any business is largely dependent on the willingness of its employees to work together in the best interests of the organization. For employees to do this, three conditions must be met: (1) they must know how to do their jobs, (2) they must have the proper tools, materials, and equipment to do their jobs, and (3) they must want to do their jobs well. This third factor is motivation.

This chapter explores the topic of employee motivation in detail.[2] First it examines the nature of motivation. Then it identifies important human needs that are relevant to the workplace and investigates various complexities of human motivation. It continues by discussing reinforcement processes and concludes with a summary of how reward systems affect motivation.

The Nature of Human Motivation

et us define **motivation** as the set of processes that determine behavioral choices.[3] Note the word *choices*. You can choose whether to study a lot, study a little, or not study at all. Most employees at Apple choose to do their best. Our concern here is how managers can help create conditions under which essentially all employees will make this same choice.

Historical Perspectives

Motivation is the set of processes that determine the choices people make about their behaviors.

Managers have been aware of the importance of employee motivation for decades. In general, their thinking about motivation has progressed through three distinct stages.[4]

The traditional view, popular during the era of scientific management, was very simplistic. The dominant opinion in those days was that employees worked only for economic reasons. Presumably, people found work unpleasant and did it only for money, so the more people were paid, the harder they would work. Although the importance of money should not be underestimated, managers soon recognized that money was only one of several factors that led to motivation.

The human relations view, which was part of the human relations school of thought, held that social forces were the primary determinants of motivation. In particular, the adherents of this view believed that the more satisfied people were with their jobs, the harder they would work. As we see later in this chapter, this assumption is also extremely simplistic and not often true.

Motivation can be enhanced through group support. Fifteen classmates of a young man diagnosed with cancer—and who would probably lose his hair during chemotherapy treatment—had their mothers shave their heads to demonstrate support. (Karen Kerckhove/Aurora Beacon-News.)

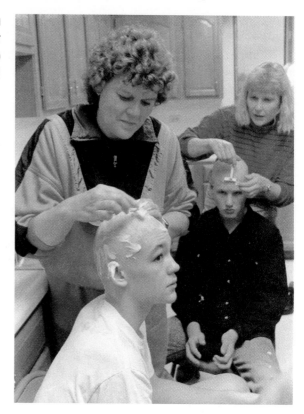

The human resources view is reflective of most contemporary thinking and takes the most positive attitude toward employee motivation. This philosophy argues that people are actually resources that can benefit the organization that they want to help, and that managers should look on them as assets. These notions relate to current interests in employee participation, workplace democracy, and so forth.

The Motivational Process

Exactly how does motivation occur? Although the complete set of processes is quite complex and not totally understood, we can devise a general framework for the motivational process, which is illustrated in Exhibit 17.1.

Needs are drives or forces that initiate behavior.

The starting point in the process is **needs,** drives or forces that initiate behavior. People need recognition, feelings of accomplishment, food, affection, and so forth. When our needs become strong enough, we engage in efforts to fulfill them. For instance, suppose you began to experience pangs of hunger at ten o'clock this morning. By noon the pangs became too great to ignore, so you went looking for a restaurant.

As a result of such efforts, people experience various levels of need satisfaction. If you had a good meal, you are no longer hungry. The extent to which people find their needs satisfied will then influence their future efforts to satisfy the same needs. If the meal was filling but not particularly tasty, you may look for a different restaurant the next time you get hungry.

Obviously, the motivational process is a dynamic one. We always have a number of needs to satisfy, and we are always at different places in the process of satisfying them. Likewise, different time frames are involved. Satisfying your hunger might take only a couple of hours, but satisfying the need to accomplish meaningful work can take months or years.

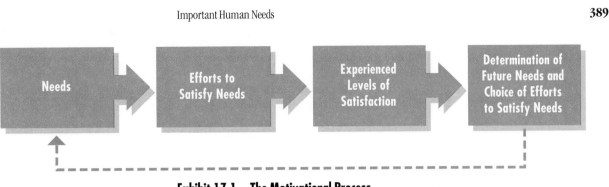

Exhibit 17.1   The Motivational Process

At any rate, the starting point is always the same — needs. Now let us explore this concept in more detail.

Important Human Needs

Needs are the starting point in all motivated behavior. Our biological craving for food and water and our emotional longing for companionship are both needs. All people have many needs, even in the workplace, and for many people work itself is an important need.[5] Several different theories that describe human needs in the workplace have been developed. Let us examine two of the more popular ones.

The Need Hierarchy

*The **need hierarchy** has five levels of needs: **physiological**, **security**, **social**, **esteem**, and **self-actualization**.*

Although several different theories about needs have been advanced, the one most familiar to managers is Maslow's **need hierarchy.**[6] Maslow argued that humans have a variety of different needs that can be classified into five specific groups and then arranged in a hierarchy of importance. Exhibit 17.2 illustrates the basic framework of the hierarchy.

At the bottom are the **physiological needs,** the things we need to survive, such as food, air, and sufficient warmth. In the workplace, adequate wages for food and clothing, reasonable working conditions, and so forth are generally thought to satisfy these needs.

Next are **security needs,** which reflect the desire to have a safe physical and emotional

Exhibit 17.2

Maslow's Need Hierarchy

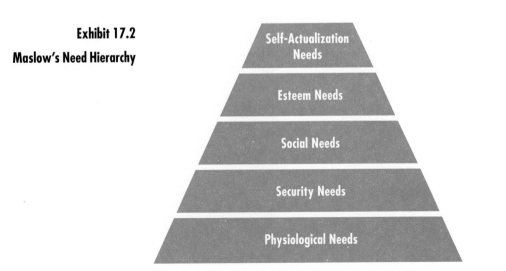

environment. Job security, grievance procedures, and health insurance and retirement plans are used to satisfy security needs.

Third in the hierarchy are **social needs,** the need for belongingness. These include the desire for love and affection and the need to be accepted by our peers. Making friends at work and being a part of the team are common ways in which people satisfy these needs.

Esteem needs come next. These actually comprise two different sets: the needs for recognition and respect from others, and the needs for self-respect and a positive self-image. Job titles, spacious offices, awards, and other symbols of success help satisfy the externally focused needs, whereas accomplishing goals and doing a good job help satisfy the internally focused ones.

Finally, at the top of the hierarchy are the **self-actualization needs,** the needs to continue to grow, develop, and expand our capabilities. Opportunities to participate, to take on increasingly important tasks, and to learn new skills may all lead to satisfaction of these needs. Many people who break away from jobs in large corporations to start their own business may be looking for a way to satisfy their self-actualization needs.

The manner in which the hierarchy is presumed to work is really quite simple. Maslow suggests that we start out by trying to satisfy the lower-level needs. As they are satisfied, they no longer serve as catalysts for motivation. If you eat a big meal to satisfy your physiological hunger, for instance, you will stop looking for restaurants. Similarly, if an employee has satisfied his or her security needs, he or she will begin to look for new friendships and other opportunities to satisfy the social needs.

In general, this view provides a convenient framework for thinking about needs. It illustrates the ideas that we have various needs, that satisfaction of those needs decreases our motiva-

Getting high levels of involvement and commitment can sometimes accomplish far more than one might expect. Vision of Dreamz was formed when Junior Achievement and McDonnell Douglas sponsored a program for at-risk high school students. In twelve weeks it returned 224 percent on equity and turned around the lives of participants Lisa Ryman (front), Jesse Richardson (right), and Nicole Woods (striped vest) pictured here with their team. (Dana Fineman/SYGMA.)

tion to get more satisfaction, and that we can become frustrated trying to satisfy needs that are unattainable. On the other hand, it is difficult for managers to use in a clear-cut fashion. For example, managers would have a difficult time assessing the need level for each of their employees, let alone figuring out how to satisfy the different and changing needs for each.

Criticisms of Maslow's need hierarchy led to the development of ERG Theory.[7] This theory collapses Maslow's into three levels—existence, relatedness, and growth—and suggests that more than one can be active at any given time (Maslow had insisted that only one need could motivate at a time). Research tends to be more supportive of this conceptualization,[8] but it, too, is of limited usefulness to practicing managers.

The Two-Factor View

*The **two-factor view** of motivation suggests that employee satisfaction and dissatisfaction are two distinct dimensions affected by different sets of factors.*

Another popular way to describe employee needs is by using the **two-factor view,** which was developed by Frederick Herzberg in the 1960s.[9] This model grew from a study of two hundred accountants and engineers in Pittsburgh. Prior to the study, it was believed that employee satisfaction and dissatisfaction and thus motivation and lack of motivation, were at opposite ends of the same dimension. That is, people were satisfied, dissatisfied, or something in between. However, the Pittsburgh study uncovered evidence that satisfaction and dissatisfaction are considerably more complex than this. The researchers found that one set of factors influenced satisfaction and an entirely different set of factors influenced dissatisfaction, hence the term **two-factor.**

The model is shown in Exhibit 17.3. At the top is the dissatisfaction dimension and some of the factors found to affect it. For example, when pay and security, supervision, working conditions, and so forth are deficient, employees tend to be dissatisfied. When these factors are adequate, however, employees are not necessarily satisfied. Instead, they are simply not dissatisfied.

The bottom of the exhibit shows the other dimension, satisfaction. Factors such as achieve-

Exhibit 17.3   The Two-Factor Model

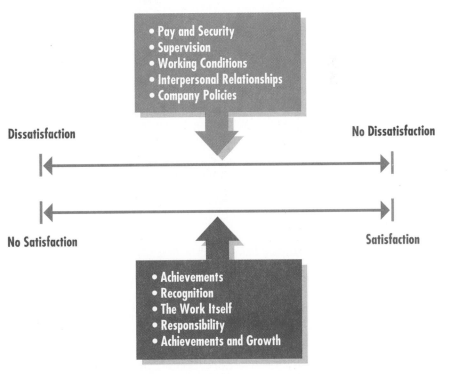

ment and responsibility influence this dimension. When these factors are present, employees should be satisfied. When they are deficient, employees are not dissatisfied but merely not satisfied.

The two-factor theory carries some very clear messages for managers. The first step in motivation is to eliminate dissatisfaction, so managers are advised to make sure that pay, working conditions, company policies, and so forth are appropriate and reasonable. Then they can address motivation itself. But additional pay, improvements in working conditions, and so forth alone will not accomplish this. Instead, managers should also strive to provide opportunities for achievement, growth, and responsibility. The theory predicts that these things in turn will enhance employee motivation.

The two-factor model has been the source of considerable debate. On the one hand, it has not always been supported by research and is somewhat arbitrary in its classification of factors. On the other hand, it does provide a useful and applicable framework for managers to use.[10]

Affiliation, Achievement, and Power

*The need for **affiliation** is the need to work with others, to interact, and to have friends.*

*The need for **achievement** is the desire to excel or to accomplish some goal more effectively than in the past.*

Three specific needs incorporated in the need perspective warrant additional discussion. One of these is the need for **affiliation,** the need that most people have to work with others, to make friends in the workplace, and to socialize. Work settings that deprive people of social interaction may lead to dissatisfaction and low morale. The need for affiliation is similar to Maslow's social need and Herzberg's interpersonal relationship.

Another important employee need is the need for **achievement.**[11] This is the desire that some people have to excel or to accomplish some goal or task more effectively than they did in the past. This need parallels Maslow's need for self-actualization and Herzberg's achievement factor. Research has indicated that people with a high need for achievement tend to have four common characteristics.

First, they set moderately difficult goals. A computer software sales representative, for instance, might set a sales goal of 115 percent of last year's sales. The goal is moderately difficult to reach but can be accomplished with hard work.

Second, they want immediate feedback. A new department manager at a Sears store who calls the store manager every morning to learn how her department did the day before might well have a strong need to achieve.

Third, people with high needs to achieve tend to assume personal responsibility. Suppose a number of plant managers at General Motors are formed into a task force to study ways to improve productivity. If one of them continually volunteers to do the work for the entire group, he might be a high achiever. In *The Quality Challenge: Merry-Go-Round Has Heads Spinning,* we can see how Merry-Go-Round trains its employees to assume personal responsibility for the quality of service provided to its customers.

Fourth, such people are often preoccupied with their task. An engineer who thinks about the job at Hewlett-Packard while taking a shower, eating breakfast, and driving to work every day might also have a high need to achieve.

Researchers have estimated that only about 10 percent of the American population has this need, but there is evidence that the desire to achieve can be taught to people.[12]

*The need for **power** is the desire to control situations and people.*

A third employee need is the need for **power,** the desire to control the situation and the behavior of others. Clearly an organization with lots of managers with high power needs would not be very effective. People with high power needs tend to be high performers and have good attendance records. Supervisors tend to have high power needs.[13] Further, there is some evidence that more successful managers have higher power needs than do less successful ones.[14] The discussion of need for affiliation, achievement, and power can seem very abstract and vague. The Skill Builder in this chapter provides you with a critical technical skill in understanding these motivating factors. It will help you see both your need for these three factors as well as the needs of two of your fellow classmates. Once you understand how to use and interpret the Thematic Apperception tool, you can use it to assess others' need for affiliation, achievement, and power.

The Quality Challenge

Merry-Go-Round Has Heads Spinning

Merry-Go-Round Enterprises of Joppa, Maryland, ranked among the top specialty stores in the 1990s, with sales in excess of $600 million. The customer focus so necessary in total quality management is achieved in two major ways at Merry-Go-Round. One way is through the use of technology. Merry-Go-Round uses high technology such as a computer-linked distribution system, sorting software, and software-integrated bar coding and scanners to link its nearly 750 outlets and to help it stay on top of what its customers want and do not want. In this way it can respond quickly to changes in customers tastes and fads. If an item is not selling, prices are slashed to clear it off the shelves fast. This is necessary since the customers are largely individual spenders in their teens who quickly learn what merchandise is "in" and what is not.

Motivating employees to have a customer focus is also critical to total quality management. This comes through the company's employee training program. New employees are taught how to treat customers, instructed on how to greet them when they come into the store, shown how to help them select an outfit, how to escort them to a dressing room, and how to close a sale. The customer is the focus of attention.

Merry-Go-Round's success is apparent. It continues to add stores, has strong sales and earnings, and its stock price has risen strongly. Achieving quality through motivation works![15] ∎

Complex Models of Employee Motivation

Although an understanding of basic human needs is a necessary starting point for enhancing motivation, managers also need to have a more complete perspective on the complexities of employee motivation. They must understand why different people have different needs, why individuals' needs change, that need frustration can lead to possibly dysfunctional behavior, and how employees choose to try to satisfy needs in different ways. There are several useful theories for understanding these complexities.

The Expectancy Model

*The **expectancy model** suggests that motivation is determined by how much we want something and how likely we think we are to get it.*

The **expectancy model** is perhaps the most comprehensive model of employee motivation, but its basic notion is simple: motivation is a function of how much we want something and how likely we think we are to get it.[16]

As an example, consider a new college graduate looking for his first job. He hears about an executive position with Weyerhaeuser with a starting salary of $200,000 per year. He wants the job, but does not apply because he knows he has no chance of getting it. He then hears about a job with a local Safeway store, carrying bags of groceries for customers. He thinks he could get the job, but again he does not apply, this time because he does not want it. Finally he hears about a management trainee position with Xerox. He will probably choose to apply for this job because it is similar to what he wants, and he thinks he stands a good chance of getting it.

The problem, of course, is that in many situations we have various outcomes—some bad and some good—to consider. Suppose the recent graduate ends up with two reasonable job offers. One pays a little more but is in a less desirable location. His choice is thus more difficult.

Exhibit 17.4 illustrates the basic expectancy model.[17] The theory holds that motivation leads to effort, which, with ability and environmental forces such as the availability of materials and equipment, leads to performance. Performance in turn has multiple outcomes. For example, high employee performance can result in several outcomes: a pay increase, a promotion, and better job assignments. However, it can also lead to stress and to the resentment of less successful colleagues. Therefore the employee must choose how much effort to exert. She may weigh the potential outcomes and decide that the raise, promotion, and better assignments are more impor-

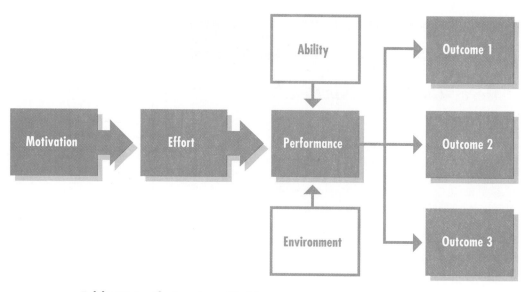

Exhibit 17.4　The Expectancy Model

tant to her than putting up with stress and resentment, so she exerts maximum effort to achieve those things. Another employee in the same situation, though, might put a higher premium on reducing stress and avoiding resentment, and he would consequently exert less effort.

A real example of how the expectancy model works can be drawn from the Chaparral Steel Company, where pay is tied directly to output, promotions are based on merit rather than seniority, all employees participate in a lucrative profit-sharing plan, and all employees have a voice in decision making. Thus Chaparral is making it easy for workers to figure out what outcomes are available to them and how best to achieve those outcomes.[18]

In summary, the expectancy model implies that managers should (1) recognize that employees have different needs and preferences, (2) try to understand each employee's key needs, and (3) help employees determine how to satisfy each of their needs through performance.

Performance and Satisfaction

Good performance, followed by rewards, leads to higher levels of employee satisfaction.

Managers must also recognize the complexity of the relationship between performance and satisfaction. In Chapter 1 we noted the belief of the human relationists that employee attitudes, such as satisfaction, would lead to changes in employee behaviors, such as performance. We also noted that this thinking is now considered inaccurate and overly simplistic.

Exhibit 17.5 illustrates the way that researchers now believe the relationship looks. Note in particular that performance is presumed to occur before satisfaction.[19] At first this seems unbelievable, but consider how you evaluate your classes each semester. When someone asks you how you feel about a certain class after the first week, you usually have a fairly neutral reaction. After you have taken the first exam, though, your attitude is somewhat more intense. If you get an A on the exam, you are likely to say the class is great. Under other circumstances, you may come up with a less favorable evaluation.

The same process occurs in work settings. During the early stages of employment, people tend to have fairly neutral attitudes toward the organization and their jobs. After they have worked a while and received various rewards (both extrinsic, like salary increases, and intrinsic, like a feeling of accomplishment), however, their attitudes become more extreme. For example, if an employee has worked hard and subsequently gets praise and a pay raise, he is likely to express favorable attitudes toward the organization. But if another employee feels she worked just as hard but received little recognition and a small raise, she will be inclined to have less favorable attitudes.

Exhibit 17.5

The Relationship Between Performance and Satisfaction

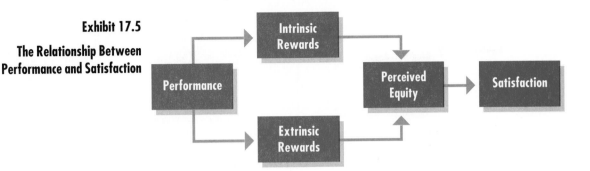

Source: Edward E. Lawler, III, and Lyman W. Porter, "The Effect of Performance on Job Satisfaction," *Industrial Relations,* Vol. 7, No. 1, October 1967, p. 23. Used with permission of the University of California.

Thus it may be more accurate to argue that performance, through the reward system, leads to satisfaction rather than the reverse. This raises the notion of equity, which, as you will note, is also part of the process shown in Exhibit 17.5. Much of how the two employees feel has to do with equity. This subject is discussed next.

Equity in the Workplace

Equity is an individual's perception that he or she is being treated fairly relative to others in the organization.

Another complex perspective on employee motivation is the role of **equity,** or fairness, in the workplace. Equity has been found to be a major factor in determining employee motivation.[20] Its power is demonstrated visibly in the sports arena. For example, until 1989, there were no baseball players being paid $3 million a year. However, when Will Clark, one of the game's top players, negotiated a new contract calling for such a salary, others followed suit almost immediately. As a result, by the end of that year, there were ten players earning a salary of over $3 million. Likewise, after an NFL team signs its first round draft choice each year, almost invariably several veteran players start demanding that their contracts be renegotiated.

Although equity in the workplace is perhaps less visible, it is also important. First, each employee contributes to and gets things from the workplace. We contribute our education, experience, expertise, time, and effort. In return we get pay, security, recognition, and so forth. Given the social nature of human beings, it should come as no surprise that as shown in Exhibit 17.6 we compare our contributions and rewards to those of others. As a result of this comparison, we may feel equity or inequity, that is, we may feel that we are fairly treated or that we are not.

We should note, of course, that everyone's contributions and rewards do not have to be the same for equity to exist. If one employee has a college degree, ten years on the job, and is a good performer and another employee has only a high school diploma, little experience, and is only an average performer, the second employee should expect to be paid less. For equity to exist, people must perceive that the relative proportion of all rewards and all contributions is equal. And if equity is present, people are generally motivated to keep everything as it is.

In contrast, if people experience inequity, they are generally motivated to change something. If someone believes that she is underpaid relative to a colleague, her only option is to decrease her contributions, since she does not control her rewards. Working harder would only exacerbate the perceived inequity. While it might lead to more rewards, it would also increase even further her contributions. Thus the employee will decrease her efforts. She might, of course, try to exercise some control over rewards by asking for a raise or for her colleague's pay to be cut. She could also try to convince the colleague that he should work harder to justify his pay, or she can rationalize the problem away in some manner. And, of course, she can quit so that the issue no longer exists. Regardless of which option she chooses, she will be uncomfortable with inequity and will try to do something about it.

This viewpoint also conveys several clear messages to managers. First, people should be re-

Exhibit 17.6

Equity Theory

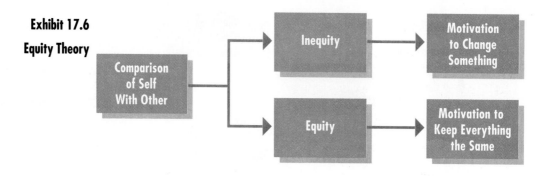

warded according to their contributions, which include their performance as well as their knowledge and skills. Second, managers should try to ensure that employees feel equity by assuring that the reward allocation system is linked to performance and is clearly understood. Finally, managers should be aware that feelings of inequity are almost bound to arise. When they do, managers must be patient and either correct the problem, if it is real, or help people recognize that things are not as inequitable as they seem.[21] Relatively recent modifications of equity theory may render it even more useful to managers in the future.[22]

Goal-Setting Theory

*According to the **goal-setting theory,** specific and moderately difficult goals may increase motivation.*

Still another useful perspective on employee motivation is **goal-setting theory.**[23] Goal setting from a planning perspective was discussed earlier in the book. Recent evidence also suggests that goal setting can be applied on an individual level as a way to increase employee motivation.[24] The starting point is for managers and their subordinates to meet regularly. As a part of these meetings, they should jointly set goals for the subordinate. These goals should be very specific and moderately difficult. Assuming they are also goals that the subordinate will accept and be committed to, the employee is likely to work very hard to accomplish them. The evidence thus far suggests that goal setting will become an increasingly important part of the motivational process in the future.[25]

High-Involvement Management

Employee participation can also increase motivation.

Finally, **high-involvement management** is also being used more and more as a way to enhance motivation in the workplace. Managers are finding that when employees are given a greater voice in how things are done, they become more committed to the goals of the organization and are willing to make ever-greater contributions to the success of the business. A first step in achieving high involvement is getting each employee involved in his or her job. The Self-Assessment at the end of this chapter examines job involvement. Quality circles, discussed later in the book, are one popular method of increasing employee participation. This approach solicits employee volunteers who meet regularly in an attempt to first identify and then recommend solutions for quality-related problems in the workplace. Many businesses are attempting to encourage participation as a means of enhancing competitiveness.[26] Honda, for instance, has already used participation to gain a competitive edge.[27]

The use of high-involvement management is more than just participation, however. It involves a total approach whereby the organization's structure, processes, reward systems, and methods of doing work all are altered to focus on information, knowledge, power, and rewards.[28] As indicated in chapters 1, 11, and 12, high-involvement management builds on horizontal organizational structures with involving work designs. A lot of group processes are involved (more will be said about the use of groups in the next chapter) and reward systems are based on skills and performance. High-involvement management holds tremendous promise as a way of tapping the enormous potential in diverse organizations. That promise is reflected in *The Entrepreneurial Spirit: Small Companies Have Big Motivational Impacts.*

The Entrepreneurial Spirit

Small Companies Have Big Motivational Impacts

Large organizations are breaking up into smaller ones. The average size of a business firm dropped significantly between 1975 and 1985 in Britain, Germany, and the United States. Large firms appear to be trying to emulate smaller firms not only in terms of flexibility and strategy but also in terms of employee motivation. Small companies are constantly demonstrating that they can evolve motivational programs equal or perhaps even superior to those found in major corporations.

At Sonic Corp., a Southwestern fast-food chain, for instance, each outlet manager owns a 25-percent stake in his or her operations. This arrangement tends to assure that the managers will be strongly motivated to draw customers and operate efficiently. Sonic feels that this practice will virtually guarantee that its managers are hard working and dedicated so that the overall organization will benefit from their efforts.

At FourGen Technologies, Inc., there are no real "bosses" and no job descriptions. FourGen uses a high-involvement, team-based approach to involve everyone in corporate decisions. This practice gives all personnel a genuine stake in the company's success or failure. Coupled with a flat, horizontal organization, this form of employee empowerment seems highly successful.[29] ∎

Reinforcement Processes

Reinforcement processes suggest that future behavior is shaped by the consequences of current behavior.

A final question about motivation concerns how and why behaviors stay the same or change. Consider the case of two new workers. One starts out as an average performer and continually gets better, the other starts out as a top performer but becomes a poor performer. What has happened? The answer probably involves reinforcement processes.

The idea of **reinforcement** suggests that future behavior is shaped by the consequences of current behavior. If people's current behavior leads to a reward, they are likely to engage in that same behavior again. But if current behavior does not lead to a reward, or if it leads to unpleasant outcomes, they are more likely to follow a different behavior pattern in the future.

Much of what we know about reinforcement can be traced to psychologists who have studied human learning processes,[30] but more and more people have come to see how clearly the concept relates to organizational settings.[31] The following sections describe kinds of reinforcement and schedules that managers can use to provide them.

Kinds of Reinforcement

*Four kinds of reinforcement are **positive reinforcement, avoidance, extinction,** and **punishment.***

As shown in Exhibit 17.7, there are four basic kinds of reinforcement: positive reinforcement, avoidance, extinction, and punishment.[32]

Positive reinforcement is a reward, or desirable outcome, that is given after a particular behavior.[33] For instance, suppose that a supervisor notices a worker doing an extra good job. She stops and tells the worker what a good job he is doing and then recommends to her boss that the worker should get a small pay raise. The praise and the pay raise are positive reinforcements. As a consequence the worker is likely to continue to work hard.

Avoidance also increases the likelihood that someone will repeat a desirable behavior, although it uses a different perspective. In this case the employee is allowed to avoid an unpleasant situation because of good performance. If a company has a policy that employees who are late for work get penalized, if all employees come to work on time, no penalties are imposed. As long as the threat continues, employees will be motivated to be on time every day.

Extinction is used to weaken behavior, especially behavior that has previously been rein-

Exhibit 17.7
Kinds of Reinforcement

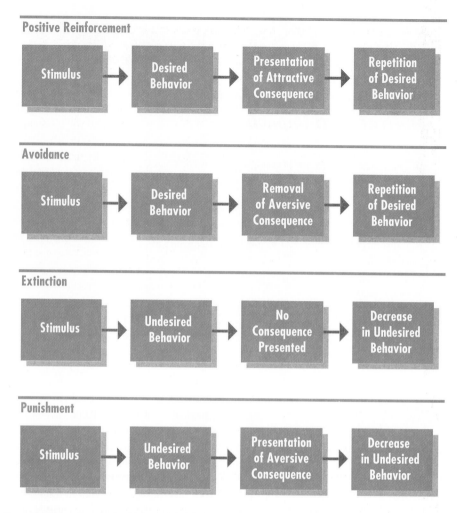

Source: Adapted from *Organizational Behavior,* 3rd ed., by Gregory Moorhead and Ricky W. Griffin. Copyright © 1992 by Houghton Mifflin Company. Used with permission.

forced. Take a manager of a small office who once allowed employees to come by whenever they wanted to "shoot the breeze." Now the office staff has grown so large that she must curtail this practice. The manager might remain cordial but will continue working at her desk until employees get the message; that is, she just ignores the undesired behavior. Of course, she must also work to guard against resentment and a loss in communication.

Punishment is also used to change behavior. Common forms of punishment in organizations include reprimands, discipline, and fines. Since punishment usually engenders resentment and hostility, managers should use it only as a last resort. Suppose that an employee has been late for work three times in the last week with no valid excuse. His boss might choose to reprimand him, explaining that another absence within the next six months will lead to a suspension.

Schedules of Reinforcement

For managers to use reinforcement effectively to enhance motivation, they must know when to provide it. Five basic schedules of reinforcement are available.[34]

Under the **continuous reinforcement schedule,** the manager provides reinforce-

Schedules of reinforcement include **continuous, fixed** *and* **variable interval,** *and* **fixed** *and* **variable ratio schedules.**

ment after every occurrence of the behavior; that is, the supervisor praises her subordinate every time she sees him doing a good job. Obviously, the power of the praise as reinforcement will rapidly diminish, since it is so common and easy to get.

Under a **fixed interval schedule,** the manager provides reinforcement on a periodic basis, regardless of performance. An example is the Friday paycheck many employees get. The check is obviously important to them, but it really does not affect their performance, since they receive it regardless of how hard they work. This schedule is therefore also of limited value as a way to enhance motivation.

The **variable interval schedule** also uses time as a basis for reinforcement, but the time intervals between reinforcement vary. If praise follows this schedule or is tied to random office visits by the manager, it will tend to be more powerful.

Under the **fixed ratio schedule,** the manager provides reinforcement on the basis of number of behaviors rather than on the basis of time. However, the number of behaviors an employee must display to get the reinforcement is constant. For example, suppose Montgomery Ward decides to get more credit card customers. Each salesclerk is asked to solicit new applicants, and the clerks are given fifty cents for every five applications that are completed. The idea is that each clerk will be highly motivated to get new applicants because each one brings him or her closer to the fifth application needed for another reward.

Finally, there is the **variable ratio schedule,** which is generally the most powerful one for enhancing motivation. Under this arrangement, the manager again gives reinforcement on the basis of behaviors, but the number of behaviors an employee needs to display to get the reinforcement varies. A supervisor might praise a subordinate after the second and fourth indications of good performance, then after the third, fourth, and fifth indications, then after the second one. Thus the subordinate is motivated to continue to work hard because each incident raises the probability (though not the certainty) that the next will bring praise. This schedule is the one used in slot machines in casinos in Las Vegas.

Reward Systems and Motivation

Regardless of what motivational model or perspective a manager uses, it is typically made operational through the organization's reward system.[35] In this section we consider what kinds of rewards are usually available, the characteristics of effective reward systems, and some interesting reward systems that are just being developed.

Kinds of Rewards

A **reward** *is anything the organization provides to employees in exchange for their services.*

From the standpoint of the employee, a **reward** is anything the organization provides in exchange for services. Clearly, however, outcomes vary in terms of their potency as rewards. One category of reward includes base pay, benefits, holidays, and so forth; these rewards are not tied to performance. A second category includes pay increases, incentives, bonuses, promotions, status symbols (bigger offices, reserved parking spaces), and attractive job assignments. These are rewards in the truest sense; they represent significant forms of positive reinforcement and satisfy many of the basic needs of most employees.

Some fairly inexpensive, simple reward systems have had good success. One of your textbook authors helped achieve outstanding performance from those involved in a three-year project by handing out stars periodically. Everyone involved got a gold star once a month, but those who made some sort of special effort during the month would get a silver star. Those who got three silver stars in a row would then get larger red stars. People kept their stars visible at their work stations and took considerable pride in showing them to others.

The Holiday Inn at Briley Parkway in Nashville, Tennessee, evolved The Apple Award to reward its personnel for outstanding service. Guests or fellow employees can nominate any employee for an award. A committee reviews nominations to assure that they were indeed for outstanding

Table 17.1

Characteristics of Effective Reward Systems

Characteristic	Examples
1. Rewards satisfy the basic needs of employees.	Adequate pay, reasonable benefits, appropriate holidays.
2. Rewards are comparable to those offered by similar organizations in the area	Pay rates of nearby companies are equal; employees receive the same holiday time as employees in comparable positions in other organizations.
3. Rewards are distributed fairly and equitably.	Employees who work overtime for a special project receive extra pay or compensatory time off; employees in comparable positions receive equal rewards for similar work.
4. The reward system is multifaceted.	A range of rewards are given: pay, benefits, promotion, privileges, etc.; rewards may be obtained in different ways.

service. If so, the employee receives a red apple pin. Five red apples earn a silver pin, five silver ones earn a gold pin, and five gold ones earn a crystal apple to display. When more than one person in a department earns a recognition, the whole department may receive a basket of real apples to share. Personnel display their pins with great pride, and the program has been so successful that it is spreading to other Holiday Inns.[36]

Effective Reward Systems

If reward systems are to serve their intended purpose, they must be effective. Effective reward systems tend to have four basic characteristics, as summarized in Table 17.1. First, they must satisfy the basic needs of the employees. Pay must be adequate, benefits reasonable, holidays appropriate, and so forth. Second, the rewards must be comparable to those offered by other organizations in the immediate area. If a Dow Chemical plant is paying its workers eight dollars an hour, and a Union Carbide plant down the road is paying nine dollars, employees at the Dow plant will always be looking for openings at the Carbide facility.

Rewards must also be distributed in a fair and equitable fashion. As we have discussed, people have a need to be treated fairly. If rewards are not distributed in an equitable fashion, employees will be resentful. Finally, the reward system must be multifaceted, which means that it must acknowledge that different people have different needs. A range of rewards must be provided, and people need to be able to attain rewards in different ways. For example, a marketing manager and a financial manager must each have an opportunity for promotion into the ranks of middle management.

New Reward Systems

In an effort to compete with other firms for good employees, many organizations have begun to experiment with new kinds of rewards and new ways to achieve them.[37] Du Pont, for instance, has worked at developing a new reward system as a way to boost productivity.[38]

One kind of contemporary system ties pay directly to performance, moreso than was done in the past. Another innovation is the all-salaried work force. Under this arrangement, all workers

Organizations and managers must be careful to reward desired behaviors, rather than undesired ones. Motorola desires quality performance and so uses training and rewards to support quality. Here a winning team celebrates its victory in the company's annual quality contest. (Michael L. Abramson.)

are paid by the month rather than by the hour, time clocks are eliminated, and people monitor their own work hours. Both Gillette and Dow Chemical have used this plan.

Skill-based job evaluation systems are also becoming increasingly popular. In this case people are paid according to their level of proficiency, or skill. Teachers with master's degrees, for instance, are paid more than teachers with undergraduate degrees, even though they do the same job. General Foods and Texas Instruments have used this approach, increasing an employee's pay whenever he or she masters a new job or skill.

Chapter Summary

Motivation is the set of processes that determine behavioral choices. The traditional view of motivation was that people worked only for economic reasons. The human relations view argued that if people were satisfied with their work, they would produce more. The human resources view suggests that people are actually resources that can benefit organizations and that managers should maintain and develop them, like other assets, for maximum productivity. The process of motivation begins with needs, drives or forces that initiate behavior. The existence of needs leads to efforts to try to satisfy those needs. The extent to which needs are satisfied leads in turn to the levels of satisfaction that people experience, which influence their choices of future efforts to satisfy needs. Hence the process begins again.

Early theories stressed needs and the need hierarchy. These theories, while important as starting points, are of limited value to practicing managers. The dominant theory today is the expectancy model, which holds that motivation is a function of how much we want something and how likely we think we are to get it.

Many early writers felt that if managers could satisfy the needs of employees, those employees would perform better. However, research has shown that satisfaction does not cause performance. It is more accurate to say that performance properly rewarded leads to satisfaction, a key element of which is equity. Whenever people perceive an inequity in their situation, they will try to do something about it, that is, they will be motivated to reduce the perceived inequity. Goal setting and high-involvement management are also important ingredients in motivation.

Reinforcement processes are very similar to the process described by the expectancy model. The theory suggests that future behavior is shaped by the consequences of current behavior. There are four basic kinds of reinforcement: positive reinforcement, avoidance, extinction, and punishment. Positive reinforcement is a reward that follows desired behavior, increasing the chances it will be repeated. Avoidance behavior is aimed at avoiding negative consequences. In extinction, nothing happens following a behavior, and the behavior is ignored. Punishment, on the other hand, means that the behavior results in an undesirable consequence.

The impact of these kinds of reinforcements on behavior is complicated, however, by their schedule, or the frequency with which the reinforcement occurs.

There are numerous kinds of rewards, both extrinsic and intrinsic. These include base pay, benefits, pay increases, incentives, bonuses, praise, recognition, work assignments, and so on. Effective reward systems tend to have four characteristics: they must satisfy basic needs, be comparable to those used elsewhere, be distributed equitably, and be multifaceted.

The Manager's Vocabulary

motivation	affiliation need	avoidance
needs	achievement need	extinction
need hierarchy	power need	punishment
physiological needs	expectancy model	continuous reinforcement schedule
security needs	equity	fixed interval schedule
social needs	goal-setting theory	variable interval schedule
esteem needs	high-involvement management	fixed ratio schedule
self-actualization needs	reinforcement	variable ratio schedule
two-factor view	positive reinforcement	reward

Review Questions

1. What are the three basic historical perspectives through which motivational theory has passed?
2. What are the five basic need levels in Maslow's hierarchy of needs?
3. Summarize the basic premises of expectancy theory.
4. What is the relationship between performance and satisfaction?
5. What are the four basic types of reinforcement? What are the five schedules of reinforcement?

Analysis Questions

1. How important do you think money is in motivation? Explain.
2. Do you agree or disagree with the basic premises of the two-factor theory? Why or why not?
3. How do you think performance and satisfaction are related?
4. Explain how you might form equity perceptions in your role as a student.
5. Which new reward system do you think holds the most potential? Why? Why might workers oppose it?

Self-Assessment

Job Involvement

Introduction When employees are given a greater voice in how things are done, they become more involved and committed to the organization. When employees enjoy their job, they become more involved in the work. This self-assessment examines your level of involvement starting with your job.

Instructions Your response to the following twenty items will enable you to describe the extent of your involvement on the job you presently have. If you are not now working, think of the job you most recently held. Respond to the items according to whether you (1) strongly disagree (2) disagree (3) agree (4) strongly agree.

1. _____ I'll stay overtime to finish a job, even if I'm not paid for it.

2. _____ You can measure a person pretty well by how good a job is done.

3. _____ The major satisfaction in my life comes from my job.

4. _____ For me, mornings at work really fly by.

5. _____ I usually show up for work a little early to get things ready.

6. _____ The most important things that happen to me involve work.

7. _____ Sometimes I lie awake at night thinking ahead to the next day's work.

8. _____ I'm really a perfectionist about my work.

9. _____ I feel depressed when I fail at something connected with my job.

10. _____ I have other activities more important than my work.

11. _____ I live, eat, and breathe my job.

12. _____ I would probably keep working even if I didn't need the money.

13. _____ Quite often I feel like staying home from work instead of coming in.

14. _____ To me, my work is only a small part of who I am.

15. _____ I am very much involved personally in my work.

16. _____ I avoid taking on extra duties and responsibilities in my work.

17. _____ I used to be more ambitious about my work than I am now.

18. _____ Most things in life are more important than work.

19. _____ I used to care more about my work, but now other things are more important to me.

20. _____ Sometimes I'd like to kick myself for the mistakes made in my work.

For interpretation, turn to the back of the book.

Source: Thomas M. Lodahl and Mathilde Kejner, "The Definition and Measurement of Job Involvement," *Journal of Applied Psychology,* February 1965, Vol. 49, Issue 1, pp. 24–33. Copyright 1965 by the American Psychological Association. Reprinted by permission.

Skill Builder

An Exercise in Thematic Apperception

Purpose All people have needs and those needs make people pursue different goals in an effort to satisfy their needs. This Skill Builder introduces you to one of the tools by which managers can identify both their own needs and those of their employees. This Skill Builder focuses on the *scientific management model* and the *human resources model*. It will help you to develop the producer role of the scientific model. One of the skills of the producer is the ability to motivate yourself. In addition, it will help you develop the facilitator role of the human resources model. One of the skills of the facilitator is the ability to motivate others.

Introduction Over the last thirty years behaviorists have researched the relationship between a person's fantasies and his or her motivation. One popular instrument used to establish this relationship is the Thematic Apperception Test (TAT).

Instructions

Step 1:

1. Examine each picture (provided by your instructor) for about one minute. Then cover the picture.

2. Using the picture as a guide, write a story that could be used in a TV soap opera. Make your story continuous, dramatic, and interesting. Do not just answer the questions. Try to complete the story in less than ten minutes.

3. Do not be concerned about obtaining negative results from this instrument. There are no right or wrong stories.

4. After finishing one story, repeat the same procedure until all six stories are completed.

Step 2: Conduct a story interpretation in groups of three persons each. Taking turns reading one story at a time, each person will read a story out loud to the other two people in the group. Then all three will examine the story for statements that fall into one of the following three categories:

*Category AC—Statements that refer to:
  High standards of excellence
  A desire to win, do well, succeed
  Unique accomplishments
  Long-term goals
  Careers

*Category PO—Statements that refer to:
  Influencing others
  Controlling others
  The desire to instruct others
  The desire to dominate others
  The concern over weakness, failure, or humiliation
  Superior-subordinate relationships or status relationship

*Category AF—Statements that refer to:
  Concern over establishing positive emotional relationships
  Warm friendships or their loss
  A desire to be liked
  One person liking another
  Parties, reunions, or visits
  Relaxed small talk
  Concern for others when not required by social custom.

To assist in the interpretation of the test results, assign 10 points to each story. Divide the 10 points among the three categories based on the frequency of statements that refer to AC, PO, and AF behaviors in the story. Once the allocation of the 10 points is determined, record the results in the following scoring table:

Divide 10 points among the following categories:

Number of Story Scored	AC		PO		AF		TOTAL
1	____	+	____	+	____	=	__10__
2	____	+	____	+	____	=	__10__
3	____	+	____	+	____	=	__10__
4	____	+	____	+	____	=	__10__
5	____	+	____	+	____	=	__10__
6	____	+	____	+	____	=	__10__
TOTAL	____	+	____	+	____	=	__60__

Divide totals by 10 times number of stories scored ____ + ____ + ____

Category percentages ____ % ____ % ____ % = _100%_

Your Thematic Apperception Test values of AC, PO, and AF indicate your mix of needs for achievement (AC), power (PO), and affiliation (AF) respectively. Due to the circumstances under which this exercise was conducted, your values should be considered as only rough estimates. If you feel uncomfortable with your results, it is suggested that you consult with your instructor.

Step 3: In small groups, discuss the following questions:
Do you agree with your TAT results?
Can you cite specific behaviors to substantiate your opinions?
Do other members of your group perceive you as having the needs indicated by your TAT results?
Can they cite specific behaviors to substantiate their opinions?
What interpersonal problems might exist between a manager and an employee who had different need mixes?
In what type of job would you place an employee with a high need for affiliation? A high need for power? A high need for affiliation?

Source: *Motives in Fantasy, Action and Society: Method of Assessment and Study*. John W. Atkinson, Ed., (Princeton, N.J.: D. Van Nostrand Co., Inc., 1958). Copyright © 1958. Used with permission .Drawings from Peter P. Dawson, *Fundamentals of Organizational Behavior: An Experimental Approach* (Englewood Cliffs, N.J.: Prentice Hall, 1985), pp. 81–95. Drawings by Della Myers and Doris Weber. Reprinted by permission.

CONCLUDING CASES

17.1   Nordstrom Branches Out

John W. Nordstrom came to Seattle, Washington, from Sweden and opened a retail store in 1901. His three sons focused on shoe selling and expanded from one store into the largest shoe chain in the United States by the late 1950s. In the 1960s Nordstrom began expanding beyond shoes. It acquired Best Apparel of Seattle in 1963 and Nicholas Ungar, a Portland fashion outlet, in 1966. By 1975 Nordstrom had eleven stores in three Western states. By 1985 it had surpassed Saks Fifth Avenue to become the leading specialty fashion retailer in the United States.

During most of these recent years, three grandsons of the

founder have run the company as a team. They even rotated the title of president among themselves. In 1991 they expanded this management by a team approach to include four nonfamily members. These four all have the title of copresident. Each copresident concentrates on a different part of the business, but together they evolve one "voice" on all business matters. This high-involvement approach seems to be working extremely well.

By stressing outstanding customer service, Nordstrom had sales in excess of $2 billion from its forty-eight stores in 1988 and was giving rivals a strong run for their money. By 1990 it had expanded its retail empire to the East coast, grown to fifty-nine stores, and was becoming a leader in the use of high technology to keep employees, buyers, and vendors in touch with one another. In 1993 Nordstrom announced plans to expand to the South with a store in Dallas.

Many loyal employees, called "Nordies," are clearly highly motivated. They have been known to write thank you notes to customers, telephone them to let them know about the arrival of merchandise, and even warm up their cars for them on cold winter days. Two hundred of them even paid their own way to move across the country when stores opened up on the East coast. These employees spend a lot of time and energy assuring that high customer service will be the hallmark of Nordstrom.

However, other employees do not always share this enthusiasm. Nordstrom's pay practices were labeled as unfair by labor unions and some employees. Those employees claimed that they were not paid for overtime work or for a lot of the service-related activities that occurred after hours. Lawsuits by shareholders and employees, coupled with adverse rulings by the National Labor Relations Board and the State of Washington during 1990, caused the firm to announce the first drop in annual profits in the history of the firm.[39]

Discussion Questions

1. What theory or theories of motivation seem useful in understanding conditions at Nordstrom?
2. In which environments might Nordstrom not be effective? Explain.
3. Explain some possible weaknesses in the motivational system of Nordstrom.
4. What motivational strategies might Nordstrom employ to make the company even more successful?

17.2 Perrier Has to Flow Uphill

Attempts to make a commercially successful spa at the naturally carbonated spring in Vergèze, France, failed despite its general popularity. Even efforts to bottle the water as a healthful beverage did not succeed until the Englishman, A. W. St. John Harmsworth, bought it from Louis Perrier early in this century (hence the official name, Source Perrier). By the 1930s the company was selling almost 20 million bottles. By 1992 Perrier was second only to BSN as a global producer of bottled water under such brands as Arrowhead, Calistoga, Contrex, Great Bear, Poland Spring, Vichy, Volvic, and, of course, Perrier. In addition, Perrier is a major producer of dairy products. It is, for instance, the number-one producer of Roquefort cheese.

Perrier prides itself on flexibility planning, and that flexibility has proven essential over and over. For instance, in 1990 benzene was discovered in the Perrier brand of bottled water. The company quickly pulled all brand Perrier bottled water from the shelves (not just those bottles that were known to be contaminated), found and fixed the problem (a dirty filter), and got the product back on supermarket shelves in less than three months. However, three months is an extremely long time in marketing, and competitors raced to take over the shelf space and, ideally, the market share as well. While many of Perrier's customers simply switched to another brand produced by Perrier, some did move to competitors. Perrier consolidated its buying and expended an enormous sum in advertising to reintroduce brand Perrier. It was motivated to protect its image for distributing only pure spring water and felt that the public would continue to be motivated to purchase the famous green-bottled beverage.

Some feel that Perrier overreacted by pulling all of its brand Perrier from store shelves and that it may never fully recover from the absence of its product for three months. Perrier counters that its motive was to demonstrate its dedication to its customers in providing nothing but the purest of product. Both views may, of course, be correct, but Perrier was damaged and, as a result, became the target of an acquisition attempt by Nestlé in 1992.[40]

Discussion Questions

1. How might an awareness of theories of motivation be useful in understanding conditions at Source Perrier?
2. Which motivational theory might best help explain Perrier's actions? Explain.
3. What are some possible weaknesses in a motivational explanation of Perrier's actions?
4. What motivational strategies might Perrier employ to make the company even more successful in the future?

CHAPTER

18

Groups and Teams

Learning Objectives

After studying this chapter you should be able to

- Characterize organizations in terms of interpersonal processes.

- Define a group and elaborate on different kinds of groups.

- Discuss the psychological character of groups, including why people join groups, the stages of development through which groups tend to move, and the nature of the informal organization.

- Identify important group dimensions — role dynamics, cohesiveness, and norms — and the relationships among them.

- Discuss the management of functional groups, task forces and committees, work teams, and quality circles.

- Describe the advantages, disadvantages, and techniques of group decision making.

mgen Inc. is a world leader in biotechnology, if not the world leader. Even though a major legal ruling ordered Amgen to share with a competitor profits earned on Epogen (EPO), one of its blockbuster drugs, Amgen continues to use its profits for technological innovation. Indeed, in the recession of the early 1990s, Amgen's emphasis on excellence and innovation helped it remain successful while competitors were struggling.

The Thousand Oaks, California, company has grown so rapidly that it sprawls over numerous buildings and has had 50-percent increases in employment several times during its existence. It has managed that growth through the use of teams. A small company atmosphere is maintained by having virtually every one of its fifteen hundred employees involved in one or more teams.

Amgen uses PDTs (product development teams) to work on bringing a new product to market and task forces for all other activities. Team members come from both the laboratories and the business side of the company. Usually reporting to senior management, the teams range in size from five to eighty members. Rather than running teams, the heads of departments, called facilitators, help the teams reach their goals.

Teams are not closed, however. Anyone can attend any meeting, and cross-departmental discussion is actively encouraged. The family business culture is further fostered through chili cook-offs, bowling tournaments, workshops, field trips, and other activities designed to increase interaction among personnel.

The only significant drawback that Amgen has reported is that sometimes people feel that they work for the product or team rather than for Amgen. Continual meetings across teams will help reduce that feeling in the future should it ever become a problem.[1] ■

mgen has developed top performance and effectiveness by capitalizing on the energy and strength provided by one of the most underutilized resources in organizations today: groups. One of the oldest maxims known is that "two heads are better than one." By applying two heads (or more) to a problem, organizations can often achieve more than if they maintain the old habit of assigning single tasks to individual employees.

Litel Telecommunications Corp. restructured to a high-involvement, teamwork approach in 1989. Within a month order processing time dropped from fourteen days to one day, and the error rate went from 40 percent to less than 5 percent. Within a year revenues nearly doubled. The Saturn automobile plant in Tennessee is organized around empowered individuals and teams. A Corning plant in Blacksburg, Virginia, is organized around self-managed teams with only three managers for a 150-person plant. Harley-Davidson, Xerox, Procter & Gamble, and Digital Equipment are all using some form of teams as well.[2]

Much of the work accomplished by an organization is a result of people working together.

Interpersonal relations and groups are a ubiquitous part of organizational life and, increasingly, so is the use of teams.[3] By definition, organizations involve networks of interactions among virtually everyone in those organizations. Therefore, a manager clearly needs to understand the dynamics of group and team activities within the organization. This chapter first describes the interpersonal character of organizations. It then explores the nature of groups, establishing their psychological character and examining three critical group dimensions. Next it investigates some guidelines for using groups and teams in organizations. After discussing group decision making, it concludes by discussing conflict.

The Interpersonal Character of Organizations

As indicated in Chapter 15, the very nature of organizations means that they are composed of people working together. Heads of groups discuss work assignments and performance issues with members of their group; peers at all levels conduct regular meetings to develop plans and solve problems; group members go to their group leaders with problems and questions; sales representatives talk to customers; secretaries take telephone calls. Indeed, research has suggested that the average manager spends around three-quarters of his or her time interacting with others.[4]

However, the nature of any given interaction can vary considerably. Two managers talking at the water cooler may be reaching agreement on how to solve a problem, setting up a meeting for later in the day, discussing the latest football polls, deciding whether or not to fire someone, or arguing about how to resolve a point of disagreement. People can interact as individuals or as members of groups and teams. Whereas Chapter 15 focused primarily on individual processes, this chapter focuses primarily on group processes. Regardless of the purpose or the consequences of interpersonal activity, much of it occurs within the context of groups and the use of groups is growing.[5]

The Nature of Groups

What is a group? First let's examine the concept of a group, and then we can identify the major kinds of groups found in organizational settings.

Definition of a Group

*A **group** is two or more people who interact regularly to accomplish a common goal.*

A **group** can be defined as two or more people who interact regularly to accomplish a common goal.[6] There are three basic elements that are necessary for a group to exist.

First, at least two people must be involved. Although there is no precise upper limit, a group that gets too large usually ceases to function as a group.

Second, the members must interact regularly. This is the reason for setting an upper limit on group size; once a group reaches a certain size—say, twenty people—it becomes so difficult for everyone to interact regularly that smaller groups tend to emerge from within the larger one.[7]

Perhaps nothing exemplifies the nature of a highly effective group more than a dance troupe. Shown here is the Alvin Ailey American Dance Theater's performance of "Hidden Rites." The dance troupe shares a common vision, coordinates its activities, and becomes a highly cohesive group through its shared norm of excellent performance. (Jack Mitchell.)

Finally, group members must have a common purpose. Managers at Mobil may create a group to develop a new plan or product; a group of workers might band together to try to change a company policy; a group of friends might go out together for dinner and a movie. In each case members of the group are working toward a common goal.

Kinds of Groups

*Three common types of groups are **functional groups, task groups,** and **informal groups.***

There are many, many different kinds of groups, but we are most concerned about groups that exist in organizations. In general, most of these are formal, that is, created by the organization, and can be classified as functional, task, or informal, as shown in Exhibit 18.1.[8]

A **functional group** is created by the organization to accomplish a range of goals with an indefinite time horizon. The operations division at Allen-Bradley Co., the marketing division of Nissan, the management department at the University of Notre Dame, and the nursing staff at Ben Taub hospital in Houston are all functional groups. Each of these was formed by the organization, has a number of goals, and has an indefinite time horizon—that is, it is not slated to disappear at a certain time in the future. As the exhibit illustrates, functional groups generally conform to departmental boundaries on an organization chart.

A **task group** is created by the organization to accomplish a limited number of goals within a stated or implied time. Hallmark Cards, for example, might appoint a design team to develop a new line of greeting cards. The group is created by the organization, has only one goal, and has an implied time horizon. After the line has been developed and approved, the group will dissolve.

Exhibit 18.1

Kinds of Groups in Organizations

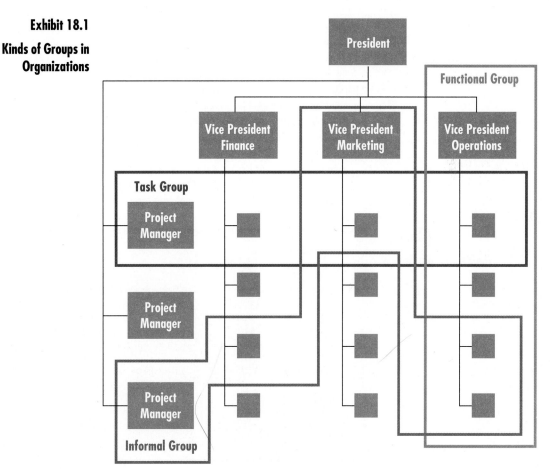

There are actually several different forms of task groups in most organizations. As shown in the exhibit, a matrix design, as discussed in Chapters 11 and 12, places task groups under the direction of a project manager. Task forces, most committees, and many decision-making groups are also task groups.

An **informal group,** also called an interest group, is created by the members of the group itself for purposes that may or may not be related to the organization, and it has an unspecified time horizon. Five coworkers who go to lunch together frequently, twelve employees who form a softball team, and three secretaries who take their afternoon coffee break together are examples of informal groups. Each person chooses to participate and can stop whenever he or she wants.

When at lunch, the first group of workers might discuss how to solve an organizational problem (relevant to and in the best interests of the organization), how to steal a machine (relevant to but not in the best interests of the organization), or local politics and sports (not relevant to the organization). As you might guess, informal groups are extremely important to managers and can be a powerful force in determining organizational effectiveness. It is therefore important to understand the psychological character of groups.[9]

The Psychological Character of Groups

Much of what is known about group processes comes from research in the field of psychology.[10] A substantial portion of this work relates to why people join groups, stages of group development, and the informal organization.

Why People Join Groups

People join groups for a variety of reasons, including interpersonal attraction, activities, goals, and instrumental benefits.

Sometimes people have no choice as to whether to join a group. Students may have to take a certain class, or employees might have to accept a specific job assignment that involves working with a designated group of other people. In many instances, though, people can choose whether to join a particular group. The four most common reasons for doing so are set forth in Table 18.1.[11]

One powerful reason for joining a group is interpersonal attraction. For instance, a new employee might find three other people who work in his department to be especially pleasant and to have interests and attitudes similar to his own, so he might start joining them for lunch most days. He thus joins the group because he is attracted to the members of that group.

Another reason for joining a group is the group's activities. Suppose that another new employee is an avid bowler. She might inquire about and subsequently be invited to join the company bowling team. Of course, she will probably not remain on the team if she dislikes all the other

Table 18.1
Why People Join Groups

Reason	Example
1. Interpersonal Attraction	An employee joins three colleagues for lunch because they share his interest in local politics.
2. Group Activities	An employee joins the company bowling team because she loves to bowl.
3. Group Goals	An employee joins a union because she believes employees should negotiate for higher wages.
4. Instrumental Benefits	A manager joins a golf club because most of his business associates are members and he will make useful contacts.

People join groups for combinations of complex reasons. As a result, when group norms evolve, they tend to be strong and changing them is not easy. The 1992 riots in Los Angeles served as a catalyst for getting the Bloods and Crips—two rival South Central Los Angeles gangs—to move from gunfire and bloodshed to handshakes. (Mark Richards.)

members, but it is not her attraction to them that prompts her to join to begin with. Rather, it is a specific activity that she wants to pursue and that is facilitated by group membership.

A third reason people choose to join groups is that they identify with and want to pursue the goals of the group. This is a common reason for joining unions. Interpersonal attraction is irrelevant, and few people enjoy tedious contract negotiations or strikes. But employees may subscribe to the goals the union has set for its members, such as high wages, better working conditions, and so forth. Similar motives cause people to join the Sierra Club and charitable groups like the United Fund and the American Cancer Society.

A final reason for joining groups is the instrumental benefits that may accompany group membership. For example, it is fairly common for college students entering their senior year to join one or more professional associations in order to be able to list it on their resume. Similarly, a manager might join a certain golf club not because he likes the other members (although he might) or because he likes to play golf (although, again, he might) but in order to make some useful business contacts.

Stages of Group Development

*Groups usually progress through four stages as they develop: **forming**, **storming**, **norming**, and **performing**.*

Regardless of the reasons that people join groups, the groups themselves typically go through a period of evolution or development. Although there is no rigid pattern that all groups follow, they usually go through the four stages portrayed in Exhibit 18.2.[12]

The first stage is **forming,** also known as mutual acceptance. As shown by the image on the left side of the exhibit, and as suggested by the term itself, forming involves the members actually coming together to create the group. During this stage the members get acquainted and begin to test which behaviors are acceptable and which are unacceptable to other members of the group.

In the **storming** stage, the members may begin to pull apart again as they disagree over what needs to be done and how best to do it. Key elements in this stage are communication and decision making to offset any conflict and hostility that may emerge. Patterns of interaction may be uneven, as suggested by the exhibit, and an informal leader often begins to emerge at this point.

Norming, a common third phase, is characterized by the resolution of conflict and the development of roles (discussed later). People have either left the group because the conflict is too

Exhibit 18.2
Stages of Group Development

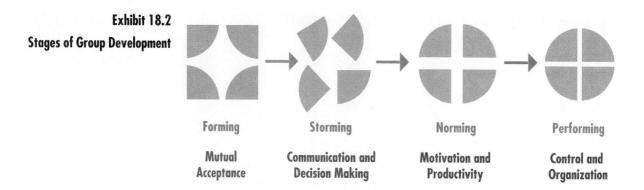

Forming	Storming	Norming	Performing
Mutual Acceptance	Communication and Decision Making	Motivation and Productivity	Control and Organization

great or accepted the group for what it is. Each member takes on certain responsibilities, and everyone develops a common vision of how the group will function. Motivation and productivity begin to emerge as a sense of unity evolves.

Finally, the group begins **performing,** moving toward accomplishing its goals, whether those are deciding which movie to see or developing a major planning document for the firm. Members enact their respective roles and direct their efforts toward the goal. Control and organization evolve as the group becomes more stable and structured.

Of course, as noted earlier, every group may not follow these exact stages in a discrete and observable sequence. All groups, however, do generally deal with the kinds of issues associated with each stage as they mature. Mature groups, then, tend to exhibit four characteristics: a role structure, behavioral norms, cohesiveness, and leadership, which will be discussed later in the chapter.

The Informal Organization

*The **informal organization** is the overall pattern of influence and interaction defined by the total set of informal groups within the organization.*

It is also critical for managers to recognize the existence and importance of the **informal organization,** the overall pattern of influence and interaction defined by the total set of informal groups within the organization.[13] As suggested earlier in Exhibit 18.1, the formal organizational structure is overlaid with informal groups. These groups actually get much of the organization's work done—that is, informal telephone calls, chance meetings at the coffee machine, and impromptu lunch gatherings go a long way toward defining the organization's goals and helping achieve them. Thus managers should not ignore the power of the informal organization as they go about their business.

Important Group Dimensions

G roups in and of themselves are of considerable importance and interest. However, managers can gain even greater insights into groups by considering their role dynamics, their level of cohesiveness, and their norms.

Role Dynamics

*A **role** is a part a person plays in a group.*

What is a **role?** In a movie or play, a role is a part played by an actor. People in groups also play roles.[14] Some people playing the role of "task specialists" might help the group accomplish its goals. Others, called "social specialists," might work to keep everyone happy. A few serve as leaders. Still others, called "free riders," might do very little.

As we have seen, everyone belongs to several different groups. Many people are part of a formal work group, one or more task groups, several informal groups, and a family. Thus each person has various roles to play. A given individual might be a task specialist in one group, the leader in another, and a free rider in a third.

*Role dynamics **are defined by** expected, sent, perceived, and enacted roles.*

Exhibit 18.3 illustrates the way in which **role dynamics** occur in a group. Role dynamics are the process whereby a person's expected role is transformed to his or her enacted role. First there is the **expected role,** the role others in the group expect a given person to play. The mem-

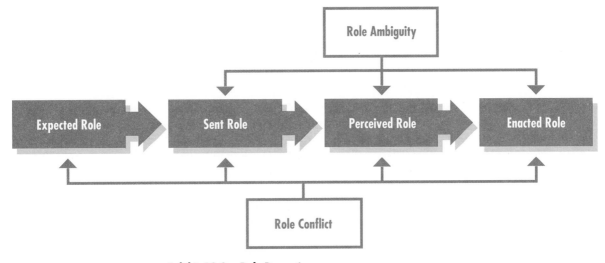

Exhibit 18.3 Role Dynamics

bers transmit these expectations in the form of the **sent role.** As we will see in the next chapter, however, communication breakdowns frequently occur, so there may be differences between the expected and sent roles.

   Perceptual factors can affect the role process, too. Therefore, still more differences may creep in as the sent role is translated into the **perceived role,** how the individual comes to think he or she should behave in the group. Finally, the **enacted role** is how the person actually behaves, and here too differences can arise. For example, the person might not be capable of executing the perceived role, or he or she might simply choose not to execute it in the way that others expect.

   The exhibit also introduces the concepts of role ambiguity and role conflict, two facets of group dynamics that warrant additional explanation.

Role ambiguity occurs when the sent role is not clear.

   Role ambiguity occurs when the sent role is unclear.[15] For instance, suppose a supervisor tells a new employee to prepare a sales forecast for the next period. It is quite possible that the employee does not know where to get the data, how many products to include in the forecast, what form to use for the report, or even what time period is involved. Thus she will probably suffer from role ambiguity.

Role conflict occurs when there is some degree of inconsistency or contradiction about the role.

   Of perhaps even greater concern is **role conflict,** which occurs when the messages about the role are clear but involve some degree of inconsistency or contradiction.[16] There are several forms of role conflict.[17]

   Interrole conflict occurs when there is conflict between two or more roles. For example, suppose an employee's leader tells him he has to work more overtime. But the employee was already feeling guilty about working so much and has just resolved to spend more time with his family. Consequently, he will now experience interrole conflict. In contrast, intrarole conflict occurs when two or more people send conflicting messages to a person in the same role. If a marketing vice president tells a sales manager to have the sales force travel more and the controller tells the sales manager to cut travel costs, the sales manager will experience intrarole conflict.

   Intrasender role conflict arises if the same person transmits conflicting expectations. Suppose that on Monday a manager tells her assistant that she can dress more casually, but on Thursday she reprimands her for not looking professional. The obvious contradiction will result in intrasender role conflict for the assistant.

Finally, person-role conflict arises when the demands of the role are incongruent with the person's preferences or values. An employee experiences this conflict if his job demands a great deal of travel, for instance, but he prefers to remain at home. Similarly, an employee who has strong feelings against military buildups and the arms race may feel uncomfortable when her company gets several defense contracts.

Cohesiveness

Cohesiveness is the extent to which members of the group are motivated to remain together.

Another important dimension of groups is **cohesiveness,** or the extent to which the members of the group are motivated to remain together.[18] A highly cohesive group is one in which the members pull together, enjoy being together, perform well together, and are not looking for opportunities to get out of the group. In contrast, a group with a low level of cohesiveness is one in which the members do not like to be together, do not work well together, and would casually leave the group if an opportunity arose.

Exhibit 18.4 shows the determinants and consequences of cohesiveness.[19] As shown, small size, frequent interaction, clear goals, and success tend to foster cohesiveness. For example, if five people (small size) are assigned to a crash project for developing a new product by the end of the year (clear goals), if they must spend virtually all of their working hours together (frequent interaction), and if they achieve a breakthrough sooner than expected (success), they are likely to emerge as a very cohesive group.

In contrast, a large group whose members are physically dispersed and that has ambiguous goals and suffers failures will be less cohesive. Suppose a firm designates eighty-five engineers (large size) located in three different plants (physically dispersed) as a task force to "explore new product ideas" (ambiguous goals). The group fails to come up with any useful ideas (failure). It will probably not be very cohesive.

The exhibit also illustrates various results of cohesiveness. If cohesiveness is high, the group tends to be more effective in attaining future goals, its members are more personally satisfied with the group, and the group will probably continue to exist. On the other hand, if cohesiveness is low, the group is less likely to attain its future goals, members will express more dissatisfaction with the group, and the group is more likely to dissolve or fall apart.

Norms

Norms are standards of behavior that the group develops for its members.

The importance of cohesiveness is accentuated when we consider it in the context of group norms. A **norm** is a standard of behavior that the group develops for its members.[20] For instance, a group might have a norm against talking to the head of the group too much. People who violate this norm may be "punished" with unpleasant looks, snide remarks, and the like. The norms themselves are, of course, socially defined and exist only in the minds of the group members.

Exhibit 18.4

Determinants and Consequences of Group Cohesiveness

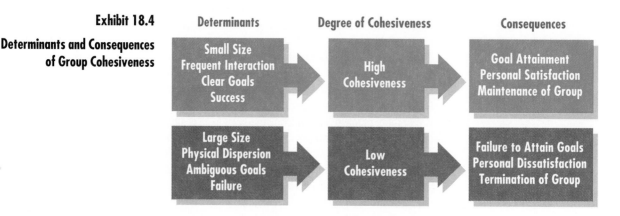

Determinants	Degree of Cohesiveness	Consequences
Small Size Frequent Interaction Clear Goals Success	High Cohesiveness	Goal Attainment Personal Satisfaction Maintenance of Group
Large Size Physical Dispersion Ambiguous Goals Failure	Low Cohesiveness	Failure to Attain Goals Personal Dissatisfaction Termination of Group

A Matter of Ethics

Ethical Treatment and Employees

The successful business organization of the 1990s considers all of its constituencies. Richard Finlay, chairman of J. Richard Finlay & Partners, argues that the very widest view of constituencies must be used — not just customers, employees, and shareholders but also the public at large must be taken into account. Each of these groups must view the organization as highly ethical and socially responsible. Small companies like Byrd Press have found that a sense of ethics pervading the company does, indeed, work.

In addition, including employees as a constituency group that must regard the organization as ethical is a highly successful Japanese management practice that these and other companies are starting to emulate. U.S. managers are recognizing that the Japanese practice of developing a dedicated, involved, and satisfied work force provides significant long-term benefits to an organization. Treating one's employees ethically has come to mean good business.

Ethical treatment of employees begins with having a fair and open selection process. After individuals are hired, ethical treatment includes involving them in decisions that impact them. And, finally, it also means developing an organizational culture that can even tolerate such activities as whistle blowing by employees.[21] ■

Norms can arise for any number of work-related behaviors. In a typical work group, there may be norms that define how people dress, the upper and lower limits on acceptable productivity, things that can be told to the head of the group and things that need to remain secret, and so forth.[22] *A Matter of Ethics: Ethical Treatment and Employees* suggests that how employees and others perceive the ethical norms of organizations is becoming increasingly important in the success of those organizations.

When confronted with a set of norms in an established group, an individual might do several different things. One common reaction is to accept and conform to the group norm. A less frequent reaction is total rebellion, in which case the person completely rejects the norm (of course, if the norm is important to the rest of the group, the newcomer will probably be ostracized). There is also creative individuality. In this situation, the person accepts some of the norms, especially the most important ones, but follows his or her own preferences within their limits. For example, if the norm is that employees will not wear jeans to work, a newcomer who prefers to dress casually might be able to get away with wearing jeans once every two or three weeks, as opposed to never wearing them (conformity) or wearing them every day (rebellion).

The norm that governs the acceptable level of performance in the group is far more important than is cohesiveness. This pattern is shown in Exhibit 18.5. When performance norms and cohesiveness are both high, the manager has a powerful vehicle for achieving high levels of performance. When performance norms are low and cohesiveness is high, however, the manager may have little choice other than to break up the group.

Managing Groups and Teams in Organizations

Since all organizations contain groups, it is obviously important for managers to understand how they should be managed.[23] This section discusses some guidelines for managing various kinds of groups. A special case of managing groups, group decision making, is considered in the section following this one.

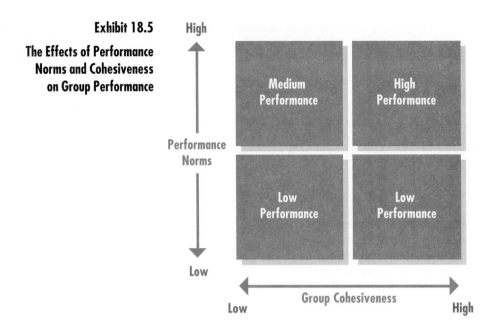

Exhibit 18.5

The Effects of Performance Norms and Cohesiveness on Group Performance

Managing Functional Groups

Virtually all aspects of interaction between a formal leader and his or her work group are related to the management of functional groups, so all of the areas of management covered in the other chapters in this book are pertinent. However, several specific implications for managing functional groups can be drawn from earlier discussions of group dimensions.[24]

For one thing, the manager should be cognizant of the importance of role dynamics. In particular, he or she should recognize the potential problems associated with role ambiguity and role conflict and strive to avoid these problems whenever possible. For another thing, the manager needs to realize the importance of group cohesiveness. As we have noted, cohesiveness can be a powerful force in organizations, especially when combined with different levels of performance norms. The manager should therefore work to enhance cohesiveness when it is in the best interests of the organization. Finally, the manager should work to establish high performance norms by adding hard workers to the group, consistently rewarding high performance, and so forth. Such actions should both reinforce current levels of performance norms and simultaneously push them higher.

Managing Task Forces and Committees

Organizations often use task forces and committees to get various kinds of tasks performed. Since both of these are task groups, they can generally be managed in similar ways. There are, however, a few subtle differences.

*Managers can follow certain guidelines in managing functional groups, **task forces** and **committees**, **work teams**, and **quality circles**.*

Managing Task Forces   Several guidelines that relate specifically to task forces have been developed.[25] A **task force** is a temporary group within an organization created to accomplish a specific purpose (task) by integrating existing functional areas. First, the majority of the group should be line managers. Since line managers are ultimately responsible for implementing the group's ideas, they should be well represented in the group. Second, the group needs to be provided with all relevant information. It will be more effective if it has access to information that affects its work.

Group members also need the legitimate power necessary to translate group needs back to their respective functional groups. Within the group, though, the emphasis should be on expert power; that is, group members with expertise in specialized areas should be placed in charge of those areas. The task force should also be properly integrated with relevant functional groups. Ideally this follows from the composition of the group, as suggested above, but special attention may be required to maintain this integration over time. A last point is to establish group membership with the goal of optimizing technical and interpersonal skills. Members need to know how to do their respective jobs, but they also need to be able to get along with one another.

Managing Committees   Another important part of almost every manager's job at one time or another is managing a committee. A **committee** is a special kind of task group. Committees may have only a few members, or they may have many. Their purpose may be broad and short term or narrow and long term. They are often given names, such as the Grievance Committee, the Steering Committee, or the President's Advisory Committee. They may appear at the bottom of the organization, or they may occur at the highest levels of the firm and have primary responsibility for its management.

Like other kinds of groups, committees can be made more effective if managers follow specific guidelines. For one thing, the goals and limits of the committee's authority need to be clearly specified in order to help keep the committee's activities focused and directed toward its intended purpose. For another, the committee should have a specific agenda. Care should also be taken to see that the committee does not interfere too much with its members' normal responsibilities; that is, people should not devote so much time to their committee duties that they neglect their regular jobs.

Finally, it is useful to specify what the output of the committee is to be. For example, suppose a manager creates a committee to locate a site for a new factory. He may want the committee to submit a list of three acceptable sites, either rank-ordered or unranked. He may need a lot of supporting materials for each site, or he may want only the recommendations. Obviously, he should clearly communicate each of these expectations to the committee before it begins to work.[26]

Managing Work Teams

A fairly recent innovation in the use of groups in organizations is the establishment of work teams. A **work team** is a small group of employees that is responsible for a set of tasks previously performed by its individual members and that takes primary responsibility for managing itself. Many firms such as A. O. Smith have adopted the work team concept.

There are several reasons for the use of work teams. Perhaps the most important is that work teams provide a natural vehicle for giving employees more say in their jobs; that is, for increasing participation. Given the general trend toward more participation, work teams are likely to be used more and more often. Moreover, they often result in increased productivity, higher quality, and better employee attitudes.

Organizations that want to use work teams need to consider several guidelines. First of all, it is often necessary to provide some initial training. People who previously did one simple task on their own may need to learn how to perform other tasks and work with others. Perhaps most importantly, organizations that use work teams must be willing to give work team members more responsibility and control over their tasks. If a first-line supervisor is always watching over their shoulders, the work team may actually be a detriment. Only if the team members have some of the responsibility previously held by their managers will they succeed. Finally, selecting new employees may need to be approached differently. New employees may need heightened interpersonal skills and the ability to work with existing group members. Considerable care, such as that taken by Mazda, should be used in building work teams.[27]

High performance teams have been shown to have both a clear understanding of the goal to be achieved as well as a belief that the goal is worthwhile.[28] Further, the structure of effective teams embodies (1) clear roles and accountability for each of those roles, (2) effective communications, (3) methods for monitoring performance and for providing feedback, and (4) objective evaluations.[29] At the end of this chapter, there is a Self-Assessment tool for determining team effectiveness.

Occidental Oil and Gas Corporation uses teams in its international exploration, acquisition, and development efforts. Here an exploration team studies maps of Oxy's land holdings in Gabon, West Africa. (Courtesy of Occidental Petroleum Corp.)

Managing Quality Circles

A final type of group with which many managers are beginning to have to contend is the **quality circle,** or **QC.** QCs will be discussed more fully in Chapter 21, but they are groups of operating employees formed for the express purpose of helping the organization identify and solve quality-related problems.[30] They are made up of volunteers from the same or related work areas who meet regularly, usually for an hour or so each week, to talk about quality issues faced by the company. Each member is free to suggest problems the group might tackle. Theoretically, the employees are so close to their tasks that they can suggest ideas and opportunities for improvement that might escape the attention of managers.

QCs are quite controversial. Many firms, such as Polaroid, Procter & Gamble, General Foods, and General Motors, have successfully adopted QCs. But other firms have had disappointing experiences with them. If an organization does decide to try QCs, it can at least increase the potential for success. Among hints given by successful companies is first to rely totally on volunteers. People who feel coerced to join will be of little value. Second, the firm should provide enough time and resources to allow the QC to do its intended job. Third, the company must provide feedback and recognition to the QC regarding its suggestions. For instance, suppose a QC recommends a new way of doing something that results in substantial cost savings for the company. Managers should, of course, tell the QC of the success of its idea, but they should also communicate that fact to others through the company newsletter, special announcements, and other means. This recognition allows the group members to develop feelings of pride and accomplishment. If an idea is not acceptable or does not really do any good, managers should also communicate this fact to the group, but in a more subtle fashion.

Mistakes to Avoid in Using Groups and Teams

There are four common mistakes made in the use of groups and teams.[31] Managers should be careful to avoid them. Calling a work unit a team but managing the members as individuals is the easiest mistake to make. In this case, the manager wants the benefits of a team without relinquishing the authority to the group. Closely related to this mistake is the simple failure to really delegate authority to the team. Managers should set the direction and the constraints but delegate the means for accomplishment to the team. The third mistake is vague delegation, or telling a group in general terms what is needed and letting them "work out the details." Teams need clear structures to be able to function effectively. Finally, setting up a team properly but not providing it with organizational support will also doom it to failure.

In addition, as discussed in Chapter 15, conflict is frequently an aspect of interpersonal relations. Such conflict may be either good or bad, so understanding it is important.[32] Remembering that interdependencies such as those that exist in teams frequently can lead to conflict suggests another reason for the careful management of teams.[33] Since conflict is quite probable when using groups and teams, it is important that managers be aware of the possibility and how to deal with it.[34]

Group Decision Making

As we have already seen, a great deal of decision making in organizations is done by groups. Executive committees make critical decisions about the company's future, project teams make decisions about which new products to introduce, and grievance committees make decisions about who is right and wrong in organizational disputes. This section outlines the advantages and disadvantages of allowing groups to make decisions and then summarizes three techniques that can be used to promote better group decisions.[35] The Skill Builder at the end of this chapter allows you not only to experience group decision making, but also to develop your skills. Apply what you learn in this part of the book to the Skill Builder.

Advantages of Group Decision Making

Group decision making has several advantages and disadvantages relative to individual decision making.

Obviously, there must be certain advantages to **group decision making.** Why else would it ever be done? Table 18.2 summarizes the four most general advantages.[36] These factors tend to lead to a higher-quality decision than a single individual working alone might have obtained. As indicated in *The Quality Challenge: Chaparral Teams Up for Quality,* Chaparral Steel seems to be deriving many advantages from its use of groups and teams.

One advantage is the fact that more information is available to the group than is available to an individual. Each member is able to draw on his or her unique education, experience, insights, and other resources and (it is hoped) contribute these to the group. Similarly, a group is likely to generate more alternatives to consider than an individual can. That is, some individuals have ideas that escape others, so the total set of alternatives should be greater in the group than for any single individual.

A third advantage is that acceptance of the decision will probably be greater than it would be if an individual made the decision alone. Since more people participated in making the decision, more people will understand its origins. Those who did not participate might well feel that the decision was reached in a democratic fashion. Finally, groups just tend to make better decisions than individuals do. The extra information and additional alternatives, when properly considered and processed, promote a better outcome.

Table 18.2
Advantages and Disadvantages of Group Decision Making

Advantages	Disadvantages
Availablility of more information	Longer decision-making process
Generation of more ideas	Too much emphasis on compromise
Easier acceptance of decisions	Dominance by an individual
Better decisions often made	Possibility of groupthink

The Quality Challenge

Chaparral Teams Up for Quality

By interrelating learning skills with management procedures and values, Chaparral Steel of Midlothian, Texas, has involved its workers with self-development educational activities to the benefit of the company. Chaparral's CEO, Gordon E. Forward, has focused on creating a "classless" organization where employees have the autonomy to keep costs down so the firm can effectively compete even in tough times. Employee involvement and the use of "mini-mills" has enabled Chaparral to be innovative and to become a strong international competitor in the steel industry during times when major steel companies have struggled just to exist.

Chaparral selected a team of workers to tour new steel facilities in Asia, Europe, and South America to learn how other steel companies were operating. After the team had learned how things were being done, the workers were put in charge of buying new equipment for a Chaparral plant. They selected the equipment, oversaw its installation, and helped get it up and running. While industry experts estimated that about three and a half years would be necessary for this process, Chaparral accomplished it in less than one year. Using work teams to learn new ways of doing things and to pass that learning along to others proved highly successful.

Teamwork, then, has become Chaparral's way to achieve total quality management and become an international competitor. Chaparral was allowed to put the Japanese Industrial Standard mark for quality on its products, the first U.S. steel company to be permitted to do so.[37] ■

Disadvantages of Group Decision Making

Unfortunately, there are also four disadvantages to group decision making. If these disadvantages did not exist, all decisions would automatically be assigned to groups. These factors, also listed in Table 18.2, serve as barriers to high-quality decisions.

One major disadvantage is that groups tend to take longer to reach a decision, because all members may want to discuss every aspect of the decision. Although this may be a plus, it adds a lot of time to the process. The group may also try too hard to compromise. Some degree of compromise may be necessary and perhaps even desirable, but compromise might be sought to the exclusion of a better decision that the group could have reached with more effort.

It is also possible that a single individual will dominate the process. If this happens, the decision may be too widely accepted because it has the appearance of having been made by the group. Besides, allowing one member to make the decision sets aside all of the potential advantages of group decision making. Groups involved in making decisions may also succumb to a phenomenon known as **groupthink.**[38] Groupthink refers to the phenomenon that happens when group members become so interested in maintaining cohesiveness and good feelings toward one another that the group's original goals become lost. In this case the group makes decisions that protect its members as individuals and the group as a whole rather than decisions that are in the best interests of the overall organization.

Techniques for Group Decision Making

Managers have come up with several techniques for capitalizing on the advantages of group decision making while simultaneously minimizing the potential harm from the disadvantages.[39] As we saw in Chapter 10, **Delphi forecasting** uses experts to make predictions about future events. These predictions are systematically refined through feedback until a consensus emerges.

The **nominal group technique** is a structured process whereby members individually suggest alternatives that are then listed on a chart for all to see. All the alternatives are discussed, and each member is asked to rank-order them. The average rankings are listed, and the process is repeated until everyone agrees.

The **devil's advocate strategy** is to assign one member the role of devil's advocate. This person is expected to challenge and take issue with the actions of the rest of the group. This is especially valuable in preventing groupthink.

Chapter Summary

Organizations are by their very nature highly interpersonal. Virtually all of the work of most organizations is accomplished by people working together increasingly in the context of groups. A group is two or more people who interact regularly to accomplish a common goal. Groups in organizations can be classified as formal (functional or task) or informal.

People usually choose to join a group because of interpersonal attraction, group activities, group goals, and instrumental benefits. Regardless of why a group is formed, it normally goes through a four-stage developmental process consisting of forming, norming, storming, and performing. The informal organization is the overall pattern of influence and interaction defined by the total set of informal groups within the organization.

In all groups people play certain parts, or roles. Role ambiguity occurs when the sent role is unclear, and the person is not sure what he or she is supposed to do. Role conflict occurs when role messages are clear but inconsistent or contradictory. Another group dimension is cohesiveness, the extent to which the members of the group are motivated to stay together. This is connected to norms, which are the standards of behavior developed by the group. Norms may relate to performance (such as the quantity and quality of goods produced) or to nonperformance (such as how to dress or what to keep secret).

Managing groups is not easy. Fortunately, several guidelines exist that can facilitate the management of functional groups, task forces and committees, work teams, and quality circles. Group decision making, which is common to American corporations, has four basic advantages and four disadvantages. Managers can use several techniques to enhance the quality of group decision making.

The Manager's Vocabulary

group	role dynamics	committee
functional group	expected role	work team
task group	sent role	quality circle (QC)
informal group	perceived role	group decision making
forming	enacted role	groupthink
storming	role ambiguity	Delphi forecasting
norming	role conflict	nominal group technique
performing	cohesiveness	devil's advocate strategy
informal organization	norm	
role	task force	

Review Questions

1. Identify and define the three basic types of groups.
2. What are the four stages of group development?
3. Describe the various kinds of role conflict.
4. How do performance norms interact with cohesiveness to determine performance?

5. What are the advantages and disadvantages of group decision making?

Analysis Questions

1. Why is there an upper limit on the number of people that can reasonably constitute a group?
2. Have you ever experienced any of the forms of role conflict described in the chapter? Describe as many as possible.
3. If you were a manager in charge of a group that had high cohesiveness but very low performance norms, what would you do?
4. What are the common elements inherent in managing the different types of groups? What are the differences?
5. Have you ever been involved in a group decision-making process? If so, how did that process compare to those described in the text?

Self-Assessment

Team Effectiveness Inventory

Introduction All organizations must have highly performing teams to be successful. Many different factors contribute to a team's effectiveness. This self-assessment measures some of the most critical team characteristics which contribute to effectiveness.

Instructions

Think of a group or team in which you are currently or have been a member. Please respond on the basis of your degree of agreement or disagreement with each statement. Use the following scale: strongly disagree (SD), disagree (D), undecided/neutral (U), agree (A), strongly agree (SA).

Statements	SD	D	U	A	SA
Task Performance					
1. We plan ahead for problems that might arise.	1	2	3	4	5
2. We are an effective problem-solving team.	1	2	3	4	5
3. We achieve high performance goals.	1	2	3	4	5
Influence					
4. Team members are willing to listen to and understand each other.	1	2	3	4	5
5. Members are active in influencing the future of the team.	1	2	3	4	5
6. Members are willing to disagree and make suggestions to each other.	1	2	3	4	5
Satisfaction					
7. I enjoy working with my team members.	1	2	3	4	5

8. I am able to make good use of my skills and abilities on this team.	1	2	3	4	5
9. Considering everything, it is a pleasure to be a member of this team.	1	2	3	4	5

Member Relations

10. I trust the members of my team.	1	2	3	4	5
11. There is no free riding by members.	1	2	3	4	5
12. We are a cooperative and cohesive group.	1	2	3	4	5

Creativity

13. Divergent ideas are encouraged.	1	2	3	4	5
14. Our norms encourage change and the exploration of new ideas.	1	2	3	4	5
15. The creative talents of member are drawn on to improve the quality and quantity of the team's outputs.	1	2	3	4	5

For interpretation, turn to the back of the book.

Source: Reprinted by permission from pp. 344–345 of *Organizational Behavior*, 6th edition, by Hellriegel, Slocum and Woodman; Copyright © 1992 by West Publishing Company. All rights reserved.

Skill Builder

The Desert Survival Situation

Purpose Many decisions in organizations are made by groups. There are advantages and disadvantages to having groups solve organizational problems. In addition, there are group decision-making techniques that have proven to be effective in helping groups make better decisions. This Skill Builder allows you to apply these techniques to an organizational problem.

This Skill Builder focuses on the *human resources model*. It will help you develop the *facilitator role* of the human resources model. One of the skills of the facilitator is the ability to make decisions. In this exercise, you expand on this skill by developing group decision-making abilities.

Introduction The situation described in this exercise is based on more than 2,000 actual cases in which men and women lived or died depending on the survival decisions they made. Your "life" or "death" will depend on how well your group can share its present knowledge of a relatively unfamiliar problem so that the team can make decisions that will lead to your survival.

This exercise will challenge your ability to take advantage of a group approach to decision making and to apply decision steps such as developing alternatives and selecting the correct alternative. When instructed, read about the situation and do Step 1 without discussing it with the rest of the group.

Instructions

The Situation It is approximately 10:00 A.M. in mid-August, and you have just crash landed in the Sonora Desert in southwestern United States. The light twin-engine plane, containing the bodies of the pilot and the copilot, has completely burned. Only the air frame remains. None of the rest of you has been injured.

The pilot was unable to notify anyone of your position before the crash. However, he had indicated before impact that you were seventy miles south-southwest from a mining camp that is the nearest known habitation and that you were approximately sixty-five miles off the course that was filed in your VFR Flight Plan.

The immediate area is quite flat and, except for occasional barrel and saguaro cacti, appears to be barren. The last weather report indicated that the temperature would reach 110 degrees that day, which means that the temperature at ground level will be 130 degrees. You are dressed in lightweight clothing: short-sleeved shirts, pants, socks, and street shoes. Everyone has a handkerchief.

Collectively, your pockets contain $2.83 in change, $85.00 in bills, a pack of cigarettes, and a ballpoint pen.

Your Task Before the plane caught fire your group was able to salvage the fifteen items listed in the following table. Your task is to rank these items according to their importance to your survival, starting with "1", the most important to, "15", the least important.

You may assume the following:
1. The number of survivors is the same as the number on your team.
2. You are the actual people in the situation.
3. The team has agreed to stick together.
4. All items are in good condition.

Please complete the following steps and insert the scores under your team's number

Step 1: Each member of the team is to individually rank each item. Do not discuss the situation or problem until each member has finished the individual ranking.

Step 2: After everyone has finished the individual ranking, rank order the 15 items as a team. Once discussion begins do not change your individual ranking. Your instructor will inform you how much time you have to complete this step.

Items	Step 1: Your Individual Ranking	Step 2: The Team's Ranking	Step 3: Survival Expert's Ranking	Step 4: Difference between Step 1 & 3	Step 5: Difference between Step 2 & 3
Flashlight (4 battery)	___	___	___	___	___
Jackknife	___	___	___	___	___
Sectional air map of area	___	___	___	___	___
Large plastic raincoat	___	___	___	___	___
Magnetic compass	___	___	___	___	___
Compress kit with gauze	___	___	___	___	___
Loaded .45 caliber pistol	___	___	___	___	___
Parachute; red and white	___	___	___	___	___
Bottle of salt tablets (1,000 tablets)	___	___	___	___	___
1 quart of water per person	___	___	___	___	___
A book entitled *Edible Animals of the Desert*	___	___	___	___	___
A pair of sunglasses for each person	___	___	___	___	___
2 quarts of 180 proof vodka	___	___	___	___	___
1 topcoat per person	___	___	___	___	___
A cosmetic mirror	___	___	___	___	___

Totals
(the lower the score the better)   ___   ___

Your Score, Step 4   Team Score, Step 5

TEAM NUMBER

	1	2	3	4	5	6
Average Individual Score: Add up all the individual scores (step 4) on the team and divide by the # on the team						
Team Score:						
Gain Score: The difference between the Team Score & the Average Individual Score. If the Team Score is lower than Average Individual Score, then gain is "+". If Team Score is higher than Average Individual Score, then gain is " − ".						
Lowest Individual Score on the Team						
Number of Individual Scores Lower Than the Team Score						

Source: *The Desert Survival Situation: A Group Decision Making Experience for Examining and Increasing Individual and Team Effectiveness,* 8th edition, by J. Clayton Lafferty, Patrick M. Eady, and Alonzo W. Pond. Copyright © 1974, 1993 by Experimental Learning Methods, Inc. Used by permission.

CONCLUDING CASES

18.1   Campbell's Continues Canning

The canned soup business of Joseph Campbell and Abram Anderson, like that of their two competitors, was struggling when Dr. John Thompson Dorrance joined the firm in the late 1800s. Dorrance invented condensed soup to enable easier transportation of the product. Campbell's condensed soup swept the nation, and by 1911 their brand was known coast to coast in the United States. In 1915 Campbell's acquired Franco-American. Fully forty years passed before its next acquisition (Swanson's, in 1955), but then a period of rapid expansion and acquisition ensued, lasting all the way through the 1980s. As a result, Campbell's is the largest U.S. maker of canned soups and a major producer of numerous other food products. Recently, however, Campbell's has been divesting itself of less profitable lines to become more competitive. Results during the early 1990s indicate that it is succeeding.

When David W. Johnson, successful Gerber Products executive, came to Campbell's in 1990, he brought about significant changes. He closed or sold twenty plants worldwide, cut unprofitable brands, and reduced the work force by more than 20 percent. Johnson followed four basic precepts: (1) act fast — once a decision has been made, act on it quickly; (2) don't change the lineup — set a direction or focus and use existing personnel to achieve it; (3) make 'em sweat — use people's pride in performance to reach high standards; and (4) manage by the numbers — empower people to be creative, but keep a scorecard (VERC: volume, earnings, return, cash) against which to measure performance.

Johnson also changed the corporate culture. Campbell's divisions had been so independent that the soup unit ran a promotion with Nabisco crackers while the Pepperidge Farm unit made a competing product. Johnson reorganized Campbell's to eliminate such "protective turf" attitudes. He tied a large proportion of managerial bonuses to overall corporate performance as a further way to reduce turf attitudes and behavior. He instituted succession planning to enable managers to know that they are constantly being evaluated for advancement and to provide them with feedback as to how well they are doing.

Elements of advanced management techniques and high-involvement management were introduced at many locations, and their success suggests that their use will be expanded throughout Campbell's. Training in communication skills and quality management were implemented. Quality circles and work teams were established. In Canadian operations, for instance,

workers quickly began to handle plant scheduling, hiring and staffing. Production went from 600 batches in three shifts over six days to 1,600 batches in three shifts over four days. Costs were also trimmed. The workers essentially freed up the equivalent of a plant's worth of capacity, which enabled the Canadian operation to expand its market. In the Maxton, North Carolina, plant the emphasis on quality led to improvements in operating efficiently enough so that manufacturing costs were reduced to less than 50 percent of the retail price as new production facilities were employed.

The use of groups and strong motivational programs has made parts of Campbell's excellent places to work. For instance, its headquarters in Camden, New Jersey, has an on-site child care center where much of the cost is covered by the company. Flextime, job sharing, and even adoption aid are offered by Campbell's to support diverse employee working situations. But other parts of the company have been different. In 1988 the Labor Department charged that the company had ignored complaints by workers about working conditions at a Pepperidge Farm facility. The changes seem to be progressing at different rates in different parts of the organization.[40]

Discussion Questions

1. What kinds of groupings of personnel (including managers) existed at Campbell's prior to Johnson's arrival? Which ones might exist now? Why?
2. Were the changes made at Campbell's positive or negative? What criteria might be appropriate in making this judgment?
3. How do group processes seem to be affecting events at Campbell's?
4. Do you think the use of groups at Campbell's is effective? Why or why not? How could it be improved?

18.2   Body Shop International PLC

The first Body Shop (see Chapter 2) opened in 1976 in Brighton, England. By 1992 there were more than eight hundred stores—more than two hundred in the United Kingdom and Channel islands, more than one hundred in the United States, nearly one hundred in Canada, and the rest scattered over forty other countries. That same year the stock value of the organization was approximately one billion dollars—not bad for a retail chain that does not believe in advertising and that stresses that it is more important to have had an interesting conversation that imparted information to a customer than for the customer to walk out of a shop having bought something. The

management style of Anita Roddick, owner and managing director, has been described as loosely structured, collaborative, imaginative, and improvisatory. She strongly believes in nurturing entrepreneurs and renegades to bring about effective groups in her organization.

Roddick pushes the education of consumers and environmental and social responsibility in her stores. Leaflets and cards offer health and beauty tips and product content information. Brochures and pamphlets about recycling and Amnesty International are scattered throughout stores. She feels that if her customers are well educated, they will not only buy her products but they will also convince their friends to do likewise. Thus, by word of mouth, her business will expand and she will not have to spend money on advertising or marketing. Of course, getting lots of free publicity by supporting social causes will not hurt either.

Employees are also educated. They are deluged with information from newsletters, videos, brochures, posters, training programs, and so on about the business. The message, however, is not about the selling or profit aspects of the business but rather about the nature and use of the products. The employee is given the knowledge to educate the customer. This education program keeps the employees learning, interested, and excited about the products, which in turn makes for better relations for customers (and finally ends up in sales but without having been stressed in the first place). The educational message may also be about a social issue — saving the rain forest or banning ozone-depleting chemicals — but again the purpose is to educate the employee so that he or she can better educate the customer.

As a result, employees understand why it is important to have good merchandise displays, clean shops, treat customers respectfully, and so on. They do not need rules about these things; they have learned why these things are important, and so they do them. And they work together as a team to get them done. Roddick is trying to forge a corporate culture that bonds employees and customers together. The common bond is a belief that businesses should do more than make money, create jobs, and sell products.

It is a belief that businesses should help solve major social problems.

That common bond enables groups of Body Shop employees to function as energetic teams of educators about its products and important social issues. The corporate staff and franchisees are strongly encouraged to work on community projects of their choice in their local areas. Groups of Body Shop personnel have worked on projects that have included cooking and serving meals in soup kitchens, working in battered women and children's shelters, and assisting in literacy programs. Employees are allowed as much as a half day of paid company time every four weeks to participate in these activities, but groups frequently spend their own time and energies on these social projects as well.[41]

Discussion Questions

1. What uses of groups are evident at Body Shop?
2. Is there any evidence of group decision making at Body Shop? Why or why not?
3. What potential sources of group conflict might be present at Body Shop? How might such conflict be managed?
4. Do you think that groups could be more effectively used at Body Shop? Why or why not? How could their use be improved?

CHAPTER

19 Managerial Communication

Learning Objectives

After studying this chapter you should be able to

· Define managerial communication and discuss its importance and pervasiveness.

· Describe the communication process and relevant behavioral processes.

· Discuss barriers to and skills for effective communication.

· Discuss oral, nonverbal, written communication, and effective listening.

· Describe formal communication in organizations, including vertical and horizontal communication, information systems, and the chief information officer.

· Describe the grapevine and discuss its nature and its advantages and disadvantages.

M ost people have heard of Wal-Mart, although a surprisingly large number of them have never shopped in a Wal-Mart store. All that is changing, however. In 1992, with sales of $55 billion and stores in forty-three of the fifty states, Wal-Mart became the nation's largest retailer, bypassing Sears.

The company has grown by more than 30 percent a year for more than twenty years and has more than eighteen hundred stores (Wal-Mart, Sam's Clubs, SuperCenters, and Hypermarts). It continues to open about one hundred fifty new stores every year and plans to be in all fifty states by the end of this decade. Wal-Mart has generated an average annual return to its stockholders of more than 40 percent a year for the past ten years. Indeed, a one-thousand-dollar investment in Wal-Mart stock back in 1970 would be worth more than half a million dollars today!

Although founder Sam Walton died in April 1992, the culture and spirit he bred into the organization are still a driving force behind the company's ongoing success. One factor that has no doubt contributed to Wal-Mart's success is the premium the company has always put on communication. Each of the company's thousands of employees, called associates, is encouraged to make suggestions, voice complaints, and do everything possible to get good ideas on the table. For example, one associate suggested that Wal-Mart hire retired persons to serve as greeters, people who stand inside the front door, welcoming shoppers and offering them the newest advertising circular. The idea was taken to Sam, who thought it was outstanding. Today, every Wal-Mart has a greeter.

Wal-Mart keeps in touch with all its stores and distribution centers through an elaborate system that would make the military of many countries envious. Every Saturday morning the company's top one hundred or so managers meet at headquarters in Bentonville, Arkansas, to discuss merchandising. They study detailed inventory and sales figures to figure out what adjustments they need to make. For example, if they are selling children's pants for three dollars and Kmart is promoting them at two pair for five dollars, the price at Wal-Mart is lowered immediately.

The company has its own six-channel satellite television system that enables company officials to broadcast live messages to every store. Sam Walton, who had the uncanny ability to make each member of his audience think he was speaking directly to him or her, often made his own personal pitch to the associates. The personal touch is not overlooked either, since Walton believed that the best way to find out what was going on in the stores was to visit them and talk to customers and employees. Therefore, every day Wal-Mart executives visit at least one hundred stores. For example, regional vice president, Andy Wilson, is on the road (or in the air) Monday through Thursday visiting ten to twelve stores a week in his region that extends from West Texas to the state of Oregon.

How far can Wal-Mart go? Most observers see no limit to the growth the company can achieve. Management, led by Sam's son Rob as chairman of the board and David Glass as CEO, is committed to maintaining the same open culture and dialogue with the associates no matter how large the company gets. [1] ■

J udged by almost every measure of success in the industry, Wal-Mart is an exemplary business. In its first year of eligibility, the company ranked ninth among more than three hundred corporations vying for a spot on *Fortune*'s list of the most admired companies in America. The next year it jumped to the number five spot. One key to Wal-Mart's success has always been the open and candid communication that occurs among everyone in the company.

This chapter explores managerial communication in detail. First, communication is defined and its importance in organizations is discussed. Then the communication process is more fully described in terms of a comprehensive model, and the influence of important behavioral processes is discussed. Several barriers to effective communication are presented, as well as several skills that result in more effective communication. The chapter then describes three important types of communication: oral, nonverbal, and written, as well as the important skills of effective listening. Finally, the chapter presents formal and informal organizational communication networks and ways in which they might be managed effectively.

The Nature of Communication

Communication has been studied from many different perspectives: as shared meaning between individuals, as the "glue" that binds an organization together, as both a one-way and a two-way process, and as the means for coordinated action in organizations. As we examine the role of communication in organizations it is important to define communication and discuss the pervasiveness of communication in the manager's job. The Skill Builder at the end of this chapter will help you develop better interpersonal communication skills by examining further one-way and two-way communications.

The Definition of Communication

*Communication is the process of transmitting information; **interpersonal communication** occurs between people. For it to be effective, the message received must be essentially the same as the message that was sent.*

In the broadest sense, **communication** is the process of transmitting information. Thus, communication can take place between organizations, between organizational units, between computer systems, and between nations. However, when communication occurs between people, it is **interpersonal communication.**[2] When two people are talking on the telephone, when a speaker is addressing a large group, and when someone is reading a letter, interpersonal communication is taking place.

Of course, the message being received might be quite different from the one that was transmitted. A person might not understand what someone else is saying, static on the telephone might interrupt a conversation, and a letter can get lost in the mail. So it is useful to differentiate between simple communication and effective communication.

Simple communication is merely the transmission of information from one person to another. Effective communication, in contrast, occurs when the message that is received has essentially the same meaning as the message that was sent. Clearly, then, it is important for managers to have the skills to communicate effectively. One of the factors that affects the meaning of a mes-

Communication includes interaction with others whether face-to-face, over the phone, through written media, on a computer, or even while doing other things. Here two employees get their exercise and communicate at the same time during a lunchtime walk. (Reprinted with permission from *Women in Business,* the national magazine of the American Business Women's Association. Photo by Jim Hoffman.)

Table 19.1

Communication in the Daily Activities of a Typical Manager

Time of Day	Activity
8:00–8:30	Read *The Wall Street Journal*
8:30–8:45	Receive telephone call from headquarters
8:45–9:30	Meet with executive committee
9:30–10:00	Read report from marketing vice president
10:00–11:00	Meet with labor committee
11:00–11:30	Review the day's mail
11:30–12:00	Meet with operations manager
12:00–1:00	Lunch with friends
1:00–2:00	Draft report for board of directors
2:00–2:30	Return three telephone calls
2:30–3:00	Interview prospective assistant
3:00–4:00	Meet with R&D task force
4:00–4:30	Dictate four letters
4:30–5:00	Read report from legal adviser

sage is the communicator's style. The communicator's style may help to get the message across clearly or it might distort the message. The Self-Assessment at the end of the chapter measures your communication style. To better understand this concept, you may wish to complete the exercise now.

The Pervasiveness of Communication

Communication is one of the major ingredients of the manager's job.[3] This is illustrated in Table 19.1, which outlines a day in the life of a typical, if hypothetical, manager. Virtually all of the activities listed involve communication in one form or another. The manager writes something that others will read, reads what others have written, talks, and listens.

Research has clearly documented the pervasiveness of communication in management. In one study, for example, it was found that the average manager spends 59 percent of his or her time in scheduled meetings, 22 percent on desk work (such as writing and reading), 10 percent in unscheduled meetings, 6 percent on the telephone, and 3 percent walking around the company premises.[4] All of these activities involve communication.

The Communication Process

Now that we have defined communication and discussed the pervasiveness of communication for managers, we can explore the communication process itself in more detail. First, we present a complete model that explains all of the dynamics of communication. We then note important behavioral processes that influence how communication occurs.

The Communication Model

*The communication process involves a **sender encoding** and transmitting a message to a **receiver** through various **channels**. The receiver **decodes** the message and gives feedback to the sender to confirm the communication.*

As noted earlier, communication involves at least two people. These are represented in Exhibit 19.1 as the **sender**—the person who transmits the message—and the **receiver**—the person who receives the message.

The starting point in the communication process is an idea. This idea may be a fact, an opinion, an observation, or anything else the sender feels a need to transmit. The idea is then translated into a message to be sent to someone else. This message may be all or part of the idea. The sender may feel that it is best to send only part of the idea in the first attempt at communication, expecting to send the rest of the idea later. The message is then **encoded** into the exact

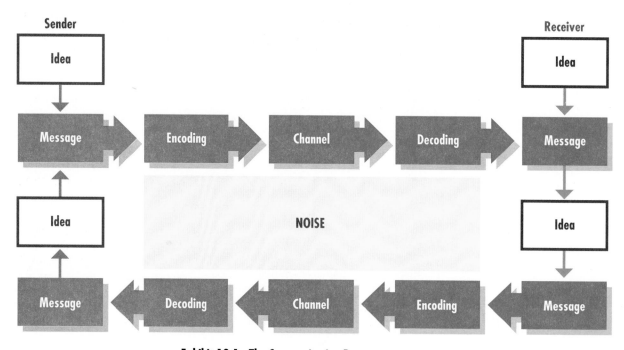

Exhibit 19.1   The Communication Process

mix of words, phrases, sentences, pictures, or other symbols that best reflect the content of the message.

The message is then transmitted through one or more **channels:** a face-to-face meeting, a letter, a telephone call, a facial expression, or any combination of these. The message is received and retranslated by the process of **decoding** into a message. The message is then combined with other ideas by the receiver, who may send a return message to the sender in the form of feedback, a response, or a new message.

The difference between simple communication and effective communication manifests itself when the symbols are decoded into a message and combined with other ideas of the receiver. If the idea formed by the receiver is similar to the one originally formulated by the sender, effective communication has occurred. On the other hand, if the ideas are different in one or more important ways, the communication was not effective.

As shown in Exhibit 19.1, the process may continue under conditions of two-way communication. That is, receivers may respond to the original message with a message of their own. Thus, the receiver becomes the sender, transmitting a new message to the original sender, who is now playing the role of the receiver.

The final part of the process is **noise.** Noise is anything that disrupts the communication process. It might be true noise, such as someone in another room talking so loudly that two people cannot hear each other speak or a radio playing so loudly that the receiver cannot hear the sender's voice over the telephone. It can also be other things, however. A letter getting lost in the mail, a telephone call being disconnected, or a typographical error in a report can all reduce communication effectiveness.

Behavioral Processes and Communication

The communication process is also influenced by a number of important behavioral processes. Two of these are attitudes and perception, which were first introduced in Chapter 15.

Attitudes and *perception* are *important behavioral processes that can affect the communication process.*

Attitudes   **Attitudes** are sets of beliefs and feelings that individuals have about specific ideas, situations, or other people.[5] Each of us has attitudes toward school, jobs, other people, movies, politicians, sports teams, and almost everything else that might be a part of our lives.

Attitudes affect how we communicate with others in a variety of ways. For example, suppose you have two subordinates. You like one subordinate a great deal and have a high regard for her capabilities and dedication to the organization. In short, you have a positive attitude toward her. You strongly dislike the other subordinate, however, and question his capabilities and dedication—a negative attitude. If the first subordinate asks for extra time off to visit a sick friend, you may respond in a favorable way and may convey feelings of concern. But if the second subordinate asks for time off for the same reason, you may deny the request and may even question his truthfulness. Attitudes about the receiver affect the sender's encoding processes, and attitudes about the sender affect the receiver's decoding processes.

Perception   The other behavioral process that strongly affects communication is perception.[6] **Perception** refers to the processes by which we receive and interpret information from our environment. Most people are familiar with real incidents or stories in which two or more witnesses observe the same accident but report different events. Such differences are attributable to perception, which, in general, affects communication through familiarity. People tend to perceive things from a frame of reference with which they are comfortable. In one classic study, for instance, executives were asked to read a case about problems at a steel mill and then to describe the nature of those problems. Five out of six sales managers said the problems were related to sales, but four out of five production managers saw the problems as being related primarily to production.[7]

Stereotyping is the process of categorizing people into groups on the basis of certain presumed traits or qualities. It is one of the ways that perception affects communication. A lot of research has been conducted on the process of stereotyping in organizations. One such study found that business students tended to stereotype older workers as less creative, more resistant to change, and less interested in learning new skills.[8] Stereotyping affects communication most in the encoding and decoding phases. When a sender encodes a message into symbols, the sender is making assumptions about what symbols the receiver will understand. The same process occurs in reverse when the receiver decodes the symbols into a message. When making assumptions about other people, we often make errors due to stereotyping the other person's ability to understand the symbols.

It follows that perception affects communication in other ways also. If managers see things from a biased perspective, they will respond accordingly. A manager who sees a problem as falling into a certain area will communicate in a certain way with other managers in that area. If the manager perceives the problem in a different way, the communication will be different.[9] In short, perceptions of the situation and the receiver affect the sender's encoding of the message into symbols, and perceptions of the sender and the situation affect the receiver's decoding of the symbols into the received message.

Barriers to and Skills for Effective Communication

As we have indicated, the message sent is not always the message received. Managers must be very skilled at trying to make both the sent message and the received message the same, whether the manager is the sender or the receiver. In general, these skills center around understanding the barriers to effective communication and knowing how to overcome those barriers.

Recognizing Barriers to Effective Communication

Among the many different kinds of barriers to effective communication shown in Exhibit 19.2, some are associated with the sender, some with the receiver, and some with both.[10]

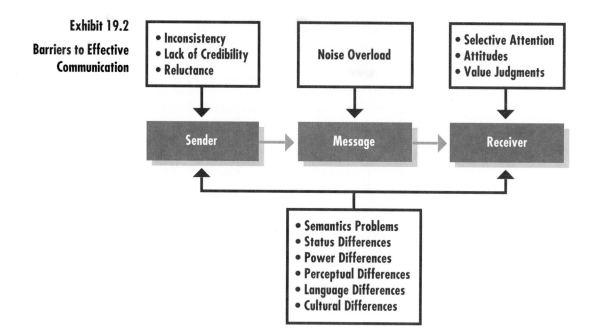

Exhibit 19.2
Barriers to Effective Communication

Barriers to effective communication are associated with the sender and/or the receiver.

From the standpoint of the sender, problems can arise because of inconsistency, credibility, and reluctance. Inconsistency occurs when the person sends conflicting messages. Credibility problems occur when the individual is considered to be unreliable. For example, when a public official makes statements that are later found to be untrue, the public official will encounter credibility problems. Dow Corning Corporation faces a major credibility problem with several relevant groups, as discussed in *A Matter of Ethics: Dow Corning Corporation and Silicone Gel Implants*. Finally, people are sometimes simply reluctant to communicate. This may be the case when the news is bad or unpleasant.

From the standpoint of the receiver, selective attention, receiver attitudes, and value judgments can be barriers. Not concentrating, letting attention wander, looking around when someone is talking, and daydreaming can all impede effective listening. Specifically, selective attention occurs when the receiver pays attention to only part of the message being sent. Sometimes people have already made up their minds about what a speaker is saying, so their attitudes get in the way of listening to the speaker's points and arguments. Making value judgments based on personal beliefs may also affect the way that the receiver hears the message.

Noise, as we have seen, can also cause difficulties with effective communication. So can

Communication overload occurs when the sender is transmitting too much information for the receiver to process adequately.

communication overload, which occurs when the sender is transmitting too much information for the receiver to process adequately.[11] When a lecturer talks too fast for students to take notes or when someone is trying to watch television while a roommate listens to the stereo, overload can occur.

Other barriers can be attributed to both the sender and the receiver. Obvious communication problems can occur when operating in a culturally diverse business situation or in the international business arena. If the receiver and the sender speak different languages, the encoding and decoding processes can be quite difficult. Anthropologists suggest that it is very difficult to understand a culture without knowing the language. The reverse is also true; it is difficult to understand the language without taking into account its cultural context. When doing business internationally, it is essential to understand the language and culture of the host country for communication efficiencies as well as for the benefit of the business.[12]

A Matter of Ethics

Dow Corning Corporation and Silicone Gel Implants

Drug companies in the United States have long-established relationships of trust with the Food and Drug Administration. The FDA has relied on the drug companies to properly test and report test results to the FDA prior to approval of a drug for marketing and public use. The FDA does not have the budget, the personnel, or the facilities to do all of the testing required to certify a new drug for use. In addition, it does not make good business sense for the companies to falsify testing documents in order to certify drugs that later may be shown to be unsafe. The costs of bad public relations and restitution to harmed patients would be too great for that. But this relationship of credibility between the FDA and drug companies may be ending.

Dow Corning Corporation announced in March 1992 that it was getting out of the silicone gel breast implant business. It was estimated that between 100,000 and 150,000 women were receiving silicone gel breast implants each year either for reconstructive purposes or for breast augmentation (about 80 percent of the women). Patients, and their lawyers, were charging that the implants were responsible for a variety of maladies, such as rashes, cancer, and even neurological disorders. In February 1992 the FDA declared a moratorium on the use of implants, although many experts claimed that they should still be available for reconstructive purposes. Although Dow Corning was the leading producer of silicone gel breast implants, with about a 30-percent market share, implants were only about 1 percent of the company's annual revenues. Faced with hundreds of lawsuits and several standing verdicts against the company, the company decided not to let a small part of the business bring down the entire company.

The credibility of the company with the FDA may be a more important issue, however. Approval by the FDA and use by the medical profession had rested on the claims of safety following the testing by Dow Corning and the other companies that produce the implants. In January 1992 the FDA asked Dow Corning to release the contents of more than ninety studies and internal memos that had not been released before and suggested that company scientists were concerned for the safety of the products. One FDA official claimed that the documents show "clear misrepresentation by the company."

This case calls into question the FDA's entire certification process. This one example of possible misrepresentation by one company shows the importance of communication between different organizations. If companies withhold information in one situation, will they do it in another? The FDA may need to make procedural changes or increase staffing. One serious miscommunication by the sender causes the receiver to question the sender's credibility.[13] ■

Jargon is the use of words that have specific meaning within a profession or group of people.

Semantics problems (problems with word meanings) involve both parties. For example, when an instructor says the course is "challenging and rigorous," the student may hear this as "hard and picky." One specific type of semantics problem arises due to professional **jargon,** which is the use of words that have specific meaning within a profession.[14] The computer industry was well known for the use of jargon particular to its industry. Status and power differences can also disrupt effective communication. For instance, a janitor may not be able to communicate effectively with a top manager, or a lower-level manager may have problems communicating with a higher-level manager in the same division. And perceptual differences, as described earlier in the chapter, can disrupt communication. If one manager perceives an employee's sloppy work habits as laziness and another manager thinks the same habits indicate creativity, the two managers could have a difficult time discussing the worker's performance.

In today's increasingly diverse workforce, both domestically and internationally, language and cultural differences can present barriers for senders and receivers of communications. Does the lack of response of a Native American coworker or the nodding of the head of a Japanese colleague indicate agreement with something that you said? Are highly participative processes

The tremendous diversity so common in U.S. organizations presents sizable opportunities but also heightens barriers to communication. At Lotus Development, diversity groups convened to discuss differences in an effort to overcome barriers. Such groups deal with sexual orientation, sexual harassment, and racial discrimination issues, among others. (Max Aguilera-Hellweg.)

equally espoused by all cultural groups? Does a pat on the back and a hug indicate the support of someone or does it suggest sexual harassment? Communication may be even more complex in the future than it is today.

Building the Skills for Effective Communication

Barriers to effective communication can be overcome by the sender, the receiver, or both.

Fortunately, there are things that managers can do to overcome some or all of these problems. The communication skills shown in Exhibit 19.3 can be used by the sender, the receiver, or both.[15]

The sender can be sensitive to the receiver's position. A manager who is telling an employee that his or her working hours are being reduced might expect the worker to be temporarily hostile. Such sensitivity can keep the manager from getting upset if the subordinate says something in anger. On the other hand, some workers might be happy if their hours were reduced. The manager needs to be sensitive to different reactions that different employees may have to communication. The sender should also solicit feedback as a way to facilitate two-way communication. Asking the receiver if the message is understood, asking for opinions, and other such actions enhance communication effectiveness.

Managers should also be aware of language and meaning. Employees almost always get concerned when they hear about major changes. Hence, a manager should not talk about an impending change as being "big" or "major" if it is in fact relatively routine or minor or if the employee will not be affected by it. The sender should also always attempt to maintain credibility. There is nothing wrong with admitting that you do not know something. Of course, it also helps to check facts and stay as up to date as possible.

There are also several things the receiver can do to improve communication. First, the receiver can work on being a good listener: on concentrating on what is being said, looking at the speaker, being patient, and paying attention to meaning. Likewise, the receiver should attempt to be sensitive to the sender's perspective. For example, few people enjoy giving bad news, so subordinates who are receiving notice of company layoffs should realize that the manager who is telling them probably is also upset. In a multicultural or international context, familiarity with the culture and the language of host nations is essential for effective communication. This means that

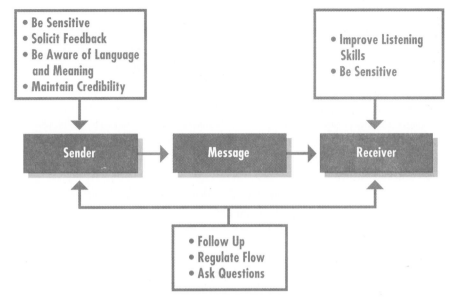

Exhibit 19.3

Skills for More Effective Communication

managers should study the language and the culture *prior* to initiating business in a different culture or country.[16]

Both the sender and the receiver can promote communication effectiveness by following up the communication and by regulating the flow of information. The sender can solicit questions, and the receiver can ask for clarification and demonstrate understanding. Suppose, for instance, that a sales executive calls a finance executive to schedule a meeting. The finance manager can send a note back to the sales executive confirming the meeting time and location. Both parties can also regulate information flows by working to prevent communication overload, the sender by making sure that he or she is not going too fast and the receiver by interrupting and asking the sender to slow down when necessary.

Forms of Interpersonal Communication

Oral Communication

*There are four basic forms of interpersonal communication—**oral, nonverbal, written,** and **listening.***

***Oral communication** is easy and facilitates **feedback;** it may also be inaccurate and provides no record.*

nterpersonal communication occurs in many different forms. In this section we will consider four primary types of communication skills that are necessary for managers: oral, nonverbal, written, and listening.

Oral communication involves the spoken word. Hall conversations, formal meetings, telephone calls, and presentations are examples. The importance of oral communication is underscored by research that found that managers often spend between 50 percent and 90 percent of their time talking to people.[17]

As noted in Table 19.2, there are advantages and disadvantages to oral communication. One major advantage is that it is relatively easy and comfortable. All people have to do is open their mouths and let words come out. (Of course, many of us can recall times when we wished we had not opened our mouths, but that issue is addressed below). There are also some people who, out of shyness or for other reasons, do have trouble with oral communication. Picking up the telephone or walking into a colleague's office to schedule a meeting are relatively simple operations, especially when compared to doing the same thing in writing. It has been suggested that more than half of all managers do not have confidence in their ability to write, so they feel more comfortable with the spoken word. Accordingly, they use oral communication whenever they can.[18]

Oral communication		Nonverbal communication		Written communication	
Advantages	**Disadvantages**	**Advantages**	**Disadvantages**	**Advantages**	**Disadvantages**
1. Is easy to use 2. Facilitates feedback	1. Causes inaccuracies 2. Provides no record	1. Gives completeness to communication 2. Can convey images without verbalizing	1. Can conflict with verbal communication 2. Can give unintended messages	1. Is fairly accurate 2. Provides a record	1. Hinders feedback 2. Is more time-consuming

Table 19.2   Advantages and Disadvantages of Oral, Nonverbal, and Written Communication

The second major advantage of oral communication is that it facilitates feedback. **Feedback** is the response from the receiver of a message to the sender of that message. If the sender wants an answer to a question or a verification that the listener understands what was said, all the sender has to do is ask. Similarly, the listener can interrupt to respond to the message or to seek clarification. An astute speaker can even tell how well the message is being received by looking at the facial expression of the listener.

Of course, there are major disadvantages to oral communication as well. For one thing, it can be quite inaccurate. As we simply talk "off the top of our heads," we can confuse the facts, omit important points, distort things, and so forth. We might also say some things that should not be said or divulge information inappropriately. Similarly, the listener may not hear everything accurately or may misunderstand or forget important details.

Finally, oral communication provides no permanent record of what has been communicated. After a conversation has taken place, the parties may have to recall details of what they said. Since memory can be quite faulty, the lack of a permanent record of the conversation can cause major problems.

Nonverbal Communication

Nonverbal communication involves settings, body language, and imagery.

Another form of interpersonal communication for us to consider is **nonverbal communication,** communication that does not use words or uses facial expressions, body movements, and gestures to convey a message.[19] It has been suggested that 55 percent of a message is transmitted through facial expression and body movement, and that another 38 percent is conveyed by inflection and tone.[20]

In general, people communicate nonverbally in three ways. First, they use the setting, which is where the communication takes place, and the nature of its surroundings. The manager who sits behind a huge desk in a big chair in front of a wall covered with awards, honors, and accolades is clearly in a position of power and authority, and this power and authority will usually influence the communication process. A visitor who sits in a small chair in front of the desk will be in a very different position in the communication process.

Second is body language. One element of body language is the distance we stand from someone when we are talking. Close contact can connote intimacy or hostility, and eye contact can convey positive or negative feelings. Body and arm movement, pauses in speech, and style of dress are also important parts of body language.

The third aspect of nonverbal communication is the imagery conjured up by language. Ross Perot, who uses colorful language and catchy phrases, conveys a certain image and meaning when he talks. Such a person can transmit messages of confidence, boldness, or aggression or of foolhardiness and recklessness. More mundane, bland language conveys images of cautiousness and thoroughness or of timidity and indecisiveness.

Another aspect of nonverbal communication that has become increasingly important in recent years relates to the cultural differences between people of different nations. We have seen that distance between people affects communication. Appropriate distances vary among countries: the English and Germans stand farther apart than Americans do when talking, whereas the Japanese, Mexicans, and Arabs stand closer together.

Nonverbal communication also has advantages and disadvantages. Nonverbal communication can provide confirming images to verbal (oral and/or written) communication. Certain facial expressions and body movements can indicate that the sender is confident in the message, thereby indicating to the reader that the sender is an expert and can be trusted. On the other hand, certain body movements or gestures can send a message that conflicts with the verbal message. When this happens the receiver can be confused about which message to believe.

Written Communication

Written communication is accurate and provides a record, but it is slow and limits feedback.

Written communication is the transmission of a message through the use of written words, including memos, letters, reports, and notes. The advantages and disadvantages of this kind of communication are essentially the opposite of those of oral communication, as Table 19.2 points out.

One key advantage is improved accuracy. If a manager chooses to use written symbols to communicate with someone, the manager can dictate the letter, proofread it, revise it, check the facts, and have the letter retyped before it is mailed.

Likewise, written communication provides a relatively permanent record of the communication. The sender and the receiver can talk about the details of their exchange over the phone several months later and still agree about the contents of the letter.

A major disadvantage of written communication is that it hinders feedback. After the manager decides to write a letter, several days can go by before it is dictated, typed, mailed, delivered, and read. If timing is critical, major problems can result from such delays. Of course, overnight delivery services and facsimile machines have reduced this factor to a great extent. However, such methods are expensive for routine correspondence, and legal documents still require original signatures.

Written communication is also more time consuming than oral communication. It takes only a few seconds to pick up the phone and call someone, but it takes days or weeks to correspond. And most managers generally do not prefer to use written communication. We have noted their lack of confidence in their writing skills. The same study found that most managers regard only about 13 percent of their mail as valuable to them, and they find almost 80 percent of it to be poorly done.[21]

Effective Listening

Listening is the process of receiving encoded symbols from a sender and decoding them into a message to be interpreted.

Listening is one type of communication that many people overlook, but yet it must occur if effective communication is to take place. **Listening** is the process of receiving encoded symbols from a sender and decoding them into a message to be interpreted. Most education and training programs focus only on what to say, not on how to listen. Talking is easier, more straightforward, and easier to measure, control, and learn. Listening, however, is harder to predict, to control, and to practice.[22]

Most errors in listening occur because the receiver is not actively listening to what the sender is sending. This may be due to several reasons. The receiver may be discounting what the sender is sending because it goes against what the receiver already believes. The receiver may be thinking about what to say next rather than really listening to what the sender is saying. The receiver may not hear what the sender is saying because of noise in the system or because the symbols sent by the sender may not mean the same thing to the receiver that they do to the sender. This confusion occurs often when the sender sends symbols that have specific meanings in a technical jargon that is not familiar to the receiver. Whatever the reason, the receiver must listen very carefully to the symbols sent by the sender and ask for clarification whenever the symbols are unclear. In addition, the sender can assist the receiver in listening better by speaking slowly, distinctly, using symbols (words) that are familiar to the receiver, and stopping periodically to ask if the receiver understands the message so far.

Skills in listening can be improved by asking others (spouse, children, manager, employees, peers) how they view you as a listener. Encourage them to be honest, listen carefully to what they have to say, and be ready to make changes in your listening habits. Second, you might tape your conversations with others (with their permission, of course), listen to the tapes critically, evaluate how much of the time you spend talking versus listening, and see how much of what others say you miss the first time.[23]

Managerial Communication

Managerial communication is a part of the formal organizational hierarchy: that is, it occurs between people in various positions. Three elements of managerial communication are communication in the formal organization, management information systems, and the position of chief information officer.

Communication in the Formal Organization

As we noted earlier, the manager's job is filled with activities that involve communication (see Exhibit 19.1). In Chapter 2 we discussed the roles that managers must fill within the organization. Recall Table 2.1 in which we showed the interpersonal roles, the decisional roles, and the informational roles. Interpersonal roles involve interacting with supervisors, subordinates, peers, and others outside the organization. Decisional roles require managers to seek out information to use in making decisions and then communicate those decisions to others. Informational roles focus specifically on acquiring and disseminating information both inside and outside the organization. Each of the ten roles discussed in Table 2.1 would be impossible to fill without communication. The new roles identified as part of the integrated framework also required extensive use of communication.

Communication within the organization is usually only experienced by employees of the organization, while external communication involves interacting with those outside the organization. This external communication is done by many different people. The sales force is often the group that does the most external communication. In addition to directing communication to potential buyers of the products or services of the organization, the sales force can be a valuable receiver of communication. Listening to the sales force can be the best way an organization can stay close to customers and their needs. U.S. Surgical utilizes its sales force to bring back valuable information from its customers that the company then uses to develop new products that solve customers' problems, as described in *The Quality Challenge: U.S. Surgical Sticks Very Close to Its Customers*.

Communication inside the organization involves information that flows both up and down and laterally through an organization. These patterns are illustrated in Exhibit 19.4, which uses the example of communication among a vice president and three division heads.

*Communication in the formal organizational structure may be **vertical** or **horizontal**.*

Vertical Communication   **Vertical communication** takes place between managers and their subordinates. It can flow both down and up the organization. Downward communication includes the assignment of new job responsibilities, information that will assist subordinates in performing their job duties, or simple information about the organization. Such communication helps subordinates know about aspects of the organization that affect them. Unfortunately, managers do not always do a good job of keeping their subordinates informed.

Exhibit 19.4

Vertical and Horizontal Communication

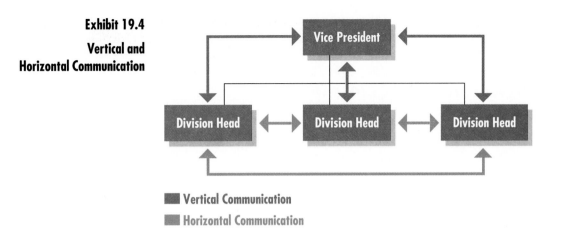

■ **Vertical Communication**
■ **Horizontal Communication**

Upward communication is also a vital part of organizational functioning. Information from employees keeps top management in touch with day-to-day operations of the company, significant successes and failures, and potential difficulties. Upward communication is also often associated with the practice of whistle blowing as occurred when Jerome LiCari discovered that his employer, Beech-Nut, was claiming its apple juice for babies was pure apple juice when in fact it was chemically modified. He went to his manager, who did not listen. Then he went to the president of the company and got the same lack of response. Finally, he resigned and told his story to the media.[24] One of the reasons that Wal-Mart executives spend so much time traveling to stores is to get upward communication from those people who are in closest contact with the customers.

Horizontal Communication   **Horizontal communication** takes place between two or more colleagues or peers at the same level in the organization. It is critical when there are high demands for coordination and integration. For instance, if the marketing manager is planning a new advertising campaign that will probably increase product demand by 10 percent, the manufacturing manager needs to be aware of this increase so that plans can be made for additional production. Similarly, if a plant manager locates a new supplier who will deliver an important raw material more reliably and at a lower price than current suppliers, it is important that this information be passed along to other plant managers in the company.

Information Systems   Another important aspect of managerial communication is the various kinds of information systems the organization creates to manage the official flow of information within the business. In recent years management information systems have changed dramatically, mainly because of breakthroughs in electronic communication capabilities. Electronic typewriters and photocopiers were early breakthroughs, but the personal computer, electronic networks, and facsimile machines are accelerating the process. The new universal wireless telephone will make it possible to be in communication with anyone in the world from anywhere in the world, instantly.[25] Information systems will be covered extensively in Chapter 23. We need only remember here that they are an important part of many organizational communications activities and should be as fully institutionalized as possible if they are to be effective.

The Chief Information Officer   A final element of managerial communication is the position of **chief information officer,** or CIO, who is the executive who oversees all aspects of information technology, such as computing, office systems, and telecommunications. Many people have never heard of the CIO because this is

The Quality Challenge

U.S. Surgical Sticks Very Close to Its Customers

Getting close to the customer is one thing, but the representatives for United States Surgical Corporation have taken it to the extreme, and the company is reaping huge benefits because of it. Its sales people have been called the green berets of the surgical selling world for the way that they attack in the field.

U.S. Surgical makes and sells a wide range of surgical supplies. It started in 1967 when the founder of the company, Leon Hirsch, developed a surgical stapler that was technically much better than the existing methods for closing surgical incisions. Hirsch decided that the lack of a superbly trained sales force was the reason his new company was losing money in spite of the superiority of his new stapler. In order to get his stapler into the hands of surgeons, he trained his representatives to be knowledgeable about surgery room procedures and comfortable enough to train surgeons to use the stapler. The training program was six weeks long and rigorous enough in such medical areas as anatomy to cause a 20-percent dropout rate. The training has paid off as representatives now scrub and join surgical teams in the operating room to demonstrate new products, observe the use of existing products, and work with operating room personnel to solve specific problems.

This closeness to the surgeon has resulted in many examples where U.S. Surgical has led the industry in the development of products for the operating room. In 1989 a company representative saw a surgeon using a handmade clip in laparoscopic gall bladder surgery. This led to the design and production of a new laparoscopic stapler that was on the market in early 1990. As a result, more than 60 percent of gall bladders are now removed laparoscopically, a procedure that is safer, cheaper, and less painful than traditional open surgery.

Company performance continues to rise, with 1991 sales of more than $930 million. Annual growth rate for the past three years has been 49 percent in earnings per share with a 22 percent return on equity. Its stock rose 211 percent in 1991. The superbly trained representatives work with operating room personnel and take information and new ideas back to the company to develop new and better products. Constant communication between customers and company has put U.S. Surgical in the lead over medical products giant Johnson & Johnson in the areas of surgical tools and equipment. Continued communication is expected to keep it there.[26] ■

The **chief information officer (CIO)** *is a new type of executive in charge of information systems within an organization.*

a very new executive position that is just being created in many organizations.[27] The CIO position is becoming important because top managers are increasingly recognizing the importance of information to the organization and of having a qualified individual responsible for managing it.

Many managers do not have the title but still fill the role of CIO; others, of course, actually are given the title. As the manager of all aspects of information technology, this executive reports to the CEO or chairperson and usually concentrates on long-term strategic issues, leaving the nuts-and-bolts part of the communication job to technicians. Numerous companies have begun to use the CIO concept, including Firestone, American Airlines, Pillsbury, Aetna Life and Casualty, Northwestern National Life Insurance, and Wells Fargo.

Informal Communication: The Grapevine

The final element of organizational communication to be addressed in this chapter is the informal communication network that exists in all organizations—the **grapevine.**[28] The nature of organizational grapevines in illustrated in Exhibit 19.5, which shows a hypothetical organization and three messages that have wound themselves through the organization.

Exhibit 19.5

The Organizational Grapevine

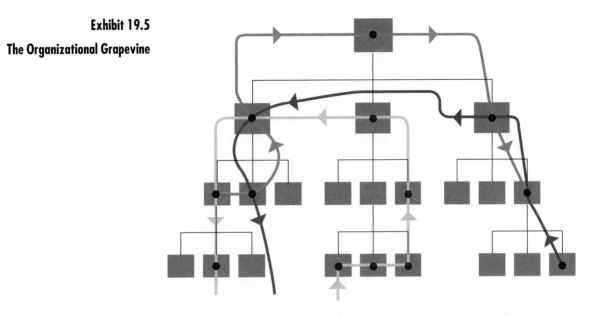

*The **grapevine** is the informal communication network within an organization.*

These paths reveal several interesting aspects of the grapevine. First, the grapevine can start anywhere; that is, any individual can start the process simply by telling someone something. Second, some people are included in virtually all of the messages. These people serve as focal points along the grapevine, receiving most messages and passing most of them on to others. Third, the grapevine flows in all directions. Messages can go up, down, or laterally in the organization. Finally, not everyone is included; some people neither receive nor pass on informal news.

The grapevine exists because being social is one characteristic of human nature. People like to interact with others. Since much of this interaction involves talking, information will naturally be passed among many different people. For another, the grapevine is often used as a way to get power. Controlling information regardless of its source makes anyone a more powerful person. And grapevines emerge in response to deficiencies in the formal communication network in the organization. If people are curious about something and do not hear about it officially, they are likely to solicit the information from others.

Advantages and Disadvantages of Grapevines

The grapevine has many attributes, some of them good and some bad. On the plus side, the grapevine can be used to transmit information quickly, it builds a sense of togetherness and a feeling of being part of the same team, and managers can use it to try out ideas or get informal reactions to potential decisions.

On the other hand, the grapevine can also be detrimental to the organization. The information carried along the grapevine can be very innacurate, or it might be information that the manager would prefer to keep confidential. Apple Computer recently had a problem with rumors and the grapevine. In the personal computer industry, where knowing "secrets" has become a status symbol, important product information was leaking out to other companies and to the media. Apple hired a manager of information security, who created an internal campaign to stop the leaks. The campaign included posters and lapel buttons reading, "I know a lot but I can keep a secret." Some insiders have reported that the campaign has not worked and may have made matters worse. In this case, the grapevine may extend beyond the organizational boundaries and may have implications for organizational success or failure.[29]

Because the grapevine is an informal communication network, it may be even more susceptible to disruption and noise. This IBM employee is on the phone, has information on her computer screen, and is talking with another employee at the same time. This is a typical, "noisy" organizational communication environment. (Courtesy of International Business Machines Corp.)

Managers should be fully aware of the potential benefits and pitfalls of the grapevine. Perhaps the best advice is to maintain open communication with employees at all levels and to respond quickly to inaccurate information. If people can come to their manager and get straight answers, they are less likely to pay attention to gossip and rumors.

Chapter Summary

Interpersonal communication is the process of transmitting information from one person to another. Simple communication is the mere transmission of information; effective communication occurs when the transmission is accurate. Communication is one of the major ingredients of the manager's job.

The communication process involves translating an idea into a message, encoding the message, sending the message through a channel, receiving the message, decoding the message, and retranslating it into an idea. Two-way communication occurs when feedback, or repeating the process in reverse, is involved. Noise is anything that disrupts the communication process. The process can also be influenced by a number of important behavioral processes, most notably attitudes and perception.

Managing communication involves understanding the numerous barriers to communication and knowing how to overcome them. Overcoming barriers involves recognizing that they exist and being sensitive to the other person in the process.

Interpersonal communication can be oral, nonverbal, or written. Effective communication generally involves a variety of forms. Interpersonal communication also involves good listening.

Managerial communication is communication that occurs as a part of the formal organization. Vertical communication occurs between bosses and subordinates and can flow downward or upward. Horizontal communication takes place between two or more colleagues or peers at the same level in the organization. The person who is in charge of information technology in major organizations is known as the chief information officer, or CIO.

The grapevine is the informal communication network that exists in all organizations. Managers sometimes use the grapevine to try out ideas or to get informal reactions to potential decisions. However, the grapevine also has several disadvantages.

The Manager's Vocabulary

communication	attitudes	written communication
interpersonal communication	perception	listening
sender	stereotyping	vertical communication
receiver	communication overload	horizontal communication
encoding	jargon	chief information officer (CIO)
channels	oral communication	grapevine
decoding	feedback	
noise	nonverbal communication	

Review Questions

1. What is the difference between simple communication and effective communication?
2. Summarize the communication model. How do attitudes and perception affect communication?
3. Note four major barriers to effective communication and four important ways to overcome those barriers.
4. What are the relative advantages and disadvantages of oral, nonverbal, and written communication?
5. What is a CIO? Why is it important?

Analysis Questions

1. Relate an incident in which your attitude affected communication.
2. Which communication form (oral or written) do you prefer? Why?
3. Describe where you have used or observed nonverbal communication taking place.
4. If nonverbal messages contradict oral statements, which do you believe? Why?
5. Think of the last "message" you picked up from the grapevine. As far as you know, was it accurate or inaccurate?

Self-Assessment

What's Your Communication Style?

Introduction Communication is all-pervasive and managers spend a great deal of their time communicating during every day. How that communication is presented has a direct impact on how effective the communication is. Communication presentation is the communicator's style. This self-assessment examines communication style.

Instructions Next to each of the following statements, respond with a *Y, y, ?, n,* or *N.* The following scale is used for each item:

YES — Strong agreement with the statement
yes — Agreement with the statement
? — Neither agreement nor disagreement with the statement

no — Disagreement with the statement
NO — Strong disagreement with the statement

_____ 1. I am comfortable with all kinds of people.

_____ 2. I laugh easily.

_____ 3. I readily express admiration for others.

_____ 4. What I say usually leaves an impression on people.

_____ 5. I leave people with an impression of me that they definitely tend to remember.

_____ 6. To be friendly, I habitually acknowledge verbally others' contributions.

_____ 7. I am a very good communicator.

(con't. on page 446)

_____ 8. I have some nervous mannerisms in my speech.

_____ 9. I am a very relaxed communicator.

_____ 10. When I disagree with people, I am very quick to challenge them.

_____ 11. I can always repeat back to a person exactly what was meant.

_____ 12. The sound of my voice is very easy to recognize.

_____ 13. I am a very precise communicator.

_____ 14. I leave a definite impression on people.

_____ 15. The rhythm or flow of my speech is sometimes affected by nervousness.

_____ 16. Under pressure I come across as a relaxed speaker.

_____ 17. My eyes reflect exactly what I am feeling when I communicate.

_____ 18. I dramatize a lot.

_____ 19. I always find it very easy to communicate on a one-to-one basis with strangers.

_____ 20. Usually I deliberately react in such a way that people know that I am listening to them.

_____ 21. Usually I do not tell people much about myself until I get to know them well.

_____ 22. I regularly tell jokes, anecdotes, and stories when I communicate.

_____ 23. I tend to constantly gesture when I communicate.

_____ 24. I am an extremely open communicator.

_____ 25. I am vocally a loud communicator.

_____ 26. In a small group of strangers I am a very good communicator.

_____ 27. In arguments I insist on very precise definitions.

_____ 28. In most social situations I generally speak very frequently.

_____ 29. I find it extremely easy to maintain a conversation with a member of the opposite sex whom I have just met.

_____ 30. I like to be strictly accurate when I communicate.

_____ 31. Because I have a loud voice, I can easily break into a conversation.

_____ 32. Often I physically and vocally act out when I want to communicate.

_____ 33. I have an assertive voice.

_____ 34. I readily reveal personal things about myself.

_____ 35. I am dominant in social situations.

_____ 36. I am very argumentative.

_____ 37. Once I get wound up in a heated discussion I have a hard time stopping myself.

_____ 38. I am always an extremely friendly communicator.

_____ 39. I really like to listen very carefully to people.

_____ 40. Very often I insist that other people document or present some kind of proof for what they are arguing.

_____ 41. I try to take charge of things when I am with people.

_____ 42. It bothers me to drop an argument that is not resolved.

_____ 43. In most social situations I tend to come on strong.

_____ 44. I am very expressive nonverbally in social situations.

_____ 45. The way I say something usually leaves an impression on people.

_____ 46. Whenever I communicate I tend to be very encouraging to people.

_____ 47. I actively use a lot of facial expressions when I communicate.

_____ 48. I very frequently verbally exaggerate to emphasize a point.

_____ 49. I am an extremely attentive communicator.

_____ 50. As a rule, I openly express my feelings and emotions.

For interpretation, turn to the back of the book.

Source: Robert W. Norton, Foundation of a Communicator Style Construct," _Human Communication Research_, Vol. 4, no. 2, 1978, pp. 99–111.

Skill Builder

Developing Communication Skills

Purpose There are several ways to give instructions to people. Some of them are quicker or more accurate than others. Some generate more satisfaction in or greater compliance by the recipient. It is important that you be able to recognize different communication models with their resulting costs and benefits. This Skill Builder focuses on the _human resources model_. It will help you develop the _facilitator role_ of the human resources model. One of the skills of the facilitator is interpersonal communication.

Introduction This Skill Builder identifies the types of behaviors that assist or interfere with effective transmission of instructions. The purpose of this exercise is to illustrate forms of communication and investigate the differing outcomes as well as the processes resulting from these means of communication. The exercise will allow you to explore possible techniques for dealing with dysfunctional communication behaviors.

Instructions

Further instructions will be provided by your instructor.

Source: Reprinted by permission from *Organization and People: Readings, Cases, and Exercises in Organizational Behavior,* 3rd edition, by J.B. Ritchie and Paul Thompson; Copyright © 1984 by West Publishing Company. All rights reserved.

CONCLUDING CASES

19.1   Union Pacific Railroad Gets Back on the Right Track

The railroads, especially the Union Pacific Railroad, are dying! NOT!! At least not anymore. Prior to 1986, Union Pacific was losing loads to truckers and other carriers. However, new management, with Drew Lewis as head of the parent company and Mike Walsh as CEO of the railroad, took over and has turned it around by investing in people, processes, and new equipment. Prior to 1986, customers were alienated, shareholders were angry, and truckers were taking away sales. Many of the changes were standard turnaround methods: cutting small and unprofitable lines of track, cutting management by 50 percent, getting tough with unions, reducing personnel on trains from four to three, reducing the bureaucracy from nine layers to four, consolidating train dispatch and customer service sites, and investing in new computerized technology in several areas. These changes have resulted in improved customer service, more on-time deliveries, increased equipment utilization, and decreases in rates, all of which have improved company financial performance.

Probably the most powerful changes, however, have occurred in the way that Mike Walsh has fostered the creation of a new organization culture of communication. Formerly, communication between employees was formal, using Mr. and Ms. and titles, mostly from manager to employees, and infrequent. Walsh started with informal town-hall-style meetings with three hundred to one thousand employees at which Walsh personally explained industry shifts and corporate strategy and their impact on employees and the company. Long question and answer sessions followed as employees asked Walsh any questions they wished.

Smaller, follow-up sessions are still held with Walsh and fifteen to twenty employees. Walsh believes that it is essential that the CEO be visible and truthful to all employees.

In addition, training has increased for middle and lower managers so that they can be better informed and serve as the primary communication contact for line workers. Information and decision-making authority have been pushed as far down the organizational hierarchy as possible. To maintain the communications links, Walsh also uses satellite transmission to communicate simultaneously with large employee groups at twenty-four remote locations. Some sessions last as long as five hours as Walsh answers questions from employees at all levels.

Walsh also holds an annual two-day Leadership Planning Conference with the railroad's top two hundred managers. The conference includes lectures, workshops, and problem-solving sessions. It concludes with a question and answer session for all participants. The session is video-taped and highlights are edited into a one-hour videotape to be used in smaller but similar conferences throughout the company.[30]

Discussion Questions

1. What forms of communication are being used by Walsh and Union Pacific Railroad?
2. Describe how Walsh uses the components of the communication model described in the text.
3. Which skills for effective communication is Walsh using?

19.2   ODS Corporation Communicates the Way No Other Japanese Company Does

The Japanese system of management has become famous for dedication of the employees to one company, lifelong employment, five-and-a-half-day workweeks that can grow up to twenty-one hundred hours per year (compared to eighteen hundred in the United States), and a strict seniority system with long times between promotions. One often

overlooked and misunderstood feature of the Japanese system is perception of equality. Job distinctions, rank, salaries, and performance evaluations are kept unclear so that employees have the perception that everyone is equal. The Japanese seem to prefer things to remain vague and do not question the authority of the organization.

The Japanese system provides job security, health insurance, adequate pay, and high expectations for performance. Unfortunately, the expectations for performance are also left unclear. Japanese workers do not talk about what is expected of them nor what or how they have done on the job. Approvals and disapprovals from senior management are rare, so the worker does not know how he (rarely she, because the work force is heavily male dominated) is evaluated. There are evidently unstated but implied indicators of approval and disapproval that put incredible pressure on employees to perform.

ODS Corporation is a Japanese company working hard to eliminate the closed-mindedness and lack of clarity. ODS is a privately held company that does research, consulting, and advertising, in addition to the importation of technical manuals that was the foundation of the company in 1964. The founder and president of the company, Takahiro Yamaguchi, believes that openness and long discussions in meetings promote fairness and team spirit and help the company adapt to rapid changes in the business environment. He believes that companies exist to serve their employees, not society or themselves. Talking with each other about job-related matters is the most important thing at ODS. ODS operates strictly by consensus among the employees, who meet as much as seven hours per week in a variety of sessions. There are weekly all-employee meetings to discuss company rules, manager meetings for strategy discussions, section meetings to go over sales, team meetings to discuss special projects, and semiannual company meetings in April and October to hash out broader management issues. In every meeting, employees at all levels state their positions and discuss the issues until consensus is reached.

No subject is taboo. Probably the most shocking meeting is the meeting to discuss the salary budget and allocate salaries for every employee in the company. At these meetings, employees state their case regarding their own performance, speak for and against salary proposals for each other (including their managers), and vote on the salaries. In a typical meeting workers might discuss the establishment and enforcement of company rules, such as proper dress for work, work rules, and tardiness. Employees freely admit when they have violated a rule, and other employees tell them what they think should be done about it. Managers in the company believe that this management by consensus inspires confidence in the company and stimulates initiative.

This open philosophy has also stimulated high turnover, since it is so different from the way that the typical Japanese company is run. On the other hand, it may also be a key factor in the performance of the company. Annual sales for the year ending March 31, 1989, were about $38 million, up 20 percent over the previous year and more than double the annual sales from three years before. Employees talk so much that outsiders claim that thousands of productive hours are lost in useless meetings where employees discuss things. Employees, however, often work late into the night to finish a project or make up for the time spent in a meeting. Although the style is not typically Japanese, who can argue with this company's success?[31]

Discussion Questions

1. What elements of the communication model are most evident in the communication within ODS Corporation?
2. What forms of communication are in use in the communication at ODS Corporation?
3. How does the type of communication at ODS Corporation affect the barriers to effective communication?
4. Do you think that a grapevine exists at ODS Corporation? Why or why not?

Part Five   Leading

Self-Assessment

Listening Self-Inventory

Introduction Communication skills are central to effective leadership. In Chapter 19, we discussed the importance of listening as a communication skill. This form of communication is often overlooked by managers, but it is just as important to effective communication as talking. This Self-Assessment examines your ability to listen effectively.

Instructions Go through the following statements, checking *yes* or *no* next to each one. Mark the inventory as truthfully as you can in light of your behavior in the last few meetings or gatherings you attended.

YES   NO

_____ _____   1. I frequently attempt to listen to several conversations at the same time.

_____ _____   2. I like people to give me only the facts and then let me make my own interpretation.

_____ _____   3. I sometimes pretend to pay attention to people.

_____ _____   4. I consider myself a good judge of nonverbal communications.

_____ _____   5. I usually know what another person is going to say before he or she says it.

_____ _____   6. I usually end conversations that don't interest me by diverting my attention from the speaker.

_____ _____   7. I frequently nod, frown, or in some other way let the speaker know how I feel about what he or she is saying.

_____ _____   8. I usually respond immediately when someone has finished talking.

_____ _____   9. I evaluate what is being said while it is being said.

_____ _____   10. I usually formulate a response while the other person is still talking.

_____ _____   11. The speaker's "delivery" style frequently keeps me from listening to content.

_____ _____   12. I usually ask people to clarify what they have said rather than guess at the meaning.

_____ _____   13. I make a concerted effort to understand other people's point of view.

_____ _____   14. I frequently hear what I expect to hear rather than what is said.

_____ _____   15. Most people feel that I have understood their point of view when we disagree.

For interpretation, turn to the back of the book.

Source: Ethel C. Glenn and Elliott A. Pood, "Listening Self-Inventory," from _Supervisory Management,_ January 1989, pp. 12–15. Reprinted, by permission of the publisher, from _Supervisory Management,_ January/1989 © 1989. American Management Association, New York. All rights reserved.

Skill Builder

Tower Building Exercise

Purpose   Throughout this part of the book, we have discussed leadership, motivation, groups and teams, and communications. While we discussed these as individual dimensions, in reality they all happen simultaneously in an organization. This Skill Builder allows you to apply all of these concepts to a single problem. The Skill Builder focuses on the _human resources model and open systems model._ It will help you develop the _facilitator role_ of the human resources model. One of the skills of the facilitator is the ability to make decisions with others. In addition, it will help you develop the _broker role_ of the open systems model. One of the skills of the broker role is the ability to develop and maintain a power base.

Introduction   Each team will be asked to plan and then build a tower. Materials will be either provided by your instructor or you will be instructed to bring certain materials to class. After the towers are built, they will be judged on the following criteria: height, stability and strength, beauty, and meaning and significance.

Instructions

Further instructions will be provided to you by your instructor.

Source: Reprinted by permission from pp. 127–128 of _Organizational Behavior: Experiences and Cases,_ 3rd ed., by Marcic; Copyright © 1992 by West Publishing Company. All rights reserved.

Organizational Control

Chapter Outline

Learning Objectives

After studying this chapter you should be able to

- Describe the nature of control and why it is necessary, as well as some areas of control and the planning-control link.

- Identify and discuss various approaches to control, such as steering, concurrent, postaction, and multiple controls.

- Identify and discuss the steps in establishing a control system.

- Describe the characteristics of effective control.

- Discuss reasons for resistance to control and how to overcome this resistance.

- Describe the responsibility for control that lies with line managers and the controller.

an a firm succeed by sitting back and waiting to see what its competitors do before taking action itself? And with little national identity? And with only modest investments in technology and research and development? It can if it is Cooper Tire & Rubber Company. Goodyear, Bridgestone, Michelin, and other large tire manufacturers fiercely compete to sell original equipment and tires to automakers. They also invest heavily in research and development, new technology and automation, and the development of new tire designs. And they advertise heavily in an effort to boost sales and market share.

But Cooper, based in Ohio, shuns each of these tactics. For example, tires sold to automakers produce relatively low profit margins. Cooper, therefore, concentrates only on the replacement tire market, where it earns much higher profits. And when Cooper needs to add capacity, it buys old plants from other companies and updates their equipment.

Cooper also minimizes research and development. It observes what other manufacturers introduce and tracks their success. It then models its own new tires after those that have succeeded. Cooper's managers argue that a Goodyear tire sold on a new car will last around four years. That four years is plenty of time for Cooper to see how customers respond to the Goodyear tire and then introduce its own version if the sales potential exists. Cooper also avoids costly advertising. Its managers express little interest in sales or market share growth. Their primary focus is return on equity and return on investment.

How well does Cooper perform? Its plants run at 99 percent capacity, compared to the industry average of 80 percent. Its profit margins are 33 percent per tire, compared to the industry average of 28 percent. Cooper's stock price also increased an amazing 6,800 percent during the 1980s. And perhaps the biggest testament to the firm's success--all seven Japanese automakers with plants in the United States buy rubber hoses, window seals, and engine mounts from Cooper.[1] ▪

ontrol was introduced in Chapter 1 as one of the four basic functions managers must perform. Organizations that neglect control are likely to face severe consequences. But they can also make a mistake by concentrating too much on control—by overcontrolling. Cooper Tire & Rubber does an exemplary job of keeping focused on its goals, keeping costs in check, and boosting profit margins, all outcomes of effective control.

This chapter, the first of four devoted to the control function, provides a general overview of control. We begin by examining the nature of control in more detail. We then discuss approaches to control and how managers establish control systems. We then distinguish between effective and less effective control. Behavioral issues in managing control are discussed next. Finally, we briefly describe who is responsible for control. Subsequent chapters in this part discuss three particularly important areas of control: total quality management, operations and technology management, and information systems management.

The Nature of Control

Controlling is the process of monitoring and adjusting organizational activities toward goals.

ontrolling is the process of monitoring and adjusting organizational activities toward goal attainment.[2] In some ways control is like the rudder of a ship. Without a rudder a ship's captain could still cause the ship to move. But it would be impossible to steer the ship in any particular direction, and it might end up going in circles and eventually run aground. Likewise, a manager can get things done without control but will eventually run into serious difficulties. Control, then, like a rudder, helps steer and guide the organization in the direction set by its managers.

Reasons for Control

IBM is in the throes of reducing its work force because its managers realized that the firm is too large and needs to shed unprofitable activities and operations. American Greetings Corp. recently instituted financial controls because it had years and years of ups and downs while its major com-

The Entrepreneurial Spirit

L. L. Bean

L. Bean, Maine's famed mail-order house specializing in outdoor apparel and sporting equipment, has long been a legend in the world of catalog selling. Its prized mailing list gets its catalogs to affluent shoppers around the world. Its retail outlet in Freeport, Maine, is open twenty-four hours a day and does a brisk business. And Bean's policies of accepting returns at any time with no questions asked and not charging for shipping have earned the firm a loyal following.

But times have been tough recently for Bean. For one thing, as postage has increased, the costs of getting its catalogs distributed has escalated significantly. And the firm was recently forced to add a small shipping charge to purchases, although the token fee does not cover all Bean's costs.

More alarmingly, returns have increased significantly. Returns traditionally ran about 5 percent of sales. But as Bean has increased its product lines and has begun selling more fashion-oriented merchandise, its returns have mushroomed to about 14 percent. Fishing boots do not go out of style, so few customers returned them. But styles in sweaters and jackets do change regularly, so some consumers take full advantage of Bean's generous policies by buying apparel, wearing it a few times, and then returning it.

Increased competition has also hurt Bean. Lands' End and Eddie Bauer, for instance, have each made inroads into Bean's loyal customer base. Still, many dedicated customers make an annual trek to Freeport just to visit the store, and many industry observers believe that Bean will bounce back. But regardless of what happens, company executives argue that they will maintain the Bean custom regarding returns.[3] ▪

---

petitor, Hallmark, was almost always profitable.[4] Ford cut its production costs so that it could make cars more cheaply than General Motors. General Electric overhauled its entire management system in order to reduce administrative costs. Each of these examples reflects a company's response to a need for greater control. IBM responded to increased competition from both domestic and Japanese manufacturers; American Greetings responded to financial fluctuations; Ford saw a need to cut costs in order to remain competitive; and General Electric had to confront rising costs and declining profits.

The environment and organizational complexity are the chief reasons for control.

In general, there are three basic reasons for control. Foremost among these is the environment. We have seen several times in previous chapters how contemporary environments change rapidly and how organizations need to respond to these changes. IBM, for example, was forced to respond because domestic competitors like Apple, Dell, and dozens of clone manufacturers were continually increasing the quality of their products while reducing their prices. At the same time, demand for mainframe computers, an IBM staple, has plummeted. Control is one of the primary channels for recognizing the need for such responses. *The Entrepreneurial Spirit: L. L. Bean* explains how L. L. Bean has struggled in recent years because of environmental shifts.

A second reason for control is organizational complexity. Contemporary organizations are so complicated that a single manager cannot hope to grasp all of their inner workings. Thus, control is necessary to help the manager monitor internal operations. For instance, a properly designed control system can provide data on raw materials inventory, work-in-process inventory, and finished goods inventory. Without such a system, the manager can never get a true fix on what the company's inventory actually is. For example, a few years ago Emery Air Freight bought one of its competitors, Purolator Courier Corporation. Emery then tried to merge Purolator into its existing operations without changing its existing control systems. The organizational complexity created by the merger almost destroyed the firm because managers were not able to effectively control operations.[5]

A final reason for control is the way that small errors and problems left unchecked can grow rapidly into much bigger ones. A satellite en route to Jupiter that is only a little off course at launch time, for example, may ultimately miss the planet by millions of miles if the error is not identified and corrected. Similarly, a small deviation in costs in a manufacturing plant can grow significantly if uncorrected. Whistler Corporation, a manufacturer of radar detectors, once confronted a small manufacturing error by deciding to simply fix the defects after assembly was complete. Defects escalated rapidly from 4 percent to 9 percent to over 25 percent. One day a manager realized that 40 percent of the plant's work force was involved in fixing defective products.[6] Control can help the manager detect and correct small problems before they grow into bigger ones.

Areas of Control

There are four basic areas of control in most organizations, as shown in Exhibit 20.1: financial resources, physical resources, human resources, and information resources. As the exhibit also shows, financial resources are usually at the center of the controlling process.

The control of physical resources deals with such areas as inventory control (having neither too much nor too little inventory), quality control (ensuring that products are being made to appropriate quality standards), and equipment control (having the proper equipment to do the job). Quality control is particularly important. For that reason, most of Chapter 21 addresses that topic more fully.

Human resources control focuses on such activities as employee selection and placement (hiring the right kinds of employees and assigning them to appropriate jobs within the organization), training (upgrading employee skills), performance appraisal (assessing employee performance), and compensation (paying neither too much nor too little). As we noted in Chapter 15, enhancing the fit between people and their jobs is in the best interests of both the organization and its employees. For example, if employees are underskilled, the firm will have to train them, sup-

Every organization has numerous areas of control. 3M's growth in the Asia Pacific region involved the contributions of long-time employees like Tatsuro Watanabe of Sumitomo 3M Limited. Watanabe helped develop traffic control materials, commercial graphics, and automotive systems. (Steve Neidorf/Reprinted with permission of 3M Corp.)

Exhibit 20.1

Areas of Control

plement their performance, or accept less work. Overskilled people may become bored and unhappy and eventually leave.

Information resources control involves making sure that various forecasts and projections are prepared accurately and on a timely basis, that managers have access to the information they need to make decisions effectively, and that the proper image of the organization is projected to the environment. Without the right information, managers cannot make decisions or else may make poorly conceived decisions.[7]

Finally, as already noted, financial resources control is all-important. First, financial resources themselves must be controlled. For instance, the organization needs to have enough cash on hand to be able to function but not so much that resources are being used inefficiently. Second, many of the other areas of control relate to financial resources. Improper inventory management costs money, as do poor employee selection, inaccurate forecasts, and so forth. More than any other resource, financial resources are needed to help maintain the other resources of the firm and to keep it on sound footing.

The Planning-Control Link

*The **planning-control link** means that planning and control are linked so that they continually cycle into one another.*

In many respects, controlling is the other side of the planning coin. This **planning-control link** is shown in Exhibit 20.2. Note in particular that planning and control continually cycle into one another, with organizing and leading serving as ways to get the actual work of the organization done. Gantt charts were introduced in Chapter 9 as a planning tool. Once a project or activity is undertaken, the Gantt chart becomes a control tool, monitoring progress of the project. The Skill Builder in this chapter will help you learn how to prepare Gantt charts.

For example, the normal cycle in establishing this cycle is for management to determine plans for the future and simultaneously to specify control conditions to keep the organization moving toward achieving those plans. That is, managers simultaneously specify where they want the firm to go and how they will know that it is headed in that direction. Organizing and leading activities also come into play as the organization implements the plans.

Control helps management determine whether to adjust plans. Suppose a firm plans to increase sales by 20 percent over the next ten years. At the end of the first year, an increase of 2 percent suggests that things are on track. No increase in sales during the second year, however, suggests that modifications to plans, such as increasing advertising or lowering the original projection, may be necessary. Subway is currently using this approach as it continues an ambitious expansion program. The sandwich shop franchisor plans to add about one hundred fifty new stores a year through 1997. If in any given year this target is not met, a reassessment of current expansion plans takes place and, in some cases, renewed efforts to make up the shortfall the next

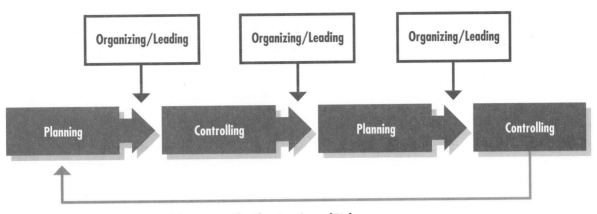

Exhibit 20.2   The Planning-Control Link

year. (In a later section we explore how to adjust things if plans are not being achieved as expected.) *The Environment of Management: Emerson Electric* shows how one firm, Emerson Electric, effectively manages planning and control.

Approaches to Control

Another important perspective that we need to consider is approaches to control. Most managers agree that there are three basic approaches: steering, concurrent, and postaction control.[8] As shown in Exhibit 20.3, steering control deals with inputs from the environment, concurrent control focuses on transformation processes, and postaction control is concerned with outputs into the environment.

Steering Control

Steering control monitors the quality and/or quantity of resources before they enter a company's system.

Steering control (also called *preliminary control* and *feed-forward control*) monitors the quality and/or quantity of various kinds of resources before they enter the system.[9] Firms like General Foods and Procter & Gamble, for instance, pay extra attention to what kinds of people they hire for future management positions. Similarly, when Sears orders merchandise to be sold under its brand, it specifies rigid standards to ensure appropriate levels of quality. Networks such as CBS and NBC monitor the commercials that potential sponsors intend to run to be sure that appropriate standards are being met. Financial inputs are thus monitored to the extent that some sponsors are rejected. And some organizations control information inputs by contracting only with the best market research firms and paying attention to only the most valid economic forecasts.

Following the lead of successful Japanese firms, more and more companies are emphasizing steering control as part of a strategy to boost product quality.[10] By requiring suppliers to provide higher-quality parts, for instance, manufacturers can enhance the quality of their own products. Each major U.S. automaker, for example, has increased numerous quality standards it demands of its suppliers. Ford alone has implemented more than one thousand tougher standards since 1988.[11]

Concurrent Control

Concurrent control involves control of the process of transforming resources into products.

Concurrent control (also referred to as *yes/no control* and *screening control*) focuses on activities that occur as inputs are being transformed into outputs. For example, a company might design various inspection stages during a production process to catch problems before too much damage is done. Likewise, the performance of employees is usually assessed at regular intervals. Care is usually taken to ensure that the information about ongoing operations that is provided to

The Environment of Management

Emerson Electric

Emerson Electric Company, based in St. Louis, is the world's seventh-largest electric products manufacturer. Emerson makes everything from thermostats to electric motors to chemical measuring devices—several thousand different products in all. Effectively linking planning and control has contributed significantly to Emerson's success.

It all started when Charles Knight became CEO of Emerson in 1973. Knight saw a small, barely growing firm and wanted to make it a giant. To do this, he launched literally hundreds of new projects. But each project was carefully planned and, at the same time, subjected to an ongoing control system to make sure its costs stayed under budget and that its product specifications remained in line with the market.

Under Knight's guidance, Emerson managers keep focused on developing new ideas and keeping costs under control. They continually strive for improvement in how they make things and how they market them. Each manager must submit a monthly report of activities, costs, and revenues. Moreover, each manager is expected to be able to defend on a moment's notice any decision he or she has made.

Emerson has been quite successful in recent years in boosting both quality and productivity. And the firm has reduced its work force only once, when Knight took over. At the time, he believed the firm's payroll was excessive. He helped find new jobs for terminated workers and promised those who remained that their jobs were secure. Today, Emerson is one of the few firms in the electronics industry to compete successfully with the Japanese. But Knight does not just want to compete--he wants to win.[12]   ■

---

managers is accurate. Financial resources are also carefully monitored through periodic audits.

Concurrent control is also becoming more widespread. As part of most employee involvement or participation programs, for example, workers are given new responsibility for halting production when problems arise. And when they point out flaws and inefficiencies managers are more willing to listen to them.

Postaction Control   **Postaction control** deals with the quality and/or quantity of an organization's outputs. When General Electric inspects finished goods before they are shipped, it is using postaction control. Re-

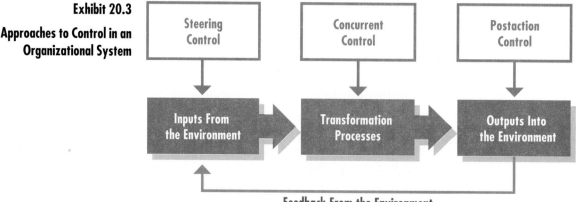

Exhibit 20.3

Approaches to Control in an Organizational System

Postaction control *monitors the quality and/or quantity of products as they leave a company's system.*

warding employees after they have done a good job is an example of postaction control of human resources. It is common for top management to screen news bulletins and press releases before they leave the organization; this represents postaction control of information. And payments of dividends to stockholders and investments in the stock market are checked in order to provide postaction control of financial resources.

As steering and concurrent control increase in usage, postaction control is perhaps becoming a bit less important. If higher-quality inputs are going into production, for example, and if more problems are caught and corrected during production, it follows that fewer problems will exist in the finished product. While some sort of final inspection is likely to always be useful, firms may be able to test somewhat fewer units and/or to test only certain aspects of them in order to assure acceptable overall quality.

Multiple Controls

Each of the various approaches to control is useful in particular circumstances. Indeed, most large organizations find it necessary to establish integrated control systems using multiple approaches. These systems include each of the three approaches to control noted above, and approach is integrated with the others for maximum effectiveness.

For example, consider a large manufacturing firm such as Boeing. Boeing carefully screens the engineers it hires, the materials it buys, the smaller firms it subcontracts with, and the financial solvency of airlines that place orders for new planes (steering control).

Boeing also carefully monitors each stage of the construction process as each new plane is assembled. Information about new technology and the overall health of the airline industry is also tracked on an ongoing basis to assure that the firm's procedures and decisions are kept current. And the performance of individual engineers and managers is assessed regularly. Cash flow is also monitored continuously to make sure the firm has sufficient capital on hand.

Quality inspection is an essential ingredient of control. At a Silgan Plastics Corporation plant in Ligonier, Indiana, bottles are inspected to assure that only top-quality products are manufactured and sold. (Keith Wood/Tony Stone Images.)

After each plane is finished, it is again subjected to numerous inspections and checks to make sure that it is flightworthy. Managers get bonuses for completing work ahead of schedule. Boeing collects its payment from the airline. And new information gleaned from its work is added to the firm's information system to assist in future development and construction projects.

Such integrated and comprehensive systems are necessary to provide adequate control for large, complex organizations.[13] This is especially true for multinational corporations with operations spread around the globe. But many smaller firms also find it necessary to create and maintain multiple control systems.

Establishing a Control System

Regardless of which approach to control a manager is taking, he or she must follow four basic steps in establishing a control system or framework.[14] A **control system** is a mechanism used to ensure that the organization is achieving its objectives. The four steps in control systems are illustrated in Exhibit 20.4.

Setting Standards

Standards should be consistent with the organization's goals and appropriate for the level at which they are being used.

The first step in control is to set **standards,** or targets against which performance will be compared. For example, a fast-food outlet such as a Burger King restaurant might set the following standards:

1. Customers will be served within four minutes of their entrance into the restaurant.
2. Drive-through customers will have their orders filled within five minutes of the time they enter the drive-through queue.
3. All tables will be wiped clean within three minutes after a customer has left.

Note that each standard is stated in objective, measurable terms. Moreover, each is very clear and specific and also has a specific time frame.

Standards are usually derived from, and therefore consistent with, the goals of the organization. Consider the Burger King restaurant. The standards given above are appropriate for an organization whose primary goals are related to customer service and satisfaction. If growth were of even more importance, however, the standards might instead reflect sales increases, increases in the number of customers served, and so forth. In similar fashion, a university coming under criticism for its overemphasis on athletic programs might attempt to offset this criticism by shifting its emphasis to academics. It might set a standard that 75 percent of all student athletes will graduate within five years of their initial enrollment, for example.

Of course, the specificity of standards will vary according to the level of the organization to which they apply. A single Burger King restaurant has many different standards, all very specific

Exhibit 20.4   Steps in Control

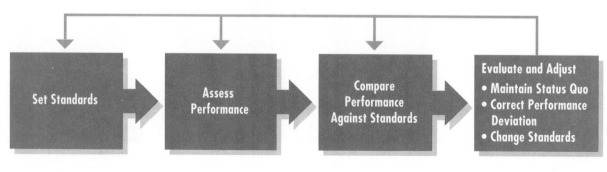

and somewhat narrowly focused on areas related to customer service, cleanliness, and efficiency. At the corporate level, on the other hand, Burger King's standards are likely to be fewer and less narrowly focused. The corporation probably has performance standards for sales growth, growth in the number of outlets, menu adjustments, and so forth.

Assessing Performance

The second step in the control process is to assess performance. This step relates specifically to those things the organization is attempting to control. That is, while assessing performance for control purposes is similar to and must obviously be consistent with the overall performance evaluation process, it must also be clearly focused on control-related standards. Thus, individual performance assessment at this stage may be a little less comprehensive than normal ongoing performance evaluations.

When managers are establishing standards, they should also specify how progress toward those standards will be assessed. Suppose that Safeway has determined that the average customer spends five minutes waiting in the check-out line before being served. Because of increased competition from Kroger, Safeway may want to reduce waiting time to three and a half minutes. Managers might decide that the best way to achieve this is to eliminate a half minute every six months for eighteen months. In a given store, then, the manager will need to measure current average waiting time, develop techniques for shortening waiting time (such as increasing the number of lines and training checkers to be more efficient), and then monitor progress to ensure continued improvement.

In many situations measuring performance is fairly easy, especially when the standards are objective and specific. In other settings, however, performance assessment is considerably more difficult. A manager taking over a struggling company might need an extended time to turn things around. Or a research and development scientist may not be able to produce consistent breakthroughs that can be immediately evaluated; instead, his or her contributions may come at irregular intervals, and their value may take some time to assess.

Finally, we should note that the appropriate time intervals for assessing performance also vary a great deal. In some areas, such as the strategic goals of General Motors or IBM, performance measurement may be appropriate every six months, or even longer. In others, such as a gambling casino or a clothing store, it is necessary to assess performance every day along several different dimensions.[15]

Comparing Performance with Standards

It is difficult to compare performance with standards because some standards are not quantifiable and judgment is often involved.

After setting standards and measuring subsequent relevant performance indicators, the manager must compare the two. Although this sounds fairly easy, it is actually somewhat difficult in many cases. For instance, some standards are relatively difficult to quantify. A standard of increasing customer or employee satisfaction is hard to measure accurately. Similarly, it may be difficult to assess a standard of achieving technological innovation.

Another difficulty relates to the fact that performance and standards are seldom precisely the same. If the standard is 10 percent and actual performance is 9.7 percent, has the standard been met or not? The answer, of course, is that it depends. The manager needs to draw on his or her experience and insight to determine whether the company needs to attain precisely 10 percent to be successful or whether a range from, say, 9 percent to 11 percent is really the same thing. If the 10 percent refers to an increase in recovery rates in a hospital, anything less than that may be unacceptable. But if it refers to improvements in the cleanliness of the company parking lot some slippage may be acceptable.

Evaluating and Adjusting

The final step in control is to evaluate and adjust standards and performance. Depending upon the circumstances, three different courses of action may be appropriate.

One response is to do nothing—to keep things just as they are. This action is clearly most appropriate when the assessed performance meets the targeted standard for performance. For example, if a manager's standard is to increase sales in her department by 12 percent this year and at the end of six months she has achieved an increase of 6.05 percent, she probably does not need to make any changes in what people in the department are doing.

More likely, some action will be needed to correct a deviation in performance from the desired standard. If the standard for another manager is to also increase sales by 12 percent this year and his department only has a 3-percent increase after six months, the department is clearly not on track to meet the standard. He may need to increase advertising, plan more promotional activities, and/or motivate his sales group. Correcting a deviation first requires giving performance feedback, a critical human skill. The Self-Assessment at the end of the chapter examines your ability to effectively provide performance feedback.

Of course, we also have problems if we are exceeding our standards by too much. Suppose our standard is to hire one hundred highly qualified new employees this year. If we end up hiring seventy-five in the first six months, we may need to cut back on recruiting and hiring. Sales of the Saturn division of General Motors recently took off, leaving many dealers with insufficient inventories and waiting lists of customers. While this was not a bad position to be in, Saturn's advertising dollars were not producing much current revenue (since it had few cars to sell), and some customers may have been annoyed by having to wait for a car.

In some situations it may be appropriate to change the standards against which performance is being assessed. Unexpectedly strong competition, for instance, may necessitate lowering an organization's expectations for growth. On the other hand, if all employees are exceeding their standards easily, the standards may have been set too low to begin with. Unfortunately, when this happens and the standards are subsequently raised, employees will probably be resentful and angry toward the organization. Therefore, it is clearly important to do a good job in the beginning.

Effective Control

Clearly, the manager's job would be greatly simplified if establishing organizational controls were easy. However, as we have seen, managing the control process is actually quite difficult and demanding.[16] What can a manager do to enhance the effectiveness of the organization's control system? In general, effective control has five attributes, which are summarized in Table 20.1.[17]

Integration

First, and perhaps foremost, control systems must be integrated into the overall organizational system. This is most critical in terms of planning. Given the cyclical nature of planning and con-

Table 20.1
Characteristics of Effective Control

Characteristics	Explanation
1. *Integration*	Establishing control systems that take into account organizational plans
2. *Objectivity*	Supplying detailed, verifiable information
3. *Accuracy*	Providing complete and correct information
4. *Timeliness*	Providing information when it is needed
5. *Flexibility*	Establishing control systems that accommodate changes in the organization or the environment

The five characteristics of effective control are integration, objectivity, accuracy, timeliness, and flexibility.

trol, as described earlier, it is logical and necessary that the planning and control systems be properly coordinated and integrated with one another for them to work smoothly.

To see how this works, consider the situation confronted by Knight-Ridder Inc., one of the largest media corporations in the United States. Although Knight-Ridder publishes some of this country's most prestigious newspapers, problems caused the company to take strong action to enhance profitability. Two interdependent actions were used: all of the company's newspapers had to prepare five-year plans aimed at boosting profit margins to 20 percent or higher, and tight controls were implemented to ensure that these targets were met.[18]

The mechanics involved in achieving proper integration are actually fairly straightforward. Managers need to consider relevant control elements as they develop plans, simultaneously using goals, strategies, and tactics to establish complementary dimensions of the control system. Similarly, results provided by the ongoing control system make very useful resources for future planning cycles.[19] A well-integrated control system will permeate the entire organization.[20]

Objectivity

A second characteristic of effective control systems is objectivity. This simply means that, to the greatest extent possible, the control system should use and provide detailed information that can be verified and understood.

For instance, suppose a sales manager asks two sales representatives to assess how their clients feel about the company and its products. One reports that he talked to fifteen customers and that ten of them liked what the company was doing, three were indifferent, and two had complaints. He also reports on the exact nature of the clients' likes and dislikes and provides an estimate of how much each intends to order next quarter. The other sales representative reports that she talked to a few people, that some were happy and some were unhappy with the products (although she is not too sure of the reasons for their attitudes), and that sales will be okay next quarter. Clearly, the data provided by the first sales representative will be more useful than those provided by the second.

Of course, the manager needs to look beyond simple numbers. A plant manager may appear to be doing a great job of cutting costs, but closer inspection might reveal that the manager is using substandard materials, pushing workers too hard, and padding reports. On balance, the control system should be as objective as possible, but not so dependent on figures that managers lose contact with what is actually going on behind the scenes.[21]

Accuracy

Obviously, the control system must be accurate in order to be effective. If it is providing erroneous information, it may be doing more harm than good. In reality, of course, any number of things can allow inaccuracies to creep into the system. A plant manager might be providing incomplete cost figures to make herself look better, or a sales representative might be padding his expense account and collecting more reimbursement than he is owed.[22] At another level, a human resource manager might overestimate the company's minority recruiting prospects in order to diminish short-term pressure to meet affirmative action goals.

The critical nature of such inaccuracies becomes apparent when we consider how managers use the control system. If a manager signs a contract to provide merchandise for a figure below what the true production costs are, the firm will lose money. Hence, managers need to take every precaution to ensure the accuracy of the information they receive from the control system.

Timeliness

It is also important that the information provided by the control system be timely. This means that the manager must have the information when he or she needs it most. The manager of a Kmart store, for example, wants and needs to know precise sales figures on a daily basis but may need inventory figures only every two or three months. And the corporate office will not need daily sales figures but only weekly or monthly figures. Timeliness does not necessarily mean speed, but it does mean that information is in the manager's hands when it is needed.

Timeliness is important not only in control but in all aspects of an organization's operations. At Topps Co., a Brooklyn company famous for its baseball trading cards, timeliness in control includes the introduction of specialty trading cards, such as the line of Desert Storm cards introduced during the United Nation's action in the Persian Gulf during the early 1990s. (Chuck Fishman 1992.)

In general, the need for timeliness is related to uncertainty. The more uncertain the situation, the greater the need for timely information. When a new product is introduced, the manager may desire daily sales reports, but for an older, more established product the manager may need them only every week or every month.

Flexibility   Finally, effective control systems tend to be flexible, that is, they are able to accommodate adjustments and change in the organization or the environment.[23] Suppose a control system is designed to manage information about two hundred raw materials that go into producing the company's products. A new technological breakthrough allows the company to produce the same products with only half as many materials. If the control system is not flexible, the managers will have to scrap the entire system and develop a new one. On the other hand, a flexible system will be able to accommodate the changes.

In summary, effective control systems generally have five basic attributes: they are integrated with other organizational systems, they are objective, they are accurate, they are timely, and they are flexible. In the next section we explore other ways to enhance control system effectiveness.

Managing Control

In addition to making control systems effective by promoting the attributes described above, managers must deal with resistance issues. Some people tend to resist control in particular, so managers need to understand why resistance occurs and what they can do to overcome it. The most common factors underlying resistance and the best ways to deal with them are summarized in Table 20.2.[24]

Understanding Resistance to Control

Overcontrol causes resistance by limiting employees' independence and autonomy.

Four of the most common reasons that people resist control are overcontrol, inappropriate focus, rewards for inefficiency, and accountability.

Organizations sometimes make the mistake of practicing **overcontrol,** or too much control. This can be particularly problematic when the control relates to employees. Employees may require a certain degree of control in the workplace, but they also want a reasonable degree of autonomy and freedom. For example, an organization may specify normal working hours and work-related expectations for its employees, but it will probably not be successful in trying to dictate personal behavior such as mannerisms, recreational preferences, and so forth. Attention is increasingly being paid to ways in which managers can get employees to exert personal control and accommodate both individual and organizational goals.[25] Personal control issues can be important to new and growing businesses.

Inappropriate focus occurs when the control is too narrowly focused or does not provide reasonable balance between different outcomes.

Another reason for resistance to control is **inappropriate focus,** which occurs when the control is too narrowly focused or does not provide a reasonable balance between different outcomes that are important. For instance, if a sales manager concentrates so much on sales increases that nothing else really matters, sales representatives may come to ignore other parts of their jobs. Likewise, if a university encourages and rewards publication and provides few incentives for professors to be good teachers, its faculty will gradually devote more and more time to research and less and less time to teaching.

In other cases, organizations end up rewarding inefficiency and perhaps not rewarding efficiency. Many departments rush to spend any of their budget that is going to remain at the end of the year because they feel that if they have money left over, management will assume they need less money next year. But if they spend all of their money, and perhaps even report a small loss, their budget might be increased next year because they ran out of funds. Obviously, this situation rewards inefficiency.

Accountability allows a manager to determine how each part of the organization is performing.

A final reason for resistance to control is that effective control creates **accountability.** That is, a properly designed control system will allow a manager to determine how each department, and in many cases how each individual manager, is performing. As a consequence, managers become more accountable for their actions, decisions, and performance. Obviously, some managers will not object to such accountability, but others—especially those who are not doing a good job—will resist.

Overcoming Resistance to Control

As also shown in Table 20.2, managers can at least partially overcome employee resistance to control in a number of ways. One obvious method is to make sure that the control system is properly designed. In particular, if it is designed to have the attributes of effective control already discussed

Table 20.2

Managing Control

Reasons for resistance	Ways to combat resistance
1. Overcontrol	1. Design the system well
2. Inappropriate focus	2. Encourage employee participation
3. Rewards for inefficiency	3. Use MBO
4. Accountability	4. Provide checks and balances

(integration, objectivity, accuracy, timeliness, and flexibility), employees will be less likely to object to it.

Second, employee participation can reduce resistance to control. If employees have a voice in designing the parts of the control system that directly affect them and also have avenues for suggesting modifications, they are more likely to accept the system as fair and reasonable. They will have a better understanding of how the control system was developed and how it contributes to overall organizational performance. And because they know it can be modified, they may be more willing to try it and see how it works, rather than resisting it out of hand.

A third approach to overcoming resistance to control is to use management by objectives, or MBO, which is described in Chapter 7 as a collaborative goal-setting technique between managers and their subordinates. Employees in a well-conceived and well-managed MBO system know exactly what is expected of them, how they should attempt to achieve those goals, and what their rewards will be if they succeed.

Finally, the control system should have a built-in provision for checks and balances. This simply means that it should provide a mechanism for checking and potentially adjusting for discrepancies. For example, suppose an employee who is dismissed for frequent tardiness denies that he was late very often. If the human resource manager can prove via thorough documentation that the employee was actually late many times, he (and other employees) will be more likely to see the control system as fair and equitable. Or suppose that a sales representative claims that she did not meet her quota because of unexpectedly high levels of competition from other companies. If the sales manager has adequate information to assess the validity of her claim, he can more easily accept or refute that claim.

Responsibility for Control

Line Managers

A final issue to consider is the responsibility for control. Exactly who needs to be concerned with control? As shown in Exhibit 20.5, this responsibility is shared between line managers and specialized managers called controllers.

In a very real sense, all managers are responsible for the control function in an organization. They all help design the system, are responsible for implementing and using it, and are at least partially governed by it.

As the exhibit illustrates, the CEO is responsible for the overall control of the total organization. Each division head is responsible for control within his or her division. In general, such managers have some degree of autonomy in adjusting the control system to fit their own preferences and views on how control should be executed.[26] No matter what variations they implement, however, the system within each division must mesh and be consistent with the overall system of the organization.

The Controller

*The **controller** helps managers, coordinates the overall control system, and gathers important information and relays it to all managers.*

In most larger organizations, control is also the specific responsibility of one or more managers who have the title of **controller.** As shown in the exhibit, a large organization may have a corporate controller as well as other controllers in each division.[27] The controller's job is to help line managers with their control activities, to coordinate the overall control system within the organization, and to gather relevant information and report it to all managers. Monsanto developed a program to train employees in controllership that it claims graduates broad-thinking, line-oriented managers.[28]

Controllers are particularly involved in the control of financial resources. This is consistent with the pervasiveness of financial concerns in control. Because of the increased importance of the control function in recent years, the position of controller has taken on added stature in many organizations. For example, controllers at Coors, Electronic Data Systems, United Parcel Service, and Hyundai have all been given more responsibility in recent years.[29]

Exhibit 20.5

Responsibility for Control

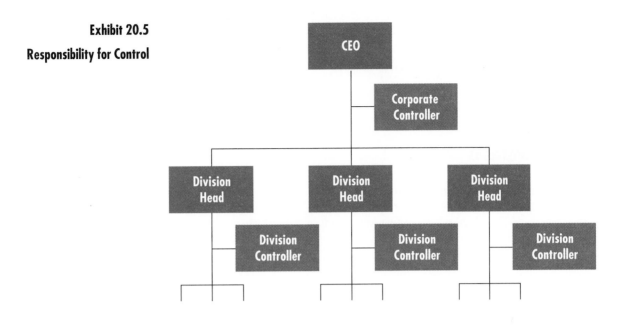

Chapter Summary

Controlling is the process of monitoring and adjusting organizational activities toward goal attainment. Most organizations have controls to deal with four areas: financial resources, physical resources, human resources, and information resources.

The planning-control link means that control is the other side of the planning coin; it helps management ensure that performance conforms to plans. Control-generated information can also facilitate future planning activities.

There are three basic approaches to control: steering control, concurrent control, and postaction control. Steering control monitors the quality and/or quantity of various kinds of resources before they enter the system. Concurrent control focuses on activities that occur as inputs are being transformed into outputs. Postaction control deals with the quality and/or quantity of an organization's outputs. These approaches to control are usually used together as multiple controls.

There are four basic steps to establishing a control system: setting standards, assessing performance, comparing performance with standards, and evaluating and adjusting.

Effective control has five attributes: it is integrated, objective, accurate, timely, and flexible. Managing control also involves dealing with resistance to control. There are four basic things a manager can do to overcome such resistance. First, he or she should make sure that the control system is properly designed and has the characteristics of effective controls. Second, the manager should encourage participation, which tends to increase acceptance. Third, the manager can use management by objectives to establish collaborative goals and to enhance acceptance of controls. Finally, he or she should ensure that the control system has a built-in provision for checks and balances, so that discrepancies do not occur or are corrected if they do.

The ultimate responsibility for control must be shared by everyone in the organization. However, control is the specific responsibility of one or more managers who have the title of controller. The controller's job is to assist line managers with their control activities, coordinate the overall control system, and gather relevant information and report it to all managers.

The Manager's Vocabulary

controlling
planning-control link
steering control
concurrent control

postaction control
control system
standards
overcontrol

inappropriate focus
accountability
controller

Review Questions

1. What is control, and why is it important to organizations?
2. What are the basic approaches to control?
3. Discuss each of the steps in establishing a control system.

4. What are the characteristics of effective control?
5. Why do people resist control, and how do managers overcome this resistance?

Analysis Questions

1. Do you ever feel that certain aspects of your life are out of control? Do you wish you could exercise more control over things that affect you? If so, describe some reasons why you might need some control, apart from those given in the text.
2. Which step in the control system is likely to be the most difficult to carry out? Why? Which is likely to meet with the most resistance? Why?

3. Do all of the characteristics of effective controls fit together? Why or why not?
4. Which characteristic of effective control do you feel is most important? Why?
5. Why would it be unwise for an organization to have just one person totally responsible for control? Who should be responsible for control? Why?

Self-Assessment

Feedback Skills Questionnaire

Introduction This Self-Assessment is designed to measure your ability to provide performance feedback. This is a critical human skill and helps implement the controlling function. Most employees report that performance feedback is one of the most important types of communication a manager can provide them. Here is a chance for you to determine your ability to provide effective performance feedback.

Instructions Circle the number that best represents your own behavior in giving feedback. Try to be as honest as you can; you will not be asked to disclose specific responses or scores. Your responses are for your own analysis and will be worth more the more accurate you can be.

1. To what extent do you use terms like "excellent," "good," or "bad" when you give someone feedback?

1	2	3	4	5	6	7
always use such terms			sometimes use such terms			rarely or never use such terms

2. How often do you provide specific examples or concrete details when giving feedback?

1	2	3	4	5	6	7
rarely give specific details			sometimes give specific details			always give specific details

3. Do you generally first ask whether the other person wants feedback?

1	2	3	4	5	6	7
assume feedback is wanted		sometimes check to see if feedback is wanted		always check to see if feedback is wanted		

4. When you give someone feedback, is it generally because you want to get a load off your chest?

1	2	3	4	5	6	7
generally I "unload" with feedback		sometimes I "unload" by giving feedback			I rarely "unload" when I give feedback	

5. Do you generally give feedback as soon as possible or do you usually wait for an appropriate time, such as an appraisal session?

1	2	3	4	5	6	7
generally I wait for a good time			usually I give feedback close to the time of the behavior			I always give feedback immediately

6. When you give feedback, is it quite clear what that person could actually do to make effective use of your feedback?

1	2	3	4	5	6	7
feedback I give is not usually focused on applications			feedback I give is sometimes focused on applications			feedback I give is always focused on applications

For interpretation, turn to the back of the book.

Source: Marshall Sashkin and William C. Morris, *Experiencing Management,* © 1987 by Addison-Wesley Publishing Company, Inc. Reprinted with permission of the publisher.

Skill Builder

Using the Gantt Chart

Purpose The ability to execute a budget, prepare a PERT chart or a Gantt chart are technical skills all managers must possess. These technical skills enable managers to control their organization's operation. This skill builder focuses on the *administrative management model.* It will help you develop the *coordinator role.* One of the skills of the coordinator is control.

Introduction This activity allows you to develop the technical skill of preparing a Gantt chart.

Instructions You are the members of the On-Time Producer's Scheduling Team. Your job is to manage work schedules and report to top management at the weekly staff meetings held every Monday morning. The company has two unwavering policies: (1) we always ship on schedule, and (2) we never work overtime. The factory works one 8-hour shift 5 days a week.

You came in early today, May 15, to prepare for the weekly staff meeting. Of concern is the important order from the Hot-Shot Corporation, on which you have collected the following information:

1. The order resulted in a schedule of eight sequential tasks (that is, a task cannot begin until the preceding task is complete), as follows:

Sequence No.	Task Activity	Days Required to Complete
1	Design change	3
2	Prepare blueprints	2
3	Purchase materials	6
4	Manufacture parts	12
5	Assemble	3
6	Paint	1
7	Test	1
8	Package	1

2. The Manufacture parts activity includes the manufacturing of five detail parts, which can be made independently within the 12-day period:

Detail Parts	Days Required
Frames	12
Flanges	10
Handles	10
Gears	5
Guides	2

3. The design change task began on May, and the order is to be packaged for shipment on June 8.

4. Engineering finished its task in just two days.

5. Blueprinting began on May 3 and took three days because of an equipment breakdown.

6. Material purchases were initiated on May 8 and were finished one day ahead of schedule on May 12.

7. Parts manufacture is scheduled to start tomorrow, although you could begin today.

At last week's staff meeting, top management announced that Gantt charts would be used to schedule and monitor work in the shops. Furthermore, updated Gantt charts were to be used as part of the staff meeting reports. All you know about Gantt charts is that they are graphic techniques applied to operations scheduling.

Your task for today's staff meeting is to apply the above data to the construction of the Gantt chart below. Prepare to present your Gantt chart in class as you would at the morning staff meeting.

Source: *Exercises in Management,* by Gene E. Burton. Copyright © 1990 by Houghton Mifflin Company. Used with permission.

Gantt Chart

Sequence no.	Activity	May																					June				
		1	2	3	4	5	8	9	10	11	12	15	16	17	18	19	22	23	24	25	26	29	30	31	1	2	5	6	7	8
1	Design change																							
2	Prepare blueprints																							
3	Purchase materials																							
4	Manufacture parts																							
	Frames																							
	Flanges																							
	Handles																							
	Gears																							
	Guides																							
5	Assemble																							
6	Paint																							
7	Test																							
8	Package																							

Symbols:

Scheduled:

Completed:

CONCLUDING CASES

20.1   Amerihost Properties, Inc.

Amerihost is a small but fast-growing Illinois firm that specializes in buying run-down, distressed motel and hotel properties, refurbishing them, and then operating them profitably. While perhaps not the most glamorous of businesses, Amerihost is fast developing a solid reputation in its industry for being a well-managed and tightly controlled enterprise.

The firm was started in 1984 as America Pop Inc., selling popcorn and sodas from kiosks in Chicago subways. The new business never earned a profit. Thus, in 1986 the founders sold the kiosk operation, changed the corporation's name to Amerihost, and began investing in hotels.

Losses mounted for three more years. The firm had to hire new managers and invest in the development of new property designs. The company also invested heavily in a computer system that it unfortunately outgrew in eighteen months. But in 1990 Amerihost earned its first profits and now seems poised for future growth and expansion.

Amerihost's strategy is a simple one. It focuses on small but growing communities in the Midwest. It buys failed motels or builds new ones. It provides limited services at each of its properties but no grand lobby, no restaurant, no laundry facilities, and so forth. At present, at least, this segment of the market is healthier than other segments.

In evaluating a potential property or building site, Amerihost relies heavily on a twenty-page checklist of criteria. For instance, one important factor is the existence of one or more so-called "demand generators." Demand generators are things like universities, new businesses, or major highways that provide ongoing potential customers.

One recent acquisition by Amerihost was a one-hundred-eighty-room former Holiday Inn in Shorewood, Illinois. The property had lost its Holiday Inn license because of substandard conditions and had been taken over by a failing savings and loan that held the mortgage. Its base room rate was twenty-six dollars a night, and occupancy was running about 30 percent.

Amerihost bought the property for $1.45 million and invested another $750,000 to renovate it. When it reopened, Amerihost promoted it heavily. For example, the firm held contests and gave away free weekend stays to local residents. Base room rates were raised to thirty-six dollars a night, and occupancy is currently running above 70 percent, considerably above the industry average for minimum service facilities.

Amerihost also practices tight control throughout its other operations. For example, it uses the same contractors and suppliers to refurbish or build its properties. And it only uses one of three basic designs, again to hold down costs. These tactics have allowed the company to build fifteen hotels without going over budget. Amerihost has no national expansion plans at the moment, but it is steadily increasing its presence throughout the Midwest.[30]

Discussion Questions

1. What forms of control does Amerihost practice?
2. What are the critical performance indicators in the motel and hotel business?
3. Do you see any problems on the horizon for Amerihost?

20.2   Gitano

Gitano is a family-owned and -operated apparel business. The firm was started by a Syrian family named Dabah in 1974. Like most apparel firms, Gitano buys materials in Asia and manufactures clothing in areas where labor is inexpensive. Gitano opened its plants in Guatemala, Jamaica, and Mississippi.

Unlike other designer firms such as Ralph Lauren, Calvin Klein, and Donna Karan, Gitano got its start by focusing on big-volume discount stores like Wal-Mart and Kmart. Its clothing, especially jeans, proved to be extremely popular, and throughout the 1980s Gitano experienced phenomenal growth.

But in the early 1990s Gitano began to unravel. And most of the blame was laid on its weak control systems and lack of professional management. One problem stemmed from the fact that the firm's CEO, Haim Dabah, refused to delegate authority and tried to oversee everything himself. When the firm was smaller, this was not too difficult. More recently, though, the organization had grown so large that Dabah simply could not stay on top of everything.

Gitano also had no budgeting system. When revenues came in they were deposited in the bank, and when bills arrived a check was written to pay them. No one really had any clear understanding of the firm's cash flow situation, nor was any thought ever given to planning ahead for future expenses.

Inventory was poorly managed as well. Gitano's plants were kept running at full capacity, and finished products were shipped to warehouses in the Midwest. When orders came in, products were pulled from stock and shipped out. If an item was out of stock, an emergency order was faxed to a plant, and finished products were shipped directly from there to the customer. But no one had any firm idea of exactly what was in inventory, nor how much the inventory was worth.

Some critics today point out that the company should probably never have gotten into manufacturing in the first place. Most apparel firms subcontract their manufacturing to other firms. But Gitano owners simply felt that they wanted to own their own factories, without really knowing why. One plant was recently running a waste rate of more than 20 percent, compared to an industry average of 4 percent.

Unfortunately, Gitano may also have lost touch with its primary market somewhere along the way. Recent sales have declined precipitously, and most customers except Wal-Mart have cut back on their orders. To turn things around, the Dabah family has finally decided to enlist the assistance of professional management. As a start, they hired a long-time executive with Levi Strauss to come in and run things. His first priority, he has said, is to get things under control. But he also said he was not sure where to begin.[31]

Discussion Questions

1. What kinds of control should be implemented at Gitano?
2. Are these problems more likely to surface in family-owned businesses? Why?
3. Do you think Gitano will survive? Why or why not?

21

Total Quality Management

Learning Objectives

After studying this chapter you should be able to

- Describe the nature of quality and productivity.

- Discuss the importance of quality and its relation to competition, costs, and effectiveness.

- Describe strategic initiatives firms use to improve quality.

- Describe operational techniques firms use to improve quality.

To some people Harley-Davidson conjures up images of black jackets and rogue motorcycle gangs. And while there may be some justification for this image, it only represents a small part of Harley. Indeed, in many ways the Harley-Davidson story represents a microcosm of what has gone bad and good with U.S. business.

For years Harley dominated the world market for large motorcycles. Its products were loud, fast, and gaudy. And they did indeed appeal to biker rebels who enjoyed the notoriety that came with riding a big Harley in a gang. But Japanese competitors were making serious inroads in Harley's more stable markets, and in the late 1970s the firm's parent, AMF, ordered management to boost output threefold. Unfortunately, without adequate planning and equipment, this boost caused product quality to erode drastically, and Harley's sales soon plummeted.

A management-led buyout in 1981 allowed the firm more autonomy in addressing its problems. In the short run it relied on cosmetic product changes to increase product appeal and sales. But over the longer term management knew the firm had to improve the quality of its products if it was to survive.

In the mid-1980s Harley management enlisted the assistance of the firm's workers. Work teams were formed and their advice solicited on everything from parts to design to marketing. Because of work teams, combined with new and improved manufacturing techniques, Harley did indeed bounce back. With higher-quality products and lower costs, profitability has been restored and the firm has, for the time being at least, beat back the Japanese.[1] ∎

The actions taken by Harley-Davidson clearly demonstrate both a major problem facing many U.S. businesses and the best way for addressing it. The problem? A serious product quality problem that has resulted in lost sales and a poor image. The solution? A renewed dedication to making product quality a cornerstone for managerial decisions and activities.

This chapter explores the concepts of quality and productivity in detail. We first describe the nature of quality and productivity. We then discuss the importance of quality and its relation to competition, costs, and long-term effectiveness. Strategic initiatives for improving quality are then introduced and discussed. Finally, we conclude by discussing operational techniques for improving quality.

The Nature of Quality and Productivity

Most people have a general sense of what the word *quality* means. Nevertheless, given both its importance and its complexities, we will start by examining the meaning of quality in detail. We then relate quality to productivity, identify levels of productivity, productivity trends, and ways to improve productivity. With this basic understanding of productivity, we can then turn back to a more detailed analysis of quality.

The Meaning of Quality

Suppose someone goes to a store and buys two pens. It turns out that one pen writes for forty hours before running out of ink, while the other writes for eighty hours. The latter is clearly of higher quality than the former, right? Not necessarily. For example, if the first pen cost the consumer sixty-nine cents and has a stated manufacturer's expectation of being able to write for thirty-five hours, it actually comes out looking pretty good. And if the second pen cost five dollars and was intended to write for ninety-five hours, it was not such a good deal after all. Thus, it is important to recognize that quality has both an absolute and a relative meaning.

Product quality refers to the quality of a real or tangible item.

It is also important to note that quality can be used in reference to products and/or to services. The example above clearly pertains to **product quality,** with the product being the pen. Product quality refers to the quality of a tangible item. Common products whose quality is particularly relevant include automobiles, electronic equipment, mechanical equipment, and consumer products.

Service quality is the quality of an intangible service.

Service quality, meanwhile, refers to the quality of an intangible service provided by an organization. Suppose a customer wants to order merchandise from a catalog. If she is given an 800 number to call, the call is answered quickly, she is treated courteously and her order taken by a trained professional, and the shipment arrives as promised, she will likely feel that she has experienced high service quality. But if she has to pay for a toll call, is put on hold, is treated brusquely by someone who has little product knowledge, and the shipment arrives much later than promised, service quality is low.

Quality is the total set of features and characteristics of a product or service that bear on its ability to satisfy stated or implied needs.

Following published guidelines established by the American Society for Quality Control, we will define **quality** as the total set of features and characteristics of a product or service that bear on its ability to satisfy stated or implied needs.[2] Thus, assuming that the two pens noted above are equivalent in all other respects, the cheaper pen that writes for forty hours is of higher quality than the pen that cost more and wrote for a while longer. Similarly, the first catalog ordering experience described above had higher service quality than did the second.

Quality can be assessed in both absolute and relative terms.

Table 21.1 lists eight specific factors or characteristics that can be used to assess or evaluate product or service quality. For example, all else being equal, the more desirable features that a product or service has, the higher its quality relative to a product or service with fewer desirable features. Likewise, all else being equal, if a particular product or service is aesthetically pleasing, it is of higher quality relative to another product or service that is less aesthetically pleasing.

Table 21.1
Eight Dimensions of Quality

Dimension	Explanation
1. *Performance*	A product's primary operating characteristic. Examples are automobile acceleration and a television set's picture clarity.
2. *Features*	Supplement to a product's basic functioning characteristics, such as power windows on a car.
3. *Reliability*	A probability of not malfunctioning during a specified period.
4. *Conformance*	The degree to which a product's design and operating characteristics meet established standards.
5. *Durability*	A measure of product life.
6. *Serviceability*	The speed and ease of repair.
7. *Aesthetics*	How a product looks, feels, tastes, and smells.
8. *Perceived quality*	As seen by a customer.

Source: Based on data in David A. Garvin, "Competing on the Eight Dimensions of Quality," *Harvard Business Review* November/December 1987.

It is important to recognize that the caveat "all else being equal" plays an important role in these quality assessments, however. For example, if a product has an abundance of features and looks beautiful but seldom works the way it is supposed to, its quality obviously suffers. Similarly, if the same product has few features and is relatively unattractive but works reliably and dependably, its quality is enhanced.

Also, we need to relate these ideas back to the previously noted dimensions of absolute and relative quality. Suppose you wanted to buy a new stereo system. You go to an electronics store and look at a portable Sony system for three hundred fifty dollars, a Sony rack system for one thousand dollars, and another Sony rack system for two thousand dollars. Regardless of which system you buy, you expect it to play a compact disk when you push the play button, to pick up the local transmission from your favorite FM radio station, and so forth. You also expect it to do so for a reasonable period of time (longer than a few days, but not necessarily twenty years). Thus, each system is evaluated in terms of some generally understood absolute level; a product or system needs to be capable of fulfilling its intended purpose.

At the same time, you also are likely to recognize that the three-hundred-fifty-dollar system will not perform as well in several ways as will the other systems. The portable system may have a limited range for FM reception, may not reproduce the bass tracks as well, does not have the same volume capabilities, may not have remote control, and may only be expected to last two or three years. On the other hand, the more expensive systems will pick up more stations, have louder and better sound, have remote control, last much longer, and so forth.

Thus, the relative component of quality must be interpreted in comparison to other alternatives in several ways. All three Sony systems may be of high quality relative to the standards they are expected to meet. The question becomes how much you want to pay in terms of what you will get. And you would also need to compare each system against comparable systems available from other manufacturers.

Quality and Productivity

From a managerial perspective, product or service quality is highly related to productivity. Thus, before proceeding further with our discussion of quality, we will first introduce the productivity construct and establish its basic principles.

__Productivity__ is a measure of efficiency that indicates what is created relative to the resources used to create it.

In a very general sense, productivity is a measure of efficiency. More specifically, **productivity** is an economic index of the value or amount of what is created relative to the value or amount of resources necessary to create it. For example, assume that two workers in the same factory are being paid the same wage to spend eight hours assembling toasters. One assembles one hundred toasters that meet standard quality tests, while the other produces one hundred twenty-five toasters of the identical quality. Clearly, the worker who makes one hundred twenty-five toasters is more productive than is the one who makes only one hundred toasters in the same period of time.

Similarly, assume that two manufacturing plants are of the same size and have identical production equipment and the same size and type of work force. One plant, however, is able to manufacture five thousand electrical instruments per day, while the other can make only forty-five hundred comparable instruments. The former plant is more productive than the latter.

In the past, managers often assumed—incorrectly—that productivity and quality were inversely related. That is, they thought they could only increase output by lowering quality. More recently, however, as shown in Exhibit 21.1, many managers have come to realize that productivity and quality are actually related in a positive way. Increased productivity often means higher quality, and higher quality results in higher productivity.

For example, if a firm can enhance its quality, several things happen. First of all, since defects are almost certain to decrease, there will be fewer returns from unhappy customers. Second, because defects are lower, fewer resources need to be dedicated to reworking or repairing defective

Exhibit 21.1
The Quality-Productivity Cycle

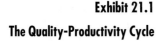

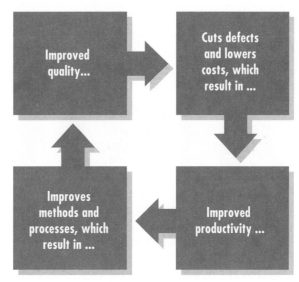

products. And finally, since there are fewer defective units being produced and since operating employees will be more involved in quality enhancement, fewer quality control inspectors will be needed. Overall, then, since fewer resources are being used to produce products and services, productivity (by definition) increases.

Levels and Forms of Productivity

As we have seen, there are different levels and forms of productivity. Indeed, there are actually several levels of productivity that can be identified.[3]

Productivity can be assessed at several different levels, including individual, unit, company, industry, and country.

Levels of Productivity   Exhibit 21.2 illustrates some of the more general levels of productivity that are of interest and concern to managers. The most basic level is individual productivity, the amount produced or created by a single individual relative to his or her costs to the organization. For example, Glen May works in a Kmart distribution center in Texas. His productivity reflects the value of the orders he fills each day relative to his wages.

One step higher on the productivity chain is unit productivity. Unit productivity might be the productivity of a manufacturing plant within a firm (as shown in the exhibit), a single restaurant within a chain of restaurants, or a group of workers within a single facility of an organization. Kmart determines the unit productivity of each of its distribution centers.

Company productivity, at still a higher level, is the total level of productivity achieved by all employees and/or units of an entire organization. All of Kmart's distributions centers, retail stores, and other operations combine to determine the corporation's overall productivity. Likewise, managers at General Motors, Boeing, and American Airlines are all concerned about their respective level of company productivity.

Industry productivity is that level of productivity achieved by all companies in a single industry. Kmart, Sears, Wal-mart, and other retailers contribute to the retailing industry's aggregate level of productivity. Likewise, Ford, General Motors, and Chrysler combine to determine the industry productivity of the U.S. automobile industry.

Finally, country productivity refers to the productivity levels achieved by entire countries. The retailing industry in the United States contributes to this country's total productivity. Industrialized countries like the United States, Japan, France, and Germany all have relatively high lev-

Exhibit 21.2

Levels of Productivity

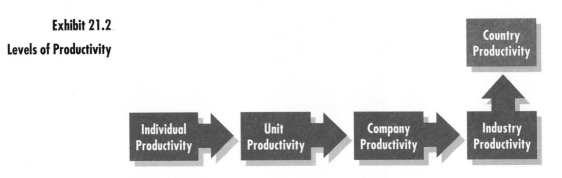

els of productivity, whereas less industrialized countries like Poland, Vietnam, Cuba, and Kenya have relatively lower levels of productivity.

Forms of productivity include
overall productivity *and* ***labor productivity.***

Forms of Productivity   In many instances it also makes sense to consider different forms of productivity. For example, **overall productivity**—technically called **total factor productivity**—is determined by dividing outputs by the sum of labor, capital, materials, information, and energy costs. That is, it includes all the inputs used by the organization.

In many instances, however, it makes sense to evaluate productivity in terms of only some of the resources used by the organization. For example, **labor productivity** is determined by dividing outputs by direct labor. Such a partial productivity index has several advantages. For one thing, resources can be expressed in different terms, such as hours of labor or units of raw materials rather than having to be transformed into a common base, such as dollars. It also allows managers to focus their efforts to enhance productivity on specific areas and to be better able to directly assess their effects.

Productivity is important because of its impact on profitability as well as on our quality of life and standard of living.

Productivity is important for both obvious and less obvious reasons. For example, the productivity of a single individual will contribute to the productivity of his or her unit. Likewise, unit productivity can help the organization determine where resources are being used wisely and where they are being used less wisely. Similarly, a firm's level of productivity will contribute directly to its profitability and, thus, to its ability to survive. The overall productivity of an industry will serve to encourage or discourage foreign competition. For example, if productivity is low for all the firms in one country in a particular industry, foreign competitors will feel that they have significant market opportunities and will enter the market aggressively. But if industry productivity is high, foreign competitors will find it much more difficult to enter the market.

Less obvious, but also very important, is the fact that productivity contributes to our overall quality of life and standard of living. For example, the more goods and services a country can create with its resources, the more goods and services its citizens will have to consume. And if those goods and services are produced efficiently enough, it will also be possible to ship them to foreign markets. The money that flows back will also add to the overall standard of living. Thus, the citizens of a highly productive country will have a better standard of living than will people who live in a less productive country.

Productivity Trends

In the preceding section we documented the clear importance of productivity. Given that importance, it is equally critical to understand trends and patterns in how productivity is changing.[4]

Trends in the United States   As far as managers in the United States are concerned, there is both good and bad news about productivity. On the plus side, the United States has the highest level

Absolute productivity in the United States is the highest in the world.

of productivity in the world. For example, the typical American worker produces goods or services worth more than $44,100 each year.[5] Canadian workers are the second-most productive workers in the world. Moreover, there is little chance that our absolute leadership in this area will disappear anytime in the near future.[6]

On the other hand, productivity growth rates in the United States have been slow in recent years. For example, from 1979 through 1990 U.S. labor productivity increased at an annual rate of only 0.5 percent. As we will see later, our major industrial competitors have been increasing their productivity at a much higher rate.

Why did overall U.S. productivity slow down to begin with? Several factors contributed to this pattern. For one thing, because of booming production levels and relatively little foreign competition, U.S. manufacturing facilities deteriorated badly during the 1950s and 1960s. This deterioration resulted in less efficient production in the 1970s. For another, more and more relatively unskilled and/or inexperienced workers (such as minorities and women) entered the work force for the first time during the 1960s and 1970s. Finally, in order to boost short-term profits, many U.S. businesses started spending less and less on long-term research and development. As a consequence, they achieved fewer breakthroughs in new technology.

Another consideration is the service sector. Productivity in the service sector has remained essentially flat for the last several years. And since the service sector has become such an important part of our total economy, stagnation in productivity in this sector has kept overall productivity from growing as much as it might have otherwise.

There are also several different explanations as to why productivity levels in the service sector have lagged. For one thing, the rapid growth in services has carried with it some inefficiencies due to rapid start-up, lack of training, poorly designed operations, and so forth. For another, measuring output in many service areas is difficult. Assessing the output of a lawyer or accountant, for example, is difficult relative to that of an assembly line worker. Hence, accurate measures of output are harder to obtain. Finally, many of the operational innovations for improving productivity (for example, robotics and automation) of the 1980s have been directed at the manufacturing sector, while fewer were produced for the service sector. Managers now have a clearer understanding

Building new plants and/or redesigning old ones are but two ways to support better quality and productivity. Another is to change the work rules that govern who does what and when. Combining the two as Union Camp did here in its Savannah paper plant can lead to very desirable results; producing twice as much paper with 20 percent fewer workers in this situation. (Michael A. Schwarz.)

of the situation, however. Thus, more and more attention is being focused on increasing productivity in the service sector in the 1990s.[7]

International Trends   A major reason that people are concerned about productivity growth rates in the United States is because workers in many other countries are becoming more and more productive. Indeed, over the last several decades, productivity growth in several industrial countries—including Japan, France, and Great Britain—has outstripped productivity growth in the United States.[8] From 1979 through 1990, for example, labor productivity increased 3 percent per year in Japan and 1.6 percent per year in the Western industrialized area of Germany.[9]

Productivity growth in the United States is lagging behind that of other industrialized countries.

Given that these countries are our major competitors in the world marketplace, concerns about their productivity growth rates are clearly well founded. Increased awareness of these trends has galvanized many business leaders in the United States to try and stem the tide. Through a variety of actions, many of which are noted in the following sections, U.S. businesses are working harder than ever to maintain their position in the world economy.[10]

Improving Productivity

Organizations that wish to enhance productivity at one or more levels have several different approaches that can be taken. As shown in Table 21.2, some of these methods are based on operations and others focus on enhanced motivation and involvement of employees.

Productivity can often be improved through a variety of techniques.

Operations and Management   Organizations can often improve productivity through various operations and basic management techniques.[11] For example, improved technological methods and facilities can be a big contributor. In 1992 the average machine tool in a U.S. manufacturing plant was seven years older than the same tool in a comparable Japanese plant. In many cases, the older equipment and plants are, the less efficient they are likely to be. Thus, by building new plants, by installing new technology and investing in new machinery, productivity may well be increased. Ford, Rubbermaid, and Caterpillar have each improved productivity through the construction of new facilities and/or the installation of new equipment.

Likewise, building new distribution systems, information systems, and office buildings may also boost productivity if they result in more efficient ways for employees to do their jobs. Wal-Mart's modern and efficient distribution centers, Federal Express's marvelous computerized communication network, and Union Carbide's efficient new corporate headquarters building have each contributed to the productivity of their respective organizations.[12]

Another approach to enhancing productivity is by increasing spending on research and development (R&D). R&D can create new products, new uses for current products, and new methods

Table 21.2
Methods for Improving Productivity

Through operations and management	Through motivation and involvement
Improve technology and facilities	Increase training
Increase research and development spending	Increase employee participation
Adopt automated and robotic systems	Improve reward systems
Enhance speed	
Enhance flexibility	

for making products. Each of these breakthroughs results in improved productivity.[13] Bausch & Lomb, 3M, Merck, and IBM all credit R&D as being a key ingredient in their overall level of organizational effectiveness.

Unfortunately, R&D is often a prime target for cutbacks when a business faces a downturn. Since R&D's dividends are usually paid "tomorrow," short-sighted managers worried about today's bottom line may inadvertently hurt a firm's future by trying to maximize short-term profits.[14] Avon, USX, and Texaco have all cut R&D spending at least once in the last decade.

Related to both technology and R&D, organizations can also increase productivity by investing in automation and/or robotics. Automated production systems, for example, can make things with much higher levels of precision and at more exacting tolerance standards than can human workers. Similarly, robots do not tire and let their concentration slip. Cummins Engine Corporation has boosted labor productivity significantly by implementing automated production systems.

Motivation and Involvement   Managers can also achieve productivity improvements by improving the motivation and involvement of its employees. Common methods for doing this are also noted in Table 21.2.

One approach is to increase training. Sometimes workers do not perform at their maximum efficiency simply because they do not know how. Training is especially important in conjunction with the operations improvements noted above. For example, installing new production technology and not appropriately training employees in how to use it accomplishes very little. And indeed, some experts speculate that service productivity has lagged because companies have invested billions of dollars in sophisticated computer systems, networks, and work stations but have not adequately trained employees and managers in how to effectively use them.[15]

Increased employee participation is also often cited as a key to improving productivity. Japanese firms like Hitachi, Sony, and Honda are held up as examples of how important employee participation can be to productivity growth. U.S. firms like Westinghouse, Ford, and General Electric have learned valuable lessons from the Japanese and have each taken steps to dramatically improve the level of participation among their employees. For example, each now gives operating employees considerably more control over how they do their jobs and has made them directly responsible for monitoring the quality of their work and correcting any defects that they happen to observe. And, as a result, their productivity has improved.

Finally, organizations can also improve productivity by modifying their reward systems. All too often, workers receive the same rewards regardless of the quality of work they perform. Thus, there are no incentives to work hard or to worry about how much one is producing. On the other hand, firms that tie significant rewards to improvements in productivity often see significant improvements. For example, Du Pont has recently implemented a new incentive system whereby employees receive bonuses if unit productivity exceeds previously agreed-upon levels. While it is too early to know the results of this program, it seems to hold considerable promise for the future.

The Importance of Quality

With the preceding introduction to quality and discussion of productivity as a foundation, we are now ready to delve more deeply into a discussion of quality and its role in businesses. We begin by investigating its fundamental importance to organizations. Indeed, quality is seen as being so important that the U.S. government sponsors an annual award for those firms that improve quality the most. *The Quality Challenge: The Baldrige Award* discusses this award and some of its recent winners. The basic factors that determine its importance are competition, cost, and long-term effectiveness.[16]

The Quality Challenge

The Baldrige Award

For years Japan has given a national award to firms that produce exceptionally high-quality products. The award is called the Deming Prize, named after W. Edwards Deming. Deming is an American who taught the Japanese how to use statistical control methods for improving quality.

To encourage American businesses to concentrate more on quality, the U.S. government recently implemented its own quality award. The award is named after Malcolm Baldrige, a former Secretary of Commerce who championed quality. The Baldrige Award is given annually to those firms deemed to have achieved the greatest quality improvements.

The Baldrige Award was first conferred in 1988. As many as six awards can be given each year—two each for manufacturing firms, service firms, and small firms. The first winners were Globe Metallurgical, Motorola, and Westinghouse's Commercial Nuclear Fuel Division.

Winning a Baldrige Award is not easy. Contestants must complete a painstaking fifty-page application form that thoroughly documents their strides in improving quality. A group of experts selects a small group of finalists and then visits each one. The experts must be allowed to see anything and talk to anyone during their inspection visits. And each finalist—winners and losers—gets a detailed analysis of its successes and shortcomings. The award has gained such importance that some large firms now require their suppliers to apply for the prize as a way to measure their quality.

In the most recent round of competition, five awards were given. The winners were Ritz-Carlton, Texas Instruments' Defense Systems & Electronics Group, Granite Rock, AT&T Network Systems Group/Transmission Systems Business Unit, and AT&T Universal Card Services.[17] ∎

Quality and Competition

Quality is important because of its impact on competition, costs, and long-term effectiveness.

In recent years quality has become an important point of competition in virtually every industry. Consumers around the world are increasingly demanding higher-quality products and services. Thus, a firm that can argue or demonstrate that its products or services are as good as or better than those offered by competitors will have an upper hand in the marketplace.

Quality has become an especially important point of competition in the automobile, computer, airline, and electronics industries. For example, Ford has always promoted its Escort line on the basis of low price. However, in 1990 the company decided to promote its Escorts on the basis that they are as good as or better than Japanese imports. (Of course, the firm did not widely publicize the fact that the Escort had been engineered by Mazda!)

Service quality has also become important in competition. American Express, for example, advertises that its cardholders get service that is superior to that provided by other credit card companies. And Lands' End has used customer service to make major inroads in the catalog sales market for outdoor clothing and accessories. L. L. Bean and Federal Express also receive high marks in customer service and satisfaction.[18]

Quality and Costs

Improved quality also results in lower costs (and thus higher profits). The earlier discussion of productivity noted several ways that quality improvement lowers costs. Direct improvements in productivity often result in both lower costs and higher quality.

But quality improvement lowers costs in other ways as well. One major cost factor is replacement parts and products. The higher the quality of original products, the lower the subsequent costs of repairing or replacing them. Following directly from this is also lower overall costs of servicing warranties and product guarantees. And still another cost that is affected is potential losses from lawsuits from disgruntled customers or customers who are injured by poorly made products.

Providing quality products and protecting the environment can go hand-in-hand. Cargill, known for its quality control laboratories assurance that its products meet exceptionally high standards, produces an environmentally sound, liquid molasses food supplement that is contributing to the health and development of cows and other animals. (Photo courtesy of Cargill, Inc.)

At one time Whistler Corporation was using one hundred of its two hundred fifty employees to repair radar detectors that did not work. After a quality improvement program was implemented, the company was able to transfer most of the workers back to the original production department, substantially lowering its labor costs attributable to quality.

Quality and Long-Term Effectiveness

Finally, quality is also very important because of its role in influencing the long-term effectiveness of the organization. Organizations have found that they can actually boost profits in the short run by neglecting research and development, by using cheap materials, and by cutting corners. But over time these measures often come back to haunt these organizations as their reputations slide and as customers come to shun their products.

But organizations that make a continual and sustained commitment to quality improvement usually find just the opposite. Their image in the marketplace becomes more and more positive, and customers realize that they get better value from the firm's products and services. Thus, long-term effectiveness is certain to be affected by the quality of a firm's products and services.

Improving Quality: Strategic Initiatives

Total quality management, or TQM, is a strategy to improve product/service quality on a continuous basis.

As is the case for productivity, organizations and managers have a number of methods they can draw on to improve quality. Some of these methods fall under the general area of strategic initiatives, while others are more specific operational techniques. In this section we discuss the strategic initiatives. Our next section addresses operational techniques.

The fundamental strategic initiative organizations pursue when they become truly committed to quality is the adoption of total quality management. **Total quality management,** or **TQM,** is a comprehensive, organizationwide strategy for improving product and/or service quality on a systematic and continuous basis.[19]

The TQM Philosophy

The basic components of a TQM strategy are illustrated in Exhibit 21.3. TQM is based on a strategic commitment to quality and relies heavily on employee involvement, materials, methods, and technology to achieve improved quality. Since TQM relies heavily on employee involvement, each

Exhibit 21.3

Total Quality Management

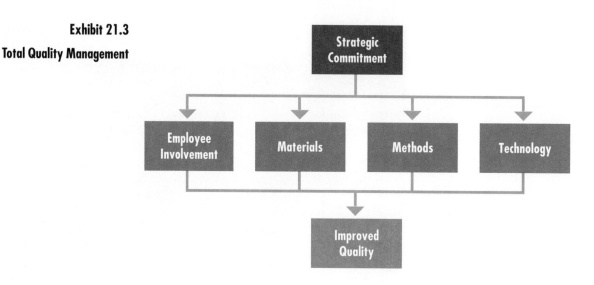

Total quality management is achieved through a combination of strategic commitment, employee involvement, materials, methods, and technology.

employee must accept the quality improvement philosophy. The Self-Assessment at the end of this chapter examines your attitude toward quality improvement.

Strategic Commitment   The starting point for any real TQM effort is a strategic commitment by the top management of an organization to make quality a top priority in every aspect of operations. Without such a commitment, quality is most likely to get only superficial consideration. And if a firm tries to promote itself on the basis of quality but that quality is eventually found to be lacking, more harm than good will have been accomplished.[20]

When James Houghton took over as CEO of Corning Glass Works in 1983, he stated publicly, clearly, and without equivocation that quality was a top priority. He then proceeded to back his assertion by committing the funds necessary to increase quality, to reward other managers on the basis of their quality improvement, and so forth. Thus, he made a firm and clear strategic commitment to quality. As a result, the TQM program at Corning has been a resounding success. Executives at Harley-Davidson also made a strategic commitment to quality following their buyout of the firm.

Employee Involvement   We noted earlier that employee involvement is often used to increase productivity. In similar fashion, employee involvement and participation are also necessary to improve quality. Without such involvement, and without the commitment to and acceptance of the program by employees, any attempt to enhance quality is not likely to succeed.

Organizations use various terms to describe employee involvement, including participation and empowerment. And it is often operationalized through work teams, as discussed in Chapter 18. Regardless of the terms used, involvement generally focuses on giving employees throughout the organization more information about what the firm is doing and more autonomy over managing their own contributions. Each work team is usually responsible for scheduling its own work, for instance, and for assessing the quality of its output.[21] Harley-Davidson relied heavily on employee involvement as part of its TQM efforts. One of the tools that employees use to get involved in the quality improvement process is called the Fishbone chart. The Skill Builder in this chapter provides you with an opportunity to develop this procedural knowledge.

Materials   Another part of improving quality through TQM is by using better and higher-quality materials. It stands to reason, for example, that if a stereo maker uses poor-quality circuitry in its stereo systems, they are likely to have quality problems. On the other hand, by demanding better circuits from suppliers, the quality of the stereo systems will improve.

Many firms today are demanding that their suppliers adopt new and more stringent quality standards. Ford, for example, recently mandated higher-quality standards for virtually all of the parts it buys from other suppliers. And some U.S. suppliers have found that by improving the quality of what they make, they have a better opportunity to sell to Japanese manufacturers. We noted in Chapter 20, for instance, that Cooper Tires sells rubber parts to Japanese automakers.

Methods In similar fashion, quality can also be enhanced through the use of more efficient and effective methods of operation. For example, L.L. Bean has an enviable reputation for customer loyalty and satisfaction. Part of the reason for this is because its telephone operators are trained to listen carefully to what customers want and to then do everything possible to satisfy those needs. In contrast, other mail-order houses have suffered because their operators are rude, ill informed, and otherwise unable to help customers. Such businesses might make the improvement of telephone assistance methods a first step in enhancing quality.[22]

Manufacturers emphasize methods through refinements in jobs and tasks and by helping workers function more efficiently. Some firms, for example, are making greater use of time-and-motion studies to again learn more scientifically how to perform jobs in the most efficient manner.[23] *The Entrepreneurial Spirit: Blue Bell* describes how one small food processor has used both materials and methods to cultivate and maintain a high-quality reputation.

Technology Related to methods, but also a distinct area, is technology. Firms can improve quality through such actions as buying new equipment, investing in automation, and so forth. Such technology provides a higher degree of standardization with fewer defective units or incomplete assemblies.

Service firms can also use technology to enhance quality. For example, restaurants can learn how to serve food faster and more efficiently. And airlines can learn how to process baggage more accurately and quickly.[24] We return to technology in Chapter 22.

Using TQM Assuming an organization wants to adopt the TQM philosophy, where does it start? We noted above that a strategic commitment is the first step. But after that step has been taken, what happens next? A recent study suggests that organizations should actually avoid moving too quickly.[25] Instead, as shown in Exhibit 21.4, they should proceed through three phases.

Phase 1 During Phase 1, the organization moving toward TQM is primarily concerned about learning about quality. Thus, it begins to invest heavily in training and tries to emulate its major competitors. It selects suppliers on the basis of price and reliability and concentrates on the fundamentals of quality enhancement.

Phase 2 After the organization has learned the basics of TQM, it moves to Phase 2. During this phase it encourages workers to find more efficient ways to do their jobs and starts to emulate market leaders and selected world-class companies. It selects suppliers primarily on the basis of quality, with price a secondary consideration. And the firm moves to make quality enhancement a fundamental part of its culture.

Phase 3 Finally, the firm that is ready to enter Phase 3 of TQM adopts self-managed work teams for most of its operations. Team members train themselves, with other training mainly reserved for new hires. Emulating the world's best companies becomes the standard way to do business. And continuous improvement become a routine and ongoing part of how the firm does business.

The Entrepreneurial Spirit

Blue Bell

Although it is sold in only three states, Blue Bell ice cream is the second-biggest brand in the United States. Three out of every five scoops of ice cream sold in Texas are Blue Bell. In Louisiana, Blue Bell has claimed more than one-third of the markets. And the firm has a similarly dominant position in Oklahoma.

What contributes to the firm's success? According to its owners, quality is critical. The firm buys only fresh and high-quality ingredients. It then maintains rigid processing procedures to ensure that the ice cream is blended and frozen according to tightly controlled specifications.

The firm also goes to great lengths to ensure that its products stay fresh. Most ice creams are blended in a processing plant, deep frozen, and then taken to a warehouse. Delivery to a supermarket might not take place for days or even weeks. But Blue Bell refuses to warehouse its products. Ice cream is taken directly from the plant and loaded into refrigerated trucks. Those same trucks then deliver it to supermarkets, where Blue Bell employees load it into the store's freezers.

How big are Blue Bell's ambitions? While the firm's owners are keeping their plans to themselves, they do promise not to expand too quickly. They do not want to disrupt their commitment to quality products. But a new processing plant in Oklahoma will allow Blue Bell to expand into the Midwest.[26] ■

Improving Quality: Operational Techniques

In addition to the strategic initiatives described above, organizations can also draw on a number of operational techniques to boost quality.

Statistical Quality Control

Statistical quality control is a set of techniques for improving quality.

One important operational approach to quality enhancement is called statistical quality control. **Statistical quality control** consists of a set of mathematical and/or statistical methods and procedures for measuring and adjusting quality levels.

For example, acceptance sampling is a process whereby finished goods are sampled to determine what proportion of them are of acceptable quality. By preestablishing the desired quality level and then statistically determining confidence levels, the manager can determine what percentage of finished goods must be checked to achieve the target level of quality.

Exhibit 21.4 Implementing Total Quality Management

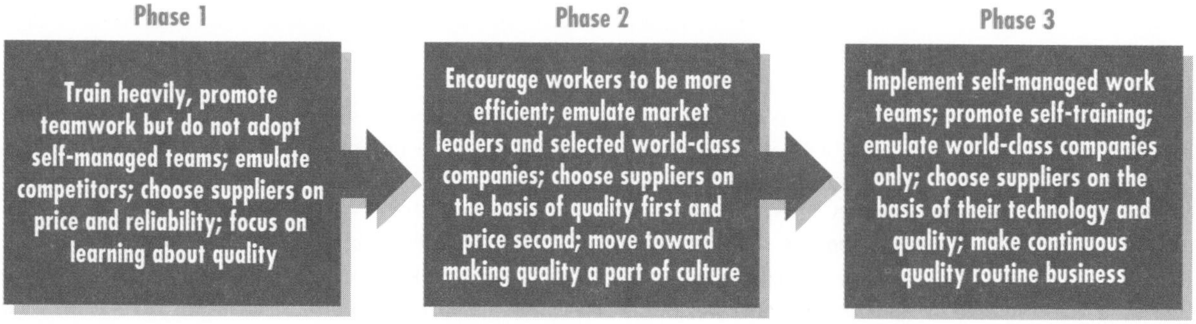

Phase 1

Train heavily, promote teamwork but do not adopt self-managed teams; emulate competitors; choose suppliers on price and reliability; focus on learning about quality

Phase 2

Encourage workers to be more efficient; emulate market leaders and selected world-class companies; choose suppliers on the basis of quality first and price second; move toward making quality a part of culture

Phase 3

Implement self-managed work teams; promote self-training; emulate world-class companies only; choose suppliers on the basis of their technology and quality; make continuous quality routine business

Benchmarking is a sound technique for improving quality. At Artistic Greetings, a five-person research and development team is constantly at work to improve benchmarking as well as to develop new techniques and processes to boost efficiency. Artistic's personalized labels (shown here) can be shipped in just five working days thanks to improvements over the years. (Michael Greenlar.)

Similarly, in-process sampling involves testing products as they are being made rather than after they are finished. In-process sampling works best for products like chemicals, paint, and so forth that go through various transformation steps.

Beyond the various statistical quality control techniques, other useful operational procedures for enhancing quality can be drawn from any of the different decision-making, control, and operations management methods discussed in Chapters 9, 20, and 22, respectively. The key, of course, is to match the technique with the situation in such a way that quality is facilitated.

Benchmarking

Benchmarking is the process of finding out, in a legal and ethical manner, how other firms do something and then either imitating or improving on it.

Benchmarking is a relatively new approach to improving quality. **Benchmarking** is the process of finding out, in a legal and ethical manner, how other firms do something and then either imitating or improving on it.[27] Sometimes benchmarking involves buying competing equipment and taking it apart to see how it works. Other times, it involves simply talking to managers at other firms to see how they do things.

For example, a manager at Convex Computer Corporation recently spent a week with Disney executives learning how that firm trains its workers and schedules its maintenance. Many firms have visited L.L. Bean to learn more about its mail-order procedures. And Xerox routinely buys competing copiers and then takes them apart to see how they are manufactured.[28]

Speed and Time

Speed and time refer to how long it takes the organization to do something.

Speed and time contribute to both productivity and quality. The major contribution is to productivity for manufacturers and to quality for service organizations. For example, if one organization can fill a customer's order in three days and another takes three weeks, the former is clearly at a competitive advantage.[29]

A recent survey of executives identified speed and time as the number one competitive issue of the 1990s.[30] It should come as no surprise, then, that many organizations are searching for ways to get things done faster. General Electric provides a good case in point. In 1985 the company needed three weeks from the time the order was received to deliver a custom-made circuit breaker.

Table 21.3

Increasing the Speed of Operations

Strategy	Explanation
1. *Start from scratch*	It's usually easier than trying to do what the organization does now but in a faster way.
2. *Minimize the number of approvals needed to do something.*	The fewer people who have to approve something, the faster it will get done.
3. *Use work teams as a basis for organization*	Teamwork and cooperation work better than individual effort and conflict.
4. *Develop and abdere to a schedule.*	A properly designed schedule can greatly increase speed.
5. *Don't ignore distribution.*	Making something faster is only part of the battle.
6. *Integrate speed into the organization's culture.*	If everyone understands the importance of speed, things will naturally get done quicker.

Source: Brian Dumaine, *Fortune,* © 1989 The Time Inc. Magazine Company. All rights reserved.

At the time, GE had six plants and several hundred workers involved. Now, the same order can be delivered in only three days—using only one plant and 129 workers.[31]

This speedup has been accomplished primarily by following the six guidelines listed in Table 21.3. For example, General Electric totally revamped one of its plants (1. start from scratch) and eliminated most supervisory jobs (2. minimize the number of approvals). Given the dramatic successes achieved by GE and similar organizations that have also promoted speed and time as major concerns, it is very likely indeed that these issues will be of major importance in the years ahead.

Flexibility

Flexibility is how easily the organization can react, respond, or change.

Finally, organizations are also realizing that the greater the flexibility they maintain, the easier it is for them to adopt new methods and approaches and to respond to shifts in technology, consumer tastes, and so forth. **Flexibility** is an organization's ability to adapt to different conditions and circumstances. For example, if a firm invests millions of dollars in a plant that is capable of making only a single product and of making it in only one way, it will be very vulnerable to obsolesence. If a new and cheaper method of making the same product is discovered, for example, the firm will either have to continue to produce at a cost disadvantage or else scrap the plant and start over.

Flexibility can be achieved in several different ways. For example, manufacturing technology can be installed so that the firm can alter work flow, add new equipment, or delete equipment without altering the overall production system too extensively. Another method is to train workers to be able to perform several different tasks. As a result, the organization can easily shift employees between different jobs when demand shifts too much. As with speed and time, flexibility is likely to become increasingly important.

Chapter Summary

Quality refers to the total set of features and characteristics of a product or service that bear on its ability to satisfy stated or implied needs. Quality can be assessed both in absolute and relative terms. Quality is closely linked with productivity. Productivity, in turn, can be assessed at several levels. The growth rate of productivity in the United States is falling behind that of other countries. There are several techniques managers can use to boost productivity.

Quality is important for several reasons. The three most important reasons are because of its role in competition, in reducing costs, and in improving long-term effectiveness.

Total quality management, or TQM, represents the fundamental strategic initiative organizations can use to enhance quality. TQM relies on a strategic commitment and uses employee involvement, methods, materials, and technology. Organizations should also implement TQM gradually.

There are also several operational techniques organizations can use to boost quality. These include statistical quality control, benchmarking, speed and time, and flexibility.

The Manager's Vocabulary

product quality
service quality
quality
productivity
individual productivity
unit productivity
company productivity

industry productivity
country productivity
overall productivity
total factor productivity
labor productivity
absolute quality
relative quality

total quality management (TQM)
statistical quality control
benchmarking
speed and time
flexibility

Review Questions

1. What are some examples of different levels of productivity?
2. What has been the trend in recent years in productivity growth in the United States, compared to that in other countries? What differences exist within the U.S. economy?
3. How are productivity and quality related to one another?
4. How can managers go about trying to improve quality?
5. What role do speed, time, and flexibility play in quality?

Analysis Questions

1. Think of a few manufacturing jobs and a few service jobs you are familiar with. What factors can you identify that might account for productivity differences between them?
2. Given that productivity and quality are related, efforts to improve them might also be related. Identify compatible ways that managers might try to boost productivity and quality simultaneously.
3. Brainstorm a list of products that U.S. companies seem to make better than foreign competitors. Now do the same for products that foreign manufacturers seem to do a better job with. Can you spot any trends?
4. Are there limits to quality improvement? That is, can absolute quality ever be attained?
5. Can you think of instances where productivity and quality are *not* related?

Self-Assessment

Quality Improvement Questionnaire

Introduction   Quality improvement is a philosophy. It is a way of thinking. This Self-Assessment determines your attitude toward continuous improvement and Total Quality Management.

Instructions

For each item circle the number that best describes your attitude or behavior on the job or at school.

Strongly Disagree	Disagree	?	Agree	Strongly Agree
1	2	3	4	5

1. I recognize the practical constraints of existing conditions when someone proposes an improvement idea.
      1   2   3   4   5

2. I like to support change efforts, even when the idea may not work.
      1   2   3   4   5

3. I believe that many small improvements are usually better than a few big improvements.
      1   2   3   4   5

4. I encourage other people to express improvement ideas, even if they differ from mine.
      1   2   3   4   5

5. There is truth to the statement, "If it isn't broke, don't fix it."
      1   2   3   4   5

6. I work at the politics of change to build agreement for my improvement ideas.
      1   2   3   4   5

7. I study suggestions carefully to avoid change just for the sake of change.
      1   2   3   4   5

8. I like to have clear objectives that support improvement, even if changes upset my efficiency.
      1   2   3   4   5

9. I constantly talk about ways to improve what I'm doing.
      1   2   3   4   5

10. I am able to get higher-ups to support my ideas for improvement.
       1   2   3   4   5

For interpretation, turn to the back of the book.

Source: Experimental Exercise from *Management,* 2nd edition, by Richard L. Daft, copyright © 1991 by The Dryden Press, reprinted by permission of the publisher.

Skill Builder

Preparing the Fishbone Chart

Purpose The fishbone chart is an excellent procedure for identifying possible causes of a problem. It provides you with procedural knowledge that you can use to improve the operations of any organization. This skill builder focuses on the *administrative management model*. It will help you develop the *monitor role* of the administrative management model. One of the skills of the monitor is the ability to analyze problems.

Introduction Japanese quality circles often use the fishbone "cause and effect" graphic technique to initiate the resolution of a group work problem. Quite often the causes are clustered in categories such as materials, methods, people, and machines. The fishbone technique is usually accomplished in the following six steps.

1. Write the problem in the "head" of the fish (the large block).
2. Brainstorm the major causes of the problem and list them on the fish "bones."
3. Analyze each main cause, and write in minor subcauses on bone subbranches.
4. Reach consensus on one or two of the major causes of the problem.
5. Explore ways to correct or remove the major cause(s).
6. Prepare a report or presentation explaining the proposed change.

Instructions

Your instructor will provide you with further instructions.

The fishbone will look something like this:

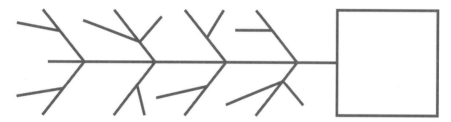

Source: *Exercises in Management* by Gene E. Burton. Copyright © 1990 by Houghton Mifflin Company. Used with permission.

Concluding Cases

21.1   Ford

For years Ford has promoted itself as the company where "Quality is Job 1." But the firm has been on rocky roads for much of the last fifteen or so years. Indeed, in the early 1980s Ford was on the verge of bankruptcy. After incurring losses of $1.5 billion in 1980, $1.1 billion in 1981, and $658 million in 1982, Ford had few cash reserves and was in danger of going under.

But today Ford has regained its footing and is currently regarded among experts as the most effective U.S. car manufacturer. It is also seen as better than most European car manufacturers and on an equal footing with the Japanese. How did it achieve this stunning turnaround? It happened primarily through a continuous commitment to improving productivity and quality.

Ford's renaissance really began with the success of the Ford Taurus and Mercury Sable. In the early 1980s Ford executives realized that they needed major new entries into the automobile market if the firm was to survive. Responsibility for creating the first new car was assigned to a group called Team Taurus. The team was a cross-functional mix of managers from operations, engineering, marketing, design, and other areas. Working together in ways never before imagined at Ford, this group created a car that would become the firm's salvation and, ultimately, the best-selling car in the United States.

One major practice adopted by Team Taurus was benchmarking. Ford had never used benchmarking before but adopted the practice wholeheartedly for the Taurus. Work began by using consumer surveys to determine the four hundred features that the team thought were most important in an automobile. Ford managers then identified specific cars that performed the best in each of these four hundred feature categories. Finally, benchmarking was used to figure out how to do the best job possible on each feature. And when the first Taurus was introduced in 1986, it was indeed a major success.

But Ford also realized that benchmarking was not a one-time activity. Thus, when it came time to update Taurus for the 1992 model year, managers went back to the drawing boards and benchmarked again. Because this model was seen as a refinement, fewer features were benchmarked. But each feature also contributed to the success of the car, which went on to become the best-selling car in the United States in 1992. Indeed, Ford feels so confident about the quality of the Taurus that it will begin exporting them to Japan soon. But Ford has not been content with one home run. While Taurus has been its biggest success, the hot-selling Explorer and line of pickups has also been important.

Ford also worked closely with Mazda to improve its manufacturing procedures and techniques. Using a variety of techniques learned from the Japanese, Ford has gradually improved the productivity of its workers at all stages of production. And as a result, in 1992 Ford became more efficient than either Toyota or Honda in making small, four-cylinder cars. If it can maintain its momentum, Ford seems on-track now to remain one of the most effective firms in the world automobile industry.[32]

Discussion Questions

1. How do you think Ford's effectiveness compares to that of Chrysler and General Motors?
2. Do you think Ford's success will continue? Why or why not?
3. What successful and less successful cars has Ford introduced lately?

21.2 Kyocera

Kyocera Corporation is not nearly as well known outside of Japan as Sony, Honda, or Nissan. But within Japan, Kyocera has a reputation for being among that country's highest-quality manufacturers. Indeed, in a recent survey Japanese executives ranked Kyocera as the firm they admired most.

Kyocera was started by a maverick. After earning his Ph.D. in chemical engineering, Kazuo Inamori went to work for a big Japanese manufacturer. But he soon found that he did not enjoy working within that firm's traditional Japanese bureaucratic system. Thus, he left his first employer and started Kyocera.

Kyocera specializes in ceramic-based electronic components. For example, one of the firm's most profitable products is a line of ceramic semiconductor-chip packages. The firm sees its competitive advantage as making the highest-quality products possible.

The thing Inamori had resisted most in his first job was having to bow to authority. He felt that individual managers should be free to pursue entrepreneurial opportunities without being constrained by a rigid bureaucracy. Thus, when he founded Kyocera one of his highest priorities was to avoid rigid channels of authority and to promote opportunities for creativity and innovation instead.

His conceptualization of Kyocera derived from the notion of amoebas. He views the organization as simply a collection of individual people without permanent job assignments or departmental affiliations. Instead, each person is assigned to a project group that grows, changes, and dissolves as dictated by its particular job assignment. Thus, each group is like an amoeba.

Each group, or amoeba, starts with the assignment of an executive or supervisor to a project. That person then scans the roster of available employees and recruits those who are best suited to the needs of the project. As the group takes shape, it takes on more and more control, and the supervisor becomes more and more a team member as opposed to the group's boss.

Ultimately, the group itself recruits new members as they are needed. Likewise, individual group members transition out of the group when their services are no longer needed. Each group also makes its own decisions about supplies, materials, and purchases, and schedules its own work assignments.

At any given time, there are several dozen amoebas at work with memberships ranging from as few as two to as many as several hundred members. This evolutionary and constantly changing structure might be hard for many people to understand, but Kyocera makes the highest-quality products in its industry. And Inamori credits his amoebas for being the critical ingredient in the firm's success.[33]

Discussion Questions

1. Why do you think the amoebas are so successful at Kyocera?
2. Would this concept work in all organizations? Why or why not?
3. What unique personal characteristics would be necessary for an individual to be comfortable working for Kyocera?

CHAPTER

22

Operations and Technology Management

Learning Objectives

After studying this chapter you should be able to

- Discuss the nature, meaning, and importance of operations management.

- Describe operations decisions and operations planning.

- Indicate what is involved in the management and organization of operations, and describe the relation of change to operations.

- Discuss operations control in its most important forms— inventory control, quality control, scheduling control, and cost control.

- Identify basic operations control techniques.

- Discuss the nature of technology management.

ike many U.S. manufacturers, Monsanto Company had to virtually remake itself during the 1980s. Several years ago Monsanto had grown into a bloated bureaucracy with inefficient manufacturing operations and a stagnant research and development unit. But the firm underwent a major transformation during the last ten years or so and has emerged as a much more efficient and effective business.

Part of the firm's success stems from its strategy for getting new products off the ground. Rather than spread its research dollars across hundreds of projects as it once did, Monsanto now concentrates on only a few relatively promising ones. And it also involves customers much earlier in the process than it once did. Several years ago, for example, Monsanto developed products it thought it could sell and worried about selling them only after they were ready for market. But now managers find out in advance what customers want and what features or characteristics are most important.

It sometimes takes ten years or more for new chemical and pharmaceutical products to get from the planning stage to actual market introduction. Thus, it is critical to firms in this industry that every product be developed correctly and that planning for actual production and marketing be undertaken early.

Monsanto faces real challenges in the next few years. Patents on two of its biggest products—Nutra-Sweet, the world's top-selling low-calorie sweetener, and Roundup, the world's top-selling herbicide—will expire soon. And increased competition from abroad will make it harder than ever to succeed. But managers at Monsanto believe that their strategic approach to developing and manufacturing new products will keep them at the head of the pack.[1] ■

y definition, business organizations provide goods and services to customers. Monsanto Company is in the business of manufacturing and selling pharmaceuticals, agricultural chemicals, food additives, and other specialty products. In similar fashion, Chevron produces and sells gasoline. Pizza Hut makes and sells pizza. And Compaq combines thousands of component parts into computers.

The various processes, decisions, and systems involved in the acquisition of resources and the transformation of those resources into the firm's products or services is the domain of operations management. In this chapter we explore the nature of operations management and discuss the connection between planning and operations. Managing operations is described, then we go on to discuss operations control and to identify a number of operations control techniques. The chapter concludes with a discussion of technology management, a related part of effective operations management.

The Nature of Operations Management

he management of operations is an extremely complex as well as a very important function. Indeed, without effective operations management, few organizations could survive for any length of time. Thus, it is important to have a clear understanding of both the meaning and the importance of operations management.

The Meaning of Operations Management

Operations management is the total set of activities used to transform resources into products and services.

We will define **operations management** as the total set of managerial activities used by an organization to transform resource inputs into products and services.[2] Exhibit 22.1 illustrates the essential nature of operations management. Recall our discussion of systems theory in Chapter 1. Systems theory holds that organizations consist of four basic parts: inputs, transformation processes, outputs, and feedback. As shown in the exhibit, operations management is primarily concerned with the transformation processes themselves. At a secondary level, it is also concerned with inputs, outputs, and feedback from the environment. Learning how to map the processes of an organization is an important conceptual skill. The Skill Builder at the end of this chapter provides you with an opportunity to map the processes of five different organizations.

Because manufacturing once dominated U.S. industry, the entire area of operations management used to be called production management. **Manufacturing** is a form of business that combines and transforms resources into tangible outcomes that are then sold to others. Monsanto Company is a manufacturer because it uses chemicals to create products. Similarly, The Goodyear Tire & Rubber Company is a manufacturer because it combines rubber and chemical compounds and uses blending equipment and molding machines to create tires. And Broyhill is a manufacturer because it buys wood and metal components, pads, and fabric and then combines them into furniture.

During the 1970s manufacturing entered a long period of decline in the United States, primarily because of foreign competition. U.S. firms had grown lax and sluggish, and new foreign competitors came onto the scene with new equipment and much higher levels of efficiency. For example, steel companies in the Far East were able to produce high-quality steel for much lower prices than were U.S. companies like Bethlehem Steel and U.S. Steel (now USX Corporation). Faced with a battle for survival, many companies underwent a long and difficult period of change by eliminating waste and transforming themselves into leaner and more efficient and responsive entities. They reduced their work forces dramatically, closed antiquated or unnecessary plants, and modernized their remaining plants. In recent years their efforts have started to pay dividends as U.S. business has regained its competitive position in many different industries. Although manufacturers from other parts of the world are still formidable competitors and U.S. firms may never again be competitive in some markets, the overall picture is much better than it was just a few years ago. And prospects continue to look bright.[3]

During the decline of the manufacturing sector, a tremendous growth in the service sector kept the U.S. economy from declining at the same rate.[4] A **service organization** is one that transforms resources into an intangible output and creates time or place utility for its customers. For example, Merrill Lynch & Co., Inc. makes stock transactions for its customers, Avis leases cars

Manufacturing organizations combine and transform resources into tangible products.

Service organizations transform resources into intangible outputs that create utility for customers.

Exhibit 22.1

The Nature of Operations Management

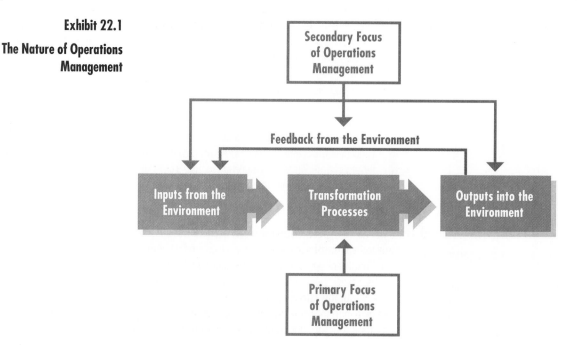

Transforming resources into output sometimes seems almost magical, as if a genie were involved. Disney used an ancient story, dozens of talented animators, computer technology, and a strong distribution network to create *Aladdin,* the most successful animated movie of all time. (David Strick/ONYX.)

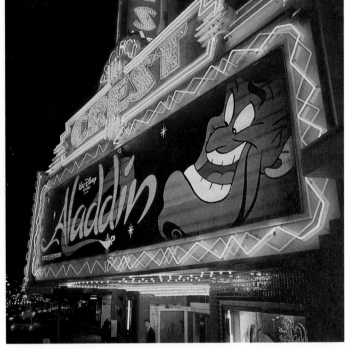

to its customers, and your local hairdresser cuts your hair. In 1947 the service sector was responsible for less than half of the U.S. gross national product (GNP). By 1975, however, this figure reached 65 percent, and by 1992 it exceeded 75 percent. The service sector was responsible for almost 90 percent of all new jobs created in the United States during the 1980s.[5] Managers have come to see that many of the tools, techniques, and methods that are used in a factory are also useful to a service firm. For example, managers of automobile plants and hair salons each have to decide how to design their facility, identify the best location for it, determine optimal capacity, make decisions about inventory storage, set procedures for purchasing raw materials, and set standards for productivity and quality.

The Importance of Operations Management

It should be clear by this point that operations management is very important to organizations. Beyond its direct impact on quality and productivity, it also directly influences the organization's overall level of effectiveness. Obviously, then, operations management needs to be addressed at every level, starting at the top. For example, the deceivingly simple strategic decision of whether to stress high quality regardless of cost, lowest possible cost regardless of quality, or some intermediate combination of the two has numerous important implications. A highest-possible quality strategy will dictate state-of-the-art technology and rigorous control of product design and materials specifications. A combination strategy might call for lower-grade technology and less concern about product design and materials specifications.

Just as strategy affects operations management, so too does operations management affect strategy. Suppose that a firm decides to upgrade the quality of its products or services. The organization's ability to implement the decision is dependent in part on current production capabilities and other resources. If existing technology will not permit higher-quality work, and if the organization lacks the resources to replace its technology, increasing quality to the desired new standards will be difficult. *The Quality Challenge: Coleman* describes how Coleman has used operations management as part of its strategy to upgrade product quality.

The Quality Challenge

Coleman

Anyone who has ever gone camping knows the name Coleman. Popular Coleman lanterns, portable stoves, and coolers, for example, are often considered standard equipment for people who spend time outdoors. The firm has been in operation for decades and was a cash cow for the Coleman family. Profits were distributed to the owners, with little reinvestment in the business.

Coleman was recently sold to investor Ronald Perelman. Perelman has a reputation for a tough-nosed management style designed to boost profits and cut costs. Under his direction, Coleman adopted a new strategy aimed at improving quality through continuous improvement. The results so far? There have been a reduction in inventory costs of $10 million, a reduction in scrappage rates of 60 percent, and an increase in productivity of 35 percent.

How does a firm achieve such dramatic improvements? Coleman rebuilt itself around conventional wisdom for quality and productivity improvement. It started by adopting a just-in-time inventory system. This allowed the firm to trim its storage costs while also uncovering production inefficiencies.

Coleman also eliminated several redundant production steps and put each worker in charge of inspecting his or her own work. Every worker was given the authority to stop the production line to correct problems. And the firm's design staff has greater freedom to modify or expand product lines. Managers at Coleman believe that future refinements will bring even higher levels of quality and productivity.[6]

Operations management is also a critically important function for specific activities within an organization. Monsanto faces problems if it cannot produce pharmaceuticals as efficiently as can its foreign competitors. Sears has problems if it has too much inventory (carrying costs, spoilage, warehousing expenses) or too little inventory (customer complaints, lost sales) on hand. It also has problems if it has the wrong merchandise or pays too much for its merchandise. Chevron has problems if it cannot refine gasoline efficiently, if it cannot deliver the gas to service stations efficiently, or if it must charge too much for its products. A Pizza Hut restaurant has problems if it has too many or too few ingredients to make pizza, if it produces poor-quality pizza, or if its service is bad.

The hallmarks of operations management, then, are efficiency and effectiveness—doing things in a way that gets the maximum value from resources, and doing the right things to begin with. Operations management helps Ford determine what parts to make and what parts to buy, when to have them delivered, how they should be combined, and how the finished product will be delivered to the showroom floor. Without an effective operations management system, few organizations would survive.[7]

Planning for Operations

The first stage in effective operations management is planning for operations. This aspect of operations management includes both operations decisions and operations planning.[8]

Operations Decisions

Operations decisions encompass virtually all aspects of the operations management system. Eight areas in particular are especially important.

*An organization's **product/service line** is the set of products and/or services it sells.*

Product/Service Line   The **product** or **service line** decision is one of the most crucial decisions an organization makes. It is almost always made by top managers from all relevant functional areas because the organization's overall strategy determines the general products and/or services on which it will concentrate. That is, Sony deals in consumer electronics, whereas Pepperidge Farm concentrates on baked goods.

Marketing and operations managers then work together to define more precisely what the product line should, can, and will be. Marketing managers at Pepperidge Farm might use consumer research to get information about what products customers want and then ask operations managers to figure out how best to produce those products. Similarly, operations managers at Sony might realize that producing another version of an existing VCR or stereo system would be very easy and efficient. They would then ask marketing managers to find out whether such a variation would sell at acceptable levels. Thus, product or service line decisions are almost always made jointly by managers from different areas.

Capacity refers to the space the organization has available to create products and/or services.

Capacity **Capacity** decisions involve determining how much space the organization needs to meet the demand for its products or services most efficiently and effectively. For example, how many automobiles does Mazda want to produce each year? How much floor space does Kmart want to devote to various kinds of merchandise? How many tables does a certain McDonald's restaurant need? These are capacity decisions.

Capacity decisions must be made with great care. If a firm has too much capacity, the result can be a dramatic underutilization of resources. If Kmart builds a new store with 150,000 square feet of floor space when 100,000 would have sufficed, the company will have to find uses for the extra space, maintain it, and keep it heated and cooled. Many recent plant closings and cutbacks in U.S. businesses have been the result of excess capacity.

Too little capacity can be just as damaging, however. For example, a manufacturing plant with insufficient capacity cannot provide an adequate quantity of merchandise and will subsequently lose customers to competitors. Likewise, if retail customers have to wait in line too long, they will get discouraged and shop elsewhere.

In general, the key is to optimize. In most cases demand fluctuates. A restaurant, for instance, might be able to fill eighty tables on Friday night and one hundred on Saturday night. The rest of the week, however, only thirty tables will be filled. Having one hundred tables is probably not efficient. Instead, the restaurant should probably have fifty or sixty tables. The excess capacity during the week will probably not be a problem, and on weekends the tables will be filled, although some people will have to wait to be seated, and a few will leave and go elsewhere. On balance, the organization will probably be most effective if it has more than the minimum capacity it needs but less than the maximum it occasionally is able to use.

A planning system determines how the operations managers get the information they need and how they provide information to others.

Planning System The planning system decision involves determining how operations managers will get the information they need and how they will provide information to other managers. For example, assume an organization uses sales forecasts as a basis for deciding how much of a particular product to make. In the middle of January the operations manager receives a sales forecast for the month of February. He or she then needs to check current inventory, including work-in-process, and set production levels for February. The information can also go in the other direction. The operations manager may need to keep the marketing manager informed about current cost and inventory levels. These figures will help the marketing manager decide what discounts to grant, what products to push, and so forth.

Organization Another operations management decision involves the organization of the operations function—that is, where in the overall design of the organization operations activities should be housed and administered. These issues are explored in a later section.

Human Resources Working in conjunction with human resource managers, operations managers must decide what kinds of employees they need. These decisions involve both the quantity and the quality of the work force. For example, suppose a toy manufacturer needs to increase its work force as it builds toys for the Christmas season. Its managers need to make decisions about how many new workers will be needed, what skills they should have, and when they should be hired. Recent trends toward automation and high-tech manufacturing have made these decisions even more critical because managers must take greater care to select just the right kinds of employees to work in such settings.[9]

Technology is the set of processes used by an organization to transform raw materials and other inputs into appropriate outputs.

Technology   **Technology** involves the actual processes used in transforming raw materials and other inputs into appropriate outputs. Some organizations, such as home cleaning services and athletic teams, tend to be **labor-intensive,** which means that people do most of the work. Other firms, such as General Electric, are **capital-intensive,** which means that machines do almost all of the work. Still other companies use a balance of people and machines. Decisions related to what form of technology to use and when to change technology are critical parts of operations management. We discuss technology management later in this chapter.

Labor-intensive organizations rely on people to do most of the work.

Capital-intensive firms rely on machines to do almost all of the work.

Facilities   Another important set of operations decisions involves **facilities,** the means of accomplishing production. Should a firm have one or two large plants or several smaller plants? Should it make all its own components and then assemble them, or buy some or all of them from other manufacturers? Where should the plants be located? And how should they be arranged?

Facilities are the physical means the organization uses to create products and/or services.

Each of these decisions requires considerable research and consideration. Suppose that a company is searching for a site for a new plant. It might be efficient to locate the plant near major suppliers, or it might be more efficient to put it close to major customers. The company also needs information about land costs, the supply of labor, construction costs, tax rates, utility rates, quality of life for employees and so forth. And considerable pressure is often put on companies to locate plants in certain cities. Small towns throughout the United States have engaged in high-stakes competition as potential sites for new manufacturing facilities. To get the predicted economic benefits, such communities offer reduced tax rates, free land, and other incentives.[10]

Controls   Decisions also must be made about operations control, including inventory control, quality control, and scheduling control. Each of these is discussed in more detail later in this chapter.

Operations Planning

Operations planning relates to the day-to-day, ongoing activities of operations management. There are many associated questions that have to be answered by managers responsible for carrying out operations activities. How much should the organization produce? When should it be produced? How often should it be produced? In general, four basic steps are involved in operations planning.

The planning horizon is the time span across which operations managers plan.

The first step in operations planning is to select a planning horizon. This decision will vary, of course, depending on what kinds of products and/or services the company provides. Research and development managers at Monsanto have a long-term planning horizon. A manufacturer of heavy construction equipment may plan over a twelve-month cycle. And a restaurant manager might plan only a few days ahead.

Once the appropriate time horizon has been chosen, the manager then needs to estimate demand for that period. For example, the manufacturer's plant manager might use marketing data to estimate construction equipment demand for each month of the next year. The restaurant manager, in contrast, will forecast customers for each meal for each of the next seven days, with higher estimates developed for special occasions and weekends and lower estimates developed for most weekdays.

The third step in operations planning is to compare projected demand with current capacity for each meaningful block of time. In the plant this might mean that comparisons are made on a monthly basis. As a consequence, materials may be ordered and labor hours scheduled on one-month blocks. For the restaurant, on the other hand, comparisons might be made for each meal. As a result, fresh ingredients might be ordered twice a day (once for lunch and once for dinner) and five table servers scheduled for lunch and nine scheduled for dinner.

The last step in operations planning is to adjust capacity to demand. If demand exceeds capacity in the plant, the manager has several options: schedule overtime, add more workers, or add another shift. Or the manager might subcontract some of the work out to other manufacturers or shift it to other plants in the same company. If capacity exceeds demand, the manager can lay off some workers and/or shut down some of the plant. Similarly, the restaurant manager might increase or decrease staff, order more or less food, and so on.

Managing Operations

Clearly, managing the various elements of an organization's operations systems is an important consideration for managers. In addition to the elements we have already discussed, two major areas of concern in managing operations are organizing and organizational change.

Organizing for Operations

The principal issue in organizing for operations is defining where the operations management function fits into the overall structure and design of the organization.[11] Directly or indirectly, operations management affects and is affected by all of the dimensions of organizational design described in Chapters 11 and 12.

For example, job design considerations permeate operations management. Specialization is one approach to designing jobs, but operations management is affected when managers turn to alternative approaches such as rotation, enlargement, or enrichment. And new efforts to use participative work teams are clearly relevant for both organization design and operations management.

Perhaps even more significant is the link between departmentalization and operations management. How the operations function looks when the organization is departmentalized by function and by product is shown in Exhibit 22.2. As we can see, operations are centralized at the top under the control of a vice president or similar top manager when departmentalization is functional. When departmentalization is by product, as in a divisional structure, operations for each product group or division are decentralized under the manager responsible for the division. Other variations are also possible. Each plant might be thought of as a separate department (departmentalization by location), or departmentalization by time might be used for different shifts within a plant.

Operations management must also address delegation and decentralization issues. Firms like General Electric and Westinghouse practice relatively high levels of decentralization. As a result, their plant managers have considerable discretion and autonomy and can make fairly significant decisions without approval from corporate managers. In settings like the distribution division of Kmart, more centralization is the norm. Warehouse managers there, for example, have relatively little discretion in decision making. In most cases they have to follow established procedures and regulations or must consult with higher-level managers before making decisions.[12]

In recent years managers have begun to be increasingly interested in how to structure their organizations to facilitate operations management, especially new-product development. For example, innovation and the creation of both new products and services and the ways to create those products and services are becoming ever more critical. When Monsanto refocused its research and

Exhibit 22.2

Organizing for Operations

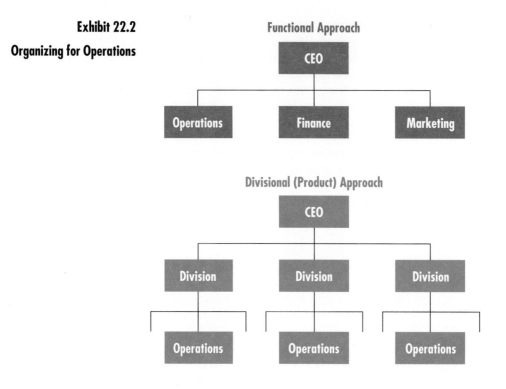

Functional Approach

CEO

Operations   Finance   Marketing

Divisional (Product) Approach

CEO

Division   Division   Division

Operations   Operations   Operations

development program in order to concentrate more on major projects, it used its organization de-sign to implement the new approach. *The Environment of Management: Modular Corpora-tions* explains how so-called modular corporations are being created to help simplify the role of operations management in organization design.

Change and Operations

Another important dimension of the management of operations relates to organizational change. As we discussed in Chapter 13, two of the major reasons for change are technology and competi-tion. Technology, of course, relates directly to operations management, so being aware of new technology and adopting it when it is appropriate are important to operations managers. Simi-larly, many (but not all) of the reasons for responding to competitors involve operations. Changes in packaging, product design, product quality, and so forth might be undertaken for competitive reasons.

Technology also provides a major way in which to change organizations. Changes in work processes and sequences, for instance, are common forms of organizational change that have di-rect implications for operations management. Several structural (for example, coordination and decentralization) and people-focused (such as selection and training) change techniques are also related to operations management.[13]

Operations Control

A major concern of operations management is the control function. In fact, many people consider operations management to be almost totally concerned with control. Although this view may be too narrow, operations and control are certainly interrelated.[14] Four areas of operations management that are especially critical are inventory control, quality control, scheduling control, and cost control.

The Environment of Management

Modular Corporations

Some of today's most effective organizations are exploring new and radical approaches to organization design that allow them to achieve greater efficiency from their operations management systems. Some experts call these firms modular corporations, while others prefer the term virtual corporations. Whatever label is used, however, the experts agree that the enhanced flexibility and responsiveness offered by these approaches allow the firms to move faster and more effectively in dealing with their competitive environment.

In years past managers believed that their companies should do as much of their own work as possible. But modular corporations take a different approach. Their strategy is to develop close linkages with suppliers and then use those linkages to collaborate on design, manufacturing, and assembly.

For example, Exabyte Corp. is a booming Colorado computer firm. But the firm does virtually none of its own manufacturing. It buys preassembled components from firms like Sony and Solectron, subcontracts assembly of these components into complete computers to other firms, and then markets them under its own label. Similarly, Nike and Reebok design shoes but produce virtually none themselves.

Firms are finding that they can outsource everything from shipping to data processing to accounting. Since they then have to spend less on these services and equipment, they have more funds available for expansion. Besides the examples noted above, other firms that are using this approach include Dell Computer, Chrysler, Corning, and Apple.[15] ∎

Inventory Control

Inventory control is making sure the organization has an adequate supply of raw materials to transform into products, that there are enough finished goods to ship to customers, and that inventory in process is adequate.

Inventory control is essential for effective operations management because inventories represent a major investment for all organizations. The goals of inventory control are to make sure the organization has an adequate supply of raw materials to transform into products, that there are enough finished goods to ship to customers, and that inventory in process is adequate to meet future needs.[16]

As shown in Exhibit 22.3, there are four basic forms of inventory. **Raw materials inventory** is the supply of materials, parts, and supplies the organization needs to do its work. Ford's raw materials include mechanical parts, electrical parts, paint, belts and hoses, upholstery fabric, and so forth. Pizza Hut's raw materials include flour, sausage, tomato paste, cheese, and other in-

Exhibit 22.3 Kinds of Inventory

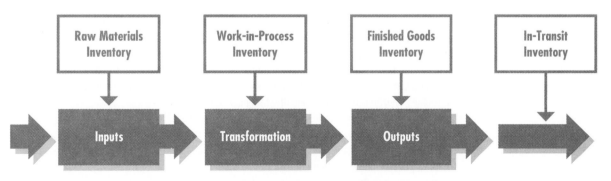

The market is the ultimate measure of how well a business is managing its quality control process. Because some people felt that the Styrofoam pellets used in shipping were harmful to the environment, Curl Pack of Suwanee, Georgia, developed an alternative—fluffy curls of paper-thin wood shavings that can be used as mulch after they have served as packaging material. Assuming that Curl Pack manages its quality control process effectively, this new environmentally friendly idea should be a big success. (John Bazemore.)

Raw materials inventory *is the supply of materials, parts, and supplies needed to do the work.*

gredients. The most important thing in raw materials inventory is to make sure that enough materials are on hand to meet production needs but not so much that materials spoil, get broken, or are stolen.

Work-in-process inventory refers to the inventory of parts and supplies that are currently being used to produce the final product or service, which is not yet complete. For example, at any given point Ford has millions of dollars' worth of materials at various stages of completion on the assembly lines of its factories. At Pizza Hut, in contrast, work-in-process is fairly minimal and consists only of pizzas as they are being cooked.

Work-in-process inventory *is the inventory of parts and supplies that are currently used to produce the final product or service.*

Finished goods inventory is the set of products that have been completely assembled but have not yet been shipped. The key concern here is to have enough goods on hand to meet customer demands but not so much that the products become obsolete, spoiled, or damaged. Boeing does not maintain an inventory of 747 jumbo jets but instead makes each plane to customer specifications, whereas Ford often has thousands of automobiles in finished goods inventory, awaiting dealer orders.

Finished goods inventory *is the set of products that have been completely assembled but not yet shipped.*

Finally, **in-transit inventory** includes goods that have been shipped from the company but have not been delivered to the customer. Again, Ford is likely always to have a lot of automobiles on trains and trucks, heading for dealer showrooms.

In-transit inventory *includes goods that have been shipped from the company but not yet delivered to the customer.*

Quality Control

Another important part of operations management control is quality control, ensuring that the inputs and outputs of the organization meet desired levels of quality. As we discussed in Chapter 21, quality control has become increasingly important in recent years, primarily because of the growing recognition that Japanese success is often due to the quality of their products.[17]

Quality control *is the attempt to make sure inputs and outputs meet desired levels of quality.*

Quality control begins with strategic planning. A strategic issue for most firms is determining how they want their products to be perceived in the marketplace. Mercedes-Benz, F.A.O. Schwarz, Rolex, and Neiman-Marcus have all decided that quality is to be their hallmark. Thus price becomes a secondary consideration. Honda, Seiko, Sears, Ford, and Sony have all determined to strike a balance between good quality and reasonable price. At the low end, Kmart, Timex, and Radio Shack strive for acceptable quality but stress low price.

Quality control systems can usually parallel inventory control systems. For example, it is quite common for companies to specify certain quality standards when they buy raw materials or supplies. The supplies are checked carefully when they are delivered, and if the standards have not been met, or if the shipment is damaged, the company either refuses the materials or accepts them subject to further review.

Work-in-process is generally the time when desired levels of product or service quality are achieved. Managers in an automobile plant make numerous checks as various parts are assembled. If the company has decided that sheet-metal parts like fenders and doors cannot deviate more than half an inch from target fittings in order to be acceptable, the managers can detect and correct a problem in a fender or door before it is compounded.

Finished goods are also checked for quality. Say that each car at an auto plant is driven from the end of the line to a holding area. During the drive, the worker can check things like the lights, radio, and brakes. In other instances, the quality of finished goods can only be assessed via sampling. Obviously, checking a flash cube or a bottle of wine makes the product unusable, so managers check samples to determine overall quality.

We should also note that quality control is as important for a service company as it is for manufacturers. A restaurant that sells poor-quality foods, a barber who gives bad haircuts, or a university that does not care about teaching will have problems.

Scheduling Control

Still another important aspect of operations management control is **scheduling control,** having the right things arrive at and depart from the organization at the right time.[18] Consider the

Chrysler's assembly plant in Bramalea, Ontario, Canada focuses on customer satisfaction as a key part of its quality program. A satellite stamping plant will use just-in-time delivery to assure that the automobiles will be ready for customers when they should be. Customer satisfaction with delivery dates is an important determinant of the overall perception of product quality. (Courtesy of Chrysler Corp.)

Making sure that the right things arrive at and depart from the organization at the right time is ***scheduling control.***

JIT (just-in-time) *scheduling involves having things arrive at designated spots just as they are needed.*

case of a contractor who is building a new house. The contractor will need a supply of two-by-four studs to use in framing the house. If the shipment arrives too soon, the wood might be stolen or scattered, but if it arrives too late, work will be delayed. Thus, one of the contractor's scheduling control problems is to have the lumber delivered on time.

A recent innovation in scheduling control is the **just-in-time** method, or **JIT.** Used by Robert E. Wood in the construction of the Panama Canal, JIT was pioneered by the Japanese but has become increasingly useful in the United States.[19] [20] As illustrated in Exhibit 22.4, the traditional approach to scheduling incoming materials is to order relatively few large shipments of materials, which are then stored in warehouses until they are needed for production. The traditional American automobile plant capable of producing one thousand cars a day requires two million square feet of space, much of it devoted to storage space, and $775 in inventory per car.

Under a JIT system, the company makes more frequent, and therefore smaller, orders of raw materials. The idea is to have resources arrive just as they are needed—just in time. Some materials go straight to the plant, while others are maintained (at a low level) in small warehouse facilities. A Japanese plant designed to produce one thousand cars a day is about one million square feet in size and uses only $150 in inventory per car.

For obvious reasons, U.S. firms have begun to copy this system. Today, automobile engines at many Ford plants are delivered daily and taken straight to the assembly line. Computers and advanced communication systems facilitate this practice a great deal.

Another dimension of scheduling applies to manufacturing itself. In traditional systems, machines in a plant are fixed, both in terms of where they are and what they do. Parts flow through the plant and are assembled into a certain final product. Changes in products necessitate major changes in the plant as well. But new types of manufacturing systems promise to change this approach. These systems rely on computers to adjust machine placements and settings automatically. This kind of change greatly enhances both the complexity and the flexibility of scheduling in a manufacturing system.

Exhibit 22.4   Traditional Versus Just-In-Time Scheduling

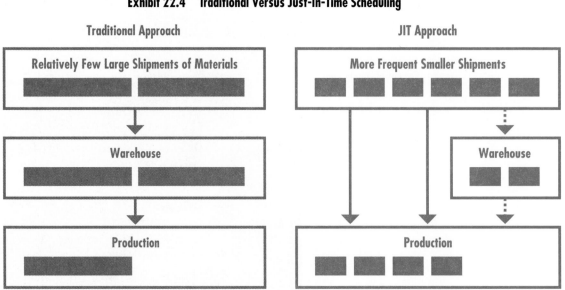

Cost Control

Cost control involves the management of expenses.

Finally, operations management control also gives considerable attention to **cost control.** Costs are the expenses incurred by the organization as it conducts its business. Obviously, payments for labor and materials frequently represent major costs, so managers using cost control attempt to identify areas in which costs are excessive and to find ways to reduce them appropriately. Cost control has become a major area of managerial attention. For example, AT&T, Xerox, Celanese, and Burlington have all undertaken major cost-cutting programs in recent years.

Operations Control Techniques

To carry out operations control most efficiently, managers rely on various control techniques. Several of these techniques were discussed earlier in Chapter 9. Two additional techniques that are particularly relevant to operations management, however, are process control charts and materials requirements planning.

Process Control Charts

*A **process control chart** is a visual representation of an operations function.*

A **process control chart** is a visual representation of an operations function. It illustrates the operation itself, shows how materials are transported to and from work stations, highlights inspection points, and details inventory and storage arrangements. The chart also shows the time and resources associated with each element of the operations function.

For example, a manager might develop a process control chart for the operations being performed by one particular machinist in a factory. The chart will first diagram where the various parts to be machined are being transported from. It will also show where they are to be stored after they arrive but before the machinist can get to them. The chart will also highlight exactly what operations the machine is capable of performing and how long it takes to perform each of those operations. It will indicate who is responsible for inspecting the work as it is completed and what happens if parts are not passing that inspection. Finally, the process control chart will show where the parts are transported to after the machinist has successfully completed working on them.

Table 22.1

The MRP Process

Step	Example
1. *Manager specifies the needed resources and decides when they must be available.*	A plant manager determines that 240 steel wire casings as well as component nuts, bolts, wires, and screws are needed to make 240 products during the next six weeks. Production is to be spaced evenly throughout the period.
2. *Manager determines the existing inventory.*	Current inventory includes 17 wire casings as well as specified numbers of nuts and bolts, wires, and screws.
3. *Computer specifies an ordering and delivery system for parts not currently in inventory.*	The specifications include details as to amounts needed, suppliers, schedules, and the like. The suppliers are all local.
4. *Computer generates reports that tell the manager what and when to order.*	The manager gets a report summarizing orders for 23 casings and sets of component items to be delivered next Monday, and 40 additional casings and sets of component items to be delivered each of the following five Mondays.

By carefully studying such charts, operations managers can develop a better understanding of work flows within a particular facility, spot inefficiencies, and make adjustments to improve the overall operations management system. Thus, process control charts are continuously being updated and refined as new and better ways of doing things are identified.

Materials Requirements Planning (MRP)

MRP (materials requirements planning) is a method for managing complex delivery schedules.

Another useful control technique for operations management is **materials requirements planning,** or **MRP.** [21] MRP is used to manage complex delivery schedules so that materials arrive as needed and in the proper quantities. Table 22.1 outlines the steps in the MRP process.

MRP is actually performed with computer software. First the manager specifies the parts and supplies that are needed for a project and figures out when they should arrive. Then he or she determines existing inventories. The MRP system then specifies an ordering and delivery system for materials and parts that are not currently in inventory. Finally, the software generates reports that tell the manager when to place orders and what quantities of each material and part to specify in each order.

Perhaps the greatest value of MRP is its ability to handle different delivery systems and lead times effectively. When a company needs hundreds of parts in vastly different quantities, and when delivery times range from a day to several months in the future, coordination by an individual manager may well be impossible. A properly designed MRP system, however, can cope with such factors fairly easily.

Technology Management

We noted earlier the importance of managing technology as an integral part of operations management. In this section we first discuss manufacturing technology and then service technology. Some people are more inclined toward technical issues than others. The Self-Assessment in this chapter examines your technical orientation. To be a successful manager, you must have a technical orientation as well as a people orientation and know how to balance the two.

Manufacturing Technology

Numerous forms of manufacturing technology are used in organizations. Two especially important new forms are automation and computer-assisted manufacturing.

Automation is the process of designing work so that it can be performed by machines.

Automation   **Automation** is the process of designing work so that it can be completely or almost completely performed by machines. Because automated machines operate quickly and make few errors, they increase the amount of work that can be done. Thus, automation helps to improve products and services, and it fosters innovation. Automation is the most recent step in the development of machines and machine-controlling devices. Machine-controlling devices have been around since the 1700s. James Watt, a Scottish engineer, invented a mechanical speed control to regulate the speed of steam engines in 1787. The Jacquard loom, developed by a French inventor, was controlled by paper cards with holes punched in them. Early accounting and computing equipment was controlled by similar punched cards.

Automation relies on feedback, information, sensors, and a control mechanism. Feedback is the flow of information from the machine back to the sensor. Sensors are the parts of the system that gather information and compare it to some preset standards. The control mechanism is the device that sends instructions to the automatic machine. These elements are illustrated by the example in Exhibit 22.5. A thermostat has sensors that monitor air temperature and compare it to a preset low value. If the air temperature falls below the preset value, the thermostat sends an electrical signal to the furnace, turning it on. The furnace heats the air. When the sensors detect that the air temperature has reached a value higher than the low preset value, the thermostat stops the furnace. The last step (shutting off the furnace) is known as feedback, a critical component of any automated operation.

Exhibit 22.5

A Simple Automatic Control Mechanism

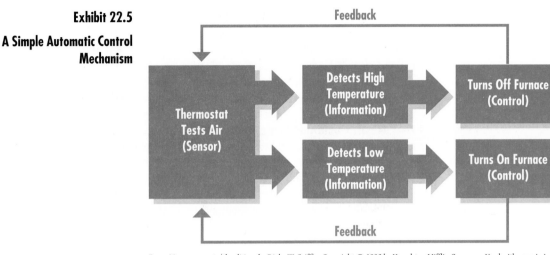

From *Management*, 4th edition, by Ricky W. Griffin. Copyright © 1993 by Houghton Mifflin Company. Used with permission.

The big move to automate factories began during World War II. The shortage of skilled workers and the development of high-speed computers combined to bring about a tremendous interest in automation. Programmable automation (the use of computers to control machines) was introduced during this era, far outstripping conventional automation (the use of mechanical or electromechanical devices to control machines).[22] The automobile industry began to use automatic machines for a variety of jobs. In fact, the term *automation* came into use in the 1950s in the automobile industry. The chemical and oil-refining industries also began to use computers to regulate production. It is this computerized, or programmable, automation that presents the greatest opportunities and challenges for management today.

The impact of automation on people in the workplace is complex. In the short term, people whose jobs are automated find themselves without jobs. In the long term, however, more jobs are created than are lost. Nevertheless, not all companies are able to help displaced workers find new jobs, so the human costs are sometimes high. In the coal industry, for instance, automation has been used primarily in mining. The output per miner has risen dramatically from the 1950s on. The demand for coal, however, has decreased; and productivity gains resulting from automation have lessened the need for miners. Consequently, a lot of workers have lost their jobs, and the industry has not been able to absorb them. In contrast, in the electronics industry, the rising demand for products has led to increasing employment opportunities despite the use of automation.

Computer-Assisted Manufacturing   Current extensions of automation generally revolve around computer-assisted manufacturing. **Computer-assisted manufacturing** is technology that relies on computers to design or manufacture products. One type of computer-assisted manufacturing is **computer-aided design (CAD),** the use of computers to design parts and complete products and to simulate performance so that prototypes need not be constructed. McDonnell Douglas uses CAD to study hydraulic tubing in DC-10s. Japan's automotive industry uses it to speed up car design. GE used CAD to change the design of circuit breakers, and Benetton uses CAD to design new styles and products. Oneida Ltd., the table flatware firm, used CAD to design a new spoon in only two days.[23] CAD is usually combined with **computer-aided manufacturing (CAM)** to ensure that the design moves smoothly to production. The production computer shares the design computer's information and is able to have machines with the proper settings ready when production is needed. A CAM system is especially useful when re-orders come in be-

*Computer-assisted manufacturing can involve **CAD**, **CAM**, **CIM**, and/or **FMS**.*

cause the computer can quickly produce the desired product, prepare labels and copies of orders, and send the product out to where it is wanted.

Closely aligned with this approach is **computer-integrated manufacturing (CIM).** In CIM, CAD and CAM are linked together, and computers adjust machine placements and settings automatically to enhance both the complexity and the flexibility of scheduling. All manufacturing activities are controlled by computer. Because the computer can access the company's other information systems, CIM is a powerful and complex management control tool.[24]

Flexible manufacturing systems (FMS) usually have robotic work units or work stations, assembly lines, and robotic carts or some other form of computer-controlled transport system to move material as needed from one part of the system to another. FMS such as the one at IBM's manufacturing facility in Lexington, Kentucky, rely on computers to coordinate and integrate automated production and materials-handling facilities.[25]

These systems are not without disadvantages, however.[26] For example, because they represent fundamental change, they also generate resistance. Additionally, because of their tremendous complexity, CAD systems are not always reliable. CIM systems are so expensive that they raise the breakeven point for firms using them.[27] This means that the firm must operate at high levels of production and sales to be able to afford the systems.

Robotics   One of the newest trends in manufacturing technology is robotics. A robot is any artificial device that is able to perform functions ordinarily thought to be appropriate for human beings. Robotics refers to the science and technology of the construction, maintenance, and use of robots. The use of industrial robots has steadily increased since 1980 and is expected to continue to increase slowly as more companies recognize the benefits that accrue to users of industrial robots.

Welding was one of the first applications for robots, and it continues to be the area for most applications. In second place and close behind is materials handling. Other applications include machine loading and unloading, painting and finishing, assembly, casting, and machining applications such as cutting, grinding, polishing, drilling, sanding, buffing, and deburring. Chrysler, for instance, replaced about two hundred welders with fifty robots on an assembly line and increased productivity about 20 percent.[28] The use of robots in inspection work is also increasing. They can check for cracks and holes, and they can be equipped with vision systems to perform visual inspections.

Robots are also beginning to move from the factory floor to all manner of other applications. The Dallas police used a robot to apprehend a suspect who had barricaded himself in an apartment building. The robot smashed a window and reached with its mechanical arm into the building. The suspect panicked and ran outside. At the Long Beach Memorial Hospital in California, brain surgeons are assisted by a robot arm that drills into the patient's skull with excellent precision.[29] Some newer applications involve remote work. For example, the use of robot submersibles controlled from the surface can help divers in remote locations. Surveillance robots fitted with microwave sensors can do things that a human guard cannot do, such as "seeing" through nonmetallic walls and in the dark. In other applications, automated farming (agrimation) uses robot harvesters to pick fruit from a variety of trees.[30]

Robots are also used by small manufacturers. One robot slices carpeting to fit the inside of custom vans in an upholstery shop. Another stretches balloons flat so that they can be spray-painted with slogans at a novelties company. At a jewelry company, a robot holds class rings while they are engraved by a laser. These robots are lighter, faster, stronger, and more intelligent than those used in heavy manufacturing and are the types that more and more organizations will be using in the future.[31]

Service Technology Service technology is also changing rapidly. And it, too, is also moving more and more toward automated systems and procedures. In banking, for example, new technological breakthroughs have led to automated teller machines and made it much easier to move funds between accounts or between different banks. Some people now have their pay checks deposited directly into a checking account from which many of their bills are then automatically paid. And credit card transactions by VISA customers are recorded and billed electronically.

Hotels use increasingly sophisticated technology to accept and record room reservations. Universities use new technologies to electronically store and provide access to all manner of books, scientific journals, government reports, and articles. Hospitals and other health care organizations use new forms of service technology to manage patient records, dispatch ambulances, and monitor vital signs. Restaurants use technology to record and fill customer orders, order food and supplies, and prepare food. Given the increased role that service organizations are playing in today's economy, even more technological innovations are likely to be developed in the years to come.

Chapter Summary

Operations management deals with the transformation of inputs into outputs; the inputs and outputs themselves are secondary components. Operations management is critically important for both strategic and operational reasons.

Planning for operations is the first stage in effective operations management. It involves both operations decisions and operations planning. Operations decisions must be made in eight primary areas, which affect all aspects of operations management but relate most significantly to the transformation process. Operations planning relates to the more day-to-day activities of operations management. There are four basic steps in operations management.

The management and organization of operations involve all of the aspects discussed under planning for operations. Managers must decide how to organize the operations function within the context of organization design. There is also a very important link between change and operations management.

Operations control involves four areas. Inventories represent a major investment for an organization and so must be carefully controlled. Quality is also important. Scheduling control involves having the right things arrive at and depart from the organization at the right time. Cost control deals with the expenses incurred by the organization in conducting its business.

Managers can use numerous techniques in operations management. Two major tools are process control charts and material requirements planning.

Technology management is a related area that is also important to organizations. Manufacturing technology has been influenced by CAD, CAM, and CIM. Robotics have also become quite important. Service technology is also an important consideration for organizations.

The Manager's Vocabulary

operations management
manufacturing
service organization
product/service line
capacity
planning system
technology
labor-intensive technology
capital-intensive technology
facilities

inventory control
raw materials inventory
work-in-process inventory
finished goods inventory
in-transit inventory
quality control
scheduling control
JIT
cost control
process control chart

materials requirements planning (MRP)
automation
computer-assisted manufacturing
computer-aided design (CAD)
computer-aided manufacturing (CAM)
computer-integrated manufacturing (CIM)
flexible manufacturing system (FMS)

Review Questions

1. Why has the term "operations management" gradually replaced the term "production management"?
2. What are the eight key operations decisions managers must make?
3. Identify the four key areas of operations control.
4. Name and describe the four types of inventory most organizations maintain.
5. What is meant by just-in-time scheduling?

Analysis Questions

1. How do you use operations management in your day-to-day activities?
2. Which operations decisions are most related to other managerial activities and which are "purely" operations management?
3. How is operations planning similar to and different from more general types of planning activities as described earlier in the planning section?
4. Are some forms of operations control more important for some businesses than for others? Support your answer with examples.
5. What steps might an organization go through in converting from a traditional to a just-in-time scheduling system?

Self-Assessment

Are You Technically Oriented?

Introduction Some people tend to be left-brain dominant, while others are right-brain dominant. Studies suggest that left-brain people are more technically oriented. That is, they solve problems systematically, work best with sequential ideas, and like to solve problems logically. This is in contrast to right-brain people, who are intuitive problem solvers. The following questions are designed to provide feedback on your preference for left- or right-brain thinking.

Instructions Answer each question as accurately as you can. It is a forced-choice test, so choose the option you like best (or dislike least), but be sure to answer each one.

1. When you solve problems, your basic approach is:
   a. logical, rational
   b. intuitive

2. If you were to write books, you would prefer to write:
   a. fiction
   b. nonfiction

3. When you read, you read for:
   a. main ideas
   b. specific facts and details

4. What kind of stories do you most like to read:
   a. realistic
   b. fantasy

5. When you study or read:
   a. you listen to music on the radio
   b. you must have silence

6. You prefer to learn:
   a. through ordering and planning
   b. through free exploration

7. You prefer to organize things:
   a. sequentially
   b. in terms of relationships

8. Which of these statements best describes you:
   a. almost no mood changes
   b. frequent mood changes

9. Do you enjoy clowning around?
   a. yes
   b. no

10. You would describe yourself as:
    a. generally conforming
    b. generally nonconforming

11. Are you absentminded?
    a. frequently
    b. virtually never

12. What types of assignments do you like best?
    a. well structured
    b. open ended

13. Which is most preferable to you?
    a. producing ideas
    b. drawing conclusions

14. Which is most fun for you?
    a. dreaming
    b. planning realistically

15. Which of these would be most exciting for you?
    a. inventing something new
    b. improving on something already in existence

16. What type of stories do you prefer?
    a. action
    b. mystery

17. Which do you like best?
    a. cats
    b. dogs

18. What do you like best?
    a. creating stories
    b. analyzing stories

19. Do you think better:
    a. sitting up straight
    b. lying down

20. Which would you prefer to be?
    a. a music composer
    b. a music critic

21. Could you be hypnotized?
    a. yes, quite easily
    b. no, I don't think so

22. Which would you prefer to do?
    a. ballet dancing
    b. interpretative impromptu dancing

23. Which are you best at?
    a. recalling names and dates
    b. recalling where things were in a room or picture

24. When it comes to getting instructions, which do you prefer?
    a. verbal instructions
    b. demonstration

25. When getting verbal instructions, how do you generally feel?
    a. restless
    b. attentive

For interpretation, turn to the back of the book.

Source: Self feedback exercise from *Organizational Behavior: Theory and Practice* by Steven Altman, Enzo Valenzi, and Richard M. Hodgetts, copyright © 1985 by Harcourt Brace & Company, reprinted by permission of the publisher.

Skill Builder

Organizations as Systems

Purpose Operations management is the total set of managerial activities used by organizations to transform inputs into products and services. To conceptualize this process, all managers must be familiar with systems theory. This skill builder focuses on the *open systems model* and the *administrative management model*. It will help you develop the *innovator role* of the open systems model and the *monitor role* of the administrative management model. One of the skills of the innovator is the ability to develop an organizational framework, while one skill of the monitor is the ability to analyze feedback data.

Introduction Systems theory provides a method for mapping the processes of any organization. In other words, you will be able to diagram the operation process for an organization. Once you understand the process of how this is done, you can develop a systems model for any organization.

Instructions Study the section on systems theory in Chapter 1. Then apply that approach to complete the Organizational Systems Model for the five organizations below. Be prepared to discuss your process for each organization in class.

THE ORGANIZATIONAL SYSTEMS MODEL

Organization	Inputs	Tranformation Processes	Outputs
Campus Bookstore	_____ _____ _____	_____ _____ _____	_____ _____ _____
Wal-mart	_____ _____ _____	_____ _____ _____	_____ _____ _____
Public Library	_____ _____ _____	_____ _____ _____	_____ _____ _____
Ford Motor Co.	_____ _____ _____	_____ _____ _____	_____ _____ _____
Microsoft	_____ _____ _____	_____ _____ _____	_____ _____ _____

Source: From *Exercises in Management,* 3rd ed., by Gene Burton. Copyright © 1990 by Houghton Mifflin Company. Used with permission.

CONCLUDING CASES

22.1   General Mills

Two of the more successful restaurant chains in the United States today are Red Lobster and Olive Garden. The former specializes in seafood and has been around for several years, while the latter serves Italian dishes and is a relative newcomer to the scene. But both are owned by the same company, General Mills, and both use the same formula for success.

The success of General Mills's restaurant operations starts with raw materials. Red Lobster buys more than 30 million tons of seafood a year from all over the world. Some of it, like shrimp, is shipped to a St. Petersburg plant where it is processed, quick-frozen, and packed. Other products, like swordfish, are shipped

fresh directly to warehouses around the country. These warehouses then ship both fresh and frozen products to Red Lobster restaurants around the country. This system saves more than twenty-five cents a pound over the average costs other seafood restaurants pay and also ensures consistent quality.

Olive Gardens take an even simpler approach by making pasta on site. By using prepacked materials and blending the pasta daily in each restaurant, its costs are around forty cents a pound. This compares with fifty-five cents a pound to buy pasta already prepared.

Each night restaurant managers predict next-day sales

using sales figures from that same day the previous week and year. Ingredients necessary to serve that many people are then pulled from the freezer and refrigerator, and work orders are prepared to get appropriate meals for the next day. This system saves $5 million a year.

By predicting customer flows using accurate historical data, both Red Lobster and Olive Garden are also able to schedule workers more efficiently. Like most restaurants, they rely heavily on part-time workers and thus have considerable flexibility regarding staffing levels on a day-to-day basis.

Cooking and presentation are also highly standardized in each Red Lobster and Olive Garden restaurant. A one-pound lobster, for example, is to be steamed exactly ten minutes. These standards, developed in home-office test kitchens, ensure that food is always prepared the same way.

And illustrated diagrams show exactly how food is to be arranged on each plate, right down to the location of the parsley.

These food placement diagrams are designed to make portions look larger and to also maintain consistency.

Each manager at Red Lobster and Olive Garden restaurants carries a pocket thermometer to spot-check food temperature. For example, coffee is never to be served at less than one hundred fifty degrees, while salads are always to be below forty degrees. If deviations crop up, this is a signal that the kitchen may be behind, a server may be too slow, or there may be a problem with the ovens.[32]

Discussion Questions

1. What aspects of operations management are illustrated in this case?
2. Are restaurants manufacturing organizations or service organizations?
3. Have you ever worked or eaten at a Red Lobster or Olive Garden? Are there elements of operations management you can recall from your own experiences?

22.2   Mercedes-Benz

Mercedes-Benz is the biggest business unit within Daimler-Benz AG, Germany's largest corporation. Mercedes-Benz is the world's largest manufacturer of heavy trucks. But it is the firm's luxury car division that is best known among consumers around the world. Indeed, driving a Mercedes was once the dream of every upwardly mobile driver.

But things have changed for Mercedes-Benz in recent years. Its biggest domestic competitor, BMW, passed it in total sales for the first time in 1992, and Japanese rivals like Lexus and Infiniti also gained market share at its expense. Previously immune to recessions and competition, the firm's total sales and profits also declined markedly in 1992.

To fight back Mercedes-Benz brought in a new boss, Helmut Werner. Werner, in turn, has announced sweeping changes in both manufacturing and marketing that will shake the firm to its roots. The new president of Mercedes-Benz has made a career of walking into bleak situations and turning them around. His most recent success was with Daimler's Freightliner truckmaking subsidiary.

One of Werner's first moves was to announce the elimination of the firm's cost-plus development and pricing strategy. In the past Mercedes-Benz engineers were given a free hand to design and manufacture cars to meet high quality standards without regard to cost. The firm simply made the cars as they were engineered and then added on their target profit margins. Customers were willing to pay the resultant high prices, in part because of the Mercedes-Benz mystique and in part because there were few alternatives.

But Werner warns that the firm must now begin to focus more on costs to offset inroads by competitors. His first effort will be directed at the new Mercedes 190E. Werner has decreed that the car must be priced below twenty-five thousand dollars (the same price as its predecessor) but include five-thousand-dollars worth of former options as standard. And it is up to the firm's engineers to figure out how to make it happen.

Mercedes-Benz is also cutting jobs (thirteen thousand in Germany alone) and expanding its markets. For the first time, the firm is also making cars outside of Germany. It is currently assembling cars in South Korea and is constructing a new plant in Spain. And Werner has suggested that yet another foreign manufacturing plant may be constructed as well.

The firm has also announced plans to dramatically expand its product line. At the low end, for example, Mercedes-Benz plans to introduce a subcompact city car to sell in the ten-thousand-dollar range. And mini-vans and sports utility vehicles are also under development. If the venerable automaker can successfully pull off these new initiatives, it may become an even more important player in the world auto industry. But if it falters, it may fall behind so far it will never be able to catch up again.[33]

Discussion Questions

1. What aspects of operations management are illustrated in this case?
2. What is the role of technology in a firm like Mercedes-Benz?
3. What advantages and disadvantages can you see in Mercedes-Benz's new strategy?

CHAPTER

23 Information Systems

Learning Objectives

After studying this chapter you should be able to

- Describe the nature of information and information systems, including their effect on the manager's job and the characteristics of effective information.

- Identify the basic components of information systems.

- Discuss the types of information systems available.

- Discuss how to determine information system needs and how to match needs with systems.

- Describe the impact of information systems on organizations.

P harmacist Charles R. Walgreen, son of a Swedish immigrant, opened a drugstore in Chicago in 1901. A second store was opened in 1909 and a third in 1911. Walgreen began serving ice cream in the summer and soup and sandwiches in the winter, thus inventing the drugstore soda fountain and restaurant business. By 1929 there were 397 stores in 87 cities. Today Walgreen is the largest drugstore chain in the United States and is still run by the Walgreen family.

To keep all of these stores plus the planned expansion in control and in communication with one another, Walgreen employs technology. It installed price-scanning equipment throughout the chain and developed its own private satellite communications system. Walgreen was one of the first retail organizations to computerize its planning and distribution systems. By the early 1980s it had installed a central computer database linking every pharmacy. It was also one of the first drugstore chains to link its pharmacy to third-party payment plans so that neither customers nor Walgreen has to fill out long insurance forms.

Most drugstores do not use scanners, which are common in supermarkets, because they are not generally economical where orders are small. However, Walgreen has installed both computers and scanners to help it monitor inventory and track demand. As a result, Walgreen is one of the longest-running successes in retailing. What it may lack in low prices it makes up for by having customers' prescriptions readily on hand at its more than sixteen hundred stores throughout the United States. Ever alert for opportunities, today Walgreen is using computer networks to expand into the mail-order business with just as much success as it has enjoyed in its more conventional store business.[1] ▪

W algreen has demonstrated the value of using high technology to manage its information systems. It found that rapid, accurate information not only about prescriptions but also about sales of all its products enabled it to respond to customers quickly. Even in a recession Walgreen was able to grow and make profits. The importance of managing information systems, then, would seem apparent. Information systems much like those at Walgreen are being used by many other organizations.

Consider the following:

Any retail organization could use such systems to monitor sales and move merchandise accordingly.

The systems could be used in service industries to more nearly match the needs of customers with the availability of personnel and supplies.

They could be used in transportation firms to better schedule aircraft, trucks, and other vehicles.

Banks and other financial organizations could use such information to better monitor extensive holdings and transfers of funds.

This chapter discusses another aspect of organizational control—information and information systems that are useful to managers. The nature and basic components of information systems are described first. Then the chapter examines how various information systems are designed to match managers' needs. Next we look at different types of information systems. Finally, managing information systems is discussed, along with the impact of these systems on organizations.

The Nature of Information

nformation consists of data organized in a meaningful way. **Data** are merely facts and figures, unorganized pieces of information.[2] Data are useless until they are processed and organized in some way. If the Dial Corporation, for example, has a list of figures that show the

*****Data** are unorganized facts and figures, whereas **information** consists of data organized in a meaningful way.***

monthly sales of a product, those data are made more useful—changed into information—when they are analyzed and organized to show seasonal fluctuations and annual trends.

Remember from Chapter 1 that a **system** is an interrelated set of elements that function as a whole. A system, then, consists of a set of components so arranged as to accomplish some purpose. If the Dial Corp. built a system to produce marketing reports from its sales data, it would have built an information system. If it further arranged for those reports to automatically go to managers who needed the information, it would have a management information system such as those introduced in Chapter 1. The keys to systems, then, are interrelatedness and purpose. An information system must accomplish a purpose through the interaction of its component parts.

Information Needs of Managers

The manager's job was discussed in Chapters 1 and 2 as consisting of functions, roles, and skills. Managers have always had to be skilled in using information. The nature and importance of information, however, have changed dramatically in recent years because the amount and variety of data coming to managers have grown tremendously. Managers, therefore, have had to become information processors. They have to decide which information to combine to form new information, which information to discard, which to pass along to others, which to put to immediate use, and which to retain for possible use later.[3]

Susan Kidder, an accounting manager for a medium-size manufacturing firm, could serve as an example. During the course of her normal day, Susan participates in formal and informal meetings on both job-related and nonjob-related topics. In addition, she receives letters, memos, notes, and other forms of written communication; she gets and makes telephone calls; and she may send or receive a FAX (electronic facsimile) message or use her company's electronic mail (EMail) system. All of the data and information she receives from all of these different sources must be processed in some way.[4]

Effective Information

Effective information is accurate, timely, complete, and relevant.

All managers use information, and the information they get should be effective; that is, it should provide them with what they need to carry out their tasks successfully. To be effective, information must be accurate, timely, complete, and relevant.[5]

As the Information Age arrives in full-swing, PepsiCo strives to be ready. Shown here is an experimental automated ordering terminal developed for PepsiCo's Taco Bell. Designed to reduce waiting lines and to improve the accuracy of ordering, such systems can also be integrated into inventory and cash management programs to further assure efficient and effective management. (Philip Saltonstall/ONYX.)

These characteristics seem obvious. Yet time after time managers make decisions based on information that is inaccurate. For example, the Japanese overbid for a piece of land in Great Britain and then found that they could not use it because a building on it had been declared historic. The information they had used was inaccurate.[6] Benetton, on the other hand, has a computerized information system that clearly provides timely as well as complete information that paper systems or centralized systems cannot provide. Knowing only the profit per item, for instance, is not enough information for deciding how many multiple items to stock, since a product that is less profitable per unit may sell far more units and hence earn more total profit for the firm.[7] Finally, information must be relevant. Data or information on sales in one region may not be highly relevant to sales managers in other regions, and yet many small-business managers try to function with such irrelevant information on the mistaken assumption that it is better than no information at all.[8]

The Information Age

In the information age, the focus is on information rather than the computer.

While computers clearly had origins dating back to the 1800s, the first true electronic computer was developed in the 1940s. Even so, it was not until the 1960s when second-generation computers using transistors came into use that the computer age was born. With the third generation using integrated circuits and the fourth using microprocessors, developments in the hardware of computing dominated its role. In the 1980s, as the emphasis began to shift from the technology to its applications, the information age was born. In the information age, the computer is simply a tool that helps managers use information as a corporate resource; it is the focus on information that is important.[9] Information, then, is becoming a competitive advantage. However, some managers have trouble accessing and using information because of computer anxiety. The Self-Assessment in this chapter measures your computer anxiety.

The use of computers seems to go through five stages. In the first stage management is enthusiastic about computers and uses them primarily for accounting applications. In the second stage management becomes aware of some of the limitations of computers and is a bit more cautious about extending applications. In the third stage the information systems tend to become overloaded, and management becomes cynical about the ability of computers to solve all of its problems. Then in the fourth stage managers begin to learn how to use the computer and information systems to bring about needed changes in the organization. Finally, the fifth stage brings about management understanding and control of information systems and computers in all areas of the organization. This, then, is the stage in which the information age comes about.[10] Many organizations are now entering the information age, and the impact and importance of information and information systems is clear. An understanding of systems is vital to effectiveness in the global marketplace.[11]

Information and Information Systems

nformation and information systems, then, are increasingly important parts of the manager's job. But just what does an information system look like, and how do managers use one?

Components of Information Systems

Every information system has five basic interrelated components. There must be some way to get the data into the system, to analyze or process the data, to store the data and information, and to make the information available to users. There must also be some overall control of the system itself. In a simple, noncomputerized system, the data are recorded on paper forms or memoranda that are stored somewhere (boxes, drawers, file cabinets). The analysis is done by people who then prepare reports that are sent to those who need them. Control is basically by exception; that is, once the system is in place it continues as is unless a problem is detected.

A computerized information system, on the other hand, would look like that shown in Exhibit 23.1 Getting the data into the system involves one or more **input devices.** Analysis and

Exhibit 23.1

Basic Components of Computerized Information Systems

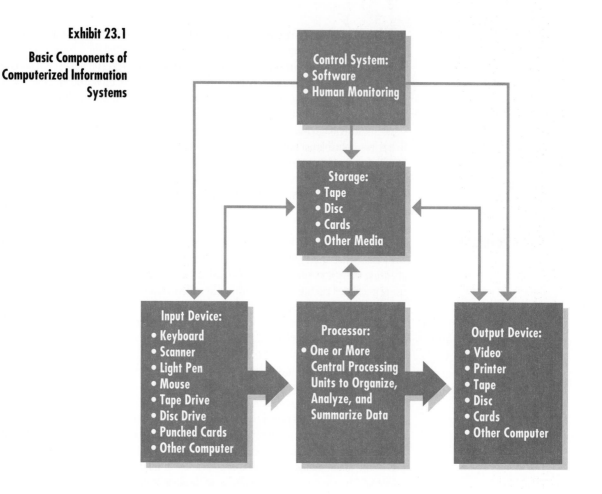

processing are done by a **central processor.** Storage is also accomplished through one or more of several media; in many cases more than one medium is used in case something should happen to one storage device. The information is made available to users through a variety of **output devices.** The central processor and these devices are known as the computer *hardware. Software* refers to the instructions (programs) that enable the hardware to function. Finally, the control system usually involves some form of computer software as well as human monitoring to ensure that the software and the system are functioning as planned. Management must assure that the information system is integrated with all operating and control systems so that individual managers and groups of managers receive relevant and timely information from the system.[12]

Designing Information Systems

The purpose of an information system is to ensure that proper information is available when needed so that managers do not have to rely on chance or guesswork.[13] Designing a good information system, then, involves knowing the information system needs as well as the kinds of systems that exist or might be developed in the future.

The needs of an organization for information are termed its ***information system needs.***

Information System Needs   The **information system needs** of an organization are determined by the kind of organization, its environment, and its size. A high-technology organization, for instance, has greater information system needs than does a low-technology organization. The more uncertain and complex the environment, the greater is the need for a formal information system. And, all other things being equal, larger organizations have greater information systems needs than do smaller ones; thus Procter & Gamble's information needs would be greater than those of a local retailer.

Within an organization, information needs are influenced by the area and level of management involved. The information systems needs of a production department are different from those of a human resources department, although each usually needs a formal system. Likewise, executive-level managers have different information needs than do supervisors. Each manager has unique information needs, and a well-designed system will tend to be tailored to each of its users rather than merely provide general information to all users.

The process of determining what information each individual needs to perform his or her job is called **information requirements analysis.**[14] The process should be conducted before the information system is developed and then be periodically repeated as part of the updating and maintenance of the system. Normally it involves interviewing individuals to obtain their views on what information they need, in what form, and when. These views must then be verified through the use of some other technique, such as a paper simulation of the individuals' activity or direct observation of them at work. If many people in similar situations are involved, surveys could also be used. In any event, once the information requirements analysis has been completed, it should be integrated into the system and periodically examined to ensure that it is still accurate.

Implementing Information Systems

Implementation of information systems, then, follows from design. Organizations must be careful to match systems with needs, since there are a variety of needs for and uses of information as well as numerous different kinds of information systems. Matching involves working through a series of questions like the following: For what goals is information needed? What information is needed? In what way can that information be readily obtained, stored, analyzed, and reported? (In a computer system this involves determining the hardware and software to use.) What are the costs and benefits of the various ways of meeting those needs? How might the information and the technology for dealing with it be integrated? After obtaining answers to these questions, the system itself must be designed, tested, implemented, and then monitored, maintained, and perhaps improved. As shown in Exhibit 23.2, matching can be thought of as a process in itself.

Exhibit 23.2   Matching Information Needs with a System

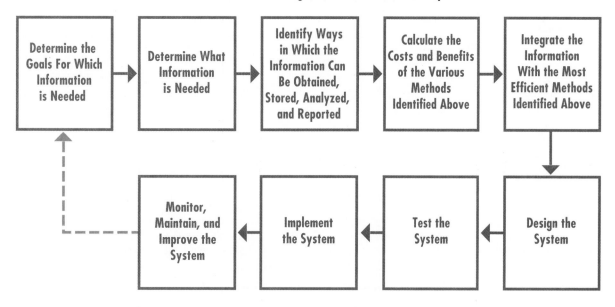

Centralized versus Distributed Systems   Just as decision making in an organization can be centralized or decentralized, so information systems also can be centralized or distributed. In the early days of computer technology, virtually all information systems were centralized. They consisted of data-processing or computer services departments built around large, expensive, main-frame computers. As computer technology changed, it became more and more possible to have the information system components scattered or distributed throughout the organization. Prudential Insurance tends to use a centralized approach, for instance, whereas The Travelers Corporation uses a distributed system.[15] Centralized information systems are better coordinated but slower; distributed systems are faster but may result in more duplication of effort. As the power of smaller computers increases and as networking software improves, information systems of the future may be able to obtain the best of both worlds.

It seems increasingly clear that in the future many members of organizations will be increasingly computer literate and have access to computers that can be interfaced to the organization's information system. This step will open up information and alter organizations in ways that we are just beginning to understand. Nevertheless, organizations must decide whether the implementation of their information systems will involve relatively centralized or distributed systems.

Types of Information Systems

Information systems may be informal and unstructured or formal and structured, and may be either paper or computer based.

Information systems can be formal or informal. Informal, unstructured information systems are a major factor in every manager's life.[16] Managers gather impressions through their interactions with others and through their travels in the organization. And there are always emotional reactions to that information. Although this kind of information system is important, it is so situationally specific that few generalizations can be developed about it.

More formal, structured information systems involve record keeping of one sort or another. Formal information systems are very ancient managerial devices. The Sumerians had a complicated tax and governance system whose records were maintained on clay tablets. The Egyptians used papyri for record keeping. Today, virtually all formal systems are computerized. Three common kinds are transaction-processing systems, basic management information systems, and decision support systems. Table 23.1 summarizes the different kinds of information systems, and

Table 23.1

Kinds of Information Systems

System	Description
1. *Informal*	Unstructured. Information is obtained from day-to-day interactions and impressions, notes, and/or diaries.
2. *Formal*	Structured. Information is gathered and communicated either on paper or by computer. Information can be either centralized or distributed.
a. Transaction-Processing	Handles routine and recurring transactions.
b. Management Information	Gathers, organizes, summarizes, and reports data for use by managers.
c. Decision Support	Searches for, analyzes, summarizes, and reports information needed by a manager for a particular decision.

A Matter of Ethics

Computers Check Abusers

Computers and information systems are aiding businesses by identifying practices that may be potentially unethical and costly. Numerous medical organizations, while still providing quality health care, are designing computerized systems to aid in cost containment. Business firms have also developed such systems. First Chicago Corporation, for instance, performed computer analyses for disability claims. It found that an HMO practice designed to save money did, but it cost First Chicago because employees took time off to wait for treatments. Further, it found that women not covered by the HMO were given more expensive procedures by their physicians, who received added income from those procedures.

Federal Express developed its own computerized database to analyze similar problems. That database integrates all disability, medical, and other personnel records so that quick cross-checking can be performed. This enables FedEx to monitor very precisely the practices of its insurance carriers and employees. Having accurate information has enabled FedEx to develop new policies and practices that have saved both time and money and seem to have improved the health of its workers.

Such extensive computerized databases raise ethical issues concerning privacy, however. Both First Chicago and FedEx attempt to limit access to medical personnel to assure that privacy will not be violated. Other companies are developing internal privacy codes to protect themselves from potential lawsuits in this area.[17] ■

A Matter of Ethics: Computers Check Abusers suggests how computer information systems are being used to hold down fringe benefit costs for organizations.

Transaction-Processing Systems

A system designed to handle routine and recurring transactions within an organization is known as a **transaction-processing system,** or **TPS.** These were the first formal, structured information systems and the first to be computerized. A TPS is most useful for tasks that involve a large number of highly similar transactions such as filing employee or customer records, handling charge cards, dues notices, subscriptions, and so on.

Recently transaction-processing systems have been combined with optical scanning equipment to strengthen their value to organizations. When a local grocery store uses automated scanners to record each unit sold and its selling price, the information is part of a TPS. Bank cards such as Discover, MasterCard, and VISA also all use a TPS to handle the huge volume of transactions with which they must deal.

Management Information Systems

*An **MIS** is a **management information system** that gathers, organizes, summarizes, and reports information for use by managers.*

A **management information system,** or **MIS,** is a system that gathers, organizes, summarizes, and reports data for use by managers. Sometimes called information reporting systems, these systems help link the several parts of an organization together. For a manufacturing firm like the Kingsport Publishing Corp., for example, a computerized inventory system might track finished goods, work in progress, and beginning materials to ensure that customer commitments are met. A marketing representative working with a customer could access the system to determine fairly precisely when an order would be shipped to that customer. Managers could also regularly access the system to obtain information necessary for effectively operating the organization.

Decision Support Systems

A newer, very powerful form of information system is known as a **decision support system,** or **DSS.** A DSS automatically searches for, analyzes, summarizes, and reports information needed by a manager for a particular decision. At the end of the chapter, the Skill Builder allows you to experience first hand the development of a DSS. In a sense, a DSS combines a TPS and an MIS with features that make the system even more automatically responsive to the needs of its users. A finance officer of a company like PepsiCo, for example, might need to know the capital recovery periods and tax consequences of several alternative investment opportunities. The DSS would have the relevant information and be able to present it in a useful way quickly so that the financial officer's decision process could be both fast and accurate. The real basis of the connection between managers and information systems, then, is turning data into decisions, which has come to be known as decision processing.[18]

Other System Technologies

The computer is at the heart of most information systems today. As indicated in Exhibit 23.3, several new information technologies are currently being developed for organizations.

Computer Software   Whether the computer is a notebook, desk model, or mainframe unit, data can be stored and manipulated by computers through software. Software that can be used in information systems comes in a variety of types: databases, spreadsheets, word processors, and electronic mail, to name the most common ones. Databases permit the user to organize and manipulate primarily numerical data in interconnected ways. Spreadsheets arrange numerical data in a matrix of rows and columns. Word processors and electronic mail deal primarily with text data.

Each of these systems can, to some degree, interrelate with others, and the power to do so is increasing every year. Most word-processing programs (WordStar, Word, and WordPerfect, for instance) can work directly with database programs (dBase, FoxPro, and Rbase, for instance). Likewise, graphic presentation programs (Power Point, Overhead Express, and Harvard Graphics, for example) can import data from word-processing programs or spreadsheet programs (Excel or Lotus 1-2-3, for instance). As networked systems become more prevalent and as modems are increasingly used to send files over long distances, integrated software and hardware will become even more important to enable information systems to evolve into the highly effective control and communication tools they are capable of being.

Telecommunications includes teleconferencing, telecommuting, and networking.

Telecommunications   Great strides have also been made in **telecommunications,** which is communication over some distance. Teleconferencing, telecommuting, and networking are three forms already in use by some firms. **Teleconferencing,** or videoconferencing, permits individuals in different locations to see and talk with one another. This visual capability clearly overcomes one limitation of other electronic communication systems. The former CEO of Wal-mart,

Exhibit 23.3   New Information Technologies

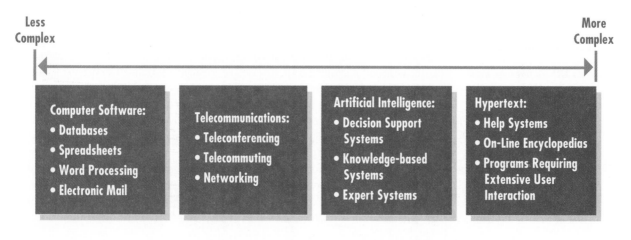

Less Complex — More Complex

Computer Software:
• Databases
• Spreadsheets
• Word Processing
• Electronic Mail

Telecommunications:
• Teleconferencing
• Telecommuting
• Networking

Artificial Intelligence:
• Decision Support Systems
• Knowledge-based Systems
• Expert Systems

Hypertext:
• Help Systems
• On-Line Encyclopedias
• Programs Requiring Extensive User Interaction

Telecommuting is becoming more and more common. One of the authors of this book used a remote linkage during the actual writing and frequently communicated with editors and others through electronic mail. An even more dramatic example, however, is shown here as Ralph Bothne trades currencies worldwide from his California home office through the use of specially designed software and satellite linkups. (Charles O'Rear/Westlight.)

Sam Walton, used teleconferences to talk directly with employees during Saturday morning meetings.[19] Boeing has also used videoconferencing to communicate more quickly and completely across its sprawling Seattle facilities.[20]

Telecommuting refers to having employees perform their work at home through the use of computers connected to the organization's computer. This is an electronic version of cottage industries, where the product is produced in people's houses and collected at a central location for distribution. Companies such as IBM, American Express, Johnson & Johnson, J. C. Penney, and Blue Cross and Blue Shield find that this approach saves them office space and enables them to obtain the productivity of good people who otherwise might resist commuting to a central workplace.[21]

Networking involves connecting independent computers directly together so that they can function in interrelated ways. Direct access to common software and databases is gained more easily in this way than through the use of telephone connections between computers. Electronic communications can also be made quicker and more responsive to individuals through the use of a network. Networks at one organizational level can then be linked to others to establish a true information system for the organization. In this way Local Area Networks (LANs) can be linked. Still to come are Integrated Services Digital Networks (ISDNs), which will link computers and other machines through the use of digital cabling with jacks much like those used for telephones, and Electronic Data Interchanges (EDIs), which enable exact copies of a company's forms to be transmitted from one unit to another.[22]

Artificial intelligence (AI) refers to attempts to have computers simulate human decision processes.

Artificial Intelligence   **Artificial intelligence (AI)** refers to attempts to have computers simulate human decision processes. Although many exciting projects are going on in this area, applications are still rather scarce.[23] However, some systems are coming into use, such as the maintenance system at Bechtel and Westinghouse's on-line diagnostics for turbines.[24] The most common ones are decision support systems, knowledge-based systems, and expert systems.[25] As discussed earlier in this chapter, decision support systems are advanced management information systems designed to provide the information needed by managers for particular decisions. Knowledge-based systems are somewhat broader systems that can provide support for more general activities. Expert systems attempt, as much as possible, to capture the expertise of a human in software.[26]

Expert systems build on series of rules to move from a set of data to a decision recommendation.

The last-mentioned systems, **expert systems,** build on series of rules, frequently if-then rules, to move from a set of data to a decision recommendation. Boeing has been developing expert systems for various uses for some time. One is known as CASE (connector assembly specification expert). CASE produces assembly procedure instructions for each of the five thousand electrical connectors on an airplane. Where it used to take more than forty minutes of searching through twenty thousand pages of printed material, it now takes only a few minutes to get a computer printout for a specific connector.[27] Working with Texas Instruments, Campbell developed an expert system to capture the expertise of a manager in one of its soup kettle operations.[28] Martin Marietta has developed an expert system to assist in air traffic control.[29] Expert systems are being developed to aid managers in a variety of tasks, including more interpersonal tasks such as providing performance feedback to subordinates.[30]

Executive information technology (EIT) is being developed to help managers improve product and process quality as well as customer service. Motorola Codex, for instance, is using such a system.[31] This technology is kind of a combination of an expert system and a decision support system to specifically assist the executive level of an organization with monitoring and managing the activities of the organization.

Hypertext   In most information systems, the user may progress from one level to another in linear fashion. In a hypertext system, the user is able to move in any direction through the information to acquire what is necessary for the particular task at hand. Although the technology behind hypertext possesses many elements associated with artificial intelligence, it should be considered a separate information technology. Hypertext systems have been used in advanced help systems, on-line encyclopedias, and some programs that require a lot of user interaction. Hypertext systems tend to be complicated to develop. However, because they are extremely easy to learn and use, they hold tremendous promise for the future.

Many of these new technologies are being combined, and some of them are being combined in devices intended to fit in the palm of your hand.[32] Sharp, EO Inc., General Magic, and Apple are introducing products during 1993 with varying combinations of software and hardware to facilitate telecommuting and networking over long distances. As interactive, multimedia devices become more commonplace, further developments are highly likely.

Managing Information Systems

Like all other aspects of organizations, information systems, once developed, must be managed. In this section of the chapter, we look at that issue.

Integrating Information Systems

Throughout this chapter, the plural *information systems* has been used because most organizations actually use more than one system. Most middle-size to large organizations, for instance, have a marketing system, a production system, and a human resources system.[33] As indicated in Exhibit 23.4, these different information systems must be integrated or linked so that the different kinds of information can merge to form even more useful information.

Integrating systems is not easy. The production system might have been installed on an IBM computer. The marketing system, on the other hand, may use special-purpose computers developed by Intel. Wang computers may be used by the human resources department. Linking these different systems that were developed and that run on different hardware and with different software may be very difficult or even impossible.[34]

Exhibit 23.4

Integrating Information Systems

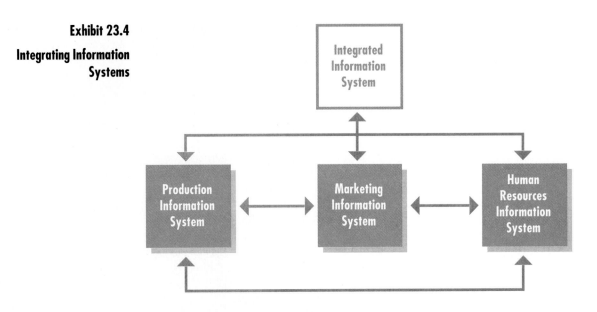

Had all the systems been developed at one time, this problem would have been avoided. But developing all of them at once is expensive, and information needs rarely occur at the same intensity. Therefore, most such systems are developed piecemeal. Again, if a common standard for hardware and software were adopted, integration would be much easier, but both hardware and software change and improve so rapidly that agreeing on a standard for even a few years at a time can be very difficult. Luckily, some more recent developments in hardware and software are making it easier to develop the necessary links across information systems. Linked systems, which could be used by virtually any company, enable managers to use electronic mail, access information needed to make decisions, and handle virtually all routine business using only a single, integrated information system.[35] Some of these systems are discussed elsewhere in the chapter.

Using Systems

Information systems must be used to be of value. You might think that information should somehow be just where you want it when you want it. The reality, of course, is that information must be sought, and learning to use the system to obtain information is critical to the success of the system. For that reason, then, organizations need to spend considerable time and effort to ensure that information systems are easy to use, or user friendly. Well-designed, user-friendly systems can quickly be used, even by those who have had no prior experience with computers, such as very senior workers.[36]

User-friendly systems are designed so that users can examine and easily modify information.

User-friendly information systems are typically designed so that users can examine and easily modify information to maximize its usefulness. The Travelers Corporation uses a team of trained nurses to review health insurance claims. They can access the system and review the medical diagnoses provided with each claim. Using this information, they can determine whether or not a second medical opinion is warranted before a surgical procedure is approved. The nurses then add their decision to the data on the claim form for other users of the information.[37]

The use of an information system is one measure of its effectiveness. However, many such systems are not, in fact, used because they require considerable computer fluency. Recent developments are changing that situation.

Robert Kidder, CEO of Duracell, can do more in one hour using a new user-friendly information system than he previously could in several hours. The system lets him begin at one level and progress into more and more detail as he desires. He can examine performance across divisions and then probe a division that is out of line with others to try to determine why. The system

Computer systems are becoming so user-friendly that you can even talk to them. One of the authors of this book has a system that enables him to run all normal Windows commands by voice. Here Caroline Chin Reisinger controls her workstation using Cite, a product of Qualix Group of San Mateo, California. (Andy Freeberg.)

makes it possible to do all this quickly and easily without upsetting the people in the division he is investigating and, thus, gets used rather than just sitting idle.[38]

The use of a remote control, a touch screen, or a mouse seems particularly appropriate where the user is not a touch typist.[39] Such devices, however, may not be needed in the future since many schools are training virtually all students to operate keyboards. Keyboard mastery is becoming a symbol of high status rather than low status, as it has been to many managers. Further, voice command systems are becoming more accessible and enable the user to access most commands orally. More importantly, though, software that enables users to browse through information in almost any direction based on their experience or even hunches makes the system more friendly and powerful. Such software, known as hypertext, is just beginning to be used for information systems and promises to be a powerful aid in the future.

Organizations and Information Systems

Whether informal or formal, information systems are clearly an important part of organizations. They are not, however, panaceas. They are only tools of management, and, although they can have very beneficial effects, they are also limited. Table 23.2 outlines some of those effects and limitations, which we will now explore.

Effects of Information Systems on Organizations

Information systems have effects at several different levels. They affect the performance of the organization, the organization's structure and design, and the people within the organization. There are a variety of measures used by organizations to assess the performance of information systems and their impact on organizations, and the appropriate one must be matched to the goals of each individual organization.[40]

Performance   There seems to be a growing consensus that information systems do enhance performance. The U.S. Forest Service recently installed an information system to assist it in evalu

Table 23.2

Effects and Limitations of Information Systems

Effects	Limitations

1. On Performance
  a. They tend to save money.
  b. They generally improve performance.
 	
2. On Organizational Structure
  a. A separate unit is created to oversee the information system.
  b. The organization becomes flatter because fewer managers are needed.
 	
3. On Behavior
  a. Some employees feel isolated.
  b. Others experience job enrichment.
  c. Some can work at home more.
  d. Some new work groups may be formed.
	1. They are costly to develop.
	2. They may be difficult to learn.
	3. Their information can be overly valued.
	4. They cannot handle all complex problems.
	5. Operators may misuse them.
	6. Operators may become discouraged and reject them.
	7. They are dependent on electric power sources.

Information systems affect performance, organizational structure, and behavior.

ating how to respond to forest fires. In the past every fire was attacked the morning after it was reported. The costs of such efforts could run to $10 million for a major fire. The new information system, however, automatically figures in such natural fire breaks as rivers, enabling some fires to be contained at far lower costs. General Electric, Kmart, and American Airlines also are companies reporting high levels of satisfaction with the performance of their information systems.[41]

So pervasive can be the effects of information systems that it is important that organizations monitor their environments carefully when developing them. *The Environment of Management: Home Depot's Environmentally Sensitive* shows how Home Depot was able to use such monitoring to tremendously benefit the organization and emerge as a dominant competitor in a highly competitive industry.

Organizational Structure   Since most organizations create a separate unit to oversee their information system, its first impact on organizational structure is the creation of that unit. In some cases the head of that unit or the person overseeing all information needs of the firm is a newly created position, the chief information officer, or CIO (discussed more in Chapter 19).[42] The more profound effect of information systems on organizational structures is, however, that with more and better information available, fewer managers, particularly those at middle levels, are needed. IBM, for instance, has eliminated a layer of management in this way, and its span of management may be greatly enlarged through the impact of information systems.[43]

Behavior   The behavioral effects of information systems are not yet well understood. Some individuals feel isolated because they spend their time interacting with computers instead of people. Others enjoy the new technology and are excited about having their jobs enriched in this way. Some will be able to work at home rather than at a central office and be able to spend more time with their families with no detrimental performance effects. New groupings of personnel may form around electronic bulletin board systems. But since there appear to be considerable learning experiences with such systems, the long-lasting behavioral effects will not be fully evaluated or understood for several years to come.

The Environment of Management

Home Depot's Environmentally Sensitive

Taking advantage of its environment, Home Depot has become spectacularly successful. Tying itself to retail consumers rather than construction-trade customers, it has garnered the largest share of the highly competitive building supplies market. With twenty-seven thousand employees and revenues in excess of $5 billion, it is the clear leader in that industry.

To accomplish its goals, Home Depot makes extensive use of technology. It has point-of-sale technology to enable it to keep close track of what is selling and what is not. It can quickly check with other nearby stores to help a customer lo-

cate merchandise that has been sold out in one store. Indeed, its customer service orientation couples very nicely with its technology to assure availability and service at reasonable prices. Home Depot can also tell manufacturers what to make, in what colors, how much to ship, and when. That ability enables Home Depot to be even more efficient. It began to outgrow its information system, however, in the late 1980s and began to replace it with a new one during the early 1990s.

Home Depot's sensitivity to its customers is also apparent with regard to employees. Employees have been known to stand up and cheer when the CEO comes around. But its sensitivity is also manifest in its approach to the environment. It is working with Mindis Recycling to erect a free-standing recycling center in a Home Depot parking lot to contribute to environmental action.[44] ∎

Limitations of Information Systems

The most obvious limitation of information systems is cost. They are expensive to develop, largely because each one must be tailored to fit particular organizational needs. This limitation is closely followed by learning difficulties. Since most information systems involve doing things differently, and hopefully better, everyone involved must learn the new and different way. Although these two limitations are relatively obvious, they are by no means the only ones.

For one thing, the information derived from an information system may be overly valued. There are those who assign great credibility to information from computers even when the information is actually very rough. Moreover, some tasks or problems simply cannot be handled by information systems. Highly complex tasks or problems may necessitate human intervention, and if people depend upon a system too much, its information can become dysfunctional.

Another problem is that some managers improperly use information systems. Many electronic mail systems when first installed become cluttered with graffiti, messages, and notes left from unknown parties saying all manner of things. This initial period of using the system as much for sport as for business may last weeks or even months. Then, if the system is not user friendly, some managers cease using it. The manager who gives up too soon may fail to eventually realize the power of the new communication system, which may be substantial. And, of course, any organization that does not provide for electrical power failures is asking for trouble.

Implications of Information Systems

We have considered some of the dramatic changes and effects on management caused by innovations in computers and information systems. Three implications are especially relevant. First, the advent of computer networks and electronic mail promises greatly to enhance productivity in the workplace. Managers will have much greater access to information, will be able to sort and process that information rapidly, and will be able to communicate with others quickly. Second, it will be even more important for managers to remain abreast of breakthroughs and changes. As new developments in information systems are unveiled and new applications developed, managers will need to assess how and to what degree their organization can effectively use these. Third, every organization will have to contend with issues of control and coordination. For instance, the Hartford

Insurance Group tried a program that allowed employees to work at home on computers, but it was soon abandoned because supervisors had trouble coordinating work and complained that they were losing touch with their work groups. Although widespread telecommuting has been slow to develop, its potential advantages—allowing the disabled to work, using less office space, providing greater work flexibility, and so forth—suggest that managers will have to work even harder in the future to make it possible.[45]

Chapter Summary

Information is data organized in a meaningful way. Data are merely facts and figures, unorganized pieces of information. A system is an interrelated set of elements that function as a whole to accomplish some purpose. Because information is so important to contemporary management, it must be accurate, timely, complete, and relevant.

There are five basic interrelated components of any information system. In a computerized system, getting the data into the system involves input devices. Analysis and processing are done by a central processor. Storage is accomplished through one or more media, and in many cases more than one medium is used for back-up purposes. Making the information available to users is also accomplished through a variety of output devices. Finally, the control system usually involves some form of computer software as well as human monitoring.

Information systems should ensure that proper information is available when needed. Designing information systems involves knowing one's information system needs as well as the kinds of systems that exist or might be developed. Information system needs are determined by the kind of organization, its environment, and its size.

Most managers maintain informal, unstructured systems of information, but formal, structured systems predominate in large organizations. Systems designed to handle routine and recurring transactions within an organization are known as transaction-processing systems. A management information system, or MIS, is a system that gathers, organizes, summarizes, and reports data for use by managers. A decision support system, or DSS, is a system that automatically searches for, analyzes, summarizes, and reports information needed by a manager for a particular decision. All these systems can further be classified as central or distributed. Organizations must be careful to match their various needs with the many systems available.

Although integrating systems is not easy, it must be done if the total information system is to be effective. Effectiveness is also increased when the systems are user friendly. Many new systems are becoming easier to learn and use. Information systems affect the performance of the organization, the organization's structure and design, and the people within the organization. There seems to be a growing consensus that information systems do enhance performance. Information systems also have some limitations. They are expensive and can be difficult to learn to use. In addition, the information derived from them may be overvalued, and they may be improperly used or not used at all. And, of course, computerized information systems depend upon electricity to operate and so are vulnerable during power outages.

The Manager's Vocabulary

information
data
system
input devices
central processor
output devices

information system needs
information requirements analysis
transaction-processing system (TPS)
management information system (MIS)
decision support system (DSS)
telecommunications

teleconferencing
telecommuting
networking
artificial intelligence (AI)
expert systems

Review Questions

1. What is the difference between information and data? Why is that difference important?
2. What are the major components of information systems?
3. What are the different types of information systems and technologies?
4. What are the key considerations in managing information systems?
5. What are the effects and limitations of information systems?

Analysis Questions

1. Should computerized information systems be duplicates of paper information systems? Why or why not?
2. Do information needs differ so much across organizational levels that different information systems have to be developed, or could an organization really get by with just one system?
3. Many people refer to the current period of economic development as the Information Age. Do you think we are really in the Information Age? Why or why not?
4. Do you think that the chief information officer of an organization could become too powerful? If so, how could that be prevented or corrected? If not, why not?
5. Comment on this quotation: "The Turing Test of a computer system is designed to evaluate whether or not a user can tell that it is a computer system rather than a human being providing advice. A system that passes is then a computer system that is indistinguishable from a human. But who would want such a system? Humans are cheaper. What I want is a computer that is readily distinguishable from a human because it is better— it has no emotional problems, does not complain about hard work or overtime, wants no bonuses or retirement, makes no errors in judgment, and won't talk back."

Self-Assessment

Computer Anxiety Index

Introduction While information has become a competitive advantage for most organizations, some managers find it difficult to use information technology. These managers suffer from computer anxiety. This self-assessment measures computer anxiety. You can use it to measure your computer anxiety and later to measure your co-workers' anxiety level.

Instructions Respond "Y" (yes) or "N" (no) to indicate how closely each of the following statements corresponds to your beliefs.

_____ 1. I think it is hard to interpret many computer printouts.

_____ 2. I look forward to using a computer at work.

_____ 3. I don't think I can learn an advanced computer programming language.

_____ 4. The more you practice with computers, the better you become.

_____ 5. You can become too dependent on computers.

_____ 6. The technical aspects of computers don't scare me.

_____ 7. I worry about hitting the wrong computer key and losing important data.

_____ 8. I think I can keep up with the advancements in computer technology.

_____ 9. You have to be a genius to understand some of the new computer software.

_____ 10. Computers are necessary tools in most work and educational settings.

For interpretation, turn to the back of the book.

Source: Robert K. Heinssen, Jr., Carol R. Glass, and Luanne A. Knight, "Assessing Computer Anxiety: Development and Validation of the Computer Anxiety Scale," *Computers in Human Behavior*, 1987, pp. 49–59. Copyright 1987, Pergamon Press, Inc. Used with permission.

Skill Builder

Decision Support for the Campus Bookstore

Purpose Decision support systems are very powerful computerized tools that can assist managers in making timely decisions. This skill builder focuses on the *human resources model* and the *administrative management model*. It will help you develop the *facilitator role* of the human resources model and the *moni-*

tor role of the administrative management model. One of the skills of the facilitator is making decisions and one of the roles of the monitor is analyzing information.

Introduction It is often difficult to develop decision support systems that provide pertinent and timely data for decision makers. But once the system is built, decisions are made more timely and effectively. In this skill builder, you will have the opportunity to try your hand at developing just such a system.

Instructions Form a group of eight to ten students. Read over the scenario below. Next, develop a decision support system that you feel will provide the bookstore manager with timely and pertinent information for making decisions. Below the scenario are some areas you might want to focus on as you prepare your report on the decision support system you have designed.

Scenario: The manager of the campus bookstore has requested that the class determine the essential features of a decision support system that would enable its book buyers to do their jobs better. Specifically how much should the book buyers pay for used books brought in by the students at the end of a particular semester? Second, how many of each book should they buy at different prices? What price should they charge students who

purchase the books for use in subsequent semesters? How many new books should the bookstore manager buy each semester? The manager indicates that the system should be compatible with the store's personal computer system, which enables each of the six book buyers to have access to a common database through the network. The manager envisions a system that would enable the book buyer to call up all the pertinent information on the personal computer whenever an individual comes into the store with a book to sell.

1. What decisions does the store manager want to support?
2. What information do the buyers need?
3. Who is the source of this information? Is the information external or internal to the bookstore?
4. How will the system be kept current?

Source: Adapted from James H. Donnelly, Jr., James L. Gibson, and John M. Ivancevich, *Fundamentals of Management,* 8th ed., published by Richard D. Irwin, Inc. © Richard D. Irwin, Inc., 1971, 1975, 1978, 1981, 1984, 1987, 1990, and 1992.

CONCLUDING CASES

23.1   Dillard's Department Store, Inc.

Based in Little Rock, Arkansas, Dillard's has grown from a single store in 1948 to one of the largest department store chains in the United States. The founder, William Dillard, was still touring more than one hundred fifty stores a year when he was seventy-six years old in 1991, and his five children all work for the company, including its president, Bill Dillard. Dillard's growth during the 1980s included numerous acquisitions. Dillard's also maintained an average gross margin of 37 percent, higher than virtually all of its competitors. By 1990 Dillard's had become a $3 billion business and was ranked among the top five national department stores along with J. C. Penney, Mervyn's, Macy's Northeast, and Nordstrom.

During the 1960s Dillard's developed its own computerized information system, known as Quick Response. With computerized point-of-sale cash registers, that system keeps track of departmental inventory on an hourly basis and automatically reorders fast-moving items. Thus, an executive can see how any given product is selling in any given store on an hour-by-hour basis in a matter of seconds. This sort of close monitoring of sales in each store has enabled Dillard's to not only keep its prices low and sales high but also to get its merchandise onto the floor faster than most competitors (hence the name of the system). Further, it enables Dillard's to keep track of how every salesperson is doing, to provide raises to those who exceed their quotas, and to assist those who do not to find employment elsewhere.

Dillard's has also benefited from advances in computer-aided design (CAD) systems. On-screen analysis has proven very useful in analyzing how store floor plans can affect sales and profit margins. Time, though, is the big advantage. A complete 200,000-square-foot floor plan can be developed in about a week using a CAD system, whereas it had previously taken four months.

As a result, Dillard's, J. C. Penney, and others are trying to reduce the number and size of promotional activities for many of their lines. Dillard's continues, though, to retain its focus on having clean, well-lit stores stocked with merchandise that appeals to middle- and upper-middle-class customers. Despite its success, however, Dillard's, like many other department store chains, has found that the high level of promotional activity has cut into its profits.[46]

Discussion Questions

1. Which concepts presented in the chapter are illustrated in the Dillard's case? Cite specific examples.
2. What are the major characteristics of the information system at Dillard's?
3. What are the strengths and weaknesses of the Quick Response system? How might the weaknesses be offset?
4. Do you feel that Dillard's success will continue? Why or why not?

23.2   United Parcel Service

Jim Casey and Claude Ryan, both teen-agers, began the American Messenger company in 1907 in Seattle. In 1913 the name was changed to reflect the business that had developed; it became the Merchants Parcel Company. By 1918 it was handling all deliveries for three of Seattle's largest department stores. It began to expand operations and changed its name to United Parcel Service. By 1930 it had expanded from the West Coast to New York City. During the 1950s UPS expanded its services to include door-to-door parcel pickup and delivery and got into the air express business. By the 1980s it had become the largest delivery service in the United States. UPS now operates in nearly two hundred countries worldwide.

Jim Casey adopted many of the time-saving methods of Frank Gilbreth, the time-and-motion study pioneer. As a result of Casey's influence (he ran the organization for more than fifty years), efficiency dominates the firm. Drivers' seats were beveled to enable drivers to get out and make pickups and deliveries more quickly, for instance. But technology has come to be a major factor in efficiency. UPS maintains computerized daily records of driver performance and, as one part of its stress on efficiency, has supervisors ride along with the worst drivers to help them improve. Even more importantly, it uses computers to monitor every aspect of performance in the firm.

By the early 1990s UPS had more than sixty thousand drivers and handled more than a million accounts in the United States alone. To conduct this vast business it used more than seventy thousand hand-held pen computers. These were linked through more than three hundred local area networks into its global communications network. This gigantic information system enabled it to trace the flow of more than 12 million packages each day.

UPS also developed its own version of the bar code to handle even more information than usual. It is called a dense code because it packs about twice as much information in about the same space. Scanners can read a package's origin, destination, contents, and price and send that information to the central computer system.

This use of technology has enabled UPS to expand into Europe, providing door-to-door service throughout the European Community countries. Through an advanced data link in airplane cockpits, it is also able to compete in the air freight business. UPS's technology is designed so that it is easy to connect to its computer information system. This kind of easy connection has enabled UPS to put package shipping centers in supermarkets to make service even more convenient for customers.[47]

Discussion Questions

1. What similarities and differences can you note between the information systems of Dillard's and of UPS?
2. What components that were discussed in the chapter can you identify in the description of UPS's information system? Cite specific examples.
3. What strengths and weaknesses can you suggest about UPS's information system? How might the weaknesses be reduced?
4. How might UPS make its information system even better in the future?

Part Six   Controlling

Self-Assessment

Who Controls Your Life?

Introduction Throughout this part of the book, we have discussed the procedure for implementing control in an organization. However, you can also exercise control over your life. This self-assessment examines your attitude toward your ability to take control over what happens to you.

Instructions Read the following statements and indicate whether you agree more with Choice A or Choice B.

1. A. _____ Making a lot of money is largely a matter of getting the right breaks.
   B. _____ Promotions are earned through hard work and persistence.
2. A. _____ I have noticed that there is usually a direct connection between how hard I study and the grades I get.

B. _____ Many times the reactions of teachers seem haphazard to me.

3. A. _____ The number of divorces indicates that more and more people are not trying to make their marriages work.

B. _____ Marriage is largely a gamble.

4. A. _____ It is silly to think that one can really change another person's basic attitudes.

B. _____ When I am right I can convince others.

5. A. _____ Getting promoted is really a matter of being a little luckier than the next person.

B. _____ In our society a person's future earning power depends upon his or her ability.

6. A. _____ If one knows how to deal with people, they are really quite easily led.

B. _____ I have little influence over the way other people behave.

7. A. _____ The grades I make are the result of my own efforts; luck has little or nothing to do with it.

B. _____ Sometimes I feel that I have little to do with the grades I get.

8. A. _____ People like me can change the course of world affairs if we make ourselves heard.

B. _____ It is only wishful thinking to believe that one can really influence what happens in our society at large.

9. A. _____ A great deal that happens to me is probably a matter of chance.

B. _____ I am the master of my fate.

10. A. _____ Getting along with people is a skill that must be practiced.

B. _____ It is almost impossible to figure out how to please some people.

For interpretation, turn to the back of the book.

Source: Julian B. Rotter, "External Control and Internal Control," *Psychology Today,* June 1971, p. 42. Reprinted with permission from *Psychology Today* Magazine. Copyright © 1971 (Sussex Publishers, Inc.).

Skill Builder

Paper Plane Corporation

Purpose Throughout this part of the book, we have discussed operations management and methods to control the operations of organizations. This skill builder allows you to put it all together and try your hand at operating and controlling a simulated organization. This skill builder focuses on the *administrative management model.* It will help you develop the *coordinator role* of the administrative management model. This skill builder expands on all three of the coordinator's skills: planning, organizing, and controlling.

Introduction This exercise is designed to specifically apply planning and control concepts to improve organizational performance.

Instructions Your group is the complete work force for Paper Plane Corporation. Established in 1943, Paper Plane has led the market in paper plane production. Currently under new management, the company is contracting to make aircraft for the U.S. Air Force. You must establish a plan and organization to produce these aircraft. You must make your contract with the Air Force under the following conditions:

1. The Air Force will pay $20,000 per airplane.
2. The aircraft must pass a strict inspection.
3. A penalty of $25,000 per airplane will be subtracted for failure to meet the production requirements.
4. Labor and other overhead will be computed at $300,000.
5. Cost of materials will be $3,000 per bid plane. If you bid for ten but make only eight, you must pay the cost of materials for those you failed to make or that did not pass inspection.

Your group should choose a manager and an inspector; the remaining participants should be employees. Your instructor will tell you when to begin.

You will report your production and profits to the class. Be prepared to explain how you planned, organized, and controlled for the production of your planes.

Source: James H. Donnelly, Jr., James L. Gibson, and John M. Ivancevich, *Fundamentals of Management,* 7th ed., published by Richard D. Irwin, Inc. © Richard D. Irwin, Inc., 1971, 1975, 1978, 1981, 1984, 1987, and 1990.

Managerial Careers

Some people spend their whole lives pursuing a single business career; others begin one career only to switch to another later in life; still others may have several careers throughout their lives. Some people work for others throughout their entire careers; others operate their own businesses. There is no single career path that leads to success. Each of you must find the one that best suits you.

You have learned that managers exist at all levels of organizations and in all areas. To understand who managers are and what they do at a more personal level, you need to know more about managerial careers. Managers work long hours; their tasks are fragmented; the activities in which they engage are brief; they are involved with other people; and most of their communications are oral.[1] They function in all walks of life, all organizations, and all environments, including foreign countries. Indeed, many young managers are deciding to pursue part or all of their careers outside the United States, since there are many career opportunities in both developed and developing economies. Moving from a nonmanagerial position to a managerial one is a very significant change in a person's career and should not be done without considerable thought.[2]

What Is a Career?

Hard work, long hours, and difficult personal adjustments are all part of a managerial career, and challenge, recognition, and a good income are usually also part of the package. If that sounds interesting, perhaps a managerial career is for you. But exactly what do we mean when we talk about a career?

Many people think of themselves as having jobs, not careers. Yet they do have careers. A **career** is the sequence of attitudes and behaviors that you perceive to be related to work experience during your life.[3] The term *career* can be applied to every walk of life; everyone can have a career. A secretary who considers how she can improve her current position and what that might lead to in a few years has a career in mind. A cook who is learning new recipes and trying to better his work situation has a career.

Careers are important because they help people shape their lives. As an ancient proverb implies: "Give me a fish, and I will eat for today; teach me to fish, and I will eat for the rest of my life."[4] Having a career enables us to respond to changing conditions in our work. It also enables us to tolerate some of the boring and frustrating parts of our jobs because they are necessary to move us to the next stage of our career.

Career Choices   Your choice of a career is important, but you must remember that careers can and do change, so no choice is forever. The career you decide to prepare for and follow when you are sixteen may very well be different from the one you select when you are twenty-six. That one in turn may be different from the one that you choose at thirty-six.

One career choice is which **economic sector** in which to work. Every sector of our economy needs qualified managers. Employment in agriculture has fallen, but in other sectors it has grown or fluctuated. The service sector, wholesale and retail trade, and state and local government have seen substantial increases in employment during the past forty years. Employment in mining and the federal government has stayed relatively stable over that same period. But no matter what the employment opportunities are, managers are needed everywhere.

You can also choose the military for part or all of your career. Military employment is substantial even in times of peace, so there is an ever-present need for competent managers in all branches of the service, as well as in the Coast Guard and the merchant marines.

Not-for-profit organizations, which have goals other than making a profit, need managers too. Religious, social service, and charitable organizations and foundations must be managed even though making a profit is not their fundamental purpose. You should consider these organizations too when you are making a career choice.

Another career decision that you may face is whether to pursue your managerial career overseas. To find out more about employment outside the United States, contact the addresses shown in Table A1.1.

A great many people in the United States want more than anything else to be their own boss, to own and operate a business.[5] This desire is part of the American dream. Owning and operating a business (usually a small one) clearly involves management, so another choice you have is whether to pursue your managerial career in this field. Small-business activity increased during the late 1970s and 1980s, and pursuing a managerial career in this area is something that many people will choose.

Managers also manage different groups of people: clerical personnel, technical personnel, and even professionals such as engineers, scientists, and physicians. If you choose to pursue your managerial career in one of these areas, you may find that specialized training is valuable. Office administration deals primarily with the management of clerical personnel, whereas hospital administration, obviously, focuses on hospitals.

Choosing a Career   As indicated in Exhibit A1.1, making a career choice involves three steps. First you must find out about yourself.[6] Next you must research possible careers. Finally, you must match yourself with a

Exhibit A1.1   Making Your Career Choice

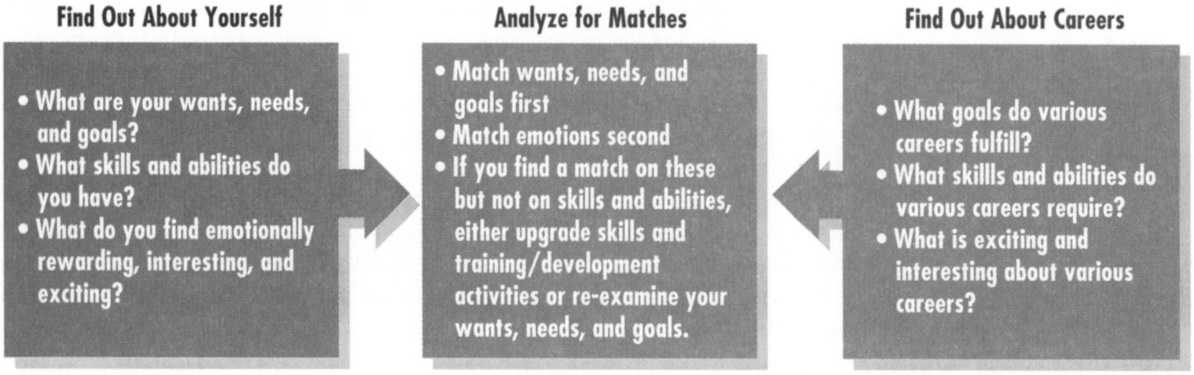

Find Out About Yourself

- What are your wants, needs, and goals?
- What skills and abilities do you have?
- What do you find emotionally rewarding, interesting, and exciting?

Analyze for Matches

- Match wants, needs, and goals first
- Match emotions second
- If you find a match on these but not on skills and abilities, either upgrade skills and training/development activities or re-examine your wants, needs, and goals.

Find Out About Careers

- What goals do various careers fulfill?
- What skillls and abilities do various careers require?
- What is exciting and interesting about various careers?

Table A1.1

Finding Jobs Abroad

Government

Department of State

For some jobs you must first pass the Foreign Service examination. Inquiries about employment in the Foreign Service should be directed to:

PER/REE/REC
P.O. Box 9317
Rosslyn Station
Arlington, VA 22209

Department of Defense

Contact the Civilian Personnel Office at any Defense installation and they can put you in touch with the Department of Defense Automated Overseas Employment Referral Program.

Peace Corps

Call toll free 1-800-424-8580.

Other Federal Agencies

Department of Commerce
Office of Foreign Service Personnel
Room 3813
14th & Constitution Avenues, NW
Washington, D.C. 20230

Voice of America
300 Independence Ave., SW
Washington, D.C. 20547

Agency for International Development (AID)
320 21st St., NW
Washington, D.C. 20523

Business

Chamber of Commerce of the U.S.
1615 H St., NW
Washington, D.C. 20062

Work, Study, Travel Abroad: The Whole World Handbook (New York: St. Martin's Press for the Council on International Education Exchange).

General reference

Aulick, June L., *Looking for Employment in Foreign Countries,* 8th ed. (New York: World Academy Press, 1990).

Source: Adapted from Gary Dessler, "How to Find Employment Outside the United States," *Bryan-College Station Eagle,* August 24, 1986, p. 5F. Reprinted by permission: Tribune Media Services.

career. Simple as this seems, it can be difficult to do, but you should try to go through this process periodically during your life.

Ask yourself what you really want out of life. What are your overall goals and aspirations? Do you want to lead a peaceful life? Do you want to invent something? Do you want to be rich? Determine what it would take to achieve your goals. Do you have the necessary skills and abilities? Finally, you need to ask yourself what you find interesting and exciting. What do you like to do?

Now you need to ask these same questions about many possible careers. What are the goals associated with various careers? A career as a professional forester may lead to very different accomplishments than a career as a politician. What do the careers that interest you require in terms of skills and abilities? What do they provide in terms of emotional involvement and excitement?

Finally, look for matches between your goals and those of different careers, as well as for matches in terms of interests. If you find one or more careers that match your goals and interests fairly well, examine the required skills and abilities. If you do not have those skills and abilities, can you get them by going to school or by reading? Counselors and books are available to help you work through these steps.[7]

Life Stages and Career Stages

Life Stages   We can think of our lives as taking place in a series of **life stages:** childhood (which consists of infancy, early childhood, play age, and school age), adolescence, young adulthood, adulthood, and senescence or old age.[8] Each of these stages is associated with an age range, although the years are only approximate. For instance, childhood lasts until about age thirteen, young adulthood until around age twenty-five, and old age until we die.

Movement from one stage to another can be turbulent, but things generally settle down again after each transition. Obviously, physiological needs are critical in infancy, whereas esteem and security may be more important in old age. Individual needs vary in these stages, although not in well-understood or predictable ways.

Career Stages   Closely related to life stages is the concept of **career stages.** There is no career stage that corresponds to childhood, but each of the others has a counterpart. Career stages are even less exact than life stages in terms of the age at which they occur. As indicated in Exhibit A1.2, there are four career stages: exploration, establishment, maintenance, and decline.

The **exploration stage** is a period of self-examination and occupational exploration. People at this stage are usually young, eager to succeed, and ready to upgrade their skills. The exploration stage begins with commitment to training of some kind—vocational school, college, or the military, for instance—and people frequently take part-time employment while they are still in school. Some schools give special help during this stage; for example, Baldwin-Wallace College runs an assessment center to help students in career planning.[9] The exploration stage continues through the first or entry-level job, which is usually nonmanagerial, even for those who have a

Exhibit A1.2

Career Stages

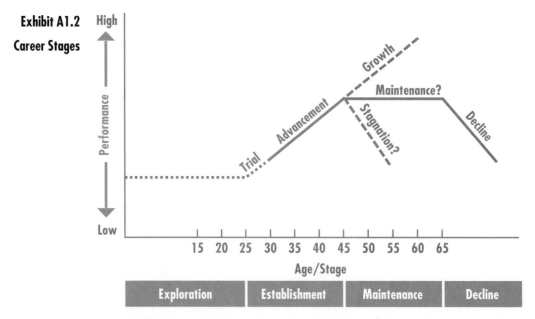

Source: Adapted from *Careers in Organizations*, by Douglas T. Hall. Copyright © 1976 by Scott, Foresman and Co. Reprinted by permission.

managerial career in mind. After all, there are about five times as many nonmanagerial jobs as managerial ones for people in the age groups usually found at this career stage.[10] Sometimes a period of learning the actual work of certain jobs is useful or even necessary before an employee moves into the managerial role in an organization. The exploration stage may also involve beginning one's own business. The dotted line in Exhibit A1.2 suggests that performance is unpredictable in this stage, although some companies, such as the New York Telephone Company, are trying to improve this situation through training.[11]

The **establishment stage** begins with a trial period, shown by the continuation of the dotted line from the exploration stage. During this period the person might hold several jobs as he or she learns more about the occupational choices available. After the trial period, accomplishment and advancement occur. Now the person is settling down in a career, learning it, and performing well. He or she is becoming less dependent on others and more independent. The person is now forming an occupational identity, establishing relationships with those in the organization, and perhaps also developing a pattern of love, marriage, and/or family relationships.

Job hopping becomes even more common throughout this stage. Many people find that they can move up faster and earn more money by changing jobs. A former top executive at Wal-Mart, Jack Shewmaker, held eight jobs in eleven years before joining Wal-Mart. He stayed with Wal-Mart and rose from district manager in 1970, when he joined the firm, to president, a position he held from 1978 until 1984.[12] Job hopping occurs partly because companies go outside for top leaders. For example, Gould, Inc. recruited James F. McDonald from IBM to be its new CEO. In 1984 Digital Equipment Corporation brought in its new finance vice president from Ford Motor Company. A major consulting firm, the Hay Group Inc., found that companies using outsiders in key jobs exceeded rate-of-return goals more often than those that relied on insiders.[13]

The **maintenance stage** can follow one or more patterns. Individuals who are "making it" may simply extend the establishment stage by continuing growth in performance. This stage can also be a period of maintenance or leveling off, or of stagnation and early decline. Career changes may result from either of these latter two patterns, and the person will start over again. People at this stage of their career frequently begin to act as mentors for younger members of the organization, showing them the ropes and helping them along. They usually begin to re-examine their goals in life and to rethink their long-term career plans. Many managers are eager for continued success but are deeply troubled by the values they have to abandon along the way.[14] The only solution is to balance the demands of their career with the satisfaction derived from skills and sources of pleasure that do not revolve around money and power. This may mean quitting a job or passing up the chance for promotion.[15]

In the **decline stage,** which usually means the end of full-time employment, the person faces retirement and other end-of-career options. The overriding question is, "What do I do now?" Some people begin new careers and others level off, but an all-too-frequent pattern is one of decreasing performance. Individuals at this stage generally begin to recognize that they are growing old, and they adjust in a variety of ways—some positive, such as helping others, and some not so positive, such as becoming indifferent or even giving up.

Career Development

Your career is important to you, and the careers of members of organizations are important to the success of those organizations. **Career development** refers to a careful, systematic approach to ensuring that sound career choices are made. It involves both an individual element, career planning, and an organizational element, career management.[16]

Career Planning

Career planning is much like career choice, but it is more detailed and involves carefully specifying how to move within a career once the choice has been made. If you decide on a managerial career and want to achieve an executive-level position, just how do you go about it? What is the route to the top? Does the area in which you begin matter? Are there certain positions in which you must be sure to gain experience? Some companies, such as the accounting firm of William Younger, provide formal assistance in career planning.[17]

In career planning the first thing you should do is develop a written plan. Think in terms of where you want to be at the end of some long time period, say, in twenty years. Now, in order to be at that point in twenty years, where do you need to be in ten years? Work backward to develop an answer; then work backward again to see where you need to be in five years and in one year. Knowing where you need to be in one year to achieve your twenty-year goal should be vital information for shaping your decision today.

As you plan your career, you may become aware of deficiencies in your skills, experience, or abilities. You may discover, for instance, that in order to accomplish your ten-year objectives, you need to acquire a foreign language. You can start learning now. Recognizing what your deficiencies are provides you with the opportunity to rectify them through training or by moving to a new job to gain additional experience.

You should review your career plan from time to time—perhaps every three or four years, but no less frequently than every five years. This review will enable you to see whether you are accomplishing your objectives, whether you need to work harder, whether you need more training, development, and experience, or whether you need to rethink your objectives. This periodic review also serves to keep your long-term objectives in your mind so that they are not driven out by short-term crises.

If you are pursuing your career within an organization, you must develop your plan in conjunction with others in the organization. Talk with your superior to get his or her advice. If your company has a formal career management system, check with those who administer it to see whether your plan makes sense within the organization.

Career Management

Career management, the organizational element of career development, is done by a number of firms, including AT&T, Bank of America, General Electric, General Foods, General Motors, and Sears.[18] Career management is distinct from training and development programs, which most companies provide either in house (that is, they do the training themselves) or by sending employees to programs conducted by trade groups, universities, or consulting firms. Career management includes career counseling, career pathing, career resources planning, and career information systems.

Career counseling can be informal or formal. Informal advice provided by a superior to a subordinate is one form; another is that provided in interviews and performance evaluation sessions. A more formal method is to have special career counseling, provided by a personnel department, that is available to all personnel or only to those who are being moved down, up, or out of the organization.[19]

Career pathing refers to the identification of coherent progressions of jobs—tracks, routes, or career paths—that are of particular interest to the organization. As with counseling, these progressions may be either formal or informal. The organization may specify a path that follows a particular sequence; an example is a university that states that the positions of assistant professor and associate professor are the normal progression toward becoming a full professor. Or the path may be informal, in which case "everyone knows" that you must first hold jobs A and B to get to job C.

Although they are useful for planning purposes, career paths should not be taken as absolutes. The organization that insists that paths must proceed in certain ways is unable to recognize unique situations and exceptional talent when they occur. In the past, for instance, most executives got to the top by working in only a single firm, whereas today many executives work in several companies on their way to the top. The increasing number of women in executive positions is also bringing changes to traditional career paths.[20] A system that is not flexible enough to permit these changes will prevent some extremely talented people from reaching the top.

As indicated in Table A1.2, there is evidence that the new generation of executives is quite different from the old one. Career management systems must be prepared to deal with those differences. In addition, career paths are not always clear and predictable. Take, for example, the career of Robert C. Wright. Wright graduated from law school and served as an infantry lieutenant before joining General Electric as a staff lawyer. He soon left GE to join first one law firm and then another, but in two years he was back at GE, where he moved into manufacturing, then sales, and then finance. Most recently, he became chief executive of NBC. Wright is the kind of executive most corporations want, but his career would have been difficult to predict.[21]

Career resources planning refers to the use of careful planning techniques in career management. The organization makes plans and forecasts of personnel needs, develops charts that show the planned progressions of employees, prepares inventories of human resource needs based on assessments of existing personnel, and monitors the implementation of these plans. As shown in Exhibit A1.3, such a system can be very complex.

Career information systems are more than just internal job markets (which means that openings within the organization are announced on bulletin boards or in newsletters and memoranda, and members of the organization have a first shot at getting these jobs). Career information systems combine internal job markets with formal career counseling and the maintenance of a career information center for employees. Thus a career information system can motivate as well as develop the organization's employees.

Table A1.2

Changing Characteristics of Managers

The old generation	The new generation
Cautious	Eager to take risks
Insecure	Optimistic
Resistant to change	Flexible
Loyal to company	Willing to job-hop
Values job security	Wants to make impact
Male	Male or female
White	Ethnically diverse
A good day's work	Workaholic
Comfortable in bureaucracies	Craves autonomy, power
Conservative Republican	Independent
People-oriented	Numbers-oriented
Slide rules, legal pads	Computers, data networks
College degree	Advanced degree
Twenty-five-year career plan	Instant gratification

Source: Teresa Carson and John A. Byrne, "Fast-Track Kids," Reprinted from November 10, 1986 issue of *Business Week* by special permission, © 1986 by McGraw-Hill, Inc.

Exhibit A1.3   A Human Resource Planning and Development System

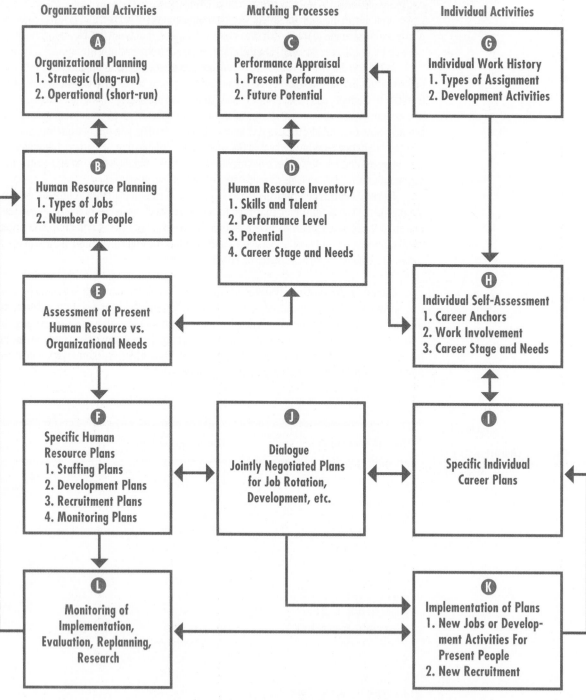

Organizational Activities   Matching Processes   Individual Activities

A Organizational Planning
1. Strategic (long-run)
2. Operational (short-run)

C Performance Appraisal
1. Present Performance
2. Future Potential

G Individual Work History
1. Types of Assignment
2. Development Activities

B Human Resource Planning
1. Types of Jobs
2. Number of People

D Human Resource Inventory
1. Skills and Talent
2. Performance Level
3. Potential
4. Career Stage and Needs

E Assessment of Present Human Resource vs. Organizational Needs

H Individual Self-Assessment
1. Career Anchors
2. Work Involvement
3. Career Stage and Needs

F Specific Human Resource Plans
1. Staffing Plans
2. Development Plans
3. Recruitment Plans
4. Monitoring Plans

J Dialogue Jointly Negotiated Plans for Job Rotation, Development, etc.

I Specific Individual Career Plans

L Monitoring of Implementation, Evaluation, Replanning, Research

K Implementation of Plans
1. New Jobs or Development Activities For Present People
2. New Recruitment

Source: Edgar H. Schein, *Career Dynamics: Matching Individual and Organizational Needs,* © 1978 by Addison-Wesley Publishing Company, Inc. Reprinted with permission of the publisher.

Women and Minorities

All too frequently, members of some groups have felt that managerial careers were closed to them, most often because people from that group had not yet entered the managerial ranks in sufficient numbers to set an example for others. When the potential pool of managerial talent is artificially or arbitrarily reduced in some way, our country suffers, because organizational effectiveness is not what it might be. Therefore, it is important to recognize that members of any group can and do become managers. Two groups—women and minorities—merit particular attention.[22] The number of women and minorities in executive and managerial positions has been steadily growing. From 1983 to 1989, women in these positions went from about 32 percent to 40 percent, blacks rose from 5 percent to 6 percent, and Hispanics went from 3 percent to 4 percent.[23]

Managerial Careers for Women

As shown in Exhibit A1.4, more and more women work every year. More than half the females over sixteen years old are now employed, and almost half of the working population now consists of women. Both of these statistics represent huge increases from conditions at the start of this century. For that matter, there has been significant growth in recent years.

As the number of working women has grown, so has the number of women managers. Many of these people own their own businesses. In fact, women-owned businesses were one of the fastest-growing parts of the American economic scene during the 1970s and 1980s. Despite the rapid growth and the fact that nearly three million businesses are owned by women, however, relatively little is known about the career pattern of successful businesswomen.[24] They certainly are not confined to small businesses; some women have excelled even in some of the largest corporations in the United States.[25]

Executive search firms have suggested that there are career differences between male and female corporate officers.[26] The men tend to be older and to have been with their companies longer. One study found that both groups worked fifty-five-hour weeks, although the men earned substantially more than the women. Further, most of the women felt that they had made great

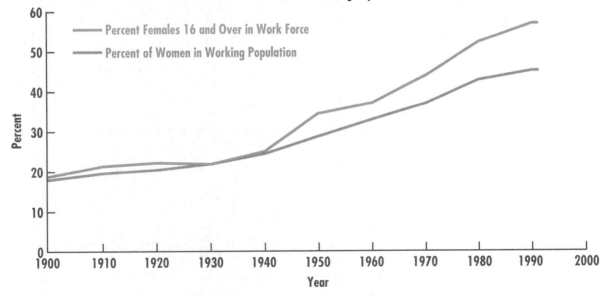

Exhibit A1.4   Women in the Working Population

Source: Data from *Information Please Almanac 1993* edited by Otto Johnson. Copyright © 1992 by Houghton Mifflin Company.

personal sacrifices to get where they were. Twenty percent had never married, as opposed to less than 1 percent of the men; 20 percent were separated or divorced, as opposed to about 4 percent of the men; 95 percent of the men had children, but more than half of the women were childless. Nevertheless, the number of women officers has dramatically risen over the past decade or so, and women have joined the boards of companies such as Black & Decker and SmithKline Beckman Corporation.[27] These women are experienced managers and do not hold these positions because they own or control the firms. Because there are different issues in the careers of men and women, women need to be particularly attentive to planning their careers.[28]

However, discrimination continues to plague women, especially in terms of salaries.[29] As of 1990, only 2 percent of top executives were women, and female vice presidents earned 42 percent less than their male counterparts.[30] By the mid-1980s women were dropping out of managerial positions more frequently than men. Lower salaries, smaller chances of making it to the top, unexciting job assignments (women most often end up in "the three p's"—purchasing, personnel, and public relations), and less autonomy than they desire seem to be the most common reasons.[31]

Companies such as Corning Glass, General Foods, General Motors, Honeywell, IBM, and Gannett are trying to do something to keep women in management. They are instituting flexible working hours and improving leave policies. Some allow employees to work at home, others help get a manager's spouse a new job when the employee is relocated. The recognition that the problem continues is itself a step toward improving conditions for women in managerial careers.[32] The number of women in management attests to the success of such efforts.

Managerial Careers for Minorities

Members of minority groups also succeed as managers and owners.[33] Table A1.3 indicates that a substantial number of businesses are owned by members of minority groups. The corporation is the most common legal arrangement for these minority-owned businesses, and partnerships are the least common form.

Government assistance exists in a variety of forms to help members of minority groups who are interested in starting and running their own businesses. The Minority Business Development Agency was begun in the Department of Commerce in 1969. The U.S. Department of the Interior, through the Bureau of Indian Affairs, began the Indian Business Development Fund in 1970 to help Native Americans secure funds for starting businesses. The Economic Development Administration began a Minority Contractors Assistance Program in 1971 to help minorities in the construction industry. Professional and technical assistance such as accounting and engineering help is provided under Section 406 of the Equal Opportunity Act. Some private groups, like the Cuban American Foundation, are also available to assist minorities in owning their own businesses.[34]

Table A1.3
Minority Business Owners*

Race	1987	1982
Blacks	14.6	11.3
Hispanics	20.9	14.3
Asian	57.0	43.2
Native Americans	11.8	8.8
* Firms per 1,000 population		

Government assistance programs exist because long-standing biases against minorities have made it especially difficult for minorities to enter the owner and managerial ranks. Despite these programs and a recognition of the problem, however, difficulties remain. Black M.B.A.s report that many in the business world are "indifferent," "patronizing," and "reluctant to accept blacks."[35]

Of course, although the route to a successful managerial career for a minority member might be circuitous, it can be followed, and the outlook is not dismal.[36] In 1986 the president and chief operating officer of AM International Incorporated was black, Jerry O. Williams. SmithKline Beckman Corporation that same year had four blacks in top-ranking positions, including Frederick C. Foard, director of marketing communications. The director of corporate resources for Xerox, John L. Jones, is black, too.[37] Increasingly, colleges and universities are providing career counseling specifically tailored to minorities.[38]

In sum, women and minorities can and do have managerial careers. In recent years it has been suggested that the most important action is to be seen, to be visible, noticed, and appreciated by your superiors.[39]

Special Career Issues

Companies that have formal career development programs are generally more effective in utilizing their human resources than those that do not have such programs. And these programs enable organizations to cope with the numerous government regulations concerning human resources and to recognize and respond to a wide variety of career issues.

Two basic dimensions affect every individual. The more obvious one is the work versus society dimension, in which work (career or job demands) pulls one way and society (family and friends) pulls another.[40] You can advance your career by putting in long hours and focusing on nothing else, but you might not be able to maintain friendships or family under those conditions. The second dimension is the internal versus external one, in which internal, personal demands pull one way while external demands (such as religion and citizenship) pull the other. People must reconcile these multiple issues, and organizations must make that reconciliation easier. The next two sections of this appendix examine some specific examples of such issues.

Dual Incomes and Dual Careers

As we have seen, more than half of all adult females now work. Since many of these women are married, this means that large numbers of households now have two sources of income; they are **dual-income families.** The economic advantages of this system are obvious. Indeed, in the absence of children, there are few, if any, financial disadvantages. Problems do occur when there are children, but, as noted earlier, many companies are taking steps to alleviate some of them by providing flexible hours, more generous personal leaves, daycare centers, and the like.

Perhaps most of the problems of dual-income families can be worked out. If a problem arises—say, a child is stricken with a long-term illness—one partner can drop out of the work force and stay at home to nurse the child back to health. If both partners are pursuing careers, however, as opposed to merely earning income, the situation changes radically. Interrupting a career is far more devastating than interrupting a series of jobs. Which career should suffer? Whose career is less important? The adjustment for the **dual-career family** is not easy or obvious, and sometimes one or both partners must make a serious sacrifice of long-term goals. Even such things as scheduling vacations can become a severe problem because both parties must be able to get off at the same time.[41]

The long-term illness of a child is not a problem faced by most dual-career couples, of course. Promotions and reassignments that involve transfers to new locations are far more common and can be extremely disruptive. One partner's career may best be served by taking the new assignment, but the other partner's career may best be served by remaining. Which career is more important?

What if both people are employed by the same organization, and one is a far better performer? That one is moving up rapidly, while the other moves slowly or not at all (or, even worse, gets fired). This kind of friction can tear a marriage apart.

Resolving these conflicts is not easy. It is particularly difficult now because not many people are experienced enough to offer advice, although some tentative advice is becoming available.[42] Obviously, a key element in dual-career families is to adopt a "family" or "we/us" view rather than an "I/me" view. This view might mean deciding to relocate to help partner A now, with the understanding that the next major career decision will help partner B. (Of course, when partner B's turn comes, partner A may get cold feet.)

Affirmative Action

Affirmative action refers to plans of action undertaken by organizations to comply with the letter and the intent of human rights legislation, part of the responsibility associated with organizational citizenship. Organizations that are acting affirmatively go beyond equal opportunity. Equal opportunity means that they avoid discrimination, as they must under the law, on the basis of race, sex, religion, color, or national origin (and age, under certain conditions). Affirmative action means that companies actively strive to recruit, hire, train, develop, and promote women and members of minority groups. Affirmative action requires a careful balancing of the personal wants of individuals against the external responsibilities of citizenship.

In terms of career development, affirmative action dictates that companies give special attention to race, sex, religion, color, national origin, and age to ensure that members of certain groups have equal access to training and development programs. Further, it ensures that they will be helped and formally counseled with their career plans.

These and other issues surround corporate career planning, just as they surround individual career planning. Companies must consider the impact of dual careers as they strive to facilitate managerial succession. Individuals must also consider the impact of dual careers on each of those careers. Affirmative action plans must be taken into account in corporate plans for managerial succession, too. From an individual viewpoint, a company with an affirmative action plan may well provide more career opportunities for women and minorities. Table A1.4 indicates some of these issues, with particular emphasis on human rights and related concerns.

Table A1.4

Issues Surrounding Corporate Career Planning

Corporate career planning
Reliable and valid personnel decision techniques
Vocational rehabilitation
Benefits
Dual careers
Hiring of minorities
Other regulatory issues
Hiring of women
Equal pay
Affirmative action
Age discrimination issues

The Manager's Vocabulary

career
economic sector
not-for-profit organization
life stage
career stage
exploration stage
establishment stage

maintenance stage
decline stage
career development
career planning
career management
career counseling

career pathing
career resources planning
career information system
dual-income family
dual-career family
affirmative action

Review Questions

1. What is a career, and what is involved in a career choice?
2. Describe career development.
3. Discuss some career issues.
4. What career opportunities exist for women and minorities?

Analysis Questions

1. In what life stage are you? In what life stage is your instructor? How do you determine which stage you are in?
2. In what career stage are you? In what career stage is your instructor? How do you determine which stage you are in?
3. Where do you want to be in your career in twenty years? Ten years? Five years? One year? Does each of your answers lead you logically to the next?
4. What strengths do you have that will help you achieve your career goals? How can you focus these strengths more clearly on a particular career?
5. What weaknesses do you have that you will have to overcome in order to reach your career goals? How can you accomplish this?

Control Techniques and Methods

This appendix first examines the role of control techniques in management. Then one of the most important and widespread techniques, the budget, is explored before going on to investigate financial analysis and other control techniques. Finally, the appendix concludes by looking at the relationship between computers and control.

The Nature of Control Techniques

Techniques are tools; control techniques are handy tools that managers can use to enhance organizational effectiveness in general and organizational control in particular.

The Importance of Control Techniques

As discussed in the text, adequate control is important for numerous reasons. The proper use of the right techniques facilitates control and also helps managers communicate with others both inside and outside the organization. Many of the techniques are used by virtually all organizations and so represent standard business practice. The techniques involve different levels of management in the control process and enable managers to know what is happening in the organization.

Financial techniques provide the opportunity to keep up with the assets and debts of a firm, and budgetary techniques can ensure that the firm will not overspend its resources. Control can be particularly important to small businesses.[1] A plumber who decided to become a plumbing contractor soon went out of business because he forgot that although he had to pay his workers weekly, he did not get paid until the job was completed. Had he used budgets and financial control techniques, he would have foreseen his cash flow problem and perhaps been able to borrow enough money to keep from going bankrupt.

Strengths and Weaknesses

Like tools used in any field, control techniques have various strengths and weaknesses. When used properly, they are a great asset to any manager. When used improperly, however, they can do more harm than good.

On the plus side, control techniques provide objective indicators of an organization's performance. Budgets, which will be covered in more detail later in this appendix, and various financial ratios, for example, are quantifiable and verifiable indications of an organization's financial situation.[2] Control techniques also provide useful road maps for action. Budgets indicate clearly where and how resources are to be allocated.

On the other hand, these techniques can be characterized by two significant weaknesses. For one thing, they can be rigid and uncompromising, especially when managers use them with no regard for flexibility or for the appropriate context. A manager could, for instance, continue to rely on a budget that had been developed on the basis of outdated government regulations. Thus, control techniques must be flexible to be truly effective.[3]

Similarly, control techniques can be misused. In particular, individual managers might be able to distort information in order to mask problems. A manager could report that, historically, personnel recruited from one region of the country turn over more than others. She could use these data to support an argument for not recruiting from that region when, in fact, the turnover stemmed from her treatment of those employees.

Thus, when using control techniques, managers need to remember that they are valuable tools but that they do not replace individual judgment and insight into organizational dynamics.

Budgets

Budgets are perhaps the most widely used and universally known control techniques available.[4] A **budget** is simply a plan expressed in quantitative terms. Budgeting, then, is the process of developing budgets.

Budgets serve four basic purposes. They help coordinate resources and projects; they define standards used in other control systems and activities; they provide clear and unambiguous guidelines about resources; and they facilitate appraisals of managerial and departmental performance.

Because of the importance and pervasiveness of budgets in organizations, we need to explore them in detail. First, let us look at the budgeting process. We can then identify types of budgets and fixed and variable costs, important parts of most budgets. Finally, we will see how to manage the budgeting process effectively.

The Budgeting Process

The **budgeting process** is unique for every organization. That is, every organization follows a budgeting process that fits its own culture and style. Thus we cannot identify a process that is representative of all organizations. However, many organizations follow the general pattern of budgeting shown in Exhibit A2.1.[5]

As a starting point, top management usually issues a call for budget requests, a step indicated in the exhibit by arrow 1. As we can see, the first demand usually goes from top to middle-

Exhibit A2.1

The Budgeting Process

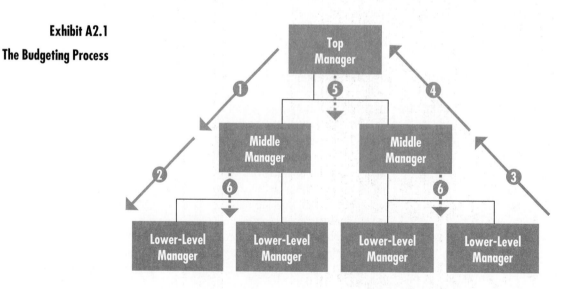

level managers. The top managers usually accompany this call with some indication of what resources are available during the coming time period. For example, they might point out that sales and profits are increasing and therefore encourage requests for budget increases. Alternatively, they could ask for cutbacks. As a part of strategic planning, the top managers might also indicate that some units will have higher or lower priorities than in the past.

Step 2 parallels Step 1 in that middle managers request budget proposals from lower-level managers. They provide the same basic information, but it pertains more to individual subunits than to the overall division.

In Step 3, the lower-level managers prepare budget requests and forward them to the appropriate middle managers. In general, these requests summarize the unit's current resources, account for how those resources have been used, and point out what resources are needed for the next period (usually one year) and how those resources will be used.

The middle manager then coordinates and integrates the various requests. For instance, two department heads in a college of business might each request ten thousand dollars to buy five computers. The dean knows that an order of ten computers carries a 10-percent discount, so the college will request eighteen thousand dollars to buy ten computers.

As indicated by arrow 4, middle managers then forward their division requests to top management, where these requests are coordinated and integrated. Some will be returned to middle management for further work. Others will be approved as is. Still others will be modified by top management with little or no input from below.

The last step, as indicated by arrows 5 and 6, is to pass final budgets back down the organization. In some cases middle managers will still have the option of modifying their subunits' budgets, whereas in other cases the final budgets are provided all the way down the hierarchy.[6]

Types of Budgets

In most organizations several different types of budgets are produced.[7] The most common of these are shown in Table A2.1. You should recognize, of course, that there are budgets for each part of an organization as well—marketing, information services, and so on.[8]

Financial Budgets   **Financial budgets** detail where the organization intends to get its cash for the coming period and how it intends to use it. Most money comes from sales revenues, the sale of assets, loans, and the sale of stock. This money is used to pay for expenses, to repay debt, to purchase new assets, and to pay dividends to stockholders.

Table A2.1
Types of Budgets

Major type	Subtypes
Financial Budgets	Cash flow budget
	Capital expenditure budget
	Balance sheet budget
Operations Budgets	Revenue budget
	Expense budget
	Profit budget
Nonmonetary Budgets	Output budget
	Labor budget
	Space budget

A **cash flow budget** outlines precisely where the money will come from and how it will be used for the coming period (usually a quarter or a year). If incoming funds will not cover needs, the organization must make other plans, such as getting loans or deferring payments. Surplus cash, in contrast, can be invested. Martin Marietta, a large defense contractor, uses cash flow budgets effectively as tools to bid for lucrative government contracts.[9]

Capital expenditure budgets are used to plan for the acquisition of such major assets as new equipment, entire plants, and land. Such assets are often paid for with borrowed funds, so even large firms like Ford and AT&T need to control their use carefully.

The **balance sheet budget** is a projection of what the assets and liabilities of the firm will look like at the end of the coming period. The balance sheet is discussed in more detail in a later section.[10]

Operations Budgets   **Operations budgets** relate to all or a portion of the organization's operations for the coming period. In particular, they present the various details of operations in financial terms.

A very important budget for all organizations is the **revenue budget.** For a business like Colgate-Palmolive or Avis, revenues come from sales, but a university derives its revenues from legislative appropriations, tuition and fees, and government contracts for research. Regardless of the source, the revenue budget is extremely important because it is the starting point for virtually all other budgeting.

The **expense budget** is the counterpart of the revenue budget. It summarizes the projected expenses for the organization over the coming period. The **profit budget** simply presents the difference between projected revenues and projected expenses.

Nonmonetary Budgets   **Nonmonetary budgets** are budgets that express important variables in terms other than dollars. For example, an **output budget** may project how many of each of the organization's products will be produced. A **labor budget** details the number of direct hours of labor that are available, and a **space budget** can be used to allocate plant or office space to different divisions or groups within the organization.[11]

Fixed and Variable Costs in Budgeting

Costs, remember, can be fixed or variable. **Fixed costs** are those incurred regardless of the level of operations. Examples include rent, taxes, minimum utility payments, interest payments, and guaranteed salaries. **Variable costs** are those that vary as a function of operations. Raw materials that go into each product, electricity used to operate machines, and commissions paid are all variable costs.

There are also **semivariable costs,** which vary as a function of output but not necessarily in a direct fashion. Advertising, for instance, varies in response to competition and seasonal sales patterns. Equipment repairs, maintenance, and labor are also semivariable costs.

When developing budgets, managers need to try to account for all three kinds of costs. Obviously, fixed costs are the easiest to assess, and semivariable costs the most difficult. If managers do not give each kind of cost adequate consideration, however, the budget may not serve its intended purpose, and the organization could end up with unexpected cash shortfalls at the end of the period. Because these types of costs are so important, managers are trying to find new ways to control them.[12]

Managing the Budgeting Process

Clearly, budgets are an important facet of organizational life in general and of control in particular. Table A2.2 summarizes the strengths and weaknesses of budgets, which managers must understand if they are to manage the budgeting process effectively.[13] Culture also has an impact on budget practices and so must be carefully considered, especially by multinational organizations.[14]

Table A2.2
Managing the Budgeting Process

Strengths	Weaknesses
Facilitates control	Subject to rigidity
Facilitates coordination	Time consuming
Facilitates documentation	Limits innovation
Facilitates planning	Reinforces inefficiency

Budgets can be characterized by four basic strengths. First, they facilitate control, as the foregoing discussion should make obvious. They also facilitate coordination because middle managers integrate the budgets of lower-level managers, and top managers subsequently integrate the budgets submitted by the middle managers for the overall organization.

Budgets also aid documentation. They are almost always written down, so there is a permanent record of expectations and actual performance. Finally, budgets help the planning process. As we have seen, planning and control are linked. Given the pervasive role of budgeting in control, it is logical that budgets are also an important part of planning. Indeed, a budget has been defined as a plan.

Of course, budgets have certain weaknesses as well.[15] For one thing, some managers make the mistake of using them too rigidly. As indicated earlier, budgets must be flexible to be really valuable.[16] If managers fail to consider the situation and look at the numbers in a mechanical way, they may lose important related information. Budgeting is also a time-consuming process. To do it right, every manager must invest considerable time, effort, and energy in making the budget as effective as possible. Third, budgets occasionally limit innovation. In a company like Texas Instruments, for example, if all funds are allocated to operating groups and divisions, the organization might have trouble raising money for unexpected opportunities.

Fourth, the way budgets are used frequently reinforces inefficiency. The manager who is efficient (who spends less than her budget) may find that her budget is reduced in the next cycle. On the other hand, a manager who is inefficient (who spends over his budget) may find his budget increased in the next cycle. This common practice occurs because higher-level managers are not carefully examining the assumptions and conditions under which the budget was developed.

A key method many managers have come to use to enhance the strengths and to minimize the weaknesses inherent in budgeting is participation. The greater the role that lower-level managers have in developing their budget, the more likely they are to make sure that it is useful. They will work hard to justify the funds they want and to use those funds wisely. Of course, the same holds true for middle managers as they develop budgets for entire divisions or operating groups.[17]

Financial Analysis

Another important technique for control is financial analysis. Whereas budgets are used to plan and control an organization's future financial expenditures, financial analysis helps managers study an organization's financial status at a given point in time. Using financial analysis, which consists of several techniques, managers are better able to understand and control the monetary aspects of an organization. Two of the most important techniques are ratio analysis and audits.[18]

Ratio Analysis

Balance Sheet and Income Statement   **Ratio analysis** involves calculating and evaluating any number of ratios of figures obtained from an organization's balance sheet and income statement.[19] This analysis can be used internally or externally to obtain information about companies' financial positions.[20] A **balance sheet** is a cross-sectional picture of an organization's financial position at a given time. A simplified balance sheet for a small manufacturing firm is present in Exhibit A2.2.

The left side of the sheet summarizes the **assets,** those things the company has that are of value. Current assets are those that are fairly liquid, or easily convertible into cash, such as cash, accounts receivable, and inventory. Fixed assets are those that are less liquid and that play a longer-term role in the organization, such as land, plant, and equipment.

The right side of the balance sheet summarizes the firm's **liabilities**—debts and other financial obligations—and **owner's equity,** or claims against the assets. Current liabilities are those that must be paid in the near future and include accounts payable and accrued expenses, such as salaries earned by workers but not yet paid. Long-term liabilities are bank loans amortized over a several-year period and payments on bonds. Stockholders' (owners') equity consists of common stock and retained earnings. Retained earnings are profits held by the company for expansion, research and development, or debt servicing. As shown in the exhibit, the totals on each side of the balance sheet must be equal.

Whereas the balance sheet reflects a point in time, the **income statement** summarizes several activities over a period of time. In general, a company prepares an income statement on an annual basis and a balance sheet for the point in time at which the income statement ends. For instance, the balance sheet in the exhibit reflects the firm's position as of December 31, 1993. Exhibit A2.3 presents a simplified income statement for the same organization for the year ending December 31, 1993. Essentially, the income statement shows how the accountant adds up all the revenues of the organization and then subtracts all the expenses and other liabilities. The so-called bottom line is the profit or loss realized by the firm.

Ratios   Data from both the balance sheet and the income statement provide useful benchmarks for assessing an organization's overall financial health, especially when expressed as any of several commonly used ratios.

Exhibit A2.2

A Sample Balance Sheet

Ajax Manufacturing
Balance Sheet
December 31, 1993

Current Assets			Current Liabilities		
Cash		$ 10,000	Accounts Payable		$ 60,000
Receivables		10,000	Accrued expenses		20,000
Inventory		140,000	Long-term Liabilities		150,000
		160,000			230,000
			Stockholder's Equity		
Fixed Assets			Common Stock		200,000
Land		60,000	Retained Earnings		190,000
Plant Equipment		400,000			390,000
		460,000			
Total Current and Fixed Assets		$ 620,000	Total Liabilities and Equity		$ 620,000

Exhibit A2.3

A Sample Income Statement

Ajax Manufacturing Income Statement For the Year Ending December 31, 1993		
Gross Sales		$ 806,000
Less Returns	$ 6,000	
Net Sales		800,000
Less Expenses and Cost of Goods Sold		
— Expenses	120,000	
— Depreciation	40,000	
— Cost of Goods Sold	400,000	560,000
Operating Profit		240,000
Other Income		20,000
Interest Expense	30,000	
Taxable Income		230,000
Less Taxes	110,000	
Net Income		$120,000

Liquidity ratios assess how easily the assets of the organization can be converted into cash. When a bank lends money to a small business, for example, it might be interested in learning how quickly it could recover its money if the business folded. The **current ratio,** the most commonly used liquidity ratio, is determined by dividing current assets by current liabilities. Thus the current ratio for Ajax Manufacturing (see Exhibit A2.2) is 160,000 ÷ 80,000, or 2. The ratio is expressed in the form of 2:1, which means that Ajax has two dollars of liquid assets for each dollar of short-term liability. This is considered to be a fairly healthy ratio.

Debt ratios are intended to reflect the firm's ability to handle its long-term debt. The most common debt ratio is found by dividing total liabilities by total assets. The debt ratio for Ajax is 230,000 ÷ 620,000, or 0.37. This indicates that the organization has 0.37 dollars in debt for each dollar of assets. The higher the ratio, the poorer the financial health of the organization.

The **return on assets (ROA)** is usually of more interest to potential investors. It tells them how effectively the organization is using its assets to earn additional profits. The normal method for calculating this ratio is to divide net income by total assets (see Exhibits A2.2 and A2.3). Thus, the ROA for Ajax is 120,000 ÷ 620,000, or 0.19. This figure is the percentage return achieved by Ajax over the twelve-month period. It means that the company earned nineteen cents of profit for each dollar in assets it controlled. Since most savings accounts earn only about 5 percent, an ROA of 0.19 is very good. Therefore, investors would probably think that Ajax was a good investment.

Other ratios are occasionally used, of course. **Return on equity (ROE)** is net income divided by owners' equity. For Ajax, ROE is 120,000 ÷ 390,000, or 0.3. This figure would then be compared with previous figures and to other companies in the industry to get an indication of how Ajax is doing.

Profitability ratios indicate the relative effectiveness of an organization. For example, $1 million in profits from sales of $10 million (.1) is quite good, whereas a profit of $1 million on sales of $100 million (.01) is not so good.

Operating ratios can also be useful. The index obtained by dividing the total cost of goods sold by the average daily inventory, for instance, provides a good indication of how efficiently the firm is forecasting sales and ordering merchandise.

Audits   Another important part of financial analysis is the **audit,** an independent appraisal of an organization's accounting, financial, and operational systems. An audit may be either external or internal,[21] and care must be taken to ensure that audits are of high quality.[22] An audit can focus on monetary or nonmonetary aspects of the organization as well.[23]

External Audits   **External audits** are conducted by experts who do not work directly for the organization. Most often these experts are employed by an accounting firm, such as Peat, Marwick, Mitchell & Co. The experts evaluate closely the appropriateness of the company's controls and reporting procedures and report their findings to relevant parties such as stockholders and the IRS. Publicly held corporations—that is, corporations whose stock is traded on public markets and can be purchased by anyone—must conduct external audits on a regular basis.

External auditors are extremely thorough. In some cases they even visit warehouses to count inventory in order to verify the accuracy of the firm's balance sheets. Auditors who are found to have made mistakes may lose their reputations and even their licenses, so they are generally very careful. Virtually all smaller firms and many medium-size ones conduct external audits at least on an annual basis.

Internal Audits   **Internal audits** are conducted by people who work directly for the organization. Their purpose is the same as that of external auditors: to verify the accuracy of the organization's reporting system. Internal audits tend to go further, however, and also deal with matters of efficiency. For example, if an organization's accounting system is technically accurate but somewhat inefficient, an external audit will verify the system's accuracy but ignore the efficiency problem, whereas an internal audit will deal with both.

Most large firms have internal auditing staffs. It is considerably cheaper to maintain these staffs than to rely totally on the services of an external accounting firm.[24] Internal auditors spend much of their time auditing various subunits or divisions of the organization.

In many ways internal auditors are more valuable than external auditors. Besides uncovering a variety of problems, they tend to be very familiar with all the inner workings of the organization. Even when an organization has an internal auditing staff, though, it periodically uses an external auditing group to provide an independent assessment of its practices. And well-kept records are crucial to both internal and external auditors and can influence a company's fortunes in many ways.

Other Control Techniques
Human Resource Control

Although financial and operations control are the primary concerns of most businesses, other important areas of control should not be neglected. Two of these are human resource control and marketing control.

Human resource control focuses on the work force of the organization. In particular, it is concerned with the extent to which members of the work force are productive and the extent to which the organization is effectively managing them.

Performance Appraisal   The primary way in which an organization controls the performance of its employees is through performance appraisal. Performance appraisal is the way the organization determines individuals' level of performance.[25] From a control standpoint, it helps managers monitor the performance of employees, compare that performance with desired standards, and address any problems or deficiencies that they find.

Indeed, the basic steps in performance appraisal parallel those in control very closely. First, using job analysis, the organization determines the exact content of each job and then assesses how much each person should produce. For example, the work of a machine operator might be defined as adjusting machine settings, working metal parts through the machine, and inspecting the final product. Management might further decide that the desired level of output per operator is 144 dozen parts per day. This standard is then used as a part of the standard performance appraisal during which the supervisor checks the output of each operator under his or her control.

The actual performance is then measured against the standard, and appropriate action is taken. Jack may be producing more than 160 dozen parts per day, so he should be complimented and perhaps given a small pay raise. Laverne may be producing around 146 dozen parts per day. The supervisor can tell her that she is doing a good job and leave it at that. If Joe is found to be producing only 98 dozen parts per day, appropriate action might include counseling, encouraging him to work harder, and training. If things do not improve, the supervisor can transfer Joe to another job or perhaps even fire him.

Human Resource Ratios   Managers can also use any of several human resource ratios to assess the degree to which the organization is managing its work force properly. Three of the more important ratios are turnover, absenteeism, and work force composition.[26]

Turnover is the percentage of the organization's work force that leaves and must be replaced over a period of time, usually one year. Companies like McDonald's and Pizza Hut experience high levels of turnover, occasionally as high as 100 percent, whereas companies like Kmart have moderate turnover and those like General Motors have relatively little turnover. The manager needs to know what the acceptable turnover is both for her firm and for the industry. If turnover increases or is higher than the industry average, the manager will need to take steps such as increasing wages to meet the industry standard to get things back in line.

Absenteeism is the percentage of an organization's work force that is absent on a given day. Absenteeism may range from only a few percent to as high as 20 or 30 percent. It is especially troublesome on Monday and Friday, when employees use sick time to extend their weekends. Again, the key is for the manager to know what the acceptable level of absenteeism is and to take steps if it gets out of line. He might issue warnings about excessive absences, for instance, or offer incentives to those who do not call in sick.

Work force composition ratios are indicators of how many of the organization's employees fall into various groups. For example, the manager may need to know how many of the organization's employees are black, Hispanic, female, handicapped, and over the age of forty-five. If the general labor market from which the firm hires its employees contains a higher proportion of such groups, the company may be guilty of discrimination. That is, if blacks make up 25 percent of the potential work force, yet only 10 percent of the firm's employees are black, discrimination may be occurring. The obvious step in this case is to eliminate such discriminatory practices.

Marketing Control

Another area that is important for control is **marketing,** the set of activities involved in getting consumers to want the goods and services provided by the organization.[27] British Airways used marketing control in an effort to revive itself.[28] Two common approaches to marketing control are test marketing and assessing important marketing ratios.

Test Marketing   **Test marketing** involves introducing a new product on a limited basis in order to assess consumer reaction on a small scale. Say that Wendy's creates a new sandwich and sells and advertises it only in Missouri and Kansas. If it is successful, Wendy's will introduce it in all Wendy's restaurants. If it is unsuccessful, the company might decide not to introduce it anywhere else, and it will be dropped from the menu in Missouri and Kansas as well.

The advantage of test marketing is that it minimizes the risk of losing large sums of money by introducing a new product nationally and then watching it fail. Test marketing also allows the firm to make adjustments and refinements based on limited consumer responses before committing itself to national introduction.

In recent years there has been a trend away from test marketing because it is slow and gives competitors time to copy and perhaps get ahead of the company with new products. The new approach being tried by some companies is shown in Exhibit A2.4.

Under the traditional approach, also shown in the exhibit, new products are developed and then test-marketed. The results are assessed quantitatively (that is, actual sales are measured), modifications are made, and the product is then introduced via a full-scale marketing effort. Under the new approach products are developed and then assessed intuitively by the firm's managers and perhaps by very limited consumer panels. If things look positive the product is introduced full-scale.

Sara Lee, Ralston Purina, and Frito-Lay have all adopted this approach.[29] The risk, of course, is that if the product fails, the company loses a lot of money. On the other hand the company may be able to get a big jump on the competition and save the expense of test marketing if it guesses right.

Marketing Ratios   There are also several ratios that are useful in marketing control. Perhaps the most common is **market share,** the proportion of the total market controlled by the firm's products. If the total market for a particular product is one million units per year and a certain company sells one hundred thousand units, its market share is 10 percent. A common goal of many organizations is to increase market share through increased advertising, promotion, and so forth. Decreases in market share, of course, are a source of considerable concern.

Profit margin on sales is another useful marketing ratio. This is determined by dividing net income by sales. The higher the ratio is, the more effective the organization is in managing its marketing function. When the profit margin is calculated for each product a firm sells, managers can learn which products are contributing the most in profits.

Exhibit A2.4

Trends in Test Marketing

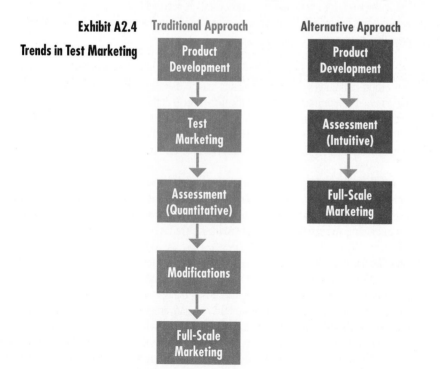

Computers and Control

Perhaps the biggest change ever to affect the control function of management has been prompted by the increased presence of computers in the workplace.[30] They are now being used to perform almost every task conceivable. For instance, they are even being used in interviewing. School systems are finding that the use of desktop computers can improve even the budget process.[31]

Kinds of Computers

In general, there are three basic kinds of computers. **Mainframe computers** are the very large, very expensive machines most people think of when they hear the word *computer*—the huge monoliths that occupy entire rooms. Such computers can handle enormous amounts of information in fractions of a second. They cost anywhere from several hundreds or thousands of dollars to millions. In reality, only the largest businesses and major research centers and universities are able to buy mainframe computers.

Minicomputers are the type that most medium-size and large businesses have. Such machines cost from around twenty-five thousand dollars to a few hundred thousand dollars and are capable of handling relatively large amounts of information very efficiently.

Microcomputers, more commonly known as personal computers, are the desktop machines that have become popular in recent years. These machines, which usually cost between several hundred and a few thousand dollars, can often handle all the information-processing needs of managers. In addition, they serve as terminals tied in to minicomputers or the company mainframe, and they can also be linked together via an information network.

Contributions to Control

The primary role of the computer in control is to give managers access to more information in ways that are faster and more accurate. For example, Shop 'n Save is a chain of grocery stores in New England. Its managers have precise figures on profit margins for more than seventeen thousand items in sixty-five different stores, thanks to a centralized mainframe computer linked to terminals in each store.

Another area of improvement has been inventory management. In the old days stores counted their inventory annually, and this was the only time they knew precisely what their total inventory was. Today's computer networks can automatically enter new orders and subtract individual sales. Thus the manager has a perpetual inventory and always knows what inventory levels are.[32] And hand-held computers linked to the company's main computer through telephone devices called modems can provide a better exchange of information between field or sales personnel and the home office.

Advantages and Disadvantages

Not surprisingly, there are both pluses and minuses to using computers in organizational control.[33] One critical strength is storage capacity. Computers can store enormous amounts of information in a very small space. They are also very fast and can process information and perform calculations many times faster than people can. And they tend to be extremely accurate. If the computer has the proper operating system and instructions and accurate data, errors are very rare.

But computers are still quite costly. A medium-range personal computer, for instance, costs about two thousand dollars. Another problem is overreliance. Many managers tend to believe everything the computer "tells" them, without considering their own experience and intuition. A third problem is that computers are complex and difficult for some people to learn to use. Such complexity can serve as a barrier to innovation and limit the potential value of the computer to the organization.

The Manager's Vocabulary

budget
budgeting process
financial budgets
cash flow budget
capital expenditure budget
balance sheet budget
operations budgets
revenue budget
expense budget
profit budget
nonmonetary budgets
output budget
labor budget
space budget
fixed costs

variable costs
semivariable costs
ratio analysis
balance sheet
assets
liabilities
owners' equity
income statement
liquidity ratio
current ratio
debt ratio
return on assets (ROA)
return on equity (ROE)
profitability ratio
operating ratio

audit
external audit
internal audit
turnover
absenteeism
work force composition ratio
marketing
test marketing
market share
profit margin on sales
mainframe computers
minicomputers
microcomputers

Review Questions

1. What are the strengths and weaknesses of control techniques?
2. Describe the budgeting process. What are the several types of budgets?
3. What is financial analysis, and how is it used by organizations?
4. What are the major types of human resource control? Marketing control?
5. What are the advantages and disadvantages of using computers in control?

Analysis Questions

1. If a frequent misuse of budgets reinforces inefficiency, why do they continue to be misused?
2. Do all organizations have to use all of the different types of budgets? Why or why not?
3. Comment on this statement: "If you want low turnover, hire incompetents and pay them well."
4. Comment on this statement: "The only real test of a product is to offer it for sale."
5. Despite careful market research, many products fail. Why is this true? What does this suggest about marketing controls?

Notes

Chapter 1 *(continued from copyright page)*

2. Henry Mintzberg, "The Manager's Job: Folklore and Fact," *Harvard Business Review*, July–August 1975, pp. 49–61. See also Brian Dumaine, "What the Leaders of Tomorrow See," *Fortune*, July 3, 1989, pp. 48–62.

3. Ibid. See Henry Mintzberg, *The Nature of Managerial Work* (New York: Harper & Row, 1973), and William Whitely, "Managerial Work Behavior: An Integration of Results from Two Major Approaches," *Academy of Management Journal,* June 1985, pp. 344–362.

4. Don Hellriegel, John Slocum, and Richard Woodman, *Organizational Behavior*, 6th ed. (St. Paul, Minn.: West, 1992). See also Ford S. Worthy, "How CEOs Manage Their Time," *Fortune,* January 18, 1988, pp. 88–97, and Thomas A. Stewart, "How to Manage in the New Era," *Fortune*, January 15, 1990, pp. 58–72.

5. Thomas M. Carroll, "Rolling Back Executive Pay," *Time*, March 1, 1993, pp. 49–50; John A. Byrne, "Comp Committees, or Back-Scratchers-in-Waiting?" in "What, Me Overpaid? CEOs Fight Back," *Business Week*, May 4, 1992, pp. 142–148; Geoffrey Colvin, "How To Pay the CEO Right," *Fortune*, April 6, 1992, pp. 60–70; "Can We Put the Brakes on CEO Pay?" *Management Review*, May 1, 1992, pp. 10–15; and "Pay for Skills: Its Time Has Come," *Industry Week*, June 15, 1992, pp. 22–31.

6. See Page Smith, *The Rise of Industrial America* (New York: McGraw-Hill, 1984).

7. See Carrie Gottlieb, "And You Thought You Had It Tough," *Fortune*, April 25, 1988, pp. 83–84.

8. "Caught in the Middle," *Business Week*, September 12, 1988, pp. 80–88. See also Rosemary Stewart, "Middle Managers: Their Jobs and Behaviors," in Jay W. Lorsch, ed., *Handbook of Organizational Behavior* (Englewood Cliffs, N.J.: Prentice-Hall, 1987), pp. 385–391.

9. See Steven Kerr, Kenneth D. Hill, and Laurie Broedling, "The First-Line Supervisor: Phasing Out or Here to Stay?" *Academy of Management Review,* January 1986, pp. 103–117.

10. "Two Wal-Mart Officials Vie for Top Post," *The Wall Street Journal*, July 23, 1986, p. 6. See also Sarah Smith, "America's Most Admired Corporations," *Fortune*, January 29, 1990, pp. 58–63.

11. See George Steiner, *Top Management Planning* (New York: Macmillan, 1969), for a classic discussion of planning.

12. See Robert C. Ford, Barry R. Armandi, and Cherrill P. Heaton, *Organization Theory* (New York: Harper & Row, 1988), for a recent review of the organizing function.

13. See Gary Yukl, *Leadership in Organizations*, 2nd ed. (Englewood Cliffs, N.J.: Prentice-Hall, 1989), for a recent review of the leadership function.

14. See William H. Newman, *Constructive Control* (Englewood Cliffs, N.J.: Prentice-Hall, 1975), for a general overview of control.

15. "Profiting from the Past," *Newsweek*, May 10, 1982, pp. 73–74.

16. Alan L. Wilkins and Nigel J. Bristow, "For Successful Organization Culture, Honor Your Past," *Academy of Management Executive*, August 1987, pp. 221–227, and Alan M. Kantrow, "Why History Matters to Managers," *Harvard Business Review*, January–February 1986, pp. 81–88.

17. See Daniel A. Wren, *The Evolution of Management Thought*, 3rd ed. (New York: Wiley, 1987), and Claude S. George, Jr., *The History of Management Thought* (Englewood Cliffs, N.J.: Prentice-Hall, 1968), for general discussions of ancient management practices.

18. See Wren, *The Evolution of Management Thought*, for details about these and other management pioneers.

19. Frederick W. Taylor, *Principles of Scientific Management* (New York: Harper and Brothers, 1911).

20. See Charles D. Wrege and Ann Marie Stotka, "Cooke Creates a Classic: The Story Behind F. W. Taylor's Principles of Scientific Management," *Academy of Management Review*, October 1978, pp. 736–749.

21. J. Michael Gotcher, "Assisting the Handicapped: The Pioneering Efforts of Frank and Lillian Gilbreth," *Journal of Management*, March 1992, pp. 5–13.

22. See Wren, *The Evolution of Management Thought*.

23. Henri Fayol, *Industrial and General Management*, trans. J. A. Conbrough (Geneva: International Management Institute, 1930.)

24. Max Weber, *Theory of Social and Economic Organization*, trans. T. Parsons (New York: Free Press, 1947).

25. Stephen J. Carroll and Dennis J. Gillen, "Are the Classical Management Functions Useful in Describing Managerial Work?" *Academy of Management Review*, January 1987, pp. 38–51.

26. Hugo Munsterberg, *Psychology and Industrial Efficiency*, 6th ed. (Boston: Houghton Mifflin, 1913).

27. Paul R. Lawrence, "Historical Developments of Organizational Behavior," in Jay W. Lorsch, ed., *Handbook of Organizational Behavior* (Englewood Cliffs, N.J.: Prentice-Hall, 1987), pp. 1–9.

28. R. G. Greenwood, A. A. Bolton, and R. A. Greenwood, "Hawthorne a Half Century Later: Relay Assembly Participants Remember," *Journal of Management*, vol. 9, no. 2 (1983), pp. 217–231. See also Elton Mayo, *The Human Problems of an Industrial Civilization* (New York: Macmillan, 1933), and Fritz Roethlishberger and William Dickson, *Management and the Worker* (Cambridge, Mass.: Harvard University Press, 1939), for details of the actual research. See Wren, *The Evolution of Management Thought*, for a summary.

29. Greenwood, Bolton, and Greenwood, "Hawthorne a Half Century Later: Relay Assembly Participants Remember," *Journal of Management*.

30. Ibid.

31. Abraham Maslow, "A Theory of Human Motivation," *Psychological Review*, July 1943, pp. 370–396.

32. Douglas McGregor, *The Human Side of Enterprise* (New York: McGraw-Hill, 1960).

33. See David D. Van Fleet, *Behavior in Organizations* (Boston: Houghton Mifflin, 1991) and Gregory Moorhead and Ricky W. Griffin, *Organizational Behavior*, 3rd ed. (Boston: Houghton Mifflin, 1992), for reviews of recent happenings in the field of organizational behavior.

34. See Robert Markland, *Topics in Management Science*, 2nd ed. (New York: Wiley, 1983).

35. See Everett E. Adam, Jr., and Ronald J. Ebert, *Production and Operations Management*, 5th ed. (Englewood Cliffs, N.J.: Prentice-Hall, 1992), for a review. See also Richard B. Chase and Eric L. Prentis, "Operations Management: A Field Rediscovered," *Journal of Management,* Summer 1987, pp. 339–350.

36. See Donde P. Ashmos and George P. Huber, "The Systems Paradigm in Organization Theory: Correcting the Record and Suggesting the Future," *Academy of Management Review*, October 1987, pp. 607–621, and Fremont E. Kast and James E. Rosenzweig, "General Systems Theory: Applications for Organization and Management," *Academy of Management Journal*, December 1972, pp. 447–465.

37. William F. Miller, "Europe 1992: Regionalism and Globalism," *The International Executive*, September 1, 1991, pp. 28–35; S. M. Jameel Hasan, "Human Resource Management in a New Era of Globalism," *Business Forum*, Winter 1992, pp. 56–59; "The New Globalism," *Nonprofit World*, January 1, 1992, pp. 22–25; Michael Porter, *The Competitive Advantage of Nations* (New York: Free Press, 1990).

38. "Buyers Respond to New GM Incentives: Questions Remain on Company Strategy," *The Wall Street Journal*, August 29, 1986, p. 2.

39. See Fremont E. Kast and James E. Rosenzweig, *Contingency Views of Organization and Management* (Chicago: Science Research Associates, 1973), for an early summary of contingency theory.

40. "Airline's Ills Point Out Weaknesses of Unorthodox Management Style," *The Wall Street Journal*, August 11, 1986, p. 15.

41. "Living: A Farewell to the Big Book," *Time*, February 8, 1993, p. 66; "Can the Man from Saks Save Sears?" *Newsweek*, February 8, 1993, p. 51; "Smaller But Wiser Now," *Business Week*, October 12, 1992, p. 28.

42. Lloyd Dobyns and Clare Crawford-Mason, *Quality or Else* (Boston: Houghton Mifflin, 1991).

43. David D. Van Fleet and Ricky W. Griffin, "Quality Circles: A Review and Suggested Future Directions," in C. L. Cooper and I. Robertson, eds., *International Review of Industrial and Organizational Psychology 1989* (New York: John Wiley, 1989), pp. 213–233.

44. E. E. Lawler, III, *High Involvement Management* (San Francisco: Jossey-Bass, 1990) and E. E. Lawler, III, *The Ultimate Advantage* (San Francisco: Jossey-Bass, 1992). For a review of participative management, see M. R. Weisbord, *Productive Workplaces: Organizing and Managing for Dignity, Meaning, and Community* (San Francisco: Jossey-Bass, 1987).

45. Lawler, *The Ultimate Advantage*, p. 25.

46. Ibid., p. 28.

47. Lawler, *High Involvement Management*.

48. "CEO of the Year: Stanley Gault of Goodyear," *Financial World*, March 31, 1992, p. 26; Peter Nulty, "The Bounce Is Back at Goodyear," *Fortune*, September 7, 1992, pp. 70–72; Gary Hoover, Alta Campbell, and Patrick J. Spain, eds., *Hoover's Handbook: Profiles of Over 500 Major Corporations* (Austin, Tex.: The Reference Press, 1991), p. 264; Zachary Schiller, "Goodyear's Miracle Man," *Business Week*, June 17, 1991, p. 35; Milton Moskowitz, Robert Levering, and Michael Katz, eds., *Everybody's Business* (New York: Doubleday, 1990), pp. 256–258.

49. Noel J. Shumsky, "Justifying the Intercultural Training Investment," *The Journal of European Business*, September 1, 1992, pp. 38–43; Shari Caudron, "Training Ensures Success Overseas," *Personnel Journal*, December 1, 1991, pp. 27–31; Kenneth Labich, "What Our Kids Must Learn," *Fortune*, January 27, 1992, pp. 64–66; Joel Dreyfuss, "Get Ready for the New Work Force," *Fortune*, April 23, 1990, pp. 165–181; Richard I. Kirkland, Jr., "Europe's New Managers," *Fortune*, September 29, 1986, p. 60; and John Naisbitt, *Megatrons* (New York: Warner Books, 1982).

Chapter 2

1. "Hard Rock Chain Hopes to Hit Pay Dirt with Casino," *The Wall Street Journal*, June 5, 1991, p. B1; Charles Bernstein, "Is Glitz More Important Than Food?" *Restaurants and Institutions*, February 26, 1992, p. 22; Stuart Greenbaum, "Clothes-Minded Marketers Find Promotion That Fits Them to a T," *Marketing News*, November 25, 1991, p. 6; Sergio Lalli, "Big Projects Boost Vegas," *Hotel and Motel Management*, November 4, 1991, pp. C2, C12; Christopher Middleton, "The Hard Rock with a Soft Sell," *Marketing*, April 25, 1991, p. 23; John Soeder, "Some Kind of Savior," *Restaurant Hospitality*, May 1990, pp. 113–118.

2. As quoted in Sheryl Hillard Tucker and Kevin D. Thompson, "Will Diversity = Opportunity + Advancement for Blacks?" *Black Enterprise*, November 1990, p. 60.

3. John Holusha, "A New Spirit at U.S. Auto Plants," *The New York Times*, December 29, 1987, pp. D1, D5.

4. "U.S. Productivity: First But Fading," *Fortune*, October 19, 1992, pp. 54–57.

5. Ibid.

6. "Anita the Agitator," *Time*, January 25, 1993, pp. 52–54; "The World Cosmetics Industry: Facing Up," *Economist,* July 13, 1992; "The Ecology of Commerce," *Inc.*, April 1992, pp. 93–100; "Changing the World," *Forbes*, March 2, 1992, pp. 83, 87; "What Selling Will Be Like in the '90s," *Fortune*, January 13, 1992, pp. 63–64; "Whales, Human Rights, Rain Forests—And the Heady Smell of Profits," *Business Week*, July 15, 1991, pp. 114–115; "New Leadership," *Executive Excellence*, March 1991, pp. 10–12; "This Woman Has Changed Business Forever," *Inc.*, June 1990, pp. 34–47.

7. Robert E. Quinn and John Rohrbaugh, "A Spatial Model of Effectiveness Criteria: Towards a Competing Values Approach to Organizational Analysis," *Management Science*, 1983, pp. 363–377; Robert E. Quinn, *Beyond Rational Management: Mastering the Paradoxes and Competing Demands of High Performance* (San Francisco: Jossey-Bass, 1988); Robert E. Quinn, Sue R. Faerman, Michael P. Thompson, and Michael R. McGrath, *Becoming a Master Manager: A Competency Framework* (New York: John Wiley, 1990), pp. 2–12.

8. Frederick W. Taylor, *The Principles of Scientific Management* (New York: Harper and Brothers, 1911), p. 44.

9. James O'Toole, *Vanguard Management* (New York: Doubleday, 1985).

10. John R. Schermerhorn, Jr., *Management for Productivity*, 4th ed. (New York: John Wiley, 1993), p. 17.

11. "One for the Gripper," *People Weekly*, August 19, 1991, pp. 95–96; Personal observation, August 1992; "The Fad of the Summer," *Time*, July 29, 1991, p. 61; "Get a Grip," *Fortune*, July 15, 1991, p. 110; "Seller of Velcro Ball and Mitts Hits Homer," *The Wall Street Journal*, July 7, 1991, p. B1.

12. Henry Mintzberg, *The Nature of Managerial Work* (New York: Harper & Row, 1975).

13. James A. F. Stoner and R. Edward Freeman, *Management*, 5th ed. (Englewood Cliffs, N.J.: Prentice Hall, 1992), p. 13.

14. See for example Larry D. Alexander, "The Effect Level in the Hierarchy and Functional Area Have on the Extent Mintzberg's Roles Are Required by Managerial Jobs," *Academy of Management Proceedings* (San Francisco, 1979), pp. 186–189; Alan W. Lau and Cynthia M. Pavett, "The Nature of Managerial Work: A Comparison of Public and Private Sector Managers," *Group and Organization Studies*, December 1980, pp. 453–466; Cynthia M. Pavett and Alan W. Lau, "Managerial Work: The Influence of Hierarchical Level and Functional Specialty," *Academy of Management Journal*, March 1983, pp. 170–177; and Allen I. Kraut, Patricia R. Pedigo, D. Douglas McKenna, and Marvin D. Dunnette, "The Role of the Manager: What's Really Important in Different Management Jobs," *Academy of Management Executive*, November 1989, pp. 286–293.

15. Pavett and Lau, "Managerial Work: The Influence of Hierarchical Level and Functional Specialty," pp. 170–177.

16. Fred Luthans, Stuart A. Rosenkrantz, and Harry W. Hennessey, "What Do Successful Managers Really Do? An Observation Study of Managerial Activities," *The Journal of Applied Behavioral Science*, 1985, pp. 255–270; Fred Luthans, "Successful Vs. Effective Real Managers," *Academy of Management Executive*, May 1988, pp. 127–132; Fred Luthans, Richard M. Hodgetts, and Stuart A. Rosenkranz, *Real Managers* (Cambridge, Mass.: Ballinger Publishing, 1988); Fred Luthans, Diane H. B. Welsh, and Lewis A. Taylor III, "A Descriptive Model of Managerial Effectiveness," *Group and Organization Studies*, June 1988, pp. 148–162; and Gary Yukl, *Skills for Managers and Leaders* (Englewood Cliffs, N.J.: Prentice Hall, 1990).

17. Quinn, Faerman, Thompson, and McGrath, *Becoming a Master Manager: A Competency Framework*.

18. Quinn, Faerman, Thompson, and McGrath, *Becoming a Master Manager: A Competency Framework*, pp. 19–20.

19. Robert L. Katz, "Skills of an Effective Administrator," *Harvard Business Review*, January–February 1955, pp. 33–42.

20. John A. Wagner III and John R. Hollenbeck, *Management of Organizational Behavior* (Englewood Cliffs, N.J.: Prentice Hall, 1992), p. 44.

21. L. Shullman, *Skills of Supervision and Staff Management* (Itasca, Ill.: F. E. Peacock Publishers, Inc., 1982).

22. Donald A. Norman, *Learning and Memory* (San Francisco: W. H. Freeman and Company, 1982); John R. Anderson, *Cognitive Psychology and Its Implications* (San Francisco: W. H. Freeman and Company, 1980); Morton Hunt, *The Universe Within: A New Science Exploring the Human Mind* (New York: Simon and Schuster, 1982); Lyle E. Bourne, Roger L. Dominowski, Elizabeth F. Loftus, and Alice F. Healy, *Cognitive Processes*, 2nd ed. (Englewood Cliffs, N.J.: Prentice Hall, 1986).

23. P. J. Guglielmino, "Perceptions of the Skills Needed by Mid-Level Managers in the Future and the Implications for Continued Education: A Comparison of the Perceptions of Mid-Level Managers, Professors of Management, and Directors of Training," *Dissertation Abstracts International*, 39(3), p. 1260A; P. J. Guglielmino and A. B. Carroll, "The Hierarchy of Management Skills: Future Professional Development for

Mid-Level Managers," *Management Decision*, 17(4), pp. 341–345; F. C. Mann, "Toward an Understanding of the Leadership Role in Formal Organizations," in R. Dubin, G. C. Homans, F. C. Mann, D. C. Miller, eds., *Leadership and Productivity* (San Francisco: Chandler Publishing Company, 1965), pp. 68–103.

24. Luthans, Rosenkrantz, and Hennessey, "What Do Successful Managers Really Do? An Observation Study of Managerial Activities," pp. 255–270; Luthans, "Successful Vs. Effective Real Managers," pp. 127–132; Luthans, Welsh, and Taylor, "A Descriptive Model of Managerial Effectiveness," pp. 148–162.

25. *The Corporate Elite* (special issue of *Business Week*, 1990).

26. Robert W. Mann and Julie M. Staudenmier, "Strategic Shifts in Executive Development," *Training and Development*, July 1991, pp. 37–40.

27. L. W. Porter and L. E. McKibbon, *Future of Management Education and Development: Drift or Thrust into the 21st Century?* (New York: McGraw-Hill, 1988).

28. "Desperate to Know Where Grads of Procter & Gamble Are Hiding?" *The Wall Street Journal*, August 20, 1986, p. 15.

29. "New Hotel Symbolizes Change at Marriott," *Hotel and Motel Management*, June 22, 1992, pp. 1, 12; "Room-Rate Structures Simplified," *Hotel and Motel Management*, April 27, 1992, pp. 3, 84–85; "Greening for Dollars," *Lodging Hospitality*, April 1992, pp. 36–38; "Marriott Reserves a Corner Suite for Steve Bollenbach," *Business Week*, February 24, 1992, pp. 37–38; "Hoteliers React to Dwindling Lounge Usage," *Hotel and Motel Management*, May 9, 1992, pp. 27, 29; "All That Lean Isn't Turning into Green," *Business Week*, November 18, 1991, pp. 39–40.

30. "Taken to the Cleaners," *Financial World*, August 4, 1992, pp. 28–30; "Maytag Corp.," *Barron's*, May 25, 1992, pp. 35–36; "A Heartland Industry Takes On the World," *Fortune*, March 12, 1990, pp. 110–112; "Wake Up, Maytag Man!" *Forbes*, November 13, 1989, pp. 308, 310; "Remaking Maytag," *Barron's*, August 21, 1989, pp. 12–13; "Can Maytag Clean Up Around the World?" *Business Week*, January 30, 1989, pp. 86–87.

Chapter 3

1. "In Search of the '90s Consumer," *Fortune*, September 21, 1992, p. 100; "Changing Clothing Limits Limited," *USA Today*, October 19, 1990, p. 3B; "Retailers Face Wild Ride to Recovery," *The Wall Street Journal*, April 9, 1992, pp. B1, B6; "Maybe The Limited Has Limits After All," *Business Week*, March 18, 1991, pp. 128–129; "Why Leslie Werner Shops Overseas," *Business Week*, February 3, 1992, p. 30.

2. Daniel A. Levinthal, "Organizational Adaptation and Environmental Selection—Interrelated Processes of Change," *Organization Science*, February 1991, pp. 140–151.

3. Danny Miller, "Environmental Fit Versus Internal Fit," *Organization Science*, May 1992, pp. 159–173.

4. See Jay B. Barney and William G. Ouchi, eds., *Organizational Economics* (San Francisco: Jossey-Bass, 1986), for an overview of current thinking about linkages between economics and organizations.

5. Robert H. Hayes and Ramchandran Jaikumar, "Manufacturing's Crisis: New Technologies, Obsolete Organizations," *Harvard Business Review*, September–October 1988, pp. 77–85.

6. "Regulation Rises Again," *Business Week,* June 26, 1989, pp. 58–59.

7. "They Don't Call It Blockbuster for Nothing," *Business Week,* October 19, 1992, pp. 113–114; "Blockbuster's Grainy Picture," *Business Week,* May 20, 1991, pp. 40–41; "After Frantic Growth, Blockbuster Faces Host of Video-Rental Rivals," *The Wall Street Journal,* March 21, 1991, pp. A1, A6; "Video Giant Got Bargain, Analysts Say," *USA Today,* November 20, 1990, pp. 1B, 2B.

8. Philip M. Rosenzweig and Jitendra V. Singh, "Organizational Environments and the Multinational Enterprise," *Academy of Management Journal,* June 1991, pp. 340–361.

9. P. Rajan Varadarajan, Terry Clark, and William M. Pride, "Controlling the Uncontrollable: Managing Your Market Economy," *Sloan Management Review,* Winter 1992, pp. 39–50; Ming-Jer Chen and Ian C. MacMillan, "Nonresponse and Delayed Response to Competitive Moves: The Roles of Competitor Dependence and Action Irreversibility," *Academy of Management Journal,* September 1992, pp. 539–570.

10. "National Firms Find That Selling to Local Tastes Is Costly, Complex," *The Wall Street Journal,* July 9, 1987, p. 17. See also Regis McKenna, "Marketing in an Age of Diversity," *Harvard Business Review,* September–October 1988, pp. 88–95.

11. Susan Helper, "How Much Has Really Changed Between U.S. Automakers and Their Suppliers?" *Sloan Management Review,* Summer 1991, pp. 15–28.

12. "What Went Wrong?" *Time,* November 9, 1992, pp. 42–50; "The Lessons GM Could Learn for Its Supplier Shakeup," *Business Week,* August 31, 1992, p. 29; "GM Tightens the Screws," *Business Week,* June 22, 1992, pp. 30–31; "Jack Smith Is Already on a Tear at GM," *Business Week,* May 11, 1992, p. 37; "Doing It Right, Till the Last Whistle," *Business Week,* April 6, 1992, pp. 58–59.

13. "Many Businesses Blame Governmental Policies for Productivity Lag," *The Wall Street Journal,* October 28, 1980, pp. 1, 22.

14. Grant T. Savage, Timothy W. Nix, Carlton J. Whitehead, and John D. Blair, "Strategies for Assessing and Managing Organizational Culture," *The Academy of Management Executive,* May 1991, pp. 61–75.

15. "Time Warner Feels the Force of Stockholder Power," *Business Week,* July 21, 1991, pp. 58–59.

16. Rob Norton, "Who Owns This Company, Anyhow?" *Fortune,* July 29, 1991, pp. 131–142.

17. John J. Curran, "Companies That Rob the Future," *Fortune,* July 4, 1988, pp. 84–89.

18. "More Competitors Turn to Cooperation," *The Wall Street Journal,* June 23, 1989, p. B1.

19. Jeremy Main, "The Winning Organization," *Fortune,* September 26, 1988, pp. 50–60; Harrison M. Trice and Janice M. Beyer, *The Culture of Work Organizations* (Englewood Cliffs, N.J.: Prentice-Hall, 1993).

20. Terrence E. Deal and Allan A. Kennedy, *Corporate Cultures: The Rights and Rituals of Corporate Life* (Reading, Mass.: Addison-Wesley, 1982).

21. Gurney Breckenfield, "The Odyssey of Levi Strauss," *Fortune,* March 22, 1982, pp. 110–124. See also "Levi Strauss . . . at $3 Billion Plus," *Daily News Record,* October 10, 1988, p. 44; John P. Kotler and James L. Heskett, *Corporate Culture and Performance* (New York: Macmillan, 1992).

22. Jay B. Barney, "Organizational Culture: Can It Be a Source of Sustained Competitive Advantage?" *Academy of Management Review,* July 1986, pp. 656–665.

23. "Hewlett-Packard's Whip-Crackers," *Fortune,* February 13, 1989, pp. 58–59.

24. James D. Thompson, *Organizations in Action* (New York: McGraw-Hill, 1967).

25. Michael E. Porter, *Competitive Strategy: Techniques for Analyzing Industries and Competitors* (New York: Free Press, 1980).

26. *Are You Ready for Disaster?* MAPI Economic Report, Washington, D.C., 1990.

27. Ian I. Mitroff, Paul Shrivastava, and Firdaus E. Udwadia, "Effective Crisis Management," *The Academy of Management Executive,* August 1987, pp. 283–292.

28. "Getting Business to Think About the Unthinkable," *Business Week,* June 24, 1991, pp. 104–107.

29. For recent discussions of how these processes work, see Barbara W. Keats and Michael A. Hitt, "A Causal Model of Linkages Among Environmental Dimensions, Macro Organizational Characteristics, and Performance," *Academy of Management Journal,* September 1988, pp. 570–598; and Danny Miller, "The Structural and Environmental Correlates of Business Strategy," *Strategic Management Journal,* Vol. 8, 1987, pp. 55–76.

30. "Why the Street Isn't Moved by Tenneco's Big Move," *Business Week,* September 26, 1988, pp. 130–133.

31. Tom Burns and G. M. Stalker, *The Management of Innovation* (London: Tavistock, 1961).

32. Keats and Hitt, "A Causal Model of Linkages Among Environmental Dimensions, Macro Organizational Characteristics, and Performance."

33. David B. Yoffie, "How an Industry Builds Political Advantage," *Harvard Business Review,* May–June 1988, pp. 82–89.

34. "Safeway Faces Brawls in Every Aisle," *Business Week,* September 7, 1992, p. 78; Gary Hector, "How Safeway Coped With the Quake," *Fortune,* November 20, 1989, pp. 101–104; Gary Hoover, Alta Campbell, and Patrick J. Spain, eds., *Hoover's Handbook of American Business 1992* (Austin, Tex.: The Reference Press, 1991), p. 471.

35. "Sweet Smell of Excess,"*Newsweek,* October 14, 1992, pp. 46–47; "Is Sony Finally Getting the Hang of Hollywood?" *Business Week,* September 7, 1992, pp. 76–77; Brenton R. Schlender, "How Sony Keeps the Magic Going," *Fortune,* February 24, 1992, pp. 76–84; Nancy J. Perry, "Will Sony Make It in Hollywood?" *Fortune,* September 9, 1991, pp. 158–166.

Chapter 4

1. "Can Wayne Calloway Handle the Pepsi Challenge?" *Business Week,* January 27, 1992, pp. 90–98; "Frito-Lay is Munching on the Competition," *Business Week,* August 24, 1992, pp. 52–53; "The Cola Kings Are Feeling a Bit Jumpy," *Business Week,* July 13, 1992, p. 112; "Pepsi Is Doing Better with Its Fast Foods and Frito-Lay Snacks," *The Wall Street Journal,* June 13, 1991, pp. A1, A2.

2. See Alvin Toffler, *Future Shock* (New York: Random House, 1970).

3. "Managing Now for the 1990s," *Fortune,* September 26, 1988, pp. 44–47.

4. "1,000 Face Layoff at American," *USA Today,* October 16, 1992, p. 1B; "As Demand Shrinks, So Does IBM," *USA Today,* October 16, 1992, pp. 1B, 2B.

5. "Companies to Watch," *Fortune,* September 7, 1992, p. 75; "Sunny Days Return for Duty-Free Chain Shop," *Barron's,* December 30, 1991, p. 52; "Ripe Young Stocks Ready for the Picking," *Business Week,* December 30, 1991, pp. 76–77; "Town & Country Jewelry," *Barron's,* October 19, 1987, p. 69.

6. "Small-Business Hiring, a Locomotive for the Economy in the '80s, Is Slowing," *The Wall Street Journal,* March 16, 1990, pp. B1, B3.

7. "The Service 500," *Fortune,* June 1, 1992, p. 201.

8. John J. Curran, "Companies That Rob the Future," *Fortune,* July 4, 1988, pp. 84–89.

9. Joel Dreyfuss, "Victories in the Quality Crusade," *Fortune,* October 10, 1988, pp. 80–88.

10. "Shoes with an Attitude," *USA Today,* August 2, 1990, pp. B1, B2; "The 'Blacktop' is Paving Reebok's Road to Recovery," *Business Week,* August 12, 1991, p. 27; "L.A. Gear Calls in a Cobbler," *Business Week,* September 16, 1991, pp. 78–82; "L.A. Gear Slips, Posts Loss for Year," *USA Today,* February 23, 1993, p. 33.

11. Joel Dreyfuss, "Getting High Tech Back on Track,"*Fortune,* January 1, 1990, pp. 74–77.

12. Christopher Knowlton, "What America Makes Best,"*Fortune,* March 28, 1988, pp. 40–53.

13. Marlene G. Fine, Fern L. Johnson, and M. Sallyanne Ryan, "Cultural Diversity in the Workplace," *Public Personnel Management,* Fall 1990, pp. 305–319.

14. Badi G. Foster, Gerald Jackson, William E. Cross, Bailey Jackson, and Rita Hardiman, "Workforce Diversity and Business," *Training and Development Journal,* April 1988, pp. 38–42.

15. Sam Cole, "Cultural Diversity and Sustainable Futures," *Futures,* December 1990, pp. 1044–1058.

16. Louis S. Richman, "The Coming World Labor Shortage,"*Fortune,* April 9, 1990, pp. 70–77.

17. *Occupational Outlook Handbook* (Washington, D.C.: U.S. Bureau of Labor Statistics, 1990–1991).

18. Ibid.

19. Michael Chisholm, "Cultural Diversity Breaks the Mold," *Geographical Magazine,* November 1990, pp. 12–16.

20. Based on Taylor H. Cox and Stacy Blake, "Managing Cultural Diversity: Implications for Organizational Competitiveness," *The Academy of Management Executive,* August 1991, pp. 45–56.

21. Cox and Blake, "Managing Cultural Diversity: Implications for Organizational Competitiveness."

22. For an example, see "Get to Know the Ethnic Market," *Marketing,* June 17, 1991, p. 32.

23. Patti Watts, "Bias Busting: Diversity Training in the Workforce," *Management Review,* December 1987, pp. 51–54.

24. See Stephenie Overman, "Managing the Diverse Work Force," *HR Magazine,* April 1991, pp. 32–36.

25. Lennie Copeland, "Making the Most of Cultural Differences at the Workplace," *Personnel,* June 1988, pp. 52–60.

26. "Firms Address Workers' Cultural Variety," *The Wall Street Journal,* February 10, 1989, p. B1.

27. "Learning to Accept Cultural Diversity," *The Wall Street Journal,* September 12, 1990, pp. B1, B9.

28. "Firms Address Workers' Cultural Variety."

29. "Firms Grapple with Language," *The Wall Street Journal,* November 7, 1989, p. B1.

30. "Flexible Formulas," *The Wall Street Journal,* June 4, 1990, pp. R34, R35.

31. "Is Your Boss Spying on You?" *Business Week,* January 15, 1990, pp. 74–75.

32. " 'Guilty, Your Honor,' " *Business Week,* May 7, 1990, pp. 32–37.

33. See Jeremy Main, "Here Comes the Big New Cleanup," *Fortune,* November 21, 1988, pp. 102–118; David Kirkpatrick, "Environmentalism: The New Crusade," *Fortune,* February 21, 1990, pp. 44–52.

34. "Eastern Europe's Big Cleanup," *Business Week,* March 19, 1990, pp. 114–115.

35. " 'I Hope My Luck Holds Out,' " *Forbes,* July 20, 1992, pp. 114–119; "A Giant That Keeps Innovating," *Fortune,* December 16, 1991, pp. 101–102; "ConAgra Turns Up the Heat in the Kitchen," *Business Week,* September 2, 1991, pp. 58–59; Russell Shaw, "Savoring Challenges," *Sky,* August 1992, pp. 61–67.

36. "Europe's Shakeout," *Business Week,* September 14, 1992, pp. 44–51; "Will the (New) Maginot Line Hold?" *Forbes,* July 8, 1991, pp. 58–61; Thomas A. Stewart, "Brace for Japan's Hot New Strategy," *Fortune,* September 21, 1992, pp. 62–74.

Chapter 5

1. "The World 'S' Ours," *Newsweek,* March 23, 1992, pp. 46–47; Gary Hoover, Alta Campbell, Alan Chai, and Patrick J. Spain, eds., *Hoover's Handbook of World Business 1992* (Austin, Tex.: The Reference Press, 1991), p. 523; "Guess Who's Selling Barbies in Japan Now?" *Business Week,* December 9, 1991, pp. 72–76.

2. Richard M. Steers and Edwin L. Miller, "Management in the 1990s: The International Challenge," *The Academy of Management Executive,* February 1988, pp. 21–22; David A. Ricks, Brian Toyne, and Zaida Martinez, "Recent Developments in International Management Research," *Journal of Management,* June 1990, pp. 219–254.

3. For a more complete discussion of forms of international business, see Arvind Phatak, *International Dimensions of Management,* 3rd ed. (Boston: Kent, 1993).

4. Alex Taylor III, "U.S. Cars Come Back," *Fortune,* November 16, 1992, pp. 52–85.

5. "The Stateless Corporation," *Business Week,* May 14, 1990, pp. 98–104.

6. Philip M. Rosenzweig and Jitendra V. Singh, "Organizational Environments and the Multinational Enterprise," *Academy of Management Review,* April 1991, pp. 340–361.

7. John Labate, "Gearing Up for Steady Growth," *Fortune,* July 29, 1991, pp. 83–102; "The *Fortune* Global 500," *Fortune,* July 27, 1992, pp. 175–232.

8. "U.S. Corporations with the Biggest Foreign Revenues," *Forbes,* July 22, 1991, pp. 286–288.

9. John D. Daniels and Lee H. Radebaugh, *International Business,* 6th ed. (Reading, Mass.: Addison-Wesley, 1992).

10. Kenichi Ohmae, "The Global Logic of Strategic Alliances," *Harvard Business Review,* March–April 1989, pp. 143–154.

11. "The Magnet of Growth in Mexico's North," *Business Week,* June 6,

1988, pp. 48–50; "Will the New Maquiladoras Build a Better Mañana?" *Business Week,* November 14, 1988, pp. 102–106.

12. Allen J. Morrison, David A. Ricks, and Kendall Roth, "Globalization Versus Regionalism: Which Way for the Multinational?" *Organizational Dynamics,* Winter 1991, pp. 17–29.

13. Ben L. Kedia and Rabi S. Bhagat, "Cultural Constraints on Transfer of Technology Across Nations: Implications for Research in International and Comparative Management," *Academy of Management Review,* October 1988, pp. 559–571; Carla Rapoport, "Japan's Growing Global Reach," *Fortune,* May 22, 1989, pp. 48–56.

14. Louis Kraar, "The Growing Power of Asia," *Fortune,* October 7, 1991, pp. 118–131.

15. "'Free Trade Isn't Painless,'" *Business Week,* August 31, 1992, pp. 38–39; "Why Some Asian Companies Are Gung Ho About NAFTA," *Business Week,* August 31, 1992, p. 39; "A Noose Around NAFTA," *Business Week,* February 22, 1993, p. 37; "Free Trade? They Can Hardly Wait," *Business Week,* September 14, 1992, pp. 24–25; Louis S. Richman, "How NAFTA Will Help America," *Fortune,* April 19, 1993, pp. 95–102.

16. "Where Killers and Kidnappers Roam," *Fortune,* September 23, 1991, p. 8.

17. Daniels and Radebaugh, *International Business.*

18. "The Face of the Global Economy," *Business Week/Reinventing America* (A special issue of *Business Week*), 1992, pp. 150–159.

19. John Paul Newport, Jr., "Texas Faces Up to a Tougher Future," *Fortune,* March 13, 1989, pp. 102–112.

20. "Firms Address Workers' Cultural Variety," *The Wall Street Journal,* February 10, 1989, p. B1.

21. "10,000 New EC Rules," *Business Week,* September 7, 1992, pp. 48–50; "Choking the Spirit of Enterprise," *International Management,* March 1992, pp. 30–39; A. H. Moini, "Europe 1992: A Challenge to Small Exporters," *Journal of Small Business,* January 1992, pp. 11–18.

22. "You Don't Have to Be a Giant to Score Big Overseas," *Business Week,* April 13, 1987, pp. 62–63.

23. "Famous Bakery Keeps Business Thriving," *Corsicana Daily Sun,* June 9, 1991, p. 1C.

24. "Euro Disney—Oui or Non?" *Travel & Leisure,* August 1992, pp. 80–115; "Mouse Fever Is About to Strike Europe," *Business Week,* March 30, 1992, p. 32; "The Mouse Isn't Roaring," *Business Week,* August 24, 1992, p. 38; "Mickey Mess," *Time,* June 22, 1992, p. 30.

25. "High-Tech Star," *Business Week,* July 27, 1992, pp. 54–58; "Users Rate PBXs," *Data Communications,* June 1992, pp. 93–100; Gedas Sakus, "A Strategy for Success," *Canadian Business Review,* Winter 1991, pp. 37–39; Graham Palmer and Sherrill Burns, "Revolutionizing the Business: Strategies for Succeeding with Change," *Human Resource Planning,* Summer 1991, pp. 77–84.

Chapter 6

1. "Tree-Huggers Vs. Jobs: It's Not That Simple," *Business Week,* October 19, 1992, pp. 108–109; "'The Spotted Owl Could Wipe Us Out,'" *Business Week,* September 18, 1989, pp. 94–99; "Growth Vs. Environmentalism," *Business Week,* May 11, 1992, pp. 66–75.

2. See F. Neil Brady, "Aesthetic Components of Managerial Ethics," *Academy of Management Review,* April 1986, pp. 337–344.

3. Thomas M. Barrett and Richard J. Kilonski, *Business Ethics,* 3rd ed. (Englewood Cliffs, N.J.: Prentice-Hall, 1990).

4. "What, Me Overpaid? CEOs Fight Back," *Business Week,* May 4, 1992, pp. 142–148.

5. Gene Bylinsky, "How Companies Spy on Employees," November 4, 1992, pp. 131–140.

6. John Huey, "Wal-Mart—Will It Take Over the World?" *Fortune,* January 30, 1989, pp. 52–61.

7. Patricia Sellers, "Winning Over the New Consumer," *Fortune,* July 29, 1992, pp. 113–125.

8. "Not Everyone Loves Wal-Mart's Low Prices," *Business Week,* October 12, 1992, pp. 36–38.

9. "The Dark Side of Japan Inc.," *Newsweek,* January 9, 1989, p. 41.

10. See Kenneth Labich, "The New Crisis in Business Ethics," *Fortune,* April 20, 1992, pp. 167–176.

11. Erik Jansen and Mary Ann Von Glinow, "Ethical Ambivalence and Organizational Reward Systems," *Academy of Management Review,* October 1985, pp. 814–822.

12. Roy Rowan, "The Maverick Who Yelled Foul at Citibank," *Fortune,* January 10, 1983, pp. 46–56.

13. "Can Ethics Be Taught? Harvard Gives It the Old College Try," *Business Week,* April 6, 1992, p. 34; "Ethics and Bottom Line at Bentley," *The Boston Globe,* September 28, 1992, pp. 17 and 19.

14. "The Ugly Mess at Waste Management," *Business Week,* April 13, 1992, pp. 76–77; Gary Hoover, Alta Campbell, and Patrick J. Spain, eds., *Hoover's Handbook of American Business 1993* (Austin, Tex.: The Reference Press, 1992), p. 575; "Recycled Accounting," *Barron's* August 6, 1990, pp. 16–17, 45; "Down in the Dumps," *Financial World,* June 23, 1992, pp. 30–34.

15. "Ethics Training at Work," *The Wall Street Journal,* September 9, 1986, p. 1.

16. "Ethics on the Job: Companies Alert Employees to Potential Dilemmas," *The Wall Street Journal,* July 14, 1986, p. 17.

17. "Companies Get Serious About Ethics," *USA Today,* December 9, 1986, pp. 1B–2B.

18. See Frederick D. Sturdivant, *Business and Society: A Managerial Approach,* 4th ed. (Homewood, Ill.: Richard D. Irwin, 1989).

19. See Archie Carroll, *Business and Society: Ethics and Stakeholder Management* (Cincinnati, Oh.: Southwestern, 1989), for a review of the evolution of social responsibility.

20. Stahrl W. Edmunds, "Unifying Concepts in Social Responsibility," *Academy of Management Review,* January 1977, pp. 38–45.

21. Page Smith, *The Rise of Industrial America* (New York: McGraw-Hill, 1984).

22. Keith Davis, "The Case for and Against Business Assumption of Social Responsibility," *Academy of Management Journal,* June 1973, pp. 312–322.

23. Milton Friedman, *Capitalism and Freedom* (Chicago: University of Chicago Press, 1962).

24. "Big Trouble at Allegheny," *Business Week,* August 11, 1986, pp. 56–61.

25. Edwin M. Epstein, "The Corporate Social Policy Process: Beyond

Business Ethics, Corporate Social Responsibility, and Corporate Social Responsiveness," *California Management Review,* Spring 1987, pp. 99–114.

26. "A Mail-Order Romance: Land's End Courts Unseen Customers," *Fortune,* March 13, 1989, pp. 44–45.

27. Alan Farnham, "Holding Firm on Affirmative Action," *Fortune,* March 13, 1989, pp. 87–88.

28. "Ashland Just Can't Seem to Leave Its Checkered Past Behind," *Business Week,* October 31, 1988, pp. 122–126.

29. Jeremy Main, "Here Comes the Big New Cleanup," *Fortune,* November 21, 1988, pp. 102–118.

30. "Ashland Just Can't Seem to Leave Its Checkered Past Behind."

31. Nancy J. Perry, "The Education Crisis: What Business Can Do," *Fortune,* July 4, 1988, pp. 71–81.

32. Anthony H. Bloom, "Managing Against Apartheid," *Harvard Business Review,* November–December 1987, pp. 49–56.

33. See S. Prakash Sethi, "A Conceptual Framework for Environmental Analysis of Social Issues and Evaluation of Business Response Patterns," *Academy of Management Review,* January 1979, pp. 63–74. See also Steven L. Wartick and Phillip L. Cochran, "The Evolution of the Corporate Social Performance Model," *Academy of Management Review,* October 1985, pp. 758–769.

34. "Ashland Just Can't Seem to Leave Its Checkered Past Behind."

35. "In 'Tobacco Smoker's Paradise' of Japan, U.S. Cigarettes Are Epitome of High Style," *The Wall Street Journal,* September 23, 1991, pp. B1, B6.

36. "A Mail-Order Romance: Land's End Courts Unseen Customers."

37. "Make the Punishment Fit the Corporate Crime," *Business Week,* March 13, 1989, p. 22.

38. "Many Businesses Blame Governmental Policies for Productivity Lag," *The Wall Street Journal,* October 28, 1980, p. 1.

39. Greg Densmore, "Scannell Brings New Look to OSHA," *Occupational Health & Safety,* January 1, 1990, pp. 18–21; William J. Rothwell, "Complying With OSHA," *Training and Development Journal,* May 1, 1989, pp. 52–54.

40. "How to Win Friends and Influence Lawmakers," *Business Week,* November 7, 1988, p. 36.

41. Wartick and Cochran, "The Evolution of the Corporate Social Performance Model"; Jerry W. Anderson, Jr., "Social Responsibility and the Corporation," *Business Horizons,* July–August 1986, pp. 22–27; and Epstein, "The Corporate Social Policy Process: Beyond Business Ethics, Corporate Social Responsibility, and Corporate Social Responsiveness."

42. Anderson, "Social Responsibility and the Corporation."

43. "Charity Doesn't Begin at Home Anymore," *The Wall Street Journal,* February 25, 1991, p. 91; "Japanese Firms Embark on a Program of Lavish Giving to American Charities," *The Wall Street Journal,* May 23, 1991, pp. B1, B5; "Good Deeds Are Good Business," *American Demographic,* September 1991, pp. 38–42.

44. "Unfuzzing Ethics for Managers," *Fortune,* November 23, 1987, pp. 229–234.

45. Janelle Brinker Dozier and Marcia P. Miceli, "Potential Predictors of Whistle-Blowing: A Prosocial Behavior Perspective," *Academy of Management Review,* October 1985, pp. 823–836; Janet P. Near and Marcia P. Miceli, "Retaliation Against Whistle Blowers: Predictors and Effects," *Journal of Applied Psychology,* February 1986, pp. 137–145.

46. Donna J. Wood, "Corporate Social Performance Revisited," *Academy of Management Review,* October 1991, pp. 691–718.

47. "A Scandal Waiting to Happen," *Business Week,* August 224, 1992, pp. 32–36; "These White Shoes Are Splattered With Mud," *Business Week,* September 7, 1992, p. 32; "Phar-Mor Disaster Shakes Private Market Investors," *Investment Dealer's Digest,* August 10, 1992, pp. 15–16; "Wait a Minute—Phar-Mor is Still Kicking," *Business Week,* March 8, 1993, pp. 60–61; "Phar-Mor's Ousted Vice-Chairman Hires Lawyer in Face of Possible Fraud Counts," *The Wall Street Journal,* August 6, 1992, p. A3; "Convenient Fiction: Inventory Is a Popular Thing to Manipulate," *The Wall Street Journal,* December 14, 1992, p. A4.

48. "Sweet Sales for Sour Mash—Abroad," *Business Week,* July 1, 1991, p. 62; "The Toast of Tokyo," *Marketing Week,* December 9, 1991, p. 20; " 'The Big Four': An Examination of the International Drinks Industry," *European Journal of Marketing,* September 1989, pp. 47–64.

Chapter 7

1. Stephen Creamer Yoder, "Intel Corp. Decides It's Time to Leave the Numbers Game," *The Wall Street Journal,* October 20, 1992, p. B6; Alan Deutschman, "If They're Gaining on You, Innovate," *Fortune,* November 2, 1992, p. 86; Robert D. Hof, "Inside Intel,"*Business Week,* June 1, 1992, pp. 86–94.

2. "ConAgra Turns Up the Heat," *Business Week,* September 2, 1991, pp. 58–63; Milton Moskowitz, Robert Levering, and Michael Katz, *Everybody's Business* (New York: Doubleday, 1990), pp. 6–8.

3. Russell Mitchell, Lois Therrien, and Gregory L. Miles, "ConAgra: Out of the Freezer," *Business Week,* June 25, 1990, pp. 24–25.

4. Seth Lubove, "ConAgra," *Forbes,* July 20, 1992, pp. 114–123; Ronald Henkoff, "ConAgra: A Giant That Keeps Innovating" *Fortune,* December 16, 1991, p. 101.

5. See Arie P. De Geus, "Planning As Learning," *Harvard Business Review,* March–April 1988, pp. 70–74.

6. Harrison M. Trice and Janice M. Beyer, *The Cultures of Work Organizations* (Englewood Cliffs, N.J.: Prentice-Hall, 1993), p. 117.

7. Henri Broms and Henrick Gahmberg, "Communications to Self in Organizations and Cultures," *Administrative Science Quarterly,* 28, pp. 482–495.

8. "Waldenbooks Peddles Books a Bit Like Soap, Transforming Market," *The Wall Street Journal,* October 10, 1988, pp. A1, A4.

9. George A Steiner, *Top Management Planning* (New York: Macmillan, 1969).

10. Jeff Bracker and John Pearson, "Planning and Financial Performance of Small Mature Firms," *Strategic Management Journal,* 1986, pp. 503–522.

11. Hugo Uyterhoeven, "General Managers in the Middle," *Harvard Business Review,* September–October 1989, pp. 136–145.

12. Ronald L. Nichol, "Get Middle Managers Involved in the Planning Process," *The Journal of Business Strategy,* May 1, 1992, pp. 26–33.

13. See Charles W. Hofer and Dan Schendel, *Strategy Formulation: Analytical Concepts* (St. Paul, Minn.: West, 1978); Richard F. Vancil and Peter Lorange, "Strategic Planning in Diversified Companies," *Harvard*

Business Review, January–February 1975, pp. 81–90; Rosemary Stewart, "Middle Managers: Their Jobs and Behavior," in Jay W. Lorsch, ed., *Handbook of Organizational Behavior* (Englewood Cliffs, N.J.: Prentice-Hall, 1987), pp. 385–391.

14. See Leonard A. Schlesinger and Janice A. Klein, "The First-Line Supervisor: Past, Present, and Future," in Jay W. Lorsch, ed., *Handbook of Organizational Behavior* (Englewood Cliffs, N.J.: Prentice-Hall, 1987), pp. 370–384.

15. Carol Davenport, "America's Most Admired Corporations," *Fortune,* January 30, 1989, pp. 68–94.

16. "CEO of the Year: Stanley Gault of Goodyear," *Financial World,* March 31, 1992, p. 26; Peter Nulty, "The Bounce Is Back at Goodyear," *Fortune,* September 7, 1992, pp. 70–72.

17. Andrew Campbell, "The Power of Mission: Aligning Strategy and Culture," *Planning Review,* September 10, 1992, pp. 10–15.

18. Edward Boyer, "Citicorp: What the New Boss Is Up To," *Fortune,* February 17, 1986, p. 40.

19. See Max D. Richards, *Setting Strategic Goals and Objectives,* 2nd ed. (St. Paul, Minn.: West, 1986), for more discussion of the goal-setting process.

20. See Michael E. Porter, *Competitive Advantage* (New York: Free Press, 1985) and Charles W. L. Hill and Gareth R. Jones, *Strategic Management: An Integrated Approach,* 2nd ed. (Boston: Houghton Mifflin, 1992).

21. Carol Davenport, "America's Most Admired Corporations."

22. Richard S. Teitelbaum, "Companies to Watch," *Fortune,* July 13, 1992, p. 91; "No Hangout Booths Here," *Restaurant Hospitality,* December 1, 1991, pp. 122–129; "Inside Wall Street," *Business Week,* October 14, 1991, p. 110; "Menu Concepts: IHOP Expands Menu Selection with Four New Chicken Sandwiches," *Restaurants & Institutions,* October 28, 1988, p. 54.

23. Gary Hector, "Yes, You *Can* Manage Long Term" *Fortune,* November 21, 1988, p. 68.

24. Michael T. Jacobs, "A Cure for America's Short-Termism," *Planning Review,* January 1992, pp. 4–9. See also Grady D. Bruce and James W. Taylor, "The Short-Term Orientation of American Managers: Fact or Fantasy?" *Business Horizons,* May/June 1991, pp. 10–15, who argue that the problem is not a short-term orientation.

25. Ricky W. Griffin, *Management,* 3rd ed. (Boston: Houghton Mifflin, 1990).

26. Donald C. Hambrick and David Lei, "Toward an Empirical Prioritization of Contingency Variables for Business Strategy," *Academy of Management Journal,* December 1985, pp. 763–788.

27. Ari Ginsberg and N. Venkatraman, "Contingency Perspectives of Organizational Strategy: A Critical Review of the Empirical Research," *Academy of Management Journal,* July 1985, pp. 421–434.

28. "Is Gatorade a Sleeping Giant?" *Beverage World,* August 1, 1992, pp. 32–35; "Business: Power Play in Sports Drinks," *Time,* June 1, 1992, p. 75; "Gatorade Energizes the Competition," *Adweek's Marketing Week,* March 2, 1992, p. 25; Stuart Elliott, "Gatorade Has Competition Bottled Up," *USA Today,* August 21, 1990, pp. B1–B2; and Kenneth Dreyfack, "Quaker Is Feeling Its Oats Again," *Business Week,* September 22, 1986, pp. 80–81.

29. George A. Steiner, *Strategic Planning: What Every Manager Must Know* (New York: Free Press, 1979).

30. Noel Tichy and Ram Charan, "Speed, Simplicity, and Self-Confidence: An Interview with Jack Welch," *Harvard Business Review,* September–October 1989, pp. 112–120.

31. "Cover Story: A Wide-Ranging Interview," *United States Banker,* February 1, 1992, pp. 20–21; Gary Hoover, Alta Campbell, and Patrick J. Spain, eds., *Hoover's Handbook: Profiles of Over 500 Major Corporations* (Austin, Tex.: The Reference Press, 1991), pp. 107, 111, 170, and 375; Bill Saporito, "Who's Winning the Credit Card War," *Fortune,* July 2, 1990, pp. 66–71; Larry Light, Leah Nathans Spiro, Peter Coy, and Suzanne Woolley, "The War of the Plastic," *Business Week,* April 15, 1991, pp. 28–29.

32. "Subaru in the Image Shop," *Business Week,* August 19, 1991, p. 86; "Long-Term Introduction: Subaru SVX," *Road & Track,* October 1, 1992, p. 158; Gary Hoover, Alta Campbell, and Patrick J. Spain, eds., *Hoover's Handbook: Profiles of Over 500 Major Corporations* (Austin, Tex.: The Reference Press, 1991), pp. 217 and 247; Milton Moskowitz, Robert Levering, and Michael Katz, *Everybody's Business,* pp. 248–249.

Chapter 8

1. "In Business This Week," *Business Week,* June 29, 1992, p. 44; Laurel Touby, "Playing with the Big Kids," *Business Week,* June 15, 1992, pp. 124–126; Richard Grey, "Tyco Toys," *Forbes,* May 11, 1992, p. 204; "Board Games: The Next Generation," *Adweek's Marketing Week,* November 25, 1991, p. 22.

2. See Charles W. L. Hill and Gareth R. Jones, *Strategic Management: An Analytical Approach* (Boston: Houghton Mifflin, 1989), for a review.

3. Richard P. Rumelt, "How Much Does Industry Matter?" *Strategic Management Journal,* 1991, pp. 167–186.

4. Jay Barney, "Firm Resources and Sustained Competitive Advantage," *Journal of Management,* 1991, pp. 99–120.

5. Arthur A. Thompson and A. J. Strickland III, *Strategic Management: Concepts and Cases,* 4th ed. (Dallas: Business Publications, 1987).

6. I. MacMillan and P. Jones, *Strategy Formulation* (St. Paul, Minn.: West Publishing, 1986).

7. Jay B. Barney and Ricky W. Griffin, *The Management of Organizations* (Boston: Houghton Mifflin, 1992), p. 216.

8. A. Tanzer, "We Do Not Take a Short-Term View," *Forbes,* July 13, 1987, pp. 372–374.

9. Jay Barney, "Organizational Culture: Can It Be a Source of Sustained Competitive Advantage?" *Academy of Management Review,* 1986, pp. 656–665.

10. Russell Mitchell, Lois Therien, and Gregory L. Miles, "ConAgra: Out of the Freezer," *Business Week,* June 25, 1990, pp. 24–25.

11. W. Olcott, "Taking Care of America: 50 Years of Philanthropy," *Direct Marketing,* May 1988, pp. 98–102.

12. Michael E. Porter, *Competitive Strategy: Techniques for Analyzing Industries and Competitors* (New York: Free Press, 1980). See also Walter Kiechel III, "Corporate Strategy for the 1990s," *Fortune,* February 29, 1988, pp. 34–42.

13. Janice Castro, "This Industry Is Always in the Grip of Its Dumbest

Competitors," *Time,* May 4, 1992, pp. 52–53; "The Risk Takers," *Maclean's,* August 31, 1992, p. 26; "Delivering Profits Through Air Cargo Operations," *Commuter Air International,* October 1, 1992, p. 23; "In Business This Week," *Business Week,* August 31, 1992, p. 34; "CAA Chairman Urges Merger Policy to Protect Smaller European Airlines," *Aviation Week & Space Technology,* February 17, 1992, p. 30; "Transportation Attorneys Favor Small Carriers in Route Cases," *Aviation Week & Space Technology,* November 4, 1991, p. 34; Thomas McCarroll, "You Too Can Run an Airline," *Time,* July 19, 1993, p. 54.

14. Leslie Brokaw, "The Secrets of Great Planning," *Inc.,* October 1, 1992, pp. 151–160.

15. Steve Glain, "L.A. Gear President Says Firm Will Recover, Will Focus on Asia," *The Wall Street Journal,* October 16, 1992, p. 3A; Kathy Tyrer, "L.A. Gear Not Thrilled with Michael Jackson," *Adweek,* September 21, 1992, p. 4; Kathleen Kerwin, "L.A. Gear Calls in a Cobbler," *Business Week,* September 16, 1991, pp. 78–82; "L.A. Gear: Tripping on Its Laces," *Business Week,* August 20, 1990, p. 39.

16. See "Personal Computers: And the Winner Is IBM," *Business Week,* October 3, 1983, pp. 76–79. See also "Mike Armstrong Is Improving IBM's Game in Europe," *Business Week,* June 20, 1988, pp. 96–101.

17. See, for example, Ian C. MacMillan, Donald C. Hambrick, and Diana L. Day, "The Product Portfolio and Profitability—A PMS-based Analysis of Industrial Product Businesses," *Academy of Management Journal,* December 1982, pp. 733–755.

18. Charles W. Hofer and Dan Schendel, *Strategy Formulation: Analytical Concepts* (St. Paul, Minn.: West Publishing, 1978).

19. Susan Benway, "Coleco: Out of the Cabbage Patch and into the Fire," *Business Week,* March 30, 1987, p. 54; Michael Porter, "Note on the Electronic Parts Distribution Industry," *Cases in Competitive Strategy* (New York: Free Press, 1979), pp. 1–19.

20. Raymond E. Miles and Charles C. Snow, *Organizational Strategy, Structure, and Process* (New York: McGraw-Hill, 1978).

21. "Masters of Innovation," *Business Week,* April 10, 1989, pp. 58–63.

22. Donald C. Hambrick, "Some Tests of the Effectiveness and Functional Attributes of Miles's and Snow's Strategic Types," *Academy of Management Journal,* March 1983, pp. 5–26.

23. Stuart Gannes, "America's Fastest-Growing Companies," *Fortune,* May 23, 1988, pp. 28–40.

24. Wayne Claycombe, "Building a Sound Management Foundation for Strategic Planning," *Industrial Management,* May 1, 1992, pp. 17–19.

25. "Disney's Epcot Center, Big $1 Billion Gamble, Opens in Florida," *The Wall Street Journal,* September 16, 1982, pp. 1, 19.

26. Donald C. Hambrick and Ian C. MacMillan, "Efficiency of Product R&D in Business Units: The Role of Strategic Context," *Academy of Management Journal,* September 1985, pp. 527–547.

27. Bernard Krisher, "A Different Kind of Tiremaker Rolls into Nashville," *Fortune,* March 22, 1982, pp. 136–146.

28. Thompson and Strickland, *Strategic Management: Concepts and Cases.*

29. For a complete discussion of strategy implementation, see J. Galbraith and R. Kazanjian, *Strategy Implementation* (St. Paul, Minn.: West Publishing, 1986) and L. Hrebiniak and W. Joyce, *Implementing Strategy* (New York: Macmillan, 1984).

30. "The 'Art' of Taking the Long View," *Industry Week,* November 18, 1991, pp. 12–23.

31. Alan Brache, "Process Improvement and Management: A Tool for Strategy Implementation," *Planning Review,* September 1, 1992, pp. 24–26.

32. Mason Tenaglia and Patrick Noonan, "Scenario-Based Strategic Planning: A Process for Building Top Management Consensus," *Planning Review,* March 1, 1992, pp. 12–19.

33. P. Lorange, M. Morton, and S. Ghoshal, *Strategic Control* (St. Paul, Minn.: West Publishing, 1986), p. 10.

34. Lorange, Morton, and Ghoshal, *Strategic Control,* pp. 35 and 53.

35. Chris Driscoll, "Bad Wednesday for DuPont," *Arizona State University State Press,* October 29, 1992, pp. 1 and 8; Joseph Weber, "DuPont: The Wollard Years," *Business Week,* August 31, 1992, pp. 70–71; Zachary Schiller and Janet Bamford, "A Tooth-and-Nail Fight Over Plastics," *Business Week,* May 4, 1992, p. 35; Gary Hoover, Alta Campbell, and Patrick J. Spain, eds., *Hoover's Handbook: Profiles of Over 500 Major Corporations* (Austin, Tex.: The Reference Press, 1991), p. 215; Milton Moskowitz, Robert Levering, and Michael Katz, *Everybody's Business* (New York: Doubleday, 1990), pp. 521–523; Christopher S. Eklund and Alison Leigh Cowan, "What's Causing the Scratches in DuPont's Teflon," *Business Week,* December 8, 1986, pp. 60–64.

36. Christopher Knowlton, "Europe Cooks Up a Cereal Brawl," *Fortune,* June 3, 1991, pp. 175–179; Gary Hoover, Alta Campbell, and Patrick J. Spain, eds., *Hoover's Handbook: Profiles of Over 500 Major Corporations* (Austin, Tex.: The Reference Press, 1991), p. 324; David Woodruff, "Winning the War of Battle Creek," *Business Week,* May 13, 1991, p. 80; "Cereal King Kellogg Feels Its Oats," *USA Today,* August 31, 1989, p. 3B.

Chapter 9

1. K. Michael Fraser, "NAFTA's Still a Natural,"*Global Finance,* Vol. 6, July 1992, pp. 29–33; "America Builds a Trade Block," *Economist,* August 15, 1992, pp. 53–54; Patrice D. Raia, "Globalizing Arizona," *World Trade,* Vol. 5, August/September, 1992, pp. 62–66; Amy Borrus, "A Free-Trade Milestone, with Many More Miles to Go," *Business Week,* August 24, 1992, pp. 30–31; Jeff Silverstein, "Culture: An Industry Exempt From Free Trade?" *Business Mexico,* Vol. 2, May 1992, p. 35.

2. Russell Ackoff, *The Art of Problem Solving* (New York: John Wiley & Sons, 1978).

3. Donald A. Marchant and Forest W. Horton, Jr., *Infotrends, Profiting from Your Information Resources* (New York: John Wiley & Sons, 1986).

4. Bill Dausses, Manager, External Communications, Phillips Petroleum, April 13, 1993.

5. Terry Trucco, "Bonjour, Bourjois," *The New York Times Magazine,* November 3, 1991, p. 70; Gretchen Morgenson, "Where Can I Buy Some?" *Forbes,* June 24, 1991, pp. 82–85; Maria Mallory, "Waking Up to a Major Market," *Business Week,* March 23, 1992, pp. 70, 73; Lisa Lebowitz, "A Rainbow Coalition," *Working Woman,* December 1991, pp. 72–74.

6. H. Skip Weitzen, *Infopreneurs* (New York: John Wiley & Sons, 1988), p. 9.

7. Peggy C. Smith, "Incorporating Public Information Systems into

Systems Analysis." In the Proceedings of the *Computers and Business Schools,* Raleigh, NC: North Carolina State University, October 1989, pp. 53–69.

8. Michael E. Porter and V. E. Millar, "How Information Gives You Competitive Advantage," *Harvard Business Review,* Vol. 63.

9. Stanley Davis, *Future Perfect* (New York: Addison-Wesley Publishing, 1987).

10. Jerry Rhodes, *Conceptual Toolmaking: Expert Systems of the Mind* (Cambridge, Mass.: Basil Blackwell Inc., 1991).

11. See Andre L. Delbecq, Andrew H. Van de Ven, and David H. Gustafson, *Group Techniques for Program Planning* (Glenview, Ill.: Scott, Foresman, 1975). See also Ruth S. Raubitschek, "Multiple Scenario Analysis and Business Planning," in Robert Lamb and Paul Shrivastava, eds., *Advances in Strategic Management* (Greenwich, Conn.: JAI Press, 1988), V., pp. 181–205.

12. Frederick P. Brooks, *The Mythical Man-Month* (Addison-Wesley, Reading, Mass., 1975).

13. Charles R. Hobbs, *Time Power* (New York: Harper & Row, 1987).

14. Charles Garfield, *Peak Performers* (New York: Avon Books, 1986), p. 227.

15. Thomas C. Hayes, "Dell Computer Net Up 76.6% in 2d Quarter," *The New York Times,* August 19, 1992, Section D, p. 4; Stephanie Anderson Forest, "Customers 'Must Be Pleased, Not Just Satisfied,'" *Business Week,* August 3, 1992; Kyle Pope, "Dell Cuts Pay of Its Chairman, 100 Aides by 5%," *The Wall Street Journal,* July 8, 1992, pp. 46–52; Claire Poole, "The Kid Who Turned Computers into Commodities," *Forbes,* October 12, 1991, pp. 318–322; Stephanie Anderson Forest, "PC Slump? What PC Slump?" *Business Week,* July 1, 1991, pp. 66–67.

16. Charles Garfield, *Second to None: How Our Smartest Companies Put People First* (Homewood, Ill.: Business 1, Irwin, 1992).

17. Marc U. Porat and Michael R. Rubin, *The Information Economy,* U.S. Department of Commerce, Washington, D.C., 1977.

18. *Time Robbers: Worries and Tension,* originally prepared by Saul W. Gellerman, unpublished manuscript.

19. Ackoff, *The Art of Problem Solving.*

20. William Oncken, Jr., *Managing Management Time* (Englewood Cliffs, N.J.: Prentice-Hall, Inc., 1984).

21. Richard Saul Wurman, *Information Anxiety* (New York: Doubleday, 1989), p. 52.

22. Robert D. Rutherford, *Just in Time* (New York: John Wiley & Sons, 1981).

23. Garfield, *Peak Performers,* p. 199.

24. Daniel Hunt, *Quality in America: How to Implement a Competitive Quality Program* (Homewood, Ill.: Business 1, Irwin, 1992).

25. Thomas McCarroll, "IBM's Unruly Kids," *Time,* February 1, 1993, pp. 54–55; Alan Deutschman, "Bill Gates' Next Challenge," *Fortune,* December 28, 1992, pp. 30–41; James Wallace, *Hard Drive— Bill Gates and The Making of the Microsoft Empire* (New York: John Wiley & Sons, 1992); "Bill Gates' Adventure," *InformationWeek,* February 4, 1991, p. 12.

26. Laurel Touby, "That Queasy Feeling at Bristol-Myers," *Business Week,* August 10, 1992, pp. 44–46; Elyse Tanouye, "Bristol-Myers Asks FDA to Approve Cancer Drug Taxol," *The Wall Street Journal,* August 3, 1992, Section B, p. 4; "Household Products Unit for Sale at Bristol-Myers," *The New York Times,* July 30, 1992, Section D, p. 5; Gene Bylinsky, "The Race for a Rare Cancer Drug," *Fortune,* July 13, 1992, pp. 100–102; Laura Bird, "Nuprin's Sales Fail to Match Its Ad's Success," *The Wall Street Journal,* June 22, 1992, Section B, p. 1; Constance L. Hays, "Bristol-Myers Pleads Guilty to Pollution," *The New York Times,* April 25, 1992, Section A, p. 25.

Chapter 10

1. Russell Shaw, "Tom Johnson," *Chief Executive,* July–August 1992, p. 23; Richard Zoglin, "How a Handful of News Executives Make Decisions Felt Round the World," *Time,* January 6, 1992, pp. 30–32; William A. Henry III, "History As It Happens," *Time,* January 6, 1992, pp. 24–27; "CNN's Commander in Chief," *Advertising Age,* April 8, 1991, pp. 36, 44; Tom Brown, "Lessons from CNN," *Industry Week,* April 1, 1991, p. 23.

2. George P. Huber and Reuben R. McDaniel, "The Decision-Making Paradigm of Organizational Design," *Management Science,* May 1986, pp. 572–589.

3. Andrew Kupfer, "The Champ of Cheap Clones," *Fortune,* September 23, 1991, pp. 115–120; John M. Dodge, "Lean PC Prices Help Gateway Fatten Corporate Customer List," *PC Week,* June 24, 1991, pp. 1, 8; Don Marks, "Gateway 2000 Inc., The Datamation 100 Company Profile," *Datamation,* June 15, 1992, p. 109.

4. G. Donaldson and J. Lorsch, *Decision Making at the Top* (New York: Basic Books, 1983).

5. M. W. McCall and R. E. Kaplan, *Whatever It Takes: Decision-Makers at Work* (Englewood Cliffs, N.J.: Prentice-Hall, 1985).

6. A. F. Osborn, *Applied Imagination* (New York: Charles Scribner & Sons, 1963).

7. Walter McQuade, "Union Carbide Takes to the Woods," *Fortune,* December 13, 1982, pp. 164–174.

8. This section is based on Ricky W. Griffin, *Management,* 4th ed. (Boston: Houghton Mifflin, 1993).

9. Kenneth MacCrimmon and Ronald Taylor, "Decision Making and Problem Solving," in Marvin Dunnette, ed., *Handbook of Industrial and Organizational Psychology* (Chicago: Rand McNally, 1976), pp. 1397–1454.

10. L. S. Baird and H. Thomas, "Toward a Contingency Model of Strategic Risk Taking," *Academy of Management Review,* April 1985, pp. 230–243.

11. Myron Magnet, "Meet the New Revolutionaries," *Fortune,* February 24, 1992, pp. 94–102; "Empowering Employees," *Chief Executive,* March/April 1992, pp. 44–49; Robert Wrubel, "Lean Management," *Financial World,* September 29, 1992, p. 50; Jo Isenberg-O'Loughlin, "Hot Steel and Good Common Sense, " *Management Review,* August 1992, pp. 25–27.

12. Watts S. Humphrey, *Managing for Innovation: Leading Technical People* (Englewood Cliffs, N.J.: Prentice-Hall, 1987).

13. Humphrey, p. 101.

14. Richard W. Woodman, John Sawyer, and Ricky W. Griffin, "Toward a Theory of Organizational Creativity," *Academy of Management Review,* April 1993, pp. 293–326.

15. Emily Thornton, "Japan's Struggle to Be Creative," *Fortune,* April 19, 1993, pp. 129–134.

16. David W. Miller and Martin K. Starr, *The Structure of Human Decisions* (Englewood Cliffs, N.J.: Prentice-Hall, 1976).

17. Amitai Etzioni, "Humble Decision Making," *Harvard Business Review,* July–August 1989, pp. 122–126.

18. Alvar Elbing, *Behavioral Decisions in Organizations,* 2nd ed. (Glenview, Ill.: Scott, Foresman, 1978).

19. Herbert A. Simon, *Administrative Behavior* (New York: Free Press, 1945).

20. See Barry M. Staw and Jerry Ross, "Good Money After Bad," *Psychology Today,* February 1988, pp. 30–33; and Jerry Ross and Barry M. Staw, "Expo 86: An Escalation Prototype," *Administrative Science Quarterly,* June 1986, pp. 274–297.

21. "ABC's 'War and Remembrance' Fails to Deliver Audience, Big Losses Loom," *The Wall Street Journal,* November 28, 1988, p. B4; "'War' Miniseries Starts Strong, But Loss Is Expected," *The Wall Street Journal,* November 22, 1988, p. A6.

22. Glen Whyte, "Decision Failures: Why They Occur and How to Prevent Them," *Academy of Management Executive,* August 1991, pp. 23–31.

23. Ibid.

24. Thomas A. Stewart, "New Ways to Exercise Power," *Fortune,* November 6, 1989, pp. 52–64.

25. Robert Markland, *Topics in Management Science,* 3rd ed. (New York: John Wiley & Sons, 1989).

26. Everett Adam and Ronald Ebert, *Production and Operations Management,* 4th ed. (Englewood Cliffs, N.J.: Prentice-Hall, 1989).

27. David Greising, William C. Symonds, and Karen Lowry Miller, "At Cargill, the Ties That Bind Aren't Binding Anymore," *Business Week,* November 19, 1991, pp. 92–96; Ronald Henkoff, "Inside America's Biggest Private Company," *Fortune,* July 13, 1992, pp. 83–90; Ronald Henkoff, "Cargill's Heir-Raising Future," *Fortune,* July 1, 1991, p. 70.

28. James R. Norman, "The Opportunities Are Enormous," *Forbes,* November 9, 1992, pp. 92–94; Christopher Knowlton, "Shell Gets Rich by Beating Risk," *Fortune,* August 26, 1992, pp. 79–82; Adrienne Linsenmeyer, "Shell's Crystal Ball," *Financial World,* April 16, 1991, pp. 58–63; Peter M. Senge, "Mental Models," *Planning Review,* March/April 1992, pp. 1–10, 44.

Chapter 11

1. Gary Hoover, Alta Campbell, and Patrick J. Spain, eds., *Hoover's Handbook* (Austin, Texas: The Reference Press, 1991); Milton Moskowitz, Robert Levering, and Michael Katz, Everybody's Business (NY: Doubleday, 1990), pp. 457–458.

2. "Retailers Sold on Unix," *Informationweek,* October 5, 1992, p. 14; "Software Superpower," *The Engineer,* November 7, 1991, p. 28; "EDS Sprouts Wings," *Informationweek,* February 26, 1990, p. 12; Milton Moskowitz, Robert Levering, and Michael Katz, *Everybody's Business* (New York: Doubleday, 1990), pp. 233 and 236; "GM + EDS = EDI," *Purchasing World,* November 1, 1990, p. 45.

3. Robert H. Miles, *Macro-Organizational Behavior* (Santa Monica, Cal.: Goodyear, 1980).

4. Henry Mintzberg, *The Structuring of Organizations* (Englewood Cliffs, N.J.: Prentice-Hall, 1979).

5. See Robert C. Ford, Barry R. Armandi, and Cherrill P. Heaton, *Organization Theory: An Integrative Approach* (New York: Harper & Row, 1988), for a more complete listing of the components of organizing.

6. For an alternative view of organization design, see Michael W. Stebbins, "Organization Design: Beyond the Mafia Model," *Organizational Dynamics,* Winter 1989, pp. 18–30.

7. Frederick W. Taylor, *Principles of Scientific Management* (New York: Harper and Brothers, 1911).

8. A. S. Miner, "Idiosyncratic Jobs in Formal Organizations," *Administrative Science Quarterly,* September 1987, pp. 327–351.

9. See Adam Smith, *Wealth of Nations* (New York: Modern Library, 1937, originally published 1776), for a classic treatment of the advantages of job specialization.

10. Ricky Griffin, *Task Design—An Integrative Approach* (Glenview, Ill.: Scott, Foresman, 1982).

11. Ibid.

12. Ibid.

13. Frederick Herzberg, *Work and the Nature of Man* (Cleveland, Ohio: Cleveland World Press, 1966); Robert Ford, "Job Enrichment Lessons from AT&T," *Harvard Business Review,* January–February 1973, pp. 96–106.

14. Al Ehrbar, "'Re-Engineering' Gives Firms New Efficiency, Workers the Pink Slip," *The Wall Street Journal,* March 16, 1993, p. A1.

15. Recent analyses of job design issues may be found in Ricky W. Griffin, "A Long-Term Investigation of the Effects of Work Redesign on Employee Perceptions, Attitudes, and Behaviors," *Academy of Management Journal,* June 1991, pp. 425–435; Roger L. Anderson and James R. Terborg, "Employee Beliefs and Support for a Work Redesign Intervention," *Journal of Management,* September 1988, pp. 493–500; Donald J. Campbell, "Task Complexity: A Review and Analysis," *Academy of Management Review,* January 1988, pp. 40–52; R. W. Griffin and D. D. Van Fleet, "Task Characteristics, Performance, and Satisfaction," *International Journal of Management,* September 1986, pp. 89–96.

16. Daniel Twomey, Frederick C. Stherr, and Walter S. Hunt, "Configuration of a Functional Department: A Study of Contextual and Structural Variables," *Journal of Organizational Behavior,* Vol. 9, 1988, pp. 61–75.

17. Ford, Armandi, and Heaton, *Organization Theory.*

18. Miles, *Macro-Organizational Behavior.*

19. Richard L. Daft, *Organization Theory and Design,* 4th ed. (St. Paul, Minn.: West, 1992).

20. Henry Mintzberg, *Power In and Around Organizations* (Englewood Cliffs, N.J.: Prentice-Hall, 1983).

21. Carrie R. Leana, "Predictors and Consequences of Delegation," *Academy of Management Journal,* December 1986, pp. 754–774.

22. John Waggoner, "Nu Skin Steps Up for a Makeover," *USA Today,* January 3, 1992, p. B1; Richard L. Stern and Mary Beth Grover, "Nu Skin International: A Great Company or a Cruel Scam?" *Forbes,* November 11, 1991, p. 139.

23. Dale McConkey, *No Nonsense Delegation* (New York: AMACOM, 1974).

24. Michael W. Miller and Paul B. Carroll, "IBM Unveils a Sweeping

Restructuring in Bid to Decentralize Decision Making," *The Wall Street Journal,* January 29, 1988, p. 3.

25. "Maverick Managers," *The Wall Street Journal,* January 29, 1988, p. 3.

26. Mintzberg, *Power In and Around Organizations.*

27. A. V. Graicunas, "Relationships in Organizations," *Bulletin of the International Management Institute,* March 7, 1933, pp. 39–42.

28. David D. Van Fleet and Arthur G. Bedeian, "A History of the Span of Management," *Academy of Management Review,* October 1977, pp. 356–372.

29. For an example, see Peter W. Barnes, "CBS Inc. Is Said to Be Planning More Dismissals," *The Wall Street Journal,* September 26, 1986, p. 4.

30. Bernard Baumohl, "When Downsizing Becomes 'Dumbsizing,' " *Time,* March 15, 1993, p. 55.

31. Brian Dumaine, "The Bureaucracy Busters," *Fortune,* June 17, 1991, pp. 36–50.

32. For additional information on the span of management, see David D. Van Fleet, "Span of Management Research and Issues," *Academy of Management Journal,* September 1983, pp. 546–552.

33. For a recent discussion of such factors, see Edward E. Lawler, III, "Substitutes for Hierarchy," *Organizational Dynamics,* Summer 1988, pp. 4–15.

34. See Vivian Nossiter, "A New Approach Toward Resolving the Line and Staff Dilemma," *Academy of Management Review,* January 1979, pp. 103–106.

35. "Lean But Not Mean," *The Wall Street Journal,* October 28, 1986, p. 1.

36. Jeff Balley, "Where the Action Is: Executives in Staff Jobs Seek Line Positions," *The Wall Street Journal,* August 12, 1986, p. 31.

37. Joseph Weber, "A Big Company That Works," *Business Week,* May 4, 1992, pp. 124–132; Hoover, Campbell, and Spain, *Hoover's Handbook,* p. 317; Moskowitz, Levering, and Katz, *Everybody's Business,* pp. 190–193.

38. Hoover, Campbell, and Spain, *Hoover's Handbook,* p. 198; Moskowitz, Levering, and Katz, *Everybody's Business,* p. 164.

Chapter 12

1. David Woodruff, "The Racy Viper Is Already a Winner for Chrysler," *Business Week,* November 4, 1991, pp. 36–37; Stephanie Losee, "Products of the Year," *Fortune,* December 2, 1991, pp. 6–67; Gary Hoover, Alta Campbell, and Patrick J. Spain, eds., *Hoover's Handbook: Profiles of Over 500 Major Corporations* (Austin, Tex.: The Reference Press, 1991), p. 167.

2. Max Weber, *Theory of Social and Economic Organization,* trans. T. Parsons (New York: Free Press, 1947).

3. These records were to be kept in drawers in cabinets or bureaus, hence the term *bureaucracy.*

4. Richard L. Daft, *Organization Theory and Design,* 3rd ed. (St. Paul, Minn.: West, 1989).

5. Daniel Wren, *The Evolution of Management Thought,* 3rd ed. (New York: John Wiley & Sons, 1986).

6. See Rensis Likert, *New Patterns of Management* (New York: McGraw-Hill, 1961) and *The Human Organization* (New York: McGraw-Hill, 1967).

7. Bruce H. Phillips, "Pledger v. Illinois Tool Works, Inc.," *Arkansas Law Review,* Vol. 45 (1992), pp. 597–630; Ronald Henkoff, "The Ultimate Nuts & Bolts Co.," *Fortune,* July 16, 1990, pp. 70–73.

8. William F. Dowling, "At General Motors: System 4 Builds Performance and Profits," *Organizational Dynamics,* Winter 1975, pp. 23–28.

9. Robert C. Ford, Barry R. Armandi, and Cherrill P. Heaton, *Organization Theory: An Integrative Approach* (New York: Harper & Row, 1988).

10. Derek S. Pugh and David J. Hickson, *Organization Structure in Its Context: The Aston Programme* (Lexington, Mass.: D. C. Heath, 1976); see also "Is Your Organization Too Big?" *Business Week,* March 27, 1989, pp. 84–94.

11. Joan Woodward, *Industrial Organization: Theory and Practice* (London: Oxford University Press, 1965).

12. Patricia L. Nemetz and Louis W. Fry, "Flexible Manufacturing Organizations: Implications for Strategy Formulation and Organization Design," *Academy of Management Review,* October 1988, pp. 627–638.

13. For example, see Tom Burns and G. M. Stalker, *The Management of Innovation* (London: Tavistock, 1961) and Paul R. Lawrence and Jay W. Lorsch, *Organization and Environment* (Homewood, Ill.: Richard D. Irwin, 1967). For a review, see Daft, *Organization Theory and Design.*

14. Henry Mintzberg, *The Structuring of Organizations: A Synthesis of the Research* (Englewood Cliffs, N.J.: Prentice-Hall, 1979).

15. Oliver E. Williamson, *Markets and Hierarchies* (New York: Free Press, 1975).

16. Michael E. Porter, "From Competitive Advantage to Corporate Strategy," *Harvard Business Review,* May–June 1987, pp. 43–59.

17. Kevin Kelly, "Newell Isn't Bagging Big Game Anymore," *Business Week,* July 8, 1991, pp. 83–84; Julianne Slovak, "Companies to Watch," *Fortune,* February 12, 1990, p. 118.

18. Mintzberg, *The Structuring of Organizations.*

19. Robert E. Hoskisson, "Multidivisional Structure and Performance: The Contingency of Diversification Strategy," *Academy of Management Journal,* December 1987, pp. 625–644.

20. Stanley M. Davis and Paul R. Lawrence, *Matrix* (Reading, Mass.: Addison-Wesley, 1977).

21. Harvey F. Koloday, "Managing in a Matrix," *Business Horizons,* March–April 1981, pp. 17–24.

22. See, for example, Jeffrey Barker, Dean Tjosvold, and I. Robert Andrews, "Conflict Approaches of Effective and Ineffective Project Managers: A Field Study in a Matrix Organization," *Journal of Management Studies,* March 1988, pp. 167–178.

23. James Owens, "Matrix Organization Structure," *Journal of Education for Business,* November 1988, pp. 61–65; Kenneth Knight, "Matrix Organization: A Review," *Journal of Management Studies,* May 1976, pp. 111–130.

24. "Matsushita Electric Industrial Company," *The Wall Street Journal,* June 29, 1988, p. 19; G. Turner, "Inside Europe's Giant Companies: Nestlé Finds a Better Formula," *Long-Range Planning,* June 1986, pp. 12–19.

25. William G. Egelhoff, "Strategy and Structure in Multinational Corporations: A Revision of the Stopford and Wells Model," *Strategic Management Journal,* Vol. 9, 1988, pp. 1–14.

26. Burns and Stalker, *The Management of Innovation.*

27. "Westinghouse Gets Respect at Last," *Fortune,* July 3, 1989, p. 92; Christopher K. Bart, "New Venture Units: Use Them Wisely to Manage Innovation," *Sloan Management Review,* Summer 1988, pp. 35–43.

28. D. Bruce Shine and Donald F. Mason, Jr., "ESOP: The American Workers' Leveraged Buy Out," *Case and Comment,* January 1, 1990, p. 24; "More Competitors Turn to Cooperation," *The Wall Street Journal,* June 6, 1989, p. B1: Tyzoon T. Tyebjee, "A Typology of Joint Ventures," *California Management Review,* Fall 1988, pp. 75–86; Howard Grindle, Charles W. Caldwell, and Caroline D. Strobel, "RDLP: A Tax Shelter That Provides Benefits for Everyone," *Management Accounting,* July 1985, pp. 44–47.

29. Edward E. Lawler, III, *High Involvement Management: Participative Strategies for Improving Organizational Performance* (San Francisco: Jossey-Bass, 1986).

30. Thomas A. Stewart, "The Search for the Organization of Tomorrow," *Fortune,* May 18, 1992, pp. 92–98.

31. Edward E. Lawler, III, *The Ultimate Advantage* (San Francisco: Jossey-Bass, 1992), pp. 67–69.

32. Ibid., pp. 69–71. See also R. Johnston and P. R. Lawrence, "Beyond Vertical Integration—The Rise of the Value-Adding Partnership," *Harvard Business Review,* 1988, pp. 94–101.

33. This section is based on Lawler, *The Ultimate Advantage,* pp. 307–312.

34. Gregory Moorhead and Ricky W. Griffin, *Organizational Behavior,* 2nd ed. (Boston: Houghton Mifflin, 1989), Chapter 16; W. Jack Duncan, "Organization Culture: 'Getting a Fix' on an Elusive Concept," *Academy of Management Executive,* August 1989, pp. 229–235.

35. Terrence Deal and Allen Kennedy, *Corporate Cultures: The Rites and Rituals of Corporate Life* (Reading, Mass.: Addison-Wesley, 1982).

36. For an excellent summary of that work, see Harrison M. Trice and Janice M. Beyer, *The Cultures of Work Organizations* (Englewood Cliffs, N.J.: Prentice-Hall, 1993).

37. See Deal and Kennedy, *Corporate Cultures,* and Vijay Sathe, "Implications of Corporate Culture: A Manager's Guide to Action," *Organizational Dynamics,* Autumn 1983, pp. 5–23.

38. "Hewlett-Packard's Whip-Crackers," *Fortune,* February 13, 1989, pp. 58–59.

39. See Sathe, "Implications of Corporate Culture," and Ralph H. Kilman, Mary Jane Saxton, and Roy Serpa, eds., *Gaining Control of Corporate Culture* (San Francisco: Jossey-Bass, 1985).

40. John P. Kotter and James L. Heskett, *Corporate Culture and Performance* (New York: Macmillan, 1992), pp. 144–149.

41. Ibid., Chapter 3.

42. Ibid., Chapter 11.

43. "Teamwork Is Key to KAD Site Management's Success," *Plant Engineering,* September 17, 1992, p. 72; Stewart, "The Search for the Organization of Tomorrow"; "Integrative Learning Speeds Teamwork," *Management Review,* December 1, 1991, p. 43; Hoover, Campbell, and Spain, *Hoover's Handbook: Profiles of Over 500 Major Corporations,* p. 218; Milton Moskowitz, Robert Levering, and Michael Katz, *Everybody's Business* (New York: Doubleday, 1990), pp. 305–307.

44. Carla Rapoport, "A Tough Swede Invades the U.S.," *Fortune,* June 29, 1992, pp. 76–79; Hoover, Campbell, and Spain, *Hoover's Handbook:*

Profiles of Over 500 Major Corporations, p. 97; Gary Hoover, Alta Campbell, Alan Chai, and Patrick J. Spain, eds., *Hoover's Handbook of World Business 1992* (Austin, Tex.: The Reference Press, 1992), p. 144; Moskowitz, Levering, and Katz, *Everybody's Business,* p. 450.

Chapter 13

1. "Rip Van Weyerhaueser,"*Forbes,* October 28, 1991, pp. 38–40; Gary Hoover, Alta Campbell, and Patrick J. Spain, eds., *Hoover's Handbook of American Business 1993* (Austin, Tex.: The Reference Press, 1992), p. 579; Bill Leonard, "Taking a Big Risk," *HR Manager,* January 1990, pp. 52–54.

2. "Leaders of Corporate Change," *Fortune,* December 14, 1992, pp. 104–114; "IBM to Cut 25,000 More Jobs, Spending," *USA Today,* December 16, 1992, pp. 1B, 2B.

3. See Roy McLennan, *Managing Organizational Change* (Englewood Cliffs, N.J.: Prentice-Hall, 1989).

4. "Managing Change," *Reinventing America* (A special issue of *Business Week,* 1992), pp. 59–74.

5. Rosabeth Moss Kanter, "Change: Where to Begin," *Harvard Business Review,* July–August 1991, pp. 8–9; Michael Beer, *Organization Change and Development: A System View* (Santa Monica, Cal.: Goodyear, 1980).

6. See Paul R. Lawrence, "How to Deal with Resistance to Change," *Harvard Business Review,* March–April, 1979, pp. 106–114.

7. "Revolt of Uncle Sam's Paper Pushers," *Business Week,* October 30, 1989, p. 156.

8. John P. Kotter and Leonard A. Schlesinger, "Choosing Strategies for Change," *Harvard Business Review,* March–April, 1979 pp. 106–114.

9. "This Marketing Effort has L'eggs," *Business Week,* December 23, 1991, pp. 50–51; "Sara Lee's Recipe for Success," *The Journal of European Business,* July–August 1992, pp. 9–35; "A Winning Global Strategy," *Institutional Investor,* May 1992, pp. 17–18.

10. Harold J. Leavitt, "Applied Organizational Change in Industry: Structural, Technical, and Human Approaches," in W. W. Cooper, H. J. Leavitt, and M. W. Shelly, eds., *New Perspectives in Organization Research* (New York: John Wiley & Sons, 1964), pp. 55–71.

11. Kotter and Schlesinger, "Choosing Strategies for Change."

12. Bro Uttal, "Texas Instruments Regroups," *Fortune,* August 9, 1982, pp. 40–45.

13. "U.S. Exporters That Aren't American," *Business Week,* February 20, 1988, pp. 70–71; "What's Behind the Texas Instruments–Hitachi Deal," *Business Week,* January 16, 1989, pp. 93–96.

14. Brian Dumaine, "The Bureaucracy Busters," *Fortune,* June 17, 1991, pp. 36–50.

15. Dorothy Leonard-Barton and William A. Kraus, "Implementing New Technology," *Harvard Business Review,* November–December 1985, pp. 102–110.

16. Richard Beckhard, *Organization Development: Strategies and Models* (Reading, Mass.: Addison-Wesley, 1969).

17. See William Pasemore, "Organization Change and Development," *Journal of Management,* June 1992.

18. Robert R. Blake and Anne Adams McCanse, *Leadership Dilemmas—Grid Solutions* (Houston: Gulf, 1991).

19. Wendell L. French and Cecil H. Bell, Jr., *Organization Development: Behavioral Science Interventions for Organization Improvement,* 2nd ed. (Englewood Cliffs, N.J.: Prentice-Hall, 1978).

20. "Welsh Coutre," *Forbes,* July 20, 1992, pp. 100–102.

21. L. B. Mohr, "Determinants of Innovation in Organizations," *American Political Science Review,* 1969, pp. 111–126; G. A. Steiner, *The Creative Organization* (Chicago: University of Chicago Press, 1965); R. Duncan and A. Weiss, "Organizational Learning: Implications for Organizational Design," in B. M. Staw, ed., *Research in Organizational Behavior,* Volume 1 (Greenwich, Conn.: JAI Press, 1979), pp. 75–123; J. E. Ettlie, "Adequacy of Stage Models for Decisions on Adoption of Innovation," *Psychological Reports,* 1980, pp. 991–995.

22. Beth Wolfensberger, "Trouble in Toyland," *New England Business,* September 1990, pp. 28–36.

23. See Alan Patz, "Managing Innovation in High Technology Industries," *New Management,* 1986, pp. 54–59.

24. An excellent guide to these kinds of management errors is Robert F. Hartley, *Management Mistakes and Successes,* 3rd ed. (New York: John Wiley & Sons, 1991).

25. See William G. Ouchi, *Theory Z* (Reading, Mass.: Addison-Wesley, 1980) for a discussion of quality circles at Oki Electric.

26. See Gifford Pinchot, III, *Intrapreneuring* (New York: Harper and Row, 1985).

27. See Steven P. Feldman, "How Organizational Culture Can Affect Innovation," *Organizational Dynamics,* Summer 1988, pp. 57–68.

28. "The New, New Thinking at Xerox," *Business Week,* June 22, 1992, pp. 120–121; Robert Howard, "The CEO As Organizational Architect: An Interview with Xerox's Paul Allaire," *Harvard Business Review,* September–October 1992, pp. 107–121; "Profiting from the Inevitable," *Forbes,* December 23, 1991, pp. 136–138; "Xerox on the Move," *Forbes,* June 10, 1991, pp. 70–71.

29. "Will Philips Sell the World on the VCR of the Future?" *Business Week,* August 17, 1992, pp. 44–45; "How Hard It Is to Change Culture," *Fortune,* October 19, 1992, p. 14; "The Sound and the Fury at Sony and Philips," *Business Week,* June 15, 1992, p. 42; "Philips' Big Gamble," *Business Week,* August 5, 1991, pp. 34–36.

Chapter 14

1. "Firms Address Workers' Cultural Variety," *The Wall Street Journal,* February 10, 1989, p. B1; "Despite the Face-Lift, Avon Is Sagging," *Business Week,* December 2, 1991, pp. 101–102; "Avon Is Calling on New Tactics," *Advertising Age,* January 7, 1991, pp. 3–4.

2. See Cynthia Fisher, Lyle Schoenfeldt, and Ben Shaw, *Human Resource Management,* 2nd ed. (Boston: Houghton Mifflin, 1993), for a more detailed treatment of the staffing process.

3. David P. Twomey, *A Concise Guide to Employment Law* (Dallas: Southwestern, 1986).

4. "The Disabilities Act Is a Godsend—for Lawyers," *Business Week,* August 17, 1992, p. 29.

5. Benjamin Schneider, "Strategic Job Analysis," *Human Resource Management,* Spring 1989, pp. 51–60.

6. Norman Scarborough and Thomas W. Zimmerer, "Human Resource Forecasting: Why and Where to Begin," *Personnel Administrator,* May 1982, pp. 55–61. See also Randall S. Schuler, "Scanning the Environment: Planning for Human Resource Management and Organizational Change," *Human Resource Planning,* October 1989, pp. 257–276.

7. Nancy Adler and Susan Bartholomew, "Managing Globally Competent People," *The Academy of Management Executive,* August 1992, pp. 52–60.

8. "When in Japan, Recruit As the Japanese Do–Aggressively," *Business Week,* June 24, 1991, p. 58; "Japanese Mind Set," *Business Credit,* August 1991, pp. 23–24; "Satisfaction in the USA, Unhappiness in Japan," *HR Focus,* January 1992, p. 8.

9. "Recruitment, Training, and Quirkiness Are Crucial to Success in Age of Talent," *Chicago Tribune,* October 5, 1992, section 4, p. 6.

10. Fisher, Schoenfeldt, and Shaw, *Human Resource Management.*

11. Laura M. Herren, "The Right Technology for Recruiting in the '90s," *Personnel Administrator,* April 1989, pp. 48–53.

12. James J. Asher, "The Biographical Item: Can It Be Improved?" *Personnel Psychology,* Summer 1972, pp. 251–269.

13. Frank L. Schmidt and John E. Hunter, "Employment Testing: Old Theories and New Research Findings," *American Psychologist,* October 1981, pp. 1128–1137.

14. Neal Schmidt, "Social and Situational Determinants of Interview Decisions: Implications for the Employment Interview," *Personnel Psychology,* Spring 1976, pp. 79–102.

15. For an interesting look at some of the legal cases regarding selection, see Kathryn E. Buckner, Hubert S. Field, and William Holley, Jr., "The Relationship of Legal Case Characteristics with the Outcomes of Personnel Selection Court Cases," *Labor Law Journal,* January 1990, pp. 31–40. For a review of recent research on selection, see Edwin A. Fleishman, "Some New Frontiers in Personnel Selection Research," *Personnel Psychology,* Winter 1988, pp. 679–702.

16. Kenneth N. Wexley and Gary P. Latham, *Developing and Training Human Resources in Organizations* (Glenview, Ill.: Scott, Foresman, 1981).

17. "Companies Use Cross-Cultural Training to Help Their Employees Adjust Abroad," *The Wall Street Journal,* August 4, 1992, pp. B1, B9; Paul Vanderbroeck, "Long-Term Human Resource Development in Multinational Organizations," *Sloan Management Review,* Fall 1992, pp. 95–104.

18. William M. Fox, "Getting the Most from Behavior Modeling Training," *National Productivity Review,* Summer 1988, pp. 238–245.

19. "Training 101: How to Win Closure and Influence People," *Training and Development Journal,* January 1990, pp. 31–35.

20. Charles D. Pringle and Peter Wright, "An Empirical Examination of the Relative Effectiveness of Supervisory Training Programs," *American Business Review,* January 1990, pp. 1–7; Stewart J. Black and Mark Mendenhall, "Cross-Cultural Training Effectiveness: A Review and a Theoretical Framework for Future Research," *Academy of Management Review,* January 1990, pp. 113–136.

21. Jeanette N. Cleveland, Kevin R. Murphy, and Richard E. Williams, "Multiple Uses of Performance Appraisal: Prevalence and Correlates,"

Journal of Applied Psychology, February 1989, pp. 130–135; Richard I. Henderson, *Performance Appraisal* (Reston, Va.: Reston Publishing, 1984).

22. William M. Fox, "Improving Performance Appraisal Systems," *National Productivity Review,* Winter 1987–1988, pp. 20–27.

23. Gary P. Latham and Kenneth N. Wexley, *Increasing Productivity Through Performance Appraisal* (Reading, Mass.: Addison-Wesley, 1981).

24. Timothy M. Downs, "Predictors of Communication Satisfaction During Performance Appraisal Interviews," *Management Communication Quarterly,* February 1990, pp. 334–354; James R. Larson, Jr., "The Dynamic Interplay Between Employees' Feedback-Seeking Strategies and Supervisors' Delivery of Performance Feedback," *Academy of Management Review,* July 1989, pp. 408–422.

25. Peter H. Lewis, "I'm Sorry, My Machine Doesn't Like Your Work," *The New York Times,* February 4, 1990, p. F27.

26. Gary Hoover, Alta Campbell, and Patrick J. Spain, eds., *Hoover's Handbook of American Business 1993* (Austin, Tex.: The Reference Press, 1992), p. 279; "Much More Than a Day's Work—for Just a Day's Pay?" *Business Week,* September 23, 1991, p. 40; "Stalking Bigger Game," *Forbes,* April 1, 1991, pp. 73–74; "Food Lion: Still Stalking in Tough Times," *Business Week,* June 22, 1992, p. 70.

27. Richard E. Kopelman, Janet L. Rovenpor, and Mo Cayer, "Merit Pay and Organizational Performance: Is There an Effect on the Bottom Line?" *National Productivity Review,* Summer 1991, pp. 299–307.

28. Allan N. Nash and Stephen J. Carroll, *The Management of Compensation* (Monterey, Los Angeles: Brooks Cole, 1975).

29. "Executive Pay," *Business Week,* May 1, 1989, pp. 46–47; Thomas H. Patten, Jr., *Employee Compensation and Incentive Plans* (New York: Free Press, 1977).

30. "The Boom in Benefits," *Personnel Journal,* Vol. 67, No. 11 (November, 1988), p. 52. See also U.S. Chamber of Commerce, *Employee Benefits 1991* (Washington, D.C.: U.S. Government Printing Office, 1992).

31. National Technical Services Unit, *Flexible Compensation: Giving Employees a Choice* (Washington, D.C.: Coopers & Lybrand, 1983).

32. For a general treatment, see Benjamin J. Taylor and Fred Witney, *Labor Relations Law,* 3rd ed. (Englewood Cliffs, N.J.: Prentice-Hall, 1979). For a view of what may be expected in the future, see "Peter Drucker Looks at Unions' Future," *Industry Week,* March 23, 1989, pp. 16–20.

33. See Casey Ichniowski and Jeffrey S. Zax, "Today's Associations, Tomorrow's Unions," *Industrial and Labor Relations Review,* January 1990, pp. 191–208; Wendell French, *Managing Human Resources,* (Boston: Houghton Mifflin, 1986).

34. See Taylor and Witney, *Labor Relations Law.*

35. James Rand, "Preventive Maintenance Techniques for Staying Union-Free," *Personnel Journal,* June 1980, pp. 497–508.

36. Taylor and Witney, *Labor Relations Law.*

37. Ibid.

38. "Cat Claws Back," *Forbes,* February 17, 1992, p. 46; "Confrontation Vs. Negotiation in Today's Economy," *Railway Age,* June 1992, p. 9; Some Secrets of Success," *Industry Week,* July 6, 1992, p. 34; Hoover, Campbell, and Spain, eds., *Hoover's Handbook of American Business 1993,* p. 182.

39. "Even Lufthansa Is Carrying Too Much Baggage," *Business Week,* September 7, 1992, p. 80; "Steering a Supertanker," *Interavia Aerospace Review,* January 1992, p. 64; "Lufthansa Cityline," *Business & Commercial Aviation,* September 1992, pp. C2–C6.

Chapter 15

1. "Employees Encouraged to Lighten Up," *USA Today,* September 23, 1992, pp. 1B, 2B; "Lighten Up," *Sky,* August 1992, pp. 16–20; "But Not So Seriously, Folks …" *Industry Week,* July 20, 1992, pp. 19–22.

2. Denise M. Rousseau, "Psychological and Implied Contracts in Organizations," *Employee Responsibilities and Rights Journal,* Vol. 2, 1989, pp. 121–139.

3. See Jennifer A. Chatman, "Improving Interactional Organizational Research: A Model of Person-Organization Fit," *Academy of Management Review,* July 1989, pp. 333–349.

4. Lawrence Pervin, "Personality" in Mark Rosenzweig and Lyman Porter, eds., *Annual Review of Psychology,* Vol. 36 (Palo Alto, Cal.: Annual Reviews, 1985), pp. 83–114; S. R. Maddi, *Personality Theories: A Comparative Analysis,* 4th ed. (Homewood, Ill.: Dorsey, 1980).

5. Lawrence Pervin, *Current Controversies and Issues in Personality,* 2nd ed. (New York: John Wiley & Sons, 1984).

6. J. B. Rotter, "Generalized Expectancies for Internal vs. External Control of Reinforcement," *Psychological Monographs,* Vol. 80, 1966, pp. 1–28.

7. T. W. Adorno, E. Frenkel-Brunswick, D. J. Levinson, and R. N. Sanford, *The Authoritarian Personality* (New York: Harper & Row, 1950).

8. "Big Brother, Pinned to Your Chest," *Business Week,* August 17, 1992, p. 38; "Electronic Mail and Employee Relations: Why Privacy Must Be Considered," *Public Relations Quarterly,* Summer 1992, pp. 37–40; "Is Greater Privacy the Key to Better Employee Morale?" *The Office,* June 1991, pp. 18–22; Kenneth A. Jenero and Lynne D. Mapes-Riordan, "Electronic Monitoring of Employees and the Elusive 'Right to Privacy,' " *Employee Relations,* Summer 1992, pp. 71–102.

9. "Who Becomes an Authoritarian?" *Psychology Today,* March 1989, pp. 66–70.

10. Edward Necka and Malgorzata Kubiak, "The Influence of Training in Metaphorical Thinking on Creativity and Level of Dogmatism," *Polish Psychological Bulletin,* Vol. 20, 1989, pp. 69–78; A. F. Kostin, "The Truth of History and Stereotypes of Dogmatism," *Soviet Studies in History,* Vol. 27, 1988, pp. 85–96.

11. Barbara Foley Meeker, "Cooperation, Competition, and Self-Esteem: Aspects of Winning and Losing," *Human Relations,* Vol. 43, 1990, pp. 205–220; Jiing-Lih Farh and Gregory H. Dobbins, "Effects of Self-Esteem on Leniency Bias in Self-Reports of Performance: A Structural Equation Model Analysis," *Personnel Psychology,* Vol. 42, 1990, pp. 835–860; Jon L. Pierce, Donald G. Gardner, and Larry L. Cummings, "Organization-Based Self-Esteem: Construct Definition, Measurement, and Validation," *Academy of Management Journal,* Vol. 32, 1989, pp. 622–648.

12. "Hey, I'm Terrific," *Newsweek,* February 17, 1992, pp. 46–51.

13. Charles E. Kimble, *Social Psychology: Studying Human Interaction* (Dubuque, Io.: Wm. C. Brown, 1990); Frank E. Saal and Patrick A. Knight, *Industrial/Organizational Psychology* (Belmont, Cal.: Brooks/Cole, 1988).

14. Leon Festinger, *A Theory of Cognitive Dissonance* (Palo Alto, Cal.: Stanford University Press, 1957).

15. For an example of attitude change effects, see Deborah A. Byrnes and Gary Kiger, "The Effect of a Prejudice-Reduction Simulation on Attitude Change," *Journal of Applied Social Psychology,* Vol. 20, 1990, pp. 341–353.

16. Patricia C. Smith, L. M. Kendall, and Charles Hulin, *The Measurement of Satisfaction in Work and Behavior* (Chicago: Rand-McNally, 1969).

17. Anne B. Fisher, "Morale Crisis," *Fortune,* November 18, 1991, pp. 70–80; Myron Magnet, "The Truth About the American Worker," *Fortune,* May 4, 1992, pp. 48–65.

18. "Controlling Absenteeism, How to Motivate Good Attendance," *Small Business Report,* September 1989, p. 30.

19. See Dennis W. Organ and Mary Konovsky, "Cognitive Versus Affective Determinants of Organizational Citizenship Behavior," *Journal of Applied Psychology,* February 1989, pp. 157–164 for recent findings regarding this behavior.

20. Organ and Konovsky, "Cognitive Versus Affective Determinants of Organizational Citizenship Behavior."

21. James L. Gibson, John M. Ivancevich, and James H. Donnelly, Jr., *Organizations—Behavior, Structure, Processes,* 6th ed. (Plano, Tex.: BPI, 1988), p. 230.

22. Hans Selye, *The Stress of Life* (New York: McGraw-Hill, 1976).

23. Ibid.

24. M. Friedman and R. H. Rosenman, *Type A Behavior and Your Heart* (New York: Alfred A. Knopf, 1974).

25. Selye, *The Stress of Life.* See also Stephan J. Motowidlo, John S. Packard, and Michael R. Manning, "Occupational Stress: Its Causes and Consequences for Job Performance," *Journal of Applied Psychology,* August 1986, pp. 618–629; James C. Quick and Jonathan D. Quick, *Organizational Stress and Preventive Management* (New York: McGraw-Hill, 1984).

26. See Anne B. Fisher, "Welcome to the Age of Overwork," *Fortune,* November 30, 1992, pp. 64–71.

27. John M. Jermier, Jeannie Gaines, and Nancy J. McIntosh, "Reactions to Physically Dangerous Work: A Conceptual and Empirical Analysis," *Journal of Organizational Behavior,* January 1989, pp. 15–33.

28. John Schaubroeck, John L. Cotton, and Kenneth R. Jennings, "Antecedents and Consequences of Role Stress: A Covariance Structure Analysis," *Journal of Organizational Behavior,* January 1989, pp. 35–58.

29. T. H. Holmes and R. H. Rahe, "Social Readjustment Rating Scale," *Journal of Psychosomatic Research,* Vol. 29, 1967, pp. 213–218.

30. Ibid.

31. Quick and Quick, *Organizational Stress and Preventive Management.* See also John M. Ivancevich and Michael T. Matteson, *Stress and Work: A Managerial Perspective* (Glenview, Ill.: Scott, Foresman, 1980). See also Paul E. Spector, Daniel J. Dwyer, and Steve M. Jex, "Relation of Job Stressors to Affective, Health, and Performance Outcomes: A Comparison of Multiple Data Sources," *Journal of Applied Psychology,* February 1988, pp. 11–19.

32. Walter Kiechal, III, "The Executive Insomniac," *Fortune,* October 8, 1990, pp. 183–184.

33. Quick and Quick, *Organizational Stress and Preventive Management.* See also Brian D. Steffy and John W. Jones, "Workplace Stress and Indicators of Coronary-Disease Risk," *Academy of Management Journal,* September 1988, pp. 686–698.

34. Quick and Quick, *Organizational Stress and Preventive Management.*

35. Leonard Moss, *Management Stress* (Reading, Mass.: Addison-Wesley, 1981).

36. Thomas A. Stewart, "Do You Push Your People Too Hard?" *Fortune,* October 22, 1990, pp. 124–128.

37. Alan Farnham, "Who Beats Stress—And How," *Fortune,* October 7, 1991, pp. 71–86.

38. C. Folkins, "Effects of Physical Training on Mood," *Journal of Clinical Psychology,* April 1976, pp. 385–390.

39. John W. Lounsbury and Linda L. Hoopes, "A Vacation from Work: Changes in Work and Nonwork Outcomes," *Journal of Applied Psychology,* May 1986, pp. 392–401.

40. Daniel C. Ganster, Marcelline R. Fusilier, and Bronston T. Mayes, "Role of Social Support in the Experiences of Stress at Work," *Journal of Applied Psychology,* February 1986, pp. 102–110.

41. Quick and Quick, *Organizational Stress and Preventive Management.*

42. Ibid.

43. Richard A. Wolfe, David O. Ulrich, and Donald F. Parker, "Employee Health Management Programs: Review, Critique, and Research Agenda," *Journal of Management,* Winter 1987, pp. 603–615.

44. See Marcelline R. Fusilier, Daniel C. Ganster, and Bronston T. Mayes, "Effects of Social Support, Role Stress, and Locus of Control on Health," *Journal of Management,* Fall 1987, pp. 517–528.

45. Stephen P. Robbins, *Managing Organizational Conflict* (Englewood Cliffs, N.J.: Prentice-Hall, 1974).

46. James Thompson, *Organizations in Action* (New York: McGraw-Hill, 1967).

47. "Two GM Auto Plants Illustrate Major Role of Workers' Attitudes," *The Wall Street Journal,* pp. A1, A4; "What Went Wrong?" *Time,* November 9, 1992, pp. 42–50.

48. "Hey, Japan! Here's a Survey!" *Industry Week,* February 17, 1992, pp. 58–60; "Japan in the Mind of America," *Time,* February 10, 1992, pp. 16–20; "America in the Mind of Japan," *Time,* February 10, 1992, pp. 20–23.

Chapter 16

1. Russell Mitchell, "Say What, Mr. Rogers?" *Business Week,* April 27, 1992, p. 38; Richard Brandt, "The Bad Boy of Silicon Valley," *Business Week,* December 9, 1991, pp. 64–70.

2. See Bernard M. Bass, *Bass & Stogdill's Handbook of Leadership,* 3rd ed. (New York: Free Press, 1990), for a thorough review of various definitions of leadership.

3. Robert P. Vecchio and Mario Sussman, "Choice of Influence Tactics: Individual and Organizational Determinants," *Journal of Organizational Behavior,* March 1991, pp. 73–80; G. Yukl and C. M. Falbe, "Influence Tactics and Objectives in Upward, Downward, and Lateral

Influence Attempts," *Journal of Applied Psychology,* Vol. 75 (1990), pp. 132–140.

4. David D. Van Fleet and Gary Yukl, "A Century of Leadership Research," in D. A. Wren, ed., *Papers Dedicated to the Development of Modern Management.* Academy of Management, pp. 12–23.

5. For a more complete review of the literature, see Gary Yukl and David D. Van Fleet, "Theory and Research on Leadership in Organizations," in Marvin D. Dunnette and Leaetta M. Hough, eds., 2nd ed., volume 3, *Handbook of Industrial & Organizational Psychology* (Palo Alto, Cal.: Consulting Psychologists Press, Inc.), pp. 147–197.

6. John P. Kotter, "What Leaders Really Do," *Harvard Business Review,* May–June 1990, pp. 103–111.

7. John P. Kotter, *A Force for Change* (New York: Free Press, 1990).

8. See Kenneth Labich, "The Seven Keys to Business Leadership," *Fortune,* October 24, 1988, pp. 58–66.

9. Cynthia Epstein, "Ways Men and Women Lead," *Harvard Business Review,* January–February 1991, pp. 150–160; David D. Van Fleet and Julie Saurage, "Recent Research on Women in Leadership and Management," *Akron Business and Economic Review,* Vol. 15 (1984), pp. 15–24.

10. Judy B. Rosener, "Ways Women Lead," *Harvard Business Review,* November–December 1990, pp. 119–125.

11. David A. Thomas, "The Impact of Race on Managers' Experiences of Developmental Relationships (Mentoring and Sponsorship): An Intra-Organizational Study," *Journal of Organizational Behavior,* November 1990, pp. 479–492; E. M. Van Fleet and David D. Van Fleet, "Entrepreneurship and Black Capitalism," *American Journal of Small Business,* Fall 1985, pp. 31–40.

12. "Older Workers Chafe Under Young Managers," *The Wall Street Journal,* February 26, 1990, p. B1.

13. John R. P. French and Bertram Raven, "The Bases of Social Power," in Dorwin Cartwright, ed., *Studies in Social Power* (Ann Arbor: University of Michigan Press, 1959), pp. 150–167.

14. Henry Mintzberg, *Power in and Around Organizations* (Englewood Cliffs, N.J.: Prentice-Hall, 1983). See also Thomas A. Stewart, "New Ways to Exercise Power," *Fortune,* November 6, 1989, pp. 52–64.

15. Eric Schine and Paula Dwyer, "America West: The Final Crisis?" *Business Week,* August 3, 1992, p. 28; Eric Schine, "Mutiny Is in the Air at America West," *Business Week,* November 25, 1991, p. 32; Stewart Toy, "America West Is Flying High Again—But for How Long?" *Business Week,* February 6, 1989, pp. 41–42.

16. Gary A. Yukl, *Leadership in Organizations,* 2nd ed. (Englewood Cliffs, N.J.: Prentice-Hall, 1989).

17. Bass, *Bass & Stogdill's Handbook of Leadership,* and Yukl, *Leadership in Organizations.* See also John W. Gardner, *On Leadership* (New York: Free Press, 1989).

18. Bass, *Bass & Stogdill's Handbook of Leadership.*

19. Shelley A. Kirkpatrick and Edwin A. Locke, "Leadership: Do Traits Matter?" *Academy of Management Executive,* May 1991, pp. 48–60.

20. Bass, *Bass & Stogdill's Handbook of Leadership,* and Yukl, *Leadership in Organizations.*

21. Rensis Likert, *New Patterns of Management* (New York: McGraw-Hill, 1961), and *The Human Organization* (New York: McGraw-Hill, 1967).

22. Ralph M. Stogdill and A. E. Coons, eds., *Leader Behavior: Its Description and Measurement* (Columbus, Ohio: Bureau of Business Research, Ohio State University, 1957). See also Bass, *Bass & Stogdill's Handbook of Leadership.*

23. Gary Yukl, Steve Wall, and Richard Lepsinger, "Preliminary Report on Validation of the Managerial Practices Survey," in Kenneth E. Clark and Miriam B. Clark, eds., *Measures of Leadership* (Greensboro, N.C.: Center for Creative Leadership, 1990), pp. 223–237, and Yukl, *Leadership in Organizations,* Chapter 7.

24. D. Hosking and I. E. Morley, "The Skills of Leadership," in J. G. Hunt, B. R. Baliga, H. P. Dachler, and C. A. Schriesheim, eds., *Emerging Leadership Vistas* (Lexington, Mass.: Heath, 1988), pp. 89–106.

25. See Bass, *Bass & Stogdill's Handbook of Leadership,* for a description of other situational approaches.

26. Fred E. Fiedler, *A Theory of Leadership Effectiveness* (New York: McGraw-Hill, 1967).

27. See Yukl, *Leadership in Organizations,* for a review.

28. Robert J. House and Terrence R. Mitchell, "Path-Goal Theory and Leadership," *Journal of Contemporary Business,* Autumn 1974, pp. 81–98.

29. Bass, *Bass & Stogdill's Handbook of Leadership.*

30. Victor H. Vroom and Philip H. Yetton, *Leadership and Decision-Making* (Pittsburgh: University of Pittsburgh Press, 1973); Victor H. Vroom and Arthur G. Jago, *The New Leadership* (Englewood Cliffs, N.J.: Prentice-Hall, 1988).

31. R. H. G. Field and R. J. House, "A Test of the Vroom-Yetton Model Using Manager and Subordinate Reports," *Journal of Applied Psychology,* Vol. 75 (1990), pp. 362–366.

32. Yukl, *Leadership in Organizations.*

33. P. B. Smith, J. Misumi, M. Tayeb, M. Peterson, and M. Bond, "On the Generality of Leadership Style Measures Across Cultures," *Journal of Occupational Psychology,* Vol. 62 (1989), pp. 97–107.

34. A. B. Shani & M. Tom Basuray, "Organization Development and Comparative Management: Action Research as an Interpretive Framework," *Leadership and Organizational Development Journal,* Vol. 9 (1988), pp. 3–10; J. Misumi & M. Peterson, "The Performance-Maintenance (PM) Theory of Leadership: Review of a Japanese Research Program," *Administrative Science Quarterly,* Vol. 30 (1985), pp. 198–223; and J. Misumi, *The Behavioral Science of Leadership: An Interdisciplinary Japanese Research Program* (Ann Arbor, Mich.: The University of Michigan Press, 1985).

35. See Abraham Zaleznik, "The Leadership Gap," *The Executive,* February 1990, pp. 7–22.

36. Robert J. House, "A 1976 Theory of Charismatic Leadership," in J. G. Hunt and L. L. Larson, eds., *Leadership: The Cutting Edge* (Carbondale, Ill.: Southern Illinois University Press, 1977).

37. J. A. Conger and R. Kanungo, "Toward a Behavioral Theory of Charismatic Leadership in Organizational Settings," *Academy of Management Review,* Vol. 12 (1987), pp. 637–647. See also J. A. Conger, *The Charismatic Leader: Behind the Mystique of Exceptional Leadership* (San Francisco: Jossey-Bass, 1989).

38. Richard Woodbury, "Prince of MidAir," *Time,* January 25, 1993, p. 55; "Shrewd Capital Planning Allows Southwest to Outperform Compe-

tition," *Aviation Week & Space Technology,* May 25, 1992, p. 56; Gary Hoover, Alta Campbell, and Patrick J. Spain, eds., *Hoover's Handbook: Profiles of Over 500 Major Corporations* (Austin, Tex.: The Reference Press, 1991) p. 503; Murray Smith, "Kelleher Builds Southwest Success with 737s," *Professional Pilot,* March 1, 1990, p. 48; Murray Smith, "Kelleher Adds 737-500s to Southwest Fleet," *Professional Pilot,* April 1, 1990, p. 38; "Crazy Like a Fox," *Business Week,* July 3, 1989, pp. 53–56.

39. James M. Burns, *Leadership* (New York: Harper & Row, 1978).

40. See Bernard M. Bass, *Leadership and Performance Beyond Expectations* (New York: Free Press, 1985), and B. J. Avolio and F. J. Yammario, "Operationalizing Charismatic Leadership Using a Levels-of-Analysis Framework," *Leadership Quarterly,* Vol. 1 (1990), pp. 193–208.

41. See Chapter 7 in Harrison M. Trice and Janice M. Beyer, *The Cultures of Work Organizations* (Englewood Cliffs, N.J.: Prentice-Hall, 1993).

42. Steven Kerr and John M. Jermier, "Substitutes for Leadership: Their Meaning and Measurement," *Organizational Behavior and Human Performance,* December 1978, pp. 375–403.

43. Jon P. Howell, David E. Bowen, Peter W. Dorfman, Steven Kerr, and Philip M. Podsakoff, "Substitutes for Leadership: Effective Alternatives to Ineffective Leaership," *Organizational Dynamics,* Summer 1990, pp. 20–38.

44. *Merck World,* October 1992, pp. 2–3; Kate Ballen, "America's Most Admired Corporations," *Fortune,* February 10, 1992, pp. 40–72; Alison L. Sprout, "America's Most Admired Corporations," *Fortune,* February 11, 1991, pp. 52–60; Hoover, Campbell, and Spain, *Hoover's Handbook: Profiles of Over 500 Major Corporations,* p. 374; Milton Moskowitz, Robert Levering, and Michael Katz, *Everybody's Business* (New York: Doubleday, 1990), pp. 162–165.

45. Kenneth Labich, "Europe's Sky Wars," *Fortune,* November 2, 1992, pp. 88–91; Richard D. Hylton, "United to BA: Take Off," *Fortune,* September 7, 1992, p. 9; "Getting Extra Mileage from British Air," *Business Week,* August 24, 1992, p. 86; Paula Dwyer, Andrea Rothman, Seth Payne, and Stewart Toy, "Air Raid: British Air's Bold Global Push," *Business Week,* August 24, 1992, pp. 54–61; Gary Hoover, Alta Campbell, Alan Chai, and Patrick J. Spain, eds., *Hoover's Handbook of World Business 1992* (Austin, Tex.: The Reference Press, 1992), p. 163; Tom Peters, *Liberation Management* (New York: Alfred A. Knopf, 1992), pp. 160–161; Nathaniel Gilbert, "British Airways' Fail-Safe I/S Takes Off," *Chief Information Officer Journal,* Spring 1990, pp. 41–44; Kenneth Labich, "The Big Comeback at British Airways," *Fortune,* December 5, 1988, pp. 163–174.

Chapter 17

1. Andrew Kupfer, "Apple's Plan to Survive and Grow," *Fortune,* May 4, 1992, pp. 68–72; C. M. Solomon, "The Loyalty Factor," *Personnel Journal,* September 1, 1992, p. 52; G. K. Kronenberger, "Out of the Closet," *Personnel Journal,* June 1, 1991, p. 40; Gloria Gordon, "This Man Knows What Diversity Is," *Communication World,* December 1, 1992, p. 8.

2. For a thorough review of motivation, see Ruth Kanfer, "Motivation Theory and Industrial and Organizational Psychology," in Marvin D. Dunnette and Leaetta M. Hough, eds., *Handbook of Industrial &*

Organizational Psychology, 2nd ed., Volume 1 (Palo Alto, Cal.: Consulting Psychologists Press, Inc., 1990), pp. 75–170.

3. See Richard M. Steers and Lyman W. Porter, eds., *Motivation and Work Behavior,* 5th ed. (New York: McGraw-Hill, 1991).

4. Craig Pinder, *Work Motivation* (Glenview, Ill.: Scott, Foresman, 1984).

5. See Walter Kiechel, III, "The Workaholic Generation," *Fortune,* April 10, 1989, pp. 50–62.

6. Abraham H. Maslow, "A Theory of Human Motivation," *Psychology Review*, Vol. 50, 1943, pp. 370–396.

7. Clayton P. Alderfer, "An Empirical Test of a New Theory of Human Needs," *Organizational Behavior and Human Performance*, April 1969, pp. 142–175.

8. Clayton P. Alderfer, *Existence, Relatedness, and Growth* (New York: Free Press, 1972).

9. Frederick Herzberg, "One More Time: How Do You Motivate Employees?" *Harvard Business Review,* January–February 1968, pp. 53–62.

10. Pinder, *Work Motivation.*

11. David McClelland, "That Urge to Achieve," *Think,* November–December 1966, p. 22.

12. David McClelland, *The Achieving Society* (Princeton, N.J.: Van Nostrand, 1961).

13. E. Cornelius and F. Lane, "The Power Motive and Managerial Success in a Professionally Oriented Service Company," *Journal of Applied Psychology*, January 1984, pp. 32–40.

14. David McClelland and David H. Burnham, "Power Is the Great Motivator," *Harvard Business Review,* March–April 1976, pp. 100–110.

15. "No longer Running in Circles," *Informationweek,* November 23, 1992, p. 40; "The Top 100 Specialty Stores," *Stores,* August 1, 1991, p. 24; Susan Caminiti, "If It's Hot, They've Got It," *Fortune,* June 3, 1991, p. 103; Michael Sullivan, "Cover Story," *Stores,* February 1, 1991, p. 14.

16. Victor Vroom, *Work and Motivation* (New York: John Wiley & Sons, 1964). See also Pinder, *Work Motivation*, and Lynn E. Miller and Joseph E. Grush, "Improving Predictions in Expectancy Theory Research: Effects of Personality, Expectancies, and Norms," *Academy of Management Journal,* March 1988, pp. 107–122.

17. See also David A. Nadler and Edward E. Lawler, III, "Motivation: A Diagnostic Approach," in J. Richard Hackman, Edward E. Lawler, and Lyman W. Porter, eds., *Perspectives on Behavior in Organizations*, 2nd ed. (New York: McGraw-Hill, 1983), pp. 67–78.

18. Kurt Eichenwald, "America's Successful Steel Industry," *Washington Monthly,* February 1985, p. 42.

19. Lyman W. Porter and Edward E. Lawler, III, *Managerial Attitudes and Performance* (Homewood, Ill.: Dorsey, 1968).

20. Richard T. Mowday, "Equity Theory Predictions of Behavior in Organizations," in Steers and Porter, eds., *Motivation and Work Behavior,* pp. 91–113. See also J. Stacey Adams, "Toward an Understanding of Inequity," *Journal of Abnormal and Social Psychology*, November 1963, pp. 422–436.

21. Jerald Greenberg, "Equity and Workplace Status: A Field Experiment," *Journal of Applied Psychology*, November 1989, pp. 606–613; Edward W. Miles, John D. Hatfield, and Richard C. Huseman, "The Equity Sensitivity Construct: Potential Implications for Work Performance," *Journal of Management,* December 1989, pp. 581–588.

22. R. A. Cosier and D. R. Dalton, "Equity Theory and Time: A Reformulation," *Academy of Management Review*, April 1983, pp. 311–319; R. C. Huseman, J. D. Hatfield, and E. W. Miles, "A New Perspective on Equity Theory," *Academy of Management Review*, April 1987, pp. 222–234.

23. "Paying Workers to Meet Goals Spreads, But Gauging Performance Proves Tough," *The Wall Street Journal*, September 10, 1991, pp. B1, B8.

24. M. E. Tubbs and S. E. Ekeberg, "The Role of Intentions in Work Motivation: Implications for Goal-Setting Theory and Research," *Academy of Management Review*, January 1991, pp. 180–199.

25. Gary P. Latham and Edwin Locke, "Goal Setting—A Motivational Technique That Works," *Organizational Dynamics*, Autumn 1979, pp. 68–80.

26. Dean Tjosvold, "Participation: A Close Look at Its Dynamics," *Journal of Management*, Autumn 1987, pp. 739–750.

27. Louis Kraar, "Japan's Gung-Ho U.S. Car Plants," *Fortune*, January 30, 1989, pp. 98–108; "The Americanization of Honda," *Business Week*, April 25, 1988, pp. 90–96; "Honda Wins USA's Heartland," *USA Today*, December 2, 1987, pp. 1B, 2B.

28. E. E. Lawler, III, *The Ultimate Advantage* (San Francisco: Jossey-Bass, 1992).

29. "More Power to Them," *Small Business Report*, November 1, 1992, p. 51; Tom Peters, *Liberation Management* (New York: Alfred A. Knopf, 1992); Kevin Maney, "Sonic Serves Up Earnings in Snap," *USA Today*, July 26, 1991, p. 3B; Seth Subove, "The Up & Comers," *Forbes*, April 2, 1990, p. 56.

30. B. F. Skinner, *Beyond Freedom and Dignity* (New York: Knopf, 1971).

31. Fred Luthans and Robert Kreitner, *Organizational Behavior Modification and Beyond: An Operant and Social Learning Approach* (Glenview, Ill.: Scott, Foresman, 1985).

32. Ibid.

33. "At Emery Air Freight: Positive Reinforcement Boosts Performance," *Organizational Dynamics*, Winter 1973, pp. 41–50.

34. C. B. Ferster and B. F. Skinner, *Schedules of Reinforcement* (New York: Appleton-Century-Crofts, 1957).

35. Edward E. Lawler, III, *Pay and Organizational Development* (Reading, Mass.: Addison-Wesley, 1981).

36. Personal interviews with employees conducted in December 1992 and the nomination form.

37. "Pay Raise Demands Appear to Be Modest," *The Wall Street Journal*, February 28, 1989, p. A2.

38. Brian Dumaine, "Creating a New Company Culture," *Fortune*, January 15, 1990, pp. 127–131; "All Eyes on Du Pont's Incentive Pay Plan," *The Wall Street Journal*, December 15, 1988, p. B1.

39. "News Briefs," *The Arizona Republican*, January 6, 1993, p. C1; Dori Jones Yang, "Nordstrom's Gang of Four," *Business Week*, June 15, 1992, pp. 122–123; "Electronic Mail," *Chain Store Age Executive*, October 1, 1992, p. 72; "Technology Leaders," *Stores*, January 1, 1992, p. 112; Milton Moskowitz, Robert Levering, and Michael Katz, *Everybody's Business* (New York: Doubleday, 1990), pp. 223–224; C. M. Solomon, "Nightmare at Nordstrom," *Personnel Journal*, September 1, 1990, pp. 76–83; "Nordstrom KnowHow," *Stores*, January 1, 1990, p. 68.

40. "Review/Preview: A Quickened Tempo in 1992 Dealmaking," *Mergers & Acquisitions*, May 1, 1992, p. 7; Gary Hoover, Alta Campbell, Alan Chai, and Patrick J. Spain, eds., *Hoover's Handbook of World Business 1992* (Austin, Tex.: The Reference Press, 1992), p. 288; Patricia Sellers, "Perrier Plots Its Comeback," *Fortune*, April 23, 1990, pp. 277–278; Daniel Seligman, "Keeping Up," *Fortune*, March 12, 1990, p. 139; Daniel Butler, "Perrier's Painful Period," *Management Today*, August 1990, pp. 72–73; "Inside Perrier's Buying Review," *Marketing & Media Decisions*, July 1, 1990, p. 28.

Chapter 18

1. "Amgen," *Chemistry and Industry*, July 6, 1992, p. 475; Andrew Erdman, "Amgen: How to Keep That Family Feeling," *Fortune*, April 6, 1992, pp. 95–96; "Churning Out Earnings," *Business Week*, July 31, 1989, p. 30; "Amgen is Hot—and Bothered," *Business Week*, January 23, 1989, p. 40.

2. This paragraph is based on Clay Carr, *Team-Power* (Englewood Cliffs, N.J.: Prentice-Hall, 1992).

3. Richard A. Guzzo and Gregory P. Shea, "Group Performance and Intergroup Relations in Organizations," in Marvin D. Dunnette and Leaetta M. Hough, eds., *Handbook of Industrial & Organizational Psychology*, 2nd ed., vol. 3 (Palo Alto, Cal.: Consulting Psychologists Press, Inc.), pp. 269–313; John J. Gabarro, "The Development of Working Relationships," in Jay W. Lorsch, ed., *Handbook of Organizational Behavior* (Englewood Cliffs, N.J.: Prentice-Hall, 1987), pp. 172–189.

4. Henry Mintzberg, *The Nature of Managerial Work* (New York: Harper & Row, 1973).

5. "A Braver New World?" *Industry Week*, August 3, 1992, pp. 48–54; Colin Coulson-Thomas, "The Responsive Organisation," *Journal of General Management*, Summer 1990, pp. 21–31.

6. Gregory Moorhead and Ricky W. Griffin, *Organizational Behavior*, 3rd ed. (Boston: Houghton Mifflin, 1992); Linda M. Jewell and M. Joseph Reitz, *Group Effectiveness in Organizations* (Glenview, Ill.: Scott, Foresman, 1981).

7. T. Kameda, M. F. Stasson, and J. H. Davis, "Social Dilemmas, Subgroups, and Motivation Loss in Task-Oriented Groups: In Search of an 'Optimal' Team Size in Work Division," *Social Psychology Quarterly*, March 1, 1992, pp. 47–56.

8. Marvin E. Shaw, *Group Dynamics—The Psychology of Small Group Behavior*, 4th ed. (New York: McGraw-Hill, 1985).

9. Ibid.

10. Dorwin Cartwright and Alvin Zander, eds., *Group Dynamics: Research and Theory*, 3rd ed. (New York: Harper & Row, 1968).

11. Shaw, *Group Dynamics*.

12. B. W. Tuckman, "Developmental Sequence in Small Groups," *Psychological Bulletin*, vol. 63, 1965, pp. 383–399. For a more recent treatment of group development stages, see Connie J. G. Gersick, "Marking Time: Predictable Transitions in Task Groups," *Academy of Management Journal*, June 1989, pp. 274–309.

13. George Homans, *The Human Group* (New York: Harcourt, 1950).

14. David Katz and Robert L. Kahn, *The Social Psychology of Organizations*, 2nd ed. (New York: John Wiley & Sons, 1978).

15. Ibid.

16. Robert L. Kahn, D. M. Wolfe, R. P. Quinn, J. D. Snoek, and R. A. Rosenthal, *Organizational Stress: Studies in Role Conflict and Role Ambiguity* (New York: John Wiley & Sons, 1964).

17. Katz and Kahn, *The Social Psychology of Organizations.*

18. Shaw, *Group Dynamics.*

19. For how to increase cohesiveness, see P. F. Buller and C. H. Bell, Jr., "Effects of Team Building and Goal Setting on Productivity: A Field Experiment," *Academy of Management Journal,* June 1986, pp. 305–328.

20. Shaw, *Group Dynamics.* See also Monika Henderson and Michael Argyle, "The Informal Rules of Working Relationships," *Journal of Occupational Behavior,* vol. 7, 1986, pp. 259–275.

21. Richard D. Arvey and Gary L. Renz, "Fairness in the Selection of Employees," *Journal of Business Ethics,* May 1, 1992, p. 331; Tim Barnett, "A Preliminary Investigation of the Relationship Between Selected Organizational Characteristics and External Whistleblowing by Employees," *Journal of Business Ethics,* December 1, 1992, p. 949; J. Richard Finlay, "Survival Ethics," *The Business Quarterly,* Fall 1990, p. 40; F. B. Green and Eric Hatch, "Involvement and Commitment in the Workplace: A New Ethic Evolving," *S.A.M. Advanced Management Journal,* Fall 1990, p. 8; "Fun and Games and Ethics," *Nation's Business,* November 1, 1989, p. 38; Stephenie Overman, "Good Ethics Is Good Business: A Longstanding No-Layoff Policy Is Part of Byrd Press's Commitment to Employees," *The Personnel Administrator,* July 1, 1989, p. 34.

22. Daniel C. Feldman, "The Development and Enforcement of Group Norms," *Academy of Management Review,* January 1984, pp. 47–53.

23. In addition to the views presented in this section, see Kim B. Clark and Steven C. Wheelwright, "Organizing and Leading 'Heavyweight' Development Teams," *California Management Review,* Spring 1992, pp. 9–20 and "Blueprint for a Successful Team," *Supervisory Management,* May 1, 1992, pp. 2–3.

24. James H. Davis, *Group Performance* (Reading, Mass.: Addison-Wesley, 1969).

25. Jay Galbraith, *Organization Design* (Reading, Mass.: Addison-Wesley, 1977).

26. Cyril O'Donnell, "Ground Rules for Using Committees," *Management Review,* October 1961, pp. 63–67.

27. "The Payoff from Teamwork," *Business Week,* July 10, 1989, pp. 56–62.

28. Carl E. Larson and Frank M. J. LaFasto, *TeamWork* (Newbury Park, Cal.: Sage, 1989), p. 27.

29. Ibid.

30. George Munchus, "Employer-Employee Based Quality Circles in Japan: Human Resource Implications for American Firms," *Academy of Management Review,* April 1983, pp. 255–261. See also Ricky W. Griffin, "Consequences of Quality Circles in an Industrial Setting: A Long-Term Field Experiment," *Academy of Management Journal,* June 1988, pp. 280–304.

31. This section is based on J. Richard Hackman, ed., *Groups That Work (and Those That Don't)* (San Francisco, Cal.: Jossey-Bass, 1990).

32. Stephen P. Robbins, *Managing Organizational Conflict* (Englewood Cliffs, N.J.: Prentice-Hall, 1974).

33. James Thompson, *Organizations in Action* (New York: McGraw-Hill, 1967).

34. Danny Ertel, "How to Design a Conflict Management Procedure That Fits Your Dispute," *Sloan Management Review,* Summer 1991, pp. 29–39.

35. Shaw, *Group Dynamics.*

36. Davis, *Group Performance.* See also John P. Wanous and Margaret A. Youtz, "Solution Diversity and the Quality of Group Decisions," *Academy of Management Journal,* March 1986, pp. 149–159.

37. Dorothy Leonard-Barton, "The Factory As a Learning Laboratory," *Sloan Management Review,* Fall 1992, p. 23; "Steelmaker of the Year," *Iron Age,* August 1, 1992, p. 14; Brian Dumaine, "Unleash Workers and Cut Costs," *Fortune,* May 18, 1992, pp. 88–91; Fred Luthans, "Conversation with Gordon Forward," *Organizational Dynamics,* Summer 1991, pp. 63–65; "Chaparral Quality Cited by Japanese," *Journal of Manufacturing,* July 1990, p. 4.

38. Irving L. Janis, *Groupthink,* 2nd ed. (Boston: Houghton Mifflin, 1982).

39. Andre L. Delbecq, Andrew H. Van de Ven, and David H. Gustafson, *Group Techniques for Program Planning* (Glenview, Ill.: Scott, Foresman, 1975). See also David M. Schweiger, William Sandberg, and James W. Ragan, "Group Approaches for Improving Strategic Decision Making: A Comparative Analysis of Dialectical Inequity, Devil's Advocacy and Consensus," *Academy of Management Journal,* March 1986, pp. 51–71.

40. "Campbell Soup Posts 29% Increase in Net For Latest Quarter," *The Wall Street Journal,* September 11, 1992, p. A7; Bill Saporito, "Campbell Soup Gets Piping Hot," *Fortune,* September 9, 1991, pp. 142–148; Bruce Hager, Lisa Driscoll, Joseph Weber, and Gary McWilliams, "CEO Wanted. No Insiders, Please," *Business Week,* August 12, 1991, pp. 44–45; Gary Hoover, Alta Campbell, and Patrick J. Spain, eds., *Hoover's Handbook: Profiles of Over 500 Major Corporations* (Austin, Tex.: The Reference Press, 1991), p. 149; Milton Moskowitz, Robert Levering, and Michael Katz, *Everybody's Business* (New York: Doubleday, 1990), pp. 19–20.

41. Various "Fact Sheets" provided in the press packet by The Body Shop Communications Office, Cedar Knolls, New Jersey, November 1992; Rahul Jacob, "What Selling Will Be Like in the '90s," *Fortune,* January 13, 1992, pp. 63–64; Tom Peters, *Liberation Management* (New York: Alfred A. Knopf, 1992), pp. 594–596; Laura Zinn, "Whales, Human Rights, Rain Forests—and the Heady Smell of Profits," *Business Week,* July 15, 1991, pp. 114–115; Bo Burlingham, "This Woman Has Changed Business Forever," *Inc.,* June 1990, pp. 34–47.

Chapter 19

1. Bill Saporito, "A Week Aboard The Wal-Mart Express," *Fortune,* August 24, 1992, pp. 77–84; Janice Castro, "Mr. Sam Stuns Goliath," *Time,* February 25, 1991, pp. 62–63; "Leaders of the Most Admired," *Fortune,* January 29, 1990, pp. 40–54; "Marketing with Emotion: Wal-Mart Shows the Way," *The Wall Street Journal,* November 13, 1989, p. B1; "Little Touches Spur Wal-Mart's Rapid Growth," *The Wall Street Journal,* September 22, 1989, p. B1.

2. Norman B. Sighand and Arthur H. Bell, *Communication for Management and Business* (Glenview, Ill.: Scott, Foresman, 1986).

3. Henry Mintzberg, *The Nature of Managerial Work* (New York: Harper & Row, 1973).

4. Henry Mintzberg, "The Manager's Job: Folklore and Fact," *Harvard Business Review,* July–August 1975, pp. 49–61.

5. Martin Fishbein and I. Ajzen, *Belief, Attitude, and Behavior: An Introduction to Theory and Research* (Reading, Mass.: Addison-Wesley, 1975).

6. E. E. Jones and R. E. Nisbett, *The Actor and the Observer: Divergent Perceptions of the Causes of Behavior* (Morristown, N.J.: General Learning Press, 1971).

7. D. C. Dearborn and H. A. Simon, "Selective Perception: A Note on the Departmental Identification of Executives," *Sociometry,* Vol. 21, 1985, p. 143.

8. B. Rosen and T. H. Jerdee, "The Influence of Age Stereotypes on Managerial Decisions," *Journal of Applied Psychology,* Vol. 61, 1976, pp. 428–432.

9. See James P. Walsh, "Selectivity and Selective Perception: An Investigation of Managers' Belief Structures and Information Processing," *Academy of Management Journal,* December 1988, pp. 873–896, for a recent study of these issues.

10. Jerry Wofford, Edwin Gerloff, and Robert Cummins, *Organizational Communication* (New York: McGraw-Hill, 1977).

11. "Information Overload Is Here," *USA Today,* February 20, 1989, pp. 1B–2B.

12. Gary P. Ferraro, *The Cultural Dimension of International Business,* Englewood Cliffs, N.J.: Prentice-Hall, 1990.

13. Philip J. Hilts, "Biggest Maker of Breast Implants Is Said to Be Abandoning Market," *The New York Times,* March 19, 1992, pp. A1, B1; Andrew Purvis, "Not for Vanity's Sake," *Time,* March 2, 1992, p. 36; Christine Gorman, "Can Drug Firms Be Trusted?" *Time,* February 10, 1992, pp. 42–46; Philip J. Hilts, "Company to Release Data Questioning Implant Safety," *The New York Times,* January 23, 1992, p. A20.

14. See Jane Whitney Gibson and Richard M. Hodgetts, *Organizational Communication: A Managerial Perspective,* 2nd edition (New York: HarperCollins, 1991) for a general discussion of semantics.

15. Wofford, Gerloff, and Cummins, *Organizational Communication*.

16. Gary P. Ferraro, *The Cultural Dimension of International Business,* Englewood Cliffs, N.J.: Prentice-Hall, 1990.

17. Mintzberg, *The Nature of Managerial Work*.

18. Walter Kiechel III, "The Big Presentation," *Fortune,* July 26, 1982, pp. 98–100. See also Michael T. Motley, "Taking the Terror out of Talk," *Psychology Today,* January 1988, pp. 46–49.

19. Michael B. McCaskey, "The Hidden Messages Managers Send," *Harvard Business Review,* November–December 1979, pp. 135–148.

20. Ibid.

21. Kiechel, "The Big Presentation."

22. Theodore Kurtz, "Dynamic Listening: Unlocking Your Communication Potential," *Supervisory Management,* September 1990, p. 7.

23. Kurtz, "Dynamic Listening: Unlocking Your Communication Potential."

24. Chris Welles, "What Led Beech-Nut Down the Road to Disgrace," *Business Week,* February 22, 1988, pp. 124–128.

25. Andrew Kupfer, "Phones That Will Work Anywhere," *Fortune,* August 24, 1992, pp. 100–112.

26. Leon Hirsch, "One of America's Best-paid Executives Defends His Check," *U.S. News & World Report,* April 6, 1992, p. 54; Eva Pomice and Warren Cohen, "The Toughest Companies in America," *U.S. News & World Report,* October 28, 1991, pp. 65–74; Jennifer Reese, "Getting Hot Ideas from Customers," *Fortune,* May 18, 1992, pp. 86–87.

27. Gordon Bock, Kimberly Carpenter, and Jo Ellen Davis, "Management's Newest Star," *Business Week,* October 13, 1986, pp. 160–172.

28. Keith Davis, "Management Communication and the Grapevine," *Harvard Business Review,* September–October 1953, pp. 43–49.

29. "At Apple Computer Proper Office Attire Includes a Muzzle," *The Wall Street Journal,* October 6, 1989, pp. A1, A5; Brian Dumaine, "Corporate Spies Snoop to Conquer," *Fortune,* November 7, 1988, pp. 68–76; "Mind What You Say: They're Listening," *The Wall Street Journal,* October 25, 1989, p. B1.

30. Faye Rice, "Champions of Communication," *Fortune,* June 3, 1991, pp. 111–120; Daniel Machalaba, "Union Pacific's High-tech Style Generates Business," *The Wall Street Journal,* June 8, 1992, p. B3; "'The Enemy Was Us,'" *Forbes,* January 6, 1992, p. 173; Andrew Kupfer, "An Outsider Fires Up a Railroad," *Fortune,* December 18, 1989, pp. 133–146.

31. Yumiko Ono, "Sick of Meetings? Then ODS Is Not the Place For You," *The Wall Street Journal,* September 12, 1989, p. A8; Michael Berger, "Now the Japanese Bring Democracy to Salary Review," *International Management,* October 1986, pp. 58–60; Phyllis Birnbaum, "What Makes Salaryman Run?" *Across the Board,* June 1988, pp. 14–21.

Chapter 20

1. "Cooper Tire & Rubber—Now Hear This, Jack Welch!" *Fortune,* April 6, 1992, pp. 94–95; "Two Disparate Firms Find Keys to Success in Troubled Industries," *The Wall Street Journal,* May 29, 1991, pp. A1, A9; Curt Holman, "The 'Overnight' Success of Cooper Tire & Rubber: More Than 70 Years in the Making," *Elastomerics,* July 1992, pp. 29–30.

2. William Newman, *Constructive Control* (Englewood Cliffs, N.J.: Prentice-Hall, 1975).

3. "Trouble in Bean Land," *Forbes,* July 6, 1992, pp. 42–44; Dennis Holder, "Lair of the Magic Bean," *American Way,* April 15, 1989, pp. 20–26; "Using the Old Bean," *Sports Illustrated,* December 2, 1985, pp. 84–88.

4. "American Greetings Is Carding Gains," *USA Today,* August 24, 1988, p. 3B; "Flounder," *Forbes,* April 25, 1988.

5. "Why Emery Is Biting Its Nails," *Business Week,* August 29, 1988, p. 34.

6. Joel Dreyfuss, "Victories in the Quality Crusade," *Fortune,* October 10, 1988, pp. 80–88.

7. Myron Magnet, "Who's Winning the Information Revolution," *Fortune,* November 30, 1992, pp. 110–117.

8. Newman, *Constructive Control*.

9. Harold Koontz and Robert W. Bradspies, "Managing Through Feedforward Control," *Business Horizons,* June 1972, pp. 25–36.

10. Thomas A. Stewart, "Brace for Japan's Hot New Strategy," *Fortune,* September 21, 1992, pp. 62–74.

11. Alex Taylor III, "Do You Know Where Your Car Was Made?" *Fortune,* June 17, 1991, pp. 52–56.

12. Bill Saporito, "Companies That Compete Best," *Fortune,* May 22, 1989,

pp. 36–44; Gary Hoover, Alta Campbell, and Patrick J. Spain, eds., *Hoover's Handbook of American Business 1993* (Austin, Tex.: The Reference Press, 1992), p. 259; "Power Alley," *Financial World,* August 9, 1988, pp. 26–32.

13. Edward E. Lawler III and John G. Rhode, *Information and Control in Organizations* (Pacific Palisades, Cal.: Goodyear, 1976).

14. Robert N. Anthony, *The Management Control Function* (Boston: Harvard Business School Press, 1988).

15. Daniel Seligman, "Turmoil Time in the Casino Business," *Fortune,* March 2, 1987, pp. 102–116.

16. P. Rajan Varadarajan, Terry Clark, and William M. Pride, "Controlling the Uncontrollable: Managing Your Market Environment," *Sloan Management Review,* Winter 1992, pp. 39–48.

17. William G. Ouchi, "The Transmission of Control Through Organizational Hierarchies," *Academy of Management Journal,* June 1978, pp. 173–192.

18. "Knight-Ridder Acts to Boost Bottom Line," *USA Today,* November 11, 1986, pp. 1B, 2B.

19. J. M. Horovitz, "Strategic Control: A New Task for Top Management," *Long Range Planning,* June 1979, pp. 28–37.

20. Paul G. Makosz and Bruce W. McQuaig, "Is Everything Under Control? A New Approach to Corporate Governance," *Financial Executive,* January 1, 1990, pp. 24–29.

21. Ronald Henkoff, "Cost Cutting: How to Do It Right," *Fortune,* April 9, 1990, pp. 40–48.

22. See Walter Kiechel III, "Managing Expense Accounts," *Fortune,* September 16, 1985, pp. 205–208.

23. Stratford Sherman, "How to Prosper in the Value Decade," *Fortune,* November 30, 1992, pp. 90–103.

24. See Lawler and Rhode, *Information and Control in Organizations,* for a thorough explanation of resistance to control.

25. David B. Greenberger and Stephen Strasser, "Development and Application of a Model of Personal Control in Organizations," *Academy of Management Review,* January 1988, pp. 164–177.

26. Cortlandt Cammann and David A. Nadler, "Fit Control Systems to Your Management Style," *Harvard Business Review,* January–February 1976, pp. 65–72.

27. Vijay Sathe, "Who Should Control Division Controllers?" *Harvard Business Review,* September–October 1978, pp. 99–104.

28. Michael A. Robinson and Donald T. Hughes, "Controllership Training: A Competitive Weapon," *Management Accounting,* May 1, 1989, pp. 20–24.

29. Al Pipkin, "The 21st Century Controller," *Management Accounting,* February 1, 1989, pp. 21–26; "The Controller-Inflation Gives Him More Clout with Management," *Business Week,* August 15, 1977, pp. 85–87, 90.

30. "Amerihost Finds Niche in Restoring Distressed Motels," *The Wall Street Journal,* June 6, 1991, p. B2; "Amerihost Properties," *Fortune,* October 5, 1992, p. 95.

31. "Is This Any Way to Run the Family Business?" *Business Week,* August 24, 1992, pp. 48–49; "Greener Pastures," *Forbes,* July 6, 1992, p. 48; "A Marketing-Driven Company," *Discount Merchandiser,* September 1991, pp. 77–78.

Chapter 21

1. Peter C. Reid, "How Harley Beat Back the Japanese," *Fortune,* September 25, 1989, pp. 155–164; "After Nearly Stalling, Harley-Davidson Finds New Crowd of Riders," *The Wall Street Journal,* August 31, 1990, pp. A1, A6; "Willie G. Davidson: Born to Ride," *Sales & Marketing Management,* April 1991, pp. 26–27.

2. Ross Johnson and William O. Winchell, *Management and Quality* (Milwaukee, American Society for Quality Control, 1989). See also "When TQM Goes Nowhere," *Training & Development,* January 1993, pp. 22–29.

3. See John W. Kendrick, *Understanding Productivity: An Introduction to the Dynamics of Productivity* (Baltimore: Johns Hopkins, 1977).

4. Brian O'Reilly, "America's Place in World Competition," *Fortune,* November 6, 1989, pp. 83–88.

5. Thomas A. Stewart, "U.S. Productivity: First But Fading," *Fortune,* October 19, 1992, pp. 54–57.

6. Louis S. Richman, "How America Can Triumph," *Fortune,* December 18, 1989, pp. 52–66.

7. Ronald Henkoff, "Make Your Office More Productive," *Fortune,* February 25, 1991, pp. 72–84.

8. See Michael E. Porter, "The Competitive Advantage of Nations," *Harvard Business Review,* March–April 1990, pp. 73–93.

9. Stewart, "U.S. Productivity: First But Fading."

10. Michael E. Porter, "Why Nations Triumph," *Fortune,* March 12, 1990, pp. 94–108.

11. Robert S. Kaufman, "Why Operations Improvement Programs Fail: Four Managerial Conditions," *Sloan Management Review,* Fall 1992, pp. 83–94.

12. Tim R. V. David, "Information Technology and White-Collar Productivity," *The Academy of Management Executive,* February 1991, pp. 55–63.

13. Gene Bylinsky, "Turning R&D Into Real Products," *Fortune,* July 2, 1990, pp. 72–77.

14. Gary Hector, "Yes, You *Can* Manage Long Term," *Fortune,* November 21, 1988, pp. 64–76.

15. William Bowen, "The Puny Payoff From Office Computers," *Fortune,* May 26, 1986, pp. 20–24.

16. See Genichi Taguchi and Don Clausing, "Robust Quality," *Harvard Business Review,* January–February 1990, pp. 65–75.

17. "5 Baldrige Awards Honor Efforts to Improve Quality," *USA Today,* October 15, 1992, pp. B1, B6; "AT&T Smacks a Double," *Business Week,* October 26, 1992, p. 37; "No Price Tag on Being Best, Winners Show," *USA Today,* October 10, 1991, pp. 1A, 2A; Rick Tetzeli, "A Day in the Life of Ed Deming," *Fortune,* January 11, 1993, pp. 74–75.

18. "Beg, Borrow, and Benchmark," *Business Week,* November 30, 1992, pp. 74–75.

19. "Quality," *Business Week,* November 30, 1992, pp. 66–72.

20. Richard J. Schonberger, "Is Strategy Strategic? Impact of Total Quality Management on Strategy," *The Academy of Management Executive,* August 1992, pp. 80–86.

21. "Building a Self-Directed Work Team," *Training & Development,* December 1992, pp. 24–28.

22. "King Customer," *Business Week,* March 12, 1990, pp. 88–94.

23. Paul S. Adler, "Time-and-Motion Regained," *Harvard Business Review,* January–February 1993, pp. 97–108.

24. "Quality is Becoming Job One in the Office, Too," *Business Week,* April 29, 1991, pp. 52–56.

25. "Quality," *Business Week,* November 30, 1992, pp. 66–72.

26. C. Kevin Swisher, "Just Desserts," *Texas Highways,* August 1991, pp. 12–17; "Bigger Markets Won't Affect Little Creamery in Brenham," *Bryan-College Station Eagle,* March 25, 1990, pp. 1A, 6A; "The Ice Cream Man Cometh," *Forbes,* January 22, 1990, pp. 52–56.

27. Jeremy Main, "How to Steal the Best Ideas Around," *Fortune,* October 19, 1992, pp. 102–106.

28. "Beg, Borrow, and Benchmark," *Business Week,* November 30, 1992, pp. 74–75.

29. George Stalk, Jr. and Thomas M. Hout, *Competing Against Time* (New York: The Free Press, 1990).

30. Brian Dumaine, "How Managers Can Succeed Through Speed," *Fortune,* February 13, 1989, pp. 54–59.

31. Dumaine, "How Managers Can Succeed Through Speed."

32. Alex Taylor III, "U.S. Cars Come Back," *Fortune,* November 16, 1992, pp. 52–85; Jeremy Main, "How to Steal the Best Ideas Around," *Fortune,* October 19, 1992, pp. 102–106; Alex Taylor III, "Ford's $6 Billion Baby," *Fortune,* June 28, 1993, pp. 76–81.

33. Gene Bylinsky, "The Hottest High-Tech Company in Japan," *Fortune,* January 1, 1990, pp. 82–88; "The Gospel According to Sun Tzu," *Forbes,* December 9, 1991, pp. 154–162; "Cult of Personality," *Business Week,* August 1990, pp. 42–44.

Chapter 22

1. "Monsanto—Learning from Its Mistakes," *Fortune,* January 27, 1992, pp. 81–82; Gary Hoover, Alta Campbell, and Patrick J. Spain eds., *Hoover's Handbook of American Business 1993* (Austin, Tex.: The Reference Press, 1992), p. 410.

2. Everett E. Adam, Jr., and Ronald J. Ebert, *Production and Operations Management,* 5th ed. (Englewood Cliffs, N.J.: Prentice-Hall, 1992).

3. "The Myth of U.S. Manufacturing's Decline," *Forbes,* January 18, 1993, pp. 40–41.

4. Richard B. Chase and Warren J. Erikson, "The Service Factory," *The Academy of Management Executive,* August 1988, pp. 191–196. See also Richard B. Chase and Robert H. Hayes, "Beefing Up Operations in Service Firms," *Sloan Management Review,* Fall 1991, pp. 15–24.

5. James Brian Quinn and Christopher E. Gagnon, "Will Service Follow Manufacturing into Decline?" *Harvard Business Review,* November–December 1986, pp. 95–103.

6. Brian Dumaine, "Earning More by Moving Faster," *Fortune,* October 7, 1991, pp. 89–94; "Coleman is Glowing Overseas," *The New York Times,* December 8, 1991, pp. D1–D2.

7. Everett E. Adam, "Toward a Typology of Production and Operations Management Systems," *Academy of Management Review,* July 1983, pp. 365–375.

8. Adam and Ebert, *Production and Operations Management.*

9. Cynthia Fisher, Lyle Schoenfeldt, and James Shaw, *Human Resource Management,* 2nd ed. (Boston: Houghton Mifflin, 1993).

10. See Louis Kraar, "Japan's Gung-Ho U.S Car Plants," *Fortune,* January 30, 1989, pp. 98–108.

11. See Ricky W. Griffin, *Management,* 3rd ed. (Boston: Houghton Mifflin, 1990).

12. See Richard Daft, *Organization Theory and Design,* 4th ed. (St. Paul, Minn.: West, 1992), for a detailed discussion of other organization design issues that are applicable for operations management.

13. Shawn Tully, "The Modular Corporation," *Fortune,* February 8, 1993, pp. 106–113; "The Virtual Corporation," *Business Week,* February 8, 1993, pp. 98–102.

14. See Michael Beer, *Organizational Change and Development—A System View* (Santa Monica, Cal.: Goodyear, 1980), for a more detailed discussion of change and its relationship with operations management.

15. Adam and Ebert, *Production and Operations Management.*

16. See John Kanet, "Inventory Planning at Black and Decker," *Production and Inventory Management,* 3rd quarter 1984, pp. 9–22, for an example of inventory management.

17. David Garvin, "Product Quality: An Important Strategic Weapon," *Business Horizons,* March–April 1984, pp. 31–36.

18. Adam and Ebert, *Production and Operations Management.*

19. James C. Worthy, *Shaping an American Institution* (Urbana, Ill.: Univ. of Illinois Press, 1984), pp. 6–8.

20. Jeanette A. Davy, Richard E. White, Nancy J. Merritt, and Karen Gritzmacher, "A Derivation of the Underlying Constructs of Just-In-Time Management Systems," *Academy of Management Journal,* September 1992, pp. 653–670.

21. Adam and Ebert, *Production and Operations Management.*

22. Paul D. Collins, Jerald Hage, and Frank M. Hull, "Organizational and Technological Predictors of Change in Automaticity," *Academy of Management Journal,* September 1988, pp. 512–543.

23. "Computers Speed the Design of More Workaday Products," *The Wall Street Journal,* January 18, 1985, p. 25.

24. Robert Bonsack, "Executive Checklist: Are You Ready for CIM?" *CIM Review,* Summer 1987, pp. 35–38.

25. M. Sepehri, "IBM's Automated Lexington Factory Focuses on Quality and Cost Effectiveness," *Industrial Engineering,* February 1987, pp. 66–74.

26. "Computers Speed the Design of More Workaday Products."

27. "How Automation Could Save the Day," *Business Week,* March 3, 1986, pp. 72–74.

28. Otto Friedrich, "The Robot Revolution," *Time,* December 8, 1980, pp. 72–83.

29. Gene Bylinsky, "Invasion of the Service Robots," *Fortune,* September 14, 1987, pp. 81–88.

30. "Robots Head for the Farm," *Business Week,* September 8, 1986, pp. 66–67.

31. "Boldly Going Where No Robot Has Gone Before," *Business Week,* December 22, 1986, p. 45.

32. "Dinnerhouse Technology," *Forbes,* July 8, 1991, pp. 98–99; "Burritos, Anyone?" *Forbes,* March 18, 1991, pp. 52–56; "Cafe Au Lait, a Croissant—and Trix," *Business Week,* August 24, 1992, pp. 50–51.

33. "Mercedes is Downsizing—And That Includes the Sticker," *Business Week,* February 8, 1993, p. 38; Gary Hoover, Alta Campbell, Alan Chai, and Patrick J. Spain, eds., *Hoover's Handbook of World Business 1992* (Austin, Tex.: The Reference Press, 1991), p. 182; "Mercedes Finds Out How Much is Too Much," *Business Week,* January 20, 1992, pp. 92–96.

Chapter 23

1. Ronald Henkoff, "Walgreen: A High-tech Rx for Profits," *Fortune*, March 23, 1992, pp. 106–107; "Walgreen Faces Down Recession," *Drug Topics*, February 3, 1992, pp. 110–113; "USA Healthnet Deal Expands Walgreen's Mail-Order Business," *Drug Topics*, August 17, 1992, pp. 81–85; Gary Hoover, Alta Campbell, and Patrick J. Spain, eds., *Hoover's Handbook: Profiles of Over 500 Major Corporations* (Austin, Tex.: The Reference Press, 1991), p. 577; Milton Moskowitz, Robert Levering, and Michael Katz, *Everybody's Business* (New York: Doubleday, 1990), pp. 230–231.

2. See the discussion in N. Ahitov and S. Neumann, *Principles of Information Systems for Management*, 2nd ed. (Dubuque, Iowa: Wm. C. Brown, 1986), or T. H. Athey and R. W. Zmud, *Introduction to Computers and Information Systems* (Glenview, Ill.: Scott, Foresman, 1986).

3. William B. Stevenson and Mary C. Gilly, "Information Processing and Problem Solving: The Migration of Problems Through Formal Positions and Networks of Ties," *Academy of Management Journal*, December 1991, pp. 918–928.

4. Lynda M. Applegate, James I. Cash, Jr., and D. Quinn Mills, "Information Technology and Tomorrow's Manager," *Harvard Business Review*, November–December 1988, pp. 128–136.

5. Charles A. O'Reilly, "Variations in Decision Makers' Use of Information Sources: The Impact of Quality and Accessibility of Information," *Academy of Management Journal*, December 1982, pp. 756–771.

6. Carla Rapoport, "Great Japanese Mistakes," *Fortune*, February 13, 1989, pp. 108–111.

7. "Fashionable Tech: How Benetton Keeps Costs Down," *Information Week*, February 12, 1990, pp. 24–25; Janette Martin, "Benetton's IS Instinct," *Datamation*, July 1, 1989, pp. 68/15–68/16.

8. George Huber, "A Theory of the Effects of Advanced Information Technologies on Organizational Design, Intelligence, and Decision Making," *Academy of Management Review*, January 1990, pp. 47–71; Carol Saunders and Jack William Jones, "Temporal Sequences in Information Acquisition for Decision Making: A Focus on Source and Medium," *Academy of Management Review*, January 1990, pp. 29–46.

9. Paul L. Tom, *Managing Information as a Corporate Resource* (Glenview, Ill.: Scott, Foresman and Company, 1987).

10. Ibid. See also Cyrus Gibson and Richard Nolan, "Managing the Four Stages of EDP Growth," *Harvard Business Review*, January–February 1974.

11. See Steven Cavaleri and Krzysztof Obloj, *Management Systems: A Global Perspective* (Belmont, Cal.: Wadsworth, 1993).

12. Robert G. Lord and Karen J. Maher, "Alternative Information-processing Models and Their Implications for Theory, Research, and Practice," *Academy of Management Review*, January 1990, pp. 9–28.

13. Robert G. Murdick and Joel E. Ross, *Introduction to Management Information Systems* (Englewood Cliffs, N.J.: Prentice-Hall, 1977).

14. Albert L. Lederer, "Information Requirements Analysis," *Journal of Systems Management*, December 1981, pp. 15–19.

15. "Managing Information: Two Insurance Giants Forge Divergent Paths," *Business Week*, October 8, 1984, p. 121.

16. J. F. Rockart, "Chief Executives Define Their Own Data Needs," *Harvard Business Review*, March–April 1979, pp. 81–93.

17. Mitchell T. Rabkin, "Cost Containment—Ethical Implications," *Journal of the American Geriatrics Society*, April 1, 1992, pp. 413–416; Philip Hubert, "Designing an Expert System in a Medical Facility," *Industrial Engineering*, March 1, 1992, pp. 60–63; Michael H. Agranoff, "Controlling the Threat to Personal Privacy," *Information Systems Management*, Summer 1991, pp. 48–53; Janet Novack, "Abuse Control," *Forbes*, June 10, 1991, pp. 98–99.

18. Gil Press, "Decision Processing," *Information Systems Management*, Winter 1993, pp. 40–46.

19. John Huey, "Wal-Mart—Will It Take Over the World?" *Fortune*, January 30, 1989, pp. 52–61.

20. "Videoconferencing: No Longer Just a Sideshow," *Business Week*, November 12, 1984, p. 117.

21. Janice Castro, "Staying Home Is Paying Off," *Time*, October 26, 1987, pp. 112–113.

22. Susan Kerr, "The Application Wave Behind ISDN," *Datamation*, February 1, 1990, pp. 64–68; Carl Edgar Law, "Update on ISDN's Progress in Europe," *Business Communications Review*, January 1, 1989, pp. 54–56; Frank Derfler, "Building Network Solutions: Is ISDN Tomorrow's Interoffice Network?" *PC Magazine*, February 13, 1990, pp. 229ff; Kate Evans-Correia, "Hot Technologies in Tomorrow's Offices," *Purchasing*, February 25, 1988, pp. 50–57; Catherine L. Harris and Dean Foust, "An Electronic Pipeline That's Changing the Way America Does Business," *Business Week*, August 3, 1987, p. 80.

23. Mark S. Fox, "AI and Expert System Myths, Legends, and Facts, *IEEE Expert*, February 1, 1990, pp. 8–22.

24. "Artificial Intelligence and Expert Systems," *Power Engineering*, January 1, 1989, pp. 26–31.

25. Tim O. Peterson and David D. Van Fleet, "Casting Managerial Skills into a Knowledge Based System," in Michael Masuch, ed., *Organization, Management, and Expert Systems* (New York: Walter de Gruyter, 1990), pp. 171–183.

26. "Computer Applications: Software—A Risky Business," *Fairplay International Shipping Weekly*, January 4, 1990, pp. 23–24.

27. Andrew Kupfer, "Now, Live Experts on a Floppy Disc," *Fortune*, October 12, 1987, p. 117.

28. "Turning an Expert's Skills into Computer Software," *Business Week*, October 7, 1985, pp. 104–108.

29. "Martin Marietta: Computers Lead the Way to Inbound Control," *Traffic Management*, January 1, 1990, pp. 50–68.

30. See, for example, Peter H. Lewis, "I'm Sorry; My Machine Doesn't Like Your Work," *The New York Times*, February 4, 1990, p. F27.

31. Chris Carroll and Chris Larkin, "Executive Information Technology," *Information Systems Management*, Summer 1992, pp. 21–29.

32. Philip Elmer-Dewitt, "A Portable Office That Fits in Your Palm," *Time*, February 15, 1993, pp. 56–57.

33. Cornelius H. Sullivan, Jr., and John R. Smart, "Planning for Information Networks," *Sloan Management Review*, Winter 1987, pp. 39–44.

34. "Linking All the Company Data: We're Not There Yet," *Business Week*, May 11, 1987, p. 151.

35. Malcolm Cole, "Network Your Way to the Automated Office," *Accountancy*, October 1, 1988, pp. 92–94; Malcolm Cole, "Less Paper—The First Step to No Paper," *Accountancy*, October 1, 1988, pp. 88–91.

36. Wendall Hahm and Tora Bikson, "Retirees Using EMail and Networked Computers," *International Journal of Technology and Aging*, Fall 1989, pp. 113–114.

37. "Office Automation: Making It Pay Off," *Business Week*, October 12, 1987, pp. 134–146.

38. Jeremy Main, "At Last, Software CEOs Can Use," *Fortune*, March 13, 1989, pp. 77–83.

39. Ibid.

40. Adolph I. Katz, "Measuring Technology's Business Value," *Information Systems Management*, Winter 1993, pp. 33–38.

41. "Office Automation: Making It Pay Off."

42. "Home Depot," *Business Week*, August 3, 1992, p. 51; Ellen Neuborne, "Home Depot Nails Down Success," *USA Today*, January 14, 1992, p. 3B; "Clout!" *Business Week*, December 21, 1992, pp. 66–72; "Environment," *Chain Store Age Executive*, October 1, 1992, pp. 33–35; "Technology Report," *Stores*, September 1, 1991, pp. 43–45.

43. John J. Donovan, "Beyond Chief Information Officer to Network Managers," *Harvard Business Review*, September–October 1988, pp. 134–140.

44. Jeremy Main, "The Winning Organization," *Fortune*, September 26, 1988, pp. 50–60.

45. "When Empoyees Work at Home, Management Probems Often Arise," *The Wall Street Journal*, April 20, 1987, p. 21.

46. "Intimate Apparel," *Stores*, May 1, 1992, pp. 42–44; "Technology Trends," *Stores*, December 1, 1991, pp. 24–31; Carol Hymowitz and Thomas F. O'Boyle, "A Way That Works," *The Wall Street Journal*, May 29, 1991, pp. A1 and A7; Hoover, Campbell, and Spain, *Hoover's Handbook: Profiles of Over 500 Major Corporations*, p. 209; "Signage," *Chain Store Age Executive*, July 1, 1991, p. 81; "Top 100 Department Stores," *Stores*, July 1, 1990, pp. 9–12; Susan Caminiti, "A Quiet Superstar Rises in Retailing," *Fortune*, October 23, 1989, pp. 167–176.

47. "UPS Ups Rates," *The Traffic World*, January 11, 1993, pp. 15–21; Frank Hammel, "A Little 'Wrap' Music," *Supermarket Business*, November 1, 1992, pp. 73–79; "Langley Data Link Systems Provides ATC Communications," *Aviation Week & Space Technology*, January 6, 1992, pp. 52–53; Dennis Livingston, "United Parcel Service Gets a Special Delivery," *Systems Integration*, November 1, 1991, pp. 54–61; Hoover, Campbell, and Spain, *Hoover's Handbook: Profiles of Over 500 Major Corporations*, p. 555; Moskowitz, Levering, and Katz, *Everybody's Business*, pp. 614–616.

Appendix 1

1. M. W. McCall, Jr., A. M. Morrison, and R. L. Hannan, *Studies of Managerial Work: Results and Methods* (Greensboro, N.C.: Center for Creative Leadership, 1978).

2. George W. Rimler, "Moving into Management," *Journal of the American Society of CLU & ChFC*, July 1, 1992, pp. 70–73.

3. Douglas T. Hall, *Careers in Organizations* (Santa Monica, Cal.: Goodyear, 1976).

4. See "Why This Book Was Written" in R. N. Bolles, *What Color Is Your Parachute?* (Berkeley, Cal.: Ten Speed Press, 1980).

5. S. L. Jacobs, "Aspiring Entrepreneurs Learn Intricacies of Going It Alone," *The Wall Street Journal*, March 23, 1981, p. 25.

6. Diane Cole, "Assess Your Skills to Reduce Career Doubts," *The Wall Street Journal, The College Edition of the National Business Employment Weekly*, Spring 1990, pp. 7–8.

7. One excellent book is Bolles, *What Color Is Your Parachute?* For a more academic treatment, see Edgar H. Schein, *Career Dynamics: Matching Individual and Organizational Needs* (Reading, Mass.: Addison-Wesley, 1978).

8. D. J. Levinson, *The Seasons of a Man's Life* (New York: Knopf, 1978); E. H. Erickson, *Childhood and Society* (New York: Norton, 1963).

9. Peter Rea, Julie Rea, and Charles Moomaw, "Skills Development," *Personnel Journal*, April 1, 1990, pp. 126–131.

10. Michael Brody, "Meet Today's Young American Worker," *Fortune*, November 11, 1985, pp. 90–98.

11. Beverly McQuigg-Martinez and Edward E. Sutton, "New York Telephone Connects Training to Development," *Personnel Journal*, January 1, 1990, pp. 64–73.

12. H. Gilman and K. Blumenthal, "Two Wal-Mart Officials Vie for Top Post," *The Wall Street Journal*, July 23, 1986, p. 6.

13. J. A Byrne and A. L. Cowan, "Should Companies Groom New Leaders or Buy Them?" *Business Week*, September 22, 1986, pp. 94–96.

14. Cary L. Cooper and Valerie J. Sutherland, "The Stress of the Executive Lifestyle: Trends in the 1990's," *Management Decision*, Vol. 30, 1992, pp. 64–68.

15. Douglas LaBier, "Madness Stalks the Ladder Climbers," *Fortune*, September 1, 1986, pp. 79–84.

16. K. R. Brousseau, "Job-Person Dynamics and Career Development," *Personnel and Human Resources Management*, Vol. 2, 1984, pp. 125–154; Mariann Jelinek, *Career Management for the Individual and the Organization* (Chicago: St. Clair Press, 1979); J. C. Arpin and D. K. Gerster, "Career Development: An Integration of Individual and Organizational Needs," *Personnel*, March–April 1978, pp. 23–29.

17. Jane Champion, "Career Planning and Development at William Younger," *Management Accounting*, February 1, 1990, pp. 50–52.

18. B. A. Duval and R. S. Courtney, "Upward Mobility: The GF Way of Opening Employee Advancement Opportunities," *Personnel*, May–June 1978, pp. 43–53; P. G. Benson and G. C. Thornton III, "A Model Career Planning Program," *Pesonnel*, March–April 1978, pp. 30–39.

19. Walter Kiechel III, "Passed Over," *Fortune*, October 13, 1986, pp. 189–191; J. C. Latack and J. B. Dozier, "After the Ax Falls: Job Loss As a Career Transition," *Academy of Management Review*, Vol. 11, No. 2, 1986, pp. 375–392; A. Bennett, "Laid-Off Managers of Big Firms Increasingly Move to Small Ones," *The Wall Street Journal*, July 25, 1986, p. 17.

20. Carol Hymowitz, "More Executives Finding Changes in Traditional Corporate Ladder," *The Wall Street Journal*, November 14, 1986, p. 25.

21. A. Taylor III, "GE's Hard Driver at NBC," *Fortune*, March 16, 1987, pp. 97–104.

22. Kenneth B. Hoyt, "The Career Status of Women and Minority Persons: A 20-Year Retrospective," *The Career Development Quarterly*, March 1, 1989, pp. 202–212.

23. U.S. Bureau of the Census, *Statistical Abstract of the United States 1991*,

111th ed. (Washington, D.C.: U.S. Government Printing Office, 1991), p. 395.

24. D. D. Bowen and R. D. Hisrich, "The Female Entrepreneur: A Career Development Perspective," *Academy of Management Review*, Vol. 11, No. 2, 1986, pp. 393–407.

25. Anne M. Russell, "High-Tech Corporate Careers: Where Career Ladders Are Like Roller Coasters," *Working Woman*, May 1, 1989, pp. 55–86.

26. "Male vs. Female: What a Difference It Makes in Business Careers," *The Wall Street Journal*, December 9, 1986, p. 1.

27. "Women Directors Now Bring Strong Management Credentials to Boards," *The Wall Street Journal*, August 19, 1986, p. 1.

28. Kathy Cannings and Claude Montmarquette, "Managerial Momentum: A Simultaneous Model of the Career Progress of Male and Female Managers," *Industrial and Labor Relations Review*, January 1, 1991, pp. 212–228; Gregory B. Lewis, "Men and Women Toward the Top: Backgrounds, Careers, and Potential of Federal Middle Managers," *Public Personnel Management*, Winter 1992, pp. 473–492; Gary N. Powell and Lisa A. Maniniero, "Cross Currents in the River of Time: Conceptualizing the Complexities of Women's Careers," *Journal of Management*, June 1, 1992, pp. 215–237.

29. D. D. Van Fleet and J. Saurage, "Recent Research on Women in Leadership and Management," *Akron Business and Economic Review*, Vol. 15, No. 2, 1984, pp. 15–24.

30. Charlene M. Solomon, "Careers Under Glass," *Personnel Journal*, April 1, 1990, pp. 96–107.

31. Alex Taylor III, "Why Woman Managers Are Bailing Out," *Fortune*, August 18, 1986, pp. 16–23.

32. Kathleen Gerson, "Briefcase, Baby or Both?" *Psychology Today*, November 1986, pp. 30–36.

33. E. M. Van Fleet and D. D. Van Fleet, "Entrepreneurship and Black Capitalism," *American Journal of Small Business*, Vol. 10, No. 2, Fall 1985, pp. 31–40. See also Erika Kotite, "The Small-Business Melting Pot," *Entrepreneur*, July 1, 1989, pp. 158–165.

34. "Winning Friends and Influencing People," *Hispanic Business*, July 1, 1989, pp. 20–25.

35. Jeffrey H. Greenhaus, Saroj Parasuraman, and Wayne M. Wormley, "Effects of Race on Organizational Experiences, Job Performance Evaluations, and Career Options," *Academy of Management Journal*, March 1, 1990, pp. 64–86; Larry Rebstein, "Many Hurdles, Old and New, Keep Black Managers Out of Top Jobs," *The Wall Street Journal*, July 10, 1986, p. 25.

36. "Economic Trends," *Business Week*, January 8, 1990, p. 26.

37. Rebstein, "Many Hurdles, Old and New."

38. Margaretha S. Lucas, "Personal, Social, Academic, and Career Problems Expressed by Minority College Students," *Journal of Multicultural Counseling and Development*, January 1, 1993, pp. 2–13; Sharon Jones, "Providing Minority Students with the Competitive Edge," *Journal of Career Planning and Development*, March 1, 1992, pp. 36–40; C. C. Campbell-Rock, "Career Planning Strategies That Really Work," *The Black Collegian*, September 1, 1992, pp. 120–121.

39. Walter Kiechel III, "The Importance of Being Visible," *Fortune*, June 24, 1985, pp. 141–143.

40. J. H. Greenhaus and N. J. Beutell, "Sources of Conflict Between Work and Family Roles," *Academy of Management Review*, Vol. 10, No. 1, 1985, pp. 76–88; S. E. Jackson, S. Zedeck, and E. Summers, "Family Life Disruptions: Effects of Job-Induced Structural and Emotional Interference," *Academy of Management Journal*, Vol. 28, No. 3, 1985, pp. 547–586.

41. Constanza Montana, "Career Couples Find Vacations Hard to Plan," *The Wall Street Journal*, August 4, 1986, p. A15.

42. Ronya Kozmetsky and George Kozmetsky, *Making It Together: A Survival Manual for the Executive Family* (New York: Free Press, 1981).

Appendix 2

1. "Small Business," *Director*, January 1, 1990, pp. 87–88; Terry J. Engle and David M. Dennis, "Benefits of an Internal Control Structure Evaluation in a Small Business Audit," *The Ohio CPA Journal*, Spring 1989, pp. 5–11; "Cashing Out and Maintaining Control; Have Your Cake and Eat It Too," *Small Business Report*, December 1, 1989, pp. 27–41; "Case History: Growing Pains," *Small Business Reports*, July 1, 1989, pp. 34–44; Ralph M. Stair, William F. Crittenden, and Vicky L. Crittenden, "The Use, Operation, and Control of the Small Business Computer," *Information and Management*, March 1, 1989, pp. 125–130; A. Shapero and L. Sokol, "Exits and Entries: A Study in Yellow Pages Journalism," in Karl H. Vesper, ed., *Frontiers on Entrepreneurship Research 1982* (Englewood Cliffs, N.J.: Prentice-Hall, 1982, pp. 72–90; *The Business Failure Record* (New York: Dun and Bradstreet, 1981).

2. Remember that the organization may be public as well as private. Clearly, budget issues are a major concern in the public sector; see, for example, Sharon Randall, "Top Issues for 1993: Budget, Education, Health Care," *State Legislatures*, January 1, 1992, pp. 20–21.

3. "Flexible Budget System a Practical Approach to Cost Management," *Healthcare Financial Management*, January 1, 1989, pp. 38–53.

4. Belverd E. Needles, Jr., Henry R. Anderson, and James C. Caldwell, *Principles of Accounting*, 4th ed. (Boston: Houghton Mifflin, 1990).

5. Joe Park, "Budget Systems: Make the Right Choice," *Financial Executive*, March 1984, pp. 26–35.

6. Jay W. Lorsch, James P. Baughman, James Reece, and Henry Mintzberg, *Understanding Management* (New York: Harper & Row, 1978).

7. Glenn A. Welsch, *Budgeting: Profit Planning and Control*, 4th ed. (Englewood Cliffs, N.J.: Prentice-Hall, 1976).

8. Nathan J. Muller, "The '93 Budget Imperative: Do More with Less," *Chief Information Officer Journal*, Fall 1992, pp. 38–42.

9. Thomas Moore, "Why Martin Marietta Loves Mary Cunningham," *Fortune*, March 16, 1987, pp. 66–70.

10. Harry Ernst, "New Balance Sheet for Managing Liquidity and Growth," *Harvard Business Review*, March–April 1984, pp. 122–135.

11. Welsch, *Budgeting*.

12. Robin Cooper, "You Need a New Cost System When . . .," *Harvard Business Review*, January–February 1989, pp. 77–82.

13. Bess Ritter May, "How Any Supervisor Can Control Company Costs: Be a Budget Watcher," *Supervision*, April 1, 1990, pp. 3–5.

14. Susumu Ueno and Uma Sekaran, "The Influence of Culture on Budget

Control Practices in the USA and Japan: An Empirical Study," *Journal of International Business Studies*, 1992, Vol. 23, pp. 659–674.

15. Thomas A. Stewart, "Why Budgets Are Bad for Business," *Fortune*, June 4, 1990, pp. 179–190.

16. David Solomons, "Flexible Budgets and the Analysis of Overhead Variances," *Management International Review*, 1992, Vol. 32, special issue, pp. 83–91.

17. Henry L. Tosi, Jr., "The Human Effects of Budgeting Systems on Management," *MSU Business Topics*, Autumn 1974, pp. 53–63.

18. Eugene Brigham, *Financial Management: Theory and Practice*, 4th ed. (Chicago: Dryden, 1985).

19. For an example of the use of ratios in the public sector, see "Selected Financial and Operating Ratios," *Public Power*, January 1, 1993, pp. 46–55.

20. Raphael Amit and Joshua Livnat, "Grouping of Conglomerates by Their Segments' Economic Attributes: Towards a More Meaningful Ratio Analysis," *Journal of Business Finance & Accounting*, Spring 1990, pp. 85–100.

21. Brigham, *Financial Management*.

22. Douglas A. Clarke and William R. Pasewark, "Establishing Quality Control for Audit Services," *National Public Accountant*, December 1, 1989, pp. 40–44.

23. "Auditors of Corporate Legal Bills Thrive," *The Wall Street Journal*, February 13, 1991, p. B1.

24. Wanda Wallace, "Internal Auditors Can Cut Outside CPA Costs," *Harvard Business Review*, March–April 1984, p. 16.

25. Wendell French, *Human Resource Management* (Boston: Houghton Mifflin, 1986).

26. Ibid.

27. William M. Pride and O. C. Ferrell, *Marketing Concepts and Strategies*, 6th ed. (Boston: Houghton Mifflin, 1989).

28. "Buttering Up Passengers," *Business Week*, March 12, 1990, p. 94; "High-Flying Image: British Airways Integrates WIIS," *Informationweek*, February 19, 1990, p. 46; "The World's Best Airlines," *Institutional Investor*, June 1, 1989, pp. 195–208; "British Airways Empire," *Business Week*, October 9, 1989, pp. 97–101; Kenneth Labich, "The Big Comeback at British Airways," *Fortune*, December 5, 1988, pp. 163–174.

29. "Companies Get on Fast Track to Roll Out Hot New Brands," *The Wall Street Journal*, July 10, 1986, p. 25.

30. See Hugh J. Watson and Archie B. Carroll, eds., *Computers for Business* (Plano, Tex.: Business Publications, 1984).

31. Thomas E. Sheeran, "Budgeting on the Cutting Edge—Using PCs to Improve Budget Management," *School Business Affairs*, October 1, 1992, pp. 14–21.

32. "At Today's Supermarket, The Computer Is Doing It All," *Business Week*, August 11, 1986, pp. 64–65.

33. Watson and Carroll, *Computers for Business*.

Glossary

A

absenteeism Percentage of the organization's work force that is absent on a given day. (Ch. 15, App. 2)

absolute quality The generally understood level of quality a product or system needs to be capable of to fulfill its intended purpose. (Ch. 21)

acceptance sampling Process whereby finished goods are sampled to determine what proportion are of acceptable quality.

accountability Answerability for actions, decisions, and performance. (Ch. 11, 20)

achievement need The desire to excel or to accomplish some goal or task more effectively than in the past. (Ch. 17)

action plan A plan that calls for actions for specific project completion. (Ch. 9)

adaptation Changes in one's behavior in adjustment to new or modified surroundings.

adaptation model The most popular view of business strategy, which suggests that managers should solve entrepreneurial, engineering, and administrative problems by either defending, prospecting, or analyzing markets. (Ch. 8)

administrative management The subarea of classical management theory that is concerned with how organizations should be put together. (Ch. 1, Ch. 2)

administrative management model Focuses on the internal operation of the organization and attempts to make administrative procedures more efficient. (Ch. 2)

administrative managers Generalists who oversee a variety of activities in several different areas of the organization. (Ch. 1)

administrative problem The managerial problem in strategic planning that involves structuring the organization. (Ch. 8)

affiliation need The need to work with others, to interact, and to have friends. (Ch. 17)

affirmative action Plans of action undertaken by organizations to comply with human rights legislation by actively striving to recruit, hire, train, develop, and promote women and members of minority groups. (App. 1)

analyzing A strategic business alternative that involves keeping a core set of products that provide predictable revenues while systematically looking for new opportunities. (Ch. 8)

ancient management The management concepts and techniques that were used by many ancient civilizations. (Ch. 1)

application blanks Printed forms that ask job applicants for information about background, education, experience, etc. (Ch. 14)

arbitrator A labor law specialist paid jointly by the union and the organization to listen to both sides of a labor dispute and then decide how the dispute should be settled. (Ch. 14)

artificial intelligence (AI) Attempts to have computers simulate human decision processes. (Ch. 23)

assessment center An employee selection technique that allows human resource managers to observe and evaluate a prospective employee's performance on simulated tasks such as decision making and time management. (Ch. 14)

assets Items of value owned by the company. (App. 2)

attitudes Sets of beliefs and feelings that individuals have about specific ideas, situations, or other people. (Ch. 15, 19)

audit An independent appraisal of an organization's accounting, financial, and operational systems. (App. 2)

authoritarianism The extent to which a person believes that power and status differences are appropriate within organizations. (Ch. 15)

authority The power to carry out an assignment. (Ch. 11)

automation The use of machinery, especially computers and robots, to replace human labor as part of the technological transformation process. (Ch. 4, Ch. 22)

avoidance 1) A method of reinforcement that allows an employee, because of good performance, to escape from an unpleasant situation. 2) Ignoring the problem, thing, or situation. (Ch. 17)

B

balance sheet A summary statement of assets, liabilities, and equity to reveal an organization's financial position at a given time. (App. 2)

balance sheet budget A projection of what assets and liabilities of the firm will look like at the end of the coming period. (App. 2)

behavioral model An approach to decision making that recognizes that managers do not always have complete information and are limited in their ability to make rational decisions. (Ch. 10)

behavioral school School of management thought that focuses on the role of the individual in the workplace. (Ch. 1)

benchmarking The process of finding out, in a legal and ethical manner, how other firms do something and then imitate or improve on it. (Ch. 21)

benefits   Indirect compensation (payments other than wages and salaries) paid to employees, such as healthcare, life insurance, vacations, sick leave. (Ch. 14)

boundary spanner   Someone who spends much of her or his time in contact with others outside the organization. (Ch. 3)

bounded rationality   Attempts at rationality are constrained by values and experiences and by unconscious reflexes, skills, and habits. (Ch. 10)

brainstorming   The process of bringing people together and encouraging a free and open discussion of creative solutions to a problem. (Ch. 10)

break-even analysis   Determines the point at which revenues and costs will be equal. (Ch. 9)

budget   A plan expressed in quantitative terms. (App. 2)

budgeting process   The activities involved in developing a budget for the organization. (App. 2)

bureaucracy   A form of organization that is based on a comprehensive set of rational rules and guidelines. (Ch. 1, 12)

burnout   A feeling of exhaustion that may develop when someone experiences too much stress for an extended period of time. (Ch. 15)

business strategy   Strategic plans that chart the course for each individual business or division within a company. (Ch. 8)

"Buy National" Legislation   Laws that give preference to domestic producers through content or price restrictions. (Ch. 5)

C

capacity   The space an organization has available to create products and/or services. (Ch. 22)

capital expenditure budget   A financial budget that outlines when and how much money will be spent for major assets such as equipment, plants, and land. (App. 2)

capital-intensive   Machines, not people, do almost all of the work.

career   A sequence of attitudes and behaviors that a person perceives to be related to work experience during his or her life. (App. 1)

career counseling   Advice and assistance provided informally or formally to the individual regarding his or her career development and planning. (App. 1)

career development   A careful, systematic approach to ensuring that sound career choices are made; involves both career planning (an individual element) and career management (an organizational element). (App. 1)

career information systems   The combination of internal job markets with formal career counseling and the maintenance of a career information center for employees. (App. 1)

career management   The organizational element of career development, involving career counseling, career pathing, career resources planning, and career information systems. (App. 1)

career pathing   Identifying coherent progressions of jobs (tracks, routes, or paths) that are of particular interest to the organization. (App. 1)

career planning   Making detailed and specific decisions and plans about career goals and how to achieve them. (App. 1)

career resources planning   Use of careful planning techniques in career management, including forecasting personnel needs, illustrating the planned progressions of employees, preparing inventories of human resource needs, and monitoring the implementation of these plans. (App. 1)

career stages   Spans of years during which an individual has different types of concerns about job and career, sometimes labeled as the stages of career exploration, establishment, maintenance, and decline. (App. 1)

cash cow   A product that controls a large share of a low-growth market, thus generating large amounts of cash with relatively little support. (Ch. 8)

cash flow budget   A precise outline of where the money for the coming period will come from and when, plus how the money will be used and when. (App. 2)

centralization   Keeping power and control at the top level of the organization. (Ch. 11)

central processor   That part of a system where the analysis and process is done. (Ch. 23)

certainty   Knowing exactly what the alternatives are and that each alternative is guaranteed. (Ch. 10)

channels   The means of transmitting an idea, such as a face-to-face meeting, a letter, a telephone call, or a facial expression. (Ch. 19)

charisma   An intangible attribute in the leader's personality that inspires loyalty and enthusiasm. (Ch. 16)

chief information officer (CIO)   The executive who oversees all aspects of information technology, such as computing, office systems, and telecommunications. (Ch. 19)

classical school   School of management thought that emerged around the turn of the century. It is composed of two subareas: scientific management and administrative management. (Ch. 1)

codes of conduct   Meaningful symbolic statements about the importance of adhering to high ethical standards in business. (Ch. 6)

coercive power   Power to force compliance through psychological, emotional, or physical threat. (Ch. 16)

cognitive dissonance   A situation that occurs when there is a conflict among the three components of an attitude. (Ch. 15)

cohesiveness   The extent to which members of the group are motivated to remain together. (Ch. 18)

collective bargaining Negotiating a written contract covering all relevant aspects of the relationships among the organization and members of a union. (Ch. 14)

commitment The favorable response of persons confronted with an attempt by their leader to influence them. (Ch. 16)

committee Special kind of task group. (Ch. 18)

communication The process of transmitting information. (Ch. 19)

communication model An illustration showing the route of a message from its beginning as an idea to its termination with the receiver.

communication overload A communication difficulty that occurs when the sender is transmitting too much information for the receiver to process adequately. (Ch. 19)

company productivity The amount produced or created by all organization members and/or units combined. (Ch. 21)

compensation Wages and salaries paid to employees for their services. (Ch. 14)

competitive advantage The component of strategy that specifies the advantages that the organization holds relative to its competitors. (Ch. 8)

competitive challenges Efforts to gain an advantage in acquiring scarce resources. (Ch. 4)

competitor intelligence The active approach of scanning information available publicly about competitors. (Ch. 9)

competitors Other organizations that compete with an organization for resources. (Ch. 3)

complexity Number of issues, problems, opportunities, and threats.

compliance Going along with the boss's request but without any stake in the result. (Ch. 16)

compounding Adding to and increasing, as in the tendency of a small error or deviation to become large if not detected and corrected.

compromise Reaching an agreement between what each of the conflicting parties wants, without either party feeling it has won everything or lost everything.

computer-aided design (CAD) The use of computers to design parts and complete products and simulate performance so that prototypes need not be constructed. (Ch. 22)

computer-aided manufacturing (CAM) Manufacturing that ensures that the design moves smoothly to production. (Ch. 22)

computer-assisted manufacturing Technology that relies on computers to design or manufacture products. (Ch. 22)

computer-integrated manufacturing (CIM) Computers adjust machine placements and settings automatically to enhance both the complexity and flexibility of scheduling. (Ch. 22)

conceptual modeling The formation of patterns and models in an efficient way for problem solving, especially in handling and even looking for information. (Ch. 9)

conceptual skills The skills a manager needs for thinking in the abstract, such as seeing relationships between forces, understanding how a variety of factors are interrelated, taking a global perspective of the organization and its environment, and defining and understanding situations. (Ch. 2)

concurrent control Monitoring the activities that occur as inputs are being transformed into outputs; also known as yes/no control and screening control. (Ch. 20)

conflict of interest A situation where the employee's decision may be compromised because of competing loyalties. (Ch. 6)

confrontation Addressing a problem or conflict directly and working together to resolve it.

conglomerate design An organization design that uses the product form of departmentalization and takes advantage of specialization based on knowledge of specific products or services, their production and marketing. Also called the H-Form. (Ch. 12)

consumer protection Buyer-oriented safeguards from unscrupulous seller practices in advertising, pricing, and warranties. (Ch. 6)

contingency approach A management theory that argues that the most appropriate managerial actions in a situation depend on, or are contingent on, the elements of each situation. (Ch. 1)

contingency events The possible conditions or events that could arise and would necessitate the use of alternative or contingency plans.

contingency planning Part of the planning process in which managers identify alternative courses of action that the organization might take if various conditions arise. (Ch. 7, 8)

continuous-process technology The set of processes used when the making of a product requires that the composition of the raw materials be changed mechanically or chemically. (Ch. 12)

continuous reinforcement schedule Providing reinforcement after every occurrence of the desired behavior. (Ch. 17)

controller A manager who has specific responsibility for control; helps line managers, coordinates the overall control system, and gathers important information from and relays it to all managers. (Ch. 20)

controlling The process of monitoring and adjusting organizational activities toward goal attainment. (Ch. 1, 20)

control system A mechanism used to assure that the organization is achieving its objectives; involves setting standards, assessing performance, comparing performance with standards, and evaluating and adjusting. (Ch. 20)

corporate culture The shared experiences, stories, beliefs, norms, and actions that characterize an organization. (Ch. 12)

corporate ownership   Issues that include the power of mutual funds and institutional investors and hostile takeovers. (Ch. 4)

corporate social audit   A formal and thorough analysis of the effectiveness of a firm's social performance. (Ch. 6)

corporate strategy   Strategic plans that chart the course for the entire organization and attempt to answer the question What business are we in? (Ch. 8)

cost control   Identifying areas in which costs are too high and reducing them appropriately. (Ch. 22)

country productivity   The amount produced or created by entire countries. (Ch. 21)

creativity   A way of thinking that generates new ideas or concepts. (Ch. 10)

credibility   Reputation as to believability.

critical path   The longest path through the entire PERT network. (Ch. 9)

culture   The set of values that helps its members understand what the organization stands for, how it does things, and what it considers important. (Ch. 3)

current ratio   A liquidity ratio determined by dividing current assets by current liabilities. (App. 2)

customers   Those people or groups that buy the goods or services produced by an organization; part of the task environment. (Ch. 3)

cutbacks   Reductions in the scope of an organization's operations. (Ch. 4)

D

data   Facts and figures; unorganized pieces of information. (Ch. 23)

debt ratios   Ratios that reflect the firm's ability to cover its long-term debt. (App. 2)

decentralization   Shifting, through delegation, some power and control from the top level to the lower levels of the organization. (Ch. 11)

decisional roles   The roles that a manager plays when making decisions while acting as an entrepreneur, a disturbance handler, a resource allocator, or a negotiator. (Ch. 2)

decision framing   The tendency of people to let the way that a decision is stated, either as a potential gain or loss, affect their choice of risky or cautious alternatives (Ch. 10)

decision making   The process of choosing one alternative from among a set of alternatives. (Ch. 10)

decision support system (DSS)   Form of information system that automatically searches for, analyzes, and reports information needed by a manager for a particular decision. (Ch. 23)

decision tree   A decision-making technique, basically an extension of payoff matrices, that helps managers define the second-

and third-level outcomes that can result from an alternative. (Ch. 10)

declarative knowledge   Deals with facts and definitions. (Ch. 2)

decline stage   The final career stage, which usually means the end of full-time employment and could mean retirement. (App. 1)

decoding   Translating an encoded message. (Ch. 19)

defending   A strategic business alternative that involves defining a market niche and protecting it from competitors. (Ch. 8)

degree of participation   The extent to which subordinates are allowed to participate in decision making.

delegation   Assigning a portion of one's task to subordinates. (Ch. 11)

Delphi forecasting   The systematic refinement of expert opinion to make predictions. (Ch. 9)

Delphi technique   Use of a group of experts to make predictions. (Ch. 18)

departmentalization   Grouping jobs according to function, product, or location. (Ch. 11)

developing economy   An economy that is relatively underdeveloped and immature, characterized by weak industry, weak currency, and relatively poor consumers. (Ch. 5)

development   Training for managers. (Ch. 14)

devil's advocate strategy   Assigning a group member the role of taking issue with the actions of the rest of the group in order to prevent groupthink. (Ch. 18)

diagnosis   Looking carefully at the system to identify all the possible consequences of a potential organizational change.

diagnostic skills   The skills a manager needs for defining and understanding situations; includes defining a problem, determining the cause, and identifying ways to reduce it.

differentiation   Setting a company's products apart from those of competitors in terms of quality, style, or service. (Ch. 8)

direct investment   A firm headquartered in one country builds or purchases operating facilities or subsidiaries in a foreign country. (Ch. 5)

disseminator   The role that a manager plays when relaying to the appropriate people the information that was obtained through monitoring. (Ch. 2)

distribution model   A quantitative decision-making technique that helps managers plan routes for distributing products by minimizing travel time, fuel expenses, etc. (Ch. 10)

disturbance handler   The role that a manager plays when resolving conflicts between groups of employees, between a sales representative and an important customer, or between another manager and a union representative. (Ch. 2)

diversity training   Training that is specifically designed to better enable members of an organization to function in a diverse workplace. (Ch. 4)

divisional design   An organization design that establishes fairly autonomous product departments that operate as strategic business units. (Ch. 12)

division head   The individual who is responsible for the management of a division. (Ch. 12)

division manager   The individual who is responsible for the management of a division. (Ch. 12)

dog   A product or business with a small share of a stable market, which makes it difficult to salvage since its growth must come at the expense of competing products or businesses. (Ch. 8)

dogmatism   The rigidity of a person's beliefs and his or her openness to other viewpoints. (Ch. 15)

domestic business   A company that acquires all its resources and sells all of its products or services within a single country. (Ch. 5)

downsizing   Planned reduction in organizational size. (Ch. 4)

dual-career family   Household in which both the husband and the wife are pursuing careers, not merely earning incomes. (App. 1)

dual-income family   Household in which both the husband and the wife earn a paycheck. (App. 1)

dynamism   Changing fast, frequently, and in many ways.

E

economic challenge   Various forces and dynamics associated with the economic system within which their organization competes. (Ch. 4)

economic community   A set of countries that agrees to significantly reduce or eliminate trade barriers among its member nations. (Ch. 5)

economic dimension   The dimension of the international environment that includes a country's economic system, financial laws, infrastructure, and economic health.

economic environment   The overall health of the economic system in which the organization operates. (Ch. 3)

economic forces   Forces of the general environment associated with economic conditions—inflation, interest rates, and unemployment, for example.

economic sector   A portion or section of the overall business world that produces, distributes, and sells the goods and services of a country. There are, for example, the private sector and the public sector; the profit and the nonprofit sectors; the agricultural, retail, wholesale, mining, and manufacturing sectors. (App. 1)

effective control   Organizational control that is characterized by integration, objectivity, accuracy, timeliness, and flexibility.

effectiveness   Doing the right things in the right way at the right times. (Ch. 1)

efficiency   Operating in such a way that resources are not wasted. (Ch. 1)

efficiency emphasis   Involves using resources in the best way possible. (Ch. 2)

employee stock ownership plans (ESOPs)   The transfer of stock ownership to employees in an effort to increase their commitment, involvement, and motivation. (Ch. 12)

employment at will   Freedom of the organization to employ someone when it desires and therefore to dismiss the employee at any time for any reason.

enacted role   How the person in a group actually behaves. (Ch. 18)

encoding   Translating a message into the exact mix of words, phrases, sentences, pictures, or other symbols that best reflect the message's content. (Ch. 19)

engineering problem   The managerial problem in strategic planning that involves decisions regarding production and distribution of goods and services. (Ch. 8)

entrepreneur   The role that a manager plays when taking the lead in looking for new or different opportunities that the organization can pursue. (Ch. 2)

entrepreneurial problem   The managerial problem in strategic planning that involves determining which business opportunities to undertake, which to ignore, and so forth. (Ch. 8)

entrepreneurship   The process of starting a new business. (Ch. 4)

entropy   The negative result, faltering and dying, that occurs when an organization takes a closed-system perspective. (Ch. 1)

environmental analysis   An investigation of the ways in which an organization and its environment affect one another.

environmental change   The extent to which forces outside the organization alter and the rate of such alterations. (Ch. 12)

environmental characteristics   Nonpersonal factors such as the extent to which a task is highly structured, the nature of the work group, and the authority system within the organization.

environmental complexity   Having many different elements in the organizational environment. (Ch. 12)

environmental context   Such situational factors as competition, government regulation, and sociocultural norms.

environmental protection   Safeguards pertaining to air and water pollution. (Ch. 6)

environmental scanning   The process of actively monitoring the environment through observation, reading, and so forth. (Ch. 3, Ch. 9)

environmental uncertainty   The condition that exists when the organizational environment is changing frequently or contains many different elements. (Ch. 12)

equifinality   The idea that two or more paths may lead to the same place, or organizations may achieve similar success by pursuing different objectives. (Ch. 1)

equity Fairness in the workplace. (Ch. 17)

equity positions Ownership positions obtained through the purchase of significant portions of stock. (Ch. 12)

escalation of commitment Tendency of people to continue to pursue an ineffective course of action even when current information indicates that the project will fail. (Ch. 10)

establishment stage The second career stage, during which time the individual may hold several jobs while learning more about occupational choices; job hopping is common during this stage. (App. 1)

esteem needs The need for recognition and respect from others, and the needs for self-respect and a positive self-image. (Ch. 17)

ethical compliance The extent to which members of the organization follow basic ethical (and legal) standards of behavior. (Ch. 6)

ethical dilemma The situation that occurs when a manager is faced with two or more conflicting ethical issues.

ethics Standards or morals that a person sets for himself or herself regarding what is good and bad or right and wrong. (Ch. 6)

ethnicity The ethnic composition of a group or organization. (Ch. 4)

European Community (EC) A mature market system that consists of Denmark, the United Kingdom, Portugal, the Netherlands, Belgium, Spain, Ireland, Luxembourg, France, Germany, Italy, and Greece. (Ch. 5)

event A point in time, such as the start or completion of a task or tasks. (Ch. 9)

expectancy model A comprehensive model of employee motivation based on the assumption that motivation is a function of how much people want something and how likely they think they are to get it. (Ch. 17)

expected role How others in a group expect a given person to behave. (Ch. 18)

expected value The sum of all the possible outcomes of alternatives multiplied by their respective probabilities. (Ch. 10)

expense budget An operations budget that projects the use and timing of outgoing funds for the coming period. (App. 2)

expert power Power based on knowledge and expertise. (Ch. 16)

expert systems Systems that build on series of rules—frequently if-then rules—to move from a set of data to a decision recommendation. (Ch. 23)

exploration stage The first career stage, during which time the individual undergoes self-examination and explores different occupations; begins with school training and continues through first job. (App. 1)

exporting Making the product in a firm's domestic marketplace and selling it in another country.

export restraint agreement Agreements designed to convince other governments to voluntarily limit the volume or value of goods exported to a particular country. (Ch. 5)

external audit Audit conducted by experts who do not work directly for the organization. (App. 2)

external environment Everything outside an organization that might affect it. (Ch. 3)

external focus Makes the organization competitive thorough such things as organization growth and productivity. (Ch. 2)

extinction No longer reinforcing (ignoring) previously reinforced behavior; used to weaken behavior. (Ch. 17)

F

facilities The physical means of accomplishing production. (Ch. 22)

factory system Systematic approaches developed by managers of the early factories to cope with the new coordinating and supervisory problems that evolved with the Industrial Revolution.

fair labor practices Equitable practices concerning hiring, wages, union relations, etc. (Ch. 6)

feedback Response from the receiver of a message to the sender of that message. (Ch. 14, 19)

figurehead The role that a manager plays when simply appearing as a representative of the organization, as in taking a visitor to dinner or attending a ribbon-cutting ceremony. (Ch. 2)

finance managers Individuals who are responsible for the financial assets of the organization, including overseeing the accounting systems, managing investments, controlling disbursements, and providing relevant information to the CEO about the firm's financial condition. (Ch. 1)

financial budgets A budget that details where the organization intends to get its cash for the coming period and how it intends to use it. (App. 2)

financial strategy The functional strategy related to monetary matters such as dividends, retained earnings, debt financing, and equity financing. (Ch. 8)

finished goods inventory The set of products that have been completely assembled but not yet shipped. (Ch. 22)

first-line managers Those who supervise operating employees. (Ch. 1)

five competitive forces Influences on an organization that include the threat of new entrants, jockeying among contestants, the threat of substitute products, the power of buyers, and the power of suppliers. (Ch. 3)

fixed costs Costs that are incurred regardless of the level of operations; e.g., rent, taxes, minimum utility payments, and interest payments. (Ch. 9, App. 2)

fixed interval schedule Providing reinforcement on a periodic basis, regardless of performance (e.g., giving a paycheck every Friday). (Ch. 17)

fixed ratio schedule Providing reinforcement on the basis of number of behaviors rather than on the basis of time. (Ch. 17)

flat organization An organization that has relatively few levels of management. (Ch. 11)

flexible manufacturing systems Systems that have robotic work units or work stations, assembly lines, and robotic carts to move material. (Ch. 22)

flexibility The ability of an individual or firm to respond or conform to changing or new situations. (Ch. 21)

flexibility emphasis Helps the manager adapt to change. (Ch. 2)

forced mobility The changing of jobs due to events over which the individual has no control, such as firing or layoff.

force-field analysis Systematically looking at the pluses and minuses associated with a planned organizational change from the standpoint of the employees, and then attempting to increase the pluses and decrease the minuses. (Ch. 13)

forecasting The systematic development of predictions about the future. (Ch. 9)

forming The initial stage of group development; involves the coming together of would-be members to form a group. (Ch. 18)

front-end-back-end organization Organizations in which product and customer departmentalization are simultaneously employed. (Ch. 12)

functional departmentalization Grouping together those employees who are involved in the same or very similar functions. (Ch. 11)

functional design An organization design that uses a unitary or uniform approach to design. Also called the U-Form. (Ch. 12)

functional group A group created by the organization to accomplish a range of goals with an indefinite time horizon. (Ch. 18)

functional strategy Strategic plans that correspond to each of the functional areas within the organization: marketing, financial, production, human resource, organization design, and research and development. (Ch. 8)

G

Gantt chart A bar chart with each bar representing a project task. (Ch. 9)

General Adaptation Syndrome (GAS) A cycle that stress usually follows. (Ch. 15)

general environment Consists of the broad dimensions and forces in an organization's surroundings that provide opportunities and impose constraints on the organization. (Ch. 3)

generic strategy An overall framework for action developed at the corporate level; also called a grand strategy. (Ch. 8)

global business A company that transcends national boundaries and is not committed to a single home country. (Ch. 5)

global challenge Challenges that come from international competition. (Ch. 4)

global design An organization design that refers to modifications of the functional, conglomerate, and divisional designs rather than to another single specific design. (Ch. 12)

global interdependence The situation that exists as the sharp distinctions between companies and country boundaries become blurred, making it difficult to answer the question of what is domestic and what is foreign.

globalization The gradual evolution to an integrated global economy composed of interrelated markets.

goal A desired state or condition that the organization wants to achieve. (Ch. 7)

goal consistency Goals should be consistent both horizontally (between functions or areas) and vertically (between levels of management) to enhance the effectiveness of goal setting.

goal optimization The process of balancing and trading off among different goals for the sake of organizational effectiveness. (Ch. 7)

goals Targets for which the organization aims. (Ch. 7)

goal setting Process involving scanning the environment for opportunities and threats, assessing organizational strengths and weaknesses, establishing general organizational goals, setting unit and subunit goals, and monitoring programs toward goal attainment at all organizational levels. (Ch. 7)

goal-setting theory Use of goal setting to increase individual motivation. (Ch 17)

governmental factors Characteristics or conditions pertaining to the government's influence on or regulations of the business environment, especially as they pertain to foreign governments.

government regulation Federal laws, concerned primarily with enhancing the social responsiveness and awareness of business, and with protecting the best interests of society from abuse by big business. (Ch. 6)

grand strategy An overall framework for action developed at the corporate level. (Ch. 8)

grapevine Informal communication network. (Ch. 19)

grievance A written statement or complaint filed by an employee with the union concerning the employee's alleged mistreatment by the company. (Ch. 14)

group Two or more people who interact regularly to accomplish a common goal. (Ch. 18)

group decision making   Choosing among alternatives by teams, committees, or other types of groups rather than by one individual. (Ch. 18)

groupthink   Phenomenon that happens when the maintenance of cohesion and good feelings overwhelm the purpose of the group. (Ch. 18)

growth strategy   A strategic plan of actively seeking to acquire other related businesses. (Ch. 8)

H

Hawthorne studies   A series of early research studies of the human element in the workplace, conducted at the Hawthorne plant of Western Electric between 1927 and 1932. (Ch. 1)

high involvement management   Refers to all forms of participative management, including reliance on self-control and self-management at the lowest levels and such techniques as quality circles, work teams, and new design plants. (Ch. 1, Ch. 17)

high involvement organization   Organizational designs based on a process, orientation, open communications, a low level of functional specialization and standardization, and cooperation. (Ch. 12)

horizontal communication   Transmission of messages between two or more colleagues or peers at the same level in the organization. (Ch. 19)

hostile takeover   One corporation or group of investors buys or trades for enough stock in a company to gain control over it. Such a takeover is considered hostile when the target company does not wish to be taken over. (Ch. 4)

hostility   Animosity, bitterness, resentment, or even hatred.

human relations   Consideration of workers as individuals with unique needs and motives that affect their satisfaction and performance in the workplace. (Ch. 1)

human resource control   Concerned with the extent to which members of the work force are productive and the extent to which the organization is effectively managing them. (App. 2)

human resource managers   Individuals who are responsible for determining future human resource needs, recruiting and hiring the right kind of people to fill those needs, designing effective compensation and performance appraisal systems, and ensuring that legal guidelines and regulations are followed. (Ch. 1)

human resource ratios   Quantitative assessments of the degree to which the organization is managing its work force properly; commonly includes employee turnover, absenteeism, and work force composition. (App. 2)

human resource strategy   The functional strategy that deals with employee-related issues such as hiring and retention options, unions, employee development, and compliance with federal employment regulations. (Ch. 8)

human resources model   Emphasizes flexibility in adapting to internal organizational changes by focusing on the people inside the organization. (Ch. 2)

human skills   The skills a manager needs to work well with other people. (Ch. 2)

hybrid designs   An organization design that includes different designs, using whatever seems appropriate to accomplish the objective. (Ch. 12)

I

importing   Bringing a good, service, or capital into the home country from abroad. (Ch. 5)

importing/exporting strategy   A planned decision to buy from or sell to companies in another country.

inappropriate focus   Control is too narrowly concentrated or fails to balance essential factors. (Ch. 20)

income statement   A summary statement of the revenues, expenses, and profit or loss of a company during a period of time. (App. 2)

inconsistency   A communication problem that exists when a person sends conflicting messages.

incremental innovation   A new product or technology that modifies an existing product or technology. (Ch. 13)

individual differences   Personal attributes that vary from one person to another. (Ch. 15)

individual productivity   The amount produced or created by a single individual relative to his or her costs to the organization. (Ch. 21)

industry productivity   The amount produced or created by all companies in a particular industry. (Ch. 21)

informal group   A group created by members of the organization for purposes that may or may not be related to the organization and has an unspecified time horizon; also called an interest group. (Ch. 18)

informal organization   The overall pattern of influence and interaction defined by all the informal groups within an organization. (Ch. 18)

information   Data organized in a meaningful way. (Ch. 23)

informational roles   The roles that a manager plays when serving as monitor, disseminator of information, or spokesperson. (Ch. 2)

information requirements analysis   Process of determining what information each individual needs to perform his or her job. (Ch. 23)

information system needs Needs of an organization for an information system of one kind or another. (Ch. 23)

information systems Management of information by gathering and organizing relevant information for managers and assisting in summarizing that information in the form most pertinent to each manager's needs. (Ch. 3)

information technology Scientific developments related to the manner and speed with which data are accessed, processed, and communicated.

innovation The process of creating and developing new products or services and/or identifying new uses for existing products and/or services. (Ch. 4, 10, 13)

in-process sampling Testing products as they are being made rather than after they are finished.

input devices Means used to get data into a system. (Ch. 23)

instrumental benefits Benefits that may accrue as the result of some other action; e.g., making useful business contacts by playing golf as a member of the country club.

integrative framework Provides a process model for the four managerial models. (Ch. 2)

interdependency Unable to perform effectively or efficiently without the aid or output of one another.

interest group Members of a group who organize to influence their organizations. (Ch. 3)

intermediate planning Planning for a time perspective between one and five years. Intermediate plans are developed by top managers working with middle managers and are building blocks for long-range plans. (Ch. 7)

internal audit Audit conducted by people who work directly for the organization. (App. 2)

internal environment An organization's culture. (Ch. 3)

internal focus Maintaining the organization through activities such as employee participation in decision making and the management of information. (Ch. 2)

international business Business that is primarily based in a single country but acquires some meaningful share of its resources or revenues from other countries.

international divisional design A common early form of organization design for the emerging international business, which involves adding a new international division, usually headed by a vice president or other top-level manager.

international environment Forces that extend beyond national boundaries. (Ch. 3)

international forces Forces of the general environment associated with the impact of international and multinational organizations.

international matrix design A form of organization design, especially useful for multinational firms, that employs two bases of departmentalization: product managers arrayed across one side of the matrix and location-based division managers along the other dimension.

interpersonal attraction Attraction to others because of similar interests and attitudes.

interpersonal communication Communication between people. (Ch. 19)

interpersonal roles The roles that a manager plays when serving as figurehead, leader, or liaison. (Ch. 2)

interpersonal skills The skills a manager needs to work well with other people, including the ability to understand someone else's position, to present one's own position, to compromise, and to deal effectively with conflict.

intervention The option chosen to implement an organizational change.

interview Face-to-face talk between a manager and a prospective employee during the employee selection process. (Ch. 14)

in-transit inventory Goods that have been shipped from the company but have not yet been delivered to the customer. (Ch. 22)

intrapreneur The role a manager plays when developing a new business in the context of an organization. (Ch. 13)

intrapreneurship The process of starting new ventures within a larger organization. (Ch. 4)

inventory control Monitoring inventory to ensure that the supply is adequate but not excessive. (Ch. 22)

inventory model A quantitative decision-making technique that helps the manager plan the optimal level of inventory to carry. (Ch. 10)

J

jargon The use of words that have specific meaning within a profession or group of people. (Ch. 19)

job analysis The systematic collection and recording of information about jobs in the organization. (Ch. 14)

job description A summarization of the duties encompassed by the job, the working conditions where the job is performed, and the tools, materials, and equipment used on the job. (Ch. 14)

job design Determining what procedures and operations are to be performed by the employee in each position. (Ch. 11)

job dissatisfaction An attitude that reflects the extent to which a person is gratified by or fulfilled by his or her work. (Ch. 15)

job enlargement Adding more activities to a worker's job. (Ch. 11)

job enrichment Giving a worker more activities to perform and more discretion as to how to perform them. (Ch. 11)

job evaluation Determining the relative value of jobs within the organization, primarily to establish the proper wage structure. (Ch. 14)

job posting   Internal recruiting that involves identifying existing employees who want to be transferred and/or promoted. (Ch. 14)

job rotation   Systematically moving employees from one job to another. (Ch. 11)

job satisfaction   An attitude that reflects the extent to which a person is gratified by or fulfilled in his or her work. (Ch. 15)

job specialization   Defining the tasks that set one job apart from others. (Ch. 1, 11)

job specification   A description of the skills, abilities, and other credentials necessary to perform the job. (Ch. 14)

jockeying among contestants   The extent to which major competitors in a market are constantly trying to outmaneuver one another. (Ch. 3, 8)

joint ventures   The sharing by two firms in the control and ownership of a new enterprise. (Ch. 5, 12)

judgmental methods of performance appraisal   Nonquantifiable, or subjective, evaluations of how well an employee is doing in his or her job. (Ch. 14)

just-in-time method (JIT)   Making frequent but small orders of raw materials to arrive just as they are needed, with most or all of the materials going straight to the plant instead of warehouses. (Ch. 22)

L

labor   People who work for the organization, especially when they are organized into unions. (Ch. 3)

labor budget   A nonmonetary budget that details the number of direct hours of labor that are available during the coming period. (App. 2)

labor-intensive   People, not machines, do most of the work. (Ch. 22)

labor productivity   A form of productivity determined by dividing outputs by direct labor. (Ch. 21)

labor relations   Dealing with employees when they are organized in a labor union. (Ch. 14)

large-batch technology   The set of processes used when a product is made in assembly-line fashion by combining component parts into a finished product; also known as mass-production technology. (Ch. 12)

leader   The role that a manager plays when hiring employees, motivating them, or dealing with behavioral processes. (Ch. 2)

leader-member relations   Relationship between the leader and the members of a group. (Ch. 16)

leadership   An influence process directed at shaping the behavior of others. (Ch. 16)

leadership behaviors   Actions that set apart effective leaders and ineffective leaders. (Ch. 16)

Leadership Grid   A Grid for assessing leadership style; uses axes representing concern for people and concern for production. (Ch. 13)

leadership style   Combination of skills and behaviors. (Ch. 16)

leadership traits   Stable and enduring characteristics that set leaders apart from nonleaders. (Ch. 16)

leading   Guiding and directing employees toward goal attainment by motivating employees, managing group processes, and dealing with conflict and change. (Ch. 1)

legal challenges   Those that reflect the judicial context in which an organization operates. (Ch. 4)

legal compliance   The extent to which the organization complies with local, state, federal, and international laws. (Ch. 6)

legitimate power   Power created and conveyed by the organization; the same as authority. (Ch. 16)

levels of strategy   Corporate strategy, business strategy, and functional strategies.

liabilities   Debts and other financial obligations that the firm must repay. (App. 2)

liaison   The role a manager plays when dealing with people outside the organization on a regular basis; usually involves the establishment of a good working relationship. (Ch. 2)

licensing agreement   The allowance by one firm to another company to use its brand name, trademark, technology, patent, copyrights, or other assets. (Ch. 5)

life stages   Spans of years of human life, commonly labeled by chronological age as infancy and childhood, adolescence, young adulthood, adulthood, and senescence or old age. (App. 1)

linear programming   A method to determine the best combinations of resources and activities for certain types of problems. (Ch. 9)

line positions   Positions that are in the direct chain of command with specific responsibility for accomplishing the goals of the organization. (Ch. 11)

liquidity ratios   Ratios that reflect the ability of a company to cover its short-term debts with its current assets. (App. 2)

listening   The process of receiving encoded symbols from a sender and decoding them into a message to be interpreted. (Ch. 19)

lobbying   An effort by a company or industry to influence agencies, groups, and committees by sending a representative to Washington, D.C.

lobbyist   Someone who works in a seat of government specifically to influence the legislators. (Ch. 16)

locational departmentalization Grouping together the jobs that are in the same place or in nearby locations. (Ch. 11)

locus of control The degree to which a person believes that behavior has a direct impact on its consequences. (Ch. 15)

long-range planning Planning for a period that can be as short as several years to as long as several decades. Top managers are responsible for these plans which are primarily associated with activities such as major expansions of products or facilities, developing top managers, issuing new stock or bonds, or the installation of new systems. (Ch. 7)

LPC model *Least preferred coworker* model; a contingency model of leadership that suggests that appropriate forms of leadership style vary as a function of the favorableness of the situation. (Ch. 16)

M

mainframe computers Very large, very expensive computers that process enormous amounts of information in fractions of a second and may occupy entire rooms and cost millions of dollars. (App. 2)

maintenance stage The third career stage, during which time individuals examine their career goals and make necessary changes. (App. 1)

management A set of activities directed at the efficient and effective utilization of resources in the pursuit of one or more goals. (Ch. 1)

management by objectives A technique specifically developed to facilitate the goal-setting process in organizations. (Ch. 14)

management excellence The practicing of eight basic management techniques that Peters and Waterman found to be characteristic of successfully managed corporations in the mid-1980s. (Ch. 23)

management information systems (MIS) 1) The branch of the quantitative school of management thought that involves the use of a system created specifically to store and provide information to managers. 2) An integrated and organized data bank that is accessible to appropriate employees and that provides relevant and timely information needed to make decisions. (Ch. 23)

management science The branch of the quantitative school of management thought that is concerned with the development of sophisticated mathematical and statistical tools and techniques that managers can use to enhance efficiency. (Ch. 1)

managerial ethics Ethics applied to management. (Ch. 6)

managerial innovation A change in the management process by which products and services are conceived, built, and delivered to customers. (Ch. 13)

managerial roles Actions a manager is expected to perform and ways in which he or she is expected to behave. (Ch. 2)

manufacturing A form of business that combines and transforms resources into tangible outcomes that are then sold to others. (Ch. 22)

maquiladoras Light-assembly plants built in northern Mexico close to the U.S. border. (Ch. 5)

market economy An economic system that is based on the private ownership of business and allows market factors such as supply and demand to determine business strategy. (Ch. 5)

market factors Characteristics or conditions related to the buyers of the firm's products or services.

marketing Activities involved in getting consumers or other companies to want the goods and services provided by the organization. (App. 2)

marketing managers Individuals who are responsible for pricing, promoting, and distributing the products and services of the firm. (Ch. 1)

marketing ratios Ratios that are related to the marketing function, such as market share or profit margin on sales.

marketing strategy The functional strategy that relates to the promotion, pricing, and distribution of products and services of the firm. (Ch. 8)

market share A company's sales (units or dollars) relative to total sales of all companies of a particular product or within a particular industry. (App. 2)

market system Clusters of countries that engage in high levels of trade with each other. (Ch. 5)

mass-production technology The set of processes used when a product is made in assembly-line fashion by combining component parts into a finished product; also known as large-batch technology. (Ch. 12)

materials requirements planning A method for managing complex delivery schedules. (Ch. 22)

matrix design An organization design that allows a firm to combine the advantages of functional and product departmentalization. (Ch. 12)

mechanistic design An organization design that is based on limited communication systems, a relatively high level of specialization and standardization, and more independence than cooperation. (Ch. 12)

microcomputers Personal computers, or desktop machines, that cost from several hundred to a few thousand dollars and can usually handle all the information processing needs of a manager; may also serve as terminals tied to minicomputers or mainframes or may be linked to other micros in a network. (App. 2)

middle managers The largest group of managers, extending from top management down to those immediately above first-line management. They implement the strategies and policies set by top management and coordinate the work of lower-level managers. (Ch. 1)

minicomputers Computers that are smaller than mainframes but larger than micros, costing from $25,000 to several hundred thousand dollars. (App. 2)

mission The way in which an organization attempts to fulfill its purpose. (Ch. 7)

monitor The role that a manager plays when actively watching the environment for information that may be relevant to the organization. (Ch. 2)

motivation The set of processes that determine behavioral choices—things that make people decide what to do. (Ch. 17)

MRP A *materials requirements planning* technique that enables managers to organize complex delivery schedules. (Ch. 22)

multinational business (MNE) A company that is primarily based in a single country but acquires some meaningful share of its resources or revenues from other countries. (Ch. 5)

multiple constituencies Different people and groups with different interests. (Ch. 16)

multiple goals The concept that organizations must simultaneously pursue a variety of different goals.

N

need hierarchy A variety of needs classified into five specific groups and then arranged in a hierarchy of importance: physiological, security, social, esteem, and self-actualization needs. (Ch. 17)

needs Drives or forces that initiate behavior—that cause people to do things. (Ch. 17)

negotiator The role that a manager plays when attempting to work out agreements and contracts that operate in the best interests of the organization. (Ch. 2)

networking Connecting independent computers directly together so that they can function in interrelated ways. (Ch. 23)

network organization Organizations that usually engage in outsourcing. Also called value-added partnership or a hollow corporation. (Ch. 12)

neutralizers Situation in which group members have considerable expertise, such that efforts by an individual to influence them may be rendered ineffectual. (Ch. 16)

new plant approach A high involvement approach that includes a long selection process of management; a physical layout designed to suggest an egalitarian and team approach; autonomous job teams; salaried employees where pay is based on skills and performance; high decentralization; and extensive training. (Ch. 12)

new venture units Also known as "skunkworks"; small, semi-

autonomous, voluntary units used to develop new products or ventures for a firm. (Ch. 12)

noise Anything that disrupts the communication process. (Ch. 19)

nominal group technique A structured process whereby group members individually suggest alternatives that are then discussed and ranked until everyone agrees. (Ch. 18)

nonmonetary budgets Budgets that express important variables in terms other than currency. (App. 2)

nonprogrammed decisions Decisions that have significant or expensive consequences or that have not occurred in the past and for which there is no established decision, rule, or procedure. (Ch. 10)

nonverbal communication Transmitting messages through body movements, facial expressions, and gestures. (Ch. 19)

norm A standard of behavior that the group develops for its members. (Ch. 18)

norming The third stage of group formation, characterized by the resolution of conflict and the development of roles. (Ch. 18)

North American Free Trade Agreement (NAFTA) An economic agreement between the United States, Canada, and Mexico that aims to form a unified North American market to allow easier movement of goods and services among the three countries. (Ch. 5)

not-for-profit organizations Organizations that do not have the making of a profit as one of their goals; e.g., religious, social service, and charitable organizations and foundations. (App. 1)

O

objective measures of performance appraisal Quantifiable indicators of how well an employee is doing in his or her job. (Ch. 14)

on-line searching The expression used for computerized literature searches using public databases. (Ch. 9)

open systems model Emphasizes flexibility in adapting to external changes. (Ch. 2)

operating ratios Ratios obtained by comparing some item in the income statement to an asset; e.g., cost of goods sold divided by inventory, sales divided by assets, accounts receivable divided by average daily sales. (App. 2)

operational planning Narrow focused, short time frame planning supervised by middle managers and executed by supervisory managers; two kinds of results are standing and single-use plans. (Ch. 7)

operations budgets A detailed presentation in financial

terms of the organization's operations for the coming period. (App. 2)

operations decisions   Choices as to product or service line, capacity, planning system, organization of the operations function, human resources, technology, facilities, and controls.

operations management   1) The processes and systems an organization uses to transform resources into finished goods and services. 2) All the activities connected with an organization's production and operating system. (Ch. 1, 22)

operations managers   Individuals who are responsible for actually creating the goods and services of the organization. (Ch. 1)

operations planning   Day-to-day activities of operations management, such as forecasting demand, comparing projected demand with current capacity, and adjusting capacity to demand.

oral communication   Transmitting messages by means of the spoken word. (Ch. 19)

organic design   An organization design that is based on open communication systems, a low level of specialization and standardization, and cooperation. (Ch. 12)

organizational citizenship   The behavior of individuals that makes a positive overall contribution to the organization. (Ch. 15)

organizational commitment   An attitude that reflects an individual's identification with and attachment to the firm. (Ch. 15)

organizational conflict   Disagreement within the context of an organizational setting between individual employees, groups, or whole departments.

organizational constituents   People and organizations that are directly affected by the practices of an organization and that have a stake in its performance. (Ch. 6)

organizational context   Such situational factors as the way in which an organization deals with ethical situations and the behavior of leaders and peers.

organizational demographics   The age, sex, education, race, ethnic background, country of national origin, and experience of the work force.

organizational dynamics   The way in which organizations structure themselves and manage their employees.

organizational goals   General goals for the entire organization.

organizational governance   Rights and privileges of organizations and of the individuals within those organizations.

organizational innovation process   The process of developing, applying, launching, and managing the maturity and decline of a creative idea. (Ch. 13)

organizational opportunities   Those aspects of the organiza-

tion's environment which, if properly acted upon, would enable the organization to achieve higher than planned levels of performance. (Ch. 8)

organizational strengths   Those aspects of the organization that let it compete effectively. (Ch. 8)

organizational threats   Those aspects of the organization's environment which, if not countered in some way, would impede the organization's progress to achieve its plans. (Ch. 8)

organizational weaknesses   Those aspects of the organization that prevent or deter it from competing effectively. (Ch. 8)

organization change   Alteration of the organization brought about by people, technology, communication, and competition. (Ch. 13)

organization chart   Pictures or maps of organizations, comprised of a series of boxes connected by one or more lines to show positions and their relationship to one another. (Ch. 12)

organization design   The overall configuration of positions and interrelationships among positions within an organization. (Ch. 12)

organization design strategy   The functional strategy that is concerned with how the positions and divisions within the organization will be arranged. (Ch. 8)

organization development   A planned, organizationwide effort to enhance organizational health and effectiveness through the systematic use of behavioral science techniques. (Ch. 13)

organization revitalization   A planned effort to infuse new energy, vitality, and strength into an organization. (Ch. 13)

organizing   Grouping activities and resources in a logical and appropriate way. (Ch. 1, 11)

orientation   A process wherein new employees are introduced to various types of information about their jobs and the organization. (Ch. 14)

output budget   A nonmonetary budget that projects how many of each of the organization's products will be produced. (App. 2)

output devices   Means used to make system information available to users. (Ch. 23)

outsourcing   Transferring production to locations where labor is cheap. Sometimes referred to as global sourcing. (Ch. 5, 12)

overall cost leadership   Trying to keep costs as low as possible so that the firm is able to charge low prices and increase sales volume and/or market share. (Ch. 8)

overall productivity   A form of productivity determined by dividing outputs by the sum of labor, capital, materials, information, and energy costs. Also called total factor productivity. (Ch. 21)

overcontrol   Too much control; so much control that employees' independence and autonomy are limited. (Ch. 20)

overload The situation that occurs when the sender is transmitting too much information for the receiver to process adequately.

owners People, organizations, and institutions that legally control an organization most commonly through owning stock in a corporation. (Ch. 3)

owners' equity Money invested in the business in return for ownership privileges. (App. 2)

P

Pacific Rim A geographic region consisting of Japan, China, Thailand, Malaysia, Singapore, Indonesia, South Korea, Taiwan, Hong Kong, the Philippines, and Australia. (Ch. 5)

participation Giving employees a voice in how things are done in organizations.

participation model A leadership model that addresses the question of how much subordinates should be allowed to participate in decision-making. (Ch. 16)

partners Two or more firms or people working together and sharing the risks and rewards of a particular project.

path-goal model A model of leadership that suggests that the purpose of leadership in organizational settings is to clarify for subordinates the paths to desired goals. (Ch. 16)

payoff matrix A decision-making technique that involves the calculation of expected values for two or more alternatives, each of which is associated with a probability estimate. (Ch. 10)

peak performers Individuals who excel at their performance. (Ch. 9)

people-focused change Changes related to the skills and performance of employees or to their attitudes, perceptions, behaviors, and expectations. (Ch. 13)

perceived role How the individual thinks he or she should behave in a group. (Ch. 18)

perception Processes by which we receive and interpret information from our environment. (Ch. 15, 19)

performance appraisal 1) The organization's evaluation of an individual's level of performance. 2) A review of how well an employee is carrying out the tasks associated with his or her job. (Ch. 14)

performance behaviors The set of work-related behaviors that a firm expects people to display. (Ch. 15)

performing The final stage of group formation, when the group moves toward accomplishing its goals. (Ch. 18)

personal ethics An employee's own values, predilections about right and wrong, and sense of justice and fairness.

personality The relatively stable set of psychological and behavioral attributes that distinguish one person from another. (Ch. 15)

person-job fit The extent to which the contributions made by the individual match the inducements offered by the organization. (Ch. 15)

personnel A department that recruits qualified applicants, trains and develops new employees, and evaluates performance. Also called human resources. (Ch. 14)

PERT A *p*rogram *e*valuation and *r*eview *t*echnique that involves identifying the various activities necessary in a project, developing a diagram that specifies the interrelationships among those activities, determining how much time each activity will take, and refining and controlling the implementation of the project using the network. (Ch. 9)

philanthropic giving The awarding of funds or other gifts to charities or other social programs. (Ch. 6)

physiological needs Things we need to survive—food, air, warmth, clothing. (Ch. 17)

plan Blueprint or framework used to describe how an organization expects to achieve its goals. (Ch. 7)

planned organizational change A systematic alteration of the organization upon sensing a need for a change ahead of time rather than waiting to be forced to respond. (Ch. 13)

planning Establishing goals and objectives, developing strategic plans, and developing tactical plans. (Ch. 7)

planning and decision making Determining the organization's goals and how best to achieve them. (Ch. 1)

planning-control link The way in which planning and control are integrated within the business cycle. (Ch. 20)

planning horizon Time frame for planning.

planning system The means by which operations managers get the information they need and then provide information to other managers. (Ch. 22)

point system A job evaluation method that involves assigning or awarding points to each job according to the factors that characterize the job. (Ch. 14)

policies General guidelines that govern relatively important actions. (Ch. 7)

political action committee (PAC) Organizations that solicit money from a variety of organizations and then make contributions to several candidates for office in order to gain their favor. (Ch. 6)

political-legal dimension The dimension of the international environment that includes government stability, policies toward foreign trade, and investment incentives.

political-legal environment Government regulation of business and the relationship between business and government. (Ch. 3)

political-legal forces Forces of the general environment associated with the governmental and legal system within which the organization operates.

poor listening Not receiving accurate or complete communication because of failure to concentrate, letting attention wander, or daydreaming.

portfolio approach Views the corporation as a collection of different businesses, each of which can be increased, decreased, or even sold. (Ch. 8)

portfolio matrix A common approach to corporate strategy that views the activities of the corporation as a portfolio of businesses, each called a strategic business unit. (Ch. 8)

position power Power vested in the leader's position. (Ch. 16)

positive reinforcement A reward or desirable outcome that is given after a particular behavior. (Ch. 17)

postaction control Monitoring the quality and/or quantity of an organization's outputs. (Ch. 20)

power differences Inability of lower-level managers to communicate with higher-level managers.

power need The desire to control other people and the environment. (Ch. 17)

power of buyers The extent to which customers can influence an organization. (Ch. 3, 8)

power of suppliers The extent to which suppliers can influence an organization. (Ch. 3, 8)

predispositions The tendency to perceive or act in a certain way because of previous experiences in one's background or environment.

probability The likelihood, expressed as a percentage, that an event will or will not occur. (Ch. 10)

problem solving Determining a course of action when faced with an unfamiliar situation for which there are no established procedures. (Ch. 10)

procedural knowledge Outlines a set of steps to be taken to accomplish a task. (Ch. 2)

process consultation Having an organization development expert observe the communication, decision-making, and leadership processes in the organization and then suggest ways to improve them. (Ch. 13)

process control chart A visual representation of an operations function. (Ch. 22)

process knowledge Provides a manager with a mental map for a specific topic. (Ch. 2)

product departmentalization Grouping together the activities associated with individual products or closely related product groups. (Ch. 11)

production factors Characteristics or conditions related to the manufacture of a firm's products.

production strategy The functional strategy that addresses questions concerning production quality, costs, techniques, lo-

cation, efficiency, and compliance with governmental regulations. (Ch. 8)

productivity A measure of efficiency—how much is created relative to the resources used to create it. (Ch. 4, 21)

product life cycle How sales volume for a product changes during the existence of the product. (Ch. 8)

product quality The quality of a real or tangible item. (Ch. 21)

product/service line The general products and/or services on which the organization will concentrate. (Ch. 22)

professionalism The status, methods, standards, or character of a particular field or activity.

profitability ratios Ratios that reflect how much a company made relative to what it took to earn that profit; calculated by dividing profit by sales, investment, or assets. (App. 2)

profit budget An operations budget that summarizes the difference between projected revenues and projected expenses. (App. 2)

profit margin on sales Net income divided by sales. (App. 2)

program Single-use plan for a large set of activities. (Ch. 7)

programmed decisions Situations that occur frequently in which the decision maker can utilize a decision rule or company procedure to make the decision. (Ch. 10)

project Single-use plan similar to program but usually with a narrower focus. (Ch. 7)

project planning tools Techniques designed to assist in the development of an acceptable solution to a problem within a reasonable time frame and at a minimum cost. (Ch. 9)

prospecting A strategic business alternative that involves seeking new markets for a product or service. (Ch. 8)

protectionist techniques Attempts by a government to control international trade across its borders through such techniques as tariffs, export restraint agreements, and "buy national" laws.

psychological contract The set of expectations held by an individual about what he or she will contribute to the organization and what it will provide in return. (Ch. 15)

punishment Reprimands, discipline, fines, etc. that are used to shape behavior by causing a reduction in unwanted behaviors. (Ch. 17)

pure domestic strategy A planned decision not to sell in another country.

purpose The reason for the existence of an organization. (Ch. 7)

Q

quality A measure of value. (Ch. 21)

quality assurance General label applied to an overall effort by an organization to enhance the quality of its products and/or services.

quality circles Groups of employees that focus on how to improve the quality of products. (Ch. 12, 18)

quality control The attempt to make sure inputs and outputs meet desired levels of quality. (Ch. 22)

quantitative school School of management thought that emerged during World War II that focuses on measurement techniques and concepts. (Ch. 1)

question mark A product with a small share of a growing market, creating a question as to whether more resources should be invested in the hope of transforming the product into a star. (Ch. 8)

queuing model A quantitative decision-making technique that helps managers solve problems involving waiting lines to determine, for instance, the best number of operators to have on duty at various times of day. (Ch. 10)

quota A limit on the number or value of goods that can be traded. (Ch. 5)

R

radical innovation A new product or technology developed by an organization that completely replaces an existing product or technology. (Ch. 13)

ranking An approach to performance appraisal wherein the supervisor compares subordinates with one another and then places them in their relative positions in a continuum from high to low performance. (Ch. 14)

rating An approach to performance appraisal wherein the supervisor compares each subordinate with one or more absolute standards and then places that employee somewhere in relation to that standard. (Ch. 14)

ratio analysis Calculating and evaluating ratios of figures obtained from the balance sheet and income statement. (App. 2)

rational model An approach to decision making that assumes that managers are objective, have perfect information, and consider all alternatives and consequences. (Ch. 10)

raw materials inventory The supply of materials, parts, and supplies that the organization needs to do its work. (Ch. 22)

reactive change Change that occurs as a result of external (environmental) events rather than being planned. (Ch. 13)

receiver Person who receives a message from its sender. (Ch. 19)

recruiting The process of attracting a pool of qualified applicants who are interested in working for the company. (Ch. 14)

referent power Power based on personal identification, imitation, and charisma. (Ch. 16)

regulators Units in the task environment that have the potential to control, regulate, or influence an organization's policies and practices. (Ch. 3)

regulatory agencies Groups created by the government to protect the public from certain business practices or to protect organizations from one another. (Ch. 3)

reinforcement Rewarding people's current behavior to motivate them to continue that behavior. (Ch. 17)

relative quality The level of quality interpreted in comparison to other alternatives. (Ch. 21)

reluctance Hesitancy or unwillingness to speak or act.

research and development limited partnerships (RDLPs) Consortia, usually among high technology firms, designed to do basic research. (Ch. 12)

research and development strategy The functional strategy that relates to the invention and development of new products as well as the exploration of new and better ways to produce and distribute existing ones. (Ch. 8)

resistance The negative, uncooperative response of persons when their boss attempts to influence them. (Ch. 16)

resource allocator The role that a manager plays when determining how resources (e.g., dollars, personnel, space) will be divided among different areas within the organization. (Ch. 2)

resource deployment The component of strategy that indicates how the organization intends to allocate resources. (Ch. 8)

responsibility A duty or obligation to carry out an assignment. (Ch. 11)

retrenchment strategy Cutting back of resources, as in worker layoffs and plant closings. (Ch. 8)

return on assets (ROA) A profitability ratio that shows how much a firm made relative to the amount it had invested in assets; determined by dividing net income by total assets. (App. 2)

return on equity (ROE) A profitability ratio that shows how much a company made relative to the amount of money invested; calculated by dividing net income by total owners' equity. (App. 2)

revenue budget An operations budget that projects the sources and timing of incoming funds for the coming period. (App. 2)

reward Anything the organization provides in exchange for services. (Ch. 16, 17)

reward power Power to grant and withhold various kinds of rewards. (Ch. 16)

risk Understanding the available options and estimating the probabilities associated with each. (Ch. 10)

risk propensity The degree to which an individual is willing to take chances and make risky decisions. (Ch. 15)

role Part a person plays in an organization. (Ch. 18)

role ambiguity Lack of clarity as to how an individual in a group is expected to behave. (Ch. 18)

role conflict Inconsistency or contradiction in the messages about a role that an individual is to play in a group. (Ch. 18)

role dynamics The process whereby a person's expected role is transformed to his or her enacted role. (Ch. 18)

rules and regulations Statements of how specific activities are to be performed. (Ch. 7)

S

safety and health guarantees Regulations designed to force companies to protect the safety and health of both employees and consumers. (Ch. 6)

salary A fixed compensation paid to an employee on a regular basis.

satisficing Selecting the first minimally acceptable alternative rather than making a more thorough search. (Ch. 10)

scheduling control Having the right things arrive and depart at the right time. (Ch. 22)

scientific management The subarea of classical management theory that focuses on the work of individuals, primarily defining the steps needed to complete a task and training employees to perform them efficiently while the manager assumes all planning and organizing responsibilities. (Ch. 1)

scientific management model Focuses on making the best product in the most efficient way. (Ch. 2)

scope The component of strategy that specifies the position the firm wants to have in relation to its environment. (Ch. 8)

security needs The need to have a safe physical and emotional environment. (Ch. 17)

selection Choosing the best people for the job. (Ch. 14)

selective perception The process of screening out information that we are uncomfortable with or that contradicts our beliefs. (Ch. 15)

self-actualization needs The needs to grow, develop, and expand our capabilities. (Ch. 17)

self-esteem The extent to which an individual believes that he or she is a worthwhile and deserving person. (Ch. 15)

semantics differences Misinterpretations that occur in communications when two persons assign different meanings to the same word.

semi-autonomous work groups Groups of workers who operate with no direct supervision to perform some specific task. (Ch. 12)

semivariable costs Costs that vary as a function of output but not necessarily in a direct fashion; e.g., equipment repairs, maintenance, and sometimes labor and advertising. (App. 2)

sender Person who transmits a message to a receiver. (Ch. 19)

sent role The role that others in the group communicate that they expect a given person to play. (Ch. 18)

service organization An organization that transforms resources into intangible outputs that create utility for customers. (Ch. 22)

service quality The quality of an intangible service. (Ch. 21)

service sector Provides some sort of utility for consumers. (Ch. 4)

services Actions that provide some sort of utility for consumers. (Ch. 4)

short-range planning Planning for one year or less; focuses on day-to-day activities. (Ch. 7)

single-use plans Form of operational plan set up to handle events that happen only once. (Ch. 7)

situational approaches An approach to leadership definition that recognizes that the same form of leadership is not appropriate in all circumstances. (Ch. 16)

small-batch technology The set of processes used when a product is made in small quantities, usually in response to customer orders; also known as unit technology. (Ch. 12)

smoothing Downplaying the importance of a problem.

social challenges Challenges that relate to prevailing social customs and mores.

social involvement Approach to social responsibility that involves not just fulfilling obligations and requests but also actively seeking other ways to help. (Ch. 6)

social needs The need for belongingness. (Ch. 17)

social obligation An approach to social responsibility in which the company meets its economic and legal responsibilities but does not go beyond them. (Ch. 6)

social obstruction Doing as little as possible to solve social or environmental problems.

social reaction A social responsibility approach in which a firm not only meets its social obligations but also is willing to react to appropriate societal requests and demands. (Ch. 6)

social responsibility Obligations of the organization to protect and/or enhance the society in which it functions. (Ch. 6)

sociocultural dimension The dimension of the international environment that includes the human, cultural, and physical characteristics of a country.

sociocultural environment The customs, mores, values and demographic characteristics of the society in which the organization functions. (Ch. 3)

sociocultural forces Forces of the general environment associated with the customs and values that characterize the society within which the organization is operating.

space budget A nonmonetary budget that details the allocation of plant or office space to different divisions or groups within the organization. (App. 2)

span of management   The number of subordinates who report directly to a given manager. (Ch. 11)

specificity   The extent to which goals are precise or general. (Ch. 7)

speed and time   How long it takes an organization to do something. (Ch. 21)

spokesperson   The role that a manager plays when acting as a company representative while presenting information of meaningful content and/or answering questions on the firm's behalf. (Ch. 2)

stability strategy   A plan to maintain the status quo of an organization. (Ch. 8)

staffing   Procuring and managing the human resources an organization needs to accomplish its goals. (Ch. 14)

staff positions   Positions that are outside the direct chain of command; primarily advisory or supportive in nature. (Ch. 11)

standard operating procedures   Specific guidelines for handling a series of recurring activities. (Ch. 7)

standards   A measure or target against which performance will be compared. (Ch. 20)

standing plans   Developed to handle recurring and relatively routine situations; types are policies, standard operating procedures, and rules and regulations. (Ch. 7)

star   A business, within a portfolio matrix, whose products have a high share of a fast-growing market, thus generating large amounts of revenue. (Ch. 8)

statistical quality control   A category of operational techniques that consists of a set of mathematical and/or statistical methods for measuring and adjusting quality levels. (Ch. 21)

status differences   Inability of persons in low-status jobs and managers of higher status to communicate effectively with each other.

steering control   Monitoring the quality and/or quantity of resources before they enter a company's system; also called preliminary control and feed-forward control. (Ch. 20)

stereotyping   The process of categorizing people on the basis of a single attribute. (Ch. 15, 19)

storming   The second stage of group formation, when members begin to pull apart as they disagree over what needs to be done and how best to do it. (Ch. 18)

strategic alliance   A cooperative agreement that does not necessarily involve ownership.

strategic allies   Two or more companies that work together in joint ventures. (Ch. 3)

strategic business unit (SBU)   A division or related set of divisions (within a firm) that has its own competitors, a distinct mission, and a unique strategy. (Ch. 8)

strategic change   A modification of an existing strategy or the adoption of a new one. (Ch. 13)

strategic control   The process whereby management assures that the strategic planning process itself is effective. (Ch. 8)

strategic planning   Formulating the broad goals and plans developed by top managers to guide the general directions of the organization. (Ch. 7)

strategic plans   Broad plans developed by top managers to guide the general directions of the organization. (Ch. 8)

strategy formulation   The set of processes involved in creating or developing strategic plans. (Ch. 8)

strategy implementation   The set of processes involved in executing strategic plans, or putting them into effect. (Ch. 8)

stress   The condition that occurs when a person is subjected to unusual situations, difficult demands, or extreme pressures. (Ch. 15)

stressor   A stimulus that causes stress. (Ch. 15)

structural change   Any organizational change directed at a part of the formal organizational system, such as its structural components, its overall organization design, or related systems such as the reward system. (Ch. 13)

subordinate's characteristics   Personal traits of a subordinate, such as perceptions of ability, desire to participate in organizational activities, and willingness to accept direction and control.

substitutes   Situations in which people know their jobs so well or the situation is so specific that they can act without the presence of a leader. (Ch. 16)

subsystem interdependencies   The dependence of subsystems within a parent system on one another, such that a change in one subsystem affects the other subsystems. (Ch. 1)

subunit goals   More specific goals for component parts of the organization.

suppliers   Providers of resources to a firm; part of the task environment. (Ch. 3)

survey feedback   Asking subordinates about their perceptions of their leader and then feeding back that information to the entire group. (Ch. 13)

symbolic leadership   Leadership associated with establishing and maintaining a strong organizational culture. (Ch. 16)

synergy   The extra results that occur when two people or units work together rather than individually. (Ch. 1, 8)

system   Interrelated parts or elements that function as a whole. (Ch. 23)

System 4   An organization design approach based on the premise that most organizations start out as bureaucracies and can be transformed to more appropriate models. (Ch. 12)

systems theory   An approach to understanding how organizations function and operate by considering the process by which an organization receives inputs, transforms them into outputs, produces outcomes, and receives feedback. (Ch. 1)

T

tactical planning   Focuses on people and action; concerned with how to implement strategic plans; has moderate scope and intermediate time frame. (Ch. 7, 8)

tall organization   An organization that has several levels of management. (Ch. 11)

targeting   Identifying and focusing on a clearly defined and often highly specialized market. (Ch. 8)

tariff   A tax collected on goods shipped across national boundaries. (Ch. 5)

task environment   Other specific organizations or groups that are likely to influence an organization. (Ch. 3)

task force   A temporary group within an organization created to accomplish a specific purpose (task) by integrating existing functional areas. (Ch. 18)

task group   A group created by the organization to accomplish a limited number of goals within a stated or implied time. (Ch. 18)

task structure   The degree to which a group's task is well defined and understood by everyone. (Ch. 16)

team building   A series of activities and exercises designed to enhance the motivation and satisfaction of people in groups by fostering mutual understanding, acceptance, and group cohesion. (Ch. 13)

technical innovation   A change in the physical appearance or performance of a product or service, or in the physical process through which a product or service is manufactured. (Ch. 13)

technical skills   The skills a manager needs to perform specialized tasks within the organization. (Ch. 2)

technological change   Alterations related to technology, such as new equipment, new work processes or sequences, automation, and revised information processing systems. (Ch. 13)

technological dimension   The dimension of the international environment that includes the availability of qualified workers as well as appropriate equipment.

technological environments   The methods available for converting resources into products or services. (Ch. 3)

technological forces   Forces of the general environment associated with scientific and industrial progress.

technology   Processes and steps used to transform various inputs such as raw materials and components into something else. (Ch. 12, 22)

telecommunications   Communication over some distance, usually by electronic means. (Ch. 23)

telecommuting   Organizational members performing their work at home through the use of computers connected to the organization's computer. (Ch. 23)

teleconferencing   Videoconferencing, which permits individuals in different locations to see and talk with one another. (Ch. 23)

test marketing   Introducing a new product on a limited basis in order to assess consumer reaction on a small scale. (App. 2)

tests   Examinations that are used to help managers select employees. (Ch. 14)

Theory X   A pessimistic view of managerial thinking that assumes that workers dislike work and responsibility, thus requiring managers to control, direct, coerce, and threaten employees. (Ch. 1)

Theory Y   An optimistic view of managerial thinking that assumes that workers enjoy work, seek responsibility, are bright and innovative, and are internally motivated. (Ch. 1)

Theory Z   A theory proposed by William Ouchi to describe the use of a successful American management approach which capitalizes on the strengths of Japanese management models while remaining flexible enough to accommodate the American cultural differences.

third-party peace making   An organization development effort concentrated on resolving conflict that has existed for a long time through the action of a consultant. (Ch. 13)

threat of new entrants   The ease with which new competitors can enter a market. (Ch. 3, 8)

threat of substitute products   The extent to which a new product might supplant demand for an existing one. (Ch. 3, 8)

time management   The act of setting priorities for how our time will be used in achieving our needs and desires. (Ch. 9)

time-series forecasting   Plotting the subject of a forecast against time for a period of several years to determine the "best-fit" line for extending into the future.

top managers   Those at the upper levels of the organization, including the chief executive officer, president, and vice presidents. They set overall goals and determine strategy and policies. (Ch. 1)

total factor productivity   Overall productivity; determined by dividing all outputs by all inputs. (Ch. 21)

TQM   Also called total quality management, this term refers to the ubiquitous quality movement. (Ch. 1, 21)

training   Preparing new employees for specific job skills. (Ch. 14)

traits   Characteristics of a person.

transaction processing systems (TPS)   Systems designed to handle routine and recurring transactions within the organization. (Ch. 23)

transformational/entrepreneurial leadership   A leadership perspective that focuses on innovation and vision to shape organizations for the future. (Ch. 16)

turnover   Percentage of the organization's work force that leaves and must be replaced over a period of time. (Ch. 15, app. 2)

two-factor view   A way of describing employee needs, viewing satisfaction and dissatisfaction as being influenced by two independent sets of factors. (Ch. 17)

Type A   Personality type of individuals who tend to be very competitive and devoted to work and have a strong sense of urgency. (Ch. 15)

Type B   Personality type of individuals who are less competitive and less devoted to their work and have a weaker sense of urgency than do Type A people. (Ch. 15)

U

uncertainty   Not being sure of the alternatives or their probabilities. (Ch. 10)

unions   Labor organizations with which firms must frequently interact; part of the task environment.

unit productivity   The amount produced or created by a single unit within the organization. (Ch. 21)

unit technology   The set of processes used when a product is made in small quantities, usually in response to customer orders; also known as small-batch technology. (Ch. 12)

user friendly   Easy to understand and use.

V

variable costs   Costs that vary as a function of operations, e.g., raw materials, electricity to operate machines, and sales commissions. (Ch. 9, App. 2)

variable interval schedule   Providing reinforcement on a time-interval basis, but the time intervals between reinforcement are not fixed. (Ch. 17)

variable ratio schedule   Providing reinforcement on the basis of behaviors but varying the number of behaviors an employee needs to display to get the reinforcement. (Ch. 17)

vertical communication   Transmission of messages between bosses and their subordinates. (Ch. 19)

VIRO framework   In strategic analysis, asking for each strength identified if it is **V**aluable, difficult to **I**mitate, **R**are, and expl**O**itable. (Ch. 8)

W

wage level   A company's wages relative to the prevailing local or industrial wages. (Ch. 14)

wages   Compensation (payment) to employees on an hourly, daily, or weekly basis, or by the piece.

wage structure   The comparison of wages for different jobs within the company. (Ch. 14)

whistle blowing   The disclosure by an employee of illegal or unethical conduct on the part of others within the organization. (Ch. 6)

withdrawal   A refusal to socialize with others.

work force composition ratio   Percentage of work force that fall into certain demographic groups, such as black, Hispanic, female, or handicapped. (App. 2)

work force diversity   A situation that exists when the members of a group or organization differ from one another along one or more important dimensions. (Ch. 4)

work-in-process inventory   The parts and supplies that are currently being used to produce the final product, which is not yet complete. (Ch. 22)

workplace challenges   The relationships among organizations, their managers, and their operating employees. (Ch. 4)

work team   Small, self-managing group of organizational members responsible for a set of tasks. (Ch. 18)

written communications   Transmitting messages by means of memos, letters, reports, and notes. (Ch. 19)

Scoring and Interpretation of the Self-Assessment Exercises

Chapter 1: How Do I Rate as a Manager?

SCORE

Section	10	20	30	40	50	60	70	80	90	100
Management Style										
Planning										
Information/Communication										
Time Management										
Delegation										
TOTALS										

(Grand Total) _____ ÷ 5 = _____ (Composite Score)

Total your score in each of the categories. Put an asterisk in each category that represents your score. Any asterisk in a column less than 50 should be circled. Those categories require a personal development plan to improve on this characteristic. Next, add all of your category scores together and divide by 5. This is your composite score. It provides you with a more general evaluation of your performance as a manager. If your composite score is 80–100, your strengths should serve you well *if utilized*. A score of 60–80 suggests unbalanced skills that may retard your professional progress. A score of 50 or less suggests a wide area for improvement.

At the end of the course, if you have participated in any group activities in which you incorporated any of these areas, take this assessment again to see if you have improved your score.

Chapter 2: Which Management Model Applies?

For each of the statements, list the value you selected, and then add each column for a score for that management model. Place each of your scores in the appropriate quadrant of the integrative framework. Your high score indicates the appropriate quadrant for the given situation.

	Human resources	Open systems	Administrative management	Scientific management
Statements	#1_____	#2_____	#3_____	#4_____
	#5_____	#6_____	#7_____	#8_____
	#9_____	#10_____	#11_____	#12_____
	#13_____	#14_____	#15_____	#16_____
	#17_____	#18_____	#19_____	#20_____
Totals:	I._____	II._____	III._____	IV._____

The Integrative Framework:

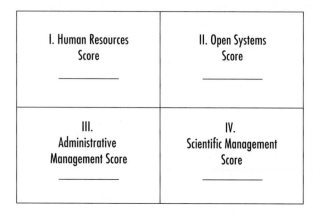

I. Human Resources Score	II. Open Systems Score
_____	_____
III. Administrative Management Score	IV. Scientific Management Score
_____	_____

Part One: A Twenty-first-Century Manager

Scoring Give yourself 1 point for each S, and 1/2 point for each G. Do not give yourself points for W and ? responses. Total your points and enter the result here:

MF = _____.

Interpretation This assessment offers a self-described profile of your *management foundations* (MF). Are you a perfect 10, or is your MF score something less than that? There shouldn't be too many 10s around. Ask someone who knows you to assess you on this instrument. You might be surprised at the difference between your MF score as self-described and your MF score as described by someone else.

Realistically speaking, most of us must work hard to contin-ually grow and develop in these and related management foundations. This list is a good starting point as you consider where and how to further pursue the development of your managerial skills and competencies. The items on the list are recommended by the American Assembly of Collegiate Schools of Business (AACSB) as skills and personal characteristics that should be nurtured in college and university students of business administration. Their success—and yours—as twenty-first–century managers may well rest on the following: (a) an initial awareness of the importance of these basic management foundations and (b) a willingness to continually strive to strengthen them throughout the work career.

Chapter 3: How Creative Are You?

Scoring To compute your percentage score, circle and add up the values assigned to each item.

	A Strongly agree	B Agree	C In between or don't know	D Disagree	E Strongly disagree
1.	−2	−1	0	+1	+2
2.	−2	−1	0	+1	+2
3.	−2	−1	0	+1	+2
4.	+2	+1	0	−1	−2
5.	−2	−1	0	+1	+2
6.	+2	+1	0	−1	−2

	A Strongly agree	B Agree	C In between or don't know	D Disagree	E Strongly disagree
7.	+2	+1	0	−1	−2
8.	−2	−1	0	+1	+2
9.	+2	+1	0	−1	−2
10.	+2	+1	0	−1	−2
11.	+2	+1	0	−1	−2
12.	+2	+1	0	−1	−2
13.	−2	−1	0	+1	+2
14.	−2	−1	0	+1	+2
15.	+2	+1	0	−1	−2
16.	−2	−1	0	+1	+2
17.	−2	−1	0	+1	+2
18.	+2	+1	0	−1	−2
19.	−2	−1	0	+1	+2
20.	+2	+1	0	−1	−2
21.	−2	−1	0	+1	+2
22.	−2	−1	0	+1	+2
23.	−2	−1	0	+1	+2
24.	+2	+1	0	−1	−2
25.	−2	−1	0	+1	+2
26.	−2	−1	0	+1	+2
27.	−2	−1	0	+1	+2
28.	−2	−1	0	+1	+2
29.	+2	+1	0	−1	−2
30.	+2	+1	0	−1	−2
31.	−2	−1	0	+1	+2
32.	−2	−1	0	+1	+2
33.	+2	+1	0	−1	−2
34.	+2	+1	0	−1	−2
35.	−2	−1	0	+1	+2
36.	−2	−1	0	+1	+2
37.	+2	+1	0	−1	−2
38.	+2	+1	0	−1	−2
39.	+2	+1	0	−1	−2
40.	+2	+1	0	−1	−2
41.	−2	−1	0	+1	+2
42.	−2	−1	0	+1	+2
43.	−2	−1	0	+1	+2
44.	−2	−1	0	+1	+2
45.	−2	−1	0	+1	+2
46.	+2	+1	0	−1	−2
47.	+2	+1	0	−1	−2
48.	+2	+1	0	−1	−2
49.	−2	−1	0	+1	+2
50.	+2	+1	0	−1	−2

Interpretation 80–100, very creative; 60–79, above average; 40–59, average; 20–39, below average, and 0–19, noncreative

    Most adults only use about two percent of their creative potential. This is the bad news. The good news is that creativity is a skill that can be practiced so that it will develop and flourish. For example, if you score average or below on this self assessment, you can improve your creativity by doing mind expansion exercises such as:

1. How many uses can you think of for a paper clip?
2. What does peak performance sound like?
3. Draw a picture of excellence.

These exercises make you use your mind in a new way and expand the way you see the world. This helps to develop creative capacity.

Chapter 4: Are You an Entrepreneur?

Scoring The scoring is weighted to determine your entrepreneurial profile. Score as follows:

1	2	3	4	5	16	17	18	19	20
a = 10	a = 10	a = 5	a = 10	a = 10	a = 0	a = 5	a = 2	a = 5	a = 8
b = 5	b = 7	b = 4	b = 5	b = 7	b = 10	b = 5	b = 10	b = 15	b = 10
c = 5	c = 0	c = 3	c = 0	c = 0	c = 3	c = 5	c = 0	c = 5	c = 0
d = 2		d = 0			d = 0	d = 5			d = 0
e = 0						e = 15			

6	7	8	9	10	21	22	23	24	25
a = 8	a = 15	a = 10	a = 2	a = 0	a = 0	a = 3	a = 0	a = 3	a = 10
b = 10	b = 2	b = 2	b = 3	b = 15	b = 15	b = 10	b = 10	b = 3	b = 2
c = 5	c = 0	c = 2	c = 10	c = 0		c = 0		c = 10	c = 0
d = 2	d = 0		d = 8	d = 0		d = 0			
			e = 4						

11	12	13	14	15	26				
a = 10	a = 0	a = 0	a = 0	a = 0	a = 8				
b = 5	b = 5	b = 10	b = 2	b = 10	b = 10				
c = 10	c = 10	c = 0	c = 10	c = 0	c = 15				
d = 5		d = 5	d = 3	d = 0	d = 0				

Add up your total points.

Interpretation Based on responses by 2,500 people who have successfully launched small businesses, your score can be interpreted as follows:

235–285 points = Successful entrepreneur

200–234 points = Entrepreneur
185–199 points = Latent entrepreneur
170–184 points = Potential entrepreneur
155–169 points = Borderline entrepreneur
Below 155   = Hired hand

Chapter 5: The Culture Quiz

1. b. Slurping your soup or noodles in Japan is good manners in both public and private. It indicates enjoyment and appreciation of the quality. (Source: Eiji Kanno, Japan Solo, Nitchi Map-Publishing Co., Inc., Ltd., Tokyo, 1985.)

2. b. Korean managers use a "divide-and-rule" method of leadership that encourages competition among subordinates. They do this to ensure that they can exercise maximum control. In addition, they stay informed by having individuals report directly to them. This way, they can know more than anyone else. (Source: Richard M. Castaldi and Tjipyanto Soerjanto, Contrasts in East Asian management practices, *Journal of Management in Practice* 2 [1], 1990, 25–27.)

3. b. Saccharin-sweetened drinks may not be sold in Japan by law. On the other hand, beer, a wide variety of Japanese and international soft drinks, and so forth, are widely available from vending machines along the streets and in buildings. You're supposed to be at least eighteen to buy the alcoholic ones, however. (Source: Eiji Kanno, Japan Solo, Nitchi Map-Publishing Co., Inc., Ltd., Tokyo, 1985.)

4. a. Family is considered to be very important in Latin America, so managers are likely to hire their relatives more quickly than hiring strangers. (Source: Nancy J. Adler, *International Dimensions of Organizational Behavior*, 2nd ed. [Boston: PWS-Kent, 1991].)

5. d. The act, by a woman, of opening the front door, signifies that she has agreed to have sex with any man who enters. (Source: Adam Pertman, "Wandering no more," *Boston Globe Magazine*, 30 June 1991, 10 ff.)

6. c. Touching one another during business negotiations is common practice. (Source: Nancy J. Adler, *International Dimensions of Organizational Behavior*, 2nd ed. [Boston: PWS-Kent, 1991].)

7. d. Approximately 45 percent of the people in Malaysia follow Islam, the country's "official" religion. (Source: Hans Johannes Hoefer, ed., *Malaysia* [Englewood Cliffs, N.J.: Prentice-Hall, 1984].)

8. a. Men holding hands is considered a sign of friendship. Public displays of affection between men and women, however, are unacceptable. (Source: William Warren, Star Black, and M. R. Priya Rangsit, eds., *Thailand* [Englewood Cliffs, N.J.: Prentice-Hall, 1985].)

9. b. This is especially an insult if it is done deliberately, since the feet are the lowest part of the body. (Source: William Warren, Star Black, and M. R. Priya Rangsit, eds., *Thailand* [Englewood Cliffs, N.J.: Prentice-Hall, 1985].)

10. c. Adler suggests that friendship is valued over task competence in Iran. (Source: Nancy J. Adler, *International Dimensions of Organizational Behavior*, 2nd ed. [Boston: PWS-Kent, 1991].)

11. b. Public discussion of business dealings is considered inappropriate. Kaplan et al. report that "the Chinese may even have used a premature announcement to extract better terms from executives" who were too embarrassed to admit that there was never really a contract. (Source: Frederic Kaplan, Julian Sobin, Arne de Keijzer, *The China Guide book: 1987 Edition*, Houghton Mifflin, Boston, 1987.)

12. a. Public praise for Hispanics and Asians is generally embarrassing because modesty is an important cultural value. (Source: Jim Braham, "No, You Don't Manage Everyone the Same," *Industry Week*, 6 Feb. 1989). In Japan, being singled out for praise is also an embarrassment. A common saying in that country is, "The nail that sticks up gets hammered down."

13. d. Whereas in the United States, being late is frowned upon, being late is not only accepted but expected in some South American countries. (Source: Lloyd S. Baird, James E. Post, and John F. Mahon, *Management: Functions and Responsibilities* [New York: Harper & Row, 1990].)

14. c. Personal space in most European countries is much smaller than in the United States. Americans generally like at least two feet of space around themselves, while it is not unusual for Europeans to be virtually touching. (Source: Lloyd S. Baird, James E. Post, and John F. Mahon, *Management: Functions and Responsibilities* [New York: Harper & Row, 1990].)

15. c. Chrysanthemums and calla lilies are both associated with funerals. (Source: Theodore Fischer, *Pinnacle: International Issue* [March–April 1991], 4.)

16. d. In Arab cultures, it is considered inappropriate for wives to accept gifts or even attention from other men. (Source: Theodore Fischer, *Pinnacle: International Issue* [March–April 1991], 4.)

17. b. In Argentina and other Latin American countries, purple is associated with the serious fasting period of Lent. (Source: Theodore Fischer, *Pinnacle: International Issue* [March–April 1991], 4.)

18. d. Private space is considered so important in Germany that partitions are erected to separate people from one another, privacy screens and walled gardens are the norm. (Source: Julius Fast, *Subtext: Making Body Language Work* [New York: Viking Penguin Books, 1991], 207.)

19. a. Whereas in the United States, political leaders especially are increasingly selected on their ability to inspire, according to international organizational behavior expert Nancy J. Adler, charisma is a suspect trait in West Germany,

where Hitler's charisma is still associated with evil intent and harmful outcomes. (Source: Nancy J. Adler, *International Dimensions of Organizational Behavior*, 2nd ed. [Boston: PWS-Kent, 1991], 149.)

20. c. Paying Mexican workers more means, in the eyes of the workers, that they can make the same amount of money in fewer hours and thus have more time for enjoying life.

(Source: Nancy J. Adler, *International Dimensions of Organizational Behavior*, 2nd ed. [Boston: PWS-Kent, 1991], 30, 159.)

The following is recommended for additional reading about conducting business outside of your own country: Nancy Adler's *International Dimensions of Organizational Behavior*, 2nd ed. (Boston: PWS-Kent, 1991).

Chapter 6: Personal Values—What Is Important to You?

Scoring

Step 1

For each question, insert your score in the appropriate space in the scoring chart that follows. Note that the letters are not always in the same column.

Scoring Chart

Question	I	II	III	IV	V	VI
1.	A ____	E ____	F ____	C ____	B ____	D ____
2.	F ____	E ____	C ____	B ____	D ____	A ____
3.	A ____	B ____	E ____	F ____	C ____	D ____
4.	D ____	A ____	F ____	E ____	B ____	C ____
5.	B ____	C ____	A ____	F ____	E ____	D ____
6.	E ____	A ____	B ____	D ____	F ____	C ____
7.	D ____	F ____	A ____	B ____	C ____	E ____
8.	F ____	C ____	D ____	A ____	B ____	E ____
9.	F ____	B ____	D ____	A ____	E ____	C ____
10.	D ____	C ____	A ____	F ____	B ____	E ____
11.	C ____	F ____	E ____	A ____	D ____	B ____
12.	F ____	B ____	E ____	D ____	C ____	A ____
13.	B ____	C ____	F ____	D ____	A ____	E ____
14.	F ____	A ____	E ____	B ____	D ____	C ____
15.	B ____	E ____	A ____	F ____	D ____	C ____
16.	B ____	F ____	C ____	A ____	E ____	D ____
17.	C ____	E ____	B ____	A ____	D ____	F ____
18.	A ____	B ____	E ____	F ____	C ____	D ____
19.	F ____	C ____	A ____	D ____	E ____	B ____
20.	E ____	F ____	B ____	C ____	A ____	D ____
Totals	____	____	____	____	____	____

Step 2

Total the six columns.

Step 3

Place the total for each personal value in the appropriate place in the graph, "Your Personal Value Orientation." Connect the scores with a straight line to form a picture of your overall value orientation.

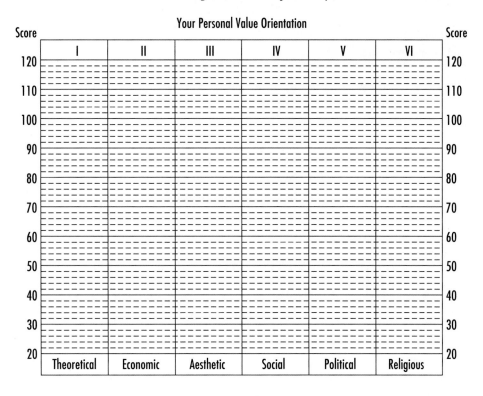

Your Personal Value Orientation

Interpretation

A brief description of each personal value follows.

Theoretical: Discovery of truth is the primary interest of the theoretical person. This type of person is very interested in explaining why things happen the way they do. They are often engineers.

Economic: The usefulness of any item or activity is the primary interest of the economic person. This type of person is very interested in producing and marketing goods and accumulating wealth. They are often business people.

Aesthetic: Harmony, beauty, and form are the primary interest of the aesthetic person. This type of person is very interested in experiencing the events of life and the symmetry in life. They are often artists.

Social: Altruistic love is the primary interest of social person. This type of person is very interested in helping other people. They are often guidance counselors.

Political: Power is a primary interest of the political person. This type of person is very interested in influencing others and the outcomes of events. They are often leaders in many different professions.

Religious: Spiritual peace is a primary interest of the religious person. This type of person is very interested in comprehending and valuing a higher meaning to life. They are often clergy.

The lists that follow show the value orientations of sample groups of American males and females with different interests and occupations. How do your values compare with these groups? How will your values affect your ethics?

Different Personal Values of Different People, in Rank Order

Engineering students (Male)
1. Theoretical
2. Economic
3. Political
4. Religious
5. Social
6. Aesthetic

Business students (Male)
1. Economic
2. Political
3. Theoretical
4. Social
5. Religious
6. Aesthetic

Personnel and guidance workers (Male)
1. Theoretical
2. Social
3. Religious
4. Political
5. Economic
6. Aesthetic

Art and design students (Male)
1. Aesthetic
2. Theoretical
3. Economic
4. Religious
5. Political
6. Social

Clergymen (Male)
1. Religious
2. Social
3. Political
4. Theoretical
5. Aesthetic
6. Economic

Nursing students (Female)
1. Religious
2. Aesthetic
3. Social
4. Theoretical
5. Political
6. Economic

Business students (Female)
1. Aesthetic
2. Political
3. Economic
4. Religious
5. Theoretical
6. Social

Personnel and guidance workers (Female)
1. Social
2. Aesthetic
3. Religious
4. Theoretical
5. Economic
6. Political

Art and design students (Female)
1. Aesthetic
2. Religious
3. Social
4. Theoretical
5. Political
6. Economic

Social Workers (Female)
1. Aesthetic
2. Social
3. Theoretical
4. Political
5. Economic
6. Religious

Different Personal Values of Different People, in Rank Order (con't.)	
College students — all majors (Male)	**College students — all majors (Female)**
1. Political	1. Aesthetic
2. Theoretical	2. Religious
3. Economic	3. Social
4. Religious	4. Political
5. Social	5. Economic
6. Aesthetic	6. Theoretical

Table Source: From *The Study of Values: Grade 10–Adult,* 3d ed., by Gordon Allport, Phillip E. Vernon, and Gardner Lindzey. Copyright © 1970 by Houghton Mifflin Company.

Part Two: International Business IQ Test

Scoring Give yourself 4 points for every correct answer.

Interpretation

1. Where in the world is:
   a. Suriname?   Northern edge of South America
   b. The Seychelles?   Indian Ocean off Africa
   c. Belize?   Central America
   d. Dar es Salaam?   Africa
   e. Lagos?   Nigeria
   f. Vientiane?   in Laos, Southeast Asia
   g. Kiev?   Ukraine
   h. Myanmar?   Southeast Asia — borders Thailand
   i. Kazakstan?   Russian state

2. What do the following acronyms stand for?
   a. EC   European Community
   b. UNDP   United Nations Development Programme
   c. ILO   International Labor Office
   d. EFTA   European Free Trade Association
   e. OAS   Organization of American States
   f. GATT   General Agreement on Tariffs and Trade
   g. IMF   International Monetary Fund

3. Define the following terms:
   a. balance of payments: a balance estimated for a given time period showing an excess or deficit in total payments of all kinds between one country and another
   b. devaluation: to lessen or annul the value of a country's currency
   c. trade barrier: barrier such as tariff or quota erected for purposes of providing protection to domestic industry
   d. floating exchange rate: Governments allow exchange rate to change as supply and demand change instead of maintaining a fixed exchange rate.

4. Match the following with the correct country:
   a. Ruled for many years by Mobutu Sese Seko — Zaire
   b. Home of the "ANC" — South Africa
   c. Home of the "Shining Path" — Peru
   d. Location of the infamous "Tianenmen" incident — Beijing, China
   e. Where Mecca is located — Saudi Arabia

With world events moving at an ever-increasing pace, it takes dedication and effort to stay informed. In the world of business and management, this is no longer just a hobby or sideline, it's increasingly a requirement of the executive suite. Take a good look at yourself and ask how well-informed you are. As a first impression, check your total score against the following summary table. Think about what you can do to get to the top.

90–100   Internationalist — globally aware
80– 89   Conversationalist — unusually aware
70– 79   Vacation traveler — limited horizons
Below 70 Homebody — nowhere (or reason) to go

Chapter 7: Job Goals Questionnaire

Scoring Add the points for items 1 through 20.

Interpretation Scores of 70 to 100 may indicate a high-performing, highly satisfying work situation. Your goals are challenging and you are committed to them. When you achieve your goals, you are rewarded for your accomplishments. Scores of 51 to 69 may suggest a highly varied work situation with motivating and satisfying attributes on some dimensions and just the opposite on others. Scores of 20 to 50 may suggest a low-performing, dissatisfying work situation.

Chapter 8: Are You a Risk Taker?

Scoring Give yourself 1 point for each true answer for items 1, 3, 4, 7, 9, 11, 13, 14, 16, and 18, and 1 point for each false answer for items 2, 5, 6, 8, 10, 12, 15, 17, and 19.

Interpretation The more points you have, the more willing you are to take risks with your money and career.

Chapter 9: Time Management Profile

Scoring Count the number of Y responses to items 2, 3, 5, 7, 8, 12. [Enter that score here. _____] Count the number of N responses to items 1, 4, 6, 9, 10, 11. [Enter that score here. _____] Add together the two scores.

Interpretation The higher the total score, the closer your behavior matches recommended time-management guidelines. Reread those items where your response did not match the desired one. Why don't they match? Do you have reasons why your behavior in this instance should be different from the recommended time-management guideline? Think about what you can do (and how easily it can be done) to adjust your behavior to be more consistent with these guidelines.

Chapter 10: Problem-Solving Style Questionnaire

Scoring

1. Add down each column of the Answer Form to obtain a total for score "A" and write it in the total box. Do the same for "B".

2. Compare the totals for columns I and II. If your highest point total is for "A", circle the letter S. "S" refers to sensation. If your highest point total is for "B", circle the letter N. "N" refers to intuitive. If your total scores for A and B are equal, circle the letter S.

3. Compare the totals for columns III and IV. If your highest point total is for "A", circle the letter T. "T" refers to thinking. If your highest point total is for "B", circle the letter F. "F" refers to feeling. If your total score for A and B are equal, circle the letter T.

Interpretation The first two columns identify your sensation-intuitive scores. Generally, people have preferred style between these two styles for gathering information. The following table presents a summary of characteristics about these two styles.

(con't. on next page)

Comparisons of Sensation and Intuitive Types of People

Characteristic	Sensation Type	Intuitive Type
Focus	Details, practical, action, getting things done quickly	Patterns, innovation, ideas, long-range planning
Time Orientation	Present, live life as it is	Future achievement, change, rearrange
Work Environment	Pay attention to detail, patient with details and do not make factual errors, not risk takers	Look at the "big picture," patient with complexity, risk takers
Strengths	Pragmatic, results-oriented, objective, competitive	Original, imaginative, creative, idealistic
Possible Weaknesses	Impatient when projects get delayed, decide issues too quickly, lack long-range perspective, can over-simplify a complex task	Lack follow-through, impractical, make errors of facts, take people's contributions for granted

The next two columns represent the thinking-feeling scores. Again people generally prefer to evaluate information based on one of these two styles. The table below summarizes the characteristics about these two styles.

Comparisons of Thinking and Feeling Types of People

Characteristic	Thinking Type	Feeling Type
Focus	Logic of situation, truth, organization principles	Human values and needs, harmony, feelings, emotions
Time Orientation	Past, present, future	Past
Work Environment	Businesslike, impersonal, treat others fairly, well organized	Naturally friendly, personal, harmony, care and concern for others
Strengths	Good at putting things in logical order, tend to be firm and tough-minded, rational, objective, predict logical results of decisions	Enjoy pleasing people, sympathetic, loyal, draw out feelings in others, take interest in person behind the job or idea
Possible Weaknesses	Overly analytical, unemotional, too serious, rigid, verbose	Sentimental, postpone unpleasant tasks, avoid conflict

Part Three: Decision Making in the Daily Life of Managers

Scoring Transfer your raw scores from the questionnaire to the grid on the next page by placing your a, b, c, d, e, and f raw scores for each incident in the appropriate box in Column S. Using the conversion Table at the bottom of the page, convert each raw score in Column S into an AS converted score and enter the converted score in Column AS.

- Total the AS columns vertically.

- Total all the AS sums horizontally.

- Divide the total by 10, the number of incidents.

- Note whether your score falls within the low (L), medium (M) or high (H) range. (Round up if .5 or over.)

Interpretation

Low scores: Scores of 0–75 indicate a self-reported intolerance for ambiguity. Despite complex or contradictory cues, you say you are able to make clear-cut, unambiguous decisions. Those with this style often appear to be able to "cut through the smoke" and recommend a clear-cut course of action when others are unwilling to move. One of the disadvantages of this style is that you may appear to be precipitous and perhaps even bullheaded.

Medium scores: Scores of 75–95 indicate a self-reported moderate tolerance for ambiguity. When the cues in a situation are complex or contradictory, you try to sort them out and narrow the alternatives so that you have identified feasible courses of action. One of the advantages of this style is that you may be seen as a sensitive, understanding person who can see many sides of a problem. One of the disadvantages of this style is that you may be seen as opportunistic or self-serving.

High scores: Scores of 96–156 indicate a self-reported high tolerance for ambiguity. You will find it easy to postpone a decision when the cues for decision making are ambiguous or not clear-cut.

	1		2		3		4		5		6		7		8		9		10	
	S	AS	S	AS	S	AS	S	AS	S	AS	S	AS	S	AS	S	AS	S	AS	S	AS
a																				
b																				
c																				
d																				
e																				
f																				
Totals		+		+		+		+		+		+		+		+		+		

÷10 = ____ Total Score

Score	0	2	4–6	7–11	12–20	21–30	31–40	41–60	61–80	81–90	91–100
AS	1	7	13	19	26	30	32	29	21	7	0

Total Score	Low	Med	High
Range	0 / 75	76 / 95	96 / 156

One of the advantages of this style is that you may often appear wise and unwilling to rush into complex or novel situations. One of the disadvantages of this style is that you may appear "wishy washy" and indecisive, surrendering your power to others.

Consider the following interpretative questions:

1. How congruent is your score with your self-perception of your tolerance for ambiguity? You can also check this perception with friends and family.

2. How congruent is your score with the level of tolerance for ambiguity required for your desired level of management?

Chapter 11: Inclinations Toward Delegation

Scoring To determine your scores, add up the points you assigned as follows: Sum of a, d, e, g, j, l, m, o, r, and s = ____. (X)   Sum of b, c, f, h, i, k, n, p, q, and t = ____. (Y)

Interpretation The higher one's X scores, the less inclined one is to delegate tasks. Theory X assumes that people are not motivated to take responsibility unless pressured. Theory Y assumes that people seek additional responsibility and the delegated tasks will be accepted.

Chapter 12: How Is Your Organization Managed?

Bureaucratic System 1				Mixed Systems 2 and 3				Organic System 4	
0-9	10-19	20-29	30-39	40-49	50-59	60-69	70-79	80-89	90-100

High scores indicate a highly organic and participatively managed organization. Low scores are associated with a mechanistic or bureaucratically managed organization.

Chapter 13: How Innovative Are You?

Interpretation The higher the score, the more willing you are to be innovative. Your attitude toward innovation is more positive than that of people who score low. A score of 72 or greater is high, while a score of 45 or less is low. People who are not innovators have a tendency to maintain the status quo. Innovative people are entrepreneurs and ones who like to create changes in their organizations.

Scoring Give yourself the following points for each circled response:

SA = 5 points
A = 4 points
? = 3 points
D = 2 points
SD = 1 point
Total your points to get your score.

Chapter 14: What Are Your Ideas About Performance Appraisal?

Add up your total points. A score of 102 or greater means that you have a positive attitude toward the effective use of performance appraisals. A score of 51 or less indicates that you believe that performance appraisals are not effective ways for managers to give subordinates accurate descriptions of their subordinates' strengths and weaknesses. A score between 51 and 102 indicates that you believe performance appraisal systems have certain strengths and weaknesses that must be addressed if they are to be successfully used by managers.

Part Four: Inventory of Effective Organization Design

Sum the point values shown next to statements one through fifteen. A score of 75 to 105 suggests a very effective organization design. A score of 70 to 89 suggests a mediocre design that probably varies greatly in terms of how specific aspects of the organization work for or against effectiveness. Scores of 0 to 69 suggest there is a great deal of ambiguity about the organization and how it operates. Scores of 15 to 49 probably suggest the design is contributing to serious problems.

Chapter 15: Behavior Activity Profile: A Type A Measure

Scoring Transfer your total scores to this chart.

Impatience (S)	Job Involvement (J)	Hard Driving and Competitive (H)	Total Score (A) = S + J + H

The Behavior Activity Profile attempts to assess the three Type A coronary-prone behavior patterns, as well as provide a total score. The three a priori types of Type A coronary-prone behavior patterns are shown:

Items	Behavior Pattern		Characteristics
1–7	Impatience	(S)	Anxious to interrupt
			Fails to listen attentively
			Frustrated by waiting (e.g., in line, for others to complete a job)
8–14	Job Involvement	(J)	Focal point of attention is the job
			Lives for the job
			Relishes being on the job
			Immersed in job activities
15–21	Hard driving/ Competitive	(H)	Hardworking, highly competitive
			Competitive in most aspects of life, sports, work, etc.
			Racing against the clock
1–21	Total score	(A)	Total of S + J + H represents your global Type A behavior

Interpretation

Score ranges for total score are:

Score	Behavior Type
122 and above	Hard-core Type A
99–121	Moderate Type A
90–98	Low Type A
80–89	Type X
70–79	Low Type B
50–69	Moderate Type B
40 and below	Hard-core Type B

Percentile Scores

Now you can compare your score to a sample of over 1,200 respondents

Percentile score	Raw score	
Percent of individuals scoring lower	Males	Females
99%	——— 140	——— 132
95%	——— 135	——— 126

Percent of Individuals Scoring Lower	Males	Females
90%	——— 130	——— 120
85%	——— 124	——— 112
80%	——— 118	——— 106
75%	——— 113	——— 101
70%	——— 108	——— 95
65%	——— 102	——— 90
60%	——— 97	——— 85
55%	——— 92	——— 80
50%	——— 87	——— 74
45%	——— 81	——— 69
40%	——— 75	——— 63
35%	——— 70	——— 58
30%	——— 63	——— 53
25%	——— 58	——— 48
20%	——— 51	——— 42
15%	——— 45	——— 36
10%	——— 38	——— 31
5%	——— 29	——— 26
1%	——— 21	——— 21

Chapter 16: Are You a Charismatic Leader?

The questionnaire measures each of the six basic behavior leader patterns, as well as a set of emotional responses. Your score can range from four to twenty. Each question is stated as a measure of the extent to which you engage in the behavior—or elicit the feelings. The higher your score, the more you demonstrate charismatic leader behaviors.

Index 1: Management of Attention (1, 7, 13, 19). Your score _____. You pay especially close attention to people with whom you are communicating. You are also "focused in" on the key issues under discussion and help others to see clearly these key points. They have clear ideas about the relative importance or priorities of different issues under discussion.

Index 2: Management of Meaning (2, 8, 14, 20). Your score _____. This set of items center on your communication skills, specifically your ability to get the meaning of a message across, even if this means devising some quite innovative approach.

Index 3: Management of Trust (3, 9, 15, 21). Your score _____. The key factor is your perceived trustworthiness as shown by your willingness to follow through on promises, avoid-

ance of "flip-flop" shifts in position, and willingness to take clear positions.

Index 4: Management of Self (4, 10, 16, 22). Your score _____. This index concerns your general attitudes toward yourself and others; that is, your overall concern for others and their feelings, as well as for "taking care of" feelings about yourself in a positive sense (e.g., self-regard).

Index 5: Management of Risk (5, 11, 17, 23). Your score _____. Effective charismatic leaders are deeply involved in what they do and do not spend excessive amounts of time or energy on plans to "protect" themselves against failure (a "CYA" approach). These leaders are willing to take risks, not on a hit-or-miss basis, but after careful estimation of the odds of success or failure.

Index 6: Management of Feelings (6, 12, 18, 24). Your score _____. Charismatic leaders seem to consistently generate a set of feelings in others. Others feel that their work becomes more meaningful and that they are the "masters" of their own behavior, that is, they feel competent. They feel a sense of community, a "we-ness" with their colleagues and co-workers.

Chapter 17: Job Involvement

Scoring Add the scores on the individual items to obtain your job involvement score.

Interpretation Your score on this self-assessment can range from 20 points to 80 points. An individual with a score less than 40 has low job involvement. These individuals feel indifferent toward work. They may be alienated from their organization. They see

work only as an instrumentality to other pleasures. On the other hand, those who score over forty are highly involved in their job. They find enjoyment in their work. They are high in achievement, desire, and drive. They enjoy going to work and willingly put in extra hours.

Chapter 18: Team Effectiveness Inventory

Scoring Add the point values for each scale: Task Performance = _____; Influence = _____; Satisfaction = _____; Member Relations = _____; and Creativity = _____.

Interpretation Point values of 12 to 15 suggest the team is effective on that dimension, whereas point values of 3 to 8 suggest

ineffectiveness. Point values of 9 to 11 suggest uncertainty and ambiguity on that dimension. Total point values for items 1 through 15 of 60 to 75 suggest a highly effective team, whereas a total score of 15 through 30 suggests a team that is probably ineffective.

Chapter 19: What's Your Communication Style?

Scoring To get your score for each item, give yourself +2 for strong agreement, +1 for agreement, 0 for neither agreement nor

disagreement, −1 for disagreement, and −2 for strong disagreement. The only exception are items 8, 15, and 21. For these three items you should reverse the scoring giving yourself +2 for strong disagreement, +1 for disagreement, 0 for neither agreement nor disagreement, −1 for agreement, and −2 for strong agreement. Next sum together the items listed for each dimension; then divide by the number of items for that dimension.

Dominant   = ——   Sum (Items 25, 28, 31, 35, 41, 43)/6.
Dramatic   = ——   Sum (Items 18, 22, 32, 33, 48)/5.
Contentious = ——   Sum (Items 10, 27, 30, 36, 37, 40, 42)/7.
Animated   = ——   Sum (Items 17, 23, 44, 47)/4.
Impression
   leaving   = ——   Sum (Items 4, 5, 12, 14, 45)/5.
Relaxed   = ——   Sum (Items 1, 8, 9, 15, 16)/5.
Attentive   = ——   Sum (Items 3, 11, 20, 39, 49)/5.
Open   = ——   Sum (Items 21, 24, 34, 50)/4.
Friendly   = ——   Sum (Items 2, 6, 38, 46)/4.

The higher your score for any dimension, the more that dimension characterizes your communication style.

Interpretation This questionnaire taps nine dimensions of communication style:

Dominant: The dominant communicator tends to take charge of social interactions.

Dramatic: The dramatic communicator manipulates and exaggerates stories, metaphors, rhythms, voice, and other stylistic devices to highlight or understate content.

Contentious: The contentious communicator is argumentative.

Animated: An animated communicator provides frequent and sustained eye contact, uses many facial expressions, and gestures often.

Impression leaving: The concept centers around whether the person is remembered because of the communicative stimuli that are projected.

Relaxed: This construct refers to whether the communicator is relaxed, tense, or anxious.

Attentive: In general, the attentive communicator makes sure that the other person knows that he is being listened to.

Open: Behavior associated with openness include activity that is characterized by being conversational, expansive, affable, convivial, gregarious, unreserved, somewhat frank, definitely extroverted, and obviously approachable.

Friendly: Friendly ranges from simply being nonhostile to deep intimacy.

Part Five: Listening Self-Inventory

The correct answers according to communication theory are as follows:

No for statements 1, 2, 3, 5, 6, 7, 8, 9, 10, 11, 14.

Yes for statements 4, 12, 13, 15.

If you missed only one or two responses, you strongly approve of your own listening habits, and you are on the right track to becoming an effective listener in your role as manager. If you missed three or four responses, you have uncovered some doubts about your listening effectiveness, and your knowledge of how to listen has some gaps. If you missed five or more responses, you probably are not satisfied with the way you listen, and your friends and coworkers may not feel you are a good listener either. Work on improving your active listening skills.

Chapter 20: Feedback Skills Questionnaire

Scoring The total of the scores on the six items is your Feedback Skill Score. Scores range from six to forty-two.

Performance Feedback Ability

Very High	31 and Above
Above Average	29–30
Average	24–28
Below Average	22–23
Very Low	21 and Below

Interpretation

Each of the items on the Feedback Skills Questionnaire is keyed to one of six basic guidelines for effective feedback. The six guidelines are:

1. Descriptive vs. Evaluative
2. Specificity vs. generality
3. Needs of the Receiver vs. Needs of the Sender
4. Asked vs. Imposed
5. Timely vs. Out of Context
6. Applicable vs. Useless

We will briefly examine each guideline.

Item 1: Descriptive Versus Evaluative

Helpful feedback is descriptive, not evaluative. Evaluation — positive or negative — creates automatic blocks to effective communication. Effective descriptive feedback is also "owned" — it is clearly attributed to the describer, rather than presented as some omniscient pronouncement. "Your reaction to my comment seemed out of character and not at all like you," may be descriptive, and is not overtly evaluative, yet a more effective statement would be, "Your reaction to my comment really surprised me, because I'd expected a very different response on the basis of our past contacts." The second statement, while it could be more specific, at least does not imply that the giver understands perfectly the "true" character of the receiver, in some godlike fashion.

Item 2: Specificity Versus Generality

Useful feedback is specific. If I'm trying to help you learn Morse code, and I say "Your last message contained three errors," this is a descriptive and, in itself, not necessarily an evaluative comment, but it is not specific enough to be of much help. "In your last message you substituted a 'P' for an 'L' once" is even less likely to be seen as evaluative and is specific enough to be useful — the re-

ceiver can practice A's, D's, P's, and L's. On a more interpersonal level, the statement "I saw your interactions with me in this group as being quite brief so that I didn't really understand what you were trying to say" is descriptive, nonevaluative, and owned by the giver but is also far more general (and proportionately less helpful) than the statement "Joe, you made that point about Bill's next assignment too quickly for me to grasp what you're getting at."

Item 3: Needs of the Receiver Versus Needs of the Sender

Helpful feedback is given on the basis of the receiver's needs, not simply the needs of the sender to be heard or to "help." Such "help" is the kind of false help Gibb (1964) speaks of in a paper entitled "Is Help Helpful?" This factor is closely related to the next one listed: is the feedback desired? Obviously, the recipient may not desire feedback yet may need it very much. In this case, the helper has a difficult task, which is probably best begun by exploring with the receiver just why it is that he or she doesn't want feedback. It can also happen that the receiver may want feedback yet not appear to need it. In this case, it would probably be easiest to give feedback and ask the recipient to explore why he or she feels a need for such feedback. Of course, the giver of feedback cannot ignore his or her own needs, but to give feedback solely on this basis, without considering the needs of the receiver, is not likely to be helpful to the receiver.

Item 4: Asked Versus Imposed

Most of the time, people do want feedback; most of us have learned that such information can be useful at times. It is also true that most of us could learn to make better use of feedback, yet the use (or disuse) we make of this information is also directly related to the manner and format in which it is given — the process of giving feedback. Most people give cues, verbal and nonverbal. We must always be attuned to and on the lookout for negative cues, such as body position (turned away) or a verbal effort to redirect the conversation by the potential recipient. When such cues are perceived, it is then important to refrain from imposing feedback. If we consider the feedback particularly important or of great value at that moment, then we should always ask whether the feedback is permissible. This need not be done in so many words, but it should certainly be done. If the feedback is then clearly not desired, we can try to explore why this is so.

Item 5: Timely Versus Out of Context

Helpful feedback is of immediate relevance, as seen by the recipient. Often, but not always, this means that specific feedback is best given in the particular context in which the behavior that the feedback concerns took place, and as soon after that behavior as possible. Naturally, this is not always true; it would be not only foolish but dangerous to give an automobile driver feedback on his steering wheel grip while he is concentrating on braking to avoid a rear-end collision. Such feedback could be useful after the car is safely stopped and the driver has calmed down. Accurate behavioral records, such as audio and videotape, can extend considerably the length of the period within which feedback is timely; these methods preserve much of the context. In general, however, the closer in time and context that the feedback is to the behavior on which it is based, the more helpful it will be.

Item 6: Applicable Versus Useless

Useful feedback concerns behavior over which the recipient has some degree of control. The movie director tells the actor that his frequent eye blinks will distract viewers from the romance of the scene, but such feedback is pointless if the actor cannot control his eye blinks. The therapist may relate to his client the precise details of certain obsessive behaviors, but such feedback is useless if the client cannot control these behaviors. There are other types of useless feedback, for example, "You're so physically powerful that I'm afraid of you" is feedback the recipient cannot use directly, since few of us can change our physical appearance at will. A similar feedback statement is "I tend to ignore advice from people with advanced educational degrees," when directed to an instructor with a Ph.D. These two examples illustrate cases in which the problem is the sender's not the receiver's, and in which actions are more properly the responsibility of the sender. That is, the feedback could be helpful to the sender (for example, "How can I become more open to advice from people I categorize as my superiors?") but is not useful to the recipient. In general, then, feedback that cannot be used by the receiver fits the old saying "A difference that doesn't make any difference is no difference," and is not helpful.

Chapter 21: Quality Improvement Questionnaire

Scoring First reverse the scores for items 1, 5, and 7. Next, add up your points for the ten items.

    Your score indicates the extent to which you are a positive force for quality improvement. The questions represent behaviors associated with the Japanese approach to companywide continuous improvement of quality.

Interpretation

40–50 points = Great. A dynamo for quality improvement

30–40 points = Good. A positive force

20–30 points = Adequate. You have a typical North American attitude.

10–20 points = Poor. You may be dragging down quality efforts.

Go back over the questions on which you scored lowest and develop a plan to improve your approach toward quality. Discuss your ideas with other students.

Chapter 22: Are You Technically Oriented?

Scoring Compare your responses to the key on the right. Circle your response to each and then add up the total of circled responses in each column.

Interpretation Column I measures your perceived preference for using right-brain functions; Column II measures your perceived preference for using left-brain functions. A high score in Column II suggests that you're technically oriented. You may, for example, be more effective in the planning and operations activities of management than in the intuitive, creative, or human relations aspects of management.

	I	II		I	II
1.	b	a	14.	a	b
2.	a	b	15.	a	b
3.	a	b	16.	b	a
4.	b	a	17.	a	b
5.	a	b	18.	a	b
6.	b	a	19.	b	a
7.	b	a	20.	b	a
8.	b	a	21.	a	b
9.	a	b	22.	b	a
10.	b	a	23.	b	a
11.	a	b	24.	b	a
12.	b	a	25.	a	b
13.	a	b			
			TOTAL ____		____

Chapter 23: Computer Anxiety Index

Scoring Give yourself 1 point for each of the following answers: 1N, 2Y, 3N, 4Y, 5N, 6Y, 7N, 8Y, 9N, 10Y. Total the number of points and subtract that number from 10; enter the result here: _____.

Interpretation This instrument is designed to indicate the degree to which you may exhibit computer anxiety. In general, the higher your score, the more computer anxiety you display. With the ever-increasing role of computers in the modern workplace, such anxiety should be a source of concern. There are many positive steps you can take in the university and elsewhere to become more familiar with computers. You can become skilled and confident in their use.

Part Six: Who Controls Your Life?

Scoring Give yourself 1 point for each of the following selections: 1B, 2A, 3A, 4B, 5B, 6A, 7A, 8A, 9B, and 10A.

Interpretation Scores can be interpreted as follows:

8–10 points = High internal locus of control
6– 7 points = Moderate internal locus of control
   5 points = Mixed
3– 4 points = Moderate external locus of control
1– 2 points = High external locus of control

The higher your internal score, the more you believe that you control your own destiny. The higher your external score, the more you believe that what happens to you in your life is due to luck or chance.

Name and Company Index

Subject Index